International Children's Rights

International Children's Rights

Sara Dillon
<small>Suffolk University Law School</small>

Carolina Academic Press
Durham, North Carolina

ISBN: 978-1-59460-115-6
LCCN: 2009932987

Carolina Academic Press
700 Kent Street
Durham, North Carolina 27701
Telephone (919) 489-7486
Fax (919) 493-5668
www.cap-press.com

Printed in the United States of America

To Kasia and Theo,
my little doves

Contents

Appendices

*(The appendices are contained in an Adobe Acrobat PDF file on the included CD. The
Acrobat Reader program can be downloaded for free at http://www.adobe.com.)*

Table of Cases

Principal cases appear in bold. Page numbers preceeded by 'A' can be found in the appendices, which are contained on the enclosed CD.

Preface

As the first chapter in this book points out, the world of international children's rights is a difficult and complex one, filled with contradictions and paradoxes. While the iconic United Nations Convention on the Rights of the Child provided children with their own human rights instrument, and in essence made children the autonomous holders of rights, what the expression "children's rights" means in any given situation remains subject to the shared understanding of the adults who have responsibility for the care and protection of those children. As is shown throughout this book, in many areas there is no consensus on what truly constitutes "international children's rights." In that sense, this is an exciting and uniquely challenging field of study.

This book is a quintessential reader; it gathers together articles and documents from a wide variety of sources: academic commentary; reports from non-governmental organizations; United Nations and Council of Europe documents; and governmental studies. In addition to structuring the subject matter, I have provided context and interpretation for these readings. The appendix, contained on a cd at the back of the book, contains all major treaties and statutes discussed in the text, as well as some additional case law. My objective has been to present a wide-ranging resource for anyone and everyone interested in the subject of children and their internationally guaranteed rights; undergraduate and graduate students, law students, activists and advocates. It is meant to be used as part of a course or program, or indeed as a guide to further study and research.

One great challenge in the teaching of international children's rights is that there is such a gap between the suffering created by the violations of these rights and the experience of merely reading about these abuses. In this sense, it is recommended that the readings be supplemented by documentary films and by guest speakers who can assist in bringing the experiences of children to life.

I have tried in each area of concern to demonstrate that there are no easy or obvious answers to such questions as whether children should have the right to work—or by contrast, the right *not* to work; the degree to which tradition and local control should give way to a generic, global vision of children's rights; or what should best be done for children who are not living with their families of origin. In each case, I have tried to present at least two sides of the story, and I invite students who use the book to approach the contrasting point of view with an open mind. A principal theme of the book is the question of whether to protect or empower children in specific situations. While the Convention on the Rights of the Child calls for both protective and empowering responses, the former approach may often be more culturally familiar than the latter. Throughout the book, I have tried to choose readings that demonstrate the complexities of applying the usual human rights template to children.

I have chosen the topics that seem to be representative of the major issues in international children's rights in the world today; specifically, the role of the United Nations

Convention on the Rights of the Child; child labor; children in the global sex industry; children living without parental care; children and punishment; children and armed conflict, including child soldiers; and finally regional approaches to international children's rights. In this regard, the final chapter argues that midway between the national and the international, regional human rights systems have shown a great capacity to articulate meaningful and effective children's rights norms. It should become obvious that the line between one cohort of children and another may be less than clear. A child who is vulnerable to one form of abuse or exploitation may well be vulnerable to another.

The book neither denounces nor glorifies the work of the United Nations; the UN has a great and central role to play in the implementation of children's rights, but its work must be assessed honestly and with objectivity. The book does invite the reader to consider the question of remedies and ask whether children and their rights are well served by the existing system of norm implementation. It is interesting to note that the United States may well be on the verge of ratifying the Convention on the Rights of the Child; the U.S. is, as is often discussed, one of only two countries in the world not to have ratified it.

Not surprisingly, I consider children as a group to be severely underserved by the international human rights system, but I am happy to acknowledge the many ways in which their rights have been promoted in recent years by intergovernmental and non-governmental organizations. In this respect, special mention should be made of the astonishing contribution of Human Rights Watch, a group which has produced reports that draw attention to the lives and suffering of otherwise invisible children in many countries. Their work also serves to keep governments and the United Nations honest, as it is all too easy to fall into platitudes when it comes to describing "progress" in the development and protection of children's rights.

This book has been a labor of love, and I was fortunate to have a number of wonderful research assistants working with me on it. I would like to thank David Dixon and Elena Mamai, who helped get me get started some years ago by piling reports in the corner of my office. My sincere gratitude also to Millie Sanders, Christy Fujio, and Jennifer Singer for their patience and indispensable help. For pulling so much together at the end, my thanks to Andrea Shannon. I would also like to thank the people at Carolina Academic Press for being so supportive of this project.

International
Children's Rights

Chapter One

Introduction to International Children's Rights and the United Nations Convention on the Rights of the Child

I. International Children's Rights as a Separate Field of Study

A. Background to International Children's Rights

Questions relating to children and their rights elicit powerful reactions across the political and cultural spectrum. One point of view holds that children cannot be seen as having rights separate and distinct from their families, or from their cultures of origin. Under this view, any attempt to extend autonomous rights to a universal "global child" constitutes a threat to traditional authority structures. Others maintain that the rights of children are indissolubly linked to the rights and progress of women, arguing that the problems of children stem directly from the social and political status of their mothers.

Still others point to the United Nations Convention on the Rights of the Child (UNCRC),[1] and its near-universal acceptance, as evidence of an emerging global consensus on clearly identifiable children's rights; consensus on the existence of a global child, holder of separate and distinct rights, a child requiring either protection and empowerment, or both, but on the child's own terms and according to his or her best interests. From the time of its promulgation in 1989, the UNCRC has provided the focal point for debate as to how contemporary societies should best protect and empower children.

Issues relating to children's rights can become proxy battles in adult conflicts. Because most writing about child rights is of necessity by adults, it is important to recognize the ubiquitousness of adult agendas in all theorizing about children. The wider the acceptance of international legal instruments relating to children, the more difficult it is to maintain a position of strong cultural relativism in the raising of children. The fact that the UNCRC has been almost universally ratified—with only Somalia and the United States not yet parties—might indicate either that an unprecedented consensus on chil-

---

1. United Nations Convention on the Rights of the Child, Nov. 20, 1989, 1577 U.N.T.S. 3, *available at* http://www.unicef.org/knowyourrights/files/crc.pdf.

dren has in fact emerged in the past decade, or simply that few countries wish to be seen as acting contrary to the interests of children. Whether the existence of the UNCRC has made a substantial impact on the well-being of children is a question that must be confronted with the greatest seriousness by its proponents. Because children have a symbolic role within the lives of families, cultures and even global legal systems, they are very likely to be described in self-serving ways by adults. In that sense, the UNCRC should be approached with some degree of caution.

That children have problems unique to their vulnerable status is impossible to deny. Children are at the mercy of decisions made by others to an extent not true of most adults. They are also uniquely unable to fully comprehend and gain perspective on their own suffering. In that regard, their inability to objectify and analyze the situations in which they find themselves is without adult parallel. The task of an international regime of children's rights must be to advocate for effective remedies in the face of often inarticulate suffering. This fact is further complicated in that the designation "child" encompasses small children as well as adolescents. While "children" have evolving abilities, as noted by the UNCRC itself, they are legally protected under Article 2 according to a straightforward "under-18" definition.

To point out that violations of the rights of children are bound up with the behavior of adults, and to prescribe genuine legal responses, is to tread on the interests of adults—families, cultures, governments. The widespread harm done to children implicates the adults responsible for that harm. Adults in turn often point to their own helplessness in the face of economic and social factors beyond their control, and argue that the problems of children can only be solved by reference to larger trends. It is a great challenge to decide at what point cultural sensitivity, and political and economic realism, should excuse a failure to protect children.

What is clear is that the scale of the violation of the rights of children is staggering; millions of children are virtually locked away as bonded laborers; hundreds of thousands work in the sex industry; millions live on the streets where they are addicted to inhalants; hundreds of thousands, and perhaps millions, live in institutions where neglect and overcrowding are endemic, and where ordinary family bonds are virtually unknown. Children in these difficult circumstances are vulnerable to abuse, neglect, and even torture. If international human rights law is to be seen as anything more than a global "consciousness raising" exercise, the development of children's rights norms must be made effective in relieving at least some of this widespread misery. Nowhere is the gap between international "norm production" and effective remedies more striking than in the case of children's rights.

Despite the recent emphasis on the "participation rights" of children, it is a fact that children are less than fully capable of arguing their own cause to any significant degree; they do not vote and cannot easily organize into groups to make themselves heard at the political level. Children, while the repository of intergenerational hopes and dreams, are also the victims of adult indifference. They are the most vulnerable of the vulnerable and lack experience of the world. They have no real access to the machinery of law or politics. They have few if any defenses against commodification and abuse, and rely almost totally on "caring" adults to intervene in light of evidence of the wrongful behavior of other adults.

Children and their unique problems have gained the attention of the international legal community in recent years. This heightened attention has produced a corresponding and intense debate over what form international legal instruments for their protection should take. In addition to the question of whether the "protection" or "empowerment" paradigms should dominate, there has also been a deep split over whether the human rights of children can be protected in any meaningful way without first providing assistance to the larger units of culture and family. If children are seen to have rights separate from their families and cultures, does this mean that these families and cultures should take the blame for not ensuring the rights of children? Does this put ever more power in the hands of international elites and professionals, to the discredit of those with direct responsibility for the child? And in a world of unequal development, can or should children's rights be considered separately from economic development?

There has also been a good deal of debate over the nature of childhood itself. If the dominant notion of childhood is a mere construction of the modern age, then the attribution of generalized rights to children loses some of its credibility. Under such a view, the notion of appropriate "rights" becomes dependant on interpretive context. Whether "childhood" represents some universal or near-universal conception of the early stages of human life—the assumption on which the UNCRC is based—is impossible to determine in any absolute sense. It is significant that the twentieth century saw the promulgation of the first international instruments calling for special consideration and treatment of children, particularly in times of conflict.

The earliest of these was the protection-oriented Geneva Declaration of the Rights of the Child, adopted by the League of Nations in 1924.[2] ("The child that is hungry must be fed, the child that is sick must be helped; the child that is backward must be helped; the delinquent child must be reclaimed; and the orphan and the waif must be sheltered and succoured" is language that highlights the protective nature of duties towards children. Other aspects of its language appear more "modern": "The child must be given the means requisite for its normal development," and "the child must be put in a position to earn a livelihood and must be protected against every form of exploitation".) In the post-World War II era, the United Nations adopted a Declaration of the Rights of the Child in 1959,[3] reflecting a new, more rights-focused conception of the child, but still far from the broad set of rights seen in the UNCRC that would be adopted in 1989. The 1959 Declaration was progressive in the sense of affirming the child's entitlement to exercise a variety of rights without discrimination; the right to normal and healthy development; to a name and nationality; social security, access to health care and special treatment for handicapped children. The Declaration also called for love and understanding for the child, adequate education, protection against neglect, exploitation or trafficking; and protection against damaging forms of employment. Thus, many of the rights spelled out more fully in the UNCRC were already present in the 1959 Declaration, albeit in nascent form.

The drafting of the UNCRC took ten years to complete and has invited emotionally-charged controversy concerning the nature and scope of children's rights. Numerous commentators have emphasized the fact that the UNCRC was qualitatively different from any instrument that came before—its sweeping and comprehensive treatment of children as the true owners of rights, rather than as appendages of families, cultures or nations. What is clear is that this instrument marked the entrance onto the world stage of the global child, the autonomous repository of rights, articulated with a breadth never before seen.

---

2. League of Nations O.J. Spec. Supp. 21, at 43 (1924), http://www.un-documents.net/gdrc1924.htm.
3. Declaration of the Rights of the Child, G.A. Res. 1386, U.N. GAOR, 14th Sess., Supp. No. 16, U/N/ Doc. A/4354 (Nov. 20, 1959), http://www.cirp.org/library/ethics/UN-declaration.

The UNCRC was embraced quickly and enthusiastically, and is one of the most widely ratified human rights conventions. Its near-universal ratification is in one sense ironic in that abuses against children seem to grow more horrific with each passing decade. Despite its positive intentions, there seems to be no area of children's rights where solid improvement can be cited as a result of the UNCRC. Whether in child labor, sexual exploitation, trafficking, numbers of street children, access to education, or poverty levels, all negative indicators seem to be worsening, some dramatically so. Insofar as children are inherently vulnerable to the failure of adults to protect them from such abuses, it is questionable how effective the United Nations human rights system has been in improving the plight of children. The professional discourse of human rights, reliant on reporting by countries and exhortation on the part of UN representatives, may seem inappropriate in the face of widespread failure to either empower or protect children at anywhere near the level set out in the UNCRC.

A brief look at the UNCRC within the United Nations human rights system

The UNCRC is the only international instrument to deal comprehensively with children's rights. Whether ratifying countries truly agree with all, or even most, of its provisions is very much open to question, but the fact is that it is almost universally accepted, at least formally, and provides a foundation for all discussion of children's rights. As an integral part of the United Nations human rights system, it relies on a state reporting mechanism, under which States Parties submit periodic reports on their own efforts to implement the Convention, reports which are reviewed and commented on by the Committee on the Rights of the Child, set up under Article 43 of the UNCRC.

What we now think of as "international human rights" date from the immediate post-World War II period. At least in theory, the conceptual shift that took place in the postwar period was that nation states were to be accountable to the international community as to how they treated their own citizens. Individuals in member states of the United Nations would now have their own internationally guaranteed rights under human rights instruments generated by the UN system. While it is clearly the case that this system was more highly developed with regard to the articulation of norms, as compared with mechanisms of enforcement and implementation, most commentators have focused on the remarkable intellectual achievement brought about in this "age of rights." No longer could states argue that the manner in which they treated their own citizens was a matter of national sovereignty. Correspondingly, individuals in these states now had a basis upon which to argue for their rights, one that transcended the legal and constitutional traditions of their particular states. In other words, there would now be a new and separate legal inheritance for citizens in the member states of the UN.

This is not to say that there was no tradition of "international human rights law" prior to World War II. However, earlier international initiatives did not emphasize to the same degree the rights of the individual vis a vis the state in which he or she lived. International humanitarian law, for example, was concerned with humane treatment of civilians and combatants during times of war, developed through the International Red Cross in Switzerland in the late nineteenth century. The League of Nations, an inter-governmental organization created in 1919 to preserve the peace after World War I, was the precursor to the contemporary United Nations, in that its aim was to settle international disputes through peaceful means. To the extent that the League was unable to prevent the outbreak of World War II, it failed in its principal aims. Many of its core concepts and intergovernmental structures, however, were incorporated into what was to become the United Nations in the late 1940s. The League did not create "human rights law" per se, but did concern itself with the rights and interests of vulnerable groups: refugees, workers, and ethnic minorities, for example.

Any description of the contemporary international human rights system must begin with the United Nations Charter,[4] the document that underpins the agenda and structure of the UN itself. Article 1(3) of the Charter, reflecting international horror over the mass slaughter of civilians during World War II, states that one of the core purposes of the UN shall be "promoting and encouraging respect for human rights." Article 55 of the Charter refers to the importance of "universal respect for human rights" on the part of member states of the UN. Article 56 mentions joint action to be taken by the membership to this end. Under Article 13(1) of the Charter, the UN's General Assembly and its Economic and Social Committee (ECOSOC) would have responsibility for making recommendations as to how this might be achieved. In this way, internationally guaranteed and universally recognized human rights became a foundational concern of the UN, despite the fact that it remained a challenge for the organization to devise a structure to transform these concerns into reality. It must be conceded that there is a significant contrast between the idealism of the UN Charter and the mechanisms that have been constructed to implement rights on the ground.

The most important of the UN bodies charged with "promoting human rights" was the Human Rights Commission, set up by ECOSOC as required under Article 68 of the UN Charter. Members of the Commission were not individual "experts", but rather member states of the UN, elected by ECOSOC for three-year terms. Among its other oversight functions, the Commission was originally given the responsibility of drafting key human rights instruments, starting with the Universal Declaration of Human Rights.[5] As a result of years of criticism that the Human Rights Commission included member countries with appalling human rights records, the UN General Assembly voted in March 2006 to dismantle the Commission and create a new body, the Human Rights Council. Whereas the Human Rights Commission had been an independent body within the UN system, the new Council is a subsidiary body of the General Assembly. The 47 seats on the new Council are distributed on a geographical basis. General Assembly Resolution 60/251 that set up the new Council states that the Council members will be elected directly by secret ballot of the majority of the members of the General Assembly. While membership is open to all states, "when electing members of the Council, Member States shall take into account the contribution of candidates to the promotion and protection of human rights and their voluntary pledges and commitments made thereto." Despite these innovations, there is some indication that the new Human Rights Council might, in common with the former Human Rights Commission, continue to draw members from among states with poor records on human rights. On the other hand, however, Belarus' bid for a seat on the Council was rejected in May 2007 due its extremely poor human rights record, generating some hope that perhaps the Human Rights Council will live up to its mandate.

The major UN Human Rights instruments

Adopted by the General Assembly in 1948, the Universal Declaration of Human Rights contains a sweeping list of rights to which all people can lay claim. Although not written as a legally binding treaty, the Declaration has taken on a unique prestige and conceptual significance over the years, to the extent that many of its provisions are now considered part of customary international law; that is, having the status of binding obligations to which all states must adhere.

---

4. 26 June 1945, 59 Stat 1031, U.N.T.S. 993, 3 Bevans 1153.
5. Universal Declaration of Human Rights, G.A. Res. 217A, U.N. GAOR, 3d Sess., 1st plen. mtg., U.N. Doc. A/810 (Dec. 12, 1948), *available at* http://www.un.org/en/documents/udhr/index.shtml.

The preamble to the Declaration speaks of the fact that "disregard and contempt for human rights have resulted in barbarous acts which have outraged the conscience of mankind, and the advent of a world in which human beings shall enjoy freedom of speech and belief and freedom from fear and want has been proclaimed as the highest aspiration of the common people." It states that the peoples of the United Nations have in the Charter reaffirmed their faith in fundamental human rights, in the dignity and worth of the human person and in the equal rights of men and women." The Declaration does not limit itself to any particular human rights topic, but rather purports to convey the sense of a dramatic historical shift, suggesting in a wide ranging manner the categories of rights to which "the peoples of the United Nations" have decided to commit themselves. The Declaration states that "all human beings are born free and equal in dignity and rights." It insists that everyone is entitled to the enjoyment of these rights, regardless of race, sex, political opinion, or any other distinguishing feature. Rights to life, liberty, and proscriptions against slavery and torture are given prominence.

The Declaration requires states to provide fair and just systems of criminal law, to protect the privacy of individuals, and allow freedom of movement. All persons are to have the right to seek asylum, the right to nationality, the right to marry and to property. Liberty interests—freedom of thought and conscience and freedom of assembly and speech, are included. Economic rights, such as the right to work, to rest, and to an adequate standard of living, are also part of the Universal Declaration, as are rights to education and to participate in the "cultural life of the community." The Declaration sets out the terms for a perfected world, freed from the repression and fear that had characterized the first half of the twentieth century.

Just as the Universal Declaration can be very roughly divided between "political" rights on the one hand, and "economic" rights on the other, the two major human rights treaties to emerge from the United Nations system were constructed around these parallel themes. Considered the two pillars of an "international bill of rights," the International Covenant on Civil and Political Rights (ICCPR),[6] and the International Covenant on Economic, Social and Cultural Rights (ICESCR),[7] were drafted by the Human Rights Commission, and adopted by the General Assembly in 1966. As its name suggests, the ICCPR contains those rights associated with political freedoms, requiring States Parties to accord to their citizens a high standard of freedom of expression and belief, fairness in criminal and judicial procedures, and freedom from discrimination, to name but a few of the obligations enumerated under the covenant. The ICCPR establishes a Human Rights Committee of eighteen members, whose task it is to review reports submitted by States Parties, evaluating State progress towards achieving the goals of the Covenant, and to make "concluding observations." An optional protocol to the ICCPR, accepted by over one hundred countries to date, allows individuals the right to petition the Committee when their states of residence have violated one or more of the rights set out in the Covenant. The result of such a petition is an investigation by the Committee, with a "view" ultimately presented by the Committee on the particular situation.

The ICCPR states in Article 2 that "Each State Party to the present Covenant undertakes to respect and to ensure to all individuals within its territory and subject to its ju-

---

6. International Covenant on Civil and Political Rights, G.A. Res. 2200A, U.N. GAOR, 21st Sess., Supp. No. 16, U.N. Doc. A/6316 (Dec. 19, 1966), *available at* http://www1.umn.edu/humanrts/instree/b3ccpr.htm.

7. International Covenant on Economic, Social and Cultural Rights, G.A. Res. 2200A, U.N. GAOR, 21st Sess., Supplement No. 16, U.N. Doc. A/6316 (Dec. 16, 1966), available at http://www1.umn.edu/humanrts/instree/b2esc.htm.

risdiction the rights recognized in the present Covenant, without distinction of any kind, such as race, colour, sex, language, religion, political or other opinion, national or social origin, property, birth or other status." This article further states that "where not already provided for by existing legislative or other measures, each State Party to the present Covenant undertakes to take the necessary steps, in accordance with its constitutional processes and with the provisions of the present Covenant, to adopt such legislative or other measures as may be necessary to give effect to the rights recognized in the present Covenant." The article concludes that each State Party undertakes to ensure that those whose rights are violated will be provided with an "effective remedy," and that the affected individual shall have access to competent judicial or other authority to determine whether there has been such a violation, and that the relevant remedies will be enforced by the competent authority. In this sense, the ICCPR is characterized by its emphasis on the duty of the State Party to take definite and concrete action in the here and now, including the duty to ensure effective mechanisms for raising claims and obtaining relief for those whose rights may have been violated.[8]

By contrast, the ICESCR states in its Article 2 that "[e]ach State Party to the present Covenant undertakes to take steps, individually and through international assistance and co-operation, especially economic and technical, to the maximum of its available resources, with a view to achieving progressively the full realization of the rights recognized in the present Covenant by all appropriate means, including particularly the adoption of legislative measures." While this should not be taken to indicate that States Parties are not required to take concrete measures towards the implementation of the Covenant's provisions, it does indicate a less resounding consensus on the concrete form of obligations that are more economic and social than political in nature. The Covenant asserts the right of people to work, to achieve a "decent living" for themselves and their families, to unionize, and to enjoy the "highest attainable" standards of health. Rights to education and to take part in cultural life are also featured. As with other human rights treaties, a Committee on Economic, Social and Cultural Rights is set up to review reports submitted by States Parties. There is no individual complaint system under the ICESCR.[9]

Over the years, a number of other human rights treaties have been created, with varying levels of international support. Of great significance for purposes of this book, given the close link between women's and children's rights, is the Convention on the Elimination of Discrimination Against Women (CEDAW),[10] adopted by the General Assembly in 1979. Like the UNCRC, CEDAW is ambitious and multi-faceted. It calls on States Parties to eliminate "any distinction, exclusion or restriction made on the basis of sex which has the ef-

---

8. The ICCPR calls for special protections for juveniles in the criminal law context, in Articles 6 and 10. Article 24 of the ICCPR states that "Every child shall have, without any discrimination as to race, colour, sex, language, religion, national or social origin, property or birth, the right to such measures of protection as are required by his status as a minor, on the part of his family, society and the State." Article 24 also states that children shall be registered after birth and shall have a name; and that every child has a right to acquire a nationality.

9. The ICESCR specifically references children in its Article 10, which states that "Special measures of protection and assistance should be taken on behalf of all children and young persons without any discrimination for reasons of parentage or other conditions. Children and young persons should be protected from economic and social exploitation." Article 10 goes on to say that States Parties should make work harmful to the health or morals of children "punishable by law," and that they should set a minimum working age for children. Article 12 of the ICESCR calls for steps to be taken to reduce infant mortality and to promote "the healthy development of the child."

10. Convention on the Elimination of All Forms of Discrimination Against Women, Dec. 18, 1979, G.A. Res. 32/180, 1249 U.N.T.S. 13, available at http://www2.ohchr.org/english/law/cedaw.htm.

fect of impairing or nullifying the recognition, enjoyment or exercise by women, irrespective of their marital status, on a basis of equality of men and women, of human rights and fundamental freedoms in the political, economic, social, cultural, civil or any other field." An Optional Protocol to CEDAW entered into force in 2000, allowing states to accept the competence of the Committee on the Elimination of Discrimination Against Women to consider complaints from individuals and groups within that state's jurisdiction.

Like CEDAW, the UNCRC is a specialized and extremely idealistic treaty on a subject of intense and universal interest. It is the one and only convention that articulates a wide range of rights for children, and is constructed, as mentioned above, around two conceptual poles—protection and empowerment. From the earliest days of the UNCRC, debate has focused on the question of whether children should be seen as needing extra protection or greater empowerment, particularly with regard to inclusion in decision-making processes that affect their lives. Common sense would tell us that they need both, but differences in emphasis on the part of various advocacy groups can become contentious. The tension between these two visions of child rights will be traced throughout this book. As we will see, the comments of the Committee on the Rights of the Child are important and influential in interpreting party obligations under the Convention.

Just as the post-World War II period gave rise to a conceptual revolution with the recognition of human rights as part of the legal heritage of each person, regardless of location, the UNCRC is unique among the UN's human rights treaties in that it recognizes rights for children as autonomous beings. Children as a group had been traditionally thought of as "belonging to" authority structures such as the state, the family, or the culture. While children had been mentioned in the generic human rights treaties as requiring special consideration and protection, the UNCRC was "their" instrument. To this extent, the UNCRC has been uniquely controversial. An international re-imagining of children as having their own rights to opinions and rights of self-expression, caused some to perceive a threat to parental and local authority, and a number of writers expressed skepticism as to what might replace traditional structures of control. What is undeniable is that with the near-universal ratification of the UNCRC (as mentioned, only Somalia and the U.S. have failed to ratify the UNCRC, but even these two countries have signed it), our collective idea of childhood is forever altered. Whether one agrees with the UNCRC's vision of childhood or not, children are now the inheritors of a separate set of legal rights; not to be exercised according to the beneficence of their States or families, but directly bestowed on them by the international community. Whether this conceptual change has brought about major improvement in the actual experience of children is questionable. The vexed relationship between international legal norms and empirical reality is a theme we will trace throughout this book.

The overall effectiveness of the UN's enforcement and implementation system has been hotly debated for many years. Since the late 1940s, this system has generated numerous human rights instruments, under which various UN enforcement bodies have acted. The most common method of treaty implementation has been the "reporting" system, like that of the UNCRC, in which States Parties to the respective treaties provide information to a specialized committee on progress in living up to the goals set out in the treaty to which they have acceded. This is the sole means of enforcement provided for in the UNCRC. In some instances, optional protocols have created individual petitioning mechanisms, allowing persons to complain about their treatment at the hands of a State Party government. Overwhelmingly, however, the UN human rights system relies on a method of "blame and shame", in the hope that national governments will recognize the compelling nature of international human rights norms and do their best to make good on these commitments within their own borders.

This book will trace the major themes of protection and empowerment of children through examining issues of paramount importance today: the role of the UNCRC, child labor, children in the global sex industry, children without parental care, children and punishment, children and armed conflict, including child soldiers, and regional remedies for violations of children's rights. The UNCRC is fundamental to understanding each of these issues, and in that sense mastery of the substance of the Convention is the necessary starting point for this book.

Notes and Questions

Read the United Nations Convention on the Rights of the Child (UNCRC), found in the appendix to this book. Take note of the wide variety of rights the Convention asserts, and the way in which the Convention covers both traditional "rights to special protection" for children, as well as the so-called "empowerment", or autonomy, rights. If the Convention must be accepted as a whole, States Parties to it take on a strikingly broad range of commitments. With this in mind, answer the following questions:

1. Why should there be a special and separate Convention dealing with the rights of children? Can you identify a clear philosophical perspective in the Convention itself?

2. How absolute is the obligation to fully implement the Convention's terms? Why do you think the Convention was ratified so quickly by such a wide range of countries?

3. What do you consider to be the most important rights guaranteed by the Convention? Which are the most clearly expressed? Are there any rights in the Convention that you feel do not belong there, or could have been left out? Which provisions are the most ambiguous or difficult to understand?

4. Why do you think there has been resistance in the United States to implementing the Convention? Why do you suppose the U.S. has not ratified it?

5. The UNCRC is one of the most widely ratified of the human rights conventions. From your general knowledge, does it seem to have had a major impact on national or international policy development with respect to children's needs? How can this be accurately reviewed?

6. What methods of implementation and enforcement do you see in the Convention? The UNCRC, as noted above, relies on a state reporting method, and does not have a separate mechanism, even an optional one, for private party complaints. How effective do you think this "blame and shame" method is at addressing human rights issues? Which groups or persons do you think are best positioned to use this method to effect change?

B. The Origins and Early Development of the UNCRC

The UNCRC is lengthy and complex. It requires States Parties to take into account the "best interests of the child" when making decisions that affect the child's life and wellbeing. Although the importance of family and identity are affirmed, the Convention does not emphasize the traditional authority of the child's parents over the child. Rather, the Convention highlights the family's role in assisting the child to exercise his or her rights under the Convention, as appropriate in light of the child's evolving abilities.

The range of rights found in the Convention is strikingly wide. Rights to identity, rights not to be separated from family against the child's will; rights of the child to be heard in all matters affecting him or her; rights to freedom of expression and association and privacy go hand in hand with more conventional protection rights, such as rights to health and education. Under the Convention, children have a right to be free from exploitation of all kinds, including rights to be free from torture and degrading treatment. As we will see later in this chapter, some writers have criticized the UNCRC as being so abstract and idealistic as to defy any real attempts at implementation.

In the articles immediately following, selected authors present their analyses of the history, application and meaning of the UNCRC. The impetus for the creation of the UNCRC, as well as the major controversies that emerged from the drafting process, are described below by writers who observed the Convention's evolution.

Nigel Cantwell, *The Origins, Development and Significance of the United Nations Convention on the Rights of the Child*

in The United Nations Convention on the Rights of the Child:
A Guide to the 'Travaux Preparatoires' 19 (S. Detrick ed., 1992)

The United Nations (U.N.) Convention on the Rights of the Child is the result of a long process that began decades before the proposal to draw up such an instrument was officially tabled in 1978. This process took place against the background of two developments: the evolution of attitudes towards, and perceptions of, children and childhood; and the progressive consolidation of international human rights law.

Attitudes towards children's rights

The first mention of the "rights of the child" as such in an internationally recognized text dates back to 1924, when the Assembly of the League of Nations passed a resolution endorsing the Declaration of the Rights of the Child promulgated the previous year by the Council of the non-governmental "Save the Children International Union". The League's members were invited "to be guided by the principles" of this five-point document, which became known as the Declaration of Geneva and retained currency for a quarter of a century. In 1948, it served as the basis for a slightly expanded, seven-point Declaration adopted by the General Assembly of the newly-constituted United Nations. Then came the Declaration of the Rights of the Child promulgated by the U.N. General Assembly on November 20, 1959, and which is still valid today. It was this text that was the springboard for the initiative to draft a convention.

The essential theme underlying all of these non-binding declarations was that children need special protection and priority care. This reflected the overwhelming concerns of the first half of the twentieth century as regards children, particularly because of the realities and ramifications of the two World Wars. That emphasis was attenuated slightly in the 1959 text, through the addition of the right to a name and nationality—the first mention of civil rights in relation to children—but it remained the hallmark of the way the international community looked upon children.

In the "North", the late Sixties and the Seventies witnessed progressive but rapid change in these attitudes. There was also a great deal of confusion as to what "the rights of the child" really implied, despite the tentative definition given in the 1959 Declaration. Indeed, the latter, for all it was to be constantly referred to later on—notably just before and during 1979, the International Year of the Child (IYC), hardly constituted a widely publicized and known text. Were "children's rights" to be seen in opposition to those of adults? Did they involve "pupil power" and/or autonomy from parents? In the Seventies, such were the questions being asked about the rights of the child, which was at that time aptly termed "a concept in search of a definition".

So the debate was on, and the advent of IYC sharpened the focus and instigated the dissemination of an unprecedented amount of information about children's issues—one famous example being the widely-publicized figures suddenly announced by the International Labour Organization, according to which there were fifty-five million child workers in the world. An IYC also, of course, marked the twentieth anniversary of the 1959 Declaration and an ideal opportunity to launch the idea of a convention on the rights of the child.

The development of international human rights law

At the same time as attitudes towards children were evolving, the body of international human rights law was growing.

Prior to the proclamation of the Universal Declaration of Human Rights, only four special human rights treaties existed: the 1926 Slavery Convention, the 1930 Forced Labour Convention, the 1948 Freedom of Association and Protection of the Right to Organize Convention, and the Convention on the Prevention and Punishment of the Crime of Genocide, which was adopted by the U.N. General Assembly just one day before it proclaimed the Universal Declaration (December 10, 1948). Since then, well over sixty human rights treaties and declarations have been adopted by the United Nations alone. An aspect of major importance in this development is that, whereas pre-1948 texts centered on acts (e.g. forced labour, genocide), as of the creation of the U.N., there was a move to also provide special rights—over and above those set out in the Universal Declaration—to specific population groups, identified either by their temporary status (e.g. refugees, prisoners) or by their essentially permanent condition (e.g. women, disabled persons). This tendency undoubtedly lent support—albeit passive—to efforts to ensure that special attention be given to children as one such group.

At the same time, it was equally true that more and more instruments were, in part at least, applicable explicitly or implicitly to children. In fact, some eighty international (not only of the United Nations) and regional texts, both binding and non-binding, have been identified as dealing in some way and to some extent with children's rights. As a result, there was a strong feeling in some quarters that a convention on this issue was unnecessary. That this view did not hold sway can be seen as particularly fortunate in terms of the protection of the human rights of children (see "The need for the Convention" below).

The Polish initiative

The proposal that the United Nations adopt a convention on the rights of the child was formally tabled[11] by the Government of Poland at the thirty-fourth session of the U.N. Commission on Human Rights, held in early 1978. Poland had in fact expressed its support for a convention when the 1959 Declaration was being discussed. Clearly at that time, however, the world community had not been ready for a fully-fledged binding human rights instrument in favor of children.

Poland has often stated its special concern for children in international fora, recalling the past sufferings of its own younger generations, as well as its pioneers in child welfare

---

11. "Tabled" in this context mean "presented."

like Janusz Korczak. The timing of this new initiative was aimed at having the Convention adopted in 1979, and therefore becoming a lasting tribute to and reminder of the International Year of the Child.

This aim goes a long way to explaining why the text of the Polish proposal was modeled so closely on the 1959 Declaration: it was based on principles already agreed by the international community, and approval could therefore, it was hoped, be ensured with very little debate, thus enabling the General Assembly to adopt the final version before the end of 1979. But there were other factors too. Firstly, the content of the Declaration leaned heavily towards economic, social and cultural rights, corresponding closely to the priorities and vision of the Polish Authorities at that time. Secondly, it seems to have been a last-minute initiative. On the one hand, the proposed text was very evidently not formulated in a style or form that had become usual for binding treaties, and on the other, minimal prior consultation or arousal of support regarding the proposal appears to have taken place.

Indeed, when the U.N. Secretary-General circulated the proposal to governments and international organizations for their "views, observations and suggestions", the response was anything but enthusiastic. Whilst few felt able officially to express doubts about the need for better ensuring access of children to their fundamental rights—although many unofficially questioned the opportuneness of a convention in doing so—they did raise several concerns regarding the proposal as it stood. The major objections were:

- that (as noted above) the language of the draft was inappropriate—as the Danish Government opined, it "lacks the preciseness and clarity which is required in the formulation of legally binding texts";
- that the text omitted to deal with a whole range of rights, the absence of which was likely to jeopardize that impact of a convention in this sphere;
- that the draft was silent on the question of implementation, fundamental to the effectiveness of an international treaty;
- that—a point made in particular by the international organizations—no text should be adopted until account had been taken of the reports, programmes and initiatives that IYC would foster.

In addition to the hesitations evidenced by such responses were those indicated by complete silence—most notably, perhaps, that of UNICEF, whose total lack of initial interest in the exercise was nonetheless happily to be remedied before the end of the drafting process.

Thus, despite the rather unexpected exhortation from the U.N. General Assembly in 1978, that the Commission on Human Rights should, at its thirty-fifth session in 1979, make discussion of the Convention one of its priorities with a view to having it adopted during IYC, it was not surprising that a rather different view prevailed. The view in question was that the proposed text should be subjected to very close scrutiny and considerable modification, and that this could not be accomplished satisfactorily in time for the Convention's adoption in 1979.

The open-ended Working Group

It was in this context that the thirty-fifth session of the Commission decided to set up an open-ended Working Group on the Question of a Convention on the Rights of the Child. The "open-ended" nature of the Working Group meant that any of the forty-three states represented on the Commission could participate. All other Member States of the

United Nations could send "observers" (with the right to take the floor), as could inter-governmental organizations. Nongovernmental organizations in consultative status with the U.N. Economic and Social Council (ECOSOC) could also participate, but with no absolute right to speak, although in practice their requests for the floor were rarely refused. Meetings were public.

The Working Group held its first meeting during the Commission's thirty-fifth session, in order to make an immediate start. As of the following year, 1980, and until 1987, it met annually as a pre-sessional Working Group, i.e. during the week immediately prior to the start of the Commission's sessions (end January/beginning February). Poland in fact presented a revised draft proposal to the 1980 meeting, a more carefully thought-out and substantial text for use as a basic working document.

By the end of 1987, however, calls for the drafting to be complete in time for the adoption of the Convention in 1989, the tenth anniversary of IYC, had become so strong that the Working Group came together for two full fortnight meetings in 1988. The first was simply an extended pre-sessional meeting to terminate the initial review of the text. The other, in November/December, was devoted to a "second reading" of that text, taking into account in particular the results of a technical review carried out, in the meantime, under the auspices of the Centre for Human Rights.

The Working Group operated on the basis of consensus. At no time during its work, in other words, was a proposal taken to a vote. Besides being important to the spirit of the drafting exercise, this had three important ramifications.

Firstly, it contributed to the fact that the drafting process was so lengthy, since it meant that every text and proposed modification had to be debated until all members of the Working Group could agree—or at least agree not to disagree.

Secondly, the consensus system resulted in the abandonment of certain proposals, notwithstanding the support of a clear majority. One casualty was a proposal to include a provision explicitly placing severe limitations on medical experimentation on children: there was general agreement on the principle, but no formulation could be found that satisfied all delegations, so the issue was quite simply dropped. Another, now infamous, example concerns the upper age-limit for the prohibition of children's participation in armed conflicts (see "Issues of controversy" below).

A positive consequence, however, was that only one provision in the draft text finally submitted by the Working Group was set in square brackets, i.e. unresolved (see Article 43, para. 11, concerning responsibility for financing the meetings of the Committee on the Rights of the Child, which went to a vote at the Fifth Committee, just prior to the General Assembly meeting that adopted the final text). This clearly facilitated the passage of the draft Convention through the higher bodies of the U.N. system.

Another major factor which affected the functioning of the Working Group, more especially in its early years, was the political climate. The change in the atmosphere of the meetings as of 1985, when East-West relations began to thaw in earnest, was remarkable. It contributed greatly to the Working Group being able gradually to move into top gear from then on, since it reduced to a minimum the purely political statements and negotiation that had previously been a hallmark of the discussions. In the early Eighties, one became resigned to seeing no more than three or four articles being adopted (and even then, often incompletely) during the week. Indeed, during a particularly tedious and sterile debate in the 1983, the USSR delegate felt prompted to announce that, at the current rate, it would take twenty-two years before the Convention was ready. By the end of the drafting process, fortunately, the pace had virtually doubled.

Very much linked with this was the fact that, during the first half of the decade, another Working Group of the Commission on Human Rights was meeting simultaneously—and literally just along the corridor—to the one drafting the Convention on the Rights of the Child. The remit of this other Working Group was to draft the Convention against Torture. The special significance of this state of affairs lay in the fact that the latter Convention had been a Western initiative, whereas the former was of course the result of a proposal by an Eastern European country. Consequently, given the climate of the era, when there were special political problems in one Working Group, they were immediately felt in the other. When the then "Eastern Bloc" was unsuccessful in making a point in the Working Group dealing with torture, for example, its representatives down the corridor would immediately start creating problems in relation to the Convention on the Rights of the Child. On one memorable occasion, word came from the Working Group on the Convention against Torture that the non-governmental organizations were demanding the same opportunities to make statements there as at the "Rights of the Child" meeting, something clearly considered undesirable by the sender of the message. For the rest of the meeting, the NGOs were hardly able to say a word....

Drafting of the Convention against Torture was complete in 1984, coinciding with the beginnings of improved East-West relations. From 1985 onwards, the debate over the formulation of the Convention on the Rights of the Child was therefore greatly eased.

Participants in the drafting process

The hesitation that characterized governments' reactions to the proposal for a convention on the rights of the child was reflected in the level of their participation. During the early years, never more than thirty countries took part in meetings of the Working Group, rising to forty as of the mid-Eighties. The industrialized countries were significantly over-represented at all stages. Fears that the outcome would be a heavily Northern-oriented text were widespread and justified. They were attenuated only by particularly active participation on the part of certain developing countries (Algeria, Argentina, Senegal and Venezuela were remarkable in this respect) as well as, in 1988, a sudden last-minute surge of delegates from the South, many from States with Islamic law.

A key feature in the successful functioning of the Working Group—for it was indeed successful, and increasingly so as time went on—was continuity in the composition of government delegations. Most of the truly active countries ensured that the least possible changes took place as regards the persons representing them. This was true of the four countries mention above as well as many others such as the then German Democratic Republic, Finland, the Netherlands, Norway, Portugal, the United Kingdom and the USSR. The result, combined with other factors, was the gradual development of what some delegates themselves qualified as a "family atmosphere". This of course made working together a far easier exercise.

The functioning of the Working Group owed a considerable amount, too, to its Chairman. From start to finish, the Group was chaired by Professor Adam Lopatka of Poland who, during the Eighties, was initially his country's Minister for Religious Affairs and subsequently President of the Supreme Court. Relatively discreet but with a quiet force, lacking neither in humor nor in warmth, and generally demonstrating virtually infinite patience, he managed to maintain—with one or two notable exceptions—a cohesion in the Group based on his acknowledged fairness and his commitment to seeing the Convention successfully and appropriately completed.

If the active participation of most individual governments generally left much to be desired, the presence and impact of intergovernmental organizations can only be qualified as scandalously weak. To be sure, the International Labour Organization made certain it was represented in particular during discussions on the child labour article (see Article 32), and UNICEF finally realized the importance of the future Convention for its work, sending strong delegations as of 1986. But the United Nations Development Programme (UNDP), United Nations Educational, Scientific and Cultural Organization (UNESCO), the United Nations High Commissioner for Refugees (UNHCR) and, most notably, the World Health Organization (WHO) (whose definition of "health" means that a wide range of the Convention's provisions are directly germane to its mandate) were rarely to be found. Their potential technical contribution would no doubt have helped to resolve, more efficiently at the very least, many of the substantive problems that came up during the debates. Their studied absence, on the other hand, remains one of the great mysteries of the drafting process.

The NGO contribution

As noted previously, the third category of participants, in addition to governments and intergovernmental organizations, was composed of recognized non-governmental organizations (NGOs). It is generally acknowledged in the international community that the NGOs had a direct and indirect impact on this Convention that is without parallel in the history of drafting international instruments.

Despite the many reservations expressed when the idea of the Convention was first mooted and the original text proposed, there was from the start considerable interest and mobilization concerning the project among NGOs, including some only partly or indirectly concerned with children's issues. A large number co-signed a written statement prior to the first Working Group meeting in 1979, and several made substantial proposals regarding the draft texts of specific articles. After a wane in overt interest in 1980–1981 (perhaps due to the fact that the 1980 meeting of the Working Group was notoriously unproductive), a significant group of NGOs submitted a further joint statement to the 1982 meeting, where twelve were physically represented as compared to just four in 1981.

But it was the 1983 meeting that proved to be the watershed for NGO participation. Several NGO representatives there began to express feelings of frustration. They knew that individually and as a group they could make a potentially major contribution to the drafting process. At the same time, they generally lacked experience and coordination in terms of making the fruits of their unique expertise known to the Working Group in the right way and at the right time. Their influence on the draft articles adopted during the first five years was very limited, restricted essentially to the results obtained by one or two well-established human rights organizations. They decided to try to change the situation.

With logistical assistance from UNICEF's Geneva office, they convened an "NGO Consultation" in mid-1983, where over twenty NGOs were represented. The major outcome of the meeting was the decision that NGOs interested in working on the draft Convention should form an Ad Hoc Group in order primarily to foster remedies to the two major ills identified in their efforts to date: lack of preparedness and lack of coherent NGO stand.

The NGO Ad Hoc Group held its first meeting later that same year and came up with a series of joint proposals on a number of draft articles due for consideration at the 1984 meeting of the Working Group. They presented these proposals in a document distributed to the government delegates. The effect was immediate and considerable. The ground was laid for substantially improving NGO input and impact.

Throughout the remainder of the drafting process, the NGO Ad Hoc Group submitted annual reports to the Working Group, setting out and explaining their proposals and concerns. In addition, they began holding briefing sessions for government representatives as well as, at a more generally level, producing materials and organizing meetings to arouse awareness about the future Convention and foster understanding of its importance.

The extent of the overall NGO contribution is, understandably, by no means always clear from the travaux preparatoires.[12] The success of the NGOs' activities to promote support for the Convention was, for example, undoubtedly instrumental in getting many governments to take the drafting process more seriously, and in giving the Working Group a renewed sense of purpose. This was all the more so when, in 1987, the NGO Group joined with UNICEF in publicly promoting the objective of having the Convention ready for adoption by the U.N. General Assembly in 1989. Furthermore, the Group's proposals were increasingly being presented by government delegates during the Working Group meetings, rather than directly by the NGOs themselves. None of these instances of NGO impact could be reflected in the reports of the Working Group. However, reviewing the final text of the Convention, the Ad Hoc Group was able to identify at least thirteen substantive articles or paragraphs for whose inclusion in the text the NGOs had been primarily responsible, and a similar number where they had had a significant impact on the formulation, form or content. It was the breadth of the expertise on which they NGO Group could draw, combined with its cohesion and careful preparation, that largely explains how it had an impact in so many of the fields covered by this unusually comprehensive treaty.

The influence of the NGO Ad Hoc Group was not limited to the substantive articles. The Group developed a draft text for what are now Articles 42 to 45, and several ideas therein are reflected in the adopted provisions. These include the obligation of States Parties to make the contents of the Convention known, not only to adults, but also and explicitly to children (see Article 42), as well as certain of the roles given to the Committee on the Rights of the Child, UNICEF and "other competent bodies" (see Article 45). Moreover, the fact that the travaux preparatoires show that the term "other competent bodies" is to include NGOs is in no small way attributable to the positive reaction of the Working Group to their contribution to the drafting process.

Issues of controversy

Whilst every paragraph of every article was the subject of debate—sometimes protracted—a number of substantive issues broached in the draft Convention caused major controversy.

The first of these in fact aroused disagreement because it was not broached: the issue in question was the definition of the minimum age of the child. There were of course two groups of countries with irreconcilably opposed standpoints as to the moment when childhood begins—at conception or at birth. Substantive discussion was pointless. Neither side could ever agree to what would have been a definition of the child in Article 1, essentially either permitting or outlawing abortion. Nor could any formulation be found for that article which would allow each society to adopt its own standard in this regard. Yet there was just one relevant point on which all could agree: that, as stated in the Preamble of the 1959 Declaration on the Rights of the Child, the child "needs special safeguards and care, including appropriate legal protection, both before as well as after birth." Such legal protection could include, but would not require, the prohibition of abortion.

---

12. The preparatory work for a treaty, similar to a legislative history.

Not without difficulty, the Working Group finally came to a consensus that explicit reference to the formulation in the Declaration would be made in the Preamble to the Convention, and that there would be no mention of minimum age in Article 1.

The second major problem area concerned freedom of religion. The initial formulation of Article 14, modeled on the text of Article 18 of the International Covenant on Civil and Political Rights, included reference to "the freedom to have or to adopt a religion (...) of his choice". It was subsequently pointed out in the strongest terms that, under Islam, a child does not have the right to choose another religion, and that the right contained in the Covenant could only be held to apply to adults. This put the drafters in a delicate situation. What attitude was to be taken towards the elimination of a right of the child in the future Convention which was already conferred by a well-established international human rights instrument without restriction as to the age of the beneficiary? Reluctantly, in the end, the proponents of retaining the full right agreed to drop all reference to choice, "in the spirit of compromise".

The third issue that provoked considerable problems was adoption. It again involved Islamic States, but in a slightly different way. The concern was to ensure that, since adoption as such is not possible under Islam, the Convention make it clear that States Parties are not obliged to recognize or set up a system of adoption. Indeed, the first draft text of Article 21 began with the words "The States Parties (...) shall undertake measures, where appropriate, to facilitate the process of adoption of the child." In fact, Article 21 was anyway due for a thorough reappraisal. Between the moment it had been formulated and the time that the full draft Convention was completed, the U.N. General Assembly had approved — in 1986 — the Declaration on Social and Legal Principles relating to the Protection and Welfare of Children, with Special Reference to Foster Placement and Adoption, Nationally and Internationally. This Declaration contained a number of fundamental principles that deserved inclusion in the Convention, and indeed translated the new thinking on inter-country adoption in particular, whereby emphasis was to be placed on guaranteeing the protection of the children concerned rather than on facilitating the process. The revised text of Article 21 took due account of all these questions.

The final example of controversial issues concerns the age at which children should be permitted to take part in armed conflict (see Article 38). There is little doubt that this was, and remains, the most hotly-debated question of the drafting process. The NGOs and many governments fought tirelessly for years to ensure that, even if it had to be conceded that children could be recruited into the armed forces as of age fifteen, at least they be prohibited from taking a direct part in hostilities until they had reached eighteen years. The final consensus was uncomfortable to say the least. At the last meeting of the Working Group, the United States delegate — ostensibly alone but clearly benefiting from the silent support of several other delegations — categorically refused to give such protection to the fifteen to seventeen age-group. Despite vociferous opposition, the Chairman declared that, since there was no consensus on the upper age limit and no delegation was arguing for an age-limit under fifteen, this clearly implied that there was consensus on age fifteen. With that, he immediately closed the debate.

Uproar ensued, together with threats of re-opening the debate at a higher level (at the Commission on Human Rights or even the General Assembly). However, all concerned quickly realized that any attempt to have this provision reviewed would open the floodgates to demands for other draft articles to be re-considered — including several whose final formulation had been the result of delicately-negotiated consensus and compromise. This would at best have severely delayed the adoption of the Convention, and maybe even jeopardized its chance of ever coming into existence at all, since there was a limit beyond which states would refuse to commit time and resources to drafting an international instrument.

So it was that the draft text of the Convention was submitted in turn to the U.N. Commission on Human Rights, ECOSOC and the U.N. General Assembly and, with no modifications, was adopted by the latter on November 20, 1989.

Adam Lopatka, *Symposium: Implementation of the United Nations Convention on the Rights of the Child: Background: An Introduction to the United Nations Convention on the Rights of the Child*
6 Transnational Law & Contemporary Problems 251 (1996)

I. INTRODUCTION

On November 20, 1989, the U.N. General Assembly unanimously adopted the Convention on the Rights of the Child (Convention). The Convention is a comprehensive, multifaceted international treaty composed of a preamble and fifty-four articles. It sets forth all of the rights of the child—civil, political, economic, social, and cultural. It is a kind of "world constitution" of the rights of the child that the international community currently accepts.

. . . .

II. OVERVIEW OF THE CONVENTION

States Parties to the Convention are required to respect and ensure the rights set forth in the Convention to each and every child within their jurisdiction. Thus, the Convention has reference beyond merely the child citizens of a given State. According to the Convention, "States Parties shall take all appropriate measures to ensure that the child is protected against all forms of discrimination or punishment on the basis of the status, activities, expressed opinions or beliefs of the child's parents, legal guardians, or family members." The Convention bans discrimination of any kind, "irrespective of the child's or his or her parent's or legal guardian's race, colour, sex, language, religion, political or other opinion, national, ethnic or social origin, property, disability, birth or other status."

The Convention is also opposed to exploitation of the child in any form. In the economic sphere, the child has the right to be protected from exploitation and from performing any work that is "likely to be hazardous or to interfere with the child's education, or to be harmful to the child's health or physical, mental, spiritual, moral or social development." Also under the Convention, the child is protected from "the illicit use of narcotic drugs and psychotropic substances as defined in the relevant international treaties." The State shall take "all appropriate measures ... to prevent the use of children in the illicit production and trafficking of such substances." The State is also obligated to protect the child from "all forms of sexual exploitation and sexual abuse." The State shall take "all appropriate national, bilateral and multilateral measures to prevent the abduction of, the sale of or traffic in children for any purpose or in any form." The State shall protect the child against "all other forms of exploitation prejudicial to any aspects of the child's welfare." In addition, the Convention also confronts parental exploitation by addressing situations where abduction is committed by one parent against the will of the other parent or the decision of a competent authority.

Implementation of the Convention is provided for in Article 4, stating that: "State Parties shall undertake all appropriate legislative, administrative, and other measures for the implementation of the rights recognized in the present Convention." Although this provision applies to all the rights defined in the Convention, with regard to economic, social and cultural rights, "States … shall undertake such measures to the maximum extent of their available resources and, where needed, within the framework of international co-operation." Thus, the Convention is aimed at the improvement of the status of the child through worldwide promotion and protection of the child's needs, interests, rights, and liberties.

In adopting the Convention, the U.N. General Assembly was convinced that it would function as a standard-setting instrument in the field of human rights by contributing to the protection of children's rights and the assurance of their well-being. The General Assembly was profoundly concerned that the situation of children in many parts of the world remains critical as a result of inadequate social conditions, natural disasters, armed conflicts, exploitation, illiteracy, hunger, and disability. The General Assembly was convinced that these conditions called for urgent and effective national and international action.

When the General Assembly adopted the Convention, it recognized, as was first proclaimed in the 1959 Declaration of the Rights of the Child, that "the child by reason of his or her physical and mental immaturity needs special safeguards and care, including appropriate legal protection both before as well as after birth." The child, much like women, the elderly, the disabled, people belonging to ethnic, linguistic and religious minorities, indigenous people, refugees, and migrant workers, needs to have additional rights guaranteed, including special care and protection, in order to be able to exercise his or her human rights and basic liberties on equal terms with others. This is the primary reason for special promotion and protection of child rights in the Convention. The Convention was adopted with the intent of protecting the basic needs, interests, and rights of all children. However, the Convention also takes into account the fact that in all States in the world there are children living in exceptionally difficult conditions and that these children need special consideration—such as children living within territories of armed conflict, children who are disabled, and the like. The Convention stipulates additional rights for these children, as they are more vulnerable than others.

The Convention expresses a modern approach to the child on account of its holistic approach to the rights of the child. It creates and spreads a new image of "childhood." The Convention assumes that the child is not merely an object of solicitude and care. Rather, the child is a subject of fundamental rights and basic liberties. The child is a human being, not a "germ" of a human being. The child is not the property of his or her parents, a local community, a political party, a church, or a State. The child is a personality with his or her own dignity and individuality. That is, among others, why the Convention proclaims that "[n]o child shall be subjected to arbitrary or unlawful interference with his or her privacy … nor to unlawful attacks on his or her honour and reputation." The child has the right to be protected by law against such interference or attacks. The articles of the Convention incorporate the latest progressive philosophy and pedagogics. In fact, Article 29 provides that the child should be fully prepared to live an individual life in society and should be brought up in the spirit of the ideals proclaimed in the Charter of United Nations.

The Convention also assumes that the family is the best environment for the proper development of the child. For this reason, the Convention proclaims that the child "for the full and harmonious development of his or her personality, should grow up in a family environment, in an atmosphere of happiness, love and understanding." The Convention goes on to provide that in all decisions and activities concerning the child, irrespective of whether they are taken by his or her parents, tutelary institutions, or authorities of a State administration, "the best interests of the child shall be a primary consideration." However, where there are conflicting opinions, the final decision as to what is in the "best interests" of the child is made by a State authority, most often by a court of law.

The Convention acknowledges that the rights of the child may be fully exercised with his or her conscious and voluntary participation. On the other hand, the Convention provides that the State shall "respect the responsibilities, rights and duties of parents ... or other persons legally responsible for the child, to provide, in a manner consistent with the evolving capacities of the child, appropriate direction and guidance in the exercise by the child of the rights recognized in the present Convention." The Convention does not make use of such traditional expressions as "parental authority" or "parental power," but instead suggests a partnership between parents and children, based on the parents' love of the child and child's love of the parents.

Emphasizing the importance of participation and respect for the personality of the child, the Convention proclaims that the State shall "assure to the child who is capable of forming his or her own views the right to express those views freely in all matters affecting the child, the views of the child being given due weight in accordance with the age and maturity of the child."

The Convention is of universal character. The rights and liberties of the child recognized in the Convention are vested in each child in every State, irrespective of the State's level of economic or political development or orientation. There is no restriction on the right of a State to grant children more rights or more broadly defined rights than are contained in the Convention. The Convention provides that nothing in it "shall affect any provisions which are more conducive to the realization of the rights of the child and which may be contained in: (a) the law of a State Party; or (b) international law in force for that State." Thus, the Convention imposes minimum requirements, below which there can be no exceptions. On the other hand, the Convention takes into consideration the importance of traditions and cultural values for the protection and harmonious development of the child. It takes into account the differing levels of development of particular States and encourages international cooperation for improving the living conditions of children in every State, particularly in developing States. The possibility of making small allowances for local conditions does not shatter the universal character of the Convention.

. . . .

III. PROSPECTS FOR THE FUTURE

To say that the Convention is the apogee of what the international community can and should do for the child would be going too far. It is easy to imagine that at some time in the future there will be a need to raise the Convention's standards and to extend the list of rights and liberties granted to the child. The expression of these trends can already be seen in the proposals to adopt two optional protocols to the Convention: an optional protocol on the sale of children, child prostitution, and child pornography, as well as an optional protocol on involvement of children in armed conflicts. The same trend can be seen in the 1996 decision of States Parties to the Convention to increase the number of members of the Committee on the Rights of the Child from ten to eighteen. The Plan of Action to strengthen the implementation of the Convention put forward by the U.N. High Commissioner for Human Rights is also a part of the trend to expand children's rights. It is highly possible that in the future the international community will ban corporal punishment of the child—even in the family, or the injuring of girls by reason of cultural beliefs still prevailing in some States. The Convention is an historic achievement of the United Nations in the sphere of promotion and protection of human rights. However, it would be too much to treat the Convention as a sanctity without the need for improvement.

Notes and Questions

1. What hurdles does Cantwell identify in his description of the UNCRC drafting process? How were political controversies resolved during this process? Which articles reflect political compromises?

2. Lopatka is undoubtedly an idealist when it comes to the role of the UNCRC, especially given his participation in its creation. What language does he use to describe the role he envisages for the UNCRC? Does he indicate how we should measure its success or failure?

C. Application and Implementation of the Convention on the Rights of the Child

1. UNCRC Committee Implementation

After the adoption of the UNCRC by a large number of states, its mechanisms of enforcement came into play. As with the promulgation of the Convention, the enforcement aspects of the UNCRC also had its enthusiasts. It is open to question whether formalized state reports to the relevant United Nations body enhances transparency or reflects national hypocrisy. The format itself—self-reflection based on the articles of the convention—is useful to the extent that it encourages a uniform method of identifying problems, yet is vulnerable to a pro-forma and platitudinous approach by the various reporting states.

As with most human rights treaties, lack of robust enforcement is a serious problem with regard to the implementation of the UNCRC as well. Some would argue that the Convention's real importance lies in its power to inspire advocates for children's rights in various countries, allowing them to rely on its prestige and comprehensiveness to bring attention to a wide array of child-related issues. Under this view, the fact that real enforcement is limited to state reporting is not the most important feature of the system. Rather, the influence of the Convention should be measured in light of the groups "on the ground" who are given tools with which to influence their own governments.

The readings that follow will first explain how the UNCRC reporting system actually works. After that, there appear several examples from the Committee's observations on state reports, as well as the "alternative" NGO reports submitted to the Committee, often far more colorful and revealing that the official version of events emanating from national governments.

Cynthia Price Cohen, *Implementing the U.N. Convention on the Rights of the Child*
21 Whittier Law Review 95 (1999)

I. Introduction

Like all other United Nations human rights treaties, the Convention on the Rights of the Child has no direct method of enforcement. Instead, the Convention has an implementation mechanism requiring the countries that ratify it to submit periodic reports, to a committee of experts, detailing the measures they have taken to implement the Convention. The role of the Committee on the Rights of the Child—the Convention's monitoring body—is to evaluate the extent to which the Convention's obligations have been met. It then advises ratifying countries—known as States Parties—on steps that they should take to better comply with the Convention's requirements.

Requirements of the Convention's implementation mechanism are laid out in Articles 43–45. Article 43 creates the Committee on the Rights of the Child. Article 44 details the reporting obligations of the States Parties. Article 45 gives the Committee additional tools with which to evaluate the truthfulness of the State Parties' reports and to assist countries in meeting the Convention's goals.

It should be noted that implementation of the Convention on the Rights of the Child is not limited to the formal treaty-monitoring process. If the Convention's rights are to be exercised by all children, its standards must be applied, not only by government officials, but by all people who deal with children: educators, doctors, social workers, lawyers, international organizations, and non-governmental organizations (NGOs).

II. States Parties' Reports

Article 44 of the Convention on the Rights of the Child explains that States Parties are "to submit to the Committee, through the Secretary-General of the United Nations, reports on the measures they have adopted that give effect to the rights recognized herein, and on the progress made on the enjoyment of those rights." The "initial" State Party report is due two years after the Convention enters into force for that nation, which is thirty days after submission to the Secretary-General of the nation's instrument of ratification. Subsequent "periodic" reports are to be submitted every five years thereafter.

. . . .

As of January 29, 1999, the Committee had received initial reports from approximately 133 States Parties and periodic (second) reports from twenty States Parties. It had completed the examination of seventy initial reports and six periodic reports, and had scheduled the examination of reports for the next three upcoming sessions. Of the 191 States Parties, fifty-eight countries have failed to submit their initial reports, while many of the submitted reports were as much as a year late.

III. Committee on the Rights of the Child

It is Article 43 of the Convention on the Rights of the Child that provides for the establishment of a Committee on the Rights of the Child to oversee implementation of the Convention. According to the second paragraph of Article 43, this Committee "shall consist of ten members of high moral standing and recognized competence in the field covered by this Convention." Members are to be elected by the States Parties and must be chosen from among their nationals. However, Committee members are to serve in their personal capacities.

The first election of Committee members took place at a meeting of States Parties in February 1991. In keeping with the Convention's requirement that "consideration be given to equitable geographic distribution as well as to the principal legal systems," the Committee's first members were from Barbados, Brazil, Burkina Faso, Egypt, Peru, Philippines, Portugal, Russia, Sweden, and Zimbabwe. Members are elected for four-year terms, with elections being held every two years. Five of the members elected at the first meeting of States Parties were given two-year terms, thus ensuring that only half of the Committee's membership would change at any given election. At the 1993 meeting of States Parties, all committee members whose terms had expired were re-elected, except the delegate from Brazil, who did not run for re-election and was replaced by another Brazilian national. The only change at the 1995 election resulted from the withdrawal of the member from Peru. All other members were re-elected and a member from Israel was elected to fill the vacancy left by the Peruvian member. The early continuity of the Committee's membership was disrupted during the 1997 and 1999 elections. In 1997, one original member chose not to run for re-election and four others did not succeed in their re-election bids. Only one of the five members who were up for re-election survived the election process. There were similar shifts resulting from the 1999 election, which resulted in the replacement of all remaining original Committee members.

The Committee's earliest sessions were devoted to drafting its Provisional Rules of Procedure and what are known as the "Guidelines on Reporting." (Guidelines). To make the reporting process less arduous, the Guidelines cluster the Convention's articles into related groupings. The Guidelines are divided into eight sections. Sections I and II ask comprehensive questions about the country (demographics, etc.), the measures that have been taken to implement the Convention and how the State Party defines the word "child." The remaining sections cover: III. General Principles; IV. Civil Rights and Freedoms; V. Family Environment and Alternative Care; VI. Basic Health and Welfare; VII. Education, Leisure and Cultural Activities; and VIII. Special Protection Measures.

The first States Parties' reports were received in 1992 and the Committee began its public formal evaluation of the reports in January 1993. At this session, the Committee examined the reports of Bolivia, Egypt, the Russian Federation, Sudan, Sweden, and Vietnam. By the end of its session in January 1999, the Committee had examined about seventy States Parties reports. In other words, the Committee averages approximately six reports per session.

Originally, the States Parties voted to give the Committee one two-week session each year to handle its work. However, due to the tremendous speed with which the Convention was ratified, it was obvious that this would not be sufficient. The schedule was quickly expanded to two three-week sessions and then to three four-week sessions. The Committee typically holds its sessions in January, May–June, and September–October. The first three weeks are devoted to State Party report hearings, which are open to the public. The fourth week is given over to what is known as a "pre-sessional" meeting, in which the Committee reviews the States Parties' reports that will be examined at the next session. It is during these pre-sessional meetings, which are closed to the public, that the Committee is able to exercise its article 45 powers to obtain information that will shed light on the accuracy of the States Parties' reports. This, in turn, enables the Committee to formulate a list of "issues" that the State Party is requested to answer in writing prior to its oral hearing.

IV. UNICEF, Other U. N. Bodies, and Non-governmental Organizations

Article 45 is unique among U.N. human rights treaty implementation processes, because it gives the Committee powers beyond simply examining States Parties' reports and transmitting its conclusions to the General Assembly. It also empowers the Committee to: a) obtain information from sources other than the States Parties themselves; b) assist States Parties in meeting their Convention obligations by providing technical assistance; and c) petition the Secretary-General to have the United Nations undertake studies "on specific issues relating to the rights of the child."

In laying out the sources with which the Committee on the Rights of the Child can exchange information, paragraph (a) of Article 45 lists: the United Nations Children's Fund (UNICEF), the specialized agencies, other U.N. organs, and other competent bodies. Drafters of the Convention on the Rights of the Child specifically intended that the words "other competent bodies" should mean NGOs. However, the Committee has given these words the broadest possible interpretation, and allows any reliable source that can provide information relating to a particular State Party's report to transmit that information to the Committee. Depending on the situation, that source may be invited to confer with the Committee during its pre-sessional meeting to explain the situation of children in that particular country. The Committee's Article 45 powers assist it in determining the veracity of the material contained in the States Parties reports.

Paragraph (b) of Article 45 similarly includes NGOs (other competent bodies), along with the specialized agencies and UNICEF, as being among the resources it can tap to assist countries that are having difficulty in meeting the Convention's standards. The Secretary-General regularly issues a report compiling the Committee's requests for assistance on behalf of these countries. The 1997 Note by the Secretary-General listed forty countries that had made such requests. Included in this Note was a request from Honduras for support from the World Bank, the International Monetary Fund, and donor countries for disaster assistance, as well as for help from the United Nations High Commissioner for Refugees, in protecting refugees. Other types of assistance requests listed in the 1997 Note were for aid in: establishing child labor standards; application of juvenile justice guidelines; vaccine sources; health aid; child rights training programs for professionals; and assistance not only in drafting child rights legislation, but also in drafting the State Party's report to the Committee.

V. Examination of State Party Reports

As explained above, the Committee uses its pre-sessional meeting for two purposes. First, it makes an effort to gain as much information as possible about the honesty of the State Party's report. It does this by obtaining information from such organizations as UNICEF, the International Labor Organization, the United Nations High Commissioner for Refugees, and the World Health Organization, as well as from international and national NGOs. Significantly, it is this latter group that frequently supplies the most important information.

At the conclusion of its pre-sessional meeting, the Committee drafts a set of "issue questions" that are based on information supplied in the State Party's report and material gleaned from informal sources that may spotlight omissions in the report. The Committee then transmits the issue questions to the State Party, which is asked to submit written responses to the questions prior to the State Party's oral hearing before the Committee. This is not unreasonable because there is usually a period of a few months between the time that the questions are transmitted to the State Party and the oral hearing. For example, the Committee's pre-sessional meeting to prepare for its Twentieth Session (January 11–29, 1999) was held October 12–16, 1998.

The Committee devotes three half-day sessions to the oral examination of each State Party's report. Typically, a government will send a delegation of several persons from different ministries to answer the Committee's questions. The dialogue tends to follow the pattern of the Reporting Guidelines, clustering the discussion of articles and issue questions into groups under headings such as Civil and Political Rights or Health and Education. At the end of these sessions, Committee members make comments and then the head of the government delegation replies. That is the conclusion of the oral examination. The final step in the reporting and examination process is the report—the Concluding Observations of the Committee—which is submitted to the U.N. General Assembly.

The Committee drafts its Concluding Observations taking into account the content of the State Party's report, the written replies to the issue questions, information from outside sources and the oral dialogue. In its Concluding Observations the Committee comments on the positive factors of the State Party's overall presentation and makes recommendations about how to improve what the Committee refers to as "areas of concern." The entire process is recorded in U.N. documents and almost all of the elements of this process are available on the United Nation High Commissioner for Human Rights web site, including: the States Parties reports, the Summary Records of the oral hearings, and the Committee's Concluding Observations.

Cynthia Price Cohen & Susan Kilbourne, *Jurisprudence of the Committee on the Rights of the Child: A Guide for Research and Analysis*
19 Michigan Journal of International Law 633 (1998)

....

B. General Trends in Committee Jurisprudence

An examination of the tables reveals trends toward increasing comprehensiveness in the Concluding Observations. The Committee's Concluding Observations for the third session, in January 1993, contained an average of sixteen paragraphs. By the sixteenth session, in October 1997, the Concluding Observations averaged forty-five paragraphs. The Committee's comments have become more detailed and complex. For example, one of the Committee's substantive recommendations to Viet Nam, during the third session in 1993, involved juvenile justice:

> The appropriate amendments should be made to the Penal Code in order to adequately reflect the provisions contained in Articles 37, 39, and 40 of the Convention as well as the relevant provisions of the Code of Conduct for Law Enforcement Officials and other international standards in this field, such as the "Beijing Rules," the "Riyadh Guidelines" and the Rules for the Protection of Juveniles Deprived of their Liberty. In this connection the Committee recommends that a training course for law enforcement personnel be organized by the Center for Human Rights in Viet Nam.

A similar paragraph found in the Committee's Concluding Observations for Lao People's Democratic Republic in 1997 provides much more detail:

> The Committee recommends that legal reform in the field of administration of juvenile justice be pursued and take fully into account the Convention on the Rights of the Child, in particular Articles 37, 39 and 40 as well as other relevant standards in this field such as the Beijing Rules, the Riyadh Guidelines and the United Nations Rules for the Protection of Juveniles Deprived of their Liberty. Particular attention should be paid to the prevention of juvenile delinquency, the protection of the rights of children deprived of their liberty, respect for fundamental rights and legal safeguards in all aspects of the juvenile justice system and full independence and impartiality of the judiciary dealing with juveniles. The Committee also encourages the State party to explore alternatives to institutional

care as well as traditional mechanisms of conciliation, as long as the principles and guarantees of the Convention are respected. The Committee also recommends that the State party avails itself of the technical assistance programs of the Office of the High Commissioner for Human Rights and the Crime Prevention and Criminal Justice Division of the United Nations.

This increased comprehensiveness probably reflects the growing familiarity of Committee members with the reviewing process, the issues involved in the Convention, and the resources available to assist States Parties. Whatever the reason, the increased comprehensiveness allows a more complete understanding of the Convention's provisions.

The tables also show a tendency for the Committee to emphasize certain sections of the Guidelines, both procedural and substantive. For example, with only three exceptions, the Committee uniformly identified paragraph 9 of the Guidelines, pertaining to general measures of implementation (e.g., harmonizing national law with the Convention and coordinating the implementation and monitoring of the Convention) as an area requiring additional measures for full implementation. In addition, the Committee almost always observed that the allocation of resources to children's programs and the training of professionals who deal with children were in need of significant improvement. Cooperation with NGOs was also frequently noted with both approval and encouragement for further measures; and beginning with the fifth session in January 1994, the Committee consistently emphasized the need for increased publicity for the Convention.

Implementation of the articles in Guidelines, Section III, dealing with the Convention's general principles, is among the substantive areas subject to regular comment by the Committee. The Committee has cited as needing improvement at least one of the articles corresponding to Section III in every State Party report reviewed. Those observations reveal a clear emphasis on the need for better implementation of the Article 2 guarantee of protection against discrimination, and an increasing concern about the implementation of the Article 12 assurance of respect for the views of the child.

In addition to these general principles, the Committee regularly comments on several other substantive subject categories. The subject categories of juvenile justice and the deprivation of liberty were often cited for improvement, as were the areas of child labor, abuse and neglect, and education. Substantive issues that have been noted by the Committee with increasing frequency include rehabilitation; birth registration; protection from harmful media, such as violent or pornographic television; and corporal punishment (usually cited as part of the issue of violence against children, Article 19).

In contrast, only one subject category was never cited in any of the Committee's Concluding Observations: the illicit transfer and non-return of the child. Two other categories have received only minimal attention from the Committee: the recovery of maintenance, which was noted only three times; and leisure and recreation, which was noted only six times.

C. Factors Influencing Committee Jurisprudence

The developing jurisprudence of the Committee on the Rights of the Child is influenced by many factors. While the most significant of these factors is probably the nature of the information made available to the Committee, other factors include trends in the jurisprudence of other treaty bodies; changes in child development theory; and the personalities and expertise of Committee members. Although most of these influences can be attributed to exterior forces, some are the result of Committee action. A typical example of the latter is the Committee's establishment of General Discussion Days as a forum for topics of general interest to States Parties. General Discussion Days grew out of the "general discussion" provision of rule 75 of the Committee's Provisional Rules of

Procedure, and have become an annual event, in which topics such as children and war, economic exploitation of children, juvenile delinquency, and children with disabilities are discussed. Another Committee practice that may have influenced its interpretation of the Convention has been a series of "on site" visits to such places as Latin America, Asia and Africa.

Perhaps the most significant outside influence is the input the Committee receives under Article 45 of the Convention. This article gives the Committee the power to obtain information from various United Nations bodies, such as the International Labor Organization, the World Health Organization and UNICEF. Article 45 also provides for information to be submitted to the Committee by NGOs and scholars.

The extent to which outside information resources were involved in the review of the United Kingdom's report illustrates the potential effect that such information can have on the Committee. In that case, the Committee was strongly urged by a British NGO, End Physical Punishment of Children (EPOCH), to take a stand against the corporal punishment of children. EPOCH is leading an international effort to make corporal punishment of children by anyone—including parents—illegal. After meeting with representatives of EPOCH, the Committee became sensitive to this issue and began calling for States Parties to consider national legislation prohibiting all corporal punishment, including within the family. Typically, the Committee has called for the State Party to:

> take all appropriate measures, including of a legislative nature, with the aim of prohibiting corporal punishment in private schools and at home. The Committee also suggests that awareness raising campaigns be conducted to ensure that alternative forms of discipline are administered in a manner consistent with the child's human dignity and in conformity with the Convention.

This is particularly notable because while the Committee has read this prohibition into the language of the Convention, the drafters of the Convention pointedly made no reference to corporal punishment.

A related influential factor is the lack of resources available to the Committee. Given the Committee's demanding workload, limited schedule, and lack of research assistance, the Committee members have little time to contemplate and develop a consistent philosophy. Under such conditions, the Committee is vulnerable to the persuasion of those who provide them with data, as occurred during the review of the report from the United Kingdom. While one may agree with the outcome from the U.K. review, future influences on the Committee may not be so positive. However, as the Committee's jurisprudence becomes more established, the dangers of undue influence will be considerably less.

Notes and Questions

1. International law is notorious for its lack of effective enforcement structures. In recent years, the rise of the post-conflict international criminal tribunals, the permanent International Criminal Court, as well as the creation of the World Trade Organization, a body with a strong enforcement arm, have led some to argue that international law is becoming more truly "legal". As mentioned above, the UNCRC relies on a system of state reporting, with review carried out by a specialized committee. What are the dangers inherent in the state reporting system? What are its strengths? Does the general public know much about the personnel of the Committee on the Rights of the Child?

2. If you had been part of the drafting process of the UNCRC, what sort of enforcement mechanism would you have wished to see?

―――――――

2. Examples from Country Reports, NGO Alternative Reports, and Concluding Observations by the Committee on the Rights of the Child

States parties to the UNCRC are required to submit an initial report, followed by revised and updated reports at intervals of five years. The Committee on the Rights of the Child has provided clear guidance to states as to how they should organize and present these reports. Parties have been told that their "Reports should provide information on the measures adopted by the state party to give effect to the rights set forth in the Convention and on progress made in the enjoyment of those rights and should indicate the factors and difficulties, if any, affecting the degree of fulfillment of the obligations under the Convention."[13] The Committee emphasizes its "supportive role in fostering effective implementation of the Convention and in encouraging international cooperation, as called for in article 45." The Committee walks through each section of the UNCRC, encouraging parties to indicate what measures they have taken to facilitate the exercise by children of the various rights set out in the Convention. The Committee asks for a "structured discussion" which proceeds in a "logical order," namely general measures of implementation, definition of the child, general principles, civil rights and freedoms, family environment and alternative care, basic health and welfare, education, leisure and cultural activities, special protection measures (including children in emergency situations and children in conflict with the law), and children belonging to a minority or indigenous group.[14]

While these reports provide access to a great deal of important information, it must be recognized that their form and content tend to be stylized and distancing. As with any form of "confession" for which there are no serious consequences, it is worth considering whether the overall function of the reports is to increase or reduce the sense of urgency around children's rights issues. To the extent that the focus is shifted from reality itself to the content of reports written according to a formula, the reports must be said to have, at best, an ambiguous function. States parties, not surprisingly, wish to emphasize their best efforts and minimize negative impressions.

What follows is a small sample taken from the reports submitted by states parties to the UNCRC to date. Most of the readings chosen are on the theme of "family environment and alternative care." After each selection, related commentary taken from the "alternative report" submitted by child welfare NGOs working within those states has been included. Following that are the reactions of the Committee to the same issues. Note that the "alternative reports" presented to the Committee by NGOs tend to be far less diplomatic than the state reports, as one would expect. Not surprisingly, NGOs use the opportunity to express frustration with the performance of the state. Presenting an "alternative report" to the Committee on the Rights of the Child is, after all, a rare chance to gain the attention of the outside world with respect to the reality of children's lives. As a creature of the United Nations, the Committee itself speaks the language of diplomacy, presenting itself

―――――――

13. See General Guidelines Regarding the Form and Content of Periodic Reports to be Submitted by States Parties Under Article 44, Paragraph 1(b) of the Convention, Committee on the Rights of the Child, 20 November 1996, available at http://www.unhchr.ch/tbs/doc.nsf/(symbol)/CRC.C.58.En?Opendocument.

14. See Overview of the working methods of the Committee on the Rights of the Child, available at http://www2.ohchr.org/english/bodies/crc/workingmethods.htm.

as a partner, and assuming the best with respect to the state's motives. At times, the horror of the underlying facts is at odds with the bland tone of the Committee's report.

As you read, consider the utility of this kind of process. What do the states parties lose or gain by the reporting system? What is the Committee trying to achieve in its concluding observations and comments on the state's progress? What if the gap between the descriptions used by the states and their NGOs is too great? Do such discrepancies cast doubt on the entire reporting process?

The following section is taken from Brazil's 2003 report to the Committee, under the heading "family environment and alternative care." Brazil has had severe problems with street children, many of whom have suffered abuse at the hands of the police and other authorities.

Brazil State Party Report
December 2003
available at http://www.unhchr.ch/tbs/doc.nsf/(Symbol)/04fd3a
430ce8f7eac1256ee60048a773?Opendocument

V. FAMILY ENVIRONMENT AND OTHER TYPES OF GUARDIANSHIP

G. Children deprived of family environment

Boys and girls who live and work in the street

242. One of the problems that most perturbs society, in the context of children and adolescents deprived of family life, concerns those that have made the street their survival zone, the so-called "street-children". This problem has manifested itself strongly, particularly since the late 1970s.

243. Various studies and surveys have been carried out in the country in order to estimate the numbers, the causes of the phenomenon and the most efficient methods "to take the children off the street". Today it is known that the number of children and adolescents who actually live on the streets, without any family ties, is much lower than the estimates which put it in the millions. In the city of São Paulo, the largest in South America, for example, a survey carried out by the Municipal Secretary for the Family and Social Welfare showed that about 3,000 children and adolescents frequented the street—but did not live in it—and that only 466 actually lived in the street.

244. The majority of them spend the day on the street, selling small items, sweets and candies, engaging in petty crimes and begging. At night, they return home, many to a family dwelling. However, the situation of those who sleep out on the street in the big cities is dramatic; there they are exposed to all kinds of exploitation, substance abuse and child prostitution. Although the basic cause is related to poverty, other factors equally play a part: ill-treatment and abuse, changes in patterns of behaviour, crises and family ruptures, and the lack of education, sport and leisure compatible with the needs and aspirations of young people.

245. The way of dealing with the problem, prior to the 1988 Constitution and the ECA, was marked by repressive action, the rounding-up of children and adolescents and their placement in homes and shelters. Only in the mid-1980s did a group of technicians from the institution then called FUNABEM, with the support of UNICEF, question Government actions, which were not only inefficient but harmful and unjust, and began to look at alternative experiences of childcare that were being carried out in the country under the auspices of non-governmental organizations. The activities of this pioneer group were

given the name of the "Project for Community Alternative Care for Street Children" by the *Pastoral do Menor* of the Archdiocese of São Paulo.

246. In 1985, one of the most influential non-governmental organizations for the enforcement of children and adolescents' rights in Brazil was created: the National Street Children Movement, which together with other human rights NGOs, particularly *Pastoral do Menor*, began to play an important role in elaborating article 227 of the Constitution, the Statute of the Child and Adolescent (ECA) and disseminating the principles and dictates of the Convention. The Movement also made a contribution, through the experiences of its militants, to reformulating public social assistance programmes. The Movement has already staged National Meetings of Street Children, which have been helping to increase the participation of children and adolescents in discussing their own problems and making society aware of the question of children who are excluded and are victims of violence.

———

Alternative Report:

Report of Civil Society on the Situation of the Rights of the Child and the Adolescent in Brazil

(2004)

available at http://blog.comunidadesegura.org/focrib/
category/government-accountability/

Organization: ANCED

THE MURDER OF CHILDREN AND ADOLESCENTS IN BRAZIL

RESPONSIBILITY

Impunity: identify and make accountable

The degree of impunity among murderers of children and adolescents in Brazil results from the authorities' failure to identify and charge the authors of murders committed against children and adolescents.

. . . .

Several Brazilian researchers have been unanimous about the undeniable impunity for persons who murder children and adolescents in Brazil.

. . . .

DEATH SQUADS

The action of death squads in murders of children and adolescents is the object of various studies, among them the dissertation "The Extermination of Children and Adolescents in Brazil", covering the period from the late 1980s to the beginning of the 90s, where Nicodemos affirms that there were three categories of exterminators of children at the time: 1) those who give the orders, usually merchants, 2) the executors, mainly military policemen or former policemen, private security guards, drug pushers and civilians, local people who live in the poor communities and 3) the advocates of the extermination, persons who occupy prominent positions and status in the community.

The Global Justice Center proves the perpetuation, until today of the homicidal action of the death squads or group of "merchants, business men and other segments of the society" to abolish undesirable social groups, that supposedly are constituted by criminals. It informs that the profile of the victims is primordially poor young men who live on the outskirts of the big cities and aged between 14 and 30.

. . . .

Adorno explains that in the 1980s, urban vigilantes who hunted bandits in the peripheries or groups of military policemen acting out of uniform formed the death squads. The Global Justice Center confirms Adorno's hypothesis regarding the shift in the profile of death squads during the 1990s, indicating that currently they are also working for the drug-trafficking organizations. They continue, however, with their mission of social cleansing, or extinction of social groups considered undesirable, especially in the outskirts of urban centers.

Police Action

. . . .

The police are responsible for many of the murders registered in the country. In his study, Cano identifies a group of policemen within the institution of the Military Police in Rio de Janeiro, which is responsible for a good part of the murders caused by firearms (PAF), in faked situations of 'armed confrontation'. Self-defense is the most common formula to guarantee impunity for the aggressors in those cases. As the Military Police is responsible for the ostensive patrolling in the city, it justifies the committed executions with simulated 'armed confrontations'. They take the corpses of the victims to the hospitals, threaten witnesses with death and register the criminal incident at the police station as "Resisting Arrest".

Inácio Cano examines the characteristics of these false armed confrontations and gathers evidence that show that the municipality of Rio de Janeiro has a routine of extrajudicial executions. He indicates that there is a "deliberate intention to kill the opponent when: a) he is already caught or dominated; b) there are other obvious ways to catch him without taking his life or c) he does not represent a threat that justifies the use of firearms. Any of these three elements characterizes an execution".

. . . .

A large number of cases documented by Amnesty International in 2003, that raised accusations of concealment and interference in the investigations by members of the police, strongly suggest that the majority of the deaths committed by policemen follow a systematic model of extrajudicial executions or, in the best case, excessive use of force.

An former Ombudsman of the State Police informed Amnesty International that when he compared police reports on a killing with the legal forensic report he often found divergent results: the police report would declare that the victim died during a shooting because he did not surrender, while the legal forensic report in general showed that the fatal bullets had entered the back and were shot from a short distance, under circumstances that suggested that the person was a victim of an extra judicial execution."

———————

CRC Committee's Report:

United Nations Convention on the Rights of the Child [CRC], Concluding Observations of the Committee on the Rights of the Child

37th Sess., U.N. Doc. CRC/C/15/Add.241 (2004)
available at http://www.unhchr.ch/tbs/doc.nsf/(symbol)/
CRC.C.15.Add.241.En?Opendocument

Special Protection Measures

Street Children

64. The Committee expresses its grave concern at the significant number of street children and the vulnerability of these children to extra-judicial killings, various forms of violence, including torture, sexual abuse and exploitation, and the lack of a systematic and comprehensive strategy to address the situation and protect these children, and the very poor registration of missing children by the police.

65. The Committee recommends that the State Party:

a) Develop a comprehensive strategy to address the high number of street children, with the aim of reducing and preventing this phenomenon;

b) Ensure that street children are provided with adequate nutrition and shelter as well as with health care and educational opportunities in order to support their full development, and provide them with adequate protection and assistance.

The selection that follows concerns the issue of juveniles in the Kenyan justice system, also found under the subject heading "alternative care." Violence against children in the educational and justice systems has been extensively covered by human rights watchdog groups, and widely documented. Note the tone taken by the Kenyan government and the Committee, respectively, and compare this with the tone of outrage and urgency evident in the alternative NGO report.

Kenya State Party Report

February 2001
available at http://www.unhchr.ch/tbs/doc.nsf/(Symbol)/a8d883af
803683a8c1256a96002f5004?Opendocument

IX. Special Protection Measures: Articles 22, 38, 39, 40, 37 (B)–(D), 32, 33, 34, 35, 36, 30

B. Children involved with the system of administration of juvenile justice

1. Article 40. Children within the system of administration of juvenile justice

. . . .

484. A child is entitled to due process rights and enjoys additional safeguards provided by the Children and Young Persons Act which is the principal statute on juvenile justice in Kenya. The Act establishes a juvenile court for the purpose of hearing all charges against persons under the age of 18 years, except where such persons are charged jointly with adults. There is only one Juvenile Court in Kenya which is situated in Nairobi. In other towns adult courts are converted to juvenile courts on an ad hoc basis.

....

486. The procedure for hearing a case involving a child is similar to that applied in other courts, both in terms of applying the law on criminal procedure and the law of evidence. The Children and Young Persons Act provides additional safeguards to a child by allowing the attendance of his or her parent or guardian if he or she can be found and resides at a reasonable distance. Furthermore, the Act protects a child's privacy firstly by restricting the categories of persons who may be allowed into a juvenile court to members and officers of the court, their advocates, witnesses and others concerned with the case; parents and guardians; and other persons specifically authorized by the court to be present. Secondly, the Act prohibits publication of the name and address of the child, the school which he or she is attending, or any other way to identify the child without authorization from the court.

....

488. In dealing with every case of a person under 18 years, the court is required to have regard to his or her welfare and must, in a proper case, take steps to remove him or her from undesirable surroundings and to ensure that proper provision is made for his or her maintenance. Words such as "conviction" and "sentence" must not be used in respect of a child.

489. A sentence of death must not be pronounced on, or recorded against a person if at the time the offence was committed he or she was under the age of 18 years. Furthermore, a person under the age of 18 cannot be sentenced to imprisonment except where the court is of the opinion that he or she cannot be suitably dealt with in any other way permitted by the law; in such cases the court should record its opinion and the reasons for it. The imprisonment must be confirmed by the High Court, and while in prison the child must be confined separately from adult prisoners and must not be allowed to associate with them. The warrant of committal must clearly show the age of the child. Other ways of dealing with a young offender include discharge of the offender, probation, corporal punishment, payment of compensation or costs, committal to the care of a fit person or an approved voluntary institution or approved school (if the child is less that 15 years of age), and committal to a borstal institution.

Constraints

490. One of the difficulties experienced in the administration of juvenile justice is the overlap of discipline and protection cases. This weakness arises from the Children and Young Persons Act which does not provide a clear distinction between a child in need of protection and a child in need of discipline. A child in need of protection may easily be processed through the juvenile justice system as one in need of discipline.

491. The child's due process rights are compromised by inadequate legal aid services throughout the criminal justice process and other support services and structures essential for the expeditious disposal of cases. For example, the inadequacy of specialized courts to handle matters affecting children reduces the time required to focus on children's cases.

492. Overreliance on institutionalization of offenders as a corrective measure has also been identified as a major weakness of the juvenile justice system. This weakness is attributable to many factors including the inadequacy of pre-sentencing reports by social workers. Besides the high cost factor in running correctional institutions the imbalance between institutions which cater for boys and girls can only mean that girls (who have been allocated one institution nationally) suffer a greater disadvantage. The use of non-institutional community options is currently being advocated.

493. The proposed Children Act provides extensive provisions on the treatment of child offenders which include the right to legal aid at public expense where the child is unable

to obtain it, and the right to expeditious disposal of a case. The proposed Act also outlaws the use of imprisonment and corporal punishment as corrective.

2. Article 37 (b)-(d). Children deprived of their liberty, including any form of detention, imprisonment or placement in custodial settings

494. Section 72 of the Constitution guarantees the individual's right to liberty. Children's personal liberty can be infringed only if it is for the purpose of their education and welfare.

495. Section 73 of the Constitution outlaws slavery and servitude. This is complemented by sections 264–266 of the Penal Code which make it a criminal offence to buy or dispose of slaves, to be a habitual dealer in slaves, or to subject a person to unlawful compulsory labour.

496. Under section 17 A of the Children and Young Persons Act, a court may make an order committing a child to the care of a fit person or approved society. Children affected include children in need of protection, discipline and care.

497. In Kenya, the police are responsible for criminal investigations and arrests. Prosecution is the responsibility of the Attorney-General. However, in practice, prosecutions are sometimes done through the police. The Kenya Police Act (Cap. 84, Laws of Kenya) contains general provisions on the conduct of criminal investigations. It has no special provisions on the conduct of the police in relation to children. However, the Children and Young Persons Act requires that accused persons under 18 years should be kept in remand homes and not in prison or police stations. The Children's Department usually provides advice in cases affecting children.

498. Under the Children and Young Persons Act, children may legally be deprived of their liberty where they have been in conflict with the criminal law, where they need social care, or are neglected or abused. In these instances, children may be placed in a juvenile remand home awaiting trial. The lack of facilities makes this difficult. For instance, there is only one officially designated Juvenile Court in the country. In many cases, normal courts are converted into juvenile courts. Normal courts lack the proper atmosphere for hearing cases involving children.

499. Kenya has 12 juvenile remand homes. These are inadequate to cater for the needs of all children in conflict with the law. This means that some children are held with adults in prison remand homes. This practice violates the spirit of the Convention on the Rights of the Child.

500. Kenya has tried to apply the United Nations Guidelines for the Prevention of Juvenile Delinquency and the Standard Minimum Rules for the Administration of Juvenile Justice in the administration of juvenile justice. There are rules and regulations for remand homes allowing for contact between children deprived of their liberty and their families. However, these institutions are few. This involves long distances between remand homes and the child's home. This compromises the child's rights. Attempts have been made to increase the number of juvenile remand homes and to bring juvenile justice closer to the child.

501. There is no law guaranteeing prompt legal assistance for children deprived of their liberty. However, children have the right to challenge a decision to deprive them of their liberty. NGOs such as the Federation for Women Lawyers (FIDA), Kituo Cha Sheria (Legal Advisory Centre) and the Law Society of Kenya (LSK) provide legal representation. To improve this capacity, children's officers are currently undergoing para-legal training at the Kenya School of Law. Approximately 60 officers are trained every year. These include children's officers, police officers, protection officers and magistrates. Some of these have

also been trained on juvenile justice administration, prevention of juvenile crimes and treatment of young offenders by experts from the United Nations Asia and Far East Institute for the Prevention of Crime and the Treatment of Offenders (UNAFEI) in Tokyo.

———————

Alternative Report:

Supplementary Report to Kenya's First Country Report on Implementation of the UN Convention on the Rights of the Child
(2001)
available at http://www.crin.org/resources/infoDetail.asp?ID=2312

Organization: **Kenya Alliance for Advancement of Children**

Chapter Eight: Special Protection Measures

2.0 Juvenile Justice (Article 40)

2.1 *Situation Analysis:* The State report describes the law relating to juvenile justice as *"satisfactory"*, and proceeds to conclude that *"the treatment of children in Kenyan criminal law promotes their sense of dignity and worth."* This description, however, contrasts with the actual situation on the ground. Up to 85% of the children who go through the system do not deserve to be exposed to the criminal justice process. Surveys have established that only 15% of the children in the juvenile justice system are actually categorized as offenders. Of these, only a small fraction fall in the category of serious offences like murder, rape or robbery with violence. However, all the children undergo the same process within the system and are confined in the same institutions where little is done to separate children by age or reason for confinement.

2.2 Of the 1,864 children who were taken to the Nairobi Juvenile court in 1997, about 80% were charged with vagrancy. The Vagrancy Act defined a vagrant as *"a person having no fixed abode and not giving a satisfactory account of himself."* Although the Act was repealed in 1997, the police continue to arbitrarily arrest and confine children. In almost 60% of the cases, the court records did not indicate what had happened to the children. The only records available indicated that 14.1% had been committed to approved schools, 16.8% repatriated to their homes, 8.7% acquitted or their cases withdrawn or handed to guardians, 0.6% fined and 0.9% caned.

2.3 There is only one permanent juvenile court in Kenya, located in the capital Nairobi. In all other areas, the normal criminal court has to occasionally convert to a "juvenile court." There is neither special selection nor training of the presiding officers on how to handle juveniles. They simply learn "on the job." There is no State-funded legal aid for children who cannot afford legal representation. Section 27 of the Penal Code allows corporal punishment for boys. (Corporal punishment is currently lawful in schools and institutional rehabilitation facilities).

2.4 Children spend the first 24–48 hours in police cells before being taken to court. Children of 15 years and above tend to be confined in adult remand centers, where they are likely to be held together with adults. The remand period is often lengthy. A study undertaken in 1998 found that about 50% of the children remanded during the period spent more than six months in custody. Children in need of care and protection are routinely lumped with those charged with offences. A survey in Nairobi has shown that police pick up both groups of children from the streets and hold them in the cells before taking them to court. At the court, they are kept in the same holding cells; called to court and share the same benches. At the juvenile remand home, no distinction is made between the two groups. Even the approved school is a destination for both groups of children.

2.5 There is, generally, over-reliance on institutional care, even for children who are non-offenders and children who are first or minor offenders. Although the state report indicates that the government is becoming more aware of the need for community-based alternatives, little is being done to change the system. Conditions in the residential facilities are pathetic and appropriate programs are lacking. For example, there are approximately 4,800 children housed in the 11 approved schools across the country. The schools are designed to "rehabilitate" children found guilty of offences, but in practice, children needing care and protection are also sent there.

2.6 Children seeking both civil and criminal justice for violation of their rights face many problems. These include lack of legal representation, difficult judicial procedures and insensitive methods of interrogation. The result is that many children continue to suffer violations of their rights, including disinheritance and sexual abuse. The unfamiliar and often unfriendly court environment makes it particularly difficult for children who have been sexually abused.

2.7 There is evidence that the child minders (police and administrative officers) frequently intimidate and manhandle the children, leaving them feeling helpless and unwanted. They come out of the system badly shaken and traumatized.

2.8 Even after the Children Bill is enacted, there will still be a need to amend 63 pieces of legislation that touch on child-related issues. Otherwise, there will be several contradictions in the law, which will stand in the way of justice for children. Certain improvements in the law, such as legal assistance for children, operations of the Family Court Division and separation of children charged with offences from those requiring care and protection will require financing.

2.9 Recommendations for the government:

- A child-friendly social policy should be instituted to rescue and re-direct children in need of care and protection before they enter the criminal justice system.

- Magistrates and other personnel who handle juvenile cases should be specially trained;

- The government should take steps to provide children with legal assistance in their cases. Magistrates should make an extra effort to ensure that children understand the nature of their cases. Family members should participate in the proceedings;

- Community-based rehabilitation as an alternative to institutional care should be given priority. Placing children in residential institutions should only be done as a last resort, and for the shortest period necessary;

- Court practice should be changed so that cases of children who are *in need of care and protection* are not treated as criminal cases. Such children should not be committed to the same institutions as children who are convicted of crimes;

- A set of guiding principles should be formulated to direct law enforcement personnel in dealing with juvenile cases, based on the CRC, the OAU Charter on the Rights and Welfare of Children and the 1985 UN Standard Minimum Rules on Administration of Juvenile Justice;

- Prevention should be the ultimate focus. This will require full government commitment and donor support. It should cover community-based vocational training centers, drug and alcohol rehabilitation centers and "Safe Houses" for emergency placement of children at risk.

CRC Committee's Report:

United Nations Convention on the Rights of the Child [CRC], Concluding Observations of the Committee on the Rights of the Child

Kenya, 28th Sess., U.N. Doc. CRC/C/15/Add. 160 (2001), *available at* http://www1.umn.edu/humanrts/crc/kenya2001.html

Special Protection Measures

Administration of juvenile justice

63. The Committee notes with concern that the juvenile justice system does not cover the entire country and that there is only one juvenile court in the State party. While acknowledging the State party's efforts to implement a Diversion Programme for children in conflict with the law, the Committee also expresses its concern about the quality of the juvenile justice system generally.

64. The Committee recommends that the State party:

(a) Take all appropriate measures, including the enactment of the Children Bill, to implement a juvenile justice system in conformity with the Convention, in particular articles 37, 39 and 40, and of other United Nations standards in this field, such as the United Nations Standard Minimum Rules for the Administration of Juvenile Justice (the Beijing Rules), the United Nations Guidelines for the Prevention of Juvenile Delinquency (the Riyadh Guidelines), the United Nations Rules for the Protection of Juveniles Deprived of their Liberty and the Vienna Guidelines for Action on Children in the Criminal Justice System;

(b) Use deprivation of liberty (institutionalization) only as a measure of last resort and for the shortest possible time and, in that regard, implement the Diversion Programme fully and with the widest scope possible, as an alternative to deprivation of liberty;

(c) Ensure that children remain in contact with their families while in the juvenile justice system;

(d) Include training programmes on relevant international standards for all professionals involved in the administration of juvenile justice;

(e) Abolish the use of corporal punishment in the juvenile justice system;

(f) Improve conditions in detention facilities;

(g) Strengthen reparation, rehabilitation and reintegration programmes;

(h) Ensure that cases involving children in need of care and protection are not treated as criminal cases; and

(i) Consider seeking technical assistance from, inter alia, the Office of the High Commissioner for Human Rights, the Centre for International Crime Prevention, the International Network on Juvenile Justice and UNICEF, through the Co-ordination Panel on Technical Advice in Juvenile Justice.

Korea continues to have a serious problem with the abandonment and institutionalization of children. Like many other countries, Korea struggles to know what to do with a population of children living outside parental care. On one hand, the UNCRC encourages States to find family-based solutions to this problem. On the other hand, the Committee is not supportive of large scale international adoption, and adequate levels of domestic adoption may be hard to achieve.

Korea State Party Report

June 2002
available at http://www.unhchr.ch/tbs/doc.nsf/(Symbol)/d691f34f4fc
5584dc1256d2b0034395c?Opendocument

V. FAMILY ENVIRONMENT AND ALTERNATIVE CARE

A. Parental guidance and responsibilities (arts. 5 and 18, para. 2)

....

83. Among the support measures for childcare is the Labour Standards Act, which ensures 60 days of paid maternity leave and paid nursing time, and the Sexual Equality Employment Act, which guarantees one year of childcare leave, as stated specifically in paragraph 79 of the initial report.

84. The Republic of Korea has passed and enforced laws ensuring that the State assists parents in carrying out their responsibilities and raising a child. These are the Mother and Fatherless Child Health Act, the Child Welfare Act, the Infant Care Act and the Protection of Minimum Living Standards Act. The concrete purposes of each Act is stated in paragraph 80 of the initial report.

E. Children deprived of a family environment (art. 20)

93. Children must be born and brought up with their family. Having a family environment is a child's right and is essential for their healthy upbringing and development. However, when a child cannot have such an environment, or remaining in the parents' home is detrimental to the child's development, a childcare institution may be a necessary substitute. In 1998, 5,112 children were placed in special care facilities or welfare institutions, accounting for 55 per cent of the total of 9,292 needy children.

94. The number of residential facilities for children, established to protect orphans resulting from the Korean War, has decreased since the 1970s. Residential care has been accepted as an alternative form of care for children in need. One reason residential care has been heavily used to care for needy children is because suitable alternative care arrangements have not been developed. To develop a broad range of alternative care environments is one of the urgent challenges Korea is facing to improve the welfare of its children in need.

95. Foster family care as an alternative to institutional care was introduced in 1985. NGOs have made efforts to develop foster care, such as by providing training for foster parents. Because of the reasons explained in paragraph 50 of the initial report, foster family care is still uncommon but the Government and NGOs continue to make great efforts. In an effort to change the primary form of welfare institution from dormitory homes to small groups, the Government has started pilot group home projects, and as of 1998 there were 10 group homes operating.

H. Abuse and neglect (art. 19), including physical and psychological recovery and social reintegration (art. 39)

....

109. The most common form of child abuse in Korea is abandonment, which has increased during the recent economic recession. Those children are placed in protection facilities and receive the necessary services from the Government.

I. Periodic review of placement (art. 25)

111. According to the Enforcement Ordinance of the Child Welfare Act, "child welfare facilities" refer to child guidance clinics, childcare institutions, child emergency protection facilities, child vocational guidance centres, juvenile reformatories, self-support facilities for those discharged from childcare institutions, foster-care facilities for adoption, and facilities for emotionally disturbed children. In December 1998, 17,820 children were cared for in the 272 residential care facilities, an average of 66 children per facility for all kinds of facilities, and 85 children per alternative facility.

112. The number of childcare institutions and children cared for in such facilities has decreased together with the decrease of abandoned and lost children. The Government expects that less than 1 per cent of needy children will be cared for in residential facilities in the future. However, as a result of the economic recession since the end of 1997, the number of children temporarily given up for care or abandoned has increased and hence the number of children cared for in the institutions will also likely increase.

113. The mayor, provincial governor and ward head are responsible for the periodic inspection of the childcare institutions under their management and their programmes, and for auditing their budgets.

Alternative Report:

Supplementary Report to the Republic of Korea's Second Periodic Report on the Implementation of the Convention on the Rights of the Child

(2003)

available at http://www.crin.org/resources/InfoDetail.asp?ID=3283

Organization: **Sarangbang Group for Human Rights**

V. Family Environment and Alternative Care

17. Children deprived of their family environment

17.1. An increasing number of children are entitled to special protection and assistance provided by the State, including abandoned, missing, and runaway children. According to the Ministry of Health and Welfare, as of the end of 2000, 7700 children were protected by the State, among which 4453 were sent to orphanages, 1406 were cared for by foster caregivers, 1337 were adopted and 564 children were protected by other means. Most children are still being sent to orphanages and large facilities. The missing children that have been found are sent to large facilities by court decision. Although they are entitled to State protection they are sent to illegal and unapproved poor facilities, beyond State supervision.

17.2. Several hundred to a thousand children previously missing children are taken to police stations and then to child support facilities in the region. Some of those children are sent to illegal and unapproved orphanages that do not use the Internet system to show pictures of the children with their unique features or identifiable points as soon as the children are admitted to their facilities. The government does not have information on the illegal orphanages so parents wander around the whole nation searching for their missing children. Some childcare facilities count missing children as abandoned children in order to receive financial support from the Government, and sometimes do not allow parents who have lost their children to enter the orphanages and look at the children housed there.

17.3. The Government has supported the residential care/group home system since 1985 as alternative care to orphanages. However, only 32 group homes are currently financially supported by the State. Group homes, administered by individuals or religious groups, are unapproved and unregistered welfare facilities that do not receive State support and supervision. Long working hours of social workers and use of partially trained employees cause problems, and the group homes are not considered proper alternative care as they are facilities without family environments. The alternative care should be foster placement and adoption as stressed by the CRC. The CRC recognizes that the child, for full and harmonious development of his/her personality, should grow up in a family environment.

The foster care system currently has 300 family members who look after the best interests of children in order to reunite them with their separated parents after temporary care. The Korean Foster Care Association provides regular foster care training and persons who have received certificates of completion of training are entitled to be foster parents. There is no direct State administration but as of 2002 the State only provides 65,000 Won (about 54$) per foster care child per month. There is the problem of follow up of children returned to their biological parents after foster care, as foster homes and group homes only provide temporary care.

17.4. According to the Ministry of Health and Welfare, the number of children who are heads of families is increasing annually; the number of them reached 13,390 in 2002. Among these, 2,600 children are living with their grandparents or relatives. Most of all, it can be considered child abuse emotionally and mentally for those children to be forced to become heads of family and financially support the family. The system of children heads of family must be abolished, and legally changed to the foster care system immediately.

The State declared that those child heads of family who are under 15 years old will be transferred to the foster care system or be sent to orphanages in its booklet of '2002 Child Welfare Plans'. Recognizing that the child, for the full and harmonious development of his/her personality, should grow up in a family environment in an atmosphere of happiness, love and understanding, Article 20 of the Convention states that institutional care is particularly inappropriate for children, especially for younger children, whose developmental needs require a one-to-one relationship with a permanent adult caregiver. The plight of large numbers of children in inappropriate institutional care has led the Committee on the Rights of Children to refer to institutionalization as a "last resort" with necessary measures. The Committee has frequently expressed concern that the assistance provided may not be of consistent quality for child development and that insufficient attention is given to preparing children for their integration into the community.

<RECOMMENDATIONS>

- Children deprived of their family and in need of protection to be entitled to special protection and assistance provided for their best interests by the State in a family environment.

- The State to monitor and supervise illegal and unregistered childcare facilities.

- Childcare that is oriented towards large facilities to be altered and avoided in favor of family environments in the best interests of children.

- The Government should support and supervise the foster care and group home systems.

- The Government should secure social workers in the fields for responsible welfare services and increase their salaries.

———

CRC Committee's Report:

United Nations Convention on the Rights of the Child [CRC], Concluding Observations of the Committee on the Rights of the Child

Republic of Korea, 32nd Sess., U.N. Doc. CRC/C/15/Add. 197 (2003), *available at* http://www1.umn.edu/humanrts/crc/korea2003.html

. . . .

5. Family environment and alternative care

Alternative care

40. The Committee notes the State party's establishment of group homes as an alternative to the institutionalization of children separated from their families. However, it is concerned that the establishment of group homes and the development of the foster care system remain limited, and that private alternative care institutions are not subject to governmental regulations or regular inspections.

41. The Committee recommends that the State party:

(a) Continue to expand the number of group homes and the foster care system, in particular by providing greater financial support to foster families and increasing the counselling and support mechanisms for foster families;

(b) Ensure a periodic review of placement of children in all public and private institutions, that takes into account the views and best interests of the child, and, wherever possible, aims to reintegrate children into a family environment;

(c) Increase the number of social workers and upgrade their skills and capacity to provide assistance to children in alternative care and to vulnerable families.

Adoption

42. The Committee remains concerned that, due to prevailing negative cultural traditions, domestic adoptions may be arranged without authorization or involvement of the competent authorities and that such arrangements do not necessarily take into account the best interests of the child or, where appropriate, the views of the child. The Committee also notes with concern the high number of intercountry adoptions, suggesting that this form of adoption is not necessarily a measure of last resort, and reiterates its concern, stated in previous concluding observations, that the State party has not ratified the Hague Convention of 1993 on Protection of Children and Cooperation in Respect of Intercountry Adoption.

43. The Committee reiterates its previous recommendation to the State party and calls for:

(a) A comprehensive review of the system of domestic and inter-country adoptions with a view to reforming legislation in order to bring it into full conformity with the principles and provisions of the Convention on the Rights of the Child, in particular article 21;

(b) The ratification of the Hague Convention of 1993 on Protection of Children and Co-operation in Respect of Intercountry Adoption.

The selection below from India's 2003 report treats the problem of caste-based discrimination and children's rights. In theory, all children should be able to exercise the rights granted under the UNCRC without discrimination—that is, without regard to their ethnic or cultural background. Does the reporting system inevitably push a country like India in the direction of featuring its laws, as opposed to its tolerance of traditional forms of discrimination?

India State Party Report

July 2003
available at http://www.unhchr.ch/tbs/doc.nsf/(Symbol)/6387247e0eeae
0c4c1256dbe004f3bf3?Opendocument

SECTION III

GENERAL PRINCIPLES

B. Non-Discrimination

Article 2

Constitutional provisions, policies and legislation

SC = Scheduled Castes

ST = Scheduled Tribes

219.The guiding principles underpinning the Constitution of India are equality before law, equal protection to all and non-discrimination. The standards set by the Constitution link to the standards set by article 2 of the CRC. Equality is a dynamic concept with many aspects and dimensions and it cannot be "cribbed, cabbined and confined" within traditional limits (E.P. Royappa vs. State of Tamil Nadu). Articles of the Constitution of India reflect this concept, in the interpretation of equality and non-discrimination. Article 14 of the Constitution, holds that "The State shall not deny to any person equality before law or the equal protection of law within the territory of India." Article 15 enjoins upon the State not to discriminate against any citizen on the grounds of religion, race, caste, sex or place of birth. Clauses 3 and 4 of Article 15 are exceptions to the general principles of non-discrimination. They empower the State to make special provisions for women and children, respectively, and for the advancement of any socially and educationally backward classes of citizens or for SCs/STs. Article 17 has abolished untouchability and forbidden its practice in any form. To enforce this solemn commitment, the Government passed the Untouchability (Offences) Act in 1955. It was amended in 1976 and is now known as the "Protection of Civil Rights Act, 1955". Articles 25–28 provide to all persons guarantees of the Right to Freedom of Religion in all aspects. Article 29 of the Constitution of India guarantees to "every section of the citizens", residing anywhere in India and "having a distinct language, script or culture", the right to conserve the same. No citizen can be denied admission to any educational institution maintained and aided by the State on the grounds of religion, race, caste or language. Article 30 states that all minorities, whether based on religion or language, shall have the right to establish and administer educational institutions of their choice.

....

221. The caste system has been a dominant feature of Indian social life for centuries. Nevertheless, several trends such as urbanisation, positive discrimination, growing literacy and economic growth have been whittling down caste barriers, particularly in urban areas. Parliament has also enacted the SCs and STs (Prevention of Atrocities) Act, 1989, as a welfare legislation, with the object of preventing atrocities against the members of Scheduled Castes and Scheduled Tribes, to provide for Special Courts for the trial of such offences and for the relief and rehabilitation of the victims of such offences and for matters connected therewith or incidental thereto. The framers of the Indian Constitution did not overlook the need to provide a separate Commission for SCs and STs. The National Commission for SCs and STs, which was reshaped in 1978, advises on broad issues on policy and levels of development of SCs and STs.

222. There is an affirmative action policy for children of backward castes and Scheduled Tribes in Tamil Nadu and many other States for admission to higher education institutions and Government service. Programmes oriented towards their welfare are monitored through the Commission for Scheduled Castes and Tribes and Commission for the Welfare of Backward Classes, Minorities and Women.

223. In order to prevent discrimination against the most disadvantaged groups of children, the GOI has enacted a wide range of laws and policies, all of which protect their rights. Some prominent laws are the Child Labour (Prohibition and Regulation) Act, 1986; the Immoral Traffic (Prevention) Act, 1986; the Juvenile Justice Act, 1986; and Persons with Disabilities (Equal Opportunities, Protection of Rights and Full Participation) Act, 1995. Similarly, some prominent policies enacted by the GOI are the National Policy for Children (1974), the National Policy on Education (1986) and National Policy on Child Labour (1987). Apart from guaranteeing equal opportunity for all under the Constitution, India also has specific laws for women. The Convention on the Elimination of All Forms of Discrimination against Women (CEDAW) has been ratified by India in 1993. The National Policy on Education, 1986, directly addresses the question of setting right the traditional gender imbalances in education and makes a strong commitment in favour of education for women's equality.

Alternative Report:

The Status of Children in India

(2003)

available at http://www.crin.org/resources/infoDetail.asp?ID=3770

Organization: Asian Center for Human Rights

IV. General Principles

Article 2: Non-Discrimination

In its periodic report, the government of India refers to various legislations prohibiting discrimination in India. While the government of India has enacted constitutional safeguards and special laws to combat the crimes against Scheduled Castes and Scheduled Tribes, implementation of these laws remains a *problematique* area.

The government of India states that "several trends such as urbanization, positive discrimination, growing literacy and economic growth have been whittling down caste barriers, especially in urban areas". It is actually skin deep. The advertisements in the matrimonial columns of the daily newspapers—which give preference to castes—provide testimonies to prevailing caste consciousness in the Indian psyche. In addition, the majority of the populations of India live in rural areas where caste discrimination is alive and kicking.

The caste system is the most visible and degrading form of discrimination in India. People of higher castes discriminate against people of lower castes. Within the circle of caste discrimination, comes discrimination based on economic means; people of lower castes have been confined to certain jobs at the bottom of the socio-economic ladder.

. . . .

While Dalits are considered as "untouchable"—too "polluted" to be touched by the upper castes—the rape of Dalit women and girls, who represent the honour of the community—by the upper caste Hindus is a commonplace. In their daily lives, untouchability results in widespread discrimination. The Dalit women and girls are paraded naked in villages. If a Dalit touches pots and pans, upper caste Hindus sprinkle 'holy water' around to purify all that has been touched by the Dalit. In some villages, Dalits are not allowed to wear shoes; if they wear shoes, they will be forced to take them off when coming into the presence of a dominant caste person. In rural areas, Dalits are not allowed to cycle through the dominant caste area of the village.

In most places, Dalits live mainly in separate villages. Dalits are not allowed to enter many Hindu temples, for fear of polluting the temples. Dalits have been chased out, abused and beaten up for daring to as much as set foot inside a temple, even though it is a temple for their religion.

. . . .

Most caste offenses in rural areas are not registered. Nonetheless, the statistics provided by the government of India clearly establish that caste violence has been increasing. 34,799 cases were registered in 1999, 36,971 cases were registered in 2000 and 39,157 were registered in 2001.

Special Courts under SCs/STs Prevention of Atrocities Act

The Committee on the Rights of the Child after consideration of India's initial report in January 2000 recommended "the full implementation of the 1989 Scheduled Castes and Scheduled Tribes (Prevention of Atrocities) Act, the 1995 Scheduled Castes and Scheduled Tribes Rules (Prevention of Atrocities) and the 1993 Employment of Manual Scavengers Act."

. . . .

While the statistics provided by the government of India state that the courts disposed of respectively 12,864 cases in 1999, 11,237 cases in 2000 and 16,203 cases in 2001, the conviction rate remains extremely low. Out of the 31,011 cases tried under the Prevention of Atrocities Act in 1998, only a paltry 1,677 instances or 5.4% resulted in a conviction and 29,334 ended in acquittal. Compare to this, under the Indian Penal Code 39.4% of cases ended in a conviction in 1999 and 41.8% in 2000.

The ineffectiveness of the existing laws primarily due to non-implementation stands exposed.

....

Despite consistent and systematic discrimination against the Dalits, in its periodic report (pages 54–64), the government of India fails to make any reference to discrimination faced by children belonging to Scheduled Castes and indigenous peoples. It focuses only on the "girl child". While the condition of "girl child" in general remains deplorable, Dalit and indigenous/tribal girls face multiple discrimination because of their caste or ethnic origin and religious belief. Therefore, the focus on girl child alone fails to present the actual status of the Dalit and indigenous/tribal girls.

CRC Committee's Report:

United Nations Convention on the Rights of the Child [CRC], Concluding Observation of the Committee on the Rights of the Child

India, 35th Sess., U.N. Doc. CRC/C/15/Add.228 (2004), *available at* http://www.unhchr.ch/tbs/doc.nsf/(symbol)/35e5ebb72fcfadbac 1256e83004a29a8?Opendocument

General principles

The right to non-discrimination

27. The Committee is deeply concerned at persistent and significant social discrimination against children belonging to Scheduled Castes and Tribes and other tribal groups, reflected, inter alia, by the many violations of the 1989 Scheduled Castes and Scheduled Tribes (Prevention of Atrocities) Act, the low number of such violations dealt with by the courts, and the fact that a majority of the states have failed to set up the special courts provided for under this Act.

28. The Committee recommends that the State party, in accordance with article 17 of its Constitution and article 2 of the Convention, take all necessary steps to abolish the discriminatory practice of "untouchability", prevent caste—and tribe-motivated abuse, and prosecute State and private actors who are responsible for such practices or abuses. Moreover, in compliance with article 46 of the Constitution, the State party is encouraged to implement, inter alia, special measures to advance and protect these groups. The Committee recommends the full implementation of the 1989 Scheduled Castes and Scheduled Tribes (Prevention of Atrocities) Act, the 1995 Scheduled Castes and Scheduled Tribes Rules (Prevention of Atrocities) and the Employment of Manual Scavengers and Construction of Dry Latrines (Prohibition) Act, 1993. The Committee encourages the State party to continue its efforts to carry out comprehensive public education campaigns to prevent and combat caste-based discrimination with a view to changing social attitudes, by involving, inter alia, religious leaders.

Notes and Questions

1. What differences in tone are apparent from comparing the state reports and the alternative NGO reports above? Are the Committee's responses to country reports useful? If you were a reporting country, how seriously would you take the committee's comments? Does the Committee seem to distinguish between very serious and relatively minor violations of the UNCRC? What difficulties do the alternative NGO reports pose for the committee?

2. Should the Committee be required to reflect the content of the "alternative" NGO reports in its own reports? Are the NGO reports completely credible? What sort of biases might they contain? What changes would you make to the reporting system?

———

D. Beyond the Committee on the Rights of the Child: How Individual States Approach UNCRC Implementation

The process established by the UNCRC, under which the States Parties report to the Committee, is of course only one aspect of the implementation of international children's rights principles. Implementation also depends on judicial interpretation of the UNCRC's provisions in each country. Jonathan Todres describes the influence exerted by national judiciaries where UNCRC provisions are less than clear and thus open to various interpretations.

1. National judicial application

Though jurisprudence on the UNCRC is in its early stages, the effect of the early case law on the development of children's rights—internationally and in the United States—is significant. The following article analyzes the manner in which some of the key concepts arising from the Convention have been taken up by courts. The issue of whether States Parties allow private parties to invoke the Convention's provisions before national courts arises frequently in the Committee's responses to national reports. The Committee sometimes notes that even in States Parties where there is a formal right to rely on the CRC's provisions in national proceedings, in practice national courts may only rarely, if ever, hear such cases.

Todres points to weaknesses in the Convention that emerge as individuals seek to rely on its provisions in national proceedings. It is to be hoped that the Convention has a great deal of as yet untapped potential to influence judicial decision making in a wide variety of countries, a view implicit in the Todres article.

Jonathan Todres, *Emerging Limitations on the Rights of the Child: The U.N. Convention on the Rights of the Child and Its Early Case Law*
30 Columbia Human Rights Law Review 159 (1998)

. . . .

III. A CLOSER LOOK AT THE CRC AND THE EARLY CASE LAW INTERPRETING ITS PROVISIONS

The CRC set out to cover four general areas: the participation of children in decisions that affect their future (which incorporates the idea of a child's "evolving capacities"); the protection of children against discrimination and all forms of neglect and exploitation; the prevention of harm to children; and the provision of assistance for children's basic needs. A closer examination of the provisions of the CRC reveals important deficiencies in the Convention. These weaknesses have been exploited in some of the early case law on the CRC.

. . . .

A. The Best Interests of the Child Principle

The primary aspiration of the CRC is to advance "the best interests of the child." The Convention aims to bring together the protections in the many scattered human rights treaties relating to children and to unite them under a single comprehensive document that focuses on the best interests of the child.

Article 3 sets forth the "best interests of the child" standard as one of the underlying principles of the CRC. This "umbrella provision" is invoked often as a guiding principle when interpreting other articles and rights in the CRC. The drafters intended this provision to establish the principle that official decisions affecting a child must be taken with primary consideration for the child's best interests, and that neither the interests of the parents nor the interests of the state should be the most important consideration.

Paragraph (1) of Article 3 merits close examination. It reads as follows: "In all actions concerning children, whether undertaken by public or private social welfare institutions, courts of law, administrative authorities or legislative bodies, the best interests of the child shall be a primary consideration."

As stated, the best interests of the child principle must be used in "all actions concerning children." This phrase is intended to be interpreted broadly, so as to encompass any action that directly or indirectly affects children. During the drafting of the CRC, an early draft of Article 3 read "[i]n all official actions concerning children," but the word "official" was dropped to broaden the scope of the provision. Geraldine Van Bueren suggests that the phrase "all actions" was intended to include not only state action but also actions by private actors. In addition, the article refers to "all actions concerning children," which implies that the CRC may be invoked not only when the action in question applies to the particular child in question, but also when the action in question affects children in general. Such an interpretation should have a positive impact on those claims brought under this article. Furthermore, the Committee has stated that the phrase should be interpreted as broadly as possible.

The domestic courts of several States Parties have adopted a broad reading of the "in all actions concerning children" phrase. Cases relating to the deportation of non-citizen parents of citizen children have been deemed to be "actions concerning children" by some courts. A criminal sentencing proceeding in which both parents of a child faced prison time has also been recognized as "action concerning children." On the other hand, an Australian court held that the CRC was not applicable to the repossession of a father's car, where the father claimed that it was in the best interests of his child to allow the father to keep the vehicle so that he could drive his child to after-school education lessons.

In all three of these situations, children were or would have been affected by the courts' decisions, yet all three determinations of whether the CRC applies seem reasonable. Courts seem to be arriving at such different decisions in large part because the CRC provides no guidance on what constitutes an "action concerning children." It has been left to states to decide, and thus left to individual judges. Though this case-by-case approach may be the best available, it has significant implications for the rights of the child.

Second, the "best interests of the child" standard itself, upon which the CRC relies so heavily, warrants examination. The standard is not new. In fact, many countries rely on the standard, and it was in use long before the advent of the CRC. The United States, for example, uses it in child custody cases. One court has stated, "without question, the paramount concern of courts in child custody proceedings is the welfare of the child." However, the "best interests of the child" principle is not without critics. Primary concerns about this principle include questions of who decides what is in the best interests of the child, and what criteria are used to determine what is in the best interests of the child. Some argue that it is not a viable standard because it relies too heavily on culture and social context....

Zimbabwe provides an excellent example of a setting where the "best interests of the child" principle can produce different results depending on the construction used. In Zimbabwe, statutory law holds that in custody cases the best interests of the child "shall be the paramount consideration." However, the construction one uses to determine what constitutes the best interests of the child—whether cultural, material, legal, or political—will shape the resulting determination. Thus, if a cultural construction is used in Zimbabwe, custody of a child rests with the family—usually the paternal family—and not with the individual. In many instances, culture dictates that custody decisions must be handled by the families outside of the formal courts. Furthermore, culture may also prescribe that a child be taught obedience, deference to elders and authority, and to act in "male" or "female" ways. In contrast, if one were to use a legal construction, custody would rest with an individual rather than a family. Alice Armstrong writes that the very act of bringing a custody case into a formal state court means, first, that "best interests" will be decided by an institution that is not recognized by [the rules, customs, and traditions of the indigenous people of Zimbabwe] and, second, that "best interests" will largely be interpreted according to the general law, based on foreign, "Western" values.

Even when culture is not an issue, a child's best interest is still a contentious topic. For example, in some instances there may be no difference between legal construction and cultural construction in a particular state, and the parties involved may share the same cultural values and beliefs with each other and with the relevant legal system. Yet, concerns would remain about the "indeterminacy, vagueness or openendedness" of the best interests standard. Some commentaries, however, maintain that the CRC itself does provide some guidance to those seeking to identify what is in the best interests of the child.

The indeterminacy of the "best interests" standard will not necessarily produce a negative result. The Zimbabwe study shows that policies adopted in the best interests of the child can differ depending on culture, and yet still benefit the child. Alston states that "identical norms can lead to very different results, but results that may well be, in light of the prevailing cultural or other circumstances, largely compatible with international norms." In these cases, child rights activists raised in the Western rights tradition must be careful not to criticize decisions as not in the child's best interests simply because the approach taken is not Western. It is possible, however, that the "best interests of the child" principle will allow governments to hide behind the veil of culture and avoid addressing human rights abuses of children in their countries.

The third, and perhaps most significant, aspect of the foundational principle of the CRC is that the "best interests of the child" is to be "a primary consideration." There was considerable debate over this aspect of the CRC. The basic working text adopted by the 1980 Working Group stated that the best interests of the child shall be "the paramount consideration."

The United States objected to this language of the working draft and introduced a revised Article 3, which mandated that the best interests of the child should be a primary consideration. Some considered the word "paramount" to be too broad. One speaker at the 1981 meeting of the Working Group stated that the interests of a child should be a primary consideration in actions concerning children but were not the overriding, paramount consideration in every case, since other parties might have equal or even superior legal interests in some cases (e.g., medical emergencies during childbirth).

Thus, although a number of the delegates agreed that the Polish proposal offered greater protection for the child, the U.S. proposal was accepted as a compromise. The final language was intended to allow for flexibility when necessary, while still asserting that any action should be taken in the best interests of the child, and with due consideration for the child's rights.

Early decisions by domestic courts demonstrate that the desire for flexibility in Article 3(1) has created a significant loophole in the CRC. Australian courts have held that by requiring that the best interests of the child be only "a primary consideration," the CRC demands that Australia only abide by the procedural fairness requirement. This interpretation of "the best interests of the child" principle as a procedural requirement not only weakens the provision, but also provides little direction for judges handling cases affecting children. The message, if any, to judges is that the requirements of the CRC are met simply by "considering" what is in the child's best interests. This interpretation allows judges to "consider" the child's best interests, but then to issue a decision that may not reflect those interests.

In New Zealand, for example, the CRC has been cited in a number of immigration cases, but the loophole has allowed the courts to adopt an approach that balances New Zealand's international obligations and its domestic laws and policies—an approach that in fact has favored its internal policies. This conflict between national and international law is a recurring one, and will be discussed in further detail below.

B. The Obligations of States Parties to the Convention

1. Article 4 of the Convention

Article 4 is the general provision outlining the obligations and duties of States Parties to the Convention. It reads as follows:

States Parties shall undertake all appropriate legislative, administrative, and other measures for the implementation of the rights recognized in this Convention. In regard to economic, social and cultural rights, States Parties shall undertake such measures to the maximum extent of their available resources and, where needed, within the framework of international cooperation.

This article, combined with the non-discrimination provision in Article 2, forms the basis of a State Party's obligations under the CRC. Since the second part of Article 4 addresses the economic, social, and cultural rights embodied in the Convention, the first sentence must therefore address all other provisions—most notably those on civil and political rights and some of the provisions on special protection measures. A state's obligations with respect to the rights and special protections covered by the first sentence of Article 4 are not subject to availability of resources. Yet, when outlining these obligations no direct reference is made to the judiciary or to judicial remedies. Furthermore, the travaux préparatoires do not reveal any discussion about judicial remedies. Perhaps the issue of judicial remedies is covered by the language "other measures," but it seems to be a significant oversight considering that "courts of law" are specifically identified in Article 3.

The second part of Article 4—specifically the phrase "to the maximum extent of their available resources"—is one of the more obvious loopholes in the CRC. This phrase parallels that of Article 2(1) of the International Covenant on Economic, Social and Cultural Rights (ICESCR). In many respects the ICESCR is a relatively weak international human rights treaty, since it generally only requires States Parties to "take steps" toward ensuring rights rather than requiring that they ensure those rights. The language of the second sentence of Article 4 of the CRC was inserted out of concern that developing countries might not ratify the Convention if no allowance were given for their limited resources. Although this reasoning is understandable and one could argue that the goal of fostering support of the CRC among developing nations has been realized, this phrase still leaves a loophole which should be of concern to human rights advocates for two reasons.

First, the Convention does not clearly delineate which provisions fall under the heading of economic, social, and cultural rights. Do special protection provisions related to child labor (Article 32) fall under the rubric of economic, social, and cultural rights? Or, are some human rights abuses suffered under child labor a violation of civil rights? One must be concerned about which provisions might fall under this category.... Some provisions of the CRC do not fit clearly in just one category, and the Committee has not published any guidelines on this issue.

Second, even if the Committee or other appropriate body defines which articles fall under the economic, social and cultural rights category, a loophole remains — States Parties can still claim that they do not have adequate resources to respect and ensure these rights. This loophole is narrowed somewhat by the additional phrase: "... and, where needed, within the framework of international cooperation." This phrase would require that States Parties without the necessary resources to ensure the rights of the child within their jurisdiction seek assistance "within the framework of international cooperation." Even with this qualification, a sizable loophole remains.

. . . .

Currently, no domestic court has analyzed or interpreted Article 4 of the CRC, but its limitations are still significant. Though Article 4 is more directly relevant to shaping legislation and public policies than to judicial decisions, domestic courts will be required to interpret and apply the new law that emerges from Article 4.

. . . .

3. Provisions for Implementation of the Rights Enshrined in the CRC

The CRC is comparatively weak with respect to provisions on implementation by States Parties. The CRC relies almost exclusively on States Parties' reports, which are to be submitted on a regular basis. It does not allow for state-to-state complaints, nor does it provide any avenue for individuals to bring complaints against a state. These limitations are a stark contrast to some of the other international human rights instruments which provide frameworks for both state and individual complaints. Without providing for its own system for handling complaints, the CRC will be forced to rely on the courts of the various States Parties to interpret and implement the provisions of the Convention. In turn, this reliance on domestic courts will open the door to a wide range of interpretations, including narrow readings that may further limit the rights of the child.

A Self-Executing or Non-Self-Executing Treaty?

Perhaps the biggest limitation to full implementation of the CRC in this context is whether the CRC is self-executing or non-self-executing. When an international agreement or treaty is self-executing, no domestic implementing legislation is needed, and the treaty is immediately applicable on a domestic level upon entry into force. If non-self-executing, then the ratification of a treaty will create international obligations for the state, but the treaty will not have domestic legal force.

Whether a treaty is self-executing often depends on the law of the country in question. In most Western parliamentary systems, treaties carry international obligations but do not have effect as domestic law. In the United States, treaties are the law of the land, and "courts in the United States are bound to give effect to international law and to international agreements of the United States, except that a 'non-self-executing' agreement will not be given effect as law in the absence of necessary implementation." The Restatement (Third) states that a treaty of the U.S. is non-self-executing "if the agreement manifests an intention that it shall not become effective as domestic law without the enactment of implementing legislation, ... if the Senate in giving consent to a treaty, or Congress by resolution, requires implementing legislation, or.... if implementing legislation is constitutionally required. Similarly, in the United Kingdom, treaties are non-self-executing and require an act of parliament to give effect to their provisions."

Article 4 of the CRC specifically states that States Parties are obligated to take steps toward implementation. This could imply that the CRC is intended to be non-self-executing. The travaux préparatoires do not provide any clear answer on this matter, thus it becomes dependent on the law of the particular country.

The early case law demonstrates that whether a state considers the CRC self-executing is particularly significant for judicial branches of governments. In Canada, a Federal Court of Appeal held that the CRC is non-self-executing, thus the courts are not required to give effect to its provisions until implementing legislation has been passed. The court stated that

> [T]he Convention on the Rights of the Child, not having been adopted into Canadian law, cannot constitutionally give rise to rights and obligations as to how the discretion given by ... the Immigration Act is to be exercised. That is the Convention cannot prescribe, in a manner enforceable by the courts, the obligation to give the best interests of children, of an alien who is under order of deportation, superior weight to some other factors. Such a prescription would give rise to a substantive, not merely a procedural, right and cannot be the subject of legitimate expectations.

The court expressed further concern that the CRC would require it to take into consideration the best interests of a convict's child. In doing so, the court did not stop at saying that the CRC does not have effect in Canadian law until implementing legislation is adopted, but went on to say that at best the CRC is a procedural requirement in cases directed at the child and not relevant for cases that merely have consequences for the child.

For states like Canada that maintain that the CRC is non-self-executing, the impact and the legal authority of the CRC are significantly minimized. However, the fact that a state considers the CRC to be non-self-executing does not absolve it of all obligations with respect to the Convention.

If the CRC is considered non-self-executing, the state still has an obligation to adhere to the provisions of the CRC. Professor Louis Henkin writes, "Rendering a treaty non-self-executing in no way reduces or significantly postpones our legal obligations." A state has an obligation to "enact necessary legislation promptly so as to enable it to carry out its obligations under the treaty." A state also has a duty, if not a legal obligation, to abide by the provisions of a treaty once it has signed the instrument. If a State Party does not take steps to fulfill its treaty obligations, it could eventually be found in default. However, this process could be lengthy, and other states may be reluctant to accuse a state of being in default.

. . . .

C. Reservations to the CRC

Reservations are another significant means by which the effects of an international human rights treaty can be minimized. Article 51 of the CRC explicitly allows for reservations, so long as they are "not incompatible with the object and purpose of the Convention." Inevitably, some tension existed in the early years following the CRC's creation. While its advocates wanted states to support all of its provisions, it was important to gain as many ratifications as quickly as possible. Thus, the CRC has achieved nearly universal ratification, but the ratifications have not been without some reservations.

For the most part, the reservations have not been detrimental to the overall quality of the document. In fact, in the rare situation where a state has made a reservation that has severe implications, other States Parties have applied strong pressure on the reserving state to withdraw it. This occurred with Myanmar's initial reservation to Article 37, which states that "States Parties shall ensure that ... [n]o child shall be subjected to torture or other cruel, inhuman or degrading treatment or punishment." Reservations to this provision can be seen as in conflict with the treaty's object and purpose. As a result, the objection to Myanmar's Article 37 reservation was strong, and Myanmar withdrew the reservation.

Although the reservations have not had an overall negative impact, they have had broad implications in a few specific areas. For example, rights under Articles 13 and 14 regarding freedom of thought and expression, and the right to education under Article 28, have raised concern about the balance between parental and children's rights. Some groups in the United States have expressed concern by objecting to U.S. ratification of the CRC because, among other things, they consider it to be anti-parent. Much of this criticism is overstated. The CRC assumes that the family environment is best for the child, and that parents play a significant role in the care of the child, a role which States Parties must respect.

Also of concern is that several States Parties to the CRC have submitted more general reservations, the actual scope of which is not clear. The most common general reservation has come from Islamic countries, many of which have reserved the right not to follow provisions that are incompatible with Islamic law or the Shariah. Several states have voiced concern that these provisions may be overbroad, that in fact these reservations could be tailored to cover only a limited number of provisions. In addition, any general reservations warrant further examination, with a view to narrowing their scope or having them withdrawn. As discussed below, an important aspect of the implementation of the CRC is to work toward the elimination of those reservations that could impair the rights of the child.

The Committee consistently recommends that States Parties review their reservations with a view toward withdrawing them. The Committee's stance could be strengthened if it receives stronger support from States Parties in the form of objections to reservations and pressure on other states to reconsider their reservations. Under international law, a State Party to a convention can object to a reservation by another State Party. Generally, however, States Parties are reluctant to criticize other states. Even when one state criticizes another, their objections usually do not challenge the legal effect of the reservation.

Finland, for example, issued the following objection:

> The Government of Finland has examined the contents of the reservation made by Qatar upon signature of the said Convention, by which Qatar expresses that "[t]he State of Qatar wishes to make a general reservation with regard to those provisions of the Convention which are incompatible with Islamic law." In the view of the Government of Finland this reservation is subject to the general principle of treaty interpretation according to which a party may not invoke the provisions of internal law as justification for failure to perform its treaty obligations. For the above reason the Government of Finland objects to the said reservation. However, the Government of Finland does not consider that this

objection constitutes an obstacle to the entry into force of the said Convention between Finland and Qatar.

Again, the tension between encouraging ratifications and establishing a strong legal instrument is evident. As a result, some States Parties may tolerate reservations by other States Parties to the detriment of children in those countries.

. . . .

VI. CONCLUSION

. . . .

Although the early years of the Convention have been marked by some great successes, we must not be content with that alone. Without monitoring of, and effective action within, the judicial branches of States Parties to the CRC, we risk permitting interpretations of the Convention that limit its effectiveness. Though the needs of the world's children cannot be addressed by law alone, the law and the courts should, and do, remain an integral part of the solution—not merely mechanisms for managing juvenile justice.

In 1994, then Executive Director of UNICEF, James Grant, stated that "the largest unified movement in pursuit of rights that the world has ever seen may be emerging around the Convention on the Rights of the Child." The importance of this stage in the international child rights movement should not be underestimated. Greater attention must be given to the role of domestic judicial systems in order to ensure the implementation and application of the CRC's provisions in ways that enable the CRC to live up to its great promise as a comprehensive human rights treaty for children.

Notes and Questions

1. How could the UNCRC have been drafted so as to avoid the legal pitfalls and inconsistencies described by Todres? Especially in light of the fact that the UNCRC is essentially universal in its reach, would it have been possible to provide more specificity to the Convention, and still gain wide acceptance?

2. Todres refers to the fact that many States Parties entered reservations—that is, broad statements indicating that their acceptance of the Convention was conditional on their continued adherence to certain cultural or religious mores. States enter such reservations to limit the effect of international obligations on certain national values and practices—in the case of children's rights, values relating to familial, religious, and community authority. As you review the States Parties reservations included in the readings in section 3 below, consider what has motivated each state in entering the reservation.

---

2. Case Study on Integrating CRC Principles into a National Constitutional Order

The following article illustrates how one state, South Africa, has integrated the UNCRC into its own Constitution, and indicates that the South African judiciary is likely to require the state to take firm steps to implement these rights through concrete measures. South Africa is an interesting case of a state in profound transition, trying to create a modern, multicultural society from the ruins of apartheid. In such a situation, might a document like the UNCRC have as special, and unifying, role to play?

Johan D. van der Vyver, *Special Spring 2006 Symposium:*
Municipal Legal Obligations of States Parties to the Convention on
the Rights of the Child: The South African Model
20 Emory International Law Review 9 (2006)

The Republic of South Africa ratified the CRC without reservations on June 30, 1995. By that time, South Africa had already included in its interim constitution of 1993 a section on children's rights, which the current Constitution incorporated and elaborated upon. South Africa's Constitution now provides:

(1) Every child has the right—

(a) to a name and a nationality from birth;

(b) to family care or parental care, or to appropriate alternative care when removed from the family environment; (c) to basic nutrition, shelter, basic health care services and social services;

(d) to be protected from maltreatment, neglect, abuse or degradation;

(e) to be protected from exploitative labour practices;

(f) not to be required or permitted to perform work or provide services that—

(i) are inappropriate for a person of that child's age; or

(ii) place at risk the child's well-being, education, physical or mental health or spiritual, moral or social development; (g) not to be detained except as a measure of last resort, in which case, in addition to the rights a child enjoys under sections 12 and 35, the child may be detained only for the shortest appropriate period of time, and has the right to be—

(i) kept separately from detained persons over the age of 18 years; and

(ii) treated in a manner, and kept in conditions, that take account of the child's age;

(h) to have a legal practitioner assigned to the child by the state, and at state expense, in civil proceedings affecting the child, if substantial injustice would otherwise result; and

(i) not to be used directly in armed conflict, and to be protected in times of armed conflict.

(2) A child's best interests are of paramount importance in every matter concerning the child.

(3) In this section "child" means a person under the age of 18 years.

The Constitution deals separately with the right to education, health care, and other rights that have special importance for children. As far as education is concerned, it proclaims the right of "everyone" to basic education, including basic adult education, and places a burden on the State to make further education "progressively available and accessible." It is interesting to note that while the State's obligation to secure the right of "everyone" to health care services, sufficient food and water, and social security was made subject to progressive implementation "within its available resources," the right of a child to "basic nutrition, shelter, basic health care services and social services" is couched in the language of immediately enforceable rights.

These constitutional provisions are amplified by the Child Care Act of 1983 and the Children's Status Act of 1987. The Children's Bill, proposing to consolidate and expand the laws dealing specifically with children, is currently before the South African Parliament. When enacted, this bill will, among other things, reduce the age of majority from 21 to 18 years.

The South African legislation, taken as a whole, contains perhaps as good a summary of the substantive clauses in the CRC as exists today in the laws of any nation. However, the practical realization of the CRC's substantive provisions is not without difficulties.... In the final section, this Essay considers means and mechanisms for the enforcement of children's rights.

....

IV. Enforcement Mechanisms

.... Sections of the South African Constitution use the phrase "to be protected from" to denote those rights of a child that involve a duty of the State. It is, therefore, a constitutional duty of the State to secure the protection of children from "maltreatment, neglect, abuse or degradation," and to protect children from "exploitative labour practices."

Other sections of the Constitution put the State under a constitutional obligation to provide housing, health care services, and basic education and educational facilities. As noted earlier, the duty of the State to provide housing and health care services to the public at large is proclaimed as a matter of progressive implementation determined by the State's available resources. In the case of children's social rights, the corollary obligation to provide shelter and basic health care services is not confined to the State in all instances. Those rights are immediately enforceable, and therefore fall squarely within the category of immediately justiciable rights depicted in Principle 8 of the Limburg Principles of 1987.

Presumably, providing appropriate alternative care for a child when the child is removed from the family environment is primarily a duty of the State; only a court of law can order the removal of a child from the care of his or her parents or family. The State is under an obligation, if needed, to provide basic nutrition, shelter, basic health care, and social services. The State must also assume the responsibility of rendering punishable the ill-treatment, neglect, abuse, or degradation of children. However, such sanctions underscore the duty of everyone to refrain from inflicting such treatment upon a child. Furthermore, the duty to provide family and parental care, and the duty to nutritiously feed, house, and secure medical treatment for a child vests primarily in the parents or other persons in loco parentis. The State's duty to provide such care is complementary to that of the parents or their substitute and would only arise if the parent or other person in loco parentis is unable to do so from their own resources.

Holding the State accountable for wrongdoing is not precluded in South Africa as it would be in the United States under the notion of sovereign immunity. The very first Act passed by the South African legislature after the formation of the Union of South Africa in 1910 confirmed that the principle of English law that "the Queen can do no wrong" is not to be part of South African law.

Enforcement of state obligations to oversee protective measures and to provide facilities, amenities, and services pertinent to the best interests of the child is perceived as a problem in several jurisdictions, especially if compliance with such obligations is made conditional upon available resources. Deciding on state expenditures from available resources is commonly perceived as a prerogative of the executive government, though the allocation of funds must be approved by the legislature. It would constitute a serious violation of the separation of powers—the argument continues—if a court of law were to dictate to the treasury how the available resources are to be allocated. This argument loses credibility in countries where preferential allocation of scarce resources derives from a constitutional duty of the State to provide.

The enforcement of economic, social, and cultural rights in cases where the State is under a constitutional obligation to provide the services, facilities, or support for their meaningful enjoyment is nevertheless problematic. In South Africa it was suggested that the Constitutional Court might follow the "French option" in the enforcement of this so-called second generation of rights: the Court could make a finding of unconstitutionality without making an order as to what is to be done about it. Subsequent South African jurisprudence, in its quest to afford meaningful relevance to the constitutionally protected economic, social, and cultural rights, has gone well beyond mere findings of unconstitutionality. The Constitutional Court has scrutinized state policies in regard to, for example, housing and health care services, to establish the constitutionality of those policies in view of the constitutional obligation of the State to provide the concerned economic and social amenities. Two of those cases had a special bearing on the interests of the child.

First, *Government of the RSA v Grootboom* dealt with the right to housing, including the child's constitutional right to shelter. The respondents had been evicted from their informal homes situated on private land earmarked for formal low-cost housing. As to the justiciability of social and economic rights, the Court stated:

> Socio-economic rights are expressly included in the Bill of Rights; they cannot be said to exist on paper only. Section 7(2) of the Constitution requires the state "to respect, protect, promote and fulfill the rights in the Bill of Rights" and the courts are constitutionally bound to ensure that they are protected and fulfilled. The question is therefore not whether socio-economic rights are justiciable under our Constitution, but how to enforce them in a given case. This is a very difficult issue which must be carefully explored on a case-by-case basis. On the merits, the Court decided that the right to housing and shelter did not entitle the respondents to claim housing or a shelter on demand; rather, the right requires progressive implementation. The Constitution did oblige the State to devise and implement a coherent, coordinated program designed to meet its obligation. The program that had been adopted at the time of the application before the Court fell short of that constitutional obligation; the program failed to provide any form of relief to those desperately in need of access to housing. The Court ordered the State to comply with its constitutional duty by devising, funding, implementing, and supervising measures to provide relief to those in desperate need.

Speaking for the Court, Justice Yacoob gave the following outline of children's constitutional rights to family and parental care, basic nutrition, shelter, basic health care services, and social services:

> They ensure that children are properly cared for by their parents or families, and that they receive appropriate alternative care in the absence of parental or family care. The section encapsulates the conception of the scope of care children should receive in our society.... It follows ... that the Constitution contemplates that a child has the right to parental or family care in the first place, and the right to alternative appropriate care only where that is lacking. Through legislation and the common law, the obligation to provide shelter ... is imposed primarily on the parents or family and only alternatively on the state. The state thus incurs the obligation to provide shelter to those children, for example, who are removed from their families. It follows that section 28(1)(c) does not create any primary state

obligation to provide shelter on demand to parents and their children if children are being cared for by their parents or families.

This does not mean, however, that the state incurs no obligation in relation to children who are being cared for by their parents or families. In the first place, the state must provide the legal and administrative infrastructure necessary to ensure that children are accorded the protection contemplated by section 28. This obligation would normally be fulfilled by passing laws and creating enforcement mechanisms for the maintenance of children, their protection from maltreatment, abuse, neglect or degradation, and the prevention of other forms of abuse of children mentioned in section 28. In addition, the state is required to fulfill its obligations to provide families with access to land in terms of section 25, access to adequate housing in terms of section 26 as well as access to health care, food, water and social security in terms of section 27. It follows from this judgment that sections 25 and 27 require the state to provide access on a programmatic and coordinated basis, subject to available resources. One of the ways in which the state would meet its section 27 obligations would be through a social welfare programme providing maintenance grants and other material assistance to families in need in defined circumstances.

The second case, *Minister of Health v Treatment Action Campaign,* arose from the refusal of the South African government to make the antiretroviral drug, Nevirapine, which counteracts transmission of the HIV virus from mother to child, available at hospitals and clinics other than those that are research and training sites. The Court found that the government's policy of confining the use of Nevirapine for research purposes was inconsistent with the Constitution and was invalid to the extent of that inconsistency. In view of the State's constitutional obligation to take reasonable measures within its available resources for the progressive realization of the right of mother and child to basic health care, the Court instructed the government to reformulate its policy so as to make the drug available to HIV-positive mothers and their newborn children. The Court here went further than merely denouncing a state policy by directing the government as to what that policy should be.

In the United States, the protection of the rights of the child and of economic, social, and cultural rights in general is not constitutionally entrenched, and complainants seeking the protection of those rights through state action would confront numerous obstacles. This is not a sufficient reason, however, for the United States to avoid international liability for the protection of the rights of the child.

Conclusion

The South African legislature and judiciary have set a commendable example of how States Parties to the CRC are to execute their international obligations under the Convention. This is no easy matter in a country where a large number of the juvenile population is exposed to socio-economic conditions that are not particularly child-friendly. Those conditions result in inadequate shelter, educational facilities, job opportunities, and health-care services for the less privileged sections of the community. They are conducive to, and exacerbated by, a startling number of homeless "street children" and children orphaned by AIDS. Those conditions are also fertile soil for the cultivation of juvenile crime. South African law represents a commendable effort in handling such problems within the parameters of good governance reflected in the spirit of the CRC.

Notes and Questions

1. The van der Vyver article above reminds us that the UNCRC is not a static document, but one that interacts with national constitutional traditions. It is national recep-

tiveness towards the norms articulated in the UNCRC that will determine whether children are actually benefited in a concrete way by ratification of the Convention. How has South Africa responded to, and been inspired by, the UNCRC?

---

3. National Reservations to the UNCRC

Reservations to human rights treaties are often controversial. In the worst case scenario, countries wish to take credit for adherence to international human rights norms, while retaining the freedom to deviate from these norms for cultural or political reasons. In theory, such reservations are only permissible to the extent that they are consistent with the spirit of the underlying treaty itself. As you review the following reservations to the UNCRC, consider how they might affect or interfere with national application of the Convention.

United Nations Treaty Collection

[As of 9 October 2001]: Reservations, *available at*
http://treaties.un.org/Pages/ViewDetails.aspx?src=TREATY&mtdsg_no=IV-11&chapter=4&lang=en

Islamic Law

Iraq

The Government of Iraq has seen fit to accept [the Convention] ... subject to a reservation in respect to article 14, paragraph 1, concerning the child's freedom of religion, as allowing a child to change his or her religion runs counter to the provisions of the *Islamic Shariah*.

Jordan

The Hashemite Kingdom of Jordan expresses its reservation and does not consider itself bound by articles 14, 20 and 21 of the Convention, which grant the child the right to freedom of choice of religion and concern the question of adoption, since they are at variance with the precepts of the tolerant Islamic Shariah.

Morocco

The Kingdom of Morocco, whose Constitution guarantees to all the freedom to pursue his religious affairs, makes a reservation to the provisions of article 14, which accords children freedom of religion, in view of the fact that Islam is the State religion.

Oman

A reservation is entered to all the provisions of the Convention that do not accord with Islamic law or the legislation in force in the Sultanate and, in particular, to the provisions relating to adoption set forth in its article 21.

The Sultanate does not consider itself to be bound by those provisions of article 14 of the Convention that accord a child the right to choose his or her religion or those of its article 30 that allow a child belonging to a religious minority to profess his or her own religion.

Right to Life, Survival, Development

China

[T]he People's Republic of China shall fulfill its obligations provided by article 6 of the Convention under the prerequisite that the Convention accords with the provisions of article 25 concerning family planning of the Constitution of the People's Republic of China and in conformity with the provisions of article 2 of the Law of Minor Children of the People's Republic of China.

France

The Government of the French Republic declares that this Convention, particularly article 6, cannot be interpreted as constituting any obstacle to the implementation of the provisions of French legislation relating to the voluntary interruption of pregnancy.

Luxembourg

The Government of Luxembourg declares that article 6 of the present Convention presents no obstacle to implementation of the provisions of Luxembourg legislation concerning sex information, the prevention of back-street abortion and the regulation of pregnancy termination.

Family and Adoption

Argentina

The Argentine Republic enters a reservation to subparagraphs (b), (c), (d) and (e) of article 21 of the Convention on the Rights of the Child and declares that those subparagraphs shall not apply in areas within its jurisdiction because, in its view, before they can be applied a strict mechanism must exist for the legal protection of children in matters of inter-country adoption, in order to prevent trafficking in and the sale of children.

Canada

With a view to ensuring full respect for the purposes and intent of article 20(3) and article 30 of the Convention, the Government of Canada reserves the right not to apply the provisions of article 21 to the extent that they may be inconsistent with customary forms of care among aboriginal peoples in Canada.

Poland

With respect to article 7 of the Convention, the Republic of Poland stipulates that the right of an adopted child to know its natural parents shall be subject to the limitations imposed by binding legal arrangements that enable adoptive parents to maintain the confidentiality of the child's origin.

Children Deprived of Liberty and Juvenile Justice

Australia

Australia accepts the general principles of article 37. In relation to the second sentence of paragraph (c), the obligation to separate children from adults in prison is accepted only to the extent that such imprisonment is considered by the responsible authorities to be feasible and consistent with the obligation that children be able to maintain contact with their families, having regard to the geography and demography of Australia. Australia, therefore, ratifies the Convention to the extent that it is unable to comply with the obligation imposed by article 37(c).

Germany

In accordance with the reservations made by it with respect to the parallel guarantees of the International Covenant on Civil and Political Rights, the Federal Republic of Germany declares in respect of article 40(2)(b)(ii) and (v) of the Convention that these provisions shall be applied in such a way that, in the case of minor infringement of the penal law, there shall not in each and every case exist:

a) a right to have "legal or other appropriate assistance" in the preparation and presentation of the defense, and/or

b) an obligation to have a sentence not calling for imprisonment reviewed by a "higher competent authority or judicial body".

Japan

In applying paragraph (c) of article 37 of the Convention on the Rights of the Child, Japan reserves the right not to be bound by the provision in its second sentence, that is, 'every child deprived of liberty shall be separated from adults unless it is considered in the child's best interest not to do so', considering the fact that in Japan as regards persons deprived of liberty, those who are below twenty years of age are to be generally separated from those who are of twenty years of age and over under its national law.

Switzerland

Reservation concerning article 37(c):

The separation of children deprived of liberty from adults is not unconditionally guarantied.

Reservation concerning article 40:

The Swiss penal procedure applicable to children, which does not guarantee either the unconditional right to assistance or separation, where personnel or organization is concerned, between the examining authority and the sentencing authority, is unaffected.

The federal legislation concerning the organization of criminal justice, which establishes an exception to the right to a conviction and sentence being reviewed by a higher tribunal where the person concerned was tried by the highest tribunal at first instance, is unaffected.

The guarantee of having the free assistance of an interpreter does not exempt the beneficiary from the payment of any resulting costs.

Economic Exploitation / Employment

New Zealand

The Government of New Zealand considers that the rights of the child provided for in article 32(1) are adequately protected by its existing law. It therefore reserves the right not to legislate further or to take additional measures as may be envisaged in article 32(2).

Singapore

The employment legislation of the Republic of Singapore prohibits the employment of children below 12 years old and gives special protection to working children between the ages of 12 years and below the age of 16 years. The Republic of Singapore reserves the right to apply article 32 subject to such employment legislation.

Media

Austria

Article 17 will be applied to the extent that it is compatible with the basic rights of others, in particular with the basic rights of freedom of information and freedom of press.

United Arab Emirates

Article 17: While the United Arab Emirates appreciates and respects the functions assigned to the mass media by the article, it shall be bound by its provisions in the light of the requirements of domestic statues and laws and, in accordance with the recognition accorded them in the preamble to the Convention, such a manner that the country's traditions and cultural values are not violated.

Miscellaneous

Botswana

The Government of the Republic of Botswana enters a reservation with regard to the provisions of article 1 of the Convention and does not consider itself bound by the same in so far as such may conflict with the Laws and Statutes of Botswana.

Netherlands

The Kingdom of the Netherlands accepts the provisions of article 26 of the Convention with the reservation that these provisions shall not imply an independent entitlement of children to social security, including social insurance.

Oman

The provisions of the Convention should be applied within the limits imposed by the material resources available.

Notes and Questions

1. Reservations to treaties should only be allowed to the extent that they are not incompatible with the goals of the convention itself. (See Article 19 of the Vienna Convention the Law of Treaties.)[15] With regard to the small sample of country reservations set out above, which appear to be consistent with the aims of the UNCRC?

2. Are general reservations—overarching ones on religious belief, for instance—to be preferred over very specific ones?

In its General Comment No. 5 of 2003, the UNCRC Committee had this to say about reservations by states parties:

> II. REVIEW OF RESERVATIONS
>
> In its reporting guidelines on general measures of implementation, the Committee starts by inviting the State party to indicate whether it considers it necessary to maintain the reservations it has made, if any, or has the intention of withdrawing them. States parties to the Convention are entitled to make reservations at the time of their ratification of or accession to it (art. 51). The Committee's aim of ensuring full and unqualified respect for the human rights of children can be achieved only if States withdraw their reservations. It consistently recommends during its examination of reports that reservations be reviewed and withdrawn. Where a State, after review, decides to maintain a reservation, the Committee requests that a full explanation be included in the next periodic report. The Committee draws the attention of States parties to the encouragement given by the World Conference on Human Rights to the review and withdrawal of reservations. Committee on the Rights of the Child, General Comment No. 5 (2003), General Measures of Implementation of the Convention on the Rights of the Child (arts. 4, 42 and 44, para.6)....

> 1. Article 2 of the Vienna Convention on the Law of Treaties defines "reservation" as a "unilateral statement, however phrased or named, made by a State, when sign-

---

15. Vienna Convention on the Law of Treaties, May 23, 1969, 1155 U.N.T.S. 331, http://www.jus.uio.no/lm/un.law.of.treaties.convention.1969.

ing, ratifying, accepting, approving or acceding to a Treaty, whereby it purports to exclude or to modify the legal effect of certain provisions of the Treaty in their application to that State". The Vienna Convention notes that States are entitled, at the time of ratification or accession to a treaty, to make a reservation unless it is "incompatible with the object and purpose of the treaty" (art. 19).

2. Article 51, paragraph 2, of the Convention on the Rights of the Child reflects this: "A reservation incompatible with the object and purpose of the present Convention shall not be permitted". The Committee is deeply concerned that some States have made reservations which plainly breach article 51(2) by suggesting, for example, that respect for the Convention is limited by the State's existing Constitution or legislation, including in some cases religious law. Article 27 of the Vienna Convention on the Law of Treaties provides: "A party may not invoke the provisions of its internal law as justification for its failure to perform a treaty".

3. The Committee notes that, in some cases, States parties have lodged formal objections to such wide-ranging reservations made by other States parties. It commends any action which contributes to ensuring the fullest possible respect for the Convention in all States parties.

3. It is clear from the quote above that the Committee would prefer that countries not enter reservations to the UNCRC. Why should that be the case? If reservations are inherently incompatible with the Convention, why didn't the Convention itself say that reservations were not allowed? Is it preferable to accept imperfect ratification, or to wait and make sure that each ratifying party really intends to commit to the realization of the rights enumerated across the Convention's text?

4. Certain kinds of reservations clearly seem to be out of keeping with the spirit of the UNCRC. Why might a state ratify the UNCRC when it had no real intention of altering its approach to children's rights post ratification?

II. Critical Perspectives on the UNCRC

The UNCRC is as much criticized as it is revered. In the selections that follow, we encounter readings that analyze the Convention from a variety of perspectives. While the preceding section dealt with problems in implementation, the articles below question whether, or in what manner, certain provisions of the Convention should be implemented at all. Some writers have denounced the UNCRC as imposing a Western set of norms on developing countries, in which views of family, culture and tradition might not be at all compatible with the individualism implicit in the Convention. Given the fact that the U.S. stands essentially alone in its failure to ratify the Convention, there has been lively debate as to its flaws and virtues within the U.S.

Wide ranging as it is, the Convention does have significant implications for the relationship of children to society and to structures of authority. It is hardly surprising, then, that there would be political resistance to a fundamental reordering of familial and social bonds through the agency of one comprehensive document. Whatever one's perspective, it is apparent that the CRC rests on a number of assumptions about the nature of childhood, and the proper relationship between the child and the child's political and social environment. The idea of a professional and specialized international elite imposing child-related norms and ideals to nations is threatening to many, and from many different points of view.

A. The UNCRC and the Developing World: Is There a "Universal Child"?

For the UNCRC to be effective, it must be seen as more than just a collection of principles and aspirations. On the other hand, if its terms are meant to be taken literally, all ratifying states must share a vision of the child as worthy of protection, empowerment and, at least to some degree, liberation. Does this mean that the developed world is attempting to dictate to the developing world what childhood ought to be? Does it mean that when the developing world fails to "deliver" on the promise of a perfect childhood, its leaders must accept the blame? Or, alternatively, should cultural relativism be understood to allow for wide discrepancies in how the UNCRC is accepted and adopted?

The writings that follow explore the dilemma of the "universal child" under the Convention. As mentioned above, the ideals of the UNCRC are often met with skepticism, and even resistance. Critiques from a developing world perspective indicate dissatisfaction with the notion that childhood should be a time of carefree enjoyment, a luxury many argue poorer countries simply cannot afford.

Vanessa Pupavac, *The Infantilization of the South and the U.N. Convention on the Rights of the Child*
University of Nottingham Centre for Human Rights Law,
Human Rights Law Review (March, 1998)

....

The Universalisation of Western Childhood

The Convention on the Rights of the Child provides universal standards to which state parties are to comply. It has been described by Richard Reid of UNICEF as acting as 'a vehicle for creating a world conscience that speaks on behalf of children'. However, to what extent is its approach appropriate to ameliorating the plight of children? Whilst there is an international consensus of concern for children, that does not mean that there is a consensus about the policies needed to bring about an improvement in child welfare. The experience and perceptions of childhood vary fundamentally in different countries, but the Convention assumes a model of childhood that is universally applicable 'based on the notion that children everywhere have the same basic needs and that these can be met with a standard set of responses'. Policies considered appropriate in one society are not necessarily useful in other societies confronted with very different circumstances.

An examination of the provisions of the Convention reveals that the universal standards of the Convention are based on a Western concept of childhood and Western social policies which emphasise the role of individual causations and professional interventions and de-emphasise the influence of the wider social, economic, political and cultural circumstances. Various accounts have attempted to emphasise that the Convention is not just a Western initiative, that it was Poland who proposed and submitted a draft convention on the rights of the child and chaired the working groups which drafted the Convention. Nevertheless Western countries ultimately dominated the drafting process. There was a lack of participation of many countries from the south in the drafting of the Convention. Nigel Cantwell, of Defence for Children International, a non-governmental organisation (NGO) which participated and was influential in the working groups which drafted the Convention, observed that, '[t]he industrial countries were significantly over-represented at all stages. Fears that the outcome would be a heavily Northern-orientated text were widespread and justified'. Delegates from developing countries were not happy with the composition of the drafting group and the fact that their cultural perspectives and economic circumstances were not sufficiently taken into account. Ironically, the greater participation of (predominantly Western) NGOs in the drafting process further marginalised the views of Eastern European and developing countries. In fact, Poland delayed ratifying the Convention because of disagreements with the final version.

The Western model of childhood is based on the idea that children should be protected from the adult world. The Western conception of childhood is a time of play and training for adulthood has become the universal standard to be enforced under the Convention to the age of eighteen. The Western 'protective view of childhood', as Aron Bar-On explains, 'has resulted from a combination of circumstances that are not part of the experience of most countries in the South'. This construction of childhood arose in the particular circumstances of the Northern developed countries late in their industrialisation which consequently led to the removal of children from the labour market into education. However, the rationale of the Convention is that, irrespective of the level of development of a country, children can have a childhood by empowering children with rights and re-orientating social policy to ensure that the best interests of the child are of primary consideration. In other words, the Convention requires the universal attainment of a modern Western childhood without the industrialisation and development that was considered a prerequisite to this modern construction of childhood as a period of dependency and protection.

Southern Perspectives

Childhood remains a luxury that is unrealisable for the majority of the population in developing countries. Children in developing countries usually have to take on adult roles at a much earlier age than in industrial countries. For example, in Britain, under-fourteen year olds are considered too young according to social services guidelines to look after children but a significant number of households in Peru are headed by six to fourteen-year olds. Therefore, in circumstances where children are the head of the household, it can be seen that outlawing child labour makes little sense, which is why developing countries oppose the idea.

Developing countries were not demonstrating any complacency about the plight of children in their states by their lack of participation in the drafting process. The issue of children is a real one in developing countries where the majority of the population is young. However, developing countries did not want to be held responsible for circumstances which they considered to be beyond their control. They believed that improvements to children's lives could only come about as a result of the amelioration of the circumstances of the whole of the population and more equal international relations. Delegates from poorer countries pointed out that it would be impossible to eradicate child labour through legislation unless poverty which drove children to work was also eradicated. They called for a convention to bring about radical changes in international relations to overcome the huge disparities between the First and Third World. They wanted the Convention to promote a new era of international cooperation to end foreign exploitation and to develop the Third World.

The final version of the Convention does emphasise international cooperation but does not discuss redistributing wealth between the North and South, which the developing countries had pressed for. During the drafting of the Convention, the United States opposed a clause on international assistance in the Convention which would have required developed countries to provide assistance to developing countries and indicated that, 'the Convention will primarily create obligations for ratifying governments to respect the rights of, and to render assistance to, their own citizens'.

The Committee on the Rights of the Child (hereinafter the Committee) acknowledges the limited resources of developing countries advising them to 'undertake appropriate measures in accordance with their available resources'. Whilst the Committee is empowered to send reports to the UN and NGOs requesting advice and highlighting the need for assistance, the reality is an unequal relation between states. The assistance provided by donor countries relates to the priorities that they set rather than the priorities of recipient countries. It is Western donors who effectively decide what is in the best interests of the child. In fact, the international initiatives on children, such as the Declaration on the Survival, Protection and Development of Children adopted by the World Summit for Children in 1990, resemble or endorse structural adjustment policies previously condemned as detrimental to the welfare of children, such as cutting health budgets and subsidies on food and introducing school fees. For example, the Organisation of African Unity, in its report *Africa's Children, Africa's Future, Human Investment Priorities for the 1990s*, discussed the necessity of introducing certain unpalatable reforms under the National Plans of Action in terms of the welfare of the children of Africa, although their welfare would be undermined by the policies proposed. Thomas Hammarberg from Sweden, one of the ten experts on the Committee, has agreed with the structural adjustment programmes. He states that 'these policies relate to the rights of the child, as a responsible, and future orientated policy is naturally in the interest of children', arguing '[f]or them it is desirable that space is created for necessary investments and foreign debts are reduced'. The best interests of the child, according to experts on the Committee, turn out to be what the World Bank and Western financial institutions consider appropriate, rather than the countries themselves.

Infantilisation of the South

. . . .

The institutionalising and globalizing of Western models of childhood under the Convention means that the experience of childhood in developing countries is outlawed. For example, children in many parts of the world have to act as adults, commonly as child soldiers or child labourers, which is condemned by proponents of children's rights. As Allison James points out, the consequence of the setting of specific age limits for children, prescribing their participation in some spheres whilst proscribing others 'means that those children whose actions take place outside the limits set for "childhood" become pathologised' and that 'the Western ideology of childhood as a period of happiness and innocence works to exclude those for whom it is not'. Southern societies are judged as having violated their children because the lives of the children do not conform to the image of childhood held in the West.

The idea of children in the South having their childhood stolen by the state ignores the reality that the experiences of children cannot be separated from the conditions in society generally. A major focus of the Committee and international organisations is on the girl child. It has been noted that girls are more likely to suffer malnutrition, poverty and be deprived of education. When one examines, for example, malnutrition studies in detail, the worst differences between boys and girls are to be found in poorer families. Since the greatest disparities are in those sections of society most disadvantaged, where all family members suffer degrees of malnutrition, awareness education or equal treatment is no solution to malnutrition but simply means sharing out hunger. However, in the process of focusing on the girl child, those problems encountered are redefined as ones of discriminatory attitudes and practise, and not poverty. Similarly, the problem of the unequal relations between the North and the South is redefined as one of unequal relations between people in the Third World, thereby narrowing issues to the cultural attitudes of Third World whilst ignoring certain problematic aspects of North-South relations, such as unequal trading terms. The singling out of the plight of children implicitly blames the adult population for their suffering. Their plight becomes a sign of the moral failings of their society. The imperative of the best interests of the child gives outside agencies the legitimacy and powers to intervene; thus Southern societies through the failure to comply with Western childhoods become permanent objects of outside intervention. In other words, the discourse on children's rights infantilises the South.

The infantilisation of society becomes clearer when one examines the programmes of international organisations which seem preoccupied with saving both adults and children from themselves and which suggest that the people of the Third World are incapable of running their own societies. Many developing countries expressed concern at the conceptualisation of children's rights as being rights separate from their parents fearing that they would undermine families and communities. Since the Convention imposes obligations on individual states, rather than on the international community and conceives children's rights as rights against both the state and individual citizens, children are invited to blame the adults of their state for their plight. Their suffering as child labourers, child soldiers or even simply as victims of war and poverty becomes understood as a form of child abuse or neglect for which the adults of their country are held responsible. At the same time, children are encouraged to identify with international organisations who point the figure at the adult population for failing to act in the best interests of their children. The encouragement of a lack of trust towards their own people can be seen in the children's rights primer being distributed in schools in Serbia funded by UNICEF and Save the Children (Sweden). The primer sees Dad as the enemy and the United Nations as saviour, not highlighting the detrimental effect of UN sanctions on children's welfare, declaring — '[t]he United Nations is not there when Dad takes out his belt. There must be someone to save me in this dark wood. There must be some power to make Dad see sense'. In this way, the discourse of children's rights boosts the moral authority of international organisations which tend to be accountable to donors rather than recipients of programmes, whilst undermining that of the people and the institutions of their own country. Dissemination of mistrust between the generations will further weaken social cohesion.

. . . .

The Convention is part of the trend towards focusing on changing individual behaviour and individual relations. This approach has not had a significant impact on improving the plight of the vulnerable in the difficult socio-economic circumstances of the South. The problems of children cannot be put down to a lack of awareness of the interests of the child in individual states nor can their plight be alleviated without taking into account the wider political, economic and international context. With the best will or parenting classes in the world, many parents and their societies are unable to ensure their children are properly fed and clothed, receive education and do not have to work. In fact, UNICEF's annual reports on *The State of the World Children* reveals that in the eight years since the adoption of the Convention the overall position of children in the world has actually become worse. Whilst there has not been a general improvement in the welfare of children in the last decade, the discourse of children's rights suggests that the plight of children in the Third World is due to the moral failings of their societies.

Eva Brems, *Children's Rights and Universality*
in Developmental and Autonomy Rights of Children:
Empowering Children, Caregivers and Communities 21
(Jan C.M. Willems ed., 2002)

. . . .

3. THE UNIVERSAL CHILD? ACCOMMODATING DIVERSITY WITHIN INTERNATIONAL CHILDREN'S RIGHTS

A risk that is inherent in any group-based emancipation movement, is that of overstressing the shared characteristics of the group members, and hence ignoring the diversity among them. Inclusive universality for children requires taking into account children's specificities.... Children's need for protection, their situation of development and their autonomy are to a large extent shared by children around the world. Yet the universality of important aspects of 'childness' should not obscure the enormous diversity of contexts in which children live, and which strongly affect their enjoyment of human rights. This is particularly so for children who are members of other non-dominant groups. A fully inclusivist protection of their human rights requires not only the accommodation of their childness, but also of their other specificities, such as their cultural context, economic circumstances or gender.

The next section will examine how international children's rights, which are an expression of children's particularities, deal with other relevant particularities. To what extent does the CRC take into account diversity among children? Discounting diversity among children may be expressed in the text of the Convention, in specific provisions addressing the experiences of subgroups of children, for example girls or children in developing countries. It may also come into play when human rights are being interpreted. Contextual interpretation is facilitated by 'elastic' language in the Convention. In the CRC, there are many provisions which are framed in terms which allow a margin of contextual interpretation. On the one hand, some central notions such as 'the best interests of the child' (Article 3(1), cf. *infra),* and 'the evolving capacities of the child' (Article 5) have a vague and general character. On the other, there are modifying words that allow for flexibility of state obligations, such as the word 'appropriate,' that is used not less than 43 times in the CRC.

. . . .

3.1.1 Expressions of cultural pluralism in the text of the CRC

Concluded in November 1989, the CRC came more than 40 years after the Universal Declaration on Human Rights, and more than 20 years after the UN Covenants on Civil and Political Rights (ICCPR) and on Economic, Social and Cultural Rights (ICESCR).

In that time, the non-Western part of the world went a long way on the road to emancipation and self-assertion. Whereas historical circumstances accounted for the severe
under-representation of the non-Western world in the drafting process of the early international human rights texts, the opportunities for participating in the drafting of the
CRC were much better. Nevertheless, like other international human rights texts, the
Convention has been criticized for being too Western. Arguably, this criticism is somewhat less justified with regard to the CRC than with regard to other texts. In Olsen's view
the Convention 'can be seen as either cultural pluralist or cultural chauvinist, depending
upon one's expectations and upon one's understanding of how the document will be interpreted.'

Ennew mentions some CRC provisions that in her view are problematic for some
parts of the world: Article l6(l) on privacy, 'which has little relevance in countries
where individual physical privacy does not have high cultural value,' and 'the 'periodic
review of placement' in Article 25, 'which is hard to envisage in the context of traditional fostering systems as in West Africa.' Even though the dynamic of cultural change
calls for a qualification of this statement, it is undeniable that the drafters of the CRC
seem more often to have had the context and circumstances of Western children in
mind than those of the rest of the world. Yet in several provisions the CRC does account for cultural diversity. The preamble contains a paragraph on 'taking due account of the importance of the traditions and cultural values of each people for the
protection and harmonious development of the child.' Although a preambulary paragraph is not legally binding, this is an encouragement for using the cultural context
in a positive way in the interpretation of the CRC. Article 5, committing states to respect the rights and duties of caregivers to give the child direction and guidance, defines the caregivers in a cultural pluralist manner as 'parents or, where applicable, the
members of the extended family or community as provided for by the local custom,
legal guardians or other persons legally responsible for the child.' In the rest of the
Convention, however, the reference to the extended family and the community is not
repeated, creating an impression of a bias in favor of 'Western' nuclear-family households. In order to remedy this, Van Bueren suggests reading the other CRC provisions
in the light of Article 5.

Another sample of cultural pluralism in the CRC is Article 20(3), which mentions the
Islamic institution of Kafala next to foster care and adoption. Moreover in considering alternative care solutions, this paragraph states that one of the factors to pay due regard
to, is the child's religious and cultural background. Article 29(c) provides that the education of children must be directed to the development of respect for his or her own cultural identity (as well as for other civilizations). And Article 30 protects the right of
children belonging to minority groups to enjoy their own culture.

Sometimes the cultural sensitivity of a provision becomes clear only by comparing the
final text of the Convention with earlier drafts. Article 21 on adoption was originally
drafted in such a way that it committed states to facilitating the adoption process. In Islamic law however, adoption is prohibited. After objections in that sense had been voiced,
a compromise text was adopted, limiting the applicability of Article 21 to 'states parties
which recognize and/or permit the system of adoption.'

....

However, the most remarkable explicit reference to cultural differences in the CRC is
one that addresses tradition as a negative factor. In Article 24 on the right to health, the
third paragraph deals with harmful cultural practices: 'States Parties shall take all effec-

tive and appropriate measures with a view to abolishing traditional practices prejudicial to the health of children.' In the dates preceding the adoption of this text, the goal of abolishing harmful practices was not questioned. Yet upon insistence of especially the Senegalese delegate, the explicit reference to FGM[16] that was proposed by the delegates of Canada, United Kingdom and the United States was omitted. In the light of the *Travaux Préparatoires* there can be no doubt that Article 24(3) applies to FGM, yet the general wording avoids targeting Africa alone, as harmful practices involving children occur throughout the world. Two aspects of the CRC approach to harmful cultural practices should be highlighted.

… The state is ultimately responsible. Its obligation is a gradual one. The state does not have to account for each case of FGM, yet it should actively work toward its abolition. The phrase 'effective and appropriate measures' leaves ample room for adapting state policy to local circumstances and cultural sensitivities.

In the second place, harmful practices are brought under the umbrella of the right to health. This is a restricted view of the harm inherent in those practices: if traditional practices violate other human rights, such as the right to privacy (including physical integrity) or the prohibition of discrimination, the CRC does not call for their abolition. Even if such practices can still be condemned under other articles of the Convention, an *a contrario* argument based on the text of Article 24(3) may support their existence. The advantage of this approach however is that the reference to health is much more objective than a reference to the child's best interest or even his or her human rights, which are interpreted in widely diverging ways in different cultural contexts (cf. *infra*). Moreover, condemnations of FGM as 'torture' by Western activists have proven counterproductive because of their lack of cultural sensitivity.

3.1.2 Elastic Language: *The best interests of the child*

Article 3(1) CRC reads: 'In all actions concerning children, whether undertaken by public or private social welfare institutions, courts of law, administrative authorities or legislative bodies, the best interests of the child shall be a primary consideration.' Because of its role as a guiding principle of interpretation underlying the entire Convention, the concept of the best interests of the child is probably the most important example of elastic language in the CRC, allowing for contextually determined interpretations. Alston, who studied the best interests principle in the light of cultural diversity, states that there is 'enormous scope' for cultural difference to be taken into account in the implementation of CRC norms at the domestic level. Yet this margin of cultural diversity is not unlimited. Article 3(1) should not be separated from its context: the CRC as a whole 'goes at least some of the way towards providing the broad ethical or value framework that is often claimed to he the missing ingredient which would give a greater degree of certainty to the content of the best interests principle. As a result, 'it must be accepted that cultural considerations will have to yield when a clear conflict with human rights norms becomes apparent.'

When traditional practices are judged according to the 'best interests' standards, in many cases the outcome will depend on the weight attached to cultural factors. If the society in which he or she lives is organized in a certain way, it may be in the interest of the child to conform to that pattern, rather than breaking with it and becoming an outcast or suffering adverse consequences in other spheres that are directly or indirectly linked to

---

16. Female genital mutilation, sometimes called female circumcision.

the rejected practice. For example in paternalistic societies, awarding custody of children to the father is often in the best in the interest of the child, as 'the customs relevant to custody of children in such traditional societies are closely related not only to marital ties but also to the formation of familial alliances and the performance of religious practices. Yet in a specific situation, this reasoning may not apply, for example if the traditional subsistence economy and family structure of the father has broken down, and the mother may override the interest based on the cultural context which has largely become irrelevant. In societies where paternal authority is very important, cultural considerations may be used to justify this practice.

'If a child refuses to comply with a decision about marriage, then she or he may endure the wrath of society which holds such strong views about authority. In a context in which the child has to continue to live in the same society, it maybe said to be in the child's best interest to comply with parental will concerning such decision.'

Yet cultures are dynamic, and when the practice becomes less imperative from the cultural viewpoint, other considerations come to the forefront. The child's freedom and autonomy and protection against the risk of an abusive marriage may then be more important to his or her best interest than the advantages of cultural conformism.

The flexibility allowed by the notion of 'best interests of the child' should not only be seen in the cultural context. Other factors, such as the available resources, can equally be taken into account. For example, custody arrangements in Africa are strongly influenced by resource factors. Armstrong found that, many if not most children, stay with a number of different relatives for periods of their lives,' and that among low-income groups this transfer of custody is 'a way of sharing economic resources among family members.' Proximity to a school is often a reason for sending children to live with relatives, where they may perform household work in return. Thus, child custody is often an informal, fluctuating arrangement within the wider family. In a context of limited resources, it may be argued that these practices are in the child's best interests 'because they ensure better schooling opportunities and better nutrition.' On the other hand, sometimes these arrangements fail to produce the desired effect.

Children may not be enrolled at school or be burdened with so much work that they fail in their studies. In those situations, the arrangement is often no longer in the child's best interests. Clearly it is not sufficient to rely on one single factor (such as culture or economic resources) to determine the best interests of the child. What counts is the interplay of several factors in the concrete situation.

Child labor is another situation that illustrates this fact. The dominant view in human rights circles is that child labor must be eradicated. Article 32 CRC recognizes 'the right of the child to be protected from economic exploitation and from performing any work that is likely to he hazardous or to interfere with the child's education, or to he harmful to the child's health or physical, mental, spiritual, moral or social development.' However there may be contexts in which child labor, even if it interferes with the child's education, may be considered to be in the child's best interests. In a study conducted in Lesotho, Letuka argues that this is the case for both cultural and economic reasons. In the first place, it is difficult for parents to regard child labor as against the interests of children, because of its positive cultural perception. 'Child work is viewed as part and parcel of the child's education, recreation and holistic development,' it is a preparation for adulthood. At the same time, child work is a way for parents to assert their authority over their children, which is vital in the cultural context. Moreover, even when in a specific case child work is against the best interests of a child, it may be justified in Lesotho society, if it is in the broader interests of the household. A collective view is taken of the child's best interest:

> 'This means that it is not just the individual child who *is* considered but account is also taken of the interests of the other siblings. For this reason, it is not uncommon to find the interests of an older child being compromised for those of younger ones but such a situation would be interpreted as being in the best interests of the child.'

In the second place, economic factors also determine the child's best interests. In the Lesotho context, education is often seen as 'secondary in view of problems such as the pervasive poverty facing the majority of people, including children. The most immediate way in which the child's best interests can he served in this context, seems to be the satisfaction of basic needs such as food and shelter.' Children hired out by their families as paid labor make an economic contribution to the family. This is seen as being in the interests of the entire family, including the child.

3.2 Other types of diversity

3.2.1 Economic circumstances

The economic resources of both parents (or other caregivers) and the state may determine the way in which children's rights are protected and may even seriously restrict the extent to which they are protected. In Freeman's words, 'much of the world has as much chance of implementing the Convention as sending its citizens to the moon.' Full implementation especially of the 'provision' rights in the CRC may indeed be very far away in many states. But this does not mean that the Convention loses its relevance in situations of resource constraints. Like cultural diversity, diversity of economic circumstances is a contextual factor that has been taken into account in drafting the CRC.

In the first place, the CRC contains a number of references to the financial resources of parents and other caregivers. Article 27(2) gives parents and other caregivers the primary responsibility to secure the conditions of living necessary for the child's development 'within their abilities and financial capacities.' The next paragraph charges the state with assisting them in this task. Thus, the interplay within the *Trias Pedagogica* between parents and state is influenced by the financial situation of the parents, when it concerns the state's task of assistance (as opposed to intervention). Two other articles illustrate how the extent of the state's duties of providing assistance varies according to the parents' means. Article 23(3) provides that assistance for disabled children 'shall he provided free of charge, whenever possible, taking into account the financial resources of the parents or others caring for the child.' And Article 26(2) states that social security benefits should be granted 'taking into account the resources and the circumstances of the child and persons having responsibility for the maintenance of the child.' Yet state resources may themselves be severely restricted. In that perspective, the CRC highlights the importance of international cooperation with developing countries. It contains provisions in that sense dealing with disabled children (Article 23(4)), and the right to health (Article 24(4)), and the right to education (Article 28(3)).

Moreover, Article 4 provides that 'in regard to economic, social and cultural rights, States Parties shall undertake such measures to the maximum extent of their available resources, and where needed, within the framework of international cooperation.' Apart from the need for international cooperation, this provision establishes the principle of progressive realization for all economic, social and cultural rights in the CRC.

A similar provision is included in the ICESCR (Article 2(1)). CESCR (the Committee on Economic, Social and Cultural Rights) describes it as 'a necessary flexibility device,' in 'recognition of the fact that full realization of economic, social and cultural rights will generally not be able to be achieved in a short period of time.' Yet the Committee emphasizes that 'even where the available resources are demonstrably inadequate, the obligation remains for a State Party to strive to ensure the widest possible enjoyment of the relevant rights under the prevailing circumstances,' and that 'even in times of severe resources constraints (...) the vulnerable members of society can and indeed must be protected by the adoption of relatively low-cost targeted programmes.' Clearly children are amongst the most vulnerable members of society. Hence the Committee on the Rights of the Child frequently emphasizes in its Concluding Comments on state reports that important obligations in the field of economic, social and cultural rights remain regardless of resource constraints. The Committee regularly blames states for not taking adequate measures for ensuring those rights to the maximum extent of their available resources. It stresses in particular the need to protect the rights of the most vulnerable groups of children, including 'girls, children with disabilities, abandoned children, children born out of wedlock, children from single-parent families, children victims of abuse and/or exploitation, and nomadic and refugee children,' as well as 'children living in rural areas, children living and/or working in the street, children involved in the administration of juvenile justice system and children affected by or infected with HIV/AIDS' and children belonging to minority groups. The Committee systematically recommends that 'in the light of Article 4 of the Convention (...) priority be given in budget allocations to the realization of the economic, social and cultural rights of children, with particular emphasis on the enjoyment of these rights by disadvantaged children.' In this regard the CmRC goes further than the CESCR, which relatively rarely comments on a state's budget allocation....

Progressive realization is a useful flexibility tool, which makes it possible to vary standards of human rights evaluation according to the economic and financial situation of the state. In fact there is no reason why this technique should not be extended to all human rights. It is now generally recognized that the strict subdivision between civil and political rights on the one hand and economic, social and cultural rights on the other does not correspond to reality. In many instances, civil and political rights require considerable expenses for their realization, just like most social, economic and cultural rights. As progressive realization by no means allows governments to use resource constraints as a total excuse, the fear of lowering human rights standards by such an extension is unjustified. Rather, legal techniques allowing for the accommodation of relevant contextual factors facilitate the assessment of states' failure to provide a sufficient degree of human rights protection.

3.2.2 Gender

Among particularities that are relevant in a human rights context, gender should not be omitted. In many situations, women and girls become the victims of human rights violations because of their gender, or they experience human rights violations in a different way than men. For example, girl children are raped and abused to put pressure on their relatives or to create a climate of terror. In some cultures the preference for male children leads to depriving girls of sufficient food, healthcare and education. Moreover, girls are the victims of harmful traditional practices, such as child marriage and FGM. In many countries, there are laws that discriminate against girls, for example denying them equal inheritance rights. In the family and in the community they are subject to sexual abuse, which is often not sufficiently addressed by the state authorities.

Although it is clear from the *Travaux Préparatoires* that certain provisions of the CRC, in particular Article 24(3) on harmful cultural practices, have girl-children as a particular target group, the CRC does not include any specific provisions on the girl child. This stands in contrast with the specific references to the girl child in more recent texts, such as the Vienna Declaration. For this reason, some commentators think that the CRC is not sufficiently equipped to tackle the specific human rights problems of girls. On the other hand, there is the opinion that considers the CRC as a feminist landmark. The CRC indeed stands out among human rights conventions as the only one using inclusive language. Where possible, the Convention avoids mentioning gender, and simply refers to 'the child.' In those instances where the use of a possessive pronoun is required, the text consistently uses the double form: 'his or her.'

Moreover, despite the gender-neutral language, many problems of specific relevance to girls are addressed in the CRC more adequately than in any other convention. The provision on harmful cultural practices is one example. Price Cohen mentions some others: Article 19 protects against interfamilial violence, and Article 39 obliges states to take measures to promote recovery and reintegration of victims of neglect and abuse. Olsen also points to the other articles protecting against sexual abuse and related violations (Articles 14 and 35), and to the strong emphasis on 'positive,' rather than 'negative rights.'

4. Conclusion

The CRC is inherently inspired by the dynamic of inclusive universality: it formulates human rights that are adapted to children's specificities. Through the use of occasional context-specific provisions and frequent elastic terminology, it moreover allows to a significant extent for the accommodation of diversity among children.

Notes and Questions

1. What does Pupavac see as problematic about the UNCRC? What does she mean by the "infantilisation of the South"? Is this a fair characterization? If she is correct, why have so many developing countries ratified the Convention? Does Pupavac imply that because child soldiers and child laborers are realities of life in some countries, that it is wrong to create international calls to end these practices?

2. Is there a universal standard of childhood upon which all states can agree? If not, does the idea of an overarching "Convention on the Rights of the Child" make sense? Should the project be abandoned in favor of narrower, more targeted norms?

3. Brems suggests that examination of the *travaux préparatoires* illustrates more cultural sensitivity than the UNCRC itself might reveal. In which articles of the Convention do you imagine significant compromise and cultural awareness must have played a role behind the scenes? Does Brems give enough weight to the idea that children are autonomous individuals, and that one of the main points of the UNCRC was to compel the societies in which they live to act quickly to ensure the realization of children's rights?

4. While both authors address similar problems with the UNCRC, Brems seems to believe that the Convention in fact has sufficient flexibility to deal with cultural variation. Which, if either of them, has it right?

Problem for Discussion

Cultural relativism and children's rights: The UNCRC, child marriage and female genital mutilation (FGM)

Article 24(3) of the UNCRC affirms the child's right to the highest attainable standard of health, stating that "States Parties shall take all effective and appropriate measures with a view to abolishing traditional practices prejudicial to the health of children." Both child marriage and female genital mutilation (FGM) are often discussed in the context of Article 24(3). The Brems article (above) discusses the fact that FGM was a very sensitive issue during the drafting of the UNCRC. Ultimately, the Convention failed to mention explicitly which traditional practices were to be discouraged by States Parties to the Convention. Was this reticence consistent with the spirit of the Convention? How might the CRC have expressed itself in clearer and easier-to-apply terms?

Read the following brief selections on child marriage and FGM. Then reconsider UNCRC Article 24(3) pertaining to harmful traditional practices. Do you think the Convention should have been more explicit about such issues, or was the more circumspect approach the correct one? Should the UNCRC attempt to take sides on cultural practices that affect the health and wellbeing of so many children, especially girls?

Child Marriage

Child marriage is common in many parts of the world, where it is identified with a wide variety of health consequences. As the short article below indicates, many girls are married by the time they are young teenagers, exposing them to the risks posed by early pregnancy. Is this a "children's rights" issue, or is it primarily a matter of cultural tradition?

For a sense of how widely accepted child marriage is in certain Indian states, see BBC news, Mass weddings for India's child brides, http://news.bbc.co.uk/player/nol/newsid _5050000/newsid_5057800/5057820.stm?bw=nb&mp=wm&news=1&nol_storyid= 5057820&bbcws=1.

The UNICEF report below created a great stir when it was published in 2001. Calling on extensive data, UNICEF was able to identify child marriage as a widespread problem, with serious implications for the health and education, not to mention personal happiness, of the children involved.

Early Marriage Child Spouses

UNICEF, Innocenti research center, No. 7. March 2001, *available at* http://www.unicef-irc.org/publications/pdf/digest7e.pdf

While early marriage takes many different forms and has various causes, one issue is paramount. Whether it happens to a girl or a boy, early marriage is a violation of human rights. The right to free and full consent to a marriage is recognized in the 1948 Universal Declaration of Human Rights (UDHR) and in many subsequent human rights instruments — consent that cannot be 'free and full' when at least one partner is very immature. For both girls and boys, early marriage has profound physical, intellectual, psychological and emotional impacts, cutting off educational opportunity and chances of personal growth. For girls, in addition, it will almost certainly mean premature pregnancy and childbearing, and is likely to lead to a lifetime of domestic and sexual subservience over which they have no control.

- Yet many societies, primarily in Africa and South Asia, continue to support the idea that girls should marry at or soon after puberty. Their spouses are likely to be a few years older than they are, but may be more than twice their age. Parents and heads of families make marital choices for daughters and sons with little regard for the personal implications. Rather, they look upon marriage as a family-building strategy, an economic arrangement or a way to protect girls from unwelcome sexual advances.

....

How Common is Early Marriage?

The practice of marrying girls at a young age is most common in Sub-Saharan Africa and South Asia. However, in the Middle East, North Africa and other parts of Asia, marriage at or shortly after puberty is common among those living traditional lifestyles. There are also specific parts of West and East Africa and of South Asia where marriages much earlier than puberty are not unusual, while marriages of girls between the ages of 16 and 18 are common in parts of Latin America and in pockets of Eastern Europe.

One problem in assessing the prevalence of early marriages is that so many are unregistered and unofficial and are not therefore counted as part of any standard data collection system. Very little country data exist about marriages under the age of 14, even less about those below age 10. An exception is Bangladesh, where the Demographic and Health Survey (DHS) of 1996–97 reported that 5 per cent of 10–14 year-olds were married.

Small-scale studies and anecdotal information fill in the picture. They imply that marriage at a very young age is more widespread than country data suggest. National statistics often disguise significant rates of very early marriage in some regions and among some sub-populations. In the Indian state of Rajasthan, for example, a 1993 survey of 5,000 women revealed that 56 per cent had married before age 15, and of these, 17 per cent were married before they were 10. A 1998 survey in Madhya Pradesh found that nearly 14 per cent of girls were married between the ages of 10 and14. In Ethiopia and in parts of West Africa, marriage at seven or eight is not uncommon. In Kebbi State, Northern Nigeria, the average age of marriage for girls is just over 11 years, against a national average of 17.

Plenty of marriage data exist for those aged 15–19, mostly in relation to reproduction or schooling. DHS data also allow some analysis of the proportion of women currently married who married below age 18.

Sub-Saharan Africa

Trends have been exhaustively examined courtesy of World Fertility Survey and DH S data. Analysts have detected two groups of countries: those where marriage age is rising, such as Kenya, Uganda, Zimbabwe and Senegal, and those where there is little change, including Cameroon, Cote d'Ivoire, Lesotho, Liberia and Mali. In several countries, over 40 per cent of young women have entered marriage or a quasi-married union by the time they reach the age of 18. By contrast, in only two countries are more than 10 per cent of boys under 19 married. Early marriage is generally more prevalent in Central and West Africa—affecting 40 per cent and 49 per cent respectively of girls under 19—compared to 27 per cent in East Africa and 20 per cent in North and Southern Africa. Many of these young brides are second or third wives in polygamous households.

In some African countries, notably Botswana and Namibia, few girls marry in their teens. However, cohabitation is relatively common. While the trend towards later marriage is clear for the continent as a whole, there are some countries, such as Lesotho and Mozambique, where the trend has been in the other direction. There are also cases where the stress of conflict or HIV/AIDS seems to be contributing to early marriage.

Asia

Marriage patterns are much more diverse. The extreme cases are Afghanistan and Bangladesh, where 54 per cent and 51 per cent of girls respectively are married by age 18.27 In Nepal, where the average age at first marriage is 19 years, 7 per cent of girls are married before they are 10 years old and 40 per cent by the time they are 15. In China, the proportion of early marriages fell by 35 per cent in the 1970s, but rose from 13 percent in 1979 to 18 per cent in 1987. In many Asian countries, such as Vietnam and Indonesia, there are vast differences among regions, states or islands; some in line with ethnographic patterns. Meanwhile some countries have managed to raise the age of marriage significantly. In Sri Lanka, for example, the average age at first marriage is 25, compared to 19 in neighboring India.

Middle East and North Africa

Early marriage is less common in this region than in South Asia or Sub-Saharan Africa. Data are scarce, but we know that 55 per cent of women under 20 in the United Arab Emirates are married, while in Sudan the figure is 42 per cent. In a number of countries, averages may again disguise major disparities. A Ministry of Health field study in Upper (southern) Egypt in the late 1980s discovered that 44 per cent of rural women married in the previous five years had been under the legal age of 16 at the time.

Caribbean and Latin America

In this region, UNICEF reports that 11.5 per cent of girls aged 15–19 are married. These figures also mask diversity, with much higher ages in the Caribbean, and lower ages in countries such as Paraguay, Mexico and Guatemala. Marriage age among rural indigenous peoples is typically much lower than that of the urbanized population, in keeping with traditional patterns. In the Dominican Republic, the proportion of early marriages actually rose during the early 1990s from 30 per cent to 38 per cent.

North America, Europe, Oceania

In industrialized countries, few women marry before age 18; only 4 per cent do so in the USA and 1 per cent in Germany, for example. But in some parts of Central and Eastern Europe, early marriage survives; notably among the Roma people and in Macedonia where 27 per cent of the women who married in 1994 were aged between 15 and 19. In most of Eastern Europe and the CIS, average age at marriage is in the low to mid-20s, implying some proportion in the teens (in the Kyrgyz Republic, 11.5 per cent).

Throughout Oceania, the average age of marriage for women is over 20. However, in Kiribati, Marshall Islands, Papua New Guinea and Solomon Islands, at least 18 per cent of women are married between 15 and 19.

Globally, it is important to note that early marriage, and early childbearing, have been more or less abandoned by the wealthiest sections of society, even in poor and highly traditional countries. Virtually everywhere, poor women in rural areas tend to marry younger than those in urban areas, and educational levels also play a critical role. An examination of the timing of marriage and the level of education ... shows consistently higher percentages of women with at least seven years of schooling marrying at age 20 or above.

Elizabeth Warner, *Behind the Wedding Veil:*
Child Marriage as a Form of Trafficking in Girls

12 American University Journal of Gender, Social Policy & the Law
233 (2004)

....

III. International Conventions Relating to Child Marriage

B. Convention on the Rights of the Child ("CRC")

The CRC, intended as a comprehensive treaty on the rights of children, contains no explicit provision on marriage, which is odd, if not downright baffling. (Perhaps the drafters thought the subject was already covered by the Marriage Convention.) However, there are a number of provisions which could arguably apply to child marriage and are worth examining.

Article 1 of the CRC provides that "a child means every human being below the age of eighteen years, unless under the law applicable to the child, majority is attained earlier." The word "majority" is deliberately not defined in the CRC and is left to local law to determine. Consider how problematic this provision is in the case of a married female child. In a society where a woman's value is defined entirely by reference to her marital status and her ability to bear children, a married female is likely to be viewed as having attained adult, or "majority," status regardless of her age, all the more so once she has borne a child of her own. One could therefore argue that the entire CRC becomes irrelevant to her at that point. And indeed, many domestic laws explicitly provide that a person attains majority upon marriage regardless of her age, thus creating an exception to the general "rule of 18" that eviscerates the CRC mandate where it is most needed.

Assuming this hurdle can somehow be overcome and the CRC remains applicable to a married girl-child, other provisions may potentially be invoked. Article 2 of the CRC prohibits "discrimination" of any form against children, including on the basis of sex, and Article 3 provides that "[i]n all actions concerning children ... the best interests of the child shall be a primary consideration," and that States Parties must "undertake to ensure the child such protection and care as is necessary for his or her well-being...." The CRC also provides that all children shall have the right to protection from all forms of physical or mental violence, injury, abuse, maltreatment or exploitation; the right to health; the right to education; the right to protection from abduction, sale or trafficking; the right to rest and leisure, the right to protection from economic exploitation and the right to protection from all forms of exploitation prejudicial to the child's welfare. Given the horrific consequences of child marriage ..., it is not inconceivable to think that the practice could be attacked as violative of at least some of these provisions.

Article 24.3 provides that States Parties shall take measures to abolish "traditional practices prejudicial to the health of children." This provision, which was probably adopted with female genital mutilation in mind, may be the best clause to invoke against child marriage, given the extreme health risks associated with sexual intercourse and childbearing before the girl's body is sufficiently mature.

But there are other provisions of the CRC that could be construed to sanctify child marriage, in direct contradiction to the provisions just cited. Article 14.2 directs States Parties to "respect the rights and duties of parents ... to provide direction to the child in the exercise of his or her right [to freedom of religion] in a manner consistent with the evolving capacities of the child." This is one of many provisions in the CRC that grants deference to the rights of parents to control aspects of their children's lives, particularly in the case of religion, education, and cultural heritage. One could argue that the CRC explicitly protects the right of a father to instruct his daughter on how to be a good Muslim (or, for that matter, a good Mormon) and to honor and obey the father's pious decision to marry off his daughter at age five. After all, at that age, isn't the parent so much wiser than the child on the child's religious obligations? And doesn't freedom of religion imply that outsiders not second-guess the father's decision to "direct" his infant daughter into marriage as sanctified by the Koran and other religious teachings?

Given all these shortcomings and ambiguities, one cannot look to the CRC as providing a strong framework for prohibiting child marriage, which is unfortunate.

....

FGM

Female genital mutilation (FGM) is one way to describe the phenomenon described below; a more neutral designation is "female circumcision." As more families from countries where the practice is widespread have moved to Europe and the United States, international awareness of FGM has risen dramatically. See for example Female circumcision on the rise, BBC news, March 24, 2004, available at http://news.bbc.co.uk/2/hi/uk_news/3564203.stm, explaining that the rise of this practice within the UK is causing consternation to the authorities.

How should the UNCRC affect our understanding of and response to the practice? Can a country that allows large numbers of young girls to be subjected to FGM be considered a State Party in good standing to the Convention, or is the Convention so vague on such matters that countries cannot be faulted for failing to act?

The following excerpt from a UNICEF report on the prevalence of FGM in various countries paints a picture of a strikingly common practice.

Female Genital Mutilation/Cutting: A Statistical Exploration
UNICEF (2005)
available at http://www.unicef.org/publications/files/
FGM-C_final_10_October.pdf

....

A violation of rights

In the absence of any perceived medical necessity, it subjects girls and women to health risks and has life-threatening consequences. Among those rights violated are the right to the highest attainable standard of health and to bodily integrity. Furthermore, it could be argued that girls (under 18) cannot be said to give informed consent to such a potentially damaging practice as FGM/C.

FGM/C is, further, an extreme example of discrimination based on sex. The Convention on the Elimination of All Forms of Discrimination against Women defines discrimination as "any distinction, exclusion or restriction made on the basis of sex which has the effect or purpose of impairing or nullifying the recognition, enjoyment or exercise by women, irrespective of their marital status, on a basis of equality of men and women, of human rights and fundamental freedoms in the political, economic, social, cultural, civil or any other field" (article 1). Used as a way to control women's sexuality, FGM/C is a main manifestation of gender inequality and discrimination "related to the historical suppression and subjugation of women," denying girls and women the full enjoyment of their rights and liberties.

As stated in the Convention on the Rights of the Child, all actions concerning children should be undertaken in the best interests of the child (article 3.1). The Convention further asserts that children should have the opportunity to develop physically in a healthy way, receive adequate medical attention and be protected from all forms of violence, injury or abuse. While 'the best interests of the child' may be subject to cultural interpretation, FGM/C is an irreparable, irreversible abuse and therefore violates girls' right to protection.

Governments have sometimes been reluctant to address FGM/C. Considered to be a sensitive issue, it has been widely viewed as a 'private' act that is carried out by individuals and family members rather than state actors. But the health and psychological consequences of the practice itself, as well as the underlying causes that reinforce it, make it imperative for societies, governments and the entire international community to take action towards ending FGM/C.

III. GLOBAL PREVALENCE RATES

FGM/C occurs throughout the world. WHO estimates that between 100 million and 140 million girls and women alive today have experienced some form of the practice. It is further estimated that up to 3 million girls in sub-Saharan Africa, Egypt and Sudan are at risk of genital mutilation annually.

... [G]lobal prevalence rates display significant regional and geographic variations. In north-eastern Africa, prevalence varies from 97 per cent in Egypt to 80 per cent in Ethiopia. In western Africa, 99 per cent of women in Guinea, 71 per cent in Mauritania, 17 per cent in Benin and 5 per cent in Niger have undergone FGM/C. Where data are available for south-eastern Africa, the prevalence rates are relatively lower at 32 per cent in Kenya, for example, and 18 per cent in the United Republic of Tanzania.

Using available survey data, countries where FGM/C is practiced can be broadly separated into three groups according to prevalence rates. Countries within each group show similarities in the way that FGM/C is practiced and in inter-regional prevalence variations. This section reflects the particular context within which FGM/C is practiced and attempts to suggest programmatic interventions and strategies to end it.

Group 1 is made up of countries where nearly all women have undergone genital mutilation or cutting. The prevalence rates for countries in this group are high, at 80 per cent or more. Data within countries display very little or insignificant variation by sociodemographic variables, including geographic location or background characteristics. In this context, programs to end FGM/C will be most effective if they target women from all regional and socio-economic groups throughout the country.

For the countries in Group 2, the FGM/C prevalence rates are at intermediate levels of 25 per cent to 79 per cent. The general characteristics of this tier are that only certain ethnic groups within the country practice FGM/C, at varying intensities.

Group 3 also consists of countries where only some ethnic groups within the country practice FGM/C. The countries in this group, however, have low national prevalence rates, between 1 per cent and 24 per cent. Strategies designed to end FGM/C in countries included in Group 3 should consider these variations in prevalence rates along ethnic and regional lines. Programmatic interventions will be most effective if they are informed by the differing attitudes and practices among the diverse ethnic communities.

For both Group 2 and Group 3, the presentation of data by socio-economic variables can significantly enhance understanding of the practice and provide a valuable entry point for programmatic interventions.

The following presents case studies for three countries—Egypt, Kenya and Benin—as they represent each of the three groups.

In Egypt, a country included in Group 1, FGM/C is almost universal among women of reproductive age. According to the most recent DHS data (2003), among women aged 15–49 who are or have been married the prevalence rate is 97 per cent. Estimates of FGM/C prevalence rates obtained from the past three DHS (1995, 2000 and 2003) are virtually constant, indicating the possibility of no change over the past decade. This can also be explained, however, by the fact that girls in Egypt generally undergo FGM/C between the ages of 7 and 11, and it would therefore take at least one generation for any decline to be reflected in the data.

… Because almost all girls in Egypt undergo FGM/C, few differences in prevalence rates can be observed at the regional or educational levels. For example, 95 per cent of women living in urban areas have undergone genital mutilation/cutting, compared to 99 per cent of women living in rural areas.

In Egypt in 1959, a ministerial decree made FGM/C punishable by fine or imprisonment. Later decrees allowed certain forms but punished others. In 1996, a Ministry of Health decree was upheld by Egypt's highest administrative court. It prohibited all medical and non-medical practitioners from conducting FGM/C in public or private facilities, except for medical reasons certified by the head of a hospital's obstetric department. In 1997, the Court of Cessation upheld this ban.

Kenya provides an example of a country where FGM/C is practiced only among certain ethnic groups and prevalence rates are intermediate (Group 2). According to the 2003 DHS, 32 per cent of women 15–49 years have undergone FGM/C; the 1998 DHS reported a similar figure, 38 per cent.

From a sub national perspective, Kenya reveals significant regional variations …, with FGM/C rates ranging from 4 per cent in the west to 99 per cent in the north-east. These regional variations reflect the presence of diverse ethnic communities. FGM/C prevalence countrywide is nearly universal among women of the Somali (97 per cent), Kisii (96 per cent) and Masai (93 per cent) groups, and significantly lower among Kikuyu (34 per cent) and Kamba (27 per cent) women.

Significant ethnic and regional variations can also be observed in the FGM/C status of daughters. While 21 per cent of all women in Kenya report having their eldest daughter mutilated or cut, the rate reported for daughters of Somali women reaches 98 per cent. Among Luhya, Luo and Swahili women, however, less than 2 per cent report having their eldest daughter circumcised.

Kenya in 2001 adopted a Children's Code stating that "no person shall subject a child to female circumcision." There are, however, no significant laws making the practice illegal. The Penal Code does contain provisions pertaining to 'Offences against Person and Health', which could be applicable to instances involving FGM/C.14

Benin is a Group 3 country in which FGM/C affects only a small proportion of the population. According to the 2001 DHS data, 17 per cent of women aged 15–49 have undergone some form of genital mutilation or cutting.

At the sub national level, however, FGM/C rates vary significantly across regional and ethnic lines …, ranging from lower than 2 per cent in the Atlantique, Mono and Oueme regions, to as high as 58 per cent in Borgou. FGM/C is highly prevalent among the Peulh (88 per cent), Bariba (77 per cent) and Lokpa and Yoa ethnic groups (72 per cent), but almost non-existent among the Fon (0.3 per cent). FGM/C is not practiced by women of the Adja ethnic group.

In Benin, similar variations in prevalence by region and ethnicity can be observed among daughters. A total of 6 per cent of women in Benin report having at least one of their daughters circumcised. In the regions of Atacora and Borgou, these numbers are 21 per cent and 20 per cent, respectively. In the rest of the country, prevalence among daughters is less than 2 per cent. FGM/C status of daughters is highest among the Bariba (30 per cent), Lokpa and Yoa (26 per cent) and Peulh (38 per cent). It is not done to daughters in the Adja ethnic group and is less than 5 per cent among the other ethnic groups.

Generational trends

The differences between the percentage of women aged 15–49 who have undergone FGM/C and the percentage of women aged 15–49 with at least one daughter circumcised indicate a change in the prevalence of FGM/C: a generational trend towards ending the practice.… This is of particular importance in countries where the prevalence among women is higher than 75 per cent. In Egypt and Guinea, for example, where almost all women aged 15–49 have undergone FGM/C, only about half of the women indicated that their daughters have undergone FGM/C.

———————

Fear of being a victim of the cultural practice of FGM has become a grounds for seeking asylum in the U.S. and Europe. See for example *Sierra Leone anger at FGM asylum in UK*, BBC news, October 19, 2006, available at http://news.bbc.co.uk/2/hi/africa/6065682.stm, describing a decision by the British House of Lords to grant a young woman asylum on these grounds.

Questions for Discussion

1. For countries with either widespread child marriage or FGM, or both, how might ratification of the UNCRC affect their domestic policies? As you read the UNCRC, how much "relativity" does the Convention leave in place for ratifying countries on such issues? In your view, do the traditional practices described above constitute clear violations of the Convention? What other traditional practices tend to violate the rights contained in the Convention?

2. Does the phenomenon of child marriage simply reflect the realities of poverty? Is it appropriate for international institutions to tell families who exist under such a cultural regime that they are violating their daughters' rights? If so, how should the issue be framed and presented?

3. Note the adoption in June 2003 of the Cairo Declaration for the Elimination of FGM, available at http://www.childinfo.org/files/fgmc_Cairodeclaration.pdf, a set of principles and recommendations agreed upon by experts from a broad range of countries in which the

practice of FGM is commonly practiced. Among other recommendations, the declaration states that governments should "adopt specific legislation addressing FGM in order to affirm their commitment to stopping the practice and to ensure women's and girl's human rights." Governments are called upon to "formulate time-bound objectives, strategies, plans of action, and programs, backed by adequate national resources, whereby FGM laws will be enforced, taking into account that legislation condemning FGM has a moral force and an educational impact that could dissuade many individuals from submitting girls to the practice."

4. Designation of the "girl child" for separate human rights consideration has been controversial. In light of the problems of child marriage and FGM, how could emphasis on the child's gender help formulate a human rights based solution for these culture-specific problems?

————

B. The UNCRC As a "Mythic" Document

The following article makes the case that the UNCRC is simply too abstract, too sweeping and too idealistic to be meaningful. David Smolin argues that though widely ratified, most ratifying states have no real intention of living up to the terms of the Convention. He places the UNCRC in what he terms its "mythic" context. Specifically, he makes the point that the UNCRC attempts to give children what disadvantaged adult groups have been given through human rights laws: the gift of liberation. He reasons that children cannot be "liberated" in this way without first ceasing to be children at all. His criticism is distinguishable from other writers', in that he is targeting not so much the content of the Convention as its inherent unattainability. In Smolin's view, the Convention purports to offer children what they can never, by virtue of their childhood itself, actually have.

David M. Smolin, *A Tale of Two Treaties: Furthering Social Justice Through the Redemptive Myths of Childhood*
17:3 Emory International Law Review 967 (2004)

I. Children as Misfits: Contemporary Mythologies of Childhood

Children are misfits within the contemporary world. Children today, as women in an earlier age, make, in Charles Dickens' words, "an ass of the law."

Globalization, built around the values and institutions of the wealthy Northern nations, centers on autonomy and efficiency. The latter serves as the primary accountability for the former. You have choice so long as you are willing and able to pay its costs.

Children do not fit because they are neither autonomous nor efficient. Children begin life helpless, and childhood is legally defined by incapacities rather than capacities. Children are terribly inefficient and costly creatures, particularly within the developed nations, which have severely limited child labor.

....

The emancipation of slaves and women (and of religious minorities) is foundational to modernization. Narratives, in which a previously enslaved and oppressed class of humanity — such as women or African-Americans — is liberated into a regimen of autonomous equality, are the modern world's redemption stories. The primary limitation we allow to this regimen of autonomous equality is that of efficiency, the requirement that you pay your own way, and bear the costs of your own choices.

The contemporary world strains to adapt this redemption narrative to children. We know how to tell the first part of the story, the tale of the oppressed, enslaved child. We use "poster children" to publicize every possible ill: disease, poverty, war, rape, abuse, and ignorance. We can tell a partial redemption story: the story of disease cured, poverty alleviated, war stopped, and children protected and taught. These narratives are deeply satisfying. Often, however, our redemption myths surrounding children are misleading in two fundamental ways. First, although we can tell individual stories of redemption from these various ills, many of them—such as poverty, disease, and war—remain problems the adult world has not yet overcome. We can use children to sentimentalize and symbolize our desire for a world of health, wealth, and peace, but we cannot truly redeem our children from disease, poverty, and war until we in fact eliminate these besetting ills. Second, we cannot tell our usual tale of redemption—the transition from bondage into a condition of autonomous equality—about children, without in fact eliminating childhood itself. So we have failed, in the global sense, to actually deliver children from oppression and bondage. The oppressive ills of the adult world continue to wreak havoc in the lives of both children and adults, and the intrinsic bondage of childhood has thus far proved virtually irremediable.

The two kinds of deliverance, moreover, are in many cases competitive and contradictory. Take, for example, the question of a twelve-year old engaged, like his father or mother, in some kind of hard and onerous work. Our desire to free the child from the characteristic hazards and ills of the adult world suggest that we "protect" the child by removing him or her from the work force. If we restrict this "child's" legal capacity to work in the name of redemption from the ills of the adult world, we at the very same time condemn the child to another kind of bondage, that of the non-autonomous minor. Ironically, it is particularly the rich Northern nations that have most extended the bondage and incapacities of childhood, by child labor laws and other restrictions on minors. The rich nations are typically attempting to force the rest of the world to accept raised ages of majority, stricter child labor laws, and other incapacities of childhood. By contrast, millions of children in the poorer, Southern nations are "liberated" into the adult work world at a relatively tender age, only to be subject more directly to the brutal ills of adult life in those countries.

Law, while ostensibly rational, is sometimes driven by deep, irrational structures of thought. We can label these larger structures of thoughts as myths, archetypes, or ideologies. These structures are "irrational" in the sense that they are not generally subject to rational evaluation. Rather, these structures form the goals and purposes against which society judges the success of its laws. These structures are sometimes also irrational in the sense of being self-contradictory.

The two redemptive myths of childhood—redemption from the ills of adult work and redemption from the bondage of childhood—are irrational in both senses. These myths drive law and policy in relation to children, particularly in the international arena. They are implicit and thus not often—or at least not often enough—subject to examination. Rather than being examined, these myths set the standards under which law and society are themselves evaluated. These myths are also irrational in the sense of being both self-contradictory and contradictory in relationship to one another.

Delivering children from the ills of the adult world is self-contradictory because children inevitably live in the world made and governed by adults, and therefore cannot escape all of its ills. Delivering children from the bondage of childhood is self-contradictory because it is biologically, socially, and legally inevitable that human beings pass through a developmental stage of dependency on adults. The two goals are contradictory to one another because our limited ability to protect children from the ills of the world is dependent on maintaining their legal and practical bondage to the authority of adults; to free them from the authority of adults is to send them into full competition with adults for the limited goods of this world, with full exposure to the ills of the adult world.

....

A. Children's Rights and Human Rights: The Convention on the Rights of the Child

There are at least two ways to read the CRC. Positively, the CRC can be read as an idealistic document describing what children, in a much improved world, would receive from the adult world. Within this improved world, children would at every stage of development receive just the right combination of protection, provision, guidance, and autonomy. Thus, children would be protected from want, war, and disease. They would be provided with caring parents, nutritious meals, excellent health care, and appropriate education. As children grew they would progressively be provided with developmentally appropriate choices regarding media, recreation, associations, religion, and culture. The state would effectively prevent current ills such as child prostitution, child pornography, child trafficking, child abuse, child labor, and children's involvement in the use, production, or trafficking of illicit drugs. The state would effectively intervene on behalf of particularly vulnerable children, acting in the best interests of the child in regard to child abuse, adoption, child refugees, children separated from their families, and disabled children. Children would be prepared for "responsible life in a free society, in the spirit of understanding, peace, tolerance, equality of sexes, and friendship among all peoples," which presumably would require all nations to constitute such free, tolerant, and egalitarian societies. While this picture seems wildly discordant with the contemporary world, it can certainly be viewed as stating very positive goals and ideals.

This positive view of the CRC resolves the apparent contradiction between protecting and freeing children through an implicit child development approach, under which the balance between protection and autonomy would shift progressively toward the latter as the child grew in age and maturity. Thus, the two redemptive myths of childhood, that of saving children from the ills of the adult world and freeing children from the bondage of childhood, are at least theoretically reconcilable. Since both parents and societies commonly grant more autonomy to children as they age and mature, this kind of resolution can have broad credence, at least as a general principle.

This apparent resolution of the paradox of "children's rights" is facilitated by the abstract nature of the CRC, which for the most part does not provide specific guidelines for when and as to what issues autonomy will trump protection. This abstractness would seem necessary to a convention designed to encompass the entire world, with its myriad of cultures. The path and timetable from childhood to adulthood is not identical in the varied cultures of the world.

....

The negative view of the CRC comes from reading it as a legally enforceable document subject to adjudication, rather than reading it as a broad set of abstract principles. Opponents of the CRC within the United States reflect this legalistic interpretation. Rather than perceiving the CRC as an idealistic document, balancing the abstractions of protection and autonomy with a developmental view of the child, the CRC is perceived as a backdoor cultural attack on traditional lifestyles.

From the negative perspective, the broad autonomy rights guaranteed by the CRC comprise a significant attack on parental rights. For example, Articles 13 and 17 of the CRC broadly guarantee children's rights to access information and media. Parents are not mentioned in these particular sections, making it unclear whether these rights may be asserted against parental, as well as state, limitations. Of course, even if one determined that parental rights were constrained by children's autonomy rights, the question of a reasonable balance would remain. Articles 13 and 17 provide for the limitation of children's autonomy rights based on public order, public health, public morals, and the well being of children.

Supporters of the treaty would probably view these sections as representing a reasonable balance, whether the conflict is between child and parent or child and state. However, social conservatives within the United States do not expect their vision of "reasonable balance" to be validated by their society's elites. Many legal and professional elites take a far broader view of appropriate children's autonomy than do social conservatives, and would probably take a very different view of the kinds of information and media that children, at various ages, should be free to access. The idea that these elites could overturn a parent's views in these matters is thus rather frightening to some. It can appear that the CRC would become a deliberately inserted wedge between parents and children, and a way for the broader society to culturally steal children from traditionalist subcultures within America.

Some social conservatives within the United States trust the United Nations even less than they trust American cultural elites. They expect international bodies such as the United Nations to be hostile to their values. The tendency of international conferences related to women's rights to engage in highly publicized controversies over culturally sensitive reproductive and sexuality issues has added to this perception. The controversy over abortion and reproductive issues at the 2002 U.N. Special Session on Children reinforced this perception and specifically applied it to children's issues.

The interpretative approach of the ... experts who function as the Committee sometimes contributes to this distrust. The Committee's country reports consistently take the position that all corporal punishment, whether in schools or within families, should be made illegal and even criminal. This concern appears to be deeply felt by the Committee. For example, the Committee's July 2002 report "deeply regrets that [A]rticle 154 of the Spanish Civil Code stating that parents 'may administer punishment to their children reasonably and in moderation' has not yet been revised." The Committee consistently interprets Article 19 of the CRC, requiring states parties to "protect the child from all forms of physical or mental violence," to require states parties to "prohibit ... corporal punishment in the upbringing of children." The Committee is so concerned about corporal punishment that it raises the matter in regard to countries, such as Ethiopia, where children suffer deeply from the ravishes of war, disease, drought, poverty, malnutrition, and the lack of even a primary education. While taking note of all of these other difficulties, the Committee still recommends that Ethiopia's new penal code include a prohibition of "all forms of corporal punishment, including in the context of school and the family," and that "children be provided with mechanisms through which they can report and complain of corporal punishment practices." Children, in other words, should be empowered to tell on their parents when they engage in the crime of corporal punishment.

Although the American Academy of Pediatrics shares the Committee's negative view of corporal punishment, it is reported that "as of 1985, 90% of parents used corporal punishment on toddlers and more than 50% continue such punishment up through early teen years, sometimes several times a week." Spanking, then, is an area where there is a gap between elite American and international human rights perspectives, on the one hand, and mainstream American practices on the other.

This kind of prioritization of a matter like corporal punishment makes the CRC look dangerous at worst, and silly at best, in the eyes of many Americans. The notion of children telling on parents when they spank, with a resulting criminal charge, appears authoritarian to some. Could the CRC be a way of getting the United Nations into America's homes, with these international experts dictating every detail of family life? Even if spanking is not viewed as a particularly significant issue, the Committee's concept of children telling on their parents about such matters suggests a wholesale alteration in the relationship between child, family, and state, not to mention an alteration in the relationship between national sovereignty and international law.

The fear that the CRC is fundamentally authoritarian, rather than libertarian, is further underscored by the document's and the Committee's interest in promoting propaganda within the schools. At first read, Article 29 of the CRC is a high-minded statement of the proper purposes of education. These purposes include developing the child's full potential and teaching respect for human rights, the child's parents, culture and national values, other civilizations, and even the natural environment. On closer inspection, however, it is possible to discern a more sinister, or at least self-serving, agenda: children throughout the world are apparently to be taught to support the United Nations, and private education will only be permitted if children are so taught. Thus, schools that oppose the United Nations become illegal under the CRC. The Committee on the CRC appears rather zealous for this principle of policing the aims of education. For example, the July 2002 report on Switzerland recommends that "the State party ... provide information in its next report on how the aims of education have been reflected into the curricula at the cantonal level." The potential authoritarian reach of the CRC can thus appear daunting. Would the Committee have jurisdiction to mandate curricular revisions in every school within the United States, if the United States were to finally ratify the CRC?

. . . .

Any comprehensive treaty on the subject of children's rights necessarily must implicate the paradox inherent in a conception of "children's rights": that of granting rights to a class that are by legal definition incapacitated. The redemptive myths of childhood, that of protecting children from the ills of the adult world and freeing children from the bondage of childhood, are endemic to elite Western culture, and thus, are inevitably implicated by such a treaty. The pervasiveness of the paradoxes and myths related to children's rights lead to two primary paths for a comprehensive children's rights treaty. If such a treaty tries to become a legally enforceable treaty subject to adjudication of particular disputes, then it necessarily risks authoritarianism because it seeks the authority to reach within the homes, schools, religious institutions, and societal structures of every cultural and religious group on the planet. It is already clear that the Committee is unable to restrain itself in the sense of only mandating minimalist, broadly accepted principles of child rearing; under the authoritarian temptation, it is the deeply felt principles of the expert, rather than the cross-cultural consensus of peoples, that becomes the justification for action. Alternatively, such a treaty can remain a largely symbolic statement, analogous perhaps to the Declaration of Independence, which reflects deeply felt ideals but is not directly enforceable. Such symbolic statements can be deeply important, and can create bureaucratic mechanisms for reviewing and implementing progress toward a better world. It is not much fun to be a scold, but it is better to be a scold than a tyrant.

Notes and Questions

1. Does Smolin justify his initial proposition to the effect that children are poor candidates for "liberation," insofar as they inevitably partake of the evils that beset the lives of their parents? Couldn't such an argument be seen as letting adults off the hook too

easily? Are you convinced by his idea that the UNCRC seeks to provide for children what "redemptive myths" have provided for other repressed groups, such as women and ethnic minorities? Is Smolin using the term "myth" as dismissive of the aims of the Convention, or does he consider it to be in some way descriptive?

2. What does Smolin mean by saying that some fear the Convention is fundamentally "authoritarian?" Isn't this just another way of saying that the Convention demands that adults respond to children's needs, even when this might not suit the immediate interests of the adults? Smolin's critique is undoubtedly creative and interesting. But does his theory cede too much to "reality," and cut off attempts to call adults to account for negative aspects of children's lives that they could in fact, with greater effort and attention, do a great deal to improve?

C. The UNCRC and American Ratification: Will It Ever Happen?

Apart from Somalia—which has little in the way of a functioning government—the United States is the only country not to have ratified the UNCRC. The articles below address distinctly American concerns about ratification; in particular, whether the Convention would interfere with the traditional parent/child relationship, and whether children ought to be given enhanced autonomy rights. It is also a matter of contention that many issues relating to children and their rights have traditionally been left up to the American states, not the federal government.

1. The Anti-Ratification Position

The first article below, by Bruce and Jonathan Hafen, typifies the negative perspective on possible American ratification. The Hafens are especially concerned over the "liberationist" dimension of the Convention, which they equate with the abdication by adults of their responsibility to guide and discipline children. As you read the article, consider whether the Hafens are presenting an accurate picture of the Convention's contents, or whether their interpretation is misleading, even inflammatory.

Bruce C. Hafen & Jonathan O. Hafen,
Abandoning Children to Their Autonomy: The United Nations Convention on the Rights of the Child
37 Harvard International Law Journal 449 (1996)

....

II. AUTONOMY IN THE UNITED NATIONS CONVENTION ON THE RIGHTS OF THE CHILD

A. Background

....

Consider ... the origins of the CRC's interest in child autonomy. Cynthia Price Cohen, an American lawyer who helped draft the CRC, describes the earlier declarations by the League of Nations in 1924 and by the United Nations in 1959 as being concerned solely with children's "care and protection" rights. The 1989 Convention, on the other hand, consciously breaks new ground, creating "an important addition to human rights jurisprudence;" namely, the notion of autonomy-based "individual personality rights" for children, a concept that includes such adult-style civil rights as "speech, religion, association, assembly and the right to privacy." This notion does not reflect prior United Nations approaches to children's needs or rights, nor did it originate in requests initiated by delegates from U.N. member nations. Rather, during the 1980s certain nongovernmental organizations (NGOs) formed an ad hoc group that located governmental sponsors for the "totally new right" of individual personality, which the NGO group promoted by taking an unusually direct role in helping to draft the CRC.

The leading proponents of this new vision for the world's children were United States children's rights advocates whose arguments for the autonomous legal personhood of children have never been fully accepted by the American legal mainstream. Some of these advocates have erroneously implied that the CRC simply restates traditionally accepted protections for children and that their positions reflect the current state of United States law. The degree of this exaggeration regarding United States law is best illustrated by the comparison that follows, which demonstrates the relationship between specific CRC provisions and current United States legal positions. To the extent that such exaggeration exists, it raises the possibility that, having failed to convince United States courts and legislature to adopt their views, certain child advocates consciously pursued and shaped the CRC in an effort to legitimize their positions in an international arena that is relatively unsophisticated and uncritical compared to traditional United States scholarly and legal forums.

To realize the significance of the CRC's emphasis on child autonomy, consider the distinction we have drawn elsewhere between rights of protection and rights of choice for children. With the exception of the choice to have an abortion by an unmarried minor whom a judge has determined to be sufficiently "mature," virtually all of the United States children's rights cases of the past generation have been concerned not with children's rights of autonomous personal choice, but with their rights to protection.

Protection rights, which do not depend on any minimum level of capacity, include such safeguards as rights to property, rights to physical care and security, and rights to procedural due process. For example, recently increased procedural protections for United States children in juvenile courts, schools, and other settings are typically designed not to increase children's personal choices, but to protect children against the abuse of unchecked adult discretion. Children's relative lack of adult-level capacity enhances the need for such protections.

Choice rights, on the other hand, grant individuals the authority to make affirmative and legally binding decisions, such as voting, marrying, making contracts, exercising religious preferences, or choosing whether and how to be educated. The very concept of minority status, reflected in statutes in every United States jurisdiction, denies underage children independent choices on such matters. This denial is not a way of discriminating against children, but is a way of protecting them, and society, from the long-term consequences of a child's immature choices and from exploitation by those who would take advantage of a child's unique vulnerability. To confer the full range of choice rights on a child is also to confer the burdens and responsibilities of adult legal status, which necessarily removes the protection rights of childhood. "One cannot have the freedom to live where and as one chooses and still demand parental support; one may not deliberately enter into contracts and yet insist that they be voidable", for lack of contractual capacity.

B. Autonomy and Civil Rights for Children in the CRC

1. Intervention Standards

Against this background, we consider some of the CRC's novel provisions. One of these is an arguably new standard for state intervention in intact families. Among the fundamental axioms of United States law is the doctrine that the parent-child relationship antedates the state just as natural individual rights antedate the state in the Constitution's political theory. Parents are not trustees who receive authority to rear their children through delegations of state power over children. Rather, as the Supreme Court held in distinguishing biological parents from foster parents, the natural parent-child tie is "a relationship having its origins entirely apart from the power of the State," while a foster placement arranged by state agents "has its source in state law and contractual arrangements." Because of this principle, the Court has said, "(t)he child is not the mere creature of the State," and the democratic structure, partly in order to limit state power, presupposes a system of family units, not just a mass of isolated individuals who all stand in the same relationship to the state.

State agents have thus never had the authority to intervene in the child-parent relationship until they establish state jurisdiction through such formal proceedings as divorce-related custody issues; adoptions; findings of serious parental unfitness, neglect, abuse, or abandonment; or child misbehavior severe enough to require state intervention. The empirical and philosophical difficulties of determining when family problems reach such jurisdictional thresholds are legion.

Article 9 of the CRC provides that children may be separated from parents when "such separation is necessary for the best interests of the child." This article does provide that such determinations may be made only by "competent authorities subject to judicial review" and "in accordance with applicable law and procedures," but its language sounds more procedural than substantive. Article 18 adds that while "parents … have the primary responsibility for the upbringing and development of the child," the "best interests of the child will be (the parents') basic concern." And article 3 provides that "(i)n all actions concerning children … the best interests of the child shall be a primary consideration." Does this language mean that any parental care that falls short of serving the child's "best interests" is sufficiently flawed to trigger intervention? Given the CRC's emphasis on considering children's own views of their interests, could a child trigger state intervention merely by requesting state review of the "reasonableness" of parental conduct compared to the child's view of his or her best interests?....

Some American proponents of the CRC note that its "best interests" language applies only in a secondary way to child placement; that is, only when custody is already in issue or neglect has been established would a judge unavoidably face placement options. Others, however, see the CRC's best interests standard as a primary jurisdictional test. Two Australian lawyers, for example, believe that under the CRC, parental childrearing rights are "subject to external scrutiny" and "may be overridden" when "the parents are not acting in the best interests of the child, or where the parents are unreasonably attempting to impose their views upon mature minors who have the capacity to make their own decisions." This interpretation is consistent with the CRC's apparent intent to place children and parents on the same plane as co-autonomous persons in their relationship with the state. To the extent that the CRC encourages such interpretations, its ambiguity, or its conscious design, risks creating a new and lower threshold for state intervention in intact families.

Subjective vs. Age-Based Determinations of Capacity

Current United States law uses an objective measure, the child's age, as a surrogate for determining a child's capacity to make legally significant choices. Age limits serve as the gateway to a wide variety of activities, including rights to vote, consent to medical treatment, drive motor vehicles, marry, consume alcohol, use tobacco, and purchase pornographic material. Justice Stevens once observed that such legislation uses "chronological age" to "protect minors from the consequences of decisions they are not yet prepared to make," even though "it is perfectly obvious that such a yardstick is imprecise and perhaps even unjust in particular cases."

Some courts in recent years have experimented modestly with legal doctrines designed to reduce the power of objective legislative classifications and to increase subjective reviews of individual merits. Individualized determinations do appear to offer greater fairness, but that promise can be more than offset by the inherent lack of reasoned generality, and, hence, the lack of neutrality, in subjective decisions. Therefore, despite some increased judicial openness to individual variations, objective categories like marriage and minority status remain as fixed stars in United States jurisprudence.

The most ardent advocates of child autonomy have still argued, if not for the removal of minority status altogether, that children should be presumed capable of legally binding action until an individualized determination shows they lack capacity. The experience of United States courts, however, reveals that customized findings of maturity are in practice not very workable. Some states, for example, allow a "mature minor" woman to make an abortion decision, if a judge finds her sufficiently mature. Absent a finding of maturity, the judge must determine whether the abortion is in the pregnant minor's best interest. A field study of 1300 minors who applied for abortions under such rules in Massachusetts found that, eventually, all 1300 received abortions. This outcome evidently resulted from the unwillingness of judges to substitute their judgment for the actual preference of an expectant teenager, regardless of her age or psychological maturity.

Rejecting age-based classifications also undermines the parental role, because it shifts to some presumably "objective" person, like a judge, the task of determining maturity, which is, in effect, the parent-like task of supervising a child's choices. Unless the parents of such a child are demonstrably unfit, long established United States juvenile law principles would prohibit shifting the basic parental role to other persons. Moreover, because judges hardly know the children whose maturity they must judge, or because "maturity" as a concept is hopelessly complex and subjective, or because so many choices are (as with abortion) laden with heavy personal value preferences, judicial supervision can abandon children to their immaturity.

Nonetheless, the CRC would grant children the right to make choices according to "the evolving capacities" of the individual child. The general rule favoring parental rights in article 5 limits parental prerogatives to "a manner consistent with the evolving capacities of the child." Similarly, article 12 assures children the right to express their views and asks that those views be "given due weight in accordance with the age and maturity of the child." Article 14 respects parents' rights in the sensitive area of directing the religious upbringing of their children, but again only "in a manner consistent with the evolving capacities of the child." Paradoxically, the CRC takes this position on choice rights despite its preference for age-based classifications in dealing with children's violations of penal laws.

....

"Civil Rights" for Children

The CRC's model of child autonomy finds its clearest expression in articles 13 through 16, its "civil rights" provisions. "Nowhere in the Convention is … the 'autonomous' view of rights more evident" than in these four articles. Although the language of these articles departs from United States law in several significant ways, some CRC advocates describe the articles as originating in U.S. legal concepts. These ideas may generally echo distinctive United States approaches to individual rights, especially when compared with earlier United Nations statements about children. It is inaccurate, however, to imply that the new and provocative personal autonomy dimensions of the CRC are consistent with the way current United States law applies to children.

Free Speech and Association

Article 13 grants children "the right to freedom of expression, including the right to seek, receive, and impart information and ideas of all kinds, regardless of frontiers … through any media of the child's choice." This broad free speech grant is subject only to restrictions that are "provided by law and are necessary to respect the rights or reputations of others" or to protect public security, order, health, or morals.

The CRC's proponents point out that article 13 reflects the breadth of Supreme Court rulings about student rights in the 1960s, notably *Tinker v. Des Moines School District*, which protected the symbolic speech of public school students who wore black armbands to protest the Vietnam War. What they fail to add is that in 1986 and 1988, before the United Nations adopted the CRC in 1989, the Court substantially clarified and limited its earlier rulings, overturning broad interpretations of Tinker in lower courts. In *Fraser v. Bethel School District* and *Hazelwood School District v. Kuhlmeier*, the Court firmly upheld a public high school's right to control not only the curriculum, but also the extra curriculum, including the content of student newspapers and speeches in school assemblies. Also, the Court last term reaffirmed Hazelwood's extensive restatement of students' rights law, upholding a school's authority to conduct random drug tests on student athletes in the absence of individualized probable cause or even suspicion. If article 13's provisions were taken literally in United States schools, teachers and administrators would have difficulty managing core educational content, let alone the larger school environment. Yet, because the CRC was adopted after the Supreme Court had decided both *Fraser* and *Hazelwood*, we can only conclude that its drafters consciously rejected the legal and educational policy choices those decisions represented. These examples further illustrate the CRC's departure from United States law.

Even *Board of Education, Island Trees Union Free School District No. 26 v. Pico*, the only Supreme Court case to acknowledge students' "right to receive information," recognized the discretionary role of school officials to determine a school's curriculum and to make initial selections of library books as well as textbooks. Perhaps by oversight, since it does not speak of educational institutions, article 13 makes no such allowance for schools. Thus, the article seems to support a child autonomy model of education that, like the early readings of Tinker by some scholars and lower courts, is fundamentally skeptical toward institutional authority in schools. Not only does the Supreme Court not share that skepticism; the Court for at least the last decade has seen public schools in an in loco parentis role, reinforcing the schools' vital institutional authority in teaching students the attitudes and skills required for both meaningful self-expression and citizenship.

….

Article 13's language about receiving "information and ideas of all kinds, regardless of frontiers" through "the media of the child's choice" also fails, except in a vague reference to "public health or morals," to recognize the risks of obscenity and pornography to children. The Supreme Court has denounced the destructive nature of child pornography, and it has upheld state laws restricting the sale of pornographic material to minors under age sixteen. The CRC does ask in article 17 for participating countries to provide media guidelines that protect children from "injurious" material, and it opposes sexual abuse in article 19. But the language of article 13 is written with such an unrestrained spirit that its relationship to these other articles is unclear.

Article 15 ensures children the right of association and peaceful assembly, subject to soft limits similar to those used in article 13. The advocates of article 15 are unable to assert that it is consistent with United States law, given the Supreme Court's opinion in *City of Dallas v. Stenglin*, which generally sustains the concept of curfew ordinances. In *Stenglin*, the Court rejected minors' freedom of association claims in upholding a local ordinance that prevented young people between age 14 and age 17 from mixing with older persons in dance halls. Rather than attacking this precedent directly, CRC proponents argue that article 15 simply extends to groups those rights of expression granted to individual children by article 13.

Religion

Article 14 affirms "the right of the child to freedom of thought, conscience and religion." It respects parents' "rights and duties" to "provide direction" in this realm, but only "to the child in the exercise of his or her right in a manner consistent with the evolving capacities of the child." In this instance, as arguably in general under article 5, the parental rights recognized by the CRC apparently extend only to giving parents a role in enforcing the rights the CRC grants to the child, without recognizing an independent parental right. This approach illustrates the tendency of the CRC's autonomy model to view parents as trustees of the state who have only such authority and discretion as the state may grant in order to protect the child's independent rights.

Rather than reflecting United States law, this article seems to reject the Supreme Court's general recognition that parental interests are independent from, not derived from, the state. More precisely, article 14 apparently rejects the Court's longstanding position that parents have their own constitutional right to rear their children within the parents' religious tradition. In *Yoder v. Wisconsin*, the Court affirmed this element of parents' "liberty" in broad terms, citing an earlier case that upheld parents' rights to send their children to parochial schools as "a charter of the rights of parents to direct the religious upbringing of their children." But article 14 prefers Justice Douglas's dissent in the *Yoder* case. Even though the record contained no evidence that the Yoder children rejected their parents' direction, Douglas believed that the majority opinion risked imposing the religious views of Amish parents on their children by allowing the parents to keep their children temporarily out of public schools against the children's will: "It is the student's judgment, not his parents', that is essential if ... (students are) to be masters of their own destiny." The majority directly refuted Douglas' autonomy-based position, but the Douglas view has since been widely quoted by child autonomy advocates.

. . . .

Privacy

Article 16 establishes child privacy rights: "No child shall be subjected to arbitrary or unlawful interference with his or her privacy, family, home or correspondence." This limited context confers little meaning on "privacy," an unfortunate omission in light of the growing complexity of privacy laws. Robert Shepherd believes article 16 grants children the same "right to privacy" from which "the constitutional protections for procreation and abortion decision-making has come." In an open-ended affirmation of autonomy principles, he regards this article as conferring on children "the right to be let alone," Justice Brandeis's 1934 phrase which now seems to capture the contemporary idea of autonomous personhood.

This broad definition of privacy is problematic for children in schools and families, because it makes little allowance either for children's minority status or for the role of adults who are unavoidably involved in a child's private world. The Supreme Court has recently upheld the right of a public school to conduct random urinalysis drug tests on student athletes, in part because students have particularly limited expectations of privacy. Illustrating that the American children's rights movement has not established adult-like rights of privacy and autonomy for children, the Court stated, "Traditionally at common law, and still today, unemancipated minors lack some of the most fundamental rights of self-determination...." Moreover, public school officials have a "custodial and tutelary" power that permits "a degree of supervision and control that could not be exercised over free adults." Thus the "nature of (students' constitutional) rights is what is appropriate for children in schools."

The notion that children may have "privacy rights" that protect them against parental intrusion short of neglect or abuse is especially difficult. In most contexts one could assume that assertions of a "right" to privacy run only against the state. However, the CRC's apparent intent to give "(g)overnment the responsibility of protecting the child from the power of parents" naturally raises the question whether the CRC's interest in privacy rights for children also intends to limit parental prerogatives.

The Supreme Court has upheld constitutional privacy rights for children in only two contexts, abortion and contraception. In a series of cases beginning in 1976, the Court has recognized that, generally, mature minors (with maturity being determined by a judge) may choose abortions without parental consent, and that immature minors may have abortions if a judge finds this choice to be in the pregnant minor's best interests. Yet, in the Court's most comprehensive analysis of minors' choice rights within the abortion context, Justice Powell spoke not of a "right of privacy," but of a specific "constitutional right to seek abortion." After explaining minors' "peculiar vulnerability" and their "inability to make ... mature (choices)," Powell explained how abortion differs "in important ways from other decisions that may be made during minority." This difference arises primarily from the extraordinary circumstance that a pregnant minor is herself a prospective parent who would not require parental consent to place her child for adoption. Therefore, the rationale for abortion-related privacy has no serious application to a minor's other choice rights and is a genuine exception to the courts' recognition of parental authority in virtually all other environments.

In 1977, in *Carey v. Population Services Int'l*, the Court held that the procreative dimension of the right of privacy prevents a state from denying minors access to contraceptives. The Court's purpose was not to authorize a maturity-based "choice" right, but to protect immature adolescents against the risks of pregnancy and venereal disease. Perhaps because of the Court's desire not to narrow adult reproductive autonomy in the post-*Roe v. Wade* era, some dicta in Carey's majority opinion may have given some readers (including proponents of the CRC) the erroneous impression that single adolescents have a constitutionally protected "privacy" interest in choosing to bear children outside marriage. That interpretation does not reflect the Court's holding. It also runs counter to well-established United States public policy interests in preventing teenage pregnancy, which the Court recognized in 1988.

For some advocates of adolescent choice, however, locating any children's right within the modern concept of constitutional privacy implies, even if the cases do not, that children may now make autonomous choices in any realm that is "private"—including sexual freedom. Ironically, however, constitutional privacy in United States law actually developed primarily to protect personal decisions regarding marriage and kinship, not as a means of furthering the sexual revolution outside marriage, whether for adults or for children. The Court has not extended constitutional "sexual rights" (as distinguished from the right to abortion or contraception) to unmarried adults, let alone to children.

Against this ambiguous background, a major risk of the CRC's vague reference to privacy rights for children is that its language can be construed to support sexual freedom for children. In fact, however, one looks in vain for serious United States scholars or policymakers—let alone courts or legislatures—who honestly believe it is wise for the nation's adolescent population to be sexually active. Most pediatricians have long agreed that "adolescent sexual activity is ... unhealthy for children—emotionally, psychologically, spiritually, and physically." Most contemporary debates over sex education and contraception policies for adolescents argue about the best means for preventing teen pregnancy, not over the desirability of adolescent sex in general.

. . . .

C. General Limitations in the CRC's Autonomy Model for Children's Rights

Children's Rights and Adult Preferences—Autonomy in Whose Interest?

In a general sense, the CRC's autonomy model ironically undermines the very autonomy-building process of education and nurturing that every child needs. A child is not "free" to play the piano just because no physical force keeps her from walking to the piano bench. She will achieve the freedom to make music only when she has developed the capacity to obey the laws of music. Similarly, a child writing a paper in a public school does not enjoy "freedom of expression" merely by being left alone at his desk. He may be free of censorship, but freedom of expression also means freedom for expression—having the capacity for understanding and self-expression. If free speech is to be meaningful, a citizen must not only be free to speak but should have something worth saying, together with the maturity, insight, and skill needed to say it intelligibly.

To develop the capacity for autonomous action, children must submit their freedom temporarily to the schoolmaster of education and training, the developmental processes that create the tools and skills that are essential for responsible and self-determined action. This educational relationship between child learners and adult parents or other teachers is that of master-apprentice, not master-slave or even master-servant. On the master or adult side of such apprenticeships, as the Supreme Court recently observed, "the tutor or schoolmaster is the very prototype of (parental) status," a status that imposes not merely a power of supervision and a duty to protect, but an affirmative responsibility to teach and nurture a child's capacities toward mature powers. Because both society and children have such a stake in the outcome of this process, the Western liberal tradition has traditionally placed parents (and those who otherwise act in parental/tutorial roles) under a heavy obligation of both nature and law to help children attain rational capacities — as John Locke wrote, "till ... (their) understanding be fit to take the government of (their) will."

To serve the interests of both society and its children, therefore, society has limited children's legal autonomy in the short-run precisely in order to maximize their actual autonomy in the long-run — assuming, of course, that adults shoulder the heavy task of teaching children how to act freely and responsibly....

As the CRC illustrates, however, an increasing number of adults prefer a short-range view of child autonomy that would liberate both children and adults from the mutual yoke of tutorial responsibilities. The emerging popular interest in greater freedom for children has arisen from a variety of recent cultural and legal developments, one theme of which is the simplistic but topical assumption that "kids are people too." Therefore society's modern tolerance for self-determined lifestyle choices now urges us to stop judging and controlling children's choices, just as American adults over the past generation have been learning to be less judgmental and controlling toward one another. In addition, a combination of judicially reduced discretion for adult caretakers and our legal system's increased reliance on procedural protection for children has sometimes created the illusion that parents, teachers, and other adults owe children only what the law procedurally demands of them.

....

State Paternalism Distinguished from Family Paternalism

Our second general concern with the autonomy-based provisions of the CRC is their failure to distinguish between state paternalism and parental paternalism. By trying to create a direct political and legal relationship between children and the state, the CRC, perhaps unintentionally, could have the long-term effect of reducing parental commitments to childrearing while concurrently increasing the dependency of children on the state....

... [P]olicies that reduce the institutional strength of parents in a family entity encourage totalitarian attitudes, not the attitudes of liberal democracy. The totalitarian cannot succeed until "the social contexts of privacy — family, church, association — have been atomized. The political enslavement of man requires the emancipation of man from all the (intermediate) authorities and memberships ... that serve ... to insulate the individual from external political power." Building a state-child tie that inherently reduces the strength of the parent-child tie creates the kind of "spiritual and cultural vacuum" that "the totalitarian must have for the realization of his design." By declaring that children are autonomous when in fact they are dependent, the CRC, perhaps unwittingly, accelerates what Peter Berger calls the "therapeutic totalitarianism" of a statist community that, perversely, does not want its individual citizens to develop the actual autonomy and capacity for personal liberty that could ultimately challenge the authority of the state. The nurturing of truly educated individualism, as distinguished from mere dependency, is only possible within the deep commitments to value-based child development found in families, not in state nurseries.

....

Notes and Questions

1. Hafen and Hafen are clearly alarmed at the implications of a possible U.S. ratification of the UNCRC. Do you find their fears realistic? How do you compare their view of the real-world potential of the UNCRC to Smolin's?

2. Do Hafen and Hafen offer compelling evidence of what they see as the primary motivations behind the drafting of the UNCRC? What do they mean by an "illusion of autonomy" for children? How does their critique of "state paternalism" fit in with their critique of the "liberationist" dimension of the Convention? Is there a way to interpret the UNCRC so as to rebut the Hafen reading? As of this writing, the new Obama administration is expressing support for the idea of reviving the prospect of U.S. ratification. What will the administration have to overcome in order for this to happen?

In the excerpt below, John Garman offers a partial explanation as to why the U.S. has not yet ratified a convention its citizens were so deeply involved in drafting. Part of his argument is that some socially conservative forces in the U.S. saw the UNCRC as a serious threat, and worked hard to prevent its ratification.

John J. Garman, *International Law and Children's Human Rights: International, Constitutional, and Political Conflicts Blocking Passage of the Convention on the Rights of the Child*
41 Valparaiso University Law Review 659 (Winter 2006)

....

The disappointing conclusion of the CRC is that the United States participated so heavily in its drafting, but now can do nothing to shape its continuing development. Because of the United States' involvement in writing the treaty, personal freedoms like freedom of expression, thought, religion, and assembly from Articles 13 through 16 have displayed to the rest of the world some of the freedoms instilled in the Bill of Rights. Without these "individual personality" articles, it is likely the rest of the world would not have had the benefit of their language.

Accordingly, it would seem that, with such heavy involvement by the United States in the construction of the treaty itself, there would be no problem with ratification. Even the rules on implementation appear to be fairly harmless. In United Nations human rights treaties, including the CRC, there "are no formal 'enforcement' procedures, … [and] no sanctions for failing to meet the treaties' standards." These treaties assume an aspect of good faith, and once a state has ratified the treaty it is presumed that, beyond a formal report to the Committee on the Rights of the Child, there is no direct penalty or punishment or criticism of domestic law that comes into play.

During negotiations for the CRC, the American delegates had to juggle a variety of influences when making their decisions. Constitutional and other policy concerns were at stake causing the delegates to respect the demands of the Department of Justice, the Pentagon, the Department of Health and Human Services, and ultimately the United States Supreme Court. But considering the time frame in which the treaty was written, there were obvious tensions between the East and West. There is clearly a taste of Western democracy in the CRC. At that time, perhaps the United States' interests were less on the side of children and more on the side opposite the Soviet Union.

Has the CRC received international legitimacy with all member nations of the world but the United States and Somalia ratifying it? The common perception around the international community is that it is not enough that 191 members to the CRC have ratified it because effective guidance of social and political actions of nations on behalf of the child requires full participation by all states. The "validity of the claims to legitimacy" for the articles of the CRC must be based "on a belief in the legality of enacted rules." In other words, the common notion is that the CRC must become a part of the administrative, legislative, and legal foundations of all states to achieve full legitimacy.

Such a transformation of international agreements and standards into the laws, practices, and belief systems of each participating nation is what is meant when the term "implementation" is used in the Convention itself. Once we disaggregate the meaning of "implementation of the Convention," the difficulties that confront such attempts become immediately apparent. At stake are not only the good intentions of legislators, government officials, and administrators to honor the terms of these international agreements, but also the values, belief systems, customs, and traditional practices, which have heretofore governed society's attitudes and behavior towards children and youth. When it is considered in its entirety, the Convention both presupposes and requires formidable changes in the political, economic, social, and cultural realities of children. These changes will often run against the grain of popular beliefs and practices of elected officials, administrators, and the generality of citizens. The task of implementing the Convention goes far beyond the legal realms of the international community and nations. The problem is to achieve legitimate authority for the Convention.

. . . .

Enforcement of the CRC, one would assume, would cause concern in the United States over possible intrusion into domestic human rights concerns. In practice, however, the CRC is essentially a toothless agreement with no formal enforcement mechanisms on participating states. Specifically, the CRC has no provisions that allow participating states to file complaints on other states. However, the CRC does create the Committee on the Rights of the Child that monitors the progress of adherence to the treaty through a series of reports submitted from states. The CRC also calls for other United Nations organs, such as the United Nations Children's Fund to submit reports that are relevant to children's rights issues. The CRC contains the assumption that all participating states intend to be responsible for their own actions when implementing the treaty and that any violations are dealt with under its provisions. As a result the CRC emphasizes "education, facilitation, and cooperation rather than confrontation." But the CRC lacks a procedure for children to make individual claims of violations and any remedies for violations. The result is that the CRC has no direct enforcement body that can influence domestic agendas through the watch of any ruling committee. Therefore, the United States' sovereignty is not at issue.

Along with international issues and the importance of United States involvement in the international community there are also domestic political issues at play perhaps holding the CRC back from ratification. In 1995, the Clinton administration announced its intentions to push to have the CRC ratified. Immediately afterward, Senator Helms submitted a resolution to the Senate Foreign Relations Committee where he announced, "If the President does attempt to push this unwise proposal through the Senate, I want him to know, and I want the Senate to know, that I intend to do everything possible to make sure that he is not successful."

Although the CRC never mentions abortion specifically, the inferences made in its words have become a heated source of right-versus-left arguments regarding ratification of the treaty. As Article 6 of the CRC recognizes an "inherent right to life" for the child, one would think that it would be supportive of the anti-abortion movement. The problem appears to be that Article 1 of the CRC recognizes a child as any "human being below the age of eighteen years[,]" but does not recognize any bottom age. So the question of whether a child becomes a viable human being at conception is not answered. Some have interpreted the provisions of the CRC to impose a position on abortion; however, "the history of the drafting process indicates that the treaty was drafted in such a way as to enable each State party to determine its own policy regarding abortion."

Education and discipline provisions of the CRC are other sources of heated domestic political debate. Article 29 of the CRC requires states to direct the child's education towards understanding "human rights and fundamental freedoms" and to develop respect for "cultural identity" of the child's own country and "civilizations different from his or her own." This led to concern by conservative groups that this would allow the state to prevent parents from teaching children according to their religious beliefs. In regard to discipline, Article 19 of the CRC requires States to take measures to end all "forms of physical or mental violence, injury or abuse, neglect or negligent treatment" and Article 28 requires states to "ensure that school discipline is administered in a manner consistent with the child's human dignity." Many have interpreted these clauses to mean an end to spanking at home and corporal punishment at school.

Abortion, education, and discipline are all major issues, but the real issue is the rights of parents to raise their children as they see fit. Senator Jesse Helms has been quoted as saying "the United Nations Convention on the Rights of the Child is incompatible with the God-given right and responsibility of parents to raise their children." The natural first place to look is at the individual rights of Article 13, freedom of expression; Article 14, freedom of thought, conscience, and religion; Article 15, freedom of association and peaceful assembly; Article 16, right to privacy; and Article 17, access to information. Conservative groups feel that "[w]hile these types of rights are acceptable for adults, they are objectionable for children." Interestingly, despite all the concerns over parents' rights to raise their children as they see fit Article 5 specifically ensures that "States Parties shall respect the responsibilities, rights and duties of parents."

Perhaps the most unfortunate aspect of the failure to ratify the CRC is that the United States had such an involved role in the CRC, but is not bringing the CRC's rules back home. Because the United States has not ratified the CRC and become a state party to the convention, it cannot take part in developing it and seeing to its adherence in the international community. No American delegate can be elected to the Committee on the Rights of the Child until the United States ratifies the CRC. As a result, any future interpretation and implementation of the articles of the CRC will take place without the United States' involvement. Finally, and perhaps the most hypocritical action by the United States, is a report published by the Department of State regarding human rights violations around the world, including violations of the CRC.

Notes and Questions

1. Clearly, Garman would like to see the United States play a key role in the development of the UNCRC. He acknowledges that social conservatives in the U.S. disliked the parts of the Convention that emphasized new freedoms and autonomy rights for children. How does Garman's view of these rights differ from that held by the Hafens, in the article immediately preceding? Which view is more compelling? Is Garman in

part arguing that the Convention would not make as big an impact as social conservatives fear?

———————

2. Advocates for U.S. Ratification

The Lozman and Rutkow article below seeks to rebut some of the arguments raised against U.S. ratification of the UNCRC. Do their arguments adequately respond to the concerns raised by Hafen and Hafen, for example? Are the arguments put forward by UNCRC advocates as passionately expressed as those of ratification opponents? If the situation of children within the U.S. legal system would not—as advocates seem to indicate—change all that much as a result of ratification, then why is ratification important at all?

Joshua T. Lozman & Lainie Rutkow, *Suffer the Children?: A Call for United States Ratification of the United Nations Convention on the Rights of the Child*
19 Harvard Human Rights Journal 161 (Spring 2006)

....

V. THE UNITED STATES' TREATMENT OF THE CONVENTION ON THE RIGHTS OF THE CHILD

A. Calls for Ratification

C. The United States' Reluctance To Ratify the Convention on the Rights of the Child

During the fifteen years since the CRC was opened for signature and ratification, the U.S. critics of the convention have posited a variety of arguments. Some of these arguments have been raised officially in Congress while others have been voiced in the legal and other academic literature. To understand why the United States has not yet ratified the CRC, it is important to review the arguments made by those opposed to its ratification. The discussion below addresses the most frequently made anti-ratification arguments.

....

1. Reproductive and Family Planning Concerns

The CRC maintains no explicit position on the issues of contraception, abortion, or other family planning services. Nevertheless, U.S. critics fear that because the CRC does not explicitly offer protection to the fetus, its ratification will endorse abortion and encourage children to have abortions.

2. Parents' Rights Concerns

The parents' rights movement is grounded in several Supreme Court cases that have affirmed certain parental rights. In 1923, the Court decided *Meyer v. Nebraska*, which concerned a Nebraska statute that prohibited the teaching of foreign languages to any student who had not graduated from the eighth grade. Although the Court struck down the statute, the parent's rights movement has found constitutional support for its cause in the Meyer Court's discussion of the Fourteenth Amendment as including the right to "establish a home and bring up children...." Two years later, in *Pierce v. Society of Sisters*, the Court affirmed the rights of parents by striking down an Oregon statute that required parents or guardians to send children between ages eight and sixteen to a public school in the district where the child resided. The Court found that the statute "unreasonably interfere[d] with the liberty of parents and guardians to direct the upbringing and education of children under their control.... The child is not the mere creature of the state; those who nurture him and direct his destiny have the right, coupled with the high duty, to recognize and prepare him for additional obligations." *Meyer* and *Pierce*, which remain good law, established broad parental rights.

In 1982, the Court again turned to the Fourteenth Amendment to expand the scope of parental rights in *Santosky v. Kramer*. This case examined a New York law that allowed the termination of parental rights when it was found that the child was "permanently neglected." The "fair preponderance of the evidence" standard was used to make a determination of "permanent neglect[ ]." In *Santosky*, however, the Court raised the evidentiary standard stating that "the Due Process Clause of the Fourteenth Amendment demands [that] ... [b]efore a State may sever completely and irrevocably the rights of parents in their natural child, due process requires that the State support its allegations by at least clear and convincing evidence." Taken together, *Meyer*, *Pierce*, and *Santosky* establish a clear line of support for certain parental rights.

Proponents of the parental rights movement have taken issue with the CRC, raising the twin concerns that the CRC elevates the rights of children to the detriment of their parents and that it endangers fundamental family relationships. Supporters of the parents' rights movement believe that the CRC grants children an unprecedented amount of autonomy. This line of reasoning finds that

> [c]hildren are not autonomous. They are, by definition, "immature"—socially, mentally, emotionally, and physically. Hence, societies keep children from driving automobiles, from shooting guns, drinking alcohol, smoking, voting, viewing sexually explicit movies and photographs, and entering into binding contracts. Such "deprivations" protect children (and others) from the consequences of their immaturity. Adults impose such limitations not from arrogance or cruelty, but from wisdom.

Critics of the CRC further emphasize the role that parents play in protecting children: "[I]t was an accepted reality of life in America that children are too immature to handle the tremendous responsibility adult 'freedoms' carry with them. Consequently, under the American model, parents determine when children are mature enough to handle adult responsibilities." As these concerns suggest, supporters of the parents' rights movement fear that the CRC legally grants "autonomous capacity to children [and] ignores the realities of education and child development to the point of abandoning children to a mere illusion of real autonomy."

A related but slightly different fear about the CRC is that it will threaten the social cohesion of the family by injecting the state into the traditional family structure. Opponents of the CRC explain that "the family, as the fundamental group of society and the natural environment for the growth and well-being of all its members and particularly children, should be afforded the necessary protection and assistance so that it can fully assume its responsibilities within the community.... Ratifying the CRC would threaten [this]." As a result, the family unit would be shattered as children looked outside of the family to the state, rather than their parents, for guidance and support.

As a direct result of these concerns, in 1995, days before President Clinton signed the CRC, opponents of the treaty's ratification introduced bills in the House and Senate entitled the "Parental Rights and Responsibilities Act of 1995." The bills, which were identical, were introduced to "protect the fundamental right of a parent to direct the upbringing of a child...." and sought to prohibit federal, state, and local governments from "interfer[ing] with or usurp[ing]" this "fundamental right." Further, the bills attempted to elevate the standard used to evaluate all cases of government interference with parental rights to strict scrutiny. Both bills died in committee and were never reintroduced.

VI. REFUTATION OF VIEWS OPPOSING THE CONVENTION ON THE RIGHTS OF THE CHILD

As already explicated, previous attempts by the United States to ratify the CRC have proved vastly unsuccessful. However, current events, recent judicial decisions, and the international political climate all support a renewed effort to ratify the CRC. Moreover, the current state of children's health and development demands that the United States pay closer attention to the inherent human rights of each child.

A. Responses to Sovereignty Concerns

Although sovereignty concerns are frequently cited as a reason to avoid U.S. ratification of human rights treaties, the manner in which these sovereignty concerns are framed must be considered. Detractors of the CRC and other international treaties believe that being subject to international law infringes on U.S. sovereignty. However, the United States can only be bound by international law through the exercise of its own legislative processes. In order for the United States to become a party to an international agreement, "a domestic decision-maker [e.g., the Senate]" must accept the agreement and "conclude[ ] that a non-U.S. rule should be a rule of decision within the United States." It is entirely possible that a domestic institution will decide that the United States' interests, both at home and abroad, are best served by ratifying a treaty or entering a trade agreement. Such a determination can be viewed "as the result[ ] of an exercise of sovereignty, not as evidence of a lapse of sovereignty." After all, [a] sovereign nation can decide that its sovereign interests are advanced ... by making agreements with other nations that limit what it can otherwise do.... Even more, a sovereign nation can decide that its sovereign interests are advanced ... by agreeing with other nations to delegate interpretive authority over treaties to some supranational body.

. . . .

Even more recently, in *Roper v. Simmons*, Justice Kennedy noted in his majority opinion, striking down the use of the death penalty on individuals convicted of capital crimes that they committed when they were juveniles, that "[i]t is proper that we acknowledge the overwhelming weight of international opinion against the juvenile death penalty...." While, of course, these developments do not alter U.S. sovereignty, they do show a growing recognition of the interconnectedness of the world's nations and an acknowledgement that the laws and practices of other nations can influence domestic law.

B. Responses to Federalism Concerns

Arguments that the CRC, if ratified by the United States, will upset the balance between the states and the federal government and violate the Tenth Amendment of the U.S. Constitution can be refuted both by the current state of the law and contemporary U.S. practice. First, federalism objections to the CRC are essentially negated by Missouri's holding that the treaty power gives the U.S. government authority over the states that is otherwise prohibited by the Constitution.

In addition, the United States has several policies in place to ensure that ratification of international agreements does not impair federalism. First, U.S. ratifications of international treaties are accompanied by reservations, declarations, and understandings ("RUDs") that "severely limit the[ ] application [of human rights treaties] in the United States." This package of RUDs traditionally includes a federalism clause, with the idea that "the United States could leave implementation [of the treaty] largely to the states." This seeming contravention of the Missouri decision is reinforced by the "the policy of the United States, when ratifying human rights treaties, that those treaties [ ] make no significant changes to the American legal system."

To further ensure that human rights treaties do not significantly alter its federal structure, the United States has declared that the human rights treaties it ratifies are non-self-executing, meaning that U.S.-ratified treaties do not automatically have legal force, "but must be implemented by legislative or other measures." This non-self-execution is designed to deny judges in the United States the ability to decide cases based upon the international standards created in human rights treaties. Opponents of the non-self-executing clause believe that the clause undermines the seriousness with which the United States should approach human rights issues.

. . . .

In light of the Supreme Court's definitive holding in Roper prohibiting capital punishment for capital crimes committed by juveniles, the CRC's prohibition on juvenile execution can no longer be cited as a reason for postponing U.S. ratification of the treaty.

Responses to Reproductive and Family Planning Concerns

The CRC does not take a position on family planning or abortion issues. Most observers assume that the CRC's authors deliberately left the CRC's provisions on family planning open to interpretation by each of the ratifying States Parties. Thus, the CRC provisions may be interpreted as recognizing a fetus as a child in need of protection. Although the CRC defines a child as a "human being below the age of eighteen years," the CRC does not establish when childhood begins. Although an individual eighteen years or older is not a "child" under the CRC, the CRC does not set a floor at which childhood starts. This omission, coupled with the statement in the CRC's preamble that "[t]he child needs special safeguards and care . . . before as well as after birth," allows nations who ratify the CRC to interpret Article 6's "inherent right to life" clause as applying to fetuses. Regardless of other nations' interpretations, U.S. law does allow the practice of abortion. Because the CRC does not violate any U.S. abortion or family planning law, its ratification by the United States would not result in any conflict between U.S. domestic policy and international law.

D. Responses to Parents' Rights Concerns

A careful parsing of the CRC reveals that objections to it based on parental rights arguments misconstrue the CRC's intentions. Critics often claim that the CRC's "participatory" rights grant autonomy rights to children that are best controlled by parents.

Yet, early on, the CRC states that the family is the "fundamental group of society" and that "parents have common responsibilities for the upbringing and development of the child." Articles 12 and 13 of the CRC focus on children's right to freedom of expression. However, Article 13 describes specific restrictions to this freedom, including a restriction "[f]or the protection of … morals." The term "morals" is not defined in the CRC, which allows each States Party to interpret the term.

Article 14 grants a child the right to freedom of thought, conscience, and religion. These are rights that are similar to those guaranteed by the U.S. Constitution to every American. Part two of Article 14 guarantees to parents the right to raise their children in accordance with the parents' religious beliefs, explaining that States Parties "shall respect the right and duties of the parents … to provide direction to the child in the exercise of his or her right.…"

The past decade has seen a rapid increase in the number of parents who use electronic devices or services to control the content their children see on television and through other mass media forums. Although this may appear to conflict with Article 17 of the CRC, which grants children the right to "access information and material from a diversity of national and international sources, especially those aimed at the promotion of his or her social, spiritual and moral well-being and physical and mental health," Article 17's intention is only to allow a child to access helpful information. For example, the CRC encourages the media to produce "material of social and cultural benefit" and encourages "the development of appropriate guidelines for the protection of the child from information and material injurious to his or her well-being." The CRC makes no suggestion on what the "appropriate guidelines" should be, leaving this task to the States Parties that ratify the CRC.

These provisions make clear that the intention of Article 17 is not to provide children with a justification for demanding access to illicit or distasteful media, but rather to aid children in accessing materials that are beneficial to their development.

VII. WHY RATIFY NOW?

….

The events of the past decade provide further reasons why the time has come for the United States to proclaim its support for the CRC to the international community. The 1990s saw large-scale human rights violations due to intra- and international conflicts in which millions of children lost their lives. Massive human rights violations against children occurred in Bosnia-Herzegovina, Chechnya, Rwanda, and the Sudan, among others, in the past decade alone. Given these occurrences, the need for passage of the CRC is as critical as ever. Ratification of the CRC by the world's only superpower, will give a needed boost to the enforcement of human rights law. This Article argues that the United States' ratification of the CRC will, as it has done with other treaties, give greater credence and international support to its principles. Ratification will commit the United States and the world to better protection and promotion of the health, welfare, and security of children.

Notes and Questions

1. Lozman and Rutkow seem to share the view expressed in the Garman article that the UNCRC is simply another manifestation of a modern recognition of the importance of freedom and democracy for all disadvantaged groups, including children. Do these writers adequately take into account the fact that children by their nature are not as capable of exercising autonomy rights as adults? Do the social conservatives in fact capture this paradox more accurately than the advocates for U.S. ratification?

The following article presents one theory of how children in the U.S. would benefit from ratification of the UNCRC. It takes as its focus the U.S. preference for "negative rights" over "positive rights." In other words, U.S. legal thought and jurisprudence has been more comfortable with the notion of the right of citizens to be left alone by government, protected against government intrusion, as contrasted with the concept of governmental obligations to guarantee the conditions under which citizens may exercise certain rights. To the extent that U.S. constitutional principles have not favored the idea of "positive rights", the author demonstrates how important these could be for the full protection of children, and how the UNCRC would introduce this concept into the U.S. legal landscape.

Tamar Ezer, *A Positive Right to Protection for Children*
7 Yale Human Rights & Development Law Journal 1 (2004)

I. Introduction

Children are an anomaly in the liberal legal order. Conceptualizations that work in other areas of human rights break down in the context of children. Children defy the conventional view of rights as implying fully rational, autonomous individuals who can exercise free choice and require freedom from governmental interference. Lacking fully developed rational capabilities, children are dependent "incompetents" by definition. Furthermore, unlike the term "individual," the term "child" does not stand alone from all others, but necessarily implies a relationship.

. . . .

Although children defy the conventional view of negative rights, they lend themselves more readily to a positive rights regime. Their very dependence and capacity for growth call for a positive right to protection and to the means necessary for their development. In fact, in the United States, while positive rights are only accepted "grudgingly and with suspicion," in connection with adults, they are much more easily accepted in relation to children. Many state constitutions have recognized children's education as a fundamental right. State legislatures have further created "welfare rights" especially applicable to children.

Not only is the adoption of positive rights for children conceptually sound, but it would help assure adequate protection for children, which the current regime fails to do. American jurisprudence is typified by the *DeShaney* case, decided in 1989, in which the United States Supreme Court held that no rights were violated when a four-year-old child was beaten by his father to the point of brain damage, while the government stood by and a social worker "dutifully recorded these incidents [of abuse] in her files." Conceptualizing the Constitution in negative terms, the Court explained that children have no right to protection from harm, even when there is already government involvement in their lives.

This paper argues for a positive right to protection for children, rooted in dignity. Protecting the psychological integrity of children requires access to education, while protecting their physical integrity requires freedom from physical harm.

. . . .

II. Positive Rights

A. The Distinction Between Positive and Negative Rights

Traditional liberal thought has developed an opposition between positive and negative rights. Negative, or non-interference rights, prevent the state from violating individual autonomy, while positive, or integrative rights, impose a duty on the state to provide certain goods and services. Thus, negative rights create distance around individuals, while positive rights connect. This differentiation also reflects two conceptions of liberty: negative liberty, or liberty from, and positive liberty, or liberty to.

The classical Western notion of rights is negative, stressing choice and autonomy. Since the rights system is rooted in Western political traditions and philosophy, this led the human rights movement to historically assume a greater emphasis on negative rights. Locke's conception of natural rights was intrinsically bound up with the individual's capacity to exercise rational choice as an autonomous human being. Thus, natural rights comprised negative freedoms to protect the individual's self-determination from violation by the state. In this way, the rights model traditionally pits the individual against the state and erects barriers to protect the individual's selfhood from arbitrary government incursion. A fear of tyranny lies at the base of restrictions on governmental power through constitutional rights.

Western liberal theory asserts the status of the individual and the individual's priority over both the state and society. Under the social contract theory, the state is a product of individual choice, and the individual precedes and justifies the state. Society is the mere sum of free individuals, organized to reach otherwise unreachable goals. As Robert Cover explains, "[T]he first and fundamental unit is the individual and 'rights' locate him as an individual separate and apart from every other individual." Thus, the human being is fundamentally individual, and the individual is seen as an end and kind of absolute.

B. International Treatment of Positive Rights

International human rights documents, such as the Universal Declaration of Human Rights (UDHR), the foundation document of the human rights movement, espouse this negative/positive rights distinction. Negative rights are regarded as the civil and political rights enshrined in the International Covenant on Civil and Political Rights (ICCPR), and positive rights are regarded as the economic, social, and cultural rights appearing in the International Covenant on Economic, Social, and Cultural Rights (ICESCR).

The "official" position, dating back to the UDHR and reaffirmed in multiple resolutions since that time, is that negative and positive rights are "universal, indivisible and interdependent and interrelated." This reveals a recognition that: (1) for civil and political guarantees to have any meaning, it is necessary to assume a base level of living conditions; and (2) as the individual is not self-sufficient, the very conditions of life are assured by society. The international approach thus connects rights with needs and reflects the understanding that the satisfaction of basic needs is essential for the realization of freedom. However, negative and positive rights are not on equal footing, and unlike the ICCPR's treatment of negative rights, the ICESCR only undertakes to realize positive rights "progressively" and "to the maximum of ... available resources."

The trend in international law has been toward the recognition of greater complexity in human rights than the simple duality between negative and positive rights. Since the adoption of the UDHR in 1948, the United Nations has continuously developed more comprehensive rights instruments, recognizing three categories of rights. "First generation," or blue rights, are the civil and political rights associated with liberal democracies. These are rights to political participation, free speech, freedom of religion, freedom from torture, and fair trial, considered important for the maintenance of democracy and individualism. "Second generation," or red rights, are the socio-economic and cultural rights preferred in socialist and communist regimes. These rights are to goods, such as shelter, medical care, education, work, and leisure. Finally, "third generation," or green rights, are group or solidarity rights of the greatest interest to developing countries. These are peoples' rights to national self-determination and to such diffuse goods as peace, environmental and cultural integrity, and healthy economic development. This last set of rights, rooted in communities, has moved the furthest from the original Western conception of rights and recognizes humanity as fundamentally social beings with social and communal needs.

C. American Treatment of Positive Rights

By contrast with the international position, the American approach reflects a more narrow understanding of government and rights. The United States prides itself on having a negative constitution that tells state officials what they may not do, rather than what they must do. This notion of the Constitution as a charter of negative liberties pervades judicial thinking and serves to exclude whole categories of individual needs and government misconduct from constitutional protection. The Supreme Court has rejected claims to housing, medical services, education, and welfare. The Court has further resisted recognizing any "affirmative right to government aid, even where such aid may be necessary to secure life, liberty, or property interests of which the government itself may not deprive the individual." Moreover, the Supreme Court accepts any justification for inequality in the distribution of basic necessities, such as food, shelter, and personal safety, that is "reasonably conceivable" and not patently arbitrary, provided that no suspect classes are involved.

This American attitude is a result of both philosophical and practical objections. First, there is an anti-government national ethos, echoing the days of colonial rebellion and the pioneers out West. The Madisonian constitutional scheme reflects a deep distrust of government action and power, including mechanisms, such as the separation of powers, to slow down government. Jeffersonian liberalism states that government is best that governs least. Americans have traditionally been suspicious of big government and skeptical about national programs to achieve social goals, preferring to place their faith in self-reliant individualism. Thus, government has been perceived in a "passive role, bound to respect pre-existing rights," rather than "as an active agent in promoting, enforcing, and interpreting them." Second, Americans have questioned whether positive rights are consistent in principle with the establishment of a free, democratic, market-oriented civil society. A third important factor is the belief that only negative rights can be fully enforced, coupled with the view that, almost by definition, constitutional rights depend on complete judicial enforceability.

Additionally, it is important to remember the age of the American Bill of Rights. Dating back over 200 years, the venerable age of the American Bill of Rights distinguishes it from the constitutions of other countries, many dating only as far back as the period post-World War II. The first ten amendments to the United States Constitution were in place long before the legislature began "to attend systematically to the health, safety, and well-being of citizens."

Nonetheless, the Constitution does not allow for a simple characterization as negative. Some constitutional provisions clearly mandate government action. For example, the Sixth Amendment requires the government to provide the accused with a speedy public trial, compulsory process, and the assistance of counsel to indigent criminal defendants. The Supreme Court has interpreted the Fifth Amendment to require Miranda warnings. The equal protection clause sometimes requires that government take affirmative steps to ensure that certain groups are not treated unequally. The Thirteenth Amendment prohibition on slavery covers private actions, and individuals are entitled to assistance from the state in enforcing it. Even conventional negative rights, like the

First Amendment, may require the government to take affirmative steps to allocate resources and ensure public access to forums and information to protect that right.

Furthermore, state constitutions specifically call for the enforcement of positive rights. Every state constitution establishes explicit substantive goals that regulate government power and provide the basis for a variety of positive claims against the state. Almost all state constitutions provide for the right to education and some states recognize constitutional rights to welfare, housing, health, and abortions.

Moreover, despite powerful resistance, the United States now has many of the characteristics of a welfare state (for instance, Social Security and Medicare programs) due to the efforts of Congress and the individual states. Ironically, negative rights stood in the way of this positive rights' development. Notions of individual rights, such as economic liberty and freedom of contract, forestalled government programs during the Lochner era. This example demonstrates that the inherent tension and contingency between rights necessitates difficult balancing choices.

. . . .

IV. Alternate Approaches Towards Children

. . . .

2. United Nations Convention on the Rights of the Child

. . . .

Unlike the 1959 Declaration, the 1989 Convention [on the Rights of the Child] "imposes binding obligations on all of the nations that have ratified it." The Convention created the Committee on the Rights of the Child to monitor the compliance of the treaty's parties, but the Committee has no enforcement power. Since the Convention has no direct method of formal enforcement and no court to assess claims, it places great weight on reporting. Two years after ratification, each government is expected to send the United Nations Committee a report detailing progress made in fulfilling obligations under the Convention.

The Convention includes a multitude of provisions affirming children's positive right to protection. Article 19 instructs, "States Parties shall take all appropriate legislative, administrative, social and educational measures to protect the child from all forms of physical or mental violence, injury or abuse, neglect or negligent treatment, maltreatment or exploitation, including sexual abuse, while in the care of parent(s), legal guardian(s) or any other person who has the care of the child." Thus, in cases of abuse, the child explicitly "has the right to the protection of the law against such interference or attacks." Article 20 further specifies cases where a child "shall be entitled to special protection and assistance provided by the State."

The Committee on the Rights of the Child has paid particular attention to a child's right to physical integrity and protection from corporal punishment in monitoring implementation of the Convention. The Committee has repeatedly stressed that the corporal punishment of children is incompatible with the Convention, and it is necessary to ban it in families in order for reporting countries to achieve treaty compliance. Guidelines for country reports require that they indicate "whether legislation (criminal and/or family law) includes a prohibition of all forms of physical and mental violence, including corporal punishment, deliberate humiliation, injury, abuse, neglect or exploitation, inter alia within the family."

As the basis for this policy, the Committee has interpreted Article 19 (above) as an absolute prohibition on the corporal punishment of children. The Committee has further pointed to Article 37's prohibition of "torture or other cruel, inhuman or degrading treatment or punishment" and to Article 24, ¶3 to support its interpretation. Article 24, ¶3 states, "States Parties shall take all effective and appropriate measures with a view to abolishing traditional practices prejudicial to the health of children," and the Committee perceives the use of physical force to educate children as such a practice.

Marta Santos Pais, the Committee's rapporteur, links the prohibition on the corporal punishment of children to their fundamental human dignity. In 1996, she explained, "The right not to be subject to any form of physical punishment ... flows as a consequence of the consideration [in the Convention of the Child] of the child as a person whose human dignity should be respected." Former High Commissioner for Human Rights Mary Robinson, echoed this notion. She stated:

> The recourse to physical punishment by adults reflects a denial of the recognition, by the Convention on the Rights of the Child, of the child as a subject of human rights. If we want to remain faithful to the spirit of the Convention, strongly based on the dignity of the child as a full-fledged bearer of rights, then any act of violence against him or her must be banned.

Despite its strong child protection language, the Convention is essentially a pro-family document, like the Declaration before it. The Convention "recognizes the family as the natural environment for child development and makes clear that parents have the primary right and responsibility to raise their own children, without interference from their government" or the United Nations. The Convention further includes numerous provisions aimed to preserve the integrity of the family. For instance, the Preamble asserts that "the family, as the fundamental group of society and the natural environment for the growth and well-being of all its members and particularly children, should be afforded the necessary protection and assistance so that it can fully assume its responsibilities within the community." Furthermore, Article 7 imbues the child with the explicit "right to know and be cared for by his or her parents." This is the flip-side of the American right for parents to control their child's custody and upbringing. In this way, "the Convention actively protects the family and the parent-child relationship as integral elements of the rights of children."

While the Convention safeguards the parent-child relationship, it maintains "the best interests of the child" to be "a primary consideration." Children's rights are not defined as antagonistic to parents' rights, but rather as their source. Of course, the question remains what the child's "best interests" actually are, and who gets to define them. However, the rest of the Convention gives content to this open-ended standard, and at least conceptually, it holds the child's best interests as the guiding principle.

. . . .

Notes and Questions

1. As an advocate for ratification, Ezer emphasizes the protective aspects of the Convention. Her hope and expectation appear to be that U.S. courts would be encouraged by the UNCRC to take a more positive, proactive approach to the rights of children, as the Convention imposes specific obligations to protect on States Parties. How might those on the anti-ratification side respond to her arguments?

2. What explains the U.S. legal tradition's preference for negative rather than positive rights? Which category of rights is more likely to benefit children? Can such entrenched national preferences be altered by ratification of a particular Convention, in this case the UNCRC?

3. In light of the readings in this section, what do you consider to be the strongest arguments for and against U.S. ratification? Does one's interpretation of specific UNCRC provisions influence one's ultimate opinion on the issue? Would U.S. ratification of the UNCRC make an appreciable difference to American children? If the Convention's provisions could not be directly argued in U.S. courts in the absence of U.S. implementing legislation, in what other ways might it exert legal influence?

III. The Convention on the Rights of the Child as a Living Document: Is It Making a Measurable Difference to the World's Children?

A. Conflicting Assessments of Effectiveness

Despite the fact that it has many critics, the UNCRC has been formally adopted by all but two nations. Some commentators believe that the Convention is having a positive effect on the lives of children; others might support the document in theory, but argue that it is failing to live up to its promises. In the readings that follow, be aware of the different ways in which the Convention's effects are either lauded or denigrated. Note that those who take a positive view often focus on Convention-related activity within the United Nations itself or on the proliferation of national legislation, whereas those of a more critical perspective highlight failures of empirically measurable implementation and enforcement "on the ground."

Cynthia Price Cohen, *Implementing the U.N. Convention on the Rights of the Child*
21 Whittier Law Review 95 (1999)

....

VI. International Application

[T]here is no doubt that the Convention on the Rights of the Child is having a major impact on how the world views children. This impact can be seen in: 1) the Committee's broad definition of its mandate; 2) the actions of governments; 3) the processes of U.N. bodies; 4) treaty drafting processes; and 5) the development of coalitions between governments and NGOs around certain child rights issue areas.

When it drafted its Provisional Rules of Procedure, the Committee chose to go beyond the mandate outlined in articles 43 and 45. One important function it added was to establish the practice of holding general discussion days at least once a year. These days are devoted to exploring a topic of interest to all States Parties. Among the topics that have been covered by the Committee are: children and war; economic exploitation; the girl child; the child and the family; the disabled child; and, most recently, children living with HIV/AIDS. Several of these general discussion days have led to further research on the topics. For example, one could argue that the Committee's General Discussion on Children and War ultimately led to the appointment of Olara Ottunu as the U.N. Special Representative of the Secretary-General for Children and Armed Conflict.

Significantly, as the periodic reports of States Parties are beginning to be submitted to the Committee, they are giving a clear indication of the actions that are being taken by countries to ensure the Convention's implementation. All countries appear to have taken the Committee's suggestions seriously—making changes in legislation and administrative procedures. To assist in this process, one of the actions taken by countries—notably both Sweden and Costa Rica—is the establishment of an office of Children's Ombudsman. In theory, the Ombudsman is a person, free of government control, who has the authority to act on behalf of children and to correct injustices.

The Convention on the Rights of the Child has affected the activities of every U.N. body. Both the Commission on Human Rights and the Fourth Committee of the General Assembly now adopt child rights resolutions every year as a part of their regular agenda. The Commission on Human Rights has also established a Special Rapporteur on the Sale of Children, whose research has been contained in numerous reports and has led the Committee to establish a working group to draft an Optional Protocol on the Sale of Children, Child Prostitution and Child Pornography. The Commission on Human Rights has established a second working group to draft an Optional Protocol to the convention regarding children in armed conflict.

Three other U.N. bodies that have changed the focus of their work because of the Convention are: the U.N. High Commissioner for Refugees, which now acknowledges that about half of the world's refugees are children, and has established special guidelines for dealing with child refugees; UNICEF, which has shifted its emphasis from child health to child rights; and the International Labor Organization, which is adding to its child labor treaties by drafting a new convention aimed at ending the worst forms of child labor.

The treaty drafting processes of three other international lawmaking bodies have also been influenced by the Convention on the Rights of the Child. The Organization of African Unity drafted its own Charter on the Rights and Welfare of the African Child. The Council of Europe drafted the Convention on the exercise of Children's Rights. Also interesting has been the subtle way in which the language of the Hague Convention on Cooperation and Protection of Children in respect of Intercountry Adoption was influenced by the Convention on the Rights of the Child. This treaty began its life as an instrument to enable parents to adopt a child from abroad, but by the time it was adopted it had become an instrument to enable a foreign child to have a family.

Finally, there is a proliferation of activity by NGOs in a number of child rights focal points. Action is being taken—often in collaboration with governments—to address such issues as: children in war; sexual exploitation; the girl child; child labor; and education. Two new areas of emphasis are child participation—which is leading to the inclusion of children on school boards and other community activities—and research that is aimed at establishing child-friendly economic policies.

VII. Conclusion

. . . .

While it is true that a human rights treaty is only as effective as its implementation, today, with the communications revolution, it will be more and more difficult for governments to exaggerate their human rights achievements. All those who care about children should become individual watchdogs, reminding governments that they have nowhere to hide. Hopefully, as the Convention's periodic reports continue to be submitted they will reveal a pattern of action supporting the notion that the world no longer looks on children as objects, but as human beings deserving of respect for their rights.

Notes and Questions

1. The late Cynthia Price Cohen was a strong proponent of the UNCRC, and a tireless advocate for children's rights. In the excerpt above, is she overly focused on, and sanguine about, the activities of the UN? Is there a danger that the enforcement procedures associated with most human rights conventions may place undue emphasis on the mechanics of state reporting?

———————

UNICEF is the acronym for the United Nations Children's Fund, created by the General Assembly in 1946 to deal with the dire situation of children in Europe in the wake of World War II.[17] It is funded through the contributions of governments and individuals. Although its primary focus is on child survival through nutrition and health programs, its work is far more complex and policy-driven than this would suggest. In recent years especially, UNICEF has taken on a "child rights" mission, which has involved the organization in almost every conceivable aspect of national policies touching on child welfare. The global UNICEF structure is characterized by decentralization, with prominence given to cooperation between regional and local offices and national governments.

Immediately following are two selections that reflect the UN perspective on the role of the UNCRC in child welfare. The first is a UNICEF retrospective on how the Convention has affected the lives of children over the course of its first decade. The second is an assessment on similar themes by Jaap Doek, Chair of the Committee on the Rights of the Child between 2001 and 2007. UNICEF and the UNCRC Committee on the Rights of the Child might be considered as the twin pillars of the UN-based child welfare establishment. As such, these two excerpts can be expected to express similar views on how to evaluate the successes of the UNCRC to date. Both place great emphasis on the fact that the UNCRC has led to greater official attention to children's rights, as framed and defined by the Convention itself.

UNICEF, *Convention on the Rights of the Child: Setbacks and Successes*

(2004)

Setbacks and Successes

More progress was made in realizing and protecting children's rights in the decade following adoption of the Convention on the Rights of the Child than in any other comparable period in human history and children's rights are now higher on public and political agendas than ever before. Gains in democratic governance and rising respect for human rights in many countries have contributed to this progress.

The near-universal ratification of the Convention on the Rights of the Child has encouraged the ratification by States of other fundamental human rights instruments and more and more States are committing to honouring and implementing human rights agendas by establishing National Plans of Action, including specific targets on the basis of which progress can be monitored.

Major achievements in the area of child rights can already be seen:

———————

17. The UNICEF homepage gives a sense of the range of UNICEF's activities worldwide, at http//:www.unicef.org.

- Special institutions, structures, agendas and measures in the interest of promoting child rights have emerged in all corners of the globe. NGOs and other actors in civil society have emerged as innovative and powerful voices for children's rights.

- Wholesale legislative reform in favour of child rights often has been the outcome of the mandatory comprehensive review of national legislation under the Convention's reporting process. Also as a result of this process, States have acquired new impetus to achieving child survival and development goals.

- States have begun to respond to the extreme violence and exploitation, abuse and neglect that is a reality for millions of children. The principles requiring that children be protected from 'all forms of physical and mental violence' have sparked new hope for reducing the many forms of adult violence against children.

- Because of the Convention's non-discrimination principle, States have moved to better realize and protect the rights of forgotten and invisible children—children who are refugees, children who have been institutionalized, children who work or are otherwise exploited, children living or working on the streets and children who have been bought and sold across borders.

- States have been obliged to ensure that their definitions of childhood meet the standards outlined in the Convention on the Rights of the Child.

- States have developed distinct systems of youth justice that focus on reintegration in society and avoid—wherever possible—criminalizing children and depriving them of liberty.

- Progress has been made in ensuring that children's views are being heard, respected and taken into account—within families, communities and States—when actions are undertaken, policies shaped and results assessed.

Challenges ahead

In spite of the remarkable achievements in advancing child rights, much remains to be done. Progress has been uneven, with some countries lagging considerably behind others in giving child rights its deserved prominence on national agendas.

- Globally, an estimated 12 million children under the age of five die every year, mostly of easily preventable causes.

- Some 130 million children in developing countries are not in primary school and the majority of them are girls.

- About 160 million children are severely or moderately malnourished.

- Some 1.4 billion people lack access to safe water and 2.7 billion lack adequate sanitation.

- Some States are moving toward increasingly punitive systems of juvenile justice, with children beaten and arbitrarily detained by police and forced to share prisons with adults in inhumane conditions.

- Many unwanted children languish in orphanages and other institutions, denied education and adequate health care. These children are often physically abused.

- An estimated 250 million children are engaged in some form of labour. There are few examples of systematic actions to end child exploitation that are sensitive to children's needs.

- Armed conflicts around the globe continue to shorten and ruin the lives of millions of children. Last year, about 300,000 children served as soldiers in national armies. Many of these children were killed or maimed in combat; and many children were forced to kill and maim others.

At the close of the 20th century, there is a growing global consciousness of the issues affecting children and a commitment to address them. New and growing problems—for example, of HIV/AIDS, which has already orphaned millions of children and daily afflicts thousands more—threaten to reverse hard-won health and other social gains in a number of countries. But the world's children have been made a promise that still stands. Millions of children's lives will be affected if that commitment is not met.

Jaap E. Doek, *The Protection of Children's Rights and the United Nations Convention on the Rights of the Child: Achievements and Challenges*

22 St. Louis University Public Law Review 235 (2003)

Achievements since 1990

....

A. Children in Armed Conflict

At the time of the drafting of the CRC, one of the most heavily debated provisions was Article 38. A number of States felt very strongly—supported by many, if not all, NGOs—that Article 38's minimum age for recruiting children to become soldiers at 15 years-old was much too low. Efforts to increase this age failed, and the States most concerned about this matter finally decided to accept Article 38 as it was (and is) because they did not want to endanger the unanimous approval of the CRC by the General Assembly. But they clearly had the intention to raise this issue again as soon as possible after the CRC was ratified by the 20 States necessary for the CRC to enter into force (on September 2, 1990). This explains why the Committee devoted its first day of General Discussion in 1992 to Children in Armed Conflicts. One of the Recommendations of this discussion was to undertake an international study on this matter. In 1993, the Secretary General appointed Graça Machel as the expert to conduct this study with the support of a secretariat provided to her by the UN. The report published in 1996 had at least two very visible consequences:

(1) The appointment of Mr. Otunu of Nigeria by the Secretary General of the UN as his special representative for children in armed conflicts. Mr. Otunu, who has an office in New York, has been and is very active visiting the countries where children are (and have been) recruited as soldiers or are (and have been) involved in armed conflicts in any other way. He also succeeded in making children in armed conflicts a topic for the agenda of the Security Council that now regularly (at least once per year) discusses the developments in this area covered by the CRC and its related Optional Protocol (see Resolution 1261(1999), Resolution 1314 (2000) and Resolution 1379 (2001) adopted by the Security Council).

(2) The drafting and adoption by the UN General Assembly (on 25 May 2000) of an Optional Protocol (OP) on Children in Armed Conflicts. This OP entered into force on February 10, 2002 and, as of March 2003, has been ratified by 46

States Parties. In this OP, the minimum age for non-voluntary recruitment (conscription) is 18 years; for voluntary recruitment the States Parties commit themselves to increase that age to above the minimum of 15 as set in Article 38 of the CRC. Another rule of this OP is that no child below 18 shall be directly involved (as a soldier or otherwise) in armed conflicts. States Parties also commit themselves to the development and effective implementation of programs for demobilization, recovery, and social reintegration of child soldiers.

The study and its follow-up (via special representative/optional protocols and other actions) have resulted in significantly more attention for children in armed conflicts, not only in terms of demobilization and social reintegration, but also in terms of prevention. Crucial in this regard have been, and still are, specialized UN agencies, in particular UNICEF and international NGOs (e.g. the Coalition against Child Soldiers) that provide technical, financial, and other assistance. Some of the concrete results of all this will be presented in the next paragraph.

B. Commercial Sexual Exploitation of Children (CSEC)

Since the end of the 1980s, the growing international attention resulted, inter alia, in the appointment by the Commission on Human Rights of a Special Rapporteur on the Sale of Children, Child Prostitution, and Child Pornography and in the establishment of an international NGO focusing on these phenomena: ECPAT (End Child Prostitution, Child Pornography and Trafficking of Children for Sexual Purposes) with branches in quite a number of countries. This NGO, supported by UNICEF, other NGOs, and governments, organized the First World Congress against Commercial Sexual Exploitation in 1996 in Stockholm. At this Congress, an Agenda for Action was adopted by 122 governments. About the same time, a working group of the UN Commission on Human Rights started the drafting of an Optional Protocol to the CRC on the Sale of Children, Child Prostitution, and Child Pornography. This work was completed in 2000, and the text was adopted by the UN General Assembly on May 25, 2000. This OP entered into force on January 18, 2002 and has been ratified by 45 States. As of March 2003, the OP requires States Parties, inter alia, to make all kinds of commercial sexual exploitation punishable under their criminal law, to introduce extra-territorial jurisdiction, to provide for the seizure and confiscation of products and benefits from such exploitation.

....

At the end of 2001, the Second World Congress against Commercial Sexual Exploitation of Children was held in Yokohama, Japan to evaluate results and to set an agenda for the next 5 years. In this agenda, the States committed themselves, inter alia, to address the root causes that place children at risk of sexual exploitation, such as poverty, inequality, discrimination, violence, armed conflicts and dysfunctioning families. Furthermore, they promoted networking among the key actors to combat CSEC, ensured adequate resources for the prevention and elimination of commercial sexual exploitation of children, and took adequate measures to address negative aspects of new technology, in particular child pornography on the internet.

C. Child Labor

At the beginning of the 1990s, the efforts to prevent and eliminate child labor were given a very strong boost, not so much because of the CRC's entering into force but due to a very substantive donation from the German government to the ILO earmarked for elimination of child labor (50 million DM for a period of 5 yrs); labor, then, it was very limited and hardly visible. This marks the beginning of the well known international program for the elimination of child labor, the International Labour Organisation (ILO-IPEC). This program is now financially supported by about 15 donor countries and different national programs carried out in about 75 Countries.

But, it is very likely that the ratification of the CRC by 191 states in 1997 contributed to the remarkable increase of international attention for child labor. The same fact may have been favorable to the ILO efforts to draft a new ILO Convention focusing on the Elimination of Worst Forms of Child Labour around 1997. These efforts were successful, and in 1999 the ILO adopted ILO Convention No. 182.

...In this regard, it is important to note that the definition of the worst forms of child labor in Article 3 of the ILO Convention No. 182 lists various forms of exploitation of children already covered in the Articles 32–36 of the CRC.

I agree with the UN Secretary General that the CRC helped to enhance existing ILO standards (first ILO Convention No. 138 and later ILO Convention No. 182). The relevant provisions of the CRC have also helped to promote a growing recognition of the connections between the protection of children from economic exploitation and the enjoyment of their rights to education, health care, rest, play, and an adequate standard of living.

The awareness of the worst forms of child labor and the need for its prevention and elimination was not limited to governments. The tripartite structure of the ILO meant and means that employers' organizations and trade unions are involved in the fight against child labour. At the same time, many national NGOs were created in the field of child labor. These NGOs, UNICEF, other UN agencies and the ILO partners (governments, employers, workers), developed and maintained a momentum which, inter alia, resulted in a Global March against Child Labour and in more awareness among consumers and international corporations. Awareness was the drive behind actions/programmes like the Rugmark initiative and agreements for the elimination of child labor from the garment industry in Bangladesh and the soccer ball stitching industry in Sialkot, Pakistan, as well as the development of codes of conduct by international corporations to include the prohibition of child labor in their production processes.

In light of the above and of many more activities which can be mentioned, it is fair to conclude that the CRC has created a movement with participants from all walks of life, from children and parents, to governments and all kind of organizations, including small, local, not-for-profit action groups, and large international corporations. The CRC has become a foundation for, and the driving force behind, a wide variety of activities aimed at improving the world of and for children. These activities have largely been devoted to increasing awareness and understanding the meaning of the child rights approach of the CRC in order to ultimately change the traditional attitudes regarding children. A change which I once summarized as "from charity to entitlement."

Although this can be considered a major and fundamental achievement, one may wonder, is this all there is? Theoretically it sounds fine, but what about the children? Did they not benefit from the CRC and all the related activities?

Improvements for Children Since 1990

For those who expected the CRC to quickly make the world a better place for children, the results may be very disappointing. This kind of expectation is not very realistic. An international human rights instrument like the CRC cannot in and of itself improve the world for children. Even a serious and rigorous implementation will only produce visible and measurable results after some time.

The CRC has been operational since September 1990, and I think it is fair to say that the results in just 13 years are quite impressive, not only in terms of international action and policies as described in the previous paragraph, but also for the children themselves. Let me briefly describe some of the improvements that can directly or indirectly be attributed to the implementation of the CRC.

A. Legal Protection and Child Participation

In the first reports on the implementation of the CRC now submitted by 175 States, one can find a wide variety of changes in laws enacted to strengthen the rights of children and their legal protection.

There is a growing trend — although not equally present in all States Parties — to recognize the child as a bearer of rights who should be given a fair opportunity to express her views and to participate in decision-making on matters relevant to her or him.

An increasing number of laws today explicitly provides the child with the right to be heard in civil procedures on e.g. custody, right of access, and child protection measures like out-of-home placements. In schools, children are increasingly being given the right to be heard and to participate in decisions relevant to their school environment. At the community level, youth councils are actively participating in the development and implementation of programmes and policies. Regional and national children and youth parliaments have been established allowing for a direct input in the political decision-making process. It may be time that some of these and other forms of participation have a high degree of decoration, tokenism, or symbolism, but it is also clear from recent developments that authentic child participation is growing at the local, national, and international level. This has been most recently illustrated by strong child participation to the Special Session on Children of the UN General Assembly.

In many States Parties, legal provisions for the protection of especially vulnerable children have been improved. This happened by increasing the minimum age for child labor through the introduction of more severe penalties and extra-territorial jurisdiction in cases of commercial sexual exploitation and trafficking.

Many legal and other measures have been taken to prevent and combat abuse of children in the family and in care institutions, including, inter alia, rules for child sensitive interviewing by well-trained professionals of victims of child abuse. The protection of girls from various forms of discrimination has improved via legal and other measures in quite a number of States Parties.

Many States Parties have changed or are in the process of changing their laws on juvenile justice in order to better protect juveniles suspected of having committed crimes throughout the prosecution process, including at the pre-trial detention stage, trial itself, and execution of sanctions stage with a growing preference for non-punitive alternatives for traditional custodial sentences.

But all these improvements of the rights of the child and his/her legal protection are not always implemented and sometimes even violated. The child therefore needs easy access to effective remedies.

It is encouraging to note that more and more children are being given a possibility to file complaints in cases of violation of their rights, either via specially created procedures (for example, the limited opportunities for children in institutions) or more generally via independent institutions for the monitoring of children's rights implementation like child commissioners or children's ombudsperson. There are a growing number of these institutions, particularly in Europe, as well as in other parts of the world.

B. Improvements in Health Care, Education and Special Protection

The improvements made during the first decade of the CRC's implementation (1990–2000) can also be presented in concrete figures and statistics. Keep in mind that factors other than the CRC, in particular the International Plan of Action of the WSC in 1990, have contributed to these improvements. While these improvements are perhaps not as good as one may want, they are nevertheless considerable. Here are a few examples:

- the mortality rate of children under 5 years of age went down from 94 (1990) to 81 (2000) per 1000 live births;

- the children suffering from malnutrition, as measured by stunting or under-weightness, decreased from 177 million in 1990 to 149 million in 2000, with about two-third of them living in Asia;

- polio has been eradicated in more than 175 countries;

- sustained routine immunization (three doses of combined diphtheria/pertussis/tetanus vaccine, DTP3) has reached a coverage of 75%.

- the reported incidences of measles have declined by nearly two thirds;

- deaths due to diarrhoea have been reduced by 50%;

- about 72% of households in developing countries are using iodized salt (less than 20% in 1990). As a result 90 million newborns are protected yearly from significant loss of learning ability;

- in more than 40 countries, over 70% of the children receive at least one high dose vitamin A supplement a year. UNICEF estimates that, as a result, the death of one million children has been prevented in the period between 1998–2000;

- access to safe drinking water and access to proper sanitation facilities has improved for 816 million and 747 million people respectively;

- enrollment in primary education has increased and the global goal set in 1990 at the WSC (80% enrollment) has been achieved;

- in 2001, 21 countries reported that school enrollment and retention of girls increased (in South Asia the gender gap in school enrollment was reduced by 20%).

From these and other figures it is clear the implementation of the right to the highest attainable standard of health and of the right to free and compulsory primary education has made considerable progress. But still a lot remains to be done;

- in the period 2000–2001 more than 300,000 working children and almost 30,000 parents have benefited from the ILO-IPEC programmes;

- thousands of child soldiers have been demobilized thanks to actions by UNICEF and those supported by other UN agencies and NGOs. For instance, 2,400 in Angola, 2,600 in the Democratic Republic of Congo (Plan of Action 2002), 6,821 in Sierra Leone (since October 1999) and 3,351 in Sudan since February 2001. Education, psycho-social, and medical support was provided to the thousands of child victims of armed conflicts.

Improvements can also be recorded in the area of special protection, although they are still very moderate given the magnitude of the problems; they are clearly less impressive than in the areas of heath and education.

Notes and Questions

1. The two selections above, broadly representative of the mainstream UN point of view, describe the Convention as an important and influential document. What sorts of evidence do the authors cite to? Do they make a convincing case for the role of the Convention in bringing about social improvements for children? Which appears to be more important in these writings—a proliferation of official statements and studies, or the reality of children for whom the "human rights" picture may not have changed a great deal? Both pieces link improvements in child welfare with the promulgation of the UNCRC itself. Can this link be assumed?

2. What criteria should one use to assess the success of the UNCRC? Who is in the best position to evaluate its successes and failures? Can or should the CRC be blamed if national governments fail to deliver on promises of enhanced rights for children?

The Human Rights Watch assessment of the UNCRC at Ten

The non-governmental organization Human Rights Watch (HRW) is the most important chronicler of human rights violations against children. Its approach can be clearly contrasted with that of the UN bodies, in that HRW's task is to investigate and expose the suffering of children in various countries, rather than to work diplomatically with governments to achieve goals set by the UN. In the article that follows, Human Rights Watch provided its assessment of how children were faring ten years after the promulgation of the UNCRC. Does Human Rights Watch go too far in using the UNCRC as a rod to measure the hypocrisy of national governments, where those governments have continued to allow heinous violations of children's rights?

Human Rights Watch, *World Report 2000: Children's Rights*
available at http://www.hrw.org/legacy/wr2k/crd.htm#topofpage

Human Rights Developments

The decade since the adoption of the Convention on the Rights of the Child was marked by some significant advances on behalf of children. Many countries used the convention as the basis on which to revise domestic legislation and improve protections for children, or have appointed special ombudspersons or envoys for children. As the Committee on the Rights of the Child evaluated country reports under the convention, it developed new standards of protection and pressed governments for specific reforms.

A 1996 United Nations report on the impact of armed conflict on children raised international concern about the plight of children in war, prompting varied initiatives to end the use of child soldiers and other wartime abuses. The number of children killed every year by antipersonnel landmines dropped in the wake of massive efforts to end the use of the weapon and the adoption of the1997 Mine Ban Treaty. The adoption of the statute for the International Criminal Court held out the hope of ending the impunity of those responsible for the recruitment of children under the age of fifteen in armed conflicts, as well as those who commit other war crimes, crimes against humanity, and genocide.

However, despite these advances, the promises of the Convention on the Rights of the Child were broken for countless children around the world. The armed conflicts that raged in all quarters of the world produced appalling abuses of children's rights. Hundreds of thousands of children were pressed into service as soldiers. Millions became refugees displaced from their homes, often separated from their families, their future and safety uncertain.

Children living outside war zones were also subjected to routine violence. Street children on every continent endured harassment and physical abuse by police. Even schools, intended to promote the healthy development of children, were the site of abuse. In some countries, the use of corporal punishment by teachers resulted in injury and even death. In others, gay and lesbian students endured harassment and violence by their peers while school authorities failed to intervene.

Millions of children had no access to education, worked long hours under hazardous conditions, or languished in orphanages or detention centers where they endured inhumane conditions and daily assaults on their dignity, in violation of the rights guaranteed to them under the convention. The issues selected for attention below represent those which were the focus of Human Rights Watch investigation and advocacy over the past half-decade.

The tenth anniversary of the Convention on the Rights of the Child marked an important milestone. The rights of children were recognized as never before. But it also posed a challenge for governments and civil society to take stronger action to implement its provisions, strengthen protections, and fulfill the promises made to the children of the world.

The Use of Children as Soldiers

In dozens of countries around the world, children were direct participants in war. Denied a childhood and often subjected to horrific violence, some 300,000 children served as soldiers in current armed conflicts. These young combatants participated in all aspects of contemporary warfare. They wielded AK-47s and M-16s on the front lines of combat, served as human mine detectors, participated in suicide missions, carried supplies, and acted as spies, messengers, or lookouts.

Physically vulnerable and easily intimidated, children typically made obedient soldiers. Many were abducted or recruited by force and often compelled to follow orders under threat of death. Others joined armed groups out of desperation. As society broke down during conflict, leaving children with no access to school, driving them from their homes, or separating them from family members, many children perceived armed groups as their best chance for survival. Others sought escape from poverty or joined military forces to avenge family members who had been killed.

Child soldiers were used in more than thirty countries around the world. Human Rights Watch investigated the use of child soldiers in some of these conflicts, including in Angola, Colombia, the Democratic Republic of Congo, Lebanon, Liberia, Sierra Leone, Sri Lanka, Sudan and Uganda....

Girls were also used as soldiers in many parts of the world. In addition to combat duties, Human Rights Watch found that girls were subject to sexual abuse and taken as "wives" by armed groups in Angola, Sierra Leone, and Uganda. Girls who were impregnated by rebel commanders were sometimes forced to strap their babies on their backs shortly after giving birth and take up arms against opposing forces.

....

Under the Convention on the Rights of the Child, the general definition of a child is any person under the age of eighteen. However, Article 38, governing children and armed conflict, uses fifteen as the minimum age for recruitment and participation in hostilities. This low standard of protection remained a glaring and troubling anomaly among the convention's other strong provisions.

. . . .

Despite these obstacles, efforts to stop the use of child soldiers continued to grow. In 1998, the recruitment of children under the age of fifteen and their use in hostilities was identified as a war crime in the statute of the International Criminal Court. Once established, the court will have jurisdiction to prosecute those responsible for the use of child soldiers. The use of children as soldiers was also recognized as a child labor issue. A labor treaty banning the worst forms of child labor, adopted in June 1999, prohibited the forced recruitment of children for use in armed conflicts.

In 1998, the Coalition to Stop the Use of Child Soldiers formed in order to campaign for a strong optional protocol to the Convention on the Rights of the Child which would prohibit any recruitment of children under the age of eighteen or their use in armed conflict. Established by six international NGOs, the coalition worked with national campaigns in more than thirty countries around the world, mobilizing political will and public pressure to end the use of children as soldiers. In addition to media campaigns, the publication of new research, and advocacy within regional and international fora, its activities included a series of high profile regional conferences focused on the use of children as soldiers in Africa, Latin America, and Europe.

Despite this growing momentum, efforts to stop the use of child soldier did not reach fruition. Recruitment of child soldiers continued around the world, those responsible for their recruitment escaped justice, and key governments continued to resist efforts to establish and enforce the prohibitions necessary to end the use of children as soldiers.

Refugee Children

Refugee children were among the most vulnerable children in the world. Not only had they suffered from war or other forms of persecution in their countries of origin, but many refugee children continued to suffer human rights abuses in countries of asylum. Children made up more than half of all refugees around the world, yet their rights and special protection needs as children were frequently neglected.

The human rights abuses that drove children into flight were only the first chapter of hardship for many refugee children. Even after traveling across an international border to seek refuge, they remained vulnerable to hazardous labor exploitation, physical abuse, denial of education, sexual violence and exploitation, cross-border attacks, militarization of refugee camps, and recruitment as child soldiers.

Article 22 of the Convention on the Rights of the Child grants special protection to refugee children. Children who are not being cared for by their parents, known as "separated children," are entitled to special protections under Articles 20 and 22. Refugee children fleeing war are also entitled to special protection under Article 38 of the convention, as children affected by armed conflict. Refugee children, like all children, are entitled to all other rights granted under the convention including the rights to life, physical integrity, adequate food and medical care, education, and to be free from discrimination, exploitation, and abuse.

Separated and unaccompanied children were particularly vulnerable. In the United States, Human Rights Watch found that unaccompanied children were held by the U.S.

Immigration and Naturalization Service in detention facilities where some were confined for lengthy periods of time before being released to family members or appropriate guardians. Rarely understanding what was happening to them, children were often denied information about their detention and their right to be represented by an attorney in immigration proceedings in a language they understood. In some cases they were housed with juvenile offenders and subjected to a rigid and punitive environment.

In 1999, Human Rights Watch conducted an in-depth investigation into the protection of Sierra Leonean refugee children in Guinea, where children made up 65 percent of the 300,000 Sierra Leonean refugees there. Most of the children interviewed by Human Rights Watch had been in refugee camps in Guinea just over a year, with little hope of returning home in the near future. Internally displaced children within Sierra Leone were thought to suffer many of the same problems on an even larger scale.

. . . .

Despite the fact that these children suffered enormously and remained extremely vulnerable, their plight was largely ignored by the international community. . . .

Although UNHCR had used the Convention on the Rights of the Child as the basis for extensive policies and guidelines designed to protect the rights of refugee children, in many cases these policies were not implemented. For Sierra Leonean children in Guinea, the international community failed to identify vulnerable children; to monitor for abuse and labor exploitation; to protect girls from sexual abuse and exploitation; to move the refugees to safe locations away from the border; to preserve the humanitarian character of the refugee camps; and to prevent refugee children from serving as child soldiers.

Police Abuse and Arbitrary Detention of Street Children

Attention to street children focused largely on their pressing economic and social plight poverty, lack of shelter, denial of education, AIDS, prostitution, and substance abuse. With the exception of mass killings of street children in Brazil and Colombia, little attention was paid to the police violence and abuse inflicted on these children, or their treatment within the justice system through which they regularly passed. Civil and political rights violations against street children were largely overlooked, symptomatic of the larger failure to take seriously the full scope of children's rights enshrined in the Convention on the Rights of the Child.

Viewed as "anti-social" or criminal elements, or a scourge on a city's tourist-filled streets and business districts, many police and ordinary citizens simply wished street children would disappear, by whatever means. Street children throughout the world were subjected to routine harassment and physical abuse by police, government, and private security forces, out to wipe the streets clean of a perceived social blight. Street children faced extortion, theft, severe beatings, mutilation, sexual abuse, and even death.

They were often arrested and jailed because of their homelessness (on vague grounds such as vagrancy or loitering) or their involvement in small businesses deemed to be illegal, such as unlicensed hawking, or were accused of petty theft, drug-related crimes, or prostitution. Some were arrested as scapegoats, or in order to finger or catch others. Many police believed street children had information about crimes committed on their beat, or attributed crimes in the area to them directly, imputing criminal associations and activities to the children generally.

They were held for excessive periods of time in police lockups, for days and even weeks, usually mixed with adults. In jails they were sometimes further beaten by police, or forced to pay bribes in order to be released. Girls were sometimes coerced into providing sexual services to police in exchange for release, or were raped. From jails, street children were transferred eventually to long-term penal institutions, sometimes euphemistically called "homes" or "schools" where they languished out of sight, for years.

. . . .

Over the years, Human Rights Watch had attempted to highlight the serious nature of the human rights abuses committed against street children by law enforcement personnel in Brazil, Bulgaria, Colombia, Guatemala, India, Kenya, and Sudan, and on the gross lack of police accountability for abusive actions. Widespread impunity and the slowness of law enforcement bodies to investigate and prosecute cases of abuses against street children allowed violence against street children to continue unchecked.

. . . .

Trial and Sentencing Practices

Far too often, children around the world were brought to trial and sentenced in ways that violated their rights. Human Rights Watch documented systemic failures to guarantee children legal representation and otherwise provide them with fair hearings in Brazil, Bulgaria, Guatemala, India, Jamaica, Kenya, Pakistan, and Russia. Of particular concern were sentences that violated the International principle that deprivation of liberty should be a measure of last resort and for the shortest appropriate period of time and prohibiting measures that constituted torture or cruel, inhuman, or degrading treatment.

In many cases, children were detained arbitrarily or indefinitely on the basis of vague legal provisions. In Kenya, Human Rights Watch's investigation found that street children were committed for years to juvenile correctional institutions after they were found to be "in need of protection or discipline" in summary proceedings without legal representation. Similarly, in Paraguay and other countries in the Americas that had not brought their laws into conformity with the Convention on the Rights of the Child, children were detained on the ill-defined basis that they were in a "state of danger."

. . . .

Conditions of Confinement

Throughout the world, children were subjected to appalling conditions of confinement that violated international standards. Often held with adults and subjected to beatings at the hands of guards and other detainees, children in confinement were frequently denied adequate food, medical and mental health care, education, and access to basic sanitary facilities. All of these children would eventually return to society, meaning that the failure to prepare them for their return was shortsighted as well as cruel, carrying enormous social costs.

The practice of holding children in adult facilities, common in many parts of the world, exposed children to abusive conditions including physical and sexual abuse far worse than those they would have experienced in juvenile facilities. In Cambodia, for example, children were housed indiscriminately with adult detainees and reportedly sexually abused and subjected to other forms of physical and psychological violence at the hands of adults. In Guatemala, Human Rights Watch interviewed children commingled with adults who reported beatings and rapes by adults, and being forced to give up their clothing to adults, or to pay money to adults in order to get a place to sleep.

The United States continued to incarcerate large numbers of children in response to a perceived upsurge in violent juvenile crime. In fact, the number of juvenile offenders consistently fell from 1994 to 1997; according to U.S. Federal Bureau of Investigation data, juvenile arrests declined each year, with an overall decrease of nearly 4 percent for the period. Juvenile arrests for violent crimes were down by 6 percent during the same time period.

....

Commendably, some countries took positive steps to acknowledge and correct abusive conditions of confinement. The South African government initiated a program in November 1997 to keep children out of the country's prisons, although delays in implementing the program threatened its effectiveness. Another deficiency in the program was that children between the ages of fifteen and eighteen who were accused of the most serious crimes would remain in adult prisons. In Bangladesh, the government accepted the need for improvements in conditions of confinement for children in conflict with the law, in particular noting in its 1997 supplementary report to the Committee on the Rights of the Child that "[t]oo many minors are held in jails and police stations alongside adult offenders." In Jamaica, following the July 1999 release of the findings of a Human Rights Watch investigation of the practice of detaining children in filthy and overcrowded police lockups, the government announced that it would move all detained children to juvenile facilities.

Orphans and Abandoned Children

Throughout the world an unknown number of children, most likely in the hundreds of thousands, if not millions, were kept in orphanages and non-penal custodial institutions. Many were condemned to live a grim existence, and subjected to shocking and at times deadly levels of abuse and neglect.

Many children who ended up in orphanages had at least one living parent but had been abandoned because their families were poor, jobless, ill, or in trouble with the law. In countries that had restrictive population control policies, or where cultural traditions valued boys more highly than girls, babies and girls in particular were abandoned. In other cases, medical personnel pressured parents at birth to give up children born with disabilities, claiming that parents would be ostracized for raising a disabled child. For this reason, healthy children who were given up for financial or domestic reasons were often assumed to be "defective."

In Russia, children were abandoned to the state at a rate of more than 100,000 per year. In a 1998 report, Abandoned by the State: Cruelty and Neglect in Russian Orphanages, Human Rights Watch found that children in Russian orphanages were exposed to appalling levels of cruelty and neglect. They were beaten, locked in freezing rooms for days at a time, or sexually abused, and often subjected to degrading treatment by staff.

Russian babies classified as "disabled" were segregated into separate rooms where they were changed and fed, but were bereft of stimulation and without medical care. At age four, these and other children faced another grave violation of their rights: those labeled retarded or "oligophrenic" ("small-brained") were sent to locked and isolated "psycho-neurological internats," which were little better than prisons. Considered "ineducable," children in these facilities were restrained in cloth sacks, tethered to furniture, denied stimulation, and sometimes left to lie half-naked in their own filth. Orphans who survived to the age of eighteen moved on to an adult internat, removed from public view.

Russian orphans who were not categorized as disabled grow up in Dickensian-like institutions where they suffered ill-treatment at the hands of staff and older children within the institutions. In the orphanages, children were physically punished not only by school staff, but by older children who were encouraged to beat up, bully, and intimidate younger ones. The use of cruel, inhuman and degrading treatment and punishment, including corporal punishment, public shaming, and isolation in freezing rooms was not uncommon. Children had no means of redress or complaint to protest ill-treatment and abuse at the hands of staff and older children.

Shocking abuses were also documented in Chinese orphanages, where infants suffered staggering mortality rates. Deprived of adequate food and basic medical care, orphans admitted into welfare institutions in 1989 faced less than a 50 percent chance of surviving for more than one year. Many institutions appeared to operate as little more than assembly lines for the elimination of unwanted orphans (especially girls), with an annual turnover of admissions and deaths far exceeding the number of beds available. At some facilities, the rate of death reached 90 percent.

. . . .

... [W]hile numerous international standards exist which protected the rights of children confined in penal or correctional institutions and settings, no comparable international standards exist to protect the rights of abandoned or orphaned children. Human Rights Watch advocated the use of alternatives to institutionalization of children wherever possible, including support for families or extended families, and foster care, with placement in small residential care facilities as a measure of last resort.

Child Labor

The International Labor Organization (ILO) estimated that 250 million children between the ages of five and fourteen were working in developing countries, at least 120 million full time. Sixty-one percent of these were in Asia, 32 percent in Africa, and 7 percent in Latin America. Most working children in rural areas were found in agriculture; urban children worked in trade and services, with fewer in manufacturing, construction and domestic service. Only an estimated 5 percent of child laborers worked in export industries.

Despite the attention devoted to child labor in recent years, those addressing the issue were divided on how to proceed and considered a range of different approaches. Some urged that child labor be eliminated quickly and aggressively, including through the use of trade sanctions when countries or industries failed to act decisively. Others called for reforming the conditions in which children worked with a view toward gradual elimination. Some believed that work plays an important and positive role in children's lives and in their relations with their families, and sought reform, but not an end to child labor.

. . . .

Child labor included a range of situations from the clearly hazardous and exploitative, as in the case of four-year-old children tied to rug looms to keep them from running away, to the benign or positive, seventeen-year-olds helping out on the family farm or working after school to earn some pocket money. In many cases, as in the latter examples, children's work was helpful to them and their families, and contributed positively to their development into responsible adults. This depended largely on the age of the child, the conditions in which the child worked, and whether work prevented the child from going to school.

What was clear, and what the international community agreed on, was that certain types of child labor were categorically hazardous to the health, safety, and morals of children and should be banned. The ILO Convention Concerning the Prohibition and Immediate Action for the Elimination of the Worst Forms of Child Labor (ILO Convention 182), adopted unanimously by the 174 member states of the ILO in June 1999, committed states party to take immediate steps to prevent, prohibit, and eliminate "the worst forms of child labor." The term child referred to anyone under the age of eighteen. Under the convention, the worst forms of child labor included the sale and trafficking of children, debt bondage, forced or compulsory labor (including the forced recruitment of children for use in armed conflict), using children for prostitution or production of pornography, using children for illegal activities, particularly drug trafficking, and other work likely to "harm the health, safety or morals of children."

. . . .

Human Rights Watch worked on the issue of child labor in areas where the rights abuses were clear and acute, and which fell within the new ILO Convention's definition of "worst forms of child labor." We worked on bonded child laborers in India; the use of children as soldiers in armed conflicts around the world; and the employment of live-in domestic child servants in Sri Lanka. Throughout, Human Rights Watch emphasized the importance of providing education and rehabilitation in assisting children removed from these worst forms of child labor to truly end the practice.

Notes and Questions

1. At its best, the UNCRC provides inspiration for the work of NGOs and politicians around the world. It sets out universal principles and goals, and assists those involved in local or national children's issues by lending them the authority and prestige of the "international community." At its worst, the UNCRC invites hypocrisy by providing cover to national governments that have no intention of radically altering their behavior towards children and families, but are able to claim credit by going through the procedure-heavy motions demanded by the United Nations of States Parties. In light of the readings above, which interpretation seems closer to the truth? Does the UNCRC inevitably try—and often fail—to be all things to all child welfare constituencies?

B. Children's Lives versus Children's Rights?

The application of children's rights to the area of child survival has raised some controversy. In 1995, Carol Bellamy, a politician, lawyer and investment banker from New York, with two years of experience as the director of the U.S. Peace Corps, became UNICEF's executive director. (She was succeeded in that position by Ann Venemen, formerly George W. Bush's Secretary of Agriculture, in 2005.) Perhaps because Ms. Bellamy's tenure fell within the early years of the UNCRC, she made great efforts to infuse the traditional preoccupations of UNICEF—child immunizations, nutrition and access to clean water—with considerations of children's rights. Gender issues and rights to information were blended with the more established UNICEF activities. This change in emphasis on UNICEF's part, combined with the fact that there seemed to be insufficient progress in the areas of basic child health and survival, led to charges that the core UNICEF mission was being compromised. Writing in the British medical journal, The Lancet, in late 2004, Richard Horton leveled strong criticism against the changes that had been made to UNICEF's agenda under Bellamy's leadership—particularly the fact that she had turned the organization in the direction of "rights", allegedly at the expense of ensuring child survival. In the article below, Horton decries this change in orientation as being dangerous to vulnerable children. If true, Horton's charges could be devastating to the credibility of UNICEF as an organization.

Richard Horton, *UNICEF Leadership 2005–2015:*
A Call for Strategic Change
The Lancet, Vol. 364, No. 9451, 2071 (2004)

In 2005, Carol Bellamy, UNICEF's executive director, steps down from a position that she has occupied for 10 years. As the world's most senior advocate for child health, she leaves at a critical time. All the indications are that the fourth Millennium Development Goal—reducing by two-thirds, between 1990 and 2015, the under-five mortality rate—will not be met in many countries. The World Bank recently reported that "progress against child mortality has so far been so slow that no sub-Saharan country in Africa is on target to reach that MDG."

. . . .

It is widely, if regrettably, accepted that UNICEF has lost its way during Carol Bellamy's long term of office. A corporate lawyer and financier for many years, Bellamy went on to become a New York politician who was thrust into a position that demanded deep experience of children's issues—and child health especially—worldwide. It was a role that she was ill-equipped for, despite her evident enthusiasm for UNICEF's ideals. While Bellamy has focused on girl's education, early childhood development, immunisation, HIV/AIDS, and protecting children from violence, abuse, exploitation, and discrimination, she has failed to address the essential health needs of children. It was left to independent child health researchers and advocates, driven by intense frustration at Bellamy's unwillingness to engage with child survival, to draw attention to UNICEF's pervasive neglect of its central mission.

The call for a reorientation of UNICEF's work came with a simple question: "Where and why are 10 million children dying every year?" Based on new data from the Child Health Epidemiology Reference Group, Robert Black and colleagues reported that half the world's deaths among children under 5 years of age occurred in just six countries—India (2·4 million deaths); Nigeria (834000); China (784000); Pakistan (565000); Democratic Republic of Congo (484000); and Ethiopia (472000). Although the highest absolute number of deaths occurred in south Asia, the highest rates were found in sub-Saharan Africa, where mortality in many countries is actually increasing.

These figures were shocking to those who believed that UNICEF had been making steady progress in improving child survival. Worse still, over 60% of these deaths were and remain preventable. Undernutrition contributes to the deaths of over half of all children. Cost-effective interventions are available for all major causes of child mortality. But coverage levels for these interventions are appallingly low in the 42 countries that account for 90% of child deaths. 80% of children do not receive oral rehydration therapy when they need it. 61% of children under 6 months of age are not exclusively breastfed. 60% do not receive treatment for acute respiratory infections. 45% do not receive vitamin A supplements. A quarter of children do not receive the diphtheria-pertussis-tetanus vaccine. And the gap in survival between the richest and poorest children is increasing. In sum, for almost a decade, child survival has failed to get the attention it deserves. Child health needs better leadership, improved coordination of services, and increased funding.

. . . .

Given this escalating evidence base for child health, but all on a paradoxical background of failure to meet the MDG on child survival, UNICEF clearly has a pivotal role to lead the world's efforts to make children a global priority. Under Bellamy's leadership, UNICEF is presently in a poor position to do so. Her distinctive focus has been to advocate for the rights of children. This rights-based approach to the future of children fits well with the *zeitgeist* of international development policy. But a preoccupation with rights ignores the fact that children will have no opportunity for development at all unless they survive. The language of rights means little to a child stillborn, an infant dying in pain from pneumonia, or a child desiccated by famine. The most fundamental right of all is the right to survive. Child survival must sit at the core of UNICEF's advocacy and country work. Currently, and shamefully, it does not.

UNICEF was created in December, 1946. The UN International Children's Emergency Fund was needed because of the threats posed to children in Europe from disease and famine after World War II. With each of the three executive directors before Bellamy, health became an increasingly important part of UNICEF's work. In 1982 came UNICEF's greatest contribution to date to the welfare of children worldwide: the child survival revolution, which was based on four simple interventions—growth monitoring, oral rehydration therapy, breastfeeding, and immunisation. The great strength of UNICEF, then and now, lies in its decentralisation. Almost 90% of the agency's highly regarded staff work within 157 countries. The organisation's concern to find "practical ways to realise the rights of children and women" is monitored by a 36-member executive board made up of government representatives elected by the UN Economic and Social Council. But during Bellamy's time at UNICEF, this board has failed badly to make sure that the agency capitalises on the legacies left by past executive directors, especially that of James Grant.

. . . .

During recent months, UNICEF has tried to change the tone of its advocacy. In response to our series last year, the agency commented that "child survival lies at the heart of everything" it did. And UNICEF has taken action to house the Child Survival Partnership. But experienced observers of UNICEF, those who have long worked in the field of international child health, take a different view. They see these words and actions as mostly rhetoric. UNICEF's claims do not reflect the reality of its work in the field. There is no organisation-wide commitment to reduce child mortality—indeed, no comprehensive strategy exists to do so. There are vague promises about early childhood care, promises that have few clear outcomes, survival targets, or programmes for their achievement.

There is an ever-pressing need for an effective UNICEF.

. . . .

Children remain one of the most marginalised groups in our world today. The predicament of children is the predicament of our futures—and the future of our predicaments. UNICEF needs a visionary leader, a person of profound ability to make the next ten years the Decade of Child Survival and Development.

Notes and Questions

1. How do you suppose Bellamy would defend her leadership of UNICEF against the criticism expressed in the Lancet article, above? Is Horton being fair to the child rights agenda, or is he guilty of using emotive rhetoric about children's survival for persuasive purposes? Is it necessary to choose between child rights and child survival?

2. What seem to be the UNCRC's greatest achievements to date? What seem to be the greatest challenges remaining in the field of children's rights? How convinced are you of UNCRC's overall effectiveness/success?

IV. Critical Perspectives on the United Nations Human Rights Regime

A. Improving the Human Rights System

Despite its resilience, the UN's human rights system has many critics. It is often derided as bureaucratic, artificial, and even irrelevant. The most often-voiced concern is that human rights norms generated by the UN system are not really being "enforced" by the available UN-based procedures, and thus these norms bear little relation to the behavior of governments in their treatment of their own citizens. In the reading that follows, Anne Bayefsky takes up the issue of the ineffectiveness of "treaty reporting" by States Parties, the most common method of UN human rights law enforcement. This is also, of course, the main method of implementation under the UNCRC, as distinct from the Convention's possible effects with respect to national legislative initiatives or judicial application.

The second article, by feminist writer and international law scholar Hilary Charlesworth, attacks the international human rights system for its failure to place sufficient emphasis on the human rights of women. Her criticisms could also apply to the failure to place children's rights at the center of the international human right system. She implies that the rights of women and children are considered to be "niche" concerns relative to what are seen as mainstream human rights issues.

Consider how the critiques put forward by these authors could apply to the UNCRC and its deficiencies.

The UN Human Rights Regime: Is It Effective?
91 American Society of International Law, Proceedings of the Annual
Meeting 460 (1997) (remarks by Anne Bayefsky at 466–472)

My subject is human rights treaties. The human rights treaty system is of central importance to the international protection of human rights because in many circumstances legal standards offer benefits that political forums cannot — in particular, the potential to generate remedies and to provide greater accessibility to human rights victims. In view of the fact that the international lawyer keenly perceives the potential for progress through the rule of law, questioning the foundation for that optimism from within the society is frequently branded as disloyal or cynical. But the overriding interest in closing the gap between rules and reality requires coming to terms with a number of unfortunate details.

First, three-quarters or more of United Nations member states have ratified five of the six human rights treaties. State reports, due to each treaty body, are overdue to an enormous extent. Specifically, an average of 60 percent of state parties have overdue reports in the case of each treaty. Ninety-five states have five or more overdue reports. Fifty states parties (approximately one-third of all states parties) to each of the Women's Discrimi-

nation Conventions and the Economic Covenant have never submitted even a single report. States having the largest number of overdue reports frequently include those with
extremely poor human rights records, such as: Togo, Liberia, the Central African Republic, Somalia, Afghanistan, Cambodia and Lebanon.

Second, the treaty bodies now meet for a total of fifty weeks per year. If all the overdue reports were actually submitted, it would take the treaty bodies an average of six-
and-a-half years to expunge the current backlog. Even on the basis of the reports that
have already been submitted, the meeting time now available to the treaty bodies means,
for example, that the Child Committee and the Economic Committee can only schedule
the consideration of a report currently in hand for their May 1999 sessions and beyond.

Third, the treaty bodies spend an average of six hours considering a single report, on
average every four years. The time spent in an actual dialogue or exchange with the state
party is often severely circumscribed by the length of a government's oral presentation,
the large number of questions posed by different treaty body members, the repetitive nature and lack of focus of many of these questions, the treaty body members' lack of familiarity with the country's circumstances, and the reluctance of many state representatives
to answer questions clearly and directly.

Fourth, the proceedings of the treaty bodies in general are poorly attended. Normally
only a handful of individuals, if any, from the country concerned observe the dialogue on
the country report. National news media rarely attend. One or two representatives of international nongovernmental organizations (NGOs) are usually present. International
news media are almost never there. The treaty bodies themselves also spend little energy
cultivating the interest of the news media or educating them. The treaty bodies' conclusions on the country report are usually only released days, if not weeks, after the report
is considered—so external reporting on the event becomes highly problematic. The
media's disinterest in the process is exemplified by the coverage of the Human Rights
Committee's consideration of the U.S. report. In March 1995, the U.S. report was considered—in contrast to the situation for every other state but Switzerland—within the
borders of the state party itself—that is, in New York. Nevertheless, the event went un-
reported, except by the Washington Post, which discussed one member's questions about
the status of Washington, D.C. This was despite the fact that in the Committee's conclusions it expressed the opinion, for the first time, that a reservation was incompatible with
the object and purpose of the treaty.

The isolation of the work of the treaty bodies is of even greater significance to individual victims or NGOs. There is considerable variation among the treaty bodies in the
relationship each has developed with NGOs. The limited resources of the UN human
rights system, combined with a failure of proactive leadership in collecting human rights
information about states parties, means that the treaty bodies heavily depend on NGOs
for alternative information on country conditions beyond what appears in the government
reports. The flow of information between the treaty bodies and NGOs is well developed
in the context of the Committee on the Rights of the Child, and very poorly developed
in the context, for example, of the Racial Discrimination Committee. But many of the
treaty body practices themselves contribute to the communication problem. Frequently
the treaty bodies fail to do the following: develop lists of national NGOs in each state
that could provide useful input; solicit information from the national NGOs well in advance of the consideration of a state report; develop guidelines for NGOs to ensure that
the information that is submitted is the most useful to the dialogue process; inform NGOs
well in advance of the dates upon which the dialogue is to be conducted; arrange oral
sessions with NGOs well in advance of the dialogue in order to better inform the ques-

tioning of states parties; take the initiative to transmit treaty body conclusions to interested NGOs.

. . . .

Fifth, the issue of the collection of reliable, independent information on human rights conditions in state parties by the treaty bodies is of central significance to the efficacy of the system. With very few exceptions, the treaty bodies do not engage in fact-finding. Nongovernmental organizations are not without their political agendas, and the information submitted by those NGOs that are aware of the process is often highly selective. The quest for information about the state has often meant that the treaty body operations have been unduly driven by such limited contributions. With the further fact that treaty body members often are nominated by governments concerned to ensure state representation in the guise of independent experts, the opportunities for straying from the legal framework for implementation cannot be ignored.

. . . .

Sixth, given the limitations — inherent and otherwise — of the state-reporting system of implementation, an ability to enforce the legal standards through individual complaints and remedies offers an important alternative. However, the alternative is not available in the case of three of the six treaties, although optional protocols creating a right of individual petition are at various stages of consideration for two of the remaining instruments. In the case of the three treaties that include a right of petition, access is also limited by the rate of ratification of this optional corollary: 47 percent in the case of the Covenant on Civil and Political Rights, 20 percent of state parties to the Torture Convention, and 12 percent of state parties to the Racial Discrimination Convention. It is therefore immediately clear that, for the majority of states, the system of enforcement of their treaty obligations does not include the empowerment of the individual to lodge complaints against the state party and to seek a remedy through international means.

Furthermore, even in the case of the most widely ratified individual petition mechanism, the Optional Protocol to the Civil and Political Covenant, there have been relatively few cases over the years. During the 1990s, an average of forty-eight cases have been registered each year, from a potential complainant population in the ratifying states of more than a billion people. While this figure is slightly on the rise — seventy complaints having been registered in 1996 — these low figures are disturbing. Not even a single case has been registered from 40 percent of state parties, including such states as Algeria, Bulgaria, Chad, Congo, El Salvador, Malawi, Namibia, Nepal, Romania, Somalia and Uganda.

. . . .

The Human Rights Committee's 1996 annual report to the General Assembly specifically highlights those states parties whose failure to comply with the reporting obligations are the most flagrant. At the top of the list is Syria, which has failed to produce the last three reports, the first due in 1984, despite twenty-four reminders. Yet no resolution of the General Assembly or of the Human Rights Commission mentions either of these two states. The recent report of the independent expert on the effective functioning of the treaty bodies, produced for the 1997 session of the UN Human Rights Commission, concludes, "The principle of holding States accountable for non-compliance with their treaty obligations by means of an objective and constructive dialogue, on the basis of comprehensive information and inputs from all interested parties, has been vindicated in practice." Unfortunately, however, the information available is not comprehensive; input is not obtained from all interested parties; the dialogue, for these reasons as well as constraints upon time, accessibility, and follow-up, is often marginally constructive, and with those states that need it most, frequently never takes place.

The question which must therefore be asked is, where should future implementation efforts be placed? The answer depends on articulation of four fundamental propositions:

1. The treaty system today includes many states that share no common democratic aspirations.

2. When NGOs are fearful of participating, or inhibited from sharing information with the treaty bodies, when individuals are prevented from criticizing their governments and complaining of violations of human rights, when a nation's news media are not permitted to monitor and reveal proceedings critical of the government, the treaty system will fail.

3. Successful implementation machinery requires expanded, mandatory rights and procedures of individual petition, adequate funding to allow sufficient familiarity with country situations, and enhanced capacity for investigation and fact-finding missions to state parties.

4. Extensive resistance to such reforms comes from nondemocratic states. Consequently, two additional questions must be asked: (1) What is the best method for securing democratic reform? Through the equal participation of nondemocracies within the treaty system? Or through alternative venues for interchange outside the treaty system, such as the marketplace—that is, economic pressure for reform? (2) Who is the system for? Is it aimed at assisting democracies, or aspiring democracies, to adjust and calibrate their laws and practices? Or is it aimed at the unrepentant social deviant, and intended to expose the depravity and provide a tool for critics everywhere?

In the European regional human rights system, democratic preconditions are—at least in spirit—applied to would-be participants. In the UN context, such preconditions for human rights machinery are dismissed out of hand. But the kinds of reforms necessary for serious improvement of the UN system's performance for democratic states, like a full-fledged judicialized individual complaint process, will discourage nondemocratic states from joining. But the inducements necessary to achieve the participation of nondemocratic states, such as continued low levels of resources, tolerance of illegitimate reservations, and feeble institutional methodologies, undercut effective implementation. The institution of reforms that would be unacceptable to states having no democratic aspirations, and their anticipated nonparticipation in the treaty system, could be offset by exposure of their human rights violations in regional bodies or UN political forums, and economic pressures or incentives outside the system. Consequently, I draw the conclusion that the price to be paid in failing to advocate far-reaching reforms is too high for the sake of adding the relatively minor voice of the treaty bodies to the volume of public criticism directed at extreme delinquents.

Hilary Charlesworth, *Not Waving but Drowning: Gender Mainstreaming and Human Rights in the United Nations*
18 Harvard Human Rights Journal 1 (2005)

I. THE IMPACT OF GENDER MAINSTREAMING ON HUMAN RIGHTS

Feminist critiques of the international human rights system in the early 1990s argued that it had effectively become a structure to protect men's rights. Scholars argued that both the substance of human rights norms and the institutions devised to protect them were skewed to give preference to the lives of men. Non-government organizations also documented the inadequacies of the human rights canon with respect to women. Perhaps prompted by these developments, the Second World Conference on Human Rights in 1993 accepted that the human rights of women should form "an integral part of the United Nations human rights activities." This commitment was then translated into the language of gender mainstreaming at the Beijing Conference.

The gender mainstreaming strategy has affected the U.N. human rights structures. For example, the Office of the High Commissioner for Human Rights has reported on efforts to integrate gender into all human rights activities, with the co-operation of the Division for the Advancement of Women. Approaches to "mainstream" gender perspectives in the U.N. human rights system were developed in 1995 by a meeting of experts. These approaches were expressed in general terms and included the collection of "gender-disaggregated data," attention to "gender-specific aspects of [human rights] violations, as well as violations of the human rights of women," and the use of "gender inclusive" language. The Commission on Human Rights has adopted several resolutions over a number of years on "Integrating the Human Rights of Women Throughout the United Nations' System." These resolutions expressed concern that the Vienna and Beijing calls for mainstreaming had little impact and renewed calls for all components of the U.N. human rights system to "regularly and systematically take a gender perspective into account in the implementation of their mandates." The resolutions specified the responsibility of the human rights treaty bodies to integrate a gender perspective, with reference to "gender-sensitive guidelines" in reviewing states' reports, preparing general comments and issuing recommendations and concluding observations. ECOSOC and the Commission on Human Rights have also requested that the country-specific and thematic Special Rapporteurs, experts, and working groups include sex-disaggregated data in their reports, to address women-specific violations of human rights and to cooperate and exchange information with the Special Rapporteur on Violence Against Women.

The response to calls for gender mainstreaming in the U.N. human rights system has been muted. This is to some extent the product of the low representation of women in the system. For example, in 2004, women made up approximately 40% of the overall membership of the human rights treaty bodies, but most of the women (74%) were concentrated in two committees: the Committee on the Elimination of Discrimination Against Women and the Committee on the Rights of the Child. The overall proportion of women in the other, mainstream committees was 15%. The call for greater participation by women, which is itself part of the gender mainstreaming strategy, has thus had little impact. Responsiveness to the gender mainstreaming mandate seems to depend on the presence of at least one or two committee members who have a strong commitment to the issue. For example, the Committee on Economic, Social, and Cultural Rights has addressed the task of gender mainstreaming to a limited degree, at least insofar as it refers to the position of women in its Concluding Observations on states parties' reports and in its General Comments. Gender mainstreaming appears in these contexts as exhortations to non-discrimination on the basis of sex and the inclusion of women in relevant decision-making, and as references to the special burdens women face with respect to access to the right in question. The Committee's reporting guidelines are uneven, however, with respect to women and gender issues. Some guidelines request information on the situation of women, but others do not. For example, the guidelines do not refer to the position of girls with respect to the right to free primary education.

The Committee on the Elimination of Racial Discrimination ("CERD") was initially reluctant to refer to gender considerations in its Concluding Observations or General

Recommendations. Indeed, the Chairman of CERD stated in 1996 that directives to integrate gender into states parties' reports were "fundamentally misconceived." In 2000, however, CERD adopted a General Recommendation on "the gender-related dimensions of racial discrimination." The document is brief and desultory. It notes that racial discrimination may not always affect women and men in the same way. It then simply announces the intention of the Committee to "enhance its efforts to integrate gender perspectives, incorporate gender analysis and encourage the use of gender-inclusive language." The General Recommendation also calls for gender-disaggregated data to be included in states parties' reports. One result of the Recommendation was the Committee's revision of its guidelines to request states to include information in their reports about the situation of women. Concluding Observations adopted by CERD since 2000 sometimes include a request for more information about the position of women, but they do not go beyond this to comment on the way that understandings of sex and gender affect racial discrimination. Overall, the Committee's approach to gender has been described as "inconclusive," and it has thus far failed to identify the gender-based aspects of racial discrimination.

The Human Rights Committee, which monitors the International Covenant on Civil and Political Rights ("ICCPR"), has adopted some General Comments on articles of the treaty that express an interest in the position of women. The most explicit is General Comment 28 on Article 3 of the ICCPR, adopted in 2000. This document examines each of the rights set out in the Covenant and comments on the way in which they might affect women's lives. In 1995, the Committee amended its reporting guidelines to request states parties to provide information on the position of women. The Committee is not, however, consistent in its concern about women or gender. For example, a General Comment on torture adopted in 1996 did not examine the gendered dimensions of the right to be free from torture, although it did refer to the need for states parties to address the issue of the infliction of torture or cruel, inhuman, or degrading treatment by private actors. A General Comment on article 4 of the ICCPR addressing derogation in times of emergency contains no reference to the position of women during public emergencies or the impact of gendered assumptions on the definition of an emergency.

The Human Rights Committee has occasionally used its adoption of Concluding Observations to raise concerns about women's lives. For example, Concluding Comments on Peru's 1996 periodic report under the ICCPR drew attention to the criminalization of abortion even in cases of rape, which had resulted in "backyard" abortions becoming the major cause of maternal mortality. The Committee stated that "these provisions not only mean that women are subject to inhumane treatment but are possibly incompatible with articles 3 [the right of men and women to equal enjoyment of the rights set out in the ICCPR], 6 [the right to life] and 7 [the right to be free from torture and cruel, degrading and inhuman treatment] of the Covenant." Generally, however, the Human Rights Committee confines itself to occasional questions and comments about the number of women in public life and seeks more statistical information on women. There is little evidence of more probing questions about the impact of gender on the enjoyment of human rights.

The records of the annual meetings of the Chairpersons of the human rights treaty bodies suggest that there is no regular discussion of gender mainstreaming. Draft guidelines on states parties' reports to the treaty bodies adopted by the Chairpersons in June 2004 also do not refer to the strategy of gender mainstreaming. The Commission on Human Rights has regularly called for the integration of women's human rights into the work of the Special Rapporteurs on human rights. The reports of these experts suggest, however, a resistance to, or misunderstanding of, gender mainstreaming. At best, they may give information about individual cases where women were victims of human rights abuses, but there is no analysis of the relationship between these harms and women's status in public and private life. The Special Rapporteurs also tend to use and refer to the category of "women and children," reinforcing women's identity and value as mothers. Indeed, by far the most significant Special Rapporteur with respect to women and gender is the specialized Special Rapporteur on the Elimination of Violence against Women. Few women are appointed to the "mainstream" Special Rapporteur positions, despite constant calls for better representation. Gender mainstreaming is most often understood as requiring attention to how many women were affected by the right or situation in question. Information about women, for example in the reports of successive Special Rapporteurs on the Situation of Human Rights in Afghanistan, has tended to be brief and broad-brushed, involving general statements without any analysis. Overall, attention to questions of women and gender in the U.N. human rights system has been haphazard. At best, there is attention to the position of women in particular contexts, mainly in statistical terms, but there is no attempt to understand the way in which stereotypes about sex and gender roles can affect the human right in question. Violations of women's human rights are typically presented as an aspect of women's inherent vulnerability, as if this attribute were a biological fact.

Notes and Questions

1. What can be done about countries that regularly report to the Committee on the Rights of the Child, but where violations of children's rights continue to be rampant? Is this merely an unfortunate aspect of state sovereignty, a problem common to all human rights treaties and their implementing structures? How could one alter the UNCRC reporting system to make it more effective?

2. Is there something about children's rights in particular that makes them less amenable to being dealt with through the UN reporting system? To return to David Smolin's point, is the "liberationist" human rights analogy between adults and children a less than perfect one? Or is it only natural that children should have their "own" branch of the UN human rights system, no better or worse than any of the other specialized convention reporting systems?

3. Could there be a "child rights mainstreaming" process to match the gender mainstreaming described by Charlesworth, above? How would it be different from gender mainstreaming, if at all? Is it likely to happen?

B. The UNCRC and Its Ultimate Paradox: Reconciling Protection and Liberation

In the essay that follows, Michael Freeman examines the ambiguities of the UNCRC, and suggests how these might be clarified in practice. In particular, he explores the conceptual challenge that children and their "rights" present to classical human rights paradigms. What does it mean to "empower" children, and how should we factor in their inherent dependency? Freeman's main interest is in assisting children to participate in their own destinies, but with a clear sense of what the traditional obstacles might be to this participation.

Michael Freeman, *Beyond Conventions—Towards Empowerment*
in The Moral Status of Children: Essays on the Rights of the Child (1997)

THE CONVENTION REVISITED

....

I would like to see more intensive policing of the Convention. If the fulcrum of enforcement is to be the Committee [on the Rights of the Child], let it have more powers. It ought to be a Permanent Bureau. Expertise in child-related disciplines ought to be a prerequisite. It ought to be proactive, with the ability to conduct strategic investigations and garner evidence. It ought to have access to children and young people. But I would go further and allow for inter-state complaints and for complaints by individuals who consider themselves aggrieved by shortcomings in the laws or practices of their own country. The model of the European Convention on Human Rights is instructive. Why not a system whereby aggrieved children can complain and seek redress when their State, though a party to the Convention, violates rights contained within it?

The Convention constitutes the end of the beginning, but we are very far from the beginning of the end of our quest to see children treated as persons accorded equal respect and concern.

We can improve the structure of the Convention by giving it more 'teeth'; we can add to the rights contained within it, for example by diluting the emphasis on adult values; we can make the rights more specific—an example might be restating Article 19 so that a child was given the right not to be hit as in the Nordic countries and Austria. All such measures would be valuable. But we have to consider also the limits of this approach. I do not, as some do, reject the rights approach. Rights are 'valuable commodities', but that does not mean they are things or possessions. They refer to doing more than having. They refer to social relationships that enable or constrain action. Rights are relationships: they are institutionally defined rules specifying what people can do in relation to one another. A child's life is not necessarily improved by giving him or her more 'rights'.

The Convention presupposes an agenda of liberal legalism and provides according to this agenda abstract legal mandates. Formal legal guarantees of the sort that the Convention envisages States Parties adopting have value, but as a catalyst rather than as a source of change. Surely we can learn from the experiences of other marginalized 'social groups'—women, for example. In how many countries with equal pay legislation is there equal pay? How well have those countries with legislation outlawing sex discrimination coped with pregnancy? Nor should we overlook the importance of interpretation and experiences of interpretation in other areas. Again, using the perspective of women as a model, look at the way the Constitution of the U.S.A. has been interpreted: there is a right to bear arms (Amendment 2), but not, if poor, to obtain an abortion, a right to sell 'artistically redeeming' pornographic magazines, but no right to equal educational expenditures.

Nor should it be overlooked that the Convention, in laying down rights for children, has to a large extent attempted to extend access rather than to alter the basic fabric of the existing institutions.

Furthermore, the Convention has done little to reduce the equation that being dependent (as to a greater or lesser extent all children must be) means being deprived of basic rights. Dependency implies a sufficient justification to suspend basic rights to privacy, respect and individual choice. Being dependent implies being legitimately subject to the often arbitrary and invasive authority of social service providers and other public and private administrators, who enforce rules with which the dependent must comply, and otherwise exercise power over the conditions of their lives. In meeting the needs of the dependent, often with the aid of social scientific disciplines, welfare agencies also construct those needs themselves....

Dependency should not be a reason to be deprived of choice and respect. An important contribution of feminist moral theory has been to question the firmly embedded assumption that moral agency and citizenship rights require a person to be independent, totally autonomous. Feminists, such as Carol Gilligan in *In A Different Voice* and Marilyn Friedman, have questioned this deeply held assumption. It is, they argue, derived from a specifically male experience of social relations which values competition and solitary achievement. It is inappropriately individualistic. Dependence is a basic human condition. We have all been dependent and many of us have passed though phases of dependency or will do so. The Convention, using largely an autonomy model, would as much as possible give children the opportunity to be independent. But it is also possible, as feminism argues, to accord respect and participation in decision-making to those who are dependent. The new English Children Act, in emphasizing 'partnership' and recognizing the value of partnership with children, takes account of this.

....

The empowerment of children is not then a question, or simply a question, of redistribution of power. Putting children on to decision-making committees — school boards or community homes — only scratches the surface and does little to undermine entrenched processes of domination. More is clearly required — ultimately a re-thinking of the culture of childhood. This has happened before: childhood is not a decontextualized construct. Concepts of childhood have undergone sea changes in early modem times and then again with the emergence of industrial capitalism. What contribution can ombudswork make to this cultural evolution?

This question can he answered on a number of levels. It can seek to discover the social and historical causes of oppression. The answers to this will sometimes be culture and economy-related (for example, child prostitution in Thailand or the Philippines), but not always so. It can foster the establishment of child-oriented institutional structures within countries. Institutions which will probe and question both existing and mooted laws and practices, which will examine critically the impact of structures and designs on the everyday lives of children and not just those institutions targeted at children (schools, youth courts, neglect and abuse procedures) but also those which hitherto have paid scant regard to the interests of children (shops, the city, the environment generally). On a third level, ombudswork can concentrate on child advocacy at grass-roots level — the representation of the child in trouble, the lawbreaker, the abused child, the child in conflict with his or her parents. The three levels are inter-related.

The first is the most theoretical, but it is also the most difficult work to sustain. It requires the collective enterprise of historians, sociologists, lawyers, educationalists, psychologists, anthropologists, theologians and other disciplines. It involves research into the past and a critical probing of existing attitudes which seek their intellectual strength in historical practices. The history of childhood, a nightmare from which we are only now beginning to awake, was, until recently, a gap in our cultural knowledge. We need revisionist history to challenge the often superficial images of childhood that appear in official versions of the truth. This first level of ombudswork is a subsidiary concern of this conference and yet its importance cannot be underestimated. From an understanding of the cultural foundations of childhood will come the ammunition to destroy the faces of oppression, and out of the rubble a reconstruction of childhood with the child de-reified and accorded the concern and respect owing to him or her as a person and as a participant in social processes. For anyone concerned with the degradation and pollution of children that we call child abuse, this should strike a chord. For, surely we now recognize that the roots of child abuse lie not in parental psycho-pathology or in socio-environmental stress (though their influences cannot be discounted), but in a sick culture which denigrates and depersonalizes which reduces children to property, to sexual objects so that they become the legitimate victims of both adult violence and lust.

The first level of ombudswork is important for three reasons. It will give us an understanding of how childhood has been constructed and reconstructed and in so doing may, as just indicated, throw light on major wrongs from which children suffer (and not just abuse and neglect, the examples just given, but attitudes to their wrongdoing, methods of social control of them and even questions such as abortion). Secondly, it will assist the tasks of those who undertake ombudswork on the other two levels. Thirdly, and in combination with the other two levels of ombudswork, it will work towards a day when its work will no longer be necessary. This day is far in the future and none of us will ever see it. It will work towards a time when with a new cultural revolution childhood is so constructed that the problems for which ombudswork is developing will no longer exist.

The second level of ombudswork concerns the establishment and development of child-oriented institutional structures. A number have been mooted and some, like the ombudsperson itself in Norway, New Zealand and Costa Rica are in operation. It by no means follows that the same model is appropriate for all countries. Different political structures and different states of development may require different responses.

A Minister for Children has often been postulated. One such suggestion was formulated by Brian Jackson in 1976. Only New Zealand and Norway have introduced a ministry as such with responsibilities specifically for children. A categorical answer to whether a Minister for Children would be a good idea is not really possible. Much clearly depends on the structure of government in the country, and if on nothing else, the relationship between the government and the governed. To argue that a Ministry for Children would be of no more than symbolic significance is to say nothing in countries where departmental responsibility is itself no more than a veneer or smokescreen. But even in those countries where there is some devolution of decision-making, would a Ministry for Children really empower children? In Britain it is feared that the Minister would necessarily be committed to Government policy. S/he might be as much concerned with excusing decisions as with making them. In reality all ministers should be prepared to see the impact of governmental decisions on children and to represent children's interests.

....

It is equally important that the actual effects of policies in action should be regularly monitored. And it is not just legislation which needs to be so examined. The policies and practices of local state institutions, education authorities, housing departments, social services committees which directly penetrate the lives of children should also be rigorously scrutinized. So should the activities of the courts (and not just juvenile or youth courts) and the police (the impact of policing on ethnic minority youth has given concern in a number of countries).

....

The third level of ombudswork is child advocacy at grass-roots level. There are different forms of advocacy, legal advocacy, legislative advocacy, administrative advocacy. But, as Knitzer has argued, the underlying assumptions of advocacy programmes are the same:

(i)   Advocacy assumes people (in this case children) have, or ought to have, basic rights.

(ii) Advocacy assumes rights are enforceable by statutory, administrative or judicial procedures.

(iii) Advocacy efforts are focused on institutional failures that produce or aggravate individual problems.

(iv) Advocacy is inherently political.

(v)   Advocacy is most effective when it is focused on specific issues.

(vi) Advocacy is different from the provision of direct services.

. . . .

It is surprising how little attention has been given to what is entailed by the representation of children in courts. Yet the concept of representation in the political arena is well-trodden. As in the political context, we may ask—what is the function of representation? Is it to represent the child's best interests (his or her welfare) or to advocate his or her wishes, to assist the furtherance of the child's autonomy? In a sense the dualism fits neatly into the debate about children's rights itself. Is this concerned with protecting children (with their 'salvation') or with protecting their rights, their 'liberation', with autonomy? An understanding of function and role is crucial in determining who the advocate should he. If the 'mandate' view is adopted (that is the representative should carry out the wishes of the child) the legal profession would seem to be the best qualified. If, on the other bend, the 'independence' view is adjudged most appropriate, social workers may be thought the ideal choices. A categorical answer is difficult to elicit: there are so many variables: the age of the child; the type of evidence being adduced; the orientation to be adopted by the representative (should it be legalistic, social work, educational?).

The question has also been asked as to whether there is 'anything unique' about the role of lawyering for the child. Three Canadian researchers have identified three models. The adversary role is traditionally combative—it envisages a lawyer using skills within the framework of a trial governed by strict rules of law and procedure to convince a court that the cause argued for has merit and should prevail. The *amicus curiae* model is, to quote Bernard Dickens, 'comparably legalistic but neutral as to outcome'. It envisages assistance to the court to resolve a conflict by presenting another perspective from the strictly partisan cases presented by the opposing parties. The social work model is intended to help the child 'by proposals, concession and collaboration to put him or her into the most satisfactory condition that can be achieved'. But should lawyers adopt the roles of other professionals? And should their roles be conceived differently when they are representing children as opposed to adults? There seems to be an assumption that they should, but this, I would suggest, is yet another instance of the way we project our reluctance to see children as participants in processes which affect them.

The conflict is well illustrated by the dilemmas faced by the lawyer who is asked to advocate a course of action by a child when those presenting the welfare case for that child would wish a different view to be presented. In England this is graphically portrayed in sex abuse cases, in particular where an adolescent girl is represented by a solicitor and a guardian *ad litem*, the latter an independent social worker. What the guardian *ad litem* deems to be in the girl's best interests may not cohere with the arguments she wishes her advocate to present.

. . . .

There are, then, three levels of ombudswork, all important. The significance of the first can all too easily be underestimated. The importance of the second is undeniable. The third is very valuable for the individual child, but of limited value to children as a whole. The system emerges intact and oppression is but little undermined.

The Vote?

A paper on empowerment which says nothing on extending the vote to children may be thought peculiarly defective. One which considers it, only to reject it may be considered self-defeating. The arguments for extending the suffrage to children are difficult to counter. Indeed, some of those postulated against voting rights for children could be used equally to disenfranchise many adults. In the past I have cautioned against seeing 'votes for children' as a panacea. It is not so much that I am opposed to the principle as that I believe we could all too readily deceive ourselves that suffrage rights amounted to empowerment. In doing so the other strategies depicted here might be given less attention, and some might fall by the wayside. Nevertheless, I believe further extensions of the suffrage are inevitable and to be welcomed and I would like to think that those countries which lowered the age of voting to 18 in the 1970s gave consideration to a further lowering to 16.

But this in itself would not guarantee empowerment. Women have had the vote for more than half a century in Britain. There has even been a government headed by a woman Prime Minister. But it has to be accepted that democracy is, as yet, far from 'engendered'. Children need, as women have and continue to need, advancement as a group, and giving more of them the vote is unlikely to achieve this.

Conclusion

Hitherto, the concentration has been on encoding rights. What we must now set our minds to is finding ways of giving children a voice. Only with empowerment will come true recognition of children as persons entitled to equal concern and respect.

Notes and Questions

1. Freeman states that the UNCRC should be seen as only the "end of the beginning" in the realization of children's rights. What does he mean by this?

Which version of childhood does Freeman accept, and what implications are there for implementation of the CRC at national level? How does he propose to reconcile the dependency and empowerment dimensions of children's rights law?

2. Freeman deals with many of the paradoxes recognized by Smolin—that children are to some extent inherently dependent, such that attempting to free them from that dependency gives rise to many forms of resistance from society at large. However, Freeman's vision is one of multi-level, profoundly engaged, and energetic enforcement of children's rights principles. Is his vision too idealistic to be useful? Is it applicable universally, or does it tend to reflect European, and specifically northern European, views?

3. Freeman is a strong advocate for ongoing "monitoring" of performance in the children's rights area. Is there enough political will to institutionalize such scrutiny at national level, across a wide variety of countries? How might traditional forms of resistance to children's rights be overcome? How does Freeman view the role of children's dependency in the oppression they experience?

Chapter Two

Child Labor: The Children's Rights Dimension

I. The Child Labor Debate: Prevention, Empowerment, and "Worst Forms"

The international debate over child labor is characterized by conflict between those who favor protecting children from the need to work, and those who call for recognition of the right of children to work in dignity, thus "empowering" working children. This is a dichotomy we have already noted in our discussion of the contents of the UNCRC, which contains both "protective" and empowering provisions. The more traditional view of children is that their vulnerability and inability to plead their own cause makes it essential that they receive special protection from the state. By contrast, at least one side of the contemporary "child rights" movement favors an approach that allows children to exercise rights on a basis similar to adults.

In many Western countries, the last hundred years has seen a movement aimed at eliminating child labor altogether, based solely on minority status and under the theory that children should be studying or playing, but not laboring. In the 1970s, many in the anti-child labor movement hoped that all countries would come around to the view that children should be removed from the labor market and put into school. In recent years, however, compelling counterarguments have been put forward to the effect that in many cultures, the labor of children has both economic and social value, such that only the "worst forms" of child labor should be outlawed, at least as a matter of urgency. These contrasting points of view are reflected in two important ILO instruments, the "Minimum Age Convention" of 1973,[1] and the Worst Forms of Child Labor Convention ("Worst Forms Convention"),[2] completed in 1999. Both of these instruments may be found in the appendix to this book, and should be consulted while reading the selections that follow. The International Labor Organization (ILO), created after World War I for the purpose of helping to establish more humane workplace conditions in Western countries, is now a specialized agency of the UN. Its important role in setting international labor standards will be discussed later in this chapter.

Ironically, those on both sides of the debate believe themselves to be advocating on behalf of children and their rights. It may well be that a middle position is possible; that the worst forms should be outlawed in every country as a priority, and as many children

---

1. Convention Concerning Minimum Age for Admission to Employment (ILO No. 138), Jun. 26, l973, 1015 U.N.T.S. 297.
2. Convention Concerning the Prohibition and Immediate Action for the Elimination of the Worst Forms of Child Labour (ILO No. 182), June 17, 1999, 38 I.L.M. 1207 (1999).

as possible sent to school for as long as the community can afford. As explored in the first chapter of this book, these questions relate in a fundamental way to our understanding of childhood itself. Under the more traditional, "abolitionist" view of child labor, such labor is an outgrowth of poverty, an unfortunate anomaly. This is an approach which depicts children as the victims of negative economic conditions. Under this view, the ultimate goal must be the abolition of essentially all labor for children under 18, with limited exceptions for light work that may act as a supplement to, not a substitute for, education. For those who believe that education and leisure are the natural elements of a happy childhood, whether children may make a contribution to society and the family through their labor is more or less irrelevant.

On the "empowerment" side, arguments are raised to the effect that the right to work is a basic human right, and one from which children should not be excluded. It is claimed that cultural views of work differ substantially, and that where children find fulfillment and societal approval through and for their work, there are not necessarily any adverse effects. The case is made that if child labor is legal and regulated, working conditions for children should also improve. Where child labor is illegal but inevitable, the argument goes, there is a far greater likelihood of child exploitation.

As with the child protection versus empowerment debate generally, there is a significant conceptual divide evident in the child labor discussion. If labor is harmful to the development of the child, then those who claim to advocate for children's rights by calling for greater access by children to the labor market must be misguided. Equally, from a children's "right to work" perspective, those who would "protect" children by keeping them out of the labor market are actually harming those they claim to want to protect. In this context, one's perspective on the UNCRC's call for children's "voices" to be heard is crucial. If adolescent child workers claim that they are participating in the labor market by choice and according to their own culture's norms and values, on what basis should international children's rights advocates oppose this? On the other hand, there is no shortage of informational material that purports to show children speaking out against the phenomenon of child labor generally.

To some extent, this polarizing debate has been set aside with the more recent approach to child labor, one that focuses on identifying and responding to its "worst forms" as a matter of priority. Under the ILO's Worst Forms Convention, only those varieties of child labor that are clearly and unquestionably harmful to children—those inherently exploitative because of health risks or moral dangers—should be outlawed by all states, and implementing measures taken in a time-bound and concrete fashion. The worst forms approach may be seen as a collective decision to accept the reality that many children do work and will continue to work. Under this approach, conflicting views on the proper role and status of children in the workplace are seen as unavoidable, but less time and energy is spent arguing over whether or not children should work as a philosophical matter. In the wake of the Worst Forms Convention, we can expect greater focus and emphasis on protecting children against the more obviously dangerous forms of labor.

In the following article, William Myers presents the "protection versus empowerment" issue in historical context, arguing that increased cultural sensitivity has led away from the doctrinaire anti-child labor assumptions that informed the ILO's 1973 Minimum Age Convention. He describes the UNCRC's provisions relating to child labor as a kind of bridge between the Minimum Age Convention and the Worst Forms Convention. Under Myers' view, there is a natural and logical progression to the development of international law principles governing child labor.

William E. Myers, *The Right Rights? Child Labor in a Globalizing World*

575 Annals of the American Academy of Political and
Social Science 38 (2001)

The Globalization of Ideas about Childhood

Current debates about the application of children's rights to child labor have their roots in the thorny problem of reconciling uniform global rules with the protection of cultural diversity and international democracy. How should a children's rights approach based on specified international standards of social conduct deal with infinite variation in how societies think about children and childhood in general and about child work in particular? On the one hand, there is today a renewed emphasis on multiculturalism, on the importance of maintaining cultural integrity, and on raising children to appreciate and fit into their own social milieu as well as in an expanding world. On the other hand, however, most thinking on children's rights has for a century been based on a homogenizing concept of childhood as a biologically driven natural phenomenon characterized by physical and mental growth stages that are everywhere roughly the same, even if culturally inflected. Recent experience and scholarship suggest that this homogenizing notion is too simplistic. Practical experience demonstrates the existence of an international divide between rich and poor societies, according to which the industrialized countries of Europe and North America (and often Western-educated elites in poorer countries) tend to conceive of childhood and raise their children differently than the less economically developed societies of Africa, Asia, and elsewhere. For instance, Northern societies tend to rigorously separate childhood from adulthood by keeping children dependent through adolescence and discouraging their participation in certain adult concerns such as economic maintenance of the family. Many Southern societies, on the other hand, stress family unity and solidarity, equip their children to play mature roles by adolescence, and include children in contributing to the family livelihood. They often reject Northern-influenced international child labor standards because the views of children and childhood implicit in such do not adequately fit with the realities of developing countries.

Diversity is also a principal theme in research from the academic disciplines of social science and social history, in which childhood is increasingly understood to be every bit as much a culturally constructed concept as it is a natural phenomenon of biological immaturity. In fact, many historians and social scientists no longer treat childhood as a universal phenomenon that merely has different cultural expressions. They find it more useful to think instead in terms of many different childhoods linked to particular contexts, "neither timeless nor universal but, instead, rooted in the past and shaped in the present." If children are raised by different methods to make their way in societies having different values, goals, and challenges, what is the legitimate basis for international children's rights standards such as those articulated in the CRC? A perspective emphasizing the diversity of childhood raises some cogent questions about whose values and what processes should orient globalized children's rights standards, and no children's rights issue has so far raised them more clearly than that of child labor.

These questions were explored by Oxford anthropologist Jo Boyden in a now classic 1990 critique of the globalization of ideas about children and childhood. She noted that European and North American urban, middle-class concepts of children and childhood have been promoted worldwide as a standardized universal model of childhood assumed to apply to all societies. It is presumed that these culture-specific notions represent universal childhood as it is rather than as it is imagined to be from a particular cultural perspective. Despite the lack of evidence that these ideas are necessarily correct or somehow better for children than other people's notions, child-raising practices from these same rich, capitalist, politically democratic, mostly Judeo-Christian societies are being held up as universal norms applicable also to societies of developing countries whose economic conditions, social structures, and cultural and religious traditions are vastly different. European and North American middle-class notions of what constitutes a proper childhood in their own societies are ethnocentrically projected globally as criteria by which to judge how well all the other world's societies tend to their own children.

Boyden contended that the ethnocentrism of industrialized countries, bolstered by their superior political and economic power, was unjustly dominating the international discourse on children's rights. She pointed out that ideas useful primarily within the cultural and economic context of northern Europe and North America end up being globally institutionalized through international instruments, such as the CRC, which was being readied for adoption at the time she wrote. Concepts and values perhaps more important in the developing world were not equally represented. Boyden intended not to defend relativism or discourage international agreements to defend children's rights but to point out that the institutionalization of a particular Western model of childhood as the basis for global rights disenfranchises poor and working-class children — by far the world's majority — by making their lives seem deviant, inferior, or even pathological just for departing from an inappropriately imposed culture-biased norm. She cited work as a central element of many developing-country childhoods, which tends to be unjustly neglected or condemned by rich-country ethnocentrism.

Seven years after her seminal article first appeared, Boyden took the occasion of a second edition to add a substantial postscript updating her observations in the light of experience with the CRC, which had by then become the primary international framework for discussing children's rights. She again called attention to child labor as an area in which Northern ethnocentrism combined with vested economic interests, imposed on the South in the name of children's rights, can easily injure the very children supposedly being protected. As an example, she cited a well-documented case in which thousands of children working in Bangladesh garment factories were summarily dismissed from their jobs when the U.S. Congress considered legislation prohibiting the importation of products made with the involvement of workers under 15 years of age, citing international child labor standards. Since the United States was by far the largest export market for the industry, which also contributed over half of Bangladesh's foreign exchange, nervous owners unwilling to risk access to their best market quickly dismissed workers thought to be under or even near that minimum age. Nongovernmental organizations concerned with the children's welfare soon reported that fired children were not returning to school as U.S. advocates of the measure had expected they would but were instead moving from comparatively safe, well-paid garment factory employment into forms of work at once less remunerative and more dangerous for children, a situation confirmed by International Labor Organization (ILO) and UNICEF follow-up studies.

Boyden held up the Bangladesh case of misguided good intentions as a warning about the consequences of simplistically applying rich-country assumptions and remedies to poor-country situations without adequate attention to differences of social and economic context. She worried that the pat formulas of much children's rights discourse would substitute for rigorous attention to the specifics of children's situations and lead to generic, simplistic solutions likely to be ineffectual or counterproductive for the children involved. She pointed out that the ultimate impact of the CRC will depend as much on the style of its implementation as on the content of its text, and she insisted on the need for basing international children's rights standards on more objective and culturally inclusive criteria. She suggested that effective protection of children from workplace abuse often depends less on preventing them from working, per the European and American solution unilaterally imposed on Bangladesh, than on protecting them in their work and creating more alternatives for economic and social advancement. Child work tends in much of the world to be more deeply embedded in family life than is typical in rich countries, and interventions in it may therefore have important consequences for how children are perceived and treated by their parents and other caregivers. Those intervening in children's work need to keep in mind likely consequences beyond the workplace.

Work has been shown by anthropologists, sociologists, and psychologists to relate to children's welfare and development in diverse ways that vary with social, economic, and cultural factors and even with the particular characteristics of children themselves. While there is no evidence that engaging in work is necessarily bad for children—in most societies, it remains an important means of teaching and socializing them—very large numbers of children are involved in kinds of work and working conditions that are clearly detrimental to them. However, often what is damaging about such work is less its intrinsic nature (for example, processes exposing children to toxins or unsafe machinery) than its organization or the social relations surrounding it (for example, working too many hours or in competition with school, harsh and demeaning supervision, or disparagement by adults for working or choice of occupation). The same kinds of work, or protective interventions in work, can and do have very different impacts on children's lives and development depending on how society constructs the meaning and value of the work in question. Even children in stressful kinds of work have been found to thrive surprisingly when they and the work they do are esteemed by family and community, and children in far less stressful work situations may become more vulnerable when they and their work are denigrated by others.

Sensitivity to culture and the way it mediates the effects of experience on children by no means invalidate the idea of global child labor standards but do suggest the need to carefully distinguish between values based on a broad representation of human experience and those that are merely Euro-American ethnocentrism projected by economic and political power onto a global arena. Modern social science thinking about children and childhood would suggest that beneficial international standards for dealing with child labor need to be able to accommodate diverse models of childhood and ways of raising children while at the same time establishing widely accepted norms by which societies can be held accountable. Also, practical experience suggests that valid global standards should also reflect widely shared values and avoid ethnocentric impositions by the rich and powerful. Many have recognized these dilemmas as the central problems of establishing meaningful children's rights. Philip Alston, a leading authority on children's rights, has said that it is necessary to point the way toward "approaches which involve neither the embrace of an artificial and sterile universalism nor the acceptance of an ultimately self-defeating cultural relativism."

Is it realistically possible to draft and negotiate international agreements to meet so demanding a criterion? Is it feasible to walk a children's rights tightrope suspended between ethnocentric cultural imperialism at one extreme and unaccountable relativism at the other? In order to find out, let us consider the history of the main international conventions pertaining to child labor.

....

The ILO Minimum Age Convention

The earliest of these three conventions is the ILO Minimum Age Convention (No. 138), which in 1973 updated and replaced a series of earlier child labor conventions going back to the founding of the ILO in 1919. This agreement perfectly exemplifies the attempt to globalize Northern ideas and values and the problems this globalization engenders. That characteristic is explainable by its roots in the early days of the ILO. The ILO was at its outset a Europe-centered agency whose original purpose included, among other things, the political objective of halting the spread of radical socialism by providing a democratic alternative based on a tripartite collaboration of government, industry, and labor. The elimination of child labor was considered such an important element of this strategy that the Treaty of Versailles authorizing establishment of the ILO mandated as one of its main tasks "the abolition of child labor and the imposition of such limitations on the labor of young persons as shall permit the continuation of their education and assure their proper physical development." During its early years of mostly European focus, the ILO logically enough drew on accumulated European concepts and experiences to create its international child labor standards and policies. However, when developing countries began somewhat later to enter the organization in greater numbers after decolonization, the ILO merely reinforced and disseminated its existing Europe-derived policies rather than reconceive them to fit new realities. As a result, the various successive ILO conventions regulating the work of children have essentially globalized European (and now also North American) history, conceiving of child labor in primarily urban-industrial terms and looking to the state for the same remedies that had been at the center of child labor reform in the rich countries. These were primarily legal mechanisms requiring a well-developed legislative apparatus credible with the public, an honest and well-organized public sector labor inspectorate for enforcement, and compulsory education in a well-developed public education system able to provide all children with a worthwhile alternative to work. It goes almost without saying that this industrial conception and legalistic approach are anachronistic in most of today's developing countries, where child employment is overwhelmingly agricultural, where social welfare laws have relatively little impact on the everyday life of the poor, where labor inspection services tend to be precarious and corrupt, and where national governments have extreme difficulty extending full primary education coverage to the rural and urban periphery areas where most working children live.

Convention 138 is best understood in this historical light. Although nowhere does it use the term "child labor," it starts from the original Northern idea, first developed in late-eighteenth-century and early-nineteenth-century England, that children have a natural right not to work and that their very presence in the workplace is the crux of the child labor problem. This position also reflects fears that the economic participation of children undermines adult jobs and income, a proposition still widely believed and asserted, although it receives little support from the available evidence, which is ambiguous. It needs to be remembered that the Minimum Age Convention was not intended to be just about children or to serve only their interests; it is equally about protecting labor markets and adult economic interests. The abolition of child labor has therefore long been understood by the ILO to mean removal of underage children from economic activity, which is felt to be properly the exclusive province of adults. Accordingly, Convention 138 prohibits children from engaging in any economic activity (child care and housekeeping chores are considered noneconomic) below certain specified minimum ages. The only exceptions are for work in educational institutions (as part of training) and on small family farms producing for local consumption. The convention standards apply even to children working for themselves in odd jobs or for their parents in small family-run businesses. A general minimum age for admission to "employment or work" is set at 15, but in no case is it to be less than the age up to which children are obligated by law to be in school. In the poorest countries, the minimum age may be temporarily set a year younger. Children may do "light work," defined as safe part-time work that does not interfere with schooling, beginning at age 13 or, in the poorest countries, at age 12. Below these ages, economic activity of any type or amount is proscribed. Children below age 18 may not engage in hazardous work, although those at least age 16 may do so if properly protected and instructed. Countries have some discretion in deciding what work activities should be covered by or exempted from minimum age laws, but this discretion is limited since the convention dictates certain kinds of work that must be covered. It should be noted that the convention's style is relatively detailed, going beyond principles and objectives to specify a variety of different universal age standards to the precise year.

....

As might be expected, Convention 138 has met resistance in societies whose child-raising values include introducing children to work at an early age rather than excluding them from it. In many traditional African societies, for example, properly raised children are supposed to be introduced to various work roles and skills at a young age, and idle children are considered to be victims of parental neglect. The precise age standards, which are widely perceived to reflect industrialized-country norms more than developing-country realities, have also caused many problems. In many developing-country rural areas, for instance, children starting school at 6 years of age can finish all the education (typically the primary level) locally available to them by age 10 or 11, well before even the reduced standard would permit them to work. In many places, girls are allowed to marry and assume responsibility for a household at an age younger than this convention would allow them to work.

Given such incompatibilities, it is hardly surprising that, for its first quarter-century, the convention languished with fewer than 50 ratifications, very few of which were from developing countries having noteworthy child labor problems. Although the huge majority of the world's working children are in Asia—half are thought to be in South Asia alone (Bangladesh, India, Pakistan, Nepal, and Sri Lanka)—no Asian country ratified Convention 138 until the Philippines did so in 1998. By September 2000, however, the convention had been ratified by 100 countries, 6 of which are from Asia but still none from the critical region of South Asia. Nor, interestingly enough, has the convention been ratified by any of the three North American countries (Canada, Mexico and the United States). Why the sudden rush of new ratifications? The only plausible explanation is a campaign of firm political pressure from the ILO, which has recently promoted this convention as one of the core conventions all of its members are expected to ratify in solidarity with basic ILO principles. Also, the ILO's International Programme for the Elimination of Child Labor (IPEC) insists that countries receiving its financial and technical assistance begin the process of ratifying Convention 138 if they have not already done so. For poor countries, this is a cheap price to pay for needed money and technical assistance. One could be forgiven, however, for questioning the practical impact of such pro forma ratifications, especially in light of the expanding ideological influence of the CRC.

The wisdom of a global child labor standard prohibiting all work below a given age has in recent years also been increasingly called into question by expert sources as varied as nongovernmental child defense agencies, the World Bank, and independent researchers. In brief, it has been observed that this approach does not work very well for protecting children and may sometimes even be counterproductive, not only in developing countries but even in Britain, where it was originally invented. The case generally is argued that economic incentives, improved education, public information about work hazards, targeted income generation projects, local monitoring of child work, the organization of working children, and other interventions are likely to be more effective in protecting the majority of working children. While this line of thinking is clearly on the rise, the Convention 138 goal of excluding children from economic participation still is fiercely defended by, most notably, the trade union movement, with support also from the ILO and some government and nongovernmental organizations in both industrialized and developing countries.

The U.N. Convention on the Rights of the Child

The CRC was adopted in 1989, 16 years after the ILO Minimum Age Convention, and one can see in it both similarities and profound differences. Like the 1973 ILO convention, it is clearly conceived along the lines of Euro-American notions of childhood and how to protect it. Even the very idea that there should be a single, formalized children's rights convention consolidating existing rights and creating new ones is entirely a product of the North; no such demand would be likely to surface from the South. Its creation was in fact largely a northern European initiative, especially from Poland and Sweden. Although it still retains the strong Northern influences that worried Boyden, it is nevertheless more accommodating of diversity than is Convention 138. Part of the reason lies in its different style; rather than prescribing details, it articulates objectives and principles, leaving more room than does the Minimum Age Convention for members to implement it in ways appropriate to their situation. Also, the opening paragraph of its main provision on child work (Article 32) proposes not to exclude children from economic participation altogether but to protect them "from economic exploitation and from performing any work that is likely to be hazardous or to interfere with the child's education, or to be harmful to the child's health or physical, mental, spiritual, moral or social development." By targeting only work that is detrimental to children, this approach fits poorer societies that are mostly agricultural (virtually all farm children have to help out with chores), and in which children often must help secure the family's survival, much better than does the ILO blanket prohibition on children working. At the same time, it prohibits children from engaging in work that is harmful to them, an objective that can be reached even in the context of poverty. Even if children must work, their safety and education can be secured. Other clauses in this article call for regulating the hours and conditions of child employment, as well as the legal penalties needed to make enforcement effective. However, one provision retreats a bit from this concept by calling for establishment of a minimum age, or minimum ages, for admission to employment, though no particular age is suggested.

....

The effect of both the specific and overarching provisions is to make the CRC application to child labor more child centered than is ILO Convention 138, partly by specifying children's rights as such, partly by granting those rights priority over adult interests, and partly by opening opportunity for working children to participate in and have effect on decisions affecting them and their work. The growing influence and extensive ratification of the CRC, in conjunction with its more contemporary and widely adaptable concepts of child labor, now seems well on the way to displacing Convention 138, which looks increasingly anachronistic, as an intellectual force. Attempts by UNICEF, the ILO, and others to semantically reconcile, or at least bridge, important differences between the CRC and Convention 138 have not been very credible. Despite some overlap, the two are widely and sensibly perceived to be in tension.

One can argue that the CRC is gradually expanding beyond its original status as primarily an international legal instrument for reorienting national child welfare and protection codes to become a cultural force rooted perhaps more solidly in civil society than in government. If one consults the thick and widely disseminated UNICEF handbook for implementing the CRC, one will note that it deals almost exclusively with legal issues of the sort that would be of interest to government lawyers writing or interpreting national legislation to bring it in line with CRC guidelines. In the case of child labor, however, it is increasingly accepted by virtually all parties everywhere that the direct impact of government is limited and that providing children with the protection against detrimental work mandated by the CRC must involve families, communities, and civil society as well....

The Worst Forms of Child Labour Convention

By the mid-1990s, the ILO had taken note of the various problems with Convention 138, delicately terming it too "complicated." It also noted that the social and political environment had been changed by the nearly universal ratification of the CRC, which also had a stronger claim as the main international guideline for child protection policy. It was increasingly clear that the ILO, stuck with an uninspiring child labor convention and competing with the more compelling vision and broader authority of the CRC, stood to lose its international leadership on child labor issues. It responded to this challenge in a highly creative and socially constructive manner, proposing an altogether new convention to focus world attention and resources with priority on "the most intolerable forms of child labor." Although the ILO may have been prodded by events, this action was not primarily a case of bureaucratic one-upmanship, for a reasonable policy basis for prioritizing the worst forms of child labor had already been laid through IPEC activities and an ILO publication—jointly produced with UNICEF—calling for such a policy priority. Moreover, the ILO took care, as did CRC advocates, to work with international nongovernmental organizations and others to lay a politically popular groundwork for a new convention. The grassroots activities came to a climax in a "global march," consisting of country-level workshops and demonstrations and a very media-friendly convergence of child delegates on the Geneva ILO headquarters when the new convention came up for adoption.

The resulting Worst Forms of Child Labour Convention (No. 182), with its accompanying Recommendation No. 190, was adopted in 1999 and commits all ratifying members to "take immediate and effective measures to secure the prohibition and elimination of the worst forms of child labor as a matter of urgency." It targets all forms of slavery, child prostitution, and the use of children in other illicit activities such as the drug trade, as well as work that "is likely to harm the health, safety or morals of children." These are forms and conditions of work that no group or country could credibly defend and that virtually all societies are able to condemn from within their own value systems. The new convention commits ratifying countries to prevent or remove children from engagement in the targeted forms of child labor and to provide education, vocational training, or other viable alternatives to inappropriate work. It directs member countries to "identify and reach out to children at special risk" and to "take account of the special situation of girls." It also demands that each member state prepare an action plan, and it calls for international cooperation in support of implementation.

The content and style of ILO Convention 182 suggest the impact of the CRC, which it specifically references as an antecedent, and of lessons learned from experience with the Minimum Age Convention. One could argue that this convention has come closer to expressing a genuinely global consensus on child labor than has either the CRC or Convention 138, and anthropologist Ben White interestingly notes that it "appears ... to represent an attempt to incorporate relativist principles in a global standard-setting exercise, and therefore perhaps to have side-stepped the issue of cultural relativism." This achievement is remarkable in several ways. First of all, Convention 182 was so skillfully negotiated to garner support from both industrialized and developing countries that it became the first ILO convention ever adopted by unanimous vote. It got there by rigorously targeting the worst aspects of a major global social problem in a way that all the essential actors can agree to, which is no small achievement. If ratification proceeds as expected—38 countries already had ratified by October 2000, a quick pace compared to the usual time lag—the new convention will rest on unusually solid political ground. Because of its broad support, it already is attracting substantial donor investment toward implementation. Second, the Worst Forms of Child Labour Convention is positioned to become one of the most basic of global human rights agreements and should encounter little trouble in being widely accepted as such. Third, it articulates its objectives and the ratifying states' responsibilities in terms that are general but able to be monitored and that leave ample room for different societies to work toward its implementation within their own concepts of childhood and child raising. Fourth, the accompanying Recommendation 190 provides for "taking into consideration the views of the children directly affected by the worst forms of child labor." Here it buys into the CRC concept that children are competent to act on their own behalf. It responds to the CRC Article 12 provision for children's participation in public decisions affecting them, as well as to pressure exerted on the ILO by international child defense organizations, working children's own associations, and others insisting that the new convention be consistent with at least key provisions of the CRC. While we have yet to see how this new convention will be implemented, it is impressive to note that national and international nongovernmental organizations, governments, and bilateral and multilateral development assistance programs are now in the process of gearing up to focus on the rights of children in the most harmful child labor situations.

Conclusion

The story of how three conventions have, in the short space of just 26 years, struggled to bring a workable children's rights perspective into global action on child labor suggests the presence of a learning process. Comparison of these three conventions in their historical sequence indicates a progression of children's rights thinking about child labor, first from globalized Northern ethnocentrism (ILO Convention 138), to a more open and culturally adaptable approach still set within Northern concepts of children's rights (the CRC), and from there to a more democratic model better structured to accommodate diversity while focusing on a realistic social objective against which progress can be monitored (ILO Convention 182). However, the sequence is one of emphasis only, for all three conventions are simultaneously in force.

. . . .

Notes and Questions

1. Read over the Minimum Age Convention, Articles 28, 29, 31 and 32 of the UNCRC, and the Worst Forms Convention. Do you agree with Myers that what we see is an historical learning curve, with Western ethnocentrism giving way to a recognition of cultural diversity in ideas of childhood? Is it possible for those who believe that children should be studying or playing to remain silent on the question of abolishing child labor generally, in order to help build a consensus on the "worst forms"?

2. Looking at the Worst Forms Convention, does it seem to be mainly about work? Doesn't it include many forms of criminal activity under the heading "worst forms of child labor"? Considering the range of activities included in the Worst Forms Convention, is the Myers theory that the Worst Form Convention is a kind of historical departure from the Minimum Age Convention less convincing?

3. The Worst Forms Convention states in its preamble that it is meant to "complement" and not replace the Minimum Age Convention. It also states that "child labor is to a great extent caused by poverty and that the long-term solution lies in sustained economic growth leading to social progress, in particular poverty alleviation and universal education." In light of this, is it possible that commentators are over-emphasizing the conceptual shift represented by the Worst Forms Convention?

4. What kinds of evidence are most relevant to evaluating the persuasiveness of arguments for and against the abolition of child labor? Should a particular social context be the main element in determining the value of a child's labor?

––––––––––

The following article takes a much more traditional "abolitionist" approach to the child labor question. It is clear that for Bozena Maria Celek child labor, seen as a general phenomenon, is tragic and undesirable, although she is also careful to distinguish between work that is harmful (what she calls "labor") and work that is not. She sees child labor as an historical anomaly, with adverse effects both socially and economically. While many, perhaps most, commentators in the Western world share Celek's perspective, others would criticize it as distorting the issue by emphasizing the supposed misery and alienation of working children, with little attention paid to the positive contribution of children's work within the context of their own societies.

Bozena Maria Celek, *The International Response to Child Labor in the Developing World: Why Are We Ineffective?*

11 Georgetown Journal on Poverty Law and Policy 87 (2004)

. . . .

You are only four years old when your parents sell you into bonded servitude for a loan of six hundred rupees, an equivalent of twelve U.S. dollars. You are forced to work in a factory for up to twelve hours per day, six days a week, tying knots in intricately designed carpets that are in high demand around the world.

You are chained to a loom most of the time, exposed to factory dust and fumes, and constantly beaten as punishment for your repeated escape attempts and occasional refusals to work. You also suffer from malnutrition. You look around and see hundreds of children like you. They all have scars on their hands and feet from wounds inflicted by sticks or sharp metal tools for falling asleep at the loom. You quickly learn that every time you make a mistake, a fine is added to the amount owed on your parents' loan. You soon realize that you will never be able to pay it off.

Six years go by before you learn that child labor is illegal in your country—a fact that is generally ignored by the local manufacturers and civil officials. You contact a human rights organization and escape from the factory. You then join the human rights organization that helped you escape, and work to liberate thousands of other bonded children in your nation. You go back to school and dream of becoming a lawyer. You are only twelve ... when someone cruelly takes your life....

The above account is the true story of Iqbal Masih, a Pakistani boy, sold by his parents when he was four years old, a common practice among poor Pakistani families hoping to pay off debts owed to landlords and local merchants. The organization that helped Iqbal escape was the Bonded Labor Liberation Front (BLLF), a human rights organization headed by labor activist Ehsanullah Khan. After six years of living as an enslaved carpet weaver, Iqbal one day saw BLLF posters declaring that child labor was illegal under Pakistani law. He secretly contacted BLLF activists. Iqbal then led the BLLF to the carpet looms and helped rescue hundreds of children.

Iqbal subsequently became a spokesman for the bonded children of South Asia. He traveled to the United States and Europe in an effort to persuade potential carpet buyers to stop purchasing Pakistani carpets until the country enforced its child labor laws. Iqbal's efforts gained international attention, and in 1994, he won the Reebok Human Rights Youth in Action Award and a future scholarship to Brandeis University in Waltham, Massachusetts. He dreamed of becoming a lawyer and helping more children in his country gain their freedom. But on April 16, 1995, Iqbal was shot to death while visiting relatives in the rural village of Muridke in Pakistan. According to local sources, Iqbal was murdered by the Carpet Manufacturers and Exporters Association, a group that greatly benefits from having child laborers in their factories. Pakistani law enforcement never investigated the crime.

. . . .

There are hundreds of stories like the one of Iqbal Masih around the world. In Bangladesh, six-year-old boys stitch garments to be exported for up to twenty hours per day in dark, dirty sweatshops. In Pakistan, ten-year-old children work in shoe factories, applying glue to pieces of leather using their fingers as brushes, earning ten cents per day. In India, five-year-old children hand knot carpets for up to eighteen hours per day.

Approximately 250 million children between the ages of five and fourteen are working around the world today, mostly in the textile, sporting goods and toy industries of the developing world. Of these children, approximately one half or 120 million work full time. It is worth noting, however, that these numbers are likely grossly underestimated, due to the fact that many violations are never reported or recorded. These children are subject to poor pay and both physical and verbal abuse, as well as hazardous and unsanitary working conditions highly detrimental to their growth and natural development.

Child Labor—What is it and Why do we Fight It?

What Is "Labor"?

[T]here are ... a number of distinct views on what constitutes "labor." Most commentators make a distinction between child "labor" and child "work" to distinguish between employment that is potentially harmful or helpful to a child. Certain types of work can actually be beneficial in that they help train children for adult life by providing relevant work experience and teaching children accountability and responsibility. By taking up work, children learn their importance in the family and feel that they are true contributors. Traditional and semi-agrarian societies view this kind of work as "a rehearsal for adult life.... Given the absence of or the limited opportunities for vocational training, it performs an indispensable function in transmitting skills and in facilitating social adaptation." Examples of such work include part-time employment delivering newspapers, babysitting, or doing simple work on a family farm.

Labor, in contrast, is defined as work that is harmful to the child. More specifically, it is work that: endangers his safety, health or welfare; [labor] that takes advantage of the defenselessness of the child; [labor] that exploits the child as a cheap substitute for adult labor; [labor] that uses the child's effort but does nothing for his development; [labor] that impedes the child's education or training and thus prejudices his future.

Such work includes full-time or part-time employment in factories, polishing diamonds and other precious stones, making garments and leather goods, and manufacturing carpets.

It is this type of harmful work that nations are trying to address, through both domestic and international legal standards and declarations. Therefore, for the remainder of this Note, child labor will be considered to be any work that exploits children and impedes their physical, psychological and emotional growth. The next section briefly discusses the negative effects of child labor on a young child.

IV. Poverty—The Cause ... and the Effect

....

B. The Effect

Various negative consequences flow from the employment of young children. While working children may contribute to the income of their immediate families, they certainly do not contribute to their country's sustained economic growth. First, when children go to work for half of adult pay or less, they depress the already inadequate adult wages and increase unemployment. Second, the less education children have, the higher the chance that they will be illiterate. Children who cannot devote their time and energy to education will become the poor, illiterate, and underdeveloped adults of the future. As one author concluded, "[i]t is abundantly clear that dependency on child labor recycles poverty and hopelessness by turning today's generation of child laborers into tomorrow's sick, unemployed, uneducated and unproductive adults who are tragic in their own lives and a burdensome weight on their countries' hopes."

The existence of child labor perpetuates a cycle of poverty in and of itself. Adults suffer unemployment and underemployment while children who work for half the wages monopolize the jobs; these same children eventually become uneducated adults without a chance for a better life. Standards of living continue to decline, and poverty continues to spread. Ultimately, the ability of a country to achieve sustained economic growth decreases, leaving no chance to escape poverty. International organizations such as the ILO believe that child labor "retards the development of human resources, reduces lifetime earnings for the individual, and lowers the level of productivity and economic growth for the society at large."

Child labor perpetuates poverty in the same way that poverty perpetuates child labor. It is therefore clear that child labor hurts not only the child but also society as a whole. Yet, despite this fact, state governments only minimally, if at all, address the issue. Generally, states either consider child labor to be a part of their culture, are unwilling to follow child labor laws in the belief that child labor actually benefits the child's immediate family, or lack the necessary resources to enforce the relevant regulations prohibiting child labor. The next section addresses each of these issues in turn.

V. Individual State Measures Regarding Child Labor and Their Inadequacies

The majority of countries where child labor is most prevalent fail to recognize the interconnectedness between child labor and continued poverty. In fact, even though most countries have some forms of child labor laws and regulations, these nations do not support strict enforcement.

In some states, the governments consider child labor to be a part of their functioning society, or sometimes even a tradition. Poor families see young children as liabilities, mere consumable goods, or an economic investment. These families perceive the opportunity to put children to work as beneficial because children begin to contribute to the family income, and help provide basic food and necessities. Wealthier families who can afford to send their children to school nonetheless may choose to have their children work. With regard to young girls, many cultures regard female education as less relevant to their futures as wives and mothers; as a result, girls are more likely to work than go to school.

In other states, governments argue that enforcement of child labor laws will harm children rather than protect them. Specifically, they argue that stricter enforcement of child labor regulations will either reduce the income of already poor families by erasing their children's contribution or even further endanger children's safety and well-being. If a family sends their child to school instead of to work, less money will be available to support the household, and the family's ability to survive will be threatened. Such a family will, out of necessity, send their children to more dangerous, underground forms of employment where regulation of child labor is beyond the authorities' reach.

For those reasons, governments in countries where child labor is particularly prevalent rarely make the effort to adhere to and enforce domestic provisions regulating the employment of children. They rarely provide the funds necessary to train and pay labor inspectors. Instead, inside government officials engage in corrupt practices and fail to develop adequate inspection machinery. In turn, the employers refuse to allow inspectors to interrogate the children about their age or hours of work, or instruct the children to either hide or tell the inspectors that they came to the factory to bring lunch to their parents. To make matters worse, the employers bribe inspectors to simply ignore the ongoing violations. In the long-term, this practice allows child exploitation to continue and promotes further corruption between officials and state industries.

Two relatively simple assertions undermine the validity of the states' reasoning discussed above. First, if children stopped working, more jobs would become available to adults. According to a study conducted in India, if child labor were eliminated in India altogether, at least twenty million new jobs would become available to adult workers. Second, if children were offered more vocational training and educational possibilities, human capital could develop significantly. Education contributes to economic development by providing the state with the expertise to develop and advance existing industries. When human capital remains underdeveloped, long-term economic growth cannot occur.

The few countries that do recognize the long-term negative consequences of child labor often confront weak judicial systems that lack the resources to respond to violations in an adequate manner. In India, for example, inspections conducted under child labor law rarely result in prosecutions. During 1991–1992, the inspectors in India launched close to 7,000 inspections, yet prosecuted less than eight hundred cases. Furthermore, of those 800 prosecutions, less than 300 resulted in convictions. Often times the inspectors lack the capability to collect sufficient evidence to prevail in courts. Courts in India, for example, decide cases on the basis of hard fact. When inspectors lack sufficient evidence, either due to their own mistakes or to a lack of cooperation from employers, the courts will not convict.

Child labor is both a cause and an effect of poverty and must be eliminated. When state governments lack the desire or capability to enforce child labor rules and regulations, international bodies must intervene in an effort to control the problem ...

Notes and Questions

1. Does Celek take into account the "participatory rights" of children for purposes of devising national child labor regulations? Although she says that she is drawing a distinction between harmful and non-harmful forms of child labor, is it clear that she is in fact doing so? Is her economic analysis of the adverse effects of child labor on the well-being of society convincing?

2. Is it appropriate for the international community to intervene when certain states do not live up to ideals of what categories of work-related activity is proper for children? How can the line be drawn between children's work that is merely difficult and demanding, as opposed to labor that is truly harmful? How should such a determination be made? Note that the ILO also publishes guidelines for the implementation of its conventions, including for the child labor conventions. See R146 Minimum Age Recommendation, 1973,[3] available at http://www.ilo.org/ilolex/cgi-lex/convde.pl?R146, and R190 Worst Forms of Child Labor Recommendation, 1999,[4] available at http://www.ilo.org/ilolex/cgi-lex/convde.pl?R190.

The two articles that follow both take a strong stand in favor of the right of children to work. The authors are squarely in the "empowerment" camp, a position which favors the maximum participation of children in decisions affecting their lives, including decisions as to whether they should be allowed to work. Note how the authors look for evidence of the children's own viewpoints on labor questions. How much weight should policy makers give to what children themselves say about the value of their work? If we do consult children's representatives, then which ones? In the first article, Hanson and Vandaele point out that advocates and critics of child labor rely on an identical human rights discourse to justify their positions.

Karl Hanson & Arne Vandaele, *Working Children and International Labour Law: A Critical Analysis*

11 The International Journal of Children's Rights 73 (2003)

Introduction

Bhima Sangha, an Indian union of working children, chose 30 April, i.e. the day before International Labour Day, to celebrate Child Workers Day. In the same vein, the African Movement of Working Children and Youth considered working children's celebration of Labour Day on 1 May as a landmark for the emergence of the movement. By adopting one of the most powerful symbols of labour movements around the world, organisations for working children—usually referred to by the Spanish acronym NATs (*Niños y Adolescentes Trabajadores*)—strongly connect their situation to the world of work and labour. In this respect, [it has been observed] that working children live in conditions of working people, and that their demands are hardly any different from those of adult workers.

Since the beginning of the nineties, national, regional and international meetings of working children's organisations were held in Asia, Africa and Latin America. The claim

---

3. Convention Concerning Minimum Age for Admission to Employment (Recommendation 146), Jun. 26, l973, 1015 U.N.T.S. 297.

4. Recommendation Concerning the Prohibition and Immediate Action for the Elimination of the Worst Forms of Child Labour (Recommendation 190), June 17, 1999, 38 I.L.M. 1211.

for the recognition of children's right to work in dignity is common to several organisa-tions of working children. They consider working in dignity as a basic human right. The organisations refer to international human rights legislation, such as the Universal Dec-laration of Human Rights (UDHR) and the Convention on the Rights of the Child (CRC), to support these outcries. The *Declaracion de Huampani,* adopted at the gathering or NATs on 6 to 15 August 1997 in Lima, Peru, supports this point of view by demanding the recognition of "the right to work as a human right for all people without distinction of age …"

On the international institutional level, the International Labour Organisation (ILO) is one of the major players dealing with child labour. As the NATs, the ILO also uses human rights as a supporting legal argument. For instance, in its *Declaration on Fundamental Prin-ciples and Rights at Work* of 19 June 1998, it stresses the right to work in dignity and hence adopts a similar human rights language. In the Declaration, the ILO qualifies seven of its conventions as core conventions and indicates that the four rights covered by these conventions are fundamental rights and principles. Not only the freedom of association and the effec-tive recognition of the right to collective bargaining, the elimination of all forms of forced or compulsory labour, the elimination of discrimination in respect of employment and occupation, but also the effective *elimination* of child labour—contrary to the claims of NATs— is one of the fundamental rights and principles covered under these conventions.

It becomes clear that both the NATs and the ILO use similar human rights discourses in defending apparently contradictory positions on child labour. Organisations of work-ing children refer to human rights to support their claims for recognition of the right to work in dignity and to participate in the discussions on regulating child labour. The ILO along with major NGOs, on the other hand, while also adopting a human rights dis-course, advocate the effective abolition of child labour as their ultimate goal.

Working children as social actors: agency and participation

It is important for legal science to know how social sciences look upon the phenom-enon of child labour … The first and most common historical response to child labour is the *abolitionist* perspective, aiming at the full abolition of child labour. The second ap-proach contends that children can work when adequate protective legislation exists. This points to the so-called regulative approach towards child labour, which is for instance the way India approaches child labour. Thirdly, the so-called empowerment perspective views children more as active subjects or agents of change and focuses on promoting self-organisation of working children. NATs' claims for participation and the right to work in dignity fall under this empowerment perspective.

The analysis of this article will use the regulatory and empowerment approaches of child labour. Both perspectives rest on an emerging approach of social scientists that do not view the relationship between children and labour as inherently negative. They view work as an important societal element, and emphasise the child as social actor, capable of doing socially acceptable work …

The value of work and children's agency

. . . .

Several studies on the place and value of work in the lives of children stress the eco-nomic and social functions of work. From this perspective the importance of work for chil-dren lies in its capacity to generate income as well as in its function to provide children with a socially useful place in society. Hence, for many children working is a source of self-esteem. Detailed research on children and their activities shows that work constitutes an integral part of the lives of children. In addition, it is argued that, in one way or another, all children work. Apprentices, children working in factories or in fields, school children and students all spend a considerable amount of their time in restricting non-leisure activities that are socially useful. The difference between studying and working relates to the question whether the activity is immediately useful or in the future, studying being considered as an investment for future productive work. [It has been stated that] "all children are working, but not under the same conditions."

The dominant approach that excludes children from the societal division of labour has been challenged also from a theoretical perspective ... Children ... contribute to society, for instance as child workers or as students contributing to the economy in the form of the production of knowledge. This theoretical departure makes it clear that "children across societies do both manual and school work and contribute to both family economies and national ones—with the proportions, meaning and significance of each varying." In studies focusing on the meanings and values of work, as well as in the development of theoretical frameworks for the 'new social studies of childhood,' "the crucial element is that children are understood as social actors who are not only shaped by their circumstances but also, and most importantly, help shape them."

Within this sociological paradigm, a central place is assigned to the notion 'child agency,' that expresses the importance of considering children as "active agents of change," rather than "passive recipients of welfare enhancing help." This notion, which is elaborated within the new social studies of childhood, is in line with approaches underlying the CRC: "[T]he Convention on the Rights of the Child and the new interest in studies of childhood are likely to represent the same movement towards abandoning an almost exclusive protectionist perspective of its monopoly to the advantage of establishing children as participants and claim-makers, indeed as humans."

. . . .

Child Labour and the ILO minimum age conventions

The study of the ILO conventions is highly instructive for the present international debate on child labour, especially since the ILO was one of the first international organisations to tackle the issue in a global manner. In particular, the study of these conventions demonstrates that the ILO Conventions have two approaches to deal with children and labour. The early conventions show that the ILO aimed at *protecting* children at work and *abolishing* children at work and abolishing children from labour.

. . . .

Abolition of child labour for young people falling under the minimum age limits—The whole concept of establishing minimum ages reflects the concern that children of too young age should especially be protected by the prohibition on child work. Labelling work below minimum ages as child labour would become the dominant paradigm to think of the relation of children and employment.

. . . .

A flexible view on abolition in the early years—This abolitionist approach, however, was not global. As explained above, the ILO originally set the minimum age at fourteen. Moreover, it had in its early days a quite flexible view on child employment. Several exceptions could override the basic age limit of fourteen years. Children of a lower age could undertake work in the course of an educational purpose, in family undertakings, or when cultural or economic conditions in certain countries required a lower age. In such cases, most conventions explicitly stated that the school obligation for children could not be violated. On the other hand, the age was raised to eighteen for heavy work. Smolin rightly states that, in early times, the rhetoric and terminology of abolishing child labour were absent from the early ILO conventions.

A stricter view on abolition later on—Throughout time, ILO Conventions created less and less space for *child work* because of a twofold reason. First, the minimum age of acceptable forms of child labour gradually raised. In the initial conventions, the age was fourteen. The succeeding conventions of the thirties raised the age to fifteen. ILO Convention No. 138 sets forth an age which, "in any case, shall not be less than 15 years." Recommendation No. 146 even recommends that Member States should take as their objective the progressive raising of the minimum age to sixteen years. This means that the scope of legitimate child work gradually diminished. The protective approach more and more resulted in the *prohibition* of child work.

A second element contributing to the conclusion that less and less forms of child work were allowed, is the general approach of Convention No. 138 on Minimum Age. As stated, this Convention established the "total abolition of child labour" as its ultimate goal. We have stated that it was unclear if this obligation also applied to child labour forms not explicity covered by Convention No. 138. In any event, Convention No. 138 connected total abolition and child labour the first time. This connection has made a neutral use of the term "child labour" impossible from that time and it has had severe consequences for the rights of children at work.

Both the gradual raising of minimum ages and the global aim of Convention No. 138 to completely abolish child labour led to the distinction between unacceptable and illegitimate child *labour* and acceptable and legitimate child *work* as it is used today and set the landmark for the second, *abolitionist* approach of the ILO towards child labour.

The current approach of the international law framework towards child labour, based on Convention No. 138, is not unproblematic. Despite several attempts to promote the ratification of this Convention, it remains the least ratified of all core ILO conventions. Establishing minimum ages is practically impossible in certain countries. When ratifying the CRC, India for example declared with respect to Article 32 of the CRC that "for several reasons children of different ages do work in India" and that it is impractical to prescribe minimum ages for admission to each and every area of employment in India immediately. The problems to entirely subscribe to the current abolitionist approach, as illustrated by the interpretative declaration of India, are precisely caused by the fact that child labour is a very complex matter in social reality. Here again, law stands in a specific relationship with social reality, in a twofold way.

The reality of working children—First, the legal system finds its limits in the practical impossibility of abolishing child labour in reality. It can be argued that an abolitionist legal approach does not take into account the reality that many children work. In this respect, the so called child labour movement has not succeeded in providing a clear definition of acceptable forms of child labour, or to create a methodology for determining the degree of harm and of value to the child. A *regulative* and *empowerment* approach would in any event have the advantage that it would in some instances better comply with reality. This realism, however, should not be considered as tame attitudes and ways of implicitly accepting causes of child labour such as poverty, or should not be used to justify intolerable practices, but should rather consist of *a pragmatic* attitude towards child labour. Therefore, the conditions under which this work has to be undertaken, have to be clearly stipulated.

The counterproductive effect of the abolitionist approach—The relation of law and social reality cannot only be made problematic because of the fact that the legal framework does not comply with social reality, but also because the legal framework aggravates child labour in social reality. Indeed, the current international labour law with regard to child labour leads to an inherent contradiction. Because of the formal ban on child labour, possibilities for working children to invoke fundamental workers rights to eliminate the exploitative character of their work are restricted. From a legal point of view, working children under the established age limits do not exist. They work clandestinely, outside the law and outside protective networks. It is even argued that legislation prohibiting child labour which is intended to protect children "often turns out in practice to be regressive and counterproductive, driving child work underground and making children even more vulnerable to exploitation."....

Reconsidering the legal framework

The analysis of work-related rights in international labour law from a perspective in which the child is considered as a social actor, now makes it possible to question the current framework of international labour law with respect of child labour. Is there, given the existing legal framework, space for the recognition of children's work-related rights and freedoms? Or does the legal framework need to be reshaped in order to reflect the importance and value of children's work? Consequently, new avenues of looking at the existing international labour law with regard to child labour will be explored.

The necessity to investigate such new avenues can be illustrated by the emphasis of the ILO on the abolition of child labour rather than the regulation, as reaffirmed by the 1999 Convention on the Worst Forms of Child Labour. At first sight, by focusing on the abolition of the worst forms of child labour, this Convention leaves space for tolerable forms of child labour. However, Convention No. 182 emphasises at the same time the pivotal role of Convention No. 138. Convention No. 182 again leaves very little space for the recognition of children's work-related rights and freedoms and risks to further alienate child labour from labour in general. In adhering to Convention No. 138, signatory parties even tend to widen the gap between the case for children's (labour) rights and the justifiable empowering merits of international labour law.

This approach is further illustrated by the IPEC. Before the adoption of Convention No. 182, the ILO stated that "(o)ne of the merits of a new ILO Convention would be to consolidate the legal underpinnings of the International Programme on the Elimination of Child Labour (IPEC)." Moreover, 77 per cent of IPEC programmes focus on forms of child labour in the 'intolerable' category. It is only the remainder of the project that is concerned with the improvement of working conditions as a transitional measure. The IPEC occupies a pivotal place in ILO actions concerning child labour. Therefore, it is doubtful whether the organisation will have much space and budget left to focus also on the improvement of working conditions of children.

This does not mean that the aim of immediate abolition of child slavery and similar practices would be superfluous—the contrary is true. However, by framing the objective of total abolition of all child labour, the IPEC further risks to make children's claims to a right to work in dignity impossible. In this sense, the position of movements of working children and youth of Africa, Latin America and Asia can be understood. In their "Declaration of Dakar" of March 1998, they debated the (then upcoming) new ILO Convention on the Worst Forms of Child Labour, by stating as follows: "We are against prostitution, slavery and drug trafficking by children. These are *crimes* and not *work*. The decision-makers should distinguish between work and crime." How the current international legal framework should be reconsidered in the way that these examples illustrate, will be explored in this section.

Within the general labour law framework, the elimination of slavery and the freedom of forced and compulsory labour are usually read together with the freedom to work. The analysis of the freedom to work shows that this right is in the first place positively formulated. The counterpart of this freedom is the prohibition of slavery and forced labour. The elimination of these practices is even a condition for ensuring a person's freedom to work.

International labour law regarding child labour contains a totally different conception of the relation between slavery or forced labour and child labour. The Convention on Slavery and Forced Labour, as well as the practice of the ILO Committee, illustrates that child labour is, via the concept of exploitation, often used as a *synonym* for slavery and forced labour. In a similar vein, Convention No. 182 qualifies slavery and forced labour as one of the worst forms of child labour. Thus, child labour and the abolition of slavery or forced labour are often put on equal footing, concealing the primarily positively defined freedom to work, and, as a consequence, considering the abolition as a goal by itself.

A different approach towards child slavery and forced labour, however, should be considered, in two ways. Firstly, in accordance with the general labour law principles, the elimination of child slavery and forced labour should be firmly related to the right to freedom to work, without rendering these activities less intolerable. Conceptually such an approach could respond both to the ambition to eliminate child slavery and forced labour and the importance and value of children's work.

Secondly, a clearer definition of the slavery and forced labour concepts is required. Below, it is argued that tackling the issue of child labour does not necessarily entail a *prohibition* on performing child labour. Hence, the slavery and forced labour concepts have to be preserved for the most severe acts of child work ... Consequently, the current monitoring bodies which interpret these concepts, such as the Working Group on Slavery and Contemporary Slavery and the ILO Committee of Experts, bear a responsibility to provide clearer definitions of slavery and forced labour regarding children.

. . . .

When analysing child labour from the perspective of specific international law with regard to child labour, however, the relation with the freedom to work has been abandoned. ILO Convention No. 138 does not contain any reference whatsoever to the principle of the right to freedom to work. The aim of the Convention, read together with the accompanying Recommendation No. 146, is the total abolition of child labour. This is presented as a goal by itself, reflecting a protectionist approach towards child labour. The 1998 ILO Declaration on Fundamental Principles and Rights at Work proclaims the effective abolition of child labour, thus granting it the status of a fundamental human right.

As discussed, on the basis of the international text and their interpretations, it is possible to argue that child labour can be permitted. However, the overall approach of these instruments is that work performed by children is an exception to the prohibition of child labour. This is most clearly illustrated in Convention No. 138. Hence, the current view is that the imposition of age limitations itself does not constitute an exception to the right to freedom to work.

Notes and Questions

1. The Hanson and Vandaele article takes a hard line against those who would like to see the abolition of child labor. How is the child's "right to work" presented? What evi-

dence is provided to show the "positive" effects of labor in the lives of working children? What do the authors mean by a child's right to work in dignity? If we were to carry the Hanson theory to its logical conclusion, what would that be?

2. For the authors, what is the role of the UNCRC in the child labor debate? Are they in turn being simplistic when it comes to discussing children's "participation" in devising child labor policy? Is their analysis fair and accurate with respect to the ILO? What is the human rights discourse that both advocates and critics of child labor rely on to justify their positions?

3. The article speaks of the ILO's successful IPEC program, described in some detail at the end of this chapter. The essence of IPEC is that it provides funding to allow children who work in some of the most difficult conditions to return to school; in other words, the focus of IPEC has been to reverse the economic incentives for families and thus altering the child labor economic calculus. Does the article seem to be critical of IPEC, as making it even less likely that positive changes in children's working conditions would be the focus of governmental attention?

4. In fact, there has been a substantial increase in ratifications of the Minimum Age Convention. As of March 2009, there have been 151 ratifications of the Minimum Age Convention, and an impressive 169 ratifications of the Worst Forms Convention.

———

In the article that follows, Invernizzi and Milne are critical of groups purporting to represent the views of children, when in fact these groups actually reflect adult hostility to child labor. The authors single out the well-known international action network, Global March Against Child Labor, for particular criticism. The authors argue that images and representations of children are manipulated by such groups to support the view that the worlds of children and adults should be kept separate, and that the assessment by these groups that children themselves do not want to work is false.

Antonella Invernizzi & Brian Milne, *Are Children Entitled to Contribute to International Policy Making? A Critical View of Children's Participation in the International Campaign for the Elimination of Child Labour*

10 The International Journal of Children's Rights 403 (2002)

I. Introduction

....

The moves to see universal adoption and implementation of the ILO Conventions 138 and 182 are being met by well articulated opposition from working children's organisations that defend their right to work and are, in general, seeking improved working conditions and fair pay. The combined international efforts of the ILO with UNICEF and the World Bank to eliminate child labour are reinforced by the NGO efforts of the Global March Against Child Labour and, increasingly, the move to alignment by previously tolerant NGOs. The effort to eliminate or, as has recently been said by ILO, abolish children's work is placed firmly in the hands of national governments to sign, ratify and then enforce and continue to police. They will, of course, be faced with the pressures of funding reductions from the World Bank and less development and aid funding from both other UN agencies and the NGO sector.

The overall losers are children. In the first line it is children who are defending their right to work, behind them those who are silently working out of sight and unheard. Further behind them are the rest of the children in any single place, then ultimately all children worldwide who at present do not appear to have a legitimate reason for expressing their opinions critically as working children do. Thus, we may be led to believe children will not generally be encouraged to have opinions that make other, comparable demands. It is not a particularly encouraging picture. However, it is far more complicated than simply looking at the containment and control of children's participation, since the situation before us is far more complicated than that. It becomes discriminatory. On the one hand, there will be some children who will be allowed and encouraged to use their participatory rights *as long as they conform* to the controls that are now subtly being imposed on them. On the other hand, those children who are attempting to claim their rights through the channel of social action that conforms to the pertinent articles of the CRC will be chastised for so doing since they are speaking out for children *who work illegally*.

The selection and rejection of children is also an intricate process. Working children's organisations are representative of only a very small minority of children worldwide, either working or not. On balance, the apparently 'active' role of children in bringing an end to child labour is far more widespread and seems to have more of the characteristics that make it universal than pro-child labour activism. Of course, the majority tend to be an amplification of the adults behind them and their participation is classically considered measurable against 'Hart's Ladder' as *manipulation* or, in many instances, *tokenism*. We shall, though, return to the question of the use of this kind of measurement of participation later. However the pro-elimination children also have the larger and more effective means of aggrandisement of the cause through: UN agency support (UNICEF, UNESCO, etc.); NGOs; agency of government such as education, health, employment, and public information services; and, generally, universal media support. Working children's organisations, whilst representing minority interest pressure groups that often work well for adults to draw attention to particular issues, are considered an outrage in even the most liberal democracy. This is very clearly because the ideology of the contemporary world is an abhorrence of child labour that is largely constructed by a highly efficient media and public relations process.

Behind the facade: The ambiguous nature of participation

....

If we begin by imagining that the Global March Against Child Labour is a children's initiative, further scrutiny would reveal that in fact very little comes from children. Website users may be misled by the fact that it uses pictures of children who appear to be in situations of great need and also others who have the appearance of children who are about to say something important or about to lead children into action. Nevertheless, until recently participation processes were not part of this NGO's activities and not one example of children's words was presented on its site. Just before we began to write, the Bal Mahapanchayat or Child Friendly Village initiative was launched, whereby children are (it would appear) organising themselves in order to fight child labour in India. It presents itself as a very overtly political action which is exactly, as we will see later, what is often most criticised when child workers use political language. Kailash Satyarthi, chairperson of SACCS, was quoted as saying in an e-mail from 1 July 2002 that announced the beginning of the project:

The Child Friendly Village model has successfully inculcated a sense of responsibility, leadership and decision-making among the children who were earlier exploited as child labourers. The aim is to involve a child in decision-making from the lowest organ of democracy, the panchayat. It is an experiment we hope to put on national as well as international agenda.

Apart from this more recent example, many of the children's views that are expressly against child labour come, in fact, from non-working and non-poor children. UNICEF's *Voice of Youth* initiative that collects children's voices via Internet and is available on UNICEF's homepage ... is a good example of what children require in order to participate: internet access, IT skills and literacy. Poor working children are very much more unlikely to be able to contribute for a number of quite apparent reasons.

Dilemmas confronting children's movements

It is with the activism of support groups that the "Achilles' Heel" of children's initiatives has been exposed, especially through the manner in which they have generalized children's views. On the one hand, children's organizations tend to represent only a minority of all working children worldwide. The majority tend to prefer to remain protected by their anonymity or the fact that their work is not classified as one of the economic activities destined for elimination. Where children unionise in any way there is a high risk that employers will dismiss them and replace them with unorganized workers. The case is often proven by groups who call themselves working children's unions, whereby one most often finds that having joined such a group a child has to then cease to work in industry or agriculture, including in many cases where even adult organisation or unionisation is equally regarded as undesirable. These organized working children may thus often be better described as ex-workers. The other dimension of this is that because children in structured, employed work thus remain unorganised, that ... working children's associations are often such children as street vendors, shoe shines and so on who cannot be dismissed by bosses. They are, to all intents and purposes, their own bosses although they may be part of a family enterprise. Through this simple examination we thus see that children's groups are either representative of only a part of the employment of children or are associations of ex-workers who have in effect, achieved what the ILO *et al.* are setting out to do. It is all but too apparent that the eliminationists are well aware of this flaw and that it is already being used psychologically against them through the gradual vilification of the adults who work with them.

On the other hand, there are some exceptions that challenge what the ILO is attempting to say. Little has been revealed to larger audiences to report organisation of children that is successful organisation of children. In parts of Latin America some NATs groups have been endorsed by trade unions, there are some affiliations to trade union movements on the Indian Subcontinent, and in Zimbabwe there is (or has been) organisation of child workers, although not as a formal, independent union. Where such schemes work children have far greater negotiating power and share in decision making, often have the cooperation of employers to include free schooling within the work area, be insured, earn comparatively good wages and sometimes reach formal education age with both a skill and work experience.

Unfortunately, within the child labour world this has itself been very carefully manipulated to entirely separate domains of adults and children. Thus, by adult decree children should be removed from a large range of economic activities using definitions of what is not permissible that are also adult. Child workers, who may well generally agree, have not been consulted in this process and will accordingly be banned from workplaces. Whilst one element of the proposition is to see all children receive at the very least a good basic education, in fact nobody has really given serious thought to children's needs. What kind of education do they want? If many of them wish to have vocational training, then regulated workplaces with fair pay would offer exactly that. How also do countries without the ability to afford to train teachers, build schools and equip pupils begin to pull the two strands of the process together? Elimination of child labour is seen as an immediate measure, but building up an education system can never be. So what will children who no longer work do with interminable, enforced leisure time? What does the world want them to do? Most importantly, what do they want? Some of the answers already exist within working children's groups but the pressure of the elimination movement that amplifies their version of 'the truth' almost entirely invalidates what the children might beneficially add to the wider debate.

Notes and Questions

1. Is it surprising that Invernizzi and Milne are so critical of groups that most people, at least in the West, would consider to be doing important work in children's rights? How do they characterize the agendas of the most prominent child labor groups? How do they evaluate the role of the ILO in standard setting and consciousness raising? In what way is the view expressed in this article similar to that set out in the Hanson and Vandaele article above? How different?

2. What do you think of asking working children their view on the right to work? To what degree should their responses determine child labor policy? Should the empowerment provisions of the UNCRC be taken literally in this context?

3. The issue of including children's "voices" in policy making is a difficult one. In what way should children be chosen for inclusion in such a process? The degree to which they are represented by interest groups? Or should they be chosen according to some idea of geographical or ideological representativeness?

II. International Labor Organization Standards

A. Overview of the ILO

The International Labor Organization (ILO) is a vital pillar in the promulgation of international labor standards. With its unique structure, involving governments, unions and non-governmental organizations, the ILO is regarded as a venerable source of expertise and policy guidance in the area of fair labor standards for adults and children. As has been seen in the readings above, the ILO's position on child labor has evolved over time, away from a total rejection of child labor towards a more nuanced perspective. The ILO's current point of view is that child labor should ultimately and ideally be eliminated, but that more attention should be paid in the here and now to doing away with the "worst forms." With respect to child labor, the ILO has also developed the IPEC system (short for International Program on the Elimination of Child Labor), which provides funding for children to leave the most harmful occupations and return to school. Although not yet applied on a mass scale, the IPEC approach has been very successful where it has been tried. IPEC is discussed in more detail in the remedies section at the end of this chapter.

The following article makes clear the enduring power and prestige of the ILO as a standard-setting body. It explains the ILO's complex structure and principal activities. It is impossible to consider international labor standards in general, or child labor issues in particular, without a basic knowledge of what the ILO is and how it functions.

Matteo Borzaga, *Accommodating Differences: Discrimination and Equality at Work in International Labor Law*

30 Vermont Law Review 749 (2006)

I. THE INTERNATIONAL LABOUR ORGANISATION: STRUCTURE AND FUNCTIONS

The Treaty of Versailles concluded World War I in 1919. During the negotiations of the Treaty, the Commission on International Labour Legislation was created and presented a project for the establishment of the International Labour Organisation. The project became part XIII of the Treaty, and today constitutes the ILO Constitution.

The ILO Constitution is composed of a preamble, which expresses the aims of the ILO, four chapters dedicated to organizational matters, and an annex, which incorporates the 1944 Declaration of Philadelphia into the constitution. The Declaration is particularly important because it fixes the mission of the ILO. As most scholars agree, this mission is essentially provided by part II(a) of the Declaration, where the International Labour Conference affirms that "all human beings, irrespective of race, creed or sex, have the right to pursue both their material well-being and their spiritual development in conditions of freedom and dignity, of economic security and equal opportunity." To reach this objective the ILO has to deal not only with labor matters but also with relationships between labor matters and the social, economic, and financial ones.

.... In 1945 the ILO Constitution was substantially amended to address the issue of membership. The amendments established that all member states of the United Nations were also members of the ILO. Countries that joined the United Nations later automatically became members of the ILO if they formally agreed to respect the principles contained in the constitution. States that are not members of the United Nations can become members of the ILO if they are admitted by a qualified majority of the International Labour Conference.

With regard to the structure of the ILO, it is important to note that the ILO "is not a supranational entity." This assertion, fundamental to understanding the problem of effectiveness of international labor standards in domestic law, means that the ILO "may not impose obligations on member states," except regarding matters to which they voluntarily agree. After the amendments to the 1945 Constitution, the ILO became "a specialized agency 'associated' with the United Nations."

In the International Labour Conference, the supreme body of the ILO, each national delegation is composed of two representatives for the government, one for the employers, and one for the workers. The Governing Body is elected by the Conference and is now composed of fifty-six members: twenty-eight represent national governments, fourteen represent employers, and fourteen represent workers. Members representing governments are divided into two groups. The first group is comprised of ten members with permanent seats whose countries are considered to be chief industrial countries. The second group is comprised of the remaining eighteen members elected by the governmental representatives of the International Labour Conference. This group does not include those representatives from countries with permanent seats. The members representing employers and workers are chosen by their own groups inside the International Labour Conference.

.... [T]he two most important organs of the ILO are the International Labour Conference and the Governing Body. The Conference is principally charged by the constitution to discuss and adopt international labor standards, in particular conventions, recommendations, and sometimes declarations, such as in Philadelphia in 1944 or in Geneva in 1998. The Conference also supervises the application of the ratified conventions into the domestic law of member states. The Conference meets once a year in order to examine the issues on the agenda prepared by the Governing Body. During its session, the Conference sits in plenary or in committees established to do a preliminary exam of the different issues on the agenda. Finally, the Conference discusses and adopts the program and the budget of the ILO.

The Governing Body is the executive organ of the ILO and has many tasks. The Governing Body prepares the agenda for the International Labour Conference; selects the Director General of the International Labour Office; supports the Director General in exercising the Director General's responsibilities; draws up the program and the budget of the ILO; and decides and supervises the policy of technical cooperation. The Governing Body meets four times a year.

The International Labour Office, the permanent secretariat of the ILO, is closely related to these two principal governing bodies. It is charged by the constitution to provide technical assistance to the International Labour Conference and to the Governing Body. It prepares the documentation for the meetings of both the International Labour Conference and the Governing Body, collects and publishes information on labor and social conditions, and prepares specialized reports to advise the International Labour Conference in adopting conventions and recommendations. In addition, the International Labour Office draws up technical reports for the committees of the Conference and gives assistance in labor matters to the member states, their trade unions, and employers' associations. The headquarters of the International Labour Office is in Geneva.

The most significant feature of the ILO's structure is certainly the tripartite composition of its internal bodies. Both the International Labour Conference and the Governing Body have a tripartite structure, which means that representatives of governments, workers, and employers of each member state compose the two organs.

Most scholars affirm that "[t]ripartism is the real strength of the ILO," and distinguish it from other international organizations. In fact, tripartism gives particular authority to ILO decisions, because the most important parties in the labor system of each state share in these decisions. However, the ILO remains an intergovernmental organization. Thus, the number of government representatives outnumbers the representatives of workers and employers. The proportion of representatives from each constituency group has been a source of contention, but the principle of tripartism has never been criticized. Worker and employer representatives provide legitimacy to ILO decisions. This legitimacy is very important, particularly in labor matters.

There are many other commissions and committees within the ILO that help the ILO do its work. Of particular importance to this Essay are the committees charged with the supervision of compliance with international labor standards in domestic law.

The Declaration of Philadelphia gives the ILO a general objective to pursue not only labor but also social, economic, and financial matters. Before the adoption of the Declaration of Philadelphia, the Permanent Court of International Justice paved the way for the ILO's very broad mission. In fact, the court was asked to decide if particular groups of people or specific issues should be excluded from the competence of the ILO. In each of these cases, concerning for example agricultural workers and self-employed people, "[t]he Court confirmed the ILO's competence."

The increase in scope of the ILO's mission also affected its principal activity: the creation of international labor standards. The ILO was established to deal with the most basic problems in the labor field. After the 1944 Declaration of Philadelphia, the situation progressively changed because the ILO began to deal not only with traditional labor law but also with the newest related challenges including human rights, employment and living conditions, development, and social welfare. The enlargement of the ILO's mission is evident in the topic of this Essay. After the Declaration of Philadelphia, the ILO began to consider not only equal pay but also discrimination and workplace equality.

The ILO was established to create internationally recognized labor standards, chiefly through conventions and recommendations. However, today it is generally recognized that the ILO has acquired two other functions. The first is technical assistance to its member states, and the second is to promote, realize, and disseminate research and studies on labor matters.

The experience of technical assistance began in the 1950s, in the period of the independency that brought the birth of many new states. These states, which were (and in most cases still are) particularly underdeveloped, progressively became members of the ILO. For this reason, the ILO assumed a new function that consists of helping these developing countries modernize their economic and social situation.

. . . .

The degree of implementation of international labor standards into domestic law or the creation of the conditions necessary to progressively guarantee this implementation became the principal criterion considered to provide technical cooperation to a member state. The link between implementation of international labor standards and technical cooperation is very important because it constitutes a fundamental instrument to improve the effectiveness of international labor law in the most underdeveloped countries.

. . . .

The [ILO's] constitution establishes the ILO monitoring system, which is based on the fair cooperation between the member states and the ILO. As established by article 22 of the constitution:

> Each of the Members agrees to make an annual report to the International Labour Office on the measures which it has taken to give effect to the provisions of Conventions to which it is a party. These reports shall be made in such form and shall contain such particulars as the Governing Body may request.

Furthermore, article 19 of the constitution requires each member state to report on the measures taken in the matters related to conventions that the member state did not ratify.

On the basis of this global reporting activity, the ILO exercises its monitoring tasks through two different bodies: the Committee of Experts and the Conference Committee on Application of Conventions and Recommendations (Conference Committee).

The first, and most important, of the two bodies—the Committee of Experts—was created in 1926 and is composed of twenty members representing the different regions of the world, chosen among experts in labor and social matters at the international level....

The Committee of Experts prepares its annual report by assessing each member state's annual report presented to the ILO as required by articles 22 and 19 of the constitution, in which national laws and practices are analyzed for compliance with the international labor standards. This activity is particularly important to the programmatic or promotional conventions for which the Committee of Experts evaluates the progression or regression of the member state in reaching the general objectives of the convention concerned....

The second significant body concerning the monitoring activity of the ILO is the Conference Committee. This body is established every year by the International Labour Conference and has a tripartite character, with participation from representatives of governments, workers, and employers. The duties of the Conference Committee are twofold. First the Conference Committee examines the Committee of Experts annual report in its entirety. Second, the Conference Committee addresses the specific, problematic instances of domestic law that failed to comply with international labor standards, as listed by the Committee of Experts. Relating to these specific instances, the Conference Committee asks the governments concerned about the reasons for noncompliance. The governments may respond and communicate the measures taken to promote the application of the ratified Conventions. After having received the answers of the governments and having discussed them, the Conference Committee prepares a report that lists the countries that did not fulfill the international labor standards. The report is then submitted to the International Labour Conference, which discusses and adopts it. While it is clear that the Conference Committee is not a court, it is also clear that the listing of a noncompliant member state certainly represents a political sanction. This is particularly severe because the report is also approved by the International Labour Conference.

Related to the ILO monitoring system, which is considered traditional because it has performed its fundamental role since 1926, is the voluntary follow-up procedure established by the 1998 Declaration of Geneva. This procedure is another instrument to supervise member states' compliance with the international labor standards....

The most significant characteristic of this follow-up procedure is that it considers the progress or regress of all ILO member states with regard to those four matters, even if they have not ratified the conventions that regulate them. The reason for this particularity is that those four matters are regarded as the constitutional principles of the ILO, which are implemented by every member state as a condition of their participation in the ILO.

The described mechanisms basically represent the monitoring system of the ILO. This is completed by a complaints procedure....

Conclusion

....

... [I]t is clear that the formal ratification of international labor standards by a member state is not sufficient to ensure their practical implementation, especially for programmatic standards. Furthermore, not even the monitoring system of the ILO is able to achieve this goal because of the difficulty in sanctioning the noncompliance of member states. Thus, the reporting activity of the ILO, the most important instrument of international labor standards' implementation provided by the Committee of Experts and the Conference Committee, can achieve only sanctions of a political nature. Moreover, the complaint procedure provided by articles 26–34 of the constitution, which foresee the existence of legally binding sanctions, has failed to yield significant results. A complaint was discussed before the International Court of Justice only once in ILO history, which is a signal that member states and the ILO itself do not consider sanctions the correct way to enforce international labor standards.

A final weakness of the ILO monitoring system, with important consequences to the efficacy of its standards, is the voluntary nature of the reporting system. Without the cooperation and honesty of each member state in preparing reports about ratified and nonratified conventions, the fundamental activity of both the Committee of Experts and the Conference Committee cannot be properly carried out. In other words, it is highly probable that a government breaching the norms of a convention is not going to be particularly collaborative and fair in reporting their noncompliance with the convention.

The second phenomenon, the increase of ILO members following decolonization, resulted in the coexistence of developed and developing countries within the ILO; countries with very different labor markets and working conditions. Until decolonization the ILO was characterized by a membership of countries with similar economies and development status.

The internal balance of the ILO was greatly modified by the new membership of many developing countries since the 1950s. In order to understand the impact of this change, it is sufficient to note that in 1946 the ILO had 52 member states, in 1958 there were 80 member states, and in 2003 there were 177 member states. This increase of ILO membership had significant consequences to both the techniques of adopting international labor standards and their implementation into domestic laws. This is due to the conditions of underdevelopment that characterized, and still characterize, in many cases, the newly associated countries and their difficulty to practically apply the ratified conventions.

One consequence of the ILO's increased membership was a great increase of flexibility in setting international labor standards with the inclusion of flexible provisions within many conventions. One example of a flexible provision allows member states not to apply a part of the convention concerned; another permits the adoption of standards that are lower than those provided by the convention itself.

....

The practical difficulties created by increased membership in the ILO have affected the ILO's adoption of international labor standards. Thus, the number of conventions adopted has declined progressively since the 1950s. Regarding the ratification process, there was an approximately twenty percent increase in ratifications in the decade ending 2004 over the previous decade. Nevertheless, it is important to point out that "three-fifths of ILO Member States ha[d] ratified fewer than one-quarter of ILO conventions ... and more than one-fifth [of Member States] ha[d] ratified fewer than 20 conventions" through September 2004.

The reason for the increase of ratifications may be the result of the Declaration of Geneva of 1998, which set forth the core labor standards, and generally had a very positive impact on the ILO and its activities. Thus, the Declaration produced a strong increase of ratifications involving the core labor standards. One example is Convention No. 111, which had been ratified by approximately ninety percent of ILO member states by the end of 2003.

Nevertheless, the formal ratification of a convention is an important start, but ratification is not a guarantee that the convention's provisions are going to be applied in practice. In this sense, the increase in ILO membership certainly produced significant changes within the ILO due to the need to adapt its role to the new situation. As previously noted, the original mission of the ILO essentially consisted of producing international labor standards, in particular through conventions and recommendations. Although this is still one of the most important tasks for the ILO, the ILO was charged with a second task after the enlargement of its membership: technical cooperation. The performance of this function has increased steadily over the years, especially because technical cooperation provides a softer alternative for promoting international labor standards in developing countries than a sanctions system. In other words, when addressing the difficulties that arise when associated countries do not respect the norms provided by ratified conventions, the ILO opted for the development of technical cooperation to help them adapt their laws to the international labor standards, rather than impose sanctions upon them.

. . . .

. . . [S]ome scholars propose a global reform of the ILO institution, with particular regard to the complaints procedures in order to create an international court with specific competence on labor matters deriving from the same complaint procedure, but having legally binding power of decision. This kind of reform could make the international labor standards more effective; it could also cause a problem. Member states could be afraid of a stricter system, causing a sharp decrease in ratifications, or worse, the denunciation of already ratified conventions. On this point it should be remembered that the augmentation in ratifications of fundamental conventions was favored in recent years by the adoption of the Declaration of Geneva, an instrument of soft law, accompanied by a voluntary follow-up procedure.

Notes and Questions

1. According to Borzaga, the rapid increase in ILO membership in the post colonial period led to great difficulties in establishing truly international labor standards. How does he explain these difficulties? How does the ILO cope with this set of problems, especially given the fact that its membership is so economically diverse? Does this fact have particular implications for the child labor question?

2. As for the "complaints procedure" mentioned by Borzaga, note the following from the ILO's own website:

The Complaints procedure—

The complaint procedure is governed by articles 26 to 34 of the ILO Constitution. Under these provisions, a complaint may be filed against a member state for not complying with a ratified convention by another member state which ratified the same convention, a delegate to the International Labour Conference or the Governing Body in its own capacity. Upon receipt of a complaint, the Governing Body may form a Commission of Inquiry, consisting of three independent members, which is responsible for carrying out a full investigation of the complaint, ascertaining all the facts of the case and making recommendations on measures to be taken to address the problems raised by the complaint. A Commission of Inquiry is the ILO's highest-level investigative procedure; it is generally set up when a member state is accused of committing persistent and serious violations and has repeatedly refused to address them. To date, 11 Commissions of Inquiry have been established.

When a country refuses to fulfil the recommendations of a Commission of Inquiry, the Governing Body can take action under article 33 of the ILO Constitution. This provision states that "[i]n the event of any Member failing to carry out within the time specified the recommendations, if any, contained in the report of the Commission of Inquiry, or in the decision of the International Court of Justice, as the case may be, the Governing Body may recommend to the Conference such action as it may deem wise and expedient to secure compliance therewith." Article 33 was invoked for the first time in ILO history in 2000, when the Governing Body asked the International Labour Conference to take measures to lead Myanmar to end the use of forced labour. An article 26 complaint had been filed against Myanmar in 1996 for violations of the Forced Labour Convention (No. 29), 1930, and the resulting Commission of Inquiry found "widespread and systematic use" of forced labour in the country. Available at … http://www.ilo.org/global/What_we_do/InternationalLabourStandards/ApplyingandpromotingInternationalLabourStandards/Complaints/lang-en/index.htm.

3. How might the ILO's complaint procedure be reformed to address situations where states violate the labor rights of their citizens? What implications would this have for the child labor question?

———————

Edward E. Potter, *The Growing Significance of International Labor Standards on the Global Economy*
28 Suffolk Transnational Law Review 243 (2005)

The Adoption of International Labor Standards

The philosophy and purpose of the ILO when it was formed was to promulgate minimum labor standards, i.e., basic labor standards below which no nation should fall. When the ILO Conference first met in Washington, DC in October 1919, it adopted six international labor standards. The standards dealt with maximum hours of industrial work, unemployment, maternity protection, night work for women, minimum age, and night work for young persons in industry. Presumably these were the most important labor standards issues of the day. In its first decade, the ILO Conference adopted twenty-six conventions and thirty recommendations. In its second decade, during the Great Depression, the ILO had its most prolific era, adopting thirty-seven conventions and twenty-six recommendations.

Beginning in the 1950s, the ILO's pace of adopting international labor standards began to slow. In the 1980s, sixteen conventions and one protocol were adopted; in the 1990s, thirteen conventions and three protocols were adopted. Notably, the great majority of conventions in the last two decades have been adopted by close voting margins suggesting the absence of a strong international consensus. Currently, over half of them (eighteen) have nine or fewer ratifications, and eight others have nineteen or fewer ratifications. Nearly eighty percent of the international labor standards adopted by the ILO Conference in the last two decades have been ratified by less then ten percent of the member states. The three conventions that were adopted by wide voting margins and addressed general principles, labor statistics, worst forms of child labor and vocational rehabilitation, have had much higher ratification levels ranging from 42 to150 or more.

In 1930, the ILO adopted its first human rights treaty concerning the abolition of forced labor (Convention No. 29). In the late 1940s and 1950s, the ILO adopted five other human rights treaties concerning freedom of association (Convention No. 87), the right to organize and collective bargaining (Convention No. 98), equal remuneration (Convention No. 100), forced labor (Convention No. 105) and equal treatment (Convention No. 111). These conventions are the most heavily ratified conventions, having been ratified by 120 to 150 nations. In June 1999, the ILO Conference unanimously adopted a convention prohibiting the worst forms of child labor (Convention No. 182). The Convention was quickly ratified by 150 member nations.

The Leveling Effect of ILO Standards is Incomplete

As multilateral treaties, conventions create no leveling effect on international labor standards unless all nations ratify them. Today, ILO conventions cover virtually every aspect of conditions of employment. ILO standards range from basic matters such as freedom of association and the worst forms of child labor to more technical issues, such as wage setting, social security, and chemical safety.

The goal of universal ratification and adoption of ILO standards to take labor standards out of competition is far from being achieved. Even for the most widely ratified conventions, primarily concerning fundamental worker rights-freedom of association, right to organize, collective bargaining, forced and child labor, and equal opportunity-it remains the case that over half of the world's workers do not work in countries that have ratified these conventions. This is because three large countries, China, India and the United States, have ratified few of the fundamental labor standards. On the other hand, 104 of the 176 ILO member countries have ratified all eight of the fundamental ILO standards. Twenty-nine have ratified seven of the core labor standards, and fourteen states have ratified six fundamental conventions.

The ratification rate and coverage for the more technical conventions, particularly those negotiated in the last twenty years, is substantially lower. More significantly, nearly seventy percent of the 176 ILO member nations have ratified twenty-five percent or less (forty-five or fewer) of all adopted ILO conventions. In sum, the strategy of taking labor standards as a factor out of international competition through ratified conventions has not succeeded as those standards are presently identified, developed and negotiated in the ILO.

ILO Declaration on Fundamental Principles and Rights at Work

As a result of the pressure to link worker rights and trade in the WTO and in recognition of the ILO's primary responsibility with respect to workers, the ILO Conference unanimously adopted on June 18, 1998, a Declaration on Fundamental Principles and Rights at Work (Declaration). Adoption of the Declaration, which is applicable to all ILO members, was a top priority for the U.S. Government and U.S. businesses.

The Declaration commits all ILO members to "respect, to promote and to realize … the principles concerning fundamental rights" that are the subject of eight ILO human rights conventions. Because the legal basis for the substance of the Declaration is drawn from the ILO Constitution, the Declaration represents a solemn commitment by virtue of ILO membership and requires no additional action by the Member nation. The Declaration has follow-up procedures to hold ILO members accountable for their commitment to seek to achieve the goals and objectives of the fundamental ILO conventions. Under annual review and global report procedures, the follow-up constitutes a political track in the ILO to address egregious or "worst case" violations of fundamental worker rights.

Under the Declaration, the 176 ILO member nations promise to seek to achieve the goals and objectives, but not the legal requirements, of the fundamental ILO conventions. It is not a new international labor standard but rather an embodiment of the fundamental principles of ILO membership. The principles are:

> Freedom of association and the effective recognition of the right of collective bargaining;
>
> The elimination of all forms of forced or compulsory labor;
>
> The effective abolition of child labor;
>
> The elimination of discrimination in respect to employment and occupation.

Although the Declaration addresses fundamental workplace human rights issues, and its follow-up reporting and accountability procedures are clearly promotional, it is significant that protectionism and comparative advantage were the dominant issues of concern for developing countries in the four years of discussions leading to adoption of the Declaration. One consequence of the adoption of the Declaration has been a substantial increase in the number of ratifications of the fundamental conventions.

The Declaration and its follow-up are based on the view that "sunshine," in the form of peer review, publicity, and targeted technical assistance will do much more, and more quickly, to promote fundamental worker rights than the sledgehammer approach of trade sanctions which developing countries would strongly resist.

. . . .

Notes and Questions

1. The Potter article describes the ILO's 1998 Declaration on Fundamental Principles and Rights At Work,[5] a set of goals considered binding on all ILO member countries and which includes a commitment to the "effective abolition of child labor." Does the inclusion of this language tilt the child labor debate in the direction of the protectionists, or should the declaration be read as a set of aspirations, within which there is room to pursue a nuanced international agenda?

2. If the ILO is promoting both its Minimum Age and Worst Forms conventions, is this a coherent position? If you were a state with widespread child labor, how would you read international signals with regard to the urgency of moving children out of the labor market and into other forms of activity—education, for instance?

3. As international standards are now, what is the degree of "blame" attached to states that find it difficult, in light of cultural and economic reality, to reduce the numbers of children in the work force?

-----

5. 37 I.L.M. 1233, CIT/1998/PR20A (June 18, 1998), available at http://www.ilo.org/public/english/10ilc/ilc86/com-dtxt.htm.

B. The Recent Emphasis on Worst Forms of Child Labor

With the "abolitionist" approach to child labor considered to be less than completely successful, there has been growing international recognition that the focus should be on the "worst forms" of child labor. As described above, labor falling into the category of "worst forms" is that with obviously harmful effects on young people; it is labor without any redeeming social or cultural features. The worst forms list is diverse: bonded labor, sexually exploitative work, and child soldiering are included, as well as types of industrial work associated with adverse health effects. Some have objected that many of these activities are not "work" per se, but rather crimes, and some working children's organizations object to associating child labor with illicit occupations.

With the more recent emphasis on "worst forms," there is a corresponding stress on urgency of governmental responses. Since the worst forms designation transcends the protection versus empowerment debate, the reasoning goes, there should be no reason for governments to drag their feet in eliminating these worst forms. Likewise, there can be no argument that the worst forms of child labor simply result from the "sad reality" of poverty, and that it will be eliminated in tandem with the eradication of poverty. These forms are too immediately harmful to allow for such a position. The view that all child labor can be abolished in the near term may be to some extent a dead letter, although whether it remains a genuine long term goal of the international community is open to question. It is unclear whether isolating the worst forms of child labor will guarantee greater governmental efforts, but in theory an intensive, time-bound set of governmental responses are demanded by the Worst Forms Convention.

The articles that follow deal with the worst forms concept, its codification in the Worst Forms Convention, and provide examples of what the "worst forms of child labor" really are. In the first excerpt, Yoshie Noguchi describes the link between the worst forms standard and ideas of fundamental human rights. In particular, the author discusses how the UNCRC relates to the notion of eliminating the worst forms of child labor.

Yoshie Noguchi, *ILO Convention No. 182 on the Worst Forms of Child Labour and the Convention on the Rights of the Child*
10 International Journal of Children's Rights 355 (2002)

1. Introduction—a quick overview of ILO Convention No. 182

The ILO Convention concerning the Prohibition and Immediate Action for the Elimination of the Worst Forms of Child Labour, 1999 (No. 182) was unanimously adopted on 17 June 1999, by the ILO Member States at the 87th annual International Labour Conference, together with supplementing Recommendation (No. 190). While its full title is as above, it is often called by its short title—the *"Worst Forms of Child Labour Convention, 1999"* or simply C.182. This Convention reflects widespread recognition over recent years and a global consensus that there should be an immediate end to the worst forms of child labour. It came into force on 19 November 2000. By October 2002, that is less than two and a half years from its adoption, 132 countries had ratified this Convention, i.e., three out of every four Member States of the ILO, and several more are expected soon. This is the fastest pace of ratifications ever—more ratifications than any other ILO Convention in a comparable period in its history of over 80 years.

This extraordinary success of one recent ILO Convention is by no means the first attack on the exploitation of children. The ILO has been setting international labour standards since 1919, including in the area of child labour. The Convention on the Rights of the Child (CRC) was adopted by the General Assembly of the United Nations by its resolution 44/25 of 20 November 1989, came into force in 1990, and has received almost universal ratification (Somalia and the U.S. are the only two countries yet to ratify it). What is the relation between the two systems—UN (CRC) and ILO? What was the value of Convention No. 182? This article aims to shed some light on these questions.

....

1.2. Economic exploitation and beyond

CRC and ILO standards on child labour are complementary to each other. A good illustration of this is Article 32 of CRC, which provides for the child's right to be protected against economic exploitation, with reference to "the relevant provisions of other international instruments" in its second paragraph. Any work carried out by children in conditions below those established by UN conventions or by the ILO should be considered as economic exploitation. This has indeed been the position of the Committee on the Rights of the Child in examining reports from countries on CRC implementation. The same Committee has always been referring to the ILO Conventions Nos. 138 and 182 as the framework in assessing the national situation of child labour, and systematic in recommending to States parties to CRC, if not yet done, to ratify them. The close linkage between the CRC and these ILO Conventions is reflected among other things in the Implementation Handbook for the Convention on the Rights of the Child, which makes an extensive reference to the two ILO Conventions.

The name "international labour" Conventions may give an impression to unfamiliar readers that they are something to do with conditions of employment and work. In fact, C.182 as well as several other so-called fundamental Conventions of ILO relate more directly to the fundamental human rights related to work, than regulation of working conditions as such.

According to C.182, the definition of the worst forms of child labour comprises:

(a) all forms of slavery or practices similar to slavery, such as the sale and trafficking of children, debt bondage and serfdom and forced or compulsory labour, including forced or compulsory recruitment of children for use in armed conflict;

(b) the use, procuring or offering of a child for prostitution, for the production of pornography or for pornographic performances;

(c) the use, procuring or offering of a child for illicit activities, in particular for the production and trafficking of drugs as defined in the relevant international treaties;

(d) work which, by its nature or the circumstances in which it is carried out, is likely to harm the health, safety or morals of children.

The last category is often referred to as "hazardous work." The list of the exact types of work to be prohibited and eliminated as hazardous work needs to be determined nationally after tripartite consultation and taking into consideration relevant international standards. This determination in each country is extremely important as a first step to clarify what is to be eliminated and to take concrete actions accordingly. This "hazardous work" is a category closely related to how the conditions of work are regulated and safety and health of workers are protected in general and especially for young workers. For children who have already reached the general working age, the removal of the hazards or increased protection of their occupational safety and health could be a solution in this category of worst forms of child labour. In contrast, the other three categories under (a) to (c) are called "unconditional worst forms" because improving working conditions would not justify, for instance, the exploitation of children in prostitution.

1.3. Linkage with the optional protocols

Convention No.182 thus confirms the wide range of issues within its scope, and is therefore under the ILO's mandate. Many of them have direct connections with CRC. In fact, they are not limited to economic exploitation (Article 32 of CRC)—traditional area of child "labour," but also comprise use of children in illicit production and trafficking of drugs (Article 33), sexual exploitation (Article 34), trafficking in children (Article 35), children in armed conflicts (Article 38). Therefore, it can never be overemphasized that the ILO is concerned not only with Article 32 of CRC but with several other areas of the rights of the child. Given such a wide scope of coverage, it may be noticed that many of the related acts are not at all normal types of employment or even "labour"—they are criminal offences in many countries.

Some people even ask: Does the ILO recognize prostitution as work, by including it among the worst forms of child "labour"?—The answer is "No." The Convention calls for immediate and effective measures to secure the prohibition and elimination of, amongst other things, the use, procuring or offering of a child (i.e., under 18, as explained above) for prostitution, for the production of pornography or for pornographic performances. An ILO report to the International Labour Conference in 1998—one of the preparatory documents for C.182 elaboration—indicated: "Child prostitution, child pornography and the sale and trafficking of children are crimes of violence against children. They must be treated as crimes ... Yet while they are crimes they are also forms of economic exploitation akin to forced labour and slavery." The ILO bodies which supervise the application of international labour standards have already been dealing with the issue of child prostitution in several countries under the Forced Labour Convention, 1930 (No. 29). The inclusion of this issue in the scope of the new instruments was generally supported by the ILO constituents throughout the process of elaboration. Other forms of illicit acts—e.g., forced labour—are dealt with in ILO standards with the sole aim of eradicating them.

....

2. Characteristics of C.182—its emphasis on immediate and effective action

2.1 Obligation beyond a simple prohibition

The Convention is explicitly action-oriented: it requires ratifying States not only to prohibit the worst forms of child labour in law, but to design and implement *programmes of action* to eliminate them as a priority (Article 6); and to establish or designate appropriate mechanisms for *monitoring* implementation of the Convention (Article 5). Ratifying States should also take *effective and time-bound* measures (Article 7(2)) for prevention; provide support for the removal of children from the worst forms of child labour and their rehabilitation; ensure access to free basic education or vocational training for all children removed from the worst forms of child labour; identify children at special risk; and take account of the special situation of girls.

It is generally the case for all ILO standards that provisions of a Convention have to be applied both in law and practice. For example, even when the Convention only sets forth a minimum age (e.g., Article 2 of Convention No. 5: "Children under the age of fourteen years shall not be employed or work in a public or private industrial undertaking ..."), ratifying States must take measures not only to fix such a minimum age in law but also to make such national legislation effectively applied in practice. However, in the case of C.182, such requirements for action are spelt out as substantive provisions, as mentioned above. This would make it easier to point to the inaction of the governments concerned, and place pressure on them, with a possibility in extreme cases of procedures under the ILO Constitution. . . .

The accompanying Recommendation (No. 190) offers a wide range of guidelines for actions for implementation, from international efforts in gathering and exchanging information, extraterritorial pursuit of related offences by nationals even when the offences are committed in another country, to a wide social mobilization. Since the ILO Recommendation does not have a legal binding effect as in the case of the ratified Conventions, it may receive less attention as an international standard. However, R.190 is also a unanimously adopted international instrument reflecting a global consensus on its contents, and should be referred to as a guideline for action in any country, irrespective of the ratification of C.182, and also for actions at local or international level.

Thus, the principle of C.182/R.190 goes far beyond a simple prohibition of the situation in question. Child labour is a complex issue, and demands a comprehensive and integrated approach, so as to break the vicious cycle of poverty, social inequality and child labour. Measures needed to eliminate child labour including its worst forms effectively and in a sustainable manner encompass a wide range of economic and social support to the children and their families. Such a comprehensive approach will serve as an example of how the protection of children's rights is to be integrated into social and economic development strategies.

. . . .

Most commentators have conceded that efforts to completely eliminate child labor, and replace it with education, solely on grounds of the child's age are not going to succeed in the near term. Merely switching gears to focus on "worst forms" is no guarantee of success, either—even in the more limited field described by that term. The following article evaluates the likelihood that this more contemporary approach will change hearts, minds and behavior towards children and labor.

Mary Gray Davidson, *The International Labour Organization's Latest Campaign to End Child Labor: Will It Succeed Where Others Have Failed?*

11 Transnational Law & Contemporary Problems 203 (Spring 2001)

I. INTRODUCTION

. . . .

According to ILO estimates, there are approximately 250 million children ages 5–14 years old employed in developing countries. Nearly half work on a full-time basis, while the rest combine their work with some schooling or other activities. Among children attending school, up to one-third (33%) of the boys and more than two-fifths (42%) of the girls are engaged in economic activities on a part-time basis. Of the 250 million children concerned, approximately 50–60 million between the ages of five and eleven are working in extremely hazardous circumstances given their age and vulnerability. C182 is addressed to those 50–60 million children who are involved in the worst and most abusive forms of child labor, which the ILO defines as modern types of slavery, sex work, illicit activities, such as drug trafficking, and any other work likely to harm the health, safety, and morals of children.

The ILO's definition of abusive child labor along with a recent report by the United Nations Children's Fund (UNICEF) highlight the common myth that abusive labor mostly occurs in factory settings where children work to produce goods, such as clothing and toys for consumers in more affluent countries. In reality, only a small minority of children work in the formal economy. A 1995 study in Bangladesh identified three hundred non-export jobs performed by children including brick-making, stone-breaking, street-hawking, and rag-picking. Seventy percent of South Asia's working children are employed in agriculture, often as bonded laborers, where entire families are enslaved to pay off a debt. India is reported to have the world's largest child labor force. According to the Indian government, there are twenty million child laborers — with two million involved in such hazardous industries as underground mining, brick-making, match and fireworks production, and construction. Many children are never counted in government statistics, because they are working for their families, are in agriculture, or are hidden away in houses, far from the reach of the official labor inspectors. UNICEF's Director, Carol Bellamy, says it would be a "grave disservice" to the great majority of children who labor in "virtual invisibility" if we perpetuated the myth that the most exploited child workers are all in the industrial export sector. C182 is one attempt to put those "invisible" child laborers in the spotlight.

Because government estimates often exclude children who work part-time or in the informal sector, the figures on the number of child laborers may be misleading. This has the effect of "obscuring the real scope and distribution of the child labor problem." Children working without pay for their parents or as domestic servants in exchange for their keep are among those who are seriously undercounted.

. . . .

IV. PREVIOUS EFFORTS TO COMBAT HARMFUL CHILD LABOR

. . . . Beginning in the early 1980s, the ILO began a new approach to combat child labor, first through its public information campaign and then, in 1991, by launching the International Program on the Elimination of Child Labor (IPEC). IPEC is currently a ninety-country alliance that provides technical and other assistance to countries to work on the phased elimination of child labor. The program's target population is "bonded child laborers, children in hazardous working conditions and occupations and children who are particularly vulnerable, i.e. very young working children (below 12 years of age), and working girls."

Believing that child labor will only be eliminated through national will, IPEC aims to strengthen "national capacities" to address the problem and to promote a worldwide movement against it. Currently, IPEC has programs in thirty-seven countries to "develop and implement measures which aim at preventing child labor, withdrawing children from hazardous work and providing alternatives, and improving the working conditions as a transitional measure towards the elimination of child labor."

One of the first countries to join IPEC was India, where government estimates range from 11.28 to 17.2 million child laborers. Private estimates from non-governmental sources range from 44 to 110 million children working. To date, approximately 100,000 children working in hazardous occupations have received IPEC assistance to leave their work and enroll in school.

The United States has been the largest contributor to IPEC providing over $112 million to the ILO program from 1995 to 2001. IPEC programs have used these funds in a variety of ways, including the creation of a $6 million grant to eliminate child labor in the coffee industry in Costa Rica, El Salvador, Guatemala, Honduras, Nicaragua, and the Dominican Republic. The goal of this Latin American program is to give alternatives to approximately twenty-one thousand children working in jobs that harm their development. These alternatives include schooling, health services, and preventing the future employment of other children in those workplaces. Additionally, in March 2000, President Clinton announced a $14 million aid package to Bangladesh. The purpose of the aid is to place thirty thousand children in schools to help remove them from hazardous industries such as construction, shrimping, leather, and weaving.

V. CONVENTION 182 ON THE WORST FORMS OF CHILD LABOUR

A. Why Another Child Labor Convention?

.... The idea for a more narrowly-focused convention grew out of the successes the ILO began to realize from its practical projects in the field through IPEC. These projects provided educational alternatives to working in areas such as "football stitching, carpet weaving, [and by] tackling sweatshop conditions in the garment industry, withdrawing children from work in mines and quarries and saving young girls from trafficking and sexual exploitation." In C182, the ILO concentrated on a much less debatable norm, namely, the abolition of the worst forms of child labor, which the ILO calls "morally abhorrent situations under any circumstance or development condition." While it only entered into force on November 19, 2000, already 106 countries have ratified C182.

B. Analysis of How C182 Differs from Previous Conventions

Article 2 of C182 is not a complete departure from previous standards. Article 2 defines "child" for purposes of C182 as "all persons under the age of 18." This is consistent with previous age conventions that set 18 as the minimum age for any work that endangers a person's "health, safety or morals." The Recommendation accompanying C182 authorizes employment "from the age of 16 on the condition that the health, safety, and morals of the children concerned are fully protected …"

One of the most striking differences between C182 and C138, the Minimum Age Convention, are the categories of labor encompassed by the conventions. C138 mentions specific industries such as mining, quarrying, manufacturing, construction, electricity, gas, and water. C182 talks in more general terms about slavery, trafficking of children, forced military recruitment, child prostitution, drug trafficking, and any work likely to harm the "health, safety or morals of children." C138 categorizes industries that are not illegal per se, however, when children are employed in those industries they are subject to C138 scrutiny. C182, on the other hand, addresses activities that are illegal in nearly every country.

….

In addition to possible criminal sanctions for violations of C182, the Convention requires governments not only to remove children from abusive labor situations, but also to rehabilitate them through free basic education or vocational training. This is appropriate, because a more educated and skilled workforce is in a country's self-interest. As the Indian government's delegate to the 1999 International Labour Conference, which passed C182, stated:

> The ultimate answer to child labor lay in the eradication of poverty, unemployment, and illiteracy by gradually securing the realization of economic and social rights. Only multidimensional strategies that provide access to educational opportunities … and ensure the protection of the child could eventually eliminate the worst forms of child labor.

C182 also differs from the older Minimum Age Convention, C138, which concerns relatively easy-to-identify industries in the formal economy such as mining, manufacturing, commercial agriculture, and construction. C182 is a pledge to root out the worst forms of child labor wherever it exists, in both the formal and informal economies. Regulating the work of young people outside the formal employment sector may be impossible in some countries for many years. Nevertheless, the ILO believes it is important for the Convention to cover all child workers, not just those under a contract of employment and that national legislation clearly protects all child workers.

1. Monitoring Compliance with C182

The core provisions for the successful implementation of C182 are contained in Articles 5, 6, and 7. Article 6 requires ratifying countries to "design and implement programmes of action to eliminate as a priority the worst forms of child labor." The ILO recognizes that most countries have child labor legislation that establishes a minimum age for employment and working conditions. However, one problem is that such legislation often "exempts from coverage precisely the kinds of work in which children are most engaged (agriculture, family undertakings, small workshops, domestic service)." Therefore, legal protection must be extended to the primary places where children work to ensure that the worst forms of child labor are included in national legislation. The ILO also notes that where national legislation exists to protect children who work, it has had the greatest effect in the urban, formal sector. This accounts for why only a relatively small percentage of total child labor exists in those urban settings. The biggest child labor problems today occur outside the urban and formal sectors where legal protection often does not extend. With ratification of C182, children who work in those sectors are now, in principle, protected.

Article 5 will be critical to the success of C182. It consists of one short statement: "Each Member shall, after consultation with employers' and workers' organizations, establish or designate appropriate mechanisms to monitor the implementation of the provisions giving effect to this Convention." Again, one of the main obstacles is in identifying children working in home-based and other informal-sector work. In Guatemala, for example, the labor inspection system is unable to adequately monitor large factories, not to mention the many family-based enterprises scattered across the country. In Lesotho's and Portugal's thriving shoe industries, and in the Philippine garment industry, entire families work at home, making inspection nearly impossible. Furthermore, monitors may be subject to legal challenges should they attempt to inspect workers' homes.

One advocate for children's rights testifying before the U.S. Senate Foreign Relations Committee said she was puzzled about the use of the word "employers" in Article 5 of C182. She said she could not imagine the U.S. government, for example, "making deals with pimps or drug dealers to improve the working conditions of the children," or even negotiating with some factory owners in India who know "full well that they are acting against the law of their country." She claimed that those factory owners will go so far as to "hire protectors to keep reporters and child labor activists away from the child laborers."

3. Results to Date of C182

Even before it entered into force on November 19, 2000, forty-three countries had ratified C182. By comparison, only seven countries had ratified the Minimum Age Convention, C138, when it entered into force June 19, 1976. In addition, only six countries had ratified the Forced Labour Convention when it entered into force May 1, 1932. The number of countries that have ratified the Worst Forms of Child Labor Convention at this early date is higher than any other convention in a comparable time during the ILO's eighty-one-year history and may bode well for universal ratification in the not too distant future.

Countries are already beginning to institute changes based on the Convention. For example, in March 2000, Nepal passed the Child Labour (Prohibition and Regulation) Act, which addresses approximately 2.5 million underage laborers. The Act improves conditions for children working in the garment and carpet industries and manufacturing bricks. The Act also helps children working in mines, as bonded laborers, or as commercial sex workers. While the ILO has no direct authority to enforce C182, former U.S. Secretary of Labor Alexis Herman recognized that there are other ways to compel countries to comply with their obligations. Herman says that with the new ILO reports on child labor within countries, "we will be able to use the moral powers, as well as the political powers, to put the spotlight on the worst actors on the world stage today when it comes to the most abusive forms of child labor."

Given the vast under-reporting of child labor in many nations, a more accurate accounting of those employed in abusive situations will be important in the growing global campaign against such child labor both at the governmental and non-governmental levels. This information, coupled with the additional scrutiny and accountability mechanisms through the ILO's reporting and supervisory procedures, will assist, for example, the enforcement of the new U.S. Trade and Development Act. The Act requires countries to implement their commitments to eliminate the worst forms of child labor, as established in C182, before receiving trade benefits. As Secretary Herman stated, "It is our view that measuring whether we are making progress in efforts to eliminate abusive child labor through periodic and accurate child labor surveys is of the highest importance."

Notes and Questions

1. Both Noguchi and Davidson seem convinced that the Worst Forms Convention is more likely to prove effective in inducing countries to take abusive child labor seriously. Do you share their optimism? What specific features of the Convention lead you to your conclusion? In the event that a state ratifies the Convention, but fails to enforce it adequately—despite the language of urgency—what are the consequences?

2. Although many people assume that the worst forms of child labor are found mainly in global manufacturing industries, this is far from the case. In fact, agriculture is the largest employer of children worldwide. In addition, agricultural work is frequently of the exploitative "worst forms" variety. For details on this phenomenon, broken down by country and sector, see Human Rights Watch, Child Labor in Agriculture, available at http://www.hrw.org/backgrounder/crp/back0610.htm. Human Rights Watch deplores the fact that these "worst forms" of child labor in agriculture do not receive the attention they deserve.

3. The Global March Against Child Labor network is a good source of statistics as to the conditions of working children in various parts of the world. Their motto is "From exploitation to education," and their website is at http://www.globalmarch.org/. Global March is a coalition of broadly based child welfare and human rights NGOs. The Global March website provides statistical breakdowns on worst forms of child labor, showing the prevalence of work in specific categories, in various countries and regions. Their website states the following:

> The Global March movement began with a worldwide march when thousands of people marched together to jointly put forth the message against child labour.

The march, which started on January 17, 1998, touched every corner of the globe, built immense awareness and led to high levels of participation from the masses. This march finally culminated at the ILO Conference in Geneva. The voice of the marchers was heard and reflected in the draft of the ILO Convention against the worst forms of child labour. The following year, the Convention was unanimously adopted at the ILO Conference in Geneva. Today, with 150 countries having ratified the convention so far, it has become the fastest ratified convention in the history of the ILO. A large role in this was played by the Global March through our member partners.

With ILO conventions 138 and 182 as well as the UN Convention on the Rights of the Child forming the base of our movement, the Global March also perceives education, and the right to free and compulsory education of good quality for all children, as non-negotiable. Therefore the Global March also considers the EFA goals under the Dakar Framework an equally important international instrument and pushes for governments to achieve the goal of education for all.

4. "Worst forms of child labor" is a category of tremendous variety and complexity. With so many countries involved and so many types of work included in the designation of "worst forms," how can a coherent campaign be mounted against these abuses? Do you agree with adding such issues as child soldiering and trafficking into the discussion of child labor via the worst forms definition?

III. Case Studies in Worst Forms of Child Labor

A. Bonded Labor in South Asia: A Tradition of Child Slavery

Bonded labor is one of the most egregious of the "worst forms of child labor." It is practiced very extensively in South Asia, notably in India and Pakistan. Both children and adults are used extensively as bonded laborers. Many artisanal sectors in India, including carpet weaving, jewelry making and silk spinning, rely heavily on bonded children. The agricultural sector and domestic servitude also employ huge numbers of virtually uncompensated child laborers.

It is clear that bonded child labor is quite literally a form of slavery, with the children enjoying neither personal freedom nor education. Once sold into a bonded labor situation, escape for these children is nearly impossible. India is a sophisticated democracy and an emerging economic leader. Given this, why does the bonded labor problem remain so intractable in a country of such high political reputation? As you read the Human Rights Watch material on South Asia, ask yourself whether India and Pakistan practice what we might call a form of child slavery, and whether bonded labor is beyond the control of the authorities. If bonded child labor is a form of slavery, why is it not identified as such in a more explicit manner by journalists and commentators on contemporary politics? Do historical and social contexts matter when it comes to identifying and holding accountable states that tolerate extensive child slavery? Do the readings below identify cultural as well as economic factors that make bonded child labor so prevalent?

India and Bonded Child Labor

India has one of the world's most intractable problems with bonded labor, particularly bonded child labor. As you read the following report, published by Human Rights Watch in the mid-1990s, consider why bonded labor flourishes in India, and what remedies are available to address it. Is it fair to think of bonded child labor in India as primarily a cultural phenomenon? Can its presence be attributed to poverty alone? Are international labor standards, including the Worst Forms Convention, likely to penetrate the cultural nexis that allows for bonded child labor? What changes would India have to commit to making before bonded labor could be effectively reduced, even if not eliminated?

Although the report below dates from the mid-1990s, it is included because of the breadth of its coverage of bonded child labor in India. It must be noted that many of the problems identified in this report remain essentially unchanged. Human Rights Watch reports rely extensively on interviews with affected persons, and are known for their graphic detail and vivid descriptions. We should contrast this classic NGO approach with the more technical and distancing language used by the United Nations in its reporting. Human Rights Watch does not hesitate to accuse the governments involved in these abuses of bad faith and indifference. For an update on the bonded child labor situation, see a later Human Rights Watch Report on the same subject, entitled *Small Change*, and available at http://www.hrw.org/en/reports/2003/01/22/small-change.

Human Rights Watch, *Small Hands of Slavery:*
Bonded Child Labor in India

(1996) *available at* http://hrw.org/reports/1996/India3.htm

....

The practice of child debt servitude has been illegal in India since 1933, when the Children (Pledging of Labour) Act was enacted under British rule. Since independence, a plethora of additional protective legislation has been put in place. There are distinct laws governing child labor in factories, in commercial establishments, on plantations, and in apprenticeships. There are laws governing the use of migrant labor and contract labor. A relatively recent law — the Child Labour (Prohibition and Regulation) Act of 1986 — designates a child as "a person who has not completed their fourteenth year of age." It purports to regulate the hours and conditions of some child workers and to prohibit the use of child labor in certain enumerated hazardous industries. (There is no blanket prohibition on the use of child labor, nor any universal minimum age set for child workers.) Most important of all, for children in servitude, is the Bonded Labour System (Abolition) Act, 1976 which strictly outlaws all forms of debt bondage and forced labor. These extensive legal safeguards mean little, however, without the political will to implement them. In India, this will is sorely lacking. All of the labor laws are routinely flouted, and with virtually no risk of punishment to the offender. Whether due to corruption or indifference — and both are much in evidence — these laws are simply not enforced. In those rare cases where offenders are prosecuted, sentences are limited to negligible fines.

Why does India — the Indian government, the ruling elite, the business interests, the populace as a whole — tolerate this slavery in its midst? According to a vast and deeply entrenched set of myths, bonded labor and child labor in India are inevitable. They are caused by poverty. They represent the natural order of things, and it is not possible to change them by force; they must evolve slowly toward eradication.

In truth, the Indian government has failed to protect its most vulnerable children. When others have stepped in to try to fill the vacuum and advocate on behalf of those children, India's leaders and much of its media have attributed nearly all "outside" attempts at action to an ulterior commercial motive. The developed world is not concerned with Indian children, this view holds, but rather with maintaining a competitive lead in the global marketplace. Holding to this defensive stance, some officials have threatened to end all foreign funding of child labor-related projects.

This nationalist rhetoric has been largely a diversionary tactic. What the government has hoped to hide is the news that, no matter how the data are analyzed, official efforts to end the exploitation of child laborers are woefully deficient. Former Prime Minister P. V. Narasimha Rao, for example, made much of his initiative, announced in 1994, to bring two million children out of hazardous employment by the year 2000. Two million represents only 1.7 to 3.3 percent of the nation's child laborers; the fate of the other 58 to 113 million children was not addressed. In a welcome move, the United Front government, elected in May 1996, has promised to eradicate child labor in all occupations and industries, and has stated that the right to free compulsory elementary education should be made a fundamental right and enforced through suitable statutory measures. It remains to be seen what measures the government will take to fulfill these promises.

OVERVIEW OF BONDED CHILD LABOR

Approximately fifteen million children work as bonded laborers in India. Most were put into bondage in exchange for comparatively small sums of money: two thousand rupees—equal to about thirty-five U.S. dollars—is the average amount "loaned" in exchange for a child's labor. To India's vast numbers of extremely poor, however, this money can be, literally, a life-saver. With scant alternative sources of credit available—few rural banks, cooperative credit schemes or government loans—the poor are forced to turn to the local moneylender, who extracts the only collateral available: the promise of their labor or the labor of their children.

Two players create the debt bondage arrangement: the creditor-employer, who offers money to an impoverished parent in an attempt to secure the extremely cheap and captive labor of his or her child, and the parent who accepts this money, agreeing to offer the child's labor as surety for the debt. The child is a commodity of exchange. She or he is powerless to affect the agreement or its terms and—whether willing or unwilling to serve the bond master—powerless to refuse.

The arrangements between parents and contracting agents are usually informal and unwritten. The number of years required to pay off such a loan is indeterminate. Many of the children interviewed by Human Rights Watch had already been working for several years, and even among those relatively new to their jobs, none said that they expected to be released prior to maturity. Some intended to walk away from their bondage when they married, leaving a younger sibling to take over the labor-payment or a parent to somehow extinguish the debt—perhaps by a new loan from a different creditor-employer.

. . . .

FACTORS BEHIND BONDED CHILD LABOR:

. . . .

"NIMBLE FINGERS," AND OTHER MYTHS OF CHILD LABOR

A number of myths underlie and perpetuate child labor, justifying it on the grounds that the system "benefits" everyone involved: the country, the community, the family, the craft and the child. Children must be trained at the right age or they will never learn a skill; children must be trained in a profession appropriate to their background and class; children are particularly suited for certain kinds of work because of their "nimble" fingers; and child labor is a natural and desirable function of the family unit. These myths have widespread support.

The "nimble fingers" theory is applied to some of the harshest industries employing children, including the carpet, silk, beedi and silver industries. It asserts that children make the best products in these occupations thanks to their nimble fingers which are, according to the myth, better able to tie the tiny knots of wool, unravel thread from boiling silk cocoons, and solder tiny silver flowers to a chain. In this view, child labor is not an evil, but a production necessity. This rationalization is a lie. In fact, children make the cheaper goods; only master weavers make the best quality carpets and saris.

The myth that children must be trained at the "right" age—at six or seven years of age, or younger—contends that children who go to school, postponing their craft training until adolescence, either will be unable to adequately learn a skill or will be at an irreparable disadvantage in comparison with those who did begin working as young children. A study on child labor in Varanasi summarized the calculation behind this logic:

> Any number of justifications are available at the community level in support of children taking up a job at an early age. It is said that in order to learn the craft properly one has to start working away from the family. Further, in order to become an accomplished artisan one has to start working at an early age. Those who start working at the "late" age of 12 years might pick up the craft within a few months but they would never be able to pick up speed in their work. As against this, those starting at the "right" age of six or seven years become very good workers after an apprenticeship of 5 to 6 years. Whatever be the truth behind the general belief, it ensures continuous availability of child labour at low wages.

CHILDREN IN BONDAGE

BEEDI

. . . .

"Beedi" is a domestically-produced and consumed Indian cigarette. Though cheaper than manufactured filter-tip cigarettes, it is a relatively expensive product—a pack of twenty-four beedies costs between ten and twenty rupees—and one that is heavily consumed, with more than 500 billion beedi cigarettes produced and smoked each year. With annual sales worth forty billion rupees, beedi is one of India's most significant domestic products.

More than 325,000 children labor in the beedi industry, most in the southern state of Tamil Nadu. Other states with beedi production are Madhya Pradesh, Maharashtra, West Bengal, Andhra Pradesh, Karnataka, Kerala, and Uttar Pradesh (in the district of Allahabad). Human Rights Watch investigated bonded child labor in the beedi industry of Tamil Nadu only.

Beedi rolling is stationary work; the children sit cross-legged on the ground or floor all day, with a large and smoothly-woven shallow basket in their laps. The basket holds a pile of tobacco and a stack of rectangular rolling papers cut from the large leaves of the *tendu* plant. The child takes a paper, sprinkles tobacco into it, rolls it up tightly, and ties it with string. The tips are closed either by the roller herself or by a younger child, typically four to seven years old; young children often begin their beedi careers by working as tip closers.

The pace is rapid, with practiced children rolling and tying each beedi cigarette in a matter of seconds. Most of the older children—those over ten—roll 1,500 to 2,000 beedies each day. In order to encourage speed, employers keep close vigil over the child workers, scolding them or hitting them if they slow down. Some children have been forced to work with a matchbox tucked between their chin and their neck; in order to hold the box in place, they must keep their head down and focused on the work. If the matchbox falls, the employer knows the child has looked away and will punish her or him.

Children working under bondage in the beedi industry work between ten and fourteen hours a day, with short breaks for lunch and dinner. They work six and a half days a week year-round, but are only paid for six—the half day on Sunday is a designated "catching up" day. When children fail to report to work, either because of sickness or out of rebellion at the harsh conditions, their employer typically will go to their house and return them to the workplace under force.

The structure of work and bondage

Entire families are dedicated to the production of beedi. Usually it is the children who work as bonded laborers, with adults managing to buy their own freedom by the time they reach maturity or marry. For these poor families, bondage is a cyclical phase, a defining characteristic of childhood and youth. Generations repeat the steps: as children they are bonded; as young adults they buy or win their release; as mature adults (thirty or thirty-five years is middle-aged in India) they face growing economic pressures—illnesses, weddings and funerals, crop failures, housing needs, alcohol addiction. At the same time that financial need increases, they find their earning power decreasing, as the years of childhood labor take their toll on physical strength and capability. The moneylender-employer offers an advance for the rights to the parent's child, the advance is accepted, and the cycle begins anew.

. . . .

Employer abuse

Punishment is common for a variety of infractions: arriving late, working slowly, making a mistake in the work, talking to other workers—even missing work because of illness can lead to punishment. With very few exceptions, the children we interviewed all complained of being beaten and severely scolded. The beatings consisted of being hit, usually by the agent's open hand, on the arms or head. A few children reported being beaten by sticks on their arms. The children clearly resent and fear their agents as a result of this verbal and physical mistreatment, and the emotional damage of long-term abuse was much in evidence. Other researchers have found more extreme examples of abuse at the hands of employers. Until the early 1990s, the matchbox-under-the-chin form of compulsion and control was quite common, and even measures such as chaining children in place were not unusual. As recently as 1993, a social worker found a fourteen-year-old beedi roller who was kept shackled in leg irons. The boy, who had been bonded for 2,000 rupees, had once attempted to escape, and his employer had kept him in shackles ever since. Although these forms of abuse have decreased significantly in villages where social activists have been working to increase public awareness, there is no evidence to suggest the practices have changed significantly in more remote villages, where outside intervention has not taken place.

Health hazards

Kumar: "Rolling beedi is so hard. We sit all day. My back hurts. I want to be able to play."

Beedi is one of the twenty-five industries classified by the Child Labour (Prohibition and Regulation) Act as hazardous. Beedi rollers suffer chronic back pain from sitting hunched over their work all day. The long hours of maintaining this unnatural position sometimes interfere with normal growth patterns, causing stunted growth or physical deformities among those who spend their childhoods rolling beedi. As adults, these children will be restricted in the types of work they are physically able to do; they will not be able to perform hard manual labor and may in fact be restricted to beedi rolling for their entire productive lives. Large muscle groups are neglected and atrophy during years of sitting six and a half days a week, for twelve or more hours a day. In the words of one local beedi activist, the children grow up "small, puny, and malnourished."

. . . .

SILK

The production of silk thread and the silk saris woven from that thread is historically one of India's most important industries. The saris, worn by many Indian women, range from relatively affordable basic saris to the intricate and expensive ceremonial, wedding, and *haute couture* saris. The latter are painstakingly handwoven of domestically-produced silk thread and adorned with elaborate designs woven in gold thread. Two Indian cities, Varanasi in the north and Kanchipuram in the south, are famous for their elegant silk saris. A moderate Kanchipuram silk sari sells for about two hundred U.S. dollars—more than the annual wage of India's poorest quarter, and a hefty amount for even the most solidly middle class.

India is the world's second largest producer of silk, but India only accounts for 5 percent of the global silk market. This market share was still enough to generate approximately $260 million in revenues during 1995. Germany, the largest consumer of Indian silk, imported DM 540 million ($231 million) in 1995. The bulk of Indian silk thread and silk cloth, however, are consumed domestically.

. . . .

It is not unusual for children as young as five to begin working in the silk industry. Some work alongside their bonded parents, assisting them as they weave fine saris. Others are contracted out to silk twisting factories or work locally as silk reelers, pulling the fine threads off the boiling cocoons. Still others are bonded to employers of relatively modest means, who may have only two looms in their houses and their own children working alongside the bonded children. All of these children earn very low wages, typically ten rupees a day or less, suffer occupational hazards and the threat of employer abuse, and are not free to leave their employer for whatever reason. They are, in the words of one researcher, "cage-birds ... condemned from their very birth to be captive workers ..."

Silk reeling

. . . . Reeling is the process by which the silk filaments are pulled off the cocoon. The cocoons are cooked in boiling water in order to loosen the sericin, a natural substance holding the filaments together. The reeler dips his or her hands into the scalding water and palpates the cocoons, judging by touch whether the fine threads of silk have loosened enough to be unwound. When they are ready, the worker finds the ends of eight to ten filaments and gently begins to reel them off. The average length of a single unbroken filament is 700 meters.

More than 80 percent of silk reelers are under twenty years of age, with most of them between ten and fifteen years old. As in other industries, the myth of children having natural advantages and skills is used to justify the exploitation of young girls and boys in this dangerous work. This myth is perpetuated not just by the employers of the children, but by society as a whole, including the educated elite. As one writer put it, "[m]uch of the manual work ... requires skills and a delicate touch, for which the supple hands of children are regarded as more suitable." The children are not permitted to use spoons instead of their hands when checking the boiling cocoons, on the theory that their hands can more easily discern when the threads are ready to reel.

. . . .

Silk twisting

Silk twisting (or twining) is the process whereby individual silk threads are twisted into a strong multi-ply thread. Twisting usually takes place in small factories with between fifty and a few hundred spindles. These factories utilize bonded child labor. In one *Taluk* (subdivision of a district) alone, there are about one hundred twining factories, together employing more than 8,000 children, all of them believed to be bonded.

The children tend to the spindles, fitting them with thread, correcting deviations, and performing other routine tasks. Many of the factories seen by Human Rights Watch were dark and stuffy, with doors shut and windows barred, filled with the deafening racket of the clacking machines.

. . . .

Work Conditions and Health Hazards of Silk Reeling and Twisting

As a consequence of the constant immersion in scalding water, the skin on the hands of the child silk reelers becomes raw, blistered, and sometimes infected. As one team of investigators described it, "thousands of children work in these factories, with hands that seem to belong to ninety year olds." In addition to the skin ailments, reelers frequently suffer from respiratory problems, caused by the constant inhaling of the sericin vapors.

The workers in the silk twisting factories suffer pain in their legs and backs from standing all day without rest. Some of them develop leg deformities over the years, including bowleggedness. The boys and girls also suffer occasional injuries—mainly cuts—from the machines, particularly to their hands and fingers. Many children mentioned injuries severe enough to warrant medical attention and prevent further work by the victims.

Employer Abuses in Silk Reeling and Twisting

Abuses common to other bonded industries are found in silk production as well: verbal abuse, including threats and harsh language; physical abuse in the form of blows for arriving late, working slowly, or annoying the employer; and physical abuse by denying the children adequate rest and recovery time.

Girl factory workers also suffer from sexual abuse at the hands of their employers. Girls are preferred by owners because they are believed to be more obedient, docile, and submissive. According to the activists and investigators in the area, girls are also frequently targeted for sexual assault by the owners inside the factories. The practice is so prevalent that it is difficult for these girls to get married when the time comes. Because of the high rate of abuse, everyone assumes that the factory girls have been "touched," that is, molested or raped by their employers.

. . . .

LEATHER

[Similarly dire conditions for child laborers in the leather industry are described.]

HANDWOVEN WOOL CARPETS

The Indian carpet industry is notorious for its exploitation of child workers. Reports of severe abuse have been surfacing from the northern Indian "carpet-belt" since the mid-

1980s. Despite the industry's claims that only small numbers of children work the carpet looms, and these under good conditions, frequent reports by journalists, academics, government commissions, and child welfare specialists continue to provide the dark details of bondage and savage mistreatment doled out by many carpet manufacturers.

On January 26, 1996, a New Delhi newspaper reported on the rescue of twenty-three bonded laborers by the Bonded Labor Liberation Front, one of the leading social activist organizations working on this issue. The children reported that they were forced to knot carpets eighteen hours a day and were beaten if they fell asleep or complained. They were given two poor meals a day, but never enough to satisfy them, "because if we ate to our fill we would feel sleepy." One of the boys was lashed with a whip; another hit so hard with a metal tool that he had to have the gash stitched closed; a third was burned with cigarettes when he asked about his parents. The news account ends with the boys' desires for the future, reporting that "[a]ll the younger boys want to be policemen, since they believe no one can hurt a policeman." News stories such as this appear frequently.

There are 300,000 children working to produce India's fine carpets. Ninety percent of these children, or about 270,000, are bonded laborers. In the carpet belt of Uttar Pradesh, where most of India's carpets are woven, the vast majority of the workers are low-caste Hindu boys. The number of girls in their ranks is increasing, however, as more children are brought in from Nepal or recruited to work in other states.

Built on the backs of these children, the carpet industry is one of India's most lucrative. Carpet exports totaled more than half a billion dollars in 1994 and reached $650 million in 1995. Germany and the United States are the two largest importers of Indian carpets, accounting for about 73 percent of the export market. Britain, Japan, and other industrialized countries also import significant amounts of the carpets. Other major importers of Indian carpets are Switzerland, Canada, Japan, Sweden, Australia, France, and Italy.

India's carpet industrialists claim to be suffering from "the negative propaganda" of Indian and international nongovernmental organizations, who have been raising the issue of abusive child labor practices for several years. To date, however, the growing international awareness of the carpet industry's abuse of children has had little effect on carpet exports and earnings. The industry, which already accounts for 2.5 percent of India's total annual exports, experienced a growth rate of 11 percent in 1994—a fall from previous years but nonetheless robust. There are currently more than 2,000 carpet exporters in India, representing a one hundred-fold increase in less than two decades.

. . . .

Conditions of Work and Health Hazards

Children work an average of ten to fourteen hours a day, six and a half or seven days a week. Again, this frequently does not apply to the trafficked migrant children, who report being forced to work as long as sixteen or even eighteen hours on a daily basis. The loom sheds are often poorly ventilated, poorly lighted, and cramped.

The long days spent in cramped positions damage the children's backs and legs, causing backaches and severe joint pain. Many of the children suffer from scabies, skin ulcers and other dermatological diseases, a result of the close and crowded conditions and the constant exposure to wool. Respiratory illnesses are rampant and eye damage is common, as are intestinal disorders. The children are also particularly vulnerable to tuberculosis and other lung diseases, which are caused and aggravated by the constant inhalation of tiny wool fibers.

Work-caused cuts and wounds are endemic and frequently become infected. When cuts occur, the loom-owners will "treat" the wounds so that the children can continue working without dripping blood on the carpets. This "treatment" consists of scraping the sulphur from match heads into the cuts and then lighting them on fire, thereby sealing the wound.

By the time the youngsters reach their mid-teens, their fingers and hands often are badly damaged from the cuts and nicks of the knives and strings used in knotting, their eyesight has grown weak from long hours of tedious work in dark rooms, and their growth often is stunted by years of sitting in uncomfortable, hunched positions at the looms.

In addition to their long hours on the loom, migrant child laborers are always subject to the demands of their master, often forced to work for the master around his house or in the field, performing whatever jobs he demands of them.

Employer Abuses

As in other industries, employers tend to treat the bonded child laborers harshly. One study of child weavers found that 71 percent reported being beaten for mistakes in weaving, and beaten even more severely if they asked for their wages or tried to escape. The following comments from Munni, a nine-year-old former carpet weaver, were echoed by the majority of children speaking to Human Rights Watch.

I got beaten if I arrived late or if I made a mistake; he was constantly abusing me. He hit me on the back and on my hand. I worked with three other children, and he hit them also. If I did not go to work, he would come to my house and catch me and beat me.

As mentioned, the migrant children suffer the worst abuses, with numerous reports of them being hit, tied up in trees, half-starved, and otherwise punished. Dozens of children taken to the looms of the carpet belt have later been reported missing, sold, or dead.

Tasleem, a seven-year-old with eyes that still shine in a hollow, emaciated face, longs to return to Bihar, her home. "Once when I cried for my mother, the mill owner hit me with a steel rod," she recalls.

Ninety-five percent of the carpet workers in the carpet belt are boys, and sexual abuse is not a common complaint. As girls begin to enter this workforce in larger numbers, however, reports of such abuse are surfacing.

....

Notes and Questions

1. The Human Rights Watch report implies that certain social myths contribute to the prevalence of bonded child labor. If this is true, can we expect international conventions or national legislation to be effective in eradicating the practice? The report also blames the Indian government for failure to protect bonded child laborers. What incentives might the government have for maintaining the bonded labor system?

———————

The article that follows describes the elaborate legal provisions governing child labor in India, and explores why these laws have made so little impact on the problem. In Neil Browne's vision, India passes legislation against child labor and has national judges acutely aware of the child labor problem. Yet, despite these positive developments, children continue to be engaged in labor across India. As with other writers, Browne seems unable to reach any definite conclusion as to why India has been so unsuccessful in its attempts to eradicate even the worst forms of child labor.

M. Neil Browne, et. al., *Universal Moral Principles and the Law: The Failure of One-Size Fits All Child Labor Laws*

27 Houston Journal of International Law 1 (2004)

....

India gained independence in 1947 and the Indian Constitution came into existence on November 26, 1949. Provisions were made within the Constitution to protect children from exploitation and early employment. Article 23 of the Indian Constitution prohibits the trafficking of human beings and forced labor. Article 24 states: "No child below the age of 14 shall be employed to work in any factory or mine or be engaged in any hazardous employment." Other articles intended for the welfare of children, protecting their freedom and dignity against exploitation, were also included in the Constitution. Furthermore, a provision was made for free and compulsory education for children.

To uphold the provisions made in the Constitution, several pieces of legislation were enacted in the years following independence. The first major act after independence was the Factories Act of 1948, restricting the age of employment to fourteen years. Legal judgments made in conjunction with the Factories Act added further restrictions to child labor. Then, the Plantation Labour Act of 1951 prohibited the employment of children under the age of twelve on plantations. Children over twelve were allowed to work based on a certificate of fitness by a doctor. The Mines Act of 1952, the Merchant Shipping Act of 1958, the Motor Transport Workers Act of 1961, the Apprentices Act of 1961, the Atomic Energy Act of 1962, and the Beedi & Cigar Workers Act of 1966 are other statutes concerning child labor in specific occupations. They were all aimed at addressing the different sectors of the economy where child labor existed.

The most comprehensive of all child labor laws passed in India is the Child Labour (Prohibition and Regulation) Act of 1986 (CLPRA). The beginnings of this Act could be traced to a nongovernmental organization based in Bangalore, India. This group argued that "poverty was the main cause of child labour and that, therefore, the attempt should be to regulate the conditions under which children work rather than prohibit such work." This argument resulted in widespread discussions between two groups of activists: While one supported the regulation of child labor, the other insisted that prohibition would be the only solution to the problem. Prior to the creation of the Act, "the Child Labour (Prohibition and Regulation) Bill was introduced in both houses of Parliament" with the following statement of objects and reason:

> There are a number of Acts which prohibit the employment of children below 14 years and 15 years in certain specified employments. However, there is no procedure laid down in any law for deciding in which employments, occupations or processes the employment of children should be banned. There is no law to regulate the working conditions of children in most of the employments where they are not prohibited from working and are under exploitative conditions.

The introduction of this Bill generated a debate in the Indian Parliament with some members voicing their apprehensions and reservations with regards to different aspects of the Bill. Even so, the CLPRA was passed in 1986, and it continues to be the principal enactment on the issue of employment of children. This Act does not call for an outright ban on child labor, but instead permits employment of children in industries that are not specified in the Act. Although the Act has been criticized for the above reason, it must be noted that the attempt to contextually address the problem of child labor in India is evident in this Act.

In the year following the passing of the CLPRA, the Government of India announced a National Child Labour Policy, following which a project-based plan of action was adopted. Some industries were identified to promote non-formal education for children, employment, and income generation schemes for poor parents of working children. These projects now constitute seventy-six industries, a big step from the initial nine. The individual projects have been largely effective in removing child labor from hazardous industries and rehabilitating them, while improving the socioeconomic conditions that prevail in these industries.

A large network of Non-Governmental Organizations (NGOs) work in close association with the National Child Labour Projects as well as with child labor projects initiated by the ILO and other organizations. These NGOs work at the grassroots level and are able to initiate programs that improve the lot of working children on a far more interactive basis. The challenge faced by most organizations, however, is their limited scope and resources. Nevertheless, these organizations are an important part of the movement against child labor in India. Furthermore, they are the breeding grounds for social activism and community awareness. These organizations help garner support and initiate legal action against businesses that continue to exploit child labor.

Not only have efforts of this kind helped defend the rights of the poor and voiceless, they have also encouraged wide-ranging interpretations of the various legal and constitutional provisions. For instance, in M.C. Mehta v. State of Tamil Nadu, the noted social activist M.C. Mehta sought to improve the conditions of the children working in the match and fireworks industries of Sivakasi, Tamil Nadu. The Supreme Court of India decided that the employers offending the CLPRA must be required to pay compensation for every child employed in contravention of the Act. Furthermore, the Court suggested that the parents of the children employed in hazardous conditions be provided with employment so as to compensate for the prospective lost income of the child. While the Supreme Court judgment was considered a landmark in the movement against child labor, the situation in Sivakasi, Tamilnadu has not vastly improved.

B. The Causes and Contexts of Perpetual Child Labor in India

. . . .

Although a lot has changed since ancient times, it is still not uncommon to find children working in most parts of India. Numerous studies have been conducted investigating the extent and conditions of child labor in India. Estimates suggest that approximately eleven million children in India work full-time. Child labor is essentially a rural phenomenon with "[c]ultivation, agricultural labour, forestry and fisheries account[ing] for 84.9 per cent of child labour." "In urban areas, [the children work in] manufacturing, service and repairs." The factories (registered manufacturing units) account for a very small percentage of child labor; child labor, in rural, semi-urban and urban areas is almost entirely a feature of the informal and unorganized sectors.

Moreover, studies indicate that the incidence of child labor in various states is highly correlated to the level of poverty. Not only is poverty a direct cause of child labor, poverty is also the genesis of many other causes of child labor. For instance, the demand for child labor often originates on account of the low profit margins of the small firms in the unorganized, informal sector. As we examine the other aspects of child labor in India, the thread of poverty linking all of the causes becomes apparent.

An essential feature of the informal sector is the lack of technology and automation implying the non-requirement of highly skilled workers. The low skill requirement increases the substitutability of adults with children in the workforce. This substitution is made more attractive by the low wages that are paid to children. In what forms a vicious cycle, the low wages paid to children further depress the adult wage, consequently reducing adults' incentive to work. Unemployed parents send their children out to work so as to augment the now impoverished family income. Furthermore, the low levels of technology imply easy entry into the industry, leading to high levels of competition and, hence, lower profit margins that only discourage any incentive to upgrade to better technologies. Even if manufacturers could invest in laborsaving technology, child labor still remains the cheapest form of production.

. . . .

Most of the industries are organized on a tier basis. The manufacturer or exporter contracts the production out to small production units or workshops, which in turn employ workers and laborers more often than not on a piece-rate system. This structure allows for the presence of many middlemen and contractors and therefore a profit-maker at each level. More often than not, the employers of child labor cannot afford to employ adults because of the marginal profits they make. Although the informal sector does not constitute formal workplaces, such as large factories, it is not representative of household production units either. Consequently, a large number of women who participated in the production processes earlier as part of the household are now displaced from the labor force because of the social stigmatization faced by women working outside the house. This effect causes parents to send children to work to make up for the lost income.

Societal pressures have worked in more ways than in the displacement of women from the work force to encourage the use of child labor. In a society that is largely illiterate and unaware of the benefits of education, the emphasis on child labor is far greater. While some parents suggest that a child going to work will stay out of trouble, others see no merit in educating their children who will ultimately have to work in a field doing work that does not require any formal education. Furthermore, the poor health facilities combined with the poor nutrition in poverty stricken areas greatly decrease life expectancy rates. Often children have to assume the responsibility of the breadwinner because of the ill health, or in some cases, the demise of a parent who is more often than not the father. Religious preferences, especially in the case of Muslims, also seem influential in the decision to send children to work.

. . . .

Although inadequate law enforcement and lack of political zeal have often been cited as the main causes for persistence of child labor in India, even by many who are well aware of the conditions that surround child labor, these causes conceal a much more complicated scenario. Furthermore, the success that the U.S. child labor laws have achieved might not be replicable in India given the vast differences in context.

C. The Failure of Child Labor Laws in India

. . . .

While passing legislation may be an approach that has been successful in removing child labor in developed nations like the United States, the same may not be true for a developing nation like India.

. . . .

Most developing nations such as India agree that the worst forms of child labor should be banned and have national laws that make illegal such forms as prostitution, employment in hazardous industries, and bonded labor. However, these nations cannot be expected to establish labor standards equivalent to those in the developed world. These standards have been established only recently in the developed world and were definitely not in existence when these nations were at a stage of development comparable to that of developing nations today.

Developing nations and some economists argue that the prevalence of child labor reflects a stage of a nation's economic development. To take this argument further, the developed world has also undergone a period of heavy use of industrial child labor. One economist observes:

> We know of no case where a nation developed a modern manufacturing sector without first going through a "sweat shop" phase. How long ago was it that children could be found working in the textile factories of Lowell, Massachusetts, of Manchester, England, or of Osaka, Japan? Should the developing economies of today be any different? If child labor is a necessary evil of industrialization, then a nation should be judged on how quickly it passes through this phase.

Those who believe that the use of child labor is part and parcel of economic development suggest that the only solution is for developing nations to pass through this stage of development as quickly as possible. Thus, the demands made of developing nations to abolish child labor may be premature and even harmful in that their pace of development may be hindered, slowing their rise out of poverty, and thereby removing the foremost cause of child labor.

Yet another argument put forth by developing nations is the lack of resources to address the problem of child labor. Not only do developing nations have to enforce laws regulating child labor, resources also have to be funneled into alternatives to work, such as schooling and vocational training, so as to make the shift from work a lucrative one for children and their families. Lack of adequate resources make it difficult for developing nations to use this multi-pronged approach to removing child labor.

Even so, many within the developed world, frustrated by the marked increase in child labor in the developing world, are afraid that developing nations are exploiting children in a way that cannot be redressed by development alone. Moreover, they argue that globalization is one of the prominent causes for child labor and, therefore, the same system of world trade should apply standards to curb the use of child labor. Thus, the setting for a linkage between world trade and labor standards is created. The developing world has traditionally been wary of such a linkage.

This controversy of associating child labor standards with trade is further fueled by the conflict of free trade and protectionism. While developing nations argue that the low cost of child labor constitutes a comparative advantage, which the world trade system should respect, developed nations argue that these lower costs are a means of illegitimate protectionism.

Developing nations worry that these low cost advantages may be prematurely liquidated by the imposition of labor standards through trade and may not whole-heartedly support the child labor movement, fearing the possible repercussions and disadvantages to their own nations. Thus, the linkage recommended by the developed world may actually work in contradiction to the child labor movement by jeopardizing the welfare of child laborers.

Attempts to remove child labor may not work as intended, and although the international child labor movement is well intentioned, care must be taken to avoid situations wherein the welfare of children is actually jeopardized by legal action intended to assist them. While there might be universal acceptance that child labor is morally reprehensible, the approach to resolve the issue is not through overarching laws or trade restrictions banning child labor, but rather a more contextual approach identifying and addressing the causes and contexts within which child labor flourishes.

Notes and Questions

1. Would forcing India to eliminate any form, or even the worst forms, of child labor constitute the 'Westernization' or 'Americanization' of a political and economic system that cannot yet function without child labor? The reading suggests that the local labor inspectors are burdened by long hours and subject to bribery. Would a total overhaul of this aspect of the labor system (more inspectors with better training, strict punishment for accepting bribes, etc.) enhance enforcement of child labor laws? Would sanctions against employers who utilized child labor be useful in protecting laboring children, or cause them further harm?

2. Are economists right in arguing that every developing nation has to go through a child labour "phase" on the way towards development; or is this another way to try to justify, or at least partly excuse, child labor?

3. How much of the Indian bonded labor problem appears to rest on governmental complicity, and how much is social and historical in nature? Note that India has still not ratified either the Minimum Age or Worst Forms of Child Labor Conventions. Why might that be?

———————

Ranjan K. Aharwal, *The Barefoot Lawyers: Prosecuting Child Labour in the Supreme Court of India*
21 Arizona Journal of International and Comparative Law 663 (2004)

. . . .

B. Legislation and Policy

. . . .

2. Targeting Systemic Problems

The child labour regime in India does not target systemic problems, including caste, religion and tradition. These systemic issues may also be related to the apathy of government officials responsible for enforcing minimum age laws. In Varanasi, the majority of child workers are Muslims or from the scheduled castes and scheduled tribes. In addition, families without land are less likely to send their children to school than families with land. Even amongst the families with land, the "advanced" castes are more likely to send their children to school. In rural communities, Muslim families and scheduled caste families are more likely to earn a poor and irregular income. Children from these groups are more likely to be at work.

Children from poor families suffer other biases. Their ability to learn is considered substandard as compared to that of children from middle-class families: "A distinction … between children as 'hands' and children as 'minds'; that is between the child who must be taught to 'work' and the child who must be taught to 'learn,' the acquisition of manual skills as distinct from cognitive skills." The Hindu concept of class and social ranking compounds this stereotype and it can inform attitudes about child labour and education. In the space of a few generations, low caste and poor Indians enter a cycle of poverty and illiteracy. Since children from poor families must be "taught to work," they often abandon school and join the workforce.

Another problematic attitude is the belief that an education, however limited, inculcates in children a preference for white-collar, urban jobs. These jobs are highly valued amongst rural families as they provide an assured income and prestige. In recent years, there has been increased competition for these jobs, resulting in underemployment and unemployment. As such, middle-class government officials believe the competition for these jobs must be culled. Their concern is that the semi-educated, when unemployed, are more likely to be exploited by radical political groups seeking to destabilize India's social and political system. As Weiner notes, "a high dropout rate in the schools can be regarded as contributing to social stability." At the same time, government officials believe that children from rural families can gain valuable skills, attitudes, and work habits by being employed at a young age. Even if only a small portion of bureaucrats hold these beliefs, there is a strong impetus for rural and poor children to enter the workforce at an early age.

. . . .

V. THE SUPREME COURT'S RESPONSE TO CHILD LABOUR

This section is an examination of the response of the Supreme Court of India to the problem of child labour. In two decisions, the Supreme Court of India attempted to tackle the failings of the legislation and the overarching problem of poverty. Though the Court could be criticized for not closing the loopholes in the legislation, its orders are still an activist approach to guaranteeing fundamental rights for Indian child labourers.

A. The Situation in Sivakasi

Sivakasi is the home of India's match and fireworks industries. . . .

Information on the number of child workers in Sivakasi is difficult to find. The 1991 census estimates thirty thousand child labourers between the ages of six and fourteen in Sivakasi. In 1994–95, the State of Tamil Nadu and UNICEF sponsored a joint study on child labour. This study revealed thirty-three thousand child labourers—three thousand in the fireworks industry and thirty thousand in the match industry.

Attention has been drawn to the industry and the employment of children by NGOs, the media, trade unions, and academics in addition to well-publicized accidents involving child workers. In 1976, a bus full of child workers employed in the match industry turned over, injuring many of the children. In 1981, an accident at the Aruna Fireworks factory in Mettupatti killed thirty-two workers, including children. These incidents prompted the Tamil Nadu government to study the issue. In 1976, a government committee, chaired by Harbans Singh, recommended the amelioration, rather than abolition, of child labour. The committee argued that abolition would negatively affect the families of child labourers and the welfare of the match and fireworks industries. In 1983, Land Reforms Commissions N. Haribhasker chaired another government committee recommending a similar approach to that of Singh.

Though these reports were well received by child labour opponents and government officials, the state failed to act on their recommendations. This inaction prompted a writ petition by Indian lawyer and social activist M.C. Mehta in 1983. The Supreme Court of India has responded to Mehta twice, in 1990 and again in 1993. On both occasions, the

Court has sympathized with the plight of child labourers in Sivakasi and attempted to craft a remedy to protect their rights and livelihood.

B. The Court's 1991 Judgment

Mehta's 1983 petition was first resolved by the Supreme Court of India in 1990. Mehta argued that the employment of children in the match and fireworks industry in Sivakasi was a violation of India's Constitution, the Factories Act, the Minimum Wages Act, and the Employment of Children Act. M.H. Kania, held that "employment of children within the match factories directly connected with the manufacturing process upto [sic] final production of match sticks and fireworks should not at all be permitted." The Court found that the employment of children in the production of matches and fireworks violated the spirit of the Constitution of India, in particular its Directive Principles.... [T]he Directive Principles cannot be enforced in any court of law. Nonetheless, it appears from the decision that the Supreme Court relied on articles 39(f) and 45 in making their final order.

The order had five elements. First, in line with the Constitution's prohibition on the employment of children in hazardous employment, the Court said that "children can, therefore, be employed in the process of packing but packing should be done in an area away from the place of manufacture to avoid exposure to accident." The Court acknowledged that the Directive Principles recommend that children should be in school until the age of fourteen, but "economic necessity forces grown up children to seek employment."

Second, the Court ordered that children be paid sixty percent of "prescribed minimum wage for an adult employee in the factories doing the same job." The Court stated that if the state should feel that a higher wage is viable, this decision "should not stand in the way."

Third, the Court believes that special education facilities (both formal and job training), recreation and socialization should be made to provide for the quality of life of working children. To pay for these facilities, the Court ordered the creation of a welfare fund, to which registered match factories would be made to contribute. Upon the recommendation of the counsel for the State of Tamil Nadu, the Court also ordered that the government should make a matching grant to the fund.

Fourth, the Supreme Court ordered the State of Tamil Nadu to provide "facilities for recreation and medical attention." These facilities were to include "provision of a basic diet during the working period and medical care with a view to ensuring sound physical growth." It was recommended that the state work with UNICEF in making these facilities available.

Finally, the Court ordered the creation of a compulsory insurance scheme for both adults and children employed in the Sivakasi match factories. All employees were to be insured for fifty thousand rupees, and the premiums were to be paid for by the employer. The Court concluded its decision by awarding Mehta three thousand rupees in costs.

In some quarters, this decision is not progressive enough and, in fact, incorrect at law. The Factories Act states: "No child who has not completed his fourteenth year shall be required or allowed to work in any factory." It is unclear how the Supreme Court reconciled this prohibition on work "in any factory" with its decision to allow children to work in factories, provided they are packing matches, and not manufacturing them.

The other concern is that the Court appeared to give credence to the "nimble fingers" theory of children's work. It stated: "We take note of the fact that the tender hands of the young workers are more suited to sorting out the manufactured product and process it for the purposes of packing." This nimble fingers theory has been criticized by a number of human rights organizations, including Human Rights Watch: "In this view, child labor is not an evil, but a production necessity. This rationalization is a lie. In fact, children make the cheaper goods; only master weavers make the best quality carpets and saris."

Finally, the Court did not create a disincentive for employers violating the law or its order. Though the Court emphasized that employers must play a role in maintaining the well-being of children at work, either through an insurance scheme or contributing to the welfare fund, it did not even mention the possible penalties they might incur for either failing to pay children a minimum wage or employing children in the manufacturing process.

These issues notwithstanding, this decision was an important first-step in protecting the rights of India's child labours. The Court recognized that poverty is the main incentive for children to enter the workforce. By ordering employers to pay these children a minimum wage and to ensure that they are insured, the Court attempted to protect against the exploitation of child workers. The order regarding the welfare fund and the facilities for recreation and medical attention was an attempt to balance the children's need to work with the Constitution's requirements that they enjoy a suitable standard of living. The Supreme Court of India could have banned child labour outright. Its failure to do so is indicative of the Court's respect for the constitutional separation of powers. Though the judiciary has, as discussed above, made policy through its PIL orders, it is loath to order the enactment of legislation. Instead, the Court in this case hoped to quell (sidestep?) the problem by using existing statutory means.

C. The Court Revisits the Issue of Child Labour

Not surprisingly, the Supreme Court of India revisited the issue of child labour in 1997. In 1991, after an accident at a Sivakasi firecracker factory, the Supreme Court took suo moto cognizance of the issue of child labour. It ordered that compensation be paid to the victims of the accident and created a three-person committee to investigate and make recommendations regarding child labour in Sivakasi.

. . . .

Before making its order regarding the Committee's recommendations, the Court reviewed the problem of child labour in India. Its summary is the most comprehensive evaluation of this issue. Most importantly, it expanded its order to include not only the fireworks and match factories in Sivakasi, but also all industries in India employing children. It held: "We have, therefore, thought it fit to travel beyond the confines of Sivakasi to which place this petition initially related. In our view, it would be more appropriate to deal with the issue in wider spectrum and broader perspective taking it as a national problem and not appertaining to any one region of the country." Unlike the 1991 decision, this order was meant to apply to all employers across India.

The Court relied on India's Constitution, India's international commitments, and domestic legislation as the basis for its decision. Article 24 of India's Constitution, which prohibits the employment of children in hazardous employment, is a fundamental right. The Court also found that Article 45, the provision for free and compulsory education, "has been raised to a high pedestal." In addition, the Court also relied upon Article 39(e) (protection of the health and strength of workers), Article 41 (right to work, to education and to public assistance in certain cases) and Article 47 (duty of the state to raise the level of nutrition and the standard of living and to improve public health) in making its decision. These provisions are Directive Principles and "it is the duty of all the organs of the state (a la Article 37) to apply these principles."

In regards to international commitments, the Court noted that India is a party to the Convention on the Rights of the Child. In its instrument of accession to the Convention, India undertook: "to take measures to progressively implement the provisions of Article 32, particularly paragraph 2(a), in accordance with its national legislation and relevant international instruments to which it is a State Party." Article 32 of the Convention states that state parties shall take action to provide for a minimum age for admission to employment, as well as to regulate the hours and conditions of employment and sanction employers that violate such provisions.

The Supreme Court then detailed the legislative history regarding the issue of child labour. It concluded: "The legislature has strongly desired prohibition of child labour." In particular, it analyzed the Child Labour Act. The Court noted that the Act provides for punishments up to one year or a fine of up to twenty thousand rupees. Nonetheless, the Court said, "it is common experience that child labour continues to be employed." It took note of the loopholes in the Act, including that children can work if they are part of a family of labour. The Court also noted that the Act, unlike the Constitution or other labour laws, does not use the word "hazardous" anywhere. To the Court, the implication is that "children may continue to work in those processes not involving chemicals." Beyond failures in the Act, the Court also identified causes of child labour. To the Court, poverty is the "basic reason which compels parents of a child, despite their unwillingness, to get it employed.... Otherwise, no parents, especially no mother, would like that a tender aged child should toil in a factory in a difficult condition, instead of it enjoying its childhood at home under the paternal gaze." This concern about poverty informed the Court's ultimate order. Rather than absolutely prohibiting child labour, the Court sought to regulate it so as to protect the dignity and the standard of living of working children. It stated: "... till an alternative income is assured to the family, the question of abolition of child labour would really remain a will-o-the wisp."

Notes and Questions

1. Human Rights Watch points to Indian customs and attitudes as a central aspect of the phenomenon of child labor. Their reports indicate that the legislative regime fails to capture the prejudice that leads to social acceptance of bonded labor in particular. On the other hand, the discussion by Ranjan Ahrwal, immediately above, of the Indian Supreme Court's approach to child labor indicates that the Indian judiciary has a progressive and human rights oriented side that provides a substantial outlet for airing grievances relating to child labor. Does there seem to be a clash between different branches of government with regard to child labor?

2. India's National Human Rights Commission has expressed its dissatisfaction with enforcement of child labor standards. See *More Convictions Essential to Tackle Bonded Labor*, The Hindu, (Feb. 18, 2006) (available at http://www.hindu.com/2006/02/18/stories/2006021814490300.htm). The Special Rapporteur of the Commission is quoted in this article as saying that the government's Labour Department "should pursue suspicious deaths of domestic child labour." He decried the "social evil" of the system of bonded labour in India, and faulted the authorities for failure to act against "atrocities" committed against bonded laborers.

––––––––––

Despite the rapid modernization of Indian in recent years, it seems that there is still no social or political consensus on the question of child labor. The news item below reports on an Indian law that restricts child labor in certain sectors, particularly domestic service. What seems to have motivated the new law?

Amelia Gentleman, *Indian Ban on Child Labor: Who Will Clean the Houses?*

International Herald Tribune, September 12, 2006, *available at* http://www.iht.com/articles/2006/09/06/news/letter.php

NEW DELHI Of course, it's really not done—to talk about it too much in polite society, but India's middle-class families have a most inconvenient problem looming over their domestic staffing arrangements.

A ban on child domestic workers will come into force next month, making it illegal to hire children under 14 in the home—with punishment of up to two years' imprisonment for employers found breaking the law.

This leaves hundreds of thousands of families wondering how they will ever replace the timidly subservient (and remarkably cheap) child maids, nannies and cleaners who prop up their households.

It is not just these employers who view the legal development with consternation.

Human rights activists have been campaigning for decades for an amendment of India's Child Labor Act, first passed in 1986.

The campaigners wanted domestic work, and serving in roadside restaurants and hotels, to be added to a list of 57 professions classified "hazardous" and therefore unsuitable for children.

But when the government finally made a change in early August, children's charities then complained that it was mere tweaking, rather than an outright ban. At best, they said, little would change; at worst, life could even get harder for the children.

Children over 14, some noted, would still receive no protection under the law.

"Who are we kidding?" asked The Hindustan Times in an editorial, arguing that the ban would just give police officers a new chance to collect bribes in exchange for turning a blind eye to abuses.

"What worries me is that it is very easy to ban things. What happens next is much more difficult," said Rita Panicker, director of a rehabilitation center for child workers in New Delhi.

"Unscrupulous middle-class employers will start throwing out their child workers because they're scared the police may come, and God only knows what will happen to the children. As usual, the employer will get off scot-free."

There is uncertainty over how the government proposes to enforce the ban.

No one knows how many children work as badly paid domestic servants, although it is clear that the phenomenon has been growing fast in urban India, as extended family structures dissolve and working women look for extra help at home.

The government estimates that, overall, India has 12.6 million child workers (although nongovernmental organizations believe the figures is closer to 40 million), of whom somewhere around a million may be employed in homes and restaurants.

Quite what will happen on Oct. 12 is unclear.

Will there be raids on private houses? What will the police do with a sudden influx of hundreds of thousands of liberated children? How will they be reunited with their families? Will new schools be built for them?

The government, activists claim, has not given proper thought to these questions.

The effectiveness of existing legislation offers little scope for optimism. Since 1986, the law has anyway failed to stop children working in factories, mines and textile workshops, and there have been few prosecutions.

Periodically, aggressive action is taken by the police to arrest employers but these high-profile operations tend to backfire.

A few months ago, about 500 boys aged between 5 and 15 were rounded up in televised raids on embroidery workshops across Delhi.

No one could decide what to do with the children once they had been freed, so they were locked up in an empty shopping mall for a week, traumatized and miserable, until the authorities found temporary shelter for them.

The harshest criticism leveled at the government is that its actions are cosmetic, with no parallel attempt to address the root problems that prompt children to take up work in India—acute poverty and lousy educational opportunities.

There is no point freeing children from employment if their families have no viable alternative source of income, campaigners say, because they will simply find themselves new work.

If the ban is to be effective, then the government must intensify its schemes to reduce rural poverty, and offer better opportunities to convince parents and children that it really is worth staying in school.

India has signed the UN's Convention on the Rights of the Child, but qualified its commitment to introducing a full ban instantly, arguing that with so many children in work in India this was unrealistic and impractical.

Harjot Kaur, director of child labor within the Ministry of Labor and Employment, pleaded for patience: "Child labor is not a problem that you can resolve overnight. It is not that today you come up with an act and tomorrow it is eradicated. This is a gradual process."

International aid workers may squirm, but, as a recent report by the Carnegie Council on Ethics and International Affairs carefully noted, in Europe "child labor did not disappear abruptly but gradually," over the course of about 150 years. Reducing poverty, the report added, was essential.

Hervé Berger, senior specialist with the International Labor Organization, suggested India's recent growth had spurred increasing official attention to the problem.

"It's seen as important because children who work are not getting an education or learning skills, which means that a large proportion of India's future work force will not be skilled," he said.

"For a country like India, which is trying to strengthen its economy, that really matters."

Despite anxieties over implementation, the recent amendments marked an important step forward, said Shireen Miller of Save the Children.

"Most of these employers think that they're doing the children a favor—looking after them, giving them a roof over their heads, perhaps a bit of food," she said. "There's no embarrassment about employing them. Now, finally, we can say, 'This is illegal.'"

Notes and Questions

1. For comparison with the situation in India, read the 1995 report by Human Rights Watch, *Contemporary Forms of Slavery in Pakistan,* available at http://www.hrw.org/reports/pdfs/c/crd/pakistan957.pdfhttp://www.hrw.org/reports/pdfs/c/crd/pakistan957.pdf. Despite many religious and cultural differences, India and Pakistan share a widespread problem of bonded labor, including bonded child labor. As you read the Pakistan report, not far distant in time from the India report reproduced above, consider what elements are shared by the two countries with regard to the worst forms of child labor. Is there any reason to be more hopeful about effective remedies in one country as opposed to the other? In either, does the government seem committed to positive change?

Aine Smith, *Child Labor: The Pakistani Effort to End a Scourge upon Humanity — Is It Enough?*
6 San Diego International Law Journal 461 (2005)

....

II. Pakistan and the Bonded Child Laborer

A. History of Child Labor in Pakistan

The Human Rights Commission of Pakistan (HRCP) conjectures that the number of child laborers is between eleven and twelve million, with at least half under the age of ten. The brick kiln, carpet weaving, and soccer ball industries utilize the largest number of child laborers. Commentators have suggested that child labor is so prevalent in Pakistan because "the child labor pool is all but inexhaustible, owing in part to a birth rate that is among the world's highest and to an education system that can accommodate only about a third of the country's school age children."

Parents are often forced to sell their children to local factories, a practice commonly referred to as bonded labor. One Pakistani mother said: "When my children were three, I told them they must be prepared to work for the good of the family. I told them again and again that they would be bonded at five. And when the time came for them to go, they were prepared and went without complaint." Despite the problem of bonded labor, the Pakistani government employs no programs to aid the impoverished and banks are unwilling to loan money to people without collateral. Thus, when a family is in dire need of money, the head of the household is forced to borrow from a local kadar (employer who owns a nearby factory). In return for the peshgi (loan), the loanee must give something of value as collateral. The collateral, often times, is a child. The child then works for the kadar until the entire loan, including interest and expenses, is paid back.

Even more deplorable than the treatment of children as chattel is the means the kadars use to gain more child laborers. Some factories hire recruiting agents who use watching agents to determine which local families are barely surviving monetarily. The watching agent introduces the recruiting agent to the head of the household. The recruiter acts sympathetic, flying in like a superhero, promising to end the family's financial woes and "[to] place" the child "in a company where he will learn a trade." Generally, parents allow their children to work in a factory only as a means of survival.

Why do factory owners employ children who lack experience, trade knowledge, and maturity? Employers have been asked that very question and have expounded upon the many virtues of the child worker. Children are "cheaper, more motivated, more efficient, obedient, don't form labor unions, and don't strike," unlike adult laborers. In Pakistan's shoe factories, children earn ten cents a day for manufacturing a shoe that the employer can export to another country for one-hundred twenty U.S. dollars. Sensing the widespread disgruntlement, some employers take a more philanthropic stance to justify their use of child labor. These employers say: "[C]hildren would starve if they couldn't go to work ... the only alternative would be worse forms of employment or prostitution." Still other employers maintain nationalist reasons for maintaining a child labor force. Shabbir Jamal, an adviser to the Ministry of Labor, stated to an interviewer: "Westerners conveniently forget their own shameful histories when they come here ... Europeans addressed slavery and child labor only after they became prosperous. Pakistan has only now entered an era of economic stability that will allow us to expand our horizons and address social concerns."

. . . .

B. International Law regarding Children and Child Labor

Pakistan law and international law both prohibit the use of bonded child labor. Under its own law and as a signatory of numerous international instruments, Pakistan is required to prohibit all forms of slavery, including debt bondage, child servitude, and forced labor, as well as to protect children from exploitation and hazardous work.

2. Treaties to which Pakistan is a Signatory

a. The Convention on the Worst Forms of Child Labor

In 2001, Pakistan ratified the International Labor Organization Convention on the Worst Forms of Child Labor (ILO Convention No. 182). The drafters hoped to protect children from any hazardous activity or occupation that leads to adverse effects on the child's safety, health, and moral development.

. . . .

b. ILO Forced Labor Convention No. 29

The International Labor Organization Forced Labor Convention (ILO No. 29) mandates that signatories suppress the use of all forms of compulsory/forced labor as soon as possible. ILO No. 29 defines forced or compulsory labor as "all work or service which is exacted from any person under the menace of any penalty and for which the said person has not offered himself voluntarily." Article IV reminds signatories that private individuals, companies, and associations are no longer permitted to utilize forced or compulsory labor. Signatories are also obligated to "ensure that penalties imposed are really adequate and strictly enforced." Pakistan agreed to abide by the terms of this convention in 1957.

. . . .

4. National Laws regarding Child Labor

International law, as well as Pakistani national law, prohibits the use of bonded child labor. International law mandates that Pakistan prohibit all forms of slavery, including debt bondage, child servitude, and forced labor. International law also expects Pakistan to protect children from economic exploitation and hazardous work. To fulfill these international obligations, Pakistan passed laws to eliminate the use of child-bonded labor.

a. The Constitution of the Islamic Republic of Pakistan

First, the Constitution of the Islamic Republic of Pakistan (Constitution) prohibits all forms of forced labor. Ulfat Hussein Kazmi, the President of the Global Foundation, stated that the Constitution prohibits the use of children under the age of fourteen in factories, mines, and other hazardous occupations. Penalties for violation of the Constitution include fines of up to 20,000 rupees or one-year imprisonment. The Constitution also states that the government "shall remove illiteracy and provide free and compulsory secondary education within a minimum possible period." Bonded child labor is also arguably prohibited under the supreme law of the land, but the military government suspended the Constitution in October 1999. President Pervez Musharraf promised that the Constitution would become effective once again after the 2002 national elections.

b. The Employment of Children Act

The Pakistan National Assembly passed the Employment of Children Act in 1991, which prohibits the use of child labor in industries hazardous to children's health. In those industries where employment is permissible, the law prohibits children under fourteen from working. The law limits the workday of a child to seven hours, including a one-hour break after three hours of labor. A working child must be given at least one day off per week, and a child may not work overtime. Employers must furthermore maintain an employment register of laboring children that labor inspectors may examine.

c. The Bonded Labor System (Abolition) Act

In 1992 Pakistan passed the Bonded Labor System (Abolition) Act, a measure that specifically abolished bonded labor. The Bonded Labor System Rules of 1995 provided penalties for those who: (1) continue the use of bonded labor; (2) omit or fail to restore property to the bonded laborer; and (3) abet in an offense. This act also established Vigilance Committees whose functions include: advising local government on how to implement the law; helping in the rehabilitation of freed bonded laborers; ensuring that the letter of the law is being carried out; and providing any assistance necessary to achieve the objectives of the act.

d. The Employment of Children Rules

The Pakistan legislature also passed the Employment of Children Rules in 1995. This act created more stringent requirements for employers to maintain a minimum standard of health and safety in a child's working environment. Violations of its provisions result in a maximum one-year prison term and/or a fine of 20,000 rupees for the offender.

While Pakistan's laws condemn the use of bonded child labor, as well as hazardous child labor, the practice nonetheless persists. The Pakistani government estimates that 3.3 million children are currently working in its borders. Nongovernmental organizations (NGOs) maintain that this figure is a gross underestimation, and the real figure is closer to ten million. Indeed, while Pakistan's ratification of international agreements and initiation of programs to help combat child labor are promising, the U.S. Department of Labor questions Pakistan's ability to abolish the worst forms of child labor.

The Department of Labor's pessimism in this regard stems from several reasons. First, Pakistan's government institutions are hesitant to enforce child labor laws due to the high levels of family poverty. Pakistani parents need their children to work to ensure familial survival. Second, the regulation and prosecution of cases involving forced and bonded child labor are nearly impossible because of their elusive character. Employers do everything in their power to conceal the use of child labor, and corruption runs rampant. Third, Pakistan lacks the "financial and human resources" to effectively enforce their anti-child labor laws. Fourth, child labor is linked to the caste system—an institution that has proven extremely difficult to eradicate. Finally, "political instability, complacency, and corruption within governments make good laws and adequate resources ineffective." Even the Federal Secretary of the Ministry of Labour, Manpower and Overseas Pakistanis stated:

"Legislation alone is not a panacea; it will work only if accompanied by measures that create a conducive national environment which promotes the eradication of child labour."

C. Steps Taken by the Pakistani Government to Eradicate Child Labor

Pakistan already has legislation in place to abolish bonded labor and the worst forms of child labor, but what means has the government implemented to achieve this noble end? Has the incidence of child labor been reduced in the country? In 1996, a journalist for The Atlantic Monthly charged that Pakistan's efforts to curb the use of child labor were practically non-existent. "Given its relative prosperity, its constitutional prohibition against child labor, and its leaders' signatures on every U.N. human- and child-rights convention, Pakistan's de facto dependency on child labor is troubling and to its critics inexcusable." Is this charge still viable?

The government has made more of a concerted effort to curb the use of child labor since 1996. The National Policy and Action Plan of May 2000 delineated three particular goals: immediate eradication of the worst forms of child labor, a progressive elimination of child labor from all sectors of employment, and implementation of programs meant to prevent children from entering the workforce.

One means to achieve these goals is through membership in the International Programme on the Elimination of Child Labour (IPEC), an International Labor Organization group whose goal is the progressive elimination of child labor. With the help of IPEC, Pakistan has established Work Pilot Programs in several provinces infamous for their use of child labor. In Peshawar, IPEC established rehabilitation centers for children rescued from the workplace. These centers include health care facilities, vocational guidance and training, and alternative income programs for families. IPEC, with the support of the Pakistan Carpet Manufacturing and Export Association, implemented a similar program to combat child labor in the carpet industry.

To further bolster its efforts, the government established Bait al-Mal, a government welfare agency. This agency operates over thirty-three rehabilitation centers throughout the country. Targeting children who have worked in hazardous occupations, the agency provides both children and their families with training and stipends for lawful income-generating activities.

The Embassy of Pakistan informed the United States Department of Labor that it is mandating strict implementation and enforcement of their labor laws and of the United Nations' Declaration of the Rights of the Child. Such efforts include regular inspections and raids of employers. The government formed the National Committee on the Rights of the Child to perform the functions elucidated in the Convention on the Rights of the Child, Article 43. This committee also serves an advisory role, informing the government of hazardous businesses utilizing child labor.

. . . .

The Constitution of Pakistan states that every child up to the age of sixteen has the right to an education. One provision in particular states that the government "shall remove illiteracy and provide free and compulsory secondary education within a minimum possible period." Despite these constitutional obligations, education is not compulsory at the national level in Pakistan. In fact, only two of the four provinces in Pakistan have compulsory primary education laws in effect.

Despite this lack of a nationwide compulsory education law, the Minister of Labour, Manpower, and Overseas Pakistanis reported that the government is working to expand educational opportunities for all Pakistani children. "The Policy envisages that 90 [percent] of the children in the primary age group (5–9) are expected to be in schools by the year 2002–03; the promulgation and enforcement of compulsory primary education law could be possible by 2004–05 ..." To garner support locally, social welfare departments in each of the provinces attempt to convince employers and parents that education is invaluable.

....

D. The Present Scope of the Problem

A Pakistani newspaper recently reported that, "unofficially, eight million children work for various employers. Approximately two million children labor in hotels, carpet factories, workshops, boot polishing stands, and vending carts throughout the country. Thus far, the government fails to institute a plan to rescue these children and provide them with an education. Bonded labor is still deeply entrenched in the agricultural sector; the government is only removing bonded labor from the industrial sector. This complacency is in complete derogation of the Bonded Labour Act of 1991. Global March, a leading NGO, reports that "even where landlords are caught red-handed with bonded laborers they still manage to escape justice." The government also fails to attack child labor in mechanic shops. An estimated 5,000 children fix engines in auto shops throughout one province of Pakistan. The transgressions continue unabated in various sectors of Pakistan's economy.

....

Though Pakistan purports to be revamping its educational system, generally speaking, these alterations are still inadequate. First, the education costs still serve as a deterrent for poor families. In fact, the expenses incurred from the primary level to the secondary level increase substantially. Many families cannot afford to pay for uniforms, books, supplies, and transportation. Second, many families rely upon the income generated by their children. Third, some parents contend that the present curriculum taught in these schools is substandard. A Pakistani newspaper stated that twenty-four percent of kids do not attend school because the quality is low and the content fails to include life-skills. The present system, essentially, is not tailored to meet the needs of the individual child laborer.

The inadequate education system indicates an even greater problem is looming in the background, which the government has failed to address. An official at the Labor Department admits: "[W]e have been concentrating on making these children aware of the hazards of labor, but their main problem is poverty, and the government has limited resources to offer alternatives to child labor." An employer states: "[W]e can't refuse parents who bring these children because of their poverty." Rashid, a child laborer, recounts what his mother told him: "[Y]ou are poor and have no right to an education, because you have to feed your two sisters."

Impoverished families are forced to pawn their children off to a willing employer in order to supplement the income needed for mere survival. Legislation alone is not a panacea. The government must accompany such labor laws with social programs meant to reduce poverty.

Notes and Questions

1. Debt bondage as a phenomenon is remarkably similar in form and technique in India and Pakistan. If anything, in Pakistan there seems to be an even greater level of violence by employers, and more active complicity of the police. Employers maintain private jails, allowing for illegal confinement of those who resist forced labor conditions.

Bonded labor is extremely prevalent in certain Pakistani industries, such as in brick making. Does "poverty reduction" strike you as a useful prescription in this context?

2. Could debt bondage exist without severe forms of discrimination? How much official complicity did you note in India and Pakistan relative to the continuance of these worst forms of child labor? How should countries be responded to in international forums when they argue that their child labor problem is attributable to "poverty"? How do cultural relativist arguments square with the empirical reality of child debt bondage in South Asia?

—————

B. Child Labor in Its Worst Forms in Ecuador's Banana Sector

The following Human Rights Watch report describes the many and severe violations of children's rights in the banana industry in Ecuador. There is no mistaking the fact that bananas coming from Ecuador are consumed in many parts of the developed world. This raises questions concerning remedies for the egregious abuse of child workers in this industry; in particular, what trade-related steps could be taken to force changes in the treatment of these children? Whereas many of the worst forms of child labor do not involve global trade in goods, and are more localized, the banana industry in Latin America is indirectly dominated by a handful of U.S.-based multinational corporations. These companies use certain contractual techniques to distance themselves from the labor rights violations that are occurring; nevertheless, the structure of the Latin American banana industry would seem to make it the obvious target for an international campaign on behalf of exploited children.

Human Rights Watch, *Tainted Harvest: Child Labor and Obstacles to Organizing on Ecuador's Banana Plantations*

(April 2002) *available at* http://www.hrw.org/legacy/reports/2002/ecuador/

. . . .

In May 2001, Human Rights Watch conducted a three-week fact-finding mission in Quito and the Guayas and El Oro provinces in Ecuador to investigate child labor and obstacles to freedom of association in the banana sector. During the investigation, Human Rights Watch spoke with seventy current and former banana workers, adults and children, whose real names are not used in this report to protect them from potential employer reprisals.

Child Workers

Human Rights Watch interviewed forty-five children who had worked or were working on banana plantations in Ecuador. Forty-one of them began in the banana sector between the ages of eight and thirteen, most starting at ages ten or eleven. They described workdays of twelve hours on average and hazardous conditions that violated their human rights, including dangerous tasks detrimental to their physical and psychological well-being. The children reported being exposed to pesticides, using sharp tools, hauling heavy loads of bananas from the fields to the packing plants, lacking potable water and restroom facilities, and experiencing sexual harassment. Children told Human Rights Watch that they handled insecticide-treated plastics used in the fields to cover and protect bananas, directly applied fungicides to bananas being prepared for shipment in packing plants, and continued working while fungicides were sprayed from planes flying overhead. Sometimes the children were provided protective equipment; most often, they were not. These children enumerated the various adverse health effects that they had suffered shortly after pesticide exposure, including headaches, fever, dizziness, red eyes, stomachaches, nausea, vomiting, trembling and shaking, itching, burning nostrils, fatigue, and aching bones. Children also described working with sharp tools, such as knives, machetes, and short curved blades, and three pre-adolescent girls, aged twelve, twelve, and eleven, described the sexual harassment they allegedly had experienced at the hands of the administrator of two packing plants where they worked. In addition, four boys explained that they attached harnesses to themselves, hooked themselves to pulleys on cables from which banana stalks were hung, and used this pulley system to drag approximately twenty banana laden stalks, weighing between fifty and one hundred pounds each, over one mile from the fields to the packing plants five or six times a day. Two of these boys stated that, on occasion, the iron pulleys came loose and fell on their heads, making them bleed.

Fewer than 40 percent of these children were still in school at age fourteen. When asked why they had left school to work, most answered that they needed to provide money for their parents to purchase food and clothing for their families, many of whom also relied on the nearby banana plantations for their income. Though important for their families, the average income contributed by the children with whom Human Rights Watch spoke was only U.S. $3.50 for every day worked — roughly 64 percent of the average wage earned by the adults interviewed by Human Rights Watch and 60 percent of the legal minimum wage for banana workers.

If applied, Ecuadorian laws governing child labor could go a long way to protecting the human rights of these children — preventing them from laboring in conditions that violate their right to health and development. If implemented, the laws could also prevent children from engaging in employment likely to interfere with their right to education. Nonetheless, the Ministry of Labor and Human Resources (Ministry of Labor) and the juvenile courts — from which employers must obtain authorization prior to hiring any child under fourteen fail to fulfill their legally mandated responsibility to enforce domestic laws governing child labor, and the other governmental entities commissioned to address children's issues do not include child banana workers in the scope of their activities. The result is an almost complete breakdown of the government bureaucracy responsible for enforcing child labor laws and preventing the worst forms of child labor in Ecuador's banana sector.

. . . .

Corporate Responsibility

These labor rights abuses underlie the production of millions of metric tons of bananas supplied to exporting corporations every year. They occur because of Ecuador's failure to enforce its labor laws and its lack of sufficient legal protections for workers' rights — governmental omissions that allow banana producers to violate workers' rights with impunity. Exporting corporations contract directly with these national producers and benefit from these violations by receiving goods produced under abusive labor conditions. Nonetheless, representatives of Dole, Chiquita, Del Monte, Noboa, and Favorita with whom Human Rights Watch spoke in Ecuador all disclaimed any obligation to demand respect for workers' rights on third-party plantations from which they purchase bananas for export. They explained, in some cases contradicting their own codes of conduct, that supplier plantations are private property over which they have no jurisdiction and that decisions regarding labor matters thereon are ultimately the prerogative of the plantations' administrators. Human Rights Watch believes that when exporting corporations fail to use their financial influence to demand respect for labor rights on their supplier plantations, the exporting corporations benefit from, facilitate, and are therefore complicit in labor rights violations.

. . . .

IV. CHILD LABOR

Human Rights Watch believes that without reliable government data documenting the scope and scale of child labor in the banana sector, it would be difficult for the government or other institutions to design programs and allocate sufficient resources to remedy violations of child banana workers' human rights. Human Rights Watch, however, was unable to obtain reliable estimates concerning the number of child laborers in Ecuador's banana sector. The Ecuadorian government does not keep such statistics. Although the National Institute of Statistics and Census (INEC) signed an agreement with the International Labor Organization's (ILO) Statistical Information and Monitoring Programme on Child Labour (SIMPOC) in June 2001 to implement a national child labor survey and began the survey in August 2001, this survey will also not disaggregate data by occupation. Other available data, however, provide some guideposts with which to estimate the scope of child labor in the banana sector. In 1994, according to government estimates, approximately 38 percent of all children in Ecuador between the ages of ten and seventeen worked, roughly 808,000 children, approximately 419,000 of whom were between the ages of ten and fourteen. In the rural sector, roughly 59 percent of children between ages ten and seventeen worked, approximately 568,000 children. In 1998, another government survey indicated that the percentage of children at work between the ages of ten and seventeen in Ecuador had risen to 45 percent. There is no breakdown of these figures by industry, however. Based on these statistics assessing the general scope of child labor in Ecuador; Human Rights Watch interviews with seventy current and former child and adult banana workers, most of whom described laboring on plantations alongside other child workers; and the ease with which child banana workers can be found in villages near plantations, Human Rights Watch believes that child labor on banana plantations in Ecuador is widespread.

The forty-five child banana workers—persons under the age of eighteen with whom Human Rights Watch spoke described the labor conditions under which they worked and the tasks they performed, many of which, under international law, rank their employment among the "worst forms of child labor."....

The average age at which these forty-five children began working on banana plantations was eleven. Only four started working at age fourteen or above. The other forty-one became banana workers between the ages of eight and thirteen, without prior juvenile court authorization, in violation of both Ecuadorian law and the ILO Minimum Age Convention. Although two of the children indicated that they worked approximately five-hour days, the vast majority worked between nine and thirteen hours a day, with an average workday of eleven hours, also in violation of Ecuadorian law, as well as the ILO Convention concerning the prohibition and Immediate Elimination of the Worst Forms of Child Labour (Worst Forms of Child Labour Convention), whose recommendation identities "work under particularly difficult conditions such as work for long hours" as one of "the worst forms of child labor."

Exposure to Hazardous Substances

I went under the packing plant roof until the [fumigation] plane left—less than an hour. I became intoxicated. My eyes were red. I was nauseous. I was dizzy. I had a headache. I vomited.

—Marcas Santos, describing an event that occurred when he was eleven and working on plantation Guabital in the canton of Balao.

The United States Environmental Protection Agency (U.S. EPA) has recognized that "[c]hildren are at a greater risk for [sic] some pesticides for a number of reasons. Children's internal organs are still developing and maturing and their enzymatic, metabolic, and immune systems may provide less natural protection than those of an adult." Similarly, according to the Natural Resources Defense Council (NRDC), an international environmental nongovernmental organization (NGO), "a sizable body of evidence has shown that children's health is uniquely threatened by environmental hazards." In particular, the NRDC has found that, when in the presence of pesticides, children are proportionately more exposed than adults, due to several factors, including that children's resting breathing rate is significantly higher than resting adults', children have a skin surface area per unit of body weight far greater than adults, and children may be less able than adults to expel toxins from their bodies due to immature kidneys.

Despite the heightened risks they face when exposed to toxic chemicals, most of the child workers with whom Human Rights Watch spoke came into contact with pesticides at one or more stages in the banana production process. Most were never told by employers of the health hazards and dangers of such exposure nor what measures to take to protect themselves from contamination. And in many cases, these often toxic pesticides had been approved for application by the banana-exporting corporations supplied by the plantations on which the children labored, which Human Rights Watch believes makes these corporations highly complicit in the violation of those children's right to health.

Insecticide-treated plastics

The banana production process involves the use of insecticide-treated plastics, which are placed on banana stalks growing in the fields to protect the developing fruit from harmful insects. Most commonly, these insecticides are applied to plastic bags that cover the entire banana stalks, from top to bottom, and to long and thin plastic strips, which are tied around the stalks at each end of the bags. Children reported being involved in placing these treated plastics on the plants, removing them in the packing plants, gathering them from the packing plant floors, and disposing of them.

From lists of the pesticides approved by Chiquita, Dole, and Noboa for use on their directly owned and supplier plantations in Ecuador, provided to Human Rights Watch by representatives of these corporations in Ecuador, Human Rights Watch learned that two of the most common insecticides used in Ecuador to treat the plastics are diazinon and chlorpyrifos. Both insecticides are classified as "moderately hazardous," category II by the World Health Organization (WHO), which measures pesticides' acute risk to human health—the risk caused by exposures over a short period of time-based on their oral and dermal toxicity to rats....

Diazinon and chlorpyifos are both organophosphates. Originally synthesized in World War II as a nerve warfare agents, organophosphates interfere with cholinesterase, "the enzyme [in the brain] that breaks down a critical nerve-impulse-transmitting chemical," causing the over-expression of certain nerve impulses and producing "an array of acute toxic symptoms." Among the symptoms of poisoning are headache, nausea, dizziness, salivation, sweating, wheezing, coughing, tightness in the chest, blurred vision, and in more severe cases, vomiting, diarrhea, abdominal cramps, and slurred speech. At particularly high toxicity levels, seizures, coma, and death may result. Chronic effects may include "impaired memory and concentration, disorientation, severe depressions, irritability, confusion, headache, speech difficulties, delayed reaction times, nightmares, sleepwalking and drowsiness or insomnia."

. . . .

Many of the children with whom Human Rights Watch spoke, including Carlos Ortiz, stated that they did not use any protective equipment, not even gloves, while handling the treated plastics. Others explained that although they used gloves, they bought them themselves because employers did not provide them. Marta Mendoza, a twelve-year-old girl who had been working since age eleven on the four plantations of Las Fincas in the canton of Balao—San Aiejandro, San Fernando, San Gabriel, and San Jose—told Human Rights Watch that she wore protective gloves to handle insecticide-treated plastics, but "I bought them with my own money. They don't give you any equipment."

Applying pesticides in the packing plants

Children had also been exposed to pesticides when they directly applied fungicides to bananas being prepared for shipment in packing plants—holding small, fungicide-filled tanks and spraying the chemicals through hoses onto the bananas. From the lists of pesticides approved by Chiquita, Dole, and Noboa for use on their directly owned and supplier plantations in Ecuador, Human Rights Watch learned that the most commonly applied pesticides at this stage of production are thiabendazole and imazalil. As with organophosphates, imazalil is classified as "moderately hazardous," category II. It has been found to cause muscle uncoordination, reduced arterial tension, tremors, and vomiting, and the International Programme on Chemical Safety, composed of the WHO, the ILO, and the United Nations Environment Programme, has noted that "a harmful concentration of airborne particles can … be reached quickly on spraying" and long-term or repeated exposure "may have effects on the liver, resulting in impaired functions and tissue lesions." The product label for imazalil indicates that the chemical may cause "eye damage" and warns, "Do not get in eyes or on clothing. Wear goggles when handling." Thiabendazole, however, is classified by the WHO as "unlikely to present acute hazard in normal use."

. . . .

Several of the children also stated that they did not wear any protective equipment—no gloves, no mask, no goggles, no apron—while applying these chemicals. Humherto Rojas, a fourteen-year-old boy who began as a banana worker at age thirteen, explained: "Sometimes I spray pesticides with the tank in the packing plant. It [the tank] has a hose. I don't [wear] protective equipment. No gloves, no mask.". . . .

. . . .

Work with Dangerous Tools

Children described using sharp knives, machetes, and *curvos*—short, thick, crescent-shaped blades with wooden handles—for a variety of tasks on the plantations. Fifteen children reported handling curvos, five machetes, and one a sharp knife used to cut yellow leaves off the banana plants. The children enumerated a variety of uses for the curvos, including cutting *piola*—the thick plastic used to stabilize banana plants by tying them to each other; cutting bananas off their stalks; making banana clusters; cutting plastic color-coded ties, used to indicate bananas' stages of development, off the banana stalks; cutting off plastic bags used to cover the banana stalks; and cutting off the long plastics interwoven among bananas to prevent them from damaging each other. They also explained that with the machetes they weeded the fields, cut *piola*, and cut yellow leaves off the banana plants.

Twelve of the children told Human Rights Watch that they had cut themselves with these sharp tools at least once. Cristobal Alvarez said that in 2001, at age twelve, working on Frutos Bellos, C.A., nicknamed "La María," in the canton of Balao, "I cut myself once. I put up with it. I didn't tell anyone. I put syrup from the banana stalk on it, and there was no more blood." Leonardo Chamorro, a thirteen-year-old boy, similarly explained, "I have cut myself, twice on San Jose [of the plantation group Las Fincas]. I was twelve. I told the boss that I cut myself, and he sent me home. There was a lot of blood. My mom healed it." Pedro Sandoval also described that when he was thirteen, "I cut myself with a *curvo* on [plantation] Porvenir. I was helping cut bananas off the stalks." He added, "It stayed like this," and he showed Human Rights Watch how the injury had not properly healed. Carla Chamorro, now eleven, also stated, "I cut myself while learning to cut the bananas off the stalk.... I was ten years old.... I was working on [the plantation group] Las Fincas."

....

Lack of Potable Water and Sanitation

Eighteen children told Human Rights Watch that at least one of the plantations on which they had worked did not have a bathroom for workers to use. Boys explained that, in such situations, if they had to urinate, they went to the banana fields to do so. Three girls, Marta Mendoza, Fabiola Cardozo, and Marta Cárdenas, explained that on San Fernando of the plantation group Las Fincas, there was no bathroom in the packing plant, and "you have to go to the canal to use the bathroom in San Fernando. There is [also] no faucet to wash your hands."

Although most children stated that in the packing plants where they had worked they had access to water they believed to be potable from wells, tanks with chlorine, sink faucets, or hoses, some told Human Rights Watch that there was no potable water for them to drink when they became thirsty while working on the plantations. Several children explained that when they were thirsty, they went home to get water, and four children told Human Rights Watch that when they wanted water, they had to purchase water from small stores on the plantations. Jorge Arrata, a thirteen-year-old who had worked on plantation San Jose, owned by Parazul, S.A. in the canton of Balao since he was eleven, explained, "There is no water to drink. You have to buy water if you are thirsty. There is a store in the packing plant.... It costs [U.S.] $0.25 for a bottle of water."

A few children described drinking water from the runoff canals that travel through the plantations. Guillermo Guerrero, a fourteen-year-old working in the fields of Balao Chico, told Human Rights Watch, "You have to bring water from home in a bottle." If that water runs out, he said, "you have to look for water in the canals.... The boss won't give you any." Similarly, Diego Rosales, age fourteen, explained that in the fields of Guabital, where he was working, there was no potable water, only water running in the canals. He told Human Rights Watch that once he broke his arm when he fell into a canal. He said he was thirsty and, like Guillemo Guerrero, was trying to get some water to drink. The canals drain excess water from the fields and catch plantation runoff, including aerially-sprayed fungicides, nematicides sprinkled around the bases of the plants to kill root-eating worms, herbicides sprayed on the ground, fertilizers, and human and animal waste."

....

Sexual Harassment

Human Rights Watch interviewed three young girls, ages twelve, twelve, and eleven, who described being sexually harassed by the "boss" of the packing plants on San Fernando and San Alejandro, plantations of the Las Fincas group. Marta Mendoza, a twelve-year-old who began working on Las Fincas at age eleven, explained, "There is a boss at the plant who's very sick.... This man is rude. He goes around touching girls' bottoms.... He is in charge there and is always there. He told me that he wants to make love to me. Once he touched me. I was taking off plastic banana coverings, and he touched my bottom. He keeps bothering me. He goes around throwing kisses at me. He calls me 'my love.'" Mendoza added, "He gave my cousin the nickname 'whore." Miriam Campos, an eleven-year-old who in 2001 began working on San Fernando and San Alejandro, started to tell Human Rights Watch that "that man" had "said something dirty to me" that "was ugly," but she stopped, looked down at her feet, and said she was too embarrassed to continue." Fabiola Cardozo, a twelve-year-old who began working on Las Fincas at age ten, similarly commented, "The boss of the packing plants ... says, 'Oh, my love.' When we bend down to pick up plastic bags, he says, *'Alli para meterle huevito'* ['There is a good place to stick my balls.'] She added that "he says, 'You are going to marry me, and you are going to kiss me.'"

....

Incomplete Schooling

The majority of the children with whom Human Rights Watch spoke had quit school before the age of fifteen. Of the forty-two children who began working under the age of fifteen, thirty-seven discussed their schooling with Human Rights Watch, and only fourteen—approximately 38 percent—were still in school at age fourteen, working primarily during their vacations. The mother of a fourteen-year-old boy who left school at age thirteen to begin working on plantation Guabital expressed her frustration with the situation, stating, "All of my children work. Working, they're not able to advance. I wish that my children could study, but they can't because they have to work."

....

School is mandatory in Ecuador for all children under fifteen and, according to the Constitution, is free through high school. The Minors' Code reiterates that "the State guarantees the right to education ... [and] basic education is mandatory and free," guaranteeing all children access to basic education." Furthermore, in the case of child workers, employers share the obligation to "ensure that [the child] attends an educational establishment and completes ... secondary instruction," and juvenile courts may only grant work authorizations to children ages twelve and thirteen if the children can demonstrate that they have completed or are completing the mandatory minimum schooling.

Nonetheless, work authorizations are rarely sought, and according to a juvenile court judge, even when they are, "in practice, it is not a requirement that school be finished. You receive authorization even if you have not completed [school]."

....

The sections of the Human Rights Watch report excerpted above set out the appalling conditions for children working in Ecuador's banana industry. The Latin American banana trade is one in which the United States and other capital exporting, and banana consuming, nations could exert a great deal of influence. Indeed, the economic and historical links between U.S. corporations and Latin American banana plantations are well known. The U.S. fruit industry has played a troubling political role in Latin American over the course of the last century, and could, if it chose, insist on higher standards of labor protection in the region.

The HRW report continues below, with emphasis in this section on issues of corporate responsibility. This part of the report makes the point that the matter of labor rights should be relevant to whether particular products are allowed to be freely traded. However, the current global trade regime, with the World Trade Organization at its center, pays little heed to such questions.

Human Rights Watch, *Tainted Harvest: Child Labor and Obstacles to Organizing on Ecuador's Banana Plantations*
(April 2002)

VI. BANANA-EXPORTING CORPORATIONS

International law establishes labor rights and standards that states are required to uphold. If states fulfilled this obligation, they would demand that corporations also respect these rights and standards. Corporations, however, are not directly regulated by international law. Nonetheless, as reflected in the United Nations Global Compact ... there is an international consensus that corporations have a duty to uphold workers' rights. There is also an emerging consensus, evidenced in various corporate codes of conduct, that corporations have a responsibility to take steps to ensure that labor rights are respected not only in their directly owned corporate facilities but throughout their supply chains as well.

When countries, like Ecuador, do not adequately enforce labor laws or lack sufficient legal protections to guarantee workers' rights, the government fails to fulfill its duty to protect labor rights. These governmental acts of omission enable employers to commit labor rights violations with impunity and thereby allow them to benefit from workers' rights abuses. Exporter corporations may enter into direct contractual relationships with these employers in whose workplaces workers' rights are violated to purchase product for export. When those financial or contractual relationships are forged and the exporting corporations fail to use their influence to demand respect for labor rights in those workplaces, in some cases contravening their own codes of conduct, the exporting corporations also facilitate and benefit from the labor rights violations because they receive goods produced under abusive conditions. Human Rights Watch believes that, in such cases, the exporting corporations have a fundamental responsibility to ensure respect for labor rights in the workplaces of their suppliers and are complicit in the workers' rights violations when they fail to do so. And when the exporting corporations sanction for use on their third-party supplier plantations pesticides that may be toxic for children, Human Rights Watch considers the corporations to be highly complicit in the human rights violations suffered by the child workers exposed to those chemicals while laboring on the supplier plantations.

As discussed below, Human Rights Watch believes that Dole and Noboa have failed to ensure respect for workers' rights by primary suppliers, from which they purchase regularly, and that Chiquita, Del Monte, and Favorita, as well as Dole and Noboa, have failed to do so on plantations from which they purchase occasionally. These exporting corporations have therefore benefited from and, Human Rights Watch believes, are complicit in labor rights abuses on these supplier plantations. In the cases of Chiquita and Dole, they have also disregarded their own policies that recognize corporate responsibility for labor conditions on supplier plantations—policies established through Dole's "signatory membership" in Social Accountability 8000 (SA8000), "a global humane workplace standard" for "company-owned and *supplier facilities*" [emphasis added], and in Chiquita's internal code of conduct, based largely on SA8000.

Because of heavy corporate reliance on third-party suppliers and because the vast majority of workers interviewed by Human Rights Watch labored on supplier plantations, when Human Rights Watch met with the Ecuadorian representatives of Noboa, Dole, Favorita, Del Monte, and Chiquita, the five corporations discussed in this investigation, the conversations focused on their policies with respect to labor practices on the plantations from which they purchase bananas—both primary suppliers with which they have long-standing contractual relationships and suppliers from which they purchase only on occasion. The companies uniformly assumed responsibility for compliance with Ecuadorian law and claimed to monitor labor conditions, including child labor and health and safety, and to allow freedom of association on their directly owned plantations. Nonetheless, although the companies' representatives in Ecuador, to varying degrees, recognized that labor rights violations may occur on their supplier plantations, they all ultimately disclaimed any obligation to mandate respect for workers' rights on those plantations.

For example, the executive president of Favorita, Segundo Wong, wrote to Human Rights Watch that "labor rights of workers hired to perform farm work in Reybanpac or Reybancorp farms are strictly within social and economic legislation in force in Ecuador, including the labor code. In particular, rights related to compensation, social benefits and ages are strictly adhered to and closely monitored by management." The executive vice president of Favorita, Vicente Wong, told Human Rights Watch, however, that, with respect to its supplier producers, "They are the bosses of their own plantations.... We cannot interfere in their administration process.... It is private land and property of the administrators."

Similarly, the head of human resources at Noboa, Francisco Chavez, stated, "The law only obligates the employers with dependent relationships. The producers are governed by the laws, but it is not for us to make them comply with that. We don't have anything to do with that.... We don't intervene in that part. It's not in the contract." Chavez continued, "We demand that they comply with quality norms. If not, we don't buy from them. There are quality ... inspectors who go to these plantations ... [to verify] quality norms and the process. Nothing with labor. We cannot intervene because they are private properties."

The general manager of Bandecua, Del Monte's Ecuadorian subsidiary, expressed a similar attitude towards suppliers, stating, "They don't have to comply with any rules of Del Monte with the exception of quality of fruit and technical procedures, [i.e.], ... chemical products. With respect to workers, nothing. Health and safety, nothing.... We don't have any rules regarding underage workers. It's the decision of each hacienda." He explained that "Del Monte's engineers supervise [the producers]," monitoring the production process and the use of pesticides, "but nothing with regards to personnel. Only with respect to production."

Ricardo Flores, general manager of Brundicorpi, Chiquita's subsidiary in Ecuador, in slight contrast, expressed company concern for the labor practices on supplier plantations, but nonetheless concluded that while Chiquita can make recommendations regarding labor policies, the recommendations are, in the end, unenforceable. For example, he noted that in May 2000, Chiquita adopted a code of conduct, but, he explained, "We are in the process of implementing it internally. Later, we have to convince suppliers that they should comply with the code of conduct, [but] we are not in a position to demand it, only to convince them that it is good.... We cannot demand [it] of anyone." Flores explained, "We have people in the fields who visit the plantations to verify the quality of the fruit ... that the fruit is protected according to standards—level of leaf infection, processing at the correct age, ... that they are using the approved chemicals.... Nothing with respect to the labor question. We don't have any right to do that." Human Rights Watch believes, however, that not only do banana-exporting corporations have the right to monitor compliance with high labor standards on their supplier plantations but the responsibility to do so, using their financial leverage to demand respect for workers' rights.

When Human Rights Watch posed similar questions to representatives of UBESA, the Dole subsidiary in Ecuador, different answers were given by the agricultural engineer, responsible for environmental safety, and the director of human resources, responsible for administering labor policies. The agricultural engineer, Ivan Bermúdez, explained that UBESA provides "guides" to its primary suppliers, which include worker health and safety standards, and that each primary supplier should develop internal regulations based on these guides. According to Bermúdez, UBESA sends personnel from its Department of Environmental Safety to primary supplier plantations to provide technical assistance and oversee compliance with the company's internal guidelines. Bermúdez commented, "We don't limit ourselves to buying fruit." With respect to child labor, Bermúdez told Human Rights Watch, "Our producers ... are conscious that they should not hire [children]. It has happened, and we have indicated that they should not do it, and they do not do it again." He noted, however, that as an agricultural engineer supervising environmental safety, he was not qualified to speak on labor matters, including child labor and worker health and safety, and that Human Rights Watch should contact the director of human resources.

When Human Rights Watch asked UBESA's director of human resources, José Anchundia, about labor conditions, including child labor and health and safety, on the plantations of the company's third-party suppliers, he stated emphatically:

> We do not have jurisdiction over that. They have to follow the law. It is their discretion. Here contracting minors is prohibited, ... [but] we do not intervene in that. Absolutely not. It's their business.... We do not have that responsibility. Nothing to do there. Our contract is limited to quality and technical assistance.... We give technical assistance to obtain the optimal quality. We have inspectors to oversee the quality of fruit.... The only obligation we have with respect to those plantations is that we buy [bananas] and pay the official price [set by] the government, but the responsibility with regard to contracting personnel and health and safety corresponds to the plantation owner, the owner of the property.

These responses are disappointing. Exporting corporations exercise the power of the purse and could insist that high labor standards be met on their supplier plantations.

....

VII. BANANA EXPORTS AND TRADE REGIMES

Human Rights Watch believes that there is an inherent link between labor rights and trade. When countries or regions engage in trade, they have a fundamental obligation to ensure that the goods being traded are not produced in violation of internationally recognized labor rights, including freedom of association and the prohibition of the worst forms of child labor. As the two largest importers of Ecuadorian bananas, importing in 2000 roughly one million metric tons and 680,000 metric tons of Ecuadorian bananas, respectively, the United States and the European Union should be able to guarantee that trade provisions governing the import of Ecuadorian bananas include provisions that en-sure respect for the labor rights of banana workers in Ecuador. Nevertheless, because of the current structure of U.S. and E.U. tariff arrangements for the importation of Ecuado-rian bananas, such conditionality is likely precluded by the terms of the World Trade Or-ganization (WTO), of which the United States, E.U. countries, and Ecuador are members.

. . . .

Under the WTO, a member country may provide more favorable treatment to an-other's products under regional free-trade agreements, like the ATPA, or under special trade regimes for developing countries, like GSP. But, under article I . . . of the General Agreement on Tariffs and Trade (GATT), a country must treat a product from one WTO member country neither more nor less favorably than that same product from another WTO member country in most other cases. Since U.S. and E.U. tariff rates governing the importation of Ecuadorian bananas are established neither by trade agreements nor by trade regimes for developing countries, the United States and the European Union are likely precluded from revoking duty-free treatment or providing less favorable treatment for Ecuadorian bananas based on labor rights abuses in that country's banana sector. Un-less article XX of the GATT, the WTO provision allowing a country to restrict importa-tion of a product to protect public morals or human health, is interpreted to permit import restriction based on the export country's failure to protect internationally recog-nized workers' rights, the United States and the European Union have little leverage with which to demand that Ecuadorian bananas eaten by their consumers are not produced by workers whose labor rights are violated.

Notes and Questions

1. Human Rights Watch has done more than any other organization to present de-tailed studies on child labor conditions in various countries. Their painstaking reports pro-vide credible evidence of the suffering of child laborers. See also their study on child labor in the sugarcane industry of *El Salvador, Turning a Blind Eye*, Vol. 16, No. 2(B) (June 2004). Many of the issues concerning abuse of young children and the complicity of multinational industry are also found in the El Salvador report. Are the U.S. companies that source bananas from Ecuador at least indirectly culpable for the conditions under which these Ecuadoran children are working?

2. To what extent is the child labor problem in Ecuador, as well as other Latin Amer-ican countries, the result of "local" conditions, and to what extent is there international responsibility? What historical and social conditions contribute to the persistence of the abuse of child laborers; for instance, insufficiently democratic political structures?

IV. Child Labor in the United States, Including Worst Forms

The phenomenon of child labor in the United States is complex. Most people are sup-portive of part time work for adolescents, and assume that there is no serious or severe prob-lem of child exploitation involved. In fact, the U.S. does have a significant child labor problem, some of which involves the "worst forms" of child labor. Although it is generally thought that the U.S. does not need a legal overhaul in the child labor area, the readings below indicate that this is not the case. As will be described, young people working with other family members in the agricultural sector are often subjected to very arduous labor conditions. It should be asked whether the U.S. public remains unaware of or indifferent towards this issue because it tends to affect immigrant children and migrant families. Many child laborers in the agricultural sector are prevented from seeking an adequate education. As you read the material that follows, consider how Congress might reconfigure national labor law so as to allow adolescents to work—whether for pocket money or to gain experience or both—while ensuring that young people who should be involved full time in the educational system are not exploited by the agricultural industry. It should be asked why, with so much data on the issue available, Congress has not yet taken these steps.

The Seymour Moscowitz article, excerpted below, points out that Americans normally associate child labor with far away places and repressive regimes, whereas the number of children working under adverse conditions in the United States is also very large. He traces the history of child labor law in the U.S., and describes the tension between federal and state laws with respect to this subject matter.

Seymour Moskowitz, *Malignant Indifference: The Wages of Contemporary Child Labor in the United States*
57 Oklahoma Law Review 465 (2004)

Introduction

.... The problems associated with child labor in underdeveloped countries have captured our nation's attention. Legislatures have passed statutes and resolutions, citizen coalitions have organized, and the media has devoted extensive coverage to the issue. School classes have petitioned Disney and Nike to stop employing child workers in their overseas factories. Global Exchange protestors recently rallied in front of M&M's World store in Las Vegas to protest Mars's use of cocoa harvested with child labor. Even portfolio managers are under investor pressure not to invest in foreign companies using child labor. Only one thing is missing from this wave of moral outrage and activism—attention to the problems of child labor here at home.

In 2001, more than 3.7 million American youths worked. Employment in the United States poses substantial, immediate, and long-term risks for youthful workers. Many are killed and injured each year. The total number of occupational fatalities from 1992–1998 for youths under eighteen was 468. An estimated 200,000 young people are injured on the job annually.

....

Contemporary U.S. child labor law and enforcement reflects a malignant indifference to the plight of American youth in the workplace. American law generally does not permit minors to make decisions with long-term consequences on their own. Yet the federal Fair Labor Standards Act (FLSA)[6] requires no consent from—or even notification to—parents before a child may work. While some minimal hour limits are set for youths under sixteen in nonagricultural employment, only jobs or equipment designated "hazardous" by the Department of Labor (DOL) are off limits for children sixteen or older. Remarkably, those hazardous designations have remained largely unchanged for decades. The

---

6. Fair Labor Standards Act of 1938, 29 U.S.C. §§ 201–219 (2000).

DOL, moreover, has imposed no other hour or place restrictions on the work of sixteen- and seventeen-year-olds.

The FLSA also has huge gaps in coverage, and private enforcement of the statute—typical of other civil rights and protective legislation—is unavailable. Despite DOL's monopoly on enforcement, its performance is extraordinarily ineffectual. In the last decade, the federal courts decided only six lawsuits involving child labor violations. The DOL underestimates the numbers of illegally employed children and rarely initiates investigations of statutory violations.

....

Any attempt to explain the current inadequacies must begin with an analysis of the past. Historically, restriction of child labor was one front in a long legal war waged to determine the constitutional boundaries between state and federal power. In many instances, and sometimes out of necessity, parents wanted children as immediate income providers, while employers desired this source of cheap and controllable labor. The enactment of state, and later federal, child labor laws was slow and bitterly contested. The original state statutes created modest restrictions on both parental ability to force young children to work and the right of employers to contract with children. Enactment of the child labor provisions of the federal FLSA in 1938 was a moral and political victory, but its practical effect was limited, as many of the FLSA's protections were eviscerated during World War II.

In an attempt to rally public support for legislative reforms, the National Child Labor Committee, in the early 1900s, used dramatic visual images to document the horrors and negative social effects of unrestricted child labor. Louis Hine, a photographer and social reformer who worked for the Committee, photographed children in textile mills, the tobacco industry, and a variety of other settings. These images were immensely important in changing public opinion. Today, modern equivalents to Hine's photos are desperately needed to focus America's attention on contemporary child labor.

Despite the extraordinary economic and social changes in the United States, the FLSA remains largely unchanged since the 1960s. Over the years, powerful interests have resisted change. The Act contains numerous exemptions and significant structural defects; moreover, enforcement is lax. State child labor laws and administration reflect similar problems. Because children are politically voiceless, there is no powerful constituency demanding change. This political powerlessness leaves America's youth largely forsaken.

....

II. How We Got Here: The History of Child Labor Regulation

A. A History of Child Labor

Child labor has a lengthy history in the United States. Children owed services to their parents, and parents could assign their children's service to others. In colonial times, children were indentured for long periods. Master craftsmen contracted with parents to train the child in a trade or craft in exchange for years of the child's services. "Bound out" orphans were taken in by strangers with the expectation that the child would provide useful labor.

Between 1860 and 1890, over ten million immigrants arrived in the United States. Often these families faced poverty and chronic underemployment; the wages from child labor were necessary to support the family. A study in Philadelphia in 1880, for example, revealed that children of Irish-born men earned between 38% and 46% of their household's total income; in families with German-born fathers, children earned between 33%

and 35%. Parents commonly made their children available for paid employment. These parents often opposed child labor reform because of the "desperate need ... for additional income."

Although the immigrant population remained largely concentrated in urban areas, work by children in agrarian areas was also frequently an economic necessity and, indeed, was seen as essential to a child's upbringing. Americans at that time believed agricultural labor provided training for adulthood and independence. After the Civil War, however, the population overall migrated from rural communities to larger industrial cities.

By 1900, one out of every six children between the ages of ten and sixteen was gainfully employed. Children between ages ten and thirteen comprised one-third of the workforce in southern textile mills. Children in the post-Civil War South were particularly encouraged to work due to the loss of men in battle.

From 1900 to 1920, the urban population in the United States grew by 80%, while rural populations correspondingly declined. Industrialization spurred employment of children in mines, mills, factories, canneries, and other manufacturing establishments. The short- and long-term hazards of work in these enterprises were often great. Unhealthy and dangerous working conditions abounded. Children's labor in nineteenth and twentieth century America was parental property, stemming from the rule that parents are entitled to their children's services. As one state supreme court justice asserted in 1888, "It is a rule as old as the common law that the father is entitled to the custody and control of his minor children, and to receive their earnings." The right of parents to children's services, however, correlated to the parent's obligation to support the child and is statutory today in a number of states.

. . . .

B. Early Regulation in the States

Ideology, laissez-faire economic policies, and the considerable financial benefit from employing children blocked any serious consideration of the effects of child labor before the Civil War. Unions supported child labor restrictions, partly for humanitarian reasons and partly for economic considerations relating to depressed wages and adult unemployment....

Legal control of child labor was agonizingly slow and piecemeal.... Momentum for child labor regulation increased near the beginning of the twentieth century. A growing "progressive" movement opposed child labor as destructive of family values and inconsistent with the child's and society's long-term interests. By 1907, forty-two states had some type of child labor legislation. Even southern states, where child labor was widespread, began passing regulatory legislation. Widespread violations of these laws occurred, however, primarily because of the lack of enforcement and ignorance.

Clearly, an irregular web of state laws could not solve this national problem. Economic concerns created disincentives for states to regulate the problem, particularly when neighboring states had less stringent laws and thus reaped an economic benefit. Employers could play one state against another....

Because of the varied state approaches to the child labor problem, federal legislation was the only realistic solution.

C. Federal Developments Until 1937

. . . . Congress passed the first federal child labor law, the Keating-Owen Act on Child Labor, in 1916. Under the Act, neither mines, where children under age sixteen worked, nor factories that employed children under fourteen, could ship commodities in interstate commerce. The Act also limited the working hours of children ages fourteen to sixteen to eight hours per day and only six days per week, and prohibited work after 7:00 p.m. and before 7:00 a.m. State officials assisted in the enforcement of the Act and, in the nine months the law was in effect, almost 700 inspections revealed 293 establishments in violation of child labor statutes.

During the Lochner era, the federal judiciary, led by the U.S. Supreme Court, aggressively protected economic rights under the Due Process Clause and used federalism concepts to limit Congress's ability to regulate the economy. In this judicial climate, the Supreme Court in Hammer v. Dagenhart declared the Keating-Owen Act unconstitutional. The suit was brought by a poor father of two employed sons, represented by a distinguished group of nationally known corporate attorneys presenting familiar constitutional arguments. Before the Court, Solicitor General John W. Davis argued that ruinous competition among the states created an insurmountable barrier to nonfederal regulation of child labor. The Court rejected the argument and held that the statute was beyond Congress's power under the Commerce Clause because it regulated "local production," not interstate transportation. Control over child labor was vested in the states under their traditional police powers, and Congress could not interfere.

. . . .

[The article here discusses the failed attempt at a Child Labor Amendment to the U.S. Constitution during the 1920s.]

The next attempt at child labor reform came in the midst of the nation's most severe depression. In 1933, Congress passed the National Industrial Recovery Act (NIRA) as part of President Franklin D. Roosevelt's New Deal. The Act's purposes included reemployment of workers, creation of decent wages, and prevention of unfair competition. Child labor was seen as a significant factor in all of these problems. The NIRA empowered trade associations, organized by industry and unions, to create voluntary regulations which, when approved by the President, would become an enforceable industrial code. Most of the codes prohibited employees under eighteen from performing "hazardous work" and set minimum age requirements for workers. The U.S. Supreme Court declared the NIRA unconstitutional in *A.L.A. Schechter Poultry Corp. v. United States*. Despite being declared unconstitutional, the NIRA child labor provisions became the model for the FLSA.

D. The FLSA

In the mid-1930s, still suffering from an economic depression, many Americans saw child labor as a cause of both low wages and underemployment of adult workers. A uniform federal law was essential to protect goods in more progressive child labor states from unfair competition. . . .

In *NLRB v. Jones & Laughlin Steel Corp.*, the Court upheld the National Labor Relations Act, effectively overruling the limits that the Court had placed on Congress's power during the Lochner era. It was thus not surprising when the Court upheld the FLSA in *United States v. Darby*, overruling *Hammer v. Dagenhart*. Although *Darby* involved no child labor issues, the Supreme Court approved the FLSA in its entirety.

While the FLSA constituted an enormous step forward in establishing national standards, the immediate gains were modest in practice. Although the Act was undoubtedly an educational and moral force, "in those areas where children are useful they continued to be employed." Jonathon Grossman, historian at the DOL, noted that "[t]he law avoided some sectors of the work force where most abuses of child labor were concentrated." Indeed, while approximately 850,000 children under sixteen were gainfully employed in 1938, only an estimated 50,000 were subject to the Act. "Children in industrial agriculture, intrastate industries, the street trades, messenger and delivery service, stores, hotels, restaurants, beauty parlors, bowling alleys, filling stations, garages, etc., were outside the law."

....

E. Child Labor During World War II

The initial version of the FLSA prohibited employment of children under sixteen. When the United States entered World War II, the work force was soon exhausted. When a labor shortage emerged as males entered the armed services, women entered the work force in large numbers. World War II also affected child labor. According to the DOL, "[c]ontrary to general belief, the early withdrawal of boys and girls from school was a greater factor in the expansion of the labor force than was the increase in the number of women working."

At the outset of World War II, the United States had historically low levels of child labor and high levels of school enrollment. Following the outbreak of the war, school enrollment fell by 24% for fifteen- to eighteen-year-olds, while the number of fourteen- to seventeen-year-olds employed increased by 200%. Illinois is illustrative: during 1943, the number of Illinois children who legally left school to go to work was 400% greater than in 1942.

Nationally, young workers who were not attending school worked an average of forty-six hours per week. The DOL recognized that many students who dropped out of school to partake in wartime labor were unlikely to return to school after the war. Other consequences quickly emerged as the number of employed youths rose. For example, work accidents involving children increased. In Michigan, there was a 183% increase in compensable injuries to children, and in Illinois, work accidents involving children rose 100% from 1942 to 1943. The DOL attributed the increase both to the rise in the number of children employed generally and to the sharp increase in children employed in hazardous jobs.

....

III. The Current Legal Regime

A. Federal Statutory Provisions

Despite economic and social transformations since World War II, the FLSA has remained substantially unchanged. The FLSA outlaws "oppressive" and "hazardous" work for minors in commerce or in the production of goods for commerce. Persons under eighteen years of age may not be employed in mining or manufacturing or "in any occupation which the Chief of the Children's Bureau in the Department of Labor shall ... declare to be particularly hazardous for the employment of children ... or detrimental to their health or well being." Sixteen is the usual minimum age for employment, but the Secretary may permit employment of fourteen- to sixteen-year-olds in work that does not interfere with schooling and is not detrimental to the child's "health and well-being." The Act restricts youths under sixteen to no more than three hours of work per day and eighteen hours per week in nonhazardous tasks in retail, food service, and gasoline service stations when school is in session. During vacations, a minor under sixteen may work a maximum of eight hours per day and forty hours per week. With the exception of barring hazardous occupations, adolescents over sixteen have no federal restrictions on the number of hours or the time of day they may work. There are no parental or school consent requirements imposed by federal law.

When an employer violates the child labor provisions of the FLSA, the DOL must determine an appropriate penalty for the violation. Although the Act originally contained only criminal penalties, the FLSA now provides for civil remedies. Employers who willfully violate the Act may be fined not more than $11,000 or, after a prior conviction for violation of the provisions, imprisoned for not more than six months or both. The Secretary of Labor, subject to the direction and control of the Attorney General, may also petition a federal district court for injunctive relief.

B. State Laws

Although the FLSA does not preempt the field of child labor legislation, state provisions tend to follow federal law. Many state statutes provide minimum age requirements, limit working hours, and prohibit employment in hazardous occupations. All states place some limits on night work for minors under age sixteen. Similar to the FLSA, sixteen- and seventeen-year-olds in most states have legal freedom to choose the number of hours they will work. State child labor laws typically impose criminal or civil penalties on employers for violating the statute.

While there are many similarities, important differences exist between state and federal law.

....

Our current legal regime reflects a remarkably laissez-faire response to the millions of youths in America's workplaces. Especially in the case of older teens, federal and state statutes create few restrictions on their labor. There is little legal protection for parental input and control of youthful decisions regarding work and school. The consequences of this legal vacuum are great.

IV. The Consequences of American Child Labor

....

C. The Youth Workforce

In 2001, 3.7 million American adolescents between the ages of fifteen and seventeen worked. Large numbers of children under fifteen also worked. One study found employed high school students worked more than twenty hours per week. Boys typically averaged more hours of paid work than girls, especially in the later years of high school. While children from lower income families were less likely to work, when they did work, they tended to work more hours. As might be expected, more children worked during summer months.

In 2001, as throughout the past decade, retail trades, such as department stores, groceries, restaurants, or retail outlets, employed about 60% of all working children. While paying somewhat more than the legally established minimum wage, these jobs typically provide few positive benefits to teenagers. Indeed, youth employment may cause more harm than good.

D. Morbidity & Mortality at Work

The weakness of child labor laws and their lax enforcement are dramatically illustrated by the physical damage sustained by working adolescents. Youth workers face the same workplace dangers as adults in similar occupations but are far less prepared to confront these hazards. Teens are "congregated in jobs that are characterized by the absence of opportunities for significant promotion," low pay, high turnover, little on-the-job training, wide variation in hours, and few benefits. Jobs with these characteristics are, in general, more dangerous than other jobs. Young workers with limited education and low earning potential increasingly bear the burdens of evening and night hours. Agricultural work is particularly dangerous for young workers as well as adults, yielding fatality rates second only to mining.

Although juvenile employees are protected by general statutes, such as the Occupational Safety & Health Act, they receive neither additional protections nor special allowances for their inexperience. Moreover, thousands of children work in the "underground" economy and other industries, where work is often performed by undocumented workers. Work in the home or in sweat shops often involves conditions and materials that increase the risk of accidents and other safety hazards. Not surprisingly, minors have higher injury rates than adult workers. More than 200,000 young people are hurt on the job annually. In 1999, 58,000 employees aged sixteen to nineteen reported occupational injuries that caused them to miss days from work.

The pattern of work-related fatalities for adolescents has remained the same over the past decade. Forty percent of children killed during the past decade worked in agriculture, primarily crop production. Retail trade and construction accounted for 20% and 14% of all fatalities, respectively.

There is good reason to believe occupational injury statistics for children substantially understate the extent of the problem....

Adolescent workers age sixteen and older suffer the great majority of work-related injuries. During the 1990s, 84% of youths were injured in the retail trade and service industries—the two industries in which young workers are most likely to be employed. Those working in eating and drinking places, food stores, general merchandise stores, and health services had the largest numbers of injuries. Working teens are also at high risk for highway accidents.

E. Negative Academic & Nonacademic Results

Limited employment—twenty hours or less per week during high school—is associated with reduced high school dropout rates, increased involvement in school activities, and higher grade point averages. In contrast, high-intensity work correlates with numerous negative educational results. For example, truancy and suspension rates increase as a student works more hours. Moreover, the adverse educational effects of early high-intensity employment extend far beyond high school, hindering postsecondary educational achievement.

....

A. The Inadequacy of the Current Legal Regime

1. Federal Law

a) Statutory Failings

While the FLSA provides some regulation of child labor, it is far from comprehensive....

Federal law has failed to keep pace with the enormous increase in the number of children working and the variety of jobs they perform. While the FLSA has been amended numerous times since its enactment in 1938, its major provisions have remained substantially unchanged.

....

While federal labor law prohibits the employment of sixteen- and seventeen-year-olds in occupations found "hazardous or detrimental" to their health and well-being, these designations have not been changed since 1975 despite new technologies, changing work conditions, and a vastly different work force. Moreover, in jobs deemed "hazardous" by the DOL, if employers fall outside the jurisdiction of the FLSA, youth workers receive no protection from federal law. Despite the large number of workplace accidents, federal law does not require youth workers to be provided with safety training before starting a job. Employed youths are not required to have adult supervision. Notably, 41% of workplace deaths occur while an adolescent is doing work prohibited by federal child labor laws.

In addition, the FLSA provides no federal remedy for youths injured while working in prohibited jobs. In *Breitwieser v. KMS Industries, Inc.*, for example, a sixteen-year-old boy was crushed to death by the forklift he was operating. The Secretary of Labor had previously declared the operation of forklifts a "particularly hazardous" occupation. Under the Georgia Worker's Compensation statute in effect at the time, the amount of recovery given to beneficiaries of deceased workers with no dependents was $750. The Fifth Circuit Court of Appeals refused to imply a cause of action from the FLSA, despite the obvious inadequacy of the state worker compensation award. The court found that the Act already contained a "comprehensive enforcement scheme." Consequently, the FLSA provided no money damages for death. Most young workers, of course, have no spouse or dependents and thus the death of a minor worker often provides minimal compensation to the parent. Even if willful misconduct or gross negligence by the employer results in injury, federal law provides no remedy for the victim.

. . . .

c) Enforcement Deficiencies

The FLSA's child labor enforcement provisions are weak. Although the FLSA provides for criminal penalties, a "one free bite" rule is in effect; thus, employers may be jailed only if they have a prior conviction for breaking child labor laws. Between 1988 and 2004, no employer faced criminal prosecution. In stark contrast to the minimum-wage and maximum-hour provisions of the FLSA and most civil rights statutes, federal law gives no private right of action for violation of the child labor provisions and makes no provision for attorney fees. The most affected parties—aggrieved minor employees and their parents—are thus unable to sue as "private attorneys-general."

Enforcement is thus left entirely to administrative processes. There are fewer than one thousand federal wage-and-hour compliance officers to enforce the FLSA and numerous other statutes.

. . . .

The DOL consistently understates the problems of child labor. The DOL has estimated fewer than 10,000 children working in violation of federal laws in every year since 1994. In a recent, thorough study, Professors Kruse and Mahony, using the Current Population Survey (CPS) and other sources, estimated that businesses employ 154,000 children in violation of federal or state labor laws in an average week; 301,000 children are illegally working during a year. Most children working in violation of the FLSA are under sixteen years old and work an average of ten hours more than allowed by law. They also work in prohibited industries and occupations. In 2001, as in the past, "minority children and children from families with annual incomes below $25,000 were more likely than other children to work illegally." Teens unlawfully employed in hazardous jobs earn, on average, $1.38 less per hour than lawful workers in the same occupations. When combined with savings derived from employing youths for excessive hours, illegal child labor results in employer cost savings of roughly $136 million per year.

. . . .

Lack of federal enforcement is particularly egregious in the agricultural industry. The statistics are themselves instructive. In 1990, the DOL reported only 138 cases of child labor violations. In 1993, the DOL reported fifty-four cases with violations involving 146 farm children, and in 1997, it reported fourteen cases with violations involving twenty-two children. In contrast, others estimate over a million child labor violations and 100,000 minors working illegally on farms each year.

2. State Laws

a) Child Labor Laws

Working children typically fare no better under current state child labor laws, which generally track the FLSA. State statutes, however, apply in the many instances when the FLSA is silent or inapplicable to a particular employment situation. The major issues covered by state child labor laws include: (1) the type of work children may perform, (2) minimum age, (3) number of hours and time of work, (4) involvement in decision making by responsible adults, (5) legal remedies after injury, and (6) administrative enforcement of existing rules.

Federal law is generally more stringent than state law in defining "hazardous work," which is barred for juveniles. More than half of the states define "hazardous" work less restrictively than federal regulations. Seventeen states either exempt agricultural employment entirely or do not identify it as a covered industry under the state's child labor laws. Another eight jurisdictions place only the minimal restrictions on agricultural employment used by federal law.

. . . .

Federal law requires no consent from parents or school authorities for children to work. State law, although varied, follows this pattern of giving parents little legal control over the child's decision to work. Only nineteen states require parental consent for children under sixteen years old to work. Only twelve require consent by parents for sixteen- and seventeen-year-olds to work.

Under the FLSA, no limitations exist on hours worked by sixteen-and seventeen-year-olds, and many states' laws are similar. Thirty-one states allow these teens to work without an employment or age certificate. Thirty-six states permit forty hours or more of work while school is in session. Arkansas, for example, restricts children to fifty-four hours per week during school. Notably, only four states limit the employment of sixteen- and seventeen-year-olds to five hours or less of paid work during a school day. Twenty-eight states impose no restrictions on the amount of work time on school days. Thirty-one states have no upper limit on the amount of hours per day, hours per week, or days per week that minors may work during school vacation. Administration of state child labor laws is generally poor.... Some state agencies have statutes with no penalties for violation or no enforcement authority. The amount collected for state child labor violations was often trivial. In many instances, where an employed minor is fatally injured in the workplace while working illegally, the only penalty is criminal, and in many states even this is not available.

b) Workers' Compensation

When youths are injured on the job, state workers' compensation systems often provide the exclusive remedy. These statutes grant employers immunity from tort actions by injured employees in exchange for limited compensation for injuries that arise out of and in the course of employment. The benefits that injured employees usually receive are typically meager—one-half or two-thirds of employees' average weekly income plus hospital and medical costs. In contrast, the employers' total cost for compensation insurance is a small fraction of their total payroll. Employers are liable for only these small amounts because compensation systems often ignore the problems of long-term disability, occupational disease, and worker rehabilitation. These problems are particularly acute for young workers injured on the job. In addition, workers' compensation awards may be less for young workers because they are more likely to work part-time, earn lower wages, lack dependents, and be illegally employed.

....

VI. Conclusion

In the end, this Article returns to the very beginning. As President Franklin Roosevelt noted in 1937, there is "no justification" for the amount and results of child labor in the United States. Although some of the original abuses have been eliminated since 1937, others remain and new problems have emerged in the modern era. In some situations, minors and their families may legitimately make the choice to work. Young people may benefit from opportunities to acquire responsibility, compensation, and knowledge in the workplace. But these opportunities should create "social capital"—opportunities for later employment or education. The current legal rules, and administration of these rules, create enormous damage to American children, their families, and society at large. The subject of child labor elicits instinctive images of a problem long since solved in the United States and confined to the developing world. Yet it is these instinctive images and lack of political will that hamper reexamination of our current public policies. It is time to begin a public conversation about this unspoken tragedy.

Notes and Questions

1. To what does Moscowitz attribute America's failure to revise its antiquated approach to child labor? What role does history play in the U.S. context? Social attitudes? How does he see the capacity of young people to make decisions about how much work is right for them? Where do his theories fall in terms of the CRC empowerment debate?

———

The article by Celeste Corlett, immediately following, chides the United States for hypocrisy in its approach to agricultural labor by minors. The article explains that the U.S. has strongly supported the principles of the Worst Forms Convention, while failing to recognize its own legal and moral support for oppressive child labor policies in the agricultural sphere. The article sets out the historical reasons for "agricultural exceptionalism," and explains the many loopholes which lead to the exploitation of children in this sector.

Celeste Corlett, *Impact of the 2000 Labor Treaty on United States Child Laborers*

19 Arizona Journal of International and Comparative Law 713 (2002)

I. INTRODUCTION

....

Former President William Clinton raised hopes that the United States would change the policies that allow children to work in the hazardous conditions of the agriculture industry. Speaking to the International Labour Organization (ILO), a United Nations agency, Clinton declared:

The time has come to build on the growing world consensus to ban the most abusive forms of child labor.... We will not tolerate young children risking their health and breaking their bodies in hazardous and dangerous working conditions for hours unconscionably long — regardless of country, regardless of circumstance. These are not some archaic practices out of a Charles Dickens novel. These are things that happen in too many places today.

The occasion for President Clinton's speech was the signing by ILO member nations of an international child labor treaty on June 16, 1999 in Geneva....

....

II. CHILD LABOR LAW IN THE UNITED STATES

B. Regulation of Child Labor During the New Deal Era

After the Great Depression, the prevailing view in the United States was that government intervention in the economy and industrial reform was needed to improve the economy and the life of the laborer. The New Deal programs included legislation providing child labor standards, fair wages and maximum work hours. Introducing his New Deal legislation, President Franklin Roosevelt proclaimed:

Our problem is to work out in practice those labor standards which will permit the maximum but prudent employment of our human resources to bring within the reach of the average man and woman a maximum of goods and of services conducive to the fulfillment of the promise of American life. Legislation can, I hope, be passed at this session of Congress further to help those who toil in factory and on farm. We have promised it.

However, an environment of discrimination and racism led to many restrictions on New Deal legislation, including child labor laws. Southerners felt that the New Deal programs would destroy the underpinnings of the entire southern economy. The climate of racism was apparent even before the introduction of the Fair Labor and Standards Act of 1938 (FLSA), which dealt with child labor. In 1935, when Congress was considering the Social Security Act, the Southern position was expressed in the *Jackson Daily News*:

The average Mississippian can't imagine himself chipping in to pay pensions for able-bodied Negroes to sit around in idleness on front galleries, supporting all their kinfolks on pensions, while cotton and corn crops are crying for workers to get them out of the grass.

Responding to Southern concerns, Congress excluded agricultural employees from the benefits of the Social Security Act.

.... This blatant racial discrimination was an accepted part of the status quo by the time Congress considered the FLSA in 1938. The FLSA is the federal statute that sets minimum ages for work, maximum numbers of work-hours per day and per week, and the minimum hourly wage. During the debates over the FLSA, Representative Wilcox of Florida expressed his opposition to the statute:

There has always been a difference in the wage scale of white and colored labor. So long as Florida people are permitted to handle the matter, this delicate and perplexing problem can be adjusted.... You cannot put the Negro and the white man on the same basis and get away with it. Not only would such a situation result in grave social and racial conflicts but it would also result in throwing the Negro out of employment and in making him a public charge.... This bill, like the anti-lynching bill, is another political goldbrick for the Negro.

Agreeing with his colleague from Florida, Senator "Cotton" Ed Smith from South Carolina added that just like the federal anti-lynching bills "the main object of [the FLSA] is, by human legislation, to overcome the splendid gifts of God to the South."

President Roosevelt acquiesced to Congress' practice of exempting agricultural workers from New Deal legislation. For instance, the Roosevelt Administration's proposed FLSA exempted agricultural workers from its protections. Notably, the majority of farm workers were either Blacks in the South or Latinos and Asians in the West. Despite Roosevelt's speech promising to help those who toiled on the farms, he later announced that "there has never been any thought of including field labor in the Wages and Hours Bill." With virtually no opposition, exemptions for agricultural workers were incorporated into the new FLSA. While the passage of the FLSA was a great victory for most workers, it offered no minimum age, maximum hours, or minimum wage protections for adults and children in agriculture.

C. Current Regulation of Child Labor in Agriculture

Over the ensuing years, Congress amended the FLSA several times, adding protections for agricultural workers and children. For instance, in 1966, the FLSA was amended to prevent children working on farms from engaging in hazardous occupations, as determined by the Secretary of Labor. The most substantial changes to the FLSA affecting child agricultural workers came in 1974. These amendments prohibited children under the age of twelve from working on any farm. Moreover, children between ages twelve and sixteen could work only on the same farms as their parents.

1. Hazardous Work

Sixty years after its enactment, the FLSA still carves out exemptions that essentially allow most children to work in agriculture under hazardous conditions, despite amendments to the statute. Section 212 of the FLSA expressly prohibits oppressive child labor, stating, "No employer shall employ any oppressive child labor in commerce or in the production of goods for commerce...." Yet, Section 213(c) exempts the agricultural business, the third most dangerous occupation in the United States, from regulations prohibiting oppressive child labor in certain situations:

(c) Child labor requirements

(1) Except as provided in paragraph (2) or (4), the provisions of section 212 [prohibition of oppressive child labor] of this title relating to child labor shall not apply to any employee employed in agriculture outside of school hours for the school district where such employee is living while he is so employed, if such employee—

(A) is less than 12 years of age and (i) is employed by his parent, or by a person standing in the place of his parent, on a farm owned or operated by such parent or person or (ii) is employed with the consent of his parent to a person standing in the place of his parent, on a farm, [description of a small business farm] or (ii) his parent or such person is employed on the same farm as such employee, or

(B) is 12 years or 13 years of age and (i) such employment is with the consent of his parent or person standing in the place of his parent, or (ii) his parent or such person is employed on the same farm as such employee, or

(C) is fourteen years of age or older.

(2) the provisions of section 212 [prohibition of oppressive child labor] of this title relating to child labor shall apply to a child employee below the age of 16 em-

ployed in agriculture in an occupation that the Secretary of Labor finds and declares to be particularly hazardous for the employment of children below the
age of sixteen, except where such employee is employed by his parent or by a
person standing in the place of his parent on a farm owned or operated by such
parent or person.

As long as the activity is merely hazardous and not "particularly hazardous," many
groups of children may work in oppressive working conditions under the above exemptions. There is no minimum age requirement to work under hazardous conditions, as
long as the child works for his parent on a farm owned or operated by the parent or as
long as the child's parent works on the same farm. The exemption in Section 213(c) of
the FLSA allows a child of any age whose parent is a farm worker to work on the same
farm as his parent. If a child is twelve or thirteen, then the child need only have the consent of the parent to work on the farm, even if working conditions are hazardous or oppressive. If a child is fourteen, he does not even need parental consent. Most importantly,
a child of any age may work under even "particularly hazardous" conditions in the agriculture industry, if the child is employed by his parent or works on a farm operated by
his parent. Children are prohibited from working in other hazardous industries, such as
mining and manufacturing, regardless who employs them. The government's recognition of the need to protect children in one hazardous industry but not another is inconsistent at best.

On the face of the law, it appears that by allowing children of any age to work in the
fields, even under hazardous conditions, the legislators are simply acknowledging the tradition of a child helping with the chores of a family farm. However, the key to the problem lies in the interpretation of the language working for a "parent on a farm owned *or
operated* by [a] parent." Farm owners often hire farm laborers as "sharecroppers" or independent contractors. The farm owner enters into an agreement with the farm worker
indicating that the farm worker will operate an independent farming operation and will
pay the farm owner a portion of the crops harvested. In reality, the farm worker, under
the guise of an "independent contractor," is an employee of the farm owner, and the farm
owner escapes the FLSA and other labor regulations. As a result, the farm worker, now
labeled an "independent contractor," or "farm operator," may allow his children, no matter how young, to work under hazardous conditions simply because the parent "operates" the farm.

Due to the exemptions under the FLSA, the case of a young child working under hazardous conditions in the fields does not automatically amount to a violation of the child
labor laws. In order for the Department of Labor to intervene, it must determine that
the exemptions under the law do not apply. Then, if the farm owner denies any wrongdoing, the case must be resolved in a court, which must determine whether the farm
worker's relationship is one of independent contractor or employee. Each situation must
be decided on a case-by-case basis, where each court determines which factors to consider.
One court may interpret the FLSA to "effectuate its humanitarian and remedial purposes"
and give a narrow interpretation of what constitutes an independent contractor. Yet, another court may provide a broad interpretation and find the worker to be an independent
contractor, even though the worker's only investment in the farm may be a pair of gloves
and a pail, as compared to the landowner's tractors, irrigation equipment, and transport
trucks.

The case of *Department of Labor v. Elderkin* illustrates the irrationality of the law. In
1995, at 9:30 p.m., Peter Gage, a ten-year-old, was working on a farm around a dangerous machine—a feeder wagon—when he had an accident. Peter describes the incident:

"It caught the strings off my snow suit, pulled me in, kept banging my head against the metal, ripped my right arm off and threw me out the other side." As a result, the Department of Labor investigated the farm owner. It found that not only Peter, but eight other children, ages seven, ten, and eleven, had worked on the farm, driving a fork lift and tractor, working in a pen with a bull, and operating a chain saw. The farm owner claimed that he had no employees and that he used only independent contractors. The farm owner asserted that Peter was an employee of his father, who was an independent contractor, and thus the farm owner had not violated the child labor laws. The court found that although some factors weighed in favor of the ten-year-old being an independent contractor, the child was actually an employee of the farm owner. The court penalized the farm owner for employing Peter and the other children in dangerous occupations, for employing another child in hazardous work after Peter's accident, and for refusing to provide records requested by the investigators. Had it not been for the accident, Peter and the eight other children may never have been discovered on the farm.

....

2. Minimum Wages, Maximum Hours

Besides allowing oppressive child labor, Section 213 of the FLSA exempts agricultural child laborers from the minimum-wage and maximum-hour requirements. The statute provides in relevant part:

(a) Minimum wage and maximum hour requirements

The provisions of sections 206 [minimum wage] ... and section 207 [maximum hours and overtime] of this title shall not apply with respect to ... (6) any employee employed in agriculture (A) if such employee is employed by an employer [describes small business employer], (B) if such employee is the parent, spouse, child, or other member of his employer's immediate family, (C) if such employee (i) is employed as a hand harvest laborer and is paid on a piece rate basis in an operation which has been, and is customarily and generally recognized as having been, paid on a piece rate basis in the region of employment, (ii) commutes daily from is permanent residence to the farm on which he is so employed, and (iii) has been employed in agriculture less than thirteen weeks during the preceding calendar year, (D) if such employee ... (i) is sixteen years of age or under and is employed as a hand harvest laborer ... (ii) is employed on the same farm as his parent or person standing in the place of his parent, and (iii) is paid at the same piece rate as employees over age sixteen are paid on the same farm, or (E) ...

(b) Maximum hour requirement

The provisions of section 207 [maximum hours and overtime] of this title shall not apply with respect to ...

(12) any employee employed in agriculture ...

These exemptions allow a child to earn less than minimum wage if the child is employed by his parent. The problems discussed with respect to the hazardous-work exemptions also apply to the minimum-wage and maximum-hour exemptions in that a court has to determine on a case-by-case basis whether an "employee ... is the child ... of the employer's immediate family." However, the minimum-wage exemptions go even further than the oppressive child labor exemption. The only conditions a farm owner must meet in order to pay piece rate wages are that the work is normally paid on a piece-wage basis, the worker is permanent (not migrant), and the work is limited to thirteen weeks. These broad conditions allow most farm owners to pay piece-rate wages. The majority of farm workers are not migrant but local workers, so they meet at least one condition. Additionally, although the rate of pay is limited to thirteen weeks at each farm, it is not limited to longer time periods at a variety of farms. According to a 1998 study, agricultural workers aged fourteen to seventeen earn an average of four dollars an hour. With a piece-rate of fifty cents per bushel of chilies, younger children make significantly less than the minimum wage, considering their small size.

The maximum hours exemption for agricultural workers contains no conditions. There are no limits to the number of hours a child may work in a day or week, as long as it is not during school hours. Moreover, regardless of the number of hours a child works, employers are not required to pay overtime. During peak season, farm owners require long hours to harvest the crops in order to avoid crop damage. Human Rights Watch reports sixteen-year-old children working fourteen-hour days, six days a week, from April to November, while harvesting lettuce in Yuma, Arizona. The children are not paid overtime for their eighty-four-hour work weeks, which are legal under the FLSA's exemptions.

In sum, after sixty years of labor law legislation, children working in the agriculture industry are virtually unprotected from long hours, low wages, and hazardous working conditions. Thus, it was with great hope that child advocates in the United States looked to the Child Labor Treaty for protections afforded to children throughout the world.

III. CONVENTION CONCERNING THE PROHIBITION AND IMMEDIATE ACTION FOR THE ELIMINATION OF THE WORST FORMS OF CHILD LABOUR (THE "CHILD LABOR TREATY")

C. Article 3(d) of the Child Labor Treaty—Hazardous Work

....

Given the detailed record regarding what constitutes hazardous work under the [Worst Forms of] Child Labor Treaty, when the United States ratified the Treaty, it agreed to eliminate hazardous child labor domestically. The Recommendation's additional clarification of what amounts to hazardous work describes the exact conditions under which child laborers work in the agriculture industry in the United States. American children working in agriculture are exposed to pesticides, which are hazardous substances. Children work in extreme weather conditions, for long hours and during the night. They utilize dangerous tools, such as feeder wagons, forklifts, and tractors. All of these conditions, and more, are prohibited child labor under Article 3(d) of the Child Labor Treaty and under the Recommendation. The members of the Committee representing workers made clear that hazardous work includes work on farms, except those farms where the children are relatives of the farm *owners*. Therefore, when the United States signed and ratified the Child Labor Treaty, it agreed to eliminate agricultural child labor as it currently exists under United States law.

Despite appearances, the United States did not implement the protective working conditions for children envisioned by the Child Labor Treaty. Because Article 4(1) of the Child Labor Treaty permits each state to define what constitutes hazardous work, and because, even upon ratification of the Treaty, the United States will not change its domestic laws, the United States has ensured that its current labor laws will not protect children from performing hazardous work.

IV. UNITED STATES RATIFICATION OF HUMAN RIGHTS TREATIES

....

D. United States Ratification Policy as it Applies to the Child Labor Treaty

The unofficial United States policy of prohibiting treaties from creating new domestic law or changing current law is perfectly illustrated by the government's treatment of the Child Labor Treaty. Article 3(d) of the Child Labor Treaty prohibits child labor in hazardous conditions, and the worker representatives of the ILO Committee on Child Labor made clear that Article 3(d)'s prohibitions include child labor on farms that are not bona fide family farms. Nevertheless, Article 4(1) allows each signatory state to apply its own interpretation of what constitutes hazardous work:

> The types of work referred to under Article 3(d) shall be determined by national laws or regulations or by the competent authority, after consultation with the organizations of employers and workers concerned, taking into consideration relevant international standards, in particular Paragraph 3 and 4 of the Worst Forms of Child Labour Recommendation, 1999.

Before the Child Labor Treaty was ever presented to employer and worker representatives for interpretation, the United States representatives had assumed they would negotiate a treaty that would not change the laws of the United States. One American negotiator, Michael Dennis, explained that the United States had to establish that Article 3(d) excludes the family farm since United States law exempts work by children "employed by a parent or by a person standing in the place of a parent on a farm owned or operated by such parent or person." This interpretation allows virtually anyone on the farm to employ children. An employer does not have to be the child's relative since such employer can "stand[] in the place of a parent." Moreover, if the farm is "operated by [a] parent," such parent is an "independent contractor" and can lawfully employ his own children. Thus, regardless how the worker representatives interpreted the Child Labor Treaty, the United States government representatives never intended that the Treaty change domestic child labor laws.

. . . .

E. Impact of the Child Labor Treaty, United States Labor Laws and Policies on Child Labor in Agriculture

Exemptions in United States labor law allow children to work in the agriculture industry under deplorable conditions, which harm their health and education. Child laborers suffer the impacts of the law. For example, in Casa Grande, Arizona, on a day when the heat rose to 110 degrees in the shade, a fourteen-year-old pitched watermelons and chopped cotton for twelve hours a day. The fourteen-year-old described the job of pitching watermelons: "Now that's some hard work. You throw it down the line, one to the other, standing about five feet apart. . . . You can faint." In another case, children, ages eight, twelve and sixteen, dragged thirty to forty pound baskets of beans around the fields from five-thirty in the morning until "they [couldn't] stand no more," working ten to twelve-hour days. Moreover, children have died from devastating accidents on the fields. A nine-year-old child was killed when he was accidentally run over by a tractor while working in a blueberry field. In Utah, a child, who had been picking fruit and pruning trees, died from a massive brain hemorrhage after being sprayed twice in one week with pesticides.

. . . . As farm workers, children use knives, work near heavy machinery, climb ladders, and are exposed to pesticides. One hundred thousand children annually endure agriculture-related injuries in the United States. They are allowed to reenter pesticide sprayed fields at the same time as adults. The Environmental Protection Agency studies on "safe reentry" into pesticide sprayed fields are based on a 154-pound adult male, not on a ten-year-old child. Farm workers frequently have no washing facilities, a fact that virtually guarantees that they will ingest the pesticides on the produce they just picked or absorb the chemicals through the skin.

By its own laws, the United States recognizes the need to prohibit oppressive child labor. Also, it seeks to eliminate hazardous child labor in other countries. Recently, Congress appropriated 167 million dollars toward eliminating child labor in foreign counties. Previous funds already helped 9,000 children in Bangladesh leave sweatshop work and obtain education, and 7,000 children in Pakistan are going to school instead of stitching soccer balls. Congress committed millions of dollars toward the elimination of labor in foreign countries because "that is what the American people want. They have said time and again they want child labor reduced, they do not want to buy articles of clothing, sporting goods, and other commodities that are made with child labor." This public sentiment is evident in the Nike, Wal-Mart and Levi's boycotts that led to substantial changes in child labor conditions in other countries.

With concern for child laborers, Congress mandated that the United States Department of Labor study the exploitation of child labor in other countries. In its second report, By the Sweat and Toil of Children Volume II: The Use of Child Labor in U.S. Agricultural Import and Forced and Bonded Child Labor (the "Report"), the Department of Labor surveyed the agriculture work performed by children in foreign countries. The Report found that ten-year-old children worked on a short-term basis during the harvest season, picking fruits and vegetables. Children worked "long hours without rest." The Report states: "Fatigue makes them more susceptible to accidents. Dangerous working conditions, excessive physical strain, malnutrition, and regular exposure to ... toxic chemicals lead to lung, skin, and respiratory diseases, back injuries, and permanent physical handicaps and deformities." The Report further informs that "children exposed to [toxic chemicals] tend to become ill or disabled much more quickly than do adults with similar exposure ... The probability of their developing cancer is greater than that of adults having equal exposure." These findings are nearly identical to the results of the Human Rights Watch study of American farm worker children. Therefore, the same exploitation of child labor the United States condemns in other countries, it exempts from protective labor laws within its own borders.

Notes and Questions

1. Corlett presents a strong and detailed indictment of the U.S. approach in its ratification of the Worst Forms Convention. In her view, does the U.S. live up to the terms of either the Minimum Age Convention or the Worst Forms Convention? If child labor is the result of "poverty," then why is it still prevalent in certain sector in the United States as well? How has U.S. agribusiness influenced the techniques of treaty ratification?

2. According to Corlett's analysis, how should we interpret U.S. "concern" for child laborers in other countries? What does she imply about the U.S. approach to ratification of human rights conventions in general?

V. Possible Remedies in the Child Labor Arena

As with any human rights issue, the primary means of "enforcing" the obligations of states towards their own citizens is via the UN's blame and shame method of treaty reporting and expert commentary. In the children's rights area, states are especially prone to neglect commitments made, and to express good intentions that are never fulfilled. With so much disagreement over the relative merits of the "abolitionist" versus empowerment views of child labor, it is not surprising that effective remedies to end even the worst forms of child labor have been hard to come by.

Often seen as merely an unfortunate aspect of endemic poverty, child labor occupies a very ambiguous and contentious place in discussions of human rights. Nevertheless, there is no lack of academic writing on the subject of possible remedies to address the most serious abuses. The final section of this chapter will look at several categories of "remedies" that go beyond, or have the potential to go beyond, the blame and shame strategies set up under the relevant treaties. General "reporting systems," such as the mechanisms of the ILO and the UNCRC Committee system, do not seem to have had much effect on the scope and scale of child labor, whether of the worst forms of not. We have seen that other methods, such as through public interest litigation in India, can be comparatively effective, even if primarily aimed at raising awareness.

In this section, the last of the chapter, there will first be an examination of recourse to the U.S. courts by foreign plaintiffs under the Alien Tort Claims Act. This statute, dating from the late eighteenth century, permits alien plaintiffs to bring actions in U.S. courts seeking damages for torts that are judged to have violated "the law of nations." This kind of remedy is, by its nature, only available in situations where there have been demonstrably gross forms of human rights violations. In that sense, it will only be relevant to a narrow band of cases, as explained below.

We will then consider what global trade regulation might have to offer by way of responding to the exploitation of child labor. Many have advocated the use of trade sanctions to encourage countries to eliminate their child labor abuses; specifically, by refusing the importation of goods made by child labor, at least in its worst forms. While much has been made of this possibility, in fact it is very unlikely that countries will prove willing or able to identify such goods and refuse them access. Nevertheless, the idea has shown resiliency and at least theoretical appeal. The fact that most child labor is not related to the global economy in the first place makes it much harder to approach this problem through international remedies. Trade-based measures are obviously ineffective where the goods produced by children are not being internationally traded

The anti-sweatshop movement managed to popularize the child labor issue for a time during the 1990s, as major U.S. importers and retail chains were forced, because of negative publicity, to certify that their products were not made from child labor. Some maintain that this type of "voluntary" compliance in the face of popular pressure offers a way forward. Immediately after the trade sanctions section, there is material on the role voluntary corporate codes of conduct might have in eliminating child labor, at least where the labor involved has some intersection with the global economy.

The final section will take a brief look at the ILO's successful International Program for the Elimination of Child Labor (IPEC) program. Although limited in its scope and scale, IPEC has created a winning formula: essentially providing funding to families to make sure their children go to school, thus reversing the economic incentives that have long inclined parents to push their children in the direction of labor. It is not clear whether this form of direct "investment" in education will be made available widely enough to bring large numbers of working children out of even the most detrimental sectors, but indications to date are impressive. By creating new economic arrangements at the community level, it is possible that parents will be persuaded to forego the short term benefits linked with removing their children from schooling.

We have already seen how the contemporary trend is to focus on the "worst forms" of child labor, rather than on abolishing child labor as such. However, this bifurcation complicates matters in that it can lead to an endless argument over what constitutes truly hazardous employment, and whether there is a universal standard to judge this by. In light of the regional case studies provided in the earlier readings in this chapter, try to determine which category of remedies might be effective in eliminating the various types of child labor described, or at least in eliminating its most abusive forms.

A. The Alien Tort Claims Approach: A Potent Remedy for a Narrow Band of Abuses

The Alien Tort Claims Act, also known as the Alien Tort Statute, dates from the Judiciary Act of 1789. It grants jurisdiction to U.S. federal courts over tort claims brought by alien plaintiffs against those who have violated "the law of nations" or a treaty of the United States.[7] The act lay dormant until it was revived in the late 1970s on behalf of the family of a young man tortured to death by a police official in Paraguay, in the famous *Filartiga*[8] case, discussed in the article below.

Since that time, the act has been used in a number of creative ways by lawyers working on behalf of victims of human rights abuses in a number of countries. In 2004, the U.S. Supreme Court clarified the scope of the act,[9] explaining that while the statute should be seen as primarily jurisdictional in nature, it could also be relied upon with respect to a very limited number of tort actions—in particular, those that "rest on a norm of international character accepted by the civilized world and defined with a specificity comparable to the features of the 18th-century paradigms we have recognized." With *Sosa*, the Court set a high, but not insurmountable, bar.

The ATCA is narrowly cast; only torts that violate the "law of nations" qualify, and of these, only those that meet the standard articulated in Sosa. In the child labor context, the ATCA would only be useful in a very limited range of complaints. The plaintiffs would ideally be alien children who had suffered at the hands of corporate employers who were in some way amenable to the jurisdiction of the U.S. courts. Such children might gain attention, as well as damages, by bringing claims in U.S. courts under the ATCA, so long as the torts complained of involved severe and widely recognized violations of the law of nations. One can imagine that only the most abusive and exploitative forms of labor—bonded, slave-like labor or extremely hazardous work—would qualify. The Act has been found to apply in cases of egregious abuses of the rights of workers. Recently, a U.S. District Court judge found that bonded child labor could indeed meet the "law of nations" standard that would qualify for treatment under the ATCA.[10]

In the article that follows, Marisa Pagnattaro explores the possible uses of the ATCA in the labor context. Describing recent ATCA cases on the subject of labor rights, she sets out a confident vision of the statute as a device for bringing attention to the obligations of corporate employers.

---

7. 28 U.S.C. § 1350 (2000).
8. *Filartiga v. Pena-Irala* 630 F.2d 876 (1980).
9. *Sosa v. Alvarez-Machain* 542 U.S. 692 (2004).
10. See *John Roe I, et al., Plaintiffs v. Bridgestone Corporation*, 492 F. Supp. 2d 988, June 26, 2007.

Marisa Anne Pagnattaro, *Enforcing International Labor Standards: The Potential of the Alien Tort Claims Act*

37 Vanderbilt Journal of Transnational Law 203 (2004)

A crucial aspect of participating in the global community is effective enforcement of international agreements, treaties and conventions. Workers who are treated in violation of international law need an effective means to redress their grievances. The Alien Tort Claims Act (ATCA) offers that potential in the realm of international labor standards. If U.S. multinational companies fail to comply with the terms of international agreements, they should be held accountable. The United States has the unique opportunity to take the high road by honoring its international commitments in the realm of labor rights. To do so, even in the face of opposition from those who fear that it might "dampen commerce," would give the United States a great deal of international credibility.

As one commentator observed, "there is a groundswell of people demanding the benefits of globalization … propelled by millions of workers who have been knocked around by globalization, but who nonetheless get up, dust themselves off and knock again on globalization's door, demanding to get into the system." At the present time, there is limited recourse for these workers…. Indeed, the position of the WTO is succinctly stated on its official web site with the caption "Labour Standards: not on the agenda" and its statement that, "for the time being, there are no committees or working parties dealing with the issue." For critics of the current course of globalization, this position is a call to action.

Where then, can workers go for enforcement of international labor standards? With increasing frequency, some advocates for improved global labor standards are looking to federal courts in the United States. The ATCA has the potential to be a new weapon in the international movement for labor rights by offering workers the ability to enforce international rules against U.S.-based multinational companies. Although it is not a substitute for domestic law, the ATCA should be used as a way of giving force to international agreements pertaining to labor standards by holding companies responsible for their treatment of foreign workers.

Ironically, the ATCA is not a new law; adopted by the first Congress in the Judiciary Act of 1789, it provides for a federal cause of action for claims brought by: 1) an alien, 2) alleging a tort, 3) committed in violation of the law of nations or a treaty of the United States. For nearly 200 years, the law lapsed into obscurity. In the last twenty years, however, it has been revived in a number of human rights contexts, including claims for egregious employment and labor practices. The ATCA has the potential to enforce human rights norms, including international labor standards.

An essential aspect of a successful claim under the ATCA is the demonstration that the acts committed violate the law of nations. This prompts many unanswered legal questions in the international labor context. What constitutes the "law of nations" with regard to labor practices? What international labor standards rise to the requisite level? Should core labor standards set forth by the United Nations, treaties, international agreements, and conventions promulgated by groups such as the ILO be a part of the "law of nations"?

Ultimately, this article concludes that there is sufficient international consensus, evidenced by treaties, conventions, declarations, and resolutions, to support ATCA worker-related claims, making this statute an important method of enforcing existing core labor rights. Specifically, there is widespread agreement that the law of nations prohibits extrajudicial murder and genocide, torture, kidnapping, unlawful detention, and slavery and forced labor.

Moreover, based on a number of official documents, there is demonstrable international agreement that the law of nations also protects freedom of association and collective bargaining, prohibitions on child labor, and discrimination, including gender discrimination.

....

II. ATCA: Developing International Labor Jurisprudence

A. History

....

The first case to test the use of the ATCA in the context of human rights was *Filartiga v. Pena-Irala*, in which Paraguayan citizens brought an action against another citizen of Paraguay who was in the United States for wrongful death of their son by deliberate torture. The Second Circuit held "that deliberate torture perpetrated under color of official authority violates universally accepted norms of the international law of human rights, regardless of the nationality of the parties." Laying important groundwork for future ATCA cases, the court elaborated: In the twentieth century the international community has come to recognize the common danger posed by the flagrant disregard of basic human rights and particularly the right to be free from torture. Spurred first by the Great War, and then the Second, civilized nations have banded together to prescribe acceptable norms of international behavior. From the ashes of the Second World War arose the United Nations Organization, amid hopes that an era of peace and cooperation had at last begun.... In the modern age, humanitarian and practical considerations have combined to lead the nations of the world to recognize that respect for fundamental human rights is in their individual and collective interest. Because of its broad human rights stance, *Filartiga* has been called the *Brown v. Board of Education* for the "transnational public law litigant," opening the door to a variety of claims.

B. The ATCA in International Labor Rights Contexts

The use of the ATCA in international labor rights cases has been spearheaded by the International Labor Rights Fund (ILRF). The Executive Director of the ILRF, Terry Collingsworth, became involved with the first case through a serendipitous set of circumstances:

The General Secretary of the Federation of Trade Unions of Burma (FTUB), U Maung Maung, had escaped Burma and was living in Thailand following his participation in the pro-democracy uprising of 1988. He enjoyed reading Reader's Digest because his parents had exposed him to the magazine when he was a child as a way to learn English. In 1994, he read an article about a lawsuit filed in the United States filed by a couple whose dog died after being over anesthetized by a veterinarian. Apparently, the couple had been successful in their case.... U Maung Maung was both amused and angered that the United States legal system provided a remedy for the accidental death of a dog but inexplicably allowed [the U.S. company] Unocal to use forced labor to build a billion dollar pipeline in Burma. Through a series of connections, U Maung Maung sought legal advice, and Collingsworth was approached about being lead counsel. He ultimately agreed, and in September 1996 the ILRF filed a complaint against Unocal.

In their complaints against Unocal, the plaintiffs alleged that Unocal directly or indirectly subjected villagers from the Tenasserim region in Myanmar to "forced labor, murder, rape, and torture" during Unocal's construction of a gas pipeline through that region. It is undisputed that the "Myanmar Military provided security and other services" for this project with Unocal's knowledge. The substance of the allegations against Unocal is grim. For example, when one plaintiff, who was forced to work on building roads leading to a pipeline construction area, attempted escape from the forced labor program, he was shot at by soldiers. Thereafter, in acts of retaliation, his wife and her baby were "thrown into a fire, resulting in injuries to her and the death of the child." Other plaintiffs testified that "while conscripted to work on pipeline-related construction projects, they were raped at knife-point by Myanmar soldiers who were members of the battalion supervising the work." Plaintiffs seek to hold Unocal liable under the ATCA as well as through other causes of action for these alleged acts. Despite motions to dismiss, the plaintiffs' ATCA claims against Unocal remain an important part of the ongoing Unocal litigation.[11]

The ILRF also has three other labor-related ATCA cases pending in U.S. federal courts. The first case, *SINALTRAINAL v. Coca-Cola Company*,[12] involves the alleged "systematic intimidation, kidnapping, detention, and murder of trade unionists in Colombia" and, in particular, the ongoing campaign of terror against trade unionists at Coca-Cola. The defendants allegedly "hired, contracted with or otherwise directed paramilitary security forces that utilized extreme violence and murdered, tortured, unlawfully detained or otherwise silenced trade union leaders" who represented workers at defendants' facilities. The ATCA claims are for murder, denial of fundamental rights to associate and organize, kidnapping, unlawful detention, torture, and crimes against humanity.

In the second case, *Aldana v. Fresh Del Monte Produce, Inc.,*[13] the allegations arise out of activities at a banana plantation (Bobos plantation) where workers were represented by SITRABI, a national trade union of plantation workers affiliated with the International Union of Food, Agricultural, Hotel, Restaurant, Catering, Tobacco, and Allied Workers' Associations. The complaint alleges, inter alia, that certain of the defendants "hired or otherwise created an agency relationship with an armed and organized security force ... to use violence to intimidate the SITRABI leadership in order to affect the outcome of the ongoing collective bargaining negotiations and the labor disputes concerning the workforce at the Bobos plantation." The complaint contains two ATCA causes of action: one for torture, kidnapping, unlawful detention and crimes against humanity; and a second claim for denial of fundamental rights to associate and organize. At this time, a motion to dismiss is pending.[14]

Similar to the other two cases, the third case, *The Estate of Rodriguez v. Drummond Co., Inc.,*[15] also deals with the treatment of union leaders. This case involves the alleged "systematic intimidation and murder of trade unionists in Colombia, South America at the hands of paramilitaries working as agents" of the defendants. The defendant companies allegedly "hired, contracted with or otherwise directed paramilitary security forces that utilized extreme violence and murdered, tortured, unlawfully detained or otherwise silenced trade union leaders of unions representing workers" at defendants' facilities. The two ATCA causes of action are for the extrajudicial killing of three union leaders and for the denial of fundamental rights to associate and organize. Both of these counts in the complaint have survived defendants' motions to dismiss.

---

11. The *Unocal* case was settled soon after the Supreme Court's decision was handed down in the Sosa case in 2004.

12. *Sinaltrainal v. Coca-Cola Co.* 256 F.Supp.2d 1345 (2003).

13. *Aldana v. Fresh Del Monte Produce, Inc.*, 305 F. Supp.2d 1285 (2003).

14. The case was dismissed on grounds of forum non conveniens. See *Aldana v. Fresh Del Monte Produce, Inc.*, 2007 WL 3054986 (S.D. Fla.).

15. *Rodriguez v. Drummond Co.*, 256 F. Supp. 2d 1250 (2003).

Another very high-profile case also involved labor issues and ATCA claims. Originally filed in January 1999, *Does I v. The Gap, Inc.*, was a class action suit brought on behalf of foreign "guest workers" from the Peoples Republic of China, the Philippines, Bangladesh, and Thailand working in the garment industry in the Commonwealth of the Northern Mariana Islands (CNMI). Plaintiffs alleged egregious working conditions, including physical abuse, intimidation tactics, forced labor, involuntary servitude, peonage, and discrimination. The ATCA claim was sweeping in nature, alleging violations of the law of nations through "forced labor, involuntary servitude, and peonage," and the forced relinquishment of [U]niversally-recognized and protected rights of association, freedom, speech, and privacy; the right to be free from workplace discrimination on grounds of gender, pregnancy, national origin, and other proscribed grounds; the right to be free from corporal punishment in the workplace; the right to organize and join labor unions and to engage in concerted protected activity; the right to attend church and practice their religions; the right to get pregnant and bear children; the right not to engage in industrial homework; and the right to be free from cruel, inhuman or degrading treatment or punishment.... [P]laintiffs' ATCA claim for involuntary servitude was dismissed because the complaint did not "contain sufficient allegations to show or give rise to an inference that the plaintiffs were forced to work by the use or threat of physical restraint, physical injury or legal coercion and that they had no other choice but to work." The case ultimately settled against all defendants except Levi Strauss & Co. Settlement terms include a total settlement fund of more than $20 million; the institution of a code of conduct of basic employment standards, including extra pay for overtime work, safe food and drinking water; factory monitoring; compensation for unpaid back wages; and repatriation—workers seeking to return to their home countries are eligible for up to $3,000 in travel and relocation costs. The settlement did not involve an admission of wrongdoing by the defendants.

In addition to these labor-related cases, there are other significant ATCA cases also pending for violations of human rights by U.S. companies such as Occidental Petroleum, Exxon Mobil, ChevronTexaco Corporation, and Dyncorp. The progression and outcome of these cases will significantly shape the landscape for all future ATCA claims, including those brought in the international labor arena. The following discussion is intended to give a sense of the current state of the law, as well as a road map for bringing ATCA cases on behalf of international workers.

III. Asserting An ATCA Labor-Related Case

A. Federal Jurisdiction Over Multinational Corporate Employers

International workers can seek redress in federal court in the United States. In accordance with *Filartiga*, a majority of courts have interpreted the ATCA as "providing both a private cause of action and a federal forum where aliens may seek redress for violations of international law." Section 1350 thus provides "both federal jurisdiction and a substantive right of action for certain violations of customary law." To maintain a claim, the worker must first demonstrate that he or she is an alien or non-citizen of the United States. Second, a tort must be alleged. With regard to this pleading requirement, "plaintiffs need not establish that every tort claim alleged constitutes an international tort within the meaning of Section 1350. Federal jurisdiction requires pleading only one such claim for each plaintiff." Lastly, the tort must be committed in violation of the law of nations....

Although the scope of the ATCA may sound expansive, one of the practical problems in international labor cases is that some potential defendants may not be subject to the jurisdiction of the federal courts. By virtue of the fact that they are incorporated in the

United States or have a principal place of business here, many multinational corporations are subject to federal jurisdiction. If a U.S. company has the right, obligation, or duty to control the labor policies of another entity, it could be subject to ATCA liability. Moreover, if a foreign company has an agent in the United States, it could subject the foreign company to personal jurisdiction in the United States in an ATCA case. However, often these companies have foreign partners over whom the federal courts cannot exercise personal jurisdiction under present legal standards.

IV. International Foundations for Labor Claims under the ATCA

....

A. General Human/Labor Rights

A number of international agreements contain general provisions regarding labor conditions, which lay the ground work for the argument that the most basic of labor rights are also human rights.

.... The ILO is an independent agency of the United Nations with 175 member countries dedicated to the promotion of fundamental principles and rights at work. It was founded in 1919 under the Treaty of Versailles and joined the U.N. system in 1946. In accordance with the 1998 Declaration on Fundamental Principles and Rights at Work, the ILO seeks to promote four basic principles:

- Freedom of association and the right to bargain collectively;

- Abolition of forced labor;

- Equal opportunity and treatment in the workplace; and

- The elimination of child labor. All of the core conventions have been ratified by at least 120 of the 175 members, and the majority have been accepted by over 150 members. In addition to the core standards, the ILO seeks to define "acceptable levels of working conditions and worker protection," such as occupational health and safety, working time, as well as social security pensions and health insurance. All of these documents, taken together, form a foundation for developing international labor rights and for determining what constitutes the law of nations for an ATCA claim.

Notes and Questions

1. Many have argued strenuously against use of the ATCA for the purpose of sanctioning U.S. multinational corporations. Is there a realistic danger that U.S. corporations would have their economic freedom of maneuver restricted by such reliance on the ATCA, or are such fears overblown? Is it possible that there is exaggeration on both sides—that the ATCA is not capable of offering significant hope for reducing international labor abuses, while the effects on U.S. corporate interests will also in fact be slight? Why do you think the ATCA has generated so much interest? Considering the child labor case studies we have reviewed in this chapter, in which situations would you want to try and rely on the ATCA?

2. Should child plaintiffs be allowed to proceed to U.S. courts in actions taken against U.S. corporations when they cooperate with repressive foreign governments in violating labor rights? Is there a danger that U.S. corporations would be asked to in essence take responsibility for the abusive actions and policies of foreign governments?

3. For a discussion of the potential of the ATCA to "tame" corporate abuses, see Ronen Shamir, *Between Self-Regulation and the Alien Tort Claims Act: On the Contested Concept*

of Corporate Social Responsibility, 38 Law and Society Review 635 (2004). As with the Pagnattaro excerpt, Shamir highlights the important, if limited, place occupied by the ATCA in educating the global public on the issue of labor rights violations by corporations. He notes the increasing popularity of voluntary codes of corporate conduct. Such codes may be seen as a response by corporations to negative publicity generated by legal actions.

4. The Alien Tort Claims Act undoubtedly has the potential to address certain labor abuses, especially where these involve the complicity of U.S. corporations. Is the Act relevant to the broader problem of child labor, whether in its worst forms or not? What are the legal limitations of the ATCA? Are you convinced by the argument put forward by some that the ATCA poses a threat to U.S. commercial interests? How much faith should be placed in the growing "corporate social responsibility movement"?

The *Sosa* decision, handed down in 2004, represented the first time the U.S. Supreme Court had interpreted the Alien Tort Claims Act. It was a much anticipated decision, as on it rested the future of many human rights-based claims by alien plaintiffs in U.S. courts. The following excerpt from an article by Virginia Gomez explains the significance of the Supreme Court's reasoning and its impact on defining the type of alien tort claims likely to succeed in the future. In general, the opinion was considered to be a moderate and balanced reading of the ATCA, allowing future claims to go forward, but only in a narrow range of circumstances. A section of the *Sosa* decision follows immediately after.

Virginia Monken Gomez, Note, *The Sosa Standard: What Does It Mean for Future ATS Litigation?*
33 Pepperdine Law Review 469 (2006)

III. Sosa v. Alvarez-Machain

A. Case Summary

After informal extradition talks broke down, the U.S. Drug Enforcement Agency ("DEA") enlisted petitioner José Francisco Sosa and several other Mexican nationals to forcibly abduct respondent Humberto Alvarez-Machain from Mexico in 1990 and bring him to the U.S. The DEA believed that Alvarez-Machain, a medical doctor allied with Mexican drug traffickers, participated in the interrogation, torture and murder of DEA agent Enrique Camarena-Salazar in 1985. Alvarez-Machain challenged his criminal indictment in U.S. courts on the ground that he was kidnapped in violation of the Extradition Treaty between the United States and Mexico. The case went all the way to the Supreme Court, and the Court concluded that Alvarez-Machain's forcible abduction did not prohibit a trial in the United States under its criminal laws. The case was remanded to the district court for trial, where Alvarez-Machain was acquitted of the criminal charges.

Still unsatisfied, Alvarez-Machain sued the United States for false arrest under the Federal Torts Claims Act ("FTCA") and DEA employee Sosa for violating the law of nations under the ATS. The district court dismissed the FTCA claim, but found in favor of Alvarez-Machain on the ATS claim and awarded him damages. The Ninth Circuit Court of Appeals affirmed the lower court's ATS judgment but reversed the FTCA holding. The Supreme Court granted certiorari and heard the case on March 30, 2004. The Sosa Court held that Alvarez-Machain could not recover (a) under the FTCA since the alleged transgressions occurred across the border, placing his case in the "foreign country" exception to the waiver of government immunity; nor (b) under the ATS because a single detention of less than one day did not violate a norm of customary international law so well defined as to create a substantive cause of action.

B. The *Sosa* Standard

In evaluating whether Alvarez-Machain brought a valid claim under the ATS, the Sosa Court articulated a long-awaited standard for ascertaining substantive claims under the ATS. Prior to Sosa, it was generally accepted that the ATS gave U.S. federal courts jurisdiction to hear claims brought forth "by an alien for a tort only, committed in violation of the law of nations or a treaty of the United States." The controversy stemmed from a dispute over first, whether the ATS was more than a jurisdictional grant, i.e., did it empower federal courts to recognize substantive claims that Congress has not specifically identified as viable causes of action? And second, if the ATS does empower courts to recognize substantive claims in violation of international law, how does a court determine what constitutes a violation of international law?

The Sosa Court directly settled the first flashpoint in the ATS debate. The Court held that the ATS is indeed more than a jurisdictional grant, and that the statute authorizes U.S. federal courts to recognize substantive violations of a small number of well-settled violations of international law. The Court concluded:

> [W]e agree that the [ATS] is in terms only jurisdictional, [but] we think that at the time of enactment the jurisdiction enabled federal courts to hear claims in a very limited category defined by the law of nations and recognized at common law.... [The ATS presumably allowed] federal courts [to] entertain claims once the jurisdictional grant was on the books, because torts in violation of the law of nations would have been recognized within the common law of the time [and] ... [t]here is too much in the historical record to believe that Congress would have enacted the ATS only to leave it lying fallow indefinitely.

The Court then turned its attention to the second hotly-debated issue in ATS litigation: what constitutes a violation of international law sufficient to give rise to a claim under the ATS? In answer to this question, the Sosa Court set forth the following two-fold standard. A claim rests on a tort in violation of international law and is actionable under the ATS where it: (1) rests on a norm of international character accepted by the civilized world; and (2) is defined with specificity comparable to those violations of international law that existed at the time the ATS was enacted. With regard to the second prong, the Sosa Court noted that it considered only three offenses to have been recognized in the eighteenth-century as violations of the law of nations: offenses against ambassadors, violations of safe conduct, and individual actions arising out of prize captures and piracy.

....

IV. Impact: Applying the *Sosa* Standard in Future Litigation

The *Sosa* decision will have varying implications for ATS cases depending on whether they are litigating "traditional" claims, such as torture or genocide, which have already passed judicial muster, or whether they are breaking new ground, such as seeking to hold a corporation liable for cultural genocide stemming from the company's degradation of the environment. A brief survey of the cases adjudicated post-Sosa supports this position. For example, on the one hand, Alvaro Rafael Saravia was held liable under the ATS using Sosa's standard for extrajudicial killing and crimes against humanity for his role in the assassination of the El Salvadoran archbishop Oscar Romero and in carrying out other atrocities against the El Salvadoran people. On the other hand, the Southern District of New York held that Nigerian nationals, who alleged serious injury from an experimental drug administered by the U.S. corporation Pfizer in violation of international law, failed to state an adequate claim under the ATS according to the Sosa standard.

Sosa v. Alvarez-Machain
542 U.S. 692, 124 S. Ct. 2739 (2004)

Judge Friendly called the ATS a "legal Lohengrin," *IIT v. Vencap, Ltd.*, 519 F.2d 1001, 1015 (C.A.2 1975); "no one seems to know whence it came," and for over 170 years after its enactment it provided jurisdiction in only one case. The first Congress passed it as part of the Judiciary Act of 1789, in providing that the new federal district courts "shall also have cognizance, concurrent with the courts of the several States, or the circuit courts, as the case may be, of all causes where an alien sues for a tort only in violation of the law of nations or a treaty of the United States." Act of Sept. 24, 1789, ch. 20, §9(b), 1 Stat. 79.

The statute has been slightly modified on a number of occasions since its original enactment. It now reads in its entirety: "The district courts shall have original jurisdiction of any civil action by an alien for a tort only, committed in violation of the law of nations or a treaty of the United States." 28 U.S.C. §1350.

The parties and *amici* here advance radically different historical interpretations of this terse provision. Alvarez says that the ATS was intended not simply as a jurisdictional grant, but as authority for the creation of a new cause of action for torts in violation of international law. We think that reading is implausible. As enacted in 1789, the ATS gave the district courts "cognizance" of certain causes of action, and the term bespoke a grant of jurisdiction, not power to mold substantive law. The fact that the ATS was placed in §9 of the Judiciary Act, a statute otherwise exclusively concerned with federal-court jurisdiction, is itself support for its strictly jurisdictional nature. Nor would the distinction between jurisdiction and cause of action have been elided by the drafters of the Act or those who voted on it. As Fisher Ames put it, "there is a substantial difference between the jurisdiction of courts and rules of decision." It is unsurprising, then, that an authority on the historical origins of the ATS has written that "section 1350 clearly does not create a statutory cause of action," and that the contrary suggestion is "simply frivolous.".... In sum, we think the statute was intended as jurisdictional in the sense of addressing the power of the courts to entertain cases concerned with a certain subject.

But holding the ATS jurisdictional raises a new question, this one about the interaction between the ATS at the time of its enactment and the ambient law of the era. Sosa would have it that the ATS was stillborn because there could be no claim for relief without a further statute expressly authorizing adoption of causes of action. *Amici* professors of federal jurisdiction and legal history take a different tack, that federal courts could entertain claims once the jurisdictional grant was on the books, because torts in violation of the law of nations would have been recognized within the common law of the time. Brief for Vikram Amar et al. as *Amici Curiae.* We think history and practice give the edge to this latter position.

1

"When the *United States* declared their independence, they were bound to receive the law of nations, in its modern state of purity and refinement." *Ware v. Hylton*, 3 Dall.

199, 281, 1 L.Ed. 568 (1796) (Wilson, J.). In the years of the early Republic, this law of nations comprised two principal elements, the first covering the general norms governing the behavior of national states with each other: *the science which teaches the rights subsisting between nations or states, and the obligations correspondent to those rights,*".... or "that code of public instruction which defines the rights and prescribes the duties of nations, in their intercourse with each other".... This aspect of the law of nations thus occupied the executive and legislative domains, not the judicial. See 4 W. Blackstone, Commentaries on the Laws of England 68 (1769) (hereinafter Commentaries) ("[O]ffenses against" the law of nations are "principally incident to whole states or nations").

The law of nations included a second, more pedestrian element, however, that did fall within the judicial sphere, as a body of judge-made law regulating the conduct of individuals situated outside domestic boundaries and consequently carrying an international savor. To Blackstone, the law of nations in this sense was implicated "in mercantile questions, such as bills of exchange and the like; in all marine causes, relating to freight, average, demurrage, insurances, bottomry ... ; [and] in all disputes relating to prizes, to shipwrecks, to hostages, and ransom bills." *Id.,* at 67. The law merchant emerged from the customary practices of international traders and admiralty required its own transnational regulation. And it was the law of nations in this sense that our precursors spoke about when the Court explained the status of coast fishing vessels in wartime grew from "ancient usage among civilized nations, beginning centuries ago, and gradually ripening into a rule of international law...." *The Paquete Habana,* 175 U.S. 677, 686, 20 S.Ct. 290, 44 L.Ed. 320 (1900).

There was, finally, a sphere in which these rules binding individuals for the benefit of other individuals overlapped with the norms of state relationships. Blackstone referred to it when he mentioned three specific offenses against the law of nations addressed by the criminal law of England: violation of safe conducts, infringement of the rights of ambassadors, and piracy.... An assault against an ambassador, for example, impinged upon the sovereignty of the foreign nation and if not adequately redressed could rise to an issue of war.... It was this narrow set of violations of the law of nations, admitting of a judicial remedy and at the same time threatening serious consequences in international affairs, that was probably on minds of the men who drafted the ATS with its reference to tort.

....

We think it is correct, then, to assume that the First Congress understood that the district courts would recognize private causes of action for certain torts in violation of the law of nations, though we have found no basis to suspect Congress had any examples in mind beyond those torts corresponding to Blackstone's three primary offenses: violation of safe conducts, infringement of the rights of ambassadors, and piracy. We assume, too, that no development in the two centuries from the enactment of § 1350 to the birth of the modern line of cases beginning with *Filartiga v. Pena-Irala,* 630 F.2d 876 (C.A.2 1980), has categorically precluded federal courts from recognizing a claim under the law of nations as an element of common law; Congress has not in any relevant way amended § 1350 or limited civil common law power by another statute. Still, there are good reasons for a restrained conception of the discretion a federal court should exercise in considering a new cause of action of this kind. Accordingly, we think courts should require any claim based on the present-day law of nations to rest on a norm of international character accepted by the civilized world and defined with a specificity comparable to the features of the 18th-century paradigms we have recognized. This requirement is fatal to Alvarez's claim.

....

Notes and Questions

1. At their best, actions brought under the ATCA to vindicate labor rights raise public awareness concerning the treatment of the world's dispossessed by corporations and governments. However, as a specific type of litigation, does it seem to you that the ATCA provides a stable basis for hopes of relief? Under the *Sosa* standard, is child labor likely to figure prominently in future ATCA actions?

A decision of the U.S. District Court for the Southern District of Indiana was handed down in June of 2007. In this case, a group of workers on Liberian rubber plantations, both adults and children, brought suit against a multinational corporation for alleged abuses associated with forced labor. While the workers failed to make out a valid claim on several of the arguments raised, the court did find that the child workers had stated a claim meeting the ATCA standard.

United States District Court,
S.D. Indiana, Indianapolis Division,
John Roe I, et al., Plaintiffs v.
Bridgestone Corporation, et al., Defendants
June 26, 2007

H. *International Norms for Child Labor*

.... Count Two also seeks relief under the ATS, asserting that work done by the child plaintiffs on the Plantation violates international law. The Complaint alleges that the Firestone supervisors on the Plantation encourage and even require the adult latex tappers to put their children to work to help meet the production quotas. Plaintiffs allege that children apply fertilizers and pesticides by hand, without protective equipment. Plaintiffs also allege that children as young as six years old work at the Firestone Plantation. The defendants deny these allegations, but the court must accept these factual allegations for purposes of the motion to dismiss under Rule 12(b)(6).

Plaintiffs have submitted for the court's consideration a United Nations report, U.N. Missions in Liberia, "*Human Rights in Liberia's Rubber Plantations: Tapping into the Future*" (May 2006), filed as Docket No. 14, Ex. A, *available at* http://unmil.org/documents/human_rights_liberiarubber.pdf (last visited June 25, 2007). United Nations human rights investigators reported that management at the Firestone Plantation and other rubber plantation stated that child labor was prohibited. Yet the investigators spoke with a number of children working on the Firestone Plantation and other rubber plantations who were 10 to 14 years old.... The UN investigators also reported that Firestone management told them that management and the Liberian government did not effectively monitor compliance with policies against child labor. This report is not admissible evidence at this point, but its filing as part of the opposition to a Rule 12(b)(6) motion enables plaintiffs to show the types of evidence they expect or hope to offer to support their allegations in the Complaint....

The question is whether Count Two alleges violations of sufficiently specific, universal, and obligatory norms of international law. Plaintiffs quote a report from the United States Department of State in 1997 stating that there is an international consensus that freedom from "child labor" is one of several "core labor standards."... Yet whatever one's initial reaction is to the broad phrase "child labor," reflection shows that national and international norms accommodate a host of different situations and balance competing values and policies.... What are the relevant age limits, for which types of work? How does access to education affect the appropriate policies? What does one say to a parent who insists that a child work so that the family has enough to eat? It is not always easy to state just which practices under the label "child labor" are the subjects of an international consensus.

One can see this in the United States' own Fair Labor Standards Act. The FLSA prohibits not "child labor" but "oppressive child labor." 29 U.S.C. § 212(c). The phrase is defined so that the law allows employment of minors aged 14 and 15 in occupations other than manufacturing and mining if the employment is confined to periods that do not interfere with schooling and under conditions that will not interfere with their health and well-being. 29 U.S.C. § 203(l). Focusing on agricultural work, such as that alleged here, in the United States minors who are 16 and 17 years old may work in any farm job at any time. Minors who are 14 or 15 years old may work a wide variety of agricultural jobs so long as the work is done outside of school hours. 29 U.S.C. § 213(c)(1)(C). Children who are 12 or 13 years old also may work on a farm with the consent of their parents, outside school hours. 29 U.S.C. § 213(c)(1)(B). The FLSA even allows the employment of a child under the age of 12 by his parent on a farm owned by the parent, or employment on another small farm, again outside school hours. 29 U.S.C. § 213(c)(1)(A). In the United States, even children as young as 10 or 11 years old may hand-harvest some crops with a special waiver from the Department of Labor. 29 U.S.C. § 213(c)(4). Liberian law on this subject is not as detailed, but defendants have come forward with evidence that Liberian law allows children under the age of 16 to be employed so long as their work does not interfere with their education....

Returning to international standards, ILO Convention 138, the Minimum Age Convention of 1973, also shows the need to draw lines that accommodate a variety of policies. ILO Convention 138 sets forth minimum ages for different types of work in different nations at different stages of economic development. Nevertheless, that convention notes that its age limits apply to certain forms of employment, including "plantations and other agricultural undertakings mainly producing for commercial purposes, but excluding family and small-scale holdings producing for local consumption and not regularly employing hired workers." Art. 5(3). In such settings, ILO Convention 138 prescribes a minimum age of 14 for employees. Yet neither the United States nor Liberia has ratified ILO Convention 138, though Japan has ratified it.

The key source of international child labor standards for present purposes is ILO Convention 182, the 1999 Convention Concerning the Prohibition and Immediate Elimination of the Worst Forms of Child Labor, which the United States, Liberia, and Japan have all ratified. The importance of the line-drawing is evident in that very title. ILO Convention 182 does not seek to outlaw child labor as such, but only its "worst forms." Those worst forms include slavery and forced or compulsory labor, prostitution and production of pornography, and drug trafficking. The worst forms also include "work which, by its nature or the circumstances in which it is carried out, is likely to harm the health, safety or morals of children." Art. 3. ILO Convention 182 leaves to member nations the identification of the jobs likely to harm health, safety, or morals. Art. 4.

Giving plaintiffs the benefit of their factual allegations, the Complaint states that defendants are actively encouraging—even tacitly requiring—the employment of six, seven, and ten year old children. Giving plaintiffs the benefit of their factual allegations, the defendants are actively encouraging that these very young children perform back-breaking work that exposes them to dangerous chemicals and tools. The work, plaintiffs allege, also keeps those children out of the Firestone schools. The court understands that defendants deny the allegations, but defendants have chosen to file a motion that requires the court to accept those allegations as true, at least for now.

The circumstances alleged here include at least some practices that could therefore fall within the "worst forms of child labor" addressed in ILO Convention 182. The conditions of work alleged by plaintiffs (and reported by the UN investigators) are likely to harm the health and safety of at least the very youngest of the child plaintiffs in this case.

As noted above, and as Firestone has argued, national child labor laws and international conventions on child labor are often written to allow even very young children to help out on family farms. Those special accommodations for family farms have no application here. Plaintiffs do not challenge labor practices on subsistence farms. They challenge the practices of a huge multinational corporate family that hires the children's parents and then (allegedly) encourages the parents to require their young children to do much of the work. Plaintiffs allege that defendants have set the daily production quotas so high that use of child labor is both necessary and inevitable, and that defendants take advantage of the parents in this situation.

The court recognizes that international legal standards for child labor do not always establish bright lines, though there are some. That is also the case with forced labor, as discussed above. Just as some practices that might be described by some as "forced labor" might not violate international law, some practices that could be described as "child labor" also do not violate international law. One must more closely at the particular circumstances, as shown by the pleadings and later by the evidence.

At least some of the practices alleged with regard to the labor of very young children at the Firestone Plantation in Liberia may violate specific, universal, and obligatory standards of international law, such that Count Two should not be dismissed on the pleadings. In light of ILO Convention 182, the court believes that the allegations of child labor in Count Two meet the *Sosa* standard for ATS claims. It would not require great "judicial creativity" to find that even paid labor of very young children in these heavy and hazardous jobs would violate international norms. Those international norms are not inconsistent with Liberian law. Those norms also are stated in an international convention that both the United States and Liberia have ratified. On this record, there is no indication that this lawsuit threatens to cause friction with the foreign policy of the United States. See *Sosa*, 542 U.S. at 725–28, 124 S.Ct. 2739 (identifying reasons for caution in recognizing new claims under the ATS). Plaintiffs may face other daunting challenges in pursuing their case, and the court will address those issues as they are raised. The court is also cautious about the practical consequences of recognizing child labor claims under the ATS and international law.... In a sufficiently extreme case, however, such as plaintiffs have alleged here, the court believes that *Sosa* leaves the ATS door open. The allegations that defendants are encouraging and even requiring parents to require their children as young as six, seven, or ten years old to do this heavy and hazardous work may state a claim for relief under the ATS. Defendants' motion to dismiss is denied as to Count Two.

Notes and Questions

1. What is the legal basis for the judge's determination that the child labor issue "qualifies" for recognition under the ATCA? What aspects of international law, and Liberian practice, did the court find to be relevant for establishing a violation under the ATCA?

B. Trade-Based Strategies to Eliminate Child Labor

Since the end of World War II, and particularly since 1995, global trade rules have made it more difficult for countries to protect their own domestic industries. Free trade theory has gained ground in virtually all parts of the world, even where socialist politics had long held sway. With the creation of the World Trade Organization (WTO) in 1995, the rules of trade became more enforceable, in the sense that countries had to either live up to their free trade obligations, or face the possibility of trade sanctions, generally in the form of retaliatory tariffs imposed by other countries. Interest in this newly "legalized" or judicialized version of trade law has also led to an increase in academic attention to the possibility of using trade methods to enforce other, non-trade, values. Among these values are the so-called ILO "core" labor values, including a commitment not to allow the worst forms of child labor. What follows is a discussion of how to apply trade rules and strategies to addressing the problem of child labor, at least where the child labor involves an industry that provides goods to a global market.

Where products are made through the agency of child labor, it becomes a question whether governments may on that basis refuse to import such goods. In the first place, it is difficult to single out goods that result from child labor, including the worst forms of child labor. Even in cases where governments are able to flag such goods and seek to keep them out, it remains an open question whether WTO rules would allow the use of such trade-related remedies as a matter of national trade policy. To argue that the WTO bodies would allow national governments to refuse importation remains largely a matter of speculation. The idea that a mere hypothetical possibility that national governments would, if they could, refuse to import certain of these products and that this could act as a significant brake on the use of child labor appears a fanciful proposition. The world trading system shows no sign of any widespread commitment to incorporating core labor standards as part of its agenda. Should that happen, the trade-child labor link might prove to be a more meaningful one than it is today.

Frank Garcia & Soohyun Jun, *Trade-Based Strategies for Combatting Child Labor*

in Child Labor and Human Rights: Making Children Matter,
(Burns Weston ed., 2005)

I. Introduction

From a regulatory standpoint, the problem of distinguishing between good and bad child work takes on special significance: which practices are appropriate targets for legal (and extra-legal) sanction and which are not? Many contributors to this volume have responded skillfully to this definitional challenge. We defer to that work and assume here that abusive and exploitative child work (hereinafter "child labor") is the appropriate regulatory target.

While domestic strategies are central to any effective elimination or reduction of child labor, complimentary international strategies of cooperation and coordination are required as well. Given the competing interests and values involved, it cannot be assumed by the world community that child labor will be eradicated solely through domestic law mechanisms and procedures. Such is the nature of our Westphalian system of international relations. Yet, despite widespread recognition of human rights doctrines, principles, and rules, there currently is no effective multilateral regime requiring states to eliminate child labor in a manner that subjects them to binding, enforceable sanctions for failure to do so. The need for international cooperation and coordination to ensure that the rights of working children will be effectively enforced remains a global policy priority of the highest magnitude.

Recognizing such coordination and enforcement problems allows us to situate properly the role of trade-based strategies to address child labor. Reform-minded states can use trade to address extraterritorially the problem of child labor occurring within other jurisdictions. For example, they can offer trade preferences to child labor states that are conditioned on compliance with international labor standards pertinent to child labor (hereinafter "child labor standards"). This approach alters the policy incentives of the target state, by linking its domestic enforcement of child labor standards to eligibility for attractive trade preferences. Alternatively, reform-minded states can follow a more punitive trade-based strategy by using trade sanctions to impose bans on the importation of products produced through the use of child labor.

. . . .

Trade sanctions are intended to eliminate or reduce producer incentives to use child labor by eliminating or reducing through law demand for their products. Social labeling, corporate codes of conduct, and other such private sector initiatives likewise seek to alter commercial conduct, but in a voluntary manner. And conditional trade preferences, also a market-oriented approach but operating in the state-to-state market for trade advantages, use the promise of preferential trade terms to cause states to alter their behavior — in the present context, relative to the more aggressive domestic enforcement of child labor standards. By their very indirection, of course, trade strategies may play a limited role in combating child labor. Sanctions are effective only with child labor industries that export. Social labeling and other voluntary approaches rely on public good will. And conditional trade preferences depend on the degree to which the target state's economy needs the preferences, supervisory and enforcement efforts are vigorous, and compliance is not waived for extrinsic political reasons. Nevertheless, trade strategies play an important role, offering readily available methods to address extraterritorial child labor problems in the absence of more effective transnational mechanisms.

The purpose of sanctions is to change the behavior of states. For this reason, if sanctions are to succeed in whole or in part, they must be recognized as legitimate in moral and legal terms. In this respect, a multilateral trade sanctions regime is better than a unilateral one because of its enhanced legitimacy. If, for lack of a multilateral alternative, a state is driven to take unilateral trade action to modify another state's behavior — say, in its use or tolerance of forced child labor — it will have squarely to face contentious debate and potential retaliation.

A. Arguments For and Against Trade Sanctions Opposed to Child Labor

When is it justifiable to impose trade sanctions to prevent the exploitation of working children or otherwise protect them? The answer to this question depends in part on the normative traditions of the sanctioning state. In a liberal state favoring Kantian notions of human autonomy, children's rights will be seen as inalienable (belonging to them simply for being human), and trade sanctions in defense of children's rights therefore as moral (assuming a meaningful link between the sanction and the infringed right). Of course, the target state may have a quite different normative tradition than the sanctioning state. For this reason, sanctions critics argue on relativist grounds that a country should not restrict trade access for internal moral reasons. Bhagwati and Srinivasan, for example, find inappropriate "GATT sanctioning of the use of unilateral state action to suspend other countries' trade access, or … their trading rights under the GATT 'treaty,' unless one's choice of ethical concerns is adopted by others through implicit harmonization in one's direction…."

Even granting this objection, however, sanctions opposing child labor cannot be easily condemned outright. Beyond the liberal community, international law ensures that certain human rights attain universal status as positive law because of their widespread recognition in consensual instruments such as International Labor Organization (ILO) conventions and other international agreements. Within international law, the goal of prohibiting certain child labor practices, e.g., indentured or exploitative child labor, is widely recognized in custom and treaties. This amounts to "explicit" harmonization and justifies sanctions even against cultural relativism objections.

. . . .

Some free traders argue also that an increased focus on reformist social policies will result automatically from rising incomes through market forces in international trade. This economic determinism ignores, however, the historical political struggle that took place in industrialized countries to win the labor standards that exist today. Others argue that contemporary free trade orthodoxy is itself the threat; workers would be much better off, it is argued, without the neo-liberal policies of trade liberalization, deregulation of the economy, privatization, and the free market ideology that force wages down and deny people work. While this argument is a legitimate global economic policy debate, we cannot wait for its resolution to implement strategies to address child labor, a necessary response within any global economic paradigm, particularly in relation to child labor's "worst forms."

Critics of a trade sanctions approach to child labor in particular perceive this strategy also as too simplistic; they believe that import bans only drive employed children from the formal to the informal sector where they are less exposed to scrutiny and more vulnerable to infringement of their rights. At the opposite extreme is the argument that any trade sanction is justified once the child labor practice in question is deemed illegal or immoral, and regardless of its actual impact on the children or whether the sanction actually reduces the offending practice — a contention that raises the central question of the effectiveness of child labor sanctions, independent of their legitimacy. Before implementing measures that are designed to ensure that children's interests are protected, one must consider whether linking labor rights to trade actually can improve the conditions of child workers (in the developing world especially) or can eliminate child labor where it should not exist. In other words, are sanctions effective or useful in protecting children against abusive and exploitative labor?

We do not undertake to answer this question definitively here. However, we do recommend some relevant considerations.

Generally it is agreed that for sanctions to be justifiable it must be possible to demonstrate that they can be more or less effective in addressing the root concern. There is less agreement as to the definition of effectiveness. A simple measure would be the elimination or substantial reduction of child labor practices in the target industry. However, this metric is by itself inadequate to measure the effectiveness of child labor trade sanctions because it fails to take a comprehensive view of the problem. Where the effect of an import ban is to increase the number of working children in the sector producing goods for domestic consumption rather than exports, or in the informal economy in which their rights are even less subject to protection, it could be argued that the sanction has failed.

Moreover, if the number of children in the sector producing for domestic consumers increases, the wages may dwindle, adversely affecting all workers.

B. Case Study: U.S. Child Labor Trade Sanctions Law

To understand better the legal and policy issues raised by a trade-based strategy opposed to child labor, we explore here a particular trade sanctions law with child labor ramifications: Section 307 of the U.S. Tariff Act of 1930, also known as the U.S. "forced labor statute." Section 307 has been amended to include forced child labor, and is therefore the leading U.S. statute on point and, given the sway of the U.S. worldwide, of obvious significance to any trade-based approach to human rights enforcement.

Section 307 prohibits the importation of all goods produced wholly or in part in any foreign country by forced labor, and authorizes the Secretary of the Treasury to prescribe such regulations as may be necessary for the enforcement of the provision. Amendments to Section 307 in 1997 barred the use of customs service funds for the importation into the United States of any goods produced by forced or indentured child labor. Additional amendments in 2000 inserted a definition of forced labor, which explicitly included forced child labor. If a customs officer has reason to believe that any merchandise being imported or likely to be imported into the United States is produced in any foreign country with the use of forced child labor, he or she must report this belief to the Commissioner of Customs. If the Commissioner conclusively determines that the merchandise is subject to the import ban, the burden is on the importer to establish by satisfactory evidence that the merchandise was not produced in any part with the use of forced child labor in order to have the merchandise released from custody.

In conjunction with Section 307 of the Tariff Act of 1930, and in order to further enforce U.S. laws on forced labor, President Clinton, in 1999, issued an executive order to prevent federal agencies from buying products made with forced or indentured child labor. "Forced child labor" is defined as involuntary work or service rendered by a person under the age of eighteen," and under the Executive Order, the Department of Labor, in cooperation with the Department of Treasury and the Department of State, is required to publish a list of products that it reasonably believes might have been produced by forced child labor. If the contracting officer of an executive agency reasonably believes that forced child labor has been used, the head of the agency will initiate an investigation. If it is found that the contractor has furnished products produced by forced child labor or uses forced child labor and has submitted a false certification or has failed to cooperate, the head of an executive agency may terminate a contract or debar or suspend a contractor from eligibility for federal contracts. This Order does show a determination on the part of the Executive Branch to enforce laws relating to child labor practices in foreign countries.

Application of Section 307 has been episodic and, from a child labor perspective, disappointing. During the 1990s, Section 307 of the Tariff Act was invoked to prohibit the importation of certain Mexican products produced with prison or forced labor and was used to ban the importation of leather imports and iron pipe fittings determined by the Customs Service to have been produced with convict or prison labor from China. However, since the 1997 amendment to Section 307 affecting child labor, petitions have been filed to halt importation of rugs from South Asia knotted by children, and cocoa picked by children in the Ivory Coast, with no action taken in either case.

III. WTO Case Law on GATT Articles I, III and XX: Room for Justifiable Child Labor Sanctions?

Those who claim the WTO downplays adult workers' rights may also conclude that the GATT contains nothing for working children. In this section, we seek to demonstrate that WTO case law allows room for distinguishing nondiscriminatory and justified child labor measures from protectionist measures purportedly based on child labor and that therefore it can accommodate a trade-based strategy of import sanctions to protect working children's rights while also safeguarding core trade liberalization principles.

. . . .

B. Guiding a Trade Based Strategy Through GATT Article XX

. . . . Article XX provides for situations in which a WTO member may deviate from its GATT obligations for certain designated policy reasons. A three-step inquiry is required to determine whether an otherwise "GATT-illegal" measure is justified under Article XX. First, the stated policy must come within the scope of one of the categories listed under Article XX—for example, as a measure to protect public morals, or human, animal, or plant life, or health. Second, the measure complained of must be either "necessary" or "related to" the policy being furthered, depending on the paragraph. Finally, the chapeau (i.e., preamble or introductory clause) of Article XX requires that the application of any measure that otherwise meets the first two tests must not constitute a means of arbitrary or unjustifiable discrimination between countries where the same conditions prevail, or a disguised restriction on international trade. In other words, Article XX permits policy-driven discrimination between countries as long as it is not arbitrary or unjustifiable.

1. Finding the Right Exception

The first step in evaluating the legality of a child labor sanction under Article XX is to determine which of the enumerated exceptions best covers the regulatory goal of the measure in question, here child labor. There are three immediate possibilities: Article XX(a) for measures protecting public morals; Article XX(b) for measures protecting human life or health; and Article XX(e) for measures banning importation of the products of prison labor. Despite the obvious similarities between products of prison labor and products of forced child labor, Article XX(e) will not be developed here as a suitable exception under which to mount the defense of a child labor trade sanction. It is our judgment that the language and negotiating history of the provision are too narrowly tied specifically to prison labor to allow extension to other forms of forced labor. This leaves two other options: articles XX(a) and XX(b).

a. Article XX(a): Public Morals Exception

Surprisingly there is no GATT or WTO case law on the public morals exception. Some have argued against interpreting this exception to cover labor rights violations on the grounds that both the reference to prison labor in Article XX(e) and the fact that the Havana Charter included explicit language on labor rights suggest that the drafters did not intend for Article XX to cover labor rights (or children's rights had they envisioned regulating child labor). A powerful counter-argument to this view is that as in the case of constitutional interpretation, it is reasonable and appropriate not to be bound by the drafters' "original intent." Instead, altogether consistent with the international law of treaty interpretation, one should take into account the evolution of thinking about the intersection of trade and human rights in the years intervening, which has developed to include the prohibition of certain labor practices that violate universal human rights, e.g., the prohibition on child labor.

This being said, the hard question remains as to how to resolve what constitutes "public morals" and whose public morals count. It is clear that the provision is intended to protect the public morality of the importing/sanctioning country. Controversy arises, however, when that country, on the basis of its own sense of public morality, seeks, through "outwardly-directed" trade measures, to protect foreigners outside its jurisdiction. The U.S. law banning goods made with forced child labor via "outwardly directed" trade measures is arguably illustrative in that it attempts to protect working children in other countries from practices the United States considers immoral and/or illegal.

. . . .

C. WTO Law and U.S. Section 307

Since international organizations tend generally to lack human rights enforcement mechanisms beyond the "mobilization of shame," the WTO stands out as an attractive if not the ideal arena in which to confront fundamental violations of internationally recognized labor rights, including the rights of working children. It is unlikely that a targeted WTO member country would protest a sanction issue in a WTO dispute settlement proceeding lest it publicize its child labor practices. Nevertheless, since legality is central to international legitimacy independently of whether or not the measure ever will be litigated, it is important to consider the trade law issues discussed above when designing and implementing a child labor trade sanction.

Taking Section 307 of the U.S. Tariff Act of 1930 as our model, we have analyzed the key features of a trade sanction which raise issues under WTO standards. Based on this analysis, we conclude that Section 307 is capable of surviving a WTO challenge. The fact that trade sanctions such as Section 307 are targeted at a production process and not at a product per se raises important interpretive issues, but we conclude that such sanctions are not or should not be a problem under current WTO law. The more difficult question is whether child labor sanctions can be excused under the existing public morals or human life and health exceptions of the GATT. As argued above, it is reasonable and appropriate to conclude that they do come within the scope of the exceptions.

The most serious issue is unilateralism. Section 307 is unilateral in nature since it allows the U.S. to act essentially on its own determination. While a unilateral sanction is inherently controversial, such sanctions can prove to be multilateral de facto when there is a multilateral legal or moral consensus underlying a de jure unilateral ban. This is to the good given that, as discussed above, a multilateral approach to trade sanctions is to be preferred over a unilateral one. The most troubling scenario, implying that there exists no international consensus whatsoever, would be a sanction that is unilateral in both law and fact. This issue presents the greatest risk to Section 307 and similar trade sanctions. In interpreting the Article XX chapeau, the WTO Appellate Body has indicated that it expects sanctioning countries to engage in bona fide multilateral negotiations before resorting to unilateral action. Section 307 is not a response by the U.S. to failed multilateral negotiations, but international standards prohibiting forced or indentured child labor do confer a de facto multilateralism on Section 307.

Given the spotty U.S. record relative to multilateral human rights instruments, it remains to be seen if this conferral would be enough under WTO law. A fully multilateral trade sanctions regime would be subject to less opposition and create less criticism on "culture specificity" and "power asymmetry" grounds, but de facto multilateralism at least is preferable to pure unilateralism.

IV. Conclusion

Trade sanctions that take aim at child labor practices to enhance the human rights of working children, such as Section 307 of the U.S. Tariff Act of 1930, have a role to play in the internationalization of fundamental values. Sanctions can influence producers in particular child labor sectors, they can attract foreign attention to the importance of protecting exploited children in various parts of the world, and they can increase multilateral pressure on the target country. In sum, they can move states and private actors "from one-time grudging compliance to habitual internalized obedience."

. . . .

Given the fact that child labor enforcement efforts under Section 307 have so far been fruitless, it is disappointing that the WTO as currently constituted has no active role to play in compelling any state to enforce international child labor standards. However, by ruling positively on any unilateral child labor sanction statute that comes before them, future WTO panels can play an important continuing role in shaping the interpretation of GATT provisions to promote fundamental human rights, in particular the human rights of working children.

Notes and Questions

1. In the "trade and child labor" debate, General Agreement on Tariffs and Trade (GATT) Article XX has been much discussed. Article XX essentially allows for the possibility of violating a GATT rule or principle (for instance, the prohibition against creating quantitative barriers to imports) on the grounds of some public policy value. The power of Article XX to achieve real results for laboring children is questionable. The text of that article is reproduced here:

> Subject to the requirement that such measures are not applied in a manner which would constitute a means of arbitrary or unjustifiable discrimination between countries where the same conditions prevail, or a disguised restriction on international trade, nothing in this Agreement shall be construed to prevent the adoption or enforcement by any contracting party of measures:
>
> (*a*) necessary to protect public morals;
>
> (*b*) necessary to protect human, animal or plant life or health;
>
> (*c*) relating to the importations or exportations of gold or silver;
>
> (*d*) necessary to secure compliance with laws or regulations which are not inconsistent with the provisions of this Agreement, including those relating to customs enforcement, the enforcement of monopolies operated under paragraph 4 of Article II and Article XVII, the protection of patents, trade marks and copyrights, and the prevention of deceptive practices;
>
> (*e*) relating to the products of prison labour;
>
> (*f*) imposed for the protection of national treasures of artistic, historic or archaeological value;
>
> (*g*) relating to the conservation of exhaustible natural resources if such measures are made effective in conjunction with restrictions on domestic production or consumption;
>
> [paragraphs describing other grounds deleted]

How difficult would it be to invoke Article XX as a defense when a trade restriction based on a labor rights rationale is challenged? Conceptually, does Article XX imply anything of significance about standards of labor or environmental protection in the international trade regime? In other words, even if the WTO bodies were to interpret Article XX very generously, allowing a large number of such trade restrictions, would that be enough to affect child labor policy in countries where the relevant products are made?

The article that follows casts doubt on the idea that reliance on GATT Article XX to effect changes in state behavior vis a vis abusive labor practices would succeed. Sara Dillon advocates a more direct approach, that would require investment in a solution to the problem, thereby avoiding academic preoccupation with narrowly-based remedies such as those linked with the WTO.

Sara Dillon, *A Deep Structure Connection: Child Labor and the World Trade Organization*
9 ILSA Journal of International & Comparative Law 443 (2003)

. . . .

It has baffled me, as a long-time observer of writing on the topic of "trade and" — trade and human rights, trade and labor, trade and the environment — that there has been a near-obsession by many academics with the question of what the WTO might, through the interpretation of GATT Article XX by panels and the Appellate Body, "allow." Or what those two bodies could be induced to "take on board" in terms of a non-economic, human dimension. Or what the Appellate Body will "come to understand" with regard to an ultimate synthesis of conflicting state obligations arising from different and opposing treaties — trade versus labor, the environment, human rights. I have no doubt that such a synthesis must be carried out, but not by any organ of the WTO. Rather, the real and inescapable need is for another, as yet undefined, global institution to carry out this synthesis; not a trade organization the sole focus of which, the sole ethos and objective of which, is to facilitate trade.

I would term the entire "Article XX" approach, with its narrow WTO focus, reductionist at best. At worst, it is a distraction that leads one to ignore the actual facts of global child abuse; the reality of child trafficking for the purposes of work in sweatshops and in the sex industry. That is why, in my view, the fact of a global economy leads inevitably to the need for a global solution to such economic outrages; at the same time, I maintain that the WTO itself, as an institution, is not the place to look for that solution.

There have been periodic bursts of academic speculation on the subject of what the WTO's Appellate Body would now do if clearly faced with a challenge to a national import restriction on imports of products made from child labor. The favored hypothetical in these discussions is the case of a WTO member country that creates an import ban on the products of child labor. (The U.S. and EC do, in fact, maintain certain restrictions on the import of products of child labor, but these are far from comprehensive and of course cannot begin to identify all incoming products that might contain elements produced through the agency of child labor).

. . . .

My dominant impression in reading such academic discussions has been: What on earth does this have to do with the broader effects of the momentum of globalization? With environmental degradation, with the frantic drive to develop, with the suffering of people caught up in these processes? And, as a very fundamental matter, it must be asked whether developed countries do in fact maintain import restrictions capable of dealing more than superficially with human rights and environmental abuses, based on consideration of the "processes" through which certain items are produced for export by trading partners in the developing world? Isn't it true that the products likely to be identified through such import bans represent only the tip of the iceberg, when it comes to child

labour and other abuses? Aren't many academic discussions of Article XX wastefully theoretical, given the scale of the problem, and of the non-trade values at stake?

. . . .

As far as methodology is concerned, there has been far too much attention paid to the
study of the WTO in isolation from other global institutions, and indeed from empirical
phenomena generally. Joseph Stiglitz has clearly identified the deeply flawed and ideologically based functioning of the IMF and World Bank, and it is plain that the WTO
cannot serve as an instrument for development in the absence of a genuine "linkage"
among all three of these institutions. It is almost unthinkable that, in the absence of targeted investment mediated by a global finance body, there could be adequate levels "spontaneous" development attained in much of the developing world.

It could be said that the creation of the WTO, with its mechanisms of enforcement, highly
unusual in the context of "international law," has generated a collective imagination in
the direction of a more structured set of global institutions. This in turn must lead to a
recognition of the need for a court-like body capable of synthesizing conflicting international obligations, including conflicts between trade rights and labor standards. Key to the
success of such a global system is a redistributive body to fund programs proven effective
in eliminating abuses like the worst forms of child labor.

I understand it when Professor Summers laments that "There is no international agency
other than the WTO able to effectively exert pressure for observance of rights on a global
basis." But this absence of an alternative body is not adequate reason for allowing or expecting the WTO to do that which it does not know how to do. Summers is surely right,
though, when he states that "freedom of international trade is subject to observance of
internationally recognized basic human rights." The concept of "subject to," however, is
both mysterious and deeply ambiguous. How can we make countries "subject to" that
which they insist they cannot afford? But how, on the other hand, can we countenance
transnational corporations, many based in the developed world, continuing to profit from
their access to resources and markets in the developing world, where widespread abuses
against children proliferate?

A significant amount of attention has been paid to attempts to take action in U.S. courts
against U.S. multinational corporations involved in serious labor/human rights abuses; as
well as to the production of corporate "codes of conduct" meant to govern the conduct of
developed world multinationals. There have been a number of actions brought against
U.S. corporations under the Alien Tort Claims Act, a statute that allows alien plaintiffs to
seek a remedy in U.S. courts where another party has acted "in violation of the law of nations or treaty of the United States." While such actions are very important devices for
drawing attention to abusive conduct by U.S. corporations, the statute is quite difficult to
use, in that it applies to only a small band of corporate acts. One must link the conduct
to international law principles; normally by demonstrating that a U.S. corporation has
been complicit in the abusive conduct of a repressive foreign regime. This kind of legal
action bears little relationship with the mass phenomenon of child labor, though it is conceivable that certain particularly egregious corporate conduct could fall within the net of
the statute. As for self-regulatory codes, these too are potentially significant, but are unlikely to have any generalized effects on the general problem of child labor. Although one
might argue over the precise figures, it should be recalled that only a certain, perhaps small,
proportion of labor abuses against children involve Western multinationals.

Without either fetishizing or ignoring the connection between international trade law
and child labor, I would propose a multifaceted approach to eliminating the worst forms

of child labor, a task which must be seen as an international obligation falling on all parties having any degree of influence over the process of globalization. First of all, the reality of the contentious divide between the views of the developed and developing worlds with regard to the fairness of relying on import restrictions as a device to promote higher labor standards must be recognized. Penalizing countries with the most vulnerable economic profiles actually makes little sense, and cannot have the desired global effect, despite the reams of academic writing on the subject of "trade and labor, and the role of GATT Article XX."

Where OECD-based multinationals are involved in the exploitation of children for economic gain, any sanctions should be against the corporations in question. This would involve the creation of a far more effective set of OECD rules, with mandatory national implementation, than anything that exists to date. I could not in good conscience state that such a development is politically likely. Nevertheless, it is clear that where developed world MNEs are directly involved in labor/human rights abuses, regardless of the minimal or nonexistent labor standards of the host country, the proper target of sanctions in most cases is the MNE, not the host country. (I make the point below that sanctions against the host country could become appropriate, but only after a transition period during which significant investment had been made in programs to eliminate the worst forms of child labor and other abusive labor practices.)

As has been pointed out, most child labor is tied to a given national economy, and does not bear any direct relationship to MNEs. Nor is most child labor related to export trade, although clearly some is. Relying on GATT Article XX to justify import bans in such cases is certain to generate more hostility, and have little effect on the underlying problem. Where there is no relationship of the labor exploitation to exports, GATT Article XX is essentially irrelevant in any case.

I would like to posit a "deep structure linkage," in which the very fact of globalization means that the global economic institutions should be required to act in a concerted manner to invest in the elimination of particular abuses. This would necessitate a reorientation of the agendas of the IMF and World Bank in particular. Whether seen in the context of human rights or long term economic development, the elimination of the worst forms of child labor would be a starting point for such targeted investment. While far too small in scale, there are model programs, such as the ILO's International program on the Elimination of Child Labour (IPEC), designed to allow countries to eliminate child labor, by giving children access to school and replacing child labor with adult labor—a far more certain route to development than waiting for market liberalization to work its magic. The IMF and World Bank should be held to the achievement of specific, empirically based goals, derived from the principles contained in international conventions, including those of the ILO.

My own perspective on the WTO is that it provides a model of international regulation; not in its substance so much as in its "non-voluntariness." Assuming that there was an international fund to assist in the elimination of child labor, at that point developing countries and developed countries should indeed have their participation in bodies like the WTO conditioned on their good faith efforts to bring about results. The expansion of global economic activity does bear a logical relationship to the impulse towards global regulation. The WTO is possessed of an unusual and even exciting non-voluntary quality, contributing to the prospect that non-trade law, including labor and human rights law, might share that same non-voluntariness. How one counters the economic forces that created the WTO with non-trade values, such that a similar urgency could inform a project to eliminate the worst forms of child labor, is a difficult political problem. For a start, there should be a redirection of the content of anti-globalization protests, through the creation of a list of firm "trade and" demands. The message of the global dissidents should be more focused, centered on the principle that the right of developed countries to profit from global business activity should depend on the contribution of those same countries to high levels of targeted investment in a global regime to protect core labor standards.

Notes and Questions

1. The Dillon article above expresses some impatience with the attention paid by scholars to the relationship, or potential relationship, between GATT Article XX and the problem of child labor. What is Dillon's major objection? Is she being fair to authors such as Garcia and Jun?

———————

There is yet another possible "remedy"—if an indirect one—to confront the problem of child labor. In recent years, voluntary codes of corporate conduct have become popular. Designed to enhance the reputation of the participating company, and to provide a practical, privatized approach to eliminating abusive child labor, the code of conduct has a great deal of popular appeal.

Frederick Jonassen, *A Baby-Step to Global Labor Reform: Corporate Codes of Conduct and the Child*
17 Minnesota Journal of International Law 7 (2008)

. . . .

I. THE MAGNITUDE OF EXPLOITATIVE CHILD LABOR

[T]he rise of the MNC most likely accounts for the increase in child labor in the third world. Typically, an MNC is based in an industrialized country that has long enforced laws against child labor. For such companies, poor, underdeveloped, third-world countries provide a competitive advantage in the form of cheap labor. Child labor is among the cheapest. The MNC, through its contractors, will pay children far less than it would have to pay workers in its home country, and pockets the differential. The arrangement is also beneficial to the underdeveloped country, for MNCs bring investment, jobs, markets, and other services that develop economic infrastructure. Hence, the economic circumstances of child labor result in a globalized "race to the bottom" in which wages are reduced as much as possible.

. . . . In its 2006 Report of the General Director, "The End of Child Labour: Within Reach," the ILO found that from 2000 to 2004, there has been a modest decrease in children involved in child labor, from 246 million to 218 million worldwide. Noting that there is a great deal yet to be done, the report reviewed many causes for this improvement, among them, the "cooperation of employers," which "is crucial in the fight against child labour because they can help to ensure that their enterprises are free of child labour … [and] play a powerful role in influencing those who hire children.…"

. . . .

IV. HISTORICAL BACKGROUND TO CORPORATE CODES OF CONDUCT

. . . .

B. Past Model Codes

There have been several modern attempts to regulate labor through codes of conduct. These include the following.

1. The Sullivan Principles for South Africa

In 1971, the Reverend Leon Sullivan, a Philadelphia clergyman and member of the board of General Motors, developed a set of principles as a guide for corporations that did business under the apartheid regime in South Africa. Sullivan had consulted with religious and labor leaders in South Africa who believed that constructive engagement with foreign investors was preferable to disinvestment. Constructive engagement, Sullivan thought, would raise the quality of life for black South Africans, help them to obtain education, and eventually overcome the barriers of apartheid, while disinvestment would only put South Africans, especially non-white South Africans, out of work. Twelve U.S. firms, including General Motors, immediately adopted the Sullivan Principles, and by 1986, approximately 200 of the 260 U.S. corporations doing business in South Africa had adopted them. The Sullivan Principles included commitments to racially non-discriminatory employment, wages, access to management programs, supportive services, affirmative action, and the use of corporate influence to end apartheid. Each Sullivan firm's performance was to be monitored by an independent accounting firm, Arthur D. Little. By 1987, however, the Reverend Sullivan himself declared his Principles a failure, largely due to the intransigence of the South African government on the question of apartheid. Apartheid eventually fell not because of the Sullivan Principles, but rather because of corporate disinvestment and international sanctions against South Africa.

In spite of Sullivan's ultimate rejection of his Principles, there is evidence that they did some good. The Sullivan Principles resulted in the desegregation of hundreds of enterprises, education, and job training for approximately 50,000 workers a year, and significant investment in the infrastructure of black and desegregated education in South Africa. The Principles increased the number of non-white managers, placed them in positions supervising whites, inspired other countries to establish similar codes for their corporations operating in South Africa, and promoted the growth of black trade unions. A study also showed that the Sullivan companies as a group out-performed the Dow Jones Industrial Average in average return on equity from 1977 to 1983. Hence, investing in the ethically sound Sullivan companies was also financially sound. Perhaps the most important effect of the Sullivan Principles was the demonstration that such ethical schemes were possible and worthwhile.

. . . .

5. Rugmark

To combat the widespread problem of child labor in the carpet industry of south Asia, an Indian child labor activist, Kailash Satyarthi, founded the Rugmark Foundation with the help of the South Asian Coalition on Child Servitude, the Indo-German Promotion Council, UNICEF, and other concerned industry and nongovernment groups. Rugmark is a labeling program. Carpet retailers and manufacturers agree to abide by the Rugmark code of conduct that provides for the replacement of child labor with adult labor and for the education of the children. Signatories pay a licensing fee and are subject to inspection by Rugmark monitors. Those who pass the inspection may attach the Rugmark label to their products, which signifies that the carpet was not produced with child labor. In Germany, which is an import center for carpets from Asia, carpet wholesalers and retailers who agree to buy only Rugmark-certified products are permitted to publicize the fact and use the label. In 1994, the U.S.-based Child Labor Coalition established the Rugmark

Foundation to promote the U.S. Consumer Education Campaign for Rugmark. Rugmark also rescues children from exploitative labor situations and places them in schools. The movement has been successful in Germany and is gaining popularity in the United States.

6. FIFA

Child labor is a serious problem in the manufacture of soccer balls. In 1996, the Fédération Internationale de Football Association (FIFA), a Swiss organization that oversees the sport of soccer, reached an agreement with international unions to incorporate child labor standards into FIFA's regulatory system. In order to attach the FIFA label to soccer balls, a manufacturer now not only had to meet FIFA's regulations as to the size, weight, and durability of the soccer ball, but also had to certify that the manufacturer was in compliance with ILO conventions, which include a ban on child labor. In 2002, however, nongovernmental organization (NGOs) reported that manufacturers using the FIFA logo were violating the FIFA code on a massive scale, including violations of child labor. FIFA itself acknowledges the difficulty of addressing the problem of child labor. In 2003, FIFA joined the ILO in a renewed effort to combat child labor in the manufacture of sports equipment called "The Red Card to Child Labor."

7. Social Accountability 8000

In 1997, The Council on Economic Priorities and Accreditation Association (CEPAA) created Social Accountability 8000 (SA 8000). This is a certification program that provides a code of standards to measure the performance of MNCs in several areas, including child labor. The SA 8000 code is based on international workplace norms such as ILO Conventions, the Universal Declaration of Human Rights, and the U.N. Convention on the Rights of the Child. The CEPAA accredits firms to certify and monitor signatories on the basis of briefs provided by local unions and human rights organizations regarding signatory work sites. Currently SA 8000 certifies more than 1,300 companies in sixty-three countries and seventy industries.

. . . .

V. THE EMERGENCE OF CORPORATE CODES

A. Of Corporations, Celebrities, the Media, and the Public

During the late 1990s, corporations and celebrities who sponsored corporate products found that the public had certain expectations of them. The idea that corporations, whether they had committed to a corporate code or not, should abide by certain standards of conduct came to have a certain enforcement power of its own. It was the media and the public response to exploitative child labor that produced this result.

1. The Gap

In early 1995, for instance, labor and religious groups mounted a campaign to protest sweatshop conditions prevalent in El Salvador among the contractors of the trendy clothing retailer, the Gap. A columnist at the New York Times related how young teenage girls were paid fifty-six cents an hour, forced to work eighteen hours a day, had to get tickets from supervisors to go to the bathroom, and were subject to firing if they formed a union. The Gap responded by suspending the contractor's orders and sending investigators. Eventually, the Gap halted all business with the contractor until it met a set of newly adopted guidelines. Further, the Gap refused to deal with any other contractors until the government of El Salvador capably investigated such abuses and resolved the labor disputes fairly.

In March 1996, the Gap established an independent monitoring system for human rights violations by its contractors. In an attempt to resolve the conflict, the clothing retailer agreed with its Salvadoran contractor and local religious, human rights, and labor organizations to monitor compliance under its revised and more specific code of conduct.

2. Levi Strauss

In September of 1991, Levi Strauss established a Sourcing Guidelines Working Group to develop standards for overseas suppliers not only for ethical reasons, but also to protect the company's brand image. The group reviewed the UN's Universal Declaration of Human Rights and other international human rights instruments. In March 1992, the company adopted the task force's guidelines after embarrassing media exposure of labor abuse at a company source factory in Saipan.

The Levi-Strauss code of conduct has two parts. The first, Business Partner Terms of Engagement, addresses "workplace issues that are substantially controllable by [the company's] individual business partners, such as environmental requirements, ethical, health and safety standards, legal regulations and employment practice." The second part, Country Assessment Guidelines, entails issues that are probably beyond the ability of the business partner to control, but that nevertheless "could subject [the company's] corporate reputation and therefore [its] business success, to potential harm." These include health and safety, human rights, legal requirements, and political or social stability.

The employment practice section includes six specific issues of employment: wages and benefits, working hours, child labor, prison/forced labor, discrimination, and disciplinary practices such as corporal punishment or other forms of coercion. It omits the right to form a union. The company has established an internal monitoring and enforcement system that begins with a questionnaire on employment practices in foreign plants, provides for audits, surprise site visits, review by company personnel, and possible termination of violators' contracts. The company rates business suppliers according to a three-tiered system: contractors who are indifferent or unwilling to improve unacceptable working conditions are terminated; contractors who can possibly improve can negotiate a plan and time-table to resolve the problems; and contractors who could do more are encouraged to improve.

At its Saipan contractor, Levi Strauss found virtually slave labor conditions. Immigrant workers were housed in padlocked barracks, their passports confiscated during the contract period. They worked for eleven hours a day, seven days a week, for $1.65 an hour. As a result of its investigation under its "Terms of Engagement," Levi Strauss canceled its contract with the Saipan factory owner and with thirty other contractors in the Philippines, Honduras, and Uruguay while improving employment practices with one hundred others overseas. In Bangladesh, Levi Strauss established an innovative program in two plants where it discovered children under fourteen were working. In an agreement with local officials, the children returned to school but continued drawing pay from the contractor while Levi Strauss paid for their tuition, books, and uniforms and agreed to offer the children jobs at the plants when they became fourteen.

In regard to its "Country Assessment Guidelines," Levi Strauss checked whether any of its facilities in China and Burma were reported to use prison labor and conducted surprise visits and inquiries. As a result, the company entirely withdrew from both countries.

3. Kathie Lee Gifford

In May of 1996, talk show host Kathie Lee Gifford felt vilified after Charles Kernaghan, the executive director of the National Labor Committee, alleged that exploited child laborers in Honduras produced her Wal-Mart fashion line. Her first response was defensive. She declared herself a victim of a smear campaign and threatened to sue the organization that accused her of taking advantage of child labor. Eventually, however, she spoke with one of the children who worked in the sweatshop that produced the line of clothing bearing her name. To her credit, Mrs. Gifford began to work with other garment-endorsing celebrities to organize a July 16 industry summit in Washington, promoting the Labor Department's "No Sweat" campaign.

B. The Effectiveness of Corporate Codes of Conduct

3. Reputation and Unpredictability

....

Though public reaction may at times be disappointing, at other times, public reaction may be surprisingly strong and effective, as the cases of the Gap, Levi Strauss, and Kathy Lee Gifford illustrate. This uncertainty of the public's response to publicity concerning exploitative child labor may actually contribute to the effectiveness of corporate codes. A high-profile corporation that either tolerates exploitative child labor in the manufacture of its products or is negligent about maintaining standards regarding child labor risks injuring its reputation and hurting its sales. It is unpredictable whether the media will expose a particular situation of exploitative child labor or whether the story will have legs: the public reaction might be anything from indifference to boycotts. To avoid this risk, it is prudent to temper the corporate interest in cheap labor with some solicitude for maintaining labor standards. This would be particularly true of standards regarding the use of child labor, since the abusive exploitation of children can potentially provoke the greatest sympathy and hence the most unforeseeable and unmanageable public response. The exercise of discovering whether losses generated by a bad corporate image will outweigh the gain of exploiting child labor is probably not worth the risk, since the corporate reputation and sales contingent upon it, once lost, may prove unrecoverable.

The concern with reputation not only justifies efforts on the part of the corporations to impose codes of conduct, but also efforts to enforce them. If a corporation creates a code of conduct because it does not wish the media to portray it as an exploitative employer, the corporation is also likely to have some interest in enforcement of the code, since the bad press will be worse if the media portrays the corporation as hypocritical in publicizing a code that has no real effect.

4. The Flexibility of Corporate Codes

Macklem and Trebilcock point out that corporate codes of conduct differ profoundly from conventional forms of labor regulation:

> [l]abour market regulation, traditionally understood, is a blend of specific rules negotiated by parties—either individually or collectively—to an employment relationship and general legislative imperatives that establish baseline entitlements to workers regardless of their bargaining power. In contrast, codes of conduct and social labeling programs rely "primarily on the participation and resources of nongovernmental actors in the construction, operation, and implementation of a governance agreement."

The implementation of codes of conduct does not depend "on an employment contract, a collective agreement, legislation, or the common law" to govern relations between employers and employees. Corporate codes depend upon internal or external monitoring chosen by the corporation itself, and not the state or government, to insure compliance with any regulations contained in the code. Corporate codes rely on the economic power of the consumer rather than the policing power of the state to enforce compliance. Indeed, much about corporate codes of conduct "runs counter to the basic tenets of domestic labour law," which assume that labor agreements are the product of negotiations between or among the relevant parties under the rules set by the state. This situation subjects the corporate code regimen to many inadequacies because the corporation is able to bypass its workers, therefore ignoring their interests. Because the corporation sets out its own code and means of monitoring it, the corporation can be arbitrary and inconsistent in its formulation and enforcement of its own code. Further, reliance on consumer power for enforcement means the corporation will often manipulate the codes for purposes of public relations.

. . . .

Ultimately, the unpredictable danger of media investigation and public scrutiny should motivate corporations to comply with their self-imposed codes. While this self-imposed compliance may not be the most efficient manner of eliminating exploitative child labor, it provides an opportunity to foster global consensus and cooperation among developed and developing countries until an international labor regimen is forthcoming.

5. The Influence of Corporate Codes

The idea that corporate codes of conduct can significantly reduce child labor has attracted the criticism that such codes can only affect a fraction of the children who work. The majority of children who work do so in agriculture, in family settings at home, the domestic manufacturing sector, or service-oriented positions in homes and restaurants, not in a factory. In fact, a manufacturing job in the export sector is likely to be a better job than most of the other employment available to poor children in developing countries. As a result, only local or national governments can effectively regulate the majority of exploitative child labor situations through enforcement of their child labor laws. Corporate codes might even be counterproductive by, in effect, distracting attention from the duties that governments must perform.

The recent ILO Report announcing reductions in the number of children who labor around the world indicates that in the teeth of increased global competition for cheap labor, the child labor situation is improving. The ILO found:

> [t]he number of child laborers in both age groups 5–14 and 5–17 fell by 11 per cent over the four years from 2000 to 2004. However, the decline was much greater for those engaged in hazardous work: by 26 per cent for the 5–17 age group, and 33 per cent for 5 to 14 year-olds ... Child work is declining, and the more harmful the work and the more vulnerable the children involved, the faster the decline.

The improvement is not attributable to corporate codes alone, though the ILO Report makes it clear that corporate codes have played a crucial role in this improvement. But the ILO report also speaks of a "growing global consensus" among the governments of developing countries on the need to set standards on child labor, and illustrates this consensus with examples of programs from various developing countries that reduce child labor.

Developing countries are realizing that poverty cannot be eliminated without the elimination of child labor, because "[child labor] is both the result of poverty and a way of perpetuating it." The toleration of child labor makes no economic sense. The ILO Report cites a study that found that the elimination of child labor and its replacement by universal education yields benefits that exceed costs at a ratio of 6.7 to 1. Children who spend their youth working grow up to become adults whose health is poorer, and whose labor, if they can work at all, will be worth much less than it would had they gone to school. The child labor standards of corporate codes, therefore, provide an impetus that nudges developing governments toward reforms, which, these governments are beginning to realize, serves their own best interests as well.

....

Because corporate codes are neither generated by government action nor motivated by government interests, their implementation sidesteps the political confrontation between developed and developing countries over core labor standards. For one thing, these codes often require that the child labor laws of the host country be respected. The host country cannot very well complain that the corporation is imposing some foreign regime, or ignoring the law of the host country, when the corporation is in fact insisting that the host country's domestic law be respected.

Corporate codes of conduct mute the objections of developing countries in another respect. The extent to which corporations seek to impose and enforce codes of conduct undercuts the argument that the global adoption of core labor standards is merely a ploy to rob developing countries of their cheap labor advantage. Unlike the governments of developed countries, the corporations that are implementing codes of conduct cannot be accused of having protectionist motivations. The main reason these corporations are in developing countries at all is to take advantage of the cheap labor markets there. Corporations have invested a great deal in cultivating these markets and cannot want to destroy them in order to return to the more expensive labor of developed countries.

In implementing corporate codes, MNCs are pursuing interests that are congruent, not adverse, to the interests of the host developing country. Developing countries must eventually face the fact that corporate implementation of codes of conduct protects their economic interests as well as those of the corporations. If a country develops a reputation for exploiting the labor of its impoverished children, that country, like any corporation, may itself become the target of consumer boycotts, which may lead not only to a loss of business, but also to a corporate exodus as well. "A potential loss of revenue from the lucrative U.S. market arguably far outweighs any potential gain to be made by hiring lower-cost child labor."

....

Notes and Questions

1. Jonassen seems to indicate that corporate codes of conduct can be a way around the impasse posed by disparate international standards on child labor, which are in turn attributable to disparate levels of development. Are you convinced by his reasoning? Are such codes likely to lead to a measurable decrease in child labor, seen in terms of the entire pool of child labor? If not, are these codes worth much time and attention? Or is the author simply describing the degree to which such codes can raise awareness among multinational corporations, and thus improve life for a certain group of children being exploited by corporations otherwise searching the world for the cheapest possible labor?

———

C. International Elimination of Child Labor (IPEC)

At first glance, the ILO's IPEC program may not seem to belong in the "remedies" section of this chapter. However, in terms of effectiveness, IPEC has achieved measurable results. Put in its simplest terms, IPEC involves investment in moving children from certain industries and back into school, a win-win for the children and for their communities. It has been, as we saw at the beginning of this chapter, the target of some critics who find it too focused on the "abolition" of child labor. However, in terms of concrete results, it is well worth studying, as it has taken thousands of children out of the workplace into education through specific forms of funding, thought by most experts to be the surest way of breaking the cycle of child labor.

IPEC (International Programme on the Elimination of Child Labour) Action Against Child Labour

(2007) available at *http://www.ilo.org/ipecinfo/product/view Product.do?productId=3764*

Part I. IMPLEMENTATION REPORT

Chapter 1. Child Labour Update

The ILO's second Global Report on Child Labour, *The end of child labour: Within reach*, published in May 2006 summarized the results of IPEC's analysis of trends in child labour worldwide from 2000 to 2004. According to the new estimates, the number of child labourers fell by 11 per cent from 2000 to 2004 to about 218 million. The 26 per cent decline in the number of children involved in hazardous work was cited as a particularly hopeful sign of progress. The impressive decline recorded in Latin America and the Caribbean is in large part behind the overall fall in child labour, as the reduction for Asia and the Pacific was more restrained and the number of child labourers in Africa actually increased. In terms of sectors, agriculture employs the largest number of children; nearly 70 per cent of all child workers are found in this category. The Report also noted that with a more determined focus on eliminating child labour in Africa the goal of eliminating all worst forms of child labour by 2016 should be attainable.

IPEC's response and strategy

The ILO Minimum Age Convention, 1973 (No. 138) and Worst Forms of Child Labour Convention, 1999 (No. 182) have now been ratified by 147 and 163 member states, respectively. The need to assist governments with the implementation of these has led IPEC to progressively reorient its strategy towards an emphasis on upstream work. This involves intensified support to the development of national plans of action, updating and enforcement of national legislation as well as strengthening of capacities of key players at the policy, planning, and implementation levels. IPEC also continues to support downstream interventions that demonstrate viable strategies for the prevention of child labour, withdrawal of children from it, and the rehabilitation of former child labourers.

It has been recognized for some time that for action to be sustainable, child labour concerns must be mainstreamed into socio-economic development frameworks on the national and global levels. Creating awareness at all levels and mobilizing a wide range of alliances and partnerships to take action remain key strategies. These concepts are built into IPEC's national time-bound programme approach for the elimination of the worst forms of child labour that has been adopted by 23 countries since 2001. IPEC's current strategy is incorporated in the Action Plan for 2006–10....

1.2 WHAT IS BEHIND THE DECLINE IN CHILD LABOUR

The Global Report noted that the overall decline in child labour is probably due to a combination of several factors. Many countries around the world have enacted policies and

Table 1. Global Trends in Children's Economic Activity by Region, 2000 and 2004 (5–14 age group)

	Child Population (millions)		Economically active children (millions)		Activity Rate (per cent)	
Region	2000	2004	2000	2004	2000	2004
Asia & the Pacific	665.1	650.0	127.3	122.3	19.4	18.8
Latin America & the Caribbean	108.1	111.0	17.4	5.7	16.1	5.1
Sub-Saharan Africa	166.8	186.8	48.0	49.3	28.8	26.4
Other Regions	269.3	258.8	18.3	13.4	6.8	5.2
World	1199.3	1206.6	211.0	190.7	17.6	15.8

programmes which have had an important impact on reducing child labour and changing attitudes about the need to respect children's rights. Since 1999, 163 of the ILO's 179 member States have ratified ILO Convention No. 182 on the worst forms of child labour. The rate of ratification of Convention No. 138 on the minimum age for admission to employment also picked up substantially over the same period and now stands at 147. The mobilization of governments, employers, workers, international agencies, parliaments, non-governmental organizations, local authorities and the public at large has engendered a true worldwide movement to eliminate child labour. The ILO, through IPEC, plays a substantial role in this global movement and has helped to keep momentum strong. Around the world the message seems to be taking hold—it is no longer acceptable for children to be deprived of their childhood and an education because they are poor and have to work.

The decline in the number of children involved in hazardous work is a particularly hopeful sign. From 2000 to 2004, the number of children from 5 to 17 years of age in this category fell by 26 per cent. There was an even greater decline of 33 per cent for younger children from 5 to 14 years old. As the Global Report observed, if such a pace can be maintained it should be possible to eliminate all worst forms of child labour by the target date of 2016. Preserving momentum is a big part of the challenge ahead and there will be no room for complacency. An estimated 126 million children are still being exploited in work that gravely endangers their safety, health and well-being, and about 74 million of them are under the age of 15. The majority of these children live in sub-Saharan Africa and Asia and are desperately poor. Most live and work in rural areas, often making them much more difficult to reach than their urban counterparts.

1.2.1. Latin America turns the corner; a redoubling of efforts needed for Africa and Asia

The new estimates allowed a regional breakdown for children in the 5–14 year age group. While the economic activity rate declined in all regions, the progress recorded in Latin America and Caribbean was unparalleled. In this region, the activity rate of children plummeted to 5.1 per cent in 2004 compared to 16.1 in 2002 (table 1). It was thus fitting that the ILO Global Report was launched in Brasilia by the Director-General of the ILO, Juan Somavia, and the representative of President Luis Inacio Lula da Silva of Brazil. The nearly 70 per cent decline child labor in the Americas registered for the period 2002–2003 represents a victory of political will and hard work by many governments and organizations in the region. Several important factors favored this decline region-wide, in particular strong national policies and programmes that have torn at the roots of child labour. Notable among these are conditional cash transfer schemes in Brazil and Mexico that target school attention and retention. Dramatic as the change in the child labor situation appears, it must be not be forgotten that there are still 5.7 million working boys and girls in Latin America and the Caribbean region who are under the minimum age for employment or are engaged in work that must be abolished to ILO Worst Forms of Child Labour Convention No. 182.

In sub-Saharan Africa, the region with the highest incidence of child labour, the small decline in the activity rate of 5–14 year olds from 28.8 to 26.4 per cent was not caused by a drop in the number of economically active children—which in fact rose somewhat. It is explained by the high rate of population growth. Extreme poverty, the effects of the HIV/AIDS pandemic and conflict have in fact exacerbated the child labour problem in Africa. There are now nearly 50 million children under the age of 15 estimated to be working in the region.

Asia and the Pacific registered declines both in the child population and the number of economically active children, but only a very small decrease in the activity rate. At 122 million, the number of working children in the Asia-Pacific area is by far the largest in the world. About 18.8 per cent of the 650 million 5–14 year olds in the region are economically active. Many worst forms of child labour are still important concerns, including child trafficking, commercial sexual exploitation, bonded child labour, child domestic labour, hazardous child labour and the recruitment and use of children for armed conflict or drug trafficking.

. . . .

1.2.2 Most working children are in agriculture

The new global estimates also provided breakdown of working children by broad sector for the first time. Agriculture, which also includes activities related to hunting, forestry and fishing, is by far the sector employing the largest number of children. Nearly 70 per cent of child workers under the age of 15 years old are found in this category. This is followed by services, including wholesale and retail trade, restaurants and hotels, transport, personal services, etc., at 22 per cent, and industry, including mining and quarrying, manufacturing, construction, account for the remaining 9 per cent.

Not only is agricultural work the most prevalent form of child labour, it is one of the most hazardous—only mining and construction are considered to be more dangerous in terms of work-related injuries or death due to accidents. Although children working on farms may not be the first form of child labour that comes to mind, the potential hazards are numerous. IPEC has been building up experience and know-how to begin confronting the problem on a large scale. Several major multi-country projects in Africa and Latin America have been undertaken over the past three years and the World Day against Child Labour 2007 has been dedicated to raising awareness about the issues involved. An overview of the specific issues associated with child labour in agriculture and IPEC's current and future work in this sector is provided in part II, Chapter 1 of this report.

1.3 IPEC's Response and Strategy

1.3.1 The goal

The ILO and its constituents are firmly committed to the elimination of child labour. IPEC was formed in 1992 to support the work of the ILO to help member States fulfill their obligations under the ILO Minimum Age Convention, 1973 (No. 138). In a Resolution concerning the elimination of child labour, the 1996 International Labour Conference (ILC) outlined the Organization's overall strategy for total elimination of all child labour while giving priority to the rapid elimination of its worst forms. This goal, which was reinforced by the unanimous adoption of Convention No. 182 on the worst forms of child labour in 1999, has been pursued by IPEC ever since.

Target group priorities:

While the goal of IPEC is the elimination of all forms of child labour, the direct interventions of IPEC seek to first reach those children who are worst off. The worst forms of child labour are defined in Convention No. 182 as:

- all forms of slavery or practices similar to slavery, such as the sale and trafficking of children, debt bondage and serfdom and forced or compulsory labour, including forced or compulsory recruitment of children for use in armed conflict;

- the use, procuring or offering of a child for prostitution, for the production of pornography or for pornographic performances;

- the use, procuring or offering of a child for illicit activities, in particular for the production and trafficking of drugs as defined in the relevant international treaties;

- work which, by its nature or the circumstances in which it is carried out, is likely to harm the health, safety or morals of children.

Also guided by Convention No. 182, IPEC gives special priority to the youngest children and pays special attention to the situation of girls.

Notes and Questions

1. The ILO speaks of IPEC as a means of assisting countries in implementing their commitments under the Minimum Age Convention. In what way does the IPEC theory deal with the "minimum age versus worst forms" dilemma described at the beginning of this chapter?

Chapter Three

Children in the Sex Industry

I. Overview of the Exploitation of Children in the Global Sex Industry

Just as children are in great demand as laborers, they are also exploited by the global sex industry in astonishing numbers. Nationally, regionally and internationally, there is an extremely lucrative market in children. To an extent that is hard to fathom, they are moved from country to country or within countries to be used as prostitutes, often held in locations known to international pedophiles, and to others who defy easy categorization. Some countries are heavily reliant on the income derived from the sexual exploitation of these children. Young girls may be trafficked along traditional routes; for instance, Nepali girls who are trafficked by the thousands into Indian brothels. Sometimes new "markets" are created as countries open up to the outside world, often after experiencing the trauma of war and economic collapse. Southeast Asia in particular has been characterized by its dependence on the sex industry, and the sale and prostitution of children in particular, as a source of profit.

The idea of "human trafficking" is one that has gained great attention in recent years, particularly after it was identified as a priority issue by the United States government in 2001.[1] Trafficking has been legally defined to include all forms of coercive movement of persons for purposes of exploitation.[2] In this chapter, we will focus on the movement of children, whether internationally or within national borders, for purposes of sexual exploitation. It should be noted that this occurs in virtually every region of the world, despite the proliferation of laws intended to prevent it. We may consider sex trafficking to be a subset of the modern phenomenon of human trafficking, described by many to be a contemporary form of slavery, with child sex trafficking as a further subset of sex traf-

---

1. See the 2001 remarks by John Ashcroft, U.S. Att'y Gen., News Conference on Worker Exploitation (Mar. 27, 2001), *available at* http://www.usdoj.gov/archive/ag/speeches/2001/032701worker exploitation.htm, where he announced that the fight against trafficking would be a top priority for the Bush Administration and U.S. law enforcement agencies. Toward achieving this goal, the Justice Department announced new guidelines for federal prosecutors to pursue trafficking cases and the State Department issued its first Congressionally mandated annual report on trafficking in persons in July 2001. *See* U.S. Dep't of St., 2001 Trafficking in Persons Report 2 (2001).

2. Congress defined the term "severe forms of trafficking in persons" as:
(A) sex trafficking in which a commercial sex act is induced by force, fraud, or coercion, or in which the person induced to perform such act has not attained 18 years of age; or
(B) the recruitment, harboring, transportation, provision, or obtaining of a person for labor or services, through the use of force, fraud or coercion for the purpose of subjection to involuntary servitude, peonage, debt bondage, or slavery.
Victims of Trafficking and Violence Protection Act of 2000, 22 U.S.C. § 7102(8) (2000).

ficking.[3] Child sex trafficking and exploitation is increasingly perceived as a human rights crisis of the most egregious kind.

There has been an undeniable proliferation of national and international "anti-trafficking" laws over the past decade. In addition to the United Nations Protocol to Prevent, Suppress and Punish Trafficking, Especially Women and Children,[4] which was completed in 2000 and entered into force in 2003, dozens of countries—including the United States—now have laws specifically aimed at human trafficking in all its forms.[5] While this indicates a welcome increase in awareness of the problem of modern-day slavery, it may be wondered whether a generic approach to human trafficking can contribute much towards eradicating child sex trafficking. Anti-trafficking laws do represent a significant development, to the extent that they strengthen the hand of prosecutors who deal with organized criminals trading in human beings.

In addition to the section on trafficking of children, this chapter will cover the related issue of sex tourism, specifically the laws passed in the United States and elsewhere to facilitate prosecution of those who travel abroad and engage in the sexual exploitation of minors. Many tourism destination countries have also passed laws explicitly criminalizing such conduct, and there has been enhanced cooperation between the "sending" and "receiving" countries in this regard.

Finally, it is impossible to study the problem of children in the global sex industry without facing up to the issue of demand. There are many regional and cultural variations on the theme of child sexual exploitation, but all share a common element of apparently huge and growing demand. Are there more children being exploited now than ever before? Was the demand always there, and is it only now facilitated and enabled because of globalization and corresponding ease of movement around the world? Has the internet "normalized" child sexual exploitation? Does our legal thinking on the issue of child pornography recognize developments in children's rights? These demand-related matters will be taken up at the end of this chapter.

A. The Generic Approach: Human Trafficking as a Unitary Phenomenon

In his 1999 book, *Disposable People: New Slavery in the Global Economy*, author Kevin Bales adopts a comprehensive view of human trafficking, and draws attention to the rapid proliferation of what he identifies as modern day slavery. Surveying the apparently unlimited supply of devalued and exploitable people in the global economy, he outlines commonalities in the manner in which these people are bought, sold, used and tossed away. Bales' conceptual contribution is in alerting readers to the fact that what might have seemed a relic of the past—trade in human beings—is still very much alive. Indeed, it is likely to flourish as the world became more economically integrated. He describes, in

---

3. "Sex trafficking" is further defined as "the recruitment, harboring, transportation, provision, or obtaining of a person for the purpose of a commercial sex act." *Id.* at §7102(9).

4. Protocol to Prevent, Suppress and Punish Trafficking in Persons Especially Women and Children, G.A. Res. 55/25, Annex II, U.N. GAOR, 55th Sess., U.N. Doc. A/RES/55/25 (Jan. 8, 2001), *available at* http://www.uncjin.org/Documents/Conventions/dcatoc/final_documents_2/convention_%20traff_eng.pdf.

5. *See, e.g.,* Victims of Trafficking and Violence Protection Act of 2000, 22 U.S.C. §§7101–7112 (2000).

a generalized manner, how slavery continues to destroy the lives of people. He writes about modern day slavery in many countries and many forms—from domestic servitude and forced industrial and agricultural labor through the brothel sex industry. Bales has been a leader in re-introducing the concept of "slavery" to the contemporary world.

Kevin Bales, Disposable People: New Slavery in the Global Economy
(1999)

. . . .

Slavery is not a horror safely consigned to the past; it continues to exist throughout the world, even in developed countries like France and the United States. Across the world slaves work and sweat and build and suffer. Slaves in Pakistan may have made the shoes you are wearing and the carpet you stand on. Slaves in the Caribbean may have put sugar in your kitchen and toys in the hands of your children. In India they may have sewn the shirt on your back and polished the ring on your finger. They are paid nothing.

Slaves touch your life indirectly as well. They made the bricks for the factory that made the TV you watch. In Brazil slaves made the charcoal that tempered the steel that made the springs in your car and the blade on your lawnmower. Slaves grew the rice that fed the woman that wove the lovely cloth you've put up as curtains. Your investment portfolio and your mutual fund pension own stock in companies using slave labor in the developing world. Slaves keep your costs low and returns on your investments high.

Slavery is booming business and the number of slaves is increasing. People get rich by using slaves. And when they've finished with their slaves, they just throw these people away. This is the new slavery, which focuses on big profits and cheap lives. It is not about owning people in the traditional sense of the old slavery, but about controlling them completely. People become completely disposable tools for making money.

"On more than ten occasions I woke early in the morning to find the corpse of a young girl floating in the water by the barge. Nobody bothered to bury the girls. They just threw their bodies in the river to be eaten by the fish."

This was the fate of young girls enslaved as prostitutes in the gold mining town of the Amazon, explained Antonia Pinto, who worked there as a cook and a procurer. While the developed world bemoans the destruction of the rain forests, few people realize that slave labor is used to destroy them. Men are lured to the region by promises of riches in gold dust, and girls as young as eleven are offered jobs in the offices and restaurants that serve the mines. When they arrive in the remote mining areas, the men are locked up and forced to work in the mines; the girls are beaten, raped, and put to work as prostitutes. Their "recruitment agents" are paid a small amount for each body, perhaps $150. The "recruits" have become slaves—not through legal ownership, but through the final authority of violence. The local police act as enforcers to control the slaves. As one young woman explained, "Here the brothel owners send the police to beat us . . . if we flee they go after us, if they find us, if they don't kill us they beat us all the way back to the brothel."

The brothels are incredibly lucrative. The girl who "cost" $150 can be sold for sex up to ten times a night and bring in $10,000 per month. The only expenses are payments to the police and a pittance for food. If a girl is a troublemaker, runs away, or gets sick, she is easy to get rid of and replace. Antonia Pinto described what happened to an eleven-year-old girl when she refused to have sex with a miner: "After decapitating her with his machete, the miner drove around in his speedboat, showing off her head to the other miners, who clapped and shouted their approval."

As the story of these girls shows, slavery has not, as most of us have been led to believe, ended. To be sure, they word *slavery* continues to be used to mean all sorts of things, and all too often it has been applied as an easy metaphor. Having just enough money to get by, receiving wages that barely keep you alive, may be called wage slavery, but it is not slavery. Sharecroppers have a hard life, but they are not slaves. Child labor is terrible, but it is not necessarily slavery.

We might think slavery is a matter of ownership, but that depends on what we mean by ownership. In the past, slavery entailed one person legally owning another person, but modern slavery is different. Today slavery is illegal everywhere, and there is no more legal ownership of human beings. When people buy slaves today they don't ask for a receipt or ownership papers, but they do gain control—and they use violence to maintain this control. Slaveholders have all of the benefits of ownership without the legalities. Indeed, for the slaveholders, not having legal ownership is an improvement because they get total control without any responsibility for what they own. For that reason I tend to use the term slaveholder instead of slaveowner.

In spite of this difference between the new and the old slavery, I think everyone would agree that what I am talking about is slavery: the total control of one person by another for the purpose of economic exploitation. Modern slavery hides behind different masks, using clever lawyers and legal smoke screens, but when we strip away the lies, we find someone controlled by violence and denied all of their personal freedom to make money for someone else. As I traveled around the world to study the new slavery, I looked behind the legal masks and I saw people in chains. Of course, many people think there is no such thing as slavery anymore, and I was one of those people just a few years ago.

. . . .

My best estimate of the number of slaves in the world today is 27 million. This number is much smaller than the estimates put forward by some activists, who give a range as high as 200 million, but it is the number I feel I can trust; it is also the number that fits my strict definition of slavery. The biggest part of that 27 million, perhaps 15 to 20 million, is represented by bonded labor in India, Pakistan, Bangladesh, and Nepal. Bonded labor or debt bondage happens when people give themselves into slavery as security against a loan or when they inherit a debt from a relative. Otherwise slavery tends to be concentrated in Southeast Asia, northern and western Africa, and parts of South America (but there are some slaves in almost every country of the world, including the United States, Japan, and many European countries). There are more slaves alive today than all the people stolen from Africa in the time of the transatlantic slave trade. Put another way, today's slave population is greater than the population of Canada, and six times greater than the population of Israel.

These slaves tend to be used in simple, nontechnological, and traditional work. The largest group works in agriculture. But slaves are used in many other kinds of labor: brickmaking, mining or quarrying, prostitution, gem working and jewelry making, cloth and carpet making, and domestic service; they clear forests, make charcoal, and work in shops. Much of this work is aimed at local sale and consumption, but slave made goods reach into homes around the world. Carpets, fireworks, jewelry, and metal goods made by slave labor, as well as grains, sugar and other foods harvested by slaves, are imported directly to North America and Europe. In addition, large international corporations, acting through subsidiaries in the developing world, take advantage of slave labor to improve their bottom line and increase the dividends to their shareholders.

But the value of slaves lies not so much in the particular products they make as in their sweat, in the volume of work squeezed out of them. Slaves are often forced to sleep next to their looms or brick kilns; some are even chained to their work tables. All their waking hours may be turned into working hours. In our global economy one of the standard explanations that multinational corporations give for closing factories in the "first world" and opening them in the 'third world" is the lower labor cost. Slavery can constitute a significant part of these savings. No paid workers, no matter how efficient, can compete economically with unpaid workers — slaves.

. . . .

What does race have to do with it?

In the new slavery race means little. In the past, ethnic and racial differences were used to explain and excuse slavery. These differences allowed slaveholders to make up reasons why slavery was acceptable, or even a good thing for the slaves. The otherness of the slaves made it easier to employ the violence and cruelty necessary for total control. This otherness could be defined in almost any way — a different religion, tribe, skin color, language, custom, or economic class. Any of these differences could be and were used to separate the slaves from the slaveholders. Maintaining these differences required tremendous investment in some very irrational ideas — and the crazier the justifying idea, the more vehemently it was insisted upon. The American Founding Fathers had to go through moral, linguistic, and political contortions to explain why their "land of the free" was only for white people. Many of them knew that by allowing slavery they were betraying their most cherished ideals. They were driven to it because slavery was worth a lot of money to a lot of people in North America at the time. But they went to the trouble of devising legal and political excuses because they felt they had to justify their economic decisions morally.

. . . .

In Europe and North America the police fight organized crime; in Thailand the police are organized crime. The same holds true for many parts of Africa and Asia: the state's monopoly on violence, the monopoly that should protect citizens, has been turned against them. This disintegration of civil order often occurs in times of rapid social and political change. A community under stress, whether caused by disease, natural disaster, economic depression, or war, can break up and descend into the horror of "might makes right." These are the conditions found in areas of rapid development such as the frontier areas of Brazil or at the rural/urban interface in Thailand. There, transitional economies drive farming families off the land and leave them destitute, while fostering a demand for unskilled labor in the cities. With destitution, traditional systems of family or community support for the vulnerable collapse — and in these countries they are not replaced with any effective state welfare measures. Without protection or alternatives, the poor become powerless, and the violent, without state intervention, become supremely powerful.

Slavery blossoms in these circumstances. To control their slaves, slaveholders must be able to use violence as much and as often as they choose. Without permanent access to violence, they are impotent. The old slavery often regulated the violence a master could use against a slave. Though often ignored, the slave codes of the American South, which prohibited the teaching of reading and writing and recommended a program of strict discipline, also protected slaves from murder and mutilation and set minimum standards of food and clothing. However, the codes gave master, as his legal right, a complete monopoly on violence short of murder. If the master needed it, the law and the power of the state would back him up, for the state was allowed to murder (execute) slaves. Today, the monopoly of violence is often decentralized. It resides not in national law but in the hands and weapons of local police or soldiers. In fact, we can say that this transfer of the monopoly of violence from central government to local thugs is essential if the new slavery is to take root and flourish. What normally brings it about is the head-on collision of the modern and traditional ways of life.

Transition zones where the world's industrial economy meets the traditional culture of peasant farming are found throughout the developing world. At the interface there are often bloody struggles over the control of natural resources. In the Amazon a small but terrible war continues over the region's mineral wealth and timber as the line of exploitation advances. The Amazonian Indians have little to fight with, and they are pushed back repeatedly, killed wholesale, and sometimes enslaved. The new open mines ripped from the forests are hundreds of miles from direct government control. Here those with the most firepower run the show, and those without weapons obey orders or disappear. The few local police have a choice: cooperate with the thugs and make a profit, or attempt to enforce the law and die. The result is the lawlessness and terror that Antonia Pinto described as the beginning of this chapter. In a mining village that does not expect the government to interfere anytime soon, the choice is clear and a brutal social order asserts itself. The situation in Brazil is dramatic, but the same trend appears from rural Ghana to the slums of Bangkok, from the highlands of Pakistan to the villages of the Philippines — and this Wild West syndrome strongly affects what can be done to end slavery.

Notes and Questions

1. Kevin Bales treats the trafficking question in terms of a general phenomenon of "modern day slavery." This means that sex trafficking and other forms of trafficking (for purposes of other kinds of labor) are conceptualized as part of the same set of problems. Is this a useful approach? What virtues does it have? What issues might it obscure? Although slavery is an historically non-specific term, in the United States it is of course closely linked with the exploitation of African slaves in the South before the Civil War. Is Bales' use of the term problematic in that sense?

2. Refer to the UN Protocol to Prevent, Suppress and Punish Trafficking in Persons Especially Women and Children[6] in the Appendix. Does the Protocol share any common traits with Kevin Bales' methodology? How does the Protocol deal with the human rights dimension of human trafficking? Does it differentiate sex trafficking from other forms of trafficking? Do you find its "unitary definition" of human trafficking helpful? What does its definition contain? The Protocol will be discussed in detail in the readings below.

Ten years after the adoption of the UNCRC, Human Rights Watch provided a summary of the multifaceted problem of child sexual exploitation. Although brief, this kind of as-

---

6. Protocol to Prevent, Suppress and Punish Trafficking in Persons Especially Women and Children, G.A. Res. 55/25, Annex II, U.N. GAOR, 55th Sess., U.N. Doc. A/RES/55/25 (Jan. 8, 2001), *available at* http://www.uncjin.org/Documents/Conventions/dcatoc/final_documents_2/convention_%20traff_eng.pdf.

sessment allows us to see the common features of the commercial exploitation of children. Significantly, Human Rights Watch places this phenomenon in the context of children's human rights, with an emphasis on state responsibility to confront and eliminate commercial sexual exploitation of children. As always, Human Rights Watch plays a consciousness raising role, setting out the often distasteful reality against the formal promises of human rights law.

Human Rights Watch, *Promises Broken: An Assessment of Children's Rights on the 10th Anniversary of the Convention on the Rights of the Child*

(1999) *available at* http://www.hrw.org/legacy/press/1999/nov/children.htm

Sexual Abuse and Exploitation

When they brought me here, it was in a taxi. I kept looking around, wondering what kind of work was going on in this area of this big city. Everywhere I looked, I saw curtained doorways and rooms. Men would go and come through these curtained entrances. People on the street would be calling out, "Two rupees, two rupees." I asked the other Nepali women if these were offices; it seemed the logical explanation. In two days I knew everything. I cried.

—Tara N., a Nepali woman who was trafficked into India at sixteen.

Children around the world are sexually abused and exploited in ways that can cause permanent physical and psychological harm. In some cases, police demand sexual services from street children, threatening them with arrest if they do not comply. In detention and correctional facilities children may be sexually abused by staff or are not protected from sexual abuse by other inmates. In refugee camps many children are exploited by adults or sometimes forced to sell their bodies for food. Children in orphanages may be abused by staff members or other children. In conflict areas children are kidnapped to serve as child soldiers and also as sexual servants for adult soldiers. Children working as domestics may be assaulted or raped by employers.

This grim picture is compounded by the use of children as prostitutes in countries throughout the world. An unknown but very large number of children are used for commercial sexual purposes every year, often ending up with their health destroyed, victims of HIV/AIDS and other sexually transmitted diseases. Younger and younger children are sought with the expectation that clients will not be exposed to HIV. Prostituted children can be raped, beaten, sodomized, emotionally abused, tortured, and even killed by pimps, brothel owners, and customers. Some have been trafficked from one country to another; both boys and girls are trafficked. Moreover, child prostitutes are frequently treated as criminals by law enforcement and judicial authorities, rather than as children who are victims of sexual exploitation.

Articles 34 and 35 of the Convention on the Rights of the Child forbid sexual exploitation or trafficking of children, and the Committee on the Rights of the Child has devoted time and efforts to the issue, urging governments to crack down on the practice. Other international instruments in human rights, humanitarian law, refugee law, and labor standards protect children against sexual exploitation. In addition, a U.N. special rapporteur on the sale of children, child prostitution and child pornography investigates these issues.

A good deal of international attention has been focused on sexual exploitation and trafficking, particularly on the practice of sex tourism, which is a relatively small part of the problem. A World Congress against Commercial Sexual Exploitation of Children was held in Stockholm in 1996, attended by representatives of governments, U.N. bodies, and nongovernmental organizations, from 125 countries. The congress issued a strong declaration against commercial sexual exploitation of children and an agenda for action; an international focal point on sexual exploitation of children was established in Geneva to coordinate reform efforts. A number of governments and NGOs are continuing their efforts to attack the problem. But vast numbers of children are still trapped in this life-threatening sex trade.

. . . .

The international community, both governments and nongovernmental groups, must make every effort to end these abuses. In some cases new laws are required; in others the political will must be mobilized to implement existing legislation and prosecute those involved in sexually abusing and exploiting these vulnerable children.

Notes and Questions

1. NGOs such as Human Rights Watch and Amnesty International have increasingly focused on sex trafficking as a major human rights violation. This brief report on the state of child sex trafficking around the world captures some of the torment associated with child sex slavery. Does sex trafficking, whether of women, children, or both, receive the kind of attention it deserves from the international community? Why does such a shocking form of abuse fail to garner sustained comment at the highest political levels?

II. Historical and Contemporary Legal Approaches to Trafficking for Purposes of Sexual Exploitation

A. Background to the United Nations Trafficking Protocol

The concept of human trafficking, of course, points to a criminal act of moving about, dealing in, and otherwise coercing human beings for profit. Sex trafficking is one very profitable branch of that activity. The term "trafficking" refers generically to a movement and sale which is inherently illegal, because of what is being bought and sold. The following articles discuss the history and scope of legal instruments enacted to address sex trafficking. This section is intended to familiarize readers with legal efforts to combat trafficking, most of which have focused on prosecution of the traffickers themselves. Sex trafficking has obvious links with other forms of trafficking—in narcotics and armaments, for instance—which often share common routes of transmission. All experts in the field concur that human trafficking is increasingly profitable, and likely to overtake other forms of trafficking as the most lucrative. As you read the followings articles, consider whether the sex trafficking phenomenon is likely to be adequately addressed by criminal law solutions.

Kathryn E. Nelson, *Sex Trafficking and Forced Prostitution: Comprehensive New Legal Approaches*

24 Houston Journal of International Law 551 (2002)

....

III. International Law

A. Early Treaties

The first international treaty regarding the trafficking of women was drafted around the turn of the twentieth century in response to the sale of women into prostitution in European cities. The 1904 International Agreement for the Suppression of the White Slave Traffic ("1904 Agreement") set up mechanisms to collect and coordinate information on the international procurement of women for prostitution. Parties to the 1904 Agreement promised to supervise train stations and ports and to provide shelter to trafficking victims, eventually returning them to their home countries. Rather than punishing the procurers, the 1904 Agreement focused on protecting the victims of trafficking for prostitution.

In 1910, the International Convention for the Suppression of the White Slave Traffic ("1910 Convention") strengthened anti-trafficking efforts by criminalizing the procurement of women for prostitution. The 1910 Convention bound the parties to punish any person who "hired, abducted, or enticed for immoral purposes any woman under the age of twenty-one, or used violence, threats, fraud or any compulsion on a woman over twenty-one, notwithstanding that the acts which constituted the offense were committed in different countries." However, the 1910 Convention still only addressed the trafficking aspect of forced prostitution and did not cover the holding of women in brothels, which at the time was considered a domestic issue.

The 1921 Convention for the Suppression of the Traffic in Women and Children ("1921 Convention") extended the protections of the 1904 Agreement and the 1910 Convention to minors of either sex and raised the relevant age limit from twenty to twenty-one in the case of non-forcible recruitment for prostitution. The 1921 Convention also changed the prevalent terminology to include all young women and children, not just whites. The 1921 Convention encouraged states to fight trafficking by taking legislative and administrative measures, specifically by the licensing and supervising of employment agencies to protect emigrating and immigrating women and children. However, the focus was still on trafficking and not on the crimes committed against the women once they arrived in their destinations.

Finally, in 1933, the International Convention for the Suppression of the Traffic of Women of Full Age declared punishable the acts of procuring, enticing, or leading away of an adult woman for "immoral purposes" in another country. It also removed consent as a defense to procurement. Still, no treaty attempted to coordinate efforts among nations regarding trafficking.

B. The United Nations

1. Convention for the Suppression of the Traffic in Persons and of the Exploitation of the Prostitution of Others

In 1949, the U.N. General Assembly adopted the Convention for the Suppression of the Traffic in Persons and of the Exploitation of the Prostitution of Others ("1949 Convention"). The 1949 Convention supersedes the 1904 Agreement and the Conventions of 1910, 1921, and 1933. Signatories are charged with three obligations under the 1949 Convention: prohibition of trafficking, specific administrative and enforcement measures, and social measures aimed at trafficked persons. The 1949 Convention presents two shifts in perspective of the trafficking problem. First, it views prostitutes as victims of the procurers. Second, it eschews the terms "white slave traffic" and "women," using for the first time race- and gender-neutral language.

Article 1 provides punishment for any person who "procures, entices or leads away, for purposes of prostitution, another person" or "exploits the prostitution of another person, even with the consent of that person." To fall under the provisions of the 1949 Convention, the trafficking need not cross international lines. Attempts or preparatory acts to the aforementioned offenses are punished as well. Moreover, states are required to establish an authority to coordinate and facilitate the nation's efforts to prevent and prosecute trafficking in persons.

The 1949 Convention does not outlaw prostitution per se; instead it targets aspects of the prostitution industry. Article 2 flatly prohibits the operation of brothels. States agree to punish any person who "keeps or manages, or knowingly finances or takes part in the financing of a brothel" or "knowingly lets or rents a building or other place ... for the purpose of the prostitution of others." In addition, under the 1949 Convention, state regulation of prostitution is prohibited.

. . . .

The 1949 Convention better addressed the problem of trafficking for prostitution than its predecessors. For one, in mentioning "traffic" and "prostitution" in its title, the 1949 Convention focuses on both the international and domestic aspects of the international trafficking in persons for prostitution. Second, the substantive terms of the 1949 Convention are, on the whole, explicit and clear, in contrast to the vague terms of subsequent conventions. For example, the 1949 Convention explicitly enumerates as a punishable offense the enticement and deception that occurs when women are forced into prostitution. The 1949 Convention also includes both preparatory acts and attempts and intentional acts as punishable offenses. Article 5 even includes a limited procedural right for victims of trafficking: the victims may be parties in proceedings against traffickers if the victims are otherwise entitled to participate under national law. Finally, for the first time, the 1949 Convention includes components of a comprehensive solution to the trafficking problem by calling for the punishment of those involved in trafficking, requesting aid for the victims of trafficking through victim-assistance programs, and asking for cooperation and coordination of anti-trafficking efforts among nations.

. . . .

The 1949 Convention also presents a conflict between articles 1 and 12. Article 1 removes the defense of consent, yet article 12 declares that the offenses shall be defined, prosecuted, and punished in accordance with domestic law, which may allow the affirmative defense of consent.

The most glaring defect of the 1949 Convention is its lack of adequate enforcement mechanisms. First, many states have not yet ratified the convention. Second, a victim of trafficking has no private remedy against her procurers and pimps; only signatory nations may bring claims against each other.

Finally, the 1949 Convention provides little incentive for victims to come forward because, in doing so, they may be expelled from the country due to their immigration status. According to article 19, a victim of trafficking shall be repatriated if the victim desires repatriation or if "expulsion is ordered in conformity with the law." Persons without legal resident status presumably fall under this category, and many victims of trafficking enter a foreign country illegally with forged documents. Although repatriation is to occur without prejudice to prosecution, few procurers will be prosecuted if the principal victims and witnesses are forced to leave the country because of their immigration status.

2. Convention on the Elimination of All Forms of Discrimination Against Women

In 1979, the U.N. General Assembly adopted the Convention on the Elimination of All Forms of Discrimination Against Women ("Women's Convention"). Where the 1949 Convention fails to take a rights-based approach to the trafficking problem, the Women's Convention begins to recognize the rights of victims of trafficking for prostitution. It was the first international agreement recognizing that women's rights are human rights. The framers of the Women's Convention state that discrimination against women "violates the principles of equality of rights and respect for human dignity." The Women's Convention also recognizes that discrimination is worsened in impoverished countries, where women have less access than men to food, health, education and training, and opportunities for employment. The risk of women being trafficked for prostitution is also greater in countries where employment opportunities are low.

The Women's Convention defines discrimination against women as "any distinction, exclusion or restriction made on the basis of sex which has the effect or purpose of impairing or nullifying the recognition, enjoyment or exercise by women ... on a basis of equality of men and women, of human rights and fundamental freedoms...." Trafficking of women for forced prostitution arguably fits this definition, because trafficking impairs women's freedom on the basis of their sex. The Women's Convention specifically addresses this issue in article 6: "States Parties shall take all appropriate measures ... to suppress all forms of traffic in women and exploitation of prostitution of women."

....

Despite its potential, the Women's Convention has been largely ineffective. First, the language in article 6 — "appropriate measures" — is not defined and is too vague to be readily enforceable. Second, many industrialized nations, including the United States, have failed to sign the Women's Convention because it is legally binding. Third, the Women's Convention has been subject to a large number of reservations, diminishing its effectiveness. Finally, the Women's Convention gives the victims of trafficking no private remedy. Only States Parties may bring claims, and only against each other, in the International Court of Justice....

The General Assembly addressed some of these concerns in the adoption of an Optional Protocol to the Women's Convention. The Optional Protocol begins by reaffirming the authority of CEDAW to monitor compliance with the Women's Convention. Then, the Optional Protocol finally gives CEDAW some muscle. Under articles 5 through 9, CEDAW is given the power to communicate directly with States Parties. For instance, after a State Party has submitted a report for consideration, but before a determination on the merits, CEDAW may request that the State Party take interim measures to prevent "irreparable damage" to the alleged victim. CEDAW may also submit comments and recommendations directly to the parties concerned, at the conclusion of the examination.

....

Although the new complaint mechanism (contained in the Protocol) appears to give power to victims of trafficking, it is laden with many obstacles. The complaining victim must first seek relief through local channels, if relief is even available in that country. Unfortunately, in the case of forced prostitution, the woman could be criminally prosecuted herself for prostitution if she seeks assistance from the local authorities. Before complaining to CEDAW, she must determine whether the right in question is addressed by the Women's Convention and whether the country is a party to both the Women's Convention and the Optional Protocol. To meet these requirements, the woman will probably require the assistance of legal counsel. It is difficult to imagine that a victim of trafficking, stranded in a foreign country without money or proper immigration documents and frightened of adverse legal action if she makes her presence known, would seek to hire an attorney familiar with the remedy outlined in the Optional Protocol.

3. Protocol to Prevent, Suppress and Punish Trafficking in Persons, Especially Women and Children

In November 2000, the U.N. General Assembly adopted the Trafficking Protocol, in part due to the ineffectiveness of the 1949 Convention. The Trafficking Protocol aims to provide a "comprehensive international approach" to the trafficking problem by punishing the traffickers and aiding their victims. It is the first international agreement to do so.

Article 5 calls on States Parties to criminalize "trafficking in persons" and the organization or direction of others in this endeavor. "Trafficking in persons" is defined as:

> the recruitment, transportation, transfer, harbouring or receipt of persons, by means of the threat or use of force or other forms of coercion, of abduction, of fraud, of deception, of the abuse of power or of a position of vulnerability or of the giving or receiving of payments or benefits to achieve the consent of a person having control over another person, for the purpose of exploitation. Exploitation shall include, at a minimum, the exploitation of the prostitution of others or other forms of sexual exploitation, forced labour or services, slavery or practices similar to slavery, servitude or the removal of organs[.]

Article 6 of the Trafficking Protocol requires States Parties to assist victims of trafficking by keeping their identities confidential, providing them with information regarding legal proceedings and victims' assistance programs, providing physical protection, and ensuring that domestic law allows recovery for trafficking victims. Article 9 mandates that States Parties adopt prevention measures, including trafficking awareness campaigns and measures to "alleviate the factors that make persons, especially women and children, vulnerable to trafficking, such as poverty, underdevelopment, and lack of equal opportunity."

Under the Trafficking Protocol's expansive definition of trafficking in persons, exploitation of a victim's economic situation can be considered "coercion" or "abuse of power or of a position of vulnerability." The requirement that States Parties adopt or strengthen measures to alleviate the economic and social problems that contribute to trafficking also indicates that the Trafficking Protocol considers economic hardship as an important factor contributing to trafficking. For the first time, the international community has recognized the prominence of poverty in the trafficking equation.

....

V. Conclusion and Recommendations

....

The Trafficking Protocol finally adopts a comprehensive approach to the worldwide scourge of sex trafficking as well. By broadening the definition of trafficking and specifically addressing the economic issues in victim assistance and prevention, the Trafficking Protocol may have a greater effect on trafficking than did previous agreements. If combined with domestic and foreign measures such as the Trafficking Act, the Trafficking Protocol will have an even greater impact, and the world someday may see a decrease in trafficking in women for prostitution.

Notes and Questions

1. Sex trafficking is an issue of overwhelming importance to women and children. As described by Nelson, what do you think of the contribution made by the Convention on the Elimination of Discrimination Against Women (CEDAW)[7] to the sex trafficking problem, and more generally?

2. How does the recent UN Trafficking Protocol relate to the earlier international instruments described by Nelson, such as the 1949 Convention? Is the UN Trafficking Protocol specific enough to be of use to trafficked women and children, or is a more targeted instrument required? What additional elements might the Protocol have covered?

3. For a clear and precise explanation of how the UN Trafficking Protocol treats human trafficking as a problem encompassing migration, criminal law, human rights and labor, see Natalia Ollus, The United Nations Protocol to Prevent, Suppress and Punish Trafficking in Persons, Especially Women and Children: A Tool for Criminal Justice Personnel (2004), available at http://www.unafei.or.jp/english/pdf/PDF_rms/no62/ Finland(1).pdf.

Ollus points out that there is an unresolved controversy around the problem of prostitution. Should prostitution that cannot be clearly shown to have been forced or coerced also be considered as trafficking? Will it be possible for law enforcement to distinguish between coerced and non-coerced prostitution?

4. The Trafficking Protocol did not impose a State obligation *not* to return trafficking victims to their countries of origin against their will. Yet the Protocol insists that the victim's safety should be ensured. Is this a defect in the Protocol? Does it reflect a fear on the part of States that anti-trafficking laws will be used as a way to liberalize national immigration rules?

B. On What Constitutes Trafficking

The following excerpt sets out key issues in international anti-trafficking law, particularly with regard to the internationally recognized definition of trafficking and the controversial issue of victim consent. The clear criminalization of human trafficking is meant to make the issue of the victim's "consent" irrelevant. While true consent is impossible in the case of a minor, the matter is more complex with respect to adult victims. Some fear that elimination of a defense of victim "consent" unduly relieves the trafficked person of any responsibility; or indeed, unduly paints adult women as incapable of making decisions on work and migration. In the brief excerpt below, Abigail Schwartz emphasizes the central element of trafficking—coerced movement—and gives a sense of the complexities involved in trying to establish a clear definition of sex trafficking.

Abigail Schwartz, *Sex Trafficking in Cambodia*
17 Columbia Journal of Asian Law 371 (2004)

Trafficking Defined

Although comprehensive, [the definition of trafficking found in Article 3 of the UN Protocol] is far from universally accepted; at the national level, definitions still vary greatly.

---

7. U.N. Doc. A/34/46 (1979), into force Sept. 3, 1981.

Of course, there is some shared ground. Generally, every definition contains three common elements: 1) the recruitment and/or transportation of a human, 2) for work or service, and 3) for the profit of the trafficker. However, confusion arises because the phenomenon of trafficking encircles other social evils such as forced labor, illegal migration, and prostitution. Some law and policy makers would distinguish trafficking from these other issues as much as possible; others see such a practice as a largely fruitless formalistic exercise. Specifically, controversy surrounds two important questions. First, does the transportation of humans within national borders qualify as trafficking? Second, must there be coercion?

A. Trafficking and the Element of Crossing Borders

Some definitions consider illegal border-crossing or illegal residence a necessary element to trafficking. Supporters of this approach argue that it is essential to distinguish between ordinary labor exploitation—covered by domestic labor laws—and the forced relocation of humans for exploitative purposes. According to this view, trafficking laws and policies are necessary to address the specific vulnerability of undocumented workers in other countries. It is the very nature of their illegal status that exposes trafficking victims to the worst forms of exploitation and leaves them without any means of protection or legal recourse. The victims are often unable to escape abusive situations on their own due to language barriers, unfamiliarity with the area, and lack of a social network. These factors have an additional effect of making victims afraid of criminal sanctions or repatriation (which would place them back in the orbit of their traffickers), preventing them from seeking police intervention. Therefore, trafficking victims require a distinct legal status, apart from both illegal migrants and domestic exploited laborers.

Others take the position that trafficking is possible without the crossing of borders, either legally or illegally, with victims in possession of a legal residence and/or working permit. Supporters of this approach insist that individuals who are relocated within national boundaries are equally defenseless against exploitation and equally unprotected by the law as those taken outside the country as those transported internationally. This is because more often than not, these people are involved in illegal activities (e.g. prostitution) and fall outside the scope of domestic labor laws, which makes them reluctant to file police reports. Moreover, because they are usually displaced far away from their homes, they may be as friendless and unfamiliar with their surroundings as if had they been taken to another country. In addition, because a large number of trafficking victims throughout the world comes from minority populations, they may encounter language barriers and, in some cases, may not have the same legal rights as other citizens. Finally, in the rare instances when victims do manage to escape, they may be unwilling to return home due to social stigmatization or fear of being re-sold by their original traffickers, who are often members of their communities or families. Thus, according to this position, trafficking laws should apply to both nationally and internationally transported victims.

The United Nations has adopted the second definition in its Protocol Against Trafficking—that is, trafficking may exist within national borders. This approach seems reasonable when one considers the practical application of trafficking laws and the overall objective of safeguarding victims' rights. First, despite the stated objective in distinguishing trafficked persons from illegal migrants, trafficking laws which require an element of border-crossing run the risk of conflating trafficking victims with illegal migrants. In so doing, they shift the focus from the trafficking of women to women's status as illegal aliens. For example, some national laws requiring an element of border-crossing obligate a victim to establish that she was trafficked as opposed to willingly smuggled across state lines. This standard of proof is extremely difficult to meet, especially in cases where a woman was deceived into traveling to another country for a "good job" and later forced to live in slave-like conditions. If she cannot meet the burden of proof, she will be placed in a worse situation than had she never crossed the border: she will be exempt from domestic laws which might offer some redress against her exploiters and subject to that country's immigration laws. Second, these laws often place domestic victims of trafficking in worse situations than their foreign peers. While a non-national may be awarded certain legal rights and social services because of her "trafficked" status, a national may find herself in trouble with the law for prostitution. In both cases, the law tends to treat the trafficked women as lawbreakers, which results in protection for traffickers rather than for the victimized women. Ultimately, trafficking laws that dispense with the border-crossing requirement offer the promise of more consistent and unilateral application. In addition, laws which focus on the exploitative conditions, as opposed to the victims' status, stand a better chance of promoting the victims' basic rights.

B. Trafficking and the Element of Coercion

Women are trafficked into commercial sex in four principle ways. They might have been lured by false promises of employment as models, dancers, waitresses, nannies, or seamstresses, but when they arrive at their destination, they are sold into prostitution or other forms of commercial sex and held captive, either literally or through a system of debt bondage. Some of them might have consented to work in the sex industry, but are deceived about the work conditions and their freedom to quit at any time. In addition, they might have been abducted. Finally, they might have been sold by their families, often into debt bondage. Most recent definitions of trafficking include an element of coercion, including, but not limited to, the first, third and fourth categories, but controversy surrounds the question of whether trafficking laws should cover women who consent to being trafficked. In keeping with the 1949 Convention for the Suppression of the Traffic in Persons and of the Exploitation of the Prostitution of Others, many modern lawmakers hold that that trafficking can occur even with the consent of the women. Women who allow themselves to be trafficked, it is reasoned, are not consenting but rather surrendering. In other words, the decision to enter the exploited workforce reflects an absolute lack of other viable alternatives and therefore little to no freedom of choice. Traffickers who prey on the economically weak engage, in the words of the Protocol, in an "abuse of power or of a position of vulnerability." Sponsors of this policy advocate a broader reading of coercion to include economic coercion. They believe that the feminization of poverty in certain areas is so extreme as to qualify as a form of gender discrimination under the Convention Against the Elimination of All Forms of Discrimination Against Women. The lack of economic freedom makes the trafficking victim more vulnerable and in need of special legal protection.

Feminist scholars and lawmakers contend that this stance is decidedly paternalistic towards women because it denies the possibility that a woman may consciously choose to use a trafficker for her own purposes. As Linda Malone points out, "Eliminating the coercion requirements … risks treating women as victims, incapable of making choices about their bodies and their means of migration." She goes on to ask, "Why should a woman who places herself in the hands of a sexual trafficker in order to feed her children be deserving of more protection than the father with the same motivation who is smuggled to another country to seek employment?" A variation of this approach accepts prostitution as a legitimate form of work and advances that the industry should be decriminzalized and subjected to the same kinds of regulations and safeguards as other industries. This way, the state and the workers, rather than crime syndicates, would reap economic benefits. Finally, some scholars insist that a line should be drawn between trafficking and forced labor. Quoting Marjan Wijers and Lin Lap-Chew, Annuska Derks writes:

> Trafficking can be a means to bring women into slavery-like situations, but this is not necessarily the case. On the one hand, women can be recruited and transported under conditions of coercion but not end up in forced labour/slavery-like conditions. On the other hand, women may find themselves in forced labour/slavery situations without having been trafficked.

Thus, Derks maintains that both forced labor and trafficking should be addressed as separate legal issues.

Seductive as the coercion requirement position may be, it somehow misses the point. First, trafficking differs from prostitution not just in the way it is entered into but the form in which the sale of sex is perpetuated. As Malone herself astutely notes, "Whether to require a coercion element in the definitions of prostitution does not determine whether coercion should be required for trafficking. A coercion requirement for prostitution could be maintained and yet coercion could be irrelevant to the question of whether one has been victimized by trafficking." The term "trafficking" connotes a state of exploitative working conditions involving some form of bondage, be it physical *or financial,* very often accompanied by violence or the threat of violence, and may therefore be irrelevant to the issue of voluntary prostitution. Second, while it may be useful to legally differentiate trafficking and forced labor, practicality dictates otherwise. In Cambodia (and other countries in Southeast Asia), trafficking of women does not end after the initial transaction. Even if a woman enters the sex industry voluntarily, she is constantly at risk of being deceived and sold to another brothel and exposed to subsequent mistreatment. In recognition of the dilemma of determining the point at which trafficking begins, Cambodian law requires neither an element of coercion nor the crossing of borders for an act to qualify as trafficking. Because of the above reasons, sex trafficking should not be isolated from forced labor and slavery-like conditions.

Notes and Questions

1. Are you convinced by Schwartz' positions on the definition of trafficking as it relates to border crossing and coercion? Why or why not? Are local law enforcement personnel likely to accept the idea that "trafficking" applies to coerced prostitution that does not involve significant movement of a victim from one geographical location to another?

2. While debates continue to rage concerning the trafficking-prostitution link for adult women, there can never be any question of children consenting to participate in the sex industry. Should sex trafficking of women and children be analyzed and attacked according to the same set of criteria? Are there reasons to consider these two problems separately?

C. How National Legislatures Should Respond

Mohamed Mattar has carried out detailed research into national anti-trafficking regimes in every part of the world. Professor Mattar is the director of the influential anti-trafficking Protection Project, part of the Johns Hopkins School of Advanced International Studies.[8] In his article, excerpted below, he sets out the elements he believes to be neces-

---

8. See The Protection Project, http://www.protectionproject.org/ (last visited Mar. 21, 2009), for more information on the organization and it's work.

sary for the creation of an effective set of national anti-trafficking laws. He provides numerous examples of varying national approaches to such legislation. Anti-trafficking laws are proliferating, as global awareness of the need to rein in this branch of organized crime grows. Does Mattar endorse the idea that adoption of these laws will guarantee improvement in the overall picture of human trafficking? Is his approach too schematic, or is it an efficient approach based on the depth of his expertise?

Mohamed Y. Mattar, *Incorporating the Five Basic Elements of a Model Antitrafficking in Persons Legislation in Domestic Laws: From the United Nations Protocol to the European Convention*
14 Tulane Journal of International & Comparative Law 357 (2006)

I. Introduction

....

In this Article, I will argue that there are five basic elements that should be incorporated into any anti-trafficking legislation. First, laws must recognize all forms of trafficking as specific crimes that are subject to serious sanctions. Second, these laws must identify the trafficked person as a victim of a crime who is entitled to basic human rights, while taking into consideration the victim, the derivative victim, the vulnerable victim, the potential victim, and the presumed victim. Third, countries should adopt a comprehensive Five P's approach to combating trafficking in persons, including prevention, protection, provision, prosecution, and participation. Fourth, laws must target all actors in the trafficking enterprise, including the natural person, the legal person, the private person, and the public person. Finally, countries should acknowledge trafficking in persons as a transnational crime that warrants transnational policies, especially extraterritoriality, extradition, and the exchange of information.

II. Historical Overview of Anti-trafficking Legislation

On June 28, 1999, Laura Lederer testified before the 106th Congress, stating: "We have found that more than 154 countries currently have legislation that at least minimally target the prosecution of traffickers by prohibiting the procuration of women or children for the purposes of prostitution or forced labor. However, these laws are poorly, if ever, enforced. In fact, we found that the prostitution laws are enforced, but the procuration laws are ignored. They're rarely invoked. So that the women and children end up in jail and the traffickers go free. This was the status of Anti-trafficking legislation in foreign countries prior to the passage of the U.N. Protocol, which supplemented the United Nations Convention Against Transnational Organized Crime (Transnational Crime Convention)."

....

III. Recognizing All Forms of Trafficking in Persons as a Crime and Providing for Serious Sanctions for Such Crime

Any Anti-trafficking legislation must first address how it defines trafficking. The U.N. Protocol offers a comprehensive definition, which many domestic laws have followed.

....

Some domestic laws follow the Protocol's definition of trafficking. Other laws use a definition that references specific forms of sexual exploitation, such as: sexually explicit performance, begging, pornography, use in criminal activities, sex tourism, commercial sex,... exploitation in armed conflicts, illegal bio-medical research, debauchery, economic exploitation, illegal adoption, forced marriage, pornography, child pornography, and nonremunerated work. Other domestic laws adopt a narrower definition than the U.N. Protocol has promulgated. Some laws define trafficking as only sex trafficking, and some laws define trafficking in relation to forced labor. Anti-trafficking legislation must also distinguish between trafficking in persons and alien smuggling. The criminal offenses involved in alien smuggling are considered to be crimes against the state, while trafficking in persons is a crime against the individual. Moreover, the smuggled alien who consented to be smuggled is treated as a criminal. Conversely, a trafficked person should be considered a victim of the crime of trafficking. Unlike with alien smuggling, the trafficked person is typically subject to the "threat or use of force or other forms of coercion, of abduction, of fraud of deception, of the abuse of power or of a position of vulnerability."

....

Anti-trafficking legislation must recognize trafficking as a serious crime. Thus, in any model Anti-trafficking legislation the crimes associated with trafficking should be viewed as serious crimes and the legislation should carry penalties similar to those of other serious crimes like rape and drug trafficking. Traditionally, the criminal or penal codes of many countries did not consider sex trafficking as grave a crime as other sexual offenses.

....

Many states have specific provisions in their Anti-trafficking legislation or criminal codes guaranteeing enhanced penalties in cases of trafficking in persons committed under aggravated circumstances, including a crime committed against a child victim; a crime committed by an organized group; a crime of trafficking committed against more than one victim; a perpetrator being a spouse, parent, boyfriend, or girlfriend; a perpetrator abusing one's role as a parent or guardian; a perpetrator abusing one's public position or as a clergyman; causing serious injury or death to a victim; transmitting the HIV virus; adopting a child for the purposes of prostitution, pornography, sexual exploitation, forced labor, slavery, involuntary servitude, or debt bondage; committing a crime of trafficking on a large scale; repeated offenses; kidnapping; causing the victim psychological damage; causing bodily injury to the victim; taking advantage of a vulnerable victim; rape; selling the victim out of the territory of a particular country; committing a crime by force, fraud, deceit, or threat of harm; committing the crime for financial gain; falsifying documents; and for the transnational nature of a crime.

....

IV. Identifying the Trafficked Person as a Victim Who Is Entitled to Basic Human Rights

One of the most important elements of any model legislation is recognition of the trafficked person as a victim who is entitled to basic human rights. The U.N. Protocol presents trafficked persons as victims, but it does not define a victim of trafficking. However, the term "victim of a crime" has been defined by the U.N. Declaration of Basic Principles of Justice for Victims of Crimes and Abuse of Power, which states that victims are "persons who, individually or collectively, have suffered harm, including physical or mental injury, emotional suffering, economic loss or substantial impairment of their fundamental rights, through acts or omissions that are in violation of criminal laws operative within Member States."

....

Recognition of the trafficked person as a victim means adopting a victim-centered approach to trafficking in persons. This means that what I call the "Five V's" must be taken into account. They are: the "victim," the "derivative victim," the "potential victim," the "presumed victim," and the "vulnerable victim."

A. The Victim

. . . .

Recognition of the trafficked person as a victim requires the application of the principle of noncriminalization. That is, the law must excuse the victim from criminal liability for the acts committed as a result of being trafficked. Victims of trafficking should be immune from such liability every time they commit an illegal act as long as those acts are related to their trafficking, whether this act is illegal entry, falsification of travel documents, or prostitution.

. . . .

However, still interpreting trafficking in persons mainly as a crime against a state and not a threat to individual security, some countries make the application of the principle of noncriminalization contingent upon the victim's willingness to cooperate with the state law enforcement officials in investigating and prosecuting the trafficking offense and testifying against the traffickers. The Dominican Republic law on trafficking falls into this category and provides for the exemption from criminal liability for victims of trafficking. More specifically, the law provides for the exclusion of victims of trafficking from prosecution for illegal entry, prostitution, illegal presence, unauthorized work, and other criminal acts that a victim might commit as a result of being trafficked. The law, however, conditions this exemption upon collaborating or providing the identity of the person responsible for trafficking.

. . . .

In August 2003, the Kyrgyz Republic became the first country in the region to decriminalize the acts committed by a victim of trafficking in connection with the act of trafficking. However, the Kyrgyz Republic's law also requires victims to cooperate with investigators to be eligible for this benefit.

The law of Romania exempts a victim of the crime of trafficking in persons "if, before the start of the criminal investigation. . . . this person has reported the offence to the competent authorities or if, after the start of the criminal investigation or after the identification of the perpetrators, this person facilitates the arrest of those perpetrators." Yet, the victim's immunity from liability for trafficking-related offenses should not be contingent upon the victim serving as a witness on behalf of the state. While the victim's testimony should be encouraged, it should not be required.

Unfortunately, the U.N. Protocol was silent as to the principle of noncriminalization of the behavior of the victim of trafficking. In contradistinction, the European Convention provides that member states should not impose penalties on victims "for their involvement in unlawful activities, to the extent that they have been compelled to do so."

. . . .

Victims of trafficking must be entitled to the right to privacy, which should extend to members of the victim's family, in accordance with the derivative victim doctrine. The U.N. Declaration of Basic Principles of Justice for Victims of Crime and Abuse of Power calls for: "Taking measures to minimize inconvenience to victims, protect their privacy, when necessary, and ensure their safety, as well as that of their families and witnesses on their behalf, from intimidation and retaliation." These measures must be explicitly recognized in any Anti-trafficking legislation.

. . . .

C. The Vulnerable Victim

The "vulnerable victim" is a victim who is unusually vulnerable due to age, physical or mental condition, or who is otherwise particularly susceptible to the criminal conduct. So, "a child victim" is always a vulnerable victim who should be entitled to special protection under Anti-trafficking laws. The U.N. Protocol recognized the "special need[s] of children, including appropriate housing, education and care." The European Convention is more detailed in providing for such special needs. The European Convention calls for a "child-rights approach" and "a child-sensitive approach in the development, implementation and assessment of all the policies and programmes."

. . . .

F. Rights of Identified Victims

1. Identifying Victims

While the U.N. Protocol was silent as to the issue of identification of trafficking victims, the European Convention specifically addressed it.

. . . .

First, a state is obligated to provide its authorities with persons trained and qualified to identify victims. Second, states have an obligation to "adopt such legislative or other measures as may be necessary to identify victims as appropriate in collaboration with other parties and relevant support organisations." In the case of child victims of trafficking, the Convention further establishes that "[w]hen the age of the victim is uncertain and there are reasons to believe that the victim is a child, he or she shall be presumed to be a child and shall be accorded special protection measures pending verification of his/her age." In addition, the Convention imposes an obligation upon the states, as soon as an unaccompanied child is identified as a victim, to provide for representation of the child, to take the necessary steps to establish his/her identity and nationality, and to try to locate the child's family if in the best interests of the child.

This kind of recognition of the trafficked person as a victim is important because it entitles such a person to basic or fundamental rights. In 2002, I declared a Bill of Rights on behalf of victims of trafficking, arguing that the following ten rights should be guaranteed to trafficking victims in any model legislation: (1) the right to safety, (2) the right to privacy, (3) the right to information, (4) the right to legal representation, (5) the right to be heard in court, (6) the right to compensation for damages, (7) the right to medical assistance, (8) the right to social assistance, (9) the right to seek residence, and (10) the right to return. In addition to these enumerated rights, victims of trafficking should be treated with dignity, fairness, compassion and respect for their human rights. I will discuss three of these rights in detail: the right to safety, the right to compensation, and the right to seek residency.

2. The Right to Safety

Victims of trafficking should be entitled to the right to safety and included in any state-sponsored witness protection program. As explained above, if the country does require the victim of trafficking to testify against one's traffickers, then the victim should be provided with witness protection as a prerequisite to coming forward and testifying. The safety of the person needs to be protected while one is testifying for the state. However, in most of the European countries that have witness protection laws, the criteria for application of such programs are so strict that victims of trafficking can rarely meet the standard. Moreover, countries such as Belgium, Denmark, Finland, France, Luxemburg, Sweden, and most of the countries in Eastern and Southeast Europe do not have any formal witness protection programs at all. Nonetheless, protection of witnesses is an internationally recognized principle provided for in both the Transnational Crime Convention and the United Nations Convention Against Corruption and should be implemented in all states.

3. The Right to Compensation

A victim of trafficking should also be entitled to the right to compensation. While this is an element that should be included in any Anti-trafficking legislation, the detailed implementation of such an element should be left to the particular legal system. For instance, the U.S. [Trafficking Victim Protection Act] provides for mandatory restitution to be ordered by the criminal court for any trafficking offense. Restitution under this section is a criminal sanction. The TVPA does not provide for a private civil action for damages, although it allows for such possibility under relevant statutes since § 1593 provides for mandatory restitution "in addition to any other civil or criminal penalties authorized by law." In 2003, the TVPA was amended by the United States Trafficking Victims Protection Reauthorization Act of 2003 (2003 TVPRA), which now provides, in § 1595, that a victim of a severe form of trafficking

> may bring a civil action against the perpetrator in an appropriate district court of the United States and may recover damages and reasonable attorneys fees.... Any civil action filed under this section shall be stayed during the pendency of any criminal action arising out of the same occurrence in which the claimant is the victim.

....

4. The Right to Residency

A victim of trafficking must also be entitled to the right to seek residency in the country of destination. The immediate return of the victims to their home countries is unsatisfactory both for the victims and for the law enforcement authorities endeavoring to combat trafficking. For the victims, this means having to start again from scratch—a failure, that in most cases, they will keep quiet about, with the result that nothing will be done to prevent other victims from falling into the same trap. A further factor is fear of reprisals by the traffickers, either against the victims themselves or against family or friends in the country of origin. For law enforcement, if the victims continue to live clandestinely in the country or are removed immediately, they cannot give information for effectively combating such traffic. The greater victims' confidence that their rights and interests will be protected, the better the information they will give. Thus, availability of residence permits is a measure calculated to encourage them to cooperate.

Under the U.S. model, a victim of trafficking is granted immigration status if such person "is or has been a victim of a severe form of trafficking in persons," "is physically present in the United States," "has complied with any reasonable request for assistance in the investigation or prosecution of acts of trafficking or has not attained 15 years of age" and "would suffer extreme hardship involving unusual and severe harm upon removal" from the United States. The United States, therefore, does not require the victim of trafficking to testify to be eligible for a residency status.

....

By comparison, the U.N. Protocol calls upon countries to "give appropriate consideration to humanitarian and compassionate factors" in considering granting victims of trafficking a resident permit. Unfortunately, the U.N. Protocol does not mandate a state obligation to grant a victim of trafficking residency status.

....

5. The Right to Assistance: The Three R's

Victims of trafficking should be entitled to the right to assistance, in the form of medical, psychological, legal, and social aid. In this context it is important to address what I call the Three R's: rehabilitation, reintegration, and repatriation. Victims of trafficking must be rehabilitated and reintegrated into society after the abuses they have suffered.

. . . .

Any assistance to victims of trafficking should not be limited to protection within the country of destination, but should also include repatriation, with dignity and respect, to their country of origin. This is what the U.N. Protocol calls for under article 8, which provides that the country of origin "shall facilitate and accept, with due regard for the safety of that person, the return of that person without undue or unreasonable delay." A country of origin "shall agree to issue. . . . such travel documents or other authorization as may be necessary to enable the person to travel to and re-enter its territory." Consequently, a state has the responsibility to ensure the safe return of trafficked victims. Most notably, this process includes the issuance of travel documents, because, in most cases of trafficking, the trafficker confiscates the travel document of the victim.

. . . .

VII. Recognizing Trafficking as a Transnational Offense that Requires Transnational Policies, Including the Three X's: Extradition, Extraterritoriality, and Exchange of Information

. . . .

Transnational policies should cover what I call the Three X's of transnational trafficking: extradition, extraterritoriality, and exchange of information. First, trafficking in persons must be recognized as an extraditable offense. It is interesting to note that under article 16(4) of the Transnational Crime Convention, if "a State Party that makes extradition conditional on the existence of a treaty receives a request for extradition from another State Party with which it has no extradition treaty, it may consider the Convention the legal basis for extradition in respect of any offence to which this article applies."

Second, Anti-trafficking legislation should also have extraterritorial jurisdiction; this means the application of domestic laws regardless of the place where the act was committed. Both the Council of Europe and United Nations have addressed these issues with regard to peacekeeping missions. There are currently fifteen U.N. peacekeeping missions operating around the world. Rule 4 of the U.N. Peacekeeper Code of Conduct says that U.N. peacekeepers should "not indulge in immoral acts of sexual, physical, or psychological abuse or exploitation of the local population or United Nations staff, especially women and children." At the same time, U.N. Peacekeepers fall under the exclusive criminal jurisdiction of their own national authorities and have immunity from local prosecution. It is up to the U.N. Board of Inquiry to find reasonable grounds for a charge of serious misconduct with a recommendation that the peacekeeper be repatriated for subsequent disciplinary action in his country. However, as I testified before Congress in 2003, of only twenty-four officers repatriated to their countries for misconduct, none has been prosecuted for violating Rule 4 of the Code of Conduct.

. . . .

Another area that should be addressed on an extraterritorial basis is child sex tourism. This was recognized by the United States in the U.S. 2003 TVPRA. This is precisely why the Prosecutorial Remedies and Tools Against the Exploitation of Children Today Act of 2003 (Protect Act) makes traveling to engage in illicit sexual activities a crime, the punishment for which is up to thirty years imprisonment. However, there are problems in the application of extraterritorial legislation. One is double criminality, where a person's actions have to be acknowledged as criminal offenses both in the country in which one committed the act as well as one's country of citizenship to be convicted. Another problem besides double criminality is double jeopardy.

. . . .

Third, exchange of information between countries of origin and countries of destination must take place. Bilateral treaties on mutual assistance in criminal matters must be a part of any transnational legal response because apprehension of traffickers, investigation of cases of trafficking, and prosecution of the traffickers sometimes require cooperation between countries of origin and countries of destination in matters including request for assistance, search, seizure, attachment and surrender of property, measures for securing assets, service of judicial decision, judgments and verdicts, appearance of witness and expert witnesses, and transmittal of information of records.

. . . .

Notes and Questions

1. Mattar provides a generic set of elements for, in his view, a successful anti-trafficking approach by national governments. To the extent that national governments have very different capabilities in terms of available resources, levels of official corruption, and influence of organized crime, is this across the board formula useful? Which aspect of Mattar's analysis seems most compelling?

Judge Nimfa Cuesta Vilches, *Trafficking of Women and Children*
Business World (Philadelphia), Dec. 17, 2003

For a considerable length of time, trafficking and sexual exploitation of women and children hardly mattered to the Filipino man and woman. This, in turn, made it difficult for the victims to seek redress in court for the violence and abuses committed against them. But with the sex trade reaching global proportions, the Philippine legislature was prompted to enact Republic Act 9208, or the "Anti-Trafficking in Persons Act Of 2003" on May 26, 2003.

. . . .

The anti-trafficking law is a milestone in the promotion of human dignity and protection of persons, especially women and children, against any threat of violence and exploitation. It seeks to eliminate trafficking, the establishment of necessary institutional mechanisms for the protection and support of trafficked persons, and provides penalties for violations of the law.

. . . .

A comprehensive law

Trafficking under the new law is interpreted in its broadest sense. It refers to recruitment, transportation, transfer or harboring, or receipt of persons with or without the victim's consent or knowledge, within or across national borders by means of threat or use of force or other forms of coercion, abduction, fraud, deception, abuse of power or of position, taking advantage of the vulnerability of the person.

....

Acts of trafficking

The following are deemed acts of trafficking committed either by a person or an entity when done for the purpose of prostitution, pornography, sexual exploitation, forced labor, slavery, involuntary servitude or debt bondage:

(a) to recruit, transport, transfer, harbor, provide or receive a person on the pretext of domestic or overseas employment, training or apprenticeship;

(b) introduce or match for a consideration any Filipino woman to a foreign national for marriage for the purpose of trading her for prostitution;

(c) offer or contract marriage;

(d) undertake or organize tours and travel plans;

(e) maintain or hire a person; and

(f) adopt or facilitate adoption.

Any undue recruitment, hiring, adoption, and movement of persons and children for removal or sale of organs or for the children to engage in armed activities in the Philippines or abroad are also considered acts of trafficking.

Unlawful acts which promote or facilitate trafficking

A person may be held liable under the law for promoting or facilitating trafficking by doing any or a combination of the following acts:

(a) knowingly lease space or building;

(b) furnish fictitious certificates to comply government regulatory and pre-departure requirements;

(c) publish propaganda materials;

(d) assist in the exit and entry of persons from/to the country with fraudulent documents;

(e) deprive or destroy passports and personal documents to prevent trafficked persons from leaving the country and for obtaining assistance; or

(f) knowingly benefit services from persons held to a condition of involuntary servitude, forced labor or slavery.

All those who create demand for trafficking of women and children that usually results in prostitution are punished under the above provisions of the law.

Qualified offenses of trafficking

No less than a penalty of life imprisonment and a fine of not less than P2 million is inflicted on the offender in special instances of trafficking such as follows:

(a) when the trafficked person is a child [below 18 years old or over but unable to care of self];

(b) when adoption is effected under the Inter-Country Adoption Law;

(c) when committed by a syndicate [group of three or more persons in conspiracy] or in large scale [against three or more persons];

(d) when committed by a person exercising parental authority over the victim or by a public officer or employee;

(e) when trafficked person is recruited to engage in prostitution with military or law enforcement agencies;

(f) when offender is a member of the military or law enforcement agencies; and

(g) when by reason or on occasion of the trafficking, the victim dies, becomes insane, suffers mutilation or is afflicted with human immunodeficiency virus (HIV) or the acquired immune deficiency syndrome (AIDS).

Worthy of note at this juncture is the recent effort of the Philippine government to include as predicate crime under the Anti-Money Laundering Law child prostitution. Predicate crimes are those which would trigger immediate investigation by the anti-money laundering council making it easier to stop the flow of money from illegal activities.

Use of trafficked persons for prostitution is an offense

Any person who buys or engages the services of trafficked persons for prostitution is penalized with six months of community service and a fine of P50,000 for the first offense. An imprisonment and fine of P100,000 are imposed for the second and subsequent offenses.

....

Repatriation and extradition

Trafficked Filipinos abroad are repatriated regardless of whether their travel to another country is documented or not. But if repatriation will expose the victim to greater risks, the Philippines make representations with the host country for an extension of residency permit and protection. However, trafficking in persons shall be included among extraditable offenses.

....

When the persons trafficked are children, the Special Protection of Children Act and the Rule on Examination of a Child Witness mandate that there must only be a single interview by a multidisciplinary group of professionals recorded in audio or video tape. In this way, the child victim does not suffer the damaging effect of feeling re-victimized through a series of repeated questioning.

Justice for the victims

Inside the courtroom, a child victim is presumed to be a competent witness and is entitled to the services of support persons such as a trained child advocate or a guardian ad litem. If there is a substantial likelihood that the child will suffer trauma from testifying in front of the offender, the Rule on Examination of a Child Witness provides for alternative ways to testify such as by live-link television or videotaped deposition.

When women or girls are the offended parties, the "sexual shield rule" bars the offender from offering evidence which tends to establish the fact that the victims engaged in other sexual behaviors or show proof of their sexual predisposition. This demonstrates good court practice by way of being gender and child sensitive when dealing with cases on women and children.

....

Notes and Questions

1. Judge Nimfa Cuesta Vilches takes the sort of "comprehensive" view of human trafficking that we have seen in both international and national legal approaches to this problem. What sorts of abuses are included in the Philippine law? Do you get a clear sense of how the law will function?

2. What do you think explains the continued proliferation of trafficking in the Philippines, given that there seems to be a comprehensive legal structure in place to eliminate it? How does the Philippine law add up when compared with the recommendations made by Professor Mattar, above? Does Professor Mattar place too much emphasis on the creation of legislation as the means of eradicating sex trafficking?

III. Commercial Sexual Exploitation of Children: The Same Issues from a Different Conceptual Angle

A. Introduction to the UNCRC's Optional Protocol on the Sale of Children[9]

Article 34 of the UNCRC states that "States Parties undertake to protect the child from all forms of sexual exploitation and sexual abuse. For these purposes, States Parties shall in particular take all appropriate national, bilateral and multilateral measures to prevent: (a) the inducement or coercion of a child to engage in any unlawful sexual activity; (b) the exploitative use of children in prostitution or other unlawful sexual practices; (c) the exploitative use of children in pornographic performances and materials."[10] In view of the acute nature of the problem of child sexual exploitation, one of the only two protocols to the UNCRC was drafted to address the global crisis. (The other, as we will see, is on the subject of children and armed conflict.) The Optional Protocol to the UNCRC on the Sale of Children, Child Prostitution and Child Pornography, reproduced in the Appendix to this book, has been widely ratified.

The history of international debate on child sexual exploitation may be seen as somewhat distinct from the international approach to sex trafficking, which tends to be reliant on prosecution of human traffickers. The following article traces the development of international concern with the "commercial sexual exploitation of children" (CSEC), and provides a brief overview of the recent history of international legal developments in this area. This narrative intersects with and complements the development of a legal consensus on human trafficking. It is interesting to note the conceptual contrast between the UN Trafficking Protocol and the UNCRC's Optional Protocol on the Sale of Children. What obligations are placed on states, and what type of remedies are featured in the Optional Protocol?

Consider how a number of separate legal instruments, setting out inter-related international norms, can work together to help governments address a problem like child sex trafficking and exploitation.

---

9. Optional Protocol to the Convention on the Rights of the Child on the Sale of Children, Child Prostitution and Child Pornography, G.A. Res. 54/263, Annex II, U.N. GAOR, 54th Sess., U.N. Doc. A/RES/54/263 (June 26, 2000), *available at* http://www1.umn.edu/humanrts/instree/childprotsale.html.

10. Convention on the Rights of the Child art. 34, Nov. 20, 1989, 1577 U.N.T.S. 3.

Amy McCoy, *UN Report: Children "Playing Sex for Money": A Brief History of the World's Battle Against the Commercial Sexual Exploitation of Children*

18 New York Law School Journal of Human Rights 499 (2002)

Since the entry into force of the CRC, the commercial sexual exploitation of children has been an ongoing battle for developing and industrialized countries, multi-national and national non-governmental organizations, and the United Nations. Last year, the United Nations Deputy Secretary-General estimated that over 30 million children were trafficked each year, in many instances for sexual exploitation, by traffickers who went relatively unpunished. For the past twelve years, recognizing the serious and sometimes insidious nature of these offenses, international organizations have struggled to identify the causes and solutions of the problem while attempting to precisely categorize these offenses. This struggle has resulted in a separate movement within children's rights organizations to address the commercial sexual exploitation of children, and the growth of an arsenal of international and state specific weapons designed to combat this growing crisis.

I. Early Developments: The First World Congress Against Commercial Sexual Exploitation of Children

Immediately following the entry into force of the CRC in 1990, the World Summit for Children first acknowledged the problem of child sexual exploitation, which led to the first United Nations initiatives, including the appointment of a Special Rapporteur on the Sale of Children, Child Prostitution and Child Pornography. The Summit's Declaration, however, made no specific mention of commercial sexual exploitation of children (CSEC), and it took several years for this issue to become fully exposed to the general public.

The First World Congress Against Commercial Sexual Exploitation of Children was held in Stockholm in August 1996, six years after the establishment of the CRC. One hundred and twenty-two nations were represented at the gathering, and for the first time, the CSEC was brought to the world consciousness as a multi-faceted international crisis.

As well as bringing attention to the plight of thousands of children, the Congress formalized the myriad of issues and challenges involved in CSEC for the first time in their Declaration. Re-affirming the guarantee of the CRC for full protection from sexual abuse and sexual exploitation, the Declaration called for action on the local, regional, national and international levels. Nation states were called to criminalize CSEC, to enforce, revise and create new laws against CSEC, to interact with other States to combat the trafficking of children, to develop community based programs disseminating information on CSEC and to mobilize political and community leaders to assist in eliminating CSEC.

....

Each country was urged to develop national agendas for reducing the number of children vulnerable to commercial sexual exploitation and given methods of gauging progress in addition to a target time frame for implementation by the year 2000. The Agenda also highlighted the key role played by international organizations, including United Nations affiliates, the World Bank, the International Monetary Fund (IMF), INTERPOL, the World Tourism Organization and non-governmental organizations, in eliminating CSEC by recognizing children's rights, and advocating for the full implementation of the CRC.

II. Progress Assessed: The Second World Congress on the Commercial Sexual Exploitation of Children

Five years later, progress in regards to CSEC was assessed in several regional conferences and in the Second World Congress on the Commercial Sexual Exploitation of Children held in Yokohama, Japan in December 2001. Over 3,000 participants attended the four-day conference, three times as many as were present at the First Congress. While participants reported on actions taken to meet the Stockholm Agenda's goals and recommitted themselves to the Stockholm Declaration, the proliferation of child pornography, and the access to children, or those operating child "sex tourism" on the Internet, raised new concerns. The necessity of a multi-national effort in preventing CSEC is now even more of a priority, as sexual exploitation of children was seen to be tied not only to children in impoverished areas, but also to those in prosperous countries.

Western European countries reported the development of computer software programs that identified child victims through facial recognition, evaluated pornographic images to determine whether they had been newly created and experimented with computer viruses that would destroy child pornographic sites on the Internet. Since the First Congress, twenty-one nations, including Japan, Korea, and United States, have adopted laws that allow the police to arrest people for paying for sex with children while overseas.

In Togo, incorporating the Convention on the Rights of the Child into the National Code was a step towards raising their nation's awareness of children's issues. Revising passport and visa procedures to carefully regulate and screen the movement of children and requiring a governmental agency to check up on children adopted out of the country were steps taken to combat CSEC. In Cambodia, the dissemination of information to townspeople and the forming of a village network for stopping the abduction of children for forced prostitution proved successful in saving children's lives. In Kenya, rehabilitation programs for young women at risk or in the early stages of involvement in the sex trade have been developed to educate on exploitation of women's rights as well as offer vocational training.

The U.S. government, recognizing that each year approximately 25,000 women and children are smuggled into the U.S. for forced prostitution or illegal adoption, enacted the Trafficking Victims Protection Act, which established penalties for those who "knowingly operate enterprises that profit from sex acts involving persons who have been brought across international boundaries … by force or fraud" equal to those for kidnapping and forcible rape.

III. The Optional Protocol to the Convention on the Rights of the Child on the Sale of Children, Child Prostitution and Child Pornography

In January 2002, one month after the Yokohama Conference, the Optional Protocol to the Convention on the Rights of the Child on the Sale of Children, Child Prostitution and Child Pornography entered into force. Signed by eighty-six nations to date and ratified by eighteen, the Optional Protocol extends the measures that State Parties can undertake in order to guarantee the protection of children from commercial sexual exploitation.

The Protocol extends the CRC's generalized protections, by defining particular offenses and criminalizing these offenses under State Party's criminal law. Specific definitions are given to the "sale of children," "child prostitution," and "child pornography." Practices, such as "offering, delivering, or accepting by whatever means a child" for purposes of sexual exploitation, the "offering, obtaining, procuring or providing" of a child for child prostitution and the "producing, distributing, disseminating, importing, exporting, offering, selling, or possessing …" child pornography are criminalized and made actionable under a State Party's criminal law.

The Protocol calls for governments to pursue citizens involved in the abuse of children abroad by strengthening State Party's extraterritorial jurisdiction and rights to the extradition of offenders. International cooperation in aiding child victims is also sought. The Protocol specifically allows signatories to the CRC to sign and ratify the Protocols even if they have not ratified the underlying Convention. The United States, which has signed but not ratified the CRC, is therefore eligible to sign, ratify, and implement the Protocol.

. . . .

It has been said that it is better to light a candle than to curse the darkness, but while international organizations have lit what seems be thousands of lights, the darkness and horror of the sexual exploitation of children remains, endures, and maybe grows stronger. Now more than ever, amid the HIV/AIDS pandemic, the proliferation of child pornography on the Internet and access to children and those who provide access to child "sex tourism" through the Internet, the international community stands threatened by those who force children to "play sex for money." Success will come through continued vigilance on the part of the United Nations and international, governmental, and non-governmental organizations by keeping these hidden secrets in the full light of day.

Notes and Questions

1. Read the UNCRC's Optional Protocol on the Sale of Children in the Appendix. Compare and contrast the conceptual framework and methodology of the Optional Protocol with the UN Trafficking Protocol. Which seems a more promising approach towards ending commercial sexual exploitation of children? Is the Optional Protocol internally coherent, or are there any parts that do not seem to fit? Is there a danger that a number of separate international instruments could confuse the situation, particularly for legislatures that must try and implement the obligations being placed on States Parties?

————————

What follows is a report by the UN's Special Rapporteur on the sale of children, child prostitution and child pornography. The United Nations creates the position of "special rapporteur" in many contexts, mainly for the purpose of carrying out fact finding on a human rights question.[11] Excerpts from the report recognize that a good law, in and of

————————

11. In 1990 the United Nations Commission on Human Rights decided to appoint a Special Rapporteur on the sale of children, child prostitution and child pornography. The Special Rapporteur is mandated to investigate the exploitation of children around the world and to submit reports to the General Assembly and the Commission on Human Rights. The Special Rapporteur is also required to make recommendations for the protection of the rights of the children concerned, which are targeted primarily at governments, UN bodies, and NGOs. Since 1990, the appointment of the Special Rapporteur has been regularly renewed, most recently by the Human Rights Council in March 2008 for a three-year period. Specifically, the Human Rights Council mandates the Special Rapporteur, through visits and exchange of communications with Governments, to: analyze the root causes of the sale of children, child prostitution and child pornography; identify new patterns of sale of children, child prostitution and child pornography; identify, exchange and promote best practices on measures to combat the sale of children, child prostitution and child pornography; continue efforts to promote comprehensive strategies and measures on the prevention of sale of children, child prostitution and child pornography; make recommendations on the promotion and protection of human rights of children actual or potential victims of sale, prostitution and pornography, as well as on the aspects related to the rehabilitation of child victims of sexual exploitation. Special Rapporteur on the Sale of

itself, is insufficient to stop trafficking. The rapporteur highlights the enforcement efforts of various countries and suggests what is needed to combat trafficking and sexual exploitation.

Report of the Special Rapporteur on the Sale of Children, Child Prostitution and Child Pornography
U.N. Doc. E/CN.4/2004/9 (2004)

...

III. Special Focus on the Prevention of Child Sexual Exploitation

...

C. Enforcement mechanisms

If legislation is a first, indispensable step, the real challenge lies in implementation. Effective enforcement of any law requires government investment in human and financial resources, and the establishment and operation of administrative and judicial structures and confidence in the system, on the part of the general public, particularly children.

There are many challenges in enforcing the law. For example, victims of sexual exploitation find it hard to find adequate legal assistance to collect enough evidence to prove their cases, to face a painful procedure marked by long delays and uncertain results. This may be coupled with gender and cultural biases of judges and lawyers and the community at large. This process of revictimization of children and adolescents who seek remedial action nourishes the vicious cycle of impunity, pernicious fuel for violence.

In Costa Rica, the NGO Casa Alianza works primarily to break the vicious cycle of impunity. A hotline was set up to receive complaints. Legal aid, among other types of assistance, is provided to bring cases before the competent judicial authorities. Approximately 65 per cent of sex crime cases reported to the Public Prosecution Service were submitted by Casa Alianza. Coordination between the NGO and the Public Prosecution Service is essential to activate the enforcement machinery effectively.

In Kenya, the Coalition on Child Rights and Child Protection provides free legal services in cases of child abuse and neglect through a network of legal volunteers. This, among other factors, contributed to an increase in the number of cases reported over the years since this service started in 1997.

In South Africa, the Child Witness Project of the NGO Resources Aimed at the Prevention of Child Abuse and Neglect (RAPCAN) prepares children and their caregivers for the court experience by providing them with information about the proceedings and skills to help them deal with the process of testifying.

UNICEF is implementing a capacity-building project in Cambodia to improve the investigative capacity of police, judges and prosecutors in cases of sexual exploitation of children.

In Lithuania, the Controller (Ombudsman) for the Protection of the Rights of the Child examines complaints of children's rights violations. The Controller can undertake investigations upon his/her own initiative.

Children, Child Prostitution and Child Pornography, Background to the Mandate, http://www2. ohchr.org/english/issues/children/rapporteur/index.htm (last visited Mar. 21, 2009).

D. Institutions and networks

Many States have made efforts to set up an institutional framework for the implementation of children's rights. To this end, they created many specialized bodies. These bodies can have advisory and promotional functions, such as collection and dissemination of information and analysis and of advice on legislation, policy implementation and monitoring of action plans. Their structure often includes both public authorities and representatives of civil society encompassing the main stakeholder groups and ensuring a multidisciplinary approach.

The Council for the Rights of the Child of the Government of the Republic of Serbia, established in 2002, was entrusted with the task of monitoring the implementation of children's rights and coordinating government policies dealing with children and youth. The Council comprises representatives of the Government, scientific and educational institutions and NGOs.

The Syrian Arab Republic has a Higher Committee for Childhood, chaired by the Deputy Prime Minister for Services and composed of representatives of relevant ministries, such as health, justice, culture, social affairs and labour, information, foreign affairs, finance and industry, as well as NGOs and trade unions.

The local level

Reaching out at the grass-roots level is both a goal and a constant challenge for institutions. An institutional presence at the community level has contributed significantly to lower rates of violence, including sexual exploitation.

In Lithuania, Children's Rights Protection Services under municipal government are responsible for the protection of children's rights at the local level. They monitor the implementation of the laws on children's rights. They also represent children's interests in court.

In Portugal, 234 commissions for the protection of children act at the local level to promote children's rights and prevent situations of danger for children. The commissions count on the participation of the community and decisions are taken in partnership with families and the participation of children.

Local councils for the protection of children in each village of the Philippines promote children's rights, encourage responsible parenting, provide assistance to abandoned, maltreated and abused children and monitor cases filed against perpetrators. To date, the country has 17,465 functional councils.

In Ecuador, the local committees on children's and adolescents' rights promote and monitor the implementation of children's and adolescents' rights at the local level.

. . . .

Transforming Long Mei into a "civilized village"

Long Mei is a small village of about 500 people in the Yunan Province of China. When the project on the prevention of internal trafficking started in 1999, as many as 70 per cent of the village population, the majority of them women, were involved in trafficking newborn babies and girls.

The idea was to transform Long Mei into a model "civilized village". According to local definition, a "civilized village" should ideally have good roads, where people are healthy, respectful and helpful to each other, citizens look after old people, women and children have their rights, children go to school, villagers acquire knowledge and technology and the village is free of crime including trafficking, quarrels, discrimination and domestic violence.

Government support helped to build a community centre and a drinking water pool. Electricity and telephone lines were improved. Training in science and technology to improve farming and livestock was provided. The NGO Save the Children provided training on children's and women's rights, purchased books for children and the community, and improved sanitation at the village primary school. In return, villagers, men and women, demonstrated their eagerness to reverse the negative image of their village. They wanted Long Mei to change from a "village of traffickers" into a "civilized village".

These are some of the achievements in that direction: (a) villagers set out regulations to run their village efficiently; (b) trafficking, stealing and beating of women and children have been substantially reduced; (c) illiterate women received basic education through evening schooling; and (d) older women feel they have a role to play in the efforts to improve the village.

The Long Mei model has now been broadcast on television 20 times. Replication of this experience is ongoing in eight counties in Wenshan prefecture. Each county set up a model village following the Long Mei example.

The following elements have been identified as factors contributing to the success of the Long Mei experience: (a) Government's commitment and leadership; (b) supportive policy directives at the provincial level; (c) interdepartmental cooperation; (d) commitment to addressing the root causes of the problem; (e) mobilization of resources from various institutions; (f) capacity-building; and (g) recognition of women's leadership.

. . . .

G. The role of the media

The mass media reflect our world. They are part of society and are imbued with the same intolerance and prejudices. At the same time, they reflect our aspirations for social justice and they voice the concerns of marginalized people who otherwise have no voice or means of portraying them. In the information age, the impact of the media is a fact; so is their potential to fight child sexual exploitation.

. . . .

The Stockholm Agenda for Action recommends initiating gender-sensitive communication, media and information campaigns to raise awareness and educate about child rights and sexual exploitation. It also encourages the media to provide information of the highest quality and reliability concerning all aspects of child sexual exploitation.

In some countries, media campaigns are still at the very initial stage, as in Lebanon, where the pioneer slogan, "Let's stop sticking our heads in the sand", was launched on television to encourage individuals to bring to light violations of children's rights.

In 1999–2000 an awareness campaign against trafficking in human beings was launched in the Czech Republic. It was an informative campaign on the risks of human trafficking specially targeted at women seeking jobs abroad. The campaign produced a manual for teachers and a video was distributed in schools. Human trafficking was introduced in the school curricula. A positive side effect of the campaign was the increased collaboration between the institutions involved in the campaign, government authorities, NGOs, the International Organization for Migration and consular authorities.

In Mexico, a national awareness campaign on pornography and child prostitution was launched in 2002. Its first phase, called "Open your eyes" ("Abre los ojos"), focused on raising the awareness of the general public with some targeted initiatives, such as the distribution of informative material on CSEC in areas frequented by truckdrivers. The second phase of the campaign, named "Open your eyes, don't shut your mouth" ("Abre los ojos, no cierres la boca"), focused on facilitating the reporting of cases through the establishment of a hotline.

. . . .

The ILO conducts regional and country workshops for journalists on how to treat CSEC in the media and how to use the potential of the media in a strategic way.

In the framework of a campaign against CSEC in Asian tourism, ECPAT produced an in-flight video to warn travellers on CSEC. The video has been shown on major airlines, such as Air France, Swiss and Lufthansa. Traveller awareness campaign materials, such as luggage tags, information kits and ticket pouches on the dangers and illegality of sex tourism were produced and disseminated through travel operators and airlines.

The campaign "Please disturb!", implemented by Terre des Hommes and aimed at preventing sex tourism, launched the web site www.child-hood.com. The site gathers information on CSEC targeted at tourists, travel operators and the media. A section on best practices outlines exemplary initiatives undertaken by the tourism industry to fight sex tourism.

Notes and Questions

1. The report of the special rapporteur is designed to draw attention to the situation on the ground with respect to a particular UN human rights initiative. Does this report seem to be a very effective attention-getting device? What methodology does it rely on? What would you criticize about the format? What part of it works well?

B. Child Sexual Exploitation in Southeast Asia

The rise in demand for children to exploit appears to transcend cultural boundaries. However, certain regions present conditions particularly favorable to the proliferation of this problem. Southeast Asia appears to have an especially intractable problem with child sexual exploitation. A combination of historical and indigenous cultural factors has given rise to a huge commercial sex industry, a significant subset of which involves the exploitation of children under 18. Cambodia has developed a reputation for the exploitation of even extremely young girls, mainly by foreign pedophiles. UNICEF has estimated that thirty five percent of Cambodia's 55,000 prostitutes are under the age of 16.[12] The lengthy Vietnam War undoubtedly created an image of Southeast Asia as a destination for Western and Japanese men seeking women to whom they could have easy sexual access. This in turn made the region heavily dependent on the sex industry as part of its larger "tourism" industry. At the same time, there is a long tradition of brothel sex, and a large proportion of Southeast Asian men, particularly Thai men, are known to seek out prostitution on a regular basis. Within this troubling

---

12. Bureau of Democracy, Human Rights, and Labor, U.S. Department of State, 2001 Country Reports on Human Rights Practices: Cambodia (2001), http://www.state.gov/g/drl/rls/hrrpt/2001/eap/8283.htm.

economic and cultural nexus, the exploitation of children provides still more problematic opportunities.

The Schwartz article, partially reproduced above, continues here with an overview of sex trafficking in Southeast Asia, particularly Cambodia. What regional characteristics, both cultural and economic, can you identify here?

Abigail Schwartz, *Sex Trafficking in Cambodia*
17 Columbia Journal of Asian Law 371 (2004)

In 1999, a Dan Sandler, an American living in Cambodia, added a live bondage sex show to his pornographic web site. The site, named "Rape Camp," featured "Asian sex slaves" who were used for "bondage, discipline and humiliation." The Cambodian women on the site were blindfolded, bound, gagged, and some had clothespins attached to their nipples. The site also advertised Cambodia's flourishing sex trade, for those who are "sick of demanding American bitches who don't know their place." It volunteered to help tourists find cheap flights, hotels, and brothels. It also offered advice for naive first timers. "Don't pay in advance," it counseled, "and don't be bashful about sending her back if she doesn't do as advertised or if there is some major attitude shift." When the site came to the attention of Mu Soucha, the Cambodian Minister of Women's Affairs, she demanded Sandler's arrest and prosecution under Cambodia's new anti-trafficking laws. Facing a five-year sentence, Sandler appealed to the United States government, which eventually intervened, arranging for him to be deported rather than prosecuted under Cambodian law.

Sandler's case is emblematic of Cambodia's pandemic sex trafficking problem. It illustrates the ubiquity of cheap sex sold throughout the country and the often violent and abusive atmosphere in which women are forced to work. For altogether too many women and girls, Cambodia has become a virtual "rape camp." The country has one of the fastest-growing sex industries in the world. It portrays the government's ambivalence and often conflicting attitude towards its burgeoning sex trade. The state tolerates the country's numerous commercial sex outlets, which are mostly based on coerced labor. Yet, in the hopes of improving its human rights reputation in the international community, it cracks down on high profile cases with a strong hand. Sandler's exoneration demonstrates the ultimate impotence of Cambodia's anti-trafficking legislation and the general immunity of traffickers from legal consequences.

. . .

II. Sex Trafficking in Southeast Asia

In March 2002, ministers of some thirty Asia-Pacific countries convened in Bali to tackle the problem of trafficking for the first time. The Bali conference indicates a growing, and long overdue, regional concern for the issue of trafficking. Indeed, nowhere else in the world has sex trafficking grown at the rate or to the degree that it has in Asia, and in particular, Southeast Asia. It is estimated that nearly one-third of the global trafficking trade, or about 225,000 women and children, are trafficked annually from Southeast Asia. Although many are taken overseas, about sixty percent remain in the region. Moreover, a staggering number of minors are engaged in commercial sex throughout the region: thirty percent of the prostitutes found in Cambodia are between the ages of twelve and seventeen; one third of Thailand's prostitutes are underage; 60,000 of Indonesia's 71,281 registered prostitutes are between the ages of fifteen and twenty; 75,000 of 300,000 prostitutes in the Philippines are children. Explanations for this phenomenon vary from country to country. However, the ubiquity of commercial sex throughout the region is no mere coincidence. Similar historical, cultural, and economic patterns offer some insight into both the demand and supply trends.

A. Explaining Demand

Two main theories explain the excessive demand for commercial sex in Southeast Asia. One asserts the historical acceptance of prostitution throughout the region. According to this theory, prostitution is a culturally embedded tradition dating back as far as recorded history. Most Southeast Asian men are regular, if not frequent, patrons of brothels, and the number of men who lose their virginity to prostitutes is so large as to render it a rite of passage. Another theory blames the upsurge in the commercial sex industry over the past fifty years on foreign, particularly Western, influence. The growth of prostitution within certain strategic locales, it is argued, coincides with the influx of foreign men into these areas. For example, Pattaya, Thailand's infamous hedonistic beach resort, sprang up during the Vietnam War to satisfy the appetites of American G.I.s. Once the war was over, tourists, who were by then familiar with Thailand's reputation as a sexual paradise, flocked to the renowned nightclubs and massage parlors that operate as fronts for sex-related businesses. More recently, the United Nation's Mission in Cambodia in the early 1990s created an instantaneous market for the bodies of impoverished young women. As in Thailand, tourists have begun to replace soldiers in Cambodia as the clientele for the sex industry.

While both views offer elements of the truth, neither fully elucidates Southeast Asia's abundant and varied commercial sex industry. A better answer lies at the intersection between the two theories. Indeed, the Southeast Asian sex market of today rests on a solid historical tradition of treating women as commodities. In traditional Asian societies, women were seen as chattels; sexual exploitation of women took the forms of concubinage and landlords' sexual access to peasant women. However, mass prostitution did not really exist in Southeast Asia until the latter half of the twentieth century when large numbers of single young men with disposable incomes moved to the region.

The first large-scale trafficking of women took place at the end of the nineteenth century when Chinese and Japanese women were imported to Southeast Asia to provide sexual services to Chinese male migrant workers. Later, the rapid pace of urbanization and industrialization provided a significant population of relatively wealthy men eager to spend their money on the purchase of sex. Louise Brown notes, "The sexual access to women that had previously been enjoyed by the powerful now came within the reach of large numbers of men, and they took maximum advantage of this new and exciting opportunity." Female rural migrants who moved to the cities in search of work discovered that they could make far more selling their bodies than their labor. Soon, brothels were sprouting like weeds in the commercial and residential neighborhoods.

The next big wave of commercial sex coincided with the Vietnam War. When armies went to war, they were often accompanied by prostitutes who set up red light districts near forts and military garrisons. What made the Vietnam War different from other wars was the flood of spend-thrifty American troops and the breadth of venues that arose to accommodate their needs. Similar events took place in the Philippines, where thousands of troops were stationed at U.S. military bases, and Cambodia, where a rotating pool of multinational UN peacekeeping forces took up residence. As the military personnel withdrew, the sex industry transferred its energies to attracting a new clientele—tourists from the developed world. An unofficial alliance grew between the sex and tourist industries and the government in these countries who elicited wealthy foreign consumers by relying on the now well-established stereotypes of Asian women. Sex tour packages offering young, beautiful, and submissive girls at low rates became a mainstay of the Thai and Filipino tourism industries.

Recent international attention to women's rights has led to stricter enforcement of anti-prostitution laws and thus a closeting of sex tour operations. Nonetheless, sex tourism is still a thriving business in Southeast Asia.

. . . .

However, the influence of domestic clientele on the Southeast Asian sex trade should not be underestimated. The majority of Southeast Asian sex clients are locals. For example, in Thailand, 4.6 million Thai men routinely use prostitutes, whereas the number of foreign tourists who do so is 500,000 each year.

. . . .

One last cultural factor that explains not only the prevalence of prostitution but also the increasing demand for younger and younger girls is the common Southeast Asian superstition about the restorative powers of virgins. With the rate of HIV/AIDS on the rise in most Southeast Asian countries, men are paying more money to have sex with virgins in the hopes of curing or preventing the spread of disease. Once a girl has been sold for these purposes, she is often forced to continue working as a prostitute either to pay off her debts or because she has nowhere else to go, or both. The same social stigmas against premarital sex which send men to prostitutes in the first place often restrict former prostitutes from returning to their communities.

B. Explaining Supply

. . . .

It is perhaps not remarkable that demand for commercial sex is so flexible, but the reciprocal elasticity of supply comes as somewhat of a shock. Who are the women who provide the labor force for this industry and where do they come from? A simple explanation for the willingness of individuals as well as families and communities to sell themselves or their daughters, wives, and neighbors into sexual servitude is poverty. However, if this is so, we would have expected the Southeast Asian sex industry to contract rather than expand as it did during the 1980s and 90s. After all, Southeast Asia is home to the some of the fastest growing economies in the world. Even despite the economic downturn of the late 90s, most Southeast Asian nations boast a higher per capita income, longer life expectancies, and better standards of living than many other developing countries around the world. Thus, a more appropriate construction of the problem combines aspects of poverty with cultural norms regarding women and the nature of economic development in these countries.

At first glance, Southeast Asian countries are less discriminatory towards women than other parts of the developing world such as South Asia. In contrast to certain places in South Asia, for example, where there are high levels of suicides by women and infanticide and where women are confined to the home under the Muslim system of "purdah," Southeast Asian women have traditionally played a major role as family breadwinners. However, upon closer inspection we see that it is this responsibility for family welfare which renders Southeast Asian women most vulnerable to sexual exploitation. In fact, the low levels of female infanticide in Southeast Asia are partially due to the dependence of aging parents on daughters. As they grow older, parents look to their daughters to tend to their physical needs and comfort. In recent years, more and more women are seeing to their parents' needs by selling their bodies.

Daughters' duties come from their status as commodities of the family. Women and girls are treated as property because they are generally economically and socially dependant upon men. Girls are socialized to accept this second-class citizenship. However, although for many families sending a daughter into prostitution can make the difference between dire poverty and survival, this is often not the case. In certain parts of Southeast Asia, the breeding of girls for prostitution has become a kind of lucrative cottage industry in which parents view their daughters as highly-valued cash crops. In northern Thailand and parts of Burma, for example, sending girls into prostitution is not considered shameful but an accepted economic enterprise. The parents of prostituted girls proudly display their winnings, in the form of TVs, concrete houses, and motorcycles, as a symbol of their daughters' loyalty and beauty. Girls whose mothers or sisters have worked as prostitutes are seen as simply entering the family business. Recruitment practices in these areas are public and traffickers resemble employment agents.

. . . .

The commercial sex sector not only provides substantial income and employment for those directly involved but a wide array of other individuals and institutions. First, the sex sector serves as a mechanism for redistributing incomes. Lim quotes statistics revealing that an annual US$300 million is transferred from urban sex workers to their families in the countryside. And, if we consider owners, managers, pimps, and other employees of the sex establishments, as well as support staff and those employed in the related entertainment businesses such as "waiters, cleaners, cashiers, parking valets, and security guards," the number of people supported by the sex industry is staggering. Second, the huge amount of easy money draws in international crime syndicates as well as corrupt government officials who hope to augment their often paltry salaries. National and international press and human rights reports all emphasize that the sector is supported by politicians, police, armed forces, and civil servants, who receive brides, demand sexual favors, and are themselves customers and often partial owners of the establishments. For example, Burmese children often speak of how policemen or border guards were involved in their trafficking into Thailand and how they had to entertain policemen. Third, the sex sector supplies a good deal of business to legitimate industries such as hotel companies, air carriers, and tour operators.

Many developing country governments perceive the sex sector as an engine of macroeconomic growth. As it has assumed the dimensions of a full-fledged industry, governments have perceived an interest in maintaining it. Although prostitution is illegal in most Southeast Asian countries, most national governments neglect policies, legislation, regulations, and welfare measures designed to stymie prostitution when they might conflict with economic growth objectives. The Philippines provides a good example of two-faced official attitudes to prostitution. The sale of sex is illegal, yet the state supports official licensing and SDT testing of sex workers. These procedures are designed to protect customers, not the prostitutes; when a sex worker is found to be infected with an STD she is "blacklisted" and forced to stop working, but is not provided with any health or social services. In addition, the Philippine government has promoted labor export as a major element of its development strategy, knowing that for many Filipina women, labor export translates into sexual slavery.

. . . .

III. Trafficking in Cambodia

A. Introduction to Trafficking in Cambodia

. . . .

Nearly 25 years later, the Khmer Rouge's legacy of sacrificial self-preservation remains ingrained in Cambodian society. Despite the ensuing political incarnations, the movement towards a market-based economy and large foreign donations, many Cambodians are still struggling to merely reach the economic poverty line. Moreover, Cambodian society is plagued by a rash of social diseases resulting from its poverty and genocidal past including drug abuse, mental illness, and homelessness. However, traditional forms of aid which once provided for the most needy are in short supply: adult children are no longer able to support their elderly and infirm parents, and, due to lack of free public education, children are working through the night as street vendors to pay for school.

....

Nowhere is Cambodia's "survival of the fittest" climate revealed more clearly than in its flourishing sex trade. Accurate figures reflecting Cambodian trends in trafficking are hard to come by, but it is generally estimated that there are a total of 80,000 to 100,000 sex workers throughout the country, many of whom have been trafficked, eighty-one percent of whom are Cambodian (the rest are primarily Vietnamese). Roughly thirty percent are below the age of eighteen, and, according to a 1999 ILO-IPEC Report, fifteen percent of all prostitutes are between the ages of nine and fifteen. In addition to prostitutes working in brothels, there are ones who work from private rented accommodations, as well as dancers in discos, beer-girls, masseuses, karaoke singers, and street-walkers. Based on a number of small surveys, the Coalition Against Trafficking estimates that there are up to 15,000 sex workers in Phnom Penh alone. Finally, thousands more women and children are sold into prostitution abroad each year.

It is not merely the size of Cambodia's trafficking problem which is so disquieting. Rather, what distinguishes Cambodia's sex trade from that of other countries' is the conditions under which women and children are sold and kept. Surveys suggest that the vast majority—roughly ninety percent—of prostitutes in Cambodia enter the sex industry against their will. Even those who enter the industry willingly are often strictly controlled and prevented from leaving. All are exposed to degrading and often dangerous situations, including exposure to STDs, abuse by patrons and brothel owners, and unhealthy living conditions.

....

B. Description of the Cambodian Sex Industry

....

3. Recruitment

Scholars of Cambodian sex trafficking agree that the recruitment and placement of women and girls into prostitution is a domestic practice, not yet governed by the international crime syndicates that operate in other parts of Asia. However, there remains contention about the level of organization amongst domestic actors. Some scholars believe that the practice is carried out by highly organized and well-established domestic criminal networks, while others maintain it is highly fragmented. Annuska Derks, who has written two of the most comprehensive studies of Cambodia's trafficking industry, takes the middle ground. She finds that "there exist links between brothel-owners and the police, between different brothel-owners and between brothel-owners and recruiters. However, they seem to be based more on a personal, sometimes familiar, set of relationships than part of a well-established criminal network."

....

... [W]omen in Cambodia are trafficked in three ways. First, they might have willingly entered the sex industry but were deceived about the conditions under which they will be forced to work. Derks states, "Voluntary entry into prostitution can bring the women and girls into slavery-like conditions such as being forced to work 24 hours a day, receiving no or very little payment, not being able to leave the brothel, being forced to have sex without a condom, and being bit hit or otherwise violated." In addition, Derks continues, "Those who have already entered prostitution are easy targets for recruiters who have connections at other brothels." Because this paper does not distinguish between sexual slavery and forced entry into the sex industry, women who are not initially coerced into prostitution but later find themselves in coercive situations are considered to have been trafficked.

Second, women might have been bonded into prostitution. Bonded entry occurs when parents, friends or other close acquaintances sell a child or woman for employment in return for cash. The current price for woman or girl is US$100 to US$200 in rural areas, and US$550 to US$700 in Phnom Penh. The woman is then required to continue working until the debt is paid off....

Thirdly, women are lured, deceived, kidnapped, or in some other way tricked into prostitution. A CWDA survey conducted in Phnom Penh in 1994 found that 64.5% of sex workers had been coerced into the profession and that of those, 53% had been lured from their homes with the promise of high paying urban jobs and subsequently sold into prostitution. Similarly, a Human Rights Task Force survey conducted a year later in thirteen provinces estimated that forty-five percent of the prostitutes interviewed were either deceived or abducted into prostitution.

....

4. Conditions

Although victims of trafficking can be taken to many different kinds of establishments, most research has focused on brothel areas. The following is a description of a typical brothel experience:

A woman or girl who has just been trafficked is usually confined within a room in a hotel or a brothel for a week or more and not allowed to leave. If she objects, she is beaten or drugged or both. She may also be raped by her captors to prepare her for her future clients. She is usually fed very little and often deprived of sleep. Her first client buys her for one week and she must do whatever he says or face more beatings from either the client or her captors. A victim may then be sold to more clients in the same room for a week at a time, or she may be moved to another hotel room or brothel. After several weeks, once she has resigned herself to her fate, she might be allowed to leave the room in which she is confined but she is not allowed to leave the premises of the hotel or the brothel.

A victim in a brothel lives in squalid conditions. Her windowless room is filthy, dark, and small. There is typically just enough space for a small bed. Former patrons of Svay Pak describe the "short time" rooms, where the women also sleep and eat, as "cramped and miserable" and "hot, musty and dirty." One former patron warns of another brothel, "If you have an allergy to molds, better try someplace else." A victim is fed whatever small amount of food her captors provide and her eating habits are irregular and unhealthy. She is not given enough water to both drink and wash herself. She may not be able to speak to the other prostitutes or anyone else besides the brothel owner and her clients. She is never allowed to sleep through the night (or day, for that matter) since clients arrive at all hours. She is forced to receive customers when she is sick or menstruating. She may also be forced to sit outside the brothel to attract customers. She receives anywhere from one to twenty clients per day. She may be beaten for any petty infraction of show of disobedience. These beatings can, in some extreme cases, lead to death. Whether or not she is beaten, she lives with the constant threat of violence.

. . . .

Health problems named by sex workers and clinicians include specific injuries from violence, headaches, fevers, skin irritations, abdominal pains, vaginal discharge, sores and warts, syphilis, gonorrhea, other STDs, and HIV/AIDS. Many prostitutes say that they try to use condoms but that most clients refuse to use them. Moreover, most prostitutes do not have access to condoms and must rely on their customers to provide them. One study found that almost forty percent of the prostitutes in Cambodia test HIV positive. . . .

C. Explanation of Cambodia's Trafficking Problem

There is one persistent question in every study of Cambodia's trafficking problem: Why are so many families and communities willing to sacrifice their daughters, wives, sisters, and friends to sexual slavery? When asked this question, most Cambodians respond with a one word answer, "poverty." Clearly, poverty plays a significant role in a family's decision, and yet economics, in itself, cannot provide a sufficient answer. Indeed, Cambodia's trafficking rate surpasses that of many of its poorer counterparts across the globe. Instead, a combination of socio-cultural, historical, and political, and economic factors contribute to the trafficking Cambodian of women and girls. This paper divides the causes into five categories: traditional views about women, disintegration of traditional society, foreign influences, lack of political will and legal means to deal with the problem, and poverty.

1. The Societal Role of Women in Cambodia

Current statistics reveal that sixty to seventy percent of Cambodian men visit prostitutes. These numbers are undoubtedly connected to the recent surge in trafficking but they also reflect Cambodia's long history of commodification of women, stemming from its patriarchal values regarding sex and power. Cultural rules and norms, including the Women's law ("chbap srey") and Men's law ("chbap proh") dictate that females should be passive and subservient to men. Violence towards women is commonplace — twenty-five percent of all Cambodian women report being abused by their husbands. Although this figure in itself is not so shocking — it is consistent with worldwide averages (including those for the United States) — the impunity afforded abusers is.

. . . .

Traditional values can be used to explain not only the broad societal acceptance of prostitution but the reason why so many families are willing to sell their daughters into the industry. Cambodian Buddhism (Theravada or Hinnayana Buddhism) requires that both men and women show gratitude towards their parents. A male fulfills this obligation through accumulating merit on his family's behalf by entering the monkhood or "Sangha" for a temporary period of time. A female child's responsibility is of a more earthly nature. She must cook and clean and generally see to her parents' physical needs. In former times, a girl's obligation to her parents required her to remain close to home. However, changing circumstances and opportunities have forced daughters to leave their homes villages and enter jobs that are not considered respectable. By working as a prostitute a girl abandons her virtue, yet she fulfills her obligation to her parents and accumulates merit for her next life. Thus, prostitution is portrayed in some ways as a morally guided decision.

Two additional Cambodian traditions should be mentioned. First is the general practice of treating children like possessions. Sin Kim Sean, one of Cambodia's top legal scholars, explains that one of the greatest human rights challenges facing Cambodia today is that most parents assume their children have absolutely no rights, despite constitutional guarantees which hold otherwise. Second is the Cambodian historical use of bonded labor. Milton Osbourne asserts that the temporary abandonment of personal freedom to pay back a debt has been a widespread practice throughout Southeast Asian history. This cultural precedent of indentured servitude perhaps makes current uses of bonded labor such as prostitution more acceptable to Cambodians.

....

3. Foreign Influence

The presence of the United States in Southeast Asia throughout the early 1970s led to the expansion of Cambodia's commercial sex industry. The closing of Cambodia's border to foreigners in 1975 stymied this influence. During the Khmer Rouge period of the mid to late 1970s, prostitution was outlawed, but resurfaced in the 80s. It was the entry of UNTAC's 22,000 international personnel in 1992 which occasioned the biggest boom for Cambodian prostitution. In 1991 Phnom Penh was home to 1500 prostitutes. By 1993 the numbers had swelled to almost 20,000. The UN has recently come under attack for allowing, if not officially condoning, the lascivious behavior of its troops in various countries, including Cambodia.

....

When UNTAC departed in 1993, the number of prostitutes dropped slightly but is rising again to meet the demands of Cambodia's growing sex tourist industry. A quick Internet search for "Sex guide and Southeast Asia" shows that Cambodia is swiftly becoming a favorite haven for both budget-conscious sex tourists and pedophiles alike. One Cambodian ex-pat offers, "Buying sex with a twelve year-old is quicker than changing money." Another gushes, "Five dollars for a short time in Cambodia is a bargain and when you consider what you would pay in Thailand it makes you wonder how much money you have wasted all this time!" Messages like these will likely generate more and more customers and ultimately more trafficking victims. Communications technology is a significant factor in this growth; with the advantage of the Internet, it is likely that Cambodia's sex tourism scene will grow as big as Thailand's in less than half the time.

4. Political and Legal Factors

Notwithstanding the passage of the 1996 Anti-Trafficking laws and intermittent brothel raids, Cambodia does not seem to have the legal capacity or the political will to address the trafficking problem. The country's legal system was devastated under the Khmer Rouge and has yet to fully recover. Courts were destroyed, judges and lawyers were killed, reeducated, or forced to flee the country. There is a general dearth of qualified legal professionals. At the time of the Vietnamese invasion, there were fewer than ten lawyers in the country, and by 1997, there were still only sixty-eight lawyers and eighty-three judges. Today the number has expanded to 200 lawyers, although many still await certification, and 120 judges, over half of whom never received any formal legal education. Most judges have no human rights training, and some did not even complete secondary school.

....

Apart from.... institutional problems, enforcement is severely hindered by widespread corruption in the judiciary and police and military forces. Judges are notorious for taking bribes both as a means of supplementing their meager salaries, which start at US$15 a month, and appeasing those in power. Police and military officers often do more to support the commercial sex industry than to thwart it. Many brothel owners are married to police officers and soldiers and have their unofficial protection. Some officers are themselves co-owners of brothels. In other cases, brothel owners pay "taxes" to law enforcement officials, either in cash or in kind, to insulate them from arrest. Arrests and brothel raids are often staged and within weeks the brothels are doing business again. It might even be argued that it is the government's unofficial policy to turn a blind eye towards trafficking because it attracts tourists and helps the economy. Regardless of whether or not there is any truth to this allegation, there does appear to be a genuine reluctance to press charges against traffickers. Prosecutions against traffickers are rare and tend to focus on small players, allowing, "the Mister Bigs of Cambodia's sex trafficking underworld [to] operate freely. As a result, impunity for the traffickers, like that for most all political elites, continues to rankle justice in Cambodia.

....

IV. Law and Policy

A. *Law*

Cambodia is bound by a number of legal instruments relevant to sex trafficking, including its Constitution, domestic trafficking legislation, and elements of family and labor laws, and international conventions. The following is a brief description of pertinent laws as well as some of their drawbacks.

1. The Constitution

The 1993 Cambodian Constitution expressly prohibits trafficking. Article 46(1) states, "commerce of human beings, exploitation by prostitution and obscenity which affect the reputation of women shall be prohibited." Furthermore, the Constitution obligates Cambodia to respect human rights, particularly the rights of women and children. Article 31(1) incorporates all international human rights law as part of the Cambodian legal framework, including the Universal Declaration of Human Rights and the covenants and conventions related to human rights and women's and children's rights....

2. Trafficking Legislation

The Cambodian National Assembly approved the Law on the Suppression of Kidnapping, Trafficking and Exploitation of Humans in 1996. The law provides penalties for any person who "lures another person, male or female, minor or adult of whatever nationality by ways of enticing or any other means, by promising to offer any money or jewelry, whether or not there is consent from that other person, by way of forcing, threatening or using of hypnotic drugs, in order to kidnap him/her for trafficking/sale or for prostitution." Consistent with the definition of trafficking used throughout this paper, the law does not require crossing borders or the use of coercion.

....

Increased penalties are provided where the victim is younger than fifteen years old. Because prostitution is illegal, the law does not propose any penalties for prostitutes, other sex workers, or victims of trafficking.

Although the anti-trafficking is an important step in addressing the country's trafficking problem, it suffers from several weaknesses. First, advocates of victims' rights believe that even though the law does not make prostitution illegal, it is often used to prosecute prostitutes who "open a place" which is used for "debauchery," namely, the rooms in which they exercise their trade. Some legal scholars also suggest that the law does not go far enough in requiring the state to take positive measures to protect victims of trafficking. In addition, the law does nothing to safeguard the identity or safety of victims who come forward with evidence against traffickers. Finally, the law suffers from serious implementation and enforcement problems resulting from legal uncertainties and corruption.

...

Notes and Questions

1. It is always problematic when extremely poor countries are expected to implement elaborate legal regimes based on international law principles. In the case of Cambodia, where the social and political fabric of society was nearly destroyed in the very recent past, is it sensible to expect that a "model" set of anti-trafficking principles will be effective? Or can any society, no matter how administratively weak and corrupt, at least be improved by its own legal efforts?

2. Journalist Nicholas D. Kristof helped to raise awareness of the problem of young girls being held captive in brothel slavery in a series of 2005 op ed columns that appeared in the New York Times. He focused particularly on the situation in Cambodia, where many of the prostitutes are extremely young. See particularly his column *Cambodia, Where Sex Traffickers are King*, N.Y.TIMES, Jan. 15, 2005, at A15, where he writes of the difficulties of removing young girls from the word of prostitution. Kristof writes, chillingly, of the establishments where young girls can be ordered by number, and comments that "Cambodia may be becoming the first sex-slavery state." *Id.* Also see his article *Sex Slaves? Lock up the Pimps*, N.Y.TIMES, Jan, 29, 2005, at A19.

3. The Schwartz article, written in 2004, mentions that the United States announced plans to cease significant amounts of aid to Cambodia if its government did not take active measures to prevent human trafficking. However, it was not until 2008 that Cambodia passed a Law on Suppression of Human Trafficking and Sexual Exploitation. The United States never actually withheld the funds despite the fact that the Cambodian government has only convicted 12 people of trafficking-related crimes to date. For an overview of the law and the 2008 Human Rights Report on Cambodia, see BUREAU OF DEMOCRACY, HUM. RTS., AND LAB., U.S. DEP'T OF ST., 2008 COUNTRY REPORTS ON HUMAN RIGHTS PRACTICES: CAMBODIA (2008), *available at* http://www.state.gov/g/drl/rls/hrrpt/ 2008/eap/119036.htm.

Earlier in this chapter, we noted that Kevin Bales had brought the idea of "modern day slavery" to the consciousness of the international community. What follows is a further excerpt from his book. Here, Bales examines the conditions of Thai brothels and seeks to explain the cultural and economic reasons why child trafficking and prostitution continue to flourish in Southeast Asia.

Kevin Bales, Disposable People:
New Slavery in the Global Economy
(1999)

...

When Siri wakes it is about noon. In the instant of waking she knows exactly who and what she has become. As she explained to me, the soreness in her genitals reminds her of the fifteen men she had sex with the night before. Siri is fifteen years old. Sold by her parents a year ago, her resistance and her desire to escape the brothel are breaking down and acceptance and resignation are taking their place.

If the pimp is away, the girls will joke around, but if not they must be constantly deferential and aware of his presence, for he can harm them or use them as he pleases. At about five p.m., Siri and the other girls are told to dress, put on their makeup, and prepare for the night's work. By seven the men are coming in, purchasing drinks and choosing girls, and Siri will have been chosen by one or two of the ten to eighteen men who will buy her that night. Many men choose Siri because she looks much younger than her fifteen years. Slight and round faced, dressed to accentuate her youth, she might be eleven or twelve. Because she looks like a child she can be sold as a "new" girl at a higher price, about $15, which is more than twice that charged for the other girls.

Siri is very frightened that she will get AIDS. Long before she understood prostitution she knew about HIV, as many girls from her village returned home to die from AIDS after being sold into the brothels. Every day she prays to Buddha, trying to earn the merit that will preserve her from the disease. She also tries to insist that her clients use condoms, and in most cases she is successful as the pimp backs her up. But when policemen use her, or the pimp himself, they will do as they please; if she tries to insist, she will be beaten and raped. She also fears pregnancy, and like the other girls she receives injections of the contraceptive drug Depo-Provera. Once a month she has an HIV test, and so far it has been negative. She knows that if she tests positive she will be thrown out of the brothel to starve.

. . . .

In Thailand prostitution is illegal, yet girls like Siri are sold into sex slavery by the thousands. The brothels that hold these girls are but a small part of a much wider sex industry. How can this wholesale trade in girls continue? What keeps it working? The answer is more complicated than we think; Thailand's economic boom, its macho culture, and its social acceptance of prostitution all contribute to it. Money, culture, and society blend in new and powerful ways to enslave girls like Siri.

. . . .

By my own conservative estimate there are perhaps 35,000 girls like Siri enslaved in Thailand. The actual number of prostitutes is certainly much higher. The government states there are 81,384 prostitutes in Thailand—but that official number is calculated from the number of registered (though still illegal) brothels, massage parlors, and sex establishments. Based on information gathered by AIDS workers in different cities, my own reckoning is that there are between a half a million and one million prostitutes. Of this number only about one in twenty is enslaved. Most become prostitutes voluntarily, though some start out in debt bondage. Prostitutes range from high-earning "professional" women who work with some autonomy, through the women working by choice as call girls or in massage parlors, to the enslaved rural girls like Siri. Enslaved girls service the lowest end of the market: the laborers, students, and workers who can afford only the 100 baht per half hour rate. The reasons that such large numbers of Thai men use prostitutes are much more complicated and grow out of their culture, their history, and a rapidly changing economy.

For most married women, having their husbands go to prostitutes is preferable to other forms of extramarital sex. Most wives accept that men naturally want multiple partners, and prostitutes are seen as less threatening to the stability of the family. Prostitutes require no long term commitment or emotional involvement. When a husband uses a prostitute he is thought to be fulfilling a male role, but when he takes a minor wife or mistress, his wife is thought to have failed. The relationship may not be formalized (polygamy is illegal) but it nevertheless will be regarded as binding, and the children still have legal claims for support.

Owners of brothels may just look at it as an investment, never coming into contact with anyone who works there. They are not really interested in their slaves at all, just in the bottom line on their investment. If they weren't slaveholders they would put their money into other businesses, but there is little incentive to do so since brothels are such solid investments, much more stable than the stock market. Contributing to the economy is the strong moral argument in Thailand, and these slaveholders might be proud of their contribution—they see themselves as providing jobs, and even as lifting the debt-bonded girls out of rural poverty. Not that these moral questions matter, since the slaveholders never need think about the women in their brothels, where they come from, or what will happen to them.

Sex with virgins: The strong preferences shown by customers to have sex with virgins has two bases. The first is the ancient Chinese belief that sex with a virgin will reawaken sexual virility and prolong life. A girl's virginity is though to be a strong source of yang (or coolness), which quenches and slows the yin (or heat) of the aging process. When a new girl is brought to the brothel, she will be placed in another room (the "room to unveil virgins"). Here she will be displayed and her price will be negotiated with the pimp—a very high price, usually between $200 and $2000 dollars. Deflowering often takes place away from the brothel in a hotel room rented for the occasion. The pimp or his assistant will often attend as well, since it is usually necessary to beat the girl into submission.

....

Enslaved prostitutes in brothels face two major threats to their physical health and to their lives: violence and disease. Their enslavement is enforced through rape, beatings, or threats, and the violence is always present. Within hours of being brought to the brothel, the girls are in pain and shock. Like other victims of torture they often go numb, paralyzed in their minds if not in their bodies. For the youngest girls, with little understanding of what is happening to them, the trauma is overwhelming. Shattered and betrayed, they often have little clear memory of what has occurred. Escape is impossible. The police serve as slave-catchers whenever a girl escapes; once captured, girls are often beaten or abused in the police station before being sent back to the brothel. For most girls, it soon becomes clear that they can never escape, that their only hope for release is to please the pimp and to somehow pay off their debt. The girls will do whatever it takes to reduce the pain—lethargy, aggression, self-loathing, and suicide attempts, confusion, self-abuse, depression, full-blown psychoses, and hallucinations. Rehabilitation workers report that the girls suffer emotional instability; they are unable to trust or form relationships, to readjust to the world outside the brothel, or to learn and develop normally.

....

The complex relationship between slave and slaveholder helps explain why a young prostitute runs back to the brothel after so much cruel treatment. When I met Siri, she had just crossed the invisible line between resistance and submission. Though only fifteen she was reconciled to life as a prostitute. She explained it was her fate, her karma, and each day she prayed to Buddha for acceptance. In the past she had tried to escape; now she dreams of earning enough money to build a house in her village. Her anger and resentment had dissolved, and she willingly accedes to the pimp's wishes. In his domination of Siri, the pimp has a powerful ally: her mother, who provides assistance by reminding Siri of her debt to the brothel and to her parents.

Thailand's government is ineffective when faced with the enslavement of its own citizens. Most Thai politicians do not take sex slavery seriously. While it is true that full and complete laws exist forbidding enslavement, trafficking, and exploitation, they are not enforced. Well, they are very occasionally enforced whenever public scandal requires that politicians need to be seen doing something—when they do occur, they take on a quality of comic opera. In 1994, a government special task force arrested 64 brothel owners, 472 Thai prostitutes, and 9 foreign prostitutes, and rescued 35 children and sex slaves—in a country with an estimated one million commercial sex workers. When police or officials are charged in connection with these offenses, they receive the lightest slap on the wrist. Punishment for the police ordinarily consists of a posting to another job. Thai cooperation with European law enforcement has improved. In 1992, Thailand passed an Act on International Cooperation in Criminal Law Matters: this allows the attorney general to gather evidence against foreigners who commit crimes in Thailand and send it to their home countries. ECPAT and other organizations have also convinced the Thai attorney general not to allow bail in future cases of foreigners accused of child sexual abuse.

At the beginning of 1997, Thailand revised the law on prostitution. The new statute dramatically increased the fines and prison sentences for anyone who has sex with prostitutes under the age of eighteen (maximum 60,000 baht and three years, respectively) or under the age of fifteen (maximum 400,000 baht and 20 years). This marked a real improvement over the 1960 Prostitution Suppression Act, which made every person involved in prostitution subject to penalties except the customer.

For girls like Siri the law will probably have little, if any, impact. In the provincial towns, the police have a firm grip on the sex industry and few concerns about national political decisions; they worry even less about international concerns.

The following report by Human Rights Watch describes the trafficking of young women and girls from Burma into Thailand to serve the sex industry. It must be noted that, despite the passage of time since the report was written, the reality of sex trafficking from Burma into Thailand has changed little. In that regard, the U.S. State Department's 2008 Trafficking in Persons Report[13] places Burma in Tier 3, the lowest possible trafficking rank, with the following comment:

> BURMA (Tier 3): Burma is a source country for women, children, and men trafficked for the purpose of forced labor and commercial sexual exploitation. Burmese women and children are trafficked to Thailand, People's Republic of China (P.R.C.), Bangladesh, India, Pakistan, Malaysia, South Korea, and Macau for commercial sexual exploitation, domestic servitude, and forced labor. Some Burmese migrating abroad for better economic opportunities wind up in situations of forced or bonded labor or forced prostitution. Burmese children are subjected to conditions of forced labor in Thailand as hawkers, beggars, and for work in shops, agriculture, fish processing, and small-scale industries. Women are trafficked for commercial sexual exploitation to Malaysia and the P.R.C.; some women are trafficked to the P.R.C. as forced brides. Some trafficking victims transit Burma from Bangladesh to Malaysia and from P.R.C. to Thailand. Internal trafficking occurs primarily from villages to urban centers and economic hubs for labor in industrial zones, agricultural estates, and commercial sexual exploitation. Forced labor and trafficking may also occur in ethnic border areas outside the central government's control. Military and civilian officials continue to use a significant amount of forced labor. Poor villagers in rural regions must provide *corvee* labor on demand as a tax imposed by authorities. Urban poor

----

13. The U.S. State Department's Trafficking in Persons Report, produced annually under the requirements of the Trafficking Victims Protection Act, will be discussed in detail in Part IV of this chapter, below.

and street children in Rangoon and Mandalay are at growing risk of involuntary conscription as child soldiers by the Burmese junta, as desertions of men in the Burmese army rises. Ethnic insurgent groups also used compulsory labor of adults and unlawful recruitment of children. The military junta's gross economic mismanagement, human rights abuses, and its policy of using forced labor are the top causal factors for Burma's significant trafficking problem.[14]

Human Rights Watch, *A Modern Form of Slavery: Trafficking of Burmese Women and Girls into Brothels in Thailand*
(1993) *available at* http://www.hrw.org/legacy/reports/1993/thailand/

IV. TRAFFICKING IN WOMEN AND GIRLS

A. RECRUITMENT

The first phase of the illicit trade in Burmese women and girls is their recruitment and sale into brothels throughout Thailand where they are compelled to prostitute themselves under conditions tantamount to slavery. The actions of the recruiting agent and the brothel owners are clearly in violation not only of international standards on trafficking and forced labor, but also of domestic Thai laws prohibiting trafficking and prostitution. Yet for the most part, these laws are not enforced.

....

All but one of the women we interviewed for this report were lured from their homes on a promise of economic benefits. But data from other sources, including police records, indicate that in Ranong in particular, the use of physical force to procure women and girls is common.

....

The process of recruitment by agents working for brothel owners is necessarily covert, because of laws restricting the freedom of Burmese citizens to leave their country and laws in both Thailand and Burma making prostitution a crime. The brothel owners thus rely on a network of "small agents" and "big agents", acting in concert—and for a price—with Thai and Burmese officials to keep a steady supply of Burmese girls coming across the border.

The Promises

The lure for the Burmese girls is the chance to escape from poverty. Twenty-nine of the thirty women and girls interviewed deliberately set out to earn money in Thailand for themselves or their families. Only four of these knew when they set out from home that they would be involved in some form of prostitution. Of the twenty-five others, eighteen thought they would be working as maids, cooks, laundresses, waitresses or some other job that required few skills. Like seventeen-year-old "Tin Tin" who was invited by a friend to go to Chiangrai to make flowers, or sixteen-year-old "Tar Tar" who was brought to Thailand by a teacher on the promise of making enough money to buy a traditional dress, most were attracted by the promise of an opportunity to help their parents or simply to escape from the grimness of their own surroundings. A Burmese girl, aged fourteen or fifteen, from the Akha ethnic group told a Thai NGO worker how the agents operate:

---

14. U.S. Department of State, 2008 Trafficking in Persons Report 79–80 (2008).

One day two women came to the village while "Par" was on her way to the fields. They talked to her about how much better it would be to live in the city and work. [They talked to her father as well.] Her father wanted to go along, as he was afraid of her being sold, but the two women said it was not necessary and would be a waste of his time. So her father did not go and her mother cried, because "Par" was her only daughter. Ah Daw [the agent] told her that the daughter would be fine. She would be taking care of children and would get to go to school. Ah Daw's husband came and said the same thing. Finally, "Par's" parents believed Ah Daw. Ah Daw told her that she would study Thai for a month, then learn to speak Thai, make necklaces, take care of children. Ah Daw gave her father 800 baht ($32).

In only two cases we investigated did the girls return voluntarily to prostitution after they had been returned home. In one case, the girl believed that since she had lost her virginity anyway, she might as well earn money for her family. In the other case, the shame of being known in her village as having worked as a prostitute was too great, and she, too, decided to help her family by going back.

In only one case out of the thirty we investigated directly was a girl lured from her home on other than a promise of economic prosperity.

. . . .

Of the thirty girls and women, eleven had been brought into Thailand by family members. The network for finding work in Thailand appears to be well-known in the rural areas of Burma that supply the women and girls. Relatives knew, for example, to take their daughters or sisters to the "Mekong shop" in Mae Sai or to a particularly well-known agent or to a certain temple. In some cases, women who have returned from Thailand provided the information to potential recruits. In other cases, relatives who live in or near Mae Sai knew the agents and directed the new recruits to them.

Of the remaining nineteen women and girls, eight were recruited by women returning from the brothels, who saw their escape as contingent on their ability to find successors. Those women were likely to reinforce the belief at home that they had worked as waitresses or maids in Thailand to save face. They would emphasize the cash rewards rather than the abuse. Four of our interviewees were recruited by someone known to them in the village, such as a teacher, who was operating as a "small agent" for the "big agent" in Mae Sai. Two set out for the border themselves, without knowing anyone at the other end. It is unclear how the remaining women were recruited.

. . . .

B. THE BROTHEL

. . . .

Working Conditions

Nearly every Burmese girl and woman interviewed had to be available to work between ten to fourteen hours a day with a only few days off each month during their menstruation. Some explained that they could get time off if they were very sick or sore, but they only dared request such days if absolutely necessary. Those interviewed had an average of ten clients a day (some with as many as twenty on weekends) with no means to negotiate who their clients were or what they did with them. Compliance was often obtained by threats and beatings from the brothel owner and pimps.

The girls and women could also be hired out for the entire day or night. Regular clients would leave a deposit and/or identification and take the girl or woman wherever they chose, with whomever and for as long they were willing to pay. Those interviewed talked of feeling vulnerable and frightened in these situations. Some girls reported that friends they knew in the brothels were in fact stolen through such arrangements and never heard of again. However, because of the owner's fear that his girls could be stolen and sold elsewhere, he was usually careful about which clients he allowed to take the women and girls out of the brothel.

As noted above, most women lived and slept in the same cubicles where they took their clients. The Ranong brothels raided in July 1993 were particularly bad:

Each of the cubicles, measuring two by two-and-a-half meters contained a cement bunk where the girls were forced to prostitute themselves. Hidden doors, concealed by secret passageways where the girls could be hidden in case of a raid.... The stench of the place was terrible. There were no proper toilets. It was a hell hole.

....

"Yin Yin" worked from noon to midnight and served ten to twenty men a day. She had to do whatever the clients wanted and never refused them. The owner only gave her and the other workers 30 baht ($1.20) each day for food and all other expenses. This was not enough for survival. She worked every day except when she was menstruating. Sometimes when she was very sore, she asked to stop for a few days, but she tried to work as much as possible so she could pay off her debt and go home. She told us, "The owner knows he doesn't have to physically force us."

One girl from Keng Tung, seventeen years old, was taken to a brothel in Hat Yai in the south, and described to an NGO worker in Chiangmai how dirty, sweaty and smelly her clients were. She did not want to sleep with any of them, but the owner beat her if she refused. She said she asked them to take a bath first, but they would not agree.

....

Notes and Questions

1. The readings included above present a complicated set of circumstances leading to the proliferation of child sex slavery in Southeast Asia. What similarities and differences did you note between Thailand and Cambodia?

2. There is a good deal of debate over the question of what makes a region succumb to reliance on the commercial sex industry, including its worst forms, brothel slavery and child sex trafficking. Is there any way to sort out the relative culpability of domestic versus foreign sources of demand? Is there any good reason to do so?

C. Sex Trafficking in India

Despite the fact that India generally enjoys an international reputation as a stable democracy with a deep concern for human rights, women and children are often abused and exploited with the full complicity of the Indian police and other authorities. Brothel sex slavery in India is particularly egregious. India's case is interesting in that it has developed this industry without much economic incentive from global sex tourism, and appears to thrive mainly on local demand. The memo that follows below was written by the U.S. Department of State; despite the friendly relations between the U.S. and India, note the harsh language used in describing India's brothel system. It should be noted that in the State Department's 2008 Trafficking in Persons Report, India remained on the Tier 2 Watch List, which indicates caution and concern, as well as a wait and see attitude on the part of the U.S. government about the level of commitment to anti-trafficking measures.[15]

Bureau of Democracy, Human Rights & Labor, U.S. Department of State, Country Reports on Human Rights Practices: India

(2001) *available at* http://www.state.gov/g/drl/rls/hrrpt/2001/sa/8230.htm

Trafficking in Persons

The law prohibits trafficking in persons; however, trafficking in persons is a serious problem. NGOs allege that corruption at the enforcement level helps to perpetuate the problem. The country is a significant source, transit point, and destination for numerous trafficked persons, primarily for the purposes of prostitution and forced labor. The country is a destination country for Nepali and Bangladeshi women and girls trafficked for the purpose of labor and prostitution. Internal trafficking of women and children is widespread. To a lesser extent, India is a country of origin for women and children trafficked to other countries in Asia, the Middle East, and the West. The country serves as a transit point for Bangladeshi girls and women trafficked for sexual exploitation to Pakistan, and for boys trafficked to the Gulf States to work as camel jockeys.

Over 2.3 million girls and women are believed to be working in the sex industry against their will within the country at any given time, and more than 200,000 persons are believed to be trafficked into, within, or through the country annually. Women's rights organizations and NGOs estimate that more than 12,000 and perhaps as many as 50,000 women and children are trafficked into the country annually from neighboring states for the sex trade. According to an ILO estimate, 15 percent of the country's estimated 2.3 million prostitutes are children, while the U.N. reports that an estimated 40 percent are below 18 years of age. Many tribal women are forced into sexual exploitation. The Situation Report India (DWCD) 1998 estimated that 61 percent of commercial sex workers in India belong to lower castes or are refugees or illegal migrants. Trafficking in, to, and through the country largely is controlled by organized crime.

There is a growing pattern of trafficking in child prostitutes from Nepal. According to one estimate, 5,000 to 10,000 children, mostly between the ages of 10 and 18, are drawn or forced into this traffic annually. Girls as young as 7 years of age are trafficked from economically depressed neighborhoods in Nepal, Bangladesh, and rural areas of India to the major prostitution centers of Mumbai, Calcutta, and New Delhi. There are approximately 100,000 to 200,000 women and girls working in brothels in Mumbai and 40,000 to 100,000 in Calcutta. In Mumbai an estimated 90 percent of sex workers began when they were under 18 years of age; half are from Nepal. A similar profile is believed to exist among female sex workers in Calcutta, although the vast majority of women who are trafficked there come from Bangladesh, as opposed to Nepal. NGOs in the region estimate that about 6,000 to 10,000 girls are trafficked annually from Nepal to Indian brothels, and that a similar number are trafficked from Bangladesh.

---

15. U.S. Department of State, 2008 Trafficking in Persons Report 139 (2008).

....

Within the country, women from economically depressed areas often move into the cities seeking greater economic opportunities, and once there are victimized by traffickers who force or coerce them into the sex trade. However, in some cases family members sell young girls into the sex trade. For example, according to a local NGO researcher, in one village in Uttar Pradesh, girls 1 to 2 years of age are purchased from their parents and adopted by persons who train them for the sex trade through the use of pornographic materials, and then sell them into the sex trade when they are 7 to 12 years old.

....

The Prevention of Immoral Trafficking Act (PITA), supplemented by the Penal Code, prohibits trafficking in human beings and contains severe penalties for violations. The Constitution also prohibits trafficking in persons. The PITA toughened penalties for trafficking in children, particularly by focusing on traffickers, pimps, landlords, and brothel operators, while protecting underage girls as victims. The PITA requires police to use only female police officers to interrogate girls rescued from brothels. The PITA also requires the Government to provide protection and rehabilitation for these rescued girls. In addition, under the PITA prostitution is not a crime; the PITA criminalizes only solicitation or engaging in sex acts in or near a public place. Some NGOs note that this ambiguity, which was intended to protect trafficking victims, instead has been exploited to protect the sex industry.

However, the country's prostitution and trafficking laws are imposed selectively by police; clients and organizers of the sex trade tend not to be penalized, while prostitutes found soliciting or practicing their trade in or near (200 meters) public places are penalized. Due to the selective implementation the "rescue" of sex workers from brothels often leads to their revictimization. Using the PITA's provisions against soliciting or engaging in sexual acts, police regularly may arrest sex workers, extort money from them, evict them, and take their children from them. Clients of prostitutes, by comparison, largely are immune from any law enforcement threat, as clients have committed a crime only if they have engaged in a sex act with a sex worker in a public place or have had sex with a girl under the age of 16 years (statutory rape). Therefore, although the intention of the PITA was to increase enforcement efforts against the traffickers, pimps, and border operators, the opposite is the reality; a Calcutta NGO reports that on average, approximately 80 to 90 percent of the arrests made under the PITA in West Bengal state in the 1990s were of female sex workers. Only a small fraction of arrests made under the PITA involve traffickers. Implementation of the PITA's provisions for protection and rehabilitation of women and children who are rescued from the sex trade is extremely poor. NGOs familiar with the legal history of prostitution and trafficking laws regard the failure of the judiciary to recognize this inequity in the law's implementation as a continuing "blind spot." Over the last several years, arrests and prosecutions under the PITA have remained relatively static, while all indications suggest a growing level of trafficking into and within the country.

The Government is proposing amendments to the PITA to increase penalties for traffickers and to decriminalize the actions of sex workers. NGOs also have demanded that special PITA courts for speedy resolution of cases allow videotaped testimony so that underage victims need not be summoned back for trial.

Social welfare agencies of the central and state governments recognize that trafficking is widespread, but most are underfunded and typically are unable to implement Anti-trafficking plans effectively. The NGO community has taken the lead on prevention, pro-

tection, and prosecution of trafficking and has a mixed record in securing the cooperation of the state and local police. An NGO helped to rescue 153 children from brothels
of New Delhi's redlight district between June and September.

....

NGOs and others allege that when police take action against brothels suspected of en-
slaving minors, the resulting police raids often are planned poorly and seldom are coordinated with NGOs or government social agencies. NGOs claim that without advance
notice of police raids on brothels, they are not able to lend valuable assistance in identifying and interviewing underage victims. Moreover, police do not seek advice or assistance
from NGOs in planning law enforcement action to protect the victims during raids. Therefore, the police action often worsens the situation of the girls and women indebted to
traffickers and brothel owners. Girls rescued from brothels are treated as criminals and
often are abused sexually by their police rescuers or by the staff of government remand
centers, where they are housed temporarily before being brought back to the brothels as
a result of the bribes paid by brothel operators, or legally released into the custody of
traffickers and madams posing as relatives. In these cases, the debt owned by the girls to
the brothel operators and traffickers further increases as the costs of bribing or legally
obtaining release of the girls is added to their labor debt. In April, in a West Bengal remand home for destitute women, two girls attempted suicide following sexual torture by
another inmate. In August another inmate tested positive for pregnancy, and it was discovered that the janitor was the inmates' baby's father. In June 2000, 14 underage rescued sex workers fled the government shelter in Mumbai, citing poor conditions and
"inhuman treatment." In August 2000, the Mumbai High Court instructed the Maharashtra government to improve conditions in its rescue homes.

Some NGOs are very knowledgeable about the trafficking situation in the brothel areas
such as Kamathipura, and can identify traffickers and the locations of girls being held
captive by brothel owners. However, most of these NGOs are reluctant to trust the police with this information due to the past conduct of police in brothel raids and the likelihood that many trafficking victims would be arrested and revictimized rather than
assisted by such raids. Cooperation among NGOs in sharing information and assessing
the magnitude and scope of the trafficking problem in Mumbai has not been significant
to date, although it continues to improve. Some Mumbai NGOs have worked aggressively
to sensitize, train, and create awareness of trafficking among local authorities. The NGO
Prerana, which has been working closely with government officials, is an example. During 2000 a Prerana pilot program trained employees of a large Maharashtra government
enterprise to identify and assist trafficking victims during their daily bus commute; Prerana also has enlisted the assistance of state police, who help train the workers. Conversely, other NGOs working to rescue trafficked women and girls from forced sexual
exploitation report that complaint-based police rescues are quite effective. These are focused attempts to rescue a small number of women and girls using specific information
about the victims locations, names and appearances, information; police responses in
such cases frequently have resulted in the rescue of the women and girls involved.

Similar efforts to improve NGO coordination are being made in Calcutta, where 10 NGOs
meet monthly as part of the Action Against Trafficking and Sexual Exploitation of Children (AATSEC) forum. Every 3 months the group attempts to meet with its Bangladeshi
and Nepalese counterparts. Calcutta NGOs such as Sanlaap also are seeking to build
stronger working relationships with local police. As a result of this coordination, Sanlaap
has built stronger working relationships with police and other law enforcement officials
in Calcutta. It has organized and sponsored meetings between representatives of the sex

workers and police to discuss such issues as violence against women and trafficking. The seminars have helped sensitize police to the fact that many of the sex workers are the victims of organized traffickers. Sanlaap is usually the first organization Calcutta police turn to when they have rescued a trafficked sex worker. The NGO has been allowed to place a counselor at the West Bengal Remand Home for Women, where rescued trafficking victims are housed. It also has been permitted to place counselors in police stations within Calcutta's red light district and has convinced the courts to release young trafficking victims into its custody, instead of sending them to the remand home. Training and informational meetings have taken place under the AATSEC forum, which works with groups in Nepal and Bangladesh. The NHRC asked the committee that oversees the Hajj (pilgrimage) to require individual passports for children instead of allowing them to be included on that of their escort, in order to reduce trafficking of children. NHRC also advised the Government of West Bengal to make efforts to educate Muslims about child trafficking.

Notes and Questions

1. In the 2001 State Department Report reproduced above, it is clear that India has a serious problem with sex trafficking and the commercial sexual exploitation of minors. Yet this phenomenon often does not feature in popular perceptions of modern India. What sort of diplomatic initiatives might lead to improvement in this area? Or is the Indian government is to some degree powerless to intervene? Does it seem that this problem has tended to be associated in the public mind with Southeast Asia and not with India? Why should that be?

2. It is clear that Indian NGOs are far more effective in and committed to bringing attention to the issue of sex trafficking than any arm of the Indian state. Is it because the Indian government turns a blind eye to trafficking, or are the NGOs simply more equipped to investigate such issues?

The Human Rights Watch report that follows describes a well established and traditional route of transmission for young Nepali girls into the brothels of India, particularly those in Bombay. Young Nepali prostitutes, living in slave-like conditions, occupy a niche in India's huge brothel sex industry. Consider what factors make young girls in this Nepal-India link so vulnerable to sex trafficking.

Human Rights Watch, *Rape for Profit: Trafficking of Nepali Girls and Women to India's Brothels*

(1995) *available at* http://www.hrw.org/legacy/reports/1995/India.htm

I. Introduction

At least hundreds of thousands, and probably more than a million women and children are employed in Indian brothels. Many are victims of the increasingly widespread practice of trafficking in persons across international borders. In India, a large percentage of the victims are women and girls from Nepal. This report focuses on the trafficking of girls and women from Nepal to brothels in Bombay, where nongovernmental organizations say they comprise up to half of the city's estimated 100,000 brothel workers. Twenty percent of Bombay's brothel population is thought to be girls under the age of eighteen, and half of that population may be infected with the human immunodeficiency virus (HIV).

Trafficking victims in India are subjected to conditions tantamount to slavery and to serious physical abuse. Held in debt bondage for years at a time, they are raped and subjected to other forms of torture, to severe beatings, exposure to AIDS, and arbitrary imprisonment. Many are young women from remote hill villages and poor border communities of Nepal who are lured from their villages by local recruiters, relatives or neighbors promising jobs or marriage, and sold for amounts as small as Nepali Rs.200 [$4.00] to brokers who deliver them to brothel owners in India for anywhere from Rs.15,000 to Rs.40,000 [$500–$1,333]. This purchase price, plus interest (reported to be ten percent of the total), becomes the "debt" that the women must work to pay off—a process that can stretch on indefinitely. Only the brothel owner knows the terms of the debt, and most women have no idea how much they owe or the terms for repayment. Brothels are tightly controlled, and the girls are under constant surveillance. Escape is virtually impossible. Owners use threats and severe beatings to keep inmates in line. In addition, women fear capture by other brothel agents and arrest by the police if they are found on the streets; some of these police are the brothel owner's best clients. Many of the girls and women are brought to India as virgins; many return to Nepal with the HIV virus.

Both the Indian and Nepali governments are complicit in the abuses suffered by trafficking victims. These abuses are not only violations of internationally recognized human rights but are specifically prohibited under the domestic laws of both countries. The willingness of Indian and Nepali government officials to tolerate, and, in some cases, participate in the burgeoning flesh trade exacerbates abuse. Although human rights organizations in Nepal have reported extensively on the forced trafficking of Nepali girls to Indian brothels, and sensationalist coverage of trafficking issues is a regular feature of the local press, the great majority of cases are never publicized, and even when traffickers have been identified, there have been few arrests and fewer prosecutions.

In India, police and local officials patronize brothels and protect brothel owners and traffickers. Brothel owners pay protection money and bribes to the police to prevent raids and to bail out under-age girls who are arrested. Police who frequent brothels as clients sometimes seek out under-age girls and return later to arrest them—a way of extorting bigger bribes. Girls and women who complain to the police about rape or abduction, or those who are arrested in raids or for vagrancy, are held in "protective custody"—a form of detention. Corrupt authorities reportedly allow brothel owners to buy back detainees.

In Nepal, border police are also bribed to allow traffickers to transport girls to India. In many districts, traffickers exploit political connections to avoid arrest and prosecution. On return to Nepal, the few women who escape the brothels and appeal to the police for help, or who are returned by the Indian police, are shuttled from one police station to another as they make their way back to their home districts. Some remain in police detention for weeks until their guardians come and collect them. Women who have managed to survive the system of debt bondage frequently become recruiters to fulfill their owners' requirement that they find another girl to take their place. If women who return home have managed to earn money, they are more easily accepted back into their communities, and may eventually marry. Those who escape the brothels before they have paid off their debts, who return without money, or who are sick and cannot work, are shunned by their families and communities. Many will return to India.

Existing laws in both countries have had virtually no effect on curbing trafficking. Poor training, corruption and the lack of political will among senior government officials on both sides of the border means that the laws go unenforced. Officials also try to evade responsibility for the problem by categorizing trafficking as purely a social problem. Lack of transborder cooperation between India and Nepal compounds the problem. Apathy on the part of both governments, the highly organized nature of trafficking networks, police corruption and the patronage of influential government officials means virtual impunity for traffickers.

....

II. Political and Economic Background

....

Economic Factors

The flourishing trade in Nepali women and girls in India must be understood in the context of economic conditions in both countries. Nepal's extreme poverty makes recruiting in its rural villages easy and profitable. Because of its economic dependence on India and the political ties between the powerful Nepali Congress Party and the Indian government the previous government of Nepal was inhibited from regulating the border or actively combating cross-border crime unless the Indian government also committed itself to stemming demand by enforcing anti-trafficking laws.

....

Border towns on both sides are bustling markets, catering to residents from both countries seeking jobs and bargains. They also provide a natural market for smuggling and prostitution, serving as a nexus for brokers and agents who take advantage of the crowds of anonymous travelers, the guest lodges, and the easy access to transportation.

A 1950 treaty with Nepal provided for free passage and trade across the Nepal/India border. Article 7 of the treaty reads:

> The Government of India and Nepal agree to grant, on a reciprocal basis, to the nationals of one country in the territories of the other the same privileges in the matters of residence, ownership of property, participation in trade and commerce, movement and other privileges of a similar nature.

Successive governments of Nepal expressed dissatisfaction with the treaty several times, but although either country could terminate the treaty with a year's notice, India has not wished to lose the privileges it enjoys, and Nepal cannot afford the consequences of a deterioration in its trade relationship with India. On February 9, 1995, India announced that it was ready to hold talks with Nepal's new government on amending the forty-five-year-old treaty.

The effect of the open border policy on the prevention of trafficking of women is clear. No passports, visas or residence permits are required for nationals traveling between India and Nepal. Because people pass freely between the two countries for work, shopping and business (according to Nepali police, up to 100,000 people per day through one popular border post), it is extremely difficult for border police to check illegal activity. Traffickers and their victims move easily across the border, and the onus is on individual police officers to stop and question suspicious-looking travellers. The problem is compounded by consistent reports of police corruption on both sides of the border.

In India's red-light districts, the demand for Nepali girls, especially virgins with fair skin and Mongolian features, continues to increase. It is impossible to say how many girls and women are employed in the sex industry in India or what percentage of the total is from

Nepal. Estimates have been based largely on the numbers of women employed by broth-els in urban areas, but prostitution exists in every city and town in India and in many vil-lages, and statistics vary enormously. Dr. I.S. Gilada, general secretary of the Indian Health Organization (IHO), estimated in various studies conducted between 1985 and 1994 that there were between 70,000 and 100,000 prostitutes in Bombay, 100,000 in Calcutta, 40,000 in Delhi, 40,000 in Pune and 13,000 in Nagpur. Based on his statistics, Nepali social work-ers estimate the number of Nepali girls and women now working in Indian brothels at about 200,000 and believe that between 5,000 and 7,000 new Nepalis end up in Indian brothels every year. The Indian Council of Medical Research estimates the total number of prostitutes in India at about one million. By contrast, the Bharatiya Patita Udhar Sabha (Indian Association for the Rescue of Fallen Women), a voluntary organization dedicated to the welfare of the country's sex workers, estimates that in 1992 there were more than 8 million brothel workers in India and another 7.5 million call girls. There is simply no way to verify these statistics, but it is clear the percentage of Nepali girls in Indian brothels is very high, that their numbers appear to be increasing, and that the average age at which they are recruited is significantly lower than it was ten years ago, dropping from fourteen to sixteen years in the 1980s to ten to fourteen years in 1994. Dr. Gilada of IHO told our researcher that the youngest girl he had seen in a Bombay brothel was nine years old.

. . . .

Although tourism is an important industry in both countries, and sex tourism ap-pears to be on the increase in India, tourism is less a factor in the sex industry than local demand. All of the women Human Rights Watch/Asia interviewed reported that most of their customers were Indian. Some were also Nepali, although in at least one case Nepali customers were discouraged, for fear they would help Nepali girls escape.

Brothels are big business. Despite expenses incurred in employing a network of agents to recruit new workers in Nepal (some procurers are reportedly paid up to Indian Rs.6,000 [about $200] per trip) and protection money that is paid weekly to police and local crime bosses (said to total Rs.200 [$6.60] per brothel inmate per week), even the cheapest of broth-els can turn a substantial profit, generally collecting from Rs.50–Rs.100 [$1.66–$3.33] per client, with much more for special services. A brothel may employ anywhere from four to fifty workers, and an inmate may serve more than fifteen clients a day, on an av-erage of twenty-six to twenty-eight days a month. The brothel owners generally provide no more than two meals a day and most workers are allowed to keep only the tips from their clients, Rs 2 to 5 (fifteen cents or less) per man. With these meager resources, they must cover their own expenses for food, clothing, and personal effects. The cost of med-ical care is typically paid by the owner, and then added to a inmate's "debt"—sometimes with interest. The owner, who frequently owns more than one brothel, clearly stands to make a profit, but agents, local police and others involved in the industry also benefit. As one former prostitute told Human Rights Watch/Asia, "Police, doctors, *dalals* (pimps), they are all fed by the brothels."

III. Patterns of Abuse

There are two distinct patterns to the trafficking of girls and women from Nepal. The best known and oldest involves the enticement of mainly Tamang girls from hill districts where the flesh trade has become an almost traditional source of income. But the inci-dence of forced trafficking from other parts of Nepal is also on the rise. Poor migrant women and children whose families have moved to Nepal's urban areas in search of em-ployment are the principal victims. These girls and women come from all castes and eth-nic groups. Human Rights Watch/Asia visited Nepal and interviewed women from several areas of Nepal who had been trafficked to India and had returned. In all cases, families, neighbors and friends play an active role in forced trafficking by concocting fictitious marriage and job offers, contacting recruiters and brokers, or simply luring girls away from home on outings or errands, kidnapping and selling them. Regardless of the victims' origins, their reports of abuse in Indian brothels are remarkably consistent.

The average age of the thousands of Nepali girls recruited every year for prostitution in brothels in India has reportedly dropped in the past decade from fourteen to sixteen years in the 1980s, to ten to fourteen in 1991, despite new laws promulgated in both countries in 1986 designed to stem trafficking and child prostitution. Police in areas with a high incidence of trafficking state that the average age of new trafficking victims is about thirteen. However, trafficking victims are frequently coached by captors to conceal their true ages. Girls forced into prostitution in Bombay's brothels may remain trapped in the brothel system for more than ten years, during which time they may be sold from one brothel to another many times.

. . . .

The Path to Bombay

The Nepali girls and women who were interviewed by Human Rights Watch/Asia were forcibly trafficked into India. They did not work as prostitutes voluntarily but were held in conditions tantamount to slavery. Promises of jobs and marriage are common techniques by which recruiters entice their victims to leave home. But other, more overtly coercive tactics such as kidnapping are also reported. Girls who are already in debt bondage in other industries, particularly carpet factories, are particularly vulnerable.

The Traffickers

Traffickers are most typically men in their twenties or thirties or women in their thirties and forties who have traveled the route to the city several times and know the hotels to stay in and the brokers to contact. Traffickers frequently work in groups of two or more. Male and female traffickers are sometimes referred to as *dalals and dalalis*, (commission agents) who are either employed by a brothel owner directly, or operate more or less independently. Professional agents who recruit for the bigger brothels reportedly may be paid up to Rs.6,000 [$200] per girl. But most traffickers are small-time, local recruiters who earn considerably less. In either case, to stay in business they need the patronage of local bosses and the protection afforded by bribes to the police.

. . . .

Girls are recruited in a number of ways. Village girls and their families are often deceived by smartly dressed young men who arrive in the village claiming to have come from Kathmandu and offering marriage and all the comforts of modern urban life. They go through a local ceremony and leave the village never to be seen again. The girls end up in Indian brothels.

Sometimes older men promise the girls employment in the city. Another avenue is through distant relatives or friends who pretend to arrange a marriage with relatives or friends in another village, but instead abduct the girl and send her to India. Sometimes a trusted individual abducts the girl on the pretext of educating her in India.

. . . .

Local women who have returned from India are also employed as recruiters. These women are exceptionally well-placed to identify potential trafficking victims because they already know the local girls and their families.

Women who are already in the sex trade and have graduated to the level of brothel keepers, managers or even owners travel through the villages of their own and neighboring districts in search of young girls.

....

Perhaps the most pernicious and lamentable examples in this category are those women who are themselves forced into prostitution and who have been told by their brothel keepers that the only way they can procure their release is by furnishing a substitute. At any given time, several of these women travel to their villages in the hope of cajoling a younger female relative, a friend or just another village woman to accompany them. Most often they are successful.... and return with another victim, in lieu of themselves. However, once free they do not make an exit from the prostitution market, they merely end up working as.... [independent] prostitutes and finally hope to set up their own little shop with five women working under them.

....

In the Brothels

Nepali women in India's red-light areas remain largely segregated in brothels located in what are known to their Indian counterparts and their customers as "Nepali *kothas*" or compounds. The concentrations of Nepalis vary from city to city, but appear to be highest in the Bombay neighborhood of Kamathipura. Brothels vary by size, physical configuration, ethnicity of sex workers, and price. But in all cases, movement outside the brothels is strictly controlled, and inmates are subjected to both psychological and physical abuse. The cheapest brothels, nothing more than dark, claustrophobic rooms with cloth dividers hung between the beds, are known among Nepalis as "pillow houses." About one-fifth of all Bombay's brothel workers, or approximately 20,000 women, work in squalid brothels like these on numbered lanes (or *gallis*) in Kamathipura. Certain lanes, like the 11th and the 13th, are known particularly as Nepali gallis. Many customers seek out Nepali prostitutes specifically, because of their looks and their exotic reputations.

....

Debt Bondage

....

Every Nepali girl or woman with whom we spoke said that the brothel owner or manager forced her to work by invoking her indebtedness. This supposed debt, and the threats and beatings that accompanied it, were the major obstacles between her and the possibility of freedom. For most of the women interviewed, the debt was the amount of money the brothel owner said she paid a broker when the girl was purchased, plus the costs of medical care and protection money or payoffs to police and local thugs. Men interviewed in Nepal who were familiar with the brothel system said the girls were also charged 10 percent interest on their purchase price.

....

Illegal Confinement

There are other aspects of the work in brothels which reinforce its non-voluntary nature. One of these is illegal confinement. Debt bondage is enforced by the near total confinement of the women and girls to the brothel premises. Women and girls are generally not allowed to leave the brothel or its immediate surroundings without escorts and are threatened with a range of consequences, including arrest by the Indian police or capture by other brothel owners, should they attempt to do so. The women and girls we interviewed explained that they would be beaten severely if they tried to escape.

With few exceptions, the Nepali women are unable to communicate with anyone outside of the brothel and some are even forbidden to take Nepali clients out of fear that the latter might be more likely to help the women escape. Even conversation with customers is sometimes forbidden.

....

Fear of beatings, arrest or recapture by other brothel agents keeps many girls from trying to escape. Devi stated that the brothel had a window so that all the girls could be observed by the management. When she was seen trying to escape, she was beaten. Whenever there was a police raid the owner would hide all the girls; those who tried to come out would be beaten. Devi said that only newcomers tried to run away; the older ones would not try to escape. "Maybe they know that those who run away would be sold to another brothel by men on the street, so they don't run." The girls were also afraid of the police. In September or October 1993, a girl who had escaped was taken into custody and raped by the police. The next day the police brought her back to the brothel and told the owner to bring out all the new girls and leave only the "licensed" ones. The owner gave the police Rs.10,000 [$333,] and they went away.

....

IV. The Role of the Nepali and Indian Governments

Despite the fact that both Nepal and India have numerous laws criminalizing trafficking and prescribing severe penalties for abusers, trafficking in women and girls flourishes between the two countries. Human Rights Watch/Asia's investigation reveals the involvement of police and other government officials at various points along the trafficking routes, but there has been little effort on the part of either government to investigate charges of official complicity or to punish those responsible.

Police demand bribes as payment for not arresting traffickers and brothel owners, or are themselves involved in trafficking. Government officials protect traffickers who are politically influential.

Police Corruption and Complicity

The Bharatiya Patita Udhar Sabha, in its letter to the Home Minister in 1993, charged that police regularly extorted large sums of money in red-light areas in the name of protection—up to Rs. 26,000 [$866] per day in Delhi alone. The organization president, Khairati Lal Bhola, complained that out of the Rs.55 [$1.83] paid by a customer in one of the city's better brothels, Rs.10 [.33] went to the police. On a daily basis, he charged, the local police station received cuts according to rank: a constable could expect Rs.25 [$.83], a head constable received Rs.40 [$1.33], and an Assistant Sub-Inspector (ASI) received Rs.80 to Rs.100 [$2.66–$3.33]. The groups charged that the Station House Officer (SHO) received Rs.500 [$16.66] per month, and the district special branch police, which addresses special categories of crimes, collected monthly payments of about Rs.300 [$10] per *kotha* [brothel compound] of ten girls, and Rs.500 [$16.66] for larger kothas.

In the case of recently trafficked girls and women, the organization charged that police were involved in the staged process called "registering" the victims. In this process, the madam would notify the police of the arrival of a new victim in her establishment and pay a bribe for their silence. The madam routinely paid between Rs.5000 and Rs.25,000

[$166–$833] to the police station on scale with her purchase price. In the case of a minor, the police took their bribe from the madam, kept the girl for a day in lock-up, and produced her in court the next day along with a falsified First Information Report (FIR) attesting to her adult status, thereby protecting the brothel owner from any future charges related to the prostitution of a minor. The released minor girl, newly registered with the authorities as twenty-one years of age or older, would be handed back to the madam. For this service, the madam paid the police Rs. 500 to Rs. 1000. [$16–$33] Sometimes the girl was given falsified papers and brought before the magistrate on a trumped-up charge of seduction in a public place, and handed back to the madam on payment of a fine of about Rs. 1000 [$33] for her release. Thus, for a fee, the madam is assured of police collusion in keeping the trafficking victim captive, while the performance of a few legal routines protects the police from complaints of negligence.

. . . .

Police Raids in India

Activists and trafficked women told Human Right Watch/Asia that although police harassment of commercial sex workers in Bombay was commonplace, the Bombay police rarely undertook formal raids or "rescues" in the city's red-light districts. Activist Preeti Pai Patkar said that when these raids did occur, they appeared to be made to fulfil police quotas or to carry out political vendettas. She thought international pressure also sometimes led to raids, but that on the whole women in prostitution were viewed as criminals by the police and by society at large and were not thought worthy of extra rescue efforts.

Police in Bombay maintained that they did conduct regular raids on brothels, although high-level criminal cases took precedence. But most law enforcement against prostitution appears to be aimed at the arrest of individual sex workers for solicitation and other public offenses, rather than against traffickers, brothels owners or pimps....

Activists who work with women in prostitution, as well as the brothel inmates interviewed by Human Rights Watch/Asia charged that local policemen regularly took advantage of their power to frequent the kothas as customers....

The Role of the Nepali Police

The Nepali police are also complicit in the trafficking of Nepali girls and women to Indian brothels. Villagers and officials in Nuwakot District told Human Rights Watch/Asia that traffickers routinely pay protection money to local police and Nepali politicians as "a sort of commission" to prevent arrests and prosecutions. "If a trafficker ends up in prison it means he or she hasn't paid off the police," one villager observed. A journalist who has researched trafficking patterns in Nepal told Human Rights Watch/Asia:

[E]very point of the border, the police come if they suspect trafficking. But they don't try to arrest, they just take bribes. You can see them go down through the bus collecting money. It's very visible."

. . . .

The Dangers of Dissent

The trafficking network is vast, reaching from India's largest cities to Nepal's most remote villages, yet the brothel owners and managers in Bombay, the brokers, the agents and the victims are frequently from the same villages and communities. Local residents in Nepal's hill villages who oppose trafficking said they were afraid of the criminal gangs that operate in their areas. The few individuals who were outspoken in their opposition complained that they were shunned and harassed by their neighbors.

One Nuwakot resident told Human Rights Watch/Asia that almost every household in his village had daughters in India, and some had three or four. In 1993 he said he had tried to start an educational campaign against trafficking, but his neighbors got angry. He gave up when he found he could not interest local police or politicians in the project. He believes the trafficking network in Nuwakot operates with police complicity.

People who protest trafficking are in the minority. It is very difficult to fight because everyone is unified—all are involved in trafficking in one way or another. The families are profiting, so no one will talk.

....

Villagers hate individuals, government agencies and nongovernmental organisations that campaign for the abolition of prostitution and girl trafficking. These villagers take the individuals and social organisations as their enemies who are trying to deprive them of a livelihood. They, in connivance with the agents, are reported to have made attempts on the lives of some social workers working for the abolition of trafficking and have often warned them not to create any obstacles to their activities.

....

V. The Applicable Law

There is no shortage of applicable law addressing trafficking in women and other abuses typical of the brothel industry. Both international and domestic laws prohibit slavery and all similar practices, including the sale of persons, forced labor and debt bondage. There are also specific prohibitions against the trafficking of adults and children for prostitution and other forms of sexual exploitation. Among those fundamental human rights guaranteed by international law but frequently denied trafficking victims are state protection against arbitrary detention, torture, including sexual assault and rape, and other cruel, inhuman or degrading treatment. International law obligates the state to protect individuals against such abuse, even when it is committed by a private actor. Such crimes are also prohibited under Indian and Nepali law. The problem lies in enforcement, which is rare and inconsistent, and in the active perpetuation of trafficking-related abuse by corrupt and complicit officials.

....

India's Laws

Trafficking in human beings and the abuses associated with it are also explicitly prohibited under a wide range of India's domestic laws, including the Indian constitution, specific anti-trafficking acts, the Indian penal code, and in state and local ordinances.

The Indian constitution specifically prohibits trafficking in persons. Article 23, in the fundamental rights section of the constitution, states, "traffic in human beings ... and other similar forms of forced labour are prohibited." Article 39 guarantees equal treatment of men and women and obligates the state to ensure "that the health and strength of workers, men and women ... and children are not abused ... and that children and youth are protected against exploitation ..." Article 42 provides protection against inhumane working conditions.

....

Notes and Questions

1. The 2003 film, *The Day My God Died*, made clear that the situation of Nepali girls and women in Indian brothels had scarcely improved at all in the ten years since the publication of this Human Rights Watch report. The film depicted the scale and scope of the brothel sex problem in Bombay, the well known routes of Nepal-India trafficking, the issue of young girls in the industry, and the profound indifference of officials. See the film's website, at http://thedaymygoddied.com/. As with countries like Thailand, the international image of India is drastically out of sync with what we read about official indifference to, and complicity with, child sex slavery in Indian brothels. To what extent is India guilty of gross violations of human rights here? Is the problem genuinely intractable, or is poverty an excuse for continued exploitation?

2. What are the common elements of government support for the child sex industry in both Southeast Asia and South Asia? How important is the role played by tradition, as opposed to globalization and modernization? The report notes that Nepali villagers are opposed to the activities of NGOs who work to free the girls from trafficking. Does this statement contradict the widely held view that families are unaware of the fates met by their daughters when they leave the village to seek work in Indian cities?

3. The process of intimidation that new entrants to brothel sex undergo seems to have common features all over the world. How are girls led to accept their condition in the brothels?

D. Sex Trafficking in Eastern Europe

A striking feature of sex trafficking in general and child sex trafficking in particular, is that the trafficking networks are busy all over the world, irrespective of cultural context. In Eastern Europe, teenagers are especially vulnerable to being forced into the sex trade. The techniques of deception and threat used in Europe are similar to those found in the readings about Southeast and South Asia

ECPAT European Law Enforcement Group, *Joint East West Research on Trafficking in Children for Sexual Purposes in Europe: The Sending Countries*

(Muireann O'Briain et al. eds., 2004) *available at* http://www.childcentre.info/projects/traffickin/dbaFile11169.pdf

Economic and Political Problems

There are many similarities between the Eastern European project countries in terms of their political, social and economic situations, all of which affect the issue of trafficking in children for sexual purposes. In every country poverty and unemployment have seriously increased in the last ten years, due to the political changes in the region, and the resulting economic instability. The statistics given in the country reports portray very difficult conditions in which young people are growing up today. In Albania, 18% of the population of working age was unemployed in 1999, and unemployment was as high as 60% among those under the age of 34. In Belarus, at the beginning of 2001, more than 30,000 women in the age range of 14 to 25 were unemployed. The Estonian report produced similar statistics, with an unemployment rate in 2002 of 10.3%, which rose to 22.5% among women in the age range of 15 to 24. In Moldova, more than half the population lives below the poverty level, and young people represent one-third of those unemployed. Economic collapse in Romania reduced 44% of the population to poverty by the year 2000, whereas it had been at only 7% in 1989. At the beginning of this century, some 30% of Russians were considered to live in poverty, while in Ukraine the official poverty rate is 27%, or almost 13 million people.

Some countries have endured particular problems, such as Albania which received an influx of more than 600,000 displaced persons from Kosovo during the late 1990s. Belarus was reported to have received an influx of up to 100,000 illegal migrants and refugees after the fall of the 'Iron Curtain', mostly from Commonwealth of Independent States (CIS) countries, not as a result of war, but because of its perceived stability. The Czech Republic's closeness to Germany and Austria, and the differences in economic purchasing power between those countries, as well as the fact that prostitution is not regulated in the Czech Republic, led to an explosion of prostitution along a border 'brothel belt' that runs for hundreds of kilometres. Estonia found itself in a similar situation, due to its proximity to the rich Scandinavian countries. In Estonia, drug trafficking, prostitution and excise fraud are seen as the main sources of organised crime today. The Russia and Ukraine reports say that prostitution began to flourish in their countries, not only because of external factors, but because of a general liberalisation of attitudes, which encouraged the growth of a highly lucrative domestic industry attracting criminal financial involvement. An IOM report was quoted in respect of Moldova to the effect that there are at least 300 brothels in Chisinau, most of them disguised as saunas and bathhouses. Prostitution is also widespread at hotels and in the areas near train and bus stations in Moldova.

. . . .

Children at Risk

The main risk group are teenagers, from 13 to 18 years of age, the majority of those trafficked being in the age group of 15 to 17 years. When poverty affects families, many social problems arise that have adverse effects on young people. The reports mention alcoholism, single-parent families, drug abuse, sexual abuse and domestic violence as alienating factors. The Moldova report also mentions risk where families are broken up because one or both parents have gone abroad to work. It is reported that some 200,000 children are left without adequate supervision in Moldova. Homeless children are also noted as a feature of post-Soviet Russia. Official figures from the General Office of the Public Prosecutor show that there are 2 to 2.5 million people homeless in Russia, but other estimates quoted in the report put the figure at 3 to 4 million. The Ukraine report says that homelessness is a serious problem and that prostitution is widespread among homeless children. Children in institutions do not escape these social problems; their situation is especially difficult, as they are often neither safe within the institution, nor after they leave it. The Czech report points to runaways from children's homes as a particular risk group, having already experienced sexual and physical violence while in the care of the state. The Russian report mentions that staff of some children's homes have been suspected of selling newborn babies, and of helping to recruit children for sexual exploitation.

Children born into or living in situations of social and economic poverty tend to drop out of school, to leave home and live on the streets, to migrate from rural areas to towns and cities. Even children who find work are at risk of exploitation because of their lack of education. Figures published in 1998 in Albania show that 38% of children of school-going age drop out of school in order to work; nearly 50,000 children under 18 years of age are working either full-time or part-time. Street children in the city of Tirana alone number more than 800. Roma children are mentioned as a particular risk group in the reports for Albania, the Czech Republic, and Romania, because their social grouping is marginalised within the societies in those countries. Roma children rarely attend school and therefore have very high levels of illiteracy.

The Czech Republic report says that drug problems, violence and theft have increased in the Roma communities, and that since the 1990s, prostitution among the Roma has become a way of making fast money, even though traditionally prostitution would be unacceptable in those communities. Nowadays, however, it is not unusual to see Roma minor girls being prostituted, and their presence is frequently justified on the basis of an earlier sexual maturity among girls in their communities. The Ukraine report shows that of the minors involved in prostitution in Ukraine, over 74% are from single-parent families, and over 20% are from residential institutions.

. . . .

In Russia, a specific category of 'at-risk' young people are minor girls working as models and participating in beauty contests or trying to get into show business. Modeling is a prestigious and highly paid job in the Russian Federation, and there are more than 2,500 agencies seeking talent. Often these agencies promise jobs and work abroad to young people, but in reality the young people end up trafficked for sexual exploitation. The Russian report also refers to refugee children from regions where there are local wars as being at particular risk of becoming victims of trafficking. Even children with an education can become victims. In the Ukraine and Moldova, for example, it is not unusual for students to prostitute themselves in order to be able to pay for their studies, or for them to migrate for study or to earn money for their studies. Children, once trafficked, run the risk of being re-trafficked, for example when reintegration in a stable family is not possible after their return. Several reports refer to the continuing vulnerability of victims in the absence of adequate reintegration programmes.

. . . .

Migration

The desire of young people to change their future by migrating and working abroad is another risk factor. Many children are not aware of their rights, lack information and do not know the legal procedures for travelling abroad, and the risks related to migration. The search for adventure, idealised notions about living abroad, and success stories from those who return from abroad encourage risk-taking. Very importantly, the reports note the risks to children who may have migrated normally with their families or voluntarily on their own, but who end up in foreign countries without any protections, and so become extremely vulnerable to exploitation and trafficking. They get involved in petty crime and move into prostitution as a survival strategy, or because they are found by someone who will exploit them. Many people, and especially young people, are migrating because of the lack of opportunities for them in their own countries. The fall of the 'Iron Curtain' and the links with countries of the European Union have opened up both borders and travel opportunities, and at the same time the increasing gap between rich and poor, the growth of international organised crime, and corruption, provide their own incentives or opportunities. The Czech Republic, Estonia and Russia have experienced migration both into and out of the country to service the sex industry. The Czech Republic report mentions the migration of Roma families to the Republic from Slovakia, who, when unable to survive, turn to prostitution and the selling of family members. Also young boys migrate to the Czech Republic from Slovakia, Ukraine, Romania and Russia, many of them runaways from children's homes in those countries. They end up in Prague and other cities of the Republic, and turn to homosexual prostitution as a survival strategy. Adults from Ukraine, Belarus and Russia have been found trafficked to Estonia, and there was one case of a Latvian minor found in Estonia. The Russian report mentions boys at risk of trafficking within Russia, and of being trafficked within the CIS countries, but not being trafficked outside of Eastern Europe.

....

The Trafficking Chain

The chain seems to be the same, whether the victims are adults or minors. Girls who have been trafficked mostly end up in prostitution. Their use in the making of pornography is also common. But children are not only trafficked for sexual purposes. The younger ones especially are used for begging and manual labour, such as agricultural work. Children are also used in criminal gangs for stealing and drug peddling. Trafficking for organ transplantation was mentioned by some countries, but they had no evidence on any such cases.

Minors are often lured into a trafficking operation with their apparent consent, but they will have been misled about the job they will do, and the working conditions. Recruiters offer jobs abroad for which no particular qualifications are needed to minors, such as modelling, serving in bars or restaurants, childminding, dancing. Children are frequently misled with offers to study abroad or to marry a foreigner.

Recruiters are usually acquaintances of the victims and are people they trust. The Internet is also used to lure youngsters. Recruitment by advertisements in magazines and newspapers seems to be less frequent. Children's homes can be fertile recruiting grounds for traffickers. The 'loverboy' syndrome is another ruse whereby girls are seduced first and then sexually exploited and coerced into prostitution. Even the sale of children, by parents or relatives, is common. Simple abduction of a minor rarely happens.

....

Transportation can be public or private (cars, trains, buses), but is rarely by plane, because of the stricter checks at airports. The travel will be made to look as normal and 'legal' as possible, using stolen, altered or forged documents.

> "On arrival in the destination country, the trafficker will provide the teenager with a place to live, clothes, hair colour, condoms and a place where he/she will work. The teenager is supervised, so that on the one hand he/she does not keep any of the money, and on the other hand to protect him/her from abuse by other pimps. If he/she does not obey, physical and mental cruelty is used: he/she is beaten, raped, threatened, or witnesses the beatings of others to terrify him/her. There is also information on the involvement of minor girls in prostitution on the highways between Russia and Belarus: "Many girls stand on the road.... There are certain parts of the roads where adults in cars show up to choose a girl they want. In certain places the girls work for a female pimp who deals with the clients and handles the money". (Country report Belarus)

In a pattern that is common in these reports, money and identity papers are taken from the victims. They are brought to a brothel or an apartment, where they are kept locked up or under close supervision. Victims will first have to pay back the travel and other expenses, with huge interest, to the traffickers. The money they earn from their sexual encounters is taken by the pimp. Sometimes victims are even forced to pay for their living expenses, which are added on to their debts. After the debt is repaid, victims can be re-sold to another pimp, and the same cycle starts all over. Children work under harsh circumstances, working many hours, servicing many clients, and living in difficult conditions. They run serious risks of sexually transmitted diseases and HIV infections, as well as pregnancy and physical abuse from clients. Violence is used as a means of intimidation. Drug and alcohol dependence are commonly used to ensure compliance.

Moldova

The experts consulted for the research believe that the younger minors are recruited for begging, and that older children are recruited for sexual exploitation, including the making of pornography. Other occupations, such as work in agriculture and animal husbandry in Ukraine are also mentioned. It is mostly girls who are recruited for sexual exploitation, but cases of boys are also known. In many cases, the children recruited initially for begging are also exploited sexually. Minors are recruited both by individuals and by legal entities. The individuals are usually people who have been abroad, have established certain contacts and have returned home to recruit girls. Former pimps blackmail earlier victims to involve them in this activity, but some of the girls start their own businesses. The legal entities are usually officially registered in Moldova (tourism agencies, employment agencies, modelling agencies, marriage agencies). Girls are recruited through advertisements that promise them a career as dancers, hotel workers or tourism workers abroad, or work as waitresses, housekeepers, or child-minders. Usually the girls agree to pay the cost of the transport to their destination from their anticipated salary: US$800–$1000. According to Save the Children, Moldova, children are kidnapped or taken under false pretences from their parents by members of the Roma community, and trafficked to Russia (Moscow, St. Petersburg), Ukraine and other countries. According to the police Anti-Trafficking Unit, however, the majority of trafficked children actually leave Moldova with their own mothers. The Italian Committee of Solidarity carried out research on the family situation of minors who had gone to Italy. They discovered that in the majority of cases parents had paid US$1,000–$1,500 to send their children abroad, being deceived by the traffickers who promised highly paid jobs, and hoping that their children could build a better future. There were also cases where parents, often addicted to alcohol, had sold their own children for less than US$50.

. . . .

One of the particularities of trafficking in Moldova is the transparency of its borders. Moldavian citizens can travel to Romania or the CIS countries without a visa. In addition, a great part of the Moldavian border with Ukraine is not under the control of the Moldavian authorities, which makes for uncontrolled migration, including that of minors.

. . . .

Children enter the destination country usually in total captivity. Traffickers take their identity papers, and personal belongings; victims have no freedom to move or communicate, and are continuously threatened. The children have to refund the traffickers the expenses of the journey. Also owners who give the children things, such as food, clothes, jewellery, cosmetics, drugs, shelter, during the period of exploitation then force the minors to repay the value of the goods from their earnings. In more than half the cases mentioned in the questionnaire responses, children were reported to have been in debt to their owners for the costs of transportation. The period they had to work to pay their debts lasted from one to two years. Most of the time the children were not paid, and in all cases they were physically abused, malnourished and were subjected to sexual perversities. Their normal working periods were from 8 to 12 hours per day/night daily, serving from 6 to 10 clients. In Italy the situation of Moldovan children was reported to be much more serious in that the number of the clients per day varies from 15 to 25. Punishments were randomly imposed, if the children didn't satisfy the client, for example. The children were forbidden to speak to other people or to call their parents. If they were allowed to talk to their parents they were forced to tell them that they had a decent job.

Russia

The Russian report says that the main purpose of trafficking children abroad is sexual exploitation, but the researchers also mention begging, drug peddling and some low skilled work as occupations. Different ways of recruiting children for trafficking to foreign countries were described by the experts. Suggestions are made to young people to work abroad as dancers, child-minders, servants, etc. Offers of opportunities in show business, beauty contests, modelling schools, and work in the service industry, such as bars, were also mentioned.

The work is usually proposed to minors by people they know and trust, or by acquaintances they do not know very well. Sometimes women who make the proposals are victims of trafficking themselves, the 'second wave' of trafficking. Recruitment can also be done through advertisements. Such announcements can include marriage proposals, or meetings with a potential husband. Parents can even be involved in trafficking, for example by coming to an agreement with a purchaser, and unknowingly selling their child to traffickers. Another well-known way of recruiting is by making proposals for exchange and educational programmes to school pupils. Minors who are trafficked within the country are often offered work in a big city, with the promise of good pay and independence by people they know, or older adolescents. It is not difficult to move children within Russia or the CIS countries, and mostly the child leaves voluntarily. Minors are brought to large cities, where it is easier to 'hide' them. Once in the city these children are exploited in pornographic films or other kinds of sexual acts. Experts mentioned the use of narcotics to remove a minor's inhibitions, and the use of violence.

. . . .

Removing children abroad can be done in a number of ways. Forged passports are made most often for girls under 14 years of age. The experts say that falsification of documents in Russia is widespread and does not entail any special difficulties. A forged passport for a 14-year-old girl can be made for a bribe of US$800. Minors younger than 14 years of age are recorded on their parent's passport. However, under the age of six, the child's photo is not attached to passport. Therefore it is easy to remove a child under six.

. . . .

Ukraine

According to the Ukrainian experts, the majority of girls trafficked abroad are deceived and trafficked under the pretence of employment, marriage, adoption and prostitution. Dubious announcements about highly paid jobs abroad appear frequently in employment columns of newspapers and on the Internet. There are notices for jobs for singers and dancers in casinos, models, tutors and child-minders, nurses, housemaids and agricultural workers. Companies that publish such advertisements hardly ever check them, and the police do not have sufficient legal grounds to do so. Another widely used method of attracting minors and forcing them into prostitution are 'lonely hearts' advertisements, and marriage agencies. A lot of young Ukrainian girls dream of marrying a foreigner and living in a Western paradise. Less frequent ways of recruiting minors are through arranged or spontaneous meetings with a dealer in a bar, night club, supermarket or even in the street. Some anonymous sources say that a large number of traffickers enjoy the protection of the law enforcement agencies. A small number of trafficked girls are girls who are already prostituting themselves in Ukraine and who consciously leave Ukraine in search of more money. Two respondents mentioned kidnapping as a trafficking method.

Notes and Questions

1. Although the situation in Eastern Europe remains grave from the point of view of trafficked children, most of these countries have followed the global trend and enacted legislation specifically focused on human trafficking. Moldova is widely acknowledged to be a hub for human trafficking in Europe, and its progress is monitored with the assistance of the Organization for Security and Cooperation in Europe. See OSCE Mission to Moldova, http://www.osce.org/moldova/13429.html.

2. While the techniques of sexual slavery may be similar all over the world, the population considered most vulnerable to trafficking differs. What are the life circumstances of most Eastern European victims of sex trafficking? Does the situation in Europe seem more amenable to legislative approaches, or it the problem of essentially the same intractability as in Asia?

3. On February 1, 2008, the Council of Europe Convention on Action against Trafficking in Human Beings[16] came into force. Since the Council encompasses most of the sending and receiving countries within Europe, it is hoped that the Convention will contribute to a uniform, Europe-wide human rights approach to human trafficking. To read the text of the Convention, visit http://polis.osce.org/library/f/2715/548/CoE-POL-RPT-2715-EN-Convention%20on%20Action%20against%20Trafficking%20in%20Human%20Beings.pdf.

For an extraordinary look into how sex trafficking functions worldwide, see Siddarth Kara, Sex Trafficking: Inside the Business of Modern Slavery (2009). His chapter on trafficking networks in Moldova is especially disturbing.

E. Sex Trafficking to and within the United States

The following article by Peter Landesman caused a great outcry when it first appeared in the New York Time Magazine in 2004. Some argued that Landesman was exaggerating, sensationalizing, or that he had relied on the revelations of unreliable persons. Despite this controversy, the article provided startling evidence of the fact that the United States is a major receiving country for children of all ages, mainly arriving through Mexico. Landesman indicated that Mexican children and Eastern European adolescents were routinely brought into the United States by criminal gangs, via well established routes through Mexico. Landesman described how the trafficking networks spread their tentacles into suburban U.S. neighborhoods, holding children in squalid conditions to be exploited by adult men.

---

16. Council of Europe Convention on Action against Trafficking in Human Beings, May 16, 2005, ETS No. 197.

Peter Landesman, *The Girls Next Door*

New York Times Magazine, Jan. 25, 2004, at 30

The house at 1212 1/2 West Front Street in Plainfield, N.J., is a conventional mid-century home with slate-gray siding, white trim and Victorian lines. When I stood in front of it on a breezy day in October, I could hear the cries of children from the playground of an elementary school around the corner. American flags fluttered from porches and windows. The neighborhood is a leafy, middle-class Anytown. The house is set back off the street, near two convenience stores and a gift shop. On the door of Superior Supermarket was pasted a sign issued by the Plainfield police: "Safe neighborhoods save lives." The store's manager, who refused to tell me his name, said he never noticed anything unusual about the house, and never heard anything. But David Miranda, the young man behind the counter of Westside Convenience, told me he saw girls from the house roughly once a week. "They came in to buy candy and soda, then went back to the house," he said. The same girls rarely came twice, and they were all very young, Miranda said. They never asked for anything beyond what they were purchasing; they certainly never asked for help. Cars drove up to the house all day; nice cars, all kinds of cars. Dozens of men came and went. "But no one here knew what was really going on," Miranda said. And no one ever asked.

On a tip, the Plainfield police raided the house in February 2002, expecting to find illegal aliens working an underground brothel. What the police found were four girls between the ages of 14 and 17. They were all Mexican nationals without documentation. But they weren't prostitutes; they were sex slaves. The distinction is important: these girls weren't working for profit or a paycheck. They were captives to the traffickers and keepers who controlled their every move. "I consider myself hardened," Mark J. Kelly, now a special agent with Immigration and Customs Enforcement (the largest investigative arm of the Department of Homeland Security), told me recently. "I spent time in the Marine Corps. But seeing some of the stuff I saw, then heard about, from those girls was a difficult, eye-opening experience."

The police found a squalid, land-based equivalent of a 19th-century slave ship, with rancid, doorless bathrooms; bare, putrid mattresses; and a stash of penicillin, "morning after" pills and misoprostol, an antiulcer medication that can induce abortion. The girls were pale, exhausted and malnourished.

It turned out that 1212 1/2 West Front Street was one of what law-enforcement officials say are dozens of active stash houses and apartments in the New York metropolitan area — mirroring hundreds more in other major cities like Los Angeles, Atlanta and Chicago — where under-age girls and young women from dozens of countries are trafficked and held captive. Most of them — whether they started out in Eastern Europe or Latin America — are taken to the United States through Mexico. Some of them have been baited by promises of legitimate jobs and a better life in America; many have been abducted; others have been bought from or abandoned by their impoverished families.

Because of the porousness of the U.S.-Mexico border and the criminal networks that traverse it, the towns and cities along that border have become the main staging area in an illicit and barbaric industry, whose "products" are women and girls. On both sides of the border, they are rented out for sex for as little as 15 minutes at a time, dozens of times a day. Sometimes they are sold outright to other traffickers and sex rings, victims and experts say. These sex slaves earn no money, there is nothing voluntary about what they do and if they try to escape they are often beaten and sometimes killed.

Last September, in a speech before the United Nations General Assembly, President Bush named sex trafficking as "a special evil," a multibillion-dollar "underground of brutality and lonely fear," a global scourge alongside the AIDS epidemic. Influenced by a coalition of religious organizations, the Bush administration has pushed international action on the global sex trade. The president declared at the U.N. that "those who create these victims and profit from their suffering must be severely punished" and that "those who patronize this industry debase themselves and deepen the misery of others. And governments that tolerate this trade are tolerating a form of slavery."

Under the Trafficking Victims Protection Act of 2000 — the first U.S. law to recognize that people trafficked against their will are victims of a crime, not illegal aliens — the U.S. government rates other countries' records on human trafficking and can apply economic sanctions on those that aren't making efforts to improve them. Another piece of legislation, the Protect Act, which Bush signed into law last year, makes it a crime for any person to enter the U.S., or for any citizen to travel abroad, for the purpose of sex tourism involving children. The sentences are severe: up to 30 years' imprisonment for each offense.

The thrust of the president's U.N. speech and the scope of the laws passed here to address the sex-trafficking epidemic might suggest that this is a global problem but not particularly an American one. In reality, little has been done to document sex trafficking in this country. In dozens of interviews I conducted with former sex slaves, madams, government and law-enforcement officials and anti-sex-trade activists for more than four months in Eastern Europe, Mexico and the United States, the details and breadth of this sordid trade in the U.S. came to light.

In fact, the United States has become a major importer of sex slaves. Last year, the C.I.A. estimated that between 18,000 and 20,000 people are trafficked annually into the United States. The government has not studied how many of these are victims of sex traffickers, but Kevin Bales, president of Free the Slaves, America's largest anti-slavery organization, says that the number is at least 10,000 a year. John Miller, the State Department's director of the Office to Monitor and Combat Trafficking in Persons, conceded: "That figure could be low. What we know is that the number is huge." Bales estimates that there are 30,000 to 50,000 sex slaves in captivity in the United States at any given time. Laura Lederer, a senior State Department adviser on trafficking, told me, "We're not finding victims in the United States because we're not looking for them."

Abduction

In Eastern European capitals like Kiev and Moscow, dozens of sex-trafficking rings advertise nanny positions in the United States in local newspapers; others claim to be scouting for models and actresses. In Chisinau, the capital of the former Soviet republic of Moldova — the poorest country in Europe and the one experts say is most heavily culled by traffickers for young women — I saw a billboard with a fresh-faced, smiling young woman beckoning girls to waitress positions in Paris. But of course there are no waitress positions and no "Paris." Some of these young women are actually tricked into paying their own travel expenses — typically around $3,000 — as a down payment on what they expect to be bright, prosperous futures, only to find themselves kept prisoner in Mexico before being moved to the United States and sold into sexual bondage there.

....

In October, I met Nicole, a young Russian woman who had been trafficked into Mexico by a different network. "I wanted to get out of Moscow, and they told me the Mexican border was like a freeway," said Nicole, who is now 25. We were sitting at a cafe on the Sunset Strip in Los Angeles, and she was telling me the story of her narrow escape from sex slavery—she was taken by immigration officers when her traffickers were trying to smuggle her over the border from Tijuana. She still seemed fearful of being discovered by the trafficking ring and didn't want even her initials to appear in print. (Nicole is a name she adopted after coming to the U.S.)

Two years ago, afraid for her life after her boyfriend was gunned down in Moscow in an organized-crime-related shootout, she found herself across a cafe table in Moscow from a man named Alex, who explained how he could save her by smuggling her into the U.S. Once she agreed, Nicole said, Alex told her that if she didn't show up at the airport, "'I'll find you and cut your head off.' Russians do not play around. In Moscow you can get a bullet in your head just for fun."

. . . .

The girls' first contacts are usually with what appear to be legitimate travel agencies.

According to prosecutors, the Komisaruk/Mezheritsky ring in Ukraine worked with two such agencies in Kiev, Art Life International and Svit Tours. The helpful agents at Svit and Art Life explained to the girls that the best way to get into the U.S. was through Mexico, which they portrayed as a short walk or boat ride from the American dream. Oblivious and full of hope, the girls get on planes to Europe and then on to Mexico.

Every day, flights from Paris, London and Amsterdam arrive at Mexico City's international airport carrying groups of these girls, sometimes as many as seven at a time, according to two Mexico City immigration officers I spoke with (and who asked to remain anonymous). One of them told me that officials at the airport—who cooperate with Mexico's federal preventive police (P.F.P.)—work with the traffickers and "direct airlines to park at certain gates. Officials go to the aircraft. They know the seat numbers. While passengers come off, they take the girls to an office, where officials will 'process' them."

Magdalena Carral, Mexico's commissioner of the National Institute of Migration, the government agency that controls migration issues at all airports, seaports and land entries into Mexico, told me: "Everything happens at the airport. We are giving a big fight to have better control of the airport. Corruption does not leave tracks, and sometimes we cannot track it. Six months ago we changed the three main officials at the airport. But it's a daily fight. These networks are very powerful and dangerous."

But Mexico is not merely a way station en route to the U.S. for third-country traffickers, like the Eastern European rings. It is also a vast source of even younger and more cheaply acquired girls for sexual servitude in the United States. While European traffickers tend to dupe their victims into boarding one-way flights to Mexico to their own captivity, Mexican traffickers rely on the charm and brute force of "Los Lenones," tightly organized associations of pimps, according to Roberto Caballero, an officer with the P.F.P. Although hundreds of "popcorn traffickers"—individuals who take control of one or two girls—work the margins, Caballero said, at least 15 major trafficking organizations and 120 associated factions tracked by the P.F.P. operate as wholesalers: collecting human merchandise and taking orders from safe houses and brothels in the major sex-trafficking hubs in New York, Los Angeles, Atlanta and Chicago.

Like the Sicilian Mafia, Los Lenones are based on family hierarchies, Caballero explained. The father controls the organization and the money, while the sons and their male cousins hunt, kidnap and entrap victims. The boys leave school at 12 and are given one or two girls their age to rape and pimp out to begin their training, which emphasizes the arts of kidnapping and seduction. Throughout the rural and suburban towns from southern Mexico to the U.S. border, along what traffickers call the Via Lactea, or Milky Way, the agents of Los Lenones troll the bus stations and factories and school dances where under-age girls gather, work and socialize. They first ply the girls like prospective lovers, buying them meals and desserts, promising affection and then marriage. Then the men describe rumors they've heard about America, about the promise of jobs and schools. Sometimes the girls are easy prey. Most of them already dream of El Norte. But the theater often ends as soon as the agent has the girl alone, when he beats her, drugs her or simply forces her into a waiting car.

The majority of Los Lenones — 80 percent of them, Caballero says — are based in Tenancingo, a charmless suburb an hour's drive south of Mexico City. Before I left Mexico City for Tenancingo in October, I was warned by Mexican and U.S. officials that the traffickers there are protected by the local police, and that the town is designed to discourage outsiders, with mazelike streets and only two closely watched entrances. The last time the federal police went there to investigate the disappearance of a local girl, their vehicle was surrounded, and the officers were intimidated into leaving. I traveled in a bulletproof Suburban with well-armed federals and an Immigration and Customs Enforcement agent.

On the way, we stopped at a gas station, where I met the parents of a girl from Tenancingo who was reportedly abducted in August 2000. The girl, Suri, is now 20. Her mother told me that there were witnesses who saw her being forced into a car on the way home from work at a local factory. No one called the police. Suri's mother recited the names of daughters of a number of her friends who have also been taken: "Minerva, Sylvia, Carmen," she said in a monotone, as if the list went on and on.

Just two days earlier, her parents heard from Suri (they call her by her nickname) for the first time since she disappeared. "She's in Queens, New York," the mother told me breathlessly. "She said she was being kept in a house watched by Colombians. She said they take her by car every day to work in a brothel. I was crying on the phone, 'When are you coming back, when are you coming back?' " The mother looked at me helplessly; the father stared blankly into the distance. Then the mother sobered. "My daughter said: 'I'm too far away. I don't know when I'm coming back.'" Before she hung up, Suri told her mother: "Don't cry. I'll escape soon. And don't talk to anyone."

Sex-trafficking victims widely believe that if they talk, they or someone they love will be killed. And their fear is not unfounded, since the tentacles of the trafficking rings reach back into the girls' hometowns, and local law enforcement is often complicit in the sex trade.

One officer in the P.F.P.'s anti-trafficking division told me that 10 high-level officials in the state of Sonora share a $200,000 weekly payoff from traffickers, a gargantuan sum of money for Mexico. The officer told me with a frozen smile that he was powerless to do anything about it.

"Some officials are not only on the organization's payroll, they are key players in the organization," an official at the U.S. Embassy in Mexico City told me. "Corruption is the most important reason these networks are so successful."

Nicolas Suarez, the P.F.P.'s coordinator of intelligence, sounded fatalistic about corruption when I spoke to him in Mexico City in September. "We have that cancer, corruption," he told me with a shrug. "But it exists in every country. In every house there is a devil."

The U.S. Embassy official told me: "Mexican officials see sex trafficking as a U.S. problem. If there wasn't such a large demand, then people — trafficking victims and migrants alike — wouldn't be going up there."

When I asked Magdalena Carral, the Mexican commissioner of migration, about these accusations, she said that she didn't know anything about Los Lenones or sex trafficking in Tenancingo. But she conceded: "There is an investigation against some officials accused of cooperating with these trafficking networks nationwide. Sonora is one of those places." She added, "We are determined not to allow any kind of corruption in this administration, not the smallest kind."

Gary Haugen, president of the International Justice Mission, an organization based in Arlington, Va., that fights sexual exploitation in South Asia and Southeast Asia, says: "Sex trafficking isn't a poverty issue but a law-enforcement issue. You can only carry out this trade at significant levels with the cooperation of local law enforcement. In the developing world the police are not seen as a solution for anything. You don't run to the police; you run from the police."

Breaking the Girls In

Once the Mexican traffickers abduct or seduce the women and young girls, it's not other men who first indoctrinate them into sexual slavery but other women. The victims and officials I spoke to all emphasized this fact as crucial to the trafficking rings' success. "Women are the principals," Caballero, the Mexican federal preventive police officer, told me. "The victims are put under the influence of the mothers, who handle them and beat them. Then they give the girls to the men to beat and rape into submission." Traffickers understand that because women can more easily gain the trust of young girls, they can more easily crush them. "Men are the customers and controllers, but within most trafficking organizations themselves, women are the operators," Haugen says. "Women are the ones who exert violent force and psychological torture."

This mirrors the tactics of the Eastern European rings. "Mexican pimps have learned a lot from European traffickers," said Claudia, a former prostitute and madam in her late 40s, whom I met in Tepito, Mexico City's vast and lethal ghetto. "The Europeans not only gather girls but put older women in the same houses," she told me. "They get younger and older women emotionally attached. They're transported together, survive together."

The traffickers' harvest is innocence. Before young women and girls are taken to the United States, their captors want to obliterate their sexual inexperience while preserving its appearance. For the Eastern European girls, this "preparation" generally happens in Ensenada, a seaside tourist town in Baja California, a region in Mexico settled by Russian immigrants, or Tijuana, where Nicole, the Russian woman I met in Los Angeles, was taken along with four other girls when she arrived in Mexico. The young women are typically kept in locked-down, gated villas in groups of 16 to 20. The girls are provided with all-American clothing — Levi's and baseball caps. They learn to say, "U.S. citizen." They are also sexually brutalized. Nicole told me that the day she arrived in Tijuana, three of her traveling companions were "tried out" locally. The education lasts for days and sometimes weeks.

For the Mexican girls abducted by Los Lenones, the process of breaking them in often begins on Calle Santo Tomas, a filthy narrow street in La Merced, a dangerous and raucous ghetto in Mexico City. Santo Tomas has been a place for low-end prostitution since before Spain's conquest of Mexico in the 16th century. But beginning in the early 90s, it became an important training ground for under-age girls and young women on their way into sexual bondage in the United States. When I first visited Santo Tomas, in late September, I found 150 young women walking a slow-motion parabola among 300 or 400 men. It was a balmy night, and the air was heavy with the smell of barbecue and gasoline. Two dead dogs were splayed over the curb just beyond where the girls struck casual poses in stilettos and spray-on-tight neon vinyl and satin or skimpy leopard-patterned outfits. Some of the girls looked as young as 12. Their faces betrayed no emotion. Many wore pendants of the grim reaper around their necks and made hissing sounds; this, I was told, was part of a ritual to ward off bad energy. The men, who were there to rent or just gaze, didn't speak. From the tables of a shabby cafe midblock, other men—also Mexicans, but more neatly dressed—sat scrutinizing the girls as at an auction. These were buyers and renters with an interest in the youngest and best looking. They nodded to the girls they wanted and then followed them past a guard in a Yankees baseball cap through a tin doorway.

Inside, the girls braced the men before a statue of St. Jude, the patron saint of lost causes, and patted them down for weapons. Then the girls genuflected to the stone-faced saint and led the men to the back, grabbing a condom and roll of toilet paper on the way. They pointed to a block of ice in a tub in lieu of a urinal. Beyond a blue hallway the air went sour, like old onions; there were 30 stalls curtained off by blue fabric, every one in use. Fifteen minutes of straightforward intercourse with the girl's clothes left on cost 50 pesos, or about $4.50. For $4.50 more, the dress was lifted. For another $4.50, the bra would be taken off. Oral sex was $4.50; "acrobatic positions" were $1.80 each. Despite the dozens of people and the various exertions in this room, there were only the sounds of zippers and shoes. There was no human noise at all.

Most of the girls on Santo Tomas would have sex with 20 to 30 men a day; they would do this seven days a week usually for weeks but sometimes for months before they were "ready" for the United States. If they refused, they would be beaten and sometimes killed. They would be told that if they tried to escape, one of their family members, who usually had no idea where they were, would be beaten or killed. Working at the brutalizing pace of 20 men per day, a girl could earn her captors as much as $2,000 a week. In the U.S., that same girl could bring in perhaps $30,000 per week.

. . . .

Crossing the Border

In November, I followed by helicopter the 12-foot-high sheet-metal fence that represents the U.S.-Mexico boundary from Imperial Beach, Calif., south of San Diego, 14 miles across the gritty warrens and havoc of Tijuana into the barren hills of Tecate. The fence drops off abruptly at Colonia Nido de las Aguilas, a dry riverbed that straddles the border. Four hundred square miles of bone-dry, barren hills stretch out on the U.S. side. I hovered over the end of the fence with Lester McDaniel, a special agent with Immigration and Customs Enforcement. On the U.S. side, "J-e-s-u-s" was spelled out in rocks 10 feet high across a steep hillside. A 15-foot white wooden cross rose from the peak. It is here that thousands of girls and young women—most of them Mexican and many of them straight from Calle Santo Tomas—are taken every year, mostly between January and August, the dry season. Coyotes—or smugglers—subcontracted exclusively by sex traffickers sometimes trudge the girls up to the cross and let them pray, then herd them into the hills northward.

A few miles east, we picked up a deeply grooved trail at the fence and followed it for miles into the hills until it plunged into a deep isolated ravine called Cottonwood Canyon. A Ukrainian sex-trafficking ring force-marches young women through here, McDaniel told me. In high heels and seductive clothing, the young women trek 12 miles to Highway 94, where panel trucks sit waiting. McDaniel listed the perils: rattlesnakes, dehydration and hypothermia. He failed to mention the traffickers' bullets should the women try to escape.

"If a girl tries to run, she's killed and becomes just one more woman in the desert," says Marisa B. Ugarte, director of the Bilateral Safety Corridor Coalition, a San Diego organization that coordinates rescue efforts for trafficking victims on both sides of the border. "But if she keeps going north, she reaches the Gates of Hell."

One girl who was trafficked back and forth across that border repeatedly was Andrea. "Andrea" is just one name she was given by her traffickers and clients; she doesn't know her real name. She was born in the United States and sold or abandoned here—at about 4 years old, she says—by a woman who may have been her mother. (She is now in her early to mid-20s; she doesn't know for sure.) She says that she spent approximately the next 12 years as the captive of a sex-trafficking ring that operated on both sides of the Mexican border. Because of the threat of retribution from her former captors, who are believed to be still at large, an organization that rescues and counsels trafficking victims and former prostitutes arranged for me to meet Andrea in October at a secret location in the United States.

In a series of excruciating conversations, Andrea explained to me how the trafficking ring that kept her worked, moving young girls (and boys too) back and forth over the border, selling nights and weekends with them mostly to American men. She said that the ring imported—both through abduction and outright purchase—toddlers, children and teenagers into the U.S. from many countries.

"The border is very busy, lots of stuff moving back and forth," she said. "Say you needed to get some kids. This guy would offer a woman a lot of money, and she'd take birth certificates from the U.S.—from Puerto Rican children or darker-skinned children—and then she would go into Mexico through Tijuana. Then she'd drive to Juarez"—across the Mexican border from El Paso, Tex.—"and then they'd go shopping. I was taken with them once. We went to this house that had a goat in the front yard and came out with a 4-year-old boy." She remembers the boy costing around $500 (she said that many poor parents were told that their children would go to adoption agencies and on to better lives in America). "When we crossed the border at Juarez, all the border guards wanted to see was a birth certificate for the dark-skinned kids."

Andrea continued: "There would be a truck waiting for us at the Mexico border, and those trucks you don't want to ride in. Those trucks are closed. They had spots where there would be transfers, the rest stops and truck stops on the freeways in the U.S. One person would walk you into the bathroom, and then another person would take you out of the bathroom and take you to a different vehicle."

Andrea told me she was transported to Juarez dozens of times. During one visit, when she was about 7 years old, the trafficker took her to the Radisson Casa Grande Hotel, where there was a john waiting in a room. The john was an older American man, and he read Bible passages to her before and after having sex with her. Andrea described other rooms she remembered in other hotels in Mexico: the Howard Johnson in Leon, the Crowne Plaza in Guadalajara. She remembers most of all the ceiling patterns. "When I was taken to Mexico, I knew things were going to be different," she said. The "customers" were American businessmen. "The men who went there had higher positions, had more to lose if they were caught doing these things on the other side of the border. I was told my purpose was to keep these men from abusing their own kids." Later she told me: "The white kids you could beat but you couldn't mark. But with Mexican kids you could do whatever you wanted. They're untraceable. You lose nothing by killing them."

Then she and the other children and teenagers in this cell were walked back across the border to El Paso by the traffickers. "The border guards talked to you like, 'Did you have fun in Mexico?' And you answered exactly what you were told, 'Yeah, I had fun.' 'Runners' moved the harder-to-place kids, the darker or not-quite-as-well-behaved kids, kids that hadn't been broken yet."

Another trafficking victim I met, a young woman named Montserrat, was taken to the United States from Veracruz, Mexico, six years ago, at age 13. (Montserrat is her nickname.) "I was going to work in America," she told me. "I wanted to go to school there, have an apartment and a red Mercedes Benz." Montserrat's trafficker, who called himself Alejandro, took her to Sonora, across the Mexican border from Douglas, Ariz., where she joined a group of a dozen other teenage girls, all with the same dream of a better life. They were from Chiapas, Guatemala, Oaxaca—everywhere, she said.

The group was marched 12 hours through the desert, just a few of the thousands of Mexicans who bolted for America that night along the 2,000 miles of border. Cars were waiting at a fixed spot on the other side. Alejandro directed her to a Nissan and drove her and a few others to a house she said she thought was in Phoenix, the home of a white American family. "It looked like America," she told me. "I ate chicken. The family ignored me, watched TV. I thought the worst part was behind me."

In the United States: Hiding in Plain Sight

A week after Montserrat was taken across the border, she said, she and half a dozen other girls were loaded into a windowless van. "Alejandro dropped off girls at gas stations as we drove, wherever there were minimarkets," Montserrat told me. At each drop-off there was somebody waiting. Sometimes a girl would be escorted to the bathroom, never to return to the van. They drove 24 hours a day. "As the girls were leaving, being let out the back, all of them 14 or 15 years old, I felt confident," Montserrat said. We were talking in Mexico City, where she has been since she escaped from her trafficker four years ago. She's now 19, and shy with her body but direct with her gaze, which is flat and unemotional. "I didn't know the real reason they were disappearing," she said. "They were going to a better life."

Eventually, only Montserrat and one other girl remained. Outside, the air had turned frigid, and there was snow on the ground. It was night when the van stopped at a gas station. A man was waiting. Montserrat's friend hopped out the back, gleeful. "She said goodbye, I'll see you tomorrow," Montserrat recalled. "I never saw her again."

After leaving the gas station, Alejandro drove Montserrat to an apartment. A couple of weeks later he took her to a Dollarstore. "He bought me makeup," Montserrat told me. "He chose a short dress and a halter top, both black. I asked him why the clothes. He said it was for a party the owner of the apartment was having. He bought me underwear. Then I started to worry." When they arrived at the apartment, Alejandro left, saying he was coming back. But another man appeared at the door. "The man said he'd already paid and I had to do whatever he said," Montserrat said. "When he said he already paid, I knew why I was there. I was crushed."

Montserrat said that she didn't leave that apartment for the next three months, then for nine months after that, Alejandro regularly took her in and out of the apartment for appointments with various johns.

Sex trafficking is one of the few human rights violations that rely on exposure: victims have to be available, displayed, delivered and returned. Girls were shuttled in open cars between the Plainfield, N.J., stash house and other locations in northern New Jersey like Elizabeth and Union City. Suri told her mother that she was being driven in a black town car—just one of hundreds of black town cars traversing New York City at any time—from her stash house in Queens to places where she was forced to have sex. A Russian ring drove women between various Brooklyn apartments and strip clubs in New Jersey. Andrea named trading hubs at highway rest stops in Deming, N.M.; Kingman, Ariz.; Boulder City, Nev.; and Glendale, Calif. Glendale, Andrea said, was a fork in the road; from there, vehicles went either north to San Jose or south toward San Diego. The traffickers drugged them for travel, she said. "When they fed you, you started falling asleep."

In the past several months, I have visited a number of addresses where trafficked girls and young women have reportedly ended up: besides the house in Plainfield, N.J., there is a row house on 51st Avenue in the Corona section of Queens, which has been identified to Mexican federal preventive police by escaped trafficking victims. There is the apartment at Barrington Plaza in the tony Westwood section of Los Angeles, one place that some of the Komisaruk/Mezheritsky ring's trafficking victims ended up, according to Daniel Saunders, the assistant U.S. attorney who prosecuted the ring. And there's a house on Massachusetts Avenue in Vista, Calif., a San Diego suburb, which was pointed out to me by a San Diego sheriff. These places all have at least one thing in common: they are camouflaged by their normal, middle-class surroundings.

"This is not narco-traffic secrecy," says Sharon B. Cohn, director of anti-trafficking operations for the International Justice Mission. "These are not people kidnapped and held for ransom, but women and children sold every single day. If they're hidden, their keepers don't make money."

International Justice Mission's president, Gary Haugen, says: "It's the easiest kind of crime in the world to spot. Men look for it all day, every day."

But border agents and local policemen usually don't know trafficking when they see it. The operating assumption among American police departments is that women who sell their bodies do so by choice, and undocumented foreign women who sell their bodies are not only prostitutes (that is, voluntary sex workers) but also trespassers on U.S. soil. No Department of Justice attorney or police vice squad officer I spoke with in Los Angeles—one of the country's busiest thoroughfares for forced sex traffic—considers sex trafficking in the U.S. a serious problem, or a priority. A teenage girl arrested on Sunset Strip for solicitation, or a group of Russian sex workers arrested in a brothel raid in the San Fernando Valley, are automatically heaped onto a pile of workaday vice arrests.

....

Imprisonment and Submission

The basement, Andrea said, held as many as 16 children and teenagers of different ethnicities. She remembers that it was underneath a house in an upper-middle-class neighborhood on the West Coast. Throughout much of her captivity, this basement was where she was kept when she wasn't working. "There was lots of scrawling on the walls," she said. "The other kids drew stick figures, daisies, teddy bears. This Mexican boy would draw a house with sunshine. We each had a mat."

Andrea paused. "But nothing happens to you in the basement," she continued. "You just had to worry about when the door opened."

She explained: "They would call you out of the basement, and you'd get a bath and you'd get a dress, and if your dress was yellow you were probably going to Disneyland." She said they used color coding to make transactions safer for the traffickers and the clients. "At Disneyland there would be people doing drop-offs and pickups for kids. It's a big open area full of kids, and nobody pays attention to nobody. They would kind of quietly say, 'Go over to that person,' and you would just slip your hand into theirs and say, 'I was looking for you, Daddy.' Then that person would move off with one or two or three of us."

. . . .

Montserrat said that she was moved around a lot and often didn't know where she was. She recalled that she was in Detroit for two months before she realized that she was in "the city where cars are made," because the door to the apartment Alejandro kept her in was locked from the outside. She says she was forced to service at least two men a night, and sometimes more. She watched through the windows as neighborhood children played outside. Emotionally, she slowly dissolved. Later, Alejandro moved her to Portland, Ore., where once a week he worked her out of a strip club. In all that time she had exactly one night off; Alejandro took her to see "Scary Movie 2."

All the girls I spoke to said that their captors were both psychologically and physically abusive. Andrea told me that she and the other children she was held with were frequently beaten to keep them off-balance and obedient. Sometimes they were videotaped while being forced to have sex with adults or one another. Often, she said, she was asked to play roles: the therapist's patient or the obedient daughter. Her cell of sex traffickers offered three age ranges of sex partners—toddler to age 4, 5 to 12 and teens—as well as what she called a "damage group." "In the damage group they can hit you or do anything they wanted," she explained. "Though sex always hurts when you are little, so it's always violent, everything was much more painful once you were placed in the damage group.

"They'd get you hungry then to train you" to have oral sex, she said. "They'd put honey on a man. For the littlest kids, you had to learn not to gag. And they would push things in you so you would open up better. We learned responses. Like if they wanted us to be sultry or sexy or scared. Most of them wanted you scared. When I got older I'd teach the younger kids how to float away so things didn't hurt."

Kevin Bales of Free the Slaves says: "The physical path of a person being trafficked includes stages of degradation of a person's mental state. A victim gets deprived of food, gets hungry, a little dizzy and sleep-deprived. She begins to break down; she can't think for herself. Then take away her travel documents, and you've made her stateless. Then layer on physical violence, and she begins to follow orders. Then add a foreign culture and language, and she's trapped."

Then add one more layer: a sex-trafficking victim's belief that her family is being tracked as collateral for her body. All sex-trafficking operations, whether Mexican, Ukrainian or Thai, are vast criminal underworlds with roots and branches that reach back to the countries, towns and neighborhoods of their victims.

"There's a vast misunderstanding of what coercion is, of how little it takes to make someone a slave," Gary Haugen of International Justice Mission said. "The destruction of dignity and sense of self, these girls' sense of resignation. . . ." He didn't finish the sentence.

In Tijuana in November, I met with Mamacita, a Mexican trafficking-victim-turned-madam, who used to oversee a stash house for sex slaves in San Diego. Mamacita (who goes by a nickname) was full of regret and worry. She left San Diego three years ago, but she says that the trafficking ring, run by three violent Mexican brothers, is still in operation. "The girls can't leave," Mamacita said. "They're always being watched. They lock them into apartments. The fear is unbelievable. They can't talk to anyone. They are always hungry, pale, always shaking and cold. But they never complain. If they do, they'll be beaten or killed."

. . . .

If anything, the women I talked to said that the sex in the U.S. is even rougher than what the girls face on Calle Santo Tomas. Rosario, a woman I met in Mexico City, who had been trafficked to New York and held captive for a number of years, said: "In America we had 'special jobs.' Oral sex, anal sex, often with many men. Sex is now more adventurous, harder." She said that she believed younger foreign girls were in demand in the U.S. because of an increased appetite for more aggressive, dangerous sex. Traffickers need younger and younger girls, she suggested, simply because they are more pliable. In Eastern Europe, too, the typical age of sex-trafficking victims is plummeting; according to Matei of Reaching Out, while most girls used to be in their late teens and 20s, 13-year-olds are now far from unusual.

Immigration and Customs Enforcement agents at the Cyber Crimes Center in Fairfax, Va., are finding that when it comes to sex, what was once considered abnormal is now the norm. They are tracking a clear spike in the demand for harder-core pornography on the Internet. "We've become desensitized by the soft stuff; now we need a harder and harder hit," says I.C.E. Special Agent Perry Woo. Cybernetworks like KaZaA and Morpheus—through which you can download and trade images and videos—have become the Mexican border of virtual sexual exploitation. I had heard of one Web site that supposedly offered sex slaves for purchase to individuals. The I.C.E. agents hadn't heard of it. Special Agent Don Daufenbach, I.C.E.'s manager for undercover operations, brought it up on a screen. A hush came over the room as the agents leaned forward, clearly disturbed. "That sure looks like the real thing," Daufenbach said. There were streams of Web pages of thumbnail images of young women of every ethnicity in obvious distress, bound, gagged, contorted. The agents in the room pointed out probable injuries from torture. Cyberauctions for some of the women were in progress; one had exceeded $300,000. "With new Internet technology," Woo said, "pornography is becoming more pervasive. With Web cams we're seeing more live molestation of children." One of I.C.E.'s recent successes, Operation Hamlet, broke up a ring of adults who traded images and videos of themselves forcing sex on their own young children.

But the supply of cheap girls and young women to feed the global appetite appears to be limitless. And it's possible that the crimes committed against them in the U.S. cut deeper than elsewhere, precisely because so many of them are snared by the glittery promise of an America that turns out to be not their salvation but their place of destruction.

Endgame

Typically, a young trafficking victim in the U.S. lasts in the system for two to four years. After that, Bales says: "She may be killed in the brothel. She may be dumped and deported. Probably least likely is that she will take part in the prosecution of the people that enslaved her."

Who can expect a young woman trafficked into the U.S., trapped in a foreign culture, perhaps unable to speak English, physically and emotionally abused and perhaps drug-addicted, to ask for help from a police officer, who more likely than not will look at her as a criminal and an illegal alien? Even Andrea, who was born in the United States and spoke English, says she never thought of escaping, "because what's out there? What's out there was scarier. We had customers who were police, so you were not going to go talk to a cop. We had this customer from Nevada who was a child psychologist, so you're not going to go talk to a social worker. So who are you going to talk to?"

And if the girls are lucky enough to escape, there's often nowhere for them to go. "The families don't want them back," Sister Veronica, a nun who helps run a rescue mission for trafficked prostitutes in an old church in Mexico City, told me. "They're shunned."

When I first met her, Andrea told me: "We're way too damaged to give back. A lot of these children never wanted to see their parents again after a while, because what do you tell your parents? What are you going to say? You're no good."

Notes and Questions

1. Landesman's article succeeded in bringing the issue of child sex trafficking home for those who believed that it was mainly occurring "somewhere else" and not in the United States. According to Landesman, how does child sexual exploitation flourish in the U.S.? What techniques do traffickers and users rely on? What should the social response to an article like this one be?

2. Specialists in the U.S. State Department are quoted in this article to the effect that the number of children being trafficked into the U.S. is very large, and that the U.S. is not doing nearly enough to seek them out once here. How would you compare the sense of impunity for traffickers in the U.S. with the situation in India, for example?

F. Legal Response to Sex Trafficking in the U.S.

In the following article, Susan Tiefenbrun describes the principal U.S. anti-trafficking legislation, the Trafficking Victims Protection Act, signed into law in 2000.[17] The law has received mixed reviews with regard to its effectiveness, although most agree that its conceptual foundations are sound. As with all modern anti-trafficking legislation, the TVPA is designed to ensure that trafficking victims are perceived as such, rather than as willing migrants, complicit in their own victimization.

Some have voiced criticism of national anti-trafficking laws for their tendency to divide "worthy" victims of sex trafficking from the "unworthy" economic migrant (considered to be "smuggled" rather than trafficked), since all these persons come from similarly vulnerable populations. Nevertheless, the U.S. law, in common with many other national laws, does reflect an increased awareness of the growing phenomenon of trafficking, as well as a commitment to facilitate prosecution against trafficking networks, and to providing assistance to victims of trafficking.

Susan W. Tiefenbrun, *Sex Slavery in the United States and the Law Enacted to Stop It Here and Abroad*
11 William & Mary Journal of Women & the Law 317 (2005)

I. INTRODUCTION

A. History of Trafficking Leading to Sex Slavery

Although statistics about trafficking are notoriously unreliable, according to a 2003 U.S. government estimate, "approximately 800,000 to 900,000 people annually are trafficked across international borders worldwide and between 18,000 and 20,000 of those victims are trafficked into the United States." In 2002, the Department of State's (DoS) Annual Trafficking in Persons Report (TIP Report) stated that "at least 700,000, and possi-

---

17. Victims of Trafficking and Violence Protection Act.§§ 7101–7112.

bly as many as four million men, women, and children worldwide were bought, sold, transported and held against their will in slave-like conditions." The 2001 TIP Report cited that "at least 700,000 persons, especially women and children, are trafficked each year across international borders," and 45,000 to 50,000 people, primarily women and children, are trafficked into the United States annually. The 2001 TIP Report admitted, however, that the numbers may be significantly higher. Earlier sources reported that in 1997 "more than two million women around the world [were] bought and sold each year for the purpose of sexual exploitation," and 50,000 of them are brought into the United States each year to support a lucrative sex trade industry.

. . . .

For many years, the United States has recognized the insufficiency of its criminal and immigration laws as they fail to protect the victims of sex trafficking and fail to result in the effective prosecution of perpetrators. Recognizing that sex trafficking is a modern form of slavery that has a global and deleterious impact on women's human rights, President Bill Clinton signed the TVPA on October 28, 2000. The purpose of the TVPA was to "combat trafficking in persons to ensure just and effective punishment of traffickers, and to protect their victims." Clinton hailed the legislation as the "most significant step we've ever taken to secure the health and safety of women around the world." The TVPA established a coordinated, transnational effort to protect trafficked persons, to criminalize the conduct of traffickers and to penalize sex trafficking as severely as rape, which is punishable by a sentence of twenty years to life imprisonment. The purpose of this far-reaching law is to eradicate trafficking in the United States and abroad, in part by influencing other nations to enact or amend sex trafficking legislation, to correct weak enforcement policies, and to harmonize legislation internationally.

. . . .

This article investigates the role that a U.S. anti-trafficking law, the TVPA, plays in eliminating the heinous crime of sex slavery practiced both in the United States and abroad.

. . . .

II. The TVPA

A. Definition of Trafficking and Sex Trafficking

The TVPA defines sex trafficking as "the recruitment, harboring, transportation, provision, or obtaining of a person for the purpose of a commercial sex act." The TVPA defines "severe forms of trafficking in persons" as "sex trafficking in which a commercial sex act is induced by force, fraud, or coercion, or in which the person induced to perform such an act has not attained 18 years of age." The TVPA defines a commercial sex act to mean "any sex act on account of which anything of value is given to or received by any person."

The TVPA "resists efforts to define 'trafficking' so broadly" as to dilute the effort to eradicate the crime. There is a "wide range of related offenses such as immigrant smuggling and unfair labor practices which require just and effective remedies. Yet, these remedies are better provided in the context of labor law or immigration law than in an anti-slavery bill."

The definition of trafficking in the TVPA is similar but narrower than that found in the United Nations Protocol to Prevent, Suppress and Punish Trafficking in Persons, Especially Women and Children. The U.N. Protocol was adopted by the General Assembly less than one month after the enactment of the TVPA. It supplements the U.N. Convention against Transnational Organized Crime and recognizes the role that organized crime plays in supporting and committing sex trafficking. The U.N. Protocol is an important tool to facilitate the type of international cooperation authorized by the TVPA because "[g]overnments that sign and ratify this protocol make a commitment to criminalize trafficking and to protect its many victims." In December 2000, the United States and eighty other countries signed the U.N. Protocol.

....

C. The Basic Features of the TVPA

1. One Crime, One Law

The TVPA establishes one specific law prohibiting sex trafficking, and this feature eliminates the cumbersome necessity of having to sue perpetrators of sex trafficking under several different statutes.

....

Recognizing the inadequacy of existing slavery and peonage laws, which are limited in jurisdictional reach and in severity of punishment, the criminal section of the DoJ's Civil Rights Division was eager to assist in the passage of the TVPA. The TVPA is much wider in scope than existing criminal law statutes because the TVPA includes international cooperative measures and increased penalties, which may act as deterrents to the crime of trafficking.

2. Increased Penalties

The TVPA has increased the penalties from ten to twenty years imprisonment for trafficking and for related crimes such as involuntary servitude, peonage, and forced labor. If the crime includes kidnapping, aggravated sexual abuse, or an attempt to kill, those convicted of sex trafficking may receive a penalty of up to life imprisonment. Increasing the penalty for sex trafficking increases the costs and risks for the trafficker and can act as an economic deterrent to the crime.

3. Protection for Women Victims in Funded Shelters

The TVPA provides protection for women who are victims of sex trafficking violence. Once a trafficking victim has been identified and placed into federal custody, the TVPA requires law enforcement agents and federal officials to protect the victim by assuring her access to information and translation services. Victims are also granted "continued presence" as alien victims in the United States.

The TVPA reauthorizes the Violence Against Women Act and allocates funds to provide shelters for victims of domestic violence. It also allocates funds for trafficked women.

4. T-Visas and Permanent Residency Status

The TVPA offers victims of "severe forms of trafficking" the opportunity to obtain a T-visa permitting them to stay in the country at least through the duration of their captors' prosecution and, perhaps, even permanently, if they are willing to assist in the prosecution of their perpetrators. To be eligible for the T-visa, the applicant must prove victimization by a "severe form of trafficking" as set forth in section 103(8) of the TVPA. A child involved in sex trafficking does not have to prove coercion, force, or fraud. In the case of an adult, coercion may be proven by physical restraint or by psychological force. Thus, a commercial sexual act involving an adult that is not induced by force, fraud, or physical coercion may still fall under the definition of a "severe form of trafficking" if the victim can prove psychological coercion. She is no longer required to prove legal or physical coercion, as was the standard established in *United States v. Kozminski*. Thus, victims of severe forms of trafficking are defined as people held against their will "for labor or services, through the use of force, fraud, or coercion for the purpose of subjection to involuntary servitude, peonage, debt bondage, or slavery" and are eligible for the T-visa.

. . . .

According to the TVPA, a victim of a severe form of trafficking and a potential witness to such trafficking may be eligible for permanent residency status in the United States as well as protection for her family who is still abroad. When the victim is a lawful temporary resident in the United States, she may be granted authorization to work and be provided with an employment authorized endorsement or work permit.

. . . .

To qualify for the T-visa, the applicant must have suffered "substantial" abuse at the hands of traffickers. In addition, the applicant must possess and be willing to share information that aids law enforcement personnel with prosecuting or investigating traffickers. Alternatively, the T-visa can be granted to a victim under age fifteen who would "suffer extreme hardship involving unusual and severe harm" if forced to leave the United States.

. . . .

Because the T-visa is essentially a deportation stay, the victim must decide immediately whether she will cooperate with investigators. The law does not allow the victim to delay or even reflect on her choice to assist in prosecution. She must agree to cooperate in order to be given "continued presence." "Continued presence" entitles victims of "severe forms of trafficking" to support and assistance on the same basis as refugees, as well as the ability to work.

. . . .

The number of T-visa applicants whose status may be adjusted to that of permanent resident is limited to five thousand per year. This number does not include family members.

. . . .

9. International Cooperation and International Programs

. . . .

To accomplish the lofty goal of eliminating sex trafficking both here and abroad, the TVPA codifies the establishment of an Interagency Task Force, chaired by the Secretary of State, to monitor and combat worldwide human trafficking. The Interagency Task Force establishes minimum standards for the elimination of trafficking and provides assistance to foreign countries to help them meet those minimum standards.

U.S. assistance to countries abroad includes advice in drafting laws to prevent and prohibit trafficking; investigation and prosecution of traffickers; establishment and maintenance of programs, projects, and activities for the protection of victims; and creation and expansion of international exchange programs to combat trafficking.

. . . .

10. Minimum Standards in Other Countries

The TVPA authorizes the Interagency Task Force to monitor the "progress of the United States and other countries in the areas of trafficking prevention, protection, and assistance to victims of trafficking...." To achieve this purpose, DoS issues an annual Trafficking in Persons Report (TIP) that ranks international governments' efforts to eliminate trafficking in persons in accordance with their compliance with minimum standards. The TVPA enumerates four minimum standards for the elimination of severe forms of trafficking in persons and sets forth criteria for evaluating serious and sustained efforts made by foreign governments to meet such standards.

The first standard requires the government of a country to "prohibit severe forms of trafficking in persons and to punish acts of such trafficking." In order to meet this standard, a country is required to have an anti-trafficking law that makes trafficking a criminal offense and provides for the adequate punishment for such a crime.

Since the TVPA defines severe forms of trafficking in persons to include trafficking for labor or services as well as sex trafficking, the TVPA requires a country to recognize all forms of trafficking as a criminal offense, whether it is committed for the purpose of prostitution or forced labor.

The second standard specifically applies to sex trafficking. It requires governments to prescribe the appropriate sentences in cases of sex trafficking involving children or which include aggravated circumstances, such as rape, kidnapping, or death. These sentences should be comparable to the punishments for grave crimes such as sexual assault.

The third standard requires governments to prescribe a punishment for any act of a severe form of trafficking in persons. The punishment must be "sufficiently stringent" to deter others from committing the same crime, and it must reflect the serious nature of this crime.

The fourth standard requires governments to make "serious and sustained efforts" to eliminate trafficking. To determine whether a government's implementation efforts are "serious and sustained," the TVPA delineates seven criteria. The first three criteria measure government efforts in the areas of prosecution, protection, and prevention. The remaining four criteria measure the degree of international cooperation, including investigation of severe forms of trafficking, extradition of traffickers, monitoring of immigration and emigration, and investigation and prosecution of public officials involved in trafficking.

11. Sanctions

The TVPA anticipates the use of economic sanctions in order to pressure foreign governments to recognize the gravity of trafficking in persons and to take the necessary measures to eliminate this form of slavery. Sanctions, which began in October 2003, include the denial of non-humanitarian aid, non-trade-related assistance, certain development-related assistance, and aid from international financial institutions, specifically the International Monetary Fund and multilateral development banks such as the World Bank. The President of the United States can waive the sanctions when necessary to avoid significantly adverse effects on vulnerable populations, including women and children.

12. Direct Foreign Aid

United States Agency for International Development (USAID) works directly with foreign countries to prevent trafficking by decreasing the vulnerability of trafficked women and children, protecting and assisting the victims of traffickers, and supporting legislative reform and implementation abroad. The goal is to help countries meet minimum standards set forth in the TVPA, with special emphasis on countries that have significant levels of severe forms of trafficking. Because poverty, lack of education, and lack of economic and political opportunities contribute to the vulnerability of trafficking victims, a substantial part of USAID's development assistance targets women in those countries that can greatly benefit from such programs. USAID programs operate in many countries including Azerbaijan, Thailand, Albania, and Romania. One of these programs brought hundreds of international visitors to the United States in 2003 to learn about trafficking. USAID also manages anti-trafficking programs funded through the DoS.

13. Monitoring Other Countries, the Interagency Task Force, and the Department of State Annual TIP Report

The TVPA authorizes DoS, with assistance from the Interagency Task Force, to monitor the status of other nations' sex trafficking activities by classifying those nations into one of three tiers. This classification is based upon the degree of their compliance with the minimum standards for the elimination of trafficking in persons, as stipulated in the TVPA, and is published in the annual TIP Report and submitted to the appropriate Congressional committees.

Tier 1 includes countries whose governments fully comply with the minimum standards set forth in the TVPA and have anti-trafficking legislation with adequate punishments for the crime. Tier 2 includes countries whose governments "do not yet fully comply with [these] standards but are making significant efforts to bring themselves into compliance." Tier 3 includes countries whose governments "do not fully comply with [these] standards and are not making significant efforts to bring themselves into compliance" with them. Since October 2003, sanctions can be levied against Tier 3 countries if they cannot prove that they have adopted and implemented concrete measures to fight trafficking.

The TVPA therefore establishes a multilateral effort to prevent trafficking, protect victims, and prosecute traffickers in the United States and abroad by allocating funds, establishing international and domestic programs to accomplish these goals, and offering real economic and social incentives to victims who are willing to assist in the prosecution of traffickers. While these goals and measures are laudatory, if they are unenforced or unenforceable, the TVPA will fail to meet its goals of deterrence or elimination of this crime.

III. The Domestic Impact of the TVPA

There is no doubt that the TVPA has led to significant changes in the United States government's effort to eliminate sex trafficking. It is relatively simple to measure the domestic impact of the TVPA on victims receiving benefits in the United States as the TVPA requires this information be published in an annual impact report:

Not later than December 31 of each year, the Secretary of Health and Human Services, in consultation with the Secretary of Labor, the Board of Directors of the Legal Services Corporation, and the heads of other appropriate Federal agencies shall submit a report, which includes information on the number of persons who received benefits or other services under this paragraph in connection with programs or activities funded or administered by such agencies or officials during the preceding fiscal year.

. . . .

Generally, the domestic measures implemented by the United States government as a result of the TVPA's enactment have been slow but dramatic. They include restructuring the government's entire approach to trafficking in an attempt to treat the trafficked persons as victims rather than criminals. This policy change is reflected in the creation of several new trafficking implementation offices within agencies of the federal government. It is also reflected in amendments to existing criminal statutes that include a specific crime of sex trafficking and increased penalties for trafficking and other related crimes.

. . . .

B. DoJ Domestic TVPA Implementation Measures

1. DoJ Creates New Statutes, New Regulations

In compliance with the mandates of the TVPA, new criminal offenses have been introduced into the United States criminal law system and have resulted in amendments to the peonage and slavery statutes under the United States Code. These new criminal offenses include trafficking (§ 1590), forced labor (§ 1589), and unlawful possession of documents (§ 1592). The TVPA also defines trafficking involving peonage, slavery, involuntary servitude, or forced labor as crimes.

Since 2000, new criminal regulations have been passed which make trafficking a crime punishable by fine or imprisonment for up to twenty years, or both. The amended criminal statutes also contain a provision for up to a life sentence in cases involving attempted or completed kidnapping or aggravated sexual abuse or an attempt to kill.

. . . .

The new criminal code provisions enacted as a result of the passage of the TVPA also criminalize conduct relating to documents in furtherance of trafficking, peonage, slavery, involuntary servitude, or forced labor. Under this section:

> Whoever knowingly destroys, conceals, removes, confiscates, or possesses any actual or purported passport or other immigration document, or any other actual or purported government identification document, of another person [in furtherance of any of the crimes related to peonage and slavery].... or to prevent or restrict or to attempt to prevent or restrict, without lawful authority, the person's liberty to move or travel, in order to maintain the labor or services of that person, when the person is or has been a victim of a severe form of trafficking in persons, as defined in section 103 of the Trafficking Victims Protection Act of 2000 shall be fined under this title or imprisoned for not more than 5 years, or both.

. . . .

As a result of the passage of new criminal law guidelines mandated by the TVPA, prosecutors may now charge traffickers with either trafficking, slavery, involuntary servitude, or forced labor, depending on which is easiest to prove. The punishment, benefits, and protections are now the same for each of these offenses as they are for trafficked persons under the TVPA.

2. DoJ Increases Number of Prosecutions and Investigations

Since the new and amended trafficking criminal provisions were enacted after 2000, there has been an increase in the number of prosecutions of traffickers. Before 2000, very few traffickers were prosecuted because of the difficulty to obtain proof, the expense and time of trial, the piecemeal nature of the U.S. criminal laws on trafficking, and the reportedly overwhelming amount of paperwork required for the prosecution of traffickers.

After the passage of the TVPA and from January 2001 through January 2003, the DoJ charged, convicted, or secured sentences against ninety-two traffickers in twenty-one cases. Sixty-five of those charged were convicted or sentenced for sex trafficking offenses in fourteen separate cases.

As of December 18, 2002, the DoJ reported having 125 open trafficking investigations, twice the number from the previous year. Moreover, the DoJ reported the prosecution of thirty-three traffickers under the criminal statutes created pursuant to the TVPA mandate. Of those thirty-three, nineteen were for sexual exploitation. Thus, between 2001 and 2002, the DoJ more than doubled its number of prosecutions and convictions to thirty-six.

According to one U.S. Attorney, since the TVPA's passage, it has become significantly easier for prosecutors to pursue a sex trafficking case by applying the TVPA and the new criminal statutes implemented as a result of the TVPA. They no longer have to apply several different criminal law statutes. Obtaining a conviction for the crime of sex trafficking, as defined in the TVPA, requires proof of fewer elements than forced labor, peonage, or involuntary servitude. For example, instead of having to prove deception, coercion, or abuse of a position of vulnerability, the crime of sex trafficking requires only proof of "recruitment, harboring, transportation, provision, or obtaining of a person.... for the purpose of a commercial sex act."

Thus, as a result of the establishment of new and amended criminal statutes and regulations pursuant to the mandates of the TVPA, the number of sex trafficking prosecutions in the United States has increased since 2000. Despite the time consuming and labor intensive nature of these cases, which require the full time dedication of many attorneys and investigators, the DoJ prosecuted thirty-four defendants in 2001, four times the number from the previous year. The DoJ "opened investigations into sixty-four allegations of trafficking in fiscal year 2001." As of May 2002, the DoJ had 111 open investigations, representing a fifty percent increase over the number of open investigations of trafficking the agency had in the previous year and a more than three fold increase since the establishment of the Trafficking in Persons and Worker Exploitation Task Force toll-free complaint line in February 2000.

....

9. DoJ Witness Protection Measures in the United States

The TVPA authorizes the establishment of witness protection measures to supplement the existing Federal Witness Security Program, which alone is insufficient to protect trafficking victims and their families who remain in the victim's home country. Under the Federal Witness Security Program, comprehensive witness protection measures are available to witnesses testifying in relation to trafficking, forced labor, slavery, involuntary servitude, and unlawful confiscation of documents. Additional witness protection measures specified under United States federal law include the right to a change of identity, housing, transport costs, financial assistance, assistance to find employment, and "other services necessary to assist the person in becoming self-sustaining." Federal law states that the immediate family of the witnesses may be protected and relocated if "endangered on account of the participation of the witness in judicial proceeding." In several trafficking cases, immediate family members of trafficked persons have been provided residence in the United States in order to guarantee their safety. For example, the victims of a prominent San Francisco landlord, Lakireddy Bali Reddy, who trafficked men, women, and children into sexual and other forms of forced labor over a decade, were provided permanent residence in the United States under the witness protection program.

Normally, however, under the witness protection program there must be a 'real' threat to trafficked persons, and that kind of requirement is difficult to prove. An additional problem arises once an individual enters the program. As one service provider to trafficked women noted, "the witness protection program is premised on the notion of blending into the community — something that is not possible when the people needing protection do not speak the language and cannot immediately function on their own as the witness protection program requires." Thus, the Federal Witness Security Program is not always suitable for trafficked persons.

....

V. INTERNATIONAL IMPACT OF TVPA

Sex trafficking is an international crime that requires an international response. Rising unemployment, poverty, and a weakened social structure in war torn countries make women and children in developing and transitioning nations particularly vulnerable to trafficking. The United States realizes that it cannot simply combat trafficking domestically. Therefore, the trafficking of women for sexual exploitation and slavery has become a significant U.S. foreign policy issue.

A. International TVPA Implementation Measures by the DoS

1. DoS Trafficking in Persons Reports

....

The TIP Reports have become an "invaluable tool" for the United States in "bilateral dialogues on trafficking." Many countries named in the 2001 TIP Report reacted with a high degree of concern and subsequently took action in response to their inclusion in the Report. Countries placed in Tier 2 or Tier 3 were prompted to engage for the first time with the United States government in programs to reduce trafficking. Countries categorized under Tier 2 naturally sought to strengthen their country's anti-trafficking image in order to avoid the risk of falling into Tier 3, which would render them eligible for economic sanctions beginning in October 2003. Many of the Tier 3 countries have asked for U.S. government assistance to implement changes that would allow names to be removed from the Tier 3 list.

The TIP Reports are more than simply the DoS's assessment of crime statistics. They have gained credibility because the DoS has chosen to omit countries from the Reports when available information was incomplete or could not be verified. Thus, other nations have come to view the TIP Reports as legitimate tools to aid them in combating trafficking rather than as a condemnation of individual countries.

In July 2001, the DoS published the first annual TIP Report. The report placed the governments of seventy nations into either Tier 1 or Tier 2, and it listed eighty-two nations as having a significant record of cases involving "severe forms of trafficking." After the release of this report, a number of Tier 2 and Tier 3 governments immediately took steps to prevent trafficking, prosecute traffickers, and protect victims. The 2001 TIP Report and a statement by the DoS provide statistically significant data to support the hypothesis that the TVPA has had an international impact on some countries engaged in trafficking.

....

B. International TVPA Implementation Measures by the DoJ

....

5. DoJ Working with Congress to Amend The Protect Act

The DoJ Criminal Division worked with Congress to overhaul the federal policy on sex tourism in 2003. The Protect Act, which President George W. Bush signed into law on April 30, 2003, allows prosecution of any American who, while abroad, attempts to or actually engages in statutory rape or sexual abuse of a child or who pays a minor to engage in sex. The Protect Act is a powerful tool in the battle against trafficking. It enables the DoJ to conduct undercover operations against American offenders engaging in illicit sexual activities overseas.

....

E. Measures Taken By Foreign Countries to Combat Trafficking

In June 2001, only eight months after the passage of the TVPA, the first 2001 TIP Report concluded that "most governments [were] in fact taking steps to curb [trafficking] and to help the hundreds of thousands of men, women, and children who are its victims." While some countries have enacted legislation prohibiting trafficking, others still do not have a specific penal code provision criminalizing the act of trafficking itself.

....

As noted in the 2002 TIP Report, "Several countries increased their efforts to combat trafficking since issuance of the Department's 2001 report." South Korea, for example, moved from Tier 3 to Tier 1 after the publication of the 2001 TIP Report. Similarly, Romania and Israel demonstrated "a stronger and clearer commitment to this issue and implement[ed] a wide range of activities to combat trafficking. Both have accordingly moved from Tier 3 to Tier 2 [in 2001]." Albania, Gabon, Kazakhstan, Malaysia, Pakistan, and Yugoslavia also moved from Tier 3 to Tier 2 in 2002 because of the impact of the 2001 TIP Report in particular and the TVPA in general. Several countries placed in Tier 2 on the 2001 TIP Report advanced to Tier 1 in the 2002 Report because they made significant efforts to fully comply with the minimum standards and are now in full compliance. Only a small number of countries dropped from Tier 2 in 2001 to Tier 3 in 2002 due to their disappointing efforts to comply with minimum standards.

....

Notes and Questions

1. Tiefenbrun writes in a fairly optimistic way about the effects of the TVPA on trafficking within the U.S.. What should our measure of success be? How many prosecutions would be necessary before describing the law as effective?

2. In the years since the establishment of the T visa program less than 2,000 T visas have been granted, although 5,000 are available per year.[18] This does not begin to reach the level allowed for in the statutory quota. Why might this be? What does it indicate about the likelihood of trafficking victims being willing to cooperate with law enforcement? Reauthorizations of the TVPA in 2003, 2005 and 2008 have all strengthened protections for trafficking victims and added tools for the facilitation of prosecution of traffickers.

––––––––––

IV. The U.S. Government and International Sex Trafficking

The Bush Administration took up human trafficking as a high priority item soon after the 2000 presidential election.[19] The issue had great appeal on both the left and right of the political spectrum, with implications for both global justice and sexual morality. Although the issue has received less attention since the invasion of Iraq in 2003, during the first Bush administration, Secretary of State Colin Powell took a personal interest in human trafficking, and sex trafficking in particular.

––––––––––

18. Lise Olsen, *Trafficking Victims' Lives in Visa Limbo: Only Half of the Rescued Women Have Gotten Papers Needed to Make a Fresh Start in the U.S.*, Hous. Chron., Nov. 24, 2008, at A1, *available at* http://www.chron.com/disp/story.mpl/metropolitan/6129019.html.

19. John Ashcroft, U.S. Att'y Gen., News Conference on Worker Exploitation, *supra* note 1 (announcing that the fight against trafficking would be a central goal of the Bush Administration).

The U.S. anti-trafficking legislation, the Trafficking Victims Protection Act, described in the Susan Tiefenbrun article above, reflects global trends in approaching human trafficking as a separate, distinct and commonly defined crime. The statute mandates a yearly report by the State Department to Congress on the relative effectiveness of anti-trafficking efforts in various countries (TIP Report).[20] The report has become a skillfully crafted document, showing the U.S. as a driving force behind the international anti-trafficking movement. Because of its highly charged political nature, and its placement of each country into a category based on how well it is responding to trafficking within its own borders, the report has generated some criticism from human rights bodies. The principal concern is that categorization of countries by the State Department has been based on considerations other than anti-trafficking efforts by those countries. Countries may be placed in one of several different "tiers" of achievement in the anti-trafficking realm, as described in the report below. Excerpts from the 2008 report have been chosen to give a sense of the wide-ranging topics covered by the annual report.

U.S. Department of State, 2008 Trafficking in Persons Report
available at http://www.state.gov/documents/organization/105501.pdf

Focus of the 2008 TIP Report

The TIP Report is the most comprehensive worldwide report on the efforts of governments to combat severe forms of trafficking in persons. This Report covers the period of April 2007 through March 2008. It includes those countries that have been determined to be countries of origin, transit, or destination for a significant number of victims of severe forms of trafficking. The 2008 TIP Report represents an updated, global look at the nature and scope of modern-day slavery and the broad range of actions being taken by governments around the world to confront and eliminate it.

Because trafficking likely extends to every country in the world, the omission of a country from the Report may only indicate a lack of adequate information. The country narratives describe the scope and nature of the trafficking problem, the reasons for including the country, and the government's efforts to combat trafficking. Each narrative also contains an assessment of the government's compliance with the minimum standards for the elimination of trafficking as laid out in the TVPA, and includes suggestions for additional actions to combat trafficking on the part of a country's government. The remainder of the country narrative describes each government's efforts to enforce laws against trafficking, protect victims, and prevent trafficking. each narrative explains the basis for rating a country as Tier 1, Tier 2, Tier 2 Watch List, or Tier 3. All rankings are accompanied by an explanation, but in particular, if a country has been placed on Tier 2 Watch List, the narrative will contain a statement of explanation, using the special criteria found in the TVPA.

The TVPA lists three factors to be considered in determining whether a country should be in Tier 2 (or Tier 2 Watch List) or in Tier 3: (1) The extent to which the country is a country of origin, transit, or destination for severe forms of trafficking; (2) The extent to which the government of the country does not comply with the TVPA's minimum standards including, in particular, the extent of the government's trafficking-related corruption; and (3) The resources and capabilities of the government to address and eliminate severe forms of trafficking in persons.

---

20. Victims of Trafficking and Violence Protection Act § 7107(b) (mandating the Secretary of State to submit trafficking in persons reports).

Some countries have held conferences and established task forces or national action plans to create goals for anti-trafficking efforts. While such activities are useful and can help to catalyze concrete law enforcement, protection, and prevention activities in the future, these conferences, plans, and task forces alone are not weighed heavily in assessing country efforts. Rather, the Report focuses on concrete actions governments have taken to fight trafficking, especially prosecutions, convictions, and prison sentences for traffickers, victim protection measures, and prevention efforts. The Report does not give great weight to laws in draft form or laws that have not yet been enacted. Finally, the Report does not focus on government efforts that contribute indirectly to reducing trafficking, such as education programs, support for economic development, or programs aimed at enhancing gender equality, although these are worthwhile endeavors.

Methodology

The Department of State prepared this Report using information from U.S. embassies, foreign government officials, nongovernmental organizations (NGOs) and international organizations, published reports, research trips to every region, and information submitted to tipreport@state.gov. This email address was established for NGOs and individuals to share information on government progress in addressing trafficking. U.S. diplomatic posts reported on the trafficking situation and governmental action based on thorough research, including meetings with a wide variety of government officials, local and international NGO representatives, officials of international organizations, journalists, academics, and survivors. To compile this year's Report, the Department took a fresh look at information sources on every country to make its assessments. Assessing each government's anti-trafficking efforts involves a two-step process:

Step one: Finding Significant Numbers of Victims

First, the Department determines whether a country is "a country of origin, transit, or destination for a significant number of victims of severe forms of trafficking," generally on the order of 100 or more victims, the same threshold applied in previous reports. Some countries, for which such information was not available, are not given tier ratings, but are included in the Special Case section because they exhibited indications of trafficking.

Step Two: Tier Placement

The Department places each country included on the 2008 TIP Report into one of the three lists, described here as tiers, mandated by the TVPA. This placement is based more on the extent of government action to combat trafficking, rather than the size of the problem, important though that is. The Department first evaluates whether the government fully complies with the TVPA's minimum standards for the elimination of trafficking (detailed on p. 284). Governments that fully comply are placed in Tier 1. For other governments, the Department considers whether they are making significant efforts to bring themselves into compliance. governments that are making significant efforts to meet the minimum standards are placed in Tier 2. Governments that do not fully comply with the minimum standards and are not making significant efforts to do so are placed in Tier 3. Finally, the Special Watch List criteria are considered and, when applicable, Tier 2 countries are placed on the Tier 2 Watch List.

The Special Watch List — Tier 2 Watch List

The TVPA created a "Special Watch List" of countries on the TIP Report that should receive special scrutiny. The list is composed of: 1) Countries listed as Tier 1 in the current Report that were listed as Tier 2 in the 2007 Report; 2) Countries listed as Tier 2 in the current Report that were listed as Tier 3 in the 2007 Report; and, 3) Countries listed as Tier 2 in the current Report, where:

a) The absolute number of victims of severe forms of trafficking is very significant or is significantly increasing;

b) There is a failure to provide evidence of increasing efforts to combat severe forms of trafficking in persons from the previous year, including increased investigations, prosecutions, and convictions of trafficking crimes, increased assistance to victims, and decreasing evidence of complicity in severe forms of trafficking by government officials; or

c) The determination that a country is making significant efforts to bring itself into compliance with the minimum standards was based on commitments by the country to take additional future steps over the next year.

This third category (including a, b, and c) has been termed by the Department of State "Tier 2 Watch List." There were 32 countries placed on Tier 2 Watch List in the June 2007 Report. Along with two countries that were reassessed as Tier 2 Watch List countries in October 2007, and seven countries that met the first two categories above (moving up a tier from the 2007 to the 2008 TIP Report), these 41 countries were included in an "Interim Assessment" released by the Department of State on February 28, 2008.

Of the 34 countries on Tier 2 Watch List at the time of the Interim Assessment, 11 moved up to Tier 2 on this Report, while four fell to Tier 3 and 19 remain on Tier 2 Watch List. Countries placed on the Special Watch List in this Report will be reexamined in an interim assessment to be submitted to the U.S. Congress by February 1, 2009.

Potential Penalties for Tier 3 Countries

Governments of countries in Tier 3 may be subject to certain sanctions. The U.S. Government may withhold non-humanitarian, non-trade-related foreign assistance. Countries that receive no such assistance would be subject to withholding of funding for participation by officials and employees of such governments in educational and cultural exchange programs. Consistent with the TVPA, governments subject to sanctions would also face U.S. opposition to assistance (except for humanitarian, trade-related, and certain development-related assistance) from international financial institutions such as the International Monetary Fund and the World Bank. Sanctions, if imposed, will take effect October 1, 2008.

All or part of the TVPA's sanctions can be waived upon a determination by the President that the provision of such assistance to the government would promote the purposes of the statute or is otherwise in the national interest of the United States. The TVPA also provides that sanctions can be waived if necessary to avoid significant adverse effects on vulnerable populations, including women and children. Sanctions would not apply if the President finds that, after this Report is issued but before sanctions determinations are made, a government has come into compliance with the minimum standards or is making significant efforts to bring itself into compliance.

Regardless of tier placement, every country can do more, including the United States. No country placement is permanent. All countries must maintain and increase efforts to combat trafficking.

How the Report Is Used

This Report is a diplomatic tool for the U.S. Government to use as an instrument for continued dialogue and encouragement and as a guide to help focus resources on prosecution, protection, and prevention programs and policies. Specific recommendations highlighted in the narrative of each ranked country are provided to facilitate future progress. The State Department will continue to engage governments about the content of the Report in order to strengthen cooperative efforts to eradicate trafficking. In the coming year, and particularly in the months before a determination is made regarding sanctions for Tier 3 countries, the Department will use the information gathered here to more effectively target assistance programs and to work with countries that need help in combating trafficking. The Department hopes the Report will be a catalyst for government and non-government efforts to combat trafficking in persons around the world.

Major Forms of Trafficking in Persons

[The Report points to forced labor, bonded labor, debt bondage, forced child labor and child soldiers.]

....

Sex Trafficking and Prostitution

Sex trafficking comprises a significant portion of overall trafficking and the majority of transnational modern-day slavery. Sex trafficking would not exist without the demand for commercial sex flourishing around the world. The U.S. Government adopted a strong position against prostitution in a December 2002 policy decision, which notes that prostitution is inherently harmful and dehumanizing, and fuels trafficking in persons. Turning people into dehumanized commodities creates an enabling environment for human trafficking.

The United States Government opposes prostitution and any related activities, including pimping, pandering, or maintaining brothels as contributing to the phenomenon of trafficking in persons, and maintains that these activities should not be regulated as a legitimate form of work for any human being. Those who patronize the commercial sex industry form a demand which traffickers seek to satisfy.

Children Exploited for Commercial Sex

Each year, more than two million children are exploited in the global commercial sex trade. Many of these children are trapped in prostitution. The commercial sexual exploitation of children is trafficking, regardless of circumstances. International covenants and protocols obligate criminalization of the commercial sexual exploitation of children. The use of children in the commercial sex trade is prohibited under both U.S. law and the U.N. TIP Protocol. There can be no exceptions, no cultural or socio-economic rationalizations that prevent the rescue of children from sexual servitude. Terms such as "child sex worker" are unacceptable because they falsely sanitize the brutality of this exploitation.

Child Sex Tourism

Child sex tourism (CST) involves people who travel from their own country—often a country where child sexual exploitation is illegal or culturally abhorrent—to another country where they engage in commercial sex acts with children. CST is a shameful assault on the dignity of children and a form of violent child abuse. The commercial sexual exploitation of children has devastating consequences for minors, which may include long-lasting physical and psychological trauma, disease (including HIV/AIDS), drug addiction, unwanted pregnancy, malnutrition, social ostracism, and possibly death.

Tourists engaging in CST often travel to developing countries looking for anonymity and the availability of children in prostitution. The crime is typically fueled by weak law enforcement, corruption, the Internet, ease of travel, and poverty. Sex offenders come from all socio-economic backgrounds and may in some cases hold positions of trust. Cases of child sex tourism involving U.S. citizens have included a pediatrician, a retired Army sergeant, a dentist, and a university professor. Child pornography is frequently involved in these cases, and drugs may also be used to solicit or control the minors.

Punishing Trafficking Offenders Adequately

Much of the analysis of foreign governments' anti-trafficking efforts contained in this Report focuses on the issues of punishing trafficking offenders and protecting victims of trafficking. The following offers a look at how this analysis is conducted, based on the standards provided in the TVPA.

The minimum standards found in the Trafficking Victims Protection Act call on foreign governments to prohibit all forms of trafficking, prescribe penalties for those acts that are sufficiently stringent to deter the crime and that adequately reflect the heinous nature of the crime, and vigorously punish offenders convicted of these crimes.

Legally Prescribed Penalties: In assessing foreign governments' anti-trafficking efforts in the TIP Report, the Department of State holds that, consistent with the 2000 U.N. Convention Against Transnational Organized Crime (which is supplemented by the U.N. TIP Protocol), criminal penalties to meet this standard should include a maximum of at least four years' deprivation of liberty, or a more severe penalty.

Imposed Penalties: The Department of State holds that imposed sentences should involve significant jail time, with a majority of cases resulting in sentences on the order of one year of imprisonment or more, but taking into account the severity of an individual's involvement in trafficking, imposed sentences for other grave crimes, and the judiciary's right to hand down punishments consistent with that country's laws. Convictions obtained under other criminal laws and statutes can be counted as anti-trafficking if the government verifies that the offenses involve human trafficking.

Protecting Victims Adequately

The TVPA minimum standards' criterion on victim protection reads:

"Whether the government of the country protects victims of severe forms of trafficking in persons and encourages their assistance in the investigation and prosecution of such trafficking, including provisions for legal alternatives to their removal to countries in which they would face retribution or hardship, and ensures that victims are not inappropriately incarcerated, fined, or otherwise penalized solely for unlawful acts as a direct result of being trafficked."

In every country narrative of the TIP Report, these three numbered elements are specifically addressed. In addition, the Department of State has decided to implement this criterion with the following guidelines:

In evaluating whether a country fully complies with this minimum standard for victim protection, the State Department considers the following to be critical factors:

1) Proactive identification: Victims should not be expected to identify themselves. They typically are afraid of coming forward and being considered criminals, irregular migrants, or disposable people by authorities. Formal screening procedures should go beyond checking a person's papers. Some form of systematic procedure should be in place to guide law enforcement and other governmental or government-supported front-line responders in the process of victim identification.

2) Shelter and temporary care: A government should ensure that victims receive access to primary health care, counseling, and shelter that allows them to recount their trafficking experience to trained social counselors and law enforcement at a pace with minimal pressure. Shelter and assistance can be provided in cooperation with NGOs. Part of the host government's responsibility includes funding for, and referral to, NGOs providing services. To the best extent possible, trafficking victims should not be held in immigration detention centers, or other detention.

The Department of State also gives positive consideration to two additional victim protection factors:

A. Victim/witness protection, rights and confidentiality: Governments should ensure that victims are provided with legal and other assistance and that, consistent with its domestic law, proceedings are not prejudicial to victims' rights, dignity, or psychological well-being. Confidentiality and privacy should be respected and protected to the extent possible under domestic law. Victims should be provided with information in a language they understand.

B. Repatriation: Source and destination countries share responsibility in ensuring the safe, humane and, to the extent possible, voluntary repatriation/ reintegration of victims. At a minimum, destination countries should contact a competent governmental body, NGO or international organization in the relevant source country to ensure that trafficked persons who return to their country of origin are provided with assistance and support necessary to their wellbeing. Trafficking victims should not be subjected to deportations or forced returns without safeguards or other measures to reduce the risk of hardship, retribution, or re-trafficking.

Prevention: Spotlight on Addressing Demand

Human trafficking is a dehumanizing crime which turns people into mere commodities. On the supply side, criminal networks, corruption, lack of education, and misinformation about employment opportunities and the degrading nature of work promised, together with poverty, make people vulnerable to the lures of trafficking—this is true of both sex trafficking and slave labor. Significant efforts are being made to address these factors that "push" victims into being trafficked, but they alone are not the cause. Increasingly, the movement to end human trafficking is focusing on the voracious demand which fuels this dark trade in human beings.

. . . .

In 2005, the UN Commission on the Status of Women adopted the U.S. resolution eliminating Demand for Trafficked Women and girls for All Forms of exploitation. This was the first UN resolution to focus on the demand side of human trafficking—the goal being to protect women and girls by drying up the "market" for trafficking victims, including by recognizing a link to commercial sexual exploitation.

Importance of Research

Indisputably, as a new field of inquiry and activism, anti-trafficking efforts will benefit from dedicated research, especially operational research designed to inform programming. An important example of the value of research, funded by the Office to Monitor and Combat Trafficking in Persons, is a groundbreaking study by Dr. Jay Silverman on sex trafficking and HIV within South Asia published in the Journal of the American Medical Association last summer. It has been estimated that half of all female sex trafficking victims in South Asia are under age eighteen at the time of exploitation. Yet, research on HIV and sexually-transmitted infections has rarely sought to identify adult or child trafficking victims. Dr. Silverman and his team partnered with major NGOs across India, Nepal and Bangladesh involved in rescue and care of sex trafficking victims to examine the phenomena of sex trafficking, HIV prevalence, and trafficking-related risk factors.

Among Nepalese women and girls who were repatriated victims of sex trafficking, the Silverman study found that 38 percent were HIV positive. The majority were trafficked prior to age 18. One in seven was trafficked before age 15, and among these very young girls, over 60 percent were infected with HIV. Why? Very young girls were more frequently trafficked to multiple brothels and for longer periods of time.

Silverman concludes that the girls at greatest risk for being infected with HIV (and for transmitting HIV) are the least likely to be reached by traditional HIV prevention models. He proposes collaboration among HIV prevention and human trafficking experts to develop efforts that simultaneously reduce HIV risk and identify and assist trafficking victims—a policy prescription supported by the U.S. Government's interagency working group, the Senior Policy Operating Group.

. . . .

Democracy and Human Trafficking

As already noted, our assessment of a country's performance is based strictly on the trafficking-specific criteria stipulated by the TVPA.

Nevertheless, our broad study of the phenomenon of trafficking corroborates that healthy, vital democratic pluralism is the single most prevalent feature of states conducting effective anti-trafficking efforts. A vibrant democracy is the best guarantor of human dignity and respect for the human rights and fundamental freedoms of all persons, including women, children, prostituted people, and foreign migrants, who are among the vulnerable populations susceptible to trafficking.

The Tiers

TIER 1

Countries whose governments fully comply with the Trafficking Victims Protection Act's (TVPA) minimum standards

TIER 2

Countries whose governments do not fully comply with the TVPA's minimum standards, but are making significant efforts to bring themselves into compliance with those standards

TIER 2 WATCH LIST

Countries whose governments do not fully comply with the TVPA's minimum standards, but are making significant efforts to bring themselves into compliance with those standards AND:

a) The absolute number of victims of severe forms of trafficking is very significant or is significantly increasing; or

b) There is a failure to provide evidence of increasing efforts to combat severe forms of trafficking in persons from the previous year; or

c) The determination that a country is making significant efforts to bring themselves into compliance with minimum standards was based on commitments by the country to take additional future steps over the next year

TIER 3

Countries whose governments do not fully comply with the minimum standards and are not making significant efforts to do so

Tier Placements

June 4, 2008

Tier 1

Australia	Finland	Lithuania	Slovenia
Austria	France	Luxembourg	Spain
Belgium	Georgia	Macedonia	Sweden

Canada	Germany	Madagascar	Switzerland
Colombia	Hong Kong	Netherlands	United Kingdom
Croatia	Hungary	New Zealand	
Czech Republic	Italy	Norway	
Denmark	Korea, Rep. Of	Poland	

Tier 2

Afghanistan	Ghana	Malta	Sierra Leone
Angola	Greece	Mauritania	Singapore
Bangladesh	Honduras	Mauritius	Slovak Republic
Belarus	Indonesia	Mexico	Suriname
Belize	Israel	Mongolia	Tanzania
Benin	Ireland	Morocco	Taiwan
Bolivia	Jamaica	Nepal	Thailand
Bosnia & Herzegovina	Japan	Nicaragua	Timor-Leste
Brazil	Kazakhstan	Nigeria	Togo
Bulgaria	Kenya	Pakistan	Turkey
Burkina Faso	Kyrgyz Republic	Paraguay	Uganda
Cambodia	Laos	Peru	Ukraine
Chile	Latvia	Philippines	United Arab Emirates
Djibouti	Lebanon	Portugal	Uruguay
Ecuador	Liberia	Romania	Vietnam
El SalvadorEstonia	MacauMalawi	RwandaSenegal	Yemen
Ethiopia	Mali	Serbia	

Tier 2 Watch List

Argentina	Congo, Rep. Of	Guinea-Bissau	South Africa
Armenia	Costa Rica	Guyana	Sri Lanka
Azerbaijan	Cyprus	India	Tajikistan
Albania	Cote d'Ivoire	Jordan	Tanzania
Bahrain	Dominican Republic	Libya	Venezuela
Burundi	Egypt	Malaysia	Uzbekistan
Cameroon	Equatorial Guinea	Montenegro	Zambia
Central African Rep.	Gabon	Mozambique	Zimbabwe
Chad	The Gambia	Niger	
China (PRC)	Guatemala	Panama	
Congo (DRC)	Guinea	Russia	

Tier 3

Algeria	Iran	Oman	Sudan
Burma	Kuwait	Papua New Guinea	Syria
Cuba	Moldova	Qatar	
Fiji	North Korea	Saudi Arabia	

U.S. Government Domestic Anti-Trafficking in Persons Efforts

The United States (U.S.) is a destination country for thousands of men, women, and children trafficked largely from East Asia, Mexico, and Central America for the purposes of sexual and labor exploitation. A majority of foreign victims identified during the year were victims of trafficking for forced labor. Some men and women, responding to fraudulent offers of employment in the United States, migrate willingly—legally and illegally—but are subsequently subjected to conditions of involuntary servitude or debt bondage at work sites or in the commercial sex trade. An unknown number of American citizens and legal residents are trafficked within the country primarily for sexual servitude and, to a lesser extent, forced labor.

The U.S. Government (USG) in 2007 continued to advance the goal of eradicating human trafficking in the United States. This coordinated effort includes several federal agencies and approximately $23 million in Fiscal Year (FY) 2007 for domestic programs to boost anti-trafficking law enforcement efforts, identify and protect victims of trafficking, and raise awareness of trafficking as a means of preventing new incidents.

. . . .

Prosecution

The USG sustained anti-trafficking law enforcement efforts over the reporting period. The United States prohibits all forms of trafficking in persons through criminal statutes created or strengthened by the 2000 Trafficking Victims Protection Act (TVPA), as amended. In Fiscal Year (FY) 2007, DOJ's Civil Rights Division and U.S. Attorneys' Offices initiated 182 investigations, charged 89 individuals, and obtained 103 convictions in cases involving human trafficking. Under the TVPA, traffickers can be sentenced to up to 20 years' imprisonment. The average prison sentence imposed for trafficking crimes under the TVPA in FY 2007 was 113 months (9.4 years). The Federal Bureau of Investigation and DOJ's Criminal Division continued to combat the exploitation of children in prostitution in the United States through the Innocence Lost National Initiative; in FY 2007, this Initiative resulted in 308 arrests, 106 convictions, and 181 recovered children.

The federal government worked to bolster efforts at state and local levels. By the end of 2007, 33 states had passed criminal anti-trafficking legislation. In 2007, the Department of Health and Human Services (HHS) further strengthened the Rescue & Restore Regional Program, employing a community-based intermediary model to regionally develop civil society networks for outreach, identification, and service activities.

Protection

The USG continued to provide strong victim protection services over the year. Through FY 2007, HHS certified or issued eligibility letters to 1,379 victims of human trafficking since the TVPA was signed into law in October 2000. HHS certified 270 adult victims in FY 2007, and issued eligibility letters to 33 minors. Thirty percent of the total 303 victims were male, a significant increase from the six percent male victims certified in FY 2006. Certified victims came from over 50 countries globally and at least 63 percent of them were victims of trafficking for forced labor. Primary sources in FY 2007 of victims were Thailand (48), Mexico (42), Guatemala (25), Philippines (23), and China (21). Certification and letters of eligibility allow human trafficking survivors to access services and benefits, comparable to assistance provided by the U.S. to refugees. The HHS Per-Capita Services Contract implemented by civil society partners currently covers 125 sites across the country providing "anytime, anywhere" services to human trafficking victims.

The Department of Homeland Security (DHS) provides two principal types of immigration relief authorized by the TVPA: 1) continued presence (CP) to human trafficking victims who are potential witnesses during investigation or prosecution, and 2) T non-immigrant status or "T-visas," a special, self-petitioned visa category for trafficking victims. In FY 2007, DHS/ICE's Law Enforcement Parole Branch approved 122 requests for CP and five requests for extensions of existing CPs. DHS U.S. Citizenship and Immigration Services issued 279 T-visas to foreign survivors of human trafficking in the U.S. and 261 T-visas to their immediate family members in FY 2007. The USG continues to work towards publishing a regulation for the adjustment of status for qualified T-visa holders, creating a pathway for citizenship.

As part of the assistance provided under the TVPA, the Department of State's Bureau of Population, Refugees, and Migration funds the Return, Reintegration, and Family Reunification Program for Victims of Trafficking. In calendar year 2007, the program assisted 104 cases. Of the cases assisted, five victims of trafficking elected to return to their country of origin, and 99 family members were reunited with trafficking survivors in the United States. Since its inception in 2005, the program has assisted around160 persons from 31 countries.

Prevention

Prevention efforts increased over the year, as HHS continued to fund the Rescue & Restore public awareness campaign and DHS/ICE produced a new public service announcement in multiple languages. HHS founded four additional Rescue & Restore coalitions. HHS restructured the National Human Trafficking Resource Center in 2007 to provide national training and technical assistance, in addition to operating a national hotline (1-888-3737-888). To improve identification and increase awareness, HHS also started: 1) a pilot program to identify trafficking among unaccompanied alien children; and 2) a domestic notification pilot program that provides suspected U.S. citizen trafficking victims with information regarding the benefits and services for which they may be eligible simply by virtue of their citizenship.

AUSTRALIA (Tier 1)

Australia is a destination country for women from Southeast Asia, South Korea, Taiwan, and the People's Republic of China (P.R.C.) trafficked for the purpose of commercial sexual exploitation. Prostitution is legal except for in the states of Western Australia and South Australia. Many trafficking victims were women who traveled to Australia voluntarily to work in both legal and illegal brothels, but were subject to conditions of debt bondage or involuntary servitude. There were reports of several men and women from India, the P.R.C., South Korea, the Philippines, and Ireland migrating to Australia temporarily for work, but subsequently subjected to conditions of forced labor, including fraudulent recruitment, confiscation of travel documents, confinement, and debt bondage.

The Government of Australia fully complies with the minimum standards for the elimination of trafficking. After holding several hearings, Australia's parliament issued 25 recommendations to address allegations that some employers abused the 457 Temporary Worker Visa Program to subject migrant workers to conditions of forced labor and debt bondage. The Department of Immigration and Citizenship (DIAC) subsequently instituted a series of reforms to improve monitoring of this migrant worker visa program, resulting in a greater number of trafficking cases found in the program. There were no visible measures to reduce the demand for commercial sex acts in the legalized commercial sex industry in Australia. The government provides substantial funding to support anti-trafficking efforts throughout the Southeast Asia region, including law enforcement training, victim assistance programs, and prevention activities.

....

Prosecution

The Government of Australia continued to demonstrate efforts to address trafficking in persons through law enforcement means. Australia prohibits sex and labor trafficking and trafficking-related offenses in Divisions 270 and 271 of the Commonwealth Criminal Code, which prescribe penalties that are sufficiently stringent and commensurate with those prescribed for other grave crimes. In August 2007, the Migration Amendment (Employer Sanctions) Act went into force, prescribing penalties of two to five years' imprisonment for persons convicted of exploiting others for forced labor, sexual servitude, or slavery in Australia. During the reporting period, the Transnational Sexual Exploitation and Trafficking Teams within the Australian Federal Police (AFP) conducted 27 investigations, of which approximately 80 percent were related to sex trafficking. As of February 2008, there were seven trafficking-related cases before the courts involving 15 defendants, with three of the seven cases in the appeal phase. During the reporting period, there were four convictions for trafficking; one defendant was sentenced to eight years' imprisonment.

[The Report here describes specific instances of Australian law enforcement efforts to combat trafficking within Australia.]

Protection

The Government of Australia continued to provide comprehensive assistance for victims of trafficking and their family members, if they were willing to aid in criminal prosecutions. The government encourages victims and witnesses to participate in the investigation of trafficking, but directly links continued assistance to victims' role in a viable prosecution. A total of 89 victims of labor and sex trafficking received assistance since 2004 through the Office of Women's "Support for Victims of People Trafficking Program." Other victims who do not qualify for this program may be eligible for a protection visa as a refugee, but the government does not generally assist with such applications. Individuals granted status under this visa regime are entitled to a package of benefits, including shelter, counseling, food and a living allowance. Australia funds two return and reintegration activities in the region. The first is for return and reintegration of trafficked women and children, and the second solely supports Thai victims. Victims are not inappropriately incarcerated, fined, or penalized for unlawful acts as a direct result of being trafficked.

Prevention

The Government of Australia demonstrated efforts to prevent trafficking in persons during the year. The Australian Agency for International Development (AUSAID) introduced a comprehensive child protection policy, covering all aspects of the agency's operations and applying both to AUSAID staff and all contractors and non-governmental organizations funded by the agency.... Australia's extra-territorial law on child sex tourism provides penalties of up to 17 years' imprisonment for Australians convicted of sexually exploiting children under the age 16 while outside of Australia. Thirty prosecutions since the introduction of Australia's child sex tourism laws have led to 19 convictions. Australian citizens were returned to Australia to face prosecution for sexually exploiting children in other countries under Australia's extraterritorial child sex tourism law. The Australian Government offers travelers a travel bulletin warning against child sex tourism through a government website. The Australian Government also produces a brochure "Travel Smart: Hints for Australian Travelers," that includes information on child sex crimes, existing legislation, and details on how to report a possible violation of Australia's child sex tourism laws to the AFP. Travel Smart is distributed with every passport renewal by the Australian Passports Office; during the reporting period 855,055 were distributed.

BRAZIL (Tier 2)

Brazil is a source country for women and children trafficked within the country and transnationally for the purposes of commercial sexual exploitation, as well as a source country for men trafficked internally for forced labor. The Brazilian Federal Police estimate that 250,000 children are exploited for prostitution, although NGOs put the number as high as 500,000. Between 25,000 to 100,000 men are subjected to slave labor within the country. Approximately half of the nearly 6,000 men freed from slave labor in 2007 were found exploited on plantations growing sugar cane for the production of ethanol, a growing trend. A large number of Brazilian women and girls are trafficked for sexual exploitation to destinations in South America, the Caribbean, Western Europe, Japan, the United States, and the Middle East. To a lesser extent, Brazil is a destination for the trafficking of men, women, and children from Bolivia, Peru, and the People's Republic of China (P.R.C.) for forced labor into factories in major urban areas of Brazil. Child sex tourism remains a serious problem, particularly in the resort areas and coastal areas of Brazil's northeast, and mostly involves tourists from Europe and the United States.

The Government of Brazil does not fully comply with the minimum standards for the elimination of trafficking; however, it is making significant efforts to do so. Over the past year, the government significantly increased efforts to rescue victims of slave labor through mobile inspection operations in the Amazon and remote locations, and also increased efforts to provide greater services for victims. At the same time, however, the government did not report any criminal investigations, prosecutions, convictions, or punishments of forced labor crimes and only limited investigations of sex trafficking crimes. A lack of government resources and dedicated personnel impeded Brazil's ability to combat its trafficking problem, although the government committed to allocate more funding to anti-trafficking efforts in its recently instituted national work plan to combat trafficking in persons and forced labor.

....

Prosecution

The Brazilian government demonstrated modest law enforcement efforts to confront human trafficking crimes during the last year. Brazil does not prohibit all forms of trafficking in persons, although transnational and internal trafficking for commercial sexual exploitation is prohibited under Section 231 of its penal code, which prescribes penalties of three to 10 years' imprisonment—penalties that are sufficiently stringent and commensurate with those prescribed for other grave crimes, such as rape. Some aspects of labor trafficking are criminalized under Brazilian law, including debt bondage, for which a sufficiently stringent penalty of two to eight years' imprisonment is prescribed. Forced labor is prohibited by Section 148 of the penal code—*trabalho escravo* ("slave labor")—prescribing penalties of one to three years' imprisonment. Fraudulent recruitment for the purpose of labor exploitation is also prohibited, with penalties of two months, to one year's imprisonment plus fines. The penalties for these labor trafficking offenses are not sufficiently stringent to deter these crimes. An October 2006 Presidential decree on human trafficking included a stated goal to amend the law so that penalties applied to labor trafficking crimes would be made commensurate with those applied to sex trafficking crimes; such amendments, while unrealized as of this writing, would assist the government's efforts to punish and deter exploiters of slave labor.

[The Report here describes deficiencies in data collection on this issue in Brazil.]

The government did not report any criminal investigations or prosecutions of forced labor crimes, although 751 civil investigations are under way, and 890 cases have been filed for prosecution in civil labor courts. Such actions typically result in back pay and fines levied against landowners and other offenders—penalties that are inadequate. A Supreme Court ruling of November 2006, which requires that all criminal complaints of "slave labor" be heard by a federal criminal court, appears to remain unimplemented. The Ministry of Labor's anti-slave labor mobile units increased their operations during the year, as the unit's labor inspectors freed victims, forced those responsible for forced labor to pay often substantial amounts in fines and restitution to the victims, and then moved on to others locations to inspect. Mobile unit inspectors did not, however, seize evidence or attempt to interview witnesses with the goal of developing a criminal investigation or prosecution because inspectors and the labor court prosecutors who accompany them have only civil jurisdiction. Because their exploiters are rarely punished, many of the rescued victims are ultimately re-trafficked. The Ministry of Labor's "dirty list" which publicly identifies individuals and corporate entities the government has determined to have been responsible for slave labor, continued to provide a modicum of punishment to those engaged in this serious crime, largely through public shame and the barring of these entities' access to loans from state financial institutions. During the year, however, a number of individuals and corporate entities were able to remove their names from the "dirty list" through court action. Throughout the year, there were reports of government officials' complicity in sex trafficking or slave labor, particularly with regards to police—directly or indirectly involved in sex trafficking rings—notably in the Amazon and northern states. Furthermore, numerous credible reports indicated that state police officials were involved in the killing or intimidation of witnesses involved in testifying against police officials in labor exploitation or forced labor hearings. There were also numerous killings of rural labor activists and labor union organizations, some of whom were active in fighting forced labor practices; some of these killings reportedly occurred with the participation or knowledge of state law enforcement officials.

[This section described modest efforts by Brazil to protect victims and prevent trafficking.]

....

CHINA (Tier 2 Watch List)

The People's Republic of China (P.R.C.) is a source, transit, and destination country for men, women, and children trafficked for the purposes of sexual exploitation and forced labor. The majority of trafficking in China occurs within the country's borders, but there is also considerable international trafficking of P.R.C. citizens to Africa, Asia, Europe, Latin America, the Middle East, and North America, which often occurs within a larger flow of human smuggling. Chinese women are lured abroad through false promises of legitimate employment, only to be forced into commercial sexual exploitation, largely in Taiwan, Thailand, Malaysia, and Japan. There are also many cases involving Chinese men and women who are smuggled into destination countries throughout the world at an enormous personal financial cost and whose indebtedness to traffickers is then used as a means to coerce them into commercial sexual exploitation or forced labor. Women and children are trafficked to China from Mongolia, Burma, North Korea, Russia, and Vietnam for forced labor, marriage, and prostitution. North Korean women and children seeking to leave their country voluntarily cross the border into China, but some of these individuals, after they enter the P.R.C. in a vulnerable, undocumented status, are then sold into prostitution, marriage, or forced labor. While it is difficult to determine if the P.R.C.'s male-female birth ratio imbalance, with more males than females, is currently affecting trafficking of women for brides, some experts believe that it has already or may become a contributing factor.

Forced labor, including forced child labor, remains a significant problem in China. Children as young as 12 were reportedly subjected to forced labor under the guise of "Work and Study" programs over the past year. Conditions in this program include excessive hours with mandatory overtime, dangerous conditions, low pay, and involuntary pay deductions. In June 2007, a Guangdong factory licensed to produce products bearing the 2008 Olympics logo admitted to employing children as young as 12 years old under similar conditions. Some children, particularly Uighur youth from Xinjiang Province, have been abducted for forced begging and thievery in large cities. Overseas human rights organizations allege that government-sponsored labor programs forced Uighur girls and young women to work in factories in eastern China on false pretenses and without regular wages. Involuntary servitude of Chinese nationals abroad also persisted, although the extent of the problem is unclear. Experts believe that the number of Chinese labor and sex trafficking victims in Europe is growing in countries such as Britain, Italy, and France.

The government of the P.R.C. does not fully comply with the minimum standards for the elimination of trafficking; however, it is making significant efforts to do so. Nevertheless, China is placed on Tier 2 Watch List for the fourth consecutive year for its failure to provide evidence of increasing efforts to combat human trafficking from the previous year, particularly in terms of punishment of trafficking crimes and the protection of Chinese and foreign victims of trafficking. Victims are sometimes punished for unlawful acts that were committed as a direct result of their being trafficked—such as violations of prostitution or immigration/emigration controls. The Chinese government continued to treat North Korean victims of trafficking solely as economic migrants, routinely deporting them back to horrendous conditions in North Korea. Additional challenges facing the P.R.C. government include the enormous size of its trafficking problem and the significant level of corruption and complicity in trafficking by some local government officials. Factors impeding progress in anti-trafficking efforts include tight controls over civil society organizations, restricted access of foreign anti-trafficking organizations, and the government's systematic lack of transparency.

During the reporting period, the Chinese government established a new Office for Preventing and Combating Crimes of Trafficking in Women and Children and released its long-awaited National Action Plan to Combat Trafficking in December 2007, which details anti-trafficking responsibilities implemented by 28 ministries and appoints the Ministry of Public Security (MPS) as coordinator of the Chinese government's anti-trafficking efforts. However, there are no plans for resources to be allocated to local and provincial governments for the implementation of the plan. Additionally, the action plan covers only sex trafficking of females, and does not address labor trafficking or male victims of sex trafficking. As host to the Second Coordinated Mekong Ministerial Initiative Against Trafficking (COMMIT) Summit in December 2007, China joined other ministers in signing a Joint Declaration to work together to implement the Sub-regional Plan of Action.

....

Prosecution

China sustained its record of criminal law enforcement against traffickers over the reporting period, though government statistics are difficult to verify. P.R.C. law criminalizes forced prostitution, abduction, and the commercial sexual exploitation of girls under 14 through Article 244 of its Criminal Code. Article 41 of China's revised Law on the Protection of Minors, in effect since June 2007, now prohibits the trafficking, kidnapping, and sexual exploitation of minors under the age of 18. Prescribed penalties under these criminal statutes are sufficiently stringent and include life imprisonment and the death penalty.

However, Chinese law does not prohibit commercial sexual exploitation involving coercion or fraud, nor does it prohibit all forms of trafficking. The law prohibits the employment of children under the age of 16, but the government had not adopted a comprehensive policy to combat child labor. While Article 244 of its Criminal Code bans forced labor by employers, the prescribed penalties of up to three years' imprisonment or a fine under this law are not sufficiently stringent. Additionally, Chinese law does not recognize forms of coercion other than abduction as constituting a means of trafficking. MPS reported investigating 2,375 cases of trafficking of women and children in 2007, which is significantly lower than the 3,371 cases it cited in 2006. These statistics are likely based on China's definition of the term "trafficking," which does not include acts of forced labor, debt bondage, coercion, or involuntary servitude, or offenses committed against male victims. In September 2007, an MPS official indicated that the number of reported cases of sexual exploitation and forced labor increased from 2006 to 2007. Chinese law enforcement authorities arrested and punished some traffickers involved in forced labor practices and commercial sexual exploitation, but did not provide data on prosecutions, convictions, or sentences.

[This section describes specific instances of forced labor in China.]

Protection

China made incremental progress in victim protection during the reporting period. The government, with the assistance of UNICEF, built a new shelter to provide trafficking victims in Yunnan Province with short-term care, but there remain overall an inadequate number of shelters for victims of trafficking. There continue to be no dedicated government assistance programs for victims of trafficking. China continues to lack systematic victim identification procedures to identify victims of sex trafficking among those it arrests for prostitution and to refer them to organizations providing services. It does not have a comprehensive nationwide victim protection service, but has taken some steps to improve intra-governmental coordination and cooperation in vulnerable southern border provinces. While both the MPS and Ministry of Civil Affairs run shelters, the two ministries do not share information or coordinate their efforts.

[The report indicates that China has done little if anything to assist foreign victims of trafficking within China.]

Prevention

China made efforts to prevent trafficking in persons this year. In July 2007, the ACWF co-sponsored a Children's Forum that brought together children from across the country to discuss ways to prevent the trafficking of vulnerable youth. The government did not conduct any broad public awareness program to inform the public of the dangers of trafficking. With the assistance of NGOs, the Ministry of Education undertook outreach efforts to some villages and schools, providing information on what trafficking is, how to avoid being trafficked, and providing emergency hotline numbers. The Chinese government, through the ACWF, has also conducted training for law enforcement agencies and border entry-exit officials to raise awareness of trafficking. Though it took some steps forward, China still has not taken adequate measures to prevent internal trafficking for sexual exploitation or forced labor, nor did it take measures to reduce the demand for commercial sex acts or child sex tourism. China has not ratified the 2000 UN TIP Protocol.

CUBA (Tier 3)

Cuba is principally a source country for women and children trafficked within the country for the purpose of commercial sexual exploitation. Some families push child victims to prostitute themselves as a means of increasing family income. Cuban children and adults also may be exploited for forced labor. The full scope of trafficking within Cuba is difficult to gauge due to the closed nature of the government and sparse non-governmental or independent reporting. However, by all accounts, the country is a destination for sex tourism, including child sex tourism, which is a problem in many areas of the country. Cuba's thriving sex trade caters to numerous European, Canadian, and Latin American tourists every year. State-run hotel workers, travel employees, cab drivers, and police steer tourists to prostituted women and children and facilitate their commercial sexual exploitation, sometimes extorting money or pay-offs from victims. Limited sex trafficking of Cuban women to Mexico, The Bahamas, and Western Europe has been reported. Some Cuban nationals willingly migrate to the United States, but are subsequently exploited for forced labor by their smugglers. Cuba also is a transit point for the smuggling of migrants from China, Sri Lanka, Bangladesh, Lebanon, and other nations to the United States and Canada. Some of these migrants may be trafficking victims, who are subject to forced labor, sexual exploitation, and abuse.

The Government of Cuba does not fully comply with the minimum standards for the elimination of trafficking and is not making significant efforts to do so. Exact information about trafficking in Cuba is difficult to obtain because the government does not publicly release information, and U.S. attempts to engage officials are viewed as politically motivated. Nonetheless, the Government of Cuba does not appear to have made tangible efforts to prosecute offenders, protect victims, or prevent human trafficking activity during the reporting period.

....

Prosecution

The Government of Cuba prohibits some forms of trafficking activity through various provisions of its penal code. Prostitution for persons over the age of 16 is legal. Article 316 bans transnational trafficking in minors or persons younger than 16 for the purposes of forced labor, prostitution, and pornography, prescribing penalties of seven to 15 years' imprisonment. Article 302 prohibits a defendant from inducing, promoting, or benefiting from prostitution. Such an offense carries penalties of up to 20 years in prison; if the crime is committed across international boundaries, penalties may be increased to 30 years. A second statute, Article 17 of Law Number 87, similarly prohibits the promotion or inducement of prostitution, and carries penalties of four to 10 years in prison; penalties increase to 10 to 20 years if the defendant uses force or threats against the victim. All the above penalties are sufficiently stringent, and commensurate with those prescribed for other grave crimes, such as rape. However, trafficking of adults for forced labor is not currently prohibited under Cuban law. No official data relating to Cuban investigations, prosecutions, and convictions of trafficking offenders in 2007 has been made available, and Cuban law enforcement actions may be more focused on disrupting alien smuggling networks, rather than curbing human trafficking activity. However, reporting from other sources indicates that some foreign nationals, including two American citizens, were convicted in Cuba last year for trafficking-related crimes. At least one sentence of ten years was imposed for the sexual exploitation of a minor. The government also assisted the U.S. Coast Guard with investigating potential human trafficking and alien smuggling activity, particularly cases of migrants compelled to work for smugglers or drug gangs. No investigations or prosecutions of public officials for complicity with human trafficking were noted, although some police officers reportedly accept and solicit bribes in connection with Cuba's sex trade.

Protection

Efforts by the Government of Cuba to aid trafficking victims were not officially reported over the last year, but appeared weak. Strong evidence suggests that victims are punished for unlawful acts committed as a direct result of being trafficked. Although prostitution for persons over age 16 is legal in Cuba, women and children in Cuba's sex trade, including those who may be trafficking victims, are occasionally rounded up and sent to "reeducation" programs; many are sentenced to lengthy prison terms for "dangerousness" or other vagrancy crimes. Detention and rehabilitation centers for women and children in prostitution, some of whom may be trafficking victims, are not staffed with personnel who can provide adequate care, and conditions at these detention centers are reported to be harsh....

Prevention

The government does not acknowledge or condemn human trafficking as a problem in Cuba, and therefore made no significant efforts to prevent incidents of trafficking throughout the year. There were no known information campaigns to prevent sex or labor trafficking, although the government ran newspaper campaigns against prostitution. In addition, police have reportedly cracked down on prostitution in tourist areas during the past year. As noted earlier, the government may have taken steps to reduce demand for commercial sex acts by prosecuting individuals engaging in sexual acts with children. In general, however, the government's efforts appear more focused on arresting women in prostitution rather than punishing clients or consumers. Cuba has not ratified the 2000 UN TIP Protocol.

IRAN (Tier 3)

Iran is a source, transit, and destination for women trafficked for the purposes of sexual exploitation and involuntary servitude. Iranian women are trafficked internally for the purpose of forced prostitution and for forced marriages to settle debts. Iranian children are trafficked internally and Afghan children are trafficked to Iran for the purpose of forced marriages, commercial sexual exploitation and involuntary servitude as beggars or laborers. According to non-governmental sources, Iranian women and girls are also trafficked to Pakistan, Turkey, Qatar, Kuwait, the United Arab Emirates, France, Germany, and the United Kingdom for commercial sexual exploitation.

The Government of Iran does not fully comply with the minimum standards for the elimination of trafficking, and is not making significant efforts to do so. Lack of access to Iran by U.S. Government officials prohibits the collection of full data on the country's human trafficking problem and the government's efforts to curb it. Iran did not provide evidence of law enforcement activities against trafficking, and credible reports indicate that Iranian authorities punish victims of trafficking with beatings, imprisonment, and execution.

....

Prosecution

There is no evidence to indicate that Iran made significant progress in prosecuting and punishing trafficking crimes this year. The government reportedly prohibits all forms of trafficking in persons through its 2004 Law on Combating Human Trafficking, which appears to prescribe severe penalties, often including death sentences for convicted traffickers. Nonetheless, the government did not publicize evidence of enforcing this law during the reporting year through arrests, prosecutions, convictions, or sentences. Previous reports have indicated that border officials may be complicit in trafficking offenses; however, Iran did not report any disciplinary action taken against government officials believed to facilitate trafficking.

Protection

There were no reported efforts by the Government of Iran to improve its protection of trafficking victims this year. The government reportedly punishes victims for unlawful acts committed as a direct result of being trafficked; for instance, victims reportedly are arrested and punished for violations of morality standards such as adultery, defined as sexual relations outside of marriage. It is unknown how many victims may have been subjected to punishment during the reporting period for such acts committed as a result of their trafficking experience. Foreign victims of trafficking do not have a legal alternative to removal to countries in which they may face hardship or retribution. Previous reports indicate that the government does not encourage victims to assist law enforcement authorities as they investigate and prosecute their trafficking cases.

Prevention

There were no reports of any advances in trafficking prevention measures by the Government of Iran during the reporting year. There were similarly no reports of measures taken by the government during the reporting period to reduce the demand for commercial sex acts, or of any public awareness campaigns targeting citizens traveling to known child sex tourism destinations abroad. It is recommended that Iran improve its efforts to prevent trafficking in persons by monitoring travel of Iranian women and girls to Middle Eastern countries where they are commonly trafficked for commercial sexual exploitation. Iran has not ratified the 2000 UN TIP Protocol.

JAPAN (Tier 2)

Japan is a destination and transit country for men, women, and children trafficked for the purposes of commercial sexual exploitation and forced labor. Women and children trafficked to Japan for commercial sexual exploitation come from the People's Republic of China, South Korea, Southeast Asia, Eastern Europe, Russia, and, to a lesser extent, Latin America. Japan is a transit country for persons trafficked from East Asia to North America. The majority of identified trafficking victims are foreign women who migrate to Japan seeking work, but are subjected upon arrival to debt bondage and forced prostitution. Male and female migrant workers are subjected to conditions of forced labor. Traffickers use debt bondage to exploit women in Japan's large sex trade, imposing debts of up to $50,000. In addition, trafficked women are subjected to coercive or violent physical and psychological methods to prevent them from seeking assistance or escaping. Traffickers also target Japanese women and girls for exploitation in pornography or prostitution. Many female victims, both foreign and Japanese, are reluctant to seek help from authorities for fear of reprisals by their traffickers, who are often members or associates of Japanese organized crime syndicates (the Yakuza). Japanese men continue to be a significant source of demand for child sex tourism in Southeast Asia.

The Government of Japan does not fully comply with the minimum standards for the elimination of trafficking; however, it is making significant efforts to do so. While Japan continued to implement reforms through its Inter-Ministerial Liaison Committee on trafficking in persons, the government's efforts to identify and protect victims of trafficking remained inadequate. In addition, prosecutions decreased from the previous year. Law enforcement authorities and other officials did not systematically employ formal victim identification procedures, resulting in the government's failure to recognize many trafficking victims. The number of victims identified and assisted by Japanese authorities fell for the second year in a row, but based on calls to victim hotlines and interviews with victims, NGOs and researchers believe the number of actual victims exceeds government statistics. Some observers attribute the decline in identified victims to the difficulty of investigating sex businesses that are increasingly moving underground due to police crackdowns on red-light districts in major cities. This increased pressure from law enforcement has eliminated visible prostitution and forced many sex businesses to thinly disguise prostitution as "delivery health" (escort) services.

....

Prosecution

There was no improvement in the Government of Japan's efforts to address sex trafficking through law enforcement during the reporting period, and the government failed to address the problem of trafficking for labor exploitation. Prosecutions for sex trafficking decreased in 2007, as 11 sex trafficking cases were prosecuted, and 12 trafficking offenders were convicted, compared to 17 prosecutions and 15 convictions in 2006. Of the 12 convictions in 2007, seven offenders received prison sentences of two to four years with labor; five offenders received suspended sentences. The only labor trafficking convictions in 2007 were for two cases prosecuted under the Labor Standards Law. While Japan does not have a comprehensive anti-trafficking law, a variety of laws, including the 2005 amendment to the criminal code, the Labor Standards Law, the Employment Security Law, the Prostitution Prevention Law, the Child Welfare Law, and the Law for Punishing Acts related to Child Prostitution and Child Pornography, cover most, but not all forms of trafficking. Specifically, Japanese law does not prohibit recruitment of laborers using knowingly fraudulent or deceptive offers for purposes of forced labor. Labor exploitation was widely reported by labor activists, NGOs, shelters, and the media. The Immigration Bureau and Labor Standard Inspection Bodies reported hundreds of abuses of the Industrial Trainee and Technical Internship Program (the "foreign trainee program"). Reported abuses included fraudulent terms of employment, debt bondage, restrictions on movement, and withholding of salary payments. While the majority of companies employ foreign trainees appropriately, participants in the first year of the three-year program were not protected by labor laws and were therefore vulnerable to trafficking. In addition, such exploitation was not limited to participants in the first year of the program. There were only two convictions for labor trafficking during the past two years despite Labor Standard Inspection Bodies having identified more than 1,209 violations of labor laws in 2006 alone, indicating a serious lack of will by the government to enforce these laws....

Protection

Despite the government's increased efforts, victim protection remained inadequate during the reporting period. The number of trafficking victims identified by the Japanese government declined for the second consecutive year. Law enforcement authorities identified 43 victims in 2007, down from 58 in 2006 and 116 in 2005. This number is disproportionately low relative to the suspected magnitude of Japan's trafficking problem. Although some observers speculate there are fewer victims identified because sex trafficking may have decreased in Japan, it is more likely the move of many sex businesses underground has made it more difficult for police to investigate and rescue potential victims. NGOs working with trafficking victims continue to assert the government is not proactive in searching for victims among vulnerable populations such as foreign women in the sex trade or migrant laborers. Of particular concern was the Japanese government's repatriation of 16 of the 43 identified trafficking victims without referring them to IOM for risk assessment and formal repatriation processing. Although police and immigration authorities take part in regular training programs, Japan has not adopted formal victim identification procedures, nor does it dedicate government law enforcement or social services personnel specifically to the human trafficking issue. During the reporting period, police and immigration authorities failed to consistently identify trafficking victims. Officials from third-country embassies reported Japanese police and immigration officers failed to recognize their citizens as trafficking victims, forcing the embassies to take charge of victim repatriation. . . .

[The Report here describes lack of effective legal assistance for trafficking victims within Japan.]

Prevention

The Government of Japan demonstrated strong efforts to raise awareness about some forms of trafficking during the reporting period. The government took efforts to reduce the demand for commercial sexual exploitation through the distribution of 500,000 brochures on the trauma of trafficking, government anti-trafficking efforts, and how to receive victim assistance. The government also produced 25,000 trafficking awareness posters portraying the link between prostitution and trafficking in persons. The posters and brochures were distributed to immigration offices, police stations, and foreign embassies and consulates throughout Japan. The government donated $79,000 to a Thai NGO to construct a dormitory for Thai students vulnerable to trafficking. A significant number of Japanese men continue to travel to other Asian countries, particularly the Philippines, Cambodia, and Thailand, to engage in sex with children. Although the Act on Punishment of Activities Relating to Child Prostitution and Child Pornography and the Protection of Children provides Japanese courts with extraterritorial jurisdiction over Japanese nationals who have sexual intercourse with a minor in a foreign country, the government has not prosecuted a Japanese national for child sex tourism since 2005. During the reporting period, the government did not take any steps to specifically reduce the demand for child sex tourism by Japanese nationals. Japanese law does not criminalize the possession of child pornography, and this continues to contribute to the demand for commercial sexual exploitation of children and child sex tourism. According to National Police Agency statistics, 773 Japanese children were either prostituted or exploited in child pornography during the first half of 2007. Japan has not ratified the 2000 UN TIP Protocol.

RUSSIA (Tier 2 Watch List)

Russia is a source, transit, and destination country for men, women, and children trafficked for various forms of exploitation. Men and women from the Russian Far East are trafficked to China, Japan, the Middle East, and South Korea for purposes of sexual exploitation, debt bondage, and forced labor, including in the agricultural and fishing industries. Russian women are trafficked to Turkey, Greece, Germany, Italy, Spain, Malta, the United States, Canada, Vietnam, Thailand, Australia, New Zealand, Costa Rica, and the Middle East for the purpose of sexual exploitation. Moscow and St. Petersburg are destination centers for children trafficked within Russia and from Ukraine and Moldova for purposes of sexual exploitation and forced begging. Moscow continues to be a significant destination for men and women trafficked within Russia and from Kyrgyzstan, Tajikistan, Uzbekistan, Ukraine, Moldova, and Belarus for purposes of sexual exploitation and forced labor, including work in the construction industry; in 2007, the number of Belarusian men trafficked to Moscow increased for purposes of forced labor in the construction, textile, and food industries. The ILO reported that an estimated one million illegal migrant workers may be victims of labor trafficking in Russia. Moscow remains a transit point for women trafficked from Uzbekistan and Armenia to the United Arab Emirates for purposes of sexual exploitation. Men from Western Europe and the United States travel to Western Russia, specifically St. Petersburg, for the purpose of child sex tourism; however, law enforcement authorities report a decrease in the number of cases of child sex tourism and attribute this to aggressive police investigations and Russian cooperation with foreign law enforcement.

The Government of the Russian Federation does not fully comply with the minimum standards for the elimination of trafficking; however, it is making significant efforts to do so. Russia is placed on Tier 2 Watch List for a fifth consecutive year for its failure to show evidence of increasing efforts to combat trafficking over the previous year, particularly in providing assistance to victims of trafficking. Comprehensive trafficking victim assistance legislation, which would address key deficiencies, has been pending before the Duma since 2003 and was neither passed nor enacted in 2007. Although a few municipalities across Russia have victim identification and referral systems, relatively few victims assisted were referred by government officials in 2007. During the reporting period, the federal government provided no funding to anti-trafficking NGOs while it gave approximately $40 million to other NGOs involved in civic and social work issues throughout Russia; during the previous reporting period, the Public Chamber reportedly provided funding to three anti-trafficking NGOs. Russia again increased the total number of trafficking investigations and demonstrated improved efforts to identify labor trafficking cases. Although modest improvements were noted in particular regions, the Russian government has yet to provide comprehensive victim assistance, covering the entire process from victim identification through reintegration and support systematically and throughout the country. Victim identification and assistance remains the weakest component of Russia's anti-trafficking efforts.

. . . .

Prosecution

The Government of the Russian Federation demonstrated progress in its law enforcement efforts over the last year. Article 127 of the criminal code prohibits both trafficking for commercial sexual exploitation and forced labor. Other criminal statutes may be used to prosecute and convict traffickers. Article 127 provides punishments of up to five years' imprisonment for trafficking crimes, and aggravating circumstances may extend penalties up to 10 years' imprisonment; these penalties are sufficiently stringent and commensurate with punishments prescribed for other grave crimes, such as rape. In 2007, police conducted 139 trafficking investigations; 104 of these investigations were sexual exploitation cases and 35 were forced labor cases. This total is a 10 percent increase from the 125 investigations conducted in 2006 and continues the annual trend of increased prosecutions since the statute was passed in 2003. It is difficult to ascertain the exact number of prosecutions and convictions conducted in 2007 because the government did not collect and maintain such statistics; prosecution, conviction, and sentencing data was obtained by analyzing media coverage of known trafficking cases. Authorities conducted at least 36 prosecution cases — involving 103 traffickers — during the reporting period, compared to 26 prosecution cases in 2007. Likewise, at least 46 traffickers were convicted in 2007, an increase from 13 in 2006. At least 45 traffickers faced imposed prison sentences. Despite this progress, some police noted that the anti-trafficking law remains underutilized because national directives on its implementation have not yet been issued. In July 2006, the Duma passed asset forfeiture legislation that permits prosecutors to seize the assets of convicted persons, including traffickers; however, there were no reports that the law was used against traffickers in 2007. Russia identified a total of four civilian government officials complicit in human trafficking. Of those four complicit officials, one was convicted and sentenced to four years and six months' imprisonment; the remaining three were arrested and their cases were still pending at the time of this report. Forced labor of young conscripts within Russia's military remained a concern. In 2007, five military officials were investigated and arrested for labor exploitation of military conscripts under their command.

Protection

[The report indicates that Russia made no significant progress in this area.]

Prevention

Russia demonstrated minimal prevention efforts during the reporting period. A few local governments provided modest funding or in-kind support to NGOs to conduct public awareness campaigns targeting at-risk populations. Various national ministries continued operating informational websites about trafficking. State-controlled media aired several documentaries about trafficking and featured frequent stories throughout Russia during the reporting period which aided public awareness. Russia actively monitors immigration and emigration patterns for signs of trafficking. The government did not take specific steps to reduce the demand for commercial sex acts. Russian law permits the government to prosecute Russian nationals who travel abroad to engage in child sex tourism. In 2007, one Russian man was charged and incarcerated by the Cambodian government for the commercial exploitation of a child; the case was pending at the time of this report.

Notes and Questions

1. The State Department's TIP Report has been both praised and criticized: on the one hand, it has encouraged countries to examine their anti-trafficking efforts; but on the other hand, categorization had been denounced as excessively influenced by geopolitical interests and strategic alliances. Reading through the selection of countries reproduced above, what is your assessment of the report's objectivity and ultimate value as a tool in the fight against human trafficking? Are the standards applied by the U.S. consistent?

2. What do you think of the report's methodology? In particular, how does the Tier 2 Watch List function? Was it wise to include the Tier 2 Watch List as a category additional to the more straightforward categories?

3. The report is a valuable and concise source of information on anti-trafficking efforts across a wide range of countries. Is the U.S. making too facile an assumption that developed countries, especially in Europe, deserve to be in Tier 1, simply based on good legislation? Although the U.S. does not "rate" itself relative to other countries, how does the report assess the efforts of the U.S.?

4. Saudi Arabia reacted negatively to being described as weak on trafficking and placed in Tier 3 in the 2007 TIP Report. See Mariam Al Hakeem, *Saudis Reject Human Trafficking Report*, Gulf News, July 9, 2007, quoting the chair of the Saudi Human Rights Commission as saying that the State Department's view was being influenced by "generalizations and stereotypes."

At least the U.S. report is being noticed and taken seriously by governments. The TVPA allows for the possibility of sanctions being brought to bear on any country consistently lax in its approach to human trafficking within its borders. Of the 23 countries receiving a Tier 3 ranking in 2003, for example, only Burma, North Korea and Cuba faced sanctions.[21] Sanctions have been waived for countries such as Qatar, Kuwait and Saudi Arabia to protect national interest.[22] Also see *Cambodia Cleaning Up Human Trafficking with U.S. Sanctions Looming,* Deutsche Presse-Agentur, April 29, 2003, describing Cambodia's reaction to being placed in Tier 3 in 2003. When the U.S. holds back on the imposition of sanctions, is it likely because the countries in question appear to be making sufficient efforts to eliminate human trafficking? Or is the issue of trafficking not worth the political capital that sanctions would entail?

5. As this book goes to print, the State Department has released its Trafficking in Persons report for 2009, the first to have been issued under the Obama Administration and selections from which may be seen in the appendix to this book. For the full text of the 2009 Report, see http://www.state.gov/g/tip/rls/tiprpt/2009/index.htm.

The new report notes that the global economic crisis has exacerbated the human trafficking situation, as more people have become vulnerable to the exploitation of traffickers. Early indications are that the 2009 Report is applying a rigorous anti-trafficking standard, with an increase of 30% in countries included on the Watchlist.

V. Sex Tourism and the Issue of the Customer

A. Traveling to Exploit

In the following sections, we will deal with the phenomenon of sex tourism, and the related issue of demand for children to sexually exploit. Although closely aligned with sex trafficking, the legal concerns relating to sex tourism are somewhat different, in that they involve devices to facilitate prosecution of the end user. (It is troubling that national anti-trafficking laws do little to link the end user to the crime of trafficking; under laws aimed at sex tourism, the customer is the target.) Transnational prosecutions are labor intensive, in that they necessarily involve the joint efforts of "sending" and "receiving" country law enforcement. These prosecutions raise questions regarding the extraterritorial reach of national criminal laws, and present complex problems of adequate evidence.

There is little question that an effective regime against sex tourism must involve the serious and ongoing commitment on the part of criminal authorities in Western Europe, Japan and the United States, the source countries for most of the world's sex tourists. Relying solely on corrupt and inefficient police, and equally weak judicial systems, Southeast Asia and Latin America cannot possibly be successful in stemming the tide of sex tourism. Indeed, tourism is often considered an indispensible element in the economic life of poorer countries; national governments are understandably reluctant to take any steps that might jeopardize that important source of foreign exchange. While

---

21. Dina Francesca Haynes, *Human Trafficking and Migration, in* Human Rights in Crisis 116 (Alice Bullard ed., 2008).

22. *See id.*

the 2003 U.S. Protect Act[23] made prosecution of sex tourists much easier, several U.S. states have also taken action against sex tour operators, in contrast to laws aimed at the tourist himself.

After an exploration of the phenomenon of international sex tourism, this chapter concludes with a discussion of the global demand for children to exploit and the role of child pornography in the generation of demand for these children. It is impossible to state with certainly that this demand has risen dramatically in the age of internet-based pornography. It is clear, however, that an explosion of hard core child pornography is being seen by police in many countries, and that this at least parallels the large scale demand for children in the sex tourism industry.

Descriptions of what actually takes place in sex tourism are sordid; the idea of adult men traveling around the world to exploit women and children for sexual purposes is difficult to come to terms with. While journalism might be accused of using inflammatory rhetoric in covering such emotive topics, it is clear that issues of power, domination, race and gender loom large in the sex tourism context.

Diane Taylor, *Preying Fields*

The Guardian (London), Aug. 13, 2005

The tourist standing on the Sisowath Quay, which runs alongside the Mekong river in Cambodia's capital, Phnom Penh, looks nothing unusual. He is dressed in navy shorts, blue T-shirt and trainers, and has a small rucksack on his back. It is a hot February evening, and street traders are selling cooling slices of mango dipped in sugar. Hundreds of other tourists are out on the noisy quay, shaking off skinny street children begging for small change, or lounging in the waterfront bars sipping beer.

After a couple of minutes, two young boys approach the tourist. Then two more appear, an older boy holding on to another of no more than four or five. He is carrying a bundle of possessions in a plastic bag. The meeting has obviously been prearranged. The tourist calmly takes the hands of two of the younger boys, one of whom is wearing the tourist's motorcycle helmet. The older boy walks slightly in front of them. Few words are exchanged and the group moves off. The children look happy, skipping along the pavement to keep up.

Cambodia is a country that has gained a reputation as a haven for sex tourists. Phnom Penh is described by some as "one giant brothel". As in other countries, there is a spectrum here. At one end are women who have decided—in the absence of other choices—to engage in sex work. At the other are children who are used against their will for the sexual gratification of adults.

....

In a country ranked among the 20 poorest in the world, dollar income from prostitution is highly valued, particularly by the pimps and brothel owners. A virgin of 12 or 13 can be sold to a brothel for $500 (£280). A foreign tourist who wants to hire her for several days can expect to pay around $1,000 (£560). The money paid to street boys and their fixers varies, but is far more than the children earn from months of begging and scavenging. So lucrative is the trade that many who should be policing or prosecuting

---

23. Prosecutorial Remedies and Other Tools to End the Exploitation of Children Today Act of 2003 (PROTECT Act), Pub. L. No. 108-21, 117 Stat. 650 (2003) (codified as amended in scattered sections of the U.S.C.).

this kind of activity accept bribes to cast a blind eye. The average salary of a police officer is around $25 (£14) per month.

Those in pursuit of girls can usually find them in brothels; those who want boys tend
to recruit them directly on the street. Phnom Penh alone has an estimated 24,000 street
children; many live with their parents, but 2,000 have little or no contact with their families and are willing to do almost anything to earn their next meal. The boys picked up
by paedophiles tend to combine this "part-time" work with shoe-shining and scavenging
for recyclable rubbish.

Sex for sale, and AIDS, became established here in 1992 when Untac (UN Transitional
Authority in Cambodia) arrived to stabilise the country following the devastation of the
Pol Pot era and the subsequent Vietnamese occupation. Nowadays, a guesstimate puts
2.6% of the 13m Cambodian population as infected with HIV — although the real figure
is likely to be higher — and at least a third are thought to be children under 18.

Bopha found herself in a brothel two years ago, at the age of 15. By that time, Untac
had gone and the soldier sex buyers had been replaced by Cambodian men and foreign tourists.
It all started for Bopha when she was 14 and fell in with a bad crowd at school who encouraged her to play truant, ride motorcycles around Phnom Penh and sing in karaoke bars.
She comes from a poor family, but her new friends always had money available.

. . . .

Cambodian men had sex with her at the brothel, while western men preferred to take
her to their hotel rooms. "The brothel owner's nephew used to accompany me with a
translator to the hotels of the white men. Sometimes they put pornographic films in the
video machine and tried to make me copy what was going on. If I didn't do what a customer wanted, he would go out of the hotel room and tell the translator.... Then the
nephew would beat me. The western men always asked for the youngest girls with the
darkest skin, and they didn't want to use condoms."

. . . .

Back at one of the bars not far from Sisowath Quay, the tourists are at play. As usual,
there are three times as many Cambodian and Vietnamese sex workers as white, male
visitors, and plentiful beer and football games on a big screen close by. For ordinary Cambodian women, it would be dishonourable to set foot in one of these places; for Cambodian
men, it would be culturally alien and very expensive. Many of the girls for sale look no
more than 15.

Bob, a thin, white-haired American man in his 60s, says that he is self-employed and
spends part of the year in the U.S. and part here. Like many of the men in the bars, he is
a regular. He tells me proudly that he has "had" half the girls at the bar and that, while
some men end up paying $10 for them, he can get them for as little as $5. "All the men
at this bar are here for one reason and one reason only." He winks. "Most of the girls are
doing this for their families. They send a lot of the money they earn home."

Does it bother him that so many of the girls look no more than 15? "Well, they're supposed to be 18 to work here, but who knows?" he says, shrugging.

At another bar, a large group of Scottish men in their 40s and 50s stand laughing
and playing pool. One by one they pair off with the girls who approach them. An American man shakes my hand. He, too, is happy to explain how things work. While he chats,
the Vietnamese girl he has selected to spend the night with sits patiently on her bar
stool, a smile soldered to her face. He is a regular visitor. His business on the U.S. east
coast is seasonal and in winter he heads for the 90 degree-plus (32°C) temperatures of

Cambodia. He is travelling with a friend who is wealthy enough to take a couple of months off for an annual visit to Cambodia. The pair visit brothels together. He makes a moral distinction between himself and his preference for "a mature woman who understands what sex is all about" and his fellow tourists who seek out eight- and nine-year-old children. "Those guys who come here for the girls and boys of that age should be taken out and shot."

Christian Guth, a former French senior police officer, now an adviser to the ministry of interior in Cambodia, believes there has been an improvement—the government is doing more than it once did to clamp down on foreign abusers. "Five years ago, the police laughed when we expressed concern about men having sex with 14-year-old girls, because it was something they did themselves. The first obstacle to change was their mindset. We haven't got 100% commitment, but we have identified a few officers in each area of the country who are really committed." In 2002 an anti-human trafficking and juvenile protection department was established.

It is, however, hard to find evidence of a crackdown. The number of arrests of men for sexually abusing children was 401 last year, but only 18 of them were foreigners. The men come from a variety of European countries, from New Zealand, Australia, North America and Japan. The youngest was 28, the oldest 69. Many are professionals, including two retired military officers, several teachers of English in Cambodia and a chemistry professor. The ages of the children abused range from seven to 15. The vast majority of charges are dropped even when the men are caught in a sex act with a child. There are currently fewer than half a dozen convicted foreign paedophiles in Cambodian jails, while three U.S. citizens have been extradited to their own country to stand trial. A handful of other men are in jail in their own countries, including two in the UK.

Guth acknowledges the pervasive corruption. "A lawyer might say to the family of a child who lodges a complaint against a paedophile that if they drop the complaint, the offender will give them anything from a few hundred dollars to $2,000." He wants to be optimistic, but admits that the number of sexually exploited children is increasing. Not only are there more tourists, there's also a new category of Khmer middle-class man who now has the money to pay for sex. Another problem is that the government seems less determined to stamp out child prostitution than the NGOs are. "The penalties here are much less harsh than in Thailand, and the sex is less expensive."

Some girls who were forced into prostitution do manage to put the rapes and beatings behind them and start a new life. Sovandara Somchan proudly points to photographs on his office wall of girls who have launched successful careers as hairdressers or seamstresses after a period at Neavear Thmey.

Pov, 17, hoped that she, too, could make a new start. She was tricked into a brothel at the age of 14 while selling lotus flowers on the riverfront in Phnom Penh. Like Neang, she was distraught when she became sick and diagnosed with HIV. "I knew that somehow I had to run away," she says. She succeeded by climbing out of a window and running to the local market. A porridge-seller helped her hide and gave her money to get a bus home to her mother.

Pov's priority now, as it was before she went into the brothel, is to earn enough to eat for whatever time she has left to live. "Because I have AIDS, getting married and having children is no longer an option for me." She has, she says, one simple dream. "If I knew I had just one week left to live, what I'd like to do most of all is go into town and buy all the fruits I adore and eat them—fruits like apples, which don't grow on the trees in my village."

(Some names have been changed.)

Notes and Questions

1. Sex tourism cannot be wholly separated from the issue of trafficking, since both involve child prostitution, and since sex tourists may in fact be exploiting trafficked children. For example, evidence suggests that many of the young girls in Cambodia's brothels are trafficked from Vietnam. The readings in this chapter have indicated that child sex trafficking is not specific to any one culture, or to any one set of geographical or political relationships. However, sex tourism — generally from wealthier to more impoverished countries — involves tourists preying on the vulnerable, and acting with a sense of entitlement to exploit. This has proven a difficult problem to overcome, in that it requires, almost by definition, a high degree of international law enforcement cooperation. Consider what level of consistent, ongoing investment would be required on the part of governments for international sex tourism to be significantly impacted.

B. Overview of Legal Efforts against Sex Tourism

The Naomi Svensson article that follows describes an international trend towards creating legislation that is extraterritorial in application, to allow for the prosecution of persons who travel abroad to exploit children. States known to be major senders of sex tourists abroad have been engaged in a process of eliminating legal impediments to the arrest and punishment of their own nationals for crimes committed while in countries that lack the will or capacity to apprehend the offender.

Naomi L. Svensson, *Extraterritorial Accountability: An Assessment of the Effectiveness of Child Sex Tourism Laws*
28 Loyola of Los Angeles International & Comparative Law Review 641 (2006)

I. Introduction

The United Nations defines child sex tourism as "tourism organized with the primary purpose of facilitating.... a commercial sexual relationship with a child," but child sex tourism may also include the "opportunistic use of prostituted children while traveling on business or for other purposes." This commercial sexual exploitation of children is a global crisis, devastating the lives of countless poor children around the world, while governments routinely fail to prosecute the perpetrators of these crimes for their abhorrent conduct.

Reasons such as inadequate laws, ineffective law enforcement, lack of resources, corruption, and immature legal systems frequently enable child sex tourists to escape prosecution in countries where the exploitation occurs. To bring these perpetrators to account, many nations have enacted extraterritorial legislation ("ET legislation"), which provides a country with the jurisdiction to prosecute its nationals for criminal conduct committed beyond its borders. Many commentators characterize ET legislation as an essential tool in combating the sexual exploitation of children. Although perpetrators may escape criminal liability in destination countries (countries where the child sex tourist travels to and where the crime physically occurs), ET legislation provides a mechanism through which governments can hold perpetrators accountable for their despicable crimes.

Over thirty countries have passed some type of ET legislation that enables sex tourists to be prosecuted for their criminal behavior overseas. While increasingly more child sex tourists have been arrested and convicted for their offenses, there are still relatively small numbers of actual prosecutions in comparison to the estimated number of child sex tourists. This indicates that current forms of ET legislation are inadequate to protect the world's children from commercial sexual exploitation.

This Comment explores the scope and effectiveness of current ET legislation used to combat child sex tourism. In its current form, most ET legislation is insufficient, facing many evidentiary and procedural obstacles that hinder its effectiveness. Without a more comprehensive effort that recognizes inherent difficulties in extraterritorial prosecution, most existing child sex tourism laws will continue to operate as an empty shell, failing to protect countless, vulnerable children all over the world.

....

II. Defining the Problem

....

B. The Victims

Typically child sex tourists target girls and boys between the ages of 10 and 18, although they have begun targeting increasingly larger numbers of even younger children. As a result of the covert nature of child sex tourism, it is difficult to measure the precise numbers of children victimized by sex tourism. Despite varying estimates provided by governments and non-governmental organizations, child sex tourism is certainly a widespread problem that devastates the lives of far too many children. The U.S. State Department estimates that each year, sex tourists and traffickers exploit more than one million children. However, according to UNICEF, this number is closer to two million. In India alone, according to one major organization, there are an estimated 270,000 child prostitutes.

....

C. The Perpetrators

Those who are involved in sex tourism range from mere tourists to businessmen, to military personnel and pedophiles, and can come from any level of society. While local or domestic perpetrators increase the demand for child prostitutes, the scope of this Comment focuses on foreign perpetrators. These foreign child sex tourists generally choose countries with widespread poverty, and take advantage of the anonymity and lack of criminal repercussions involved in committing sexual offenses overseas. The number of men and women who engage in child sex tourism is uncertain, since most escape criminal liability in countries where they commit the offenses.

D. Destination Countries

The countries in Asia, Latin America, Africa, and Eastern Europe (where most child prostitution exists) generally lack a stable economy, with high unemployment rates, great disparities between the rich and the poor, and a large underage population. Because many such countries rely heavily on tourism as a vital means for economic development, revenues from sex tourism, now an unfortunate part of many countries' tourist attractions, form a significant portion of many national economies. With such economic reliance on sex tourism, it is no wonder that nations with a well-developed sex tourism industry have little to no incentive to prosecute wealthy foreigners who pour their foreign currency into the local market. With so few local incentives for prosecution, there is a clear need for ET legislation that sending countries can use to hold their own nationals accountable.

III. Existing Legislation—International and Country-Specific Efforts to Prosecute Sex Tourists

There are a number of international and domestic legal instruments that aim to protect children from commercial sexual exploitation. If enforced effectively, these laws can work to protect children, deter child sex tourism, and allow for the prosecution of offenders.

A. International Efforts to Combat Child Sex Tourism

. . . .

In response to the need for more specific measures to better protect the rights of children guaranteed by the CRC, the General Assembly ratified the Optional Protocol on the Rights of the Child on the Sale of Children, Child Prostitution, and Child Pornography ("Protocol on the Sale of Children") on May 25, 2000. Thus far ratified by 101 nations, the Protocol on the Sale of Children requires member states to ensure that its domestic legislation allows the prosecution of its nationals for crimes of child sexual exploitation regardless of whether committed domestically or internationally. In addition, the Protocol states that parties may take measures to establish jurisdiction over such offenses when either the perpetrator or the victim is a national of that party state. Although not as far-reaching as prior drafts of the Protocol (the scope having been narrowed as a result of compromise and the need for consensus), the Protocol clarifies vague obligations under the CRC to require member states to enact ET legislation to prosecute child sex tourists.

. . . .

2. Extraterritorial Legislation of "Sending Countries"

Growing international pressure, along with increasing media attention surrounding child sex tourism, have caused many nations to implement some type of ET legislation that prohibits the sexual exploitation of children. ET legislation may be based on the personality principle (where jurisdiction is exercised in the interest of the victim, who is a national, or the perpetrator, who is a national or resident), the protective principle (where a state exercises jurisdiction to protect its own interests), or the universality principle (where a state is willing to prosecute because of the universally punishable nature of the crime, such as in cases involving piracy, genocide or torture).

While over thirty countries have implemented such ET laws, the requirements, effectiveness, and level of enforcement of such laws vary greatly. For example, in terms of enforcement, Japan has yet to prosecute anyone under its extraterritorial law, whereas the United States has charged at least twenty U.S. citizens under its most recent ET law. Canada recently convicted its first Canadian citizen under its revised criminal codes granting extraterritorial jurisdiction. In addition, ET laws also vary in their scope and requirements. The crimes for which nationals can be charged, as well as the age of protection vary from country to country.

The following section focuses on the content and enforcement of various countries' ET legislation.

a. Canada

In 1997, the Canadian Parliament amended its criminal code to extend criminal liability to Canadian nationals who commit sexual offenses outside of the country. Bill C-15A added several sections to the code, making prosecution of child sex tourists easier by removing procedural prerequisites for prosecution. Prior to the amendment, the Canadian government could not proceed with prosecuting the offender until the government of the country where the offense occurred requested such prosecution. Amended sections 7(4.2) and (4.3) of the criminal code now permit the Canadian government to prosecute the national simply after receiving the consent of the Attorney General.

While the amendment facilitates the prosecution of child sex tourists, Canada has thus far only convicted one person under this law. One major reason for the lack of convictions is the difficulty involved in obtaining evidence to prosecute a crime committed outside the country's territory. Prosecutors must overcome linguistic, cultural, and territorial barriers to obtain witnesses and other physical evidence necessary to effectively prosecute....

b. United Kingdom

The United Kingdom's ET legislation, the Sex Offenders Act 1997, permits the prosecution of British nationals in the United Kingdom for sexual offenses committed overseas. While several British citizens have been prosecuted under this law, the Sex Offenders Act 1997 is problematic because it requires that the offense in question be recognized as a crime both in the foreign country and in the United Kingdom (known as double criminality). Unfortunately, this encourages child sex tourists to choose destination countries that fail to criminalize child prostitution, thereby escaping prosecution under ET laws that require double criminality. In one case, a British national escaped prosecution for sexually assaulting boys in Nepal because Nepal did not have legislation protecting against the sexual exploitation of children.

In addition to double criminality, the Association of the Chief of Police Officers in the UK noted several additional factors making convictions under its ET law difficult. These factors included evidentiary obstacles such as the difficulty of tracking down victims, the challenge of determining the victim's age, and other challenges involving transnational fact-gathering. It is no wonder that convictions are a rare phenomenon.

c. Japan

Effective as of 1999, Japan's Law for Punishing Acts Related to Child Prostitution and Child Pornography, and for Protecting Children, makes any person "who engages in child prostitution" punishable by imprisonment. Article 10 specifies that this allows for the prosecution of Japanese nationals who commit such acts abroad.

Japanese men "are thought to make up the largest number of child sex tourist perpetrators in many Asian countries." Japan's law does not contain a double criminality requirement nor requires the complaint of the victim or the victim's country to initiate investigation and prosecution, making it one of the most structurally complete ET laws. However, the state rarely convicts Japanese nationals. Japan's ET legislation fails to protect children because the government does not effectively enforce its law, not because the law itself is structurally deficient. It is difficult to say whether sending countries such as Japan fail to invest in enforcement because of the difficulties of implementing the laws or because such countries are not truly committed to solving this crisis.

d. United States

Recently, the United States enacted the PROTECT Act, which makes it a crime for any person to travel abroad with the purpose of engaging in child sex tourism. Under the PROTECT Act, the government can establish the offender's culpability by proving one of the following: (1) that the accused traveled with the intent to engage in sexual conduct with a minor, (2) actually engaged in sexual conduct with a minor overseas, or (3) otherwise attempted to violate the law.

Since its passage, there have been over 20 indictments, and more than a dozen convictions. Because the PROTECT Act targets both citizens and residents, and because a violation of this law can be established through one of three possible means, this law will likely prove more successful at prosecuting criminals than under prior versions of United States ET legislation.

e. Australia

Australia's Parliament passed the Crimes (Child Sex Tourism) Amendment Act in 1994, which introduced a new section into the pre-existing Crimes Act. The Act permits prosecution of an Australian citizen or resident for engaging in sexual activities with a child under 16 outside of Australia, and may result in penalties ranging from 12 to 17 years in prison.

The Australian ET legislation possesses several strengths, including stiff penalties and provisions to overcome some of the evidentiary obstacles of extraterritorial prosecutions. For example, in 1999, a child sex tourist was convicted and sentenced to 12 years of imprisonment which, to date, was the "heaviest sentence imposed anywhere in the world for extraterritorial child sex offences." In addition, the law permits the child victim or other witnesses to testify via video link, thereby facilitating prosecution. Further, the law allows prosecution to proceed without evidence from the destination country if sufficient evidence can be found in Australia....

However, one major shortcoming is that the law only protects children under the age of 16. Having ratified the Convention on the Rights of the Child, which protects the rights of children under the age of 18, Australia should extend the application of its ET legislation to protect children under the age of 18 from commercial sexual exploitation.

f. Denmark

In response to obligations imposed by Article 4 of the Optional Protocol, Denmark also passed its own ET legislation. Denmark's ET legislation extends criminal jurisdiction to acts committed outside Denmark by a national or a resident, provided that the act is also punishable under the laws of the country where it is committed. Like other countries that have maintained double criminality requirements, Denmark's ET laws likely will not have the effect of deterring criminal activity, but will rather encourage sex tourists to commit their sexual acts in destination countries that do not criminalize their behavior.

On the up side, similar to the video link provision in Australia's law, Denmark has recently amended the Administration of Justice Act to grant express authority for the use of video interviews of children as evidence in a trial. This provision addresses both the needs of the child victim and the general evidentiary obstacles present in extraterritorial cases.

....

IV. Extraterritorial Legislation: Recommendations for Improvement

Current ET legislation, while an effective tool in the war against child sex tourism, can be improved in a number of ways. The following sections outline some suggested areas of improvement in the content and implementation of these laws. Changes in the laws' content (such as expanding the application of ET legislation and removing double criminality requirements) and implementation (such as addressing evidentiary obstacles) can enhance the effectiveness of ET legislation and help to better protect children from sexual exploitation....

A. Structural Amendments to Current Extraterritorial Legislation

1. Expand Scope of Application to Nationals and Residents

Most ET legislation applies only to nationals, but several countries have extended the scope of its extraterritorial jurisdiction to apply to permanent residents or even to those merely passing through their country. For instance, under the extraterritorial laws of France, Belgium, and the United States, both citizens and permanent or "habitual" residents are punishable for acts of child sexual exploitation committed outside each country's territory. Similarly, Denmark's criminal jurisdiction extends to include Danish nationals and persons "residing within Danish territory."

Commentators urge that ET legislation should apply both to nationals and residents of the legislating country. Although most documented cases of child sex tourist prosecutions involve nationals, there are undoubtedly resident aliens that would escape extraterritorial jurisdiction in countries such as Switzerland where their ET legislation only applies to Swiss nationals. Although some countries have amended their ET legislation to permit jurisdiction over foreigners passing through their country, commentators only support such universal jurisdiction as long as it does not invoke double criminality requirements.

2. Eliminate Double Criminality Requirements

As discussed, the ET legislation of many countries stipulates that the crime committed must constitute an offense both in the destination and sending country. Such requirements of double criminality pose significant obstacles to the successful prosecution of child sex tourists. Experts state that imposing double criminality requirements are inconsistent with "the international legal norms established by a near universal ratification of the Convention on the Rights of the Child." Since all CRC member states have committed to protect the children of the world, the issues of national sovereignty that arise from doing away with double criminality pale in comparison to fulfilling international obligations to protect vulnerable children. Further, double criminality encourages a type of forum shopping among child sex tourists looking for destination countries with weaker laws. Because of these drawbacks, the double criminality requirements should be discarded.

....

4. Offenses

The ET legislation of some countries currently contain provisions that criminalize not only sexual conduct with a child, but also criminalizes traveling with the intent to commit sexual acts with a child. For example, the United States' PROTECT Act allows for prosecution based solely on evidence of intent to travel abroad for the purpose of engaging in sexual conduct with a minor. This type of provision allows prosecutors to charge child sex tourists without evidence that any sexual misconduct took place. Prosecutors can obtain and rely on evidence available in the sending country, thereby removing the difficult task of collecting evidence overseas. While proving an offender's state of mind may appear difficult, the United States government has achieved some positive results.

For example, government agents arrested John W. Seljan, age 85, in Los Angeles as he attempted to board a flight to the Philippines. Officers had intercepted a letter Seljan had sent to Filipino girls indicating his intent to have sex with two underage girls. At the time of his arrest, officers found pornographic materials, sexual aids, chocolate, and currency in his luggage. The PROTECT Act enabled prosecutors to proceed to charge him based on this demonstration of intent. As a result, Seljan was convicted and sentenced to 20 years in prison.

As such, some commentators suggest that ET legislation enacted to combat child sex tourism should include provisions, like that in the PROTECT Act, that allow for the prosecution of those traveling with the intent to commit acts of engaging in sexual activities with children. While this permits opportunistic offenders (those that don't "intend" to engage in sex with a minor, but find themselves presented with the opportunity to do so) to escape liability under this provision, they nonetheless are subject to basic provisions prohibiting the act of engaging in sex with minors.

5. Enact Provisions to Punish Sex Tour Operators

While current ET legislation allows governments to prosecute acts of child sexual exploitation committed extra-territorially, domestic legislation should include provisions that criminalize the activities of sex tour operators, travel agents, and others involved in procuring children for sex tourists. The governments of Australia and New Zealand have both included provisions in their ET legislation that permit the prosecution of sex tour operators and others. For example, Australia's Crimes (Child Sex Tourism) Amendment Act 1994 provides that a person who acts with the intent of benefiting from or encouraging conduct that would constitute a violation of the Act is subject to imprisonment of up to 17 years. Similarly, New Zealand's Crimes Amendment Act 1961 prohibits conduct that facilitates others in the commission of acts of child sex tourism, such as making travel arrangements or printing or publishing information intended to promote child sex tours. Such activities are punishable by up to seven years imprisonment. Other countries should similarly include provisions that will allow for strict penalties to those who aid in exploiting children.

6. Time Limitations

The length of time that a government has jurisdiction over a crime of engaging in sexual conduct with a child varies from country to country. For example, under a prior version of Japan's ET legislation, the government could no longer prosecute a Japanese national after a mere five years since the crime had been committed. In other countries, the time limitation only starts to run after the child attains majority age. Commentators agree that time limitations should be harmonized to run from the time the child reaches majority age, rather than from the time the offence is committed.

B. Overcoming the Obstacles to Effective Enforcement

. . . .

The Association of the Chief of Police Officers stated that in the United Kingdom, obtaining evidence sufficient to secure a conviction in an extraterritorial prosecution is difficult. This is due to factors such as distance, difficulties involved in identifying the location of the offenses or the victims involved, possible language barriers, and the amount of time that has passed since the commission of the offense.

A closer look at the facts surrounding the conviction of Canadian Donald Bakker gives great insight into these evidentiary problems surrounding the enforcement of ET legislation. While Canadian police had seized videotapes that Bakker had made of his sexual acts with underage Cambodian girls, they were unable to identify either the location of the crime or the specific children involved. However, in an astonishing coincidence, an investigator involved in the case happened to watch a Dateline NBC broadcast that showed footage taken during an investigation of a brothel in Svay Pak conducted by a non-profit organization, International Justice Mission. The investigator recognized both the location and the girls that were in Bakker's videotape. As a result, Bakker was successfully convicted.

In most circumstances where such coincidences do not occur, investigators are faced with the difficult task of identifying the victim and gathering evidence in a foreign country, all of which is likely to require a substantial investment of time, staffing, and resources. The Honorable Amanda Vanstone, Australian Minister for Justice and Customs, stated that "[P]rosecutions are not easy under this legislation. Investigators and prosecutors face difficulties." It is no wonder the number of actual convictions under ET legislation remains relatively small.

However, Australia's ET laws have attempted to resolve some of these evidentiary problems. For example, in *The Queen v. Jesse Spencer Pearce*, the defendant was successfully prosecuted for offenses of child sex tourism based on photographs in his possession that depicted him engaging in indecent acts involving Asian girls and boys. Based on the photographs and Pearce's accompanying confession as to the details of the photograph, the state convicted Pearce without any evidence from the destination country.

Similarly, in the Lee case, while police were unable to locate the children involved in Cambodia, they were able to obtain photographs of Lee engaged in sexual activities. Although the photographs did not show Lee's face, forensic scientists matched the perpetrator's fingers in the photograph with Lee's fingerprints, which led to Lee's conviction. Australia's ET law, containing provisions to deal with some of the evidentiary difficulties of extraterritorial prosecutions, demonstrates that ET legislation can be remarkably effective.

In addition, as discussed above, Australia's law makes specific accommodations for foreign witnesses, including the child victim. Where obtaining the witness' presence would be too costly or distressing, the witness in a sex tourism case may testify from the foreign country by video link.

Denmark has also implemented similar provisions in their laws. Accommodations such as these can help lead to convictions where evidence gathering would otherwise be too difficult. However, these accommodations may not be permitted everywhere, especially where they have the possibility of conflicting with domestic constitutional laws.

In addition, governments can alleviate the evidentiary difficulties of establishing the age of the victim by allowing age to be proved through a variety of means. For example, Australia's Crimes (Child Sex Tourism) Amendment Act 1994 considers all of the following as evidence of a child's age: (a) the person's appearance, (b) medical or other scientific opinion, (c) a document that is or appears to be an official or medical record from a country outside Australia, and (d) a document that is or appears to be a copy of such a record.

By creating more than one way to prove a child's age, or by loosening standards for establishing age, governments can more easily overcome the evidentiary hurdle of proving the crime of child sex tourism.

Finally, improving international cooperation between police, prosecutors, non-governmental organizations, and others is vital to effective prosecution. Without an integrated effort between officers and prosecutors from both the destination country and the sending country, governments will have a difficult time obtaining the necessary evidence to move forward with a successful prosecution.

....

Notes and Questions

1. Anti-trafficking laws are focused on the prosecution of traffickers, those who deal in human brings as a kind of business venture. This section deals with laws that attempt to facilitate prosecution of end users on the international plane. Anti-sex tourism laws present difficult challenges, in part because of the time intensive and resource intensive nature of international criminal cooperation. With differing levels of national commitment to eradicating child prostitution, and with different levels of police corruption, is it realistic to think that transnational cooperation in the realm of sex tourism will lead to significant reduction in the phenomenon?

2. As described in the Svensson article, how impressive have the prosecutor's efforts been within the "sending" countries? How can we explain the fact that Japan has such principled and coherent laws on the subject, yet that these laws are almost never used to prosecute offenders?

———————

The main provisions of the U.S. Protect Act aimed at facilitating prosecution of the sex tourist are set out below. What flaws, if any, do you see in the language used?

The PROTECT Act

Pub. L. No. 108-21, § 105, 117 Stat. 650, 653 (2003)
(codified as amended at 18 U.S.C. § 2423)

Section 2423: Transportation of minors

(a) Transportation With Intent To Engage in Criminal Sexual Activity—A person who knowingly transports an individual who has not attained the age of 18 years in interstate or foreign commerce, or in any commonwealth, territory or possession of the United States, with intent that the individual engage in prostitution, or in any sexual activity for which any person can be charged with a criminal offense, shall be fined under this title and imprisoned not less than 10 years or for life.

(b) Travel With Intent To Engage in Illicit Sexual Conduct—A person who travels in interstate commerce or travels into the United States, or a United States citizen or an alien admitted for permanent residence in the United States who travels in foreign commerce, for the purpose of engaging in any illicit sexual conduct with another person shall be fined under this title or imprisoned not more than 30 years, or both.

(c) Engaging in Illicit Sexual Conduct in Foreign Places—Any United States citizen or alien admitted for permanent residence who travels in foreign commerce, and engages in any illicit sexual conduct with another person shall be fined under this title or imprisoned not more than 30 years, or both.

(d) Ancillary Offenses—Whoever, for the purpose of commercial advantage or private financial gain, arranges, induces, procures, or facilitates the travel of a person knowing that such a person is traveling in interstate commerce or foreign commerce for the purpose of engaging in illicit sexual conduct shall be fined under this title, imprisoned not more than 30 years, or both.

(e) Attempt and Conspiracy.—Whoever attempts or conspires to violate subsection (a), (b), (c), or (d) shall be punishable in the same manner as a completed violation of that subsection.

(f) Definition.—As used in this section, the term "illicit sexual conduct" means

(1) a sexual act (as defined in section 2246) with a person under 18 years of age that would be in violation of chapter 109A if the sexual act occurred in the special maritime and territorial jurisdiction of the United States; or

(2) any commercial sex act (as defined in section 1591) with a person under 18 years of age.

(g) Defense—In a prosecution under this section based on illicit sexual conduct as defined in subsection (f)(2), it is a defense, which the defendant must establish by a preponderance of the evidence, that the defendant reasonably believed that the person with whom the defendant engaged in the commercial sex act had attained the age of 18 years.

———————

The article that follows presents the problem of exploitative sex tourism as one of shared global responsibility. Is it likely that the international community will come to accept the commercial sexual exploitation of children as a "crime against humanity", as recommended by Jullien? Why or why not?

Karene Jullien, *The Recent Efforts to End Commercial Sexual Exploitation of Children*

31 Denver Journal of International Law & Policy 579 (2003)

On February 15 1995, English writer John Stamford faced charges in Belgium for illicit publication and encouraging sexual exploitation of children. How could an ex-Anglican Pastor be involved with child pornography or child prostitution?

Stamford was the publisher and editor of Spartacus, the first tourist guide catering to homosexuals. Available since 1970, the book was an instant success. It was presented in more than 150 countries, translated into five languages and sold more than 60,000 copies per year for 25 years. Even with the original controversy surrounding the publication, it was not apparent that Stamford was involved with commercial sexual exploitation of children until an encoded message, hidden within the guide, was later discovered to be oriented toward pedophiles.

Stamford's indictment was one of the first public legal efforts to deter sexual exploitation of children in the world. However, it took 13 years for the authorities to take action. From 1981, the organization Terre des Hommes had been denouncing Stamford's activities and had repeatedly asked Interpol to investigate. Today, it has been established that Stamford was not only the editor of Spartacus, the tourist guide, but was also the head of "Spartacus," a pedophile organization. With approximately 30,000 members worldwide, the ring shared addresses, home movies, photos, etc. Stamford never lived to be convicted; he died of a heart attack in jail in December 1995. With his death, all investigation on the "Spartacus Organization" ended. Moreover, there is nowadays a new edition of Spartacus, from Berlin, which is available over the Internet or in different bookstores in Europe. We are then inclined to wonder if any real progress has been made in the effort to end the commercial sexual exploitation of children.

Commercial sexual exploitation of children is not a recent problem but it has gained more public interest over the last decade. Up until the late 80s, with a mixture of indifference, apathy, denial, or even cynicism, child labor and more specifically child prostitution was not an issue of major concern, at either national or international levels. However, in 1989, the United Nations adopted the Convention on the Rights of the Child ("UNCRC") explicitly prohibiting child prostitution and illegal sexual practices with children under the age of 18. Since then, an increasing number of governmental and non-governmental organizations have been pressuring both governments and the general public to take steps against the commercial sexual exploitation of children.

. . . .

Developing countries' responsibilities

It has been argued that child prostitution of a massive nature originated in Thailand, the Philippines, and Taiwan during the Viet Nam War. While the troops were stationed in these countries they made use of bars and massage parlors for rest and recreation. These places were often frequented by underage prostitutes. Just after the war, the governments used the sex industry to promote tourism. They made no effort to limit prostitution at that time and tourists from Japan, Europe, and Australia came to experience the "charms" of the countries. Nobody talked about pedophilia then. In the late 70s, early 80s, travel agencies started to organize sex tours catering to men from industrialized nations. They went to Asia to engage in sexual intercourse with minors at a minimum risk. Such practices were unlawful and a great risk in their home countries. Thailand became popular for its young girls and Sri Lanka for its young boys. Prostitution was not only legal but became a great source of revenue for the states which therefore did not really care about the age of the prostitute or the consequences to the children. Rapidly, surrounding countries used the same niche to attract tourism to their countries. Children were purchased or abducted and then sold in Asia to serve men from the western world. Today, China, Burma, Laos, Vietnam, India, Bangladesh, and Pakistan are all involved in the commercial sexual exploitation of children one way or another.

Unlike the Asian market, the Latin American market developed mostly because of the local demand and then spread to cater to North American customers. Street children became engaged, voluntarily or involuntarily, in prostitution to service the upper class of their home countries. Many adolescents, bought or kidnapped from Paraguay, Bolivia, Brazil, or El Salvador, ended up in brothels located in the gold mining regions of the Amazon, highly populated by males. Sex tourism happens in major cities in Latin America, like Rio de Janeiro, where businessmen from the United States, Canada, and Europe, while visiting or making deals seize the opportunity offered by the sex market.

The Eastern European market is newer, starting after the downfall of the communist regimes at the beginning of the 90s. Sex rings were organized by local mafia, between Bulgaria, Russia, Romania, Poland, and Hungary. The demand is local or from businessmen from Western Europe. Again sex is not the main objective for the trip, but the opportunity is easily accessible. The European market is also more "high tech," and available on the Internet. On special web pages, you can book company for your trip the same way you reserve a hotel room.

For many years, industrialized countries did not take any action to prevent or control the behavior of their nationals in other countries. Adopting the "ostrich tactic," developed nations denied any responsibility. They could be embarrassed, even ashamed, but since the crimes took place far from their territorial limits, they believed that it was the receiving countries' responsibility to act. Since the adoption of the Convention and the implication of many child advocacy organizations, western governments are acting against sexual exploitation of children worldwide. The first regional organization to face up to its responsibility was the Council of Europe, which in 1988 addressed the problem of child prostitution and the involvement of Europeans. The Council made recommendations to all European countries to establish extraterritorial jurisdictions in order to allow courts to prosecute nationals for crimes committed outside their countries. In May 1990, in Thailand, churches, women's rights organizations, and charitable services organized ECPAT. The campaign openly blamed the developed countries for providing the demand necessary to maintain the sexual exploitation of children and asked the governments to join and help the fight against child prostitution around the world.

....

III. Amending The Laws: Actions Taken By Receiving And Sending Countries To Implement International Standards

Legal measures taken in receiving countries

Due to international pressures, and depending on the economical, political, and social status of the receiving country, some governments have modified their legislatures to take action against sexual exploitation of children. However, in order to be able to pass new laws and to enforce them, the country needs a certain political and economic stability.

Only developed countries can afford the time and resources needed to approve and apply new laws. Under-developed countries are too poor and do not have enough political support to concentrate on child exploitation.

Thailand

Thailand has ratified the UNCRC and ILO C 182, but reports estimate the number of child prostitutes anywhere between 25,000 and 800,000. ECPAT believes the figure to be between 200,000 and 250,000 children below the age of 18. Until 1956, prostitution was legal in Thailand, which highly profited from sex tourism.

Today, the Thai Penal Code prohibits prostitution. However, children involved in the sex trade are not prosecuted and are treated as victims rather than as suspects, even if they consented. In 1996, the government enacted the Prostitution Prevention and Suppression Act ("Act") allowing the prosecution of customers having intercourse with child prostitutes. The Act also permits the prosecution of parents allowing their child to enter the sex trade. In 1997, the government adopted the Prevention and Suppression of Trafficking in Women and Children Act, which increased prison time and penalties for people guilty of abducting and bringing to Thailand, women and children from China, Burma, Laos, or Cambodia for slave labor or prostitution. Today, the country has passed a statute, similar to statutory rape in the United States, that punishes sexual intercourse with a minor under the age of sixteen by a fine and a prison term up to twelve years.

. . . .

Thailand has taken important steps to prevent children from being victims of the sex trade; it has enacted stronger laws against prostitution and trafficking. Penalties are harsher on brothel procurers and parents guilty of profiting from children engaged in the sex trade. However, the government faces the major problem of corruption. Since the 1996 Act, 355 persons have been arrested for violating this law; only 14 have been convicted and sentenced.

Brazil

Reports estimate the number of child prostitutes in Brazil to be 250,000. However, because most of the children involved in the sex trade are street children or come from Amazonian tribes—and therefore not counted during the national census—real data are impossible to get. Helia Barbosa, working for ECPAT Brazil, argues that millions of young girls and adolescents exchange sexual favors for food and shelter. Brothel keepers and providers lie to the young women by promising them work as nannies or household servants. Instead, they are sold by auction in brothels until the owner releases them to the streets where they continue to prostitute themselves in order to survive.

Even if the laws in Brazil prohibit sexual exploitation of children and promote the Rights of the Child, the country lacks enforcement power and experiences too much corruption to be able to bring them into full effect. In addition, prostitution rings are well organized involving the complicity of nightclubs, motels, hotels, taxi drivers, travel agencies, and the parents. It is very hard for the police to find people who are willing to talk.

Brazil has not yet implemented efficient legal and social instruments to prevent the sexual exploitation of children. The state has not formulated public policies for protection, defense and childhood promotion. It neglects public services for family, health and home assistance. The Children and Adolescents Defense Center (CEDECA) admitted that the governmental efforts to better protect children were fruitless since crime against children is increasing. There exist some programs created in partnerships between NGOs and governmental entities, but they lack monetary resources and human power to be totally effective. Two states, however—Pernambuco and Bahia—have adopted the legislation called Specialized Criminal Justice of Childhood and Youths to prosecute and judge crimes against children and adolescents. Unfortunately, they are the only states which dedicated special courts to such crimes and have implemented, with the collaboration of NGOs, psychotherapeutic programs for the child victims. We can hope that other states will follow.

Sri Lanka

Sri Lanka counts between 10,000 and 15,000 child prostitutes, most of whom are young boys. Because of that factor, the government of Sri Lanka denied the facts for a long time. It had to face up to the reality after the publication in 1980 by Terres des Hommes, of Tim Bond's report on child prostitution. The government immediately appointed a Review Committee to create new laws prohibiting and preventing commercial sexual exploitation of children. Though, when a draft of the new legislation was presented in 1987, the Minister of State denied the necessity to adopt new laws curbing the commercial sexual exploitation of children.

Until 1995, efforts and pressures made by national and international organizations were fruitless. In 1995, however, the Ministry of Media, Tourism and Aviation created a special task force to study the problem of sex tourism and related offenses. The task force was abolished in 1997 and was replaced by a presidential task force. A year later, the Parliament enacted the Child Protection Authority ("CPA") statute and committee. The CPA encompassed all previous laws for the protection of children, integrated the principles of the UNCRC and made unlawful all forms of abuse against a child under the age of 18 years. The law prohibits any form of abuse—sexual, violence, traffic, cruelty, and even involvement in wars. It also proscribes the use of children in exploitative labor or illegal activities, or in any way contrary to compulsory education, which is obligatory to the age of 12.

. . . .

In general, the government of Sri Lanka is committed to protecting the welfare and rights of children. It made education free, including university, and compulsory up to the age of 12. It also provides free health care, including immunization programs. It welcomes UNICEF and any child advocacy organizations to work toward the abolition of child exploitation. It has ratified the UNCRC and ILO C 182, hoping to resolve the problem. However, the major obstacle the government has to face is a lack of enforcement due to the many internal conflicts between ethnic groups, and with India. Resources are diverted; law enforcement forces have many other pressing issues to solve.

Legal measures taken in sending countries

In 1987, 11 or 12 year-old Rosario Baluyot died in Philippines, after Dr. Ritter, from Austria, forcibly inserted an electric vibrator in her vagina where it broke. Rosario endured seven months of agonizing pain and infection before she collapsed in the street, with green bile coming out of her mouth. The doctors removed a nine-centimeter rusty screw from her vagina. She died less than a week later. After the Philippine Supreme Court reversed his life sentence, Dr. Ritter returned to Austria where he never faced charges.

To prevent such injustices, international organizations and NGOs have pressured governments of industrialized countries to extend their legislatures in order to allow prosecution of nationals acting outside their boundaries. Today, over 20 countries apply extraterritorial laws (ET) to sex tourists. However, not all nations strictly apply their ET legislations and different countries have taken different approaches. The ET legislations vary—some are extended application of the countries' penal codes while others are new laws specifically created to target sex tourism. Some laws require double criminality, while others enable the sending country to prosecute a sex tourist regardless of whether or not the person was already tried in the receiving country.

European Union

All European countries have ratified the UNCRC and are bound by its obligation under article 34, to take all appropriate measures to end child sexual exploitation. After the Council of Europe condemned sex tourism and alleged the responsibility of sending countries, it recommended to its member States to establish extraterritorial jurisdiction to allow prosecution of nationals engaged in sexual relations with minors in other states. Many European states complied; France, Switzerland, the Netherlands, Ireland, Italy, Spain, Denmark, the UK, Sweden, Norway, Finland, Belgium, and Germany have adopted ET legislation in hope to control their citizens' behavior outside their borders. All those countries also have statutory rape status; however, the consenting age varies from 15 to 18 year-old.

Sweden used its own existing ET laws to prosecute Bengt Bolin, 66 year-old, arrested in Thailand in bed with a 14 year-old boy. The laws were not constructed to apply specifically to sex tourists. Sweden extended its penal code extraterritorially in 1962. The original purpose was to protect Swedish nationals and to ensure them a fair trial and sentence in case of crimes committed outside the country. However, the law holds Swedish citizens and residents who travel outside the borders liable for any sexual activity with children that would constitute a crime within Sweden.

Nonetheless, the Swedish law is limited. It includes the requirement of double criminality. Therefore, in order to be prosecuted in Sweden, the national's activity must constitute a crime in both Sweden and the receiving country. Additionally, the court will not impose a penalty greater than the maximum penalty allowable under the laws of the country in which the crime occurred. Critics also find the law too lax since the Swedish penal code carries a maximum sentence of four years imprisonment for sexual intercourse with a minor under the age of 15. Lastly, a person will not be prosecuted in Sweden in cases where the destination country already held a trial to determine the guilt or innocence of that person.

The positive aspect of the Swedish approach is that it is "child-friendly." Courts will allow videotaped testimony of the child victim rather than requiring their physical presence. They also will appoint free judicial counsel to children and permit victims to recover damages from the defendant.

The United Kingdom extraterritorially extended certain legislation to cover British citizens and residents involved in sex tourism by enacting the Sex Offenders Act in 1997. The Act however, requires double criminality for any prosecution in British courts. In addition, the country has implemented training programs in destination countries, teaching police officers questioning techniques used with children, and providing Thailand with child-friendly rooms in which to interview the children.

United States

In 1996, the United States actively participated in the ECPAT World Congress Against Commercial Sexual Exploitation of Children, which aimed at (1) giving international visibility to the issues, (2) bringing together decision-makers from the relevant major disciplines, and (3) devising a plan of action to end this form of abuse in all countries in the world. America also participated in the Second World Congress held in Japan in December 2001. Despite the fact that the United States has not ratified the UNCRC, it is involved with the international community in order to fight sex tourism.

Amidst these international efforts, the Clinton Administration amended the Mann Act of 1910, by adding the Child Sexual Abuse Prevention Act, to enable American courts to prosecute nationals traveling to foreign countries for the purpose of engaging in sexual acts with minors. The law does not explicitly prohibit sexual intercourse with minors but traveling in foreign commerce, or conspiring to do so, for the purpose of engaging in any sexual act with a person under 18 years of age. Therefore, in order to get a conviction, a prosecutor does not need to prove that actual sexual act happened, but only the defendant's intent to engage in such act with a minor. The law allows the United States to prosecute a child sex tourist even before he can harm a child. In addition, the prosecution does not have to prove that sexual activity was the sole purpose of traveling in foreign commerce; it only must show that "one of the defendant's motives in traveling in foreign commerce was to engage in a sexual act with a minor." Since many sex tourists go overseas for other purposes other than engaging in sexual activities with minors, this interpretation of the statute grants a wider jurisdiction over potential defendants. Finally, the amendment does not contain a double criminality requirement. The major disadvantage of the U.S. statute is that it does not fully protect children ages sixteen and seventeen, unless the sexual conduct involves force, the serious threat of force, or other means to incapacitate the victim.

Section 2423(b) has been successfully used in many cases against nationals who travel in interstate commerce to engage in sexual acts with minors. It has also been used once against a U.S. citizen who traveled to Honduras to engage in sexual activity with an underage boy and once against a permanent resident who traveled to Mexico to rape a 13 year-old girl. Both trials resulted in conviction of multiple sexual offense charges.

. . . .

[T]o facilitate evidence collection and successful prosecutions, some suggest that countries adopt the Mutual Legal Assistance Treaty ("MLAT"). The suspect is usually arrested in the receiving nation, where the criminal sexual act happened, where the witnesses are and where evidence can be gathered. Therefore, if the sending country, the home of the suspect, is to try him, there must be collaboration between the two countries. Most often, the lawyers and prosecutors will have to go on site to interrogate people and verify the facts, which raises the issues of translation and interpretation. The process depends heavily on the diplomatic relations between the two countries and is also very costly. Until now, voluntary and individual action has reduced the costs to a certain extent. Conversely, if the sending country decides to import the witnesses and evidence rather than going to the receiving country, other issues are raised. Cost is still high and the children involved might be scared off. Without MLATs, countries must rely on these individual efforts to persuade courts and law enforcement to cooperate. To be fully effective, the system should not depend on occasional volunteers but on professionals, permanently working against sexual exploitation of children, who are knowledgeable about the sex industry and sensitive to the situation of the children. Special agencies could be created—composed of police officers, child psychologists, interpreters, lawyers, and social workers—who would dedicate their efforts and resources to dismantle the sex trade and protect the children.

. . . .

Model ET legislation

Countries that have already adopted ET legislation must ensure their consistency with the UNCRC and ILO C 182 principles. Such laws are to enable countries to prosecute a child sex tourist for activity in a receiving country which would constitute a crime against a child in the sending country; they must be enforced unanimously. Unfortunately, too many offenders go unpunished. It has been suggested that all sending countries should implement a model ET legislation. Such legislation would apply to both citizens and permanent residents of a country, to establish jurisdiction over a greater population. It would not have a double criminality requirement, which frustrates the purpose of ET legislation. With this constraint, many children are left unprotected since the consenting age significantly varies between countries. In addition, ET laws should not require that victims make a formal complaint or that the receiving government request prosecution. On the contrary it should be child-friendly, allowing video-link testimony, in order to limit the psychological harm to the child victim. Children are often unaware that they may access the court system to help their situation; they are often scared as well and not willing to collaborate with the judicial system. Not all destination countries will file requests for prosecution—sex tourism is too profitable for their economy. Finally, the ET legislation should be modeled after the U.S. Child Sexual Abuse Prevention Act. Such a statute penalizes persons traveling overseas with the intent to sexually exploit children. There is no need of actual sex conduct and the sex tourist may be inculpated even if sex was not the only reason for the trip; conviction can happen even before a child is harmed.

In addition to applying jurisdiction over their nationals, sending countries should enact ET legislation that would allow them to punish businesses and corporations that benefit from sex tourism. Today, only Australia provides for the prosecution of corporations and of nationals who operate brothels, bars, or any businesses promoting sexual exploitation of children, regardless of their location.

Making commercial sexual exploitation of children a crime against humanity

In 1993, France and Australia presented the Draft Optional Protocol ("Draft") to the UN Convention on the Right of the Child. Under the Draft, states are obligated to collaborate on the issue of commercial sexual exploitation of children. In addition, Article 1 categorizes sexual exploitation and trafficking in children as a crime against humanity. If that were the case, commercial sexual exploitation of children would be under universal jurisdiction, in the same category as genocide, torture, slave trade, piracy, attacks and hijacking of aircraft, and war crimes. Any state would have jurisdiction over the suspect, no matter his nationality or the place of the sexual act. Universal jurisdiction would resolve the issues of dual criminality and discrepancy in the age of consent. It would also facilitate the prosecution of many more sexual crimes against minors.

. . . .

Notes and Questions

1. The Jullien article sets out a complex vision of economic, political and legal factors contributing to the phenomenon of child sex trafficking and child prostitution. Does the author's explanation help us to understand the phenomenon? Does she leave anything out of the picture?

2. Jullien describes both the ILO Worst Forms of Child Labor Convention and the UNCRC's Optional Protocol on the Sale of Children, instruments that we have analyzed in the context of child labor. Review these instruments in the appendix. How are they

organized? How is their approach different from the UN Trafficking Protocol? What do you think of placing child sex exploitation in the context of "worst forms of child labor" on the one hand, or "sale of children" on the other? Which is the better approach? What are the flaws in these two approaches? What are these various international legal instruments meant to accomplish?

3. It is difficult to escape the idea that official, albeit unexpressed, policy in many countries is to promote all aspects of the sex trade, even where that involves child exploitation. For a discussion of these strong economic motivations and how these interact with the determined Western tourist, see Crista Foster Crawford, *Cultural, Economic and Legal Factors Underlying Trafficking in Thailand and Their Impact on Women and Girls from Burma*, 12 Cardozo Journal of Law & Gender 821 (2006).

Is it possible to eradicate child prostitution in countries where prostitution has a long history and is generally accepted? The sex tourism "hot spots" around the world change as child abusers communicate with one another and seek out the "easiest" destinations. Are we making too much of the cultural dimension, when in fact the question for exploiters is how many vulnerable children can be exploited with the least amount of risk?

4. Many sex tourists seem to feel a sense of entitlement, and behave as though the countries in which they travel are obliged to show them a good time. They are also adept at seeking new sources of children to exploit. As an example of the many articles on this subject see Alice Leuchtag, *Human Rights Sex Trafficking and Prostitution*, Humanist, Jan.–Feb. 2003.

5. A survey of the international press reveals the presence of the sex tourist in all parts of the world, always seeking out the easiest locations to exploit children. For a sense of the entrenched nature of child prostitution in Brazil, see Louise Rimmer, *Underage Sex, Driven by Poverty, Lures Paedophile Gringos to a Place in the Sun*, Independent (UK), November 22, 2003. The article states that "aid workers reckon two million children are sexually exploited in Brazil," but that the nature of the problem makes trustworthy figures hard to come by. For a report on a relatively new "market" for these activities, see Paul Jeffrey, *Sex Tourism Plagues Central America*, available at http://gbgm-umc.org/response/articles/sextourism.html. The article refers to Central America as having been recently "invaded" by smart sex tourists. Is it the case that prosecuting sex tourists will simply chase them out of one region and into another? What are the factors that make a region most vulnerable to becoming a site for large numbers of sex tourists? Are there legal initiatives that would be more effective against sex tourists than international cooperation to prosecute them after the fact?

C. United States Efforts at Prosecuting Sex Tourists

In the domestic context, U.S. efforts have been squarely aimed at the trafficker, as opposed to the customer or user of trafficked women and children. Internationally, efforts to deter sex tourism have taken a different focus; namely, the prosecution of the individual sex tourist. Whereas that approach would be very fruitful in the domestic context, where it can be assumed large numbers of those exploiting trafficking victims could be located and charged, each prosecution of an international sex tourist requires a high level of investment in international cooperation and the search for adequate evidence. In order to measure the success of laws aimed at sex tourists who travel abroad to exploit children, is there a rough sense of what the relation between numbers of perpetrators and the number charged should be? Is there a danger of the process stopping at a few high profile and symbolic cases?

Karen D. Breckenridge, *Justice Beyond Borders: A Comparison of Australian and U.S. Child-Sex Tourism Laws*
Pacific Rim Law & Policy Journal (2004)

I. Introduction

The clandestine billion-dollar sex tourism industry, which victimizes hundreds of thousands of children, is a global human rights problem with devastating consequences. In one horrific case, Michael Lewis Clark, a sixty-nine-year-old U.S. citizen and military veteran, was arrested by Cambodian police in June 2003 for engaging in sexual acts with two Cambodian boys. After Clark's extradition to the United States in early September, federal prosecutors filed a complaint in Seattle, charging Clark for engaging in illicit sexual conduct in Cambodia. Clark is believed to be the first person to be prosecuted under the Prosecutorial Remedies and Other Tools to End the Exploitation of Children Today Act of 2003 ("PROTECT Act"). The PROTECT Act seeks to strengthen laws punishing individuals who travel abroad and sexually exploit children.

Like the United States, Australia must also confront the reality that its own citizens engage in such acts. Robert Marlow, a fifty-five-year-old Australian, pleaded guilty in April 2000 to sexually abusing boys during several business trips to Fiji. The government sentenced Marlow to three years in jail under Australia's Crimes (Child-Sex Tourism) Amendment Act of 1994 ("CST Act").

Clark and Marlow's prosecutions represent two of the disappointingly limited number of successful child-sex tourism convictions. Child-sex tourism is the exploitation of children by individuals who travel to foreign countries to engage in sexual acts with children. A 1996 United Nations report estimated that a total of one million children were sexually exploited in Asia alone.

Unlike Clark and Marlow, however, most sex tourists escape identification and prosecution. Because a large percentage of sex tourists originate in the United States and Australia, both countries adopted laws that permit the prosecution of sex tourists. In 2003, the United States strengthened its existing sex tourism law by adopting the PROTECT Act, designed to prevent Americans from sexually abusing children while traveling abroad.

Unfortunately, the PROTECT Act is unlikely to achieve the objective of its design. Australia has had limited success in preventing child-sex tourism under nearly identical legislation. Further, the Sixth Amendment to the U.S. Constitution, which guarantees a criminal defendant's right to confront his accuser, is likely to significantly hinder the U.S. government's ability to successfully prosecute American child-sex tourists.

....

III. Passage of the PROTECT Act Is a Significant Step Forward After a Decade of Ineffective Legislation

Despite increased efforts by the United States to curb child-sex tourism over the past decade, attempts to apprehend and prosecute child-sex tourists have been largely ineffective. The United States first adopted a child-sex tourism law in 1994; yet in the ensuing decade, the federal government successfully convicted only two individuals under this legislation. In an attempt to strengthen existing sex tourism legislation, Congress passed the PROTECT Act, which expands the bases on which the U.S. government can prosecute individuals and organizations involved in sex tourism.

A. History of U.S. Sex Tourism Legislation: A Decade of Futility

The first U.S. attempt to combat sex tourism occurred when then President Clinton signed the Child Sexual Abuse Prevention Act of 1994 ("1994 Act") into law. The 1994 Act made it a crime for any U.S. citizen or permanent resident to travel to a foreign country with the purpose of engaging in a sexual act with a person under the age of eighteen. Convictions under the 1994 Act carried a maximum ten-year prison sentence per count.

The 1994 Act was described as "a powerful blow against the growing international child-sex trade." Under the 1994 Act, sex tourists could be convicted for their sexual acts abroad, as long as there was evidence of the tourist's intent before leaving the United States. In addition, the 1994 Act contained no double criminality requirement. Thus, even if the sexual act was legal in the foreign country, the sex tourist could still be prosecuted domestically.

The 1994 Act, however, did not result in the powerful blow against sex tourists that legislators envisioned. Over the past decade, the government has convicted only two U.S. citizens under the 1994 Act. Because of the unexpectedly low number of convictions under the 1994 Act, legislators subsequently sought to expand its scope.

B. The PROTECT Act of 2003 Expands the Reach of the Law

After failing to convict even a handful of child-sex tourists under the 1994 Act, U.S. lawmakers made another legislative attempt to curb child-sex tourism by adopting the PROTECT Act in 2003. U.S. Representatives originally proposed the child-sex tourism provisions of the PROTECT Act as separate legislation in 2002. At that time, the House Committee on the Judiciary reported that the amendments would "close significant loopholes in the law that persons who travel to foreign countries seeking sex with children are currently using to their advantage in order to avoid prosecution." The sex tourism provisions were eventually incorporated into the PROTECT Act and signed into law by President George W. Bush on April 30, 2003.

While preserving the ability to prosecute based on an individual's intent, the PROTECT Act expands the 1994 Act by criminalizing two additional categories of sex tourism. First, the PROTECT Act enables the prosecution of a person who engages in "illicit sexual conduct in foreign places." Requirements under this section are merely that the person "travel in foreign commerce" and engage in "illicit conduct." Unlike the 1994 Act, there is no requirement that the defendant intend to commit the act before or upon leaving the United States, a feature that may have constitutional implications.

Second, the PROTECT Act subjects operators of sex tours to criminal prosecution. The PROTECT Act provides for the prosecution of any individual who, for "commercial advantage or private financial gain, arranges, induces, procures, or facilitates the travel" for others to engage in sexual conduct with minors. Prosecutors must prove that the organizer had knowledge of the tourist's illicit purpose. Attempting or conspiring to organize or facilitate child-sex tourism or to engage in prohibited sexual activity outside the United States is punishable to the same extent as completed offenses.

The PROTECT Act also significantly increases the maximum sentence previously allowed under the 1994 Act. Violators may now be imprisoned for up to thirty years per sexual act. Accordingly, the U.S. Department of Justice claimed that the PROTECT Act "strengthens laws punishing offenders who travel abroad to prey on children." While it is too early to be certain about the PROTECT Act's overall success, several recent arrests of alleged child-sex tourists may bolster this claim.

1. Recent Arrests of Individuals Under the PROTECT Act Are Encouraging

Since its adoption in April 2003, prosecutors have invoked the child-sex tourism prong of the PROTECT Act on several occasions. In September 2003, prosecutors charged a sixty-nine-year-old man in Seattle, Washington for allegedly traveling to Cambodia to engage in sexual acts with two Cambodian boys, ages ten and thirteen. Michael Lewis Clark was first arrested in Cambodia in June 2003. Clark was extradited to the United States in early September 2003, where he was arrested. Investigators learned that Clark spent a significant amount of time in Phnom Penh over the past five years, sexually exploiting boys between the ages of ten and eighteen. It is estimated that Clark may have molested as many as fifty children. According to the U.S. Attorney's Office in Seattle, Clark was "believed to be" the first person charged under the sex tourism provisions of the PRO-TECT Act.

In October 2003, federal prosecutors in Los Angeles, California charged eighty-five-year-old John Seljan with attempted travel with intent to engage in illicit sexual conduct with minors, the second indictment under the PROTECT Act. Seljan was apparently preparing to travel to the Philippines to sexually exploit two young girls, ages nine and twelve. He was arrested at the Los Angeles International Airport after customs officials discovered his luggage filled with "pornographic materials—some apparently involving children—sex aids, 100 pounds of chocolate and candy and thousands of dollars in U.S. and Philippine currency." Officials first suspected Seljan after a routine inspection of overseas mail revealed correspondence from Seljan suggesting his intent to engage in sexual acts with the two girls.

The third indictment under the PROTECT Act occurred on November 20, 2003. Gary Evans Jackson, a fifty-six-year-old man from Bainbridge Island, Washington, allegedly met three boys in Phnom Phen, Cambodia, and paid them US$20 for sexual acts. All three boys were under the age of sixteen. Jackson allegedly took digital photos of his activities with the boys, some of which he loaded onto computers at a Phnom Phen internet café, which sparked an investigation of the café by a U.S. government agent, leading to Jackson's arrest.

2. Prosecution of Child-Sex Tour-Related Organizations Under the PROTECT Act May Also Be on the Rise

In addition to the initial indictments of individual travelers under the PROTECT Act, prosecutors now have the additional power to charge organizers of sex tours. Prosecutors have yet to utilize this new provision of the PROTECT Act, but a case in New York is potentially the first example.

Feminist organizations have been monitoring a New York travel agency, Big Apple Oriental Tours ("Big Apple") for years, contending that Big Apple organizes tours for men seeking prostitutes, some underage, in Southeast Asia. In 2000, advocates called upon New York prosecutors to file criminal charges against Big Apple. At that time, however, Big Apple's actions were beyond the reach of prosecutors because the 1994 Act only criminalized the acts of individuals and had no provision for sex tour organizers. The state finally turned to a civil remedy under state law. On August 20, 2003, New York Attorney General Eliot Spitzer announced that the state had filed a civil lawsuit against Big Apple. The state successfully sought a temporary order to prevent Big Apple from advertising or promoting its sex tours. The ultimate goal of such litigation is to force the closure of the agency via the imposition of financial penalties.

With the adoption of the PROTECT Act, a civil action is no longer the only option available to New York prosecutors. A spokesperson for Attorney General Spitzer suggested that the state may also file criminal charges in the future. Under the new provisions of the PROTECT Act, Big Apple could be criminally charged for encouraging or organizing travel designed to enable its clients to engage in illicit sexual conduct. A criminal conviction for organizing sex tours could result in up to thirty years imprisonment for Big Apple's operators.

The flurry of arrests and indictments following the PROTECT Act's adoption evidences the U.S. government's commitment to the prevention of child-sex tourism, but must nonetheless be viewed cautiously. It remains to be seen whether any convictions will result from these charges. Before U.S. prosecutors herald the PROTECT Act as the ultimate weapon against child-sex tourists and their operators, they should examine Australia's experience under a law very similar to the PROTECT Act. Such examination indicates that the PROTECT Act is unlikely to significantly deter sex tourism.

IV. Australia's Child-Sex Tourism Act Highlights the PROTECT Act's Limitations

A. The PROTECT Act Closely Parallels Australia's CST Act

Australia's response to child-sex tourism began with the passage of the CST Act. The CST Act criminalized sexual intercourse or acts of indecency with a child under age sixteen committed outside of Australia by an Australian citizen or resident. Under the CST Act, crimes involving sexual intercourse carry a maximum sentence of seventeen years imprisonment, while crimes involving indecent acts with a child are punishable by up to twelve years imprisonment. Australian prosecutors may also charge organizers of sex tours under the CST Act. The CST Act makes it an offense to benefit from or encourage any conduct that would violate the aforementioned provisions. Some examples of barred activities include "profiting from an arrangement that facilitates an offense" and "assisting a person to travel outside Australia in order to commit an act that would constitute an offense." Finally, the CST Act has an additional evidentiary provision allowing for witness testimony by video link in court proceedings for offenses under the Act.

. . . .

With the adoption of the PROTECT Act, the United States amended its sex tourism legislation and broadened its scope to more closely mirror Australia's CST Act. Both countries now allow for the prosecution of sex tourists based only on evidence of sexual acts abroad. Additionally, both statutes provide for the prosecution of sex tour organizers. Indeed, procedural differences between the U.S. and Australian laws—such as the maximum sentence allowed with a conviction, treatment of double jeopardy, and Australia's specific accommodation for remote testimony by foreign witnesses—stand out as the remaining material differences.

While the PROTECT Act may substantially increase the potential reach of U.S. prosecutors, the United States should be guarded in its optimism. After a decade of enforcement of its sex tourism legislation, Australia has only convicted a small number of sex tourists and operators under the CST Act. Given the similarities between the CST Act and the PROTECT Act and the U.S. and Australian sex tourism industries, it is likely that the U.S. law will have a similarly limited impact on child-sex tourism.

B. Ten Years, Eleven Convictions: The Limited Success of Australia's CST Act

In the ten years since its adoption, Australia has charged only sixteen individuals with violating the CST Act. Of the sixteen individuals charged, eleven were convicted, one case is still pending, and four cases were dismissed. Given the estimated number of sex tourists from Australia, eleven convictions reflect a very low percentage.

Examples of Australian convictions include John Arthur Lee, age forty-three, who was arrested in 1997 and charged with sexually assaulting young girls in Cambodia. Lee's arrest came after he bragged to colleagues about his sexual activities, even going so far as to showcase photos of the young girls. Lee was convicted in 1999 and sentenced to fourteen years in prison. Similarly, Robert Marlow, a fifty-five-year-old Melbourne man, pled guilty in 2000 to sexually abusing boys while on business trips to Fiji. Marlow was convicted and sentenced to three years in jail.

In 2001, Jonathan Kaye, a seventy-year-old man from Perth, was charged under the prong of the CST Act that allows for the prosecution of individuals who promote or encourage sex tourism. Kaye, a former schoolteacher, advertised his travel services in a local newspaper. While meeting with a customer regarding a tour to Thailand, Kaye offered to arrange services for the man to engage in sex activities with children "of any age," and showed the man photographs of boys under age fifteen who could provide sex. Kaye was convicted in 2003. Kaye's case marked the first time in Australia that a charge for encouraging sex tourism had gone to trial. In addition to the convictions of Lee, Marlow and Kaye, just eight other Australian men have been convicted under the CST Act. The small number of convictions under the CST Act should be of concern to advocates of the PROTECT Act, given the many similarities between the two laws. If the PROTECT Act is to be more successful than its Australian counterpart, sufficient distinctions must exist between the laws. The limited distinctions between the two laws, however, are unlikely to be the source of greater success for the U.S. prosecutors.

C. Child-Sex Tourism Laws Have Not Deterred Sex Tourists

PROTECT Act advocates may argue that the law is largely meant to serve as a deterrent, and that actual convictions of individual sex tourists, while an added benefit, are not the true measure of its success. Indeed, neither Australian nor U.S. officials, in framing their respective laws, actually expected that the legislation would yield large numbers of prosecutions. In 1994, in anticipation of the adoption of the CST Act, an aide to the Australian Attorney General stated, "[w]hile we do not expect large numbers of prosecutions, the law sends a message that this country will not tolerate its citizens going offshore to abuse the children of other countries." Likewise, a U.S. Congressional Budget Office cost estimate for the Sex Tourism Prohibition Improvement Act of 2002 suggested that the increase in costs under the new legislation would be minimal "because of the small number of additional cases likely to be affected."

The argument that child-sex tourism laws are most powerful as deterrents, however, is not supported by the statistical trend in child-sex tourism. Since Australia's adoption of the CST Act a decade ago, the number of sex tourists continues to be appallingly high; Australians continue to represent a significant percentage of this number.

Australia's experience over the past ten years does little to support the belief that the PROTECT Act is the ultimate answer to combating sex tourism originating in the United States. In virtually all material respects, the PROTECT Act and the Australian CST Act are identical. In addition, one procedural distinction between the U.S. and Australian child-sex tourism laws—the availability of remote testimony in Australian proceedings—may in fact render the PROTECT Act less effective than the CST Act.

. . . .

Sex Tourism: Big Apple Oriental Tour Operators Indicted for Promoting Prostitution

Women's Action Update (Equality Now, New York, N.Y.), Mar. 2004,
available at http://www.equalitynow.org/english/actions/action_1202_en.html

On 27 February 2004, following a year-long investigation by the New York State Attorney General, Norman Barabash and Douglas Allen, the owner/operators of Big Apple Oriental Tours were indicted by a grand jury for promoting prostitution, in violation of Section 230.25 of the Penal Law of the State of New York. This indictment, the culmination of a seven-year campaign by Equality Now to stop the activities of Big Apple Oriental Tours, marks the first criminal action of its kind in the United States against a sex tourism company and will send a strong message to other sex tour operators that promoting prostitution can and will be considered a serious criminal offense. If convicted, Barabash and Allen could face up to seven years in prison. This criminal indictment follows an unprecedented civil case against Big Apple Oriental Tours initiated by New York State Attorney General Eliot Spitzer, leading to a temporary restraining order against Big Apple Oriental Tours in July 2003, which severely restricted the company from organizing or advertising any future tours and effectively disabled their website.

In 1996, Equality Now launched its Women's Action campaign calling for the prosecution of Big Apple Oriental Tours, an agency in New York operating sex tours to the Philippines and Thailand. At the time, Big Apple Oriental Tours advertised a twelve-day trip to the Philippines for $2,195, which included transportation, airfare, hotel room and the ability of the sex tourist to "select your companion upon arrival in Angeles City." Big Apple further advertised, "you are not obligated to remain with the same companion. You may select a different companion at any time during your stay." Among the Frequently Asked Questions on the website of Big Apple Oriental Tours was the question, "Do you run sex tours?" with the answer, "The American Heritage dictionary defines sex tours as travel to locations where sexual services are available to tourists. For example, prostitution under certain rules is legal in Israel and Italy. Therefore, if our tours are sex tours, so is every religious pilgrimage to the Holy Land and Vatican City." In response to inquiries for further information, Norman Barabash provided the names and phone numbers of individuals who had previously traveled with Big Apple Oriental Tours and invited the prospective traveler to sample his video collection, which he characterized as "an Encyclopedia Britannica of raunch." The Big Apple Oriental Tours list of pornographic movies for sale includes descriptions such as "unbelievable scenes of lewdness and debauchery" and "the finalists get even with the funniest gang rape on video."

Conversations with Mr. Barabash and previous Big Apple Oriental Tours travelers more explicitly detailed what occurs on a sex tour. The traveler would be picked up at the airport by a car or bus to take him to Angeles City where he would be met by the Big Apple Oriental Tours representative in the Philippines. This representative would accompany the traveler to numerous bars in Angeles City. The traveler would select a girl or woman from among those working in the bars, and the Big Apple Oriental Tours representative would negotiate the cost of prostitution, called a "barfine", with her "mamasan" (the business manager). The mamasan would check with the traveler in the morning to ensure that the woman was "satisfactory."

Equality Now's campaign initially urged the Queens District Attorney to take action against Big Apple Oriental Tours. Despite ample evidence showing that the company was promoting prostitution contrary to New York Penal Law Section 230.25, as well as protests by members of Equality Now's Women's Action Network from around the world, it was only after Equality Now brought the issue to the attention of Attorney General Eliot Spitzer in 2002, with support from Gloria Steinem, U.S. Congressional Representative Carolyn Maloney and the New York Women's Agenda, a coalition of which Equality Now is a member, that a thorough official investigation was launched and the temporary restraining order against Big Apple Oriental Tours obtained.

Sex tourism is a form of exploitation that preys on sex inequality and contributes to the demand for trafficking of women. It is a human rights violation. Big Apple Oriental Tours is not the only operator of sex tours in the U.S.; other sex tour companies such as Dexterhorn from California, Bendricks from Florida, Men's Travel from Washington and G&F Tours from Louisiana still offer such tours to countries such as Thailand, the Philippines and Costa Rica. Holding the operators of Big Apple Oriental Tours criminally accountable will be an important step in state recognition of the need to take action to stop the illegal activities of sex tour companies and address the severe impact they have in promoting violence and discrimination against women around the world.

Notes and Questions

1. In January 2009, Norman Barabash and Douglas Allen were ultimately acquitted on charges of promoting prostitution. For a discussion of the case, see Larry Hertz, *Jury Finds 2 Not Guilty of Running Sex Tours*, Poughkeepsie Journal, Jan. 27, 2009.

2. The first successful conviction of a sex tour operator occurred in New York in May 2007. Saeed Ahmed of Jump Off Destinations was found guilty of three counts of promoting prostitution and could be imprisoned for up to three years. It is also interesting to note that Ahmed's tour company advertised on Craig's List. See Press Release, Equality Now, Manhattan Sex Tour Operator Found Guilty of Three Counts of Promoting Prostitution in the Third Degree (May 24, 2007), *available at* http://www.equalitynow.org/english/pressroom/press_releases/sextour_20070524_en.html, for additional information on this case.

3. In March 2008, the public learned that crusading New York governor Eliot Spitzer, famous for his tough approach to sex tourism during his time as Attorney General, had been purchasing the services of a prostitution ring. Despite having won high praise from anti-sex trafficking groups for his unflagging support of their cause, in his initial public remarks, Spitzer referred to his own actions as a "private matter." Spitzer was forced to resign the governorship. The sense of shock and disappointment on the part of anti-trafficking activists was profound. For a detailed description of the reaction of anti-trafficking advocates, see Nina Bernstein, *Foes of Sex Trade Are Stung by the Fall of an Ally*, NEW YORK TIMES, Mar. 12, 2008, *available at* http://www.nytimes.com/2008/03/12/nyregion/12prostitute.html?_r=1&hp. For a sense of the strong economic motives leading tour businesses in the direction of promoting travel-for-sex, see Pete Alfano, The Shadowy World of Sex Tours, Star-Telegram (Fort Worth), August 6, 2006.

4. The individual stories of U.S. and European sex tourists are variations on a theme. In 2007, Michael Koklich pleaded guilty to one count of traveling to Cambodia and engaging in illicit sexual conduct with a 13-year-old girl. He admitted to attempting to bribe witnesses in the case, including the young victim. Ultimately, Koklich was sentenced to five years and four months in prison. In addition, the judge ordered him to pay $5,000 in

restitution to each girl and required him to register as a sex offender.[24] The U.S. government is justly proud of successful prosecutions of U.S. sex tourists who prey on children. But with an estimated 25% of the world's sex tourists believed to be American men, is there some more drastic mode of prevention that should be attempted? For more on U.S. determination to pursue American sex tourists abroad, see Eric Lichtblau & James Dao, *U.S. is Now Pursuing Americans Who Commit Sex Crimes Overseas*, New York Times, June 8, 2004, at A1.

5. Not surprisingly, those charged with child sexual exploitation under the Protect Act have mounted constitutional challenges to the extraterritorial reach of the law. Fortunately, these arguments have not convinced courts that these activities by Americans should be left to the weak and often corrupt judicial systems in developing countries. Legal challenges to the extraterritorial applications of the Protect Act against American sex tourists have, not surprisingly, failed. See Amy Messigian, *Love's Labor Lost: Michael Lewis Clark's Constitutional Challenge of 18 U.S.C. 2423* (C), 43 American Criminal Law Review 1241 (2006). It is ironic that American men seeking sex with underage prostitutes within the U.S. are not identified and prosecuted as rigorously as those traveling abroad for the same purposes. Within the U.S., the prosecutorial focus remains on the "traffickers", rather than on the end user.

D. Understanding Demand: The Role of Images

Charles Miranda, *A Webcam World of Depravity*
Advertiser (Australia), Sept. 22, 2007

Police across the world are forming international partnerships to combat rising internet pornography, pedophilia and abuse, writes London correspondent Charles Miranda.

In a dark, grubby backroom of an apartment in Baltimore in the U.S., Roderick Gene Parks' face only can be seen illuminated by the on-screen glow of his computer.

He logs on to his favourite internet chat site and announces embraceu has entered the cyber room.

A live webcam clicks on and, in the background, a small boy can be seen standing by a table and chair.

A light goes on, the action begins and, with a global audience in the thousands, Parks takes on the role of actor, director and narrator of a movie most foul.

Internet pornography, pedophilia and abuse is rising so dramatically, police forces across the world are taking the unprecedented step of forming new international partnerships specifically to combat the trade.

The Virtual Global Taskforce operates independently of international law enforcement partnerships created to combat terrorism and organised crime.

---

24. Press Release, Dep't of Justice, Bay Area Man Pleads Guilty to Traveling to Have Sex with a Minor in Cambodia (Dec. 12, 2006), *available at* http://www.projectsafechildhood.gov/docs/psc_usao_121206.htm; Julia Cheever, *Bay Area Man Sentenced for Sex with a Child in Cambodia*, Bay City News Serv., Apr. 12, 2007, *available at* http://www.fogcityjournal.com/news_in_brief/bcn_cambodia_sex_tourism_070412.shtml.

The Australian Federal Police has seconded agents to the U.S. and the United Kingdom to work full-time with online child exploitation teams looking at identifying, tracking and arresting pedophiles and their networks.

What they have found has so alarmed police in Canberra, the federal police have taken a $43 million government grant and set up exchange programs to boost the number of agents working overseas to enhance their expertise to fight the crime back home.

The exploits of Parks, 42, have gone a long way to getting authorities to take notice. As Parks performed his vile abuse of a boy, 11, across the globe in Sydney a computer user logged on to the internet and, moving about an Australian-registered webcam internet site, stumbled on to the live abuse movie.

That person contacted the webcam site which recorded still images and called the federal police who, in turn, contacted their own on-line child sex exploitation team and the Federal Bureau of Investigation in the U.S.

"We had to move on it pretty quickly because obviously someone was being abused in the most vile way," Australian hi-tech crime centre director Kevin Zuccato said of the November 8, 2006, alert.

"We conducted our own investigation, contacted the Immigration and Customs Enforcement in the U.S. who identified this person and he was arrested."

Parks was arrested on December 1, pleaded guilty to sexually exploiting a minor this July and last week was sentenced to 30 years in jail. The pedophile was supposed to be watching the boy after school while his mother worked but instead was feeding a worldwide demand.

"This case is a remarkable example of how international co-operation among law enforcement agencies can stop the production of child pornography throughout the world," U.S. Attorney Rod Rosenstein said.

"The police in Australia received a complaint and immediately co-ordinated with the international community in order to apprehend the offender and rescue the child."

Mr. Zuccato knows better than some the vile nature of such abuse.

The father of four young children says when he has to watch an on-line video with sound the "image stays with you".

His admiration goes to those who have to watch it daily as part of their duties, such as former drug squad colleague and 15-year law enforcer Richard Chin.

Mr. Chin last week was seconded to London as part of a program to have the best and brightest agents sent overseas for short-term operations and training to learn new best-practice techniques and help fight the borderless crime.

Some of his work involves posing as a child and a pedophile and waiting as abusers come to him.

It's flypaper stuff but the volume surprised even him. "I think we all know the internet is linking the whole world and you get a variety of people on the net who have certain social interests," he said. Mr. Chin was speaking from a secret location in London from where he is working with the British Child Exploitation and Online Protection Centre.

That was created last year and consists of a 100-strong squad of police, intelligence officers, psychologists and technical experts.

"People who conduct offences against children are using the net in the same way we would socially network with a common interest like cars or sport," he said. "They are interested in offences against children, trading images and looking for children for webcam abuse."

Gone are the days when men walked about in parks wearing trenchcoats and carrying brown bags with poor quality videos in them for exchange.

Now, men and women around the world are watching each other live on webcams and in some cases directing the abuse of victims from 20,000km away and streaming the footage to audiences which law enforcers say easily are in the hundreds of thousands.

When asked how many abusers he thinks are in Australia, Mr. Zuccato's voice rises with intensity. "There are thousands," he says.

"It is difficult to put a number on it but if you go online posing as a child you get approached in minutes if not seconds and not by just one person but several. These aren't people who are isolated by society; they are parents, teachers, judges, solicitors. They are normal people leading normal lives but using the internet to feed their fantasy."

The webcam site, which inadvertently broadcast the sex abuse, has more than 1.6 million subscribers.

So, even if a very small portion is looking for such images that still would be high. This is only one website.

Of particular concern to the federal police is the supply and demand nature of the abuse.

Realising there is a booming market, organised crime groups are kidnapping children and offering pay-per-view abuse. Many groups operate out of Eastern Europe where the children are abused and tortured with the video posted on the net.

New Federal Government funding to tackle net abuse means the OCSET staffing levels can double to 70 with 15 new investigators and 21 specialists in intelligence and technical assessments.

Many of these agents will work directly with the Virtual Global Taskforce.

New laws also were introduced in Australia in March that allowed for hefty penalties for all online child sex exploitation, including 10 years' jail for accessing and transmitting online.

"It's a shared responsibility and parents have to take an active role," Mr Zuccato says. "You don't take your children to a soccer game and say you will come back in two hours. It's the same for the net."

Major Busts, Stings and Operations

Kids the Light of Our Lives was an internet chat forum. It hosted images and live streaming videos of children being subjected to sexual abuse as part of an international pedophile ring of more than 700 individuals. British pedophile Timothy Cox ran the forum from his bedroom at his parents farm in Suffolk. Acting from information from the Virtual Global Taskforce, British police discovered Cox's computer hard disk contained 75,960 illegal images, and he had distributed up to 11,491 images to other users. The 10-month police operation resulted in the arrest of 700 men and the rescue 31 children.

Operation Avalanche was a major U.S. investigation of child pornography on the internet. Launched in 1999, it was made public in early August 2001 at the end of the operation, that 100 arrests were made out of 144 suspects.

Operation Ore is a large-scale ongoing international police operation begun in 1999 and intending to indict thousands of users of websites featuring child pornography. In the UK it has led to 7250 suspects identified, 4283 homes searched, 3744 arrests, 1848 charged, 1451 convictions, 493 cautioned, 879 investigations underway and 140 children removed from suspected dangerous situations.

Operation Predator is an initiative started in 2003 by the U.S. Immigration and Customs Enforcement to protect children from sexual predators. It targets foreign national sex offenders, child traffickers, child-sex tourists, and people involved in all levels of child pornography, from producers to distributors to consumers. As of January, 2007, there have been more than 9300 arrests.

A central aspect of sex tourism is the issue of demand. While focus on the victim is necessary and appropriate, and while laws allowing prosecution of sex tourists are noble efforts, the "best" solution would lie in diminishing demand. What might be the cultural or other explanations for the high level of demand evident in men from such diverse backgrounds? This question requires analysis of the consumer/customer and what it is that motivates him to seek out sex with vulnerable women and children. It should be considered whether the analysis of demand for women to abuse and exploit matches our understanding of the demand for children. Are these two issues merely the two sides of a coin, or is the worldwide demand for exploitable children something distinct? The following articles raise the general issue of demand, describe the U.S. response, and explain how legislative efforts have fared.

Michelle R. Adelman, *International Sex Trafficking: Dismantling the Demand*

13 Southern California Review of Law & Women's Studies 387 (2004)

I. INTRODUCTION

....

In response to increased recognition of the violence associated with international trafficking, "governments, such as the United States, and international organizations, like the United Nations, have begun to focus financially and strategically on combating this immense human rights problem." United States efforts at countering international and domestic trafficking have focused on the prosecution of traffickers and the aiding of victims, with increasing success. Both United States and international legal efforts have diluted the illegal sex industry's stream of supply by increasing the number of traffickers prosecuted and broadening the scope of political forums in which victims can vindicate their rights. However, as this paper will examine, the United States regrettably does so by defining victims as women who are trapped in seemingly repressed economic and social conditions, which are a function of their cultural heritage. The relative factual foundations of such portrayals and the ability of such realizations to fuel effective efforts at combating "the supply," the U.S. legislative efforts, scholarly debates, and mass media depictions have exaggerated the extent of such cultural oppression. This, in turn, enforces racist beliefs and overshadows the extent of American cultural oppression, which fuels the demand for illegal sex workers. U.S. legislation ignores the cultural foundations that support an increasing demand for illegal sex workers in America. Although current U.S. law provides a strong foundation from which to build, new regulations and legislation must be drafted that contend with the increasing U.S. demand for illegal sex workers.

....

II. Victimization Of Women Precludes An Effective Solution

A. The Success of International and U.S. Law: Attacking the "Supply" Through Increased Prosecution Rates of Traffickers and Greater Resources for Victims

....

2. United States' Legal Efforts

....

The Victims of Trafficking and Violence Protection Act of 2000 (VTVPA), enacted in October of 2000, amended the slavery statutes to make prosecution efforts more effective by increasing the statutory maximum sentences that traffickers will face, in addition to creating new protections for trafficking victims. Senator Paul Wellstone (D-Minnesota), who co-sponsored the bill along with Senator Sam Brownback (R-Kansas), stated: "This bill will take immediate action against international sex trafficking, before the lives of more women and girls are shattered." Simultaneously, a new immigration statute, a special "T" visa for trafficking, will be created "in order to give victims a better chance to bring charges against traffickers. The victims, instead of being deported, will be granted 'interim immigration relief' for up to three years." The U.S. Department of State reported that as of January 31, 2002 in accordance with statutory limits, there will be 5,000 T visas available annually.

Despite the increase in the number of traffickers prosecuted and the expansion of the legal remedies available to victims, the United States has failed in its attempts to successfully curb the trafficking of 50,000 women and children into the United States each year. While U.S. legislators focus on the efforts of suppliers, they have ignored the increasing demand of U.S. consumers for trafficked sex slaves.

....

III. The Ineffectiveness of Current Law Remains Embedded in the Perpetuation of Racist Perceptions

....

A. The Characterization of the Victim Through Racist Imagery

....

Trafficking victims are described using racist language and imagery, facilitating the U.S. perception that women are abused, objectified, and humiliated by "certain countries" whose "third world," allegedly "backward" cultures "force [women] to work in the sex trade." In an effort to respond to the "estimated one million children [who] are currently trafficked for coerced sexual exploitation or labor," U.S. media efforts have identified the problem with racist undertones. The New York Times, cited the example of girls in southeastern Ghana who are often offered by their families to priests as "slaves of gods" to appease the gods for family sins, yet failed to comment on the increasing demand for these children in western cultures.

Racist portrayals of women in other, seemingly economically depressed, "third-world" cultures are rampant in U.S. media, and are rarely accompanied by any suggested parallel of such conditions in American society. For instance, the television program, 60 Minutes, told the story of a Filipina woman who supported her daughters' efforts to become mail-order brides and find wealthy foreign husbands so that they could send money home to support her. Rather than go on to examine the receiving sector of the U.S., specifically the men who demand and pay exorbitant prices for such mail-order brides, the program showed the woman's previous home, a "ramshackle hut," and then the big concrete house she acquired following the sale of her daughters.

....

The over-generalized racist claims that attempt to define the victims of sex trafficking thwart attempts at effectively protecting trafficked women and children. "These generalizations efface the problems, perspectives, and political concerns of women marginalized because of their class, race, religion, ethnicity, and/or sexual orientation." Scholars in the United States, to the detriment of victims, continue to attribute the violent and primitive nature of the international sex trade to cultural values entrenched in third-world nations. "Women in the Third World are portrayed as victims of their culture, which reinforces stereotyped and racist representations of that culture and privileges the culture of the West." Using the Third World as a scapegoat, Americans are never confronted with their own social, political, and economic shackles, which invigorate the demand for the trafficking of women and children.

B. U.S. Racist Perceptions Enable the United States to Ignore U.S. Parallel Contributions to Sex Trafficking

Racist perceptions have continued to color the U.S. position on and response to international trafficking of persons, specifically the sex trade. "Latin American and Asian women were trafficked into the United States for many years prior to the influx of Russian traffickers and trafficked women." But it was not until Russian and Ukrainian women began to be trafficked to the United States in the early 1990s that governmental agencies and many non-governmental organizations (NGOs) began to recognize the problem. The fact that it took blonde and blue-eyed victims to draw governmental and public attention to trafficking in the United States gives the appearance, at least, of racism.

Americans, through the use of media and political propaganda, including print, online, and television sources, avoid association with and acceptance of responsibility for the type of violence against women that we harshly criticize in other countries. In the U.S., "trafficking in women for prostitution and related forms of sexual entertainment is so widespread yet so invisible." News media continues to focus its attention on the deplorable behavior of the traffickers who ostensibly entice foreign women into the sex industry. Commentators make no mention of those "valued customers" that are providing the U.S. sex industry with the demand necessary to maintain its current vitality. *The Houston Chronicle*, recently reporting on the numerous U.S. cities that have become the home to "sex rings," focused the article on the women who were allegedly "lured" to the United States with promises of good jobs. The article made no mention of the increasing demand that placed those cities as the bustling centers of such "sex rings."

While the United States disparages the maltreatment of women in other cultures, stories about the maltreatment of women in the United States rarely make national headlines. The stories not often told are the stories unveiling hyper-masculine elements, including the degradation of women in advertising, male-dominated arenas like the military, and attitudes in popular culture. Those stories explain that "receiving countries (i.e., where women end up in the sex industry) tend to be wealthier" and that sites of military conflict "are popular destinations for trafficking victims." Although U.S. social and political commentary, in addition to U.S. and international legislative efforts, continue to debate the most effective social programs to empower victims in their countries of origin, we have failed to examine the extent to which our own hyper-masculine behavior contributes to the same objectifying and violent conditions we condemn.

Despite criticism of African, Arab, eastern European, and Southeast Asian countries whose military conflict fosters the type of hyper-masculine environments that seem to breed demand for the illegal sex trade, a recent article entitled "Porn Stars Film Appreciative Video for Troops" detailed the efforts of U.S. adult entertainers "[who] want to raise spirits [of U.S. military personnel].... Busting out of barely there outfits and grasping a disturbingly long microphone, porn actresses took turns [being] taped at the recent Adult Entertainment Expo in Las Vegas."

....

IV. The Solution Must Commence At Home

U.S. lawmakers ought to note that "sexual exploitation is the basis of women's oppression ... [and] rape, abortion, and pornography [constitute] the primary human rights violations against women."

A. Social Demand for Pornography

U.S. popular culture has become so entwined with pornographic images and depictions of women as sexually exploitive creatures, that it has become difficult to separate images of sex from the most fundamental media outlets of U.S. society. The pornography industry is cited as one of the largest thriving industries in the United States and continues to broaden in scope to include videos, phone-sex businesses, adult toys, magazines, and web sites. Additionally, pornographic and sexually exploitative images dominate advertising and news media (as discussed supra).

Although the U.S. adamantly criticizes the objectification of women as objects of sexual gratification abroad, Bill Asher, president of Vivid Entertainment, reports that his adult entertainment company has "'gone from a market of hundreds of thousands to hundreds of millions'" over the past twenty years. "The film, television, and Web-based products produced by Vivid alone grossed one billion dollars in retail sales last year. A 1998 study by Forrester Research in Cambridge, [Massachusetts] estimated that the industry generates $10 billion a year." The porn industry glorifies and romanticizes those acts which foster the demand for illegal sex workers, and U.S. society financially embraces the industry, as is evidenced by the emergence of pornographic video producers as "star-making machinery much like the old Hollywood studios." Actors like Jenna Jameson, the "reigning star of adult films have big-dollar contracts with filmmakers who promote them on Web sites, movie display boxes and public appearances."

The internet hosts more than 40,000 sex-related sites, and it is commonly known that "the adult entertainment industry drives the internet." During the crash of the dot-com industry, some technology specialists who found themselves unemployed leaped at the opportunity to join the porn web sites culture, which:

> shows little sign of slowing. According to New York-based market research firm Jupiter Media Metrix, Inc., the number of individual visitors at sex sites grew nearly 30 percent in about two years, from 22 million in December 1999 to nearly 28 million [in 2001].

....

Despite the financial boom of the internet porn industry, "as the internet sprawls into one massive (cyber-) mall, the growth in the transnational sex industry is spurred by the immense promotion and marketing of women and children for sex tourism, as electronic mail-order brides, and in pornography."

Pornographic images also dominate mainstream popular culture through advertising and other forms of media, which the U.S. has come not only to accept, but also to embrace. Currently, a new beer advertisement is rousing debate as "two buxom women [debate over the beer] ... tear each other's clothes off and end up wrestling in wet cement." Organizations, like the Association for Women in Communications, made a poignant statement that "these blatant displays of sexism simply reinforce ... attitudes that keep women from achieving equal treatment in pay and career opportunities."

However, this does not seem to hold true for the 50,000 women who have been abducted into the U.S. sex trade and whose business unfortunately flourishes. The proliferation of the legalized commercial sex industry in the U.S. provides unwavering evidence of the demand associated with the use of women as sexual objects. U.S. legislators must combat the proliferation of sexually explicit images and legalized sexual acts that serve to endorse the use of women as mere objects of sexual conquest.... U.S. trafficking laws must be expanded to include harsher punishment for consumers in addition to traffickers, and U.S. First Amendment protections must be narrowed in order to more effectively regulate the reinforcement of objectifying social standards.

Studies continue to link the use of pornography with the rape and molestation of women and children. The relationship of pornography to sexual abuse is compelling. A review study of eighty-one studies published in peer-reviewed journals found that "with fairly impressive consistency" exposure to pornography negatively affects attitudes towards women and increases the likelihood of rape. In addition, the crimes that international trafficking laws are attempting to prosecute continue to be glorified by pornographic materials. One study of adult sex offenders found that 86% of convicted rapists said they were regular users of pornography, with 57% admitting direct imitation of pornographic scenes they enjoyed, in the commission of their rapes. In addition, both pornography itself and the projection of sexual imagery in the media connote and validate the perception that "women have one value—to meet the sexual demands of men." It is no coincidence that a society that fosters sexual objectification of women is also one whose economy thrives on the legal commercial sex industry. Efforts to thwart illegal trafficking of women and children have failed to surpass the demand for these illegal slaves, and violence against women (including those trafficked into the United States) continues to occur.

....

Notes and Questions

1. In this provocative article, Adelman criticizes U.S. lawmakers for neglecting to focus on demand. A demand-side approach could mean more attention to prosecuting customers and users, or to the means by which demand is generated in the first place. Arguably, provisions of the PROTECT Act that attempted to crack down on child pornography, discussed below, did focus specifically on the creation of demand. But the legislation ran into problems when the U.S. Supreme Court found the ban on "virtual" child pornography to be a violation of the First Amendment, as described in detail in the readings that follow.

———

As this chapter has shown, vulnerable children are at enormous risk of commercial sexual exploitation. It is unclear whether our approach to child pornography, as at least one major element in the overall picture of child sexual exploitation, truly reflects its enormous potential to harm children. In the readings that follow, we explore the Supreme Court's reaction to a significant attempt by Congress to impose restrictions on the freedom to create and possess "virtual" child pornography; that is, computer-generated child pornography, made without the use of any real children. As technology has progressed, it has become increasingly difficult to distinguish between these types of pornography. If there is reason to believe that child pornography normalizes and thus promotes the sexual exploitation of children by raising demand, isn't is appropriate to restrict both types of images with similar severity?

Kate Dugan, *Regulating What's Not Real: Federal Regulation in the Aftermath of* Ashcroft v. Free Speech Coalition
48 St. Louis University Law Journal 1063 (2004)

I. Introduction

Pornographic images created using real children raise serious concerns about the sexual exploitation of children. Tragically, pedophiles and child molesters prey on young children by using them to create images that "feed their sexual obsessions, ... stimulate their sex drive and validate their desire to actually assault children." Philip Jenkins, author of Beyond Tolerance, recounts the following painful and disturbing story of a young female victim:

> [A] British girl..., tragically, may be one of the best-known sex stars on the Web. In the late 1980s, as a little girl of seven or eight, [she] became the subject of a photo series that depicted her not only in all the familiar nude poses of hardcore pornography but also showed her in numerous sex acts with [a young boy] of about the same age. Both are shown having sex with an adult man, presumably [the young girl's] father ... [These images] are cherished by thousands of collectors worldwide. They seem to be the standard starter kit for child porn novices.

It should be no surprise that a child's participation in the production of such images severely impacts that child's psychological well-being. There is ample evidence to suggest that children used in the production of such images struggle to develop healthy relationships as adults, endure sexual dysfunction, have a tendency to become sexual abusers themselves, and engage in drug and alcohol abuse, prostitution, or other self-destructive behavior later in life. The premature introduction of sexuality to a child might result in a lasting unhealthy emotional reaction to normal sexual experiences. In addition, "the child may be programmed to use sex to acquire recognition, attention, and validation ... [and] the child may learn that sex is something basically improper that needs to be cloaked in secrecy." Further, the impact of the abuse is not limited to the actual experience; a child victim who bravely discloses the experience to family or authorities finds him or herself reliving the stress and anxiety of the experience before and during disclosure.

To add further pain to the inevitable psychological injury resulting from a child victim's participation in the creation of child pornography, these victims are left with "a permanent record of [their] participation and the harm to the child is exacerbated by [the materials'] circulation."

Before society's relatively recent technology boom and the resulting widespread use of the Internet, child pornographers were limited to using real children to create their material. Today, unfortunately, technological advances have given child pornographers a new set of tools for the development of pornographic images that depict children in sexually explicit ways. Some say that computers have "emancipated pedophiles from having to exploit and abuse real children." Further, the computer and the Internet have become the nearly-exclusive means by which child pornography is viewed and exchanged by other child pornographers and child molesters. As one commentator noted:

Child porn is extremely difficult to obtain through non-electronic means and has been so for twenty years ... It is a substantial presence, and much of the material [on the Internet] is worse than most of us can imagine, in terms of the types of activity depicted and the ages of the children portrayed.

One unfortunate result of society's technology boom and widespread use of the Internet is the introduction of virtual child pornography to the child pornographer's production capabilities. Virtual child pornography involves methods by which computer-savvy child pornographers use technology to create computer-generated images of children that look real and, even more frighteningly, to disguise images of real children so that they appear computer-generated. For example, child pornographers and pedophiles can use 3-D modeling programs to create images of children that are indistinguishable from real children. In addition, innocent pictures of actual children can be altered by inexpensive graphics programs to create a sexually explicit image of the same child.

These technological advances and the resulting introduction of virtual child pornography have muddled the already murky landscape of child pornography regulation and have challenged courts and Congress to more precisely define what images fall outside the boundaries of protected speech under the First Amendment. On April 16, 2002, the Supreme Court rejected Congress's first attempt to regulate virtual child pornography in *Ashcroft v. Free Speech Coalition*. In this case, the Court faced a challenge to sections of the Child Pornography Prevention Act of 1996 (CPPA) and held that it was "overbroad and unconstitutional," stressing that the CPPA prohibited speech that might have "serious literary, artistic, political, or scientific value." The Court emphasized that the "CPPA prohibited speech that records no crime and creates no victims by its production." Further, the Court held that otherwise-protected speech cannot be suppressed simply because it might be used for criminal acts in the future.

The *Free Speech Coalition* decision has been interpreted as marking the Court's rejection of a complete ban on virtual child pornography. Further, the decision appears to protect the production of non-obscene, computer-generated images of children engaging in sexually explicit conduct so long as no actual child was used in the production of the image.

This result is understandably unsettling to those who cannot fathom a scenario in which an image (virtual or not) of a child engaging in sexually explicit conduct has social, literary, artistic, or scientific value. On the other hand, those who support the *Free Speech Coalition* decision applaud the Court for rejecting what was perceived to be an unconstitutional, overly broad regulation of speech. While supporters of the decision concede that certain categories of expression, including child pornography, are beyond the protection of the First Amendment because of their "slight social value," they argue that, if Congress must regulate virtual child pornography, it must do so in a manner that does not inadvertently silence speech that would otherwise be protected by the First Amendment.

Congress has struggled to draft legislation that both captures the truly objectionable virtual child pornography and stays within the boundaries of the Court's First Amendment jurisprudence. For example, in *Free Speech Coalition*, the Court held that one of the major flaws in the CPPA was Congress's failure to define precisely what harm results from virtual child pornography when no actual child is used to create the sexually explicit image. The Government argued that virtual child pornography fuels the proliferation of the child pornography market and emphasized the negative secondary effects that virtual child pornography might have on subsequent viewers of the material. This argument was flatly rejected by the majority in *Free Speech Coalition*, which held that "virtual child pornography is not "intrinsically related' to the sexual abuse of children … The causal link [between virtual child pornography images and actual instances of child abuse] is contingent and indirect." Without such a causal link between speech and its resulting harm, the Court said, the Government may not suppress speech simply because it may "encourage" pedophiles and molesters to abuse children.

In the wake of the *Free Speech Coalition* decision, both the House and Senate have made new attempts to draft legislation that targets the evils associated with virtual child pornography. Determined to ensure the effective enforcement of established child pornography laws, Congress has enacted legislation in response to—and, as this Note will consider, potentially consistent with—the *Free Speech Coalition* decision. On April 30, 2003, President George W. Bush signed into law the Prosecutorial Remedies and Other Tools to End the Exploitation of Children Today Act of 2003 (PROTECT Act 2003). Whatever the fate might be for the PROTECT Act 2003, Congress has made notable progress in crafting legislation that respects the free speech guarantees embodied in the First Amendment, while targeting the specific evils associated with virtual child pornography.

. . . .

II. Obscenity and Child Pornography — Leading Cases

A. *Miller v. California*

In *Miller v. California*, the Court tightened up the then unworkably-loose definition of obscenity. In *Miller*, the Supreme Court reaffirmed its longstanding view that obscene material is not protected by the First Amendment. Precisely defining obscenity, however, proved to be more difficult for the Court. In this landmark decision, the Court provided the following three-prong test for determining whether something is obscene:

> (a) Whether "the average person, applying contemporary community standards" would find that the work, taken as a whole, appeals to the prurient interest; (b) whether the work depicts or describes, in a patently offensive way, sexual conduct specifically defined by the applicable … law; and (c) whether the work, taken as a whole, lacks serious literary, artistic, political, or scientific value.

Whether something appeals to the "prurient interest" or is "patently offensive" is a question of fact and must be determined based on the standards of the particular community. The Court rejected the implementation of national standards, noting that such standards would ultimately prove "hypothetical and unascertainable." The majority in *Miller* emphasized that "the First Amendment protects works which, taken as a whole, have serious literary, artistic, political, or scientific value, regardless of whether the government or a majority of the people approve of the ideas these works represent."

B. *New York v. Ferber*

Nine years after the Court decided *Miller*, the Court decided *New York v. Ferber*, the leading case on the regulation of child pornography involving the use of real children in its production. At issue in *Ferber* was the constitutionality of a New York statute that prohibited the promotion and distribution of material that depicted a child younger than sixteen engaging in a sexual performance. Holding that "states are entitled to greater leeway in the regulation of pornographic depictions of children," the Court found that: (1) there is a compelling governmental interest in ""safeguarding the physical and psychological well-being of a minor;'" (2) "the distribution of photographs and films depicting sexual activity by juveniles is intrinsically related to the sexual abuse of children.… [because] the materials produced are a permanent record of the children's participation and the harm to the child is exacerbated by their circulation," (3) "advertising and selling of child pornography provide an economic motive for ... the production of such materials," and (4) "the value of permitting live performances and photographic reproductions of children engaged in lewd sexual conduct is exceedingly modest, if not *de minimis*."

The *Ferber* Court explicitly rejected the respondent's argument that the *Miller* obscenity standard should apply to child pornography. The Court maintained that the *Miller* standard did not adequately support the State's "more compelling" interest in protecting children from sexual exploitation. In reviewing pornography that involves the use of an actual child, a court should not consider the work as a whole and need not determine that the material appeals to the prurient interest or that the sexual conduct portrayed is patently offensive. Note, however, that the "serious literary, artistic, political, or scientific value" prong of *Miller* remains intact for the purposes of child pornography after *Ferber*.

In sum, *Ferber* makes clear that child pornography involving the use of real children "bears so heavily and pervasively on the welfare of children engaged in its production [and therefore,] ... it is permissible to consider these materials as without the protection of the First Amendment." Therefore, under *Ferber*, if a child was involved in the production of a sexually explicit image, that image receives no First Amendment protection even if the image would not be deemed obscene under the Miller three-prong test.

The *Ferber* Court, however, did provide the following guidance to legislators of future child pornography statutes: "Here the nature of the harm to be combated requires that the ... offense be limited to works that visually depict sexual conduct by children below a specified age." Further, the Court emphasized that "depictions of sexual conduct, not otherwise obscene, which do not involve live performance or photographic or other visual reproduction of live performances, retain First Amendment protection."

C. Post-*Ferber* Regulation of "Real" Child Pornography

After *Ferber*, there is virtually no debate regarding the constitutionality of legislation that targets the use of real children engaged in sexually explicit conduct in the production of pornographic materials.

As a result, neither the Free Speech Coalition nor the other parties who challenged the constitutionality of the CPPA challenged the categories of speech prohibited by 18 U.S.C. 2256(8)(A) and (C). Section 2256(8)(A) prohibits any visual depiction of sexually explicit conduct where "the production of such visual depiction *involves the use of a minor* engaging in sexually explicit conduct." In addition, 2256(8)(C) prohibits "visual depictions [that] have been created, adapted, or modified to appear that an identifiable minor is engaging in sexually explicit conduct." This provision prohibits the computerized "morphing" of innocent images of actual children into sexually explicit depictions of the same children.

....

III. Past Federal Child Pornography Regulation

[Here the article describes pre-1996 legislation designed to crack down on the production and possession of child pornography.]

....

The Child Pornography Prevention Act of 1996 was one of Congress's earliest forays into the regulation of virtual child pornography. Concerned with the growing use of then-advanced computer and photographic technologies to produce real and virtual child pornography, Congress passed the CPPA to criminalize the production, distribution, possession, sale, or viewing of both real and virtual child pornography. Specifically, the Congressional findings accompanying the CPPA noted that new technologies "make it possible to produce by electronic, mechanical, or other means, visual depictions of what appear to be children engaging in sexually explicit conduct that are virtually indistinguishable to the unsuspecting viewer from unretouched photographic images of actual children engaging in sexually explicit conduct." Further, the Senate's findings emphasized the danger of child pornographers' computer alteration of sexually explicit images so that it becomes impossible to detect if the images were created using actual children.

The Congressional findings also focused on the negative secondary effects of both real and virtual child pornography and maintained that harm occurs to a child viewing a sexually explicit image whether or not the child depicted in the image is real or "virtually indistinguishable" from a real child. In sum, this component of the CPPA's rationale is based primarily on the idea that child abusers who use a computer-generated image of a child engaging in sexual conduct to seduce a real child into engaging in sexual conduct should not go unpunished. In this context, any distinction between images that portray actual children and images of computer-generated children involves a "mere technicality" as the damaging influence on the real child is the same no matter how the image was created.

To target these evils, Congress expanded the definition of child pornography to include two new categories of prohibited speech in 18 U.S.C. 2256. First, 2256(8)(B) prohibited visual depictions of sexually explicit conduct where "such visual depiction is, or appears to be, of a minor engaging in sexually explicit conduct." Second, 2256(8)(D) prohibited anyone from advertising, promoting, presenting, describing, or distributing visual depictions of minors engaging in sexually explicit conduct in a manner that "conveys the impression that the material is or contains a visual depiction of a minor engaging in sexually explicit conduct."

The effect of Congress's expansion of the definition of child pornography in the CPPA was to create new categories of forbidden speech under the Court's broad prohibition of child pornography articulated in *Ferber*. It was these two provisions that were specifically challenged in *Ashcroft v. Free Speech Coalition*.

IV. The Circuit Split and the *Ashcroft v. Free Speech Coalition* Decision

A. The Circuit Split

Before the Supreme Court heard *Ashcroft v. Free Speech Coalition*, five circuits passed on the issue of the constitutionality of 18 U.S.C. 2256(B) and (D). Of the five circuits, four upheld the provisions as constitutional and one did not.

One of the first circuit cases was *United States v. Hilton*, where the First Circuit reversed the District Court for the District of Maine and held the CPPA to be constitutional. At issue in *Hilton* was the constitutionality of 2256(8)(B)'s prohibition of sexually explicit images that "appear to be a minor" engaging in sexually explicit conduct. Hilton was indicted by a grand jury for the criminal possession of computer disks that contained three or more images of child pornography in violation of 2252A(5)(b). In *Hilton*, the First Circuit Court of Appeals boiled down the issue of the provision's constitutionality into four main "lessons." First, the court held that material that appears to depict a minor engaging in sexually explicit conduct must be afforded some level of constitutional protection. Second, the court held that acceptable governmental objectives regarding child pornography included more than the protection of actual children. Efforts aimed at stamping out the child pornography market, preventing the possession and viewing of pornographic materials involving children, and ending the use of child pornography to seduce children into the production of pornographic materials were all held to be legitimate Congressional objectives. Third, the court emphasized the importance of carefully describing "the type of condemned sexual depiction." Finally, the court held that, because these regulations were aimed at protecting children, greater discretion and leeway ought to be given to state legislatures and Congress "to set out the parameters of anti-pornography restrictions."

The *Hilton* court focused on what the proper interpretation of the "appears to be" standard should be and, relying on the legislative record before the passage of the Act, held that the phrase "appears to be" was synonymous with visual depictions that were ""'virtually indistinguishable to unsuspecting viewers from unretouched photographs of actual children engaging in identical sexual conduct.'"

Further, the *Hilton* court held that the CPPA included a built-in objective standard by which a jury would be required to make its ultimate determination of guilt under the statute. "A jury must decide, based on the totality of the circumstances, whether a reasonable unsuspecting viewer would consider the depiction to be of an actual individual under the age of 18 engaged in sexual activity."

In sum, the *Hilton* court refused to second-guess Congress's findings regarding the dangers associated with virtual child pornography and held that the government's interest in regulating virtual child pornography was just as compelling as the government's interest in regulating child pornography created using actual children.

The next circuit to consider the constitutionality of the CPPA was the Eleventh Circuit in United *States v. Acheson*, which involved a defendant who was found to have downloaded more than five hundred images of child pornography from the Internet. Once again, the defendant in this case challenged the "appears to be" language of the CPPA and maintained that the statute was unconstitutionally overbroad, unconstitutionally vague, and in violation of the First Amendment.

Noting the CPPA's minimal overbreadth, the *Acheson* court held that the CPPA worked to eliminate child pornography and protected children from sexual exploitation. The court relied on the legislative record of the CPPA and took into account the nature of surrounding provisions of the statute to find that the "CPPA rests on solid footing" regardless of whether or not the material contains a depiction of an actual child or of a computer-generated image of a child.

To support its view that the statute was constitutionally sound, the court pointed to the affirmative defense provided in 2252A(c), which allowed the defendant to assert that he or she used actual adults who were adults at the time of the production in the sexually explicit material.

The court was also comforted by the burden imposed on the Government to prove that the defendant "knowingly" possessed the child pornography.

In the end, the court held that, despite the "legitimate sweep of the CPPA[,] ... the demand driving the child pornography market is primarily for images falling far from any constitutional protection [and concluded that] the legitimate scope of the statute dwarfs the risk of impermissible applications."

[Here the article goes on to describe other cases, *United States v. Mento* in the Fourth Circuit and *United States v. Fox* in the Fifth Circuit, where the courts similarly found sufficient governmental interest in regulating the secondary effects of virtual child pornography, and let stand the CPPA.]

....

B. The Ninth Circuit Court of Appeals Decision

Sandwiched between the Eleventh Circuit's *Acheson* opinion and the Fourth Circuit's *Mento* decision, the Court of Appeals for the Ninth Circuit sharply diverged from the views of its fellow circuits in *Free Speech Coalition v. Reno* and held that the contested provisions of the CPPA were unconstitutionally vague, overbroad, and not in line with established First Amendment jurisprudence. The categories of speech at issue in the case were the same as those addressed in the First, Fourth, Fifth, and Eleventh Circuit opinions — the "appears to be" language of 2256(8)(B) and the "conveys the impression that" language of 2256(8)(D).

The court acknowledged the compelling interests of curbing child pornography using real children, but refused to hold that *Ferber* extended beyond the protection of real children. As a result, the court summarily rejected Congress's secondary effects rationale and held that "Congress has no compelling interest in regulating sexually explicit materials that do not contain visual images of actual children."

In two telling footnotes, the court defended its position by stating that "the critical fault in the secondary effects analysis ... [is that it] shifts the argument focus from whether the questioned speech or images are constitutionally protected to a focus on how the speech or image affects those who hear it or see it." The court further explained its position as follows: "Many innocent things can entice children into immoral or offensive behavior, but that reality does not create a constitutional power in the Congress to regulate otherwise innocent behavior."

In addition, the court relied on *American Booksellers Association v. Hudnut* as supporting precedent for its decision. At issue in *Hudnut* was a city ordinance that prohibited pornography that portrayed women as subordinates or showed women in submissive and degrading ways. The *Hudnut* court invalidated the ordinance and held that while "depictions of subordination tend to perpetuate subordination ... if the fact that speech plays a role in a process of [mind] conditioning were enough to permit governmental regulation, that would be the end of freedom of speech."

Obviously concerned about criminalizing images created entirely by the imagination, the *Reno* court concluded that "because the 1996 Act attempts to criminalize disavowed impulses of the mind, manifested in illicit creative acts[,] ... censorship through the enactment of criminal laws intended to control an evil idea cannot satisfy the constitutional requirements of the First Amendment."

Ultimately, the Court held that the phrases "appear to be" and "conveys the impression that" were unconstitutionally vague because they provided no clear standard by which to determine if something "appears to be" or "conveys the impression" of a child engaged in sexually explicit conduct.

C. The *Ashcroft v. Free Speech Coalition* Decision

In *Ashcroft v. Free Speech Coalition*, the Supreme Court granted certiorari to the Ninth Circuit Court of Appeals' *Free Speech Coalition v. Reno* decision to determine the constitutionality of the CPPA.

Justice Kennedy delivered the opinion for the Supreme Court and held that: (1) "The CPPA prohibits speech ... [that may have] serious literary, artistic, political, or scientific value;" (2) "the CPPA prohibits speech that records no crime and creates no victims by its production;" (3) the affirmative defense provided in the CPPA is "incomplete and insufficient," and (4) 2256(8)(D) is overbroad because the provision does not consider the content of the material being pandered and therefore "the CPPA does more than prohibit pandering. It prohibits possession of material described, or pandered, as child pornography by someone earlier in the distribution chain."

1. PPA Prohibits Speech that May Have Serious Value

At the core of the Supreme Court's concern with the CPPA was its effect of chilling speech that may have "serious literary, artistic, political, or scientific value." The Court focused on the valuable role that literary themes such as teenage sexuality and the sexual abuse of children have played in our society for ages. In fact, the Court warned that:

> Art and literature express the vital interest we all have in the formative years ... If these films ... explore those subjects [or] contain a single graphic depiction of sexual activity within the statutory definition, the possessor of the film would be subject to severe punishment without inquiry into the work's redeeming value. This is inconsistent with an essential First Amendment rule: The artistic merit of a work does not depend on the presence of a single explicit scene.

To further demonstrate its concern with the limitations imposed by the CPPA, the Court mentioned such movies as "Traffic" and "American Beauty," and speculated that these films would probably be in violation of the CPPA because they contain images that arguably "appear to be" minors engaging in sexually explicit conduct.

2. The CPPA Prohibits Speech that Records No Crime and Creates No Victims

In *Free Speech Coalition*, the Government argued that Congress could legitimately regulate virtual child pornography because child pornographers and child molesters might use the images to seduce future victims, that virtual child pornography "whets the appetites of pedophiles and encourages them to engage in illegal conduct," and the Government has an interest in curbing virtual child pornography because it has become a near-substitute for real child pornography and thereby fuels the child pornography market.

The Court rejected the Government's secondary effects and market proliferation arguments and held that the causal link between virtual child pornography and subsequent instances of child abuse was "contingent and indirect" and "depended on some unquantified potential for subsequent criminal acts." This holding is anchored in the Court's critical finding that *Ferber*'s focus was to prohibit child pornography made using *actual children* in its production. Further, regarding the argument that virtual child pornography "whets the appetites" of child abusers to engage in criminal activity, the Court held that "the mere tendency of speech to encourage unlawful acts is not a sufficient reason for banning it."

The Court also held that *Ferber* did not hold that all child pornography is inherently without value. In fact, the Court held that *Ferber* explicitly relied on the distinction between pornographic images produced using real children and those that did not to support its holding.

In response to the Government's argument that virtual child pornography had become a near-substitute in the "real" child pornography market, the Court flatly disagreed and held that if the Government's contention were true, then potentially "legal" virtual images would have taken over the market long ago and would have driven out the illegal images of real children. Any sensible child pornographer, the Court hypothesized, would have forgone the risk of creating illegal images using real children and simply created computer-generated images.

3. The Affirmative Defense is Incomplete and Insufficient

The Government argued that prosecuting child pornographers who use real children in their material had become increasingly difficult because of the possibility that an image might have been computer-generated. The Government warned that even experts might not be able to discern whether or not a real child has been used in an image. Therefore, the Government reasoned that the best solution to this prosecutorial problem was to prevent both virtual and real images of child pornography and provide defendants with an affirmative defense that allowed them to show that the material was created using only adults. The Court disagreed with the Government's solution and held that "protected speech does not become unprotected merely because it resembles [unprotected speech]."

The Court held that the CPPA's affirmative defense was "incomplete and insufficient" for two reasons. First, the affirmative defense did not apply when the defendant faced a possession charge, and second, the affirmative defense did not provide protection to defendants who "used computer imaging, or through other means that [did] not involve the use of adult actors who appear to be minors."

While the Court confirmed that the particular affirmative defense in the CPPA was incomplete and insufficient, the Court left open the possibility that the CPPA could have been saved by a more complete and sufficient affirmative defense.

4. Section 2256(8)(D) is Overbroad

The Court's primary concern with the pandering provision of the CPPA was that it did not require an inquiry into the actual content of the image that the defendant was accused of pandering; rather, a person violated 2256(8)(D) merely by conveying the impression that a particular image was of a child engaging in sexually explicit conduct. At bottom, the Court held that the First Amendment required a "more precise" restriction than that which was provided in 2256(8)(D). Further, the Court stated that 2256(8)(D) "prohibited possession of material described, or pandered, as child pornography by someone earlier in the distribution chain."

D. The Concurring and Dissenting Opinions

Justice Thomas's concurrence in the Court's holding reflects his concern that at some point in the near future, technology might exist to make it difficult, if not impossible, to prove that child pornography was created using a real child....

Justice O'Connor concurred in part and dissented in part with the holding. She found that the "appears to be" language covered two types of images: (1) those that appear to be children because they are created using youthful-looking adults, and (2) those that appear to be children because they are created using a computer. With this dichotomy in place, Justice O'Connor agreed that the statute's ban on pornography created using youthful-looking adults was unconstitutionally overbroad. However, she, along with Chief Justice Rehnquist and Justice Scalia, did not agree with the majority that the statute's ban on child pornography created using a computer (virtual child pornography) was overbroad.

Citing the overwhelming governmental interest in halting the activities of sexual offenders, the three Justices were persuaded by the Government's arguments that virtual child pornography is used to "whet the appetites of child molesters" and to seduce children into engaging in sexually explicit conduct. These Justices were also troubled that a child pornographer who uses real children to create sexually explicit images might successfully avoid prosecution by asserting a false but unverifiable claim that the images were computer-generated when they, in fact, were not.

These Justices also found that the language "appears to be"—as applied to virtual child pornography by Justice O'Connor and as applied across the board by Justices Rehnquist and Scalia—was best interpreted as meaning "'virtually indistinguishable from'.... [because] the narrowing interpretation avoids constitutional problems such as overbreadth and lack of narrow tailoring." Central to this argument was the Justices' assessment that the possible conflicts involved in deciding from whose perspective "virtually indistin-guishable from" should be based would be minimal. Justice O'Connor stated, "This Court has never required 'mathematical certainty' or 'meticulous specificity' from the language of a statute."

In a separate dissenting opinion, Chief Justice Rehnquist and Justice Scalia noted that they would have upheld the statute in its entirety and said that a fair reading of the statute shows that its language does not unnecessarily prohibit the youthful-looking adult pornography that Justice O'Connor would have protected. The dissenting Justices were unconvinced by the Free Speech Coalition's doomsday view of the CPPA's effect on free speech: "We should be loath to construe a statute as banning film portrayals of Shakespearian tragedies.... The CPPA has been on the books, and has been enforced, since 1996. The chill felt by the Court has apparently never been felt by those who actually make movies."

....

V. Congress' Response: The PROTECT Act 2003

....

Despite ongoing disagreement, and presumably in the interest of the prompt passage of meaningful legislation, both houses compromised and passed the PROTECT Act 2003 on April 10, 2003. President George W. Bush signed the PROTECT Act 2003 on April 30, 2003, and stated that "this important legislation gives law enforcement authorities valuable new tools to deter, detect, investigate, prosecute, and punish crimes against America's children."

But does it? While it is hard to imagine anyone opposing Congress's good intentions, the question regarding whether the PROTECT Act 2003 is meaningful and constitutionally viable remains. In other words, what has Congress done differently this time to ensure that America's children will not suffer another successful constitutional challenge to well-meaning but ineffective legislation?

From the time immediately following *Free Speech Coalition* until the present, both the House and Senate have made clear that their desire is to respond to, not rehash, the problems identified by the Court in the *Free Speech Coalition* decision with regard to virtual child pornography regulation. In fact, Senator Leahy made the following statement regarding the objectives for the PROTECT Act 2002: "The harder task is finding those kinds of legislative solutions that are not merely designed to be tough on child pornography in the short term, but can withstand the test of time and the scrutiny of the courts.... The PROTECT Act ... is a response to the [*Free Speech Coalition*] decision, not a challenge to it." Supporters of the Protect Act 2003 argued that "the last thing we want to do is to create years of legal limbo for our nation's children.... Our children deserve more than a press conference on this issue. They deserve a law that will last rather than be stricken from the law books."

While it remains to be seen how courts will handle future constitutional challenges to the PROTECT Act 2003, what follows is a look at this purported "response to the [*Free Speech Coalition*] decision." This section presents an overview of Congress's findings that accompanied the PROTECT Act 2003 and highlights key provisions, including how the Act: (1) changes the definition of virtual child pornography; (2) changes the offense of pandering and solicitation of virtual child pornography, and (3) changes the affirmative defense. Finally, this section will briefly analyze the PROTECT Act 2003's constitutional viability in light of the Court's decision in *Free Speech Coalition*.

A. Congressional Findings Accompanying the PROTECT Act 2003

As expected, the PROTECT Act 2003 cites a rapidly growing need to protect children from child molesters and child pornographers. It states that "technology already exists to disguise depictions of real children to make them unidentifiable and to make depictions of real children appear computer-generated. The technology will soon exist, if it does not already, to computer [-]generate realistic images of children."

Notably, the PROTECT Act 2003 abandons the secondary effects and market proliferation rationales that accompanied the CPPA and instead emphasizes the perceived need to strengthen the Government's ability to prosecute child pornography offenders.

Specifically, Congress warns that there is nothing to indicate that child pornography bought, sold, and possessed in today's child pornography market is produced in any way other than through the use of an actual child. Congress insists that many criminal defendants claim that the image in question is computer-generated, and therefore require that the Government prove beyond a reasonable doubt that the image is of a real child. Apparently, some prosecutors feel this to be an insurmountable burden in some cases. In fact, "prosecutors in various parts of the country have expressed concern about the continued viability of previously indicted cases as well as declined potentially meritorious prosecutions."

. . . .

In a hearing before the House Judiciary Subcommittee on Crime, Terrorism, and Homeland Security, Associate Deputy Attorney General Daniel P. Collins testified that many experts are willing to testify to the uncertainty of whether an image was created using an actual child on behalf of defendants. He forecasts that, without a change in the law, "trials will increasingly devolve into jury-confusing battles of experts arguing over the method of generating an image that, to all appearances, looks like it is the real thing."

What follows are key provisions from Congress's effort to combat these perceived obstacles and to protect the nation's children from sexual exploitation.

B. How the Act Changes the Definition of Virtual Child Pornography

The PROTECT Act 2003 heeds the Court's warning in *Free Speech Coalition* regarding the unconstitutionality of the CPPA's "appears to be" language found at 2256(8)(B), and amends this section to read:

> "Child pornography" means any visual depiction, including any photograph, film, video, picture, or computer, or computer-generated image or picture, whether made or produced by electronic, mechanical, or other means, of sexually explicit conduct, where ...
>
> > (B) such visual depiction is a digital image, computer image, or computer-generated image *that is, or is indistinguishable from, that of a minor* engaging in sexually explicit conduct...."

In addition, the PROTECT Act 2003 creates a special definition for "sexually explicit conduct" applicable to the newly amended 2256(8)(B) by dividing 2256(2) into subsection (A), which includes the previous definition of sexually explicit conduct, and subsection (B), which houses the following definition applicable only to 2256(8)(B):

> "Sexually explicit conduct" means—
>
> > (i) *graphic* sexual intercourse ... whether between persons of the same or opposite sex, or lascivious simulated sexual intercourse where the genitals, breast, or pubic area of any person is exhibited;

    (ii) graphic or lascivious simulated;

        (I) bestiality;

        (II) masturbation; or

        (III) sadistic or masochistic abuse; or

    (iii) graphic or simulated lascivious exhibition of the genitals or pubic area of any person[.]

The PROTECT Act 2003 adds to 2256 to define "graphic" (as used in the new 2256(2)(B)) and "indistinguishable" (as used in the amended 2256(8)(B)) as follows:

> (10) "Graphic," when used with respect to a depiction of sexually explicit conduct, means that a viewer can observe any part of the genitals or pubic area of any depicted person or animal during any part of the time that the sexually explicit conduct is being depicted; ...

> (11) ""Indistinguishable" ... means virtually indistinguishable, in that the depiction is such that an ordinary person viewing the depiction would conclude that the depiction is of an actual minor engaged in sexually explicit conduct. This definition does not apply to depictions that are drawings, cartoons, sculptures, or paintings depicting minors or adults.

First, regarding the changes to 2256(8)(B), it would seem at first glance that the PROTECT Act 2003 follows the Court's criticisms of the "appears to be" language in *Free Speech Coalition*. Most notably, the definition now limits the images that fall within its purview to "digital images, computer images, or computer-generated images." Further, the sexually explicit conduct depicted must be either graphic or lascivious, and the depiction must be "virtually indistinguishable" from an actual minor engaging in graphic or lascivious actual or simulated sexual conduct.

However, recall that the Court specifically stated that *Ferber* "reaffirmed that where the [child pornography] is neither obscene nor the product of sexual abuse, it does not fall outside the protection of the First Amendment." Further, the Court stated, "*Ferber* did not hold that child pornography is by definition without value." While the PROTECT Act 2003 unquestionably narrows the definition of virtual child pornography, it is unclear whether these amendments sufficiently foreclose constitutional challenge.

....

C. How the PROTECT Act 2003 Changes the Criminalization of Pandering and Solicitation

The PROTECT Act 2003 completely eliminates 18 U.S.C. 2256(8)(D), the CPPA provision that defined child pornography as the advertisement, promotion, presentation, description, or distribution of any visual depiction in such a way that "conveys the impression that" the material contains a visual depiction of a minor engaging in sexually explicit conduct. In *Free Speech Coalition*, the Court held that this provision was substantially overbroad and in violation of the First Amendment.

The new pandering and solicitation provision in the PROTECT Act 2003 amends 18 U.S.C. 2252A by breaking up 2252A(3) into two subsections. The original provision remains at 2252A(a)(3)(A), while the PROTECT Act 2003 adds the following new pandering provision at 2252A(a)(3)(B):

> (3) [Any person who] knowingly ...

>   (B) advertises, promotes, presents, distributes, or solicits through the mails, or in interstate or foreign commerce by any means, including by computer,

any material or purported material in a manner that reflects the belief, or that is intended to cause another to believe, that the material or purported material is, or contains —

> (i) an obscene visual depiction of a minor engaging in sexually explicit conduct; or

> (ii) a visual depiction of an actual minor engaging in sexually explicit conduct.

In the PROTECT Act 2003's Conference Report, Congress explains that "this provision prohibits an individual from offering to distribute anything that he specifically intends to cause a recipient to believe would be actual or obscene child pornography.... [and] prohibits an individual from soliciting what he believes to be actual or obscene child pornography."

. . . .

... [T]he *Free Speech Coalition* Court required that the Government explain the evils posed by pandering images that simply "look like child pornography." Notably, Congress has somewhat flimsily articulated a reason why the mere pandering of otherwise legal images should be prohibited. In the PROTECT Act 2003's Conference Report, Congress mentions that "even fraudulent offers to buy or sell unprotected child pornography help to sustain the illegal market for this material." This appears to be a resurrection of the market-deterrence theory advanced by the Government in *Free Speech Coalition*. The Court summarized and disposed of this argument as follows: "It is said, virtual images promote the trafficking in works produced through the exploitation of real children. The hypothesis is somewhat implausible."

Once again, Congress has failed to articulate specifically how the pandering and solicitation of *legal* images fuels the market for *illegal* images of children engaging in sexually explicit conduct. Put simply, in what way would a trailer for "Traffic," "Romeo and Juliet," or "American Beauty" fuel the market for images of actual children engaging in sexually explicit conduct or obscene images of children (actual or real) engaging in sexually explicit conduct?

Finally, it is important to note, the PROTECT Act 2003 does include an affirmative defense; however, 2252A(c) excludes from its purview 2252A(a)(3)(B). Congress explains that the PROTECT Act 2003's affirmative defense is "comprehensive ... for anyone charged with distributing or possessing child pornography ... [but the PROTECT Act] ensures [that] the defense does not apply to the pandering provisions." As previously explained, 2252A(a)(3)(B)(ii) potentially criminalizes the promotion of materials that are not obscene and do not involve the use of an actual child. As such, the PROTECT Act 2003's affirmative defense can hardly be characterized as "comprehensive."

For these reasons, the pandering and solicitation provision of the PROTECT Act 2003 seems especially vulnerable to constitutional challenge.

D. How the PROTECT Act 2003 Changes the Affirmative Defense

The PROTECT Act 2003 provides the following amended affirmative defense to be codified at 2252A(c):

> (c) It shall be an affirmative defense to a charge of violating paragraph (1), (2), (3)(A), (4), or (5) of

> subsection (a) that—

(1)(A) the alleged child pornography was produced using an actual person or persons engaging in sexually explicit conduct; and

(B) each such person was an adult at the time the material was produced; or

(2) the alleged child pornography was not produced using any actual minor or minors ...

A defendant may not assert an affirmative defense to a charge of violating paragraph (1), (2), (3)(A), (4), or (5) of subsection (a) unless ... the defendant provides the court and the United States with notice of the intent to assert such defense.

In *Free Speech Coalition*, the Court held that the affirmative defense provided in 18 U.S.C. 2252A of the CPPA was incomplete and insufficient and that it failed to protect a significant amount of lawful speech. Specifically, Justice Kennedy held that the affirmative defense provided in the CPPA was "incomplete and insufficient" because the defense did not extend to possession offenses, nor did the defense protect defendants who could prove that the images in question were not produced using actual children.

In response to the Court's concern that the affirmative defense failed to protect defendants who could prove that no child was used in the production of the material in question, the PROTECT Act 2003 now protects defendants in two situations: (1) when the alleged child pornography was produced using an actual person engaging in sexually explicit conduct and that person was an adult at the time of production, or (2) when the alleged child pornography was not produced using an actual minor.

Both scenarios seem to answer the majority's immediate concerns regarding the ineffectiveness of the CPPA's affirmative defense, but critics raise an important point: the PROTECT Act 2003's affirmative defense arguably presupposes that a real child was used in the production of the image. Is it not the government's burden to prove beyond a reasonable doubt that the image is of an actual child?

Some say the PROTECT Act 2003's "relaxed definition of child pornography," together with its affirmative defense, unfairly requires a defendant to "prove the government's case." Further, it is argued that the PROTECT Act 2003's affirmative defense "ignores the reality that most defendants lack the resources or the ability to prove that a 'fictional' character is not a real minor. If the government ... is purportedly having trouble ... then how can criminal defendants, many of whom are indigent, be expected to do so?"

Others argue that the affirmative defense is fair and affords (at least for a producer-defendant) the opportunity to prove that adults were used in the material or that the material was made without the use of an actual minor....

Finally, some support the PROTECT Act 2003's affirmative defense on the ground that it is unreasonable to expect some prosecutors with limited access to sophisticated investigative tools to review every pornographic image involving children for evidence that a real child was used. Indeed, some feel that this task might be "overwhelming" for prosecutors.

....

VII. Conclusion

While it remains to be seen whether the PROTECT Act 2003 will survive the scrutiny of the Supreme Court, it is clear that Congress has made progress in crafting legislation that presents a more comprehensive solution to the child pornography problem.

Despite the great debate that ensued while finalizing its legislative response to the *Free Speech Coalition* decision, one thing is certain: Congress is not willing to compromise in its mission to protect children from the evils of child pornography and child molestation. Crafting legislation that both targets specific Congressional objectives and respects the speech freedoms guaranteed by the First Amendment will help secure the legislative protection that child pornography and molestation victims not only deserve, but also so desperately require.

———————

As you read the text of the *Ashcroft* opinion, below, consider what alternatives there might be in the attempt to balance the interests of free speech on the one hand, and the need to protect children against actual and potential harms from child pornography on the other. What are the main pillars of the decision? Does the majority show any real concern with indirect effects on the lives of vulnerable children? If not, why not?

Ashcroft v. The Free Speech Coalition
535 U.S. 234 (2002)

JUSTICE KENNEDY delivered the opinion of the Court.

We consider in this case whether the Child Pornography Prevention Act of 1996 (CPPA), 18 U.S.C. §§ 2251 *et seq.*, abridges the freedom of speech. The CPPA extends the federal prohibition against child pornography to sexually explicit images that appear to depict minors but were produced without using any real children. The statute prohibits, in specific circumstances, possessing or distributing these images, which may be created by using adults who look like minors or by using computer imaging. The new technology, according to Congress, makes it possible to create realistic images of children who do not exist....

By prohibiting child pornography that does not depict an actual child, the statute goes beyond *New York* v. *Ferber*, 458 U.S. 747, 73 L. Ed. 2d 1113, 102 S. Ct. 3348 (1982), which distinguished child pornography from other sexually explicit speech because of the State's interest in protecting the children exploited by the production process. As a general rule, pornography can be banned only if obscene, but under *Ferber*, pornography showing minors can be proscribed whether or not the images are obscene under the definition set forth in *Miller* v. *California*, 413 U.S. 15, 37 L. Ed. 2d 419, 93 S. Ct. 2607 (1973). *Ferber* recognized that "the *Miller* standard, like all general definitions of what may be banned as obscene, does not reflect the State's particular and more compelling interest in prosecuting those who promote the sexual exploitation of children."

While we have not had occasion to consider the question, we may assume that the apparent age of persons engaged in sexual conduct is relevant to whether a depiction offends community standards. Pictures of young children engaged in certain acts might be obscene where similar depictions of adults, or perhaps even older adolescents, would not. The CPPA, however, is not directed at speech that is obscene; Congress has proscribed those materials through a separate statute. 18 U.S.C. §§ 1460–1466. Like the law in *Ferber*, the CPPA seeks to reach beyond obscenity, and it makes no attempt to conform to the *Miller* standard. For instance, the statute would reach visual depictions, such as movies, even if they have redeeming social value.

The principal question to be resolved, then, is whether the CPPA is constitutional where it proscribes a significant universe of speech that is neither obscene under *Miller* nor child pornography under *Ferber*.

Before 1996, Congress defined child pornography as the type of depictions at issue in *Ferber*, images made using actual minors. 18 U.S.C. §2252 (1994 ed.). The CPPA retains that prohibition at 18 U.S.C. §2256(8)(A) and adds three other prohibited categories of speech, of which the first, §2256(8)(B), and the third, §2256(8)(D), are at issue in this case. Section 2256(8)(B) prohibits "any visual depiction, including any photograph, film, video, picture, or computer or computer-generated image or picture" that "is, or appears to be, of a minor engaging in sexually explicit conduct." The prohibition on "any visual depiction" does not depend at all on how the image is produced. The section captures a range of depictions, sometimes called "virtual child pornography," which include computer-generated images, as well as images produced by more traditional means. For instance, the literal terms of the statute embrace a Renaissance painting depicting a scene from classical mythology, a "picture" that "appears to be, of a minor engaging in sexually explicit conduct." The statute also prohibits Hollywood movies, filmed without any child actors, if a jury believes an actor "appears to be" a minor engaging in "actual or simulated.... sexual intercourse." §2256(2).

These images do not involve, let alone harm, any children in the production process; but Congress decided the materials threaten children in other, less direct, ways. Pedophiles might use the materials to encourage children to participate in sexual activity. "[A] child who is reluctant to engage in sexual activity with an adult, or to pose for sexually explicit photographs, can sometimes be convinced by viewing depictions of other children 'having fun' participating in such activity." Congressional Findings, note (3) following §2251. Furthermore, pedophiles might "whet their own sexual appetites" with the pornographic images, "thereby increasing the creation and distribution of child pornography and the sexual abuse and exploitation of actual children." Under these rationales, harm flows from the content of the images, not from the means of their production. In addition, Congress identified another problem created by computer-generated images: Their existence can make it harder to prosecute pornographers who do use real minors. As imaging technology improves, Congress found, it becomes more difficult to prove that a particular picture was produced using actual children. To ensure that defendants possessing child pornography using real minors cannot evade prosecution, Congress extended the ban to virtual child pornography.

Section 2256(8)(C) prohibits a more common and lower tech means of creating virtual images, known as computer morphing. Rather than creating original images, pornographers can alter innocent pictures of real children so that the children appear to be engaged in sexual activity. Although morphed images may fall within the definition of virtual child pornography, they implicate the interests of real children and are in that sense closer to the images in *Ferber*. Respondents do not challenge this provision, and we do not consider it.

Respondents do challenge §2256(8)(D). Like the text of the "appears to be" provision, the sweep of this provision is quite broad. Section 2256(8)(D) defines child pornography to include any sexually explicit image that was "advertised, promoted, presented, described, or distributed in such a manner that conveys the impression" it depicts "a minor engaging in sexually explicit conduct." One Committee Report identified the provision as directed at sexually explicit images pandered as child pornography.... ("This provision prevents child pornographers and pedophiles from exploiting prurient interests in child sexuality and sexual activity through the production or distribution of pornographic material which is intentionally pandered as child pornography"). The statute is not so limited in its reach, however, as it punishes even those possessors who took no part in pandering. Once a work has been described as child pornography, the taint remains on the speech in the hands of subsequent possessors, making possession unlawful even though the content otherwise would not be objectionable.

Fearing that the CPPA threatened the activities of its members, respondent Free Speech Coalition and others challenged the statute in the United States District Court for the Northern District of California. The Coalition, a California trade association for the adult-entertainment industry, alleged that its members did not use minors in their sexually explicit works, but they believed some of these materials might fall within the CPPA's expanded definition of child pornography. The other respondents are Bold Type, Inc., the publisher of a book advocating the nudist lifestyle; Jim Gingerich, a painter of nudes; and Ron Raffaelli, a photographer specializing in erotic images. Respondents alleged that the "appears to be" and "conveys the impression" provisions are overbroad and vague, chilling them from producing works protected by the First Amendment. The District Court disagreed and granted summary judgment to the Government. The court dismissed the overbreadth claim because it was "highly unlikely" that any "adaptations of sexual works like 'Romeo and Juliet,' will be treated as 'criminal contraband.'"

The Court of Appeals for the Ninth Circuit reversed. See 198 F.3d 1083 (1999). The court reasoned that the Government could not prohibit speech because of its tendency to persuade viewers to commit illegal acts. The court held the CPPA to be substantially overbroad because it bans materials that are neither obscene nor produced by the exploitation of real children as in *New York* v. *Ferber*, 458 U.S. 747, 73 L. Ed. 2d 1113, 102 S. Ct. 3348 (1982). Judge Ferguson dissented on the ground that virtual images, like obscenity and real child pornography, should be treated as a category of speech unprotected by the First Amendment. The Court of Appeals voted to deny the petition for rehearing en banc, over the dissent of three judges.

While the Ninth Circuit found the CPPA invalid on its face, four other Courts of Appeals have sustained it. See *United States* v. *Fox*, 248 F.3d 394 (CA5 2001); *United States* v. *Mento*, 231 F.3d 912 (CA4 2000); *United States* v. *Acheson*, 195 F.3d 645 (CA11 1999); *United States* v. *Hilton*, 167 F.3d 61 (CA1), cert. denied, 528 U.S. 844, 145 L. Ed. 2d 98, 120 S. Ct. 115 (1999). We granted certiorari. 531 U.S. 1124, 121 S. Ct. 876, 148 L. Ed. 2d 788 (2001).

II

The First Amendment commands, "Congress shall make no law.... abridging the freedom of speech." The government may violate this mandate in many ways, *e.g., Rosenberger* v. *Rector and Visitors of Univ. of Va.*, 515 U.S. 819, 132 L. Ed. 2d 700, 115 S. Ct. 2510 (1995); *Keller* v. *State Bar of Cal.*, 496 U.S. 1, 110 L. Ed. 2d 1, 110 S. Ct. 2228 (1990), but a law imposing criminal penalties on protected speech is a stark example of speech suppression. The CPPA's penalties are indeed severe. A first offender may be imprisoned for 15 years. § 2252A(b)(1). A repeat offender faces a prison sentence of not less than 5 years and not more than 30 years in prison. *Ibid.* While even minor punishments can chill protected speech, see *Wooley* v. *Maynard*, 430 U.S. 705, 51 L. Ed. 2d 752, 97 S. Ct. 1428 (1977), this case provides a textbook example of why we permit facial challenges to statutes that burden expression. With these severe penalties in force, few legitimate movie producers or book publishers, or few other speakers in any capacity, would risk distributing images in or near the uncertain reach of this law. The Constitution gives significant protection from overbroad laws that chill speech within the First Amendment's vast and privileged sphere. Under this principle, the CPPA is unconstitutional on its face if it prohibits a substantial amount of protected expression. See *Broadrick* v. *Oklahoma*, 413 U.S. 601, 612, 37 L. Ed. 2d 830, 93 S. Ct. 2908 (1973).

The sexual abuse of a child is a most serious crime and an act repugnant to the moral instincts of a decent people. In its legislative findings, Congress recognized that there are subcultures of persons who harbor illicit desires for children and commit criminal acts to gratify the impulses. See Congressional Findings, notes following §2251; see also U.S. Dept. of Health and Human Services, Administration on Children, Youth and Families, Child Maltreatment 1999 (estimating that 93,000 children were victims of sexual abuse in 1999). Congress also found that surrounding the serious offenders are those who flirt with these impulses and trade pictures and written accounts of sexual activity with young children.

Congress may pass valid laws to protect children from abuse, and it has. *E.g.*, 18 U.S.C. §§2241, 2251. The prospect of crime, however, by itself does not justify laws suppressing protected speech. See *Kingsley Int'l Pictures Corp.* v. *Regents of Univ. of N. Y.*, 360 U.S. 684, 689, 3 L. Ed. 2d 1512, 79 S. Ct. 1362 (1959) ("Among free men, the deterrents ordinarily to be applied to prevent crime are education and punishment for violations of the law, not abridgment of the rights of free speech"). It is also well established that speech may not be prohibited because it concerns subjects offending our sensibilities. See *FCC* v. *Pacifica Foundation*, 438 U.S. 726, 745, 57 L. Ed. 2d 1073, 98 S. Ct. 3026 (1978) ("The fact that society may find speech offensive is not a sufficient reason for suppressing it"); see also *Reno* v. *ACLU,* 521 U.S. 844, 874, 117 S. Ct. 2329, 138 L. Ed. 2d 874 (1997) ("In evaluating the free speech rights of adults, we have made it perfectly clear that 'sexual expression which is indecent but not obscene is protected by the First Amendment'") (quoting *Sable Communications of Cal., Inc.* v. *FCC,* 492 U.S. 115, 126, 106 L. Ed. 2d 93, 109 S. Ct. 2829 (1989); *Carey* v. *Population Services Int'l,* 431 U.S. 678, 701, 52 L. Ed. 2d 675, 97 S. Ct. 2010 (1977) ("The fact that protected speech may be offensive to some does not justify its suppression").

As a general principle, the First Amendment bars the government from dictating what we see or read or speak or hear. The freedom of speech has its limits; it does not embrace certain categories of speech, including defamation, incitement, obscenity, and pornography produced with real children. See *Simon & Schuster, Inc.* v. *Members of N. Y. State Crime Victims Bd.,* 502 U.S. 105, 127, 116 L. Ed. 2d 476, 112 S. Ct. 501 (1991) (KENNEDY, J., concurring). While these categories may be prohibited without violating the First Amendment, none of them includes the speech prohibited by the CPPA. In his dissent from the opinion of the Court of Appeals, Judge Ferguson recognized this to be the law and proposed that virtual child pornography should be regarded as an additional category of unprotected speech. See 198 F.3d at 1101. It would be necessary for us to take this step to uphold the statute.

As we have noted, the CPPA is much more than a supplement to the existing federal prohibition on obscenity. Under *Miller* v. *California*, 413 U.S. 15, 37 L. Ed. 2d 419, 93 S. Ct. 2607 (1973), the Government must prove that the work, taken as a whole, appeals to the prurient interest, is patently offensive in light of community standards, and lacks serious literary, artistic, political, or scientific value. The CPPA, however, extends to images that appear to depict a minor engaging in sexually explicit activity without regard to the *Miller* requirements. The materials need not appeal to the prurient interest. Any depiction of sexually explicit activity, no matter how it is presented, is proscribed. The CPPA applies to a picture in a psychology manual, as well as a movie depicting the horrors of sexual abuse. It is not necessary, moreover, that the image be patently offensive. Pictures of what appear to be 17-year-olds engaging in sexually explicit activity do not in every case contravene community standards.

The CPPA prohibits speech despite its serious literary, artistic, political, or scientific value. The statute proscribes the visual depiction of an idea—that of teenagers engaging in sexual activity—that is a fact of modern society and has been a theme in art and literature throughout the ages. Under the CPPA, images are prohibited so long as the persons appear to be under 18 years of age. 18 U.S.C. §2256(1). This is higher than the legal age for marriage in many States, as well as the age at which persons may consent to sexual relations.... It is, of course, undeniable that some youths engage in sexual activity before the legal age, either on their own inclination or because they are victims of sexual abuse.

Both themes—teenage sexual activity and the sexual abuse of children—have inspired countless literary works. William Shakespeare created the most famous pair of teenage lovers, one of whom is just 13 years of age. See Romeo and Juliet, act I, sc. 2, l. 9 ("She hath not seen the change of fourteen years"). In the drama, Shakespeare portrays the relationship as something splendid and innocent, but not juvenile. The work has inspired no less than 40 motion pictures, some of which suggest that the teenagers consummated their relationship. E.g., Romeo and Juliet (B. Luhrmann director, 1996). Shakespeare may not have written sexually explicit scenes for the Elizabethan audience, but were modern directors to adopt a less conventional approach, that fact alone would not compel the conclusion that the work was obscene.

Contemporary movies pursue similar themes. Last year's Academy Awards featured the movie, Traffic, which was nominated for Best Picture. See Predictable and Less So, the Academy Award Contenders, N. Y. Times, Feb. 14, 2001, p. E11. The film portrays a teenager, identified as a 16-year-old, who becomes addicted to drugs. The viewer sees the degradation of her addiction, which in the end leads her to a filthy room to trade sex for drugs. The year before, American Beauty won the Academy Award for Best Picture. See "American Beauty" Tops the Oscars, N. Y. Times, Mar. 27, 2000, p. E1. In the course of the movie, a teenage girl engages in sexual relations with her teenage boyfriend, and another yields herself to the gratification of a middle-aged man. The film also contains a scene where, although the movie audience understands the act is not taking place, one character believes he is watching a teenage boy performing a sexual act on an older man.

Our society, like other cultures, has empathy and enduring fascination with the lives and destinies of the young. Art and literature express the vital interest we all have in the formative years we ourselves once knew, when wounds can be so grievous, disappointment so profound, and mistaken choices so tragic, but when moral acts and self-fulfillment are still in reach. Whether or not the films we mention violate the CPPA, they explore themes within the wide sweep of the statute's prohibitions. If these films, or hundreds of others of lesser note that explore those subjects, contain a single graphic depiction of sexual activity within the statutory definition, the possessor of the film would be subject to severe punishment without inquiry into the work's redeeming value. This is inconsistent with an essential First Amendment rule: The artistic merit of a work does not depend on the presence of a single explicit scene. See Book Named "John Cleland's Memoirs of a Woman of Pleasure" v. Attorney General of Mass., 383 U.S. 413, 419, 16 L. Ed. 2d 1, 86 S. Ct. 975 (1966) (plurality opinion) ("The social value of the book can neither be weighed against nor canceled by its prurient appeal or patent offensiveness"). Under Miller, the First Amendment requires that redeeming value be judged by considering the work as a whole. Where the scene is part of the narrative, the work itself does not for this reason become obscene, even though the scene in isolation might be offensive. See Kois v. Wisconsin, 408 U.S. 229, 231, 33 L. Ed. 2d 312, 92 S. Ct. 2245 (1972) (per curiam). For this reason, and the others we have noted, the CPPA cannot be read to prohibit obscenity, because it lacks the required link between its prohibitions and the affront to community standards prohibited by the definition of obscenity.

The Government seeks to address this deficiency by arguing that speech prohibited by the CPPA is virtually indistinguishable from child pornography, which may be banned without regard to whether it depicts works of value. See *New York* v. *Ferber*, 458 U.S. at 761. Where the images are themselves the product of child sexual abuse, *Ferber* recognized that the State had an interest in stamping it out without regard to any judgment about its content.... ("As drafted, New York's statute does not attempt to suppress the communication of particular ideas"). The production of the work, not its content, was the target of the statute. The fact that a work contained serious literary, artistic, or other value did not excuse the harm it caused to its child participants. It was simply "unrealistic to equate a community's toleration for sexually oriented materials with the permissible scope of legislation aimed at protecting children from sexual exploitation."

Ferber upheld a prohibition on the distribution and sale of child pornography, as well as its production, because these acts were "intrinsically related" to the sexual abuse of children in two ways.... First, as a permanent record of a child's abuse, the continued circulation itself would harm the child who had participated. Like a defamatory statement, each new publication of the speech would cause new injury to the child's reputation and emotional well-being.... Second, because the traffic in child pornography was an economic motive for its production, the State had an interest in closing the distribution network. "The most expeditious if not the only practical method of law enforcement may be to dry up the market for this material by imposing severe criminal penalties on persons selling, advertising, or otherwise promoting the product." Id. at 760. Under either rationale, the speech had what the Court in effect held was a proximate link to the crime from which it came.

Later, in *Osborne* v. *Ohio*, 495 U.S. 103, 109 L. Ed. 2d 98, 110 S. Ct. 1691 (1990), the Court ruled that these same interests justified a ban on the possession of pornography produced by using children. "Given the importance of the State's interest in protecting the victims of child pornography," the State was justified in "attempting to stamp out this vice at all levels in the distribution chain.".... *Osborne* also noted the State's interest in preventing child pornography from being used as an aid in the solicitation of minors.... The Court, however, anchored its holding in the concern for the participants, those whom it called the "victims of child pornography.".... It did not suggest that, absent this concern, other governmental interests would suffice....

In contrast to the speech in *Ferber*, speech that itself is the record of sexual abuse, the CPPA prohibits speech that records no crime and creates no victims by its production. Virtual child pornography is not "intrinsically related" to the sexual abuse of children, as were the materials in *Ferber*. 458 U.S. at 759. While the Government asserts that the images can lead to actual instances of child abuse, see *infra*, at 13–16, the causal link is contingent and indirect. The harm does not necessarily follow from the speech, but depends upon some unquantified potential for subsequent criminal acts.

The Government says these indirect harms are sufficient because, as *Ferber* acknowledged, child pornography rarely can be valuable speech. See 458 U.S. at 762 ("The value of permitting live performances and photographic reproductions of children engaged in lewd sexual conduct is exceedingly modest, if not *de minimis*"). This argument, however, suffers from two flaws. First, *Ferber*'s judgment about child pornography was based upon how it was made, not on what it communicated. The case reaffirmed that where the speech is neither obscene nor the product of sexual abuse, it does not fall outside the protection of the First Amendment.... ("The distribution of descriptions or other depictions of sexual conduct, not otherwise obscene, which do not involve live performance or photographic or other visual reproduction of live performances, retains First Amendment protection").

The second flaw in the Government's position is that *Ferber* did not hold that child pornography is by definition without value. On the contrary, the Court recognized some works in this category might have significant value, ... but relied on virtual images — the very images prohibited by the CPPA — as an alternative and permissible means of expression: "If it were necessary for literary or artistic value, a person over the statutory age who perhaps looked younger could be utilized. Simulation outside of the prohibition of the statute could provide another alternative." Id. at 763. *Ferber,* then, not only referred to the distinction between actual and virtual child pornography, it relied on it as a reason supporting its holding. *Ferber* provides no support for a statute that eliminates the distinction and makes the alternative mode criminal as well.

III

The CPPA, for reasons we have explored, is inconsistent with *Miller* and finds no support in *Ferber*. The Government seeks to justify its prohibitions in other ways. It argues that the CPPA is necessary because pedophiles may use virtual child pornography to seduce children. There are many things innocent in themselves, however, such as cartoons, video games, and candy, that might be used for immoral purposes, yet we would not expect those to be prohibited because they can be misused. The Government, of course, may punish adults who provide unsuitable materials to children, see *Ginsberg* v. *New York*, 390 U.S. 629, 20 L. Ed. 2d 195, 88 S. Ct. 1274 (1968), and it may enforce criminal penalties for unlawful solicitation. The precedents establish, however, that speech within the rights of adults to hear may not be silenced completely in an attempt to shield children from it. See *Sable Communications of Cal., Inc.* v. *FCC,* 492 U.S. 115, 106 L. Ed. 2d 93, 109 S. Ct. 2829 (1989). In *Butler* v. *Michigan,* 352 U.S. 380, 381, 1 L. Ed. 2d 412, 77 S. Ct. 524 (1957), the Court invalidated a statute prohibiting distribution of an indecent publication because of its tendency to "incite minors to violent or depraved or immoral acts." A unanimous Court agreed upon the important First Amendment principle that the State could not "reduce the adult population.... to reading only what is fit for children." Id. at 383. We have reaffirmed this holding....

Here, the Government wants to keep speech from children not to protect them from its content but to protect them from those who would commit other crimes. The principle, however, remains the same: The Government cannot ban speech fit for adults simply because it may fall into the hands of children. The evil in question depends upon the actor's unlawful conduct, conduct defined as criminal quite apart from any link to the speech in question. This establishes that the speech ban is not narrowly drawn. The objective is to prohibit illegal conduct, but this restriction goes well beyond that interest by restricting the speech available to law-abiding adults.

The Government submits further that virtual child pornography whets the appetites of pedophiles and encourages them to engage in illegal conduct. This rationale cannot sustain the provision in question. The mere tendency of speech to encourage unlawful acts is not a sufficient reason for banning it. The government "cannot constitutionally premise legislation on the desirability of controlling a person's private thoughts." *Stanley* v. *Georgia*, 394 U.S. 557, 566, 22 L. Ed. 2d 542, 89 S. Ct. 1243 (1969). First Amendment freedoms are most in danger when the government seeks to control thought or to justify its laws for that impermissible end. The right to think is the beginning of freedom, and speech must be protected from the government because speech is the beginning of thought.

To preserve these freedoms, and to protect speech for its own sake, the Court's First Amendment cases draw vital distinctions between words and deeds, between ideas and conduct. See *Kingsley Int'l Pictures Corp.*, 360 U.S. at 689; see also *Bartnicki* v. *Vopper,*

532 U.S. 514, 529, 149 L. Ed. 2d 787, 121 S. Ct. 1753 (2001) ("The normal method of deterring unlawful conduct is to impose an appropriate punishment on the person who engages in it"). The government may not prohibit speech because it increases the chance an unlawful act will be committed "at some indefinite future time." *Hess* v. *Indiana*, 414 U.S. 105, 108, 38 L. Ed. 2d 303, 94 S. Ct. 326 (1973) *(per curiam)*. The government may suppress speech for advocating the use of force or a violation of law only if "such advocacy is directed to inciting or producing imminent lawless action and is likely to incite or produce such action." *Brandenburg* v. *Ohio,* 395 U.S. 444, 447, 23 L. Ed. 2d 430, 89 S. Ct. 1827 (1969) *(per curiam)*. There is here no attempt, incitement, solicitation, or conspiracy. The Government has shown no more than a remote connection between speech that might encourage thoughts or impulses and any resulting child abuse. Without a significantly stronger, more direct connection, the Government may not prohibit speech on the ground that it may encourage pedophiles to engage in illegal conduct.

The Government next argues that its objective of eliminating the market for pornography produced using real children necessitates a prohibition on virtual images as well. Virtual images, the Government contends, are indistinguishable from real ones; they are part of the same market and are often exchanged. In this way, it is said, virtual images promote the trafficking in works produced through the exploitation of real children. The hypothesis is somewhat implausible. If virtual images were identical to illegal child pornography, the illegal images would be driven from the market by the indistinguishable substitutes. Few pornographers would risk prosecution by abusing real children if fictional, computerized images would suffice.

In the case of the material covered by *Ferber*, the creation of the speech is itself the crime of child abuse; the prohibition deters the crime by removing the profit motive.... [W]here there is an underlying crime, however, the Court has not allowed the suppression of speech in all cases.... We need not consider where to strike the balance in this case, because here, there is no underlying crime at all. Even if the Government's market deterrence theory were persuasive in some contexts, it would not justify this statute.

Finally, the Government says that the possibility of producing images by using computer imaging makes it very difficult for it to prosecute those who produce pornography by using real children. Experts, we are told, may have difficulty in saying whether the pictures were made by using real children or by using computer imaging. The necessary solution, the argument runs, is to prohibit both kinds of images. The argument, in essence, is that protected speech may be banned as a means to ban unprotected speech. This analysis turns the First Amendment upside down.

The Government may not suppress lawful speech as the means to suppress unlawful speech. Protected speech does not become unprotected merely because it resembles the latter. The Constitution requires the reverse. "The possible harm to society in permitting some unprotected speech to go unpunished is outweighed by the possibility that protected speech of others may be muted...." *Broadrick* v. *Oklahoma*, 413 U.S. at 612. The overbreadth doctrine prohibits the Government from banning unprotected speech if a substantial amount of protected speech is prohibited or chilled in the process.

To avoid the force of this objection, the Government would have us read the CPPA not as a measure suppressing speech but as a law shifting the burden to the accused to prove the speech is lawful. In this connection, the Government relies on an affirmative defense under the statute, which allows a defendant to avoid conviction for nonpossession offenses by showing that the materials were produced using only adults and were not otherwise distributed in a manner conveying the impression that they depicted real children. See 18 U.S.C. §2252A(c).

The Government raises serious constitutional difficulties by seeking to impose on the defendant the burden of proving his speech is not unlawful. An affirmative defense applies only after prosecution has begun, and the speaker must himself prove, on pain of a felony conviction, that his conduct falls within the affirmative defense. In cases under the CPPA, the evidentiary burden is not trivial. Where the defendant is not the producer of the work, he may have no way of establishing the identity, or even the existence, of the actors. If the evidentiary issue is a serious problem for the Government, as it asserts, it will be at least as difficult for the innocent possessor. The statute, moreover, applies to work created before 1996, and the producers themselves may not have preserved the records necessary to meet the burden of proof. Failure to establish the defense can lead to a felony conviction.

We need not decide, however, whether the Government could impose this burden on a speaker. Even if an affirmative defense can save a statute from First Amendment challenge, here the defense is incomplete and insufficient, even on its own terms. It allows persons to be convicted in some instances where they can prove children were not exploited in the production. A defendant charged with possessing, as opposed to distributing, proscribed works may not defend on the ground that the film depicts only adult actors. So while the affirmative defense may protect a movie producer from prosecution for the act of distribution, that same producer, and all other persons in the subsequent distribution chain, could be liable for possessing the prohibited work. Furthermore, the affirmative defense provides no protection to persons who produce speech by using computer imaging, or through other means that do not involve the use of adult actors who appear to be minors. In these cases, the defendant can demonstrate no children were harmed in producing the images, yet the affirmative defense would not bar the prosecution. For this reason, the affirmative defense cannot save the statute, for it leaves unprotected a substantial amount of speech not tied to the Government's interest in distinguishing images produced using real children from virtual ones.

In sum, § 2256(8)(B) covers materials beyond the categories recognized in *Ferber* and *Miller*, and the reasons the Government offers in support of limiting the freedom of speech have no justification in our precedents or in the law of the First Amendment. The provision abridges the freedom to engage in a substantial amount of lawful speech. For this reason, it is overbroad and unconstitutional.

IV

Respondents challenge § 2256(8)(D) as well. This provision bans depictions of sexually explicit conduct that are "advertised, promoted, presented, described, or distributed in such a manner that conveys the impression that the material is or contains a visual depiction of a minor engaging in sexually explicit conduct." The parties treat the section as nearly identical to the provision prohibiting materials that appear to be child pornography. In the Government's view, the difference between the two is that "the 'conveys the impression' provision requires the jury to assess the material at issue in light of the manner in which it is promoted." ... The Government's assumption, however, is that the determination would still depend principally upon the content of the prohibited work.

We disagree with this view. The CPPA prohibits sexually explicit materials that "convey the impression" they depict minors. While that phrase may sound like the "appears to be" prohibition in § 2256(8)(B), it requires little judgment about the content of the image. Under § 2256(8)(D), the work must be sexually explicit, but otherwise the content is irrelevant. Even if a film contains no sexually explicit scenes involving minors, it could be treated as child pornography if the title and trailers convey the impression that the scenes would be found in the movie. The determination turns on how the speech is presented, not on what is depicted. While the legislative findings address at length the problems posed by materials that look like child pornography, they are silent on the evils posed by images simply pandered that way.

The Government does not offer a serious defense of this provision, and the other arguments it makes in support of the CPPA do not bear on § 2256(8)(D). The materials, for instance, are not likely to be confused for child pornography in a criminal trial. The Court has recognized that pandering may be relevant, as an evidentiary matter, to the question whether particular materials are obscene. See *Ginzburg* v. *United States*, 383 U.S. 463, 474, 16 L. Ed. 2d 31, 86 S. Ct. 942 (1966) ("In close cases evidence of pandering may be probative with respect to the nature of the material in question and thus satisfy the [obscenity] test"). Where a defendant engages in the "commercial exploitation of erotica solely for the sake of their prurient appeal," id. at 466, the context he or she creates may itself be relevant to the evaluation of the materials.

Section 2256(8)(D), however, prohibits a substantial amount of speech that falls outside *Ginzburg*'s rationale. Materials falling within the proscription are tainted and unlawful in the hands of all who receive it, though they bear no responsibility for how it was marketed, sold, or described. The statute, furthermore, does not require that the context be part of an effort at "commercial exploitation." As a consequence, the CPPA does more than prohibit pandering. It prohibits possession of material described, or pandered, as child pornography by someone earlier in the distribution chain. The provision prohibits a sexually explicit film containing no youthful actors, just because it is placed in a box suggesting a prohibited movie. Possession is a crime even when the possessor knows the movie was mislabeled. The First Amendment requires a more precise restriction. For this reason, § 2256(8)(D) is substantially overbroad and in violation of the First Amendment.

V

For the reasons we have set forth, the prohibitions of §§ 2256(8)(B) and 2256(8)(D) are overbroad and unconstitutional. Having reached this conclusion, we need not address respondents' further contention that the provisions are unconstitutional because of vague statutory language.

The judgment of the Court of Appeals is affirmed.

It is so ordered.

Notes and Questions

1. What view does the majority take towards the relationship between pornography and the demand for children to exploit? Does the inherent "dangerousness" of increasing demand play any part at all in the Court's analysis? How do you think the Court would respond to the suggestion that protection of children is so important that we must err on the side of caution and restrict the use even of virtual child pornography?

2. Even apart from the now-familiar computer generated "virtual" child pornography, there is yet another problem emerging, in the form of child sexual abuse in the realm of so-called "Second Life." See for example David Rising, *German Investigators Probe Use of 'Second Life' to Trade Child Pornography,* Associated Press, May 11, 2007, describing a situation in which an avatar, or "Second Life" character, offers real child pornography to others using the online service. This is in addition to the problem of depicting children in Second Life being abused. This indicates a whole new world of exploitative images,

with corresponding difficulties in identifying and pursuing criminals. How should legislatures and courts deal with the question of virtual child pornography and its effects?

3. It is an undeniable fact of life in a globalized and technology-oriented world that child pornography has become extremely prevalent. There are many thousands of users of child pornography, and yet there has been little public attempt to understand the possible link between these images and the search for real children to exploit. Is the main problem a legal, a social, or a cultural one? Or is there something in the nature of child sexual exploitation that the legal system has not yet come to grips with; namely, an understanding that there is an apparently limitless number of people, almost always men, who are seeking children to exploit sexually?

———————

Chapter Four

Children Living on Their Own: A Global Cohort

I. A World of Orphans: "True" Orphans, "Social" Orphans and Quasi-Orphans

At the heart of the children's rights debate are disputes over the nature of children's vulnerability and the degree to which they require special protection. Early instruments on the subject of children's rights emphasized the child's need for a high level of adult protection and care; as noted in Chapter One, at least half of the UNCRC is devoted to issues of protection. It can be said that the least controversial provisions of international children's rights law are those that focus on the need for protection. Among children, including very poor or marginalized children, the most vulnerable of the vulnerable are those who must grow up without the care of a family. Most children living out of family care have living parents, or at least close relatives. They are often called "social orphans" to distinguish them from supposedly "true" orphans—that is, those who have lost both parents to death. All children living out of family care are especially likely to fall prey to exploitative forces. They might find themselves used for their labor or abused in the sex industry. Many will have to eke out a living on the streets as they grow older. It should be borne in mind, though, that a large number of these children maintain links to adults who remain part of their "families," even when these structures do not fit a predictable pattern. All agree that children growing up without any family ties are in an unusually difficult and dangerous situation.

What constitutes, or qualifies as, "family", is a difficult question, and the answer often culture-specific. All agree that when families fall apart, family reunification is the most desirable solution. But can international child welfare bodies accomplish such goals on a mass scale? Where social factors lead to family breakdown, can the state, or the UN, act as guarantor of the child's safety? Can these entities provide adequate alternatives when original families fail to function? How well do national social services perform in supplementing or providing substitutes for the traditional family? Or does "family," in all its many forms, provide something unique and essentially irreplaceable for young children? It is clear that virtually no state has done a good job of providing non-family care that protects and nurtures the child over the long term. All institutional care is inferior to a functioning family. A debate currently rages over the value of hybrid forms of alternative care such as small group homes and foster care. If permanency is necessary to the child's well being, does any other form of care besides the family represent genuine permanency?

The provisions of the CRC relating to children living out of family care are notoriously ambiguous. Since the question of adoption was contentious during the drafting of the UNCRC (and remains contentious today), it is not surprising that the Convention should have left a good deal of room for states to maneuver in finding alternatives for children requiring out-of-family care. Article 20 states that a child deprived of the family environment "shall be entitled to special protection and assistance provided by the State." All States must provide such alternative care "in accordance with their national laws." Article 20 then sets out the possible modes of alternative care: "inter alia, foster placement, kafalah of Islamic law, adoption or if necessary placement in suitable institutions for the care of children." It concludes by stating that "When considering solutions, due regard shall be paid to the desirability of continuity in a child's upbringing and to the child's ethnic, religious, cultural and linguistic background." This provision has generated much debate as to what the CRC allows States Parties to do when making alternative plans for children living out of family care. The UN bodies have, in a general sense, come around to the view that large scale institutions are the worst possible places for children to be raised. On the other hand, the relative merits of foster care versus adoption have not been confronted in a straightforward manner by the child welfare and child rights bodies. While all states agree with the idea of reuniting families through investments in social services, there is little international monitoring of the effectiveness of such programs.

Since the UNCRC is generally believed to be a holistic document, one in which each provision must be read in the light of every other, it bears reminding that the state must live up to its obligations to prevent violence to and exploitation of the child, at the same time as it attempts to create alternative care arrangements for children in need of special protection. In other words, states allowing children to languish in traditional institutions, or to spend long periods of times in foster care and group homes, must take responsibility for the fact that these children often end up in dangerous situations, being susceptible to many forms of violence as they mature.

This chapter will first cover the issue of children on their own, or, put another way, children without parents and families. The United Nations has been attempting to devise a set of guidelines to assist States in following "best practices" when it comes to caring for children living out of the family structure, and these draft guidelines are included in the readings that follow. It will be suggested that the UN guidelines are less than easy to apply.

This chapter then covers issues related to public—often institutional—care. This issue is intimately linked to the controversial matter of intercountry or international adoption. Where countries are revealed to be warehousing vulnerable children, demands to allow these children to be placed in families inevitably grow louder. International adoption purports to link children without any appropriate family support in their country of origin with adoptive parents in other countries, typically in Europe or the United States. From the positive point of view, this process allows children to grow up in an atmosphere of safety and love; from the skeptical point of view, it involves wealthy countries "stealing the resources" of the developing world, in yet another manifestation of neo-colonialism. Several international child welfare bodies argue that international adoption lets national governments off the hook with regard to devising a domestic child welfare system that meets the needs of children in marginal and vulnerable families. It is clear, however, that as of now there is a large cohort of children without significant family or social support, surviving as best they can, whether on the streets of their own countries or in motion across borders. Intercountry adoption provides one form of solution—albeit on a modest scale—for some of these children. Both sides of the intercountry adoption debate will be explored below.

This chapter will also deal extensively with the problems of street children. Street children may be seen as a category of children who live, work and survive on the streets, almost completely unattached to mainstream social structures. However, it must be kept in mind that there are distinct categories of street children; crucially, some street children maintain contact with their families; some do not. A common characteristic is that street children are treated with contempt by their respective societies and are often subject to official and unofficial forms of violence. The debate among child welfare advocates, again reflecting the "empowerment versus protection" theme discussed throughout this book, is whether street children should be provided with services where they live and work, or whether the life of a street child is so inherently dangerous and unhealthy that the phenomenon of street children should be prevented at all costs.

A further topic to be explored is that of children crossing borders on their own, often seeking asylum. When children attempt to move across national borders, they may get caught up in another cycle of mistreatment as they face the immigration systems of other countries. Sometimes these children are fleeing persecution, sometimes migrating to escape unhappy personal circumstances. Unaccompanied migrant children, along with street children, tend to be considered the weakest and least powerful people on earth — doubly disadvantaged in that they are considered of little social value in both their countries of origin and destination, and are too young to be able to advocate for themselves.

Clearly the issue of children living out of family care cannot be separated from other topics already covered in this book: the worst forms of child labor and child sex trafficking, for example. Also, though legal instruments tend to delineate populations according to a dominant characteristic, street children have a great deal in common with abandoned and institutionalized children, since both groups lack supportive adults as protectors. As obvious as it might sound, a viable family is the protective device most likely to prevent children from falling into these extremely negative situations.

A. Defining the Problem

In the article that follows, Lynn Wardle presents the problem of children on their own in terms of "parentlessness." While seemingly obvious, her article reminds us of the dire consequences for children who lose their immediate families. As will be explored below, these children find themselves at the mercy of national public policy, though many states lack coherent methods to protect them.

Lynn D. Wardle, *Parentlessness: Adoption Problems, Paradigms, Policies, and Parameters*
4 Whittier Journal of Child & Family Advocacy 323 (2005)

Introduction: Parentless in the World Today

A. Definition and Types of Parentlessness

Parentlessness is a great problem of global concern as well as of domestic interest. Parentlessness refers to the condition of children who lack the present and long-term care and direction of their parents. Parents are the father and mother of a child who have and exercise legal and social responsibility for children — to support, educate, love, nurture, and rear them as members of their family. The most needy and vulnerable parentless children are orphans who have lost both mother and father. Orphans are often the left-behind victims of war, crime, famine, or disease that have killed one or both of their parents. Children growing up with only one parent are a second category of partially parentless children. While their vulnerability is generally less severe than that of children who have no living parents, children raised by just one parent are generally at significant disadvantage in terms of economic, educational, and social opportunity and well-being.

While death causes the most permanent and extreme form of involuntary parentlessness (the parents did not choose to leave), there are other causes of partial or total parentlessness, including legal and social barriers that separate one or both parents from the child and individual adult choices by which they become unable or unwilling to provide consistently for the needs of their child....

When relatives, communities (such as religious, tribal, ethnic, and other socio-cultural subgroups), or nations do not provide some effective form of substitute parenting for parentless children, the children are at extreme risk. Often, they become "homeless persons" or "street children." Groups of parentless children may provide some care and protection for the individual members, and "many street children feel that other children within their street child group are 'like a family.'" Likewise, parentless children in refugee camps "[o]ften ... band together to form new care groups ... led by an elder girl child for their protection and survival."

B. Scope of Parentlessness

(1) Global Involuntary Parentlessness

The scope of global parentlessness today is staggering. While the exact number of parentless children today is not known, "UNICEF estimates about 100 million street children exist in the world today. About forty million are in Latin America, twenty-five to thirty million in Asia, and ten million in Africa." In Bogota, Colombia, 200,000 abandoned street children roam the streets. "The number of street children is predicted to grow by tens of millions as poverty in the Third World becomes increasingly urban-based." "In Mexico City, ... with a population of 23 million, ... 13,000 children ... live on the streets."

The plight of parentless children is extreme. Many parentless children are unable to survive—they die, and often not tidily, not antiseptically, not with dignity, but horribly of starvation, with bloated bellies, listless, bony bodies, and huge pain-drenched eyes, with cries of hunger and fear. Their suffering and death stuns us and shames us. The United Nations estimates that approximately 50,000 human beings die every day as a result of poor shelter, water, or sanitation, and parentless children are especially vulnerable to these ravages.

Disease and starvation are not the only mortal threats that parentless children face. It is reported that "in Colombia, over 2,190 street children were murdered in 1994, an average of six children per day." Likewise, the "U.S. State Department reports ... that street children in Honduras are often tortured and killed by Honduran police officers." Similarly, Guatemalan street children often experience violence including beatings and sexual assault by private security guards who report to the Interior Ministry. These children are persecuted for their homeless status under the auspices of what the police deem to be 'creating a public scandal.' 'In December 1999, the Inter American Court of Human Rights ruled that two police officers were responsible for the 1990 deaths of five street youths and that the Guatemalan government had failed to protect the rights of the victims.' In Albania, children are exploited rather than protected by the police. 'There are approximately 800 street children in Tirana. Trafficking in children for sex and, to a lesser degree, for begging rings was a serious problem.... Albania is a country of origin and a transit country for trafficking. Police corruption and involvement in trafficking was a problem.' Reports have been made of abuse of Brazilian, Colombian, Indian, Kenyan, Egyptian, and Sudanese street children. Human Rights Watch notes in some countries the 'notion of social cleansing' is applied to street children even when they are not distinguished as members of a particular racial, ethnic, or religious group. Branded as 'anti-social' or demonstrating 'anti-social behavior,' street children are viewed with suspicion and fear by many who would simply like to see street children disappear.

Death is not the only danger facing parentless children. Somehow, millions of parentless children survive—but when deprived of security, of education, and of protection, many parentless children join the illiterate masses that live only from day to day. Unable to develop skills, many are incapable of providing more than subsistence for themselves and their families, much less to contribute to the strength and improvement of their nation and society. Parentless children are easy targets for exploiters, and often they are victims of child labor. According to the International Labor Organization (I.L.O.), there are now approximately 250 million working children aged five to fourteen, of which at least 120 million children are involved in full-time work that is both hazardous and exploitative. In the year 2000, it was estimated that "111 million children [employed] in hazardous occupations were below fifteen years old, a majority of them boys. Beyond hazardous work, about 5.7 million children work in forced or bonded labor situations."

Parentless children also are prey for child sexual exploitation (both prostitution and pornography). They are the fodder of illicit enterprise, used, abused, and discarded. The I.L.O. estimates that globally about 1.8 million children work "in prostitution or pornography, and about 600,000 in other illicit activities. Of these, at least 1.2 million children were probably 'trafficked,' that is, sold into slavery as economic goods." One study of street children in Guatemala reported that ninety-three percent of the street children surveyed had sexually transmitted diseases, and ninety percent of the children were drug users. Parentless children are also exploited in times of war:

> A global survey conducted by the Coalition to Stop the Use of Child Soldiers reported that 'more than half a million children were subject to recruitment into national armed forces, paramilitaries, or non-state armed groups in a total of eighty-seven countries, and at least 300,000 of these children were actively participating in armed conflicts in forty-one countries.'

In short, "[t]o be a poor child who lives with little or no family guidance or support is to live daily with the threat of murder, disease, malnutrition, physical and sexual abuse, prostitution, drug abuse, and exploitation."

Notes and Questions

1. Wardle paints a dire portrait of the lives of the "parentless." Is it useful to present the problem in generic terms as she does? Why are so many children who have not lost parents to death being abandoned? Is this an inevitable state of affairs or does it represent some sort of historical anomaly? To what degree should a child be separated from parents before being considered "parentless?" How large a role should the parent play in making that determination? What standards should the state use in establishing that a child is indeed "parentless?"

Child welfare organization UNICEF (discussed in Chapter One) often acts as a clearing house for information on children's lives. The short piece that follows is a plea to nations to stop placing children separated from families in institutions. Although highly critical of institutional care, UNICEF has often placed itself in opposition to international adoption, as will be explored later in the chapter.

UNICEF, *Child Protection Information Sheet: Children without Parental Care*

2006, *available at* http://www.unicef.org/protection/files/Parental_Care.pdf

Millions of children around the world are growing up without one or both of their parents. Many more are at risk of separation due to the impact of poverty, disability and HIV/AIDS or such crises as natural disaster and armed conflict. Children without parental care find themselves at a higher risk of discrimination, inadequate care, abuse and exploitation, and their well-being is often insufficiently monitored. Many children are placed unnecessarily and for too long in institutions, where they receive less of the stimulation and individual attention needed to grow to their full potential. Inadequate care environments can impair children's emotional and social development and leave them vulnerable to exploitation, sexual abuse and physical violence.

FACTS AND FIGURES

- About 1.5 million children in the CEE/CIS [Central and Eastern Europe and Commonwealth of Independent States, i.e. former Soviet Republics] live in public care. In Europe and Central Asia, over one million children live in residential institutions.

- In 93 countries of sub-Saharan Africa, Asia, and Latin America and the Caribbean, the number of orphans (children aged 0–17 who have lost one or both parents) was estimated to be 143 million at the end of 2003; of those children 15 million were orphaned by AIDS, more than 12 million of them in sub-Saharan Africa.

- Asia has the highest number of orphans due to all causes, with 87.6 million children (2003).

BUILDING A PROTECTIVE ENVIRONMENT FOR CHILDREN

Government commitment and capacity

Extended child welfare services and poverty-reduction initiatives are needed to help prevent separation. Government support—through appropriate policies, funding and legislation—is vital for establishing and promoting family-based alternatives to institutional care. For children who remain in public care, regulation and monitoring of institutions, in line with agreed national and international standards and the Convention on the Rights of the Child, are essential.

Legislation and enforcement

Laws must protect children from unnecessary separation from families. Children without parental care need to be protected from discrimination, violence and abuse and should have full access to education and health care. Inheritance laws must not discriminate against girls or against any children who have lost a parent to HIV/AIDS.

Attitudes, customs and practices

Discrimination based on gender, disability, ethnicity or HIV status, which contributes to children being institutionalized, must end. Positive attitudes to domestic adoption and well-monitored foster care can ensure that children who cannot be cared for by their families still grow up in a family environment.

Open discussion

The media can help dispel myths about the benefits of institutional care and educate the public about domestic adoption, foster care and respect for a child's right to grow up in a family environment.

Children's life skills, knowledge and participation

These are crucial, particularly when parental care is not available. Children should be provided with opportunities to express their views and wishes with regard to their care arrangements. They need to be aware of their rights and helped to protect themselves from exploitation, abuse and the dangers of trafficking and HIV/AIDS.

Capacity of families and communities

Community-based social services, such as day care, parenting education and home support for children with disabilities, are needed to strengthen the capacity of families to care for their children and of extended families and communities to provide alternative forms of care.

Monitoring, reporting and oversight

Mechanisms are needed to ensure oversight of institutions providing public and private care, as well as foster care arrangements. Data collection and analysis on the situation of children without parental care is key to changing public attitudes, promoting better practices and increasing accountability.

Notes and Questions

1. Being a child without functioning family ties is a highly dangerous condition, as the readings above indicate. Handling high levels of family breakdown and separation is a daunting challenge to national governments and NGOs. How does UNICEF frame the question? Which of the UNICEF suggestions seems to be the most practical?

2. Is it possible to devise an international "child welfare policy" for children living without parental care? What should it include?

3. There have been many policy initiatives in recent years designed to assist countries in getting children out of institutions. Why has this form of care been relied upon so heavily? How easy is it to replace institutions with other forms of care? What other forms of care would be better? Does Wardle pay enough attention to the importance of extended family and informal care givers?

B. Confronting the Problem: In Search of Best Practice

The debate over what constitutes the best solutions for children living out of parental care has been contentious in virtually all countries, whether developed or developing. The debate confronts national governments with the economically and socially marginalised, as it is ultimately the task of the state to decide the means by which to repair broken families, as well as the extent to which this should be attempted through state intervention. Some family reunification simply cannot and will not take place, no matter what level of effort is made. The relative benefits of foster care versus adoption for children who do not return to birth families is also part of this contentious mix, and will be explored later in the chapter.

The United Nations has recently published draft guidelines, excerpted below, designed to assist States in devising policy to deal with children living without parental care. As you read the selected guidelines, consider what priorities the UN is asking national governments to adhere to. Are the guidelines clear enough? Will they be easy for countries to understand and apply? If you were part of the government in a country with a large "social orphan" population, how would you interpret the guidelines?

Draft UN Guidelines for the Protection and Alternative Care of Children without Parental Care

available at http://www.iss-ssi.org/2007/Resource_Centre/
Tronc_DI/documents/DraftGuidelinesMay06.pdf
Submitted by
International Social Service and UNICEF
in collaboration with the NGO Working Group on
Children without Parental Care
and revised by the
Committee on the Rights of the Child
at its May 2006 Session

PART 1: PURPOSE

1. The present Guidelines are founded on, and seek to enhance the practical effects of, the provisions of international human rights law, including in particular those of the Convention on the Rights of the Child, as well as of the developing body of knowledge and experience in this sphere as reflected in other instruments and norms relating to the rights, interests, well-being and protection of children.

2. Against the background of these texts, the Guidelines are:

a. directed towards supporting efforts to keep children within, or return them to, their family of origin and, where this is not possible or in the best interests of the child, to identify and provide the most suitable forms of alternative child care, under conditions that promote the child's full and harmonious development, as part of an integrated national child protection policy;

b. designed to assist and encourage governments to assume their responsibilities and obligations in these respects;

c. equally designed to be made known to all concerned with child care, in both the public and private sectors, including civil society, and at all levels, and to be taken fully into account by them in their policies, decisions and activities.

PART 2: FUNDAMENTAL PRINCIPLES

3. Every individual child and young person should be given the opportunity to develop into a self-reliant, responsible and participating member of society, through living in a supportive, protective and caring environment that promotes his/her full potential.

4. Children must be treated with dignity and respect at all times and must benefit from effective protection from abuse, neglect and all forms of exploitation, whether on the part of care providers, peers, or third parties, in whatever care setting they may find themselves.

5. Children with inadequate or no parental care are at special risk of being denied a nurturing environment.

. . . .

8. The family being the fundamental group of society and the natural environment for the growth, well-being and protection of children, efforts should primarily be directed to enabling the child to remain in or return to the care of his/her parents, or when appropriate, other close family members. Ensuring that families have access to necessary forms of support in their care-giving role is the responsibility of the State.

9. Where the child's own family is unable or unwilling, even with support, to provide adequate care for the child, or abandons or relinquishes the child, the State is responsible for ensuring appropriate alternative care, with or through competent local authorities and community organisations. It is the role of the State to ensure the supervision of the safety, well-being and development of any child placed in alternative care and the regular review of the appropriateness of the care arrangement provided.

10. States should develop and implement comprehensive child welfare and protection policies, with attention to the improvement of existing alternative care provision, reflecting *inter alia* the principles contained in these Guidelines and instituted at every level of government.

11. All decisions related to alternative care for a child or sibling group, including those regarding family preservation and reintegration initiatives, the forms and contexts of alternative care, and after-care support, should be made on a case-by-case basis. They should be grounded in the best interests and rights of the child concerned and should respect fully his/her right to be consulted and to have his/her views fully taken into account in accordance with his/her evolving capacities, and on the basis of his/her access to all necessary information.

12. The provision of alternative care should never be undertaken with the primary purpose of furthering the political, religious or economic goals of the providers.

13. Decisions regarding children in alternative care, including those in informal care, should have due regard for the importance of ensuring children a stable home and consistent caregiver, with permanency generally being a key goal.

14. Financial and material poverty alone, or conditions directly and uniquely imputable to such poverty, should never be a justification either for the removal of a child from parental care or for receiving a child into alternative care, but should be seen as a signal for the need to provide appropriate support to the family.

15. Attention must be paid to promoting and safeguarding all other rights of special pertinence to the situation of children without parental care, including but not limited to access to education, health and other basic services, the right to identity, language and protection of property and inheritance rights.

16. Recognising that most children without parental care are looked after informally by relatives or others, States should devise appropriate means, consistent with these Guidelines, to ensure their welfare and protection while in such informal care arrangements.

17. No child should be without the support and protection of a legal guardian or other recognised responsible adult at any time.

18. Use of residential care should be limited to cases where this setting is specifically appropriate, necessary and constructive for the individual child concerned.

19. In accordance with the predominant opinion of experts, alternative care for young children, especially those under the age of 3 years, should be provided only in family-based settings. Where the placement is of an emergency nature, or is for a pre-determined and very limited duration with planned family reintegration or other long-term care solution as its outcome, exceptions to this principle may be warranted.

20. Where large child care facilities (institutions) remain, alternatives should be actively developed in the context of an overall de-institutionalisation strategy that will enable them to be phased out. No new facilities of this nature should be established under any circumstances.

21. States should make all possible efforts to allocate sufficient human and financial resources to ensure the optimal and progressive implementation of these Guidelines. When necessary, international assistance should be sought in this regard; the enhanced implementation of these Guidelines should figure in developing co-operation programmes.

22. While the degree to which these Guidelines can be fully and immediately implemented may depend on the economic, social and cultural conditions prevailing in the country or society concerned, the fundamental principles and overall orientations they contain should be respected in all cases.

. . . .

PART 4: FAMILY PRESERVATION

Promoting family preservation

31. Governments should ensure that their general policies promote family preservation. These policies should address *inter alia* poverty, inadequate housing, lack of access to basic health, education and social welfare services, discrimination, marginalisation and stigmatisation, as well as violence and substance abuse, which are the root causes of child abandonment, relinquishment and separation of the child from his/her family.

32. Special efforts should be made to tackle discrimination on the basis of any status of the child or parents, including ethnicity, religion, gender, sexual orientation, disability, HIV/AIDS status, birth out of wedlock, and socio-economic stigma, all of which can give rise to relinquishment, abandonment and/or removal of a child.

33. Governments should develop and implement policies designed to support family preservation by: a) preventing the need for alternative child care and b) ensuring that, wherever possible, children in alternative care placements may be reintegrated with their family under appropriate conditions.

37. Special attention should be paid to the establishment and promotion of support and care services for single and adolescent parents and their children. States should ensure that adolescent parents retain all rights inherent to their status both as parents and as children, including access to all appropriate services for their own development, allowances to which parents are entitled, and their inheritance rights. Efforts should also be made to reduce stigma attached to single and adolescent parenthood.

38. Support and services should be available to children who choose to remain together with their siblings in a child-headed household following the loss of their parents or caregivers. States should ensure that such households benefit from mandatory protection from all forms of exploitation and abuse, supervision and support on the part of the local community and its competent services, with particular concern for the children's health, housing, education and inheritance rights. Special attention should be given to ensuring the head of such a household retains all rights inherent to his/her child status, including access to education and leisure, in addition to his/her rights as a household "head".

Specific measures to prevent family separation

42. Services should be established, at maternity clinics and other appropriate places, to identify and counsel mothers who are at risk of relinquishing or abandoning their child and to refer them to further supportive services.

43. Safe havens should be established where a mother may abandon or relinquish an infant without risk to the child's safety, and without compromising the confidentiality of the parent.

44. Specific training should be provided to teachers and others working with children, in order to help them identify situations of abuse, neglect or risk of abandonment and refer such situations to competent bodies.

45. Any decision to remove a child against the will of his/her parents must be made by competent authorities, in accordance with applicable law and procedures and subject to judicial review.

Specific measures for family reintegration

47. In order to prepare and support the child and the family for his/her possible return to the family, his/her situation should be assessed with the different actors involved (the child, the family of origin, the alternative care giver), so as to decide whether the reintegration of the child in the family of origin is possible and in the best interests of the child, which steps this would involve and under whose supervision.

. . . .

49. Regular and appropriate contact between the child and his/her family specifically for the purpose of reintegration should be developed, supported and monitored.

50. The reintegration of the child in his/her family should be designed as a gradual and supervised process, accompanied by follow-up and support measures taking account of the child's age and according to his/her evolving capacities, and the cause of the separation.

PART 5: FRAMEWORK OF CARE PROVISION

51. In order to meet the specific and diverse needs of each child without parental care, States should ensure that the legislative, policy and financial conditions exist to provide for adequate alternative care options, with priority to family- and community-based solutions. These options should be adapted to the respective social and cultural environment of the child and give special attention to the situation of girls.

52. These options should comprise suitable family-based and non-family-based responses for emergency, short-term and long-term care.

PART 6: DETERMINATION OF THE MOST APPROPRIATE FORM OF CARE

56. Decision-making in the best interests of the child should be based on rigorous assessment, planning and review, through established structures and mechanisms. It should be carried out on a case-by-case basis, by suitably qualified persons, preferably in a multidisciplinary team. It should involve full consultation at all stages with the child, according to his/her evolving capacities, and with his/her parents or legal guardians.

57. Assessment should be carried out rapidly, thoroughly, and carefully. It should take into account the child's immediate safety and well-being, as well as his/her longer term care and development, and should cover the child's personal and developmental characteristics, ethnic, cultural, linguistic and religious background, family and social environment, medical history, and any special needs.

59. Permanency for the child should be secured without undue delay through, wherever possible, reintegration in his/her nuclear or extended family or in an alternative stable family setting, including *kafala* and adoption.

. . . .

61. Continual changes in care setting are detrimental to the child's development and ability to form attachments, and should be avoided. Short-term placements should aim at enabling an appropriate permanent solution to be arranged.

62. Planning should take account of, notably: the level of the child's attachment to the family of origin; the family of origin's capacity to protect the child; the child's need or desire to feel part of a family; the desirability of the child remaining within his/her community and country; his/her cultural, linguistic and religious background; and relationships with siblings, with a view to avoiding their separation.

. . . .

64. To determine the most suitable form of alternative care, the child and his/her parents or legal guardians should be fully informed on the alternative care options available and their implications.

65. The preparation, enforcement and evaluation of a protective measure for a child should be carried out, to the greatest extent possible, with the participation of his/her parents or legal guardians and potential foster carers, with respect to his/her particular needs, convictions and special wishes. At the request of the child, parents or legal guardians, other important persons in the child's life may also be consulted in any decision process, at the discretion of the competent authority.

66. Any decision on the care of the child should take account of the desirability of continuity in his/her life course, avoiding disruption and contradictory decisions. The location of the care setting should avoid distancing the child from his/her habitual surroundings.

67. Siblings with existing bonds should not be separated by placements in alternative care, unless there is a clear risk of abuse or other justification in the best interests of the child. In any case, siblings should be enabled to maintain contact with each other, unless this is against their wishes or interests.

PART 7: PROVISIONS OF ALTERNATIVE CARE

General conditions of care

79. When a child is placed in alternative care, contact with his/her family of origin, as well as with other persons close to him or her, such as friends or neighbours, should be encouraged and facilitated, in keeping with the child's protection and best interests. States should pay special attention to ensuring that children in alternative care because of parental imprisonment have the opportunity to maintain contact with their parents.

. . . .

Legal guardianship

103. States should seek to establish a mechanism for the appointment of a legal guardian vested with both the right and responsibility to make day-to-day decisions in the best interest of the child where the child's parents are absent or are incapable of making such decisions.

Foster care

119. The competent authority or agency should devise a system to assess and match the needs of the child with the abilities and resources of potential foster carers and to prepare all concerned for the placement.

120. A pool of competent foster carers should be identified in each locality who can provide children with care and protection while maintaining ties to family, community and cultural group.

Residential care

124. Facilities providing residential care should be small and organised around the rights and needs of the child, in a setting as close as possible to a family or small group situation. Their objective should generally be to provide temporary care, and to contribute actively to the child's family reintegration or, if this is not possible, to securing his/her stable care in an alternative family setting.

....

126. States should ensure that there are sufficient carers in residential care settings to allow individualised attention and to give the child, where appropriate, the opportunity to bond with one of their number. Carers should also be deployed within the care setting in such a way as to implement effectively its aims and objectives and ensure child protection.

....

Inspection and monitoring

128. Agencies and facilities providing alternative care services should be held legally responsible for ensuring that the quality of care provided is in keeping with these Guidelines and with applicable national law and policy.

129. Entities and professionals involved in care provision should be accountable to a specific public authority, which should ensure *inter alia* frequent inspections comprising both foreseen and unannounced visits, involving discussion with and observation of the staff and the children.

....

PART 8: CARE PROVISION FOR CHILDREN OUTSIDE THEIR COUNTRY OF HABITUAL RESIDENCE

[This section refers to medical care, vacations and "other" reasons for such travel, but does not reference intercountry adoption.]

PART 9: CARE IN EMERGENCY SITUATIONS

Application of the Guidelines

155. All principles set out in the present Guidelines should continue to apply in situations of emergency arising from natural and man-made disasters. Individuals and organisations wishing to work on behalf of children without parental care in emergency situations are expected to endorse and operate in keeping with these Guidelines.

156. Preventing separation

157. Organisations and authorities should make every effort to prevent the separation of children from their parents or primary caregivers, unless the best interests of the child so require, and ensure that their actions do not inadvertently encourage family separation by providing services and benefits to children alone rather than to families.

158. Deliberate separations should be prevented by:

a. ensuring that all households have access to basic relief supplies and other services, including education;

b. limiting the development of residential care options, and restricting their use to those situations where it is absolutely necessary.

Care arrangements

....

162. Children in emergency situations should not be removed to other countries for alternative care except temporarily for compelling health, medical or safety reasons. In that case, this should be as close as possible to their home, they should be accompanied by a parent or care-giver known to the child, and a clear return plan should be established.

163. Should family reintegration prove impossible within an appropriate period, or be deemed contrary to the child's best interests, other long-term options such as foster care, appropriate residential care or adoption should be envisaged.

Tracing and family reintegration

164. Identifying, registering and documenting unaccompanied or separated children are priorities in any emergency and should be carried out as quickly as possible.

....

168. The validity of relationships and the confirmation of the willingness of the child and family members to be reunited must be verified for every child. No action should be taken that may hinder eventual family reintegration such as adoption, change of name, or movement to places far from the family's likely location until all tracing efforts have been exhausted.

Notes and Questions

1. How does the term "permanency" fit into the UN draft guidelines scheme, above? How do the guidelines treat institutions? If family reunification does not prove to be possible, what are the next steps to be taken, according to the draft guidelines?

2. Do the draft guidelines provide a clear sense of what the priorities should be in devising solutions for children living without parental care? Do they set realistic, attainable goals for governments? Ideally, what bodies and groups should have a say in the drafting of international child welfare policies such as these?

3. Given the sheer number of parentless children, as outlined in the first readings in this chapter, would adherence to the guidelines overwhelm or burden governments that do not have the resources to provide such services? It seems likely that more children find themselves out of family care where national resources are most limited. If that is the case, is it realistic that states should carry out detailed case-by-case monitoring of care situations? What if states are not capable of that kind of follow up?

4. There are detailed provisions relating to the care of children separated from families during times of natural disasters. Where family members are not found within a reasonable period of time, what do you imagine happens to most children in such situations?

II. Children in State Care and the Intercountry Adoption Debate

These topics can be dealt with together, since revelations of children in state care almost inevitably revive interest in the issue of international adoption. Where there are many children in state institutional care, states often try and keep them hidden. Where this strategy is not successful, orphanage children become the focus of acrimonious debate over what should be done with them. Institutional care is acknowledged by almost everyone to be detrimental, even where it continues to be relied upon. The domestic adoption option may be difficult in societies where blood relations are central and adoption an unfamiliar or unattractive concept. Although adoption can become culturally acceptable through a process of social education, this process may take too much time to reach children in immediate need. International adoption advocates argue that this option offers immediate and extremely positive care for many, if not most, children. The United Nations bodies (including UNICEF and the UN Committee on the Rights of the Child), generally associated with opposition to international adoption, appear to be encouraging states to develop large scale systems of foster care as a "family based alternative." The growth of foster care must be examined and analyzed as a matter of urgency; one difficulty is that children placed in foster care are dispersed among the general population and become even more inaccessible to outside scrutiny than children housed in traditional orphanages.

A. Children Out of Family Care

The reasons for family breakdown and child abandonment differ greatly from region to region. National governments do not have impressive records when it comes to fully documenting and accounting for the children who come into state care due to the inability or unwillingness of biological parents to care for them. Historically, governments have been resistant to providing even approximate numbers of children living in state or other institutional care. Social orphans have tended to be a hidden population; their conditions of life are not generally accessible to the outside world. Whether willfully, or due to inadequate resources, the state often fails to properly provide for and protect those children in its care. Frequently, the state's treatment of children rises to a violation of their most basic human rights. The modern trend is away from approval of orphanages as a site for the care of children living without parents; in reality, though, it is often extremely challenging for states to come up with valid alternatives to this traditional mode of care. While the United Nations is currently encouraging foster care and small group homes, it remains to be seen how successful these will be in dealing with the widespread crisis of children living without families.

While there has been increased discussion of children without families as a cohort in recent years, the question of where adoption fits into the overall child welfare picture remains unresolved. Many countries simply do not have a tradition of formal adoption; more do not allow intercountry adoption. Even those that do countenance international adoption tend to impose artificial restrictions on the number of children who may be adopted. The United Nations child welfare bodies have not offered any proactive support for international adoption, instead emphasizing in-country foster care and "family like" alternatives. The well-known NGO, Save the Children, is strongly opposed to intercountry adoption. As noted above, it is not possible to create large-scale domestic adoption programs in a short time where social attitudes are not favorable towards adoption. This is a problem faced in many countries, where the numbers of social orphans is high, but social acceptance of adoption is low. This is almost as likely to be the case in wealthier countries as in poorer ones. In South Korea and Japan, for instance, many children find themselves out of family care, but there is entrenched social resistance to adopting non-relative children.

1. Human Rights Watch Revelations from Orphanages in China and Russia: The 1990s

The following two reports by Human Rights Watch were of enormous importance in gaining attention for the crisis of children in institutions. In the mid-1990s, the organization carried out extensive research in China and Russia, discovering worlds of abuse and neglect that were difficult for most people to fathom. Thus, these articles represent the roots of our modern international conversation on the subject of social orphans. It should be noted that large numbers of abandoned children in both these countries continue to live in institutions. The recent trend towards foster care is as yet very difficult to evaluate and analyze.

The Chinese report, along with the film, *Return to the Dying Rooms*, caused an international sensation and generated strong denials from the Chinese government. For film information, see http://www.truevisiontv.com/dying_rooms/index.htm. The allegations made by Human Rights Watch were of the most serious kind: that the Chinese authorities were knowingly, and deliberately, targeting orphan girls to die through neglect in the state's orphanages. Undercover researchers brought video cameras into the orphanages to prove what had been rumored, but always denied, by the Chinese authorities: that baby girls were being systematically allowed to die. This tradition of hidden camera work in orphanages continues sporadically today, uncovering abuses in a wide variety of countries.

Even today, there remains a striking lack of data available on how many children are living in institutions in China. China's "one child policy," implemented to stave off a population explosion, has been responsible for the abandonment of millions of girls. As is well known, Chinese families have shown a traditional preference for boy children, and the birth of a girl is frequently met with dismay. China appears to be arguing these days that the number of adoptable baby girls is greatly decreased, although without explaining why this should be so. It may be that China is referring to the fact that many are now in paid foster care, rather than the old-style orphanages.

In the wake of revelations about orphanage conditions in the early to mid-1990s, China opened up to foreign adoptions. However, due to recent restrictions, the numbers of Chinese girls being adopted internationally appears to have peaked, and is falling back sharply. In 2005, China announced drastic changes to its policies on intercountry adoption, to the effect that prospective adoptive parents would have to meet specific criteria; the most significant of these changes was that single women would no longer be able to adopt from China. China maintained that this was because there were many more adoptive parents than available children, a position that has not been authenticated by any objective international body. The fact remains that we know little about child abandonment or about the fates of children living out of family care in China, a situation that—apart from the Human Rights Watch efforts over a brief period of time—international human rights entities have paid little attention to since the mid-1990s.

Human Rights Watch, *Death by Default:*
A Policy of Fatal Neglect in China's State Orphanages

1996, *available at* http://www.hrw.org/en/reports/1996/01/01/death-default

SUMMARY

China's Orphans and Human Rights

In response to widespread criticism of its human rights record, the Chinese government has frequently argued that the international community places too much emphasis on civil and political rights, while neglecting the more basic rights to food, shelter, and subsistence rights which China claims to have secured for its citizens more effectively than some democratic countries. In accordance with the country's post-1949 political tradition, China's leaders assert that economic well-being forms the basis for the enjoyment of all other rights, and that the protection of economic rights can therefore justify restrictions on civil liberties.

In some important respects, China's record in protecting social and economic rights may serve as a model for the rest of the developing world. Levels of well-being, as measured by social indicators such as literacy and life expectancy, are considerably higher in China than in other countries at comparable stages of development, and in some cases higher than those in much wealthier nations.

But China's claim to guarantee the "right to subsistence" conceals a secret world of starvation, disease, and unnatural death a world into which thousands of Chinese citizens disappear each year. The victims are neither the political activists nor the religious dissidents who dominate the international debate over human rights in the People's Republic; they are orphans and abandoned children in custodial institutions run by China's Ministry of Civil Affairs. This report documents the pattern of cruelty, abuse, and malign neglect which has dominated child welfare work in China since the early 1950s, and which now constitutes one of the country's gravest human rights problems.

. . . .

A Nationwide Crisis

Abandonment of children surged in China during the 1980s, in part due to the one-child population control policy and in part due to policies restricting adoption by Chinese couples who are not childless. The national statistics on mortality cited in this report do not contain a gender breakdown, but anecdotal and journalistic reporting on orphanages nationwide reveals that the vast majority of children in orphanages are, and consistently have been during the past decade, healthy infant girls; that is, children without serious disabilities who are abandoned because of traditional attitudes that value boy children more highly. The financial and social problems that these children are perceived to constitute are made more acute by the fact that Chinese couples are not permitted to adopt them, for the most part.

Reports of inhumane conditions in Chinese orphanages have attracted growing international concern in recent years, prompted chiefly by the country's greater openness to foreign press coverage and charitable work financed from abroad, as well as a dramatic increase in overseas adoptions from the People's Republic. Although some scattered allegations have succeeded in bringing to light grave abuses against China's orphans, there has been virtually no effort to place these charges in context through systematic research on the country's institutional welfare system.

The Chinese government's own statistics reveal a situation worse than even the most alarming Western media reports have suggested. In 1989, the most recent year for which nationwide figures are available, the majority of abandoned children admitted to China's orphanages were dying in institutional care. Many institutions, including some in major cities, appeared to be operating as little more than assembly lines for the elimination of unwanted orphans, with an annual turnover of admissions and deaths far exceeding the number of beds available.

In any case, the majority of abandoned children in China never reach the dubious security of a state-run orphanage. Many are sent instead to general-purpose state institutions, where they are confined indiscriminately with retarded, disabled, elderly, and mentally disturbed adults. Although the statistical evidence is unclear, the limited eyewitness information available suggests that death rates among children held in these facilities may be even higher than in China's specialized orphanages.

In addition, Chinese official records fail to account for most of the country's abandoned infants and children, only a small proportion of whom are in any form of acknowledged state care. The most recent figure provided by the government for the country's orphan population, 100,000, seems implausibly low for a country with a total population of 1.2 billion. Even if it were accurate, however, the whereabouts of the great majority of China's orphans would still be a complete mystery, leaving crucial questions about the country's child welfare system unanswered and suggesting that the real scope of the catastrophe that has befallen China's unwanted children may be far larger than the evidence in this report documents.

Evidence From Shanghai

In addition to nationwide statistics on the condition of China's institutionalized children, Human Rights Watch/Asia has recently obtained a large quantity of internal documentation from one of the most prominent specialized orphanages in the country, the Shanghai Children's Welfare Institute. Based on these documents, which include medical records and other official files recording the deaths of hundreds of children, and on the testimony of direct witnesses who left China in 1995, Human Rights Watch/Asia has concluded that conditions at the Shanghai orphanage before 1993 were comparable to those at some of the worst children's institutions in China, several of which have already been exposed in journalistic accounts in the West. Since 1993, a program of cosmetic "reforms" has transformed the Shanghai Children's Welfare Institute into an international showcase for China's social policies, while an administrative reorganization of the city's welfare system has largely concealed the continuing abuse of infants and children.

Ironically, the Chinese government has praised Shanghai's municipal orphanage extensively as a national model for the care of abandoned and disabled children. In addition to frequent flattering coverage in China's official media, the Shanghai Children's Welfare Institute receives considerable financial support from Chinese and international charities and hosts a steady stream of private and official visitors. Behind the institution's glossy official image, however, lies a pattern of horrifying abuse. The brutal treatment of orphans in Shanghai, which included deliberate starvation, torture, and sexual assault, continued over a period of many years and led to the unnatural deaths of well over 1,000 children between 1986 and 1992 alone. This campaign of elimination could be kept secret through the complicity of both higher- and lower-level staff, and because the city's Bureau of Civil Affairs, responsible for the orphanage, also runs the crematoria, where starved children's corpses were disposed of with minimum oversight, often even before a death certificate had been filled out by the attending physician. In addition, officials of various Shanghai municipal agencies knowingly suppressed evidence of child abuse at the orphanage, persistently ignored the institute's high monthly death figures, and in 1992, quashed an investigation into orphanage practices.

Conditions in the Shanghai orphanage came close to being publicly exposed in the early 1990s as a result of pressure by concerned orphanage employees, local journalists and sympathetic Shanghai officials. By 1993, however, virtually all the critical staff members were forced out of their positions and silenced. The orphanage leadership was assisted in its efforts to cover up the truth by three of the city's top leaders: Wu Bangguo, Shanghai's Communist Party secretary; Huang Ju, the city's mayor; and Xie Lijuan, deputy mayor for health, education, and social welfare. Wu, Huang, and Xie were fully informed of the abuses occurring at the Children's Welfare Institute, but took no action to halt them or to punish those responsible, acting instead to shield senior management at the orphanage and to prevent news of the abuses from reaching the public. Meanwhile, Wu Bangguo and Huang Ju have risen to positions of national prominence in China's ruling Politburo.

The cosmetic changes at the Shanghai orphanage since 1993 have been engineered by Han Weicheng, its former director. Although he was a major perpetrator of abuses there, Han was promoted to an even more senior position within the municipal welfare bureaucracy. At about the same time, the orphanage was opened to visitors and large numbers of children from the city's orphanage began to be transferred to another custodial institution, the Shanghai No. 2 Social Welfare Institute. Located on Chongming Island, a remote rural area north of Shanghai, the No. 2 Social Welfare Institute, which is ostensibly a home for severely retarded adults, has been transformed since 1993 into a virtual dumping ground for abandoned infants delivered to the orphanage. While the city government has aggressively promoted the adoption of healthy or mildly disabled orphans by visiting foreigners, reports from visitors to the orphanage in 1995 indicate that infants with more serious handicaps are generally diverted to the Chongming Island institution within weeks or months of their arrival. Human Rights Watch/Asia has not been able to ascertain the mortality rates of children at the No. 2 Social Welfare Institute, but has collected credible reports of severe mistreatment and of staff impunity. Extreme secrecy surrounds the functioning of the Chongming Island institution, raising serious suspicions and fears as to the likely fate of children transferred there.

Perversion of Medical Ethics

Some Western observers have charged that the phenomenally high death rates among China's abandoned children result from neglect and lack of medical training on the part of orphanage employees. Anecdotal evidence from foreign charity workers and adoptive parents has painted a grim picture of decrepit and poorly financed institutions run by demoralized and unskilled nursing staff.

However, medical records and testimony obtained by Human Rights Watch/Asia show that deaths at the Shanghai orphanage were in many cases deliberate and cruel. Child-care workers reportedly selected unwanted infants and children for death by intentional deprivation of food and water a process known among the workers as the "summary resolution" of children's alleged medical problems. When an orphan chosen in this manner was visibly on the point of death from starvation or medical neglect, orphanage doctors were then asked to perform medical "consultations" which served as a ritual marking the child for subsequent termination of care, nutrition, and other life-saving intervention. Deaths from acute malnutrition were then, in many cases, falsely recorded as having resulted from other causes, often entirely spurious or irrelevant conditions such as "mental deficiency" and "cleft palate."

The vast majority of children's deaths recorded at the Shanghai orphanage thus resulted not from lack of access to medical care but from something far more sinister: an apparently systematic program of child elimination in which senior medical staff played a central role. By making unfounded diagnoses of mental retardation and other disorders, these doctors have helped to disseminate the widespread belief which appears to be quite inaccurate that virtually all of China's abandoned children are physically or mentally handicapped. Worse, the Shanghai orphanage's medical staff then used these supposed disabilities as a justification for eliminating unwanted infants through starvation and medical neglect. Such unconscionable behavior by doctors in China's most advanced and cosmopolitan city points to an ethical crisis of immense proportions in the country's medical profession. This corruption of medical ethics reflects broader trends in Chinese law and health policy, including recent debates in the National People's Congress, the country's nominal legislature, on legalizing euthanasia for the incapacitated elderly. Official press reports indicate that the Chinese government may also have given serious consideration to allowing euthanasia for handicapped children, but has declined to do so for fear of the international repercussions. The medical evidence suggests, however, that just such pseudo-eugenic practices may have been carried out at the Shanghai Children's Welfare Institute. At the very least, the city's abandoned infants, even when not genuinely disabled, became the victims of a policy of deliberate and fatal neglect resulting in their wholesale death by default.

Reports from the Shanghai orphanage also indicate that medical staff there misused their authority in other ways. In several cases, children who were accused of misbehavior or were in a position to expose abuses at the orphanage were falsely diagnosed as "mentally ill" and transferred to psychiatric hospitals against their will; in one case, a teenage girl named Chou Hui was imprisoned for four months to prevent her from testifying that she had been raped by orphanage director Han Weicheng. Many other children were given powerful drugs without any apparent medical justification, in order to control their behavior. Human Rights Watch/Asia calls on the leaders of the Chinese medical profession to denounce these gross ethical violations and to take urgent steps to improve standards of medical ethics in China.

Notes and Questions

1. What ought to have been the consequences for China of its treatment of these abandoned children? The Human Rights Watch team was able to actually film inside some of the orphanages, making it more difficult for China to credibly deny the content of the report. How accessible are Chinese orphanages — or for that matter any orphanages — to the outside world in recent times? Should they be? What international body ought to have routine access to institutionalized children?

Russia has a massive problem with institutionalized children and street children. The fall of the Soviet Union, coupled with a vast national crisis of substance abuse, led to a situation of severely overcrowded state orphanages. As is clear from the Human Rights Watch report that follows, Soviet medical practices, particularly over-diagnosis of mental and cognitive problems, have been relied on extensively in the state orphanage system, where many of the children are treated as inherently damaged and incapable of rehabilitation. Despite the fact that the report is ten years old, there is little indication that Russia has managed to get its social orphan problem under humane control. If anything, there is good reason to believe that the number of parentless children in Russia continues to grow.

In Russia, as in other countries, one of the recent responses to outside pressure has been to develop a network of domestic foster care. As in other countries, it remains to be seen how successful such initiatives will be in serving the needs of children separated from their original families.

Human Rights Watch, *Abandoned to the State: Cruelty and Neglect in Russian Orphanages*

1998, *available at* http://www.hrw.org/reports/pdfs/c/crd/russ98d.pdf

SUMMARY

It is seven years since the declining Soviet Union released the last of its most renowned political dissidents, and closed a chapter of notorious human rights abuse in psychiatric hospitals and GULAG prisons. Yet today, in another archipelago of grim state institutions, the authorities of the Russian Federation are violating the fundamental rights of tens of thousands of innocent citizens: children abandoned to state orphanages.

Human Rights Watch has found that from the moment the state assumes their care, orphans in Russia—of whom 95 percent still have a living parent—are exposed to shocking levels of cruelty and neglect. Infants classified as disabled are segregated into "lying-down" rooms, where they are changed and fed but are bereft of stimulation and lacking in medical care.

Once officially labeled as retarded, Russian orphans face another grave and consequential violation of their rights around the age of four, when they are deemed "ineducable," and warehoused for life in psychoneurological *internaty*. In addition to receiving little to no education in such *internaty*, these orphans may be restrained in cloth sacks, tethered by a limb to furniture, denied stimulation, and sometimes left to lie half-naked in their own filth. Bedridden children aged five to seventeen are confined to understaffed lying-down rooms as in the baby houses, and in some cases are neglected to the point of death. Those who grow to adulthood are then interned in another "total institution," where they are permanently denied opportunities to know and enjoy their civil and political rights.

The "normal" abandoned children—those whom the state evaluates as intellectually capable of functioning on a higher level—are subjected to cruel, inhuman and degrading treatment by institution staff. They may be beaten, locked in freezing rooms for days at a time, abused physically and sexually. They may be humiliated, insulted and degraded, and provided inadequate education and training.

Staff members may also instigate or condone brutality by older orphans against younger and weaker ones, incidents such as beatings and humiliation. Some children describe treatment as outrageous as being thrown out a window while nailed in a small wooden chest. When orphans finally leave their institutions, they suffer its damaging effects and the second-class status as orphans for the rest of their lives.

It is ironic and deplorable that the very state that is charged with the care and nurture of these vulnerable children condemns them to a life of deprivation and cruelty. Moreover, far too many children are consigned to Russian institutions in the first place. Of a total of more than 600,000 children classified as being "without parental care," as many as one-third reside in institutions, while the rest are placed with a variety of guardians. Thousands more are temporarily quartered in various public shelters and institutions under police jurisdiction simply waiting for an available space in an orphanage.

Humane alternatives to institutions exist and should be used, such as sending children with moderate disabilities home with their parents at birth; providing help for families to cope with their children's disabilities; and providing foster care for children who cannot return to their families. As Russian experts told Human Rights Watch in the body of this report, these alternatives do not require additional resources, but rather a reallocation of existing funds now devoted almost exclusively to expensive institutional care.

Abandoned Children as an Underclass

Human Rights Watch has found that from the moment Russian children are left in state institutions, they become victims of long-held prejudices that all abandoned children are in some way "defective." One source of this discriminatory assumption is the tradition that infants born with severe congenital defects have been abandoned in local maternity wards under pressure and warnings from the medical staff that the family will be ostracized for raising a disabled child.

Even if abandoned infants do not display severe physical or mental disabilities, however, they often come from families with chronic social, financial and health problems— including alcoholism—and they cannot escape the stigma applied to that past. A clear summary of this point appeared in an article in the *Moscow Times* of November 2, 1996, which explored the biases against adopting a baby abandoned by a stranger:

> The fear that the child will in some way be "damaged goods" stems from the knowledge that mothers of mentally and physically handicapped children are routinely advised by doctors to put their baby in an orphanage and "try again." Consequently, healthy babies who are given up for financial or domestic reasons are unfairly branded "defective."

The result is that abandoned children are consigned to the status of "orphan," and further labelled in their medical charts with physical and psychological "risk factors" in their medical charts owing to their background. Testimonies collected by Human Rights Watch are corroborated by the findings of expert investigators from the Swiss-based Comité pour la Dignité de l'Enfant (C.I.D.E.), published in 1995. They found that while Russian professionals used strict criteria in performing psychological evaluations, they also recorded factors in the child's medical history which would be considered as "risk" factors in the West, but commonly become labels of illness for an abandoned Russian child. According to the C.I.D.E. report, these include:

- babies born to alcoholic parents or whose mothers suffered depression during pregnancy will be labeled encephalopathic and remain so until they come of age.
- orphans will be classed as being mentally deficient.
- children with a single physical malformation (a harelip or speech defect ...) become subnormal in the eyes of Russian doctors.

International human rights law forbids discrimination on a variety of grounds, including "birth or other status." Under the United Nations' "Principles for the Protection of Persons with Mental Illness and the Improvement of Mental Health Care," Principle number 4 provides that, "A determination of mental illness shall never be made on the basis of political, economic or social status, or membership of a cultural, racial or religious group, or any other reason not directly relevant to mental health status."

In practice, however, the Russian system violates this principle as well as the fundamental tenets of the International Covenant on Economic, Social and Cultural Rights, by branding children of lower socioeconomic origins and children with genetic abnormalities as a class apart.

It does so by attributing to them a propensity for social deviance stemming from their background, and by imposing upon them a life-long stigma and formal restrictions on participation in society. Abandoned children who are diagnosed as "*oligophrenic*," or mentally retarded, carry that label in their official dossier from institution to institution. They have virtually no channels through which to seek a reassessment or reversal of this diagnosis, and even "mild" *oligophrenics* who graduate from technical training schools told Human Rights Watch that they had difficulty appealing for the word to be removed from their file.

Human Rights Watch concludes that the Russian state fails to provide sufficient protection and opportunities to thousands of children who are abandoned to the state at a rate of 113,000 a year for the past two years, up dramatically from 67,286 in 1992. The evidence gathered reveals several systematic disadvantages imposed on young Russian orphans, which violate their fundamental rights to survival and development, and place them in an underclass.

. . . .

Orphans in Russia have no one to appeal the state's special medical-developmental evaluation, which is performed on virtually all institutionalized children approaching the first year of school and older children at the time of abandonment.... [A] diagnosis of severe *oligophrenia* for orphans means a greater likelihood of premature death in an institution that is little more than a warehouse.

According to this "diagnosis," which is delivered by a state-run commission of doctors, psychologists, and educators based at the Chief Psychiatric Hospital No.6 in Moscow, children in Russian institutions face a "*triage*" into one of two tunnel-like systems apart from Russian society at large.... [I]n the best case, they are deemed educable, and proceed to a *dyetskii dom* run by the Ministry of Education, and attend regular Russian schools. In the worst case, they are deemed severely oligophrenic—either *imbetsil* or *idiot*—and condemned to a system of "total institutions" run by the Ministry of Labor and Social Development. There they receive little to no education and only a minimum of maintenance until they reach the age of eighteen, when they move on to an adult institution of the same kind. As the later chapters of this report show, independent child welfare experts in Russia denounce these institutions, claiming that the death rate for children is twice that of children living at home.

The comparatively fortunate orphans who make it into the educable group are still more likely to receive harsher discipline than children whose parents have left them only temporarily in state custody and continue to have contact with the orphanage.

Orphans in state institutions are less likely to be referred for needed medical services than are children with parents. Should orphans happen to be transferred to a hospital for services, they are less likely to receive proper medical treatment than children whose families can cajole and bribe hospital staff to carry out their work appropriately.

Failure to Live Up to National Commitments

The Russian government and its predecessor, the USSR, have long taken pride in the education and upbringing of their children. Its separate world of giant orphanages reflects the Soviet philosophy of collective action and discipline that guided the institutions erected to house millions of war orphans during the first half of the 20th century.

Since the break-up of the Soviet Union in 1991, however, the increased access to orphanages by journalists and charitable volunteers has unveiled a tableau of horrific conditions and malign neglect in institutions from the heart of Moscow to remote rural provinces. The Russian and international media have widely disseminated the shocking images from the orphanages during the past few years, and at least two international human rights delegations have issued damning reports of their findings, which are cited in the body of this report. Yet deplorable conditions still persist.

Officially, the Russian authorities, starting with President Boris Yeltsin, have repeatedly declared the rights of children a high national priority. The Russian Federation was among the first nations to sign and ratify the U.N. Convention on the Rights of the Child in 1990.... Russia has subsequently submitted two periodic reports of its implementation of the Convention on the Rights of the Child, in 1992 and late 1997.

Also during the 1990s, Russia passed a raft of legislation and decrees affirming children's rights to education, health, and special protection against the hardships and upheaval wrought by economic reform. By mid-decade, President Yeltsin had launched two federal programs, "Children of Russia," and "Fundamental Directions of State Social Policy for Improving the Position of Children in the Russian Federation to the Year 2000." These programs are aimed at increasing the efficiency of state programs for children at the federal and local levels, and helping poorer families to provide a stable environment in which a child may develop.

In practice, however, the reaction of the Russian authorities to the critique of their orphanages has been to block access to the institutions; punish or threaten to fire workers if they speak about abuses; and, in some instances, pardon those who are responsible for the wrongdoing.

Senior officials of the three ministries charged with maintaining the orphanages have impeded the efforts of Russian human rights organizations to investigate reports of neglect and malfeasance. Members of such groups and child welfare experts told Human Rights Watch that senior officials flatly rejected their requests to visit the particularly degrading and unhealthy psychoneurological *internaty* run by the Ministry of Labor and Social Development for orphans diagnosed as *imbetsily* and *idioty*.

Failure to Comply with International Obligations

Although the Russian government has signed the Convention on the Rights of the Child, the evidence gathered and presented in this report shows that Russian policies toward abandoned children violate as many as twenty of the convention's first forty-one articles, which comprise a sweeping array of basic rights.

....

Contrary to the precepts set forth in Article 23 of the Convention on the Rights of the Child, specifically concerning children with mental and physical disabilities, Russian orphans with severe disabilities are denied virtually every right to medical care, education, and individual development.

Such orphans are officially classified as "ineducable," and are excluded from opportunities to learn to read, write, and in some cases, to walk. In addition, abandoned babies and children of sound mind, but with physical disabilities, are routinely confined to areas in state institutions known as "lying-down" rooms. They are passed over for corrective surgery of conditions such as cleft palate as a result of the compound stigma of being abandoned and being diagnosed as "*oligophrenic*" (mentally retarded).

During a visit to the lying-down room of one psychoneurological *internat*, Human Rights Watch noticed a beaming blond, five-year-old boy walking on the callused sides of his club feet. We asked the *sanitarka* who was playing with him what his diagnosis was. "*Oligophrenia*," she replied. But when we asked specifically about his feet, she replied, "Well, it's the same ... *imbetsilnost*."

In addition to the appalling violation of the rights of orphans with severe congenital disabilities, critics of the state's diagnostic procedure also expressed their concerns time and again to Human Rights Watch that too many children were, in fact, wrongly diagnosed. Even the staff at two institutions told Human Rights Watch that they believed that nine to ten percent of the children transferred to them as *imbetsily* and *idioty*, actually had the ability to enjoy productive lives.

. . . .

In view of the known and suspected cases of misdiagnosis among orphans, Human Rights Watch finds the violation of Article 27 of the Convention on the Rights of the Child particularly relevant. It accords children undergoing medical care the right to periodic review of their treatment and surrounding conditions. In practice, however, Russian orphans with diagnoses of *oligophrenia* have extreme difficulty seeking a re-assessment of their status, which is also a violation of Russian law. Even those classified as "lightly" *oligophrenic* (*debil*) carry the burden of that classification in their official file when they embark on their search for jobs and homes.

The most severe discrimination faced by Russian orphans is suffered by children interned in psychoneurological *internaty* for children with disabilities who are aged five to seventeen years. Article 39 of the convention calls for the promotion of "physical and psychological recovery and social reintegration following neglect, exploitation or abuse ... or any other form of cruel, inhuman or degrading treatment or punishment."

Far from receiving treatment towards recovery or rehabilitation, however, Russian orphans consigned to lying-down rooms suffer further deterioration from neglect. Agitated orphans are confined to barren day-rooms where they are tethered, restrained, and given powerful sedatives without medical supervision.

Such examples of inhuman and degrading treatment and punishment are all too common features of Russian orphanages, both for children with severe disabilities, and as well for those diagnosed as "educable." In the latter case, Human Rights Watch discovered elaborate patterns of dehumanizing discipline in the *dyetskiye doma* of the Education Ministry, in which the orphanage directors and staff strove to humiliate children in front of their peers, and at times encouraged their peers to take part in the demeaning punishment.

Such choreography of cruelty by orphanage staff is often devised for the purpose of punishment-by-proxy, through which older or stronger children are delegated to maintain order. The resulting disciplinary pattern alarmingly resembles that found in the Russian military and prisons, both state institutions notorious for their elaborate systems of violence and debasement. Whether for punishment or for simple sadism, this practice amounts to a training module in physical and mental violence.

Moreover, the common practice of interning older children in psychiatric hospitals for rule-breaking behavior such as running away from the orphanage is a perversion of medical ethics and an alarming throwback to the gross misconduct of the Soviet psychiatric profession. Children returning from two weeks to several months in the *psykhushka* report the use of heavy tranquilizers, and appear disoriented and confused to their peers.

These preeminent uses of violence against Russian orphans violate the Convention against Torture and Other Cruel, Inhuman or Degrading Treatment or Punishment, as well as other international standards pertaining to medical ethics and the treatment of persons with mental illness.

. . . .

Notes and Questions

1. Cultural, historical and of course economic factors play a large part in how parents decide whether or not to parent a particular child. What are the motivating factors behind child abandonment in China? By contrast, how does the orphanage as a social institution function in Russia and the former Soviet Union? What might a process of deinstitutionalization look like in each country?

2. How do the documented abuses in Chinese orphanages differ from the documented abuses in Russian orphanages? How are they similar? The level of interest shown by Human Rights Watch in orphanages seemed to peak in the 1990s. Does it seem that these reports generated a broad interest by the international community in institutionalized children?

3. Both articles discuss the role of medical professionals in caring for the children in Chinese and Russian orphanages. In China, the cause of death for many children has been linked to deliberate policy choices, while in Russia, couples who give birth to a handicapped child are advised by doctors to put their baby in an orphanage and "try again". Are medical professionals in both countries partly to blame for the treatment of these children? Is there any way to influence the actions of medical professionals with regard to the protection of these children? Would a focus by the international community on the role played by medical professionals be a more effective approach than attempting to achieve a general alteration of each state's child welfare policies?

---

2. More Hidden Camera Revelations

Despite the fact that Human Rights Watch has not been active in exposing problems in orphanages in recent years, other groups have continued to document abuses. Some of the most dramatic work of this kind has been done by Mental Disability Rights International (MDRI). MDRI was founded by Eric Rosenthal in 1993, and has attempted, through its skilled hidden camera work, to raise awareness of the adverse conditions in which mentally disabled people are often forced to live. It should be noted that MDRI's work has also made clear that many of the "disabilities" of children in institutions are often very minor ones that are made infinitely worse by neglect.

The report that follows was particularly galling to the Romanian government, as the Romanians had made strenuous efforts, in the run up to EU membership, to show that they had phased out the notorious state institutions associated with the "bad old days" of the brutal Ceausescu regime. MDRI was able to demonstrate that in fact, behind closed doors, criminal neglect of children continues to occur in Romania.

Mental Disability Rights International,
Hidden Suffering: Romania's Segregation and Abuse of Infants and Children with Disabilities

2006, *available at* http://www.crin.org/docs/mhri_rom.pdf

Preface: Goals and Methods of this Report

Hidden Suffering: Romania's Segregation and Abuse of Infants and Children with Disabilities describes the findings of an 18-month investigation in Romania by Mental Disability Rights International (MDRI) on the human rights of people with mental disabilities (this is a broad term that includes people with a diagnosis of mental illness and people with an intellectual disability such as mental retardation). This work is the product of visits to Romania in February, June and December 2005 and February 2006. MDRI's visits to adult facilities were conducted jointly with the Center for Legal Resources (CLR). MDRI conducted all site visits to children's institutions and interviews with child protections authorities on its own.

Introduction

Romania inherited an extensive system of segregated services for children and adults with mental disabilities from the former regime of Nicolae Ceausescu. Since1989, there has been extensive international attention and assistance to bring an end to the problem of Romania's orphanages. Over the last decade, model community-based programs have been established in Romania, demonstrating that children and adults with mental disabilities can live successfully in the community. Romania has created an extensive "maternal assistance program" to provide substitute family (foster) placement for many children once left in orphanages. A family support program has also been created to assist families of children with disabilities.

As of 2006, however, Romanian's National Authority on Child Protection statistics state that there remain more than 31,000 children in institutions under their supervision. In addition, at least 9,000 babies are abandoned each year—a rate of abandonment that has not changed over thirty years. At least 700 abandoned children have never left the maternity wards of hospitals. Most maternity wards do not allow new mothers to stay with their infants while they are in the hospital. Authorities at the National Authority for Children's Rights told MDRI in 2006 that doctors still encourage parents to give up a child when the child is born with a disability. UNICEF concludes from a recent study of child abandonment that "[t]he acceptance and perpetuation of such situations constitutes not only a violation of the law, but also an acute lack of understanding of the child's developmental needs."

Once a child is abandoned, government action further increases the likelihood that the child will be institutionalized. According to UNICEF, "two-thirds of the children abandoned in maternity wards are transferred at least once to pediatric/recovery wards before any protection measures are taken." Of the total number of abandoned babies, 64% in maternity wards and 30% in pediatric hospitals have no name or identity papers. Without identity papers, children cannot receive community-based services or even basic medical care.

MDRI is concerned that the actual number of institutionalized children may be much higher than officially recognized. MDRI's investigation found children detained outside the child protection system in psychiatric facilities, institutions for adults with disabilities, and other hospitals. A complex division of responsibilities for these facilities—divided between the Ministry of Health, the Ministry of Labor, Social Solidarity and Family, as well as local governments—means that no one authority makes policies or can be held accountable for conditions in these institutions. The National Authority for Persons with Handicap (NAPH) reports to the Ministry of Labor about the facilities under its authority, but there is no system in place for holding anyone accountable for the implementation of standards within this system. In February 2006, the Ministry of Health reported to the Prime Minister's office that they could not plan for service system reform because they do not know the number of people in psychiatric facilities, why they are there, or what their needs are.

MDRI has found serious human rights violations in facilities that are out of public view. These findings have been corroborated in reports published by the Center for Legal

Resources, Amnesty International, ABC News, and numerous Romanian journalists. MDRI is particularly concerned about the abandoned infants and young children who are at an extremely vulnerable time of development and will bear scars from this neglect over their lifetimes.

I. Hidden Babies: Infants in Institutions

In January 2005, Romania's Law 272, providing for the protection and promotion of the rights of the child, entered into force. Included in this law was the ban of the placement of children two years old and younger in residential institutions.

> *The placement of the child who has not yet reached the age of 2 years old may only be decided with the extended or substitute family, and it is forbidden to place him or her in a residential service.* — *Article 60, paragraph 1*

However, this law does not extend protection to babies with disabilities.

> *As an exception to the provision stipulated under paragraph (1), the placement in a residential service of the child who has not yet reached the age of 2 years old may only occur in the case in which the child has a severe disability and is dependent on specialized residential care services.* — *Article 60, paragraph 2*

In each of the site visits described below, MDRI investigators have found a disparate pattern of children and babies being labeled with "severe disabilities." The phrase apparently can be used whenever it is administratively convenient, and it is often applied to children with little or no disability.

A. Visit to an institution for newborns in Timisoara

In the city of Timisoara, MDRI investigators asked the local child protection authorities about the placement of newborn children with disabilities. At first, they denied the existence of institutions outside their authority. When asked about infants with severe disabilities, however, authorities informed investigators that there might be children in an institution under local health authorities. Authorities stated they did not know how many such children there were, however, or what forms of treatment they received. They said they were unable to arrange a visit to the facility.

MDRI investigators then visited a ward for newborns in a general hospital. When investigators asked about abandoned babies, nurses said that there was an institution for them several blocks away. At this institution, staff told investigators that the facility housed 62 children from newborns through age two. Investigators counted 65 babies at the institution. The youngest was a three-week old infant. Despite being referred to as the *Sectia De Recuperare Nutritionala*, or a nutritional recuperation center, staff informed investigators that most infants abandoned in this facility were not placed there for nutritional reasons.

MDRI learned that most of the babies were permanently abandoned and had resided there since birth. According to the nurse, reasons for abandonment include "abuse, brain injury, heart disease, poverty and premature birth." None of the children, the nurse reported, had a "severe disability," other than the disabilities they acquired from being institutionalized.

> *Some children are here because their parents do not have enough heating fuel. When it gets cold, we have more babies.* — *Staff, Timisoara baby institution*

The facility's entire staff consisted of one nurse and three caregivers. Each staff member works a 12 hour shift. According to the nurse on duty, there was no specialized medical care available at the institution and staff were only able to treat simple ailments such as a cold. During MDRI's visit, the caregivers were feverishly involved in feeding and changing the babies. Overwhelmed with this task, staff said they could do little else. Under the circumstances, the facility was strikingly clean. Without more staff, however, the children live for years without leaving their cribs. Of 65 children, investigators observed only 2 children out of their cribs sitting in doughnut-shaped walkers located near the changing station, where staff could keep an eye on them as they changed diapers.

After a while, they just stop crying. — Nurse, Timisoara baby institution

Children who do not receive attention when they cry learn to stop crying. During MDRI's visit, there was an eerie silence about the facility. Only one baby on the ground floor was crying; staff informed investigators that this child had been placed in the institution the day before. While about one-third of the babies were sleeping, two-thirds were awake but there were no sounds of cooing or babbling, normal developmental sounds of babies that age.

We do our best, but it is impossible for us to stop the spread of lice and contagious diseases.... I give an injection and a baby cries and I have to keep going. There are too many. They get disabled from being here. — Nurse, Timisoara baby institution

The facility was organized with the youngest children on the first floor and the older children on the second floor. Walking through the facility, investigators witnessed how the children abandoned in the facility had become more disabled the longer they had been in the institution. The older children in the facility, aged one to two years, were able to sit up in their cribs, but there was no talking or other sounds as would be developmentally appropriate. As investigators entered the rooms with slightly older children, the children were rocking back and forth, with little or no reaction to investigators' presence in the room. By age two, some of the children had begun to bang their heads against the walls as a form of self-stimulation. Others were making the rhythmic sounds from dislocated jaws common in children left lying down for extended periods with no opportunity to leave their cribs.

Many of the babies had no identity papers and therefore "do not exist" according to the state, said the nurse, remarking, "Many are Roma." Staff informed MDRI investigators that some children with little or no disability could easily be adopted, but they are trapped in the facility only because they lack identity papers.

I have worked here for twenty years and my heart has turned to stone. I thought it would be better after the revolution, but it is not. — Nurse, Timisoara baby institution

MDRI was extremely impressed by the staff's dedication and caring for the children at this facility, despite the impossible job they had of attending to so many children.

B. Findings of other studies

. . . .

Care France is one organization that has investigated the institutionalization and abandonment of newborns and children in Romania. Their most recent report was based on visits to 12 different facilities in October 2005. The report expressed concern that maternity wards were slowly becoming orphanages and quoted one doctor in a maternity ward as saying that babies there "never leave their cribs." Additionally, they found "deplorable conditions" in many of the orphanages they visited. This included plumbing that did not function, "boys and girls indistinguishable [from each other]," children "crammed in tiny rooms," and in winter, "not enough heat." They found some children "reduced to the state of animals."

. . . .

The majority of Romanian leaders, both in Bucharest and in the provinces, are perfectly aware of the senselessness of this situation and are desirous of taking measures to remedy the situation. But none of them dare publicly express their opinion for fear of reprisals from Brussels, which would threaten the process of Romania's accession to the European Union.—Care France 2005 report

II. Dangerous Conditions of Children in Adult Institutions

In February 2006, Romania's national health authorities flatly denied the existence of children in adult facilities. The State Secretary for Medical Assistance, the chief authority on mental health at the Ministry of Health, vehemently denied the existence of any infants or children under age two in health care institutions—apart from the 700 officially acknowledged children in maternity wards—stating that this was prohibited by Law 272. In MDRI's limited survey of adult facilities conducted between February 2005 and February 2006, MDRI found children in five institutions outside the child protection system (in addition to the health care facility for infants described above). The following represents a sample of what MDRI believes exists in institutions across Romania.

A. The horrors of Braila: June 2005

This is like the middle ages. We are ashamed at what is happening here.—Psychiatrist on the children's neuropsychiatric ward, St. Pantelimon Psychiatric Institution

In June 2005, a team of MDRI investigators, along with staff of the Center for Legal Resources (CLR), a Romanian non-governmental organization that monitors psychiatric institutions, documented the abusive conditions of 46 children at the St. Pantelimon adult psychiatric facility in Braila. Several months prior to MDRI's June 2005 visit, CLR filed a written complaint with the national child protection agency but received no response.

I have visited institutions in twenty countries around the world. What I witnessed in Braila was the most disturbing horror I have ever seen. These children were close to death.—MDRI investigator

MDRI investigators found children between the ages of 7 to 17 in this facility.

The children were so emaciated many of them looked like they were 3 or 4 years old. Their spindly arms and legs were twisted into contorted positions from disuse and atrophy. Their eyes were deeply sunken into their skulls, and they stared blankly at us when we entered the room. Ribs and other bones stuck out from their skin, which seemed to sag from their bodies without any extra flesh. Some children were missing patches of hair, others were bald.—MDRI investigator

A large portion of the children investigators observed were self-abusive.

They were biting down hard on their fingers and forearms, leaving bloody patches or raw stubs for fingertips. One child sat stabbing himself in the eyes during our entire visit. Another ingested a long string, spat it out, and ingested it again over and over. We observed one child who sat with his entire hand up to his wrist shoved into his mouth. Many of the children sat rhythmically rocking back and forth in their cribs.—MDRI investigator

According to one MDRI investigator, a nurse who is an expert in children with disabilities:

Self-abuse is created and exacerbated among children who receive no love and attention and who are left abandoned to beds or cribs with no attention. Psychological experts agree that they crave some form of stimulus, so they cause themselves pain just to feel something.—Karen Green McGowan, RN, expert on children with complex developmental disabilities

MDRI investigators interviewed staff who revealed that many of the children never leave their beds or cribs. Those few who were dressed and sitting in chairs never go outside or have any form of activity. Investigators interviewed staff who were completely unaware of any of the common behavioral treatments for self-abuse. They did not know that stimuli, attention or activity would help alleviate the self-abuse.

Instead of giving these children attention, staff tied them down. In the first room investigators visited, children sat staring into space or nearly immobile around a barren table. There were torn strips of cloth on their small chairs. When investigators asked the staff, they confirmed that these strips of cloth are used to tie the children to chairs.

In the next room, where children were detained in cribs, almost all the children were still restrained. In addition to having their arms and legs tied to the bars of their cribs, some children were wrapped head to toe in bed sheets. When MDRI investigators unwrapped the sheets, they found many children left sitting in their own urine and feces. The stench of human excrement was overpowering.

Some children were tied so tightly in bed sheets investigators could not remove them. As one investigator related:

> *Staff agreed to unwrap several of the children. One girl, whose name was Adinana, looked to be about 4 or 5 years old, but was actually17 and weighed no more than 25 pounds (about 10 kilos). As the staff removed the restraint, her skin came off with the sheet, leaving a raw open wound beneath it. Another boy looked to be the size of a baby, but was seven years old. He too, when unwrapped, was wasting away, his legs covered with sores and his fingers chewed and swollen. — MDRI investigator*

Many of the children's arms and legs were atrophied and twisted into pretzel-like shapes from disuse. A 12 year-old boy, who appeared to be no more than 6, lay in a crib with his legs and feet tied up over his head.

After MDRI and CLR brought the dire situation of these children to government attention, the children were moved to two smaller institutions for children. With a grant from UNICEF, CLR brought in Karen Green McGowan, an expert in the treatment of children with complex developmental disabilities and one of the top nurses in her specialty from the United States. In addition to her assessment, Ms. McGowan developed a habilitation plan for each child. In her opinion, *none* of these children needed to be in an institution for medical reasons. Indeed, each of them needed to be in a home-like setting with a family who could give them love and attention.

. . . .

When MDRI returned to Romania in December 2005, all of the children in Braila had been moved to two, much improved institutions with considerably more staff attention. In this short time, they had gained a significant amount of weight. Their lives have clearly been saved by this intervention. Yet all of these children remained in institutions despite McGowan's recommendations. . . .

. . . .

C. Harmful effects of "smaller" institutions

As described above, in recent years the reform of Romania's child protection system has included the establishment of 200 new institutions with 50 or fewer children. As site visits to the facility in Timisoara demonstrate, smaller institutions retain many or all of the harmful characteristics of larger facilities.

There is a parallel process that explains the apparent decline in numbers of large adult facilities. At a meeting of the Intersectorial Committee for Coordination in Mental Health in February 2006, this process of re-classifying patients into smaller institutions—without actually moving them—was confirmed by a representative of the National Authority for Persons with Handicap (NAPH). He justified the value of the practice and defended the importance of smaller administrative units, even if the same number of patients shared a building. At least, he said, the smaller facilities would have two directors rather than one, and this would facilitate more effective administration.

Throughout Romania, children have been shuffled from one institution to another. While smaller institutions may appear to be an improvement, they do not provide the family-like environment that a child needs and deserves. Twenty, 30 or 50 children living together in a congregate setting will be denied the close emotional ties that are established in a true family setting.

Over the last 50 years, researchers have documented the damaging consequences of placing children in institutions. When infants are placed in institutions, there is a significant risk of death from diarrhea and other contagious diseases. While dangers are particularly great during infancy, children placed at an older age are also vulnerable. These dangers include cognitive problems, severe emotional and behavioral disorders, a syndrome that mimics autism, sensory integration issues, speech and language delays, serious medical problems, and deficiencies in physical growth. While it is hard to document, children in institutions in any country are likely at a higher risk of physical and sexual abuse than other children. Clinicians working in U.S. institutions in the 1960s observed a high rate of death among newly placed infants. Children born with a disability, who need specialized care, are even more at risk when placed in an institution.

. . . .

Notes and Questions

1. Just as in the early 1990s, we are still reliant on "hidden camera" work to gain access to children locked away in institutions. What methods did Mental Disability Rights International use in Romania? What did they manage to reveal about the child welfare system in that country? What does it say about children's rights that we continue to learn about parentless children through the efforts of groups working undercover? Recently, the British television station, BBC Four, documented similar abuses in Bulgarian child welfare institutions. See http://www.bbc.co.uk/bbcfour/documentaries/features/bulgarias-children.shtml.

2. In 2007, a woman at a maternity hospital in Yekaterinburg, Russia, noticed that abandoned babies had had their mouths taped shut by staff frustrated by their crying. Her video of these children, captured on her cell phone, set off a firestorm of criticism, and revived the debate on Russia's huge and grossly underserved population of social orphans. See http://www.guardian.co.uk/world/2007/feb/02/russia.lukeharding. With regard to the fall-out within Russia from that event, the editor of the local newspaper explained that he often heard about babies being mistreated in hospitals, but that people were afraid to expose the problem and lose their jobs. He told the BBC that abandoned children are often left for months in maternity hospitals, because of lack of places at local child welfare institutions. See Patrick Johnson, *Russia's unwanted babies in hospital limbo*, 2007, *available at* http://news.bbc.co.uk/2/hi/europe/6335201.stm.

Russia has struggled to find solutions to this immense set of problems. A 2005 report indicates that the yearly adoption rate within Russia is only 7,000 children, a very small fraction of the total requiring homes. *See Recommendations on the Results of the Round Table Meeting "Right of a Child to Have a Family: Problems Connected with Family Placement"*, March 28, 2005, *available at* http://www.pravorebenka.narod.ru/eng/docs/fin_rt_280320005.doc. There is anecdotal evidence to suggest that Russia attempts to maintain a "balance", such that international adoptions should not exceed the number of domestic adoptions.

3. In early 2008, researchers led by Dr. Charles Nelson of Harvard Medical School published the results of their years-long study on the effects of institutional life on the developing child's brain. The Bucharest Early Intervention Project, as it is called, has provided the clearest data yet that the young infant is seriously damaged when not raised in a family setting. The project's published results are invaluable in providing scientific certainly to what many had already assumed: that waiting to place a child in an alternative family when the original family is not available is disastrous in child welfare terms. Nelson and his team trained special foster carers in Romania to provide family life to children who had been institutionalized. The improvements were, not surprisingly, dramatic. The team cautioned however, that after two years of age, it is increasingly difficult to say whether the early effects of institutional neglect can be undone. A summary of Nelson's results may be found at: http://www.newsdesk.umd.edu/sociss/release.cfm?ArticleID=1568.

----

3. Damaging Effects of Residential Care

It is well known that thousands of children live in abusive conditions in residential institutions. All parties involved in child welfare now acknowledge that national policy on social orphans should include institutional care only to the smallest degree possible. However, the more difficult questions arise when it comes time to decide how national policy should be framed when the residential institutions are phased out. While child welfare bodies like UNICEF and Save the Children have been adamant in their insistence on a greater role for in-country solutions, such as family reunification, extended family care, and small group or foster care homes, it is difficult to determine the degree to which these bodies have been successful in bringing about positive changes on a broad scale. Even where the opposition to intercountry adoption by the international child welfare bodies has been toned down, they continue to press for a reduced role for international adoption in the overall set of solutions for problems faced by social orphans.

The brief article that follows makes clear that, in addition to the various forms of physical and cognitive impairments that result from institutionalizing of children, these children are also vulnerable to abuse by other residents and staff.

UNICEF Press Center, *Children in Residential Institutions Desperately Vulnerable to Abuse*

2005, available at http://www.unicef.org/infobycountry/media_27185.html

Violence against children in residential institutions can be found across Europe and Central Asia, according to research gathered by UNICEF in the run-up to a major conference on violence against children. The research also reveals glaring gaps in knowledge and data.

"Children in residential institutions—from children's homes to detention centres—are desperately vulnerable," said Maria Calivis, UNICEF Regional Director for Central and Eastern Europe and the Commonwealth of Independent States. "They are vulnerable because they are separated from society in a 'closed' environment. And the more closed that environment is, the greater the risk of violence and the smaller the chance that it will be reported.

"We have to remember that things have already gone badly wrong for the children who end up in institutions," she added. "They are already scarred by family troubles and that only increases their vulnerability."

. . . .

Nobody knows exactly how many children are living in institutions in Europe and Central Asia. The most conservative estimates put the figure at around one million.

"There is a serious and fundamental knowledge gap on the numbers," said Calivis "which makes the issue 'invisible' and undermines the chance of an effective response."

The research is likely to fuel debate at the forthcoming Regional Consultation:

- Ongoing investigations in Ireland testify to abuse over decades: an inquiry has received 3,000 complaints, 60 per cent of them from those over 50 who were abused as children in institutions;

- The Committee on the Rights of the Child has expressed concern at the lack of a clear ban on corporal punishment in institutions in Belgium, Czech Republic, France, Kyrgyzstan and Moldova;

- A report on Kazakhstan shows that 80 per cent of children in residential schools are treated "cruelly";

- Interviews with children in institutions in the UK found that 62 out of 71 reported physical violence between children. Half had experienced physical violence ranging from knife attacks, kicks and punches to damage to their personal property and threats.

- UNICEF sounds the alarm on juvenile justice, with research suggesting that juvenile offenders may face the greatest risk of violence in the earliest, pre-trial stages. The Committee on the Rights of the Child has raised the issue of police officers ill-treating children and young people in police custody in Albania, France, Georgia, Romania, Switzerland, Ukraine and Uzbekistan. Young people may also be kept in pre-trial custody alongside adults, increasing the risk of abuse. In Germany there is evidence that they have been threatened, blackmailed and even raped. In Croatia, custodial staff have been seen to punch, kick or hit young people with batons. . . .

UNICEF calls on . . . [government ministers] to:

- Legislate to ban all forms of violence against all children in all settings—institutions, schools, the home and the community;

- Ensure that the institutionalisation or detention of children is a measure of last resort;

- Set in motion the region-wide gathering of consistent, comparable and disaggregated data on children in institutions;

- Screen staff working with these children, pay them properly and ensure that they are qualified to deal with the tensions and conflicts that can erupt into violence;

- Create effective complaints channels for children in institutions and make sure that the children know about them;

- Ensure that these children have regular contact with their own families, unless this would put them at risk.

B. The Heated Debate over Intercountry Adoption: What Place Should It Have in National Child Welfare Policies?

A very small percentage of the world's social orphans have found families through international adoption. Especially in countries where domestic adoption is not culturally familiar or acceptable, yet where there are large numbers of children living out of parental care, children in need of families have been matched with adoptive parents, mainly in the United States and Europe. Sweden is said to have the highest per capita rate of international adoption of any nation, but the largest number of children are adopted into the United States. International adoption, or intercountry adoption as it is often called, is far from problem free, however. It is vehemently opposed by many sectors, including nationalists in "sending" countries from which many children are adopted, as well as many international child welfare professionals. The UN child rights bodies have been lukewarm at best towards the phenomenon of intercountry adoption. While avoiding blanket denunciation, these bodies, including the UNCRC Committee and UNICEF, have often been critical of intercountry adoption, and have been notoriously reluctant to support it, let alone promote its proliferation.[1] For some, the child's right to a family, through intercountry adoption if necessary, stands at odds with the child's other rights to culture and identity. Others believe that international adoption involves such stark economic differentials (as between the family of origin and the adopting family) that it is difficult, perhaps impossible, to construct ethical intercountry adoption practices.

Advocates for international adoption point to its direct benefits for vulnerable children; how it brings love, hope and permanency to children who would in all likelihood not otherwise have enjoyed any of these. Critics point to the potential for corruption, and argue that international adoption might also act as a "safety valve" for national governments, absolving those governments from responsibility for devising family reunification and community-based child welfare policies. Many are troubled that international adoption has the effect of cutting children off from their cultures of birth. As mentioned above, some have argued that international adoption simply cannot be purged of its tendency to involve economic inducements. In the recent past, some international adoption programs have closed down because of allegations that birth families were either manipulated into allowing the adoption to occur, or offered economic inducements. In other cases (Cambodia and Vietnam) the U.S. authorities have stated that, without greater accountability and ethical reform, the U.S. will no longer allow Americans to adopt from these countries.

The articles that follow explore the intercountry adoption debate in the context of international children's rights. Before beginning this section, reread the relevant portions of the UNCRC dealing with children in state care and the child's right to culture (Arti-

---

1. UNICEF published an "official" position on intercountry adoption in 2003. While it did not state outright opposition to the practice, it certainly offered no endorsement. UNICEF has apparently continued to work with countries to promote in-country foster care in preference to international adoption. Their 2003 statement is available at http://www.unicef.org/media/media_41118.html.

cles 20–21, 30–31). Also refer to the widely ratified 1993 Hague Convention on Intercountry Adoption[2] (reproduced in the appendix to this book), a product of the Hague Conference on Private International Law, and designed to assist contracting states in devising ethical and consistent procedures to safeguard children, birth families and adoptive parents in intercountry adoption. The United States has recently taken steps to finalize its ratification of this convention.

The three articles that follow explore a core difficulty in evaluating international adoption: whether internationally adopted children are truly benefited by the practice, or whether such adoptions involve unavoidable exploitation and inequality. This depends, of course, on what measures one uses to make this determination. The first two articles explore the problem of racial and cultural identity in international adoption, reaching very different conclusions as to the validity of family formation through these adoptions.

Kathleen Ja Sook Bergquist, *International Asian Adoption: In the Best Interest of the Child?*

10 Texas Wesleyan Law Review 343 (2004)

Domestic and international adoption legislation and practice has purported to take into account the "best interests of the child." More specifically, the United Nations Convention on the Rights of the Child (CRC) and subsequently the Hague Convention on the Protection of Children and Cooperation in Respect of Intercountry Adoption specifies as a goal, "To establish safeguards to ensure that intercountry adoptions take place in the best interests of the child...." Given the significant increase in parents who adopt for reasons of infertility or as single parents, and the market demand which has arisen, it would be difficult for anyone to argue that international adoption today exists solely to find homes for parentless children. The purpose of this Paper is to examine the sociopolitical assumptions and implications that are inherent in the placing of children in the diaspora as involuntary immigrants, and whether in fact it is the best interests of the children that are considered. Asian adoption is herein positioned within the history of international adoption, transracial adoption, and shifting parental motivations for adoption.

International adoption in the United States began with the placement of children from Europe following World War II. It grew out of the need to find families for orphans and was viewed as a humanitarian solution. This precedent paved the way for Korean orphans beginning in 1954. These children were largely the products of the United States and other allied nations' presence in Korea, and President Rhee initiated the overseas adoption program in an effort to deal with the problem of thousands of illegitimate biracial children. The media's ability to cover the Korean War and carry the plight of the orphans into the homes and hearts of Middle America fueled rescue fantasies in a way that was not possible during World War II. Harry Holt, an Oregon farmer and devout Christian, took on the personal mission to find families for the thousands of parentless children. Holt International continues Harry Holt's work, placing more children from Korea than any other agency. The social upheaval and poverty of a country torn apart resulted in the continuation of Korean overseas adoption. Remarkably, by the mid-1980s, South Korea experienced rapid economic solvency through industrialization and urbanization, while overseas adoptions also reached a peak with over 6,000

---

2. Hague Convention on Protection of Children and Co-operation in Respect of Intercountry Adoption (Hague Adoption Convention), May 29, 1993, *available at* http://www.hcch.net/index_en.php?act=conventions.pdf&cid=69.

children placed in the United States. China and Russia have since surpassed South Korea as sending countries. In 1991, China constituted twenty-five percent and Russia twenty-two percent of all international adoptions in the United States. Since 1998, between 4,000 and 5,000 Chinese children, mostly girls, have been adopted per annum by U.S. families. It is important to note that international adoption programs exist in many other Asian, Latin American, and Eastern European countries, although they are less significant as far as number of children placed. Particular recent media attention has been given to Romania and Cambodia because of accusations of institutional deprivation and/or corruption.

The compassionate response of American families in opening their homes to Korean War orphans superficially resembles the international adoption of European children following World War II. However, there are several factors that make both experiences qualitatively different. First, the orphans from World War II were all children from countries, viewed by most Americans to be "equal" but for the immediate circumstances, first-world white European. Interethnic differences aside, British, Italian, and German children were considered to be capable of assimilating and were often adopted by families who shared their ethnic heritage. In contrast, Korea was a third-world country with a long history of occupation and colonization by China, Japan, and the United States. The U.S. presence in Korea was largely to protect its own interests, namely military holdings, and the people of Korea were not in a position of power. This fact defined the relationship between the two countries, and families who adopted Korean children were seen as extraordinarily benevolent. Prospective parents tended to make their decisions based on religious or moral dictates to save the children from their fate as orphans and to rescue them from the poverty and third-worldness of their country.

The social unrest and change of the Civil Rights Movement and Women's Movement in the 1960s brought about a new consciousness of brother/sisterhood, global citizenship, and social responsibility. An idealistic fervor and awakening among university students, ethnic communities, and feminist camps demanded that the United States face its legacy of racial and gender politics. Families who adopted Korean and other non-white children during the late 1960s and early 1970s often attributed their decision, in part, to their commitment to promoting social justice. Joe Kroll, executive director of the North American Council of Adoptable Children and a parent of a Korean adopted daughter, in his testimony before the Subcommittee Hearing on Interethnic Adoptions stated:

> As transracial adopters in the 70s, my wife and I (and many others) went blissfully into the process thinking we would save children and integrate society by integrating our family. No one asked our infant daughter what she thought. As white adults we had certain privileges that allowed us to pick and choose from where our children would come.

The National Association of Black Social Workers (NABSW) in 1972 vehemently opposed the transracial adoption of African-American children into white homes arguing for same-race placements and stating that:

> Black children belong physically, psychologically and culturally in Black families in order that they receive the total sense of themselves and develop a sound projection of their future.... Black children in white homes are cut off from the healthy development of themselves as Black people.... We ... have committed ourselves to go back to our communities and work to end this particular form of genocide.

....

Similarly, indigenous children were being placed outside of tribal context into white homes. Prior to 1978, it is estimated that between twenty-five to thirty-five percent of Native American children were transracially placed. The Indian Child Welfare Act (1978), predicated on tribal sovereignty, attempted to decrease the prevalence of transracial adoptions, but met with limited success. Meanwhile, Korean children continued to be placed transracially and in increasing numbers, with a dramatic peak of almost 5,000 children between 1975 and 1976.

Motivation to adopt internationally had shifted from child-focused to parent-focused. The charitable inclinations to provide families for parentless children seemed to transition to a more pseudo-altruistic need to make a social statement about participation in and responsibility to crossing racial boundaries. Families and communities were often singularly integrated by these adoptees. The increasing number of couples in the United States during the 1980s who were delaying having children to begin careers accompanied a rise in infertility and a decrease in the number of available healthy white infants due, in part, to accessible abortions, rising acceptance of single parenthood, and more effective birth control. International adoption became a matter of finding children for childless couples. Motivation for adoption had shifted from the altruistic, finding a home for a parentless child, to the supply and demand economics of finding children for childless couples.

Considering the desire for couples to adopt healthy infants and the lack of availability of white children, one might wonder why couples made the leap from domestic to overseas adoption. The practice of transracial placement of African-American children into white homes continues and is projected to increase with the passage of the Interethnic Adoption Provisions and the Adoption and Safe Families Act of 1997. Nonetheless, the placement of Korean children hit an all-time high in 1986 and may have continued to today if not for the 1988 Olympics in Seoul. Bergquist, Campbell, and Unrau conducted a study of adoptive parents that indicated the primary motivations to adopt from Korea rather than domestically were (1) shorter waiting periods, and (2) an interest in international adoption. These findings reflect the pragmatism and parent-centered motivations in adoption and perhaps suggest a romanticization or exoticization of the country of origin.

Asians have a history of otherness in the United States, characterized as the perpetual foreigner while at the same time held up as the model minority. Hegemonic recreations of Asianness into orientalness commodifies and essentializes Chinese, Japanese, Korean, and other Asian realities—and in many cases contrived realities—into consumable entities. Orientalist representations in marketing, fashion, coffee house chai, and Asian fusion cuisine abound. Where do Korean and other Asian adoptees fit into this context? I would argue three points. First, international transracial adoption represents, in part, a misguided attempt to soothe the national conscience and allay the collective guilt of centuries of racism and oppression to people of color. Secondly, the relative success of Asian adoption has been held up as a validation of the model minority myth, positioning adoptees as diversity mascots—especially to the African-American and indigenous communities. Finally, international adoption represents a form of neocolonialism. I will address each point below.

The United States has yet to come to terms with its legacy of racism and oppression, although many Americans feel that it is finished business and often wonder, "why can't we just move on?" The willingness of white Americans to open their homes to Korean and Chinese orphans is often lauded as markers of a color blind multicultural society. The good intentions and genuineness of those parents and families are not being challenged in this analysis, rather this Paper attempts to deconstruct international adoption and the assumptions of privilege that facilitate and sustain these crosscultural/crossnational placements. Transracial adoptive parents in general, not just those with Asian children, tend to be publicly acknowledged for their selflessness and courage in taking on the challenge of raising children of color, which seems to be a curious response if the United States is truly multicultural and inclusive and if racism has been relegated to vague historical references to slavery and possibly the Japanese internment.

The precarious position that Asians find themselves in the United States as the model or positive minority is at the same time misrepresentative, divisive, paternalistic and a myth. It disregards the socioeconomic diversity between and within ethnic groups and the role that the United States immigration policies have played in determining who are allowed to enter. It also deepens racial divide and feeds interethnic competition: "Asian-Americans also find themselves pitted against and resented by other racial minorities and even whites. If Asian-Americans can make it on their own, pundits are asking, "why can't poor blacks and whites on welfare?" Frank Wu purports that Asian-Americans' vindication of the American Dream serves as a reminder of the failure of race relations in the United States, stating that "the myth is abused both to deny that Asian-Americans experience racial discrimination and to turn Asian-Americans into a racial threat." The model minority myth is predicated on paternalistic and condescending assumptions that Asian-Americans are remarkable, given that they are a racial minority. Korean and other Asian adoptees are positioned as pawns or trump cards in the perpetuation of this myth.

Early adoption research documented the successful adaptation of minority children into their white middle class families, and more recent studies have indicated that these children do well in school, attach to their adoptive families, and have relatively few psychosocial or behavioral problems in comparison to their white peers. Researchers have consistently been conservative in their interpretation of these results, suggesting that the studies may not address relevant measures of success, i.e. racial identity development, and are often limited to self-selection in sampling, parental reports, and lack of consideration for the long term impact across the life span. Crossracial comparisons have also been made between adoptions of African-American and other children, finding for the most part that Asian-American adoptees are better adjusted and encounter less problems behaviorally and socially—serving to bolster the model minority myth and creating divisive tension. What deserves more attention are the mitigating or contributing factors, such as racial stratification and the more virulent racism experienced by African-Americans.

Critiques of transracial adoption research, which includes the placement of Asian children into Caucasian homes, have identified fundamental methodological flaws in earlier research and have suggested strategies for promoting greater cultural relevance in adoption practice. Park and Green argue that transracial adoption research has been Eurocentric, implicitly and explicitly utilizing measures of success and well-being as defined from a majority perspective. Moreover, Goddard points out that such measures are predicated on the conceptualization of self-esteem as individualistic and therefore incongruent with a collective identity and the reality that racialized groups in the United States are positioned as members of an ascribed identity.

Adoption usually involves an exchange between a resource rich and resource limited community or country. Economic necessity is one of the dominant factors in relinquishment, whether it be by a birth parent or a country whose social services infrastructure cannot support the number of children in care, at least initially. The neocolonialism inherent in that exchange is striking. The acquiring of a country's or people's resources as a necessary function of colonialism is arguably the case in international adoption, with children being a national resource. Notably, Korean children who are internationally adopted tend to be the easiest to place—being for the most part healthy infants—while the less adaptive children are left to linger in orphanages. As one adoptee argues:

> International adoption isn't the answer to improving the overall plight of children in developing countries. Even the strongest supporters admit the movement of adoptees across international borders represents only a tiny fraction of the neglected, abused and abandoned children in these countries. And supporters of international adoption are quiet about the children who are left behind.

. . . .

The practice of international adoption at best does not address precipitating social conditions, providing instead a short term and arguably minimal impact on the problem of homelessness and poverty for children. At worst, it allows countries to abdicate responsibility for enacting sociopolitical change to secure the well-being of all children, thereby positioning receiving countries as complicit in the problem.

Notes and Questions

1. The Berquist article sets out some of the ideological objections to intercountry adoption. Many writers oppose the practice on the grounds that it involves an assertion of power by wealthy, white families in the United States over disadvantaged families in developing countries. Should the system of intercountry adoption take these issues into account? If so, how? Are there good arguments to the effect that the practice should be stopped? What might result from the cessation of international adoption?

2. The Berquist article above is highly critical of the motivations behind intercountry adoption. What evidence does the author provide that these adoptions are more about the needs of adoptive parents than adopted children? Does she make this case convincingly?

3. For further reading in the child's "right to culture," see Barbara Stark, *Children as Refugees and Displaced Persons: Lost Boys and Forgotten Girls: Intercountry Adoption, Human Rights and African Children*, 22 St. Louis University Public Law Review 275 (2003). In Stark's view, the UNCRC accepts that the child's right to culture trumps any right to a family where that involves intercountry adoption. She explores how this conflict has played out in Africa, a continent with a huge number of orphans, and extremely strong views against the practice.

4. Many people do not realize that there is also a substantial number of U.S.-born children adopted internationally, mainly to Canada and Europe. These children are voluntarily placed by birth mothers who believe it will be better for their children to be raised in those countries. For the background to this phenomenon, see Galit Avitan, *Protecting Our Children or Our Pride? Regulating the Intercountry Adoption of American Children*, 40 Cornell International Law Journal 489 (2007).

Elizabeth Bartholet was one of the first U.S. academics to confront the critics of international adoption with serious arguments as to why, in many situations, it offers the best possible outcomes for vulnerable children. When faced with balancing problems of identity with a wide variety of enhanced opportunities, she has always come down unequivocally on the side of placing children in families, wherever they may be found, at as early a stage as possible.

Elizabeth Bartholet, *International Adoption: Propriety, Prospects and Pragmatics*

13 Journal of American Academy of Matrimonial Lawyers 181 (1996)

Loss of Roots Versus Opportunities for Better Lives

Critics of international adoption often voice concern that children will not receive appropriate care in their new families and countries. Arguments are made that it is unfair to separate children from their racial, ethnic, cultural, and national groups of origin. Loss of the group link and sense of group heritage is said to be a deprivation in itself. And growing up in a foreign land is said to pose risks of discrimination.

Those who voice these concerns again ignore the realities of children's current situations. International adoption represents an extraordinarily positive option for the homeless children of the world, compared to all other realistic options. Most of these children will not be adopted otherwise. They will continue to live in inadequate institutions or on the streets. Foster care is available only to a limited degree and sometimes results in little more than indentured servitude. The homeless children who survive to grow up often will face virulent forms of discrimination in their own country, based on their racial or ethnic status, or simply on the fact that they are illegitimate or orphaned.

The empirical studies that have focused on international adoption provide no basis for concern as to the welfare of the vast majority of international adoptees and their families. The studies show these children and their families functioning well, and comparing well on various measures of emotional adjustment with other adoptive families, as well as with biologic families. This is rather strikingly positive evidence since most international adoptees have had problematic preadoptive histories that could be expected to cause difficulties in adjustment. The studies show that adoption has for the most part been extraordinarily successful in enabling even those children who have suffered extremely severe forms of deprivation and abuse in their early lives, to recover and flourish. Thus one major study involved children caught up in the Vietnamese War who arrived in Norway for adoption at ages ranging from two to five. "Many could not walk. They were passive, apathetic, retarded and malnourished." At ages seventeen through twenty-two, these children were found to be in remarkably good shape: they were basically well-adjusted and strongly attached to their families.

Some of the studies illuminate special challenges that many of these families face—challenges that have to do with adjusting to a new language and culture, or with overcoming the effects of traumatic preadoptive experiences and of early health problems. Other studies hint at the complex issues involved in being part of a biracial, bicultural, binational family. These families do have to deal with issues of discrimination. And the children do have to deal with complex identity issues in working through what it means to be an "Asian American" or a "Peruvian American" or a "Mexican American." But the problems of discrimination are not different in nature than the problems many of these children would face in their own lands. The challenges involved in developing an appropriate sense of group identity are not different in nature from those that all immigrants face. The studies provide no evidence that the challenge of establishing a satisfactory ethnic and cultural identity causes psychological harm to the international adoptee.

These findings are consistent with the findings in the transracial adoption studies involving racial identity issues. Those studies have shown transracial adoptees emerging with an apparently strong sense of black identity. They have also shown, however, that many of the adoptees have what might be characterized as a bicultural or multicultural orientation. They exhibit an unusual degree of comfort in both black and white worlds, and appear unusually committed to a future life in which they would relate to both those worlds. The studies thus indicate that transracial adoptees may be likely to develop "group identities" and attitudes about racial relations that are somewhat different, on the whole, from those of black children raised in a same-race family and environment. But the studies indicate that there is no apparent detriment to the children involved in growing up with a less exclusively black group identity orientation. These children are flourishing in all the terms in which psychic health and social adjustment can be measured.

. . . .

So the studies reveal no real negatives inherent in international adoption as compared to domestic adoption. From a real-world perspective, that is of course not the most relevant comparison. The key comparison would be between children adopted internationally and children denied the possibility of adoption—children destined for the most part to grow up in institutions or on the streets. But there is no need for comparative studies of this kind. They would simply bolster what common sense and professional opinion tell us already. A permanent adoptive family is vastly preferable from the child's perspective to even the best foster or institutional care. Most of the children without permanent families in the poor countries of the world are not living in "the best" temporary care situations, but rather in situations ranging from seriously inadequate to desperate.

. . . .

It seems clear that the debate over international adoption has little to do with genuine concerns over risks to children. Children are being sacrificed to notions of group pride and honor. As Tizard has described:

> It is argued that the practice is a new form of colonialism, with wealthy Westerners robbing poor countries of their children, and thus their resources. National pride is involved. However poor the country, they find the implication that they cannot care for their own children to be undignified and unacceptable. Thus poor countries feel pressure to hold on to what they term "their precious resources," and rich countries feel embarrassed to do anything that looks like colonialist exploitation.

But there is no real conflict between the interests of the sending and those of the receiving nations. International adoption simply serves a symbolic function for those in power. Sending countries can talk of their homeless children as "precious resources," but it is clear that the last thing these countries actually need is more children to care for. At the same time, the well-off countries of the world have no burning need for these children. Their governments might be willing to permit the entry of adoptees from abroad to enable those struggling with infertility to parent, but international adoption is not seen as serving any strong national interest. So the homeless children end up as "resources" that the receiving countries of the world are quite willing to forgo to improve relations abroad.

Notes and Questions

1. Compare the Bergquist and Bartholet articles. Whose perspective is more convincing? How ought a child's "right to culture" play into the intercountry adoption process? Are there situations in which the "right to culture" ought to be subordinated to other human rights? Is there a good way to balance the values expressed in Berquist's article on the one hand and in Bartholet's articles on the other, and still keep intercountry adoption as an option? Which author better reflects the terms of the UNCRC?

2. Elizabeth Bartholet was one of the original defenders of intercountry adoption, and has continued to identify with this issue over many years. See her influential book Family Bonds: Adoption, Infertility, and the New World of Child Production, (1999). What do you think of her idea that the only meaningful comparison is between the situation of an internationally adopted child, and the life that child would have lived in the absence of international adoption? Among many other writings, see a recent editorial in the Washington Post, criticizing the role of UNICEF in curtailing adoptions from Guatemala, *Slamming the Door on Adoption; Depriving Children Abroad of Loving Homes*, November 4, 2007.

In addition to the child's right to culture, another major issue in intercountry adoption involves the illicit profit made by many "players" in the adoption picture. David Smolin's article offers a challenging and thought-provoking critique of intercountry adoption. He asserts that, based on the economic disparities inherent in intercountry adoption, there is an unavoidable tendency for such adoptions to become corrupt. In his view, the manner in which international adoption is structured creates incentives that inevitably liken adoption to child trafficking. His objections are obviously of a different nature to those expressed in the Berquist article above, although Smolin also expresses an aversion to "stripping" children of their original culture and language.

David Smolin, *Intercountry Adoption as Child Trafficking*
39 Valparaiso University Law Review 281 (2004)

. . . .

I. WHY IT IS DIFFICULT TO DISTINGUISH CHILD TRAFFICKING FROM INTERCOUNTRY ADOPTION: PROBLEMS OF IDEOLOGY AND ETHICS

The association of child trafficking with intercountry adoption will likely strike some readers as obvious, others as offensive. To some, intercountry adoption in itself is more or less a form of child trafficking, as it involves the transfer of children from poor nations to rich nations in order to meet the demand of those in rich nations for children. The fact that those seeking to adopt want daughters and sons, not sex or labor, seems to make little difference for those most ideologically opposed to intercountry adoption. In broad terms, it is still a matter of the citizens of rich countries using their wealth and power to "buy" the vulnerable children of the poor. From this perspective, those who really care about the suffering of children in developing nations should provide assistance and help to children within their own societies, rather than spending inordinate sums to strip children of their national identity, native culture, and language.

By contrast, those most supportive of intercountry adoption perceive literally millions of children in need of intercountry adoption in developing and transition economy nations. Children abandoned, killed, left in dismal orphanages, or living on the streets bear horrific testimony to the pressing need for adoption. From this perspective, ethical or political objections to intercountry adoption lack legitimacy, since they sacrifice the concrete good of children to ideological idols.

These sharply conflicting views of intercountry adoption engender confusion. When one group views intercountry adoption as a form of child trafficking, while another views intercountry adoption as a beautiful act of compassion, the actual operation of our system of intercountry adoption becomes obscured. Continuing the ideological debate over whether intercountry adoption is inherently good or evil is a fool's errand, like so many other ideological debates leading further and further afield into conflicting worldviews. The resolution of such worldview conflicts cannot be found in the realm of brute facts — if there even is such a realm — because facts are viewed through the lens of worldviews, and often seem powerless to conquer strong ideological commitment.

Fortunately, it is possible to bring some clarity to the debates concerning intercountry adoption, despite the inability to resolve the core ideological conflicts. We can seek broadly acceptable definitions for when adoption has clearly denigrated into child trafficking, even if we cannot agree on whether intercountry adoption is per se a form of trafficking. We can seek reform of intercountry adoption, even as some argue that intercountry adoption is an evil that should be abolished.

Initially, it is helpful to guide the ethical inquiry over intercountry adoption by reference to two adoption "triads." The first triad, intrinsic to adoption itself, is the set of complex relationships between birth family, adoptive family, and child. The second triad, specific to intercountry adoption, is the complex set of relationships between the child and sending and receiving nations.

The ethical touchstone of intercountry adoption should be the imperative to respect the dignity and rights of all members of both triads. This imperative comes not merely from the broad ethical mandate to respect all human persons, and all nation-states, but it also follows from the unique nature of the adoption triads. In each adoption triad, the child is the central figure because the child is inherently and permanently connected in profound ways to all of the other triad members and links the triad members to one another. The child's inherent and permanent relationship to all triad members means that the child's best interests cannot be considered in isolation from the rights of the other triad members. An adoption built upon a severe deprivation of the rights of the birth family, for example, intrinsically harms the child as well, because of the child's profound and permanent connection to her birth family. The same can be said about all of the other members of each triad. Thus, to the degree that adoption seriously harms a triad member, the child also is harmed. From this perspective, the only kind of adoption that can serve the "best interests of children" is adoption that honors all triad members. Of course this does not mean that all triad members receive everything they demand, but it does mean that attempts to save children at the expense of the dignity and well-being of birth or adoption families or nations are inherently flawed. Ethical adoption, therefore, is adoption that respects the dignity and rights of all triad members.

The adoption triad reminds us that the legal fiction of no continuing relationship between adopted child and birth family is just that — a fiction. Indeed, the contemporary experience of adoption indicates that even adopted individuals with excellent relationships with their adoptive families yearn to know, or at least know about, their birth families. Reunions are attempted and arranged across the barriers of oceans, cultures, and language. In intercountry adoption, moreover, the continuing psychological link to the birth family is closely related to the continuing link to the birth nation. Consider, for example, the common instance of a Korean girl adopted by a white American family. It would take a willful blindness to deny the Korean adoptee's family ties to Korean parents and the nation of Korea. Indeed, the Korean adoptee cannot escape the obvious — that her physical body did not descend in any way from her adoptive parents. Every part of her physical appearance points back to Korea. No matter how American she is, she is also inevitably, permanently, and inescapably Korean. Thus, any system of adoption built upon denying her Korean identity — or demeaning, dishonoring, or victimizing the family and nation from which she came — in principle harms the adoptee herself.

From this perspective, intercountry adoption is neither an inherent good nor an inherent evil but rather it is a potential or conditional good. To the degree that an adoption, or system of adoption, meets the criteria of treating all triad members fairly—giving them their "due"—then the system has positive merit. To the degree that an adoption, or system of adoption, victimizes or demeans one or more triad members, adoption is no longer a good, but becomes—at least in significant part—an evil, and one that is generally harmful to the child.

....

DEFINING ADOPTION AS CHILD TRAFFICKING: THE LEGAL STANDARDS

....

B. International Definitions of Trafficking Specifically Addressing Adoption

1. Adoption as the Prohibited Sale of a Child Under the 2000 Optional Protocol to the Convention on the Rights of the Child on the Sale of Children, Child Prostitution, and Child Pornography ("OP-CRC").

In recent years, scandalous and illicit activities associated with intercountry adoption, along with the growing ideological controversy concerning intercountry adoption, have once again come to the attention of the international community. Given the growing international concern with child trafficking, the problem of abusive intercountry adoption practices has increasingly been defined in terms of the notorious problem of international child trafficking. Under these circumstances, the gap between the common sense concept of child trafficking and the strict legal definitions has become significant. Thus, international legal materials have cautiously begun to specifically address the question of when intercountry adoption has descended into a form of illicit child trafficking. While these developments are likely incomplete, they are significant.

The primary international document directly addressing intercountry adoption as a form of child trafficking is the OP-CRC. Significantly, the United States has ratified the OP-CRC, even though it has not ratified the CRC. Therefore, the OP-CRC is not merely international law, but it constitutes international law that is binding within the United States.

The OP-CRC defines the "sale of children" as "any act or transaction whereby a child is transferred by any person or group of persons to another for remuneration or any other consideration." In defining the situations where the "sale of children" must be legally prohibited, the OP-CRC includes "improperly inducing consent, as an intermediary, for the adoption of a child in violation of applicable international legal instruments on adoption." The term "applicable international legal instruments on adoption" is understood to refer to the Hague Convention on Intercountry Adoption ("Hague Convention"). The Hague Convention explicitly includes as one of its "objects" the prevention of "the abduction, the sale of, or traffic in children." Although the Hague Convention contains no definition of the sale of, or trafficking in, children, the OP-CRC has effectively made the Hague Convention's sections on consent to adoption into a critical part of the definition of illicit child selling. Thus, where an intermediary induces consent to adoption in a manner that violates the Hague standards, and a child is transferred "for remuneration or any other consideration," then the illicit sale of a child has occurred. Moreover, although there is no separate definition of "child trafficking," the term presumably would include any illicit sale of a child, particularly where the child is moved geographically.

Thus, as a matter of international law, intercountry adoption constitutes illicit child selling and child trafficking where an intermediary induces consent to adoption in violation of the standards of the Hague Convention and when the child is transferred for remuneration or any consideration. As a technical matter, both elements—inducement of consent by an intermediary in a manner violating Hague standards and the transfer of children for remuneration or consideration—must be established to constitute the kind of "sale of children" that literally violates the standards of the OP-CRC.

. . . .

2. Hague Standards for Valid Consent to Adoption as Applicable to the OP-CRC

The Hague Convention standards for a valid consent to adoption are extensive and yet are ultimately a matter of broadly-held ethical adoption standards. The standards have three requirements for consent by those, like birth parents, with custodial responsibilities and rights in relation to the child. First, those parents giving consent to adoption must have received the equivalent of informed consent, including counseling "as necessary," and being informed as to the legal effect of the consent, "in particular whether or not an adoption will result in the termination of the legal relationship between the child and his or her family of origin." Second, the consent must not have "been induced by payment or compensation of any kind and have not been withdrawn." Third, consent must be given "freely, in the required legal form, and expressed or evidenced in writing."

It is clear, therefore, that "inducing" birth family members to relinquish children for adoption through the payment of money would violate the terms of the Hague Convention. Moreover, such "inducing" monetary payments would also appear to constitute the separate definition of "sale of children," under the OP-CRC, because they constitute the transfer of the child for "remuneration or any other consideration." Hence, where an intermediary induces consent to adoption through monetary payments or financial benefit, such acts would clearly constitute the prohibited sale of children under the OPCRC.

. . . .

3. Money as the Root of All Evil (or Much Uncertainty) Under the OP-CRC and the Hague Convention

We have seen that the developing international law definitions of illicit child trafficking, or the sale of children, do not yet address all situations within the common sense or dictionary definition of those terms. The law has been reluctant to label all sales of children as prohibited forms of child trafficking and has failed to demand penal sanctions for all abusive adoption practices. Yet, it is encouraging that the law has been moving in the direction of clearly labeling certain abusive adoption practices as prohibited forms of child trafficking or sale of children. Certainly, it seems to be the intent of the OP-CRC to clearly and definitively label some abusive adoption practices as the illicit sale of children subject to penal sanction.

Unfortunately, further analysis will demonstrate that the kinds of wrongs addressed by the OP-CRC, which involve an illicit transfer of a child for "remuneration or other consideration," are not effectively prohibited by law. The difficulty, as we shall see, is that the law is not in a position to clearly differentiate, in the context of adoption, between licit and illicit payments of money. Once the law loses its capacity to distinguish clearly between prohibited and permitted provisions of financial benefit, the effectiveness of legal prohibitions against the "sale of children" virtually collapses.

Under the OP-CRC, there are essentially two points at which illicit consideration may be involved: (1) in inducing consent to adoption; or (2) in a subsequent transfer of the child. In both instances, difficulties arise from the fact that payment of money in itself may be viewed as customary and licit. Upon closer examination, distinguishing between licit and illicit payment of money in each instance may be difficult, not only theoretically but also in practice.

C. Inducing Consent from Birth Parents

1. The Domestic Adoption System Creates an Unstable Baseline for Distinguishing Between Licit and Illicit Payments of Money

The letter and spirit of international law, and domestic law within the United States, forbids the payment of money or other consideration to birth parents to induce relinquishment of the child or consent to adoption. Such payments are tantamount to buying a child. However, state laws governing domestic adoption within the United States generally permit the provision of very significant "birth parent expenses," including temporary living expenses, medical expenses, and counseling fees. These payments are viewed as a gift, rather than legal consideration for consent to adoption. Indeed, payment of such expenses in most states cannot be conditioned, or made reimbursable, based upon the birth mother actually consenting to the adoption. Moreover, birth parents cannot be bound to any pre-birth agreement to relinquish or place their child.

The net effect of these rules in practice is unclear and casts a certain ethical cloud over domestic adoption. The intent of the law is to prohibit, and generally even criminalize, the sale of children. In practice, however, prospective adoptive parents provide financial assistance to birth parents, directly or through intermediaries, precisely based on the hope and expectation of obtaining the child. Certainly most prospective adoptive parents lack the funds or motivation to lavish financial assistance on birth mothers for the mere sake of compassion or kindness. Everyone understands that prospective adoptive parents are, in crude terms, "in it for the baby." The fact that the birth parents are free to accept the aid, and then ultimately keep the baby, does not ultimately change the truth that the assistance is provided at least in the hope that the birth parents will relinquish the child.

. . . .

2. Money and Birth Parents in the Intercountry Adoption System

. . . .

The first issue is whether financial assistance toward keeping the family together must be offered prior to accepting a relinquishment. Given that many birth mothers will be among the segment of humanity living on less than two dollars per day—and some among those living on less than one dollar per day—it could be argued that relatively small amounts of money might help keep the child with the birth family. Indeed, it may be that the travel expenses involved in an intercountry adoption would be more than sufficient to avoid relinquishment, if such a sum were available to assist the birth family rather than to remove the child. Thus, it could be argued that consent to intercountry adoption should only be considered valid where financial assistance to keep the child with the birth family was offered and available. As an ethical matter, it is perverse to spend thousands of dollars taking a child from the birth family, when a much smaller sum would have kept the family intact.

Neither the OP-CRC nor the Hague Convention, however, require the offer or availability of such financial assistance to birth families to validate consent to adoption. It is legal to accept the relinquishment of a child for purposes of intercountry adoption even where the provision of a very modest sum of assistance would have kept the child with the birth family.

From a legal perspective, therefore, the financial issues related to relinquishment only arise when birth parents receive some kind of money or assistance. Under the combined standards of the OP-CRC and the Hague Convention, any amount of remuneration or consideration that "induces" consent to adoption is sufficient to constitute child selling. This rule is important, particularly given reports of birth families being induced to relinquish children for as little as twenty dollars. When such small sums actually are "inducements," however, proof and enforcement issues become difficult. Even if it is possible to document the receipt of money and corollary relinquishment by a birth parent—a difficult matter, when such small sums are involved, and intermediaries to send and receive are available—the distinction between assistance and inducement can be difficult to define. Given a poverty-stricken birth parent, the failure to provide some small amount of assistance would seem itself a cruelty, and yet once such assistance is given it can be difficult to tell whether it served as an inducement.

Unfortunately, the international rules governing consent to adoption are not prophylactic, in that they permit situations where inducement is likely. For example, the international rules apparently allow aid to be offered only to those birth parents who relinquish their children, rather than requiring aid to birth parents to be unconditional. Thus, the international rules permit patterns of aid that create incentives to relinquish. It is only an actual inducement that is apparently illegal. The difficulty with this rule is that proof of an inducement, or a quid pro quo, ultimately turns on the inner motivations and understanding of the parties. Because birth parents frequently will not be cooperative with investigative authorities, given their own legal, social, and financial vulnerabilities, proof of inducement will often be difficult even where children were in fact sold. If the "buyer and seller" (agency and birth parent) maintain their story that no sale occurred but that the consent to adoption and provision of assistance were each independent acts, proof of inducement becomes extraordinarily difficult even where receipt of money is proven.

. . . .

The intercountry adoption system should create a rule forbidding all assistance to birth parents that is conditioned on relinquishment or placement of the child. This kind of prophylactic rule would clarify, to some degree, the critical distinction between assistance and buying children. There is precedent for such a rule within the domestic adoption system, although the international ban would have to be broader and clearer than the domestic ban to be effective. Until the international adoption system adopts such a rule, it will be difficult to prevent both notorious and inadvertent inducement to relinquish.

In the longer term, the intercountry adoption system should require that birth parents be offered some degree of financial help to keep the child with the family. Under this rule, a relinquishment or consent to adoption by a birth parent to a licensed agency would only be valid within the intercountry adoption system if the birth parents had been offered a certain measure of financial assistance to keep the family intact. The amount offered could be relatively modest—for example, approximately one hundred U.S. dollars for adoptions in nations like India, Cambodia, and Guatemala, where relinquishing parents often earn less than two dollars per day. The funds would come from intercountry adoption fees.

. . . .

D. Money and Intermediaries

. . . .

In intercountry adoption, as in domestic adoption, the theory is that adoptive parents are paying for "services," and perhaps "gifts" to others, but they are not buying a child. The nature of those "services" and "gifts" within intercountry adoption remains quite obscure, however, due to the vague breakdown of intercountry adoption fees. Intercountry adoption can be quite expensive, but it is not always clear exactly where the money is going. Fees are often broadly designated as "agency fees," "international fees," or fees going to those within the foreign nation (i.e., "India Fee"). In many intercountry adoptions, all of the fees are paid by the adoptive parents to the U.S. placement entity, which then channels portions to various entities and persons within the sending nation. In some countries, the adoptive parents are required to bring significant amounts of cash with them into the foreign nation, and pay various entities directly. In either event, it is common for five thousand dollars to ten-thousand dollars per child to be paid to various individuals, agencies, and entities within the foreign nation. When this kind of money goes to nations with per capita incomes of less than one thousand dollars, often less than five hundred dollars, it becomes extraordinarily difficult to prevent adoption from descending into a form of child trafficking. I have elsewhere described at great length how the Indian adoption system has been corrupted by large amounts of American dollars, but doubtless the story could be repeated in the various nations plagued by adoption scandals.

. . . .

As a practical matter, the U.S. practice of spending five thousand dollars to ten-thousand dollars per child in the foreign countries generally creates a large "profit" or excess beyond any actual, legitimate costs related to adoption services. Indeed, in nations where social workers traditionally earn a few thousand dollars per year, and orphanage workers can be paid a few dollars a day or less, it seems probable that the vast bulk of the fees are sheer profits. The ultimate destinations of these profits seem to vary from nation to nation. Some argue that the Chinese, with their centralized systems of control, have successfully used most of their adoption fees to significantly improve their orphanages and services for abandoned children, most of whom will remain in China. By contrast, in Guatemala, India, and Cambodia, it appears that the exorbitant fees have enriched individual intermediaries.

The Hague Convention specifically requires contracting States to take "all appropriate measures to prevent improper financial or other gain in connection with an adoption...." But what is "improper" gain? The best definition would include compensation disproportionate to services rendered, based on the Hague Convention's prohibition of remuneration that "is unreasonably high in relation to services rendered." For example, if an individual in a developing nation spends ten hours working on an adoption, and a person in his field (social work, child welfare, law, etc.) would normally receive two hundred dollars for such work, then receipt of three thousand dollars beyond expenses should count as "improper" gain.

One difficulty with enforcing such a norm is that the foreign agencies and individuals receiving "adoption fees" often claim that those sums are funding an orphanage, including the costs of caring for children who will never be adopted. In many instances there does not seem to be a clear system of accountability to determine the degree to which such fees are truly spent on child welfare or are simply to enrich individuals. In those circumstances, it becomes very difficult to document whether the "profit" is used to fund the operation of the orphanage or is pocketed by the individual.

. . . .

III. CONCLUSION: INTERCOUNTRY ADOPTION AS CHILD TRAFFICKING

. . . .

Where the law permits orphanages to become profit centers generating wealth far beyond normal compensation for services, the concept of "payment for services" is a legal fiction ineffectively hiding a commercial trade in children. Where the law permits adoptive parents to be charged for "orphanage donations," but has no effective means of ensuring that these funds are spent on children, rather than being pocketed by intermediaries, "donations" become a legal fiction facilitating a trade in children. Similarly, the distinction between gifts to birth parents and illicitly inducing consent through financial consideration has little meaning in an intercountry adoption system in which aid to assist birth families to stay together is not required and in which it is permissible to offer aid only to birth parents who consent to adoption.

Thus, where parents give up their children for the lack of a few hundred dollars, or less, but the intercountry adoption system spends tens of thousands of dollars completing the adoption of the child, the concept of compassionate adoption becomes a cruel hoax. Moreover, where impoverished parents in developing nations are offered financial assistance only when they relinquish their children, and the law considers this a licit "gift" unless agency and parent virtually confess to intending a sale, as a result a ban on child selling becomes illusory. Similarly, within the domestic system the concept of paying for services, but not for children, becomes illusory when agencies charge far more for high-demand white infants, evidencing the development of a market in children. The willingness of the law to label such an obvious sign of a market as a mere "payment of permissible services" indicates that the adoption system is mired in legal fictions with little relationship to the underlying commodification of children.

. . . .

Intercountry adoption is a conditional good; intercountry adoption as child trafficking is an evil. Only when the law, society, and intercountry adoption system are reformed will the conditions under which intercountry adoption can flourish as a good be established. Unfortunately, the prospects for such reform are poor because there are few within the current intercountry adoption system with the motivation to demand it. Hence, the recurrent cycle of scandal, excuse, and ineffective "reform" will probably continue until intercountry adoption is finally abolished, with history labeling the entire enterprise as a neo-colonialist mistake. It does not have to be this way, but it will take more than legal fictions and illusory restrictions on child trafficking to prevent the ultimate demise of the intercountry adoption system.

Notes and Questions

1. Smolin carefully builds a case that intercountry adoption is often in practice indistinguishable from child trafficking. Are you convinced by his reasoning? What do you think of Smolin's prediction for the future of intercountry adoption?

2. Does Smolin provide any empirical basis for his conclusions? In his view, does it matter whether one can prove that these abuses are common, or only that they are likely to occur? If international adoption were ended, as he seems to imply should happen, what alternatives does he propose for the many children living out of parental care? Does it matter whether there are good alternatives immediately available for children affected by the termination of intercountry adoption?

3. Smolin proposes that an aspect of intercountry adoption should be to offer a sum of money to a family considering putting a child up for adoption. His rationale is that, since many families look to adoption because they cannot afford to feed their children, the addition of this amount of money might allow the child to remain with the family. Do you think this proposal captures the real dynamic at work in abandonment? What

are the advantages and disadvantages of his proposal? Could abuse of this system lead to the same problems Smolin has with the current intercountry adoption process? What do we make of the fact that in the U.S. international surrogacy, for instance, has not been banned, at least to date?

———————

The following article could be read as a response to the criticisms expressed by Smolin and even Bergquist. Does the author do an adequate job of refuting claims made by those authors?

Note that the article calls for a conceptual shift, and demands that national governments be placed under a human rights obligation to address the needs of young children. Can this position be squared with the calls for ethical reform voiced by Smolin, for instance?

Sara Dillon, *Making Legal Regimes for Intercountry Adoption Reflect Human Rights Principles: Transforming the United Nations Convention on the Rights of the Child with the Hague Convention on Intercountry Adoption*
21 Boston University International Law Journal 179 (2003)

I. Introduction: The Ideological Morass at The Heart of International and National Adoption Law

Popular conceptions of intercountry adoption are confused and confusing, despite the existence of an "adoption revolution." With the global imagination and non-governmental organizations ("NGOs") devoted to child welfare divided over the necessity and propriety of transnational adoption, it is not surprising that the legal regimes, international and national, that make such adoption possible are in a similar state of confusion. Have we attained global agreement, if not consensus, to facilitate intercountry adoption? Or have we decided to restrict intercountry adoption to certain narrowly defined situations? Or can we identify a broadly expressed preference to eliminate intercountry adoption altogether? Can there be meaningful international agreement on such a contentious topic? Does intercountry adoption contribute to the welfare of children, or add to their already great global suffering? Much writing on the subject reflects the inability to choose between these two highly conflicted notions of adoption. This article will argue that by making strenuous investments to eliminate the abuses characteristic of some intercountry adoption, more people and organizations involved in children's issues should feel free, and should be expected, to advocate for adoption as a method of giving a new life to children in dire need of families....

I will argue in this article that what is most urgently needed is data—hard facts—about how many children are in institutions (public and private orphanages) on a long-term basis, how and why they came to be there, as well as how many children are in alternative forms of groups care, how many are living on the streets with little or no family contact, and as a related matter, how many are working in the sex industry or are engaged in other forms of hazardous and unacceptable work. Much of what is said about international adoption is shrouded in mystery, ideology, and innuendo. What is said to be best for children is often a function of the speaker's or organization's pre-existing viewpoint. Even with the recent widespread acceptance of the principles of the Hague Convention on Protection of Children and Co-Operation in Respect of Intercountry Adoption ("Hague Convention"), we cannot devise appropriate and just national or international legal regimes for international adoption unless we come to a better, clearer, more transparent understanding of which children should be, and must be, considered truly adoptable. The trend in international law, in the human rights and other contexts, is for national political needs to give way to universal principles; this should be no less the case in the context of intercountry adoption.

It is especially difficult to find out how many children are living out their childhoods in private and state-run orphanages. There are an estimated 600,000 institutionalized children in Russian and over a million in China. Each country in the developing world has a network of orphanages housing many children. In the industrialized West, the United States is particularly notorious for keeping foster children in a web of often impermanent and substandard substitute homes. Childhope and Casa Alianza, both advocacy groups for street children, agree that there are approximately 100 million street children worldwide, with 40 million in Latin America alone. According to estimates, approximately 25% of these children truly live on the streets and without meaningful family ties. In Asia alone, there are estimated to be hundreds of thousands of child prostitutes; in South Asia, literally millions of child bonded laborers. Even leaving out of account children who are killed through infanticide, or the matter of sex-selective abortions, it is clear that literally millions of children will never be brought up in their biological families of origin, at least not until such time as social, economic, and cultural conditions giving rise to this state of affairs have been totally and truly transformed. In the meantime, the world has a massive and often underreported problem of genocidal significance. This article will argue that "children without families" must be seen as a cohort and their problems must be addressed in the near term and as a matter of urgency, in light of the psychological demands of childhood.

....

This article will discuss the legal confusion surrounding the relationship between the venerable and almost universally ratified United Nations Convention on the Rights of the Child ("UNCRC") and the more recent Hague Convention on Intercountry Adoption. While the former is ambiguous on the question of whether children should be sent to other countries for purposes of adoption, the latter focuses on how to eliminate opportunities for corruption in intercountry adoption, and on how to create procedural protections for children and their birth families where the practice is followed. Both instruments leave a substantial degree of discretion to participating states. In this regard, neither instrument comes firmly to grips with the question of whether a country can validly decline intercountry adoption when the country maintains large numbers of children in institutions—children who are extremely unlikely ever to be reunited with birth families or to be adopted domestically.

....

A. Who will articulate a child's right not to be institutionalized? How to articulate a child's right to a family of his or her own?

One missing link in the heated debate over intercountry adoption is a clearly articulated right of children not to be institutionalized, assuming that there are genuine alternatives. One such alternative is intercountry adoption. In the context of adoption, the rights of individual children have become enmeshed in discussions of the larger trends of history. Specifically, many organizations that work for children's interests tend to see the issue of intercountry adoption in the contexts of colonialism and imperialism, rather than in the context of children's rights per se. It is understandable that many have taken this view; however, there is no evading the fundamental principle that the rights of particular children exist apart and distinct from these political considerations.

At the outset, it should be stated that ethical intercountry adoption only includes adoption of those children who would have been in the system in any event, children who would have been abandoned and without family care even in the absence of a system of intercountry adoption. The difficulty of identifying these children (those who would be in the system in any event) with certainty is what I term the "adoptability conundrum." What seems to be needed above all other interventions in this area is an empirically-oriented, rigorous, objective search to identify who is in the public or group child care systems of each country, how they got there, and what options are truly (not just in the realm of ideological speculation) available to them.

The profitability of intercountry adoption has probably tended in some jurisdictions to bring children into the system who would not otherwise have been there. Such corruption has had the perverse effect of threatening the reputation and viability of transnational adoption in a much more general sense. This article will seek to address the distinction one might draw between genuine child trafficking and profiteering from adoption, as well as the question of how we might tell whether children would have been institutionalized and waiting, without a legal mechanism for intercountry adoption.

. . . .

The most important international legal instrument on children's rights, the UNCRC, both reflects and adds to the confusion surrounding the right of children to a home and family, especially where the only available means of obtaining these is intercountry adoption. While articulating the great importance of family and identity to a child, the Convention fudges the issue of whether in-country institutional care may be relied upon when no in-country alternative family exists for a child without his or her family of origin. This lack of clarity reflects the great discomfort of human rights specialists to state directly that in-country institutional care is impermissible and violates the fundamental rights of small children. Since there is little chance that most of these children will be adopted locally, if the drafters had acknowledged the unacceptability of institutional care, it would have amounted to a concession that intercountry adoption could provide at least a partial solution to widespread violations of children's rights. Few in the international human rights community appear willing to draw this conclusion. Their motivations may be correct, but their conceptual framework and resulting conclusions are faulty.

The UNCRC is frequently described as the instrument that represented a revolution in international children's rights—the instrument that showed children as subjects of rights, as autonomous beings, as more than the possessions of their parents and of their cultures or nations. Obviously, the immaturity and vulnerability of the child require us to conceive of these rights in a more circumscribed fashion than would be the case with respect to adults. Nonetheless, the general principle is a valid one: children possess inalienable rights and they must be seen in terms of rights they deserve by virtue of their humanity and indeed by virtue of their vulnerability.

B. Identifying Acceptable and Unacceptable Forms of Care

At least with regard to the adoption issue, the UNCRC does not clarify what sort of care meets a human rights standard in the case of a child without a family. If the UNCRC is stating that institutional care is a matter of national choice, and may be a valid method of childcare where intercountry adoption is not a preferred option of the state in question, this assumption must be queried as to its human rights foundation. Does this assumption not militate against the revolutionary conceptual nature of the Convention itself?

The question of where to look for a source of rights is a difficult one in the intercountry adoption context. Having named children as the bearers of rights, it is to the nature of children that one must look in defining these rights. In this sense, the effects of certain care options must be examined quite apart from ideological or national analyses. It is my contention that only non-legal studies in the areas of child psychology and the measurable effects of institutionalization can really assist us in determining the degree to which the UNCRC is flawed, or at least inadequate, when it comes to adoption. The understanding gained will help us sort out the proper interpretive relationship between the UNCRC and the Hague Convention on Intercountry Adoption.

. . . .

If there is such a thing as human psychology, I argue that cultural relativism cannot apply to issues such as the effect of institutionalization on the psychological development of small children. Although psychology obviously has a cultural dimension, it is primarily an individual matter—or a matter of the species. In the case of small children, psychological health and emotional development have a meaning and a reality quite distinct from questions of cultural autonomy and identity, even recognizing that there is a fairly broad range of normal in this context. The inquiry into whether an orphanage can provide an adequate form of protection for children in human rights terms has little to do with the important, though separate, debate on cultural relativity and human rights generally. . . .

[M]ost of the rights-oriented writing on intercountry adoption concerns the problems of adoption-related trafficking and profiteering—terrible problems, to be sure. Devoting resources to address these problems, however, does not provide a rationale for failing to confront the global phenomenon of institutionalized children without families. One might even say that institutionalized children are more fortunate than street children, of whom there are estimated to be millions. There is an obvious disproportion of concern—that is, far more concern over adoption profiteering than over the plight of children without families living in poor conditions.

It could be that some who write about intercountry adoption from the point of view of abuses in the existing system of adoption, without paying a corresponding attention to the evils of neglect and institutionalization, are engaged in a kind of wishful thinking: that if intercountry adoption and its abuses were stopped, then somehow the children would be less likely to exist in their present state (i.e., without adults "of their own"), there would be family reunification, and the children could lead successful lives in their country of origin, though if absolutely necessary adopted by their own nationals. I see no evidence to support making this causal link, and many critics of adoption fall short of providing evidence to this effect.

What seems to be most urgently required is a separation of the larger, longer-term social and economic problems that lead to children being abandoned, killed, or sold, and the more immediate problems of psychic damage caused by the institutionalized or homeless child's condition. While it is completely appropriate to prescribe remedies for these problems in tandem, there is no valid argument for highlighting one at the expense of the other.

. . . .

Unfortunately, the transformation of ethical adoption into unethical adoption often leads to thoroughgoing and sweeping denunciation of intercountry adoption generally, even (or especially) by many involved in child welfare issues. Such hostility towards the idea of intercountry adoption could result in children without families being condemned to institutional life. Thus, a clear balance must be struck—in conceptual and legal terms—

between our concern for ethical procedures in adoption to avoid child trafficking, on the one hand, and the often overlooked fact of thousands of children without families waiting for a fair and humane international response to their isolation.

. . . .

II. The International Human Rights Picture: The Hague Convention vs. The Convention on the Rights of the Child

. . . .

B. The Hague Convention and its Relationship to the UNCRC

Most legal discussions of intercountry adoption begin with an analysis of the Hague Convention on Intercountry Adoption, since it is the principal international instrument purporting to set standards and define norms in this area. It is important to note that the Hague Convention is not a human rights convention per se; it is an agreement on the standards to be observed where intercountry adoption occurs, and says relatively little on the issue of whether human rights law demands that intercountry adoption be available, at least as a second or third best option. The Hague Convention does undoubtedly set the stage for tackling endemic problems of corruption and profiteering, as it seeks to eliminate the profit motive from adoption-related legal structures. In this sense, it represents an extremely important methodological consensus designed to save intercountry adoption from abuses too often associated with it, even if these abuses are frequently overstated by critics.

. . . .

[F]rom the point of view of this article, the most significant, and certainly one of the most ambiguous, provisions of the UNCRC concerns the child's right to a certain standard of adult care when the family of origin cannot care for him or her. Article 20(1) states that when the child is deprived of the family environment, or when the child in its best interests cannot be allowed to remain in that environment, he or she "shall be entitled to special protection and assistance provided by the State." Article 20(2) says that states parties must ensure "alternative care" in accordance with the relevant national law.

Article 20(3) elaborates on what that care could include, namely, "foster placement, kafalah of Islamic law, adoption or if necessary placement in suitable institutions for the care of children." States are told that "due regard shall be paid to the desirability of continuity in a child's upbringing and to the child's ethnic, religious, cultural and linguistic background." Article 20 then suggests that it is a matter of national will, and not a human rights imperative, whether institutional care is chosen for the child for whom foster care or adoption is not available in the country of origin. I would question whether this level of national discretion continues to represent a valid approach, given our understanding of human psychology and attachment theory, and in light of the Hague Convention coming into effect.

Article 21 of the UNCRC addresses the situation of states parties that do allow adoption, and sets out standards to govern the adoption process. It states, sensibly, that the best interests of the child must be the paramount concern in the adoption system, ensuring that the competent national authorities have authorized the adoption, that the biological family has given informed consent to the adoption, and that those involved in the adoption process have not reaped improper financial gain. Article 21(b) inserts a UNCRC preference for in-country care of virtually any "suitable" kind in lieu of intercountry adoption, by stating that parties shall "recognize that intercountry adoption may be considered as an alternative means of child's care, if the child cannot be placed in a foster or an adoptive family or cannot in any suitable manner be cared for in the child's country of origin."

This article will try to determine what the human rights of children, as articulated most extensively in the UNCRC itself, demand regarding rights to family life, and regarding the right to avoid care in an institution. A more difficult question, as indicated above, is whether non-institutional forms of care, such as foster care and group home care, sufficiently recognize the human rights of children. It seems fair to say that the UNCRC allows for intercountry adoption, but leaves states parties a great deal of discretion as to whether they wish to recognize intercountry adoption.....

In analyzing whether international human rights law "allows" the institutionalization of children without families, we must address the confusing intersection of the UNCRC and the Hague Convention on Protection of Children and Co-Operation in Respect of Intercountry Adoption. While not a human rights convention, the Hague Convention on Intercountry Adoption is undoubtedly a "best interests convention." It addresses itself to the potential for corruption and profiteering in intercountry adoption, and places a burden on participating countries to root out such procedures and practices. In this light, it can be said that the Hague Convention is primarily an agreement on proper procedures for those countries choosing to maintain intercountry adoption programs. But what does the Hague Convention have to say about whether or not countries are free to refuse intercountry adoption when the only alternative is institutional care, or foster care?....

....

The right of a child not to be placed in a manner involving corruption is a very important one, but it should not be seen as a self-contained issue. It is a cause for frustration that so much writing on the subject suggests that intercountry adoption is inherently corrupt, and therefore must be eliminated, and the in-country alternatives made as humane as possible. In such a scenario, if there is continued neglect in institutional settings, that neglect is not considered to be an international human rights concern. However, it is precisely in such a scenario that the most important human rights inquiry should begin.

....

In its insistence on Central Authorities in all participating states, the Hague Convention makes a plea for regulation and oversight, based on a set of completely commonsensical principles. It attempts to eliminate possibilities for profiteering, thereby "rehabilitating" the intercountry adoption process. It would seem therefore a logical extension of the actual words of the Convention that there should be a global agency charged with keeping at least informal surveillance over the level and degree of adherence to its principles in participating countries. Both national centralization and the need for global oversight by a sympathetic but skeptical agency also imply investment. A sensible and efficient approach would be to use a portion of the fees for each adoption to assist poorer countries to fully implement the Hague Convention, and also to create a small, efficient, and highly specialized global agency to ensure the full functioning of the Convention.

....

III. Conceptualizing Intercountry Adoption: Correcting Misperceptions, Balancing Caution and Facilitation

A. Negative Rhetoric and the Human Rights Imperative: Intercountry Adoption Dismissed as a "Market"

There is a serious and persistent problem with respect to the manner in which international adoption is described in both journalism and academic writing, including legal academic writing. Perhaps due to the many and complex forms of hostility towards adoption, and particularly towards intercountry adoption, writers appear comfortable speaking of a "market" in children. Many are contemptuous of adoptive parents and describe them as craving some illicit prize, rather than as engaging in a beneficial and legitimate process to ensure a home for children without families. Most articles on the subject describe astronomical sums "paid" for children without differentiating between legitimate costs of adoption and profiteering from adoption, and without explaining adequately the relationship of costs to the various means of adoption. Adoption costs rarely receive rational treatment in the press, and there is a strong and persistent undercurrent of opinion that costs taint the adoption itself. This creates an impression of adoptive parents, desperate to gain their undeserved prize, racing about paying huge sums in bags to "agents." This is a grotesque misrepresentation of most adoptions, but, as an intellectual phenomenon, demonstrates that for many writers there is little interest in separating out the beauties from the abuses of the adoption process.

....

Many writers, including journalists, make the implicit assumption that intercountry or intercultural adoption inherently partakes of a negative history, that assumptions of superiority that characterized many forms and modes of adoption in the past have simply evolved into contemporary adoption via a new ideological code: the need to "save" children from a terrible fate. But, growing up in an institution might well be a terrible fate. Certain types of foster care, with its uncertainties, might be seen as a terrible fate. Living on the streets is unquestionably a terrible fate. We should confront the question of whether these assertions are just a matter of opinion and of point of view, or whether there are facts concerning human development that lead us to state with confidence that the outcome for some children, based on their environmental conditions, are good and positive, while others are not. This article maintains that child psychology allows us to identify good and bad, as well as better and best, in this context and, thus, can lead us towards the articulation of a child's right not to be left to grow up in an institution when true alternatives exist. In this regard, we must also confront a hierarchy of desirable modes of care, one that neither denigrates traditional or culturally specific forms that really work, nor overlooks or explains away the deprivations suffered in institutional environments.

....

E. Children Without Families as a Global Cohort: Complex Social, Economic, and Cultural Pressures

....

Unfortunately, the matter of intercountry adoption tends to be cast in purely economic terms. Poor countries, the typical description goes, produce children they cannot pay for, leading to a situation where these children become the "possessions" of persons in wealthier countries. But the problem is not at all this simple, as the rate of abortion and the continued need for foster care within the wealthier states make plain. A great deal of writing on the subject spurns the view that adoption can be the happiest possible outcome for many children, even where unfortunate loopholes in a particular national legal system might continue to allow for profiteering and corruption. Rather, the issue is often presented as if adoption itself were exploitation, and this represents a thoroughly mistaken analysis. A wide range of phenomena in all parts of the world leads to the creation of children who are not wanted in the lives of particular biological parents at a particular time. The reasons are often economic at their root, but are not simply or purely economic. Biological parents from all walks of life, including biological parents in the highest economic brackets, may not be in a position to parent at a given time.

. . . .

It is troubling that a good deal of writing on the subject of international adoption implies that children are available for adoption precisely because someone is willing to "pay for" them. This implies that large numbers of children would not be institutionalized, and would be with their families of origin, were it not for unscrupulous parties preying on birth families in order to feed a "market." In this regard, the market discourse often used to describe adoption is both misleading and destructive. There are homeless children by the hundreds of thousands all over the world. Much of the academic and non-academic writing on the subject suffers from a failure to pursue empirical approaches to such questions as: which children are homeless, for what set of reasons, and how their existence relates to those who might attempt to profiteer on the phenomenon of adoption. Drawing a distinction between profiteering and the artificial creation of a market in children is a primary task, one which has to be dealt with in light of international sociological reality. Assumptions about imperialism and exploitation and the relative merits of biological and adoptive families cannot possibly elicit an appropriate set of legal responses.

At the same time, the question of whether the children who really need homes are the children who are being adopted must be faced, and faced squarely, if intercountry adoption is to survive....

IV. The Psychological Basis for a Human Rights Approach to Intercountry Adoption

. . . .

B. Ideal Legal Regimes for Sending and Receiving Children: What Characteristics These Would Have

1. Best Interests, Child Psychology, and International Human Rights

. . . .

National legal regimes should not be constructed on the belief that complex relationships with cultural environments are the equivalent of the psychological problems that arise from long-term residence in institutional or other inadequate care. Providing food, shelter, and even some degree of affection in institutional settings is simply not the equivalent of good parenting. One can only speculate on the influence exerted by the primary international organizations concerned with children's rights and interests, insofar as they appear to have frequently set themselves against the concept of intercountry adoption, in favor of forms of in-country care that simply cannot compare with the advantages of "a family of one's own." The fact that developing children will experience some confusion and upset over issues surrounding adoption and movement from one culture to another cannot be compared to the profoundly debilitating effects of life in an institution or even in foster care, where the fostering relationships are less than the total commitment of family members to one another.

. . . .

It is fairly obvious, though not provable in the strict sense, that many countries are not allowing as many adoptable children to be adopted as they could. More often than not, the process goes forward enveloped in layers of ambiguity. It is unclear to what degree sending countries are truly suspicious of the adopters and of their own officials, or even to what degree sending countries are supportive of or hostile to intercountry adoption. This article calls for concrete measures to eliminate some of this ambiguity and mystery from the system through a sort of "global negotiation" forum. To those familiar with social conditions in a country, it should be quite apparent whether a particular child is likely to be reunified with a family of origin, or to be adopted domestically. Where both are highly unlikely, the human rights imperative urged here requires us to find an out-of-country solution for that child in the form of adoption. Where national caution is manifest in a de facto quota system, tens of thousands of children could be arbitrarily forced to languish in inferior forms of care. On the other hand, failure to control the system can lead to thousands of newborns who might not actually require intercountry adoption at all to find their way into the system, at the expense of the children who more genuinely require adoption.

. . . .

It appears that no country is willing to facilitate the adoption process while there is a risk of harming the national reputation. Negative publicity surrounding intercountry adoption has created an aura of the illicit, and each national jurisdiction currently operates in social and political isolation, despite the objectives of the Hague Convention. To break out of this state of affairs would require the creation of a truly impartial international body dedicated to examining the child welfare situation in each sending and receiving country. Such a body would have the credibility to respond to rumors or to other crises that might threaten particular programs. By combining advocacy and skepticism, such a body could be relied on by all sides to sort out the factual situation, and thereby to guarantee the full promise of the Hague Convention principles.

. . . .

B. General Conclusions

. . . .

International human rights principles, applied in light of the demands of the human psyche, require a global regime to deal with children without families. The current piecemeal, politically confused and confusing, nationally-based, under-or wrongly regulated system has led to tens of thousands of children languishing in orphanages on the one hand, and charges of the artificial creation of a "market" in children on the other. A global agency such as UNICEF has the capacity to take on the task of providing oversight for the ethical adoption of children but it, like other agencies charged with the care of children, has frequently articulated an at best ambiguous, and at worst implicitly hostile, view of international adoption. Despite protestations of neutrality, there is a basis to suspect that UNICEF has bought into and perpetuates the idea that intercountry adoption is essentially a vestige of colonialism. It is this author's contention that a separate, objective, and specialized agency, acting under the Hague Convention principles, should be set up through a widely representative conference. The underlying ethos should, as mentioned above, reflect both advocacy of adoption and a healthy skepticism with regard to the possibilities for abuse.

The Hague Convention will never be broadly ratified and properly implemented unless there is a global fund to assist in the creation of national adoption departments or official agencies. A genuinely global regime, with the expertise and capacity to respond to national political furors on the subject of adoption, is necessary in order to bring an end to the uncertainty and uneven benefits to children. Individual countries should be relieved of the burden of devising their national adoption regimes in light of nationalistic passions and historical grievances. Clearly, the human rights dimension of, and basis of, the Hague Convention lacks clarity; its preamble's stated preference for adoption over other forms of in-country care such as foster care and institutional living is too feebly articulated to overcome the vast reservoir of prejudice against intercountry adoption.

. . . .

Notes and Questions

1. If the UNCRC does not require countries to allow adoption, and if the Hague Convention encourages adoption, but also does not impose any obligation on countries to allow it, is there any basis in human rights law for saying that countries must find permanent family solutions for children living out of family care? What would that legal basis be? The Dillon article is skeptical about substituting long term foster care for institutionalization of children. Can or should foster care be seen as a valid alternative mode of care, taking into account the contextual principles of rights to identity?

2. After being presented with both sides of the debate on intercountry adoption, do you think it should be expanded, restricted, or even eliminated? Each option carries with it certain dangers and difficulties; which option most clearly comports with a proper understanding of "children's rights"?

C. Intercountry Adoption — The Case of Romania

Romania has been, in recent years, a focal point for the debate over intercountry adoption. Following a barrage of scathing criticism by Baroness Emma Nicholson, former rapporteur on Romanian accession to the EU for the European Parliament, Romania decided to halt all international adoptions out of Romania, except in very exceptional circumstances. Whereas the Romanian orphanages that developed during the repressive years of the Ceaucescu regime became a symbol of the worst forms of institutional neglect, many argued that the kind of international adoption that flourished with the fall of the Communist regime was itself thoroughly corrupt. In the years that have followed the cessation of adoption from Romania, advocates and critics of international adoption have argued over whether its new system of child welfare is humane and effective or not. There are strong views on both sides. It does seem clear that child abandonment rates have remained discouragingly high, despite the profound reforms that have taken place at EU insistence, particularly with regard to the closure of the large orphanages. Recall as well the revelations contained in the MDRI report, set out earlier in this chapter.

Elisabeth Rosenthal,
Law Backfires, Stranding Orphans in Romania
The New York Times, June 23 2005, *available at*
http://www.nytimes.com/2005/06/23/international/europe/23adopt.html

A new law here on the "protection and promotion of the rights of the child" has done little to protect Vasile, a 7-year-old who has lived his whole life in an orphanage in Botosani.

More than two years ago, Becky Hubbell, a pharmaceutical executive from Overland Park, Kan., submitted the required papers to adopt the wide-eyed, dark-haired boy, whom she and her husband had met during medical missions here.

But before that process was completed, the government passed its new child welfare law, which essentially forbids international adoptions. The measure has left hundreds of families without children they had counted as theirs. More important, critics say, the sweeping law leaves thousands of abandoned Romanian children stranded indefinitely in institutions or foster care.

"You have a child in your heart and you've made all the arrangements, and it's clear that child wants a family, too," Ms. Hubbell said. "But for Vasile, time is passing without the stability of a home. And that's harder and harder to make up for."

When, in 2002, officials in Brussels demanded that Romania clean up a chaotic and sometimes corrupt child welfare system as a condition for admission to the European Union, Romanian politicians jumped into action. Law 272, written in collaboration with European Union advisers, aimed to halt decades of mismanagement with edicts that critics say were overzealous and impractical.

In response to criticism that orphans were growing up in sterile institutions, the government mandated that no child under 2 could live in one; the new law, it noted, favored reuniting children with biological relatives or placing them in foster care. In response to charges that foreign adoptions were so poorly managed that they sometimes resembled child trafficking, the government declared there would be no more.

Experts applaud the central goal: to encourage Romanian families to stay together and to end the longstanding practice here of abandoning unwanted children. But many child advocates doubt that this poor country, just 15 years removed from a brutal dictatorship, will be able to find good living situations quickly for its huge population of orphaned and abandoned children. Many children currently in orphanages and hospitals, they say, will be stranded.

"There are good impulses behind the law — to provide more assistance to mothers, to keep children out of institutions — and we all felt the system needed more standards," said Gabi Mihaela Comanescu, program director of the ProChild Romania Foundation. "But there are problems. For example, there are older children who are as adoptable as ever, but there is no one to adopt them now. Also, the law says every abandoned child under 2 should be in foster care, but as far as I know there aren't nearly enough foster homes."

The unintended result is that deserted infants are now passing their precious first years in a hospital ward. There are close to 10,000 children abandoned at hospitals each year in Romania, according to a new study by UNICEF, and up to 50,000 children in the care of the state.

Romania's unusual tradition of child abandonment began with a ban on birth control imposed in 1966 by Nicolae Ceausescu, the former dictator, to increase the population. Within a year, women began dropping off unwanted children at state orphanages or hospitals. Their logic was that "the government wanted them, so the government should raise them," according to the UNICEF report.

Child abandonment has continued at the same level for 40 years, said Pierre Poupard, head of the Unicef office in Bucharest, even though birth control is widely available in post-Communist Romania. Now, mothers desert babies because they feel they cannot afford to raise them.

Before Law 272 took effect on Jan. 1, politicians from France, Italy and the United States, among others, vigorously lobbied the government to rethink the ban on international adoptions, or at least to allow cases already started to proceed. In January the new Romanian prime minister, Calin Popescu-Tariceanu, said he would "not forget foreign families" who had taken steps to adopt Romanian children. To date, however, nothing has been done.

According to the Romanian Adoptions Office, 467 babies were adopted by foreigners in 2002, although a partial moratorium was already in effect. Before that, several hundred Romanian children were adopted annually by families in Italy, France, Israel and the United States, according to adoption groups in those countries. Today the number is zero.

Instead, Romanian county child welfare officials are now required to "reintegrate or integrate the children into their biological or extended families or to place them with a Romanian foster family," said Theodora Bertzi, head of the adoption office.

New families are being trained in foster care to meet the need, she said. Romanian couples (or grandparents living overseas) are being encouraged to adopt unwanted children. Orphanages, called "placement centers," can take children over 2 when no home is available.

Florin Catanescu, 28, grew up in the centers after being abandoned at birth by a schizophrenic mother. Handsome and articulate, he carries his past in one small photo album decorated with a child's glittery stickers. He is skeptical about Law 272, at least in the short term.

"I just don't think the resources are sufficient in our country for this new law, and attitudes will not change that quickly," said Mr. Catanescu, who is starting a nongovernmental organization to help graduates of the centers integrate into society: find jobs, rent apartments, order food in a restaurant. "Children will be stuck—there are still so many families who abandon children."

Because so many of the children are given up for economic reasons, they continue to have contact with their mothers even if they live in orphanages for years, making it hard to define their family status.

Under the old law, if a mother disappeared for more than six months, the child could be put up for adoption. But the new law, with its emphasis on maintaining biological families, stipulates that a mother's right to her child is indefinite, extending through years of separation.

In order for a child to be put up for adoption, the mother must sign a paper formally ending the relationship, which is impossible in cases like Vasile's, in which the mother has long since disappeared. Other relatives have to decline the child as well.

At the Sunbeam Complex of Community Service, a placement center 60 miles from Bucharest, 15 of the 16 children (aged 4 to 9) have had some contact with their biological families. Only one girl, who is 4, is technically adoptable. The tidy two-story house, lying amid dusty fields, is far superior to the huge, impersonal orphanages that made the child welfare system of Communist Romania so notorious.

On a recent afternoon, young residents busied themselves drawing pictures at low tables and playing with blocks. But before Law 272, five children left here each year, adopted by foreign families, said Letitia Stefanescu, the home's director.

The new law "has many good aspects," Ms. Stefanescu said, like offering preventive counseling and financial assistance to young mothers deemed at risk of abandoning babies. But she acknowledged the downside for the children in her care: "International adoptions gave them a chance for a family."

A cute 9-year-old with pigtails, who can only be identified as M.S., said, "I like being here, but I would like more to be with my mom." The girl's mother, who lives nearby, has not visited for several years.

Ms. Stefanescu has faith that the faults of the new system will be dealt with: New programs will encourage or force some mothers to pick up abandoned children; other children will find foster homes. The four-year-old, she hopes, will be adopted by Romanians, even though they traditionally do not adopt older children.

The Unicef report said it was crucial to take steps to prevent future abandonment, like allowing mothers to start rooming with their newborns in order to encourage bonding and prevent desertion.

Becky Hubbell, who spends holidays volunteering at the Botosani orphanage, says it is great that the government is now helping families stay together. But in the meantime, she said, "there are kids like Vasile who have no options but adoption abroad.

"We already provide support for him," she said. "We will be his family, no matter what."

————————

UNICEF Romania Media Center, *Letter to Prime Minister Regarding Inter-Country Adoption*

2004

Baroness Emma Nicholson of Winterbourne, MEP, Rapporteur for Romania

—Mr. Jonathan Scheele, Ambassador, Head of Delegation, Delegation of the European Commission

—Ms. Elena Dumitru, Minister of Labor, Social Solidarity and Family

—Ms. Gabriela Coman, Secretary of State, National Authority for Child Protection and Adoption

February 6, 2004

Dear Prime Minister,

UNICEF has been carefully following the recent debate on the issue of inter-country adoption and wants to express its position and make suggestions for the Government and your counterparts, thus contributing to find adequate solutions to this very sensitive and compelling problem.

Your recent statements, deploring the mounting pressure on the government under the circumstances surrounding the moratorium, and expressing clearly that Romania is on its way to find national solutions to the phenomena of abandonment of children coincide perfectly with UNICEF's standpoint on the issue. In our view, as stipulated by the proposed legislation package and the international conventions, inter-country adoption is to be considered as an exceptional measure and last resort within the alternative forms of child protection.

All over the world, UNICEF's work is geared to the fullest possible implementation of the Convention on the Rights of the Child and is directed solely towards helping to ensure that conditions in each country and community are such that all children can receive appropriate care, in line with the provisions of that Convention and other relevant international standards.

In this context, UNICEF supports all efforts to:

- ensure that children can, wherever possible, remain in the care of their parents;

- prevent abandonment;

- secure placement with family members or others in the community if parental care is impossible for whatever reason;

- identify a permanent in-country, family-based care solution as quickly as possible;

- implement measures that preclude the need for recourse to institutional placements.

UNICEF recognises that the rights and best interests of some children may nonetheless best be served through inter-country adoption, in which case the pertinent international standards must be systematically and strictly applied on a case-by-case basis.

UNICEF has been deeply disturbed by the flagrant violation of these standards in and by many countries world-wide in recent years. Such have been the gravity and frequency of these violations that in many cases the countries concerned and/or the countries where their children were being adopted have had to suspend adoptions for the period necessary to take effective measures to prevent recurrence of illegal practices. Central and Eastern European countries have regrettably experienced such problems on a possibly unprecedented scale since "transition" began. In addition to Romania, no less than six other countries in the region—Albania, Belarus, Georgia, Moldova, Russia and Ukraine—have consequently had to resort to declaring moratoria on inter-country adoptions at certain junctures during this period.

When Romania itself was first obliged to impose a moratorium in July 1991, UNICEF was among those supporting the efforts of the competent Romanian Authorities to put in place legislation, structures and procedures that would ensure that adoption of Romanian children by foreigners took place in accordance with internationally-accepted norms. Regrettably, and for various reasons, serious abuses nonetheless continued.

The decision to suspend inter-country adoptions once more in 2001 was inevitable in the circumstances. UNICEF believes that the decision taken at that time to carry out a thorough reappraisal of the child protection legislative framework, including that pertaining to inter-country adoption, was undeniably necessary. As is the case for law reform in virtually all countries, the drafting, consultations, enactment and preparation for implementation of new and fundamental legislation is a lengthy process. In the light of experience, UNICEF also believes that the moratorium has to remain in effect for as long as that process takes.

The UNICEF position is fully in accordance with the recommendations of the UN Committee on the Rights of the Child, in its Concluding Observations issued in February 2003, which advised Romania to "*expedite the adoption of the new law, ensure that sufficient human and other resources are made available for the effective implementation of the law, ensure that the cases of inter-country adoption still under consideration are dealt with in full accordance with the principles and provisions of the Convention on the Rights of the Child and the Hague Convention, and explore ways to encourage the national adoptions so that the recourse to inter-country adoption is a measure of last resort*".

UNICEF deplores the pressure brought to bear by some quarters which could considerably prejudice the basis and aims of the moratorium and of the legislative review. It believes that such pressure may not be consistent with respect for the provisions of the Convention on the Rights of the Child. In this regard, UNICEF notes that in recent years it has proved possible to effect significant improvements in the child protection system in Romania. The largest and most inappropriate institutions for children are progressively being closed, levels of child abandonment are decreasing, and appropriate forms of alternative care are being developed. UNICEF is among those supporting these efforts. Clearly, the number of children benefiting from such developments is immeasurably greater than that of children who, had the moratorium been lifted, might have been deemed available for adoption abroad. Indeed, it is UNICEF's view that the need for recourse to inter-country adoption is now declining very rapidly, and that within two to three years, Romania should not have to envisage the adoption of its children abroad in all but the most exceptional cases. UNICEF believes that this is a goal towards which each and everyone should be working.

In this regard, therefore, UNICEF would respectfully suggest that Romania avoids legislating the imposition of an unqualified and definitive ban on any future adoption of a Romanian child abroad. European States generally leave open the possibility for inter-country adoption from their territory, recognising that there may be given circumstances—such as extended family members abroad—where the child's best interests might be served by such a solution. Indeed, such adoptions do take place, albeit in extremely limited numbers, from and between these States. At the same time, they understandably place clear and often very severe restrictions on the kind of situation where inter-country adoption may be considered and, in particular, they ensure that full control is exerted by the competent authorities. UNICEF believes that such an approach is more consistent with the spirit and letter of the Convention on the Rights of the Child and the 1993 Hague Convention on Inter-country Adoption than total prohibition. UNICEF nonetheless fully agrees, of course, that an immediate stop has to be imposed on the spontaneous submission of dossiers by prospective adoptive parents from abroad, whether individually or via agencies, which is a major factor fuelling the pressure on Romania to allow significant numbers of its children to be adopted abroad.

UNICEF will continue to provide needed support to the Government of Romania, to ensure that the best interest of the child and the provisions of the CRC on inter-country adoption are fully respected. Inter-country adoption, as is well recognised, is intrinsically linked to the wider child protection/alternative care question. UNICEF has identified three timeframes in this regard:

– 2004, equivalent to the minimum period during which the moratorium is currently expected to apply;

– 2004–2007, assuming that Romania's application to join the EU is on track;

– 2005–2009, Romania-UNICEF's next programme period.

For 2004 specifically, UNICEF will strongly and clearly defend the justification for the moratorium. It will also contribute to monitoring, and to discussing with the National Authority for Child Protection and Adoption and any other appropriate Romanian or foreign authorities, recourse to inter-country adoption while the moratorium is in effect. It will provide support to ensure that the content of the proposed legislation will be well understood and internalized by the different stakeholders.

For 2004–2007, UNICEF will place major emphasis on supporting efforts to reduce recourse to abandonment, maintain/reintegrate children with their families, and provide valid in-country non-institutional forms of out-of-home care. It will also contribute to countering effective demand regarding the adoption of Romanian children abroad. The overall aim will be to ensure that, by end 2007, conditions are such that inter-country adoption from the country is very rarely required and that it is therefore no longer a "phenomenon" as such but a truly exceptional and individualised practice.

For 2005–2009, the strategic intent of UNICEF presence in Romania will be to support Romania in ensuring that all children and youth can grow up in a caring family or a family like environment and that their fundamental rights for survival, development, participation and protection are fully realized. The program will focus on policy development, in the areas of health and fight against HIV/AIDS, education and child protection. Many of the proposed interventions will aim at reducing the level of abandonment of children, fight against child trafficking, and ensure adequate care to vulnerable children, families and communities. Additional efforts will be provided to ensure a proper monitoring of the Convention on the Rights of the Child, and an appropriate response to the Committee on the Rights of the Child, for which UNICEF has expressed its interest in supporting the creation of an inter-ministerial body, to monitor the implementation of the Convention, in partnership with civil society organizations.

Reasserting my entire availability for meeting you, should you need any further discussion, I avail myself of this opportunity to renew to you, dear Prime Minister, the assurances of my highest consideration.

Pierre Poupard,
UNICEF Representative

Notes and Questions

1. The debate over Romanian adoptions has been bitter and intense. As the readings above make clear, UNICEF weighed in on the side of the Romanian moratorium; the New York Times article seems to suggest that the Romanian "reforms" were not as successful as advertised. (Refer back to the selections from the report by Mental Disability Rights International on ongoing neglect in Romanian institutions, above.) In light of the relevant international law and the historical situation in Romania, what was the right approach for that country? Why did the international child welfare bodies seem to come down so heavily in favor of stopping international adoption from Romania?

2. It is significant that in its June 2009 Concluding Observations on Romania, the UN Committee on the Rights of the Child recommended that Romania should withdraw its existing moratorium on international adoption. Interestingly, the Committee stated that the moratorium is acting as a "barrier to the full implementation of Article 21 of the Convention." Available at http://www2.ohchr.org/english/bodies/crc/docs/co/CRC-C-ROM-CO-4.pdf, at paragraph 55.

III. Sex-Selective Abortion and Abandonment of Girls

It is a sad fact that children are often rejected because of their gender or some other characteristic, such as a disability. It is not uncommon in some societies to go so far as to kill unwanted girls or other children on the assumption that they are a drain on family resources. Gender-related infanticide is often called "gendercide"; some may include gender-based pregnancy terminations in this term. Gendercide is widely practiced in societies where boys are more valued than girls, generally because of the belief that boys remain in their family of origin to take care of the parents, whereas girls eventually take up residence in their husbands' families. Thus, for many people in poor and rural areas of India and China particularly, having male children appears to be a matter of life and death. Where for a variety of reasons the number of children a family can have is limited, then there is an even greater incentive to retain sons at the expense of daughters. (A variation on this theme is the widespread abandonment of girls in China, due to the "one child policy" begun in 1979.) The issue appears here because rejection based on gender is yet another way in which children either disappear or find themselves left to grow up without the protection offered by the biological family.

Gender-selective abortion, though nominally illegal in many countries, is popular and widely practiced. This procedure has led to serious and growing gender imbalances in many parts of Asia, which in turn has given rise to increased trafficking of girls as brides to serve the needs of young men otherwise unable to find wives. Gendercide and gender selective abortion, as well as the abandonment of disabled children, implicate children's rights in general, as well as the rights of the "girl child" and the rights of children with disabilities. The UNCRC has provisions relevant to each of these issues. Of particular relevance are Articles 2 (on the right of the child to exercise his or her rights without discrimination), 6 (on the right to life), 7 (on the obligation to register the birth of children), 23 (on the rights of disabled children), and 24 (on the right of the child to the highest attainable standard of health care). Although governments, notably in India and China, have been stung by international attention to the problem of gender-selective abortion and have moved to criminalize the practice, there is little indication that it has been discouraged in any meaningful way at the local level. Wherever boys are more highly valued, and technology exists to determine gender before birth, gender selective abortions have continued apace.

The selections that follow present in chilling outline the problem of "daughter discrimination." It is hard to see how children's rights principles have penetrated the entrenched cultural views that have led to the mass disappearance of girls described below.

Lesley Wexler, *Allowing Girls to Hold Up Half the Sky: Combining Norm Promotion and Economic Incentives to Combat Daughter Discrimination in China*
7 Chicago Journal of International Law 79 (2006)

Introduction and Background

In 1990, Amartya Sen uncovered a global epidemic of over one hundred million missing women—women that, given statistically normal birth rates, should exist in the world but do not. Sen and others have suggested three main contributors to this crisis: sex selective abortions, the related practices of female infanticide and abandonment, and inadequate medical care for female children. China provides an interesting and particularly important challenge in combating the missing women phenomena for a few reasons. First, a focus on China provides more potential value than addressing the problem elsewhere. Sen has suggested that over fifty million Chinese women are missing which accounts for 45 percent of the missing women worldwide. Even given undercounting and other problems in data collection, Chinese and foreign demographers alike agree that a significant problem exists. Second, most regions in the world are experiencing a relative improvement in the eradication of the missing women phenomena, but China's male to female sex ratio at birth is rising. Third, given the ongoing restructuring of the Chinese government and reformation of the country, the active liberalization of reproductive policy provides an "important experiment in state-society relations." Unlike many countries, China has created a separate agency for reproductive policy, and the government has a long-standing tradition of dictating desired outcomes in this area. Policy changes here can provide a model for the reformation of other Chinese agencies.

Despite the Chinese government's vocal commitment to women's rights, China is experiencing an increasing shortage of girls and young women. In a world with no widespread preference for either boys or girls, we should expect to see about 104 male births for every 100 female births—yielding a sex ratio of 1.04. Yet at the time of the 2000 China census, national statistics revealed about 118 male births for every 100 female births. The sex birth ratio is particularly skewed for second and successive births. So while some Chinese couples may not demonstrate a significant preference for their first child to be a son, most demonstrate a marked preference for sons as second children if their first child is a girl. While much variation exists among provinces, as a whole, the disparity in the sex ratio is growing in both rural and urban areas as well as in both rich and poor provinces.

. . . .

Chinese families possess multiple mechanisms for daughter discrimination. While Chinese couples once relied on faulty folk methods for determining fetuses' sex, advancements in reproductive technology allow most couples to accurately assess their fetuses' sex relatively early in the pregnancy. The active governmental role in promoting family planning means that even the poorest, most rural facilities possess ultrasound equipment. Armed with a definitive outcome, a couple with a strong son preference may elect to abort its female fetus(es). For those without access to doctors willing to reveal the sex of the fetus, a couple may instead choose to terminate a female child shortly after birth. While such practice may seem strongly objectionable, few Chinese families or communities view this practice as murder. Other families may abandon their female children shortly after birth. Finally, for those couples with a son preference but unwilling to engage in sex selective abortion or female infanticide, they may decide to under-invest in their female children's development. This underinvestment may include a failure to provide adequate health care, a reluctance to educate, and the creation of a second class status for daughters within the family. Additionally, daughters may be forced to sacrifice their development to free up resources or directly contribute to their brothers. For instance, a daughter might be pulled out of school and put to work in the fields to facilitate her brother's education.

A strong son preference and the resultant skewed sex ratio create three types of harms: to the individual girls, to families, and to society as a whole. From both Western perspectives and universal human rights approaches, female infanticide constitutes murder. Sex selective abortions are not costless either—women suffer from the health and emotional harms of abortions as well as from the additional pregnancies which risk maternal mortality and morbidity. Relatedly, abandoned children, of whom an overwhelming majority are girls, face a very high mortality rate even if they eventually make it to an orphanage. Moreover, those undesired girls who are kept by their natal families often receive fewer physical and emotional resources than other family members. Their undervaluation within both their natal and marital families often leads to severe psychological harms and affects the development of the overall society. For instance, China is unique in the world with its high rates of female and rural suicides. Many suggest this deviation from normally low female suicide rates stems from females' feelings of worthlessness in a patriarchal society and more specifically, the difficulties of living in a patrilocal kinship structure. For instance, women from China's provinces and urban areas believe that they will face discrimination if they bear only daughters. Such discrimination may extend to physical abuse and even murder. Similarly, wives living with their husbands' families experience extreme levels of conflict in trying to fulfill their in-laws' expectations.

Despite a logic that would suggest otherwise, imbalanced sex ratios are not self-correcting. One might predict that a dearth of female children would eventually lead to a rise in women's value since their scarcity enhances the difficulty of men in finding wives. The marriage market, however, does not respond in this manner. Although some women may make substantial one-time economic gains in the marriage market, their families seem unlikely to prefer them to sons since the marriage will just be a possible one-time monetary transfer while sons provide ongoing support. Moreover, both in historical and modern times, such a shortage has contributed to the rapid increase of kidnapping and sexual trafficking of women in China. In addition, the growing population of young men unable to find wives creates conditions that foster high crime rates, engagement in vice, and general societal instability. Thus the strategy of waiting out the problem until daughter discrimination naturally declines is not a viable option.

Unfortunately, daughter discrimination is deeply rooted in the Chinese family kinship structure and parts of the Confucian value system. Many Confucian practices value and honor men over women—only men may perform many religious and ancestral rituals. For most of Chinese history, only men could continue a family's lineage through the family name and only men were allowed to hold property. In addition, the practice of patrilocality, in which women generally left their natal families at marriage and joined the husband's family, created separate reasons for families to undervalue their daughters. As a daughter would not contribute to the care of her natal family once her marriage had taken place, her birth was viewed as a double loss to the family.

Similar reasons exist for the ongoing son preference in China. Non-economic considerations include the ability to carry on the family name and particular forms of ancestor worship—both of which must still be carried out by a son. The presence of a strongly enforced family planning policy exacerbates these underlying rationales. For instance, citizens who have children in violation of birth policies must pay a social compensation fee that often exceeds their annual incomes. So, rather than have several children until a boy is born, some families kill, abort, or abandon female children. Although some very wealthy provinces view social compensation fees as a mere inconvenience, they too display a high level of son preference—whereas some very poor provinces display comparatively lower sex ratios. Evidence from multiple countries indicates that greater wealth can enhance the son preference as couples prefer smaller families. This suggests economic development and greater wealth alone cannot effectively combat son preference or sex selective abortions.

. . . .

A. Limitations of Existing Proposals

1. Changing Family Planning Targets

Some scholars advocate the loosening or abandonment of China's one child policy. Total renunciation of family planning goals, however, defies existing political realities. China still cares deeply about maintaining a low and stable fertility rate into the foreseeable future, as the government is wedded to a neo-Malthusian belief that low population rates are essential to protect the environment as well as to maintain strong economic growth. Persuading the government otherwise would be a Herculean task.

As for loosening family planning targets, the Chinese government has already informally abandoned the one child policy in rural areas in favor of something better described as permitting either (1) one son or (2) one first born daughter and a second child. Some signs suggest societal pressures for even more exemptions. Such exemptions may help, but no consensus exists on the relative importance of the one child policy to China's missing women. Although a few scholars believe that lifting governmental fertility restrictions would virtually eradicate the imbalanced sex ratios, the strength of the son preference would likely still create significant numbers of missing women, to say nothing of other forms of pervasive daughter discrimination.

. . . .

2. Enhancing Enforcement of Criminal Schemes

Other scholars advocate stronger penalties for law-breaking families and increased enforcement of China's existing ban on sex selective abortions and female infanticide. Some legal activity may occur on this front. The Chinese government recently debated a revision to the criminal law that would impose monetary fines and a three-year jail sentence on any-one who assists sex selective abortions. Yet under the existing prohibitions, the government rarely prosecutes families for seeking out information to facilitate sex selective abortions, and no doctors or technicians have been convicted for providing such information.

Enforcing criminal sanctions on such actions proves quite difficult. For instance, most family planning clinics own ultrasound scanners making information about the fetus's sex quite accessible. Law enforcement officials will have a hard time knowing if doctors performed ultrasounds for legitimate medical reasons or to determine the sex of a child. Rather than openly flout the ban on assistance, doctors have already taken to coding their responses to surreptitiously let families know whether they are expecting girls or boys. Similarly, police may encounter substantial difficulty in distinguishing between cases of female infanticide and other common causes of infant death. Of course, devoting re-sources to catching and prosecuting sex selective abortions and female infanticides may yield some benefit, but given the practical difficulties, a serious change in practices seems unlikely. As an empirical matter, similar laws in India have not deterred sex selective abor-tion or other instances of daughter discrimination.

. . . .

3. Promoting Anti-Caste Principles

The first generation approach to the problem of missing women, as typified by Amartya Sen and Cass Sunstein, suggests that improving women's status through equal access to education, employment, and property ownership should help weaken the son preference. For instance, Sunstein encourages governments to promote anti-caste principles, such as sex equality, and to seek these changes through alterations of markets and social norms, rather than just through top down command and control regulations. These abstract ad-monitions complement the predictions made in the 1980s that expanding women's eco-nomic opportunities would diminish the son preference.

Notes and Questions

1. How should ratification of the UNCRC affect national policies on gendercide? Has China paid any significant price for its one child policy, or has the policy found tacit ac-ceptance in the international community? Prominent international thinkers like Amartya Sen have devoted scholarly attention to the problem of severe gender imbalance in Asia; has the topic received any corresponding attention at the level of international relations? For further discussion of gendercide in China, see Susan Tiefenbrun, *Gendercide and the Cultural Context of Sex Trafficking in China*, 32 Fordham International Law Journal 731 (2009). For a discussion of the geographical and social range in sex-selective abor-tions, also see *China Perspectives, Where Have All the Young Girls Gone: Fatal Discrimi-nation of Daughters—A Regional Comparison*, 2005, available at http://chinaperspectives .revues.org/document1120.html.

———————

The readings that follow suggest that the disappearance of girl children is nothing new. Rather, technology has allowed for early abortion, in lieu of the even more drastic female infanticide. Writers on the topic of disappeared female infants are clearly at a loss with respect to how to most accurately describe the phenomenon—can it be seen as an aspect of "reproductive freedom," when it is so obviously based on severe discrimination? If pass-ing national laws criminalizing participation in gender determination seems to be inef-fective, will UN pamphlets be any more effective?

Uma Girish, *For India's Daughters, A Dark Birthday: Infanticide and Sex-Selective Abortion Yield a More Skewed Gender Ratio*

2005, Christian Science Monitor, *available at*
http://www.csmonitor.com/2005/0209/p11s01-wosc.html

The oleander plant yields a bright, pleasant flower, but also a milky sap that, if ingested, can be a deadly poison. It's one of the methods families use to kill newborn girls in the Salem District of Tamil Nadu, a part of India notorious for female infanticide.

Though the government has battled the practice for decades, India's gender imbalance has worsened in recent years. Any progress toward halting infanticide, it seems, has been offset by a rise in sex-selective abortions. Too many couples—aided by medical technology, unethical doctors, and weak enforcement of laws banning abortion on the basis of gender—are electing to end a pregnancy if the fetus is female.

The consequence of female infanticide and, more recently, abortion is India's awkwardly skewed gender ratio, among the most imbalanced in the world. The ratio among children up to the age of 6 was 962 girls per 1,000 boys in 1981, but 20 years later the inequity was actually worse: 927 girls per 1,000 boys.

Infanticide is illegal in India (though never prosecuted), and laws are also in place to stop sex-selective abortions. But in some places, national rules don't hold enough sway to overcome local religious and social customs—which remain biased in favor of sons over daughters.

"Factors like dowry, imbalance in the employment sector whereby the male is seen as breadwinner, and societal pressure to abort female fetuses conspire to increase the antigirl bias," says Ajay K. Tripathi of the Advanced Studies in Public Health Programme, of the Institute of Health Systems in Hyderabad. Government and the medical profession, he says, need to put more resources—and more political will—into strengthening and enforcing the laws.

A case in point is legislation—introduced last year but now stalled—that would prohibit all genetic-counseling facilities, clinics, and labs from divulging the sex of the fetus. The hope is that if parents don't know "it's a girl," fewer will resort to abortion. But the proposal, which would amend a 1994 law, is opposed by medical groups. They argue that technology used to monitor fetal health—such as ultrasound scans and amniocentesis—cannot be put under such intense scrutiny.

Others, though, see another reason for the opposition: Abortion is a lucrative business that many doctors do not want to see curtailed. "Abortions are a low-risk, high-profit business. As a specialist in fetal medicine, I can tell you that no pregnant woman would suffer if the ultrasound test were banned," says Puneet Bedi, a gynecologist at Apollo Hospitals in New Delhi. "Right now, it is used to save 1 out of 20,000 fetuses and kill 20 out of every 100 because [it reveals that the baby] is the wrong gender."

India stipulates that only a government hospital, registered facility, or medical practitioner with appropriate qualifications may perform an abortion. The reality, however, is that only about 15 percent of all abortions take place under such circumstances, according to the Indian Medical Association. About 11.2 million illegal abortions are performed each year off the record. Such abortions are often "female feticide," experts say.

In Salem district, for instance, signs posted in towns reinforce the societal message: "Pay 500 rupees and save 50,000 rupees later," a suggestion that aborting a female fetus now could save a fortune in wedding expenses in the future.

. . . .

Nearly 60 percent of girls born in Salem District are killed within three days of birth, according to the local social welfare department. That doesn't count the growing number of abortions there to ensure a girl baby won't be carried to term.

. . . .

In pockets of India where female infanticide persists, the practice is rooted in a complex mix of economic, social, and cultural factors. Parents' preference for a boy derives from the widespread belief that a son lighting his parents' funeral pyre will ensure that their souls ascend to heaven; that he will be a provider in their later years (India has no form of social security); and that he will preserve the family inheritance.

Conversely, a daughter is considered an economic burden. Pressure to conform can be intense in rural areas, and some families borrow heavily to pay for the rituals prescribed for a girl—the ear-piercing ceremony, wedding jewelry, dowry, and presents for the groom's family on every Hindu festival.

The Tamil Nadu government has started several programs to protect girls—with mixed results. One urged families to hand over their baby girls to local officials, who saw that they were adopted by childless couples. Between May 2001 and January 2003, officials received 361 baby girls. An informal survey by CSG, however, found that many women would abort rather than have a baby and give her up for adoption.

Tamil Nadu's "Girl Protection" program may be more practical. Here, the government opens a bank account in a girl's name at her birth, depositing between 15,000 and 22,000 rupees during her childhood, depending on the number of girls in the family.

"The only way to wipe out this evil is by an attitudinal shift," says CSG's Mr. Prasad. "Educate a girl beyond eighth grade and encourage her to find her voice."

Alison Wood Manhoff, *Banned and Enforced: The Immediate Answer to a Problem without an Immediate Solution—How India Can Prevent Another Generation of "Missing Girls"*
38 Vanderbilt Journal of Transnational Law 889 (2005)

I. INTRODUCTION

In 2001 the Supreme Court of India ordered state authorities to begin enforcing a law, which had been on the books for years, banning the use of technology to determine the sex of fetuses. This order stemmed India's 2001 census, which showed a dramatic drop in the number of young girls in the country. For every one thousand boys under the age of six there are only 927 girls. This latter number represents a drop from the 1991 statistic of 945 girls. Some speculate that this decrease is largely the result of the abortion of female fetuses, determined to be so after a sex determination ultrasound or amniocentesis procedure. It is commonly believed that this disparity is the result of the desire of Indian parents to avoid paying a dowry at the time of their daughter's marriage. The dowry is a payment from the bride's family to the groom's family in money, property, or goods. Although India outlawed dowries in 1961, the social custom still flourishes.

Commentators suggest that the solution to the problem is not passing more laws, such as banning sex determination ultrasounds, but raising the social and economic status of women. These commentators argue that while banning sex determination ultrasounds may appear to help eliminate the problem of selectively aborting female fetuses, it is questionable whether this is a step in the right direction because such a ban will not prevent the neglect of young girls or prevent female infanticide. Moreover, they emphasize that both these tragedies are cited as potential causes of the disparity in the ratio of boys to girls ages six and under. What will the effects of banning sex determination be? While it is clear that dowries present a substantial financial burden for the parents of females, can the blame be placed on the dowry, and is increasing the social and economic status of women the answer?

. . . .

India must address this problem through a two-pronged approach. The first prong involves the immediate imposition of a strict ban on sex determination. The second prong requires the implementation of long-term solutions that involve increasing the value of women in Indian society. This approach will help India immediately start to address the problem of its "missing girls."

II. Background

A. The History of Sex Selection and the Role It Plays in India

While relatively recent technological improvements have made sex selection a viable guarantee to ensure the birth of a child of the desired sex, the quest to be able to select the sex of a child is in no way a recent phenomenon. According to one author, "because sex historically has been linked to economic entitlement, social privilege, and person status in most societies, attempts to control or predict the sex of one's offspring also date back to ancient times." The earliest post-conceptive method of sex selection was infanticide. The first written record of female infanticide dates back to the Tokugawa period in Japan (1600 to 1868), when there were nine times more male than female births recorded. It is believed, however, that the practice had already been in existence for thousands of years.

. . . .

Sex determination of fetuses became possible in India during the 1970s with the arrival of amniocentesis. Amniocentesis involves analyzing cells drawn from a hollow needle inserted by a doctor through the mother's abdominal wall into the amniotic fluid surrounding the fetus. This procedure was developed to discover genetic abnormalities but is also used to determine the sex of the fetus. In 1975, when the procedure was first available at a Delhi medical institute, "only one of the thousands of tests performed that year was performed for a purpose other than discovering the fetus's gender. And almost all of the women who found out they were carrying a female fetus aborted her." Although the government of India banned the use of amniocentesis for sex selection in 1976, the ban was not all-encompassing. The ban was applied only to government facilities and did not prevent private clinics from offering the procedure for sex-determination. The first private sex determination clinic was opened in Amritsar in 1979. Despite the weakness of the ban, the use of amniocentesis for sex selection in India remained a controlled phenomenon that was limited largely to a few urban areas.

It was not until the 1980s and the increasing availability of ultrasounds that sex determination became a widespread method of sex selection in India. . . . All areas of India, even small rural towns, gained access to the procedure through the formation of private clinics. . . . Recently, a new ultrasound technique that produces a 3D/4D image of the fetus, instead of a flat unclear image produced by most ultrasounds, has arrived in India. This technology, if used for sex determination purposes, will further enable doctors to guarantee the accuracy of the sex of the fetus.

The state of Maharashtra enacted the first ban on the use of ultrasound for sex determination in 1988. Three other states enacted similar prohibitions shortly thereafter. This legislation resulted in a decline in the number of sex determination clinics and appeared to be a step in the right direction....

The 1991 census indicated the severity of the decline in female children. The ratio had declined to a national average of 945 girls to every one thousand boys. The numbers could no longer be ignored. For the first time, the central government of India began to notice the problem. The use of ultrasounds and other sex selection technologies were banned throughout India in 1994 through the Pre-natal Diagnostic Techniques (Regulation and Prevention of Misuse) Act. This Act banned the use of prenatal technology to determine a fetus's sex, prohibited the communication of sex information to the patient or her relatives, allowed the devices to be used only in registered genetic testing clinics, and limited the tests only to women who met certain criteria for genetic counseling.

This nationwide Act, while bringing attention to the issue, was weak compared to legislation that had been enacted in some states. The Act mainly applied to government hospitals and clinics and consequently failed to address the problem adequately. The requirement for private clinics to register with the government in order to conduct "genetic counseling" did little to prevent doctors from informing patients of the sex of their child under the guise of genetic counseling. A Dehli doctor has admitted that doctors simply use code words, such as "the sky is blue" and "your baby is fine and will play football" (indicating that the fetus is male) or "you are in the pink of health" and "your child is like a doll" (indicating a female fetus), to communicate the sex of the fetus to the mother. Further, such action requires no written record, and as a result, the detection and punishment of doctors employing these practices is difficult. The Act also applied only to pregnant women, so it was not effective against the use of preimplantation techniques to engineer the sex of the child. These loopholes prevented strict enforcement of the ban. The detection of female feticide in India is made more difficult because often sex determination is conducted at one clinic and the abortion is performed at another. Further, between the enactment of the Act in 1994 and 2000, there were no convictions of individuals who did not comply with the ban. Finally, despite the implementation of the Act, it was still possible to obtain an ultrasound sex test for as little as $12.42 from any number of clinics in India.

B. The Increasing Severity of the Sex Selection Problem

....

Certain areas of India are now being described as "a Bermuda Triangle where millions of girls disappear without a trace." The decline is not a recent phenomenon. The number of females represented in the child sex ratio fell from 976 in 1961, to 964 in 1971, and then to 962 in 1981. As stated by Vibhuti Patel, the leader of a Women's Center in Bombay, "For us, it's the survival of women that's at stake. The social implications of sex-selection are disastrous. It's a further degradation of women." The practice of female feticide, long prevalent in small villages throughout India, is now an urban reality as well. The Indian census commissioner, J.K. Banthia, estimates that over the course of the decline of females, as many as 25 million female fetuses and babies have been killed before, during, or after birth in India.

....

Alarmed by India's recent census data, the Supreme Court of India in 2001 ordered the central government and state authorities "to implement with all vigor and zeal" the Pre-natal Diagnostic Techniques (Regulation and Prevention of Misuse) Act of 1994. In February 2002 state governments were ordered to impound ultrasound machines from unregistered clinics that advertise the use of ultrasound testing for sex selection. While the actual effect of this measure by the Supreme Court is unknown, after the order was issued there was a significant decrease in signs advertising the availability of ultrasound testing.

. . . .

The systematic eradication of females in the areas that have been employing the practice for the longest period of time has led to men purchasing brides from other locations or even sharing a wife with their brothers. Ravinder Bhalla, a sociologist, remarks, "the young woman is formally married to only one brother. Neither she nor her parents have any idea of their real intentions. Later, her husband's brothers also have sex with her." Another problem found in these areas is bride kidnapping. Bride kidnapping is most prevalent in small villages where it is not uncommon for a baby girl not to have been seen in years. One woman, Sandhya Khajur, escaped to tell her story. Khajur was approached on the street by a woman claiming to have a job prospect for her. After showing interest in the job, Khajur was offered a cup of tea. The next thing Khajur remembers is waking up in an unfamiliar location and realizing she had been abducted. Khajur was subsequently sold to a farmer who needed a wife for his son. After paying 35,000 rupee for Khajur, this farmer noted that "there are hardly any girls in our community. My son is 28 and it was high time he got married. Other people in my community have done the same thing. I didn't know it was illegal." Luckily for Khajur, after being kidnapped and sold into marriage, she found a support group that arranged for her release. Many other women, however, are not so fortunate. Another consequence of the lack of women in India is that men are marrying younger and younger girls. An increase in sexual violence toward women has also occurred among frustrated single men.

. . . .

Despite arguments that a lack of women will enhance the social value of daughters, it does not appear that a decrease in the percentage of females in the population has led to greater value being placed on the women present. Further, it is interesting to note that the women in India who deliver female children are "blamed" for not producing male offspring, despite the fact that it is an established medical fact that the man's semen determines the child's sex.... Women forced by their husbands and in-laws to abort female fetuses often suffer psychological harm. One woman, Sunita Shankar, is currently suffering from severe depression thought to be the result of six abortions after sex determination tests determined the fetuses to be female. Shankar has already had three daughters, and her family wants her to produce a son. The pressure has led Shankar to attempt to take her own life on two separate occasions.

. . . .

C. India's Dowry System

. . . .

The family of the bride is expected to give the groom's family a significant amount of money and goods, regardless of the family's financial ability to do so. The demands of dowry are not confined to the middle and upper classes. Although the bride brings these goods into the relationship, these gifts are usually not in the bride's name and are not under her control. According to one author, the dowry custom has "degenerated into a sordid commercial transaction in which monetary considerations receive priority over the merits of the bride." This same author explains how this practice is justified: "Parents who demand dowry justify it on several grounds. Firstly, since they have to pay dowry for their daughter, why not take it for their sons? Secondly, fathers of educated boys want to get back the money spent on the son's education."

The dowry custom has come with more costs than the dowry payment itself. When the family of the bride is unable to satisfy the desires of the groom's family, the new wife is often verbally and physically abused. Young wives are frequently driven to suicide by this abuse or murdered by their new husband's family. It is estimated that dowry payment trouble leads to the deaths of more than 13,000 young brides each year.

. . . .

D. Is the Custom of Dowry to Blame for India's Gender Imbalance?

As mentioned above, the dowry system is often blamed for the prevalence of female feticide and infanticide in India. The bias against females, however, is more deeply rooted than simply in the dowry tradition itself. This is evident by the growing trend of wealthy families' participation in sex selection. For these middle to upper class Indian families it cannot be the dowry alone that encourages the use of sex selection to produce male offspring. While the dowry can pose a burden regardless of a family's wealth, new research suggests that the answer to the gender ratio imbalance in India may not be the enforcement of antidowry statutes.

Recent research shows that the "most pronounced drop in the number of girls under the age of six was no longer in rural areas but in the cities. And not just any neighborhoods, but in the wealthiest enclaves, where the educated elite live." Educated women are assisting the perpetuation of discriminatory attitudes. A recent census showed that the number of girls under six in Delhi has dropped to 865 per one thousand boys. Some of the most exclusive neighborhoods, however, were represented by only 796 girls per one thousand boys. As noted by a senior census official, "these are the areas best-equipped with medical technology and these wealthy, educated people are misusing it to ensure they don't have girls."

This new research also seems to suggest that the education of women, an often proposed remedy to the gender imbalance problem, may not be enough to end female feticide and infanticide. Dr. Gautam Sehgal, treasurer of the Indian Healthcare Federation, notes that "education has got nothing to do with it. . . . I have received requests for sex determination from friends, people who have studied and lived abroad, people for whom money is the least of problems." The leader of the Family Unit at the Tata Institute of Social Sciences in Mumbai recognizes that "education, exposure and affluence have not brought values such as equality. . . . It has brought consumerism and commodification of relationships. Women prefer sons, as it is often the only way to increase their status in the otherwise subordinate life."

. . . .

V. Will a Ban on Sex Determination Ultrasounds Return India's "Missing Girls?"

A. An Immediate Answer to a Problem Without an Immediate Solution

Eliminating females because of their sex before or after birth is "the ultimate manifestation of gender violence and discrimination, abuse of human rights, and infringement of values of equity, equality, justice, dignity, and quality of life for all." Indeed, female feticide is clearly a practice that must end. India needs to take active steps to eradicate this devastating practice sooner rather than later.

Current discourse suggests that the ban on sex determination ultrasounds will simply push the practice underground and lead to further undesirable actions. According to Shanti Conly, former director of policy research at Population Action International in Washington, D.C., passing laws banning prenatal sex determination ultrasounds is easy and important for the government to do, but "to actually enforce these laws is very difficult." Conly advocates that the "key is changing attitudes and the value of women. It is not really a law and order problem where you can ... arrest women for murder. I think reporting and punishing selective abortions will just drive these practices underground." Some have also expressed concern that if the clinics resort to underground sex determination and abortion, regulating the safety of clinics will become impossible and the health of women will be placed in jeopardy.

More strikingly, some women argue that the "unwanted" female is better off not being born. The scarcity of women in India has not led to the improved treatment of women.

. . . .

B. India's Government Must Display the Political Will Necessary to Effect Change

In the words of one Indian news writer, "the human rights of women are always secondary to all other issues taken up by successive governments." In order to advance beyond a tradition in which women are devalued even before their birth, societal attitudes must change. The Indian government can no longer be unsympathetic to the needs of women if India's "missing girls" are to obtain the chance they deserve. Currently the Indian government does not appear to be wholeheartedly pursuing its goal to decrease gender imbalance. This is illustrated by the fact that despite the call to enforce the ban on sex determination with "vigor and zeal," not one conviction of a medical practitioner who violated the law had occurred as of December 2003.

. . . .

It is necessary for the Indian government to place further pressure on medical groups to more vocally support the ban. Some experts have argued that part of the problem with enforcing the ban on sex determination tests is that the enforcement agencies are often headed by doctors who are willing to break the law to protect others in their profession.

. . . .

D. Effective Current and Proposed Long-Term Actions to Support and Sustain Change

. . . .

India's Health Minister, Sushma Swaraj, has also recognized that "if enactment of a law was the only thing needed to curb this menace, this would have stopped long ago." Despite the statistics that tend to suggest the problem is impossible to deny, most people do not think the problem affects them or their class. Further, it is suggested that the problem is "invisible" because women are not willing to openly admit what has happened to them. Another predicament is that those who are willing to recognize the problem are not willing to participate in the solution actively.

. . . .

Notes and Questions

1. It might seem as if modernity alone would provide natural solutions to the problems of female child abandonment or infanticide, but in fact these practices have proven to be quite resistant to change. According to the article above, what kinds of efforts are being made by the Chinese and Indian governments? Are these governments serious about bringing these practices to a halt?

2. Is sex-selective abortion really an aspect of reproductive freedom, or should it be classified as an aspect of gendercide? Are there reasons, apart from the practical desirability of natural gender balance, for making sex determination tests unlawful? Is there any human rights dimension to the problem at all? If so, whose human rights are at stake?

3. What do you think of the argument that the spread of sex determination techniques and the resulting increase of single males will lead to high levels of crime and social disorder? What other problems are likely to result from an imbalance in the sexes? Should other governments be concerned about the growing imbalances in China and India?

4. Is it possible that a strict ban will lead to unsafe medical conditions for women and their unborn children by driving medical procedures underground, given the demand for sex selection and its role in Chinese and Indian culture?

IV. Children Living on the Streets

A. Setting the Scene: Introductory Articles

Although no one knows exactly how many, it is undisputed that there are millions of children living on the streets as best they can, in cities and towns of all kinds around the world. This population does exhibit some common survival techniques and lifestyle characteristics, but it should not be assumed that the designation "street child" has only one meaning. There is great variation with respect to the links these children maintain with their families, communities and cultures. Some go to the streets to earn a living, but stay in touch with adults who, at least to some degree, exercise control and supervision over the child's life. Others are largely disconnected from any consistent adult contact.

How best to prevent children from having recourse to living on the street, and how best to help them once there, are difficult questions, the proper answers to which are not as obvious as might first appear. As in other sections of this book, we must confront the opposition between ideas of protection and empowerment, and ask ourselves to what extent street life can possibly be seen as a "choice" made by children in certain difficult circumstances.

The selections that follow provide readings that describe street children as both a coherent and varied cohort. Experts emphasize that street children exist in virtually every country. Where social dislocation and economic inequality are most severe, the numbers of street children rise correspondingly. In the former Soviet Union the numbers are strikingly large. Street children are in many ways at the mercy of the societies in which they live, and subject to changes in attitudes towards them. Wherever they are found, they are plagued by drug and alcohol abuse and subject to random and systematic violence, sexual exploitation and squalid living conditions.

Mona Pare, *Why Have Street Children Disappeared?*— *The Role of International Human Rights Law in Protecting Vulnerable Groups*
11 The International Journal of Children's Rights 1 (2003)

....

2.1. *Street children: Multiple portrayals, common concerns*

The notion of 'street child' has different meanings for different people: from cute little things begging on the sidewalk alone or accompanied by siblings, to rude youngsters drinking, smoking and harassing passers-by. Indeed, street children are not all the same, and each child has a different story to tell. Some street children are born in the city they live in, some migrate there with their families, whereas others come on their own looking for a job, either sent by their parents or from their own initiative. In general terms, the street child phenomenon has to do with poverty, rapid urbanisation and industrialisation. Urban poverty and the urban way of life lead to the dilution of social values, to stress within the family and family break-up. Since only a small minority of children living in difficult conditions decide to leave their family, a crucial factor is undoubtedly the perception of the situation by the child, who decides to change his/her life. When referring to their pre-street experiences, street children tend to present themselves as victims of misunderstandings and violence to explain their presence on the street. What makes children stay on the street is a combination of factors, possibly including an abusive stepfather or an alcoholic caretaker, the knowledge that parents will send them back to work, the convenience of making their own money and using it on themselves, having time for leisure, having friends who are in a similar situation and who seem to be the only ones not to reject them, getting used to a new way of life—both hard and fun, surviving a day at a time and living by their own rules. Some causal and statistical differences exist in different parts of the world, although no accurate data is available.

Developing countries tend to refer to poverty and the weakening of the traditional family structure as the main reasons for the street child phenomenon, while European countries talk about immigration, the weakening of public welfare structures and family break-up. All these are caused by urbanization and its socio-economic consequences, and by the inability of communities and states to cope with those consequences. Even if taken separately, all these causes lead to exclusion and the search for alternative lifestyles and means of survival. An interesting similarity in all street children's back-grounds tends to be their initial problematic relationship with their family.

[More of this article is reproduced below.]

Notes and Questions

1. While systematic studies of the lives of street children are rare, a survey of the international press reveals common features to life on the street. For a description on the devastating effects of the collapse of communism in Mongolia, see *Out in the Cold: The Street Children of Mongolia*, A People's News Agency Dispatch, 1997, available at http://www.prout.org/pna/mongolian-street-children.html. The intensely cold winters in Ulaan Baataar make survival in Mongolia particularly challenging for street children there.

Family breakdown, substance abuse and the paucity of alternative housing for children are aggravating factors.

View the UNICEF-produced film on street children in Mongolia, *What's Going On? Street Children in Mongolia*. http://www.un.org/works/goingon/mongolia/homeless.html. Does its content square with the reading on Mongolia? What unique features are there in the situation of Mongolian street children? What does the presence of the street children say about the social and cultural situation in Mongolia?

2. In Zimbabwe, street children orphaned by AIDS are likely to become prostitutes and themselves contract AIDS. See *Sex and Sisterhood in Harare, Zimbabwe*, New Internationalist, 2005, available at http://newint.org/features/2005/04/01/harare-zimbabwe/.

In Haiti, as in many other countries, police abuse of street children is common. Political turmoil, a climate of violence and aversion to street children by Haiti's elites place these children in grave danger. See *Killings of Haitian Street Kids Soar, Rights Workers Say*, Pacific News Service, 2005, available at http://news.pacificnews.org/news/view_article.html?article_id=06d4c197ce91ab1f417b67c14a10dc36.

Street children everywhere become addicted to readily available inhalants and other cheap drugs. The misery of their situation has been well documented in news accounts and on film. See for example *Nepal: Street children sniff glue to beat hunger pains*, IRIN Asia, 2007, http://www.irinnews.org/Report.aspx?ReportId=74899. The near universal prevalence of drug addiction among street children is indisputable.

These and countless other readings from the international press come together to present a picture of dire living conditions on the streets in a wide variety of countries. It is clear that there are street children in virtually every country, certainly in every major region of the world, especially of course where there is widespread economic marginalization. Even from this set of brief readings, can you identify any common features to the street child "lifestyle"?

3. A number of important and revealing films have been made in recent years on the subject of street children. Along with the readings above, please review the 2001 documentary *Children Underground*, on Romanian children living in a subway station. See the film described at http://www.npr.org/programs/watc/features/2002/mar/children_underground/. The 2005 film *Children of Leningradsky*, portrays Russian children who live in a railway station, and who have many problems in common with the Romanian children shown in the earlier film. See the Russian film's official website at http://www.childrenofleningradsky.com/.

————————

B. UN Recognition of the Problem of Street Children

As has been discussed throughout this book, the United Nations tends to attach great importance to its own act of placing items "on the agenda." While this might be significant in the area of international peace and security, it seems doubtful whether a General Assembly resolution on the subject of international concern for street children makes any difference at all. Indeed, it must be asked whether such declarations could have a numbing effect on public consciousness, as they give the impression of action being taken, even where no such meaningful investment of time, money or policy development is forthcoming.

United Nations, The Plight of Street Children

G.A. Res. 49/212, 49 U.N. GAOR Supp. No. 49 at
236, 94th plen. mtg., U.N. Doc. A/49/49, (Dec. 23, 1994), *available at*
http://www1.umn.edu/humanrts/resolutions/49/212GA1994.html

94th plenary meeting
23 December 1994

49/212. The plight of street children

The General Assembly,

Recalling its resolution 48/136 of 20 December 1993,

Recalling also Commission on Human Rights resolution 1994/93 of 9 March 1994,

Welcoming the special attention given to the rights of children in the Vienna Declaration and Programme of Action, in particular in section I, paragraph 21,

Recalling the Convention on the Rights of the Child, adopted by its resolution 44/25 of 20 November 1989, as a major contribution to the protection of the rights of all children, including street children,

Reaffirming that children are a particularly vulnerable group in society whose rights require special protection, and that children living under especially difficult circumstances, such as street children, deserve special attention, protection and assistance from their families and communities and as part of national efforts and international cooperation,

Recognizing that all children have the right to health, shelter and education, to an adequate standard of living and to freedom from violence and harassment,

Deeply concerned about the growing number of street children worldwide and the squalid conditions in which these children are often forced to live,

Profoundly concerned that the killing of and violence against street children threaten the most fundamental right of all, the right to life,

Alarmed at continuing serious offences of this nature against street children,

Recognizing the duty and responsibility of Governments to investigate all cases of offences against street children and to punish offenders,

Recognizing also that legislation per se is not enough to prevent violations of human rights, including those of street children, and that Governments should implement their laws and complement legislative measures with effective action, inter alia, in the fields of law enforcement and in the administration of justice, and in social, educational and public health programmes,

Welcoming the efforts made by some Governments to take effective action to address the question of street children,

Welcoming also the publicity given to and the increased awareness of the plight of street children, and the achievements of non-governmental organizations in promoting the rights of those children and in providing practical assistance to improve their situation, and expressing its appreciation of their continued efforts,

Welcoming further the valuable work of the United Nations Children's Fund and its National Committees in reducing the suffering of street children,

Noting with appreciation the important work carried out in this field by the United Nations, in particular the Committee on the Rights of the Child, the Special Rapporteur of the Commission on Human Rights on the sale of children, child prostitution and child pornography and the United Nations International Drug Control Programme,

Bearing in mind the diverse causes of the emergence and marginalization of street children, including poverty, rural-to-urban migration, unemployment, broken families, intolerance, exploitation and war, and that such causes are often aggravated and their solution made more difficult by serious socio-economic difficulties,

Recognizing that the prevention and solution of certain aspects of this problem could be facilitated in the context of economic and social development,

Bearing in mind that in the Vienna Declaration and Programme of Action all States are urged, with the support of international cooperation, to address the acute problem of children in especially difficult circumstances, and that national and international mechanisms and programmes should be strengthened for the defence and protection of children, including street children,

1. Expresses grave concern at the continued growth in the number of incidents worldwide and at reports of street children being involved in and affected by serious crime, drug abuse, violence and prostitution;

2. Urges Governments to continue actively to seek comprehensive solutions to tackle the problems of street children and to take measures to restore their full participation in society, and to provide, inter alia, adequate nutrition, shelter, health care and education;

3. Strongly urges all Governments to guarantee the respect for fundamental human rights, particularly the right to life, and to take urgent measures to prevent the killing of street children and to combat torture and violence against them;

4. Emphasizes that strict compliance with the provisions of the Convention on the Rights of the Child constitutes a significant step towards solving the problems of street children, and calls upon all States that have not done so to become parties to the Convention as a matter of priority;

5. Calls upon the international community to support, through effective international cooperation, the efforts of States to improve the situation of street children, and encourages States parties to the Convention on the Rights of the Child, in preparing their reports to the Committee on the Rights of the Child, to bear this problem in mind and to consider requesting technical advice and assistance for initiatives aimed at improving the situation of street children, in accordance with article 45 of the Convention;

6. Commends the Committee on the Rights of the Child for the attention it pays in its monitoring activities to the situation of children who, to survive, are forced to live and work in the streets, and reiterates its invitation to the Committee to consider the possibility of a general comment on street children;

7. Recommends that the Committee on the Rights of the Child and other relevant treaty-monitoring bodies give attention to this growing problem when examining reports from States parties;

8. Invites Governments, United Nations bodies and organizations, including the United Nations Children's Fund, and intergovernmental and non-governmental organizations to cooperate with each other to ensure greater awareness and more effective action to solve the problem of street children by, among other measures, initiating and supporting development projects that can have a positive impact on the situation of street children;

9. Calls upon special rapporteurs, special representatives and working groups of the Commission on Human Rights and of the Subcommission on Prevention of Discrimination and Protection of Minorities, within their mandates, to pay particular attention to the plight of street children;

10. Decides to consider the question further at its fiftieth session under the agenda item entitled "Promotion and protection of the rights of children".

C. Street Children and International Human Rights

Mona Pare, in the article immediately following, sets out a challenging theory of street children as a vulnerable group worthy of separate recognition under international human rights law. In essence, she asks us to think of the life led by street children as an option, a choice, and a reality to be accepted on its own terms. Pare offers a counterpoint to the conventional notion that street life is an aberration, a pathological condition, that must be eliminated. Is Pare being fatalistic or realistic when she describes street children as the architects of their own destiny? Why does Pare pay so little attention to the issue of preventing children from seeking out the streets in the first place?

Mona Pare, *Why Have Street Children Disappeared?* — *The Role of International Human Rights Law in Protecting Vulnerable Groups*
11 The International Journal of Children's Rights 1 (2003)

1. Introduction

Street children and their appalling human rights situation have become common knowledge worldwide. The media and research in social sciences have provided them with a relative period of fame during the 1980s and 1990s. And yet they have rarely been mentioned in scholarly legal articles.

The reason seems to be that street children have not been officially recognized as a vulnerable group in human rights law. Initially, lack of knowledge about them and the late development of the rights of the child explained this omission. Now, general demotivation from those who have worked with and for street children and the lack of interest from decision-makers have made street children disappear from all scenes.

This article describes how initial interest in street children developed alongside the rights of the child, yet how street children were not able fully to benefit from the development of children's rights and have actually ended up in oblivion. It attempts to show how the special condition and status of street children have not led to special rights that would normally be required for the protection of vulnerable groups. Other groups have benefited from group recognition and have been able to move towards an equal standing point with other people. Although street children should be protected by the principle of non-discrimination, non-discrimination measures cannot lead to *de facto* equality unless special needs of people are addressed. These are not addressed when people do not belong to a vulnerable group whose special situation is recognised in international law. While programmes addressing street children's needs exist, these are adopted and carried out on a voluntary basis. They are therefore without guarantees and are often short-lived due to difficulties in funding and monitoring.

Deficient interest in street children can be seen from different angles, ranging from the lack of common understanding of the concept of *street children* and the complexity of those children's lives, to the lack of pressure groups advocating for street children. However, using research on street children as a basis, many of these obstacles could be overcome and street children could be endowed with a vulnerable group status without much complication. The recognition of this status is essential to help them exercise their human rights without discrimination, and only calls for a more effective use of international human rights law. To come to these conclusions, this article first explains why special attention to street children as a vulnerable group is justified, then explores how they have been taken into account in international human rights law, and finally suggests realistic solutions that could be applied to this group, and that could be useful to any groups without specific legal protection.

2. Defining concepts: Street children and vulnerable groups

. . . .

Poverty alone can drive children to the streets, but it usually will not break up family ties. It is true that poverty easily leads to stress and tensions within the family, thereby becoming an indirect but important cause of the street child phenomenon. Other scenarios also exist, and include cases of abandoned, lost or orphaned children. For instance in Angola and Sierra Leone, war is the main cause, as children become separated from their parents and find themselves wandering alone or with their siblings. In many sub-Saharan countries AIDS has become an important factor. But the consequences of war and disease can lead orphans to the same lifestyle as other street children if they spend a certain period of time on the street. As long as children are without legal guardians and live on the street with a group of other street children for a certain period of time, the outcome usually becomes identical. Indeed, while these children have different backgrounds and live in different countries, the phenomenon is surprisingly similar all over the world, as proved by a range of case studies.

These children share not only difficult social and economic conditions, but the same daily necessities and even the same perception of life and society, as a result of the place that has become their home: the street. It is a source of resilience and of problems which they have to face in their daily lives: need of food, shelter and health care, need to find a loving environment, need to get education and a source of income; fear and distrust of authority and officials, fear of violence and the multiple dangers of the street, problematic relationships with drugs and drug users, lack of access to basic social services, lack of viable opportunities leading them sometimes to resort to criminal activities. It is also the major source of marginalisation in society: "Street children who are genuinely *of* the street are outcasts everywhere, even in their own minds."

Are there street children who are not 'genuine'? The term 'street children' is used in everyday language to describe a wide category of children, all those whom we can picture on the urban scene of the developing world. However, not all those children are 'real' street children and not all street children live in developing countries. Although it would be prejudiced to deny these children their various characteristics and identities (age, culture, geographic location, nationality, level of education, family ties, etc.), something fundamentally similar links the lives of 'real' street children. They usually come from poor and/or broken families, and have started using the street as a place to live and a means of survival. Most importantly they have become accustomed to the independence that such a life entails. This characteristic overrides differences between street children, for instance in the events that led them to street life. Although descriptions of the causes of the phenomenon and of street children's characteristics can seem simplistic, all studies about street children—whatever their approach, methodology and definitions—ultimately arrive at similar conclusions concerning the situation and needs of 'hard core' street children. These are different from children who are on the street because of poverty alone, and who keep a closer relationship with their families and help them by providing for them through their work on the street. The phenomenon is similar with children of street families. The difficult living conditions seem to tighten bonds between family members even if those children can be seen on the street alone or with groups of friends. It is thus important to avoid using the blanket term 'street children' for all urban children working on the street.

It is the independence and self-sufficiency of those children that makes them different from other poor and marginalized children, including other children with a street connection. Children, who spend most of their time outside, those who run away for a short period of time, or those whose work on the street contributes to the family economy and who return home more or less regularly, are thus not be considered as subjects of this article. Although these children are part of the same urban picture as street children strictly speaking, and outnumber the latter by far, they lack the essential characteristic that determines street children's specificity, which is their independence caused by a lack of adult support and model, leading to extreme marginalisation.

Many scholars and practitioners have written about this distinction. Reference is usually made to children 'on' or 'of' the street. These terms denote different degrees within the widest category of street children, helping essentially to define links that exist between the child and his/her family. These distinctions have been adapted from UNICEF's typology according to which:

> Children *on* the streets are those whose family support base has become increasingly weakened [who] must share in the responsibility for family survival by working on city streets and marketplaces. For these children, the home ceases to be their centre for play, culture and daily life. Nevertheless while the street becomes their daytime activity, most of these children will return home most nights. While their family situation may be deteriorating, they are still definitely in place, and these children continue to view life from the point of view of their families. Children *of* the streets are a much smaller number of children who daily struggle for survival without family support, alone. While often called "abandoned", they too might also have abandoned their families, tired of insecurity and rejection and aged up with violence: [Their] ties with home have been broken de facto [they] are without families.

However, most authors have criticized the rigid and artificial character of this distinction, which makes it difficult to apply to the variety of situations existing in different countries. For example, some street children might work on the streets for extensive periods because they are far from home. Others' lives might fluctuate between street and home because of conflicting attractions: friends and independence versus family and shelter. Although it is true that individual situations cannot be easily compartmentalised due to changing circumstances, different analyses—however elaborate—provided by most researchers boil down to similar categorisations. It does seem that the major distinction between children who spend most of their time on the streets lies in degrees of attachment to the family, which makes UNICEF's definition acceptable. In light of that definition, the children considered in this study are thus children *of* the street, as they are not supported by their legal guardians.

Other attempts have been made to offer working definitions of street children. One of the most appropriate ones is the very first one, introduced by the Inter-NGO Programme for Street Children and Street Youth, according to which street children are "those for who the street (in the widest sense of the word) more than their family has become their real home, a situation in which there is no protection, supervision or direction from responsible adults". This definition has also been criticised for its simplicity, but it is precisely this simplicity that makes it functional as a legal definition, especially as it embodies the most important element, which is street children's independence.

....

For example, the Committee on the Rights of the Child describes street children as "children who, in order to survive, are forced to live and/or work on the streets". This points at the group of 'street and working children', which is too broad, and inaccurate because of the wording "... in order to survive, are forced to ...". In any case, one must recognise that all definitions, including the one chosen for this study, have to be understood in light of the definition of the child provided by the CRC and, as the latter suggests, are liable to fail standards of universality.

2.2. Street children as a vulnerable group

Some conceptual clarifications are necessary before addressing the issue of street children as a vulnerable group. The term 'vulnerable group' is not to be found in international legal instruments. Nevertheless, it seems to be the most appropriate way to designate groups of people who are treated separately by human rights law because of their vulnerable position in society that can restrict their enjoyment of human rights. People belonging to a group have specific characteristics that give them that 'group membership' and all vulnerable groups share the fact that their members are vulnerable to discrimination because of that membership. The concept does, however, require further explanation, since it can lead to confusion because of its vagueness and of the effects its use has on individuals and groups.

Individuals are not categorised into groups in international human rights law for the general purpose of labelling people, but to give them separate rights that respond to their specific condition and activities better than general human rights instruments. In general, the purpose of those separate sets of rights is to protect the individual members of groups by conferring them a special status. Not all groups are in need of protection and individuals belonging to a category might just need to have their activities regulated because of their membership to a certain group. This is the case for some professional associations, for example. In most cases, their status and rights are regulated by national law. Only if they are found to be 'vulnerable' are they also treated as a group in international law. Human rights law is thus interested in groups that find themselves in a weaker position than the rest of society and need enhanced protection because of this vulnerability. Vulnerable groups are those groups whose members need protection in all aspects of their lives, because their status and/or condition puts them in a weaker position than other individuals in the same situation. This is the case for children (because of the legal, psychological, physical and social consequences of their age), persons with disabilities, the elderly, and national minorities, for example. Not all of these groups are vulnerable at all times, in all contexts and all societies, but if a separate set of rights has been developed for them, it is based on widely noted phenomena, which show that members of those groups at least face the risk of being in a weaker position in society than other individuals. The observation of these phenomena usually confirms both historical experience and present values, thus validating the role of law in responding to social realities.

International law has not dealt equally with all vulnerable groups and there are groups it has not even considered yet, such as street children. The first groups to be treated as vulnerable groups in international law were national minorities that benefited from a protection system developed by the League of Nations. Vulnerable groups that have received significant attention as such since the creation of the UN are women, children, ethnic minorities, and refugees. Other minorities and indigenous populations have also received considerable attention. People with disabilities, the elderly, and more recently people with HIV/AIDS can also be added to the list of recognised vulnerable groups. Probably the greatest attention has been given to the situation of women, which has been addressed in an integrated way across all UN programmes. In addition to a Convention protecting their specific rights, several bodies have been established throughout the UN system to make sure that their situation and the question of their equality with men is addressed in all spheres of action. Improvements in the condition of women also ensure that their problems are being taken care of, as they have gained influence as a pressure group. As for children, those belonging to vulnerable groups that include adults have been given granted special attention. An exception to this rule exists with children temporarily or permanently deprived of their family environment, who are entitled to "special protection and assistance" by the state (CRC articles 20, 21, 25). Street children belong to this group *prima facie*. However, closer analysis reveals that street children are often not literally *deprived* of their family environment and that the provision targets children who need to be placed in care.

Street children are currently largely regarded as individual children who are in a vulnerable position, as their specificity has not been seriously tested in the international fora, where a child choosing to live on his own terms is still considered an aberration. In spite of many common characteristics and a widely used denomination, professionals and organisations dealing with street children avoid giving clear definitions of them and prefer using over-lapping terms, so as not to limit their scope of action and sources of funding. Therefore, street children have been included in different categories of groups of vulnerable children for enhanced protection. That is why terms such as 'street and working children', 'runaway or homeless children and youth', or 'urban children in difficult circumstances' are used interchangeably.

These categories associate street children with their living environment and their activities. Street children are also encompassed in more general terms with a wide variety of vulnerable children. These are 'marginalized youth', 'children at risk', 'neglected children', and even 'problem children'. A common term within the UN framework is 'children in especially difficult circumstances', introduced by UNICEF in 1986 and incorporated in the Declaration of the 1990 World Summit for Children. UNICEF recognises that street children differ from working children, destitute and abandoned children, and children living with their family on the street. However, the organisation adopts a wide conception of street children inclusive of children *on* and *of* the street. Moreover, in UNICEF's policies and projects, street children fall into the category of 'children in especially difficult circumstances', leading to further confusion.

. . . .

All street children are working children (using a broad definition of work), but not all working children—even if on the street—are street children. A problematic consequence is that because such wide categorisations, it might be impossible to address street children's specific condition and needs. Of course, the problem can be similar for other children who might need special protection as a separate group. None of these sub-categories of children are formal vulnerable groups, and this explains the flexibility of categories, memberships and denominations.

The main characteristic of vulnerable groups is the risk for their members of being treated differently because of illegitimate reasons based on social stigma. This differential treatment makes it impossible for them to exercise their rights as efficiently as other people, and this in turn contributes to their subordinate position in society. In order to protect the rights of those vulnerable people, states are bound to intervene and facilitate their enjoyment of their rights through non-discrimination measures. Indeed, simply refraining from adopting discriminatory laws and policies is not sufficient, as there is ample proof that equality before the law does not necessarily lead to *de facto* equality. Discrimination can be found in all aspects of people's lives and discriminatory practices occur without supporting legislation. This is why the state needs to adopt positive measures to combat discrimination and change the negative perception of a specific group. The utmost form of positive measure is positive discrimination, which international law does not consider as discrimination. On the contrary, it can be seen as necessary to restore the right balance and equitable treatment of all groups in society, thus combating discrimination and the conditions that lead to it.

. . . .

3. Street children and international law

3.1. *The evolution of the rights of the child*

Street children have substantially contributed to the notion of childhood, with consequences on the treatment of children and on their rights. The conception of children as separate from adults dawned in the West towards the end of the eighteenth century. Philosophers and writers, such as Rousseau, contributed to a new image of children as being innocent, close to nature and victims of society, instead of as extra mouths to feed or pairs of hands to work. They created the notion of childhood, which had previously been unknown to all societies, and the need to protect this childhood. This notion found expression in biographical and fictional stories about children, and in the appearance of literature for children. Street children inspired many of these child characters, who were pictured as clever and touching little tramps and vagabonds.

The ultimate goal of child protection was thus linked to general public interest and the rights of the child were even referred to as "identical with the interests of the State", and required "the minimum clothing, shelter, food, and training needed to fit it [the child] for becoming in due time a self-supporting member of the community".

. . . .

In the 1960s, a developmental dimension was added to the protective and humanitarian emergency approaches to the rights of the child. Children were priority targets of development assistance, and the notion of child development became part of mainstream development planning. Children were the future of those new countries, the prosperity of which depended on the physical, psychological and intellectual development of children. Once again, the rights of children were closely linked to the interests of society at large.

As street children were economically and socially disadvantaged, they could easily be integrated in developmental programmes alongside other children in need. They could also, of course, fall through the cracks of programming. A binding legal instrument on the rights of the child could have been the solution for more guaranteed protection.

The International Year of the Child marked the beginning of the drafting of a convention on the rights of the child in 1979. That year helped to draw attention to the situation of children worldwide and served as a catalyst for action and further research about children. It also showed the first signs of international concern for street children with a first international conference on street children held in Bombay in 1979 and subsequently, in 1982, the creation of an International Programme of Non-Governmental Organisations on Street Children.

....

The major innovation of the CRC was therefore its new approach to the rights of the child, a participatory one, allowing children to be heard. Article 12 of the CRC exemplifies this approach. Yet, the participatory approach had not been adopted as part of the drafting of the Convention itself and children had voiced their concerns only on rare occasions. The fact that children's participatory or 'autonomy rights' have not received unanimous support proves the challenging nature of that principle. Participatory rights have been much criticized by some legal scholars, who do not believe that children are capable of making decisions and of expressing themselves coherently, and that such rights might conflict with children's protection and development interests. Others, on the contrary, have criticised the CRC for being too weak on participation rights compared to protection and provision rights.

3.2. *Impact of the international rights of the child on street children*

Whether one finds that the CRC focuses too much or insufficiently on participation, it is noteworthy that street children had an active role in the advancement of the rights of the child in certain instances, and therefore benefited from, or contributed to the development of participation as a principle of child rights. Indeed, even though street children were not expressly included in the CRC, the international rights of the child have had an impact on these children, especially through the general changes which the child rights movement brought about. Since the CRC entered into force, views on children generally have changed and their situation has received sustained attention. As human 'beings' and not just human 'becomings' they have become more integrated into society. They are not seen as completely separate from the adult world as vulnerable things needing to be kept in a cocoon for protection, and yet their special needs are recognised. The attention they have received has also helped to bring to light new or hidden forms of violations of children's rights, such as those affecting street children: indirect forms of discrimination in access to education or health care, discrimination through status offences, the sale of organs, trafficking, the exploitation of children through begging, prostitution and drugs, etc. These new developments have again contributed to a change in the image of childhood.

This new image has most importantly translated itself into dialogue and participation. Many countries, either at national or local level, have seen the emergence of street children's congresses, associations, networks, etc. In Brazil, street children were even consulted in relation to the drafting of a new constitution and legislation. Another result of these developments is that institutions where street children used to be locked up for everybody's protection are seen as an inappropriate response to children who have become used to thinking for themselves, creating their own rules and rejecting restraint. It is becoming more accepted that street children should not be integrated into mainstream society without their consent and preferably not without their own initiative. Participation has thus become a key element for the opportunity to change traditional approaches to the issue of street children.

From another angle, children are no longer always seen as poor and vulnerable, but also as individuals who should take responsibility for their actions. These new attitudes are reflected in the administration of juvenile justice and the treatment of children deprived of their liberty in many countries, among a growing number of exceptions to minors' legal incapacity in national legislation and practice of courts. The situation can be highlighted in the case of street children, who have started to be seen as individuals having rights as persons and not only because their life is pitiful or because society could benefit from an improvement in their situation. This has brought about more research on them, especially psychological and sociological aspects, in order to understand their behaviour.

However, this new image has had some adverse consequences. In Brazil, for instance, it is since the adoption of the CRC that so many street children have been killed by the notorious death squads. Such practice has been tolerated by a population that has become afraid of these children who are left free in the streets and who seem dangerous to people from other social classes. Brazil ended its long-standing practice of institutionalising children only after it adopted the Child and Adolescent Statute in 1990, which many saw as encouraging child crime. Street children have to pay the price for their rights with the perception of them as a threat. They are now seen less as a threat to the welfare of the society—which would reflect the old view of children as budding adults instead of full-fledged human beings—and more as these "outcast, vicious, reckless" children who will "come to know their power and use it". The real problem is, however, completely opposite. Those children have no power, lack self-confidence, and are unaware of their own potentialities and life choices. Nevertheless, the result is that correctional measures are favoured again and this approach is no longer even moderated by a romantic vision of childhood. Today, because of childhood-related research and because of the message contained in the rights of the child, children are not seen as innocent any more and are expected to be more responsible for their actions. Whether the increase in responsibilities will ultimately contribute to or subvert children's best interests depends on the possibility of finding a balance between the saving and liberating concepts of child rights.

Many would consider that it is the protection provided by the CRC to children that has the most important impact on street children. If one were to consider street children as they traditionally were as orphans or victims of neglect and abuse to be rescued, or as rebels or idlers to be forced back into society, one would have to admit that street children are adequately covered by the Convention. Articles that are most often referred to in relation to street children are those for the prevention of the street child phenomenon, articles related to separation from parents, to the protection from exploitation, and the right to life (articles 6, 9, 18–20, 32–36). Prevention is fundamental, but it is not useful to children who already are on the street. Provisions on separation assume the child's need to be reunited with his/her family or to be placed into some form of institutional care. Yet, experience of work with street children has proved that family integration is not a viable option for most street children who have become used to an independent way of life and have usually run away to escape very difficult family relations. The prevention of exploitation is important, but less relevant to street children than one might think. Because of their love of freedom, street children avoid exploitative situations more easily than other vulnerable children. And it is regrettable that street children tend to get attention only when they have been murdered. The unprecedented case of murdered street children in which the Inter-American Court sentenced Guatemala to provide reparations to the families of the victims represents of course a great development. Unfortunately, it is still hard to imagine a similar decision concerning the violation of other street children's rights, and which would benefit them directly. Focusing on killings devalues street children's lives, as does limiting the description of their lives to exploitation and abuse. The Committee on the Rights of the Child has adopted this limited approach to street children's rights, despite its otherwise holistic view on child rights. The CRC reporting procedure has mainly focused on street children under the category of exploited children, or children separated from parents, without concentrating on specific aspects of street children's lives, such as access to shelter, health care, education and other basic services.

. . . .

4. Street children's non-recognition: Reasons and remedies

....

4.2. *Importance and practicalities of group recognition*

....

It is clear that the child rights movement and the CRC offer great potential for street children, especially through the general principles identified by the Committee on the Rights of the Child as 'umbrella rights': non-discrimination, the best interest of the child, life survival and development, and respect for the child's views (articles 2, 3, 6, 12). This child rights approach has replaced paternalistic and repressive approaches in most programmes for street children. However, the Convention's focus on a protected view of childhood and its use of the family as the child's focal point make it difficult to apply to street children. Using research about street children to adapt human rights to them would greatly benefit these children and improve measures taken for them. There are specific issues linked to their lifestyle that ought to be taken into consideration, most of these being linked to street children's autonomy.

First of all, street children avoid any kind of lifestyle that includes set rules that they would have to follow. Generally speaking, they avoid social conventions. This does not mean that they live in total disorganisation. Street children are usually found to live by their own rules which apply to their groups of friends and which are implicitly or expressly agreed. These are rules that street children accept, because they correspond to their values. They include principles of loyalty, solidarity, justice and survival.

....

These children have their own views and life experience to share and are more likely to commit to projects if they have a major role in designing and running them. Some of the general and most 'universal' articles in the CRC could thus be interpreted as including alternative options. For example the right to education could imply the right to non-formal education, instead of the right to compulsory primary education strictly speaking, when non-formal education is in the child's best interest and when this is the most conducive way to achieving the purposes of education listed in article 29. Different organisations and programmes could benefit from such an approach, as street children's participation would offer alternatives to traditional ways of providing solutions and services to marginalized children.

Second, street children's peers clearly have a special role in their lives, as they tend to live in informal groups with other street children. Even though these groups are informal, their friends easily become their new 'family' whose members take care of each other. This gives importance to the role of peer influence in their choice of lifestyle and their preference for the street over institutions and family. These peers and other important contacts on the streets, such as street educators, should thus be considered for the importance they have in each child's life.

This is, for instance, where the flexible meaning of 'family' in the CRC could be used to cover people who are especially important to street children, where necessary. Therefore, the concept of separation from the family could be interpreted as separation from the group that acts as a family for a child. In the same way, street children's relations with their significant peers would be protected by article 8 on the preservation of identity and family relations.

Third, street children's fears that are constantly present and linked to their lifestyle need to be addressed appropriately. These include the fear of arrest, reprisals, hunger, sickness, sexual abuse, unwanted pregnancies and lack of job opportunities. Their basic needs thus have to be met, and it is important to ensure that they get access to health care and social services without discrimination. These services thus need to be available to them even if they do not possess identity papers or do not meet other requirements, such as the presence of legal guardians. It also means that services need to reach them, instead of expecting street children to be aware of and willing to approach officials themselves. Once again, this requires the interpretation of the CRC so as to include the option of alternative and, preferably, street based services. As to street children's protection from abuse, exploitation, inhuman and degrading treatment, this would require special attention to the conduct of the police and other officials who have authority over street children, either on the streets or in institutions. This can already be understood as being covered by the CRC, but without specific mention of it, it can be overlooked, as focus is often on the neglect and abuse of children at home, or on exploitation of children through harmful forms of child labour.

Fourth, street children rarely have concrete plans for the future and they tend to accept life as it is, living day-by-day. However, if they are asked about their aspirations, their answers always include such 'normal' things as education, job, and family. They actually strive for stability and reintegration into society, the very society they ran away from and keep avoiding. These aspirations are key to providing appropriate life options for street children. It is impossible to succeed by applying our concepts of perfect childhood to street children, and we should accept the need to extend certain adults' rights to street children, such as those concerning the right to work and working conditions (such as articles 6 and 7 of the ICESCR).

Street children often dream of being able to earn a living in an honest way, being able to live in a house, to have a family and to help their mothers. However, current programmes see street children running away because of the strict rules applied by many organisations and probably because of the inappropriate nature of many solutions designed for them, such as school and family integration, or training in trades that have little market value. None of these considerations are specifically taken into account in the CRC, but with sufficient will, the Convention can lend itself to more flexible interpretation that can suit the needs of street children, enabling them to exercise their human rights without discrimination. This can even be taken as a necessity, since the CRC's guiding principles are to be used for the interpretation of all the other articles of the Convention. With the combination of research on street children and the principles of the best interests of the child, non-discrimination, participation and the child's right to life and development, it should be possible to reach the type of solutions mentioned earlier. It is fortunate that no new convention is needed to recognise street children as a vulnerable group. An optional protocol to the CRC specifying street children's rights is a possibility, but an even better (though not legally binding) option could be the adoption of guidelines by the Committee on the Rights of the Child for the application of the Convention to street children.

This could be the outcome of a 'day of general discussion' on street children and combined with a 'general comment' on street children. These guidelines could be subsequently used by the Committee in its monitoring procedure, enabling States Parties to the CRC to be guided as to the implementation of the Convention in a more detailed way, complementing the current 'list of issues' drawn by the Committee for each state report. It is important that such interpretation be formalised by the Committee for it to acquire enough weight for the protection of street children's rights. This could later lead to the drafting of an instrument on street children, similar to the Standard Rules on the Equalization of Opportunities for Persons with Disabilities. Other options should also be considered, for example the establishment of the office of a Special Rapporteur or working group on street children. Examples of such initiatives already exist with other vulnerable groups, including the girl child, children with HIV/AIDS, and most notably children with disabilities.

Using similar approaches with street children would have important consequences in practice. Aside from a contribution to the furtherance of the use of the principles of the rights of the child and the development of international human rights law, programmes on street children could finally address street children's specific needs. Moreover, current programmes that are already specific to street children and based on the principles of the CRC would have a better chance of surviving and dealing with street children's needs that are currently controversial, as they are in contradiction with these children's minority status. Today, the relatively successful programmes are few and are run by NGOs. The fact that specific action for street children is not based on legally binding provisions means that street children have to depend solely on the will of certain individuals to provide the right kind of help for them, and the NGO itself depends on the will of funders and the government to support the cause. Because of this, street children's programmes tend to be very short-lived and insufficiently monitored. Donors prefer concrete results that can be backed by illustrative and impressive figures, such as numbers of school enrolments, which are nearly impossible for NGOs to provide. Many NGOs, therefore, prefer to widen their target group or limit themselves to 'trendier' topics to get funding, while governments are happy to see NGOs tackle the street child issue.

5. Conclusion

Street children have had their hour of fame, but because of a lack of legal support for their cause, they have now disappeared. They are equated with other children living in difficult circumstances, and unless certain individuals and organisations stay committed to their cause, they will have to depend on action for poor children in general. However, such action is unlikely to reach them, which will marginalize them even further.

. . . .

It is a shame that street children are not in a position to speak for themselves, that they do not represent important interests for lobbyists and decision makers, and that the general public dislikes them. Street children should neither be blamed for that, nor suffer adverse consequences. It is time to give street children real protection through human rights. This requires only simple solutions through a formal recognition of their vulnerability as a group and the interpretation of current international human rights instruments, especially the CRC, to suit their situation and thereby combat discrimination against them. In particular, this entails understanding street children's autonomy that can clash with their minority status in national law. Acting through the Committee on the Rights of the Child would be the most effective way to influence states' implementation of international child rights and to reach street children. Insufficient understanding and motivation are the obstacles to the enforcement of street children's rights, not the lack of realistic options.

Notes and Questions

1. In many ways, Mona Pare challenges conventional wisdom on the issue of street children and the value of their lifestyle. How does she characterize street children? Why does she consider it so important that street children be designated as a vulnerable group under international law? It is clear that she does not seek this designation for its own

sake, but in order to bring about specific changes in international perceptions of street children and their lifestyle.

2. Pare suggests that functioning groups of street children should be protected from separation under article 8 of the UNCRC, based on a flexible interpretation of family and the 'preservation of identity and family relations.' Is this a realistic viewpoint? If so, would the CRC afford the same protection to a gang of children who perceive each other as family, including in cases where a child is negatively influenced by the group to which he belongs? Pare also suggests that eliminating the abuse, exploitation, and negative treatment of street children can be changed by examining the conduct of those who are supposed to protect them, such as police officers and officials in institutions. But, given the negative social stigma associated with street children, would it be more effective to work towards changing society's negative perception of the children?

3. Having viewed the Romanian film, *Children Underground*, how does the Pare theory apply to its contents? Do you consider Pare's central concept compelling? Is it likely to be widely accepted? Why or why not? Is there any downside to offering street children recognition as a separate and distinct group?

The following article adopts a far more conventional tone when describing the lives of street children. Not only are abuses of street children presented as tragic—a point of view Mona Pare would of course share—but the very fact of *being* a street child is likewise presented as tragic. Marc Seitles focuses primarily on the street children of Latin America, who have been the targets of "social cleansing" efforts by the police in a number of countries. Seitles usefully sets out the provisions of the UNCRC relevant to responding to the plight of street children.

Marc D. Seitles, *Effect of the Convention on the Rights of the Child upon Street Children in Latin America: A Study of Brazil, Colombia, and Guatemala*
16 Buffalo Public Interest Law Journal 159 (1997)

....

I. THE STREET CHILDREN OF LATIN AMERICA

A. Who are the Street Children?

....

Estimates of the number of street children vary considerably because of the difficulty in assessing the number of children who consistently live on the street. However, it is estimated that in the cities of Rio de Janeiro, Brazil and Bogota, Colombia over 4,000 children reside on the street each night. These children vary between ten and seventeen years of age, with the average child's age being around twelve years old. Due to the large numbers of street children and the conditions that have brought them there, a social stigma has been inflicted upon them. They are frequently seen as nuisances, criminals and general threats to society. As a result, street children are likely to be met with repression rather than help, because their presence in the streets is perceived as being harmful to public safety.

B. The Rights of Street Children: Poverty and Death

Unfortunately, the perception of Latin American street children is not the worst concern that these young people must face. To be a poor child who lives with little or no family guidance or support is to live daily with the threat of murder, disease, malnutrition, physical and sexual abuse, prostitution, drug abuse, and exploitation. For example, in Colombia, over 2,190 street children were murdered in 1994, an average of six children per day. A significant number of child murders are the direct responsibility of the State, thus it is not surprising that only twelve of these killings have come to trial. Ironically, law enforcement officials are the greatest threat to these children, particularly in Colombia, Guatemala, and Brazil. In fact, the government-supported policy of "social cleansing" is often carried out in Colombia by military officials and police officers who eliminate groups identified as worthless or dangerous to society, including, but not limited to, street children. In Brazil, police death squads, typically consisting of current, off-duty, or former policemen, have systematically killed street children without cause or justification. Meanwhile, in Guatemala, thousands of children living on city streets routinely face beatings, thefts, and sexual assaults at the hands of the National Police and private security guards working under the jurisdiction of the Interior Ministry. In 1996, numerous murders of children took place on the streets of Guatemala, including the horrific rape of a sixteen year old girl by two National Police officers in Guatemala City, as a third officer watched.

Finally, it must be noted that homicides, while constituting a violation of the most basic human right — the right to life — are day-to-day realities that affect street children. Other types of violations of the rights of street children include police beatings, unsanitary living and health conditions, child prostitution, and drug abuse. Children typically suffer from a variety of health problems, including skin problems, respiratory disease, dental problems, and gastro-intestinal problems. Most of these young people have cuts and scars, and improperly healed prior injuries. The rampant problems of sexually transmitted diseases (STDs) pose a serious health problem for these children. In a study of 143 street children in Guatemala, 93% of those studied reported having STD's, and none of the children reported using condoms. Of equal concern is the rampant drug use of street children, 90% of whom in Guatemala are dependent on glue, paint thinner, or other more powerful drugs. In fact, glue and paint thinner are more physically addictive than cocaine or alcohol because they become part of the blood tissue. Not only does such an addiction make it more difficult to the leave the street, but glue has "serious health consequences" and has been linked to irreversible brain and kidney damage, lung damage, malnourishment, and a general decline in health.

....

III. ADDRESSING THE RIGHTS OF STREET CHILDREN THROUGH THE CONVENTION ON THE RIGHTS OF THE CHILD

The Convention on the Rights of the Child protects a broad range of children's rights, and although not without criticism, the potential of the Convention is unparalleled, at least to the degree it recognizes the basic needs of children as having fundamental human rights which must be protected under international law. The Convention creates both guidelines and directives for action, and is a tool for promoting knowledge and understanding of children's issues. Yet the Convention's foremost objective is to change and improve the lives of children. Therefore, its success in this regard must be gauged by its ability to enforce and improve the lives of those children most disadvantaged — street children. Several substantive articles of the Convention are particularly relevant to the plight of street children in Latin America, addressing issues that these children are faced with each day. These relevant articles include: best interests of the child (Article 3); right to life (Article 6); adequate standard of living (Article 27); recovery of abused children (Article 39); illicit use of narcotic and psychotropic drugs (Article 33); and torture and inhumane punishment (Article 37). The following procedural articles, as discussed earlier, assist in carrying out the substantive articles that impact street children, including: application without discrimination (Article 2); implementation (Article 4); establishment of the Committee on the Rights of the Child (Article 43); reports (Article 44); and participation by specialized Agencies of the U.N. (Article 45). The following section discusses the responses of Brazil, Colombia, and Guatemala to these critical provisions of the Convention. The responses of these countries will be scrutinized in detail because of the countries' notoriously poor treatment of street children.

A. Best Interests of the Child

Article 3 provides that the best interests of the child will be the primary consideration in all circumstances and requires members of the Convention to provide adequate care when parents or others fail to do so. This standard places an affirmative duty upon each State party to take appropriate legislative and administrative measures as necessary, to provide protection and care for a child's welfare Consequently, the Convention makes numerous references to these governmental duties, implying that the best interests of the child is the standard by which to measure a particular nation's compliance with all of the Convention's articles. Although this article is fundamental to the whole Convention, it has a special importance for solving the problematic conditions of street children because the child's best interests, "must be a primary consideration." In fact, even under difficult economic conditions or situations of political strife, States Parties must consider the child's best interests of great importance when decisions affecting children are made. Therefore, each article in the Convention must be measured by the best interest of the child standard, particularly when determining solutions for the those children whose lives weigh in the balance of meaningful governmental action.

. . . .

B. The Right to Life

One of the most important articles of the Convention on the Rights of the Child is Article 6, the right to life. The right to life is not a preventive measure alone, but ensures that State signatories take steps to prolong the life of the child; thus it encompasses both the survival and development of street children. Implicit in this requirement are the issues of safety, health, and welfare of the child. These are areas that clearly affect street children and must be addressed in order to satisfy the goal of lengthening the life span of all young people, particularly those in poverty. In fact, States Parties are under the "highest obligation" to take affirmative action to guarantee each child an opportunity to develop his or her personality, a far greater objective than mere survival. Unfortunately, the provision declaring a right to life for all children has fallen upon deaf ears in numerous Latin American countries. In Colombia, the policy of "social cleansing" has resulted in the murder of one street child every four hours. Meanwhile, in Brazil, an estimated four street children per day are murdered, most the result of "death squad homicides." Guatemala has been the subject of international scrutiny, as National Police Officers and other government security force members have been implicated in dozens of assaults against street children, including fourteen murders in a single eighteen month period. Although it is difficult to deem such killings the policy of their respective governments, there is convincing evidence that the killings transpire with the participation or approval of some local authorities, including police and military commanders.

A 1991 report in Brazil by the special commission formed by the Rio de Janeiro state legislature, found "many irregularities that look like complicity on the part of the judiciary" in death squad killings. State party involvement in the murder of street children was also acknowledged by the Committee on the Rights of the Child in its report about Colombia. The Committee acknowledged the "discriminatory and adverse social attitudes, particularly among law enforcement officials, towards vulnerable groups of children." Furthermore, the Committee expressed its "grave concern" over life-threatening situations faced by street children, many of whom are victims of social cleansing campaigns. Since many of the murders of street children in Latin America are carried out by agents of the State, they are rarely investigated or properly prosecuted. Although there have recently been a number of high profile convictions of police officers for the murders of Latin American street children, few investigations result in more than dismissal for implicated officers. Without a doubt, the State parties of Brazil, Colombia, and Guatemala are not providing street children the right to survival and development as mandated by Article 6 of the Convention. Although the Committee on the Rights of the Child has investigated these abuses and provided public recommendations to expose this grave situation to the international community, the Committee has been unsuccessful in reducing these abuses because of local government inaction and the Committee's lack of enforcement authority, which as with so many other treaties, is devoid of any mechanism to compel state compliance. Thus, the inherent inadequacies of the Committee, coupled with the complete apathy of these Latin signatories, has led to a violation of one of the most fundamental principles of the Convention—the right to life of its children.

C. Adequate Standard of Living

Assuring an adequate standard of living for all children is particularly relevant for street children. Article 27 of the Convention on the Rights of the Child addresses this issue and obliges States Parties to ensure that children are provided with food, clothing, and housing according to the financial resources available and the norms of the particular culture. However, unlike other treaties, the Convention links the child's standard of living to aspects of a child's moral and social development. Thus, the right to an adequate standard of living extends beyond the basic physical provisions fundamental to the child's survival. This article exemplifies the necessity of state assistance in the areas that will improve the living conditions and maintenance of the child, including social security, free education, and accessible health care, each outlined in more specific articles in the Convention. Although not a novel concept, this article provides another step in the progression toward requiring nations, at least to the extent of their economic means, to assure that impoverished children obtain the necessities to survive and develop both physically and emotionally.

The objective of providing adequate standards of living for children has failed miserably throughout parts of Latin America. In Brazil, children are often forced onto the streets, either to work or to live, because of Brazil's extreme poverty. Ironically, despite having a relatively high per capita income compared to other developing nations, Brazil has one of the highest poverty rates in Latin America. Thus, it is not surprising that the statistics relating to children's health, education, and housing are abysmal. For example, even of those children who reside at home, 55% live in houses without adequate sanitation and water supplies. Only 20% of the children who enter primary education finish the mandatory eight years of schooling.

Recognizing that a nation's living standards are commensurate with their cultural norms and economic situations, Guatemala has still failed to ensure its most vulnerable children a modicum of the "basics" necessary for human survival. For example, more than 37% of the children between the ages of five and nine suffer from malnutrition; more than 50% of the families share one small room for the entire family; and over half the population lives in dirt houses without floors, latrines, or adequate water supplies. Equally inadequate standards of living for children exist in Colombia, and have been addressed by the Committee on the Rights of the Child. The Committee expressed its grave concern over the large proportion of Colombian street children who live in extreme poverty. These children have been "economically and socially marginalized and have limited or no access to adequate education or health care." Consequently, poverty and inadequate living conditions force many children into the streets.

Even considering the poor economic situations in these countries, or at least the vast differences in the wealth of its population, it is still clearly unacceptable and in direct contravention of international norms that great numbers of children have ended up living on city streets. Neither the countries themselves nor the Committee on the Rights of the Child have responded adequately. Under the overstated guise of insufficient resources, these Latin American nations have failed to effectively implement even minimal measures to improve the standard of care for impoverished children, clear violations of Article 27 of the Convention. Thus, it is critical to begin to re-emphasize the importance of international and local coordination with appropriate non-governmental organizations that could provide expertise, immediate assistance, and effective long-term care to those children most in need.

....

E. Illicit Use of Narcotic and Psychotropic Drugs

Article 33 of Convention on the Rights of the Child contains a specific reference to the illicit use of narcotic drugs and psychotropic substances, particularly because of their prevalent use among children. Unquestionably, street children are the group of children most seriously affected and exploited by this problem. Unfortunately, the majority of such street children frequently reject traditional institutions of recovery. One suggestion is to develop more informal communities which are able to meet the "child's health, social and psychological needs and are able to listen actively to children." Another recommendation involves the prohibition on the sale of glue and solvents to children. As with all other child victims of abuse and exploitation, States Parties should take measures to promote the recovery and reintegration of children who have abused narcotics or substances.

As suggested in Part I, the problem of substance abuse by street children in Latin America may be categorized as overwhelming and provides a significant challenge towards realistically improving the lives of street children. The vicious cycle of poverty and abuse instigates the use of drugs, including glue-sniffing, and makes it more difficult for these children to leave the streets. In Guatemala, governmental response to this severe problem has been non-existent. In fact, there are no government programs dealing with childhood drug addiction, and only the NGO Casa Alianza offers a drug rehabilitation program for those street children most seriously addicted to narcotics.

The recommendation to stop the sale of glue to children had received little reaction in Latin America until a recent lawsuit was filed by the parents of a Guatemalan teenager who died from the effects of sniffing glue. Along with the assistance of Casa Alianza, the parents fought back against their government's inaction. They launched a civil action in a United States federal court against H.B. Fuller, an industrial products manufacturer who produces the glue to which thousands of street children are addicted. The corporation was accused of being responsible for the street child's death because the product's fumes were addictive and deadly in nature. The case was thrown out of court, but after five years of substantial protests from street children's advocates, H.B. Fuller finally agreed to no longer sell its glue over the counter. In addition, in the midst of world attention, another international glue manufacturer has also changed its formula to make its product less attractive to children.

....

F. Torture and Inhumane Punishment

Article 37 of the Convention on the Rights of the Child prohibits the subjection of children to torture or other inhumane treatment. This includes a prohibition against capital punishment and life imprisonment for those under the age of eighteen. To the extent that some of the language is a repetition of standards in other documents, it may yet benefit street children since it is the first time such an express prohibition of torture and inhumane punishment has been made on the behalf of children. Moreover, the greater the repetition of standards, the more easily it may be argued that the standards themselves reflect customary international law. Consequently, by accepting such standards, States Parties may be likely to incorporate them into their domestic law, increasing the likelihood that the flagrant mistreatment towards street children will be enforced in their respective countries.

Nevertheless, such abusive mistreatment of street children continues to occur without government condemnation. The torture of street children detained by the police and military continues to be the norm in Colombia. In a 1994 report by Human Rights Watch, there was substantial evidence of "beatings, rape, electrical shocks, near-drownings in filthy water, and near-suffocation." Torture remains an ugly and daily reality for street children in detention in Colombia. For example, Frankie, who has lived on the streets of Colombia since age eight, has been tortured by police officers on numerous occasions. In one such encounter, he was kept naked in a cold basement cell, beaten with a water-soaked stick, punched in the stomach after having a plastic bag put over his head, and forced to have electric cable wires attached to his testicles.

In Guatemala, such torture and abuse have made street children's lives even shorter due to "the sadistic tendencies of members of the Guatemala's National Police and the country's thousands of private security guards." A legal aid clinic for street children has documented hundreds of incidents of abuse, torture, sexual abuse and illegal detention of street children. In one case, a group of female street children was arrested while watching an Easter parade because they did not have identification papers. The girls were taken to an isolated soccer field, where they were gang raped by the officers. The policemen then gave the girls change for the bus. The girls filed a complaint, but later refused to testify because they feared police retaliation.

Illegal arrests, beatings, and torture are also common problems for the impoverished children living on the streets in Brazil. In fact, four-fifths of the prison population in the city of San Paolo, are made up of those once categorized as street children. The prisons and juvenile detention centers are in horrendous conditions with reports of severe overcrowding and poor sanitation, while the abusive treatment of children detained in these facilities is almost routine.

Although inhumane treatment and torture is generally accepted throughout the world as intolerable, street children continue to survive under an umbrella tarnished with abuse. Without more pressure from the international community to curb such government supported action, the reality for street children will grow far worse, increasing the alarming number of street children who are subjected to such degrading mistreatment. Therefore, it is indisputable that Brazil, Colombia and Guatemala are in violation of the obligations imposed upon them by Article 37 of the Convention on the Rights of the Child.

. . . .

CONCLUSION

. . . .

A cynic may now find the Convention, after eight years of existence, to be an agreement devoid of substance because the document lacks sufficient enforcement mechanisms. In fact, the Convention has been compared to a "domestic society" that has no police or judicial authority, but which nevertheless "requires each member of the society to report periodically on the measures [they have taken] to comply with society's rules." However, the Convention is still in its youth and remains the only widely recognized international agreement that actually addresses the rights and needs of street children. Therefore, considering the importance of the Convention, and its lofty objectives, it is time to focus on strengthening the existing international mechanisms, condemning those nations that consistently violate these provisions, and working to improve the lives of street children in Latin America.

Notes and Questions

1. The Seitles article takes a much more traditional or predictable approach to the issue of street children than that of Mona Pare. What is Seitles' principal message? What is he suggesting national governments do, based on the UNCRC? As between Pare and Seitles, which approach is more likely to assist in improving the lives of street children? To some degree, states are faced with two main policy options: prevent the family breakdown that leads to child homelessness, or accept the reality of street children, and provide mobile services, as advocated by Pare. How does framing the issue in terms of "child rights" affect the policy debate? Which approach is more in line with our general understanding of child rights?

Casa Alianza is the Latin American branch of the American NGO, Covenant House. Like its American counterpart, Casa Alianza provides a wide range of services to street children and youth, including residential and mobile facilities. In addition to food, shelter and health care, the organization has been active in providing advocacy and legal help for many abused street children throughout Latin America. As is the case with Covenant House, Casa Alianza staff have themselves on occasion been accused of exploiting street youth for sexual favors.

In terms of its philosophy, Casa Alianza has been strong and effective in its defense of street children. It has spoken out against government repression of homeless youth, and drawn attention to the frequent violence perpetrated by police against them

Casa Alianza, *Our Integrated Approach*

available at http://www.casa-alianza.org.uk/northsouth/CasaWeb.nsf/
Street-Children/Street_Outreach?OpenDocument

Casa Alianza has developed a five stage core programme that starts on the streets and ends in kids having a home and hope for the future.

We start with street outreach and pre-community work and then offer access to crisis centres, transition homes and finally group homes.

1. Street Outreach

The very first step is to reach out to the children. We find them on the streets, in parks, darkened hallways and around garbage dumps and in bus terminals . . .

Our outreach teams provide emergency medical care, counselling, informal education and friendship. Children are then encouraged to leave the streets and come to our Crisis Centres ("Refugios"). These offer immediate, round-the-clock care and someone to talk to. Each year our Outreach Teams work with around 1,000 street children in Guatemala, Honduras, Mexico and Nicaragua.

2. "Pre-Community" Services

Our pre-community services offer a means of transition away from life on the street. It consists of a non residential day service for kids who may have become addicted to drugs or who have been destabilised from the harsh realities of street life. Pre-community services help tackle high risk behaviour, get kids to deal with drug problems and help prepare them for entry to our residential programmes.

3. Crisis Centres

Our Crisis Centres offer food, clothing, a clean bed, medical attention, education, security and most importantly ... love. We follow up on work started in our "pre-community" programme with continued drug counselling and other services.

Many of the kids only stay for a few nights but of those that do return to the streets about half return to our centres at a later date for a longer stay. For each of those that stay we help them develop a "plan de vida"—a life plan for the future. This sets attainable goals for the short, medium and long term and encourages children to think about the future. Children also participate in informal educational activities, which prepare them for the public school system.

Once children have become more stable, regain their self-respect and some hope we then offer access to our transition homes.

4. Transition Homes

Our transition home staff are specially trained to help children develop long term goals and to think positively about the future. Young children are enrolled at schools and older teenagers are offered vocational training. The average residency in a Transition Home is about four months—children then move to a group home.

5. Group Homes

The final step in the long journey from despair to an independent life away from the streets is residency in one of our Group Homes. Here children are nurtured by a carefully chosen team of counsellors who try to create a positive family environment. Children learn to bond with their new "surrogate family" while pursuing further educational or professional opportunities.

Each home houses an average of 14 boys or girls. The children remain at the home until their eighteenth birthday or until they have completed their education. Leaving the home as young adults, armed with new vocational and life skills we encourage them to pursue further education or more advanced job training.

Notes and Questions

1. Where does Casa Alianza's approach fall, with respect to the visions presented by Pare and Seitles respectively? How do the substitute homes described by Casa Alianza differ from the street children groups described by Pare as substitute families?

D. Response of State Law Enforcement to Street Children

The following reports demonstrate the often brutal response of law enforcement personnel to the problem of street children. Such behavior on the part of the police is sometimes tacitly approved of; at others, more openly encouraged by the state. The reports focus on such abuses as arbitrary arrest and detention, extortion, and violence. Where street children represent a feared and disrespected minority, they are likely to be subject to all these forms of ill treatment on the part of police, generally in the name of protecting the public. In many countries street children are scorned and feared by the general population, leading to an atmosphere of impunity with regard to police brutality.

Egypt: Arbitrary Arrest and Detention

Human Rights Watch, *Charged with Being Children: Egyptian Police Abuse of Children in Need of Protection*
2003, *available at* http://www.hrw.org/reports/2003/egypt0203/

. . . .

THE CHILD LAW: ARBITRARY ENFORCEMENT AND VAGUE LAWS

"We conduct arrest campaigns to demonstrate the government's presence. Because if we didn't have arrest campaigns then quickly the streets would fill up with kids selling tissues and wiping cars and begging."

— Police Officer, Bulaq al Dakrur Police Station, July 24, 2002

According to Ministry of Interior statistics, more than 25 percent of all children arrested in Egypt in 2001 were arrested on charges of being "vulnerable to delinquency." The Egyptian government argues that the provision is intended "to protect children exposed to delinquency before they ever commit an offence." In reality, police effectively treat these children as criminal suspects, detaining them in police lockups until it is determined that they have no warrants for their arrest, or until the Public Prosecution Office or the juvenile courts order them released, remanded to a social welfare institution, or placed under judicial probation. While not criminal sentences, these orders can result in children being placed in institutions or monitored weekly by armed social welfare experts for up to three years with little or no judicial review of the prosecution order or the placement.

. . . .

The number of arrests of Egyptian children on charges of being "vulnerable to delinquency" has more than doubled since 2000, rising from 4,197 arrests to 10,958 in 2001. Arrests of children "vulnerable to danger" went from zero cases in 2000 to 185 cases in 2001. Three thousand three hundred sixty of the 2001 arrests took place in the Cairo governorate, in comparison to four cases listed in 2000. Ministry of Interior officials credit the rise in arrests to the October 2000 decision to increase the status and resources allocated to the General Administration for Juvenile Welfare Investigations, and told us they wanted additional resources to allow them to increase the number of arrests and expand arrests of children who are truants from school.

Defining Children "Vulnerable to Delinquency" and "Vulnerable to Danger"

Egypt's Child Law (Law 12 of 1996) borrows the concept of children "vulnerable to delinquency" with only minor modifications from earlier legislation that considered such children to be socially dangerous and in need of the intervention of the criminal justice system. According to Egyptian officials, the Child Law is intended to prevent children "vulnerable to delinquency" from becoming criminals by holding parents or guardians criminally accountable for their failure to ensure the child behaves properly, and by authorizing judicial authorities to order rehabilitative measures and custody by the state when necessary. This approach contravenes international standards, which specify that children should not be charged with a crime or act of delinquency for any offense that would not be a crime if committed by an adult.

....

Following the passage of the Child Law, and in partial recognition of the failure of the law's provisions to address Egypt's international legal obligations toward children in need of protection, the government added a category of children "vulnerable to danger" when it issued the Child Law's implementing regulation in 1997. However, police, prosecutors, and judges rarely invoke the provisions on children "vulnerable to danger," and both legal concepts encompass extremely broad categories of ill-defined conduct and status that, while not crimes, nevertheless subject children to arrest and in practice rarely result in genuine rehabilitative measures.

The Child Law defines as "vulnerable to delinquency" any person under eighteen who begs, including selling or performing for small amounts of money; collects cigarette butts or rubbish; engages in immoral conduct or works for those who do; lacks a stable place of residence; associates with suspect persons or others vulnerable to delinquency; is a habitual truant; is incorrigible; lacks a legal source of income or support; suffers from a mental defect or illness; or, in the case of children under seven, commits any felony or misdemeanor. The law provides virtually no information on when authorities should take such a child into custody or how the various elements of the definition relate to each other.

The vague language of this definition invites selective enforcement and stigmatizes children by making them subject to arrest for conduct that in many cases would not be a criminal offense if committed by an adult and is often direct evidence of the child's need for protection. This is particularly apparent when considering the provisions on begging, mixing with suspect persons, sleeping in the streets, and truancy, which together account for more than 98 percent of all arrests of children "vulnerable to delinquency" in 2001. Truancy, like incorrigibility, is a status offense—an act that would not be criminal if committed by an adult. Begging is a criminal offense in Egypt, but the Begging Law only applies to persons at least eighteen years old. Egypt's Vagrants and Suspect Persons Law criminalizes persons who lack a legal means to support themselves, but excludes from this category women and children under fifteen who do not actively pursue an illegal means of living. It also specifies that a person must be over eighteen years old to be considered a suspect person, and does not criminalize association with suspect persons.

The Child Law's implementing regulations state that a child is "vulnerable to danger" if "found in a state that threatens the sound rearing he requires, and especially" in situations where the child's security, morals, health or life are in danger, where his environment exposes him to danger, where the person responsible for his support abandons him, where the child is in danger of not completing his education, or where the child is exposed to incitement to illicit use of drugs, alcohol, violence or immoral acts. These categories are essentially status offenses and subject children to arrest not for criminal acts they have committed but for others' failure to provide them with the care and protection they require. Like the provision on children "vulnerable to delinquency," these categories are so ill-defined as to encourage selective enforcement, and indeed enforcement jumped suddenly from no cases in 2000 to 185 in 2001.

Arrest Campaigns

Egyptian law requires that police making arrests have a warrant from the Public Prosecution Office or, in cases of suspects apprehended while committing a serious crime, "sufficient evidence" to charge. Both requirements are frequently violated in practice. The Child Law lowers this standard by allowing police and officials appointed by the Ministry of Justice in cooperation with the Ministry of Insurance and Social Affairs to arrest children who are not suspected of crimes but who are considered "vulnerable to delinquency."

The director of Cairo Governorate Police Directorate's al Azbekiya juvenile lockup, Brigadier Yasir Abu Shahdi, described his interpretation of these arrest powers: "We arrest kids in parks who look like they are homeless. We arrest kids selling tissues in the street. These kids become known to us, so it isn't hard. [Sometimes] we arrest kids walking down the street during school hours with their school books, but I don't have enough officers to make as many of these arrests as I would like. I am asking for more officers, because in the future we want to conduct campaigns to search for and arrest truants." While some of these arrests involve small numbers of children, more often they take the form of arrest campaigns involving tens of children in a targeted neighborhood. "Our daily work is to gather up children from the streets and arrest any who are in violation of the law."

. . . .

In reality the arrest campaigns are even broader in their scope that this description suggests. Juvenile justice experts, social workers, and activists at nongovernmental organizations providing services to street children and working children consistently said that during the campaigns police simply grab any child they find on the street. "[T]he campaigns to gather children can happen as a result of an important conference," said Dr. 'Azza Kuraym, the leading expert on juvenile justice and street children at the government-funded National Center for Social and Criminal Research. "They send police vehicles to gather children the way they send vehicles to collect dogs from the street. . . . There is no consideration for which children [they arrest,] street children, those in school or not, those begging or not; all that is important is that they collect the children on the street." Another expert told us, "The police don't distinguish between the child who works as a mechanic's assistant and is coming back from work in dirty clothes and the child who is actually begging. They arrest first and then they wait for the social worker to find the family so that the family can come to the station to get the child."

Nongovernmental organizations providing services to street children told us that these campaigns seriously impair their work by preventing children from reaching their centers, and some children complained that they had been arrested while on their way to nongovernmental organizations' drop-in centers. In some cases, police even waited outside nongovernmental organization drop-in centers to arrest street children and working children when they arrived. The director of one drop-in center told us that on normal days twenty-five to thirty children visited his center, but on days when there was a police arrest campaign "the numbers might drop to four or five children, either because they have been arrested or because they are afraid that if they come to the center they will be arrested outside the center."

....

In other cases, police appeared to target for arrest children whose accent, dress, or location may have identified them as being originally from areas outside of Cairo. Many of these arrests took place in the vicinity of the main train station in Ramsis Square, near the al Azbekiya police lockup. Mansur N., fifteen, is originally from Banha but has been living in Cairo for five years. He described his most recent arrest, three days before our interview. "I was in Alexandria for a few days and I had just returned to the Ramsis train station in Cairo. I was with a friend and I had my shoe shine box with me. The police grabbed me and took me to al Azbekiya and put me in the 'refrigerator'—it is a small room about three meters by three meters, with two windows, while they were waiting for the *kashf* [computer search] to say if I had any outstanding warrants. I was handcuffed to my friend. The computer said I was a juvenile so they sent me upstairs to the left with the kids." He was released after two days.

....

Arrest campaigns frequently involve large numbers of children and therefore increase the likelihood that children arrested during these sweeps will be subjected to overcrowding, detention with adult criminal detainees, and other abuses during detention and transport. The director of the Ministry of Interior's General Administration for Juvenile Welfare Investigations acknowledged the connection between the policy of mass arrests and abuses of children's rights, but placed the blame on the local police directorates. "In the [adult] police stations there may be problems when they are facing the pressures of many arrests [of children] due to arrest campaigns," he said. "There are written instructions sent to all officers, but our staff capacities are not sufficient to supervise the entire country. We do trainings for the [governorate-level] police directorates. Some learn, and some don't."

Detention without Prosecution Office Review

Egyptian law requires that any person arrested by police be presented to the Public Prosecution Office within twenty-four hours. When arresting children the police must present the Public Prosecution Office with a social report on the child in addition to the police investigative report. These requirements are intended to prevent arbitrary arrest and detention and to ensure that the Public Prosecution Office has sufficient information on the child to make a decision in the child's best interests. Children we interviewed said that police regularly detained them for longer than twenty-four hours without presenting them to the prosecution office. In several cases we investigated police detained children for up to two weeks without police ever presenting them to the Public Prosecution Office.

....

Public prosecutors are also required by law to conduct regular visits to all places of detention. Justice Mohammad al Gindi, a former attorney general who is widely credited as the author of the Child Law, told us, "The prosecution office for juveniles is responsible for supervising all places of detention, including police stations. The problem is that the attorney general must ask for regular reports on police stations, prisons, and other institutions where children are held. When I was attorney general I asked for such reports, but it doesn't happen now." When asked about their last visit to the al Azbekiya juvenile lockup, prosecutors in the Cairo Public Prosecution Office for Juveniles told us they had never inspected that lockup or visited other police stations to inspect detention conditions for children, and said that they did not as a rule inspect any detention centers for children. "Who has the time?" one deputy prosecutor told us. "I'd lose the whole day coming and going."

Children who are detained without prosecution office review are deprived of an important mechanism intended to minimize arbitrary arrest or detention and provide detainees an opportunity to make complaints against ill-treatment in police custody. They also lose access to the few potentially protective measures the Child Law specifies for children "vulnerable to delinquency" or "vulnerable to danger," because these measures must either be ordered by the prosecutor or by the court following a referral from the prosecutor.

Notes and Questions

1. How do the Egyptian officials justify their arrest of children who have not yet committed a crime? Whose interests do you think they believe they are serving and why? It seems clear that Egypt is attempting to prevent its street children problem from growing larger. Does it seem that the Egyptian technique will achieve that goal? What principles are violated by arresting children who are "vulnerable to delinquency" or "vulnerable to danger"?

2. Read the Human Rights Watch report entitled *Police Abuse and Killings of Street Children in India*, available at http://www.hrw.org/en/reports/1996/11/01/police-abuse-and-killings-street-children-india. How can human rights advocates make any progress in an area where police corruption and violence against children are so entrenched? For a recent report on the situation of street children in Kigali, Rwanda, see Human Rights Watch, *Swept Away: Street Children Illegally Detained in Kigali*, 2006, *available at* http://www.hrw.org/en/reports/2006/05/14/swept-away. The report describes the unjustified detention of street children under harsh and abusive conditions, similar to those reported in many other parts of the world.

Just as Egypt has taken a rigid, controlling approach to street children by swift recourse to detention, the authorities in Vietnam see the rise of street children as a negative side effect of recent economic liberalization. In the following article, the harsh conditions of life for Vietnam's street children are set out in vivid detail. This narrative describes a street child caught between the chaos of emerging capitalism and the arbitrary repression of an earlier authoritarian regime. The contempt felt by the authorities towards street children is obvious.

Vietnam: One Child's Story

Human Rights Watch, *"Children of the Dust": Abuses of Hanoi Street Children in Detention*
2006, *available at* http://hrw.org/reports/2006/vietnam1106/

Background on Street Children in Hanoi

In Vietnam children who live or work on the streets are often called *bui doi*, which means "children of the dust," or "the dust of life." Street children are also referred to as "wandering" or "roaming" children.

While Vietnam's policy of *doi moi* (the economic reform program launched in 1987) and its transition to a market economy have been credited with helping to lift many Vietnamese citizens out of poverty, economic reform has also been linked by Vietnamese government officials to a rise in "social evils" (*te nan xa hoi*). The problem of street children is included as a target of mass mobilization campaigns by the government, along with drug abuse, prostitution, HIV/AIDS, human trafficking, gambling, and vagrancy.

Street children have been described by a government official as one of the "negative phenomena arising from the revival of state-sanctioned capitalism." A 1998 directive by the prime minister attributes the problem not only to poverty, but government inattention to factors pushing children onto the street:

> The increasing numbers of street children and labor-abused children are posing a burning social problem today. They are the subjects [who are] highly vulnerable to social evils. The above-mentioned situation is partly attributed to such socio-economic reasons as unemployment, illiteracy, increasingly widened gap between the rich and the poor, moral degradation in some families ... and also partly to the improper, incomprehensive and ineffective coordination among various branches and levels [of government] as well as the lack of their concentrated efforts in addressing this problem.

. . . .

While poverty is a significant factor driving children to leave home to work on the streets, others reportedly come from families who have enough money to provide for them. These children leave home because of family or social problems such as death of a parent, domestic violence, alcoholism, divorce, or abandonment.

. . . .

Relief, juvenile justice, and administrative policies for children in Vietnam

. . . .

Trang's Story: From Dong Dau to Ba Vi and Back to the Streets Again

The following is an account from a boy we will call Trang, who was arrested and detained at Dong Dau twice during 2004, when he was 17. He was subsequently sent to Ba Vi for three months. He spoke to us two weeks after his release from Ba Vi.

First arrest (March 2004): "They never gave me any reason"

I was shining shoes at the lake [in Hanoi]. I didn't see him coming, but a man in plainclothes came up behind me and grabbed me. He took me to the police station. I was there until 11 a.m., when they took me to Dong Dau center.

When he was taking me to the station I was struggling to get free. He held me very tightly, and when we entered the station he beat me. He punched me in the head ... three or four times with his fist, and he kicked me in the legs a few times. Then I was handcuffed.

They never gave me any reason, but I knew I was arrested because I was shining shoes. When I was in the police station, they made a list of the items in my tool box and confiscated it. They took me in a truck, like a van, to Dong Dau.

Dong Dau was very dirty and smelly. We were locked in rooms all day, and the blankets had not been washed for a long time. There was a bucket used as the toilet — it was there in the room with us all the time. Every day, we were allowed out only twice, for a maximum of almost an hour. But most days, it was just half an hour at a time.

The room had just some plank beds on the floor for us to lie on. The window was always closed. It was in the door, with bars across it ...

When we were let out, all we could do was to go to the toilet and eat ... We could also shower, but usually we did not have enough time. Anyway, the water was very dirty. The conditions were filthy. When people arrive at Dong Dau, usually they get so sick because of the conditions that they cannot eat for the first few days. They just vomit. But after a few days you get used to it.

"They beat me more when I asked them to stop"

There are all kinds of people in Dong Dau, including students and soldiers, and anyone who is picked up sleeping in parks or on the street late at night. There were ten people in my room. The oldest was age 50, and the youngest was 16 years old.

The prison staff saw my hairstyle was fashionable—they beat many people for that. If you had an unusual hair style, they would beat you and cut it. Also they would beat you for many silly reasons, like talking too loudly. If a new person arrived at the center and was recognized by somebody already there, they would be excited and talk loudly. The guards would go into the room, make everyone kneel down, and then beat everyone. They even beat a boy with deformed legs and made him kneel in the hot sun.

Ninety-nine percent of the people wanted to escape. I tried, too. On the third day, they let me out to sweep the courtyard. I tried to jump over the fence, but when I jumped back down I landed on shards of glass. It was put there to stop people escaping. Some people saw me, so I ran into the center to hide. They found me.

They took me to a courtyard, and then went to find a truncheon. First they kicked me twice in the chest, and I couldn't breathe. I was sitting down. Almost everybody was watching, because all the rooms faced this courtyard. They used the clubs to beat me. They hit me so much and so hard that at the end, the club was bent out of shape.

They stood in a circle around me. Two people were beating me at the same time. After they were finished, one more came with another truncheon. He held it with both hands [he demonstrates the technique: the club is held over his head with two hands, and swung down]. I don't know how many times they hit me, but it went on for a long time.

I screamed a lot, begging for them to stop. But they just beat me more when I asked them to stop. They hit me everywhere, except my head. They hit me on the front and back.

When they sent me back to my room, I couldn't walk. The three men carried me back. For one week after, a boy named Hai had to help me go to eat and walk about.

They didn't even give me a bandage. I was bleeding so much, and they didn't even give me a bandage. My legs were covered in blood, but it was blood from the cut on my foot [he shows the scar on his foot from the glass]. I was bleeding so much that the nurse secretly brought me bandages and told me not to tell anyone.

I had bruises everywhere—all over both my arms and on my chest and legs and back—everywhere. I was in very bad condition. Some other [prisoners] helped me ...

"I have read in the newspapers ... they help you go home"

After two weeks, when they were getting ready to release me, I had to write a commitment that I would do no more shoe shine. I have read in the newspapers that when you leave these centers, they help you go home, and the government gives your family 150,000 dong [US$9] a month for the next three months. That's totally wrong. It's fiction. It never happens. Sometimes the prisoners had no money, so someone else would give them some to help them get the bus. And they'd get a beating from the guards. Nobody was even allowed to share money.

When I left, I went back to shining shoes. I was very afraid, but I need the money to go home to my family.

Second arrest (June 1, 2004): "How bad could 15 days be?"

The second time I was arrested was on Children's Day, June 1. I was sitting by the lake. I wasn't shining shoes. The security guards and the ward police came to arrest everyone ... They saw me holding a plastic bag and knew I had shoeshine tools inside ... I saw them and ran across the road into the market. They followed me in and caught me.

They said nothing—they just grabbed me and put me on the truck to Dong Dau. I was never told why I had been arrested. As I entered the grounds [of Dong Dau], all the staff recognized me. They didn't do anything but asked a lot of questions and checked to see if I was a drug addict. I filled in a form, and they locked me in a room. I was there for 14 days.

I saw a lot of people beaten. Some people wanted to get out of their room, and they were banging loudly on the door. The guards came in, and they beat everyone in the room. There was one man who was joking when he first got arrested. He joked, 'How bad could 15 days be?' So the guards showered him with blows from clubs. It was very serious—he couldn't even walk.

I saw a mother and son—the son was three or four years old. The guard sent his mother away somewhere, I don't know where, and put the child into my room. He was crying so much. The guards asked us to keep the child. He cried all night. This happened after I had been there for one week, and he was still there when I left.

Nobody in my room was sick. But in the women's section upstairs, someone had a really bad stomach ache. She was screaming so loudly, but nobody came to help.

The room was just like the last time: dirty. It was kind of cold. There were two fans and one light—both stayed on 24 hours a day—and one window in the door. There was nothing to do. We just talked all day to pass the time. When we weren't talking, we slept.

The food was terrible. Most people just nibbled at it ... The food was old; the rice was often left-over or burnt. We ate twice a day—usually rice and two pieces of meat about the size of my thumb. It was never enough, and it didn't taste good. It's cooked by other prisoners and they are not used to cooking for so many people. The staff doesn't have to do anything—they just call us and we do the work.

On the day I was arrested the second time, I was sure I would be sent right to Ba Vi, but they kept me for 14 days at Dong Dau. I thought I'd be released after that, but I wasn't. They sent me to Ba Vi.

To Ba Vi (June 14, 2004): Another commitment

I arrived at Ba Vi in a truck with 19 other people. At first I thought everything would be the same as Dong Dau, but it was very different. In each room, people vote for the head of the room. In the first few days I was there, everything was fine.

Every day there was just two hours work outside. Then I could go back to the room and play chess. The water was better and there were more showers. But if you showered too much, you'd develop a rash. One time I had a fever and the staff gave me some medicine. There is a hospital nearby.

I wouldn't say I liked Ba Vi, but staying there was okay. But there was no freedom.

The staff were okay. They talked to us like normal people. If we didn't do anything to them, they didn't do anything to us. But if the staff beat someone, they beat them a lot. I saw this a lot, but only when people didn't want to wash their dishes after eating, or if we were fighting with each other. I was beaten three times with a stick because I saw a beehive and threw rocks at it. The staff saw and told me to stop, but I threw one more. They called me over and beat me three times on my arm, wrist, and butt.

Afterwards, my wrist was swollen a little, so I put some ointment on it. I went to ask some women prisoners for medicine and they helped me out.

I saw many people beaten. The youngest was 14 or 15. No one was seriously injured—they were left with some bruises. They would beat us in the head or put us against the wall and beat us on our butts with their clubs.

Release (September 14, 2004)

When I was leaving, I signed another commitment that I wouldn't go to do shoe shine. They advised me to go to the countryside. They used to give people 20,000 dong (US$1.25) when they were leaving, but now they only give 10,000 ($0.62). We got all of our possessions back. I walked one kilometer to the highway and caught a bus from there.

Now, I am shining shoes again. I want to go home, but I don't have enough money.

Notes and Questions

1. The question of remedies is particularly difficult in the context of street children. To some extent, there appears to be an increasing awareness that street children are subject to intolerable levels of violent abuse, often at the hands of the police. Yet, as has been discussed above, it often happens that street children are on the receiving end of complex social prejudices, and the police are allowed, even expected, to treat them with a harshness that not infrequently leads to death. An article by Uché U. Ewelukwa, *Litigating the Rights of Street Children in Regional or International Fora: Trends, Options, Barriers and Breakthroughs*, 9 Yale Human Rights & Development Law Journal 85 (2006), discusses a resounding decision of the Inter-American Court of Human Rights which brought attention to horrific police violence against street children in Guatemala. The author finds great significance in the fact that the lives of street children and the suffering of their families found vindication in this important decision of a prestigious international court. (Note that this same case is also discussed in the context of regional remedies for violations of the rights of children in Chapter Seven of this book.)

V. Unaccompanied Minors — Juvenile Refugees and Asylum Seekers

Economic migrants of all kinds continue to cross borders in search of opportunity regardless of restrictions created to stop them, a certain number of these migrants being juveniles. International legal protections for these children are to some extent indirect; the UNCRC is often cited as the best source of "comprehensive" rights, including the rights of migrant children. The UNCRC, as we have seen in Chapter One, requires that the best interests of the child be taken into account in all decision making. It offers protection from improper detention, and mandates that the child be offered special protection when separated from family members.

A significant number of unaccompanied minors are refugees and asylum seekers. In 1988, the United Nations High Commission for Refugees published guidelines to assist in the proper treatment of juvenile refugees. The guidelines were updated in the 1994 publication, *Refugee Children: Guidelines on Protection and Care.*[3] The publication makes the point that "usually more than half of any refugee population are children." It notes that all the protections available to refugees under the 1951 Refugee Convention[4] and 1967 Protocol[5] (Relating to the Status of Refugees) are equally available to children, including the idea that children with a well founded fear of persecution should be considered refugees in the same manner as adults; also that children with refugee status cannot be forced to return to their countries of origin. The guidelines invoke the UNCRC, and tell decision-makers to apply all relevant rights of children found in the Convention, including protection against discrimination and the right to be heard.

A further document published by the UNHCR in 1997, entitled *Guidelines on Policies and Procedures in Dealing with Unaccompanied Children Seeking Asylum,*[6] provide national authorities with clear, child friendly methods of evaluating children's needs at the time they enter the territory and beyond.

E. Unaccompanied Minors in the United States

It is a fact that many unaccompanied child migrants, frightened and confused, find themselves without any protection once they reach their destinations. The United States, as an economic magnet, receives hundreds of these unaccompanied minors, and often fails to provide them with appropriate forms of protection.

The article that follows traces problems and abuses in the traditional U.S. approach to unaccompanied alien children, and summarizes recent initiatives to improve the situation. As with many writers in this field, Nugent criticizes insufficient attention paid to child welfare principles in the development of immigration and asylum policies.

Christopher Nugent, *Whose Children Are These?* *Towards Ensuring the Best Interests and Empowerment of Unaccompanied Alien Children*

15 Boston University Public Interest Law Journal 219 (2006)

Over the last several years, the plight of over 8,000 unaccompanied refugee and immigrant children has received significant attention by Congress, policy-makers, the media, the public and academia. These children arrive on our shores without parents or guardians, facing arrest, detention and removal. Both experts and stakeholders have amassed substantial recommendations for systemic reform in policies, practices and procedures affecting unaccompanied children. The significant amount of attention may be attributable to the vulnerability of these children by virtue of their status as unaccompanied, meaning that they are without parents or legal guardians.

---

3. United Nations General Assembly, United Nations High Commission for Refugees, *Refugee Children: Guidelines on Protection and Care*, 1994, *available at* http://www.unhcr.org/protect/ PROTECTION/3b84c6c67.pdf.

4. United Nations Convention Relating to Status of Refugees (Refugee Convention), Jul. 28, 1951, 19 U.S.T. 6577, *available at* http://www2.ohchr.org/english/law/refugees.htm.

5. United Nations Protocol Relating to the Status of Refugees (Refugee Protocol), Jan. 31, 1967, *available at* http://www2.ohchr.org/english/law/protocolrefugees.htm.

6. United Nations High Commissioner for Refugees, Guidelines on Policies and Procedures in dealing with Unaccompanied Children Seeking Asylum, Feb. 1997, *available at* http://www.reliefweb.int/ rw/lib.nsf/db900SID/LGEL-5S5BY7?OpenDocument.

This may be due to the United States' societal, cultural and legal construction of a child under the Immigration and Nationality Act[7] as a subordinate quasi-appendage to an adult familial caretaker, lest he or she become a public charge. Unaccompanied children represent an oxymoron because of the presumption that children do not and cannot have an independent existence and agency absent their relationship to adult familiar caretakers.

Despite this attention, the children's actual voices, experiences, and perspectives have rarely been directly consulted to explicitly inform and shape legislative proposals or larger policy decisions by the United States Congress or agencies charged with responsibilities over them. This may be attributable to reflexive protective paternalism predicated on an unspoken assumption that children are incapable of making rational, effective contributions to larger questions about policy. This may also reflect an unspoken assumption about the propriety of alien children's participation, as they are vested stakeholders and would be potential beneficiaries of such policy changes. Additionally, this may reveal nongovernmental stakeholders' limited time and resources to engage the children in reflection concerning policies. Finally, on a psychoanalytic level, this may reflect the adult surrogates' fear of deep listening and direct learning from the children based on their unique, individual experiences.

. . . .

The paramount need is to change the discourse and approach from an inherently "alienating" immigration paradigm to a child welfare and child-centered paradigm that gives primacy to the child's perspectives, needs and involvement. These are children first and foremost, before their status as either aliens or unaccompanied. They, in turn, need and deserve holistic, child-centered approaches premised on their individual facts and circumstances. These children further merit a shift from paternalism to youth empowerment approaches so that they may actively inform and drive the policy debates that shape their lives and futures in the United States and abroad. Paternalism may be a comfortable and instinctive antidote to the legacy Immigration and Naturalization Service's treatment of the children as "juveniles" and "minors" or law enforcement's view of the children as young adults with the agency and mens rea to violate the immigration laws. Still, youth empowerment represents the next and necessary frontier for advocacy, policy-development and service delivery for these children.

In this article, I first provide a panorama of the improving state of affairs for unaccompanied children and the innovative new efforts that are underway to serve them. I then identify the current intractable issues in need of policy resolution accounting for both institutional stakeholders' and children's perspectives so as to chart possible harmonization and meaningful reform.

I. A PARADIGM SHIFT IN THE CARE FOR UNACCOMPANIED ALIEN CHILDREN

The number of unaccompanied children arriving in the United States has risen from 4,600 in 2000 to over 7,000 in 2005. These children vary in age and ethnicity, but all are seeking protection within the United States' borders. While the majority of these children are teenaged, some are toddlers. Most have traveled from the Central American countries of Honduras, Guatemala and El Salvador, but others' roots are in Mexico, Brazil, Ecuador and China. During the 2005 fiscal year, 73% were boys and 27% were girls.... Twenty six percent were below the age of 14. Some of these children are refugees who are

---

7. Immigration and Nationality Act, 8 U.S.C. § 1101.

fleeing from persecution; some have experienced abuse, neglect and abandonment; some may have been brought by adults to the United States intent on exploiting them; and still others are looking to reunify with their parents or relatives.

After their arrest by the Department of Homeland Security (DHS), the children are placed in the care and custody of the Office of Refugee Resettlement (ORR) Division of Unaccompanied Children's Services (DUCS) which inherited care, custody and placement responsibilities for these children pursuant to the Homeland Security Act of 2002 ("HSA"). The children face administrative removal proceedings before the Executive Office for Immigration Review (EOIR), an agency of the Department of Justice (DOJ). These proceedings are administrative and adversarial, and pit the lone child, carrying the same burden of proof as an adult alien, against a trained DHS trial attorney before an immigration judge. According to the American Immigration Lawyers Association, approximately 90% of the children lack representation when they are tried before the immigration court, since there is no right to government-appointed counsel and pro bono resources are scarce and relatively untapped in most areas of the country.

In the HSA, Congress transferred the responsibilities for care, custody and placement of these children from the former Immigration and Naturalization Service (INS) to the ORR. Congress had acknowledged that the INS had a poor track record in caring for the children over the last two decades, while the ORR had a demonstrated history of expertise in working with child refugees through their Unaccompanied Minor Program. The INS suffered from a fundamental conflict of interest when acting as police officer, prosecutor and guardian of the children at the same time. Additionally, the INS typically prioritized law enforcement considerations over child welfare considerations. For example, the INS placed one third of unaccompanied children, including those children with very minor behavioral problems and those lacking any serious physical threat, in secure detention juvenile jails due to the lack of bed space in shelter facilities.

Even though the ORR inherited a dysfunctional de facto detention program from the INS, the ORR has made substantial progress for reform by prioritizing child welfare considerations despite limited resources. For example, the ORR decreased the use of juvenile detention centers from twenty-three in the 2003 fiscal year to three in the 2005 fiscal year. Furthermore, the ORR developed a continuum of care for unaccompanied children by adding a variety of housing options, such as shelter care, staff secure, foster care, and more innovative secure settings, as well as residential treatment care. As of November, 2005, the ORR had 1150 children in its care on a daily basis. The ORR contracts with 34 facilities around the country, the majority of which are shelters operated by non-profit organizations. About 500 of the children are held at several facilities in Texas. Children in the shelters receive education, health care, socialization/recreation, mental health services, family reunification and case management, including mental health and victim of trafficking assessments. On average, the children spend forty-five days in custody. Approximately 70% of the children are released from custody into the care of family or other sponsors, pending continued immigration proceedings in their detention site. During the 2005 fiscal year, 21% of the children were either ordered removed or returned voluntarily to their country of origin from ORR custody.

Conditions for the confinement and the release of the children to sponsors are governed by *Flores v. Reno* Settlement Agreement. *Flores* ultimately provided children with limited, enforceable rights and remedies in federal court. For example, the DHS detention standards enacted in 2000 provide for rights and protections to adult detainees in immigration custody, including prohibitions against strip searches after attorney visitations absent reasonable suspicion of contraband, liberal phone access rights, and rights to legal materials which children are not entitled to under *Flores*.

Regulations for *Flores* are being drafted by ORR and are in the process of review within HHS. Enforceability of *Flores* was limited to federal court actions and, even then, there has been only one reported case litigated under *Flores* involving Alfredo López-Sánchez, an indigenous Guatemalan Mayan Indian youth from the Mam ethnic group who was detained in an adult facility in Florida in contravention of *Flores*. There, the court held that, despite finding a violation of *Flores*, it could not order the child to be transferred to a children's facility. Advocates hope that in promulgating regulations for *Flores*, *Flores* will be treated as a floor, rather than a ceiling, to provide a panoply of enforceable rights for unaccompanied children.

Conditions of confinement for unaccompanied children have greatly improved now that ORR is responsible for their care; however, the system ORR inherited from INS warehoused children in remotely-located, medium-security shelters, beyond the regular access of counsel and observers. This puts ORR in a deficit of sorts, because INS saw all bed space as within their national governance, it often transferred children away from their counsel without notice in order to accommodate new arrivals in the facilities. Given bed space and funding constraints, ORR still detains significant numbers of children together, particularly along the Southern border. Some facilities house over 100 children in fairly institutionalized settings. The children receive on-site education and have supervised access to the local community. ORR's reliance on the institutional model is driven by a variety of factors including the consideration of time since the average stay in ORR custody is 45 days coupled with history, cost, and convenience since ORR inherited this economy-of-scale approach from INS. Nevertheless, ORR is open to experimenting with facility models; their facility in Houston is much like a campus, consisting of smaller cottages, while in their Queens, New York facility, there are only twelve children at any given time. Additionally, ORR has increased its use of foster care by 100% compared to INS by granting 100 placements intended for children who have long-term immigration cases.

Congress has become engaged in this programming issue, as evidenced by the 2005 Labor/HHS appropriations bill directing ORR to deinstitutionalize facility care and move towards more child-centered, age-appropriate, small group, homelike environments with access to pro bono counsel. Indeed, in Western Europe and Canada, unaccompanied children with pending immigration proceedings are often integrated into local communities and attend school with local children.

The prospect of legal representation for unaccompanied children has grown increasingly challenging post-September 11th and after the passage of the Homeland Security Act of 2002. At both the local and the national level, immigration enforcement officials often express little sympathy for unaccompanied children's predicaments and their cases for a variety of reasons. Some immigration enforcement officials carry the perception that unaccompanied children are a byproduct of, and contribute to, chain migration and greater illegal migration. Additionally, there is a notion that treatment under the law of unaccompanied children has become too lenient. Consider, for example, DHS' challenge in Seattle to the Executive Office for Immigration Review's (EOIR) jurisdiction to conduct bond redetermination hearings for unaccompanied children. DHS argued that the Homeland Security Act of 2002 conferred exclusive jurisdiction to ORR over the custody and release of children, notwithstanding the *Flores* settlement which explicitly provided for EOIR jurisdiction to conduct bonding hearings over unaccompanied children. Although the immigration judge initially adopted DHS' argument, the Board of Immigration Appeals reversed, finding that EOIR retained jurisdiction "over the threshold issue of whether an unaccompanied minor should be detained" at all.

While entrusted to uphold justice and international refugee law, DHS often appeals the rare grants of asylum by immigration judges for unaccompanied children. Even though asylum cases are adjudicated on a case-by-case basis and opinions by individual immigration judges are not published or considered as precedent, DHS often applies a strict enforcement lens to children's asylum claims in their policies. In particular, DHS may fear opening the borders to other children seeking asylum based upon novel arguments such as whether street children, gang resisters, and children facing domestic violence constitute cognizable particular social groups for asylum eligibility. In the absence of settled case law or guidelines for child asylum-seekers to bind DHS trial attorneys and immigration judges, the perennial fear of opening the floodgates may explain the paucity of asylum grants to unaccompanied children.

While unaccompanied children's cases are more exacting and more difficult to prepare by virtue of the child's development, sometimes DHS resistance and skepticism often makes representing children even more challenging, time-consuming and expensive than representing adults. Individual cases can easily become polarizing and politicized.

Unfortunately, stakeholders compete from a deficit of child welfare expertise in elements of the adjudicatory system among non-governmental, pro bono attorneys, DHS trial attorneys and immigration judges. Ensuring actual comprehension by the child and involvement of the child in all legal actions taken in his or her case remains an essential priority for advocates. Child-specific training, albeit without the direct participation of children, has been augmented for the bench and private bar in order to address this deficit. EOIR has published procedural guidelines for immigration judges' treatment of unaccompanied alien children's cases, but these guidelines are not binding, do not address substantive law, and are not always followed. In its 2006 appropriation to EOIR, Congress commended EOIR for issuing these guidelines and indicated its expectation that EOIR continue to improve these guidelines and train judges and pro bono attorneys in this area.

To address the legal representation crisis, several laudable efforts have been launched which strive to ensure competent pro bono counsel for unaccompanied children in removal proceedings. For example, a generous donation by the United Nations High Commissioner for Refugees Goodwill Ambassador Angelina Jolie helped create the National Center for Refugee Immigrant and Children ("National Center"). The National Center is a joint project of the United States Committee for Refugees and Immigrants and the American Immigration Lawyers Association. It recruits, trains, and mentors pro bono attorneys to represent unaccompanied children released from custody to sponsors at their destination site. In less than one year of operations, the National Center has trained several hundred attorneys in major metropolitan cities, matched over 200 children with competent counsel in over 25 states, and helped over 300 children whose cases may require a motion for a change of venue.

. . . .

II. MAPPING THE INTRACTABLE REMAINING ISSUES CONCERNING UNACCOMPANIED CHILDREN

There are intractable and unresolved issues concerning unaccompanied children arising from particular DHS immigration enforcement policies, and activities. Per the Homeland Security Act of 2002, DHS is responsible for arresting unaccompanied children, notifying and transporting children to ORR, prosecuting their removal cases and repatriating the children when they are ordered removed or granted voluntary departure. On the other hand, ORR is responsible for the placement, care, and legal and physical custody of unaccompanied children, as well as their release to suitable sponsors pending removal proceedings.

However, DHS's role and responsibilities vis-à-vis unaccompanied children remains significant and expansive including the arrest and treatment of unaccompanied children in DHS custody, age-determinations, the separation of families, the lack of confidentiality in connection with children's information regarding immigration enforcement, emergency trafficking benefits, authority for consent for placement of unaccompanied children in dependency proceedings as a predicate for Special Immigrant Juvenile Status and repatriation. Both singularly and taken together, law enforcement interests may trump child welfare and protection concerns, possibly to the detriment of unaccompanied children.

A. DHS as Gatekeeper

As the arresting agency that first interacts with unaccompanied children, DHS acts as a gatekeeper to determine which children will ultimately be referred and transported to ORR care within seventy-two hours, as required by *Flores*. DHS has the authority to determine whether the children are in fact under the age of eighteen and whether the children are unaccompanied or accompanied by a parent or legal guardian, triggering DHS jurisdiction over the custody. Finally, DHS has authority to release children within the first seventy-two hours in their custody to sponsors.

DHS's fulfillment of its responsibilities to determine children's custody has been the subject of criticism. To determine children's ages, DHS utilizes dental and wrist bone forensics, which medical experts criticize as scientifically fallible because of margins of error of several years. This practice has led to the erroneous placement of children in facilities, commingled with adults and detainees pending removal proceedings. These children often are detained in remote facilities beyond the reach of attorneys and advocates who could help them both challenge the age determination and represent them in their removal claims.

. . . .

In order to implement effective policy changes, DHS should recognize its lack of knowledge in child welfare, and develop its infrastructure and capacity to temporarily house children and families. While DHS is well suited to enforce immigration laws (i.e. by arresting unaccompanied children and families and conducting background checks), DHS does not have sufficient or adequate law enforcement resources to permit it to also be in the business of child or family care. Moreover, DHS detention of unaccompanied children has not been proven to have a deterrent effect on unauthorized migration. From a child's perspective, even seventy-two hours in jail-like conditions, without access to education and recreation, feels like an eternity and can have adverse mental health consequences. Policy solutions should maximize core competencies of federal agencies, such as DHS contracting with ORR or reputable nongovernmental agencies for secure, safe and supervised temporary shelters along the border for the first seventy-two hours as well as for family detention.

B. Lacunae for DHS Advantage

There are several lacunae in existing law which DHS may use to exercise a law enforcement advantage over the children in the areas of confidentiality of children's records, its insertion into the process of determining a child's eligibility for emergency trafficking benefits, and its inconsistent placement of unaccompanied children in state dependency proceedings as a predicate for Special Immigrant Juvenile Status.

....

The Homeland Security Act vests ORR with responsibility as guardian acting in loco parentis of the children to act in the child's best interests. Nevertheless DHS has retained the authority to consent to detained children's placement in state juvenile dependency proceedings and foster care as abused, neglected or abandoned children. This placement allows children access to Special Immigrant Juvenile Status and lawful permanent residence. DHS has yet to promulgate regulations regarding such consent, and there are no written or known operating policies on consent to access state dependency proceedings. Advocates claim they have difficulty acquiring DHS consent. These advocates find law enforcement considerations trump what should be a child welfare process run by welfare professionals. Congress has stepped in to urge ORR to allow individual abused, abandoned or neglected children to access these dependency proceedings.

Repatriation is another black hole where unaccompanied children easily fall through the cracks. There are no published, publicly available regulations, protocols or standards to ensure the safe and secure repatriation of children to their country of origin. While DHS clearly has a repatriation function under its sovereign authority to expel aliens, no agency has the role or responsibility to determine whether repatriation is in the child's best interest. This determination is irrelevant concerning a child's removal under the Immigration and Nationality Act. Thus, cases occur where children are removed to adverse and life-threatening circumstances without any intervention by United States authorities.

Once in the United States, unaccompanied children should benefit from all procedural and legal protections available to them by their legal and physical custodian, ORR. DHS should recognize its limitations in earning the trust and confidence of children. This lack of trust can impact psychological evaluations, benefits and repatriation purposes. Trust is essential for any cooperation whether for clinical evaluations or prosecution for trafficking. Additionally, children should not be victimized because of their status as children who have failed to secure immigration relief in the United States. The relief available is limited and may not be suitable to all children facing life-threatening harm.

Notes and Questions

1. How are the difficulties presented by unaccompanied minors different from those of street children or social orphans? Should unaccompanied minors be granted the right to counsel when they are tried before the immigration court?

2. Nugent points out that there is no governmental entity that has the responsibility of determining whether repatriation is within the unaccompanied child's best interest or not. Should the U.S. interest in regulating the number of immigrants entering the country, particularly those who require full state support and resources for survival—such as unaccompanied minors—trump the interests of the child? To what extent does the U.S. have a responsibility to take care of everyone who crosses its borders?

The "*Flores* settlement" referred to grew out of a 1997 class action suit brought against the Immigration and Naturalization Service, alleging poor treatment of juvenile migrants. The resulting settlement established that unaccompanied immigrant children should be released to family members if possible; and where this is not feasible, they should be held in the least restrictive setting available, with full access to educational, health and social benefits. For details on how the immigration authorities implemented *Flores*, see http://www.usdoj.gov/oig/reports/INS/e0109/exec.htm.

3. For a discussion of how social disadvantage, the vulnerability of childhood and the need to escape from an unendurable situation came together in the case of one unaccompanied minor, see Matthew D. Muller, Deborah E. Anker, Lory Diana Rosenberg, *Practitioners' Section: Representing Undocumented Minors in U.S. Courts: Escobar v. Gonzales: A Backwards Step for Child Asylum Seekers and the Rule of Law in Particular Social Group Asylum Claims*, 10 University of California at Davis Journal of Juvenile Law & Policy 243 (2006). By way of comparison with U.S. policy, also see Emily Benfer, *In the Best Interests of the Child? An International Human Rights Analysis of the Treatment of Unaccompanied Minors in Australia and the United States*, 14 Indiana International & Comparative Law Review 729 (2004), writing on the mandatory detention of unaccompanied asylum seeking children in Australia. For data on the situation of unaccompanied minors entering the UK, see Wendy Ayotte and Louise Williamson, *Separated Children in the UK: An overview of the current situation*, Save the Children, British Refugee Council, 2001, *available at* http://www.asylumsupport.info/publications/refugeecouncil/separated.pdf.

Are any of the "magnet" countries getting it right?

4. For a critique of U.S. failures to adjust immigration policy to the particular needs of children, see Ani Ajemian, *Alone and Ignored: Unaccompanied Alien Children Seeking Asylum in the United States, Canada and Australia*, 2007, available at http://works.bepress.com/ani_ajemian/2/.

Ajemian writes that "another inconclusive and ongoing debate in the U.S. concerns the requirement that children show a well founded fear of persecution in the same manner as adults. One author theorizes that by requiring children, including infants, to demonstrate subjective apprehension to a decision maker creates an insurmountable barrier to effective legal protection. While some procedural exemptions have been included in U.S. administrative policy for children in this regard, one author stresses that this procedural exemption must be strengthened and formalized into a singular objective risk test. In addition, because the subjective apprehension analysis is utilized by the United States, Canada, the United Kingdom, Australia, Ireland and Hong Kong, a streamlined approach may be best implemented by the UNHCR and across all jurisdictions that are signatories to the Convention and Protocol.

The present approach in the U.S. also ignores those dangers children flee that are special to them because of their age and respective positions in their home state's culture and society. As previously discussed, children face dangers specific to them as children: recruitment as child soldiers, child marriage, bonded labor, child sex trafficking and persecution by police forces when pushed onto the streets for reasons related to abuse or poverty, to name a few. Based on this short list alone, a powerful argument can be made that children, unaccompanied minors in particular, who experience child-specific persecution could constitute a particular social group under U.S. asylum laws."

F. Unaccompanied Minors in Spain: A Case Study

Unaccompanied children appear in all parts of the world, in developed and developing countries alike. Lack of documentation, lack of family ties, economic resources, and other tangible benefits of group membership often lead to tragedy as children struggle to navigate immigration systems that lack responsive mechanisms to serve their needs.

The case of Moroccan children in Spain is a particularly important one. Spain is on the front line where the EU meets North Africa; cultures and standards of living collide. Large numbers of youths try over and again to gain entry to Spain as a gateway to a better life; they are mistreated and repeatedly expelled. The problem has been well documented by Human Rights Watch and taken up for criticism by the Committee on the Rights of the Child, as seen in the following documents.

Human Rights Watch, *Nowhere to Turn: State Abuses of Unaccompanied Migrant Children by Spain and Morocco*

2002, *available at* http://www.hrw.org/reports/2002/spain-morocco/

SUMMARY

Every year thousands of Moroccan children, some as young as ten, enter Spain alone, without proper documentation. Sneaking past Moroccan and Spanish police at ports and border posts, they put their lives at risk to pursue their dreams for a better life. Some flee abusive families; others flee poverty and the lack of educational and employment opportunities at home. All too often they find violence, discrimination, and a dangerous life on the streets of unfamiliar cities. When apprehended in Spain they may be beaten by police and then placed in overcrowded, unsanitary residential centers. Some are arbitrarily refused admission to a residential center. The residential centers often deny them the health and education benefits guaranteed them by Spanish law; in these centers, children may be subjected to abuse by other children and the staff entrusted with their care. If they are unlucky, they may be expelled to Morocco, where many are beaten by Moroccan police and eventually turned loose to fend for themselves.

All this takes place in two countries that have undertaken to provide all children within their jurisdictions the rights and guarantees specified in the Convention on the Rights of the Child.

In the case of Spain, this undertaking has been codified in legislation guaranteeing unaccompanied foreign children care and protection on the same basis as Spanish children, including the right to education, health care, temporary residency status, and protection from repatriation if repatriation puts the child or the child's family at risk. The Spanish government has failed to ensure that these provisions are uniformly enforced, and the Spanish regional governments that implement the law selectively or choose to ignore it altogether are not called to account.

For its part, the Moroccan government does not routinely monitor the situation of Moroccan children in Spain, facilitate repatriation from Spain when it is in the child's interest, or ensure that unaccompanied migrant children receive protection and care when they are returned to Morocco.

. . . .

CONTEXT

. . . .

Conservative estimates suggest that at least 1,500 unaccompanied migrant children are present in Spain at any given time. True numbers are likely to be much higher. The vast majority are Moroccan; children typically range in age from twelve through seventeen, although some younger children also cross into Spain on their own.

Many of these children enter Spanish territory by crossing the land border between Morocco and the cities of Ceuta and Melilla. Located on the Mediterranean coast, these cities have been under Spanish control since the sixteenth century; they are the subject of an ongoing dispute with Morocco, which considers them occupied territories. Both are duty-free ports with significant military presences and economies largely dependent on fishing, tourism, trade with Morocco, illicit drug trafficking, and profits gleaned from the smuggling of undocumented migrants into Spanish territory. Ceuta is the larger of the two cities, with an area of approximately twenty square kilometers.

Spanish authorities and human rights activists in these cities estimate that each has a permanent population of approximately 150 unaccompanied migrant children, who are joined by hundreds more during the peak season for crossing to the mainland. The total population of each city is approximately 70,000. "We have a volume of kids on the scale of Barcelona or Madrid in a smaller city," said Melilla's fiscal for minors. "During the September holidays we are flooded."

Spanish law provides for the care of these children on the same basis as Spanish nationals. The law includes provisions for the care, legal guardianship, and residency of abandoned children.

. . . .

The Reaction in Ceuta and Melilla

Government officials in Ceuta and Melilla have promoted the summary expulsion of unaccompanied migrant children as a solution to the growing number of migrant children present in the two cities. Such proposals enjoy wide public support. For the most part, the public associates unaccompanied migrant children, particularly those living on the streets, with a reported increase in the crime rate. In both cities, members of the public have accused unaccompanied children of robbing businesses in the city center, and some of those who live near residential centers have protested the decision to house migrant children in their neighborhoods.

. . . .

The Pressures on Children to Migrate

Children in Morocco are exposed to a variety of factors that encourage migration. Many unaccompanied migrant children we interviewed told us that they saw no future for themselves in Morocco, a stark response to Morocco's demographic and economic reality. Almost one fifth of the total population lives in poverty, up from 13 percent in 1991, and the World Bank classifies almost half the population as "economically vulnerable." Forty-four percent of the poor are children under fifteen. The majority of those living in poverty are concentrated in rural areas, where many of the children we interviewed had lived. Official unemployment rates at the end of 2001 stood at 13 percent, with unemployment rates for youth aged fifteen to twenty-four at 20 percent. Legislation mandating free, compulsory education from ages six to fifteen and World Bank-financed educational reforms have increased school attendance, but primary enrollment rates remain low compared to other lower-middle-income countries. Despite significant rural/urban and gender disparities in access to education, survey data show poverty to be the "single most important obstacle for non-enrollment of school-age children in both urban and rural areas."

In contrast to this bleak landscape of poverty and lack of opportunity at home, European television broadcasts and a regular influx of adult migrants returning on annual leave provide children with a window on the opportunities for a better life in Europe. World Bank data for Morocco suggest that worker remittances play a significant role in keeping people out of poverty, and that the decline in remittances during the 1990s have contributed to the rise in poverty.

....

During our interviews, children frequently cited poverty and lack of opportunities in Morocco as their motivation for migration. Sixteen-year-old Ra'id I. explained that he had come to Ceuta in August 2001 because "I want to go to Spain to work and to help my family. My family is very poor." Fifteen-year-old Shawqi M. told us, "I came to Ceuta because my family is poor and I want to find my life in Spain." Seventeen-year-old Mamduh H. came to Melilla two years ago and lives in a residential center there. "Before Melilla I was in Nador for a while. You have to work to live in Morocco but there is no work.... The best thing [at the residential center] is the opportunity to study."

....

Some Moroccan families expressly or indirectly encouraged their children to migrate. Lutfi M., a twelve year-old from Rincon del Mediaq, a town about twenty-five kilometers from Ceuta, told Human Rights Watch that he had come to Ceuta a few months earlier because "my mother told me to look for my life in Ceuta." Other children said they were fleeing broken or abusive homes: "I had a lot of problems with my family," Munsif M. explained. "My father hit me. I don't know why he hit me." Fifteen-year-old Samir A. traveled to Melilla from Fés. "My father is married to another wife, and my mother is alone," Although he has a sister living in Ceuta, "it was too far away" and too expensive a trip to risk making.

....

RESIDENTIAL CENTERS

When Spanish authorities encounter unaccompanied migrant children, they have the responsibility to place them under the care and protection of the Department of Social Welfare (Consejería de Bienestar Social), a branch of the autonomous provincial government. Melilla's Department of Social Welfare and Health oversees the operation of five residential centers (centros de acogida) for unaccompanied migrant children, the day-to-day operations of most of which are handled by nongovernmental organizations. Ceuta's Department of Social Welfare operates one facility for unaccompanied minors. Despite the existence of these facilities, the majority of unaccompanied migrant children in Ceuta and significant numbers of unaccompanied migrant children in Melilla live on the street, sometimes for years at a time.

Officials in Ceuta and Melilla initially did not respond to and eventually denied our repeated requests for access to these facilities. Nevertheless, we were able to gather information about key aspects of life in these residential centers by speaking with children who had lived in the facilities. Nearly all of the thirty-seven youth we spoke with had stayed in one or more facilities; some were current or recent residents of a center in which they had lived for periods ranging from two months to one year or more.

In both cities, we found numerous instances where the authorities' treatment of unaccompanied children fell far short of international human rights standards and also failed to comply with relevant provisions of Spanish law....

Police Abuse During Apprehension

....

Unaccompanied children are generally apprehended by one of three police units: the Civil Guard, the National Police, or the Local Police. Children report being beaten by officers in all units, often with a *porra*, a rubber baton with a metal core. They told us that police become more violent if a child attempts to escape. "Yes, they hit you," Ra'id I. said of the Local Police. "They hit you on the legs, the knees, the face. They use *porras* and their hands. They'll hit you if you've escaped and they've caught you again. Or if they catch you the first time and you try to escape." "If they catch you, they hit you," Shawqi M. said. "They hit you in the face. They don't treat you well. More than the police, it's the Civil Guard." He spoke of one officer who set dogs on the children living in the streets. "The dogs bite the kids. One is a Doberman. The other one, I don't know. It's big."

....

Abusive Disciplinary Practices

....

Some residential center staff—known in both cities as "educators"—hit and threaten children for fighting, escaping, or committing other infractions. Children who had stayed at the Purísima Concepción Fort in Melilla and the San Antonio Center in Ceuta reported the most serious instances of abuse, but even children at smaller centers reported beatings and insults at the hands of staff. "They treated me badly," Khalil M. said of staff at the Avecina Center in Melilla. "They insulted me, they hit me, there were kids fighting there and they hit me too."

....

Physical Conditions in the Centers

Residential facilities in both Ceuta and Melilla are overcrowded, particularly from May to September, when they may have two or three children for every bed. "We have serious problems of insufficient places," the director general of Melilla's Department of Social Welfare and Health, told us in late October, 2001. "The centers are overcrowded now. Ninety-six children need places."

Conditions are especially bad in the two largest centers, the San Antonio Center in Ceuta and the Purísima Concepción Fort in Melilla. Both facilities are converted military installations located at a distance from their respective city centers.

....

Children who had stayed at San Antonio described the facility as overcrowded, dirty, and lacking in privacy. Wafiq H., thirteen, estimated that "there were 100 kids there, more or less" during one stay at San Antonio in September 2001. "When I first got there, I slept with two sheets on the floor and another one to cover me," he said. "About fifteen days later, a boy gave me his place. He went to go sleep with the older kids, the kids who are fifteen and sixteen. There were about twelve of us in the room, including the four on the floor." Ra'id I. told us it was so crowded "I spent the night once in the dining hall, a few months ago. We slept on the tables. Six of us slept on the tables that time."

With the exception of very long-term residents, children said they had to change bed assignments every night. "Those who have been there a long time have their own beds," Shawqi M. said. "We have a sheet, that's all, a very thin one. We just sleep on the floor, without a mattress or anything."

....

Health Care

Unaccompanied migrant children in Ceuta and Melilla suffer a variety of health problems, many of which are exacerbated by poor nutrition and, in some cases, addiction to sniffing solvents, gasoline, or other chemical substances for the short term "high" they provide.

Spanish law guarantees foreign children the right to health care on the same basis as Spanish nationals. In practice, unaccompanied migrant children's access to health care varies tremendously. The situation is especially bad in Ceuta, where children we interviewed reported being denied care arbitrarily by staff at both public health clinics and residential centers.

Residential centers provide the majority of medical care unaccompanied migrant children receive. Based on our interviews, none of the residential centers in Ceuta and Melilla appear to have doctors on the premises, and nurses are not always available. We found no evidence that centers were providing routine preventive care, maintaining files with children's medical histories, or even providing routine medical examinations upon entry. "They take your name and they pat you down," Majid A. said. "That's it."

....

Education

....

The vast majority of unaccompanied migrant children in Ceuta and many children in Melilla are not enrolled in school even though Spanish law provides for compulsory education for children age six to sixteen, including foreign children. The education children do receive varies considerably. Only a few children in Melilla attend courses with Spanish children, and none of the children in Ceuta appeared to attend such courses. The deputy director of Ceuta's Department of Welfare told us, "Some children go to school and others are receiving a more basic education in the center and may then go on to the school level."

The government's reliance on residential center staff to provide basic education is troubling. Low-quality basic education is a barrier to advancement to regular coursework in Spanish public schools and deprives children of the Spanish language and literacy skills needed to understand and demand rights guaranteed them under Spanish law, including the ability to present effectively complaints about abuses. Statements by government officials also suggest that children's fluency in Spanish is a key determinant in decisions regarding residency and citizenship.

....

EXPULSION AND LEGAL RESIDENCE

[The report includes an extensive interview with a youth who described being brought back to Morocco from Spain and essentially dumped there by the authorities.]

....

Between July 27 and September 18, 2001, authorities in Melilla conducted at least thirty-two expulsions using this summary procedure—which fails to comply with Spanish law—according to the local human rights organization Prodein (Asociación por Derechos de la Infancia). The youngest of the children expelled was eleven years old; seventeen of those expelled were fourteen years of age or under. Human Rights Watch wrote to the Spanish government on October 12, 2001 requesting clarification of Spanish policies and practices affecting unaccompanied migrant children, including the legal authority for these expulsions and the steps the government had taken to ensure that the expulsions complied with Spanish law. We also raised these cases in meetings with officials at the Ministries of the Interior and Foreign Affairs in November 2001. At the time of this writing we had not received a response to our request. Prodein reported that the total number of unlawful expulsions had risen to at least seventy by February 2002.

. . . .

The official term for the expulsions is "family reunification," in accord with the principle of Spanish law that unaccompanied children should be reunified with their family members if possible. The law provides that if reunification is not possible, Spanish authorities should place the child with a children's social service agency in the child's country of origin. The implementing regulations clarify that "[o]nce the child's family is located, or in its absence, the child protective services of [the child's] country, repatriation" may take place only "after verification that no risk or danger exists to the child's health and safety or of his persecution or that of his family members."

. . . .

Spanish officials frequently claimed that all of the children deported from Ceuta and Melilla were returned to family members....

Local officials offered a more realistic assessment of how expulsions take place. "The law is clear that a child should be returned to his family, or to a social service group, but it is very difficult to implement. For example, the border has many problems; there aren't enough Moroccan police at the border for them to take a child to his family. If the family is not known, we give the child to the police at the border. The police don't have the qualifications to reunite the child with his family," a fiscal for minors in Melilla told us.

. . . .

Spain and Morocco have signed bilateral agreements on migrant workers and readmission of foreigners, but these instruments do not address the treatment of unaccompanied migrant children. A Ministry of Foreign Affairs official told us his ministry had no responsibilities for unaccompanied migrant children and that the Ministry of Interior was responsible for gathering information about their families. "I think that this should be included in our bilateral contacts with Morocco, and perhaps a separate agreement on children should be signed," he added. "[But] we haven't received any suggestions from the Ministry of Labor and Social Affairs on actions to take. They have authority on this issue."

Asked what Spanish officials do to verify that returning an unaccompanied migrant child to Morocco will not place him or her at risk, the director general of Melilla's Department of Social Welfare explained, "The north of Morocco is poor, and there are thousands of kids from abusive homes. We are not able to investigate cases of children's treatment in Morocco. It is up to the Delegate to do that and to take that information into account."

. . . .

... [N]one of the children we interviewed had been given access to legal counsel or interpreters. They were not told about their right to appeal in terms that would be understandable to most children. We saw no evidence that Spanish officials regularly notify children that they are facing expulsion, and there appears to be no formal mechanism for children to contest their expulsion.

The lack of procedural guarantees violates the right of these children to have "the opportunity to be heard in any judicial or administrative proceedings affecting the child, either directly, or through a representative or an appropriate body, in a manner consistent with the procedural rules of national law."

More fundamentally, these expulsions have enormous consequences for the children who endure them. Removed from residential centers or rounded up on the street, many are then detained in inhumane conditions in Moroccan lockups and subjected to beatings. If they were attending school before their expulsions, they face interruptions in their education. Few are actually returned to their families; when they are, neither Spanish nor Moroccan authorities have determined whether they will be safe in their homes. Those who have lived in Spanish territory for years face deportation to a country that they barely remember.

. . . .

MOROCCO'S FAILURE TO PROVIDE CARE AND PROTECTION

Morocco, like Spain, has ratified the major international human rights treaties providing for the protection and care of children. Recent legislation and draft legislation seeking to improve some aspects of child protection has thus far been incomplete and limited in its implementation. Morocco's failure to fulfill its obligations to ensure children the protection and care necessary for their well being exposes unaccompanied child migrants to abuses prior to their departure and following their return. In many cases it has also contributed to the pressures some children feel to undertake the dangers of clandestine migration. A full discussion of Morocco's implementation of international standards regarding children is beyond the scope of this report. Instead, this chapter will focus on the most serious abuses faced by unaccompanied child migrants immediately prior to or following their being in Spain, including abuse by Moroccan police and the Moroccan authorities' failure to provide children with adequate protection and care.

Abuse in Police Custody Upon Return to Morocco

Moroccan police detain unaccompanied children expelled from Ceuta and Melilla at one of several police stations. Border posts at the Ceuta/Fndeq and Melilla/Beni Ansar crossing have small police stations, with larger police stations located in town. Moroccan police also sometimes take children expelled from Melilla to a main police station at Nador, the adjacent city.

When we interviewed him in October 2001, fifteen-year-old Samir A. told us that he had been expelled from Melilla seven times in the three years he had lived in the city. He described his most recent expulsion in 2001. "The police came and picked us up," he said. "We went to the station. They talked for a while, and they took us to the border. They handed us over to the Moroccan police. We went to the Moroccan police station." He was held in the single holding cell at the station, a room about three meters by four meters. "I spent an entire day there—they didn't give us anything to eat," he said. "There were three Iraqis, five Senegalese, a mix of people, all together eleven people." Samir estimated their ages at between twenty-three and thirty-five. "I was the smallest of them all," he said. "I entered the cell at two in the morning. A policeman put his foot on my back and pushed me in." He remained there for the rest of the day. "If you asked to go to the bathroom, the police would come in and beat you," he said. "At one o'clock in the morning they threw us out onto the streets." He returned to Melilla the following day.

Unaccompanied children we interviewed in Ceuta and Melilla consistently told us that they suffered beatings and other ill-treatment at the hands of Moroccan officials when expelled to Morocco, often showing us scars or marks to corroborate their accounts....

Police Release of Children to the Streets

Only three children, two of whom were expelled from mainland Spain to Tangier, told us that Moroccan police handed them over to the custody of their guardians or brought them before a judge who could order their placement in a residential facility. Instead, most children expelled from Ceuta and Melilla told us that after being held for a matter of hours, Moroccan police released them on unfamiliar streets, sometimes late at night.

Moroccan police in Fndeq held thirteen-year-old Amal M. and her friend Hiba for a day before releasing the girls late at night. The girls admitted to the police that they were from Fndeq and answered questions about their families, but the police did not return them to their homes. "It was about 10 p.m. Moroccan time," Amal said. "They let us go by ourselves. No one from our families came to get us, we just went home."

Once out of police custody, children typically spent hours and sometimes days or weeks first traveling back to the border and then waiting, in view of Moroccan police, for an opportunity to sneak past Spanish border guards. Fourteen-year-old Fares S. spent twenty days in August 2001 on the Morocco side of the Ceuta/Fndeq border, waiting to cross into Spain. Samir A., a fifteen-year-old from Fés, told us, "At one o'clock in the morning [the Moroccan police] threw us out onto the streets. I spent that day and the following night trying to get back in to Melilla. I went to one of the border posts, but they wouldn't let me enter. I tried at another border post, but they wouldn't let me enter there either. Finally I got through at 9 a.m. the next day."

Failure to Protect Children Living Outside a Family Environment

Unaccompanied child migrants often spend significant periods of time living on the street in Morocco, whether in transit from their homes to a border or port city, while attempting to cross to Spain for the first time, or while attempting to return to Spain after being forcibly returned to Morocco. Recent research suggests that the majority of children living on the streets in Moroccan port and border cities may be unaccompanied child migrants. A March 2000 survey of northern Morocco sponsored by the United Nations Children's Fund (UNICEF) estimated that only a small proportion of these children were truly street children. Instead, the UNICEF study "found that many of the children are not street children of Tangier but children waiting to cross [to Spain] or children who have been returned from Spain and are trying to cross back."

Despite the large numbers of children living on the street, Morocco has no system in place to ensure that these children are returned to appropriate guardians or placed in institutions capable and willing to care for them. Moroccan law provides little guidance on what actions should be taken when a child is found outside of a family environment and in need of protection and care, and which government agencies are obligated to act in these circumstances. Children's rights activists, representatives of international government organizations present in Morocco, and even some Moroccan government officials acknowledge that existing child protection facilities are insufficient to meet demand, and for the most part fall far short of international standards for care.

Moroccan legislation provides two primary avenues for unaccompanied migrant children to be placed in protective care. One requires the court to declare a child to be abandoned; the other requires a child to be convicted of a criminal offense. Both are heavily reliant on judicial and police discretion and fall short of international standards for protection and care of children living outside a family environment.

. . . .

Only three of the thirty-five unaccompanied migrant children Human Rights Watch interviewed had ever come before a Moroccan judge or been placed in a Moroccan residential facility. Two of the children had been expelled from Spain roughly a year earlier, but had only come before a judge when police arrested them on robbery charges months later. They were being held at a Ministry of Youth and Sport-operated Child Protection Center pending a final court review of their cases at the time of the interview. The third child, fifteen-year-old Shihab R., had been expelled to Tangier from mainland Spain three times, and had come before a judge each time.

. . . .

Lack of Appropriate Facilities

Many unaccompanied migrant children face tremendous difficulties upon their return to Morocco. Children often find themselves abandoned in unfamiliar cities, where they are vulnerable to sexual exploitation and to recruitment by gangs. Children who have been in Spain for longer periods of time, whether living on the street or in residential centers, may find the transition especially difficult. As an activist working with street children in Morocco noted, "There is a big difference between society in Spain or France and society here. They don't accept easily [re]joining their own society. It is like a shock."

Government officials working with children at risk acknowledge that Moroccan child protection facilities are insufficient to meet the demand. The Tangier Child Protection Center is considered to be among the best of Morocco's sixteen facilities. Center Director 'Abd al Hamid Azibou told Human Rights Watch that his center was the only one serving the roughly two million people in the Tangier/Chechaouene/Tétouan region, and was already functioning at capacity with a heavy case load of children charged with theft, burglary, drug or sex-related offenses. "If all the children in Melilla and Ceuta were returned there wouldn't be space for them," he said. "In fact, there is not space for all the children in Morocco who need this kind of specialized care."

Judges have few alternative placements available when the Ministry of Youth and Sports facilities are full. Children arrested on criminal charges may be placed in facilities run by the Minister of Interior. UNICEF officials familiar with some of these facilities describe them as "inappropriate places of detention for children." Intended to provide a speedier resolution than the ordinary court process, these centers function as holding cells until a child's guardians come to take custody. "There is no education project, they shower and shave the kids and the kids escape as soon as they can and no one runs after them."

. . . .

International Standards for Protection and Care

Like Spain, Morocco has ratified the Convention on the Rights of the Child and the International Covenant on Civil and Political Rights, which require states parties to provide all children with the protection and care necessary for their well-being.

Among the rights the Convention on the Rights of the Child guarantees all children is the right to protection from violence and neglect, whether at the hands of private individuals or government agents. This protection should include preventive social programs and the "identification, reporting, referral, investigation, treatment and follow-up of instances of child maltreatment described heretofore, and, as appropriate, for judicial involvement."

In cases where a child is deprived of his or her liberty, the deprivation must not be unlawful or arbitrary, and "shall be used only as a measure of last resort and for the shortest appropriate period of time." The child "shall be treated with humanity and respect for the inherent dignity of the human person, and in a manner which takes into account the needs of persons of his or her age. In particular, every child deprived of liberty shall be separated from adults unless it is considered in the child's best interest not to do so."

The convention also recognizes the special needs of children who have suffered abuse or neglect, or who are living outside a family environment. Article 20 requires that "[a] child temporarily or permanently deprived of his or her family environment, or in whose own best interests cannot be allowed to remain in that environment, shall be entitled to special protection and assistance provided by the State." States must "ensure alternative care for such a child," which "could include, inter alia, foster placement, kafalah of Islamic law, adoption or if necessary placement in suitable institutions for the care of children." Article 39 requires states to take all appropriate measures to promote the rehabilitation of children who are victims of "any form of neglect, exploitation, or abuse; torture or any other form of cruel, inhuman or degrading treatment or punishment; or armed conflicts," and to do so "in an environment which fosters the health, self-respect and dignity of the child."

Concluding Observations of the Committee on the Rights of the Child: Spain

U.N. Doc. CRC/C/15/Add.185 (2002),
available at http://www1.umn.edu/humanrts/crc/spain2002.html

COMMITTEE ON THE RIGHTS OF THE CHILD

Thirtieth session

CONSIDERATION OF REPORTS SUBMITTED BY STATES PARTIES UNDER ARTICLE 44 OF THE CONVENTION

Concluding Observations of the Committee on the Rights of the Child: SPAIN

. . . .

8. Special protection measures (arts. 22, 38, 39, 40, 37 (b)–(d), 32–36 of the Convention)

Unaccompanied foreign children

44. The Committee is deeply alarmed about the conditions of unaccompanied foreign children, mostly Moroccans, especially in the autonomous cities of Ceuta and Melilla. In particular, it expresses its concern at reports of:

(a) ill-treatment of children by police during forced expulsion to the country of origin where, in some cases, they were deported without access to legal assistance and interpretation;

(b) failure to provide to these children the temporary legal residency status to which they are entitled to under the law because the Department of Social Welfare, as their legal guardian, did not apply;

(c) overcrowding and bad conditions of residential centres and cases of ill-treatment by residential centres staff and other children;

(d) denial of access to health care and education, although guaranteed by law;

(e) summary expulsions of children without controlling that they are effectively returned to family or social welfare agencies in their country of origin.

45. The Committee recommends that the State party urgently take the necessary measures in order to:

(a) ensure the implementation of Organizational Act 4/2000 and other laws by providing to unaccompanied foreign children access to residential care, education, emergency services and other health care, and temporary residency documents;

(b) provide the Autonomous Cities of Ceuta and Melilla with the necessary financial and human resources for the care of these children;

(c) coordinate with the Government of Morocco to ensure that when children are repatriated from Spain to Morocco, they are returned to family members willing to care for them or to an appropriate social service agency;

(d) take all measures to prevent irregular procedures in the expulsion of unaccompanied foreign children;

(e) investigate in an effective way reported cases of ill treatment of these children;

(f) provide unaccompanied foreign children with information about their rights under Spanish and international law, including the right to apply for asylum;

(g) take all necessary measures to improve conditions and safety of residential centres and train adequately residential centres staff;

(h) establish effective mechanisms to receive and address complaints from children in care, to monitor standards of care and, in light of article 25 of the Convention, establish regular periodic review of placements;

(i) consider signing and ratifying the International Convention on the Protection of the Rights of All Migrants Workers and Members of Their Families, as previously recommended (ibid., para.23).

Notes and Questions

1. The Spain-Morocco case study is an interesting one, as Spain is a modern, advanced member of the European Union, while North African Morocco, literally within touching distance of Spain, is much poorer and has many impoverished young men seeking entry into Europe. Is it entirely clear that Spain is most to blame in this situation? What alternatives does Spain actually have? What share of responsibility does Morocco bear?

2. For further information on Spain's treatment of young African migrants, see Human Rights Watch, *Unwelcome Responsibilities: Spain's Failure to Protect the Rights of Unaccompanied Migrant Children in the Canary Islands*, available at http://www.hrw.org/reports/2007/spain0707/index.htm. This report describes conditions in the reception center in Spain's Canary Islands for youth from Morocco as well as other parts of Africa, including sub Saharan Africa. As in the earlier report, Spain's harsh treatment and neglect is denounced by Human Rights Watch as a violation of Spain's obligations under international human rights and refugee law.

3. Although not covered in detail in this chapter, there are many reports of unaccompanied children mistreated in developing countries. See for example Refugees International, *Malaysia: Undocumented Children in Sabah Vulnerable to Statelessness*, 2007, *available at* http://refugeesinternational.org/policy/field-report/malaysia-undocumented-children-sabah-vulnerable-statelessness. The report informs us that

[T]he Government of Malaysia has been cracking down on irregular migrants in the country. In Sabah, raids are conducted in housing areas where the migrants live and in markets and public areas where many work. Those arrested are deported back to their country of origin. Many children whose parents have been deported and who do not have any other family or guardian in Sabah end up living and working on the street at a very young age, often in fish markets. A local community worker told RI, 'It's those who have nobody who are there [in the fish markets].'

The exact number of street children in Sabah is unknown, but they are estimated to be in the thousands, mostly of Filipino descent. There is strong local resentment of undocumented migrants in Sabah, and the street children are portrayed as a criminal element by authorities and the media. The children working at the fish markets are wary of outsiders and are under constant threat of raids by police. In 2006, the police arrested about 160 street children who were placed in detention. Those with family contacts were eventually released, but there is no information on the whereabouts of the others.

Chapter Five

Children and Punishment

I. Introduction to Children and Punishment: The Anti-Corporal Punishment Movement and Juvenile Justice Issues

This chapter confronts the overarching question of what to do about children when they go wrong, when they require adult discipline, and even when they commit crimes. It is a sometimes uncomfortable truth that adults are charged with the training of children; societies are charged with protecting their members from potentially violent or disruptive juveniles. Children are, on the one hand, the lifeblood of social continuity; on the other hand, children are not always convenient, and certainly not always cooperative. "Equal rights" of children must take into account the essential role of adults in shaping the developing child. Yet, to what extent can the nuclear family always be trusted in this role? To what extent should the state intervene when discipline takes on a physical, though not overtly abusive, form? To what extent should societies create a separate set of procedures and protections for juveniles who commit even the most serious crimes? Do international law principles translate well into these culturally specific zones? In light of these questions, the chapter sections that follow may be linked together under the broad heading of "children and punishment." The transcendent question is the degree to which societies should be constrained by international legal principles in their choice of form and method in disciplining children.

The revolutionary change said to have been brought about by the UNCRC was that children would no longer be seen as mere extensions of the family, community or nation. They were to be viewed as possessors of rights, autonomous agents capable of influencing the course of their own lives. The traditional view of children as little beings greatly in need of stern correction was made, in theory, passé. Unprecedented attention has been paid in recent years to the question of how children are punished and there has been a corresponding movement to eliminate, through legal means, corporal punishment as an instrument of discipline. This movement has been most successful in Europe, where many countries now have laws against any physical punishment of children as a disciplinary tool. In this sense, the child rights revolution has led, in the family setting, to a position of greater equality for children. In those jurisdictions, children are to be treated on an equal footing with adults, who are protected by law from physical assaults by other adults, even in the domestic context.

At the same time, and by contrast, the criminal justice system is supposed to recognize the particular developmental realities of childhood and make sure that underage defendants are provided with a separate set of protections from those to which adult defendants are entitled. Children's rights cannot always be achieved, of course, by simply treating children in a manner equivalent to adults. In the realm of juvenile justice, legal principles have been developed to require countries to treat child criminal defendants with special care and leniency. As we saw in Chapter Four, in countries where children are routinely detained for offenses relating to homelessness, for instance, they are often treated with appalling brutality. In the worst cases, such children are considered to be social nuisances and their treatment by the authorities reflects this belief.

There are several key provisions of the UNCRC relating to the issue of children and punishment. With greatest relevance to the issue of corporal punishment, Article 19 states that "States Parties shall take all appropriate legislative, administrative, social and educational measures to protect the child from all forms of physical or mental violence, injury or abuse, neglect or negligent treatment, maltreatment or exploitation, including sexual abuse, while in the care of parents, legal guardians, or any other person who has the care of the child." It could be argued that the language of this provision should not be applied to sub-abusive disciplinary techniques such as mild spanking. However, the United Nations Committee on the Rights of the Child, as well as many national governments, have taken the view that a proper interpretation of Article 19 is that it does not allow for physical discipline of any kind. With regard to the treatment of children at school, Article 28 (2) states that "States Parties shall take all appropriate measures to ensure that school discipline is administered in a manner consistent with the child's human dignity and in conformity with the present Convention."

As far as the criminal justice context is concerned, Article 37 of the UNCRC says that "States Parties shall ensure that ... no child shall be subjected to torture or other cruel, inhuman or degrading treatment or punishment." Capital punishment and the imposition of a life sentence without the possibility of parole are explicitly disallowed in the context of offences committed when the person is under eighteen years old. Article 37 goes on to state that children in the criminal justice system and "deprived of liberty" must have the special needs of their age taken into account. In particular, they must be detained separately from adults.

Article 40 expands on state obligations to make special provisions for children accused of crimes. It demands that children accused of crimes receive dignified and fair treatment, and obliges states to "promote the establishment of laws, procedures, authorities and institutions specifically applicable to children alleged as, accused of, or recognized as having infringed the penal law," in particular the "establishment of a minimum age below which children shall be presumed not to have the capacity to infringe the penal law." More detailed international principles on state obligations with respect to juvenile offenders will be explored in the second half of this chapter.

The readings in this chapter are divided into two major themes involving the punishment of children: the international anti-corporal punishment movement, and juvenile justice issues which relate to children in conflict with the criminal law. As mentioned, the section on juvenile justice has some themes in common with readings in Chapter Four that dealt with street children and their treatment by national authorities. For obvious reasons, it is often street children and children from other marginalised groups who find themselves in direct contact with the police and other officials. One issue raised by the topic of "children and punishment" is the capacity of juveniles to take responsibility for wrongdoing, and the proper response of adults in these situations. As always, the theme of protection versus empowerment looms large. The methods by which children are punished reveal much about the interface between children and their societies. The readings that follow will explore the role of international law in the evolution of national beliefs about children and punishment.

II. The Anti-Corporal Punishment Movement

A. Whether to Ban the Practice of Physical Punishment

The global anti-corporal punishment movement is surprisingly strong and organized. In country after country, laws have been enacted making the physical punishment of children, including smacking and spanking, illegal. Most countries with such laws have not chosen to bring heavy criminal penalties to bear against parents who do continue to smack children, but where such laws are enacted, parents who spank children may become enmeshed in various forms of corrective action by official bodies. The UNCRC Committee in particular has consistently identified the elimination of corporal punishment as a children's rights goal, despite the fact that the CRC does not itself explicitly state that all corporal punishment violates the Convention as such. As mentioned in the introductory section, Article 19 of the Convention states that "States Parties shall take all appropriate legislative, administrative, social and educational measures to protect children from all forms of physical or mental violence, injury or abuse, neglect or negligent treatment, maltreatment or exploitation, including sexual abuse, while in the care of parents, legal guardians or any other person who has the care of the child." Article 37 states that "No child shall be subjected to torture or other cruel, inhuman or degrading treatment or punishment." While these provisions clearly prohibit extreme and abusive methods, it is at least debatable whether milder forms of physical punishment ought to be read into the mix. It is certainly worth considering whether sub-abusive corporal punishment "deserves" to be discussed alongside such children's rights topics as child labor, sex trafficking, and child soldiering, just to name a few of the more egregious violations that millions of children endure.

This brings us to a core issue relating to the corporal punishment debate—distinguishing between different degrees of physical punishment, since it is undeniable that some forms are far more severe than others. For example, a firm swat on the bottom with the palm of one's hand presumably carries less potential for harm than a caning. But while we recognize these differences intuitively, is there any effective way for the law to distinguish between them, making some permissible and others not? Or is it better to be on the safe side and prohibit all forms? In any case, if we accept some milder forms of corporal punishment, doesn't this lead us back in the direction of disciplinary "defenses" to charges of assault, the very outcome the anti-corporal punishment movement has sought to avoid? For the anti-corporal punishment movement to achieve real results, it must target even minor forms of physical punishment, since laws against abusive forms already exist in most countries. In societies where this strict abolitionist approach is taken, there arises the question of what is gained by criminalizing parental conduct that is not abusive *per se*; to what degree should parents become ensnared in state oversight because of spanking, for instance?

As indicated above, many national governments—mainly but not exclusively in Europe—have outlawed corporal punishment altogether. Some countries, including the U.S., distinguish between corporal punishment in schools as opposed to in the home, and are generally less tolerant of corporal punishment in the educational setting. As will be discussed in the readings below, there is no uniform ban on the practice of corporal punishment in school across the U.S. Not surprisingly, regions vary widely in their view of this matter. As far as discipline within the home is concerned, for a variety of historical and religious reasons, American parents have been particularly resistant to being told which forms of discipline are acceptable, and state laws within the U.S. reflect this reality. The U.S., of course, has not yet ratified the UNCRC, so in one sense U.S. attitudes towards corporal punishment have not been exposed to a formal "child rights" perspective. Social conservatives in the U.S. maintain that Europeans and Americans simply have conflicting views on sub-abusive corporal punishment in the home, even if there has been somewhat more of a convergence of attitudes when it comes to corporal punishment in schools. While many U.S. states have banned corporal punishment in public schools, only one state, Minnesota, even comes close to a ban on all corporal punishment of children.

As you read this section, consider what place you think corporal punishment ought to have in children's rights discourse and practice. Is this an area in which absolute international principles should be brought to bear? Is there more room here for cultural relativism than in some other areas of children's rights? Wouldn't the drafters of the UNCRC have used more explicit language if they had wished the Convention to prohibit mild forms of physical punishment? On the other hand, isn't it standard practice to interpret a broad and principled convention in accordance with evolving norms and social standards?

The following two articles present opposing viewpoints on the issue of whether all forms of corporal punishment are so inherently bad that they should be legally prohibited. Deana Pollard seeks to convince the reader, by citing various studies, that corporal punishment should be declared illegal in the United States. Philosopher David Benatar, on the other hand, attempts to cast doubt on both the research methods and the conclusions of those who seek a ban on all forms of corporal punishment. Which of these writers is more convincing to you? If what Pollard says is true, what might account for the fact that such a high percentage of Americans still use corporal punishment as a means of disciplining their children?

Deana Pollard, *Banning Corporal Punishment*
77 Tulane Law Review 575 (2003)

. . . .

Current Prevalence of Child Corporal Punishment in America

Not surprisingly, child corporal punishment, such as spanking, is an extremely popular form of discipline in American families today. Most studies have shown that more than ninety percent of American parents spank their toddlers; one survey showed a rate of physical punishment for children around three years of age to be one hundred percent. A 1995 Gallup Poll found that seventy-four percent of children under the age of five were hit or slapped by parents. Most of this practice does not rise to the level of "child abuse" that is prohibited by every state in this country. Boys are hit more than girls; smaller and younger children who are too small to fight back are hit more than older children; and children whose parents are uneducated and belong to lower socioeconomic classes hit more than children from educated, middle- and upper-class families. A 1992 Ohio study "showed that 70% of 800 family physicians and 59% of 400 pediatricians supported spanking." Juxtaposed to this data are surveys indicating that more and more Americans report feeling that spanking is unnecessary or wrong; yet, the vast majority continue to spank. As one social psychologist put it, "The inconsistency between attitudes and prevalence rates [of spanking] is typical of the process of social change."

Although no state has banned corporal punishment perpetrated by parents or legal guardians that does not rise to the level of "child abuse," the public at large is becoming less and less supportive of corporal punishment. For example, in 1962, fifty-nine percent of parents used spanking as the "main disciplinary method," whereas by 1993, that figure had dropped to nineteen percent, with thirty-eight percent of parents preferring time-outs and twenty-eight percent favoring lecturing. In 1968, ninety-four percent of U.S. adults agreed with the statement that it is "sometimes necessary to discipline a child with a good hard spanking," yet by 1992, only sixty-six percent agreed with this statement. The leading child psychologists and pediatricians, including Dr. Benjamin Spock, recommend against spanking, and numerous professional organizations have taken official positions against the use of all forms of child corporal punishment.

Spanking is "transgenerational"; it is passed down from generation to generation. The practice is thus entrenched in legacy and family values, making it resistant to change. However, more and more Americans, particularly child psychologists and other health care professionals, are speaking out against all forms of child corporal punishment. And, studies reveal that Americans are becoming less and less supportive of spanking. Interestingly, one study has shown that to the extent that a family member breaks the transgenerational cycle of hitting or slapping a child as a disciplinary method, that family member is most likely to have a much higher educational level than the general population, to have borne children later in life, and to have been hit solely or primarily by a mother, not a father.

. . . .

Global Trends on Child Corporal Punishment

The worldwide trend is to ban child corporal punishment, including disciplinary use of spanking by parents in the privacy of their homes. Many foreign countries have banned spanking either legislatively or judicially. In addition, the United Nations has taken a formal position opposing child corporal punishment, and several national professional organizations in America have formally expressed their positions opposing child corporal punishment.

. . . .

American Institutions Formally Opposed to Corporal Punishment

There is also a clear trend opposing corporal punishment among American professional organizations. Originally, the trend began in relation to corporal punishment in public schools. This trend is now moving toward opposing corporal punishment in the home as well.

In 1974, only two states had banned corporal punishment in public schools. However, the trend against corporal punishment in schools had begun, and a number of American professional organizations contributed to this trend by adopting formal policy statements against the use of corporal punishment in schools. For example, the American Bar Association Resolution of June, 1985, states: "Be It Resolved, That the American Bar Association opposes the use of corporal punishment in institutions where children are cared for or educated and urges that state laws which permit such corporal punishment be amended accordingly." Similarly, the Policy Statement of the American Humane Association states:

> Corporal punishment of children in schools and in custodial settings is a form of child abuse. American Humane therefore advocates for the elimination of corporal punishment in schools and other child-serving institutions and the adoption of alternative forms of discipline.

By the end of 1994, twenty-seven states had banned corporal punishment in public schools, and an additional eleven states had banned it against most public school children by local rules.

. . . .

The Consequences of Spanking Children

Over the past forty years, the majority of psychology and pediatric studies addressing the consequences of child corporal punishment have linked the use of corporal punishment and subsequent problems for the corporally punished child. A large portion of the research has revealed correlations between the use of corporal punishment and subsequent antisocial and, or alternatively, violent behavior by the children subjected to such punishment. The research has revealed correlations between corporal punishment and other problems as well, including lower self-esteem, physiological and psychological disorders, and emotional problems. Many European countries have relied on this research in making social policy decisions to ban child corporal punishment in all forms.

There is strong resistance to banning corporal punishment in the United States. The resistance comes primarily from religious groups and parents' rights advocates. In addition, while most professional organizations dedicated to child welfare oppose corporal punishment, the American Academy of Pediatrics (AAP) and some child care professionals have had a difficult time reaching a position on the issue. The stumbling block is whether the scientific research establishes sufficient proof that corporal punishment causes the problems associated with it to warrant banning the practice altogether.

. . . .

1. Corporal Punishment Causes Aggression and Other Antisocial Behavior

"One of the most reliable predictors of children's level of aggression is the heavy use by parents of harsh, punitive discipline and physical punishment."

. . . .

In 1997, researchers in New Hampshire and Texas released the results of a study that sought to clarify the causal relationship between corporal punishment and antisocial behavior by considering the level of antisocial behavior at the outset of the study. They found that when parents use corporal punishment to reduce antisocial behavior in children, the long-term effects were the opposite. The findings also suggested that if parents replace corporal punishment with other forms of discipline, it could reduce antisocial behavior in children and eventually reduce the level of violence in society.

The researchers first noted that previous research had found positive correlations between corporal punishment and aggression at all age levels. To clarify the cause-and-effect relationship, they controlled for the children's level of aggression prior to the study so that they could compare it to the level of aggression subsequent to corporal punishment. In addition to controlling for a baseline of aggressive behavior, the researchers controlled for parental involvement, especially warmth and cognitive stimulation, gender differences, socioeconomic status differences, and different age groups (three through five, six through nine, and ten and older).

The researchers tested the level of antisocial behavior (such as cheating or telling lies, bullying or exhibiting cruelty to others, not feeling sorry after misbehaving, breaking things deliberately, and not getting along with or obeying teachers) and aggression at the beginning of the study and two years later. They found that, regardless of the level of antisocial behavior at the outset, the use of corporal punishment caused an increase in the level of antisocial behavior, controlling for parental involvement, socioeconomic status, ethnic group, or child gender. There were stronger associations between corporal punishment and subsequent aggression for boys than for girls, and for European-American kids than for minority kids. However, all groups demonstrated increased antisocial behavior after corporal punishment, and corporal punishment was found to be a "statistically significant predictor" of antisocial behavior two years later.

. . . .

The researchers noted that not all children who are spanked will demonstrate antisocial behavior and likened this to the fact that nearly seventy percent of heavy smokers do not die of a smoke-related illness. Just as the fact that most smokers do not die of a smoke-related illness does not prove that smoking has no negative health consequences, the mere existence of people who were spanked that do not demonstrate antisocial behavior does not prove that spanking is not likely to cause greater antisocial behavior or other harms. The researchers concluded: "The more frequent the [corporal punishment], and the longer it lasts in the life of the child, the greater the probability of behavior problems."

. . . .

Recent research also indicates that boys who are corporally punished are much more likely to physically assault their girlfriends when they become adults. Researchers at Iowa State University published results of their 1998 study concerning the most popular explanation for dating violence — that it is learned in the family of origin. They studied 113 boys in a rural area of Iowa, beginning when they were in the seventh grade (or about age thirteen), to determine, inter alia, whether spanked children were more likely to engage in dating violence as young adults. The parents were asked how often they spanked or slapped their children and how often they used a belt or paddle. They were asked these questions again twice during the five-year study. More than half of the boys experienced corporal punishment during the study, i.e., between ages thirteen and eighteen.

The study controlled for parental warmth and affection, as well as parental support and communication such as explaining rules to their children. It also controlled for witnessing parental violence and for the child's level of delinquency at the outset of the study. The boys' delinquency at the outset of the study was measured by asking them how often they had engaged in a list of twenty-four delinquent acts, such as skipping school, stealing, using drugs and alcohol, and attacking someone with a weapon. The information about dating violence came from the boys, who answered the question: "When you had a disagreement with your girlfriend, how often [did] you hit, push, grab, or shove her?"

. . . .

Other studies have shown that exposure to corporal punishment increases the chances that the child will later hit his or her own children, as well as his or her own spouse. One such study relied on criminology research. Criminologists believe that antisocial tendencies tend to emerge in childhood, which makes assessing early antisocial behavior and its origins important to understanding adult deviant behavior. Criminologists believe that, in general, parents are likely to engage in ineffective parenting when they have antisocial tendencies — such as excessive drinking or confrontations — and that it is a general pattern of antisocial behavior, more than specific lessons regarding dating or family violence, that is transmitted across generations in violent families. In addition, a number of studies have shown that antisocial behavior is stable over the life course and that types of deviant acts tend to be correlated; this supports the theory that dating violence is likely to be an expression of a general antisocial behavior pattern. The results of this study provide strong support for the criminology perspective. Both dating violence and spousal abuse appear to be components of a more general antisocial orientation, which appear to be caused, in part, by subjection to corporal punishment as a child.

. . . .

Many explanations for the relationship between corporal punishment and antisocial behavior have been advanced over the past forty-five years. As just explained, spanked children may have negative self-images because spanking conveys the message that they are bad. A negative self-image often manifests itself in acts of misbehavior. Another long-standing explanation is that spanking does not teach children why their behavior is wrong, so it fails to help the child develop a strong conscience. In a study from 1957, researchers found that spanking was associated with a less adequately developed conscience. Very recent research supports this theory. It appears that spanking may teach a child to avoid misbehavior specifically to avoid punishment, but will not teach children to internalize the reasons not to engage in misbehavior. Thus, the child is not inhibited from engaging in the behavior in circumstances where being caught is unlikely. This may be because parents who spank do not speak to their children about right and wrong as frequently as those who do not spank, displacing conversation with hitting.

An additional explanation for the association between spanking and antisocial behavior may be that, by spanking, a parent deprives a child of experiences in conflict resolution because spanking silences the child and shuts down his or her feelings and perspective. While explanations accompanying spanking may help the child to understand why what he or she did was wrong, the act of spanking nonetheless reduces the child's participation in sorting out the conflict, because children receiving spankings often will not speak out for fear of increased or more severe spankings. Life situations often require negotiation and compromise, and spanking is more akin to a dictatorship, leaving the child with less practical experience than a child who is allowed to participate and verbalize frustrations during the disciplinary process. The loss of negotiation skills may contribute to a child later responding to stressful situations in antisocial ways, lacking more socially acceptable skills for dealing with conflict.

2. Spanking Causes Developmental/Cognitive Damage

Recent research indicates that corporal punishment disadvantages children cognitively. In 1999, researchers released the results of a longitudinal study testing the relationship between corporal punishment and cognitive development. Prompted by prior studies that have shown that talking to children, including prespeech infants, is associated with an increase in neural connections in the brain and in cognitive performance, these researchers theorized that if parents avoid corporal punishment, they are more likely to engage in verbal methods of behavior control, such as explaining and reasoning, and that the increased verbal interaction with the child will, in turn, enhance the child's cognitive ability.

. . . . Children who were hit the most had the lowest increase in cognitive development one year later, while the children who were never hit had by far the greatest increase one year later; children exposed to intermediate levels of corporal punishment fell in between the other two groups on the scale of cognitive development.

. . . .

The most important finding was that the girls were more vulnerable to cognitive damage resulting from harsh discipline than the boys. On average, girls who experienced high levels of physical punishment between one and three years of age scored an average of eight I.Q. points lower at age three than girls who did not receive harsh punishment. Maternal warmth was an important factor, and low maternal warmth coupled with harsh punishment depressed the girls' I.Q. scores further, to an average of twelve points below girls who were not subjected to harsh punishment and had warm mothers. The researchers also found that a mother's educational level, family structure, and family income were significant variables explaining a mother's use of harsh discipline. Further, boys received more harsh discipline than girls, and black children were more likely to receive harsh discipline than white children.

Research on cognitive functioning in general may provide insight into why spanking could interfere with optimal cognitive development. Fright, stress, and other strong negative feelings can interfere with cognitive functioning and result in cognitive deficits such as erroneous or limited coding of events and diminished elaboration. It is clear that being slapped or spanked is frightening and potentially painful and arouses strong negative emotions, such as anger, humiliation, and sadness. Research has demonstrated that children experience corporal punishment as highly stressful, and stress interferes with cognitive functioning....

3. Spanking Causes Psychological/Psychiatric Disorders

Many psychological problems, such as depression, begin in childhood and are associated with corporal punishment. Depression is sometimes defined as aggression or anger that is turned toward the self. Many psychologists have long believed that punishment in childhood is "one of the most powerful generators of depression in adulthood." The most serious danger of depression is suicide, which some researchers believe is the ultimate manifestation of aggression and anger resulting from physical punishment that is turned against the self....

In 1999, Canadian researchers released the results of a study with nearly 10,000 participants ages fifteen to sixty-four to determine whether there was a "relation between a history of slapping or spanking and the lifetime prevalence of 4 categories of psychiatric disorder." The subjects were asked whether they were slapped and/or spanked "often," "sometimes," "rarely," or "never" during childhood, with responses of 5.5%, 33.4%, 40.9%, and 20.2%, respectively. They specifically controlled for physical abuse (that is, abuse beyond subabusive corporal punishment, such as a typical spanking) and excluded data from physically abused subjects.

Interviewers administered a questionnaire to measure psychiatric disorders. They measured anxiety disorders (simple phobia, social phobia, agoraphobia, panic disorder, and generalized anxiety disorder), alcohol abuse or dependence, externalizing problems (including illicit drug use or dependence and antisocial behavior), and major depression. They found a linear association between the frequency of being slapped and spanked as a child and anxiety disorders, alcohol abuse or dependence, and externalizing problems. The strongest associations were between exposure to slapping and spanking and alcohol abuse or dependence and (one or more) externalizing problems such as drug abuse.

. . . .

A substantial amount of prior research has found an increased probability of depression among children subjected to corporal punishment. Other prior research has demonstrated an increased probability of substance abuse and suicide among persons who were corporally punished as adolescents. In addition, receiving corporal punishment is believed to cause lower self-esteem, which in turn may lead to self-destructive behavior. It is obvious that spanking is very stressful to a child, and stress per se is associated with many psychological disorders, anxiety, and depression. The newer research helps to clarify the association between corporal punishment and specific individual and societal problems.

4. Spanking Damages the Parent-Child Relationship

Research has shown that most children resent being spanked and feel anger toward the spanking parent. Indeed, spanked children are more likely to physically assault their parents than children who are not spanked. One study found that "nearly 86% of the parents recognized that their children felt resentment, anger, sadness, and hurt feelings, and were moderately to extremely upset when physically punished." Most of the parents (eighty-five percent) expressed moderate to high anger, remorse, and agitation while punishing their children. The researchers concluded: "Our data show that high negative emotion surrounding the use of corporal punishment is the rule."

Many parents who spank continue to spank until the child is twelve or thirteen years of age. Continuous corporal punishment over time breaks the natural bond between parent and child. Strong child-parent bonding is important for the child to accept parental restrictions and internalize the parents' behavioral guidelines, which leads to the development of a strong conscience. A number of empirical studies have found a link between a weak parent-child bond and juvenile delinquency. Weakened family relationships are hard on the parent, child, and society at large.

....

5. Spanking Is a Precursor to Child Abuse

It is a known fact that corporal punishment can lead to child abuse. When a child does not respond favorably to corporal punishment, parents often increase the force used, which can escalate into child abuse. Research indicates that parents move through a progression of parenting skills in which physical aggression (hitting, beating) represents the final strategy. Nearly seventy percent of child abuse cases in child protective services agencies result from corporal punishment going too far. Statistically, if a child is to be seriously harmed or killed as a result of corporal punishment, it will happen when the child is under five years of age. The defense of "discipline" is raised in forty-one percent of homicide prosecutions against parents who "accidentally" killed their child through discipline. Since before 1970, some researchers believed that "culturally determined permissive attitudes toward the use of physical force in child-rearing seem to constitute the common core of all physical abuse of children in American society." They argued that prohibitions against corporal punishment and changing societal attitudes toward the use of corporal punishment would be the single most effective way of reducing child abuse. The link between corporal punishment and child abuse per se supports banning corporal punishment on public policy grounds.

....

7. Corporal Punishment Is Not Efficacious

It has long been established that positive reinforcement of good behavior, such as verbal praise, smiles, hugs, extra privileges, or material benefits, is more effective than any form of punishment in producing future good behavior in children. Animal trainers have learned this and, therefore, do not use or recommend physical punishment in training animals, but rather recommend training with positive reinforcement for good behavior, such as snacks the animals enjoy.

To the extent that some form of punishment is necessary to stop certain behavior, the majority of studies have demonstrated that nonviolent strategies work at least as well as spanking, if not better. These nonviolent strategies include providing verbal explanations to a child, saying "no," depriving a child of a privilege, or putting a child in a "time-out" chair. Indeed, research indicates that time-out is the most effective method of controlling temper tantrums, fighting, aggression, and disobedience in children from eighteen months to ten years old.

....

Indeed, of the eight studies considered the strongest in support of the efficacy of corporal punishment, seven refer to short-term compliance with a parent's request. Of these seven, five compared corporal punishment with alternative forms of discipline, and all five found the alternatives to be just as "beneficial" as corporal punishment. One study concluded: "[B]oth spank and barrier procedures were equally effective at increasing compliance ... [and t]here was no support for the necessity of the physical punishment...." Thus, while a few studies have found spanking to be effective to some degree, at least in the short term, they also generally found that spanking was not necessary, and no more effective than other methods of punishment that did not carry the risks associated with spanking.

....

Conclusion

Our society's rate of violence is currently declining in many ways. Yet American law supporting violence aimed at children remains unchanged, despite a wealth of recent scientific research that indicates that child corporal punishment is not only ineffective, but counterproductive to raising happy, healthy citizens. Compelling new research demonstrates that child corporal punishment causes numerous societal and individual problems, including increased rates of violence, illness, and other social problems. America lags behind most industrialized countries that have already taken action to modify their child corporal punishment laws in response to the recent research.

It is time for American law to protect America's most vulnerable citizens so that they may maximize their physical, intellectual, and spiritual potential. The privilege to discipline children by use of physical force and pain must be abolished in recognition of the reality that child corporal punishment is harmful to children, counter-productive for parents, dangerous for society, and bad for the future of America.

———————

Those who oppose a ban on the physical punishment of children are skeptical towards arguments like those raised by Pollard, above. There are certainly religiously-based rationales for corporal chastisement, but it is difficult to sustain these arguments in the secular realm. In the article that follows immediately below, David Benatar sets out a point-by-point rebuttal of the main criticisms of physical punishment. Does his critique amount to a coherent theory in its own right? Does Benatar provide a positive basis for supporting physical punishment, or is his objective merely to advocate for leaving this question up to parents and communities?

David Benatar, *Corporal Punishment*
24 Social Theory & Practice 237 (1998),
available at http://www.corpun.com/benatar.htm

1. Introduction

....

a. What is corporal punishment?

Corporal punishment is, quite literally, the infliction of punishment on the body. Even once it is differentiated from "capital punishment," "corporal punishment" remains a very broad term. It can be used to refer to a wide spectrum of punishments ranging from forced labor to mutilating torture. My focus in this paper will be on a form of corporal punishment that seems to me to be the pivotal area of controversy—the infliction of physical pain without injury. I am not suggesting that this is the most problematic form of corporal punishment, but I shall focus on it because it seems to be the mildest level of corporal punishment at which the disagreement enters. Furthermore, the infliction of pain without injury appears to be the variety of corporal punishment that is at stake in the debate, even though opponents of corporal punishment make frequent reference to those instances of corporal punishment that result in injury.

....

2. Responding to Arguments Against Corporal Punishment

....

The arguments raised by those who believe that corporal punishment should never be inflicted are that corporal punishment 1) leads to abuse; 2) is degrading; 3) is psychologically damaging ... 5) teaches the wrong lesson ... and 7) does not deter. I shall now consider each of these arguments in turn.

....

a. Corporal punishment leads to abuse

Opponents of corporal punishment make regular reference to the frequency and severity of physical punishments that are inflicted upon children. They suggest that corporal punishment "escalates into battering," or at least increases the risk that those who punish will "cross the line to physical abuse."

Clearly there are instances of abuse and of abusive physical punishment. But that is insufficient to demonstrate even a correlation between corporal punishment and abuse, and a fortiori a causal relationship. Research into possible links between corporal punishment and abuse has proved inconclusive so far. Some studies have suggested that abusive parents use corporal punishment more than nonabusive parents, but other studies have shown this not to be the case. The findings of one study, conducted a year after corporal punishment by parents was abolished in Sweden, suggested that Swedish parents were as prone to serious abuse of their children as were parents in the United States, where corporal punishment was (and is) widespread. These findings are far from decisive, but they caution us against hasty conclusions about the abusive effects of corporal punishment.

The fact that there are some parents and teachers who inflict physical punishment in an abusive way does not entail the conclusion that corporal punishment should never be inflicted by anybody. If it did have this entailment, then, for example, the consumption of any alcohol by anybody prior to driving would have to be condemned on the grounds that some people cannot control how much alcohol they consume before driving. Just as we prohibit the excessive but not the moderate use of alcohol prior to driving, so should we condemn the abusive but not the nonabusive use of corporal punishment.

b. Corporal punishment is degrading

....

In order to respond satisfactorily to the objection that corporal punishment is degrading, clarification is required about whether the term "degrade" is taken to have a normative content, or, in other words, whether it is taken to embody a judgment of wrongfulness. If it is not, then it will not be sufficient to show that corporal punishment is degrading. It will have to be shown that it is unacceptably so before it can be judged to be wrong on those grounds. If, by contrast, "degrade" is taken to embody a judgment of wrongfulness then a demonstration that corporal punishment is degrading will suffice to show that it is wrong. But then the argumentative work will have to be done in showing that corporal punishment is degrading because it will have to be shown that it amounts to an unacceptable lowering of somebody's standing.

Either way, the vexing question is whether corporal punishment involves an unacceptable lowering of somebody's standing. Here it is noteworthy that there are other forms of punishment that lower people's standing even more than corporal punishment, and yet are not subject to similar condemnation. Consider, for example, various indignities attendant upon imprisonment, including severe invasions of privacy (such as strip-searches and ablution facilities that require relieving oneself in full view of others) as well as imposed subservience to prison wardens, guards, and even to more powerful fellow inmates.... It is true that corporal punishment involves the application of direct and intense power to the body, but I do not see how that constitutes a more severe lowering of somebody's standing than employing indirect and mild power in the course of a strip-search, for example. It is true too that the prison invasions of privacy to which I have referred would be inflicted on adults whereas corporal punishment would be imposed on children, but again I fail to see how that difference makes physical punishment of children worse. In the case of young children especially, it seems that the element of shame would be less than that of adults given that the capacities for shame increase between the time one is a toddler and the time one becomes an adult. Therefore, if we think that current practices in prison life are not wrong on grounds of degradation, then we cannot consistently say that all corporal punishment is wrong on these grounds.

c. Corporal punishment is psychologically damaging

It is claimed that corporal punishment has numerous adverse psychological effects, including depression, inhibition, rigidity, lowered self-esteem and heightened anxiety.

Although there is evidence that excessive corporal punishment can significantly increase the chances of such psychological harm, most of the psychological data are woefully inadequate to the task of demonstrating that mild and infrequent corporal punishment has such consequences. One opponent of corporal punishment who has provided data on even mild and infrequent physical chastisement is Murray Straus. His research, which is much more sophisticated than most earlier investigations into corporal punishment, does lend support to the view that even infrequent noninjurious corporal punishment can increase one's chances of being depressed. However, for two reasons this research is inadequate to the task of demonstrating that mild corporal punishment is wrong. First, the studies are not conclusive. The main methodological problem is that the studies are not experiments but post facto investigations based on self-reports. Murray Straus recognizes this but nevertheless thinks that the studies are compelling. The second point is that even if Professor Straus's findings are valid, the nature of the data is insufficiently marked to justify a moral condemnation of mild and infrequent corporal punishment. For instance, the increase of depression, according to his study, is not substantial for rare physical punishment. The increments on his Mean Symptoms Index of depression are only slight for one or two instances of corporal punishment during one's teen years. The increments are somewhat more substantial for three to nineteen incidents of corporal punishment but, surprisingly, for twenty to twenty-nine incidents the Mean Symptoms Index falls again nearly to the level of two episodes of corporal punishment. The chances of having suicidal thoughts, according to this study, decreases marginally with one incident of corporal punishment during adolescence, then rises slightly for three to five episodes of corporal punishment. For ten to nineteen instances of physical punishment the likelihood of having suicidal thoughts is approximately the same as it is for those who are not beaten at all during adolescence. The probability increases markedly for more than twenty-nine episodes of physical punishment during one's teens, as one would expect when many beatings are administered. Professor Straus does not provide data about how physical punishment during (preteen) childhood affects the likelihood of depression, which would have been interesting given that one might expect corporal punishment to be psychologically more damaging to adolescents than to younger children.

Given that even the data suggesting that very rare instances of mild corporal punishment do have some negative effects also suggest that the effects are not substantial, there is a strong likelihood that they could be overridden by other considerations in a consequentialist calculation. In other words, showing some negative effects is not sufficient to make a consequentialist case against all corporal punishment. Other considerations, including possible advantages of corporal punishment, would have to be taken into account. Moreover, because the available evidence shows no serious harm from mild and infrequent corporal punishment, there seem to be poor grounds for suggesting that for retributivists the punishment should be regarded as unacceptably severe.

e. Corporal punishment teaches the wrong lesson

It is often said that punishing a wrongdoer by inflicting pain conveys the message that violence is an appropriate way to settle differences or to respond to problems. One teaches the child that if one dislikes what somebody does, it is acceptable to inflict pain on that person.

This implicit message is believed to reach the level of a contradiction in those cases where the child is hit for having committed some act of violence—like assaulting another child. Where this happens, it is claimed, the child is given the violent message that violence is wrong. The child is told that he was wrong to commit an act of violence and yet the parent or the teacher conveys this message through violence.

Not only are such messages thought to be wrong in themselves, but it is claimed that they are then acted upon by the child who is hit. In the short term, those who are physically punished are alleged to commit violence against other children, against teachers and against school property. As far as long term effects are concerned, it is alleged that significant numbers of people who commit crimes were physically punished as children. It is these arguments that lie behind the adage "violence breeds violence." Three defenses of (limited) corporal punishment can be advanced against this objection.

First, there is a reductio ad absurdum. The argument about the message implicit in violence seems to prove too much. If we suggest that hitting a wrongdoer imparts the message that violence is a fitting means to resolve conflict, then surely we should be committed to saying that detaining a child or imprisoning a convict conveys the message that restricting liberty is an appropriate manner to deal with people who displease one. We would also be required to concede that fining people conveys the message that forcing others to give up some of their property is an acceptable way to respond to those who act in a way that one does not like. If beatings send a message, why don't detentions, imprisonments, fines, and a multitude of other punishments convey equally undesirable messages? The argument proves too much because it proves that all punishment conveys inappropriate messages and so is wrong. It is a reductio because this conclusion is absurd. Those who want to replace punishment with therapy would not be immune to the reductio either. Providing therapy would convey the message that people with whom one disagrees are to be viewed as sick and deserving of treatment.

This leads to the second argument. The objection takes too crude a view of human psychology and the message that punishment can impart. There is all the difference in the world between legitimate authorities—the judiciary, parents, or teachers—using punitive powers responsibly to punish wrongdoing, and children or private citizens going around beating each other, locking each other up, and extracting financial tributes (such as lunch money). There is a vast moral difference here and there is no reason why children should not learn about it. Punishing children when they do wrong seems to be one important way of doing this. To suggest that children and others cannot extract this message, but only the cruder version that the objection suggests, is to underestimate the expressive function of punishment and people's ability to comprehend it.

There is a possible response to my arguments. Perhaps it is true that, conceptually, the message that punishment conveys is more sophisticated. Nevertheless, those who are beaten do commit violence against others. It might not be that they got this message from the punishment, but that being subject to the willful infliction of pain causes rage and this gets vented through acts of violence on others. This brings me to my third response. There is insufficient evidence that the properly restricted use of corporal punishment causes increased violence. Although Murray Straus's study suggests that there is a correlation between rare corporal punishment and increased violence, the study has some significant defects, as I noted earlier, and the significance of his findings has been questioned in the light of other studies. Nevertheless, Professor Straus's findings cannot be ignored and they suggest that further research, this time of an experimental sort, should be conducted. Note again, however, that even if it were shown that there is some increase in violence, something more is required in order to make a moral case against the corporal punishment that causes it. On a consequentialist view, for example, one would have to show that this negative effect is not overridden by any benefits there might be to corporal punishment.

. . . .

g. Corporal punishment does not deter

. . . .

Deterrence is not an all-or-nothing matter. A punishment might have some deterrent effect without being extremely effective. Once this is recognized, the mere continued existence of wrongdoing does not demonstrate the failure of punishment as a deterrent, as many have thought. To know how effective punishment is one must know what the incidence of the wrongdoing would be if prior punishments for it had not been inflicted. To establish this, much more research needs to be done. However, there is already some evidence of the deterrent effect of corporal punishment, at least with very young children. Such findings cannot be considered decisive, but neither can they be ignored.

Finally, while we might expect increased frequency to improve the deterrent effect, there is good reason to think that the reverse might be true. The expressive function as well as the aura surrounding a particular form of punishment might well be enhanced by inflicting it less often. If one uses physical punishment infrequently, it can speak louder than if one inflicts it at every turn. The special status accorded it by its rare use might well provide psychological reason to avoid it out of proportion to its actual severity.

Notes and Questions

1. Is there any way to resolve the corporal punishment question based on research data? Will parents be dissuaded by an empirical demonstration that spanking, for instance, is ineffective, or even harmful, or is corporal punishment a matter of culture and habit? Even if corporal punishment should be shown to be not harmful in any quantifiable way, is there still a human rights argument against allowing its use?

2. No state in the U.S. makes it overtly illegal for parents to strike children for purposes of discipline. Some states even maintain laws positively affirming the right of parents to do so. All U.S. states except Minnesota allow for a discipline-based parental defense to

charges of child abuse. In light of the two articles above, does this mean that there is a positive view of corporal punishment in the U.S. and that the Pollard view has been rejected as unsound, or is it simply the fact that the full range of legal options has not been explored in the public domain?

B. Europeans Out in Front on Banning Corporal Punishment

Perhaps relying on data or opinions such as those expressed in the Pollard article, a number of countries, mainly in Europe, have banned corporal punishment of children in all its forms. The following section presents a selection of readings on the European perspective on the use of corporal punishment in the home. This perspective is clearly characterized by high seriousness, making the problem of physical punishment part of a much larger European debate on human dignity. In Europe, the debate over corporal punishment partakes of the discourse on human rights. Assuming that the problem of sub-abusive corporal punishment is treated with less care and attention in the United States, how can we account for this difference? Is it purely cultural or religious in nature? Or does the European acceptance of subjecting many problems to regulatory solutions inform the European approach to corporal punishment as well?

The formal recommendation reproduced below was drafted by the Parliamentary Assembly of the Council of Europe, the intergovernmental organization of which the European Court of Human Rights is an organ. Founded in 1949, the Council is older and larger than the European Union, and creates agreements on a wide variety of subjects.[1] In the Parliamentary recommendation, note the relationship that is posited between the respective roles of the Council of Europe and the United Nations, and consider whether the United States Congress would ever express itself in such terms on this kind of topic.

The European Social Charter referred to below was first promulgated by the Council of Europe in 1966, and revised in 1996. It guarantees a wide variety of rights relating to the standard of living and labor rights of persons in Europe. It also established a special complaints procedure. Of particular relevance to this debate is the Charter's Article 17, which states that children have a right to social, legal and economic protection, and that the states of the Council will protect them against "negligence, violence and exploitation."

Europe-Wide Ban on Corporal Punishment of Children

Doc. 10199 (June 4, 2004), *available at*
http://assembly.coe.int/main.asp?Link=/documents/
workingdocs/doc04/edoc10199.htm

Summary

Striking a human being is banned in European society. Children are human beings. Yet hitting and deliberately humiliating children remains a common practice approved in a

---

1. There are currently forty seven members of the Council of Europe, including all the EU Member States, Albania, Andorra, Armenia, Azerbaijan, Bosnia, Herzegovina, Croatia, Georgia, Iceland, Liechtenstein, Moldova, Monaco, Montenegro, Norway, Russia, San Marino, Serbia, Switzerland, The former Yugoslav Republic of Macedonia, Turkey and the Ukraine.

majority of member states. The social and legal acceptance of corporal punishment of children must be ended.

The Parliamentary Assembly invites member states to enact legislation prohibiting the corporal punishment of children, particularly within the family.

It notes the success the Council of Europe has had in abolishing the death penalty in Europe and the Assembly calls on its member states to make Europe, as soon as possible, a corporal punishment-free zone for children.

I. Draft recommendation

1. The Parliamentary Assembly notes that, according to the European Committee of Social Rights, in order to comply with the European Social Charter and the Revised Social Charter, states must ban all forms of corporal punishment and any other forms of degrading punishment or treatment of children. Five member states fail to meet these requirements because they have not effectively prohibited all forms of corporal punishment. Collective complaints have been lodged against five other member states on the same grounds.

2. The Assembly also notes that the European Court of Human Rights has found in successive judgments that corporal punishment violates children's rights under the Convention for the Protection of Human Rights and Fundamental Freedoms. These decisions applied initially to corporal punishment in young offenders' institutions, then in schools, including private schools, and most recently within the family home. Moreover, both the European Commission of Human Rights and the Court have emphasised that banning all corporal punishment does not breach the right to private or family life or religious freedom.

3. All member states have ratified the United Nations Convention on the Rights of the Child which requires them to protect children from all forms of physical or mental violence while in the care of adults. The Committee on the Rights of the Child, which monitors compliance with the Convention, has consistently interpreted the latter as requiring states both to prohibit all forms of corporal punishment of children and to educate and inform the public on the subject.

....

5. The Assembly considers that any corporal punishment of children is in breach of their fundamental right to human dignity and physical integrity. The fact that such corporal punishment is still lawful in certain member states violates their equally fundamental right to the same legal protection as adults. Striking a human being is prohibited in European society and children are human beings. The social and legal acceptance of corporal punishment of children must be ended.

6. The Assembly is concerned to note that, so far, only a minority of the 45 member states have formally prohibited corporal punishment in the family and in all other settings. While they have all banned corporal punishment in schools, including private schools and other educational institutions, this does not necessarily extend to residential and all other forms of child care. Nor are such bans systematically and universally respected.

....

8. It invites the Committee of Ministers and the other Council of Europe bodies concerned, as a matter of urgency, to establish strategies, including technical assistance, for achieving this objective in conjunction with member states....

9. [T]he Assembly invites the Committee of Ministers to recommend that the member states:

i. enact appropriate legislation prohibiting the corporal punishment of children, particularly within the family;

ii. monitor the effectiveness of abolition through regular research into children's experience of violence at home, in the school and elsewhere, the effectiveness of child protection services and parents' experience of and attitudes to violence against children;

iii. ensure that relevant judgments of the European Court of Human Rights and conclusions of the European Committee of Social Rights are fully applied.

II. Explanatory memorandum by Mrs Bargholtz

Introduction

1. Hitting people is wrong. Hitting people breaches their fundamental rights to respect for their physical integrity and human dignity. Children are small people who share these human rights with adults. Yet hitting and deliberately humiliating children remains a common practice, socially and legally approved, in a majority of member states of the Council of Europe. This Parliamentary Assembly recommendation promotes action to achieve as quickly as possible a Europe-wide ban on all corporal punishment and all other degrading punishment or treatment of children. Its first and urgent purpose is to uphold children's human rights.

. . . .

4. Ending corporal punishment is a key to improving children's status and an essential strategy for preventing all other forms of violence and exploitation. In many member states there has been no research into violence against children in the family; where there have been studies they reveal very high prevalence of corporal punishment, including severe assaults causing injuries.

5. The process of eliminating corporal punishment requires explicit legislation linked to awareness-raising of children's rights to protection and promotion of positive, non-violent forms of discipline.

The importance of the issue

6. The persisting legal and social acceptance of corporal punishment is now recognised as a breach of children's human rights. Available research suggests that where corporal punishment has not been clearly challenged by law reform and public education, it remains extremely common. Across Europe, the fundamental rights of millions of children are being systematically breached on a gigantic scale. All corporal punishment breaches children's rights to respect for their human dignity and physical integrity. Corporal punishment frequently results in physical injury, disability and in some cases death; research suggests it may also cause psychological damage to children; its use is associated with the development of violent attitudes and actions, in childhood and later life. It is extraordinary that children, whose developmental state makes them particularly vulnerable to physical and psychological injury should have less legal protection from assault in a majority of member states than adults have.

7. Traditional attitudes to slaves, servants and women were also reflected, only a century or two ago, in the legal "rights" of their masters and husbands to beat them. There is no more symbolic demonstration of the persisting low status of children in many European societies than the widespread belief that corporal punishment is legitimate. The implication that children's physical integrity and human dignity can be invaded with impunity makes other forms of violence against children, including sexual abuse, exploitation and trafficking, more likely. Ending legalised violence against children — corporal punishment — is a key strategy for the prevention of all other forms of violence.

The scale of the problem

....

Croatia: a sample of 1000 university students were surveyed in 1997/98 on their childhood experiences of physical and sexual abuse; 93% reported corporal punishment; 27% reported assaults causing injury. Croatia explicitly prohibited corporal punishment in 1999.

Greece: in a national cohort of 8,158 children aged seven, one in three was spanked at least once a week and one in six daily (1993).

Poland: a nationwide survey of adults in 2001 found that 80% had experienced corporal punishment.

Romania: of a sample of 423 children aged 11–13, 75% had been subject to corporal punishment, with 5% reporting they needed medical treatment following it. In another study 84% of a sample of children stated they had been subjected to corporal punishment by their parents, including 20% who had been beaten with objects and 15% who were afraid to go home because of the beatings.

Slovakia: Attitudinal research among a sample of adults in 2002 found 75.3% believing that parents should be allowed to use "occasional slaps"; 41.7% believing that occasional beating with an implement is acceptable, and 22.9% believing that repeated beating is acceptable.

UK: A large-scale interview study in the 1990s found that overall 91% of the children had been hit; only 25% of babies aged under one had never been smacked by their mothers, and 14% of one year olds had been smacked with "moderate severity". In two-parent families where both parents were interviewed, one fifth of the children had been hit with an implement and over one third had experienced a punishment rated as "severe" (punishment which was intended to, had the potential to or actually did cause physical and/or psychological injury or harm to the child).

The European Social Charter of the Council of Europe

10. The European Committee of Social Rights, monitoring member states' compliance with the European Social Charter and Revised Social Charter, stated in 2001 that: "Article 17 requires a prohibition in legislation against any form of violence against children, whether at school, in other institutions, in their home or elsewhere. It furthermore considers that any other form of degrading punishment or treatment of children must be prohibited in legislation and combined with adequate sanctions in penal or civil law."

....

13. Emphasising the inequality of legal protection available to children as compared with adults in many countries, the Committee states: "The Committee does not find it acceptable that a society which prohibits any form of physical violence between adults would accept that adults subject children to physical violence. The Committee does not consider that there can be any educational value in corporal punishment of children that cannot be otherwise achieved."

14. Moreover, in a field where the available statistics show a constant increase in the number of cases of ill-treatment of children reported to the police and prosecutors, it is evident that additional measures to come to terms with this problem are necessary. To prohibit any form of corporal punishment of children, is an important measure for the education of the population in this respect in that it gives a clear message about what so-

ciety considers to be acceptable. It is a measure that avoids discussions and concerns as to where the borderline would be between what might be acceptable corporal punishment and what is not.

The Convention for the Protection of Human Rights and Fundamental Freedoms

15. Successive decisions of the European Commission on Human Rights and the European Court of Human Rights have found that corporal punishment of children breaches the Convention for the Protection of Human Rights and Fundamental Freedoms: first in the 1970s as a sentence of the courts for juvenile offenders; then in schools, including private schools; and most recently within the family home. Decisions and judgments have emphasised the state's duty to protect children and their human rights wherever they are. Other decisions have confirmed that banning all corporal punishment in the home is a legitimate interference and does not breach parents' or others' rights to respect for family life or religious freedom.

16. In September 1998, the European Court unanimously found that corporal punishment of a young English boy by his stepfather had breached article 3. Prosecution of the stepfather in a UK court had failed on the grounds that the punishment was "reasonable chastisement". The Court found that the UK was responsible because the domestic law allowing "reasonable chastisement" failed to provide children with adequate protection, including "effective deterrence". The Court ordered the UK to pay £10,000 compensation to the boy, who had been repeatedly hit with a garden cane.

....

The United Nations Convention on the Rights of the Child

18. The United Nations Convention on the Rights of the Child (UNCRC) was adopted by the UN General Assembly in 1989. By 2001 this Convention had been ratified by 191 States—including all member-states of the Council of Europe. It is the most ratified international human rights treaty and this gives its detailed principles and standards a particular authority in international law.

19. The UNCRC is the first treaty to address directly protection of children from violence. Article 19 of the Convention requires states to take "all appropriate legislative, administrative, social and educational measures to protect the child from all forms of physical or mental violence, injury or abuse, neglect or negligent treatment, maltreatment or exploitation including sexual abuse, while in the care of parent(s) legal guardian(s) or any other person who has the care of the child …".

....

21. The Committee [on the Rights of the Child] has consistently stated that corporal punishment of children, within the family and in any other setting, is not compatible with the Convention and has recommended prohibition of all corporal punishment and education campaigns to encourage positive, non-violent child-rearing and education to more than 130 States in all continents, including industrialised and developing countries.

The Council of Europe Committee of Ministers Recommendations Condemning Corporal Punishment

22. The Committee of Ministers first condemned corporal punishment of children in a recommendation to member states on violence in the family adopted in 1985. The recommendation notes in its preamble that "the defence of the family involves the protection of all its members against any form of violence, which all too often occurs among

them". Violence affects "in particular children on the one side and women on the other, though in differing ways" and "children are entitled to special protection by society against any form of discrimination or oppression and against any abuse of authority in the family and other institutions". The recommendation proposes that member states should "review their legislation on the power to punish children in order to limit or indeed prohibit corporal punishment, even if violation of such a prohibition does not necessarily entail a criminal penalty". The explanatory memorandum to the recommendation describes corporal punishment as "an evil which must at least be discouraged as a first step towards outright prohibition. It is the very assumption that corporal punishment of children is legitimate that opens the way to all kinds of excesses and makes the traces and symptoms of such punishment acceptable to third parties."

. . . .

The Progress of Law Reform Prohibiting All Corporal Punishment

25. The human rights standards established by the Council of Europe mechanisms and by the UN Convention on the Rights of the Child require abolition of all corporal punishment and other degrading treatment or punishment. By March 2004, it appears that at least 12 member states have legislation which clearly prohibits all corporal punishment of children, including in the family: Austria (1989), Bulgaria (2000), Croatia (1999), Cyprus (1994), Denmark (1997), Finland (1983), Germany (2000), Iceland (2003), Latvia (1998), Norway (1987), Sweden (1979), Ukraine (2002). In at least another nine states, the penal law prohibits assault and there is no defence in legislation for assaulting children in the name of discipline—but in practice the law is not interpreted as prohibiting all parental corporal punishment.

26. These are the essential legal steps for prohibiting all corporal punishment:

a. Ensuring there are no existing defences, in statute or common law, that justify corporal punishment by parents or others;

b. Ensuring that the criminal law on assault applies equally to punitive assaults on children;

c. Enacting an explicit prohibition of all corporal punishment and of all other degrading or humiliating treatment or punishment of children, normally in civil law;

d. Providing guidance on appropriate enforcement of these laws which focuses on protection and promotion of the human rights of children in general and on the best interests of affected children in particular.

27. Corporal punishment in schools and in penal systems for young offenders has been prohibited throughout Europe, although enforcement is not uniformly effective. Many states have also prohibited corporal punishment in residential institutions. All states have legislation prohibiting severe assaults by parents and other carers, but in many there are defences for parents who use less severe forms of corporal punishment, and where parental corporal punishment remains lawful, this will extend to foster-carers and some other informal carers, unless there is legislation explicitly prohibiting it.

The process of eliminating corporal punishment

28. The process of law reform to end parental corporal punishment in Europe started almost 50 years ago in 1957 in Sweden, when the criminal law provision excusing parents who caused minor injuries through physical punishment was removed. In 1966 Sweden removed a provision allowing "reprimands" from its parenthood code. Sweden went on to become the first country in the world to explicitly prohibit all corpo-

ral punishment in its family law in 1979, when a provision was added to the Parenthood and Guardianship Code which now reads: "Children are entitled to care, security and a good upbringing. Children are to be treated with respect for their person and individuality and may not be subjected to corporal punishment or any other humiliating treatment".

....

31. First, the law needs to be well-publicised and clearly and positively interpreted by politicians, community leaders and the judiciary as prohibiting all corporal punishment and other degrading punishment or treatment of children. There needs to be ongoing awareness-raising of children's rights to protection and public and parent education to promote positive, non-violent forms of child-rearing and discipline. The United Nations Convention on the Rights of the Child requires states which have ratified it (all member states of the Council of Europe) to "make the principles and provisions of the Convention widely known, by appropriate and active means, to adults and children alike" (article 42).

Notes and Questions

1. What do you think of the statement that the Council of Europe should be prescribing "essential legal steps" in the area of corporal punishment? According to the report and recommendation excerpted above, the first two such steps should be to "Ensure there are no existing defenses, in statute or common law, that justify corporal punishment by parents or others"; and "Ensure that the criminal law on assault applies equally to punitive assaults on children." What if a country in Europe wants to pursue some other approach to corporal punishment? Should such a country be vilified for not accepting these two steps as "essential"? Or is this level of uniformity just one aspect of being part of a number of intersecting systems of law in Europe?

C. Creating a European Consensus against Physical Punishment

Continuing our look at European attitudes towards corporal punishment, the following article describes condemnation against Portugal by the World Organization Against Torture and the European Committee on Social Rights. The World Organization Against Torture is a large and active network of NGOs that works towards the eradication of torture in various countries. The current president of the group is Kofi Annan, former Secretary General of the United Nations.

The occasion for the criticism was a Portuguese judicial decision, holding that the imposition of moderate physical punishment against children by persons entitled to do so is not unlawful. As the issue is being framed in terms of fundamental human rights, is there any room for European countries to take a separate approach on these matters? Do you find the title of the article on Portugal proportionate to the facts as described? That is, is the matter so clear and obvious that Portugal should be accused of breaching human rights obligations, simply because a judge allowed for the imposition of moderate physical punishment? Or is it high time the problem was expressed and understood in these terms?

Portugal: Condemned for Tolerating
Violence against Children

(May 24, 2007) *available at* http://www.crin.org/
violence/search/closeup.asp?infoID=13466

[GENEVA, 24 May 2007] — Portugal has breached its human rights obligations by failing to ban all corporal punishment of children at home and in care, a rights watchdog has ruled.

The European Committee of Social Rights said the country is in breach of its obligations under the European Social Charter. Article 17 of the European Social Charter requires a prohibition in legislation against any form of violence against children in all settings.

The World Organisation Against Torture (OMCT) lodged a collective complaint against Portugal after the Portuguese Supreme Court decided, in April 2006, that, "moderate punishments administered to the minor by the person entitled to do it and whose purpose is exclusively educational and adequate to the situation, are not unlawful."

The case concerned an allegation of cruelty and ill treatment against children.

OMCT complained on the grounds that the new interpretation of the law, by Portugal's highest Court, amounts to a toleration of corporal punishment and sets a dangerous precedent.

"OMCT is pleased with this decision, and we wish that, from now, Portugal will fully conform to its obligations under the European Social Charter by explicitly and effectively prohibiting all corporal punishment of children" said Cécile Trochu Grasso from OMCT.

'Portugal and the rest of Europe must take note'

Peter Newell from the Global Initiative to End All Corporal Punishment of Children, said: "Hopefully, Portugal's parliamentarians will take note of this very clear decision. Changes to the Penal Code currently being discussed in the Parliament fail to give children full protection from corporal punishment and need amendment to satisfy Portugal's human rights obligations.

"It is important that all the other European States parties to the European Social Charter which still fail to comply with article 17 reform their legislation in order to achieve the right of all European children to equal protection from being hit."

OMCT originally lodged a complaint against Portugal in 2003, arguing that the law in question failed to protect children from corporal punishment and other humiliating treatment. However, in its response in June 2005, the European Committee of Social Rights decided that Portugal's caselaw did in fact prohibit all corporal punishment.

Second Complaint

OMCT complained again in 2006, but its second complaint was declared admissible. The Portuguese Government maintained that its Criminal Code explicitly prohibits violence against children. It added that the Criminal Code is currently being revised to establish a new offence, in articles 152 and 152A, for inflicting physical or psychological ill-treatment, including corporal punishment, in cases where the infliction is "intense or repeated".

However, the new ruling by the European Committee of Social Rights, who decided unanimously that Portugal does not ensure the satisfactory application of Article 17 has been welcomed as a significant step forward.

In 2007, European countries such as Belgium, Czech Republic, France, Greece, Luxembourg, Malta, Netherlands, Poland, the Slovak Republic, Slovenia, Spain, Switzerland,

Turkey and United Kingdom remain in breach of article 17 for not prohibiting all corporal punishment.

Notes and Questions

1. The Global Initiative to End All Corporal Punishment of Children is likewise an international network of human rights agencies and NGOs, united in opposition to corporal punishment. It advocates for an interpretation of the problem in strong human rights terms. See the network's website at http://www.endcorporalpunishment.org/. Global Initiative's point of view and that of the United Nations bodies dealing with child welfare issues are mutually reinforcing.

Note the strong and unequivocal nature of the presentation in the report by the Global Initiative group below. In Global Initiative's view, there is no doubt that nations in the modern world are on an inevitable journey away from the use of physical punishment, and that legal prohibitions are central to this evolution. Again, while there is truly universal condemnation of any abusive forms of punishment, do the narratives below leave any room for countries to adopt a position like that of the U.S.; i.e., that it is the job of parents to decide whether or not they will use corporal punishment, with a line being drawn between abusive and non-abusive forms? Is it simply better, more efficient, and more protective of children to frame the issue as many European, and a number of non-European, countries do—that is, to declare that physical punishment should be, must be, *per se* unlawful?

The selections that follow are not included merely for informational purposes. Rather, they are set out here to invite analysis of the manner in which the issue of corporal punishment has been framed by the Global Initiative network. The tone is one of inevitability; the context one of core human rights. Does this indicate that the U.S. is hopelessly out of step?

Global Initiative to End All Corporal Punishment of Children

States with Full Abolition, available at
http://www.endcorporalpunishment.org/pages/frame.html

States with Full Abolition:

Austria (1989); Croatia (1999); Cyprus (1994); Denmark (1997); Romania (2004); Finland (1983); Germany (2000); Israel (2000); Iceland (2003); Bulgaria (2000); Latvia (1998); Norway (1987); Sweden (1979); Ukraine (2004); Hungary (2005); Greece (2006)[2]

Sweden

Sweden was the first country in the world to prohibit all corporal punishment of children. In 1979 a provision was added to the Parenthood and Guardianship Code which now reads: "Children are entitled to care, security and a good upbringing. Children are to be treated with respect for their person and individuality and may not be subjected to corporal punishment or any other humiliating treatment".

. . . .

---

2. In 2007, Venezuela, New Zealand, Spain, Uruguay, The Netherlands, and, tellingly, Portugal, joined the list of countries with laws abolishing corporal punishment of children. In 2008, Costa Rica and Moldova followed suit.

The Ministry of Justice led a very large-scale education campaign. A pamphlet distributed to every household with children emphasised that "the law now forbids all forms of physical punishment of children, including smacking etc, although it goes without saying that you can still snatch a child away from a hot stove or open window if there is a risk of its injuring itself".

The legal provision forms part of Sweden's family (civil) law. But its purpose is to emphasise beyond doubt that the criminal code on assault covers physical punishment, although trivial offences remain unpunished just as trivial assaults between adults are not prosecutable.

. . . .

Statement from Sweden's First Children's Ombudsman, Louise Sylwander:

The anti-spanking law has influenced Swedish Society

"The UN Convention on the Rights of the Child, which every European country has accepted, strengthens the position of children within the family and in society as a whole. Everyone who meets a child has the responsibility to treat the child with respect. Children are in a vulnerable situation in relation to adults, and therefore they must be guaranteed a safe childhood: a childhood without violence including physical chastisement.

"Physical punishment is not in accordance with the UN Child Convention. And the European Court of Human Rights recently unanimously found the physical punishment of a young English boy by his stepfather breached article 3 of the European Convention. It is very important, therefore, that society clearly underlines that children and young people have a right to an upbringing based on parental support and encouragement rather than chastisement.

"In Sweden, there has been a ban on subjecting children to spanking since 1979. It goes without saying that this ban has not ended all forms of violence to children in our country. But it is obvious that attitudes towards violence and the use of physical punishment have changed for the better and today there is strong public opinion in favour of the Swedish anti-spanking law.

"No more than 11 per cent of the adult population in Sweden are positively inclined to even minor forms of physical punishment. Recent studies by Statistics Sweden show that spanking has become less common in our society. Attitudes have changed substantially since 1965 when a similar study was done. Only two per cent of today's middle school pupils report being spanked every other week, and 78 per cent report that they have never been spanked. The change in the Swedish Parental Code prohibiting spanking of children has played an important role in this positive development.

"During the last two decades, reporting of child abuse and neglect has increased. There is no clear evidence which indicates a corresponding increase in actual cases of child abuse in Sweden. Everything points to other explanations such as better awareness and knowledge of children in vulnerable situations. As mentioned above, attitudes in society have also changed: people today are less willing to accept violence against children. Another reason is that the reporting obligations under the Social Welfare Act have been strengthened and many more groups of professionals are now obliged to report children at risk—so less cases of child abuse and neglect fail to come to the attention of the social welfare authorities.

Louise Sylwander, Sweden's Children's Ombudsman, December 1993–2000

Finland

In Finland, the ban on physical punishment formed part of a comprehensive reform of children's law. The Child Custody and Right of Access Act 1983 begins with a statement of positive principles of care for children, and continues: "A child shall be brought up in the spirit of understanding, security and love. He shall not be subdued, corporally punished or otherwise humiliated. His growth towards independence, responsibility and adulthood shall be encouraged, supported and assisted". This reform in family law puts beyond doubt that the criminal law applies equally to assaults committed against children by parents and other caregivers.

. . . .

A public information campaign was launched by the Ministry of Justice and National Board of Social Affairs, including a leaflet entitled *What is a good upbringing?*, made available through health clinics, social welfare offices and so on. A large-scale campaign was also launched by the Central Union for Child Welfare, an NGO, together with the National Boards of Health and Social Affairs, including a leaflet *When you can't cope, find help: don't hit the child.*

There were also brief spots on national television at peak viewing time before the main evening news programme as the law came into effect. This is a translation of the commentary on one of them:

> Do you hit your child? Is that how you bring him up? All physical punishment deflates a child's ego. Even a slap makes him or her feel worthless. A worthless person becomes indifferent. Through slapping you are raising a bully. Talk to the child. Settle your differences through discussion. Make the child party to an agreement. That way you both win. Decide to deserve your child's respect. As a person.

Denmark

In May 1997 the Danish Parliament agreed an amendment to the Parental Custody and Care Act which reads: "A child has the right to care and security. He or she shall be treated with respect as an individual and may not be subjected to corporal punishment or other degrading treatment".

. . . .

As the proposer of the 1997 Bill to amend the law told Parliament, "Danes are increasingly turning away from corporal punishment ... A fresh opinion poll in January 1997 showed a clear majority—57 per cent of the population—were against physical punishment. This shows an unmistakable shift against such punishment".

The proposer emphasised the educational purpose of the change: "In the opinion of the advocates of the change in the law, it is important for those groups who work with families to have firm, clear and unequivocal legal grounds for being able to say that under no circumstances may one use violence in the upbringing of a child ... Doctors, the police and social workers come into contact with families where children are regularly beaten. These groups will—if the law is changed—be able to point out that it is wrong to hit a child and instead give advice on other ways to resolve conflicts". The purpose of the change was not to penalise more parents—on the contrary. But "clear legislation and a plainly worded explanation of the reasons for it are vital if we are to change public opinion on the issue of the corporal punishment of children".

. . . .

Austria

On March 15 1989 the Austrian Parliament voted to amend its family law and the Youth Welfare Act to state explicitly that in bringing up children "using violence and inflicting physical or mental suffering is unlawful". The new law was passed unanimously and without controversy. The Austrian Minister for Environment, Youth and the Family stated: "The motive for this reform is our knowledge of the immeasurable harm children suffer when parents are not willing or able to avoid physical punishment as a way of bringing up their children. I hope other countries will follow us in ruling out physical punishment".

. . . .

Germany

In July 2000 the Bundestag added a new provision to the German Civil Code which states: "Children have the right to a non-violent upbringing. Corporal punishment, psychological injuries and other humiliating measures are prohibited".

. . . .

The Federal Government and NGOs have collaborated to launch a public campaign to accompany the law reform and encourage parents to raise their children by non-violent means.

The objective of the campaign is not to pillory parents—rather to sensitise them in measured ways as to how they can raise their children with due respect and care. The campaign is two-tiered. One part consists of posters, advertisements and television spots. The other consists of individual projects and community initiatives all around Germany, geared towards supporting parents in the raising of their children. To raise the public profile of the campaign, prominent personalities, including the Federal Minister for Family, Senior Citizens, Women and Youth have been appointed as ambassadors to promote childrearing by non-violent means.

How Germany banned smacking—a brief summary

This briefing provides a few headlines on what the law reform actually means for children and families and on how and why the ban was introduced. Prepared by Phil Taverner, National Society for the Prevention of Cruelty to Children (NSPCC) Area Children's Services Manager (UK), who recently visited Germany to investigate the background to its smacking ban.

. . . .

How the law was introduced

Childcare professionals, children's rights workers and others had been campaigning for some time for a ban on smacking. The breakthrough came shortly after the general election of 1998 when the coalition of the Social Democratic Party and the Greens that formed the new Government included a commitment to ban corporal punishment in their coalition agreement. There was little opposition in either half of the German Parliament or in public, despite the fact that public opinion polls at the time were showing a majority of people opposed to a ban. The only concern expressed was the worry that parents would be criminalised, but this was overcome by writing the ban into the Civil Law. In the event the change was passed in the National Parliament on the 6th July 2000, ratified by the Federal Assembly on 29th September and came into force on the 2nd November.

The Government's aims in taking this step closely matched those of the Swedish Government more than twenty years earlier. By banning all forms of corporal punishment they hoped to:

• Give children the same legal protection from being hit as adults.

- Change public attitudes to make all forms of violence against children unacceptable in the population as a whole, leading eventually to a break in the "cycle of violence".

- Reduce child abuse by allowing professionals to identify with more confidence families whose children may be at risk and to provide help before more serious abuse takes place.

. . . .

How the change in law was communicated to the public

One of the slogans that accompanied the legal change from the beginning was "Help instead of punishment", stressing the fact that the intention was to change public opinion and provide families with the means to move away from reliance on use of force as a way of resolving conflict.

To this end the introduction of the law was accompanied by a public education campaign entitled "More Respect for Children". . . .

Greece

On 19 October 2006, the Greek Parliament passed Law 3500/2006 on the Combating of Intra-family Violence, under which corporal punishment of children within the family is prohibited. Article 4 of the new law states:

"Physical violence against children as a disciplinary measure in the context of their upbringing brings the consequences of Article 1532 of the Civil Code."

Article 1532 of the Civil Code provides for various consequences for abuse of parental authority, the most serious being the removal of parental authority by the courts. An explanatory report issued to Parliament by Ministers responsible for the introduction of the bill confirmed that "corporal punishment is not included in the permissible disciplinary measure of article 1518 of the Civil Code". Article 1518 enshrines parents' right to use "corrective measures" but "only if these are necessary from a pedagogic point of view and do not affect the child's dignity".

. . . .

Progress towards prohibition

2002

February: The Committee on the Rights of the Child, in its concluding observations on the initial Greek state party report, expressed concern that corporal punishment was not prohibited in the family and that "about 60 per cent of parents practice corporal punishment of children" (CRC/C/15/Add.170, para. 42 (a)). The Committee recommended that the Greek government "prohibit all forms of violence against children, including corporal punishment, by law in all contexts, including in the family" and "undertake education and awareness campaigns to inform, among others, teachers, parents and medical and law enforcement personnel about the harm of violence, including corporal punishment, and about alternative, non-violent, forms of educating children" (para. 43 (a and b)).

2003

July: The World Organisation against Torture (OMCT) lodged a complaint against Greece under the Collective Complaints procedure of the European Social Charter alleging, in relation to article 17 of the Charter (the right of mothers and children to social and economic protection), that legislation in Greece did not effectively prohibit corporal punishment of children (Collective Complaint No. 17/2003, *OMCT v Greece*). The European Committee of Social Rights declared the complaint admissible in December 2003.

2004

April: An informal group of experts was established, including the Greek Ombudsman (Department of Children's Rights) to promote the abolition of corporal punishment of children in Greece and to prepare for establishing a Network for this purpose.

December: Under the Collective Complaints procedure, the European Committee of Social Rights concluded that there was a violation of article 17 of the Charter because of the absence of explicit prohibition in law of corporal punishment of children within the family, in secondary schools and in other institutions and forms of childcare (7 December 2003, Complaint No. 17/2003 *Decisions on the merits*).

. . . .

2006

October: the Greek Parliament passed Law 3500/2006 on the Combating of Intra-family Violence, under which corporal punishment of children within the family is prohibited. Article 4 of the new law states: "Physical violence against children as a disciplinary measure in the context of their upbringing brings the consequences of Article 1532 of the Civil Code."

November: The new law was announced in a press release issued by the Greek Ombudsman (Department of Children's Rights) on 1 November.

2007

January: The new law comes into force on 24 January 2007.

Notes and Questions

1. The report by the Global Initiative to End All Corporal Punishment of Children mentions how several of these countries focused heavily on educating the public about these new laws, the negative effects of corporal punishment, and alternative methods of disciplining that do not involve physical punishment. What seems to have been the effect of these educational programs on public opinion? What effect did the enactment of the law itself have on public opinion? Consider in general the role that public opinion plays in influencing the law, and, on the other hand, the role that the law plays in influencing public opinion. What, in your opinion, is the proper role of each with respect to the issue of corporal punishment? Consider these questions as you read the following excerpts, discussing the court case that changed Israel's legal approach to corporal punishment.

2. Review the process by which Greece enacted its anti-corporal punishment law. Is it your impression that there existed a genuine consensus in Greek society against all forms of corporal punishment? Does it matter whether there was or not? Will the new law reorient parents towards non-physical means of discipline?

3. Is it appropriate to separate the issue of corporal punishment from other matters relating to child rearing and family culture? Are there other contextual elements one would need to know more about before arriving at a conclusion that corporal punishment is always negative in its effects?

D. Ending Corporal Punishment by Judicial Decision: Israel and the *Plonit* Case[3]

If corporal punishment is to be seen in terms of the human rights of children, it is not surprising that courts should have a significant role in placing limits on parental authority to carry out physical punishment. The 2000 *Plonit* decision of the Israeli Supreme Court, described in the Tamar Ezer article below, relies on a general understanding of human dignity as the basis for declaring corporal punishment of children to be unlawful. The decision rejects the need for social consensus in advance of the adoption of such a blanket prohibition. Is a court decision of this kind likely to influence attitudes and behaviour in a sustainable way?

Tamar Ezer, *Children's Rights In Israel: An End to Corporal Punishment?*

5 Oregon Review of International Law 139 (2003)

Introduction: The *Plonit* Decision

On January 25, 2000, the Supreme Court of Israel issued the landmark *Plonit* decision, which prohibited the use of corporal punishment as an educational tool by parents. In this case, the Court rejected an appeal by a mother, convicted of assault and abuse for slapping and striking her two minor children with shoes and a vacuum cleaner. The mother denied that her actions constituted abuse and further excused them as "disciplinary measures" imposed on her children "in order to educate and improve them." The Court both declared the mother's actions abusive and rejected the parental defense for corporal punishment. Maintaining that "corporal punishment as an educational method not only fails to achieve its goals, but also causes physical and psychological damage to the child, that is liable to leave its mark on him even in maturity," the Court proclaimed a strict policy against the physical punishment of children and imposed a duty of protection upon the state. While carving out a narrow exception permitting the use of force to prevent injury to children or others, the Court held that "corporal punishment of children, or humiliation and the derogation from their dignity as a method of education by their parents, is entirely impermissible." This decision caused a splash in the media and sparked debates on proper methods of child-rearing, both amongst secular child specialists and within the religious community. It was highly controversial for three reasons. First, it calls for state intrusion into family privacy. Second, it gives children's right to be free from violence the constitutional status of a basic right. Third, it appears to draw a distinction between the norm-setting role of law and enforcement.

. . . .

Norm-Setting and Enforcement of the Law

The decision seems to differentiate between the norm-setting function and enforcement of law. While it takes a hard line, virtually abolishing the corporal punishment of children, it nevertheless counsels prosecutorial restraint. The Court stressed, "the criminal law includes enough 'filters,' ensuring that petty cases will not be included in its sweep." First, "the prosecution has discretion not to go to trial in the absence of the public interest." Moreover, "the criminal law contains the 'de minimis' defense, which may also be used to pre-

---

3. See Israel Supreme Court, Criminal Appeal 4596/98 Plonit v A.G. 54(1) P.D. 145. http://www.endcorporalpunishment.org/pages/pdfs/Israel_Judgment.pdf.

vent the imposition of criminal liability for the use of mild force." The Court thus reassured that "acts which an ordinarily constituted individual would not complain about" and "routine physical contact between a parent and child" will not serve as a basis for criminal liability. This brings up the question of how judgments weeding out the trivial cases will be made. Is this a recipe for discriminatory and arbitrary enforcement? But, perhaps these same concerns are implicated with all laws, as most pertinently, with the prohibition on assaults against adults. Here, however, the Court was explicit about the impossibility and even undesirability of complete enforcement. The Court emphasized its role in shaping citizens' internal concepts of right and wrong and not just the external laws regulating behavior, backed by the might of the state.

As is customary, the *Plonit* case was decided by a panel of three judges. Justice Dorit Beinisch wrote the decision, in which she both defined abuse and declared that "no corporal punishment is permitted." Justice Aharon Barak concurred with Justice Beinisch's opinion without further comment. Justice Yitzhak England wrote a partial dissent in which he took issue with Justice Beinisch's characterization of abuse, but did not address the Court's rejection of all corporal punishment. However, he joined the other justices in condemning the mother's actions as an assault. He stated, "[T]he violent manner in which the mother punished her children was neither reasonable nor can be defined as de minimis."

. . . .

Reception

. . . .

Concerns Raised by the *Plonit* Decision

This section explores some of the public concerns raised by the *Plonit* decision. Material is drawn from both newspaper articles and internet sources. It is important to interpret the reaction to the *Plonit* decision against the background of the incidence of corporal punishment in Israeli homes. NCC published the results of a survey based on a state-wide representative sample of 502 men and women from ages 18 and up. About a quarter of the participants (24.3%) admitted that it was customary in their homes to use corporal punishment against children. About 44% of the participants responded that in their childhood, their parents used to punish them corporally. Thus, the use of corporal punishment appears to be declining, but it remains widespread.

The *Plonit* decision was challenged both for systemic reasons and for its wisdom. The Court was first accused of overstepping its bounds and intruding into the family. Some parents saw the decision as a direct threat to their autonomy since "[t]he right to educate one's children according to one's own understanding is among the most precious rights that a free society grants its members." Naomi Baum, a child psychologist and the director of psychological services for Gush Etzion Regional Council, complained, "What the court is doing is undermining to some degree the authority of the parents in the family." Jonathan Rosenblum took this a step further, expressing the fear that "[s]oon we'll be told that the only protection for our children is that they be raised by the benevolent state. . . ." This fear loses credibility, however, when taking into account that the state already actively participates in shaping family relations, and even the most vigorous opponents of the *Plonit* decision do not advocate giving parents absolute control over children.

The Israeli Supreme Court has also been accused of usurping legislative functions and of dangerous counter-majoritarianism in the *Plonit* decision. Knesset Member Rabbi Gafni, who submitted a bill to counter the Court's ruling which was subsequently defeated, perceived the decision as "opening the door to judicial dictatorship," criticizing the Court for its "dangerous arrogance." Jonathan Rosenblum mocked, "Our Supreme Court has once again experienced an infusion of the god-like wisdom to which it is periodically subject." This conveys a notion of the Supreme Court as a dictatorial voice determining policies from above. He then went on to ask "[w]hy the court—and not the Knesset, which has the ability to conduct extensive hearings and which more closely reflects the values of Israel's citizens—should be the body to establish these norms." He concluded that "[c]hild raising is too important a subject to be confined to the pronouncements of three justices with no self-evident qualifications in the area." Evelyn Gordon is indignant that "[w]ith supreme arrogance, a panel of three people ... decided that it knows better than the majority what 'is forbidden today in our society.'" She made this criticism part of a general critique of the Supreme Court, protesting that "this is hardly the first time the court has ruthlessly rewritten Israel's legal system to suit its own 'enlightened' values," and "the fact that a majority of the country might disagree has never stopped the court from declaring itself the sole arbiter of society's values." However, Gordon herself conceded that "[t]he ruling did produce a ... debate on the pros and cons of spanking one's child, but there was virtually no discussion of the court's right to issue such a verdict." Thus, while Israelis hotly debated the decision's implications for child raising, they generally accepted the Supreme Court's norm-setting role for society.

The third systemic issue raised with regards to the *Plonit* decision centers on its enforceability. As Barak Barfi said, "It will be very difficult to enforce the ruling." Even worse is the fear that *Plonit's* unenforceable standard will open "the way for arbitrary and unequal applications of the law. Social workers, for instance, will now have a tool with which they can institute proceedings to remove virtually any child they want from his home." The Court took pains to assure that de minimis cases will not be pursued, but its critics find this far from reassuring. As Motti Scherzer, the chairman of Education Counselors explained, "When even the court's supporters claim that a ruling it has issued is not meant to be implemented, its status as a legal authority is in trouble." Thus, paradoxically, according to *Plonit's* opponents, while the Court is aggrandizing its power, it is at the same time threatening the very basis of its authority. Evelyn Gordon warned, "[I]ssuing a decree 'that the public will not be able to abide by' is a sure way to breed disrespect for the law and most especially for the court itself." But, does this logic also apply to de minimis assaults against adults, which are also legally prohibited?

Some parents took the decision as a personal attack against their policies and status as parents. Evelyn Gordon sharply criticized the Court for issuing a "ruling, based on the flimsiest legal premises, which declared the overwhelming majority of Israeli adults to be criminals." She lamented, "A large number of Israelis are probably criminals now—even though they weren't a few weeks ago." And, she warned parents dramatically, "you'll never know when the knife might descend." To claims that corporal punishment is harmful to children, parents defensively point to their own upbringing, asserting that corporal punishment did not hurt them. Yafa Ha'Ozer quoted this common refrain: "I was also slapped, and nothing happened to me. I didn't feel a miserable and beaten child. On the contrary, I learned that if I do something bad, I deserve a punishment"

These parents are most uncomfortable by the connection drawn by corporal punishment and abuse in the decision. Jonathan Rosenblum maintains that "Beinisch's entire argument against any physical punishment was that anyone who spanks their child even once may become a child abuser.... She assumes, without support, that every parental spanking is a microcosm of what child abusers do on a continuous basis." He is quick to reassure that "[t]he means, intent, and psychological makeup of the child-abuser bear no relation to those of a normal parent who occasionally spanks a child."

. . . .

Reaction to the decision is further complicated by religious considerations. Judge Strashnov of the Tel Aviv District Court based his support of corporal punishment on Biblical and rabbinical citations. Proponents of corporal punishment commonly cite the proverb, "He who spares the rod, hates his child." The Talmud and later commentaries also seem to justify corporal punishment. Chaim Budnick explained that "in the correct circumstances and within the correct boundaries, corporal punishment is not only condoned but rather prescribed." Thus, Jonathan Rosenblum wrote, "Most religious Jews would likely be numbered among the skeptics when it comes to the absolutist position against any physical punishment." However, even among the religious, views are not unanimous. Rabbi Israel Meir Lau points out that the Hebrew word for rod, shevet, not only means rod, but it is also used in the Bible to denote authority and fear. Frimet Roth argues that since the second half of the quoted proverb is "But he who loves him reproves him early" with no mention of a rod or hitting, this supports the view that King Solomon was merely exhorting parents to teach and discipline their children.

Notes and Questions

1. How much power does one judicial decision have to change a divided society? What are the relative merits of the European and Israeli approaches to the problem of physical punishment?

2. In the *Plonit* case, Justice Beinisch, writing for the majority, reviews the history of parental defenses in the context of corporal punishment. He asks whether a defense based on reasonable corporal punishment exists, and states that "The court examining the normative aspect of the parent's behaviour towards his or her child must bring into its consideration the current judicial attitude to the position of the child and his or her rights. This is currently done in many of the world's states. . . ." He refers to the fact that Israel has ratified the UNCRC and continues, ". . . we decide that corporal punishment of children, humiliation and derogation from their dignity as a method of education by their parents, is entirely impermissible, and is a remnant of a socio-educational outlook that has lost its validity." Isn't there a certain logic to the fact that, having accepted the idea that corporal punishment should be seen in the light of human rights norms, there is no further need for true social consensus on the subject, and that it may be outlawed by judicial decision?

———————

E. The Argument for a U.S. Anti-Spanking Statute

Even if corporal punishment is seen by many as a human rights violation that must be stopped, the issue arises as to how best to accomplish this. As you read the next several articles, consider whether public opinion on corporal punishment might be swayed from tacit, or even active, support as a result of (a) public education on the negatives of corporal punishment or (b) a federal law banning corporal punishment at school and home. Will social attitudes, and thus behaviour behind closed doors, change as a result of legislative initiatives?

In the following article, Susan Bitensky urges the United States to follow the lead of those countries that have banned corporal punishment. Are you troubled by the fact that the U.S. is out of the global mainstream in allowing corporal punishment of children? Is it possible that there is a wide divergence between global rhetoric and reality in the corporal punishment context? Is there any way to accurately measure this, without engaging in a massive intrusion into family life? Bitensky advocates for a comprehensive statute banning corporal punishment in the U.S.; she also states a preference for a strict version of such a law, with the possibility of prosecution for those who defy the prohibition.

Susan H. Bitensky, *The United Nations Convention on the Right of the Child and Corporal Punishment of Children: Ramifications for the United States*
5 Georgetown Journal on Fighting Poverty 225 (1998)

. . . .

Corporal Punishment and the Convention on the Rights of the Child

Although the Convention on the Rights of the Child does not mention corporal punishment or spanking, the Convention does clearly forbid all corporal punishment of children. The Committee on the Rights of the Child (Committee), the body that monitors compliance with the Convention and issues authoritative interpretations of its provisions, has advanced the idea that the Convention as a whole is inconsistent with corporal punishment of children. In an official report issued in 1994, the Committee declared:

> In the framework of its mandate, the Committee has paid particular attention to the child's right to physical integrity. In the same spirit, it has stressed that corporal punishment of children is incompatible with the Convention and has often proposed the revision of existing legislation, as well as the development of awareness and educational campaigns, to prevent child abuse and the physical punishment of children.

The Committee has articulated and elaborated this idea many times in its concluding observations following examination of progress reports submitted by various countries.

. . . .

Both semantics and authoritative interpretation make clear that the Convention forbids all corporal punishment of children. But, one must consider what this means for nations that become parties to the Convention, most pertinently, what the implications would be for the United States if it were to ratify the Convention. In its concluding observations and elsewhere, the Committee on the Rights of the Child has urged states parties to engage in educational campaigns against corporal punishment of children. This stands to reason. If a country is going to forbid corporal punishment, its leaders had better educate the populace that this is their national policy. However, the Committee has urged an even more dramatic step. The Committee has urged nations to adopt legislation outlawing all corporal punishment of children.

Existing Laws That Prohibit Corporal Punishment

. . . .

Nor is the prohibition of all corporal punishment of children purely a foreign phenomenon. America's best kept secret is that Minnesota also prohibits all such punishment. Unlike its European counterparts, Minnesota does not have a single statute that explicitly forbids parental corporal punishment of children. Rather, the state's ban must be teased out of four statutory provisions read together. These statutes have removed the use of reasonable force, including corporal punishment, as a defense to assault charges.

That is, if parents use "reasonable force" on a child as a disciplinary tactic, they may be prosecuted by Minnesota for assault and may not hide behind the excuse that they were just using "reasonable" corporal punishment. As one expert has noted, "corporal punishment is considered a crime to the same extent as any assault" in Minnesota.

Although Minnesota has lived with this prohibition for many years, there are no reported cases of a parent being prosecuted for administering mild corporal punishment to children. As in the European countries that have banned corporal punishment of children, it appears Minnesota exercises prosecutorial restraint in relation to this issue.

Prosecutorial Restraint and the Efficacy of Anti-spanking Laws

Although governments use prosecutorial restraint, anti-spanking laws are not meaningless and the Committee on the Rights of the Child shows much wisdom in promoting them. Aristotle said that the essence of law is not that it commands conduct but that it creates a habit of obedience to itself over time. In other words, law has a pedagogical role. Law has an educative effect because it crystallizes and makes visible in an impressive way, at the level of governmental authority, those norms that constitute a society's priorities and aspirations. Law tells us who we are and should be.

Many European countries are accustomed to laws that are mere pronouncements without reference to penalties. In the Scandinavian countries and Austria, the anti-spanking laws fit this mold. Because these laws are so clear, they can and do play a pedagogical role that creates a habit of obedience to their legal mandate over time. Moreover, it is arguable that the educative effect of these laws is enhanced by the knowledge that although prosecution for corporal punishment is highly unlikely, such prosecutions or adverse custody decisions are still possible. For example, a few isolated prosecutions of parents for spanking their children have occurred in Sweden.

Minnesota's laws have less potential to carry out a pedagogical role because they do not explicitly state a ban on all corporal punishment of children. Rather, these laws, through obtuse and intricate statutory construction, achieve a ban by removing reasonable force as a defense to assault. The result is that the notice function of these Minnesota laws has been virtually lost on laypersons and even on the non-prosecutors in the legal community.

An Anti-Spanking Statute for the United States

Despite the educational and, therefore, deterrent effect of the anti-spanking laws adopted in Scandinavia and Austria, my own preference, especially for the United States, is the Cypriot model which makes clear on its face both that corporal punishment is forbidden and that offenders may be subject to prosecution. This model is preferable because the United States has a legal system that does not make laws merely to announce preferred policies without creating adjunctive enforceable rights, duties, or liabilities. I also prefer this model for our country because it seems Americans are highly resistant to the idea of restraining adults from spanking. Combining clearly articulated prohibitory language with the penalty language in one statute may be preferable in the United States because it is in a format that is both familiar and unequivocal and, therefore, more accessible to the average citizen.

Naturally, an offender could be prosecuted under such a statute. The existence of criminal liability does not mean, though, that the main purpose of the statute would be to haul parents into court. As in Minnesota and the European countries that have banned corporal punishment of children, prosecutorial restraint would be the most advisable policy. Nothing is lost by such restraint. The existence of the law and threat of prosecution should serve the law's pedagogical goals. A conservative prosecutorial strategy would take cognizance of the fact that the new statute proscribes adult behavior that may be impulsive and difficult to control. Such a policy would also probably make the statute more politically acceptable and prevent the courts from being clogged with armies of parents facing criminal charges. One possible version of a statute that would carry out the intended purposes might read as follows:

(1) (a) Corporal punishment is defined as the use of physical force with the intention of causing a child to experience bodily pain so as to correct, control, or punish the child's behavior.

(b) Any person who uses corporal punishment on a child shall be guilty of the crime of battery provided that such physical force would be a battery if used on an adult.

(2) The penalties for conviction pursuant to subsection (1) shall be the same as those for conviction under any other criminal battery provisions or, in lieu thereof in appropriate cases, shall be a post-trial or post-plea diversion program.

(3) Nothing stated in subsections (1) or (2) herein shall preclude or limit further prosecution under any other applicable laws for the use of corporal punishment described in subsection (1).

(4) The proscription set forth in subsection (1) shall not apply to the use of such physical force as is reasonably necessary to prevent death or imminent bodily pain or injury to the child or others.

. . . .

Note that subsection (2) makes the penalties for hitting a child the same as for hitting an adult, thereby communicating that children are not chattel worthy of less protection. Subsection (2) also offers diversion as an alternative to traditional criminal penalties in jurisdictions where such programs are available. This option is offered in recognition of the fact that it would probably be more productive for offenders to be counseled about better parenting skills than to be fined or incarcerated. Subsection (3) is designed to ensure that the statute will not be used to preclude prosecutions for more serious child abuse if they would be appropriate. And, finally, subsection (4) recognizes that physical force may be used in emergencies to restrain the child from injuring herself or others.

. . . .

The Feasibility of an Anti-spanking Statute

"Reasonable" corporal punishment of children by their parents or guardians is currently legal in every state except Minnesota. Approximately half of the states permit school personnel to use "reasonable" corporal punishment on students as well. Thus, law reform on this issue in the United States would require enactment of new statutes prohibiting all corporal punishment of children and repeal of existing state statutes permitting such punishment. Should such an undertaking seem overwhelming, it is worth recalling that similar law reform was needed and implemented to bar husbands from physically chastising their wives.

[I]t may be objected that what is practically feasible is not necessarily constitutionally permissible. The U.S. Constitution is supreme such that no other laws may contravene its provisions and survive judicial challenge. Laws forbidding corporal punishment would, therefore, need to be consistent with federal constitutional doctrine.

The Constitution is silent on corporal punishment of children. The United States Supreme Court has never characterized such punishment as a constitutionally-protected activity. Indeed, the Court has addressed the subject of corporal punishment of children only with respect to its constitutional permissibility in the schools. In 1977, in *Ingraham v. Wright*, the Court held that the Eighth Amendment does not apply to the paddling of children as a means of maintaining discipline in public schools. The result is that while elementary and secondary schools are not forbidden by the Eighth Amendment from corporally punishing students, states are still permitted to ban the practice from educational facilities.

However, some will no doubt argue that prohibition of corporal punishment of children by parents or other adults in the family circle raises constitutional concerns arising out of parental or familial prerogatives. It may be anticipated that these naysayers will raise four arguments: first, that prohibition arguably would violate parents' substantive due process right to rear their children as the parents see fit; second, the prohibition could be viewed as violating parents' free speech right to communicate with their children; third, the prohibition could be interpreted to constrict parents' right of free exercise of religion insofar as physical chastisement is religiously based; and fourth, the prohibition may be regarded as infringing familial privacy rights.

There are separate counterarguments to each of these contentions. For example, the Supreme Court has repeatedly held that violence against another person cannot be a part of anyone's free speech rights. The reach of the Free Exercise Clause typically protects religious beliefs rather than religiously motivated conduct burdened by laws of general applicability. And, privacy rights may be more personal than they are familial. But, there is no need to explore separate counterarguments because each of the four previously mentioned constitutional arguments suffer from the same defect. That is, like wife beating or other physical assaults, corporal punishment is so egregious in its effects and so ethically unpalatable that in a civilized society it must be outside the definitional parameters of any constitutional right—be it child-rearing, religious or other expression, or family privacy. It follows that if corporal punishment is not part of any constitutional right, legislatures may prohibit it without showing a compelling interest or any other justification beyond what rational legislative discretion and wisdom dictate.

This conclusion is strengthened by the fact that the Supreme Court has not held that under the Constitution familial or parent-child relations must be free of all governmental regulation. The Court has acknowledged "that the state has a wide range of power for limiting parental freedom and authority in things affecting the child's welfare" and that "the family itself is not beyond regulation in the public interest."

. . . .

CONCLUSION

The key to understanding the human condition may be in looking at behaviors that are so much a part of daily life for so many, that no one steps back to question them. One such key behavior is corporal punishment of children—a behavior that may help to account for what is cruel and vengeful in the human heart. The U.N. Convention on the Rights of the Child has given us the immense advantage of clearly putting corporal punishment into its proper perspective as a serious human rights issue and of mandating abolition of such punishment. If the United States were to ratify the Convention, the Committee on the Rights of the Child would probably recommend that we take educational and legal measures to achieve abolition. The American legal system presents no significant obstacles to such measures. Indeed, abolition by legislative fiat would comport with some of our most enlightened legal history.

Notes and Questions

1. Which of the justifications that Bitensky proposes for a spanking ban is most convincing to you: that children should have equal protection and treatment under the law; that spanking harms children; or that spanking unfairly equates children with chattel / property? Is there any justification for distinguishing between spanking children on the one hand, and hitting adults—women, for example—on the other?

2. Bitensky explains the importance of prosecutorial restraint in a context such as this, and mentions that some countries have anti-spanking laws that generally do not lead to prosecution of parents. How high a likelihood of prosecution should attach to anti-corporal punishment laws? What strengths and weaknesses do you see with Bitensky's proposed law for the United States?

III. Corporal Punishment in the Educational Context: Physical Discipline in Schools

A. Corporal Punishment in U.S. Schools

In the U.S., laws against corporal punishment in schools have gained relatively broad, if not universal, acceptance. The next readings address problems of corporal punishment in the context of school discipline. In what sense are the issues arising from school discipline distinct from questions of corporal punishment in the home? Although some U.S. states still allow corporal punishment in school, why are Americans generally more tolerant of prohibitions on the practice in school, as opposed to in the home?

The Andre Imbrogno article, excerpted below, reflects the reality that the matter of corporal punishment in American schools has been left up to state and local control. Imbrogno appears to be strongly against the idea of centralized imposition of one view on corporal punishment; he prefers to await the development of social consensus on inflammatory issues of this kind. Contrast his opposition to legislating without what he sees as the "consent" of the population, with Bitensky's belief in the inherent efficacy of a national anti-spanking statute.

Andre R. Imbrogno, *Corporal Punishment in America's Public Schools and the U.N. Convention on the Rights of the Child: A Case for Nonratification*
29 Journal of Law & Education 125 (2000).

Introduction

Currently, the only state-sanctioned corporal punishment in the United States exists in our public schools. Approximately half of the states permit their elementary and secondary schools to use reasonable corporal punishment in the disciplining of students. Schools in these states exercise this disciplinary right with some regularity. The United States Department of Education's most recent estimates put the number of school-administered instances of corporal punishment at over 600,000 per year. The United States remains one of only a few industrialized nations which permit corporal punishment in their schools.

At the same time, respect for the rights of children appears to be growing throughout the world. The United Nations Convention on the Rights of the Child (hereinafter "Convention"), which contains several provisions either explicitly or implicitly prohibiting the use of corporal punishment on children, has been ratified by 191 nations, making it the most quickly and universally ratified human rights treaty yet. Although some have argued strongly in favor of the treaty's ratification in the United States, ratification appears unlikely. Even if ratification were to occur, reliance upon international law as a means of undoing the long-standing practice of corporal punishment in America's schools is seriously misplaced. A new norm rejecting corporal punishment may yet emerge, but only by changing attitudes at the community and state level.

The U.N. Convention on the Rights of the Child

....

Article 28(2) [of the UNCRC] provides, in part, that "States Parties shall take ... measures to ensure that school discipline is administered in a manner consistent with the child's human dignity and in conformity with the ... Convention." The United Nations Committee on the Rights of the Child has advised that this provision of the Convention is intended to outlaw the use of corporal punishment in schools.

....

Corporal Punishment and the Courts

An examination of the courts' treatment of school discipline issues reveals a long history of judicial deference to local officials with respect to corporal punishment and other disciplinary matters. This deference notwithstanding, some civil actions have met with a measure of success. However, for a variety of reasons, the elimination, or wide-spread reduction, of corporal punishment through judicial action is not likely. While parental choice is, at least arguably, a fair resolution to the corporal punishment debate, for judicial and moral reasons, it is an unattractive solution from the standpoint of corporal punishment's strongest opponents.

A. Deference to Local Officials

In a series of decisions since 1969, the United States Supreme Court has invited judicial scrutiny of school district disciplinary decisions. At the same time, the Court has consistently articulated in these cases a rule of substantial deference to decisions made by locally elected school officials. The Supreme Court's seminal decision on corporal punishment is *Ingraham v. Wright*, handed down by the Court in 1977.

In *Ingraham*, the Supreme Court held that the Eighth Amendment's Cruel and Unusual Punishment Clause does not apply to corporal punishment imposed as discipline in public schools. Although the Court found a liberty interest implicated, due process did not require notice and a hearing prior to the imposition of corporal punishment. In the Court's view, the openness of the public schools, the supervision of these schools by the community, and the legal constraints on corporal punishment imposed under the common law and criminal law obviated the need for the constitutional protections sought by the students in this case.

Underlying the Court's decision in *Ingraham* was its perception of corporal punishment as an issue best left to local educational policymakers. According to the Court, imposing additional constitutional safeguards would unduly intrude into areas of educational responsibility that rest primarily with local school authorities. As David Pedersent notes, the *Ingraham* Court's quoting of Justice Black's concurring opinion in *Powell v. Texas* is revealing:

> This Nation is too large, too complex and composed of too great a diversity of peoples for any one of us to have the wisdom to establish the rules by which local Americans must govern their local affairs. The constitutional rule we are urged to adopt is not merely revolutionary—it departs from the ancient faith based on the premise that experience in making local laws by local people themselves is by far the safest guide for a Nation like ours to follow.

The *Ingraham* Court also recognized that extensive due process protections would burden, to an unacceptable extent, the use of corporal punishment as a disciplinary measure. The Court acknowledged that the elimination of corporal punishment would be welcomed by many Americans; it stressed, however, that the decision to eliminate corporal punishment was not its to make. According to the Court, "when such a policy choice may result from this Court's determination of an asserted right to due process, rather than from the normal processes of community debate and legislative action, the societal costs cannot be dismissed as insubstantial."

The Supreme Court's deference to local officials in matters of school discipline extends beyond the corporal punishment issue to other educational matters having substantial constitutional implications, including search and seizure and free speech. Repeatedly in its opinions the Supreme Court expresses deference to local authorities, quoting with approval its opinion in *Epperson v. Arkansas*, wherein the Court stated "judicial interposition in the operation of the public school system of the Nation raises problems requiring care and restraint.... By and large, public education in our Nation is committed to the control of state and local authorities."

Research indicates that the tone of deference established by the Supreme Court is reflected in judicial decisions from the lower federal courts and the states. A study by David Pedersent examined a wide variety of student discipline cases handed down by lower federal and state courts since 1995. Pedersent writes that "it is apparent from a review of these cases that the lower federal courts and the state courts have generally taken to heart the admonition of the ... Supreme Court to grant deference to decision-making of local school officials." In three-fourths of the cases examined, the courts either decided the case in favor of the school district or, for those cases in which school officials were not directly involved, in favor of a decision that would give school officials greater discretion in school discipline matters.

B. Available Causes of Action

The Eighth Amendment, which after *Ingraham* provides only minimal protection against corporal punishment, is not the only constitutional vehicle by which to challenge the practice in court. Other possible causes of action include substantive due process, equal protection, and free exercise of religion under the First Amendment. First Amendment challenges have not yet been brought. The other causes of action have met with varying degrees of success in recent years. However, as a basis for eliminating corporal punishment from the nation's public schools, each has severe limitations.

One question left open by the Supreme Court's decision in *Ingraham* was whether or under what circumstances corporal punishment of a public school child will give rise to an independent federal cause of action to vindicate substantive rights under the Due Process Clause of the Fourteenth Amendment. The federal courts of appeals are not of one mind on this question. Even in those circuits that recognize a substantive due process claim for unreasonable corporal punishment, the existence of the claim does little to placate corporal punishment's harshest opponents because the claim generally requires corporal punishment so excessive that it "shocks the conscience." While providing a separate federal claim, in most cases the substantive due process claim will not cover acts of punishment not already prohibited under state criminal law or actionable under state common law.

Those bringing civil rights actions for the discriminatory application of corporal punishment face similar challenges in establishing their claims. The issue of discrimination is hardly academic in nature. Studies have demonstrated that "proportionately, black children are subjected to corporal punishment many times oftener than white or Asian children in almost every school district in the nation." Although this equal protection issue has not been frequently litigated, one federal court recently held that a claim for discriminatory imposition of corporal punishment brought under the federal civil rights law states a valid cause of action. However, as this same court noted, it is well-established that the Constitution is not violated solely because a state action has a racially disproportionate impact. Plaintiff must demonstrate a racially discriminatory intent or purpose. African-American school children thus face a substantial evidentiary burden in these civil rights actions.

One possible cause of action which has not yet been brought by opponents of corporal punishment, but which could meet with some success, is one based on the First Amendment's religion clauses. While current religious doctrine overwhelmingly supports the practice of corporal punishment, some new-thought religions and even parts of the Bible itself advocate compassion toward children. Although case law addressing the relationship between the First Amendment and corporal punishment is scarce, it appears that at least some courts will entertain First Amendment challenges to state-mandated bans on corporal punishment. These decisions could, perhaps, be analogized to cases involving state-sanctioned imposition of corporal punishment.

For instance, in *North Valley Baptist Church v. McMahon*, a religious group operating a preschool challenged the constitutionality of California's Child Care Facilities Act, which, *inter alia*, prohibited corporal punishment in child care facilities. Although the court ultimately upheld the statute, it noted that where a group's religious beliefs mandate corporal punishment, a state-imposed burden on the practice could run afoul of the First Amendment's Free Exercise Clause. The problem for the plaintiffs in *McMahon* was that they failed to show that corporal punishment was mandated by their religious beliefs.

There is no apparent reason why such a holding could not be analogized to genuinely held religious *opposition* to corporal punishment. However what makes this First Amendment action a poor vehicle for the eradication of corporal punishment is the fact that few contemporary religions oppose corporal punishment. Therefore, few challenges to corporal punishment are likely to be brought on these grounds. Indeed, corporal punishment finds considerably more support in religion than it does opposition.

C. Parental Choice

A number of school districts, by local rule, permit individual parents to determine whether their children will be subject to corporal punishment. Although there is a basic fairness underlying this approach to the controversial issue of corporal punishment, courts have shown an unwillingness to recognize a constitutional basis for this compromise. Again, as with the corporal punishment issue more generally, this parental choice model has its roots in local political processes, as opposed to federal law.

In one of the few cases addressing the issue of parental choice, *Baker v. Owen*, plaintiff parents had told local school officials that they did not want their child subjected to corporal punishment. The parents' wishes notwithstanding, the child was given two licks with a drawer divider that was just slightly thicker than a ruler. While the court accepted the parents' argument that the Fourteenth Amendment embraces the right of a parent to determine and choose between means of discipline of children, that right was overborne by the countervailing and greater state interest in maintaining school discipline. Two years later in *Ingraham*, the Supreme Court put its imprimatur on the *Baker* holding when it cited its summary affirmation of *Baker* for the proposition that "parental approval of corporal punishment is not constitutionally required."

Thus, while the parental choice model is an expedient, and perhaps fundamentally fair, manner in which to deal with the corporal punishment controversy, it can do little to satisfy corporal punishment's strongest opponents. At bottom, the existence of parental choice is the end result of decisions made by local officials and, without a grounding in federal law, is vulnerable to all the vagaries of such decision-making. Moreover, to the extent corporal punishment is a moral issue, as many urge, an approach that allows the practice to continue, even as against only those children whose parents expressly allow it, is an unacceptable resolution of the issue.

Undoubtedly, those opposed to the use of corporal punishment in America's public schools have been frustrated by the deference the federal and state courts have shown local school administrators, the overall inadequacy of judicial action, and the deficiencies of the parental choice model. Compounding this frustration is the uneven treatment the issue has received in the states, as a number of jurisdictions continue to allow corporal punishment in their public schools. Accordingly, those opposed to the practice have, in recent years, increasingly looked to the Convention, hopeful that ratification will jettison corporal punishment from America's public schools.

The [UNCRC]: Challenges to Ratification and Enforcement

. . . .

... [R]atification of human rights treaties like the Convention is often accompanied by the imposition of several impediments to domestic enforcement. In the past, when the United States has ratified a human rights treaty, it has usually been on the condition that the treaty does not furnish a rule of decision to be applied in domestic litigation. As a result, the provisions of the treaty are not self-executing. Put another way, the provisions of the treaty cannot be invoked in the courts. The treaty will have domestic legal effect only if the treaty is later implemented by domestic legislation.

The device of "reservations" is another means by which the Senate can ensure that a ratified treaty will not be domestically enforceable. "Upon ratifying a treaty, a country may declare that it chooses not to accept all of the duties imposed by the treaty." The result of a reservation is the same as if the United States did not ratify the reserved part of the treaty. A reservation precludes domestic enforcement of that provision reserved. Thus, the Convention could be ratified with the United States entering a reservation on those provisions prohibiting corporal punishment. The United States thus retains the right to emasculate some or all of the Convention's provisions.

. . . .

A. The Consequences of Ratification

. . . .

Ratification without consensus would likely be a hollow victory for the Convention's proponents, at least with respect to those states which currently allow corporal punishment in their public schools, which, in fact, are the only systems that concern supporters of the Convention. This is true even if ratification occurs without qualification and the Convention is made directly enforceable in the courts of the United States. Many question the ability of the courts to vindicate fundamental rights in the face of significant popular opposition. For the most part, the courts are practically powerless to insure that their decisions are supported by local administrative officials, which means that courts are largely dependent on popular support to implement their decisions. "Courts are ... only modestly endowed with coercive capabilities — adequate, perhaps, for dealing with re-calcitrant individuals, but probably insufficient for bringing large groups or powerful in-stitutions into line."

Law enforcement pays a price for the legislating of morals without popular consen-sus. Where popular support for a law is absent, the law is unlikely to be regularly en-forced and is even less likely to be obeyed. Classic instances of the failure of moral legislation, unsupported by popular consensus, are the prohibition fiasco and today's anti-adultery laws. The moral message intended to be communicated by the law is con-tradicted by the absence of compliance and enforcement; "for while the public sees the conduct condemned in words, it also sees in the dramatic absence of [compliance and en-forcement] that it is not condemned in deed."

Moreover, the spectacle of popular nullification of the government's commands has an unhealthy effect on law enforcement generally. "It tends to breed cynicism and an indif-ference to ... [legal] processes which augment tendencies toward disrespect for those who make and enforce the law." As social and legal historian E.P. Thompson once noted, "the essential precondition for the effectiveness of law, in its function as ideology, is that it shall display an independence from gross manipulation." Similarly, those in the contem-porary communitarian movement urge that "successful policies are accepted because they are recognized as legitimate, rather than imposed."

.... [T]he question of whether corporal punishment is to be permitted in America's pub-lic schools should, as the courts have suggested, be left to the evolving standards of the local communities. A new norm in opposition to corporal punishment may yet emerge, or it may not. What is key is that if opponents of the practice are intent on waging a war for the hearts and minds of the American public on this issue, they will have to fight in-dividual battles at the grassroots level, changing attitudes and laws one community at a time. Reliance on the Convention is likely to produce only a short-lived symbolic victory destined to degenerate into a disrespected legal nullity.

B. An Alternative to Ratification: Changing Attitudes at the Grassroots Level

The roots of corporal punishment in America's schools exist at the micro level of Amer-ican society and politics. Because educators stand in the place of parents, the practice is linked to the family, the most basic unit of society. Moreover, as noted, corporal pun-ishment has roots in religion, one of the most private of human affairs. Finally, decades of judicial deference to local officials and parents with respect to this and other matters of education create the legitimate expectation among the public that policy change in this area will be the product of local political processes. Accordingly, if a new norm re-jecting corporal punishment is to emerge, it must be forged not through international law, the most global level of policymaking available to humankind, but through the chang-ing of individual attitudes at the local, grassroots level. This need for grassroots change is a product of the process by which society defines — i.e., labels — human behaviors.

Opponents of corporal punishment often equate the practice with child abuse or other forms of physical violence condemned by society. For instance, in an article supporting ratification of the Convention, Susan Bitensky draws an analogy between child abuse, wife beating, and corporal punishment. Such statements beg the ultimate question of whether corporal punishment in America's public schools is good or bad policy. In those jurisdictions in which reasonable corporal punishment is still permitted, should it now be criminalized just as spousal abuse has been criminalized? Is corporal punishment a form of child abuse or is it properly distinguishable? In equating corporal punishment with child and spousal abuse, opponents of corporal punishment convey their bare opinions on these questions, but do little more.

. . . .

By and large, our society defines child/spousal abuse and corporal punishment differently, reserving the label "deviant" for the former, but not the latter. "Deviancy" is socially defined and is a fluid concept. Today's accepted behavior may be tomorrow's deviancy. Those who urge that corporal punishment is akin to child or spouse abuse must really be arguing for a redefining of corporal punishment as deviant behavior.

Although spousal abuse and corporal punishment are by no means perfectly analogous, the history of spousal abuse in the United States can tell us quite a bit about this process of redefinition. Until fairly recently, spousal battering was viewed as falling within the private sphere of the family and largely beyond the law's reach. The "problem" of battering and the social and legal construct of the "battered woman" did not exist in this country until the woman's movement identified it. Through the years, the battered woman's movement has played a critical role in providing services for battered women, lobbying state governments for legal remedies to end the violence, and, perhaps most importantly, developing public education efforts to change perceptions about battering.

Through the efforts of the feminist leaders behind the battered woman's movement, spousal abuse was redefined as deviant behavior. With this redefining came a plethora of state civil and criminal remedies addressing the plight of battering victims. It was only after attitudes about spousal abuse were changed at the state level that the federal government addressed domestic violence in the Violence Against Women Act of 1994, putting a national gloss on policy which emerged in the states.

For corporal punishment to be effectively banished from America's public schools, the practice must experience a similar redefining. The process should begin not with the imposition of international law on local schools, but rather, with the changing of individual attitudes at the local community level. Neither the redefining of corporal punishment, nor any other social undertaking for that matter, should be assigned to an institution that is larger than necessary to do the job. What can be done at the local and state level should not be passed on to the federal or international level. The creation of a new norm rejecting corporal punishment in America's public schools must be the product of a process of redefinition that takes place one community and state at a time.

Of course, from the standpoint of corporal punishment's opponents, it appears more efficient to wage and win one battle in the United States Senate than fifty in the states. In the long run, however, the efficient course may not produce the best substantive results for opponents of corporal punishment. Without the hearts and minds of a majority of Americans behind it, the quick, efficient victory achieved through ratification of the Convention is likely to be an empty one at best.

Notes and Questions

1. Do you agree that grassroots change—which is perhaps most consistent with the American preference for deference to local control in education—is a more effective way

to alter opinions on corporal punishment than future U.S. ratification of the UNCRC? How does this square with prior readings that purport to demonstrate that, in other countries, public opinion shifted once the law was changed to outlaw corporal punishment? Is there anything unique about the U.S. that suggests its public would not respond in a similar manner?

B. Contrasting Judicial Views of Punishment and the Educational System: The United States and South Africa

The following two cases provide contrasting examples of judicial thinking from the highest courts of two nations: the U.S. Supreme Court and the Constitutional Court of South Africa. In the case of the U.S., local control over educational policy is well established; guarantees deriving from the U.S. Constitution have not overcome entrenched ideas of federal-state relationships so as to afford extra protection to children in school. In the South African case, we see the court struggling to accommodate a wide variety of social, cultural and religious elements. In the end, which values did the South African court decide were transcendent?

Ingraham v. Wright
430 U.S. 651 (1977)

MR. JUSTICE POWELL delivered the opinion of the Court.

This case presents questions concerning the use of corporal punishment in public schools: First, whether the paddling of students as a means of maintaining school discipline constitutes cruel and unusual punishment in violation of the Eighth Amendment; and, second, to the extent that paddling is constitutionally permissible, whether the Due Process Clause of the Fourteenth Amendment requires prior notice and an opportunity to be heard.

I

....

Petitioners' evidence may be summarized briefly. In the 1970–1971 school year many of the 237 schools in Dade County used corporal punishment as a means of maintaining discipline pursuant to Florida legislation and a local School Board regulation. The statute then in effect authorized limited corporal punishment by negative inference, proscribing punishment which was "degrading or unduly severe" or which was inflicted without prior consultation with the principal or the teacher in charge of the school. The regulation, Dade County School Board Policy 5144, contained explicit directions and limitations. The authorized punishment consisted of paddling the recalcitrant student on the buttocks with a flat wooden paddle measuring less than two feet long, three to four inches wide, and about one-half inch thick. The normal punishment was limited to one to five "licks" or blows with the paddle and resulted in no apparent physical injury to the student. School authorities viewed corporal punishment as a less drastic means of discipline than suspension or expulsion. Contrary to the procedural requirements of the statute and regulation, teachers often paddled students on their own authority without first consulting the principal.

Petitioners focused on Drew Junior High School, the school in which both Ingraham and Andrews were enrolled in the fall of 1970. In an apparent reference to Drew, the District Court found that "[t]he instances of punishment which could be characterized as severe, accepting the students' testimony as credible, took place in one junior high school." The evidence, consisting mainly of the testimony of 16 students, suggests that the regime at Drew was exceptionally harsh. The testimony of Ingraham and Andrews, in support of their individual claims for damages, is illustrative. Because he was slow to respond to his teacher's instructions, Ingraham was subjected to more than 20 licks with a paddle while being held over a table in the principal's office. The paddling was so severe that he suffered a hematoma requiring medical attention and keeping him out of school for several days. Andrews was paddled several times for minor infractions. On two occasions he was struck on his arms, once depriving him of the full use of his arm for a week.

. . . .

II

In addressing the scope of the Eighth Amendment's prohibition on cruel and unusual punishment, this Court has found it useful to refer to "[t]raditional common-law concepts," *Powell v. Texas*, 392 U.S. 514, 535 (1968) (plurality opinion), and to the ["attitudes] which our society has traditionally taken." *Id.*, at 531. So, too, in defining the requirements of procedural due process under the Fifth and Fourteenth Amendments, the Court has been attuned to what "has always been the law of the land," *United States v. Barnett*, 376 U.S. 681, 692 (1964), and to "traditional ideas of fair procedure." *Greene v. McElroy*, 360 U.S. 474, 508 (1959). We therefore begin by examining the way in which our traditions and our laws have responded to the use of corporal punishment in public schools.

The use of corporal punishment in this country as a means of disciplining school children dates back to the colonial period. It has survived the transformation of primary and secondary education from the colonials' reliance on optional private arrangements to our present system of compulsory education and dependence on public schools. Despite the general abandonment of corporal punishment as a means of punishing criminal offenders, the practice continues to play a role in the public education of schoolchildren in most parts of the country. Professional and public opinion is sharply divided on the practice, and has been for more than a century. Yet we can discern no trend toward its elimination.

. . . .

III

The Eighth Amendment provides: "Excessive bail shall not be required, nor excessive fines imposed, nor cruel and unusual punishments inflicted." Bail, fines, and punishment traditionally have been associated with the criminal process, and by subjecting the three to parallel limitations the text of the Amendment suggests an intention to limit the power of those entrusted with the criminal-law function of government. An examination of the history of the Amendment and the decisions of this Court construing the proscription against cruel and unusual punishment confirms that it was designed to protect those convicted of crimes. We adhere to this longstanding limitation and hold that the Eighth Amendment does not apply to the paddling of children as a means of maintaining discipline in public schools.

. . . .

C

. . . .

The schoolchild has little need for the protection of the Eighth Amendment. Though attendance may not always be voluntary, the public school remains an open institution. Except perhaps when very young, the child is not physically restrained from leaving school during school hours; and at the end of the school day, the child is invariably free to return home. Even while at school, the child brings with him the support of family and friends and is rarely apart from teachers and other pupils who may witness and protest any instances of mistreatment.

The openness of the public school and its supervision by the community afford significant safeguards against the kinds of abuses from which the Eighth Amendment protects the prisoner. In virtually every community where corporal punishment is permitted in the schools, these safeguards are reinforced by the legal constraints of the common law. Public school teachers and administrators are privileged at common law to inflict only such corporal punishment as is reasonably necessary for the proper education and discipline of the child; any punishment going beyond the privilege may result in both civil and criminal liability.... As long as the schools are open to public scrutiny, there is no reason to believe that the common-law constraints will not effectively remedy and deter excesses such as those alleged in this case.

We conclude that when public school teachers or administrators impose disciplinary corporal punishment, the Eighth Amendment is inapplicable. The pertinent constitutional question is whether the imposition is consonant with the requirements of due process.

IV

The Fourteenth Amendment prohibits any state deprivation of life, liberty, or property without due process of law. Application of this prohibition requires the familiar two-stage analysis: We must first ask whether the asserted individual interests are encompassed within the Fourteenth Amendment's protection of "life, liberty or property"; if protected interests are implicated, we then must decide what procedures constitute "due process of law." *Morrissey v. Brewer*, 408 U.S., at 481; *Board of Regents v. Roth*, 408 U.S. 564, 569–572 (1972). See Friendly, Some Kind of Hearing, 123 U. Pa. L. Rev. 1267 (1975). Following that analysis here, we find that corporal punishment in public schools implicates a constitutionally protected liberty interest, but we hold that the traditional common-law remedies are fully adequate to afford due process.

A

....

The Due Process Clause of the Fifth Amendment, later incorporated into the Fourteenth, was intended to give Americans at least the protection against governmental power that they had enjoyed as Englishmen against the power of the Crown. The liberty preserved from deprivation without due process included the right "generally to enjoy those privileges long recognized at common law as essential to the orderly pursuit of happiness by free men." *Meyer v. Nebraska*, 262 U.S. 390, 399 (1923); see *Dent v. West Virginia*, 129 U.S. 114, 123–124 (1889). Among the historic liberties so protected was a right to be free from, and to obtain judicial relief for, unjustified intrusions on personal security.

While the contours of this historic liberty interest in the context of our federal system of government have not been defined precisely, they always have been thought to encompass freedom from bodily restraint and punishment. See *Rochin v. California*, 342 U.S. 165 (1952). It is fundamental that the state cannot hold and physically punish an individual except in accordance with due process of law.

This constitutionally protected liberty interest is at stake in this case. There is, of course, a de minimis level of imposition with which the Constitution is not concerned. But at least where school authorities, acting under color of state law, deliberately decide to punish a child for misconduct by restraining the child and inflicting appreciable physical pain, we hold that Fourteenth Amendment liberty interests are implicated.

B

"[The] question remains what process is due." *Morrissey v. Brewer, supra,* at 481. Were it not for the common-law privilege permitting teachers to inflict reasonable corporal punishment on children in their care, and the availability of the traditional remedies for abuse, the case for requiring advance procedural safeguards would be strong indeed. But here we deal with a punishment—paddling—within that tradition, and the question is whether the common-law remedies are adequate to afford due process.

. . . .

1

. . . .

The concept that reasonable corporal punishment in school is justifiable continues to be recognized in the laws of most States.... It represents "the balance struck by this country," *Poe v. Ullman,* 367 U.S. 497, 542 (1961) (Harlan, J., dissenting), between the child's interest in personal security and the traditional view that some limited corporal punishment may be necessary in the course of a child's education. Under that longstanding accommodation of interests, there can be no deprivation of substantive rights as long as disciplinary corporal punishment is within the limits of the common-law privilege.

This is not to say that the child's interest in procedural safeguards is insubstantial. The school disciplinary process is not "a totally accurate, unerring process, never mistaken and never unfair...." *Goss v. Lopez,* 419 U.S. 565, 579–580 (1975). In any deliberate infliction of corporal punishment on a child who is restrained for that purpose, there is some risk that the intrusion on the child's liberty will be unjustified and therefore unlawful. In these circumstances the child has a strong interest in procedural safeguards that minimize the risk of wrongful punishment and provide for the resolution of disputed questions of justification.

. . . .

2

Florida has continued to recognize, and indeed has strengthened by statute, the common-law right of a child not to be subjected to excessive corporal punishment in school. Under Florida law the teacher and principal of the school decide in the first instance whether corporal punishment is reasonably necessary under the circumstances in order to discipline a child who has misbehaved. But they must exercise prudence and restraint. For Florida has preserved the traditional judicial proceedings for determining whether the punishment was justified. If the punishment inflicted is later found to have been excessive—not reasonably believed at the time to be necessary for the child's discipline or training—the school authorities inflicting it may be held liable in damages to the child and, if malice is shown, they may be subject to criminal penalties.

Although students have testified in this case to specific instances of abuse, there is every reason to believe that such mistreatment is an aberration. The uncontradicted evidence suggests that corporal punishment in the Dade County schools was, "[w]ith the exception of a few cases, ... unremarkable in physical severity." Moreover, because paddlings are usually inflicted in response to conduct directly observed by teachers in their presence, the risk that a child will be paddled without cause is typically insignificant. In the ordinary case, a disciplinary paddling neither threatens seriously to violate any substantive rights nor condemns the child "to suffer grievous loss of any kind." *Anti-Fascist Comm. v. McGrath*, 341 U.S., at 168 (Frankfurter, J., concurring).

In those cases where severe punishment is contemplated, the available civil and criminal sanctions for abuse—considered in light of the openness of the school environment—afford significant protection against unjustified corporal punishment. Teachers and school authorities are unlikely to inflict corporal punishment unnecessarily or excessively when a possible consequence of doing so is the institution of civil or criminal proceedings against them.

....

V

Petitioners cannot prevail on either of the theories before us in this case. The Eighth Amendment's prohibition against cruel and unusual punishment is inapplicable to school paddlings, and the Fourteenth Amendment's requirement of procedural due process is satisfied by Florida's preservation of common-law constraints and remedies. We therefore agree with the Court of Appeals that petitioners' evidence affords no basis for injunctive relief, and that petitioners cannot recover damages on the basis of any Eighth Amendment or procedural due process violation.

Affirmed.

———————

Note the complex web of legal and social considerations faced by the South African court, below. In *Christian Education South Africa*, the plaintiffs are parents who wish, on religious grounds, to be allowed to send their children to a school where physical punishment will be part of the educational regime. They object strongly and persistently to the across-the-board ban on corporal punishment in school brought about by a South African legislative act of 1996.

Christian Education South Africa v. Minister of Education

(Case No CCT 4/00) Constitutional Court, South Africa,
2000 (4) SA 757 (CC)

INTRODUCTION

1. The central question in this matter is: when Parliament enacted a law to prohibit corporal punishment in schools, did it violate the rights of parents of children in independent schools who, in line with their religious convictions, had consented to its use?

2. The issue was triggered by the passage of the South African Schools Act (the Schools Act) in 1996 (Act 84 of 1996), § 0 of which provides:

'Prohibition of corporal punishment

(1) No person may administer corporal punishment at a school to a learner. (2) Any person who contravenes subsection (1) is guilty of an offence and liable on conviction to a sentence which could be imposed for assault.'

The appellant, a voluntary association, is an umbrella body of 196 independent Christian schools in South Africa with a total of approximately 14,500 pupils. Its parent body was originally established in the USA 'to promote evangelical Christian education' and the appellant has been operating in South Africa since 1983. It says that its member schools maintain an active Christian ethos and seek to provide to their learners an environment that is in keeping with their Christian faith. They aver that corporal correction — the term they use for corporal punishment — is an integral part of this ethos and that the blanket prohibition of its use in its schools invades their individual, parental and community rights freely to practise their religion.

3. When the Schools Act was being debated in Parliament, the appellant made submissions to the effect that the prohibition of corporal punishment violated its rights to freedom of religion and cultural life, as guaranteed in the then applicable interim constitution, but it failed to secure an exemption from the prohibition for its schools. After the Schools Act was adopted, the appellant sought direct access to this court for an order challenging its constitutionality. This application was refused on procedural grounds. The appellant then applied to the South-Eastern Cape Local Division of the High Court for an order declaring § 10 of the Schools Act unconstitutional and invalid in that it interferes with the right to freedom of religion and to cultural life to the extent that it prohibits corporal punishment in those independent schools. In the alternative the appellant sought to have § 10 declared unconstitutional and invalid to the extent that it prohibits corporal punishment in independent schools where parents have consented to its application. The appellant eventually abandoned its first claim and relied solely on the alternative claim.

4. The appellant cited the following verses in the Bible as requiring its community members to use 'corporal correction':

'Proverbs 22:6

Train up a child in the way it should go and when he is old he will not depart from it.

Proverbs 22:15

Foolishness is bound in the heart of a child, but the rod of correction shall drive it far from him.

Proverbs 19:18

Chasten thy son while there is hope and let not thy soul spare for his crying.

Proverbs 23:13–14

Do not withhold discipline from a child, if you punish with a rod he will not die. Punish him with a rod and save his soul from death.'

. . . .

It contends that corporal punishment is a vital aspect of Christian religion and that it is applied in the light of its biblical context using biblical guidelines which impose a responsibility on parents for the training of their children.

5. It has further claimed that according to the Christian faith, parents continue to comply with their biblical responsibility by delegating their authority to punish their children to the teachers. By signing a document entitled 'Consent to Corporal Punishment', they indicate that they understand corporal punishment to be inseparable from their understanding of their Christian faith and an expression of their religion. They further acknowledge that if they do not wish a child of theirs to be subjected to corporal punishment they are at liberty to remove such child from the school; otherwise they authorise the school to apply corporal correction. The correctional procedure to be followed includes giving the parents themselves the option to apply corporal punishment should they so

wish. Should such option not be exercised, the correction is to be applied in the form of five strokes given by the principal, or a person delegated by him, with a cane, ruler, strap or paddle. (The prescribed procedure is set out in the appellant's affidavit as follows: '(a) Know the offence. Investigate and get the facts. The child must deserve the punishment. Know without a doubt that it was intentional not careless. (b) Get a witness. Men give hidings to boys, ladies to girls and the witness should be the same sex as the child. (c) Discuss the offence. The child must know exactly what they did and why they are being punished. Give them the benefit of any doubt. (d) Get an admission. The child should admit to doing wrong. If you know the offence and the child will not admit it, he [sic] is dishonest and this compounds the offence. (e) Identify the biblical principle that has been violated. Identify a principle from scripture that has been violated by the child's behaviour. (f) Position the child, have them lean forward with feet spread apart. Put their hands on the desk. You want them to be stationery [sic]. You don't want to hurt the child. Discipline is one thing, damage is another. (g) Review the offence, discuss the seriousness of the offence and the objective in building character. (h) Love the child, smile and tell them that you love them. (i) Pray with the child and have the child pray first and ask for forgiveness then [sic] you pray for the child and for his/her growth. (j) Men should hug boys and ladies should hug the girls. Reaffirm your relationship with that child. When the child leaves they need to know that the slate is clean.')

6. While not doubting the sincerity of the appellant's beliefs, Liebenberg J in the High Court found that the scriptures relied on provided 'guidelines' to parents on the use of the rod, but did not sanction the delegation of that authority to teachers. He held that the authority to delegate to teachers was derived from the common law and the approach adopted by the appellant was merely 'to clothe rules of the common law in religious attire'. He held that in the circumstances it had not been established that administering corporal punishment at schools formed part of religious belief. The judge, however, decided that as it was a test case he should consider the other arguments raised by the appellants. He assumed for the purposes of those arguments that administering corporal punishment at schools concerned a serious religious belief. He concluded that § 10 of the Schools Act did not constitute a substantial burden on religious freedom. He also held that corporal punishment in schools infringed the children's right to dignity and security of the person and was accordingly not protected by s 31 of the constitution. He therefore dismissed the application.

7. The appellant applied for and was granted leave to appeal to this court on the grounds that the blanket prohibition in § 10 of the Schools Act infringes the following provisions of the constitution:

Section 14
Privacy

Everyone has the right to privacy …

Section 15
Freedom of religion, belief and opinion

(1) Everyone has the right to freedom of conscience, religion, thought, belief and opinion …

Section 29
Education …

(3) Everyone has the right to establish and maintain, at their own expense, independent educational institutions …

Section 30
Language and culture

Everyone has the right to use the language and to participate in the cultural life of their choice, but no one exercising these rights may do so in a manner inconsistent with any provision of the Bill of Rights.

Section 31
Cultural, religious and linguistic communities

(1) Persons belonging to a cultural, religious or linguistic community may not be denied the right, with other members of that community—(a) to enjoy their culture, practise their religion and use their language; and (b) to form, join and maintain cultural, religious and linguistic associations and other organs of civil society. (2) The rights in subsection (1) may not be exercised in a manner inconsistent with any provision of the Bill of Rights.

8. The respondent is the Minister of Education. He contends that it is the infliction of corporal punishment, not its prohibition, which infringes constitutional rights. More particularly, he contends that the claim of the appellant to be entitled to a special exemption to administer corporal punishment is inconsistent with the following provisions in the Bill of Rights:

Section 9
Equality

(1) Everyone is equal before the law and has the right to equal protection and benefit of the law ...

Section 10
Human dignity

Everyone has inherent dignity and the right to have their dignity respected and protected ...

Section 12
Freedom and security of the person

(1) Everyone has the right to freedom and security of the person, which includes the right ... (c) to be free from all forms of violence from either public or private sources; (d) not to be tortured in any way; and (e) not to be treated or punished in a cruel, inhuman or degrading way ...

Section 28
Children

(1) Every child has the right ... (d) to be protected from maltreatment, neglect, abuse or degradation

....

9. In an affidavit submitted on behalf of the respondent, the Director General of the Department of Education contends that corporal punishment in schools is contrary to the Bill of Rights. He points out that, in 1996, Parliament adopted the National Education Policy Act which, its preamble declared, was:

'... to facilitate the democratic transformation of the national system of education into one which serves the needs and interests of all the people of South Africa and upholds their fundamental rights.'

Section 3(4)(n) of that Act provides that the Minister of Education shall determine national policy for the—

'control and discipline of students at education institutions: Provided that no person shall administer corporal punishment, or subject a student to psychological or physical abuse at any education institution.'

10. The affidavit states that the Schools Act passed later that year provided a single framework for public and independent schools and learners, based upon the rights, freedoms and responsibilities inherent in the constitution, including the dignity and equality of all persons (see the preamble to the Schools Act). During the drafting process of the Schools Act, the respondent received support for the abolition of corporal punishment at schools from all the national student representative bodies, and the two largest national teacher unions. Although not accepted, the appellant's submissions on the Bill were indeed taken note of and seriously considered when Parliament consulted with interested parties during 1995 and 1996.

11. The affidavit avers further that the advent of the new constitution requires persons and groups to desist from practices which, according to their beliefs and traditions, may previously have been regarded as generally acceptable. In the past, public institutions had inflicted physical assaults upon citizens and other forms of abuse of their physical, emotional and psychological integrity. State policy and public practice had formerly permitted corporal punishment to be administered to children in schools, and also to juvenile and other offenders in prisons and other correctional institutions. In the light of the new constitutional order, state policy is now different.

12. According to the affidavit, corporal punishment is inherently violent, and involves a degrading assault upon the physical, emotional and psychological integrity of the person to whom it is administered. South Africans have suffered, and continue to suffer, a surfeit of violence. The state has an obligation to ensure that the learner's constitutional rights are protected. It has an interest in ensuring that education in all schools is conducted in accordance with the spirit, content and values of the constitution. The affidavit avers that corporal punishment is incompatible with human dignity....

13. Finally, the respondent states that the trend in democratic countries is to ban corporal punishment in schools. South Africa's international obligations under the Convention against Torture and Other Cruel, Inhuman or Degrading Treatment or Punishment, and the United Nations Convention on the Rights of the Child require the abolition of corporal punishment in schools, since it involves subjecting children to violence and degrading punishment....

14. The respondent indicates that he does not doubt the sincerity of the beliefs of the parents, nor does he dispute their right to practise their religion in association with each other. Furthermore he does not challenge the right of these parents to administer corporal punishment at home, even if he does not necessarily approve of it. He asserts, however, that such conduct is not appropriate in schools or the education system.

15. It is clear from the above that a multiplicity of intersecting constitutional values and interests are involved in the present matter—some overlapping, some competing. The parents have a general interest in living their lives in a community setting according to their religious beliefs, and a more specific interest in directing the education of their children. The child, who is at the centre of the inquiry, is probably a believer, and a member of a family and a participant in a religious community that seeks to enjoy such freedom. Yet the same child is also an individual person who may find himself 'at the other end of the stick', and as such be entitled to the protections of §§ 10, 12 and 28. Then, the broad community has an interest in reducing violence wherever possible and protecting children from harm. The overlap and tension between the different clusters of rights reflect them-

selves in contradictory assessments of how the central constitutional value of dignity is implicated. On the one hand, the dignity of the parents may be negatively affected when the state tells them how to bring up and discipline their children and limits the manner in which they may express their religious beliefs. The child who has grown up in the particular faith may regard the punishment, although hurtful, as designed to strengthen his character. On the other hand, the child is being subjected to what an outsider might regard as the indignity of suffering a painful and humiliating hiding deliberately inflicted on him in an institutional setting. Indeed, it would be unusual if the child did not have ambivalent emotions. It is in this complex factual and psychological setting that the matter must be decided.

....

JUSTIFICATION OF THE LIMITATION OF THE RIGHT TO RELIGIOUS FREEDOM AND RELIGIOUS COMMUNITY PRACTICE

....

30. Our Bill of Rights, through its limitations clause, expressly contemplates the use of a nuanced and context-sensitive form of balancing. Section 36 provides that:

'(1) The rights in the Bill of Rights may be limited only in terms of a law of general application to the extent that the limitation is reasonable and justifiable in an open and democratic society based on human dignity, equality and freedom, taking into account all relevant factors, including—(a) the nature of the right; (b) the importance of the purpose of the limitation; (c) the nature and extent of the limitation; (d) the relation between the limitation and its purpose; and (e) less restrictive means to achieve the purpose.'

31.

....

[L]imitations on constitutional rights can pass constitutional muster only if the court concludes that, considering the nature and importance of the right and the extent to which it is limited, such limitation is justified in relation to the purpose, importance and effect of the provision which results in this limitation, taking into account the availability of less restrictive means to achieve this purpose. Though there might be special problems attendant on undertaking the limitations analysis in respect of religious practices, the standard to be applied is the nuanced and contextual one required by § 36 and not the rigid one of strict scrutiny.

32. One further observation needs to be made, however. In the present matter it is clear that what is in issue is not so much whether a general prohibition on corporal punishment in schools can be justified, but whether the impact of such a prohibition on the religious beliefs and practices of the members of the appellant can be justified under the limitations test of § 36. More precisely, the proportionality exercise has to relate to whether the failure to accommodate the appellant's religious belief and practice by means of the exemption for which the appellant asked, can be accepted as reasonable and justifiable in an open and democratic society based on human dignity, freedom and equality.

33. Before setting out to apply the above approach to the facts of this case, I feel it necessary to comment generally on difficulties of proportionality analysis in the area of religious rights. The most complex problem is that the competing interests to be balanced belong to completely different conceptual and existential orders.... Religious conviction and practice are generally based on faith. Countervailing public or private concerns are usually not and are evaluated mainly according to their reasonableness.... To the extent that the two orders can be separated, with the religious being sovereign in its domain and

the state sovereign in its domain, the need to balance one interest against the other is avoided. However religion is not always merely a matter of private individual conscience or communal sectarian practice. Certain religious sects do turn their back on the world, but many major religions regard it as part of their spiritual vocation to be active in the broader society.... Not only do they proselytise through the media and in the public square, religious bodies play a large part in public life, through schools, hospitals and poverty relief. They command ethical behaviour from their members and bear witness to the exercise of power by state and private agencies; they promote music, art and theatre; they provide halls for community activities, and conduct a great variety of social activities for their members and the general public. They are part of the fabric of public life, and constitute active elements of the diverse and pluralistic nation contemplated by the constitution. Religion is not just a question of belief or doctrine. It is part of a way of life, of a people's temper and culture.

34. The result is that religious and secular activities are, for purposes of balancing, frequently as difficult to disentangle from a conceptual point of view as they are to separate in day to day practice. While certain aspects may clearly be said to belong to the citizen's Caesar and others to the believer's God, there is a vast area of overlap and inter-penetration between the two. It is in this area that balancing becomes doubly difficult, first because of the problems of weighing considerations of faith against those of reason, and secondly because of the problems of separating out what aspects of an activity are religious and protected by the Bill of Rights and what are secular and open to regulation in the ordinary way.

35. The answer cannot be found by seeking to categorise all practices as religious, and hence governed by the factors relied upon by the appellant, or secular, and therefore controlled by the factors advanced by the respondent (see paras 7–13, above). They are often simultaneously both. Nor can it always be secured by defining it either as private or else as public, when here, too, it is frequently both. The underlying problem in any open and democratic society based on human dignity, equality and freedom in which conscientious and religious freedom has to be regarded with appropriate seriousness, is how far such democracy can and must go in allowing members of religious communities to define for themselves which laws they will obey and which not....

(b) The nature of the rights and the scope of their limitation

36. There can be no doubt that the right to freedom of religion, belief and opinion in the open and democratic society contemplated by the constitution is important.... The right to believe or not to believe, and to act or not to act according to his or her beliefs or non-beliefs, is one of the key ingredients of any person's dignity. Yet freedom of religion goes beyond protecting the inviolability of the individual conscience. For many believers, their relationship with God or creation (not all religions are deistic) is central to all their activities. It concerns their capacity to relate in an intensely meaningful fashion to their sense of themselves, their community and their universe. For millions in all walks of life, religion provides support and nurture and a framework for individual and social stability and growth. Religious belief has the capacity to awake concepts of self-worth and human dignity which form the cornerstone of human rights. It affects the believer's view of society and founds the distinction between right and wrong. It expresses itself in the affirmation and continuity of powerful traditions that frequently have an ancient character transcending historical epochs and national boundaries.

37. As far as the members of the appellant are concerned, what is at stake is not merely a question of convenience or comfort, but an intensely held sense about what constitutes

the good and proper life and their place in creation. No one in this matter contested that the appellant's members sincerely believe that parents are obliged by scriptural injunction to use corporal correction as an integral part of the upbringing of their children. Furthermore, it has set up independent schools with the specific purpose of enabling parents to have their children educated in what they regard as a true Christian ethos. The impact of § 10 of the Schools Act on their religious and parental practices is, in their view, far from trivial.

38. Yet, while they may no longer authorise teachers to apply corporal punishment in their name pursuant to their beliefs, parents are not being deprived by the Schools Act of their general right and capacity to bring up their children according to their Christian beliefs. The effect of the Schools Act is limited merely to preventing them from empowering the schools to administer corporal punishment.

(c) The purpose, importance and effect of the limitation, and the availability of less restrictive means

39. The respondent has established that the prohibition of corporal punishment is part and parcel of a national programme to transform the education system to bring it into line with the letter and spirit of the constitution. The creation of uniform norms and standards for all schools, whether public or independent, is crucial for educational development. A coherent and principled system of discipline is integral to such development.

40. The state is further under a constitutional duty to take steps to help diminish the amount of public and private violence in society generally and to protect all people and especially children from maltreatment, abuse or degradation....

41. Courts throughout the world have shown special solicitude for protecting children from what they have regarded as the potentially injurious consequences of their parents' religious practices. It is now widely accepted that in every matter concerning the child, the child's best interests must be of paramount importance.

....

[The Court here cites to the U.S. Supreme Court in the *Prince v. Massachusetts* case, to the effect that the rights of freedom of religion and of parenthood may sometimes be limited by the state, when the child's wellbeing is at stake.]

42. The respondent contended that, in line with the above considerations, the state had two powerful interests in the matter. The first was to uphold the principle of equality. It contended that to affirm the existence of a special exemption in favour of religious practices of certain children only, would be to violate the equality provisions contained in § 9 of the Bill of Rights. More particularly, it would involve treating some children differently from others on grounds of their religion or the type of school they attended. I think this approach misinterprets the equality provisions. It is true that to single out a member of a religious community for disadvantageous treatment would, on the face of it, constitute unfair discrimination against that community. The contrary, however, does not hold. To grant respect to sincerely held religious views of a community and make an exception from a general law to accommodate them, would not be unfair to anyone else who did not hold those views....

43. The second and more persuasive argument is to the effect that the state has an interest in protecting pupils from degradation and indignity. The respondent contended that the trend in Europe and neighbouring African countries was firmly in the direction of abolition of corporal punishment, and that the core value of human dignity in our Bill of Rights did not countenance the use of physical force to achieve scholarly correc-

tion. Accordingly, respondent was under an obligation to prohibit such punishment, and to do so without exception and for the benefit of all children. The appellant replied that for believers, including the children involved, the indignity and degradation lay not in the punishment, but in the defiance of the scriptures represented by leaving the misdeeds unpunished; subjectively, for those who shared the religious outlook of the community, no indignity at all was involved. It argued further that internationally there was widespread judicial support for the view that physical punishment only became degrading when it passed a certain degree of severity.... [The Court here discusses the approach to corporal punishment taken by the European Court of Human Rights.] The appellant would be bound by limits set by the common law, and these limits would establish the standards to be applied. It did not contend that corporal punishment should be permitted in all schools, but asserted that its use should be allowed within reasonable limits in independent schools where parents, out of their religious convictions, had authorised it. The state interest, accordingly, did not extend to protecting the children in the appellant's schools.

....

45. Similarly, although not called upon to decide the constitutionality of corporal punishment meted out to school children, Dumbutshena CJ in *S v. a Juvenile* 1990 (4) SA 151 at 161, nonetheless indicated that he would agree with the dissenting opinion of Mr Klecker in the European Commission of Human Rights decision in *Campbell v. UK* (1980) 3 EHRR 531 at 556:

'Corporal punishment amounts to a total lack of respect for the human being; it therefore cannot depend on the age of the human being ... The sum total of adverse effects, whether actual or potential, produced by corporal punishment on the mental and moral development of a child is enough, as I see it, to describe it as degrading within the meaning of Article 3 of the Convention.'

....

47.... [T]he trend in southern Africa has been strongly in favour of regarding corporal punishment in schools as in itself violatory of the dignity of the child. At the same time, they do indicate that the issue is subject to controversy, and in particular, that the express delegation of consent by the parents might have a bearing on the extent of the state interest....

48. The present matter does not oblige us to decide whether corporal correction by parents in the home, if moderately applied, would amount to a form of violence from a private source. Whether or not the common law has to be developed (under § 8(3) of the constitution) so as further to regulate or even prohibit caning in the home, is not an issue before us. The Schools Act does not purport to reach the home or practices in the home.

....

PROPORTIONALITY ANALYSIS

50. The measure was part and parcel of a legislative scheme designed to establish uniform educational standards for the country. Educational systems of a racist and grossly unequal character and operating according to a multiplicity of norms in a variety of fragmented institutions, had to be integrated into one broad educational dispensation. Parliament wished to make a radical break with an authoritarian past.... As part of its pedagogical mission, the department sought to introduce new principles of learning in terms of which problems were solved through reason rather than force. In order to put the child at the centre of the school and to protect the learner from physical and emotional

abuse, the legislature prescribed a blanket ban on corporal punishment. In its judgement, which was directly influenced by its constitutional obligations, general prohibition rather than supervised regulation of the practice was required. The ban was part of a comprehensive process of eliminating state-sanctioned use of physical force as a method of punishment. The outlawing of physical punishment in the school accordingly represented more than a pragmatic attempt to deal with disciplinary problems in a new way. It had a principled and symbolic function, manifestly intended to promote respect for the dignity and physical and emotional integrity of all children. It might in appropriate cases be easier to carve out exemptions from general measures that are purely administrative, regulatory or commercial in character than from those that have principled foundations and are deliberately designed to transform national civic consciousness in a major way.... Even a few examples of authorised corporal punishment in an institution functioning in the public sphere would do more than simply inconvenience the state or put it to extra expense. The whole symbolic, moral and pedagogical purpose of the measure would be disturbed, and the state's compliance with its duty to protect people from violence would be undermined. There is a further factor of considerable practical importance. It relates to the difficulty of monitoring the administration of corporal punishment. It will inevitably be administered with different force at different institutions, or by different teachers, and there is always the possibility that it will be excessive. Children are put in a very vulnerable situation because they (and their parents possibly) can only complain about excessive punishment at the risk of angering the school or the community.

51. I do not wish to be understood as underestimating in any way the very special meaning that corporal correction in school has for the self-definition and ethos of the religious community in question. Yet their schools of necessity function in the public domain so as to prepare their learners for life in the broader society. Just as it is not unduly burdensome to oblige them to accommodate themselves as schools to secular norms regarding health and safety, payment of rates and taxes, planning permissions and fair labour practices, and just as they are obliged to respect national examination standards, so is it not unreasonable to expect them to make suitable adaptations to non-discriminatory laws that impact on their codes of discipline. The parents are not being obliged to make an absolute and strenuous choice between obeying a law of the land or following their conscience. They can do both simultaneously. What they are prevented from doing is to authorise teachers, acting in their name and on school premises, to fulfil what they regard as their conscientious and biblically-ordained responsibilities for the guidance of their children. Similarly, save for this one aspect, the appellant's schools are not prevented from maintaining their specific Christian ethos.

52. When all these factors are weighed together, the scales come down firmly in favour of upholding the generality of the law in the face of the appellant's claim for a constitutionally compelled exemption. The appeal is accordingly dismissed. No order for costs was asked for and none is made.

ORDER

The appeal is dismissed.

Notes and Questions

1. How does the South African court weigh the religious interest in this case? Does the court give any hint as to what the result might be if national law forbade corporal punishment in the home, and parents challenged that law on religious grounds? In the unlikely event that the United States adopted a federal law banning corporal punishment

in all schools, and were parents of children in religious schools, and/or the schools them-selves, to challenge such a law on the basis of freedom of religion, how would the U.S. Supreme Court react?

C. Changing an Educational Culture: The Case of Kenya

The Human Rights Watch Report immediately following, written in the late 1990s, shows the degree to which corporal punishment of a severe kind was endemic in the ed-ucational system of Kenya. Yet, despite social divisions on this point, and despite the prominent place occupied by caning in school discipline, the notes and questions that follow this Human Rights Watch report indicate that corporal punishment can be successfully outlawed, even under such circumstances. Given the reliance on corporal punishment by teachers across the Kenyan educational spectrum, it is a tribute to the growing global consensus on the deleterious effects of violence against children that Kenya would have been moved to enact a blanket ban on these practices in the schools.

Human Rights Watch, *Spare the Child: Corporal Punishment in Kenyan Schools*

September 1999, *available at* http://www.hrw.org/reports/1999/kenya/

. . . .

Historical and Cultural Context

Various forms of corporal punishment (and other punishments like manual labor) have a long pedigree in Kenya. Many Kenyans told Human Rights Watch that physical chastisement has long been accepted in Kenyan homes. The Kenyan government school system arose in the days of British colonial government, and adopted nineteenth-century British traditions of school discipline, including the widespread use of the cane.

Most adult Kenyans were caned frequently when they were children, and many Kenyans believe firmly in the validity of the Biblical precept, "Spare the rod and spoil the child." A high level of domestic violence against women and children is a constant concern for Kenyan rights groups, and school corporal punishment occurs in this context. One primary school headteacher told Human Rights Watch firmly that violence is "what the African child understands, and women too. They have to be beaten."

Although most Kenyans we met told Human Rights Watch that corporal punishment should never be so severe as to cause lasting injury to a child, few of those interviewed perceived corporal punishment as a human rights issue, or even as a major cause for con-cern. This is changing, as several Kenyan rights groups have added corporal punishment to their advocacy agendas, and as newspapers like the Daily Nation have begun a con-certed effort to investigate and report on cases of severe beatings in schools. Likewise, top officials in the Kenyan Ministry of Education, including the minister himself, have begun to focus increased attention on children's rights issues, singling out corporal punishment as an area of particular concern.

Nonetheless, awareness of the problems associated with corporal punishment is low, and children, parents, or teachers who complain about corporal punishment still run a serious risk of facing ridicule or retaliation. This causes most to remain silent except in the face of particularly appalling abuses.

School corporal punishment in Kenya has a high degree of cultural acceptance, even approval. Although some teachers inflict severe forms of corporal punishment on students out of deliberate cruelty, probably the great majority of teachers genuinely intend to "educate" children by caning or whipping them. To the extent that children are seriously injured, many Kenyans are willing to write such incidents off as tragic exceptions in a generally acceptable system, the result of the occasional sadistic teacher or of unfortunate but unavoidable accidents. Some teachers dismissed abuses by noting that serious injuries usually occurred only if a student disobediently thrust out an arm to ward off the cane, and thus ended up with a broken wrist or similar injury. This was viewed as the equivalent of a self-inflicted injury. Others said that authorities should not hold teachers responsible for injuring or killing children who had preexisting medical conditions that made them particularly susceptible to physical punishment, because other students could have withstood the abuse.

. . . .

CORPORAL PUNISHMENT IN KENYAN SCHOOLS

Caning

Caning is the only form of corporal punishment permitted by the Kenyan Ministry of Education's regulations, and visits to Kenyan schools by Human Rights Watch suggest that caning is by far the most common kind of corporal punishment. As discussed in the earlier background sections of this report, caning is strictly regulated by Kenyan law. Corporal punishment is reserved for the most serious disciplinary infractions; no more than six strokes may be given, and only by or in the presence of the headteacher; a full inquiry must have been conducted before corporal punishment is administered; a written record must be kept; and children can only be hit on the buttocks or the palm, and not in the presence of other children.

As noted, despite the regulations permitting corporal punishment, the Ministry of Education has sent mixed messages as to whether teachers should cane at all. Although the 1972 regulations allow corporal punishment under particular circumstances, the reported Director's statement of 1996 was touted as prohibiting the practice as a matter of policy.

Nonetheless, our research indicates that caning is regularly imposed, and it is often administered in a manner inconsistent with the regulations. In most schools, virtually every classroom teacher has a cane, and uses it. In many schools, teachers routinely carry canes with them, or have them easily accessible in their classrooms; canes lean against the walls in many headteachers' offices, and adorn teachers' desks in some classrooms.

. . . .

Frequency of Caning

The reported frequency of caning varied considerably from school to school. At some schools, caning was relatively rare, and reserved for serious infractions; students might witness a caning once a week, or even as rarely as once a month. At most other schools, however, schoolchildren reported that students in their class might be caned every day, sometimes more than once.

. . . .

Reasons for Caning

Teachers caned students for a wide range of infractions, some serious, some extraordinarily minor. As reasons for punishment, students, teachers and head teachers frequently cited tardiness, making noise or talking in class, truancy or absenteeism, bullying, fighting, stealing, disobedience or rudeness, and leaving the classroom or school when the teacher is away. Less frequent grounds for punishment include selling or using drugs, smoking cigarettes, jumping on tables, not paying attention or falling asleep in class, and using profanity. A Standard Two boy told us that all the Standard One through Three students had once been caned for "spoiling the toilet."

Failure to complete homework and not being prepared for class were other common reasons for punishment. Other behavior that was sometimes cause for punishment included "wearing an improper uniform," having an "unkempt appearance" or being "dirty," and "failure to clean the classroom in the morning."

. . . .

At many schools, children also told us that they are caned for speaking in their native language. Kenyan public schools teach primarily in English (the official language), and at times in Kiswahili (the national language), but most Kenyans speak a local tribal language, such as Kikuyu or Kalenjin, as their first language.

Caning, sometimes accompanied by hitting, slapping, and other forms of violence, was widely used to punish children for academic problems such as poor exam performance. Margaret M., an eleven-year-old student at an elite primary school in Coast Province, told us, "Sometimes when you answer a question wrong you are beaten . . ." "In the mathematics class, there's a lot of caning," said Ethel A., a fifteen-year-old pupil at a another primary school in Coast Province. Elizabeth B. told us "[If] you are given a test and you fall below the average, you may be beaten. Carol T., a fifteen-year-old enrolled in yet another primary school in Coast Province, said, "When it is time of failing the exams, every teacher of the subject canes you."

. . . .

Number of Strokes

The severity of punishments also varied greatly, and many children viewed the number of strokes as somewhat arbitrary: while most children agreed that the more serious the infraction, the higher the number of strokes, the most important factor seemed to be the "harshness" of the particular teacher. A gentle teacher might cane rarely, and give only a few light strokes even for relatively serious offenses, while a harsh teacher might routinely administer six or more heavy strokes.

A particularly harsh teacher, some children told us, might even hit harder or administer more strokes to a child who cried when hit. In a way, expressing pain is viewed as an act of further disobedience, an expression of a child's unwillingness to silently accept punishment. Susan S., fifteen, a student at a poor rural primary school in Central Province, told us, "If you are beaten very hard, sometimes you cry, and then they are angry and beat you harder still." James E., a boy at a suburban Central Province primary school, reported, "There are some that when you cry, they hit you more. There are some that try to make you hurt." Phillip T., his classmate, agreed: "You may cry. They hit you again if you move or if you cry. Mary F., a ten-year-old attending an elite primary school in Coast Province, told us, "sometimes if the teacher has punished you, you may start crying, and she adds more strokes."

. . . .

Public Caning

For the most part, children are caned in front of their classmates, although in a few cases children reported that they were typically taken to the staff room to be caned. At some schools, students were caned in front of the entire school, during school assemblies or parades. As Janet K. from Coast Province told us, "if you did a very serious mistake ... you will be beaten by the headmistress before the whole school." An eighteen-year-old student at an urban secondary school in Central Province said to us, "In Kenya, [corporal punishment] has ... become conventional law or something. You can find students hit ten, twenty, or thirty times, in the classroom, which means you are very humiliated.... The humiliation is the worst. In some cases, they use iodine on the cane so that you do not get an infection if the cane breaks the skin."

. . . .

Parts of the Body Hit

The regulations governing corporal punishment also state that children may only be hit on the buttocks, if a cane is used, or on the palm, if a strap is used. In practice, we found that boys were mostly caned on the backside, and girls were mostly caned on the palm or back of the hand. Nonetheless, several teachers and headteachers openly acknowledged that they hit children on other parts of the body, as well, and children at schools throughout Kenya reported that at times they are hit on the back, the calf muscles, the soles of the feet, the toes, the shoulders, the front and back of the thighs, the knees, and even on the face and head.

. . . .

Other Forms of Corporal Punishment

Although caning is the only form of corporal punishment in Kenya permitted under the Education (School Discipline) Regulations, many children told Human Rights Watch that at times they are slapped, pinched, hit, whipped or kicked by their teachers. Teachers and headteachers also acknowledged that such "unofficial" punishments are used at times.

After caning, slapping was the most commonly reported form of school corporal punishment. Children recalled being slapped on the face, the head, the back, and on "every part" of the body. Slapping was considered by some to be less severe than caning: "sometimes also they slap in the face, but that is a less serious punishment."

Many students also reported that teachers pinched them, and one at primary school in Rift Valley Province explained that they were pinched on the cheeks. Fifteen-year-old Carol T. from Coast Province reported being elbowed in the back by her teachers, and in several cases children said that the teachers "boxed" and "hit" in addition to slapping. One teacher told us that she sometimes punished students by "snatching," which she described as grabbing the students.

Whipping is also not infrequent as a form of corporal punishment. A deputy headteacher at Mirera Primary school in Naivasha told us that "even this morning I had to punish eighty students" by whipping them. He showed a Human Rights Watch researcher the whip, which was made of heavy rubber, cut from a car tire. The whip was about three feet long and three inches wide, and he demonstrated its use by slamming it down on his desk. At an urban secondary school in Central Province, a whip adorned the headteacher's desk, and several students told us that the headteacher both whipped and caned to punish students. In Nyanza Province, Harold D., eighteen, reported being whipped with a garden hose, and in Coast Province, Maryanne P., fifteen, told us that she had been whipped with a length of rope.

....

Resulting Physical Injuries, Including Deaths

Much corporal punishment in Kenyan schools is inflicted by well-meaning teachers who were taught no other means of maintaining classroom discipline and promoting academic performance. For the most part, there is little reason to doubt that most teachers administer corporal punishment in a manner that seems to them to be fair, reasonable, and pedagogically valuable. Nonetheless, when the use of corporal punishment becomes an acceptable and regular part of the teaching process, severe injuries and abuses inevitably occur.

First, accidents happen: a stroke of the cane aimed at a child's backside may inadvertently strike another part of the body—the head or the kidneys, for instance—causing severe injuries. Similarly, some children have medical conditions that render them vulnerable to serious injuries from strokes of the cane that would not seriously injure another child: a child with a heart or lung condition, for instance, may faint or even die out of a combination of pain and fear.

Second, when corporal punishment is permitted, there is virtually no way to prevent some teachers from inflicting corporal punishment in a fashion that is sadistic, cruel, and intended to cause grievous injury. At virtually every one of the twenty Kenyan schools visited by Human Rights Watch, it was clear from interviews with children that some teachers, at least, inflicted corporal punishment in a disproportionate, arbitrary, and cruel manner.

....

CONCLUSION

....

Many nations throughout the world have recognized that school corporal punishment violates the provisions of the U.N. Convention on the Rights of the Child, and constitutes a cruel, inhuman, or degrading practice. Recognizing this, many nations have ended the practice of school corporal punishment, and aggressively sought to train teachers in alternative means of maintaining discipline and motivating children.

Kenya's children are its future, and there is no excuse for permitting another generation of children to be subjected to violence in the name of education. The Kenyan government and the Kenyan educational community should take immediate and strong action to eliminate corporal punishment and other forms of cruel, inhuman or degrading treatment in schools.

Notes and Questions

1. Even a country like Kenya, where physical punishment was integral to the educational process, was able to enact a total ban on corporal chastisement in schools. See David Aduda, *Minister outlaws caning in schools,* Daily Nation, Nairobi, April 1, 2001, available at http://www.corpun.com/kes00104.htm#7165. The article explains that the Kenyan education minister issued an order to the effect that corporal punishment in the schools was to end completely as of that time. Interestingly, the article makes note of the fact that Kenya had been under intense international scrutiny for the pervasiveness of corporal punishment as a means of maintaining discipline in schools. Obviously, the attention

was unwelcome, and Kenya was eager to join the mainstream of nations in its approach to teachers striking students.

Several years later, a secondary school teacher, Nicholas Kaloki Kasolya, filed a lawsuit to attempt to have the new law changed. It appears that he brought his action in order to bring attention to what he called the breakdown of discipline within Kenya, decrying this overreaching by the education minister. In a further irony, Kasolya complained that the introduction of free compulsory education led to massive class sizes, a situation in which lack of discipline was a very serious matter. See Bob Odalo, *Why Teacher Backs Caning in Schools,* Daily Nation (Nairobi), April 5, 2006, available at http://www.corpun.com/kes00604.htm.

2. What kind of pressure do you think Kenya was reacting to? Given the division of opinion that undoubtedly remains within the country, is it likely that the ban will be widely enforced over the long term?

D. The State and the Family: From Non-Intervention to Absolute Bans on Corporal Punishment

The following article describes the range of possible approaches to corporal punishment, seen in terms of degrees of state intervention in the life of the family; more particularly, intervention in the disciplinary techniques relied on by parents. Benjamin Shmueli takes a comparative and historical view of the problem, and ultimately advocates for an international middle ground that can accommodate the needs of parents, children and societies in general.

Benjamin Shmueli, *Who's Afraid of Banning Corporal Punishment? A Comparative View on Current and Desirable Models*
26 Pennsylvania State International Law Review 57 (Summer 2007)

I. Foreword

Who's afraid of banning corporal punishment of children?

The use of corporal punishment for the education of a child is one of the most loaded, difficult, and disputed questions among jurists, psychologists, sociologists and educators and, indeed, the general public. Modern approaches hold that the use of corporal punishment should be prohibited because of the physical and emotional damage it causes, its inefficiency, and because if the conduct reaches the point of an assault, the parent is not to be granted protection. Other approaches provide otherwise, namely, that if corporal punishment is administered moderately and with due composure, it is not harmful and could even be useful in setting boundaries for children.

. . . .

How does the law in different countries treat corporal punishment? In most countries of the world, corporal punishment is permitted so long as it is moderate and reasonable. Some sixteen countries, mostly in Europe, have prohibited by law, in one form or another, the use of corporal punishment for the education of children. In about ten of these countries, the prohibition was passed between 1998 and 2006. In most countries, the prohibition was enacted into legislation, while a few countries prohibited corporal punishment through a ruling of the Supreme Court. A small number of countries enacted the prohibition into criminal law. Most countries, however, enacted the prohibition as a human right of children not to be exposed to physical punishment, specifically as a matter of civil law through Family Acts and the like.

....

II. Two Dominant Approaches in Parent/Child Relationships and their Impact on Shaping Legal Models

In modern society, unequivocal attitudes are being heard more and more against the use of parental behaviors that harm children, even if allegedly undertaken for the interest of children, but inflict damage on them in different plains and different ranges, harm their self-respect, and are contrary to justice and equality. The behaviors are also ineffective and the harm they cause can exceed their benefit. Unlike the traditional view of society, the individualistic approach views the individual in the family unit per se and not solely the family as a whole. The individualistic approach aspires to seeing the child as an independent entity for almost all purposes, even at the expense of gnawing at the parents' authority, despite the natural inequality inherent in the structure of the classic family unit, at the center of which are "strong" parents and "weak" children. This approach follows from the human rights approach. If the actions of the parents hurt the child, the individualistic approach holds that the parents should be restricted, even when acting for the benefit of the child and out of a positive educational motive. In other words, there is an attempt to shake free from traditional paternalistic approaches, which leave to the parents the decision as to what is in the interest of their child, even if such is done apparently in the name of a positive goal of forging children as independent entities who know boundaries and learn to accept discipline and values, and also if the injury is mild, not serious.

....

III. The Prevailing Legal Models: Description and Critiques

A. The Minimal Legal Intervention Model: Roman Law

The first model presented is one of minimal legal intervention in parent/child relationships that will be illustrated by Roman law. This system of law espoused a minimal to zero legal intervention in the acts of parents vis-à-vis their children, even if the acts were very grave. Roman rule invested most of its efforts in public management, including international and inter-religious relations, paving roads, and constructing bath-houses and houses of pleasure, but did not view itself as able and willing to handle and arrange the small daily issues of every family unit throughout the empire. Roman rule left the internal management of each family in the hands of the father of the family, virtually undisturbed: "The Rule of the Father" (Patria Potestas).

Because of its weakness and limitations, which did not permit it to deal with family affairs, the Roman government decided to leave extensive powers to the father of the family. Fathers had almost total control over their children, which continued beyond their reaching maturity and even after their marriage. Except in rare cases, fathers enjoyed both extensive ownership over their children and non-intervention of the government in their deeds vis-à-vis members of their families. Injuries to children through violence (or neglect) were not amongst those rare cases and so did not merit legal recognition, leaving fathers unexposed to sanctions.

....

B. The Moderate Legal Intervention Model: Reservations for License — English, American, and Canadian Law

According to this intermediate model, the moderate legal intervention model, the state does indeed have to intervene in parent/child relationships and not leave it to Patria Potestas and the like. However, such intervention must not be absolute. The law has to provide balances between the individual approach and the family approach and permit corporal punishment with certain reservations, but not in any instance and at any price. The law has to understand that parental activity to educate children is important and its wings should not be clipped. At the same time, the law must not ignore children's rights, lest the parents misuse their dominant status. The rule underlying this model, therefore, is the dynamism of the family unit, but is restricted (unlike the minimum intervention model) by the rights of the child.

Moderate and reasonable corporal punishment in the family framework is permitted in most countries of the world. Such is the situation in the countries of North America, South America, Africa, New Zealand, and most of Europe. In some of these countries, a general section has been enacted permitting light corporal punishment. In other countries, mainly the common law states, the permit for parents to use corporal punishment on their children is slightly more detailed (in court rulings or legislation) and contains the foundations of being moderate and reasonable in the use of force. In other countries, however, this is even more detailed or explicit in judicial decisions which have delineated it and specified what the actual parameters are that comprise these foundations.

This model leads to creating a special orientation for the family, which while not being as extreme as the Patria Potestas, nevertheless takes into account the importance of not putting the brakes on the dynamic of the family unit in consequence of exaggerated legal intervention. The understanding that a massive reduction of parental authority would hurt the family, and that this authority is not to be sacrificed on the altar of children's rights, is a proper understanding. The application of this model, however, is problematic. The focus will be on a number of legal systems that have adopted moderate intervention in the matter: English law, American law, and Canadian law.

. . . .

The American Model Penal Code, which serves as a basis for penal legislation in many United States jurisdictions, permits parents to use corporal punishment vis-à-vis children so long as the force is applied for the purpose of "promoting the welfare of the minor" and the force is not exaggerated. Sixteen states in the United States have legislation explicitly permitting corporal punishment in the family unit, while judgments of the courts in other states permit corporal punishment. Corporal punishment is not prohibited in any United States jurisdiction.

The law permitting corporal punishment also revolves around reasonableness, moderation, and necessity, which are all requirements specifically for an educational purpose in a form that recalls the path of English law. Among the restraints enumerated in the different states, one can find the preparedness of the child to accept the punishment, the age of the child, the physical and mental state of the child, and the force and necessity of its use. In some of those states, it is emphasized that the purpose of the restraints is to differentiate between corporal punishment and child abuse or any other cruel or inhumane conduct. In foster families, however, corporal punishment has been prohibited in the majority of United States jurisdictions.

The confusion and uncertainty in many of the states are great. For example, a court in Florida noted that it is very difficult to draw the line between light corporal punishment which is permitted and child abuse which is, of course, prohibited. Bitensky justifiably criticizes the existing law because in various United States jurisdictions, if a child is beaten and the beating leaves no marks on their body, it can be assumed that the parent will be acquitted. It is no wonder that the vast majority of the American public still supports educational spanking in the family unit and very high percentages of those asked in surveys point to support for this method and actual use of it. For example, research has indicated that ninety percent of parents in the United States justify the use of corporal punishment for the sake of educating their children, while eighty-five percent of them would prefer not to utilize this method if they had some other reliable and effective method. At the same time, other research indicates a decrease in support for this phenomenon in recent years.

. . . .

There is room to critique the moderate legal intervention model, although in principal it constitutes an appropriate legal balance between the family and individualistic approaches. American, English, and Canadian law represent legal systems that provide a certain defense to parents who have adopted physical punishment for the education of children. Canadian law chose to set an explicit permit for corporal punishment, as an exception to the general prohibition of hitting, but this permit is qualified with various reservations. The reservations mirror the restraints pointed out by scholars in social science literature supporting the family approach.

. . . .

C. The Strict-Penal Legal Intervention Model: Criminal Ban — Israeli and Cypriot Law

The strict-penal legal intervention model intensively intrudes in parent/child relationships, which is to a large extent an outcome of the individualistic approach that makes allowances mainly for the rights of the child.

. . . .

The strict-penal legal intervention model will be demonstrated by way of two legal systems that have adopted penal intervention, the most sweeping form of legal intervention. Israeli law, which is relatively young, has clearly switched to the model of strict-penal intervention. The criminal prohibition imposed on corporal punishment by the Israeli Supreme Court, as it will be seen below, also has ramifications for the interpretation of earlier legislative measures on different judicial levels. Details of the various implications for existing legislation will point to the impact, which is often most problematic. Cypriot law has also prohibited corporal punishment through criminal law. Unlike Israel, this prohibition was made in orderly legislation accompanied by a public campaign to inculcate the norm. The importance of these differences will be examined below.

. . . .

Israeli law, which banned corporal punishment in a penal court judgment that constitutes a binding precedent, will be examined first. Israel is a common law country. The Supreme Court, whose rulings are law, and therefore constitute binding precedent, has recently and clearly eaten away at the right and authority of parents in favor of the rights of children because it has almost totally forbidden the use of corporal punishment of children. At first, corporal punishment was forbidden in the educational system and later expanded to the framework of the family unit. Thus, after almost fifty years, the legal situation addressing corporal punishment changed following the 1953 decision of *Rassi*, a criminal judgment that permitted the use of corporal punishment in the family unit and, with certain reservations, in the educational system. Arguing that it was a matter of lacuna, this ruling relied on English law and was based, inter alia, on agency relationships between parent and teacher, who is in loco parentis, for the purpose of the child's education. The Supreme Court ruled that parents and educators may impose physical punishments on their children in order to educate them in the right way but such is to be done with great caution, for the sake of education alone, and not for the satisfaction of any lust for revenge, in accordance with the principles of proportionality and reasonableness as distinct from acts of cruelty and abuse. Rassi constitutes an example of moderate legal intervention, with the law leaving parents with discretion whether to adopt corporal punishment so long as it is reasonable and moderate, in a way similar to the English and American law. Rassi constituted binding and guiding penal case law for decades. Section 24(7) of the Torts Civil Wrongs Ordinance in Israel sets forth a defense against a legal action for the civil tort of battery for parents and teachers who used moderate and reasonable force for the education of the child.

....

In January 2000, a judgment was given in *Plonit*. This case involved a mother accused of frequently hitting her two small children on various occasions and on different parts of their bodies with various objects and, in effect, turning them into her servants or slaves. The children were harshly beaten by her when they did not do her bidding. The mother admitted some of the acts, did not express regret over them, and claimed that although she adopted an educational path which differed from what was usual, this was done for the sake of educating the children to be obedient and disciplined. In the appeal, written by Justice Dorit Beinish with which the President, Aharon Barak, concurred, the majority opined that the acts fell into the category of battery and physical abuse. The court sentenced the mother to a period of probation and a suspended prison sentence, but not actual imprisonment.

....

Through her comments, Justice Beinish also supports the requirement of examining the legitimacy of the methods of education in accordance with changes in societal values. In her opinion, attitudes that were correct at the time of the Rassi judgment have changed and are no longer relevant. Nowadays, the use of corporal punishment as a way of education is outdated. The source of this argument is not clear. Are the Israeli and non-Israeli public, its judges and scholars, really of the opinion that there is no longer a place for such a method of education and that it should be thoroughly condemned? That this was the situation is most doubtful, mainly in view of some schools that continued to make their presence felt into the end of the 1990s, and in light of the legal systems in many countries where moderate and reasonable corporal punishment is still permissible. Also representing the ongoing life of corporal punishment is the view in social science disciplines of the familial approach, which still exists. Thus, Justice Beinish, in effect, revokes the Rassi judgment in all matters dealing with the family. The Plonit decision is the binding ruling in Israel today on the issue of corporal punishment in the family unit. The lower courts are bound by this judgment of the Supreme Court, which is binding on every court except the Supreme Court itself.

....

Justice Beinish … calls for reliance on the discretion of the prosecution not to press charges in the absence of any public interest. In her opinion, these reservations on criminal liability express a fitting distinction between the use of force by parents for unacceptable and prohibited purposes and the reasonable use of force intended to prevent harm to the child himself or to others, or to maintain order. According to Justice Beinish, there are sufficient and proper filters through which no criminal liability will be imposed on a parent in instances of little value that do not justify enforcement in the framework of the penal laws. This, however, is surprising in view of her extensive explanation about corporal punishment being harmful to the child and the importance of prohibiting it, even where it is a matter of a light punishment.

Can the de minimis defense be used in a case of light corporal punishment? In my opinion, it is difficult to see such a result after the unequivocal judgment in the *Plonit* case and the statement that no corporal punishment is permissible. If light, moderate and reasonable corporal punishment nevertheless fits into the de minimis defense, then there is an internal contradiction in the *Plonit* judgment, because all corporal punishment is forbidden. Hence, the only way that this defense could be upheld would be in those cases of light but firm contact with the body of the child for the sake of retaining order, although Justice Beinish certainly referred to two different defenses. Moreover, as noted above, the boundaries of those cases of "light but firm contact" are altogether unclear from what she says. The defense is fuzzy and its application, therefore, problematic. Apparently, there is no alternative but to construe the two defenses that have arisen here as a matter of the amount of the force used and its proportionality, reasonableness, and nothing more than that, although such was not Justice Beinish's purpose. Such an interpretation will, of course, remove the ground from under the sweeping renewal of the *Plonit* judgment.

Justice Beinish also recognized prosecutorial discretion as a defense. Such defense places the onus on the prosecutorial authorities not to take to trial cases of light corporal punishment. With all due respect, this is not a defense because it refers to a process preceding the pressing of charges. In view of the forceful determinations in the *Plonit* case, it is not clear to what extent the prosecutorial authorities will decide not to press charges in cases of light corporal punishment. That is to say, in a situation in which case law explicitly determines that light corporal punishment is an outmoded educational method and is nowadays prohibited, with a clear statement that this also includes light corporal punishment, one should not be surprised if the main points of the *Plonit* judgment are literally internalized by the prosecutorial authorities. This possibility, together with the element of an edict with which the public is unable to comply, will result in a change of the status quo and a mass pressing of charges with respect to corporal punishment. It may be noted that some criticize the very granting of such extensive discretion to the prosecutorial authorities.

The true test of the *Plonit* judgment could actually be whether the prosecution and enforcement authorities and the Courts relate, in light of the new situation, to a parent who inflicted light, moderate and reasonable corporal punishment on their child. Pressing charges, particularly after use of temporary remedies, could destroy the family ...

....

Cypriot Law took a different path of penal prohibition in legislation. This is neither a prohibition through court ruling nor civil legislation, as will be seen below in the law of some other European countries. Section 7(1) of the Cypriot Constitution grants every child a right to life and dignity, and this section also impacted the situation regarding corporal punishment in Cyprus as it did in Israel.

In 1994, the Cypriot legislature enacted the Prevention of Violence in the Family and Protection of Victims Law. This law prohibited any form of corporal punishment by a parent or other caretaker and the punishment for it was an increased fine or imprisonment. In 2000, this law was replaced with a new law, Law 119(I), the Law which Provides for the Prevention of Violence in the Family and Protection of Victims. This law is part of the Cyprus Criminal Code. The innovations it contains against its predecessor mainly concern victims' testimonial matters of domestic violence. The law determines that, "[f]or purposes of this Law, violence means any unlawful act, omission or behavior which results in the direct infliction of physical, sexual or mental injury to any member of the family by another member of the family."

. . . .

There are two main problems with the application of the strict-penal intervention model. One is the negative incentive for a parent not to educate and discipline his children if he knows that using light corporal punishment could result in charges against him and possibly destroy his family. The other problem is the intrusion of the law into the family by way, specifically of the penal law, with all its ramifications, particularly in the pointed fashion made in Israel. The judgment in *Plonit* has overly sweeping repercussions on all subsequent judgments, but the danger is also and mainly in extreme and unbalanced interpretations of the previous legislation. The judgment unequivocally decided in fact that the right of parents to educate their children as they see fit, recognized more than once in case law, takes a back seat, according to the new interpretation, to any injury, even the slightest and even for educational purposes, to the body of a child. Interpretation in accordance with that sweeping prohibition results in parents who punish their children with light corporal punishment being exposed to the operation of temporary criminal and other (such as detention or restraint) remedies against them which exist in each country and could be used against parents. As noted, mandated reporting exists with respect to everyone in Israel like in many United States jurisdictions. The detention could be either an investigative detention or detention until completion of proceedings. In addition, a restraining order against approaching the home could be imposed. The incidence of these remedies could be in certain cases for days, weeks, or even months.

The opening up of all these processes could derive from an overly literal use of mandated reporting on offenses of domestic violence, both by professionals that treat the family and by the general public. Thus, not only the basic rights of the parent might be prejudiced, to which thought should also be given, but first and foremost, the damage is to the whole family

. . . .

It is true scholars point out that several years is too short a time to examine the extent of the prohibition's acceptance and assimilation among the public, since this has to be examined over many years. Already now, as noted, one can point to a great problem, at least theoretically, particularly for the Israeli method. Thus, strict-penal intervention, mainly through a judgment without any preparatory educational campaign readying the soil, is unsuitable for the unique nature of the family unit and the desire to give it some autonomy, albeit delineated and limited, and to permit it a certain internal dynamic without outside interference. The model relates to the rights of the individual, i.e. the child, as to those of any other individuals, and this, in principle, is only right. However, it does so often, without a necessary sideways glance to the child's place in a family unit. The intention of this model is certainly desirable, but its actions are problematic because it goes much too far and does not foresee the possible damage to the family unit and the various ramifications in the spheres of law and society. One cannot view parent/child relationships only through an individualistic approach at the center of which is an individual versus an individual. Family considerations also have to be taken into account....

. . . .

D. The Civil-Rights Legal Intervention Model: Gap Between Sweeping Declaration and Moderate Enforcement—Several European Countries

In order to create an opening for a principled legal attitude with the purpose of educating the public in stages and in a way that will create empathy for a judgment or legislation forbidding corporal punishment and lead towards an edict with which the public is able to comply and to fill it with content, there is possibly room to adopt a rationale of a structured gap between a sweeping declaration and moderate enforcement. This approach will be able to create a gap between a clear declaration, consistent with the individualistic approach and with strict-penal legal intervention, and moderate enforcement. The latter means light punishment for the parent or even his non-conviction in mild cases, as follows from the family approach and from moderate legal intervention ...

....

Sweden was the first Scandinavian country and apparently of the World to prohibit corporal punishment in legislation. Corporal punishment had been accepted as a way of education in Sweden, as in most countries of the world mainly in order to drive or beat the devil out of the child. This resulted in many cases of child abuse. However, in 1949, Sweden enacted the New Parental and Guardianship Code. This code limited parental rights to administer physical punishment and determined that such was reprehensible. Even if it was not a matter of an effective remedy, it can be assumed that, for that period, this was a revolutionary law. In 1958, Sweden prohibited corporal punishment in schools and in 1969, repealed the penal defense against the battery offense for parents who hit their children for their education and caused light injuries. In 1979, the 1949 law, a civil rather than penal law, was amended in the parliament by a vast majority of 250 yeas with only 6 nays, in the wake of a public committee on behalf of the parliament. The current formulation, after a further amendment in 1983, provides that: "[c]hildren ... are to be treated with respect to their person and individuality and may not be subjected to physical punishment or any other humiliating treatment."

....

Germany has perhaps the most impressive method, even if theoretically, for handling the issue of corporal punishment. Corporal punishment in the German educational system is subject to resolution in the sixteen federal states that comprise Germany. With respect to the family unit, various attempts to pass legislation that would forbid corporal punishment began in the 1980s. In 1998, however, the legislature prohibited any form of demeaning punishment, including physical and psychological abuse, but no prohibition had yet been legislated against corporal punishment. Scholars have construed the law such that it does not apply to corporal punishment so long as it is administered in response to an act of the child and does not go beyond an educational purpose. Here too, the new situation has created confusion for the public and it was not known exactly what was allowed and what was forbidden. The lack of clarity ended in 2000 with the legislation of a civil statute, which declares that, "[c]hildren have the right to be brought up without the use of force. Physical punishment, the causing of psychological harm and other degrading measures are forbidden." One defense, non-punitive physical contact, exists. An, example of non-punitive physical contact is the act of saving a child from some form of danger such as running into the street or possessing matches.

The German government and private bodies also greatly invested in a public education campaign. The campaign included placing large posters on the streets, leaflets for distribution at clinics and other public sites, the distribution of an explanatory booklet about the development of children by social workers, and monthly distributions on the development of children and ways to avoid corporal punishment for parents, from birth until the child reaches the age of five years. Teachers further speak about the prohibition in all classes.

There is also a dispute in Germany between scholars as to whether a parent can be charged with corporal punishment through various penal sections or whether these sections only apply with respect to levels of gravity and intensity that go beyond mild punishment. An argument also exists on the question of whether a criminal defense allowing parents to punish their children in general terms and that applied to corporal punishment prior to the explicit prohibition of 2000, still applies now so long as the punishment is moderate, reasonable, and intended for educational purposes. There are those who argue that the forbidden punishment is specifically punishment that hurts, is dangerous, harmful to health, and immoral because it is destructive for the education of children.

. . . .

That being so, the revolution, led by Sweden, has clearly impacted other European countries. As stated by Bitensky, "[i]t only stands to reason that people need to be aware of a law before they can obey and/or internalize it." This path seems sensible since it understands that judicial force is problematic in the education of the public and it believes in the power of declarative educational legislation through civil family laws, integrated fully with education and advertising in order to inculcate the new norm.

However, is the civil rights legal intervention model compatible for every modern society and legal system? The answer to this question is not simple. The civil rights model proves that the existing and the desirable can be drawn together under a single roof in the form of creating a certain gap between declaration and enforcement. This is a smart interim solution between strict-penal intervention focusing on the individual and seemingly not taking the family unit as a whole into account, and moderate intervention which makes the correct balances but "sins" in an overly paternalistic overview which does not explicitly state the importance of children's rights. Unlike the moderate legal intervention model, the civil rights model indeed opts to focus on children's rights, rather than sanctions for parents. The civil-rights legal intervention model contributes to making up the missing parts of the intervention puzzle in parent/child relationships.

Should the Scandinavian model be adopted in every country and is it worth doing so or does this model still require proof as to its suitability? Are we looking at a unique model that is suitable locally for certain countries only, in accordance with the composition of the population, the stability of the government and so on? There are those who support this model as a universal solution and hold that, through a not entirely legal (and certainly not a penal law) method of an educational campaign pointing to alternatives to corporal punishment, parents can be motivated to change their ways, and the law will not be able to influence with the same force. This approach can be agreed with in principle, but the method of Scandinavian law should be examined in depth, from the decision to introduce reforms to the successful completion of the task.

. . . .

IV. Integrated Model Proposal

. . . .

B. The Integrated Model—A Collection of Proposals for a Solution

1. An Educational Publicity Campaign

Law is not a magic wand that creates miracles of metamorphosis overnight. When evaluating the effects of the 1979 ban (in Sweden B.S.) in particular, one should be mindful that even its twenty-five-years tenure is not that long a time for profoundly entrenched, nationwide attitudes and practices to undergo extensive modification.

How true this is, particularly with respect to countries such as Israel and Cyprus where the process did not take decades as in Sweden. Unlike Finland, the Israeli public was not prepared to accept the prohibition. In Finland the parliament set about enacting a law after a survey that showed the majority of the public wished to have such a law. It was also accepted in the penal law and, as noted, in Israeli law by the judiciary and not through legislation.

Psychologist Alice Miller explicitly calls on all countries of the world to prohibit corporal punishment but not for social condemnation of parents, rather for the education of the public and inculcation of the matter into the public awareness through the use of legal tools. This would seem to be an explicit plea for strict-penal legal intervention, but it is tantamount to a recommendation to the legislature to think in different directions and create a gap between a declaration and enforcement of the law. The purpose of thinking outside the box is, first and foremost, to educate the public and implement actual enforcement on the criminal level.

. . . .

As mentioned, the civil-rights model attributes special importance to ground work in educating the public, but not only through the law. It is recommended to use a publicity campaign while attempting to inculcate the prohibition into law. Such a campaign was undertaken by the Ministry of Justice in Sweden and other countries. This shows that a certain space is possible for mild corporal punishment in terms of not pressing criminal charges against the parent, and at the same time explaining to the public why corporal punishment is unacceptable and should not be used to educate children, what damage it causes and the proposed alternatives. Many parents would be surprised to know there are other systems of education, no less effective than corporal punishment and less harmful. The law can participate in the process with statements in judgments (for example, by pointing out in an obiter dictum what is desirable) and by justices giving lectures and writing articles on the subject. The legal norm should be inculcated gradually from an understanding that norms really cannot be changed overnight even with a binding rule from the Supreme Court or legislation.

Some creativity can be shown in solution proposals including lectures, written information material, information material broadcast by radio and television, advertising on consumer products, information material on Internet sites, mailing of information material to homes, free training courses or at a low, subsidized price, advanced study courses and training of new parents as a condition for receipt of the maternity grant.

. . . .

The strict-penal intervention model would seem to have reversed the order and gone immediately to the stage of sweeping legal prohibition. However, it is still important that information be disseminated even in those countries which have already accepted a legal prohibition on corporal punishment if such prohibition has not yet been assimilated amongst the population and no decline in the phenomenon can be noted.

2. Achievement of Social Consent through Postponing Implementation of the New Norm

Another sophisticated way to inculcate the norms into society, which could be suitable for each society contemporaneously with the educational campaign, is to obtain social consent regarding the undesirability of certain parental conduct by postponing the date for implementation of the new legal norm. It has been suggested that a prohibition on corporal punishment, and other parental conduct, be determined but that the law states that the prohibition will come into force some time later, say after two years.

Apart from these suggestions (and not in their stead), it can be said that the law creates a gap not only between legislation of the norm and the date on which it will come into effect, but also between the declarative nature of the norm and its actual enforcement, even if only for the interim period before the new norm becomes operative....

3. Creation of a Reasonable Gap Between Sweeping Declaration and Moderate Enforcement

....

If declarative legislation causes parents to fear being indicted the legislation has served its purpose. But one has to be careful and exercise caution not only over excessive enforcement, such as with the strict-penal intervention model, but also over excessive forgiveness in cases where there is no justification for such. When severe punishment has to be administered, such should be done without concern or fear, lest there be no deterrence and matters remain at a declarative level only. How can the prosecutorial authorities and the courts know which cases necessitate enforcement of the sweeping declaration? General sections of law do not suffice. The determination relies on a list of guiding criteria....

V. Conclusion

....

Corporal punishment is a classic example of the question of the impact of social changes on the law and society. Should the law not take a daring step forward because it does not find support for such a step in public sentiment, for example, in the United States and seemingly also in England, or should the law opt to try and change the reality and go forth as a vanguard before the camp through civil-human rights statutes and with a public-social campaign to introduce the norm, as is done in Scandinavia and other countries in Europe, or in a severe manner as was done in Cyprus through criminal legislation and in Israel through criminal court rulings.

This Article integrates advantages from existing models with some new concepts. As far as possible the proposal safeguards the rights of the child without seriously harming the nuclear family. The Article moves cautiously between two poles, with one rejecting intervention and proposing leaving the family dynamic as is, and the other supporting massive intervention because of the damage to the rights of the child, all from an understanding that legal intrusion into the family has to be intelligent both in nature and in scope....

Notes and Questions

1. Shmueli makes an extraordinary effort to take into account all aspects of the corporal punishment problem, and devise a nuanced approach for countries to follow. Is he successful in this, or is his article too equivocal for practical application? He makes the point that "A dispute in the family cannot be treated as a dispute between two strangers." Does a doctrinaire children's rights perspective on physical punishment tend to do just that? Which end of the spectrum appears to worry Shmueli the most: a too lenient or too strict and legalistic approach? He is clearly seeking a blended set of guidelines, but are societies capable of such hybrid methods on emotive questions like corporal punishment?

IV. Juvenile Justice —
Children in Conflict with the Law

A. International Principles and Social Realities

There are relatively well developed international principles intended to guide state behaviour towards juvenile offenders caught up in national criminal justice systems. Arising from the "era of the child" that led to the promulgation of the UNCRC, the United Nations Minimum Rules for the Administration of Juvenile Justice (the "Beijing Rules")[4] of 1985 and the United Nations Guidelines for the Prevention of Juvenile Delinquency (the "Riyadh Guidelines")[5] of 1990 establish comprehensive, if broad, norms for the disposition of young criminal defendants. The UNCRC also devotes certain articles to the articulation of similar ideas of protective and humane conditions of police custody for juveniles. Sadly, though, for the many thousands of children who find themselves on the outside of protective family and educational structures, states often act with both harshness and impunity, despite the existence of these principles. Because the population of affected children is often the same, there is clear overlap between the sections of this book dealing with children on their own and street children, and the following readings on juvenile justice issues.

The objective in providing the excerpts below is to introduce the reader to the evolution of modern ideas on the fair and humane treatment of children who come into contact with the juvenile justice system; that is, ideas on the correct understanding of juvenile culpability and responsibility, and on the requirement of a separate track in the legal system to reflect awareness of the child's need for special protection. At least on paper, consensus has been reached on governmental responsibility to ensure that children, whatever crimes they may have committed, are nonetheless perceived of and treated as children, a class of persons deserving of special consideration.

The Geraldine Van Bueren article excerpted below provides an overview of the emerging consensus on how children in custody should be treated. It also notes that the United States is in many ways out of step with developments at the international level, resistant to an otherwise discernible international trend. We have seen throughout this book that the United States often insists on its own version of children's rights, and consequently its own unique constitutional concepts, rejecting attempts to frame questions of rights in *international* human rights terms. It could be said that the U.S. is unusually firm in its desire to "go it alone" when it comes to the rights of children.

Because the population of children in custody anywhere in the world is likely to be drawn from the most disadvantaged social groups, the juvenile justice area may be one in which there is a striking gap between rhetoric and reality. Are children without family connections or economic resources likely to receive the special consideration and protection of the state? How do most societies feel about youthful offenders?

---

4. United Nations Standard Minimum Rules for the Administration of Juvenile Justice, G.A. Res. 40/33, U.N. GAOR, 40th Sess., Supp. No. 53, U.N. Doc. A/40/53 (Nov. 29, 1985).

5. United Nations Guidelines for the Prevention of Juvenile Delinquency, G.A. Res. 45/112, U.N. Doc. A/Res/45/112 (Dec. 14, 1990) available at http://www.un.org/documents/ga/res/45/a45r112.htm.

Geraldine Van Bueren, *A Curious Case of Isolationism: America and International Child Criminal Justice*
18 Quinnipiac Law Review 451 (1999)

I. A QUIET REVOLUTION

Since the 1980s there has been a quiet revolution spreading through the world of child criminal justice. It has spread globally as far as Australia and New Zealand in the South Pacific, Canada and Costa Rica in the Americas, Ghana, South Africa and Uganda in Africa, and Bangladesh is currently considering reform. What is strange is that in the United States of America, the country which proudly instituted one of the world's first juvenile courts, children have been left stranded behind.

One of the reasons for America's isolationism is its determination to remain one of only two countries in the world which have not become party to the United Nations Convention on the Rights of the Child—the first global treaty protecting children's rights. The other country is America's traditional ally—Somalia. Hence America is simply not party to many of the discussions on the development of child criminal justice and the quiet revolution taking place.

The advantage of the Convention is that, as a human rights treaty, it removes the debate about child criminal justice from the bitter sphere of party politics and places the discussions and campaigns firmly in the arena of legal commitments which a country is under a binding duty to implement. Hence, in the 191 countries bound by the Convention on the Rights of the Child, the provisions of child criminal justice are taken out of party politics and instead are used by campaigners to help shape the political debate, particularly when drafting bills of rights and children's statutes.

. . . .

II. THE BENEFITS OF USING A HUMAN RIGHTS APPROACH

The international laws on child criminal justice also act as powerful but peaceful catalysts for change. The Convention on the Rights of the Child takes the argument beyond who should have priority, children or society. The international law is clear—the best interests of the child indicate that children have priority and it is through prioritizing children that society benefits. According to the United Nations Standard Minimum Rules for the Administration of Juvenile Justice, known as the Beijing Rules, Rule 1.4 recommends that child criminal justice should "be conceived as an integral part of the national development process of each country." It is no longer permissible under international law to place child criminal justice at "the bottom of the pile" of resource allocation. States are under an immediate legal duty to ensure that children's civil, economic, social, and cultural rights in child criminal justice are fully protected, and this can only be done if sufficient resources are allocated for all stages of the justice system, not only in court proceedings but also in prevention and detention. A well resourced child criminal justice system, operated in accordance with international law, should not be regarded as a drain on national resources but ought to be perceived as one facet of national development. According to international law, a well resourced child criminal justice system is in society's interests, as it reduces the risk of reoffending. The Convention calls for the establishment of a child-oriented system recognizing the child as the holder of rights and freedoms and stressing the need for all actions in child criminal justice to be guided by Article 5 of the Convention, which provides that the best interests of the child should be a primary consideration. Indeed the United Nations Committee on the Rights of the Child, the body entrusted with implementing the Convention, criticized Mongolia because Mongolian legislation ranked the recovery and reintegration of children as only the third goal behind the protection of society and the punishment of the child.

One of the attractions of the international law on child criminal justice is that it requires a psychological shift for society. International law now merges what were once the punishment and rehabilitation functions of juvenile justice with the service provision and protections of child welfare. The trend is changing fundamental perceptions, and much of child criminal justice is governed by the same principles as child protection. This is a unified child rights approach, which is the same for the civil and the criminal justice fields. This is even reflected in the legislation of some states, such as Uganda, which has only one children's statute governing both areas of justice. It is also reflected in the return, albeit with modification, of indigenous values and approaches such as the creation of Family Group Conferencing developed from Maori traditions in New Zealand, which places child criminal justice within the family unit. Family Group Conferencing in New Zealand is a very different approach to punitive penalties for parenting.

The international laws on child criminal justice have also been used by states when drafting their constitutions. The 1996 South African Constitution cites word-for-word provisions from the Convention on the Rights of the Child in relation to detention. Hence the international laws on child criminal justice have helped inspire legislative reform and innovative and creative thinking. This has not only occurred at the legislative and judicial level. More and more personnel throughout the world, including social workers, child rights personnel, detention personnel, judges, lawyers, police, policy makers and probation officers are being trained in how to apply these international principles. The United Nations is currently printing a manual on child criminal justice so that these international laws can be used as a training tool.

There is still a long way to go, but the Convention on the Rights of the Child has operated as a very effective catalyst.

III. THE INTERNATIONAL FRAMEWORK

Because of this new approach to child criminal justice, states wanted more detail and guidance than could be incorporated into a treaty such as the Convention on the Rights of the Child. States were receptive to drafting new detailed rules applying and developing these principles in practice. The first set of rules focus on prevention, and despite the appalling titles, the United Nations Guidelines for the Prevention of Juvenile Delinquency 1990 ("The Riyadh Guidelines") contain much progressive and practical detail.

The Riyadh Guidelines focus on early protection and preventive intervention paying particular attention to children in situations of "social risk," children "who are demonstrably endangered and in need of non-punitive measures because of the effects of their circumstances and situation on health, safety, education … and it is this concept which underpins the Guidelines." Social risk can be produced by factors related to the inherent characteristics of children such as mental disabilities, by the relationship between the child and the family, and the socioeconomic circumstances in which the child lives. In many cases children at social risk are affected by the interplay of all of these factors; the more adverse the factors, the greater the chance that the child will drift towards delinquent activities.

The Guidelines recommend that states pay particular attention to the children of families who are affected by rapid or uneven economic and social change. Such change can disrupt the child rearing and nurturing capacity of families, and states are recommended to design innovative and socially constructive modes for these children's integration. In particular, the Guidelines recommend that prevention programs should give priority to children who are at risk through being abandoned, neglected, exploited and abused.

The advantage of a social risk approach is that it places emphasis on social and personal factors, and changes the focus of intervention previously concerned with defining morality to confronting directly the issues while allowing society to tolerate a degree of youthful deviance.

. . . .

The Riyadh Guidelines also recommend to states that children should have an active role and partnership within society. The standards recommend that children should be accepted by states as "full and equal partners" in the integration process, and should be entitled to participate in crime prevention policies. The participation of children in the formulation and implementation of prevention policies will assist both in making the policies relevant and in reducing the risk of indoctrination. Providing the children's participation is effective, it also ought to make such policies more attractive.

The standards recognize that if a state labels a child as a delinquent or deviant, the labeling can unwittingly contribute to a child's anti-social behavior. Youthful behavior does not always conform to social norms and can often disappear with the transition into adulthood. The Guidelines aim at preventing the stigmatization and marginalization of children whose behavior does not conform to prevailing social norms not only through the avoidance of labeling, but also by recommending a wide range of measures including recommendations to the media and the abolition of status offenses. However, the Guidelines also recognize that there is the risk that the identification of a child as being at social risk may become a self-fulfilling form of stigmatization.

The underlying principle of the Riyadh Guidelines is that the prevention of child crime should utilize both the child's family and the school. The Guidelines recommend that states develop community based interventions and programs to assist in the prevention of child crime. The intervention of institutions or agencies should only be utilized as "a means of last resort." The Guidelines' principal aim is to help socialize and integrate children through the family and through the active involvement and support of the community.

Following on from the Riyadh Guidelines are The Beijing Rules. They provide a framework within which a national child criminal justice system should operate and a model for states of a fair and humane response to children who may find themselves in conflict with the law. The Beijing Rules, which are divided into six parts, cover the whole range of the child justice processes: General Principles; Investigation and Prosecution; Adjudication and Disposition; Non-institutional treatment; Institutional Treatment and Research and Planning; Policy Formulation; and Evaluation.

The Beijing Rules are gender sensitive and advocate the fair treatment of girls drawing states' attention to research, which demonstrates that girls are more harshly treated and are more vulnerable to sexual assault in custody by predominately male personnel. The Beijing Rules require gender specific facilities and services. The rules also call for trained and professional personnel, inter-agency coordination and the use of research as a basis for program development, evaluation of policy and decision-making.

The Beijing Rules place much emphasis on diversion. The desirability of diverting children away from formal trial procedures is another principle which is incorporated into the Convention on the Rights of the Child. Diversions are one aspect of promoting the child's sense of well-being, as it avoids the negative effects of child justice proceedings, including the stigma of conviction and sentence. Diversions may be used at any stage and are not necessarily limited to minor offenses. Therefore, they have great potential and practical scope. In one sense, however, the term "diversion" is misleading as children are not diverted away from the legal system itself but merely from its more formal aspects.

. . . .

These standards have now been reinforced by Article 40(3)(b) of the Convention on the Rights of the Child, which places states parties under a duty to seek to promote "[w]henever appropriate and desirable, measures for dealing with such children without resorting to judicial proceedings, providing that human rights and legal safeguards are fully respected."

. . . .

Where separate systems of justice are established they should still be in conformity with international human rights law. The Convention on the Rights of the Child places a duty on states parties to maintain a balance between the informality of proceedings and the protection of the fundamental rights of the child. Regardless of whether law enforcement officials are in specific child institutions or not, the Beijing Rules recommend that all law officials who come into contact with children should "avoid harm to her or him with due regard to the circumstances of the case." In defining the avoidance of harm the commentary specifically cites as examples "the use of harsh language, physical violence or exposure to the environment." The Beijing Rules prohibition of "harm" is broader than the customary prohibition of torture, cruel, inhuman and degrading treatment and punishment. Both the Beijing Rules and the Convention on the Rights of the Child are based on the principle that any involvement in the child criminal justice system can be "harmful" per se, even though, as the commentary points out, compassion and kind firmness ought to be important elements in any such process.

Another principle fundamental to the administration of justice is that of speed. Although the international law on the administration of child criminal justice does not expressly place a duty on states to take account of a child's sense of time, Article 10(2)(b) of the International Covenant on Civil and Political Rights provides for juveniles to be brought "as speedily as possible" to adjudication. The United States is equally bound by this article. This is reinforced by Rule 20 of the Beijing Rules recommending that each case from the outset should be handled, "expeditiously without any unnecessary delay." There is an element of repetition in the phrasing of Rule 20, and this serves to emphasize that speed is consistent with the best interests of the child. The phraseology of both instruments appears to indicate that the well-being of the child is consistent with issues being decided at a pace, which is over and above that which is generally applicable to adults.

. . . .

The Beijing Rules, although aimed at the protection of the rights of children in the administration of justice, were never intended to provide a thorough, systematic and practical approach to the conditions under which children could be deprived of liberty. The United Nations Standard Minimum Rules for the Protection of Juveniles Deprived of Their Liberty apply to all children deprived of their liberty in any situation including child welfare institutions. They set out principles, which universally define the specific circumstances under which children can be deprived of their liberty, emphasizing that deprivation of liberty is a means of last resort. The rules also specify the conditions under which a child may be detained, which are consistent with respecting children's human rights.

Article 37(b) of the Convention on the Rights of the Child enshrines for the first time in binding international law, "[t]he arrest, detention or imprisonment of a child ... shall be used only ... for the shortest appropriate period of time." A provision which has been cited word for word in section 28 of the Constitution of South Africa 1996. The duty on states parties to impose arrest, detention and imprisonment on children for the shortest appropriate period of time applies to both pre-and post-trial detention. In relation to adults, this limitation is only applicable to pre-trial detention and hence the new international law creates a higher standard for children. Rule 13.1 of the Beijing Rules also recommends that detention pending trial should only be used for "the shortest possible period of time" and that Rule 19.1 recommends the placement of a child in an institution should always be "a disposition of the last resort" and for the "minimum necessary period."

It is because of the rule that states are under a duty to impose imprisonment only for the shortest appropriate period of time that states parties to the Convention on the Rights of the Child are expressly prohibited from imposing sentences of life imprisonment without the possibility of release. Sentences of life imprisonment without the possibility of release do not fulfill the criteria of the shortest appropriate period of time. In addition, the objective of reintegration is regarded as so fundamental to the deprivation of children's liberty that the rules seek to incorporate this objective into all aspects of the children's lives. Rule 29 recommends that the number of children detained in closed detention facilities should be sufficiently small to enable individualized treatment, and the detention facilities should be integrated into the social, economic and cultural environment of the community.

According to the rules, the design of the detention facilities should also be in keeping with the "rehabilitative aim of residential treatment" and states are recommended to pay attention to children's need for privacy, sensory stimuli, sport and leisure, and opportunities for peer association. Specific aspects of the child's dignity and right to privacy are highlighted including the right "to the extent possible" for children to wear their own clothing and retain possession of their personal effects.

Throughout the rules there is an emphasis on the child's continuing access to the community and the community's access to the child. Hence the rules recommend that opportunities to perform remunerated labor, as a complement to vocational training, should, if possible, be in the local community. The rules also recommend that competent authorities should assist in both re-establishing the children in society and in lessening the prejudice against them.

Under Article 37(c) of the Convention on the Rights of the Child, all children who are deprived of their liberty are entitled throughout their period of deprivation of liberty to be treated "with humanity and respect for the inherent dignity of the human person, and in a manner which takes into account the needs of persons of their age." The right to be treated with humanity and with respect for the dignity of the human person is a common standard applicable to adults and children, which is also enshrined in Article 10(1) of the International Covenant on Civil and Political Rights. According to the Human Rights Committee, it is a "basic standard of universal application which cannot depend entirely on material resources." The Convention on the Rights of the Child adds a new element. For the children of states parties deprived of their liberty, account has to be taken of the needs of their age. This is another application of the concept of the evolving capacities of the child incorporated as an umbrella principle in the Convention.

The Convention expressly highlights two aspects of respect for the child's humanity and dignity: the separation of child detainees from adult detainees, unless it is not in the best interest of the child, and the right of the child to maintain contact with his or her family. It achieves this by linking all three concepts, dignity, family contacts and separation in the same article.

The rules go beyond implicitly recognizing the negative effects of deprivations of liberty. They recommend that states should counteract these detrimental effects on children and should recognize that the care of children deprived of their liberty is a "social service of great importance" requiring the fostering of contacts between the child and the community.

Importantly, the rules apply to anyone under the age of eighteen. They therefore have the advantage of applying to all individuals under eighteen years of age who are deprived of their liberty, without any reference to national definitions of childhood and without being dependent upon the jurisdiction of special proceedings. Even if children are not tried by a special child hearing the deprivation of liberty rules apply.

. . . .

IV. USING INTERNATIONAL CHILD CRIMINAL JUSTICE IN AMERICAN COURTS

So how can the international law be used in the United States when it is not party to the Convention? First of all, even though the treaty itself is not binding on the United States, some of the principles in it and in the child criminal justice rules have become binding. As with some of the provisions of the Universal Declaration of Human Rights, they have evolved into principles of international customary law through consent, history and usage.

. . . .

The Convention on the Rights of the Child focuses states' attention on children as victims of crime, an aspect of criminal justice which with the demonization of children in some countries, is often overlooked. Article 39 obliges all states parties to take appropriate measures to promote "physical and psychological recovery and social reintegration" for child victims of abuse, neglect, torture, cruel, inhuman and degrading treatment and punishment. Such recovery and reintegration services ought to occur in an environment which fosters the health, self-respect, and dignity of the child.

The principle of non-discrimination under Article 2 is also applicable to the child criminal justice system. In particular, the committee has noted discrimination against socially and economically disadvantaged children. In relation to Bolivia, the United Nations Committee on the Rights of the Child recommended that alternatives to institutional care for economically and socially disadvantaged children should be created.

Governments have been, and will continue to be, criticized in relation to child criminal justice but still they remain part of the treaty system. Admittedly some states become party to human rights treaties for cynical reasons; remaining party to a human rights treaty helps conceptualize states as pro-human rights and it is therefore more beneficial when seeking aid and trade. Some states, however, genuinely value their children above a narrow sense of national pride and regard scrutiny by the United Nations Committee on the Rights of Child as a part of a continuing dialogue on how to improve their society for children.

. . . .

V. CHILDREN NOT JUVENILES

There is even beginning to be a shift away from the use of the term juvenile. The United Nations Programme of Action is not on juvenile justice but on children in the criminal justice system. If as Rorty and others argue, experience is shaped by language, then the adoption and use of the term juvenile justice by a number of English speaking jurisdictions also has to be queried. Because of international legal developments, the time has come to question the rationale behind describing a young person in conflict with the law as a juvenile offender, while a person under age eighteen in need of state protection is described in terms of child welfare. It is as if an inappropriate judgmental layer is added which makes it harder to argue against the more punitive suggestions being made in the American Counter Reformation. When adults breach the law they are simply adult offenders. Similarly, when those under age eighteen offend they should be referred to as child offenders without the need for an additional vocabulary. The distinction is an outmoded one, resulting from differences in approaches between the civil and the criminal legal systems in relation to children. However, as the international laws on children make clear, all of the special protections apply to children under the age of eighteen in the justice system, regardless of whether the field is civil or criminal. In international law, the special protections attach because of childhood and childhood is defined solely in regard to age.

. . . .

The philosophy behind the international law on child criminal justice is not a loose and flabby notion of the best interests of the child. Children who are in, or are at risk of being caught within, the criminal justice system are not seen as being on the margins of society, rather they are perceived as being central to creating social cohesion within the society.

Notes and Questions

1. The Van Bueren article argues that many countries have come around to the policy view that the treatment of juveniles in the criminal justice system is a matter of global standards; and that the United States is peculiarly "isolated" from this process. As in other areas of children's rights, we must ask whether the human rights gloss illuminates the true nature of the problem, or provides a fig leaf for governments that fail to alter their behaviour despite declaring their allegiance to international children's rights. Do you accept the argument that the situation for the many thousands of underage criminal defendants in the United States would be markedly different if the U.S. signed onto the UNCRC and fully accepted the relevance of children's rights in this context?

2. As described above, building on the UNCRC, several international documents set forth standards of juvenile justice. Excerpts from United Nations Standard Minimum Rules of the Administration of Juvenile Justice ("The Beijing Rules") and the United Nations Guidelines for the Prevention of Juvenile Delinquency ("The Riyadh Guidelines") are included in the appendix to this book. How do the Riyadh Guidelines and the Beijing Rules, described by Van Bueren above, reflect the "human rights of children"? How unequivocal are they? How are the Guidelines and Rules different from one another? Do the Riyadh Guidelines create a foundation for the operation of the more practical Rules?

During the period in which the UNCRC was being drafted, nations expressed a wish to have clearer guidance on how to treat juvenile offenders consistent with the larger principles set out in the UNCRC. What is the "legal status" of these rules and guidelines on juvenile justice? Do they impose binding commitments, as treaties and conventions do? If not, are they of any real significance? Do the guidelines and rules appear to genuinely represent the consensus of the international community? Keep these guidelines in mind as you read the remainder of this chapter.

3. Human rights norms are often said to be most effective when they inspire civil society in various countries to make demands on their own governments. In that sense, these norms provide a credible basis for advocacy. How do the international principles of juvenile justice play such a role, especially where they leave a wide margin of discretion to states?

———————

B. The Reality of Juvenile Justice Standards

The remainder of this chapter is devoted to examining how international principles of juvenile justice interact with social and political reality in various countries. Not surprisingly, the level of economic development and the degree of regard for the international rule of law generally determine the level of adherence to these principles. Juvenile criminal defendants are a population with a unique "image problem," as they are burdened with the dual disadvantages of immaturity and criminality. In order to live up to international law norms on juvenile justice, nations must be unusually committed to the protection of children, even when there is little organized social support for it.

The article that follows, describing juvenile justice systems in Western countries, makes the point that there is far more variety in national approaches to the juvenile criminal system than the adult system. Whereas all the countries described treat adult and juvenile offenders somewhat differently, they operate on a sliding scale of leniency. Despite the convergence of international law principles outlined in the readings above, it is not an easy matter to impose uniform notions of youth culpability.

———————

Anthony N. Doob and Michael Tonry,
Varieties of Youth Justice
31 Crime & Justice 1 (2004)

I. Separate Systems?

Youth justice systems vary much more between countries than do adult systems. Adult systems vary in many detailed ways but are broadly similar in most important respects. There is a good deal of consensus about what constitutes an offense. The exact nature of the prosecution process and court structures differs (especially between common-law and European countries), but there is widespread agreement that, at the end of the process, the sentence should, to a large extent, reflect the seriousness of the offense. Whatever else a sentence was said to accomplish, it would be seen unambiguously as punishment by the community and by the person subject to it. Sentencing systems in many countries have changed in the last thirty years — sometimes dramatically — but the focus of the sentence is more likely to be on the severity of punishment, rather than its purposes.

Youth justice systems do not have these same basic similarities. To give one illustration, what are commonly known as "status offenses" — behavior that is prohibited only because of a person's status as a youth (e.g., curfews, truancy) exist in some jurisdictions (e.g., in many U.S. states) but not in others (e.g., Canada, Denmark, or Germany).

Nor do all youth justice systems feature the same core features. In England and many U.S. states, youth justice systems closely resemble adult courts in their organization and their focus on punishment as a primary aim. In Scandinavian countries, people below age fifteen are legally incapable of committing crimes, and their serious misconduct is dealt with by social welfare agencies. At and after age fifteen, young offenders are processed by the same courts as process adults. In Scotland, a strong social welfare ethos dominates handling of young offenders. In New Zealand, nearly all cases are handled by conferences that many see as premised in part on ideas akin to those embodied in restorative justice.

The most notable aspect of the treatment of youths who offend in Western countries is that every country appears to have laws or policies reflecting the belief that youths should be treated differently from adult offenders. Exactly how they should be treated differently varies from country to country. What constitutes a "youth" also varies from country to country. And the rigidity of the demarcations between a child who is not criminally responsible and a youth who might be, and the demarcations between youthfulness and adulthood, also vary. But those responsible for criminal laws in all countries examined in this volume seem to agree that there should be some form of separation in how youthful and adult offenders are treated.

Accounts of juvenile justice history in the United States often focus on 1899 (the date of the founding of the first American separate court for juveniles in Chicago), just as Canadian juvenile justice is seen as dating from the first comprehensive "delinquency" legislation in 1908 or the first juvenile court in 1894. The experience of others, however, instructs that the formal beginnings of a "separate" youth justice system may not be especially important. The formal creation of a juvenile court is not necessary for there to be what is, from an operational standpoint, a separate youth justice system. Formal separation of juvenile from adult systems, exemplified by the "founding" of a juvenile court, may be no more than a North American idiosyncrasy and less important than the administrative structures and practices that determine a society's responses to youthful offending.

In Denmark, there is no formally separate system for young offenders. There are no special courts, and there are no special offenses (i.e., there are no status offenses). Denmark does not appear to have had a formally separate system (with distinct youth justice laws and a completely distinct set of youth justice institutions) for youths who offend. A naive American, therefore, might think that Denmark had not progressed even as far as reforms introduced in the early twentieth century in Chicago.... [H]owever, that does not mean that Danish youths are treated as if they are adults. Clearly they are not.

The Swedish system of youth justice has similar characteristics. Early twentieth-century American reformers would be dismayed to find that those over the age of criminal responsibility (fifteen) in Sweden are dealt with in the criminal courts. The system that existed at the end of the twentieth century—with shared responsibility between the welfare system and the justice system—for those between ages fifteen and twenty—does not sound like a "separate justice system." Nevertheless, various rules ... differentiate the treatment of a sixteen-year-old from that of a twenty-one-year-old and add up to, in effect, a separate system. Youths between ages fifteen and seventeen, for example, cannot normally be sent to prison.

. . . .

But all of these "systems" have one important common element: all reflect the view that youths should be dealt with differently from adults. And, generally speaking, the assumption is that the youthfulness of an offender mitigates the punishment that youths should receive and that youths should be kept separate from adult offenders.

II. Age Limits

Many countries—Canada and Germany, for example—appear to have quite rigid demarcations between the system for dealing with youthful offending, the adult system of criminal justice, and the welfare system. One might suppose that these demarcations had meaningful referents—that youths are different the day after their eighteenth birthdays from the way they were the day before, or that the homeless seventeen-year-old who steals something to eat is different from the homeless seventeen-year-old who obtains food through some legal process. When the more fluid systems of Denmark and Sweden are compared to the more rigid systems of Canada or many American states, it is clear that there are advantages and disadvantages to each.

Countries vary widely in both minimum ages of criminal responsibility, before which a young person cannot be charged with a crime, and jurisdictional ages of youth courts.

. . . .

In Canada, the minimum age (twelve) was established in 1984. Prior to that, it had been seven. Until 1985, the maximum age had varied between provinces, with some provinces declaring youths to be adults at any age between sixteen and eighteen, or, in the case of Alberta, different ages had been set for girls and boys. Until April 2003, youths aged fourteen and above could be transferred into adult court. Indeed, presumptively they were to be transferred into adult court if they were at least sixteen years old at the time of the offense and were charged with certain serious violent offenses. If they were transferred, they would, for almost all purposes, be treated as if, by judicial decision, they had aged instantly into adulthood.

Since April 2003, youths charged with serious offenses remain youths for criminal justice purposes and remain in youth court but can, on application from the prosecutor, be sentenced as an adult if a judge determines that a proportionate youth sentence is not possible because the maximum permissible youth sentence is not long enough. Even then, the judge can sentence the youth to serve his or her sentence in a youth facility. To imply, then, that the juvenile justice law in Canada has always maintained jurisdiction over youths for six years beginning at the youth's twelfth birthday is an oversimplification, given that transfers were possible before April 2003 and adult sentences are permissible after that date.

. . . .

Chronological ages are relatively easy to define. What becomes more murky, however, are situations where youths are deemed to be adults because of what they did. As Junger-Tas notes, the Netherlands' 1995 Juvenile Justice Act changed the manner in which sixteen- and seventeen-year-olds could be transferred into the adult system. Earlier, three conditions had to be met before a youth could be transferred: the offense had to be serious, there had to be aggravating factors such as the offense having been committed with adults, and the offender had to be seen as, effectively, having the maturity of an adult. The legislation that came into effect in 1995 changed this: only one of the conditions had to be present, and the "age" criterion apparently became more focused on the age of the offender at the time that the offense was committed rather than the youth's maturity. As an additional complication related to the issue of age, the maximum period of detention was changed with the new act so that those aged twelve through fifteen are liable to receive a maximum of a one-year sentence and those ages sixteen or seventeen at the time of the offense are liable to receive a two-year sentence.

. . . .

The German Youth Court Law came into effect in 1923 and provided the framework for the state's response to offending by those between their fourteenth and eighteenth birthdays. Special courts and prisons for youths had existed before that time. Germany ... has endorsed for approximately a century the idea that punishment is not the best approach to youthful offending. Nevertheless, in 1943, the Nazi government lowered the age of criminal responsibility to twelve and allowed the transfer to the adult system of offenders aged sixteen and over. These changes lasted only three years, however. But the age limits set out in the legislation are not quite as firm as would be implied by a table of minimum and maximum ages. Young adults, aged eighteen to twenty, can be prosecuted as if they were juveniles. In effect, there is the possibility of a transfer down because of variation in "maturation, social and moral development, and integration into the adult world".... Germany's maximum age of seventeen is, then, very different from those ages found in American states.

The "age jurisdiction" for England appears to be fairly simple. However, within the range of juvenile jurisdiction, variation does exist. Until 1998 there were special restrictions on the use of custody for those under fifteen, but these restrictions were relaxed by the 1998 legislation. In addition, youths in England can be dealt with by the Crown (adult) Court rather than by the youth court. In serious cases, the youth is in jeopardy of receiving the same sentence an adult would receive. In the case of a homicide offense, committal to the Crown Court is mandatory. That is why probably England's most famous recent youth offense—the case involving two ten-year-old youths who killed James Bulger in 1992—was held in Crown Court and received full publicity. Interestingly, when the two youths found guilty of the offense were released as young adults, the government felt it necessary to protect their identities so that they could integrate into civil society.

....

The age jurisdiction of the juvenile system in the United States varies from state to state, though the modal ages would appear to be similar to those in the United Kingdom. However, that is where the similarity ends. In particular, two factors must be considered. Even at the lowest age, in certain states, youths under twelve years old can be prosecuted as if they are adults.

More common is the ambiguity about the age jurisdiction at the top end. It is estimated that as many as 200,000 youths a year under the age of eighteen are processed in the adult courts in the United States as if they were adults.

In comparison, Canada, with about one-tenth as many youths as the United States, transferred fewer than 100 youths per year to adult courts even though the overall use of youth court appears to be relatively comparable in the two jurisdictions.... Most of the American youths who end up in adult court are not there as a result of judicially ordered waivers. In a few states (e.g., New York), there is no "judicial waiver" to adult court....

Instead, two mechanisms account for most of these "instant adults." In many states, prosecutors have the power to decide that an offender should be dealt with as an adult. If the indictment is filed in the adult court, the youth is, then, for criminal justice purposes, an adult. Alternatively, some state legislatures have decided that, for certain serious offenses, a youth is to be considered to be an adult and the case is automatically processed through the adult criminal courts. The idea that the youth court jurisdiction is ages ten through seventeen, then, applies in many states only if the youth is lucky enough to avoid being deemed to be an adult for criminal justice purposes.

....

If nothing else, the variation on what the upper and lower age limits mean should demonstrate the complexity and the interrelatedness of the various youth justice provisions that exist in Western countries. A seventeen-year-old would be a youth in five countries we have mentioned. But if that seventeen-year-old were to offend, he or she might well be treated in quite different ways—and decisions would be guided by quite different principles—depending on the country.

....

IV. Welfare and "Justice"

The conflict between what are generally referred to as welfare principles and criminal law principles appears to have featured in at least some of the changes that have taken place in the latter part of the twentieth century. Criminal law, however, incorporates a number of quite independent concepts. As contrasted with welfare, criminal law can mean a greater focus on the offense rather than the offender, more focus on due process issues, proportional responses to offending, or a focus on punishment as a justification for intervention.

Every jurisdiction has had to grapple with this distinction in some way. Even Germany, which had a criminal law basis for its youth justice system throughout the twentieth century, had to consider whether social welfare concerns should be integrated into it. The prolonged consideration in the 1960s and 1970s of whether to "shift" delinquency into the welfare system ... was never implemented and has since disappeared as an issue. Other countries—like Canada—have moved from a system that gave priority to one principle (welfare, under the law in effect from 1908 to 1984) to a law that came into effect in 2003 that focuses initially, and perhaps primarily in most cases, on the offense. Still others, as in many states in the United States, focus on welfare issues within the juvenile court, but focus on the offense (and criminal justice approaches) when dealing with relatively serious offenses.

....

We are not suggesting that a major focus on the welfare of children can be assumed in the long term to be in unrelenting decline in Western juvenile justice systems. However, as a generalization, its overall importance as an organizing principle in many (but not all) systems appears to be on the decline.

....

Youth crime is an attractive territory for political opportunism since tough legislation (e.g., the automatic processing as adults of youths who murder, or mandatory sentences for very serious violent offenses) can be enacted with relatively few political or financial costs. Few people—or at least few of those who appear to influence political agendas—view tough youth crime measures as being tough on youths. Instead, they are seen as being tough on crime. But tough youth crime measures have another political advantage. Compared to legislative changes that affect sentencing generally (e.g., three-strikes laws for adult offenders), a shift from a welfare orientation to a tough offense-based system for the most serious offenders will not be likely to affect many youths and, therefore, will not cost a great deal.

V. Law in Books and in Action

....

The latter part of the twentieth century and the early part of the twenty-first century have been times when people in many countries have been searching for the "right" solutions to youth justice problems. Compromises abound.... [In] one of the newest popular innovations in youth justice, restorative justice initiatives, there will always be tensions between the social welfare and social control approaches. More important, however, is [the] observation [by L. Walgrave] that "this tension is inevitable because juvenile justice jurisdictions try to combine what cannot be combined satisfactorily."... [T]he so-called Beijing rules expressed in the United Nations Declaration on the Rights of Children, which are meant to act as a guide to how young people are dealt with in all countries, "reflect a fundamental ambivalence" and, in attempting to combine approaches, might best be described as an attempt to sound good but gloss over basic incompatibilities between the approaches. The grafting of restorative justice principles onto the unresolved conflict between welfare and punishment goals obviously leads to other difficulties.... [R]estorative approaches, when added to this mix of goals, may be vulnerable to all of the existing criticisms of punishment and treatment approaches.

....

We tend to know less than we should about the involvement of the state in the lives of children during adolescence. Though we know that in some jurisdictions youths who are heavily involved in the youth justice system also are likely to have welfare needs, we know little about the decisions that are made which determine which system is invoked when both systems could be used and each might be seen as being relevant. Longitudinal studies of youths with representative samples are not terribly helpful in this regard because relatively few youths ever come in contact with the formal youth justice or child welfare systems. Although comparative data across jurisdictions on the relative use of the two systems do not exist (even where there are separate systems), these might be useful in understanding the ways in which states intervene in the lives of children. It might be, for example, that jurisdictions that have low rates of youth court, or criminal law, involvement have relatively higher rates of some form of state intervention into the lives of children for welfare purposes. Alternatively, it might be that the social policies that are likely to affect the level of welfare needs among children are the same as the policies that affect the level of involvement in offending. If this were the case, one could expect youth justice and child welfare rates to be positively correlated across jurisdictions.

In a similar vein, neither within jurisdictions nor across them do we know much about the reaction of youths to different types of interventions. Little is known about the relative efficacy of interventions in the two processes.

... [T]here is not likely to be a single best approach to responding to youthful offending. There is a good argument for seeing youthful offending and the youth justice system that responds to it as quite separate phenomena. Youthful offending may affect the youth justice system, but youth justice systems probably have very little impact on youthful offending. Some might see this hypothesis as a pessimistic one. Alternatively, it may free those who are responsible for modifying youth justice systems to focus more clearly on what is important about society's responses to crime. What is clear ... is that relatively similar Western countries have not arrived at a consensus on how best to respond to youth crime.

Notes and Questions

1. In the West, there is an obvious tension between the "welfare" and punishment objectives within the juvenile justice system. Even where the resources are greatest, public

attitudes towards crime will influence the degree to which the system shows leniency to juvenile offenders. Doob and Tonry attempt to summarize the historical back and forth between these two poles of concern. How does what the authors call "political opportunism" affect the outcomes for children in the justice system?

India, as we have seen in the child labor context, is a country of enormous contrasts and contradictions; having both energetic NGOs, and endemic problems of social and economic marginalization. In the article that follows, Erika Rickard describes the transmission of international principles into the juvenile justice context in India.

Erika Rickard, *Paying Lip Service to the Silenced: Juvenile Justice in India*
21 Harvard Human Rights Journal 155 (2008)

I. Background

As a State Party to the Convention on the Rights of the Child ("CRC") and various other rules and guidelines on children's rights, the Government of India is bound to fulfill the duties set out in these instruments. International agreements on children's rights, as they concern juveniles in conflict with law, promote a holistic approach, concerned with the development, care, and protection of children throughout their interactions with the juvenile justice system. Juvenile justice is more concerned with the rehabilitation of its charges than is adult criminal justice. When discussing juveniles in conflict with law, international agreements generally emphasize the importance of preventing juveniles from coming into conflict with the law in the first place, as well as an expectation of complete rehabilitation by the time they leave the juvenile justice system. Throughout the proceedings within the system, "States Parties recognize the right of every child alleged as, accused of, or recognized as having infringed the penal law to be treated in a manner consistent with the promotion of the child's sense of dignity and worth."

India's original Juvenile Justice Act (1986), written before many of these international instruments were promulgated, did not align with their requirements. In response to the U.N. Committee on the Rights of the Child's recommendation that India incorporate the aims of the Convention on the Rights of the Child into domestic legislation, a new law was passed. The Juvenile Justice (Care and Protection of Children) Act (2000) ("JJ Act"), amended in 2002 and 2006, covers all aspects of interaction between children and the legal system. From adoption to abuse and neglect to children in conflict with the law, the Act is far-reaching in its scope and intent. The provisions within the JJ Act, like its international predecessors, are intended to preserve the dignity and best interests of the child.

II. From Ideal to Implementation

A. Legal Proceedings

According to the JJ Act, the rights of juveniles conform to the general rights of the accused under Indian criminal procedure. The international community is concerned with the standard litany of "basic procedural safeguards such as the presumption of innocence, the right to be notified of the charges, the right to remain silent, the right to counsel, the right to the presence of a parent or guardian, the right to confront and cross-examine witnesses and the right to appeal to a higher authority." In addition to these basic protections, particular attention must be paid to the special needs of the juvenile. As stated by the

Karnataka Rules, which implement the JJ Act, juvenile justice proceedings shall be conducted "in an informal and child friendly manner."

To address the particular needs of children, the Government of India has devised entities separate from the traditional justice system: Juvenile Justice Boards ("JJBs"). The second three-year term of Juvenile Justice Boards just began in January 2007, and the JJBs have not yet been established in all districts. Each JJB consists of a three-person panel, with one magistrate and two social workers. The goal of this composition is to have a legally recognized body that is also sensitive to the needs of children. To some degree, this has been successful, but there are also limitations; by assembling these groups of people, the government has absolved itself of much responsibility in terms of training. As a result, the magistrates have limited understanding of child welfare and child psychology, and the social workers rarely have any legal expertise.

The JJB is intended to be a non-adversarial, child-friendly environment. This implies that each Board acts as both prosecutor and arbiter, a difficult combination that the state attempts to justify on the basis that juvenile proceedings are not intended to be criminal proceedings, but rather records of offenses that took place. Juvenile judicial proceedings differ notably from ordinary criminal proceedings. The room is typically occupied by the following: the three JJB members hearing the case; probation officers serving as courtroom clerks; a court reporter; a guard from the Observation Home (where children are provisionally incarcerated); a police officer or two; possibly the victim and his or her family; and the child, sometimes with his or her family. Some districts have shifted proceedings from courthouse to Observation Home; rather than make the proceedings more child-friendly, however, this simply removes trained courtroom staff from the proceedings and replaces them with (usually untrained) probation officers. These alternative proceedings do not significantly diminish the sense of formality and criminal suspicion. Regardless of the location of the proceedings, the overwhelming feeling imposed on the child is that of intimidation and fear.

1. The Issue of Innocence

The JJ Act classifies all children who interact with the legal system together, which alleviates some of the stigma attached to those in conflict with law. Furthermore, although the age of criminal responsibility is approximately seven years old, because juveniles are not considered capable of the requisite mens rea according to ordinary criminal procedure, they are not considered capable of guilt. Juvenile Justice Board inquiries therefore merely endeavor to create a record of offense and offender. To that end, the records of JJB proceedings are not kept permanently, and do not follow the children into adulthood, to prevent any child from being labeled as a criminal based on offenses committed before the age of eighteen, regardless of the offense.

The presumption of innocence is a crucial element of criminal judicial proceedings in India, but becomes complicated in juvenile proceedings. Per the Committee on the Rights of the Child, the presumption of innocence "means that the burden of proof of the charge(s) brought against the child is on the prosecution." This is a conundrum for the JJB, which does not generally have a separate prosecutor. The JJB therefore acts as both arbiter and prosecutor. Moreover, the fact that guilt and retribution are not intended to be elements of the proceedings means that for any crime, all children receive the same punishment (if any). The impotence of the JJB and the insignificance of its outcomes are criticized by government officials, and have also led to an indifference on the part of all actors in the system as to whether the child actually committed the offense in question. As a result, children generally cannot be found innocent of a crime. In addition, because juveniles are not punished, there is no perceived need to create a probation system or diversion opportunities. The orders that Juvenile Justice Boards may issue with respect to children include detention in a Special Home, probation, and community service, but these are rarely utilized. The vast majority of cases end with a disposition of "admonish and release." All juveniles, regardless of guilt or innocence, undergo the same experience: waiting, either on bail or in an Observation Home, to be processed and released.

. . . .

B. Accountability Concerns

Children have difficulty developing their own political voice, and often adults charge themselves with acting in the best interests of children, which presumes that adults can determine what the best interests of children actually are. In the criminal justice context, children cannot hold the system accountable because they have no voice or representation of their own. The system as devised under the JJ Act does not adequately address this issue, as few mechanisms exist to ensure accountability.

One severely under-utilized mechanism of accountability is the court system itself. As India's is a common law system, appellate courts should hear cases brought on appeal from Juvenile Justice Board proceedings. However, owing to the scarcity of resources for appeals proceedings, and the fact that few children are represented by lawyers at the initial proceedings (making the prospect of an appeal unlikely), significant case law has yet to develop.

Under the JDL Rules as well as the United Nations Guidelines for the Prevention of Juvenile Delinquency ("The Riyadh Guidelines")—instruments addressing the protection of persons subject to detention or imprisonment—an independent body that oversees the various institutions responsible for juveniles in conflict with law is a crucial mechanism for maintaining the best interests of children. The Government of India has not embraced this concept, as Observation Homes and probation officers remain vaguely subject to oversight by the Department of Women and Child Development, a national administrative agency that is minimally involved in observing probation officers or Home staff at the local level. The JJ Act also establishes home inspection committees and state-level advisory boards to oversee the administration of juvenile justice, but they have no authority or required meeting dates. These committees, in fact, generally do not conduct meetings or reviews of Homes. The police, meanwhile, are only held accountable within their own departments, and are subject to limited supervision combined with unlimited discretion as to when to get involved and what course of action to take.

One of the more pernicious of the Government of India's flaws, lack of oversight, flourishes in the juvenile justice system. Physical abuse, corruption, and abuse of power dominate the system, from police to incarceration to legal proceedings.

1. Police Brutality and Abuse in Observation Homes

The relationship between police and juvenile offenders is a precarious one. When the police apprehend a child for allegedly committing an offense, it is generally the first point of contact between the child and the juvenile justice system. The U.N. Standard Minimum Rules for the Administration of Juvenile Justice ("The Beijing Rules") advise that interactions between police and juveniles should "promote the well-being of the juvenile and avoid harm to her or him." The Riyadh Guidelines go further, suggesting that police "should be trained to respond to the special needs of young persons."

However, rather than avoiding harm, police interactions with juveniles tend to involve abusive interrogation techniques, sometimes bordering on torture. As the children who undergo such interrogations understand it, police want them to confess to other crimes.

Police are reputed to have an arrest quota, so they pin cases on children they can torture without repercussions. These children are generally targeted based on their poverty and vulnerability. The common refrain from children is that if they "make one mistake" by committing one crime, they can expect to be brought in for questioning by police indefinitely, for any or no cause.

Police discretion under the JJ Act is intended to reduce the number of children that are brought into the system, but that is not how it is being utilized. According to the Model Rules, which were established by the Government of India to direct implementation of the JJ Act at the state level, police should only apprehend children in cases of serious crimes. However, the demographics of the children in Observation Homes throughout the country clearly demonstrate that the vast majority of juveniles have been arrested for petty theft, and police arrest many of those on far less than a reasonable suspicion.

Abuse of children occurs within the Observation Homes as well. Lack of supervision and limited staff, combined with a lack of training, strain relations between Home staff and children. Boys in an Observation Home in Shimoga report that all but one of the staff at the Home are verbally and physically abusive, and the boys and guards are mutually distrustful of one another. The guards fear the older boys, who are similar in size to the guards, but the younger boys receive beatings on a regular basis. Abuse in Madivala Home, Bangalore, is likewise pervasive. Human Rights Watch documented some of these abuses in a 1996 report. According to a source within the Indian juvenile justice system, the staff member described in the report as particularly abusive still works at the Home today.

. . . .

III. Solutions

[The article states that The Ministry of Women and Child Development is creating Model Rules as an addendum to the Juvenile Justice Act, in the hope that these rules will be adopted by the various Indian states.]

. . . .

A. The Model Rules

The Model Rules are mildly controversial among children's rights non-governmental organizations ("NGOs") in India, as the Ministry did not consult with NGOs during the drafting of the Rules. One of the primary criticisms of the Rules is that they invest too much authority in the police, something that most child-friendly legislation seeks to minimize. The Rules also limit the pool of people that will be eligible to serve on the Juvenile Justice Boards, for example by requiring that Board members be at least thirty-five years old, hold a post-graduate degree in social science, and have seven years of experience in child welfare. NGOs are concerned about excessive restrictions, as Juvenile Justice Boards already have difficulties filling positions. One oddity of the Model Rules is that they have a set of "principles," as if the document were a Convention or Act, as opposed to a set of procedures or protocols. It is unclear who will enforce these principles, which is of concern because enforcement and implementation of legislation were a key problem in the first place.

Despite these criticisms, the Model Rules may have a tremendous impact on ameliorating the current problems within the system. The Rules advocate for a stronger relationship between NGOs and government agencies, an acknowledgement of the positive impact NGOs can have within the Observation Homes and throughout the system. There are also two key changes that may prove important: the elimination of the charge-sheet requirement, and the clarified requirement of ending case proceedings after a maximum of six months.

....

"Openness and transparency" is a new goal emphasized by the Model Rules. As such, one form of independent oversight that will be established by the Rules that may generate change is a social audit, essentially a detailed review of the workings of individual Observation Homes, to be conducted by the government in conjunction with NGOs. In order for the social audit to work, the process will need a government official (not an independent body) to oversee it, as well as strong initiative and significant resources contributed by those conducting the audit.

The recognition of the right to legal representation for all juveniles may alleviate the problems of the lack of child participation and accountability of the judicial proceedings by providing juveniles with an advocate who can object to inordinate delays or inappropriate behavior on the part of the Board, as well as through the establishment of a body of case law. Children are likely to be represented by free legal aid, such as a district legal services authority, not all of which may have the time or resources to be able to appeal cases. However, an increase in attorneys required to be involved in juvenile proceedings may mean an increase in support from either the Government of India or NGOs. This may lead to more challenges and appeals, bringing the juvenile justice system increased attention from the courts.

....

Notes and Questions

1. India is clearly engaged in a process of modernizing its approach to juveniles caught up in the criminal law system. How do these efforts square with Rickard's statement that police interrogation methods, even with regard to juvenile defendants, are often tantamount to torture?

2. Contrast juvenile justice in India with the problematic situation in Pakistan, where, despite ratification of the UNCRC, juveniles may experience severe punishment for what seem to be relatively minor violations of religious codes of conduct. For one perspective on Pakistan's historical treatment of youthful offenders, see Andrea Geiger, *International Law — Juvenile Justice in Pakistan,* 23 Suffolk Transnational Law Review 713 (2000). For information on recent Pakistani efforts to create a separate and more humane track for juvenile defendants, see the AMAL Human Development Network's 2004 report, *Street Children and Juvenile Justice in Pakistan,* available at http://www.streetchildren.org.uk/reports/Pakistan%20JJ%20report%20-%20FINAL%204.04.pdf.

The brief excerpt below on the situation in Georgia confirms the view that, despite international exhortations to the effect that juveniles deserve special protection within the criminal justice system, states tend to react harshly when threatened with a perceived juvenile crime wave. Indeed, the problem of criminal activity by minors, and a draconian police response, is endemic throughout the former Soviet Union. Also see Amnesty International, *Russia Campaign — Take Action: Appeals — Children's Rights Abused* (2002), available at http://www.amnesty.org/russia/actions/children.html, decrying the "vast numbers" of children arrested by the police in Russia and held in special colonies for youthful offenders.

Matthew Solis, et al., *International Legal Updates*

15 Human Rights Brief 28 (2008)

GEORGIA LOWERS AGE OF CRIMINAL RESPONSIBILITY

President Mikheil Saakashvili signed a set of amendments to the Georgian Criminal Code reducing the age of criminal responsibility from 14 to 12. The amendments will enter into force on July 1, 2008, and were introduced in response to a recent increase in juvenile crime in the former Soviet state.

Juvenile crime in Georgia has been steadily rising recently, with an almost 50 percent increase since 2005, mostly attributed to petty theft. According to the United Nations Children's Fund's 2007 Juvenile Justice Assessment, the percentage of juvenile offenders imprisoned more than doubled between 2000 and 2006. Experts attribute the rise in teenage crime to a breakdown of traditional values following Georgia's post-Soviet transition during the 1990s.

The change in Georgian law contradicts international and European norms that generally advocate using 18 as the age of criminal responsibility and emphasize that imprisoning children should be a last resort. The United Nations (UN) has issued several guidelines, including the Standard Minimum Rules for the Administration of Juvenile Justice (the Beijing Rules) and the Rules for the Protection of Juveniles Deprived of their Liberty. Several other international guidelines, including the Convention on the Rights of the Child and the European Social Charter, exemplify the profound international consensus against the imprisonment of children except under extreme circumstances.

Georgian practice, in adopting a widely criticized zero-tolerance policy towards young offenders, runs counter to international standards. Through this policy, the Georgian government is attempting to deter young people from criminal behavior by showing them that they will face punishment for their actions. Emphasizing the deterrent purpose of this law, the Georgian government claims that judges, prosecutors, and investigators with special training in dealing with youth will prosecute and try the juvenile offenders, who will then be imprisoned in penitentiaries that are separate from adult facilities.

Critics note that Georgia has yet to produce these separate facilities and specialists. The amendments contradict the UN Committee on the Rights of the Child's February 2007 recommendation that countries should not lower their age of criminal responsibility to 12. Although Georgia signed the Convention on the Rights of the Child, it still has not implemented its guidelines. Critics believe that while lowering the age of criminal responsibility will result in the imprisonment of more children, it will not deter juvenile crime.

Organizations advocating children's rights, including the UN and European Network of Ombudspeople for Children, suggest that juvenile offenders imprisoned at an early age are more likely to continue on a criminal path throughout their lives. These organizations suggest that a more effective strategy for dealing with Georgia's rise in juvenile crime would be to adopt measures to educate, reintegrate, and rehabilitate young offenders, as suggested in the Convention on the Rights of the Child. In this way, juveniles could still understand the gravity of their behavior, but learn how to become adults that contribute to Georgian society.

———————

Amnesty International has been active over many years in identifying the often brutal treatment of children in detention facilities around the world. See, for example, *Juvenile Jus-*

tice: Every Child's Basic Human Rights, available at http://web.amnesty.org/library/Index/ENGACT760041998?open&of=ENG-MWI, describing the harsh treatment of aboriginal children in police custody in Australia and official indifference towards juvenile detainees in Indonesia. Also see *AI raises alarm over child detainees in Burundi,* available at http://www.amnestyusa.org/business/nigeriareport/NovemberWireArticle.pdf, describing severe beatings of children by police officers and conditions of overcrowding and widespread abuse.

Brazil, a major developing country, and a leader in the development of international trade policy, is justly sensitive on the subject of its reputation in juvenile justice matters. Brazil has for many years been criticized for official callousness towards street children and youth; many children have allegedly been killed by police in a long running process of "social cleansing". The brief article that follows is indicative of the conditions in which juvenile defendants continue to be held.

Human Rights Watch, *In the Dark: Hidden Abuses against Detained Youths in Rio de Janeiro*
(June 2005) *available at* http://hrw.org/reports/2005/brazil0605/

. . . .

Conditions of Detention

In December 2004, when Human Rights Watch released its last report on juvenile detention in Rio de Janeiro, DEGASE director general Sérgio Novo told the press that he was "indignant" at our findings, which he described as "an injustice." "They show a reality that is completely different from what we have today," he declared to the *Folha de S. Paulo* newspaper. In fact, Human Rights Watch's six-month review of Rio de Janeiro's juvenile detention centers found that little has changed. If anything, detention conditions have worsened in several important respects.

Overcrowding

The Educandário Santo Expedito is a case in point. It held 181 youths the week we visited in July 2003, 9 percent over its official capacity of 166. When we returned in May 2005, it held 207 youths, 24 percent more than it was designed for. On both occasions, we found that its true capacity was closer to 90—entire cellblocks destroyed in a November 2002 fire were not repaired until late 2004, and they are not currently used to house youths. The only notable improvements were the fresh coats of paint on the doors leading into each cellblock, which are now yellow instead of a peeling, dingy blue, and on the basketball court.

Overcrowding is the rule at most other detention centers as well. CAI-Baixada is at 179 percent of its capacity. Padre Severino is at 175 percent of capacity. Santos Dumont was not filled to capacity when we visited, but officials there told us that it periodically reaches 150 percent. Only João Luiz Alves, the closest thing Rio de Janeiro has to an adequate detention center, consistently holds fewer youths than it is designed for.

. . . .

Living Conditions

Rio de Janeiro's detention centers fail to meet basic standards of health and hygiene. Detention centers report shortages of soap and toiletries; in some, youths wear a single change of clothing for up to a week before it is washed.

The youths we interviewed were particularly critical of the unhygienic conditions in Padre Severino. "The cells were all filthy" in Padre Severino, said André S., detained in Padre

Severino in early 2004, when he was seventeen. Asked if the showers were clean in Padre Severino, seventeen-year-old Marcos G. responded, "No way. It was filth. It stunk like hell." Reports of rats in Padre Severino were common among youths and parents we interviewed. "There were rats and centipedes," André S. told us. "There were rats," Marcos G. reported. "At night we would see lots of them running around."

The public defender's office described CAI-Baixada in similar terms in a lawsuit filed in March 2005:

> The infrastructure is precarious. The dormitories are dirty, fetid, and unhealthy, with leaks that have produced mold on the walls, making the place prone to respiratory illnesses and the dissemination of other infections, aggravated by the fact that the adolescents do not receive enough clothes to change them daily, as well as not having adequate facilities for their physiological needs and for daily bathing.

In addition, youths in Padre Severino and other facilities often do not have bedding and mattresses; when they do, they are often old and worn. João T., seventeen, compared conditions at Padre Severino with those at João Luiz Alves. "There [in Padre Severino] ... the mattresses were old. The foam was all worn down. Not like here [in João Luiz Alves]. Here they're good. There you ended up with your back hurting." André S. told us that he didn't have a mattress during the forty-five days he spent in Padre Severino in early 2004. The public defender's office has complained of a shortage of mattresses and bedding in CAI-Baixada, João Luiz Alves, and Santos Dumont as well.

Those detained in Padre Severino told us that they did not regularly receive items such as toothpaste and soap. Marcos G. depended on his mother to bring him soap and toothpaste when he was in Padre Severino. "My mother brought it, but once they told her that toothpaste couldn't come in," he recounted. André S. told us that getting toothpaste there "was difficult. We got it every once in a while, like that, on our fingers." Silvia R. brought her son soap when he was in Padre Severino, but she said that the guards also issued soap to the youths periodically.

The situation in CAI-Baixada is similar, according to a suit filed by the public defender's office in March 2005. Among other shortcomings, the suit charged that youths in CAI-Baixada "do not have the use of necessary items for personal cleanliness (soap, a place to bathe, towel, toothpaste, toothbrush, etc.)," lacked clean clothing, did not receive needed medications, and did not all have mattresses and bedding. In fact, the director of CAI-Baixada wrote to DEGASE's central office in February 2005 saying, "We face difficulties in obtaining supplies of all kinds for the adolescents' personal hygiene."

Clothing is changed once a week in Padre Severino and other detention centers. Silvia R. described what this meant in the close quarters of a detention center:

> Their clothing takes on a revolting smell. They stay in those clothes. They sweat. They stay in dirty rooms, a lot of them in each room. They start to reek. So the guards call them, "You stinking bunch, you filth."

Some youths in CAI-Baixada go barefoot because the center does not have shoes or sandals for them, the public defender's office reported, characterizing this situation as "not rare." And when some of the parents we interviewed tried to bring their children clothing and other items, their children did not always receive what they brought. "They didn't give him his clothes. They didn't give him many things we brought," said Gerson J., the father of an eighteen-year-old held in Santo Expedito until February 2005.

As one consequence of the lack of hygienic conditions in Padre Severino and other detention centers, we heard reports of skin conditions likely caused by scabies and other parasitic diseases, which the public defender's office describes as "constantly" present in Rio de Janeiro's detention centers. "Many get itchy sores," Silvia R. told us. "They stay there in those dirty cells, wet too." She told us that she brought her son a special antibacterial soap so that he would not get the condition. André S. gave a similar account. When he was in Padre Severino, he said, "There were many people with itches. They stayed separated from the rest.... I still have marks here on my feet, some little black bumps that don't go away." Marcos G., in Santo Expedito when we interviewed him in May 2005, reported that his hands itched. He pointed out tiny bumps on one hand. "Many people have them," he said. He told us that he had not received treatment for the condition.

C. The Death Penalty for Juveniles

A diminishing number of countries continue apply the death penalty to persons who were under the age of eighteen at the time they committed the relevant crime. While the vast majority of nations prohibit by law the application of the death penalty to juveniles, some countries do not. Still others execute juveniles in violation of their own domestic laws.

In 2005, the United States Supreme Court ruled that application of the death penalty to juveniles violated the Eighth Amendment to the U.S. Constitution, thereby ending the United States' long association with such countries as Iran, Pakistan, Saudi Arabia and Yemen, countries in which juvenile executions still occur. The judgment in question, *Roper v. Simmons,* provides an historical overview of the development of U.S. law regarding juveniles and the death penalty. While the Court based its decision primarily on a particular interpretation of the Eighth Amendment to the U.S. Constitution, it also discussed international law and the international community's widespread condemnation of the juvenile death penalty. Several justices wrote vigorous dissents, and the portions of those dissents addressing international law are also included below. What weight do you believe the U.S. and its courts ought to give to international standards? Did the majority strike a proper balance in its reliance on the U.S. Constitution on the one hand, while allowing for the influence of international law on the other? If not, what balance would be more appropriate?

Roper v. Simmons
543 U.S. 551 (2005)

Justice Kennedy delivered the opinion of the Court.

This case requires us to address, for the second time in a decade and a half, whether it is permissible under the Eighth and Fourteenth Amendments to the Constitution of the United States to execute a juvenile offender who was older than 15 but younger than 18 when he committed a capital crime. In *Stanford* v. *Kentucky*, 492 U.S. 361, 106 L. Ed. 2d 306, 109 S. Ct. 2969 (1989), a divided Court rejected the proposition that the Constitution bars capital punishment for juvenile offenders in this age group. We reconsider the question.

I

At the age of 17, when he was still a junior in high school, Christopher Simmons, the respondent here, committed murder. About nine months later, after he had turned 18, he was tried and sentenced to death. There is little doubt that Simmons was the instigator of the crime. Before its commission Simmons said he wanted to murder someone. In chilling, callous terms he talked about his plan, discussing it for the most part with two friends, Charles Benjamin and John Tessmer, then aged 15 and 16 respectively. Simmons proposed to commit burglary and murder by breaking and entering, tying up a victim, and throwing the victim off a bridge. Simmons assured his friends they could "get away with it" because they were minors.

The three met at about 2 a.m. on the night of the murder, but Tessmer left before the other two set out. (The State later charged Tessmer with conspiracy, but dropped the charge in exchange for his testimony against Simmons.) Simmons and Benjamin entered the home of the victim, Shirley Crook, after reaching through an open window and unlocking the back door. Simmons turned on a hallway light. Awakened, Mrs. Crook called out, "Who's there?" In response Simmons entered Mrs. Crook's bedroom, where he recognized her from a previous car accident involving them both. Simmons later admitted this confirmed his resolve to murder her.

Using duct tape to cover her eyes and mouth and bind her hands, the two perpetrators put Mrs. Crook in her minivan and drove to a state park. They reinforced the bindings, covered her head with a towel, and walked her to a railroad trestle spanning the Meramec River. There they tied her hands and feet together with electrical wire, wrapped her whole face in duct tape and threw her from the bridge, drowning her in the waters below.

By the afternoon of September 9, Steven Crook had returned home from an overnight trip, found his bedroom in disarray, and reported his wife missing. On the same afternoon fishermen recovered the victim's body from the river. Simmons, meanwhile, was bragging about the killing, telling friends he had killed a woman "because the bitch seen my face."

The next day, after receiving information of Simmons' involvement, police arrested him at his high school and took him to the police station in Fenton, Missouri. They read him his *Miranda* rights. Simmons waived his right to an attorney and agreed to answer questions. After less than two hours of interrogation, Simmons confessed to the murder and agreed to perform a videotaped reenactment at the crime scene.

The State charged Simmons with burglary, kidnapping, stealing, and murder in the first degree. As Simmons was 17 at the time of the crime, he was outside the criminal jurisdiction of Missouri's juvenile court system.... He was tried as an adult. At trial the State introduced Simmons' confession and the videotaped reenactment of the crime, along with testimony that Simmons discussed the crime in advance and bragged about it later. The defense called no witnesses in the guilt phase. The jury having returned a verdict of murder, the trial proceeded to the penalty phase.

The State sought the death penalty. As aggravating factors, the State submitted that the murder was committed for the purpose of receiving money; was committed for the purpose of avoiding, interfering with, or preventing lawful arrest of the defendant; and involved depravity of mind and was outrageously and wantonly vile, horrible, and inhuman. The State called Shirley Crook's husband, daughter, and two sisters, who presented moving evidence of the devastation her death had brought to their lives.

In mitigation Simmons' attorneys first called an officer of the Missouri juvenile justice system, who testified that Simmons had no prior convictions and that no previous charges had been filed against him. Simmons' mother, father, two younger half brothers, a neighbor, and a friend took the stand to tell the jurors of the close relationships they had formed with Simmons and to plead for mercy on his behalf. Simmons' mother, in particular, testified to the responsibility Simmons demonstrated in taking care of his two younger half brothers and of his grandmother and to his capacity to show love for them.

During closing arguments, both the prosecutor and defense counsel addressed Simmons' age, which the trial judge had instructed the jurors they could consider as a mitigating factor. Defense counsel reminded the jurors that juveniles of Simmons' age cannot drink, serve on juries, or even see certain movies, because "the legislatures have wisely decided that individuals of a certain age aren't responsible enough." Defense counsel argued that Simmons' age should make "a huge difference to [the jurors] in deciding just exactly what sort of punishment to make." In rebuttal, the prosecutor gave the following response: "Age, he says. Think about age. Seventeen years old. Isn't that scary? Doesn't that scare you? Mitigating? Quite the contrary I submit. Quite the contrary."

The jury recommended the death penalty after finding the State had proved each of the three aggravating factors submitted to it. Accepting the jury's recommendation, the trial judge imposed the death penalty.

Simmons obtained new counsel, who moved in the trial court to set aside the conviction and sentence. One argument was that Simmons had received ineffective assistance at trial. To support this contention, the new counsel called as witnesses Simmons' trial attorney, Simmons' friends and neighbors, and clinical psychologists who had evaluated him.

Part of the submission was that Simmons was "very immature," "very impulsive," and "very susceptible to being manipulated or influenced." The experts testified about Simmons' background including a difficult home environment and dramatic changes in behavior, accompanied by poor school performance in adolescence. Simmons was absent from home for long periods, spending time using alcohol and drugs with other teenagers or young adults. The contention by Simmons' postconviction counsel was that these matters should have been established in the sentencing proceeding.

The trial court found no constitutional violation by reason of ineffective assistance of counsel and denied the motion for postconviction relief. In a consolidated appeal from Simmons' conviction and sentence, and from the denial of postconviction relief, the Missouri Supreme Court affirmed. *State v. Simmons*, 944 S.W.2d 165, 169 (en banc), cert denied, 522 U.S. 953, 139 L. Ed. 2d 293, 118 S. Ct. 376 (1997). The federal courts denied Simmons' petition for a writ of habeas corpus. *Simmons v. Bowersox*, 235 F.3d 1124, 1127 (CA8), cert denied, 534 U.S. 924, 151 L. Ed. 2d 206, 122 S. Ct. 280 (2001).

After these proceedings in Simmons' case had run their course, this Court held that the Eighth and Fourteenth Amendments prohibit the execution of a mentally retarded person. *Atkins v. Virginia*, 536 U.S. 304, 153 L. Ed. 2d 335, 122 S. Ct. 2242 (2002). Simmons filed a new petition for state postconviction relief, arguing that the reasoning of *Atkins* established that the Constitution prohibits the execution of a juvenile who was under 18 when the crime was committed.

The Missouri Supreme Court agreed. *State ex rel. Simmons v. Roper*, 112 S.W.3d 397 (2003) (en banc). It held that since *Stanford*,

> "a national consensus has developed against the execution of juvenile offenders, as demonstrated by the fact that eighteen states now bar such executions for juveniles, that twelve other states bar executions altogether, that no state has lowered its age of execution below 18 since *Stanford*, that five states have legislatively or by case law raised or established the minimum age at 18, and that the imposition of the juvenile death penalty has become truly unusual over the last decade." ...

On this reasoning it set aside Simmons' death sentence and resentenced him to "life imprisonment without eligibility for probation, parole, or release except by act of the Governor."

....

We granted certiorari, and now affirm.

II

The Eighth Amendment provides: "Excessive bail shall not be required, nor excessive fines imposed, nor cruel and unusual punishments inflicted." The provision is applicable to the States through the Fourteenth Amendment. *Furman* v. *Georgia*, 408 U.S. 238, 239, 33 L. Ed. 2d 346, 92 S. Ct. 2726 (1972) *(per curiam); Robinson* v. *California*, 370 U.S. 660, 666–667, 8 L. Ed. 2d 758, 82 S. Ct. 1417 (1962); *Louisiana ex rel. Francis* v. *Resweber*, 329 U.S. 459, 463, 91 L. Ed. 422, 67 S. Ct. 374 (1947) (plurality opinion). As the Court explained in *Atkins*, the Eighth Amendment guarantees individuals the right not to be subjected to excessive sanctions. The right flows from the basic "'precept of justice that punishment for crime should be graduated and proportioned to [the] offense.'" 536 U.S., at 311, 153 L. Ed. 2d 335, 122 S. Ct. 2242 (quoting *Weems* v. *United States*, 217 U.S. 349, 367, 54 L. Ed. 793, 30 S. Ct. 544 (1910)). By protecting even those convicted of heinous crimes, the Eighth Amendment reaffirms the duty of the government to respect the dignity of all persons.

The prohibition against "cruel and unusual punishments," like other expansive language in the Constitution, must be interpreted according to its text, by considering history, tradition, and precedent, and with due regard for its purpose and function in the constitutional design. To implement this framework we have established the propriety and affirmed the necessity of referring to "the evolving standards of decency that mark the progress of a maturing society" to determine which punishments are so disproportionate as to be cruel and unusual. *Trop* v. *Dulles*, 356 U.S. 86, 100–101, 2 L. Ed. 2d 630, 78 S. Ct. 590 (1958) (plurality opinion).

In *Thompson* v. *Oklahoma*, 487 U.S. 815, 101 L. Ed. 2d 702, 108 S. Ct. 2687 (1988), a plurality of the Court determined that our standards of decency do not permit the execution of any offender under the age of 16 at the time of the crime. *Id.,* at 818–838, 101 L. Ed. 2d 702, 108 S. Ct. 2687 (opinion of Stevens, J., joined by Brennan, Marshall, and Blackmun, JJ.). The plurality opinion explained that no death penalty State that had given express consideration to a minimum age for the death penalty had set the age lower than 16. *Id.,* at 826–829, 101 L. Ed. 2d 702, 108 S. Ct. 2687. The plurality also observed that "[t]he conclusion that it would offend civilized standards of decency to execute a person who was less than 16 years old at the time of his or her offense is consistent with the views that have been expressed by respected professional organizations, by other nations that share our Anglo-American heritage, and by the leading members of the Western European community." *Id.,* at 830, 101 L. Ed. 2d 702, 108 S. Ct. 2687. The opinion further noted that juries imposed the death penalty on offenders under 16 with exceeding rarity; the last execution of an offender for a crime committed under the age of 16 had been carried out in 1948, 40 years prior. *Id.,* at 832–833, 101 L. Ed. 2d 702, 108 S. Ct. 2687.

Bringing its independent judgment to bear on the permissibility of the death penalty for a 15-year-old offender, the *Thompson* plurality stressed that "[t]he reasons why juveniles are not trusted with the privileges and responsibilities of an adult also explain why their irresponsible conduct is not as morally reprehensible as that of an adult." *Id.,* at 835, 101 L. Ed. 2d 702, 108 S. Ct. 2687. According to the plurality, the lesser culpability of offenders under 16 made the death penalty inappropriate as a form of retribution, while the low likelihood that offenders under 16 engaged in "the kind of cost-benefit analysis that attaches any weight to the possibility of execution" made the death penalty ineffective as a means of deterrence. *Id.,* at 836–838, 101 L. Ed. 2d 702, 108 S. Ct. 2687. With

Justice O'Connor concurring in the judgment on narrower grounds, *id.*, at 848–859, 101 L. Ed. 2d 702, 108 S. Ct. 2687, the Court set aside the death sentence that had been imposed on the 15-year-old offender.

The next year, in *Stanford* v. *Kentucky*, 492 U.S. 361, 106 L. Ed. 2d 306, 109 S. Ct. 2969 (1989), the Court, over a dissenting opinion joined by four Justices, referred to contemporary standards of decency in this country and concluded the Eighth and Fourteenth Amendments did not proscribe the execution of juvenile offenders over 15 but under 18. The Court noted that 22 of the 37 death penalty States permitted the death penalty for 16-year-old offenders, and, among these 37 States, 25 permitted it for 17-year-old offenders. These numbers, in the Court's view, indicated there was no national consensus "sufficient to label a particular punishment cruel and unusual." *Id.*, at 370–371, 106 L. Ed. 2d 306, 109 S. Ct. 2969. A plurality of the Court also "emphatically reject[ed]" the suggestion that the Court should bring its own judgment to bear on the acceptability of the juvenile death penalty. *Id.*, at 377–378, 106 L. Ed. 2d 306, 109 S. Ct. 2969 (opinion of Scalia, J., joined by Rehnquist, C. J., and White and Kennedy, JJ.); see also *id.*, at 382, 106 L. Ed. 2d 306, 109 S. Ct. 2969 (O'Connor, J., concurring in part and concurring in judgment) (criticizing the plurality's refusal "to judge whether the '"nexus between the punishment imposed and the defendant's blameworthiness"'" is proportional").

The same day the Court decided *Stanford*, it held that the Eighth Amendment did not mandate a categorical exemption from the death penalty for the mentally retarded. *Penry* v. *Lynaugh*, 492 U.S. 302, 106 L. Ed. 2d 256, 109 S. Ct. 2934 (1989). In reaching this conclusion it stressed that only two States had enacted laws banning the imposition of the death penalty on a mentally retarded person convicted of a capital offense. *Id.*, at 334, 106 L. Ed. 2d. 256, 109 S. Ct. 2934. According to the Court, "the two state statutes prohibiting execution of the mentally retarded, even when added to the 14 States that have rejected capital punishment completely, [did] not provide sufficient evidence at present of a national consensus." *Ibid.*

Three Terms ago the subject was reconsidered in *Atkins*. We held that standards of decency have evolved since *Penry* and now demonstrate that the execution of the mentally retarded is cruel and unusual punishment. The Court noted objective indicia of society's standards, as expressed in legislative enactments and state practice with respect to executions of the mentally retarded....

The inquiry into our society's evolving standards of decency did not end there. The *Atkins* Court neither repeated nor relied upon the statement in *Stanford* that the Court's independent judgment has no bearing on the acceptability of a particular punishment under the Eighth Amendment. Instead we returned to the rule, established in decisions predating *Stanford,* that "'the Constitution contemplates that in the end our own judgment will be brought to bear on the question of the acceptability of the death penalty under the Eighth Amendment.'" 536 U.S., at 312, 153 L. Ed. 2d 335, 122 S. Ct. 2242 (quoting *Coker* v. *Georgia*, 433 U.S. 584, 597, 53 L. Ed. 2d 982, 97 S. Ct. 2861 (1977) (plurality opinion))....

Just as the *Atkins* Court reconsidered the issue decided in *Penry*, we now reconsider the issue decided in *Stanford*. The beginning point is a review of objective indicia of consensus, as expressed in particular by the enactments of legislatures that have addressed the question. This data gives us essential instruction. We then must determine, in the exercise of our own independent judgment, whether the death penalty is a disproportionate punishment for juveniles.

III

A

The evidence of national consensus against the death penalty for juveniles is similar, and in some respects parallel, to the evidence *Atkins* held sufficient to demonstrate a national consensus against the death penalty for the mentally retarded. When *Atkins* was decided, 30 States prohibited the death penalty for the mentally retarded. This number comprised 12 that had abandoned the death penalty altogether, and 18 that maintained it but excluded the mentally retarded from its reach. 536 U.S., at 313–315, 153 L. Ed. 2d 335, 122 S. Ct. 2242. By a similar calculation in this case, 30 States prohibit the juvenile death penalty, comprising 12 that have rejected the death penalty altogether and 18 that maintain it but, by express provision or judicial interpretation, exclude juveniles from its reach.... *Atkins* emphasized that even in the 20 States without formal prohibition, the practice of executing the mentally retarded was infrequent. Since *Penry*, only five States had executed offenders known to have an IQ under 70. 536 U.S., at 316, 153 L. Ed. 2d 335, 122 S. Ct. 2242. In the present case, too, even in the 20 States without a formal prohibition on executing juveniles, the practice is infrequent. Since *Stanford*, six States have executed prisoners for crimes committed as juveniles. In the past 10 years, only three have done so: Oklahoma, Texas, and Virginia....

There is, to be sure, at least one difference between the evidence of consensus in *Atkins* and in this case. Impressive in *Atkins* was the rate of abolition of the death penalty for the mentally retarded. Sixteen States that permitted the execution of the mentally retarded at the time of *Penry* had prohibited the practice by the time we heard *Atkins*. By contrast, the rate of change in reducing the incidence of the juvenile death penalty, or in taking specific steps to abolish it, has been slower. Five States that allowed the juvenile death penalty at the time of *Stanford* have abandoned it in the intervening 15 years—four through legislative enactments and one through judicial decision. Streib, *supra*, at 5, 7; *State v. Furman*, 122 Wn.2d 440, 858 P.2d 1092 (1993) (en banc).

.... The number of States that have abandoned capital punishment for juvenile offenders since *Stanford* is smaller than the number of States that abandoned capital punishment for the mentally retarded after *Penry*; yet we think the same consistency of direction of change has been demonstrated. Since *Stanford*, no State that previously prohibited capital punishment for juveniles has reinstated it. This fact, coupled with the trend toward abolition of the juvenile death penalty, carries special force in light of the general popularity of anticrime legislation, *Atkins*, *supra*, at 315, 153 L. Ed. 2d 335, 122 S. Ct. 2242, and in light of the particular trend in recent years toward cracking down on juvenile crime in other respects....

Petitioner cannot show national consensus in favor of capital punishment for juveniles but still resists the conclusion that any consensus exists against it. Petitioner supports this position with, in particular, the observation that when the Senate ratified the International Covenant on Civil and Political Rights (ICCPR), Dec. 19, 1966, 999 U. N. T. S. 171 (entered into force Mar. 23, 1976), it did so subject to the President's proposed reservation regarding Article 6(5) of that treaty, which prohibits capital punishment for juveniles. Brief for Petitioner 27. This reservation at best provides only faint support for petitioner's argument. First, the reservation was passed in 1992; since then, five States have abandoned capital punishment for juveniles. Second, Congress considered the issue when enacting the Federal Death Penalty Act in 1994, and determined that the death penalty should not extend to juveniles. See 18 U.S.C. § 3591 [18 U.S.C.S. § 3591]. The reservation to Article 6(5) of the ICCPR provides minimal evidence that there is not now a national consensus against juvenile executions.

As in *Atkins*, the objective indicia of consensus in this case—the rejection of the juvenile death penalty in the majority of States; the infrequency of its use even where it remains on the books; and the consistency in the trend toward abolition of the practice—provide sufficient evidence that today our society views juveniles, in the words *Atkins* used respecting the mentally retarded, as "categorically less culpable than the average criminal." 536 U.S., at 316, 153 L. Ed. 2d 335, 122 S. Ct. 2242.

B

A majority of States have rejected the imposition of the death penalty on juvenile offenders under 18, and we now hold this is required by the Eighth Amendment.

Because the death penalty is the most severe punishment, the Eighth Amendment applies to it with special force. *Thompson*, 487 U.S., at 856, 101 L. Ed. 2d 702, 108 S. Ct. 2687 (O'Connor, J., concurring in judgment). Capital punishment must be limited to those offenders who commit "a narrow category of the most serious crimes" and whose extreme culpability makes them "the most deserving of execution." *Atkins*, *supra*, at 319, 153 L. Ed. 2d 335, 122 S. Ct. 2242. This principle is implemented throughout the capital sentencing process. States must give narrow and precise definition to the aggravating factors that can result in a capital sentence....

Three general differences between juveniles under 18 and adults demonstrate that juvenile offenders cannot with reliability be classified among the worst offenders. First, as any parent knows and as the scientific and sociological studies respondent and his *amici* cite tend to confirm, "[a] lack of maturity and an underdeveloped sense of responsibility are found in youth more often than in adults and are more understandable among the young. These qualities often result in impetuous and ill-considered actions and decisions." *Johnson*, *supra*, at 367, 125 L. Ed. 2d 290, 113 S. Ct. 2658; see also *Eddings*, *supra*, at 115–116, 71 L. Ed. 2d 1, 102 S. Ct. 869 ("Even the normal 16-year-old customarily lacks the maturity of an adult"). It has been noted that "adolescents are overrepresented statistically in virtually every category of reckless behavior." Arnett, Reckless Behavior in Adolescence: A Developmental Perspective, 12 Developmental Review 339 (1992). In recognition of the comparative immaturity and irresponsibility of juveniles, almost every State prohibits those under 18 years of age from voting, serving on juries, or marrying without parental consent. See Appendixes B–D, *infra*.

The second area of difference is that juveniles are more vulnerable or susceptible to negative influences and outside pressures, including peer pressure. *Eddings*, *supra*, at 115, 71 L. Ed. 2d 1, 102 S. Ct. 869 ("[Y]outh is more than a chronological fact. It is a time and condition of life when a person may be most susceptible to influence and to psychological damage"). This is explained in part by the prevailing circumstance that juveniles have less control, or less experience with control, over their own environment. See Steinberg & Scott, Less Guilty by Reason of Adolescence: Developmental Immaturity, Diminished Responsibility, and the Juvenile Death Penalty, 58 Am. Psychologist 1009, 1014 (2003) (hereinafter Steinberg & Scott) ("[A]s legal minors, [juveniles] lack the freedom that adults have to extricate themselves from a criminogenic setting").

The third broad difference is that the character of a juvenile is not as well formed as that of an adult. The personality traits of juveniles are more transitory, less fixed. See generally E. Erikson, Identity: Youth and Crisis (1968).

These differences render suspect any conclusion that a juvenile falls among the worst offenders.

. . . .

IV

Our determination that the death penalty is disproportionate punishment for offenders under 18 finds confirmation in the stark reality that the United States is the only country in the world that continues to give official sanction to the juvenile death penalty. This reality does not become controlling, for the task of interpreting the Eighth Amendment remains our responsibility. Yet at least from the time of the Court's decision in *Trop*, the Court has referred to the laws of other countries and to international authorities as instructive for its interpretation of the Eighth Amendment's prohibition of "cruel and unusual punishments."

. . . .

As respondent and a number of *amici* emphasize, Article 37 of the United Nations Convention on the Rights of the Child, which every country in the world has ratified save for the United States and Somalia, contains an express prohibition on capital punishment for crimes committed by juveniles under 18. United Nations Convention on the Rights of the Child, Art. 37, Nov. 20, 1989, 1577 U. N. T. S. 3, 28 I. L. M. 1448, 1468–1470 (entered into force Sept. 2, 1990); Brief for Respondent 48; Brief for European Union et al. as *Amici Curiae* 12–13; Brief for President James Earl Carter, Jr., et al. as *Amici Curiae* 9; Brief for Former U. S. Diplomats Morton Abramowitz et al. as *Amici Curiae* 7; Brief for Human Rights Committee of the Bar of England and Wales et al. as *Amici Curiae* 13–14. No ratifying country has entered a reservation to the provision prohibiting the execution of juvenile offenders. Parallel prohibitions are contained in other significant international covenants. See ICCPR, Art. 6(5), 999 U. N. T. S., at 175 (prohibiting capital punishment for anyone under 18 at the time of offense) (signed and ratified by the United States subject to a reservation regarding Article 6(5), as noted, *supra*, at 1194,); American Convention on Human Rights: Pact of San Jose, Costa Rica, Art. 4(5), Nov. 22, 1969, 1144 U. N. T. S. 146 (entered into force July 19, 1978) (same); African Charter on the Rights and Welfare of the Child, Art. 5(3), OAU Doc. CAB/LEG/24.9/49 (1990) (entered into force Nov. 29, 1999) (same).

Respondent and his *amici* have submitted, and petitioner does not contest, that only seven countries other than the United States have executed juvenile offenders since 1990: Iran, Pakistan, Saudi Arabia, Yemen, Nigeria, the Democratic Republic of Congo, and China. Since then each of these countries has either abolished capital punishment for juveniles or made public disavowal of the practice. Brief for Respondent 49–50. In sum, it is fair to say that the United States now stands alone in a world that has turned its face against the juvenile death penalty.

. . . .

It is proper that we acknowledge the overwhelming weight of international opinion against the juvenile death penalty, resting in large part on the understanding that the instability and emotional imbalance of young people may often be a factor in the crime. See Brief for Human Rights Committee of the Bar of England and Wales et al. as *Amici Curiae* 10–11. The opinion of the world community, while not controlling our outcome, does provide respected and significant confirmation for our own conclusions.

. . . .

The Eighth and Fourteenth Amendments forbid imposition of the death penalty on offenders who were under the age of 18 when their crimes were committed. The judgment of the Missouri Supreme Court setting aside the sentence of death imposed upon Christopher Simmons is affirmed.

It is so ordered.

DISSENT: Justice O'Connor, dissenting.

. . . .

II.

....

D

I turn, finally, to the Court's discussion of foreign and international law. Without question, there has been a global trend in recent years towards abolishing capital punishment for under-18 offenders.... While acknowledging that the actions and views of other countries do not dictate the outcome of our Eighth Amendment inquiry, the Court asserts that "the overwhelming weight of international opinion against the juvenile death penalty ... does provide respected and significant confirmation for [its] own conclusions.".... Because I do not believe that a genuine *national* consensus against the juvenile death penalty has yet developed, and because I do not believe the Court's moral proportionality argument justifies a categorical, age-based constitutional rule, I can assign no such *confirmatory* role to the international consensus described by the Court. In short, the evidence of an international consensus does not alter my determination that the Eighth Amendment does not, at this time, forbid capital punishment of 17-year-old murderers in all cases.

Nevertheless, I disagree with Justice Scalia's contention.... (dissenting opinion), that foreign and international law have no place in our Eighth Amendment jurisprudence. Over the course of nearly half a century, the Court has consistently referred to foreign and international law as relevant to its assessment of evolving standards of decency. See *Atkins*, 536 U.S., at 317, n. 21, 153 L. Ed. 2d 335, 122 S. Ct. 2242; *Thompson*, 487 U.S., at 830–831, and n. 31, 101 L. Ed. 2d 702, 108 S. Ct. 2687 (plurality opinion); *Enmund*, 458 U.S., at 796–797, n. 22, 73 L. Ed. 2d 1140, 102 S. Ct. 3368; *Coker*, 433 U.S., at 596, n. 10, 53 L. Ed. 2d 982, 97 S. Ct. 2861 (plurality opinion); *Trop*, 356 U.S., at 102–103, 2 L. Ed. 2d 630, 78 S. Ct. 590 (plurality opinion).... At least, the existence of an international consensus of this nature can serve to confirm the reasonableness of a consonant and genuine American consensus. The instant case presents no such domestic consensus, however, and the recent emergence of an otherwise global consensus does not alter that basic fact.

Justice Scalia, with whom The Chief Justice and Justice Thomas join, dissenting.

....

III

Though the views of our own citizens are essentially irrelevant to the Court's decision today, the views of other countries and the so-called international community take center stage.

The Court begins by noting that "Article 37 of the United Nations Convention on the Rights of the Child, [1577 U. N. T. S. 3, 28 I. L. M. 1448, 1468–1470, entered into force Sept. 2, 1990], which every country in the world has ratified *save for the United States* and Somalia, contains an express prohibition on capital punishment for crimes committed by juveniles under 18." Ante, at 1199 (emphasis added). The Court also discusses the International Covenant on Civil and Political Rights (ICCPR), December 19, 1966, 999 U. N. T. S. 175, *ante*, at 1194, 1199, which the Senate ratified only subject to a reservation that reads:

"The United States reserves the right, subject to its Constitutional restraints, to impose capital punishment on any person (other than a pregnant woman) duly convicted under existing or future laws permitting the imposition of capital punishment, including such punishment for crime committed by persons below eighteen years of age." Senate Committee on Foreign Relations, International Covenant on Civil and Political Rights, S. Exec. Rep. No. 102-23, (1992).

Unless the Court has added to its arsenal the power to join and ratify treaties on behalf of the United States, I cannot see how this evidence favors, rather than refutes, its position. That the Senate and the President—those actors our Constitution empowers to enter into treaties, see Art. II, §2—have declined to join and ratify treaties prohibiting execution of under-18 offenders can only suggest that *our country* has either not reached a national consensus on the question, or has reached a consensus contrary to what the Court announces. That the reservation to the ICCPR was made in 1992 does not suggest otherwise, since the reservation still remains in place today....

It is interesting that whereas the Court is not content to accept what the States of our Federal Union *say*, but insists on inquiring into what they *do* (specifically, whether they in fact *apply* the juvenile death penalty that their laws allow), the Court is quite willing to believe that every foreign nation—of whatever tyrannical political makeup and with however subservient or incompetent a court system—in fact *adheres* to a rule of no death penalty for offenders under 18.

. . . .

More fundamentally, however, the basic premise of the Court's argument—that American law should conform to the laws of the rest of the world—ought to be rejected out of hand. In fact the Court itself does not believe it. In many significant respects the laws of most other countries differ from our law—including not only such explicit provisions of our Constitution as the right to jury trial and grand jury indictment, but even many interpretations of the Constitution prescribed by this Court itself.

. . . .

The Court responds that "[i]t does not lessen our fidelity to the Constitution or our pride in its origins to acknowledge that the express affirmation of certain fundamental rights by other nations and peoples simply underscores the centrality of those same rights within our own heritage of freedom."... To begin with, I do not believe that approval by "other nations and peoples" should buttress our commitment to American principles any more than (what should logically follow) disapproval by "other nations and peoples" should weaken that commitment. More importantly, however, the Court's statement flatly misdescribes what is going on here. Foreign sources are cited today, *not* to underscore our "fidelity" to the Constitution, our "pride in its origins," and "our own [American] heritage." To the contrary, they are cited *to set aside* the centuries-old American practice—a practice still engaged in by a large majority of the relevant States—of letting a jury of 12 citizens decide whether, in the particular case, youth should be the basis for withholding the death penalty. What these foreign sources "affirm," rather than repudiate, is the Justices' own notion of how the world ought to be, and their diktat that it shall be so henceforth in America. The Court's parting attempt to downplay the significance of its extensive discussion of foreign law is unconvincing. "Acknowledgment" of foreign approval has no place in the legal opinion of this Court *unless it is part of the basis for the Court's judgment*—which is surely what it parades as today.

Notes and Questions

1. What role does the "overwhelming weight" of world opinion play in the majority opinion? Does the Court connect the dots between a growing consensus within the American states and a growing consensus internationally? What is the principal factor influencing the Court to state clearly that any execution of those who commit crimes under the age of 18 is wrong? How do the dissents treat the issue of an "international consensus"? Is there

any suggestion by the majority that the U.S. is bound to honor evolving international principles in the area of the death penalty, or only that international views confirm a developing American perspective? Is this a distinction that matters?

2. For an interesting discussion of the Supreme Court's holding in *Roper* and whether juvenile enemy combatants in the U.S. "war" on terror could be executed, see Suzanne Farley, *Comment: Juvenile Enemy Combatants and the Juvenile Death Penalty in U.S. Military Commissions*, 47 Santa Clara Law Review 829 (2007). Farley decries the ambiguous legal status of these juveniles and calls for clarification by the U.S. authorities that they are protected from imposition of the death penalty.

––––––––––

In the Philippines, the juvenile death penalty has been contrary to domestic law for some time. Nevertheless, as the Amnesty International report below demonstrates, several juveniles have been sentenced to death in recent years. To what does Amnesty attribute this inconsistency between law and reality?

Amnesty International, *Philippines: Something Hanging Over Me—Child Offenders under Sentence of Death*

(Oct. 3, 2003) *available at* http://web.amnesty.org/
library/Index/ENGASA350142003

3.2 Philippine domestic law

When the death penalty was reintroduced in 1993 its imposition on children was explicitly prohibited. Section 22 of Republic Act (RA) 7659, which amended the Revised Penal Code in order to provide for the death penalty, states:

> *"The death penalty shall be imposed in all cases in which it must be imposed under existing laws, except when the guilty person is below eighteen (18) years of age at the time of the commission of the crime or is more than seventy years of age or when upon appeal or automatic review of the case by the Supreme Court, the required majority vote is not obtained for the imposition of the death penalty, in which cases the penalty shall be reclusion perpetua."*

. . . .

In addition to Section 22 of RA 7659, the imposition of the death penalty on children is also prohibited by Article 68 of the Revised Penal Code which sets out sentencing procedures for youth offenders. Under Article 68, offenders between the ages of nine and fifteen (who demonstrate 'discernment') shall receive a sentence "two degrees lower" than an adult, and those under eighteen but above fifteen shall receive a sentence of "one degree lower." By "degree" the law refers to different gradations of severity in the same type of crime. The crime of theft, for example, is divided into several categories based on the value of the goods stolen and consequently, the law provides for differing sentences based on the "degree" of the crime. A serious crime such as forcible abduction with rape with aggravating circumstances, for example, which would be punishable by life imprisonment or death for an adult offender, would then be reduced by one degree to a sentence of ten to seventeen years if committed by a youth offender over the age of fifteen but under the age of eighteen.

[By law, it is impossible that seven youth offenders have been sentenced to death. Yet for Ramon Nicodemus, Saturani Panggayong, Roger Pagsibigan, Larina Perpinan, Elmer Butal, Christopher Padua, and Ronald Bragas this 'legal impossibility' is a very unfortunate reality. All were reportedly under the age of 18 at the time the crimes were committed and all are currently under sentence of death. Amnesty International has received information indicating that there may be more youth offenders under sentence of death.]

One vital oversight in the Philippine juvenile justice system is the absence of any requirement to inquire into or establish whether or not a suspect is below the age of eighteen. Amnesty International is concerned that the lack of such a provision means that many children in conflict with the law may be treated and detained as adults until they are brought before a judicial authority. Amnesty International believes that this omission effectively constitutes a violation of article 10.3 of the United Nations (UN) Standard Minimum Rules for the Administration of Juvenile Justice which requires that "[c]ontacts between the law enforcement agencies and a juvenile offender ... be managed in such a way as to respect the legal status of the juvenile." In addition, it appears to seriously undermine the effectiveness of domestic legal provisions and regulations aimed at providing human rights safeguards for child suspects.

4. Cases: child offenders under sentence of death

As of September 2003, Christopher Padua, Ronald Bragas, Elmer Butal, Ramon Nicodemus, Saturani Panggayong and Roger Pagsibigan are held in Cell 215, Medium Security Compound, New Bilibid Prison. Larina Perpinan is held in the Women's Correctional Institution. All remain under sentence of death. The six male youth offenders are separated from other inmates because of the severity of their sentences, and until recently were locked in their cells for more than 23 hours a day. Now in their twenties, the seven were convicted for crimes committed between 1995 and 1998 when each of them were reportedly under the age of 18. They have been detained since that time in adult facilities. Until August 2002 they were held on death row with convicted adults.

On 30 July, 2002, the Supreme Court of the Philippines ordered that the above seven youth offenders be transferred from death row.... The decision, which for some of the detainees came as many as seven years after their arrest, was made on the basis of the submission of documentation proving they were juveniles at the time the crimes in question were committed.

. . . .

Since the Supreme Court's decision, their cases were referred to the regional trial court in order for evidence of minority to be presented. Some of the youth offenders have now submitted their proof of minority to the regional trial court and have had it accepted; some have encountered complications and some have not yet had hearing dates assigned. Once proof of minority is accepted the case is then forwarded once again to the Supreme Court where the documentation is presented for the second time. At this stage, sentencing will be revised. Although more than one year has passed since documentation establishing minority was presented to the Supreme Court, all seven remain under sentence of death.

The crimes for which these individuals have been convicted are serious ones. The charges include rape, murder, attempted murder, aggravated robbery and kidnap for ransom. Amnesty International has the greatest sympathy for the victims of these crimes and for their families. Some of the youth offenders deny the charges against them and are appealing or intend to file appeals. Amnesty International does not take a position on whether they are innocent or guilty of the charges for which they have been convicted. The organization, however, believes that the manner in which these individuals were treated and the sentences that were imposed are inconsistent with Philippine and international law with respect to youth offenders. The delay in rectifying these breaches is an additional cause for concern that Amnesty International feels necessary to highlight in order to accelerate the pace with which this matter is resolved.

4.1 Proving minority: a necessary prerequisite

The best juvenile justice system in the world is of little use to a youth offender if they are assumed to be and treated as an adult. Establishing the age of possible youth offenders may appear to be both an obvious and a straightforward point. In many ways it is. In the Philippines, the lack of a requirement to inquire into the age of a suspect at the time of arrest is a serious hindrance which could be easily rectified. An inquiry should be made as a matter of course in all cases where a suspect could reasonably be expected to be near or below the age of eighteen.

The matter is further complicated when it is taken into consideration that youth who come into conflict with the law tend to come from disadvantaged, marginalized and impoverished sectors of society. While not all youth in detention come from such sectors, it has been established that, for instance, street youth are consistently over-represented in the juvenile justice system.

For children who are born into the least advantaged sectors of society traditional indicators of age may be less easily accessed and less readily available. Not all births are registered, and for those that are there may be discrepancies in details such as the spelling of names, or the listed last names if both parents are not legally married. School records may start late, end early, be sporadic or non-existent. Children may not understand the law and the advantage of proving their minority and may claim to be older than they are for a variety of reasons. Families break up and children become estranged from their parents. Street children may not remember their birthdates, may not know their true ages and may have travelled great distances from where their records are kept.

Children from disadvantaged backgrounds who have committed crimes may also not be readily believed when they claim to be under the age of eighteen. Others may erroneously decide that the acts child offenders have committed disqualify them from the benefits of minority. Many of these factors came into play for the child offenders sentenced to death.

. . . .

4.2 Conditions of detention

From the time of arrest the seven youth offenders were treated as adult detainees. They were held in police stations and, unfortunately, as with many child and adult detainees in the Philippines, some were subjected to torture and ill-treatment on arrest and in detention.

Some of the seven youth offenders under sentence of death report being physically ill-treated at the time of or immediately following arrest. Following arrest one youth offender reported that he was "physically beaten by the police because they were forcing me to admit to the shooting . . ." and that he was "treated like punching bags, hit with fists, kicked and beaten." Another youth stated "I was beaten by those who arrested me." A third youth offender stated that he was "pistol whipped" (beaten with a firearm). One youth offender described being "[forced to] drink a lot of water and [being] made [to] sleep handcuffed to a flagpole standing up."

Once in detention several of the youth offenders reported actual or fear of ill-treatment from adult detainees with whom they were imprisoned. One individual stated: "I thought I myself was going to get killed because there were fights among all of the inmates and each had sharp weapons." Another reported: "I was put in a cell together with the older inmates. When I was still new there, they touched me sexually and when I resisted, they punched me."

After the intervention by a number of governmental and non-governmental agencies and the submission of documentation establishing minority to the Supreme Court in July 2002, the court ruled to transfer the youth offenders from death row on 30 July 2002. They were transferred on 18 August 2002. Unfortunately, however, the youth offenders felt that their conditions of detention actually worsened as a result of the transfer. While on death row they had had free movement around the death row building during the day. In the medium security wing one youth offender reported "we are always in our cell like birds in a cage." Investigations by governmental and non-governmental bodies indicated that the youth offenders were locked in their shared cell for all but 15 to 30 minutes a day. They also did not have access to schooling or other social, educational or religious activities held in the prison.

....

Notes and Questions

1. The Philippines did enact a comprehensive law on juvenile justice in early 2006. To the great satisfaction of children's rights activists, the law specifically adopted an approach based on restorative justice. It increased the age of criminal responsibility from 9 to 15 years, exempted minors from facing charges for "status" crimes like vagrancy, and explicitly exempted minors from the imposition of the death penalty. The Philippines' Commission on Human Rights has the task of monitoring the implementation of the law. See *Philippines enacts law on juvenile justice system*, 16 May 2006, *available at*: http:// www.unicef.org/philippines/archives/news/060405.html.

To what extent was the Philippine government reacting to negative publicity by groups like Amnesty when it enacted the new law?

───────────

D. From Punishment to Child Rights: The Case of South Africa

As the following article by Julia Sloth-Nielsen makes clear, during the apartheid era, many juveniles were detained as a result of their political activities. When South Africa made its historical break from apartheid, it needed to alter its approach to and conception of youthful criminal defendants in a dramatic way. One advantage of being offered a "clean slate" of this kind is that laws tend to be drafted in a highly self conscious and targeted manner. As we saw with respect to the South African approach to corporal punishment in schools, the evolution of a new legal regime required the application of international human rights principles to vexed issues arising from historical divisions. The article that follows sets out the major issues in creating a new regime for South Africa's juvenile offenders in the late 1990s.

According to Sloth-Nielsen, what methods has South Africa chosen in order to remake social reality in the area of juvenile law and practice? As you read, consider the way in which a nation's political and social history influences its approach to juvenile justice, and the tremendous difficulty entailed in drafting a juvenile justice law that is both fair and workable.

Julia Sloth-Nielsen, *The Juvenile Justice Law Reform Process in South Africa: Can a Children's Rights Approach Carry the Day?*

18 Quinnipiac Law Review 469 (1999)

I. BACKGROUND TO THE SOUTH AFRICAN LAW REFORM PROCESS

The impetus for juvenile justice law reform sprang originally from concern for the plight of child detainees in the dark days of apartheid in the 1980s. Children, who were at the forefront of the struggle for democratic rule and against apartheid, were liable to be detained without trial as punishment for their political activism. Many hundreds of children were detained without trial under the infamous security legislation of the time. However, in the early 1990s, the political climate changed: detention without trial for political activity abated; a moratorium was placed on the execution of the death penalty; Nelson Mandela was released from prison; and negotiations for the transition to democracy began to get underway. Because the focus during the struggle had been to achieve basic human rights and the franchise for all South Africans, it was only after this period that attention turned from children as political detainees to securing procedural rights for children caught up in the conventional criminal justice system.

Historically, children charged with criminal offenses were treated in much the same way as their adult counterparts, with limited concessions being made in the course of criminal proceedings to account for their youth and immaturity.

The impetus for the present day endeavor aimed at drafting legislation for the creation of a separate and new juvenile justice system had its origin in the early 1990s. Following upon the easing of political repression against children, human rights oriented non-governmental organizations launched campaigns to focus the public attention on children who were in detention for offenses not linked to the struggle. An influential role was played by the Community Law Center, then headed by Advocate Dullah Omar, now Minister of Justice. Under his leadership, children's rights, and juvenile justice in particular, were a key area of research and advocacy of the Center. The advocacy had a practical basis as well as a research focus. Thus, university law students were contracted by the Center, designated "youth advocates," and dispatched to courts where juveniles were being tried in the Cape Town region, with the aim of intervening informally in the criminal process to provide aid to arrested children. They helped to track down their parents and guardians, and advocated for their release from custody in the pre-trial phase. Throughout this period, the major focus of the efforts of organizations involved in the campaigns was attempting to secure the release of children awaiting trial from prisons and police cells. Two of the most prominent of these campaigns were the "Release a Child for Christmas Campaign" and the "No Child Should Be Caged" initiative.

. . . .

A parallel initiative, which can be regarded as a second key factor in South Africa's juvenile justice history, commenced in 1992. The National Institute for Crime and the Rehabilitation of Offenders (NICRO) took the step of launching programs specifically targeted at young offenders, which were offered to courts as alternative sentencing options, or, something novel at the time in South Africa, as diversion options. . . .

In the initial period before South Africa's first democratic elections in 1994, therefore, the development of juvenile diversion can be tracked chiefly through two parallel and complementary initiatives. The first is public awareness of the plight of children in prison (at first confined entirely to attention on children awaiting trial, but over time, focusing to a limited extent on children sentenced to serve periods of imprisonment as well). Second is the development of diversion for juvenile offenders charged with petty offenses.

A third crucial signifier of impending change, occurring within a year of the transition to democratic rule, was the judgment of the newly established Constitutional Court in the case of S. v. Williams. In a constitutional challenge based mainly on violation of the right to freedom from cruel, inhuman, and degrading treatment or punishment, juvenile whipping was outlawed. Hitherto, judicially ordered strokes with a rod were a common penalty in juvenile criminal cases in South Africa, with some 35,000 children being sentenced to this form of punishment annually before the ban imposed by the Constitutional Court took effect. The abolition of the sentence of whipping as the routine "default option" for convicted children lent its own impetus to the movement to overhaul the juvenile justice system in the country. It left a gaping hole in the armory of sentencing options available to judicial officers, accompanied by a recognition that new options for children in conflict with the law would have to be devised.

As will be seen, the two prime concerns of the reformers of the early 1990s detailed above—limiting incarceration in prison and promoting diversion—form the backbone of the model juvenile justice statute that has been developed under the auspices of the South African Law Commission. Key themes in the draft statute are described more fully in the second section of this paper.

However, there is no denying that the political conditions for child rights-based law reform in relation to juvenile justice have changed markedly in some respects from the position that prevailed in 1994. The idealistic notions about "saving children from prison" that prevailed when elections for a democratic government took place have given way to a more realistic assessment of the seriousness of some juvenile offending, and the concomitant need to ensure a more nuanced approach to juvenile justice (as opposed to the blanket slogans of the early campaigns).

Also, non-governmental organizations ("NGOs"), government departments, and key Ministries involved in the administration of juvenile justice have learned some important practical lessons over the last while, derived chiefly from the saga of legislative attempts between 1994 and 1998 which were aimed at limiting the imprisonment of children awaiting trial. One academic has described this history as "an illustration of an attempted reform that failed."

A short summary of this recent history will suffice. As many of the new parliamentarians had themselves experienced imprisonment under apartheid, and probably as a consequence of the high profile accorded the campaigns for the release of children who were awaiting trial in prisons in the lead up to the 1994 elections, one of the first bills passed by the incoming government was one dramatically affecting children in prison. In a now oft-cited speech in Parliament, the President too, had, shortly after taking office, committed himself to improving the plight of detained children. Parliament therefore passed an amendment to the Correctional Services Act (which regulates prisons) to prohibit any detention of children in a prison while awaiting trial. The amendments put a blanket ban on pre-trial detention of any person under the age of eighteen, after the initial forty-eight hour period in police custody, which was permissible pending a first appearance in court. Children under fourteen years cannot be held in a prison at all, and their detention in police cells was confined to the twenty-four hour period before a first appearance in court. Apart from these limited concessions, it was intended that pre-trial detention in prisons be prohibited for all children under the age of eighteen years, irrespective of the offense with which the child had been charged or prior criminal history. It was envisaged that children awaiting trial would be detained in a more humane welfare institution (place of safety), rather than prisons.

This new arrangement was unanimously agreed to by all political parties and greeted with acclaim by individual members of parliament. But the new legislation lay dormant, paper on the statute book, for some months after its passage through Parliament. However, in 1995, the press began again to profile the plight of vulnerable and impoverished child detainees who were being held in appalling conditions in some prisons, and, probably in response, the legislation was suddenly promulgated without warning, literally overnight, on May 10, 1995. Some 1500 children were released immediately from prisons and from police cells, and the new ban on pre-trial detention (other than in welfare facilities) plunged the entire child and youth care system as well as the criminal justice system into chaos. It is now established wisdom that some of the released children committed serious offenses within days of their release....

It soon became clear that the issue of pre-trial incarceration of juvenile offenders was to constitute the first public backlash against the new government. The prohibition on the detention of children in prison became linked, in the public mind, with the early signs of a rising crime rate. In a remarkable volte face, the media headlines now depicted children who were formerly "poor incarcerated urchins" as "teenage thugs." Urgent steps needed to be taken in the face of one of the most severe crises to hit the present government.

Consequently, the government was forced to backtrack, indicative of wavering political will where children's rights were in conflict with fears about crime. Only six months after the 1994 amendment had come into operation, a Private Members Bill put forward by a stalwart of the African National Congress proposed that, as a temporary and extraordinary measure, courts should be empowered to order that certain children be held in prison to await trial. Thus a second amendment was made to the Correctional Services Act, as it became clear that the infrastructure to replace prisons with welfare facilities could not be obtained overnight. The second amendment, which took effect in May 1996, provided for limited circumstances when children over fourteen years, but younger than eighteen years, could be detained in prisons while awaiting trial. The 1996 amendments were intended to be temporary given the morally uncomfortable position that government had been compelled to adopt. A legislative provision was included which was supposed to ensure that the authorization to detain children would lapse after two years. However, due to a drafting error, the legislation did not cease to have effect in May 1998, and it continues to regulate the position of children awaiting trial today.

. . . .

The same parliamentarians who in 1994 declared the plight of children awaiting trial in prisons to be the "highest priority" of government were, when the drafting error became a matter of public record in early1998, somewhat more cautious about the wisdom of bold steps to set things right. There was a palpable sense of relief that the state would still have the authority in law to detain juvenile offenders in prison, and even NGOs that had the capacity to do so failed to challenge the state's reliance on a technical drafting mistake to save the day.

The political mood has changed, and in the intervening four years, crime has become the dominant concern of the government. The charter of rights accorded that arrested, detained, and sentenced people in the new constitution are increasingly being viewed as constituting a "free ticket" for criminals. In response, harsh legal measures recently have been, and are still being, rushed through Parliament in an attempt to abridge and curtail the perceived criminal justice "black holes" that the constitution has allegedly brought about. In this climate, parliamentarians are understandably anxious about provisions that might allow children charged with serious and violent offenses to be released into communities that are vociferously expressing their disaffection with crime and the failings of the criminal justice system. Thus children's rights organizations have by and large refrained from challenging the status quo and, in particular, the steadily rising child detention figures. But, arguably, the organizations that originally championed the release of children from prisons have been forced to develop a different (more pragmatic) agenda in the present climate of crime control. These organizations have come to accept the inevitability of detaining serious offenders in prison even where they are of tender years; however, NGOs continue to draw attention to the view that the continued spotlight on a few children in prison detracts from the systematic overhaul of the entire juvenile justice system. The shifting sands of media attention on children awaiting trial in prisons have indeed created an arena in which progressive reform towards the creation of a new juvenile justice system is all the more difficult to achieve.

II. THE PARALLEL PROCESS: DEVELOPING A NEW JUVENILE JUSTICE STATUTE FOR SOUTH AFRICA

Alongside the parliamentary endeavors described above, a Project Committee of the South African Law Commission has been undertaking the task of drafting a separate juvenile justice statute for South Africa. The appointment of the Project Committee was a culmination of the early efforts by NGOs to secure separate legislation on juvenile justice. It was also linked to South Africa's ratification of the 1989 United Nations Convention on the Rights of the Child that requires a ratifying country to draft child-specific legislation in relation to juvenile justice.

. . . .

The remainder of this paper will focus on the content of the Draft Bill proposed by the Project Committee, its vision, and the model that has emerged. In particular, the influence of some of the socio-political factors identified above upon both the content and contours of the draft legislation will be highlighted. The proposals have, after all, been centrally affected by the practical developments since 1994, as well as by what the drafters perceive as being realistic and achievable—both politically and economically. Thus, rather than an academic or "ivory tower stance" so often found in Law Commission proposals, the Project Committee has striven to draft legislation that is not only rooted in a child-rights framework, but is also likely to garner support from the government and politicians alike.

A. Drafting Legislation for a Child Justice System

. . . .

The experiences with the precipitous release of children from prison in 1995, and the inter-sectoral coordination that occurred following this crisis to improve and extend the capacity of the welfare system by providing alternative care facilities for use instead of prisons, have provided valuable lessons. The Project Committee concluded that at a purely practical level, implementing a new juvenile justice system would in all likelihood continue to be an inter-departmental affair, such that the drafters of any legislation would have to provide legal provisions easily understood by police, social workers and lawyers. Therefore, a coherent overall vision (or game-plan) would enhance its effectiveness.

A second reason for seeking to design a system, rather than a set of disparate procedural rules, was that our comparative research seemed to indicate that successful juvenile justice systems indeed followed this route. In particular, the project committee examined the literature on juvenile justice from New Zealand, Uganda, and Scotland, all of whose legislative provisions seem to indicate a coherent model.

B. Diversion

An obvious challenge that has faced the project committee from the outset, arising from the specific juvenile justice history that South Africa has so recently experienced, has been the need to balance the legal requirements pertaining to children detained in prison with the plight of the many other children in the country who are arrested, charged, processed through the adult court system, and sentenced. And, until now, only statistical records of children awaiting trial in prison have been reasonably well documented and accessible. There is, by contrast, no reliable information indicating what proportion of juveniles in conflict with the law the numbers of children in prison represent. In short, whilst it has been loosely estimated that some 15,000 children might be admitted to prison to await trial each year, analysts have been unable to determine with any clarity how many children are actually arrested annually in the country. It has been asserted that a possible figure is between 60,000 to 160,000 children, a far greater number than those admitted to prison.

. . . .

. . . [T]he Draft Bill proposes that diversion be given formal legislative definition and content, and that a set of minimum standards apply to those bodies or institutions offering such opportunities. The opportunities for diverting cases at the earliest possible stage are greatly increased in the proposed legislation. The Draft Bill proposes the introduction of a formal police caution for the first time if this is recommended by a probation officer, and proposes that probation officers could have the authority to divert cases of their own accord (without reference to the prosecuting authorities), where children are charged with petty offenses listed in a schedule attached to the draft legislation.

The recommendations concerning diversion in the proposed legislation have been further influenced by the reality that services, programs, and alternative diversion possibilities are in somewhat short supply at grass-roots levels, especially outside the larger urban areas. The contribution of NICRO towards the development of diversion options has been alluded to, but from within the state, no explicit moves to develop further diversion options or new alternative sentences to underpin a new child justice system has yet occurred. The approach of the drafters of the proposed bill has been to include a range of measures aimed at stimulating an increase in the availability of diversionary options. So, for example, the Draft Bill develops a set of new orders which can be used either as diversion options, or as alternative sentences. They include supervision and guidance, a positive peer association order, a family time order, and so forth.

It is clearly expressed that these orders can be monitored by a designated person in the community such as a teacher, religious leader, or any other suitable adult. Human or financial resources from the State are therefore not an essential requirement. This is intended to ensure that these orders can be utilized in even remote rural areas, where probation officers or social workers are not necessarily available.

Further, a provision has been included in the Draft Bill to the effect that if a judicial officer has decided diversion to be an appropriate option in a particular case, where formal programs are not available, that judicial officer must "as far as possible, develop a diversion strategy which meets the standards and requirements of diversion . . . and which is appropriate to the circumstances of the child, his or her family, community of origin and the alleged offense."

....

E. A New Jurisdiction: The Envisaged Child Justice Court

South Africa has a three-tiered criminal court system: the first tier is comprised of the district courts, which have jurisdiction over all offenses save murder, treason, and rape. The district courts have sentencing powers of up to two years imprisonment. The next tier is comprised of the regional courts, which have wider geographical jurisdiction, sentencing powers of up to fifteen years imprisonment, and criminal jurisdiction for all offenses including murder and rape, but excluding treason. At the highest level are the high courts, which have geographical jurisdiction broadly similar to provincial boundaries, unlimited sentencing powers, and the jurisdiction to try all offenses. At present, there is no dedicated juvenile court system in South Africa, although in large urban jurisdictions, one court room is usually utilized for juvenile hearings, so that there is an administrative arrangement which results in a quasi-juvenile court. Other than in large urban centers, children are generally tried in the same courts in which adult hearings are conducted.

The Draft Bill grants jurisdiction for juvenile criminal cases to a new child justice court, which would be placed at the lowest level of jurisdiction in the hierarchy as possible, that is, at the district court level. After the preliminary inquiry, the usual adversarial trial (with appropriate legal representation for the child accused) would ensue. However, it is proposed that the child justice courts would have increased sentencing jurisdiction of up to five years imprisonment. This is to ensure that as many criminal trials as possible, where children are defendants, would then be able to be dealt with by a more specialized forum at the lower level. Serious cases that would ordinarily be transferred to higher courts because of the possibility of higher sentences could therefore be retained at the lower court level. This was deliberately framed with the intention of promoting specialization in juvenile justice matters, and to ensure that as many children as possible have access to the more specialized forum.

In this regard, it is worth pointing out that the Draft Bill does not allow for waiver of juvenile status where a child is under the age of eighteen years, even where the charges against such a child are regarded as serious, and even where the penalty is likely to be severe. Instead the Draft Bill proposes that where a sentence may be imposed which may exceed the proposed five-year sentencing jurisdiction of the child justice court, the matter may be tried in a regional court or high court. However, any such higher-level court must nevertheless follow the principles and procedures applicable to the child justice court, and most especially the principles applicable to sentencing. This does not, it is submitted, amount to waiver of juvenile court jurisdiction.

F. A System Which Accommodates Serious and Petty Cases

The Draft Bill clearly attempts to create a new system which can address juvenile justice in a comprehensive manner. Thus, because of the fact that transfer to the adult system is not a feature of the proposed model, provisions on sentencing in particular have been drafted to allay concerns that the proposed Bill is primarily oriented towards first time and petty offenders. Therefore, a prison sentence of a maximum of fifteen years may be imposed on a child in terms of section 78(9), although such a sentence may only be imposed where the seriousness of the offense and the protection of the community requires such a sentence, or where the child has previously failed to respond to non-custodial sentences.

....

G. The Minimum Age of Criminal Responsibility

Most contentious of all has been the question of the minimum age of criminal responsibility, which in practice is inevitably linked to perceptions and preconceptions about serious juvenile crime. Cardinal principles related to children's rights and international law underpin the proposed South African legislation, so that it is reasonably clear that the upper limit of the new juvenile justice system will be eighteen years, as stated in the United Nations Convention on the Rights of the Child, and reiterated in the South African Constitution. The problem of drafting legislation within a children's rights framework to regulate the position where younger children are accused of serious offenses is not novel to South Africa. This may prove to be a dominating theme in the political debates about the new juvenile justice system that lies ahead. There are indications of a reluctance to forecast with too much finality on this issue at this interim stage, because of the risk of the ripple effect it might have on other aspects of the proposed legislation.

Therefore, the Project Committee has not proposed a definitive solution for the minimum age of criminal capacity. Rather, the Draft Bill presents three possible choices for debate. The first option proposed is a fixed minimum age of twelve or fourteen years. Second, the Draft Bill frames a provision with a fixed minimum age of prosecution, with exceptions for serious offenses such as murder, rape, and armed robbery. The third possibility involves retaining some vestige of the Roman Law presumption that a child under the age of fourteen is presumed incapable of forming a criminal intent, which can be rebutted by the state on production of evidence concerning the maturity of the child and his or her ability to form a criminal intent. The minimum age could then be set at ten or twelve years, with the presumption applicable to children between this age and fourteen years.

III. CAN A CHILDREN'S RIGHTS APPROACH CARRY THE DAY?

The Project Committee members have been acutely aware that the final legislation that will be introduced to Parliament will occur against a backdrop of an ever-increasing fear of crime. Media reports (even "scientific studies") draw attention to an alleged increase in youth crime, and (in one study) hold youth accountable for substantial proportions (up to eighty percent) of criminal activity in the country. All the while that the drafting process towards a children's rights oriented criminal procedure has been underway, Parliament has been adopting a range of harsh legislative provisions in relation to the criminal justice system in general.

So, in recent months, South Africa has seen the introduction of statutory minimum sentences (from which children are not excluded) and tough anti-bail provisions implemented in 1998. The introduction of RICO-type legislation aimed at throttling the gangs, which too sweeps children into its ambit, is imminent. It has been suggested that many of these new provisions are part of a pre-election strategy, designed to address the public backlash against crime before the May 1999 elections. The Project Committee is well aware that the tough new crime control atmosphere may ultimately compromise or dilute the proposed draft legislation.

The Draft Bill released by the Project Committee represents, it is submitted, an attempt to tread a middle path without compromising the ideal of a children's rights framework. Indeed, the non-governmental sector and welfarists are likely to complain that the Draft Bill reneges on the promise to ban pre-trial detention in prisons, and moreover, contemplates abandoning children charged with serious crimes to the mercy (if one can call it that) of superior courts with vast sentencing jurisdiction. On the other hand, though, those presently campaigning for ever harsher prison sentences, the return of the death penalty, and so forth, may view the proposals as constituting a "soft approach" to child offending, particularly as diversion and the philosophy of restorative justice form central pillars of the model. There may well be objections from these quarters to the proposed outright ban on the use of imprisonment as a sentence for young persons under the age of fourteen years.

The challenge for the future, however, is to ensure that the proposed system survives the cut and thrust of the political process more or less intact. A key element of this would be acceptance of the fundamental principle that the criminal code for juveniles should apply to all children under eighteen years, without exception. If exceptions were to be contemplated—for children charged with serious offenses, or children above a certain age—there is a risk that a philosophy of crime control rather than children's rights will determine the future of juvenile justice in South Africa.

Notes and Questions

1. In fact, South Africa did enact a wide-ranging new "Child Justice" law in November of 2008. As indicated in the Sloth-Nielsen article, the bill was under consideration for many years, and met with many obstacles. In the end, it was based on certain compromises. For instance, the bill states that children under 10 should not be brought to trial, but provides only a presumption that children between the ages of 10 and 14 lack criminal responsibility. One of the key goals of the drafters, limitation on the practice of pre-trial detention of children, was included in the new law. See Edwin Tshivhidzo, *Justice Bill makes allowance for minors,* available at http://www.southafrica.info/services/rights/child-241108.htm.

2. The ideas and ideals of children's rights are placed under great strain in the area of juvenile justice, since the larger community tends to see violent juvenile offenders as extremely frightening and dangerous persons. Thus, there tends to be little in the way of an organized constituency advocating for the humane treatment of juvenile offenders. Seen historically, socially and legally, what ingredients are required in order for states to devise effective protections for the population of youthful criminal defendants?

Chapter Six

Children and Armed Conflict

I. The Machel Report and Its Fallout—
An Introduction to Children and Armed Conflict

Since the end of the Cold War, many civil wars and regional conflicts have been characterized by their extreme brutality and by their reliance on children as valuable military "assets". Across Africa, and from Asia to Latin America, children have become the irresistible targets of recruiters for both rebel armies and government forces in a variety of conflicts. Children have been used as messengers and servants, as well as front line soldiers. Girls have been exploited for sexual purposes, and given to military men as "wives" for the duration of the conflict. Many states that were sites of "proxy wars" sponsored by the United States and Soviet Union during the Cold War have since that time experienced economic collapse and resurgent local tensions. Armed conflicts arising from such situations have relied to an unprecedented extent on young children.

Of course, there is nothing new about using young people to carry out military tasks during periods of armed conflict. It does appear, though, that we have recently witnessed an unprecedented global trend towards the recruitment of children to serve directly in combat situations, especially civil wars. While it is difficult to identify any particular set of reasons why young children have become so popular as "soldiers" in these conflicts, it is clear that once involved, it is nearly impossible for these children to escape. Recruitment techniques of desensitization and brutalization have been common across continents. Despite the proliferation of international laws designed to address the issue, it appears that the number of conflicts in which child soldiers figure prominently has actually increased. The readings that follow in this chapter will document many of these conflicts and the conditions under which children are fighting.

Tens of thousands of children have been recruited into these armies, often forcibly, but sometimes with their apparent consent, bearing in mind that true consent in such circumstances is impossible. Underage soldiers are said to make excellent soldiers by virtue of their obedience and willingness to take risks. Often given drugs and provided with light weapons, children have found themselves in situations where they must kill or be killed. Not infrequently, they have been asked to prove their loyalty by committing atrocities against people from their own communities, leaving behind an appalling legacy of trauma and confusion. The process of rehabilitating these children into normal society is daunting in the extreme. Many have lost their childhoods, as well as all connection to their places of origin. Rehabilitation of child soldiers is time consuming and labor intensive. For countries struggling with a wide variety of social and economic problems, the resources required to address the psychological effects of battlefield trauma on children are likely to remain out of reach.

In 1994, the United Nations asked Graça Machel, former Minister for Education and Culture in Mozambique, to compile a comprehensive report on the burgeoning problem of children and armed conflict. It was her amazing report, issued in 1996, that opened the eyes of the world to the scope and scale of the global phenomenon of the child soldier. As described by Machel, with the end of the Cold War, many regional conflicts shared a common theme of child exploitation. As an internationally recognized child advocate, Machel set out the complex effects of armed conflict on children, identifying the characteristics of contemporary warfare in a wide variety of geographical regions. Over time, her report led to international legal initiatives to establish principles protective of children in combat situations.

This chapter will begin with an analysis of Machel's famous report and its impact. It will also provide an overview of the reactions of the international community, in the form of new laws, official reports and statements of intent. As the chapter will demonstrate, the problem of the child soldier is now regularly on the agenda of the Security Council, and recruitment of children as soldiers has been recognized under international law as a war crime. Finally, the chapter will provide a number of case studies to facilitate analysis of the contrasts and commonalities in armed conflicts that rely heavily on the use of children as soldiers.

A. Machel and Her Report

In 1994, Graça Machel was named by former UN Secretary General Boutros Boutros Ghali as the expert in charge of producing a comprehensive report on the child soldier phenomenon emblematic of post-Cold War conflicts around the world. Besides having been a brilliant government minister, Graça Machel was the widow of President Samora Machel of Mozambique, who died in a plane crash in 1986. She went on to marry Nelson Mandela in 1998.

Her 1996 report drew attention to the brutal features of these conflicts and spoke in gripping terms of the moral abyss represented by the forced participation of children in combat. International legal developments in this area cannot be understood without reading the no-holds barred language of the report itself. As you consider the following selections from the report, consider what sort of worldview Machel presented, and why her report gained so much attention. It should be noted that its contents went well beyond the issue of child soldiers, and dealt extensively with all forms of violence against children in the context of armed conflict.

Graça Machel, *Impact of Armed Conflict on Children*
U.N. Doc. A/51/306 (Aug. 26, 1996), *available at*
http://www.unicef.org/graca/a51-306_en.pdf

Report of the expert of the Secretary-General, Ms. Graça Machel, submitted
pursuant to General Assembly resolution 48/157.

I. Introduction

A. The attack on children

1. Millions of children are caught up in conflicts in which they are not merely bystanders, but targets. Some fall victim to a general onslaught against civilians; others die as part of

a calculated genocide. Still other children suffer the effects of sexual violence or the multiple deprivations of armed conflict that expose them to hunger or disease. Just as shocking, thousands of young people are cynically exploited as combatants.

2. In 1995, 30 major armed conflicts raged in different locations around the world. All of them took place within States, between factions split along ethnic, religious or cultural lines. The conflicts destroyed crops, places of worship and schools. Nothing was spared, held sacred or protected—not children, families or communities. In the past decade, an estimated two million children have been killed in armed conflict. Three times as many have been seriously injured or permanently disabled, many of them maimed by landmines. Countless others have been forced to witness or even to take part in horrifying acts of violence.

3. These statistics are shocking enough, but more chilling is the conclusion to be drawn from them: more and more of the world is being sucked into a desolate moral vacuum. This is a space devoid of the most basic human values; a space in which children are slaughtered, raped, and maimed; a space in which children are exploited as soldiers; a space in which children are starved and exposed to extreme brutality. Such unregulated terror and violence speak of deliberate victimization. There are few further depths to which humanity can sink.

4. The lack of control and the sense of dislocation and chaos that characterize contemporary armed conflicts can be attributed to many different factors. Some observers point to cataclysmic political upheavals and struggles for control over resources in the face of widespread poverty and economic disarray. Others see the callousness of modern warfare as a natural outcome of the social revolutions that have torn traditional societies apart.

. . . .

5. Whatever the causes of modern-day brutality towards children, the time has come to call a halt. The present report exposes the extent of the problem and proposes many practical ways to pull back from the brink. Its most fundamental demand is that children simply have no part in warfare. The international community must denounce this attack on children for what it is—intolerable and unacceptable.

. . . .

B. Course of the study and its methodology

9. At its forty-eighth session, the General Assembly adopted resolution 48/157, entitled "Protection of children affected by armed conflicts", in which it requested the Secretary-General to appoint an expert to undertake a comprehensive study with the support of the Centre for Human Rights and the United Nations Children's Fund (UNICEF). The expert was asked to make recommendations in five areas: (1) the participation of children in armed conflict; (2) the reinforcement of preventive measures; (3) the relevance and adequacy of existing standards; (4) the measures required to improve the protection of children affected by armed conflict; and (5) the actions needed to promote the physical and psychological recovery and social reintegration of children affected by armed conflict.

10. In accordance with the resolution, the expert submitted progress reports to the forty-ninth and fiftieth sessions of the General Assembly (A/49/643 and A/50/537). The expert, Ms. Graça Machel, hereby transmits her final report on the impact of armed conflict on children, pursuant to resolution 48/157. The report sets out the findings and recommendations of the expert, who used the Convention on the Rights of the Child throughout her work as a guiding source of operative principles and standards. The Convention on the Rights of the Child represents a new, multidisciplinary approach to protecting

children. It demonstrates the interdependence of all children's rights, and the relevance of those rights to the activities of a whole host of actors at all levels. In accordance with the Convention on the Rights of the Child, this report uses the term "child" to include everyone under the age of 18.

. . . .

21. While the present report is formally submitted for the consideration of the United Nations General Assembly and its Member States, it is also addressed to regional institutions, United Nations bodies, specialized agencies and other competent bodies, including NGOs, relevant special rapporteurs and working groups, intergovernmental bodies and civil society.

C. Patterns and characteristics of contemporary armed conflicts

22. Violent conflict has always made victims of non-combatants. The patterns and characteristics of contemporary armed conflicts, however, have increased the risks for children. Vestiges of colonialism and persistent economic, social and political crises have greatly contributed to the disintegration of public order. Undermined by internal dissent, countries caught up in conflict today are also under severe stress from a global world economy that pushes them ever further towards the margins. Rigorous programmes of structural adjustment promise long-term market-based economic growth, but demands for immediate cuts in budget deficits and public expenditure only weaken already fragile States, leaving them dependent on forces and relations over which they have little control. While many developing countries have made considerable economic progress in recent decades, the benefits have often been spread unevenly, leaving millions of people struggling for survival. The collapse of functional Governments in many countries torn by internal fighting and the erosion of essential service structures have fomented inequalities, grievances and strife. The personalization of power and leadership and the manipulation of ethnicity and religion to serve personal or narrow group interests have had similarly debilitating effects on countries in conflict.

23. All of these elements have contributed to conflicts, between Governments and rebels, between different opposition groups vying for supremacy and among populations at large, in struggles that take the form of widespread civil unrest. Many drag on for long periods with no clear beginning or end, subjecting successive generations to endless struggles for survival.

24. Distinctions between combatants and civilians disappear in battles fought from village to village or from street to street. In recent decades, the proportion of war victims who are civilians has leaped dramatically from 5 per cent to over 90 per cent. The struggles that claim more civilians than soldiers have been marked by horrific levels of violence and brutality. Any and all tactics are employed, from systematic rape, to scorched-earth tactics that destroy crops and poison wells, to ethnic cleansing and genocide. With all standards abandoned, human rights violations against children and women occur in unprecedented numbers. Increasingly, children have become the targets and even the perpetrators of violence and atrocities.

. . . .

26. Unbridled attacks on civilians and rural communities have provoked mass exoduses and the displacement of entire populations who flee conflict in search of elusive sanctuaries within and outside their national borders. Among these uprooted millions, it is estimated that 80 per cent are children and women.

27. Involving children as soldiers has been made easier by the proliferation of inexpensive light weapons. Previously, the more dangerous weapons were either heavy or com-

plex, but these guns are so light that children can use them and so simple that they can be stripped and reassembled by a child of 10. The international arms trade has made assault rifles cheap and widely available so the poorest communities now have access to deadly weapons capable of transforming any local conflict into a bloody slaughter. In Uganda, an AK-47 automatic machine gun can be purchased for the cost of a chicken and, in northern Kenya, it can be bought for the price of a goat.

. . . .

II. Mitigating The Impact Of Armed Conflict On Children

29. Armed conflicts across and between communities result in massive levels of destruction; physical, human, moral and cultural. Not only are large numbers of children killed and injured, but countless others grow up deprived of their material and emotional needs, including the structures that give meaning to social and cultural life. The entire fabric of their societies—their homes, schools, health systems and religious institutions—are torn to pieces.

30. War violates every right of a child—the right to life, the right to be with family and community, the right to health, the right to the development of the personality and the right to be nurtured and protected. Many of today's conflicts last the length of a "childhood", meaning that from birth to early adulthood, children will experience multiple and accumulative assaults. Disrupting the social networks and primary relationships that support children's physical, emotional, moral, cognitive and social development in this way, and for this duration, can have profound physical and psychological implications.

31. In countless cases, the impact of armed conflict on children's lives remains invisible. The origin of the problems of many children who have been affected by conflicts is obscured. The children themselves may be removed from the public, living in institutions or, as is true of thousands of unaccompanied and orphaned children, exist as street children or become victims of prostitution. Children who have lost parents often experience humiliation, rejection and discrimination. For years, they may suffer in silence as their self-esteem crumbles away. Their insecurity and fear cannot be measured.

32. This section of the report documents some of the most grave impacts of armed conflict on children. The presentation is not intended to be exhaustive, but to signal major concerns and to suggest practical steps for improvement. It attempts to demonstrate that the impact of armed conflict on children cannot be fully understood without looking at the related effects on women, families and communities. It strives to illustrate how children's well-being is best ensured through family and community-based solutions to armed conflict and its aftermath, and that those solutions work best when they are based on local cultures and drawn from an understanding of child development. This section also emphasizes the importance of considerations of age—in particular, that adolescents have special needs and special strengths. Young people should be seen in that light; as survivors and active participants in creating solutions, not just as victims or problems.

33. The discussion that follows necessarily includes specific examples. It is not an effort to single out specific groups, Governments, or non-state entities. Countries are named representatively and on the basis of what is widely known. In reality, the impact of armed conflict on children is an area in which everyone shares responsibility and a degree of blame.

A. Child soldiers

34. One of the most alarming trends in armed conflict is the participation of children as soldiers. Children serve armies in supporting roles, as cooks, porters, messengers and spies. Increasingly, however, adults are deliberately conscripting children as soldiers. Some

commanders have even noted the desirability of child soldiers because they are "more obedient, do not question orders and are easier to manipulate than adult soldiers".

35. A series of 24 case studies on the use of children as soldiers prepared for the present report, covering conflicts over the past 30 years, indicate that government or rebel armies around the world have recruited tens of thousands of children. Most are adolescents, though many child soldiers are 10 years of age or younger. While the majority are boys, girls also are recruited. The children most likely to become soldiers are those from impoverished and marginalized backgrounds and those who have become separated from their families.

1. Recruitment

36. Child soldiers are recruited in many different ways. Some are conscripted, others are press ganged or kidnapped and still others are forced to join armed groups to defend their families. Governments in a few countries legally conscript children under 18, but even where the legal minimum age is 18, the law is not necessarily a safeguard. In many countries, birth registration is inadequate or non-existent and children do not know how old they are. Recruiters can only guess at ages based on physical development and may enter the age of recruits as 18 to give the appearance of compliance with national laws.

37. Countries with weak administrative systems do not conscript systematically from a register. In many instances, recruits are arbitrarily seized from the streets or even from schools and orphanages. This form of press ganging, known in Ethiopia as "afesa", was prevalent there in the 1980s, when armed militia, police or army cadres would roam the streets picking up anyone they encountered. Children from poorer sectors of society are particularly vulnerable. Adolescent boys who work in the informal sector, selling cigarettes or gum or lottery tickets, are a particular target. In Myanmar, whole groups of children from 15 to 17 years old have been surrounded in their schools and forcibly conscripted. Those who can subsequently prove they are under-age may be released, but not necessarily. In all conflicts, children from wealthier and more educated families are at less risk. Often they are left undisturbed or are released if their parents can buy them out. Some children whose parents have the means are even sent out of the country to avoid the possibility of forced conscription.

38. In addition to being forcibly recruited, youth also present themselves for service. It is misleading, however, to consider this voluntary. While young people may appear to choose military service, the choice is not exercised freely. They may be driven by any of several forces, including cultural, social, economic or political pressures.

39. One of the most basic reasons that children join armed groups is economic. Hunger and poverty may drive parents to offer their children for service. In some cases, armies pay a minor soldier's wages directly to the family. Child participation may be difficult to distinguish as in some cases whole families move with armed groups. Children themselves may volunteer if they believe that this is the only way to guarantee regular meals, clothing or medical attention. Some case studies tell of parents who encourage their daughters to become soldiers if their marriage prospects are poor.

40. As conflicts persist, economic and social conditions suffer and educational opportunities become more limited or even non-existent. Under these circumstances, recruits tend to get younger and younger. Armies begin to exhaust the supplies of adult manpower and children may have little option but to join. In Afghanistan, where approximately 90 per cent of children now have no access to schooling, the proportion of soldiers who are children is thought to have risen in recent years from roughly 30 to at least 45 per cent.

41. Some children feel obliged to become soldiers for their own protection. Faced with violence and chaos all around, they decide they are safer with guns in their hands. Often such children join armed opposition groups after experiencing harassment from government forces. Many young people have joined the Kurdish rebel groups, for example, as a reaction to scorched earth policies and extensive human rights violations. In El Salvador, children whose parents had been killed by government soldiers joined opposition groups for protection. In other cases, armed forces will pick up unaccompanied children for humanitarian reasons, although this is no guarantee that the children will not end up fighting. This is particularly true of children who stay with a group for long periods of time and come to identify it as their protector or "new family".

42. In some societies, military life may be the most attractive option. Young people often take up arms to gain power and power can act as a very strong motivator in situations where people feel powerless and are otherwise unable to acquire basic resources. In many situations, war activities are glorified. In Sierra Leone, the expert met with child soldiers who proudly defended the number of "enemies" they had killed.

43. The lure of ideology is particularly strong in early adolescence, when young people are developing personal identities and searching for a sense of social meaning. As the case of Rwanda shows, however, the ideological indoctrination of youth can have disastrous consequences. Children are very impressionable and may even be lured into cults of martyrdom. In Lebanon and Sri Lanka, for example, some adults have used young people's immaturity to their own advantage, recruiting and training adolescents for suicide bombings. However, it is important to note that children may also identify with and fight for social causes, religious expression, self-determination or national liberation. As happened in South Africa or in occupied territories, they may join the struggle in pursuit of political freedom.

   2. How child soldiers are used

44. Once recruited as soldiers, children generally receive much the same treatment as adults—including the often brutal induction ceremonies. Many start out in support functions which entail great risk and hardship. One of the common tasks assigned to children is to serve as porters, often carrying very heavy loads of up to 60 kilograms including ammunition or injured soldiers. Children who are too weak to carry their loads are liable to be savagely beaten or even shot. Children are also used for household and other routine duties. In Uganda, child soldiers have often done guard duty, worked in the gardens, hunted for wild fruits and vegetables and looted food from gardens and granaries. Children have also been used extensively in many countries as lookouts and messengers. While this last role may seem less life-threatening than others, in fact it puts all children under suspicion. In Latin America, reports tell of government forces that have deliberately killed even the youngest children in peasant communities on the grounds that they, too, were dangerous.

45. Although the majority of child soldiers are boys, armed groups also recruit girls, many of whom perform the same functions as boys. In Guatemala, rebel groups use girls to prepare food, attend to the wounded and wash clothes. Girls may also be forced to provide sexual services. In Uganda, girls who are abducted by the Lord's Resistance Army are "married off" to rebel leaders. If the man dies, the girl is put aside for ritual cleansing and then married off to another rebel.

....

47. While children of both sexes might start out in indirect support functions, it does not take long before they are placed in the heat of battle. Here, their inexperience and

lack of training leave them particularly exposed. The youngest children rarely appreciate the perils they face. A number of case studies report that when the shelling starts the children get over-excited and forget to take cover. Some commanders deliberately exploit such fearlessness in children, even plying them with alcohol or drugs. A soldier in Myanmar recalls: "There were a lot of boys rushing into the field, screaming like banshees. It seemed like they were immortal, or impervious, or something, because we shot at them but they just kept coming."

48. The progressive involvement of youth in acts of extreme violence desensitizes them to suffering. In a number of cases, young people have been deliberately exposed to horrific scenes. Such experience makes children more likely to commit violent acts themselves and may contribute to a break with society. In many countries, including Afghanistan, Mozambique, Colombia and Nicaragua, children have even been forced to commit atrocities against their own families or communities.

3. Demobilization and re-integration into society

49. Clearly one of the most urgent priorities is to remove everyone under 18 years of age from armed forces. No peace treaty to date has formally recognized the existence of child combatants. As a result, their special needs are unlikely to be taken into account in demobilization programmes. In Mozambique, for example, where recruitment of children was well known, child soldiers were not recognized in demobilization efforts by the Resistência Nacional de Moçambique (RENAMO), the Government or the international community. Official acknowledgement of children's part in a war is a vital step. Peace agreements and related documents should incorporate provisions for the demobilization of children; without this recognition, there can be no effective planning or programming on a national scale.

50. The process of reintegration must help children to establish new foundations in life based on their individual capacities. Former child soldiers have grown up away from their families and have been deprived of many of the normal opportunities for physical, emotional and intellectual development. As article 39 of the Convention on the Rights of the Child emphasizes, recovery and reintegration should take place in an environment that fosters the health, self-respect and dignity of the child.

51. Reintegration programmes must re-establish contact with the family and the community. Even children who are successfully reunited with their families, however, have little prospect of smoothly taking up life as it was before. A formerly cheerful 12-year-old may return home as a sullen 16-year-old who feels newly assertive and independent. Re-unification may be particularly difficult for girl soldiers who have been raped or sexually abused, in part because cultural beliefs and attitudes can make it very difficult for them to stay with their families or to have any prospects of marriage. With so few alternatives, many children have eventually become victims of prostitution.

52. In many cases, reunification is impossible. Families may have perished in the conflict or may be untraceable. For some children, a transitional period of collective care may be necessary. Institutional approaches have proven ineffective, but one way to provide such care is through peer-group living arrangements that are strongly integrated into communities

53. Effective social reintegration depends upon support from families and communities. But families are also worn down by conflict, both physically and emotionally, and face increased impoverishment. The field visits and research for the present report repeatedly stressed the importance of links between education, vocational opportunities for former child combatants and the economic security of their families. These are most often the deter-

minants of successful social reintegration and, importantly, they are the factors that prevent re-recruitment.

54. Education, and especially the completion of primary schooling, must be a high priority. For a former child soldier, education is more than a route to employment. It also helps to normalize life and to develop an identity separate from that of the soldier. The development of peer relationships and improved self-esteem may also be facilitated through recreational and cultural activities.

....

57. Child soldiers may find it difficult to disengage from the idea that violence is a legitimate means of achieving one's aims. Even where the experience of participating in "the cause" has been positive, as was often the case for youth who identified with and drew meaning from their part in the struggle against apartheid, the transition to a non-violent lifestyle will be difficult. This is particularly true where the frustrations of poverty and injustice remain. The challenge for Governments and civil society is to channel the energy, ideas and experience of youth into contributing in positive ways to the creation of their new, post-conflict society.

....

B. Refugees and internally displaced children

63. Armed conflict has always caused population movements. During full-scale conflicts, whether or not they cross national boundaries, people flee in large numbers. Their destinations determine whether those who flee will become internally displaced people in their own countries or refugees who have crossed national borders. Africa and Asia have been most affected by massive population upheavals but no region has escaped either the phenomenon itself or its ramifications. Wherever it occurs, displacement has a profound physical, emotional and developmental impact on children and increases their vulnerability. Except where otherwise distinguished in the present report, refugees and internally displaced persons, as well as persons in refugee-like situations, are referred to collectively as displaced persons.

64. At the beginning of the 1980s, there were 5.7 million refugees worldwide. By the end of the decade, the number had increased to 14.8 million, and today there are more than 27.4 million refugees and "persons of concern" to UNHCR, that is, some returnees and people living in "safe havens".

65. According to the report of the Representative of the Secretary-General on Internally Displaced Persons (E/CN.4/1996/52/Add.2), the number of internally displaced people has also escalated in recent years, now reaching an estimated 30 million—more than the number of refugees. The protection and assistance needs of the internally displaced are similar to those of refugees in nearly all respects, and yet their situation can be worse. While refugees have often moved outside the war zone, internally displaced persons usually remain within or close to the scene of conflict and they are often likely to be displaced repeatedly.

66. At least half of all refugees and displaced people are children. At a crucial and vulnerable time in their lives, they have been brutally uprooted and exposed to danger and insecurity. In the course of displacement, millions of children have been separated from their families, physically abused, exploited and abducted into military groups, or they have perished from hunger and disease.

1. Vulnerability of children in flight

....

68. During flight from the dangers of conflict, families and children continue to be exposed to multiple physical dangers. They are threatened by sudden attacks, shelling, snipers and landmines, and must often walk for days with only limited quantities of water and food. Under such circumstances, children become acutely undernourished and prone to illness, and they are the first to die. Girls in flight are even more vulnerable than usual to sexual abuse. Children forced to flee on their own to ensure their survival are also at heightened risk. Many abandon home to avoid forced recruitment, only to find that being in flight still places them at risk of recruitment, especially if they have no documentation and travel without their families.

2. Unaccompanied children

69. Unaccompanied children are those who are separated from both parents and are not in the care of another adult who, by law or custom, has taken responsibility to do so. Children are often separated from parents in the chaos of conflict, escape and displacement. Parents or other primary care-givers are the major source of a child's emotional and physical security and for this reason family separation can have a devastating social and psychological impact. Unaccompanied children are especially vulnerable and at risk of neglect, violence, military recruitment, sexual assault and other abuses. An essential goal of relief programmes must be to provide assistance to families to prevent separations.

....

71. While families are sought, procedures must be set up to prevent further separation and to provide each unaccompanied child with continuous alternative care. Alternative care is most appropriately found with the extended family, but when this is not possible, it can come from neighbours, friends or other substitute families. Nevertheless these arrangements need careful supervision. Many foster families take excellent care of a child, but where economic and social situations have been undermined by war, children may be at risk of exploitation....

....

74. At the height of a conflict, tracing is particularly difficult. Precisely because that is the case, unaccompanied children should not be considered available for adoption. Adoption severs family links permanently and should not be considered unless all family tracing efforts have been exhausted. This principle is safeguarded by a recommendation adopted in the Convention on Protection of Children and Cooperation in respect of Intercountry Adoption signed at The Hague on 29 May 1994.

....

4. Children in camps

77. Ideally, camps for refugees or the internally displaced should be places of safety, offering protection and assistance. However, displaced populations are complex societies that often reproduce former divisions and power struggles. At the same time their traditional systems of social protection come under strain or break down completely and there are often high levels of violence, alcohol and substance abuse, family quarrels and sexual assault. Women and adolescent girls are particularly vulnerable and even the youngest children can be affected when they witness an attack on a mother or a sister. The UNHCR guidelines on sexual violence against refugees outline practical protection measures such as careful lighting, arrangement of latrines and the organizing of people into groups for tasks such as gathering firewood. These and the UNHCR guidelines on the protection and care of refugee children should be applied to all internally displaced women and children.

78. One important aspect of relief that particularly affects women and children is the distribution of resources such as food, water, firewood and plastic sheeting. Control of these resources represents power. Men are usually in charge of distribution and often abuse their power by demanding bribes or sexual favours. This puts women at risk and especially female heads of households. As recommended in the UNHCR Guidelines on the Protection of Refugee Women, UNHCR and WFP should be in the forefront of ensuring that women are the initial point of control in distribution systems and that appropriate support systems are established for female-headed households.

79. The first days and weeks of a mass displacement of people usually result in high mortality rates for children. Among displaced children, measles, diarrhoeal diseases, acute respiratory infections (ARI), malaria and malnutrition account for 60 to 80 per cent of reported deaths. Factors contributing to high mortality include overcrowding and lack of food and clean water, along with poor sanitation and lack of shelter. Pregnant and lactating women require particular attention, as do displaced children living with disabilities. Children coming from armed conflict are likely to have injuries that require special medical attention. In these circumstances, only a multi-sectoral approach to health and nutrition can protect young children.

80. Camp environments are often highly militarized. In some instances, children have been taken, either forcibly or fraudulently, from camps to a third country for "political education" or military training. In several cases, host Governments have recruited refugee children for military service.

. . . .

6. Asylum and the right to identity and nationality

84. Statelessness is a risk for refugee children as they may have difficulty in establishing their identity and nationality. As article 7 of the Convention on the Rights of the Child provides, all children should be registered and receive citizenship at birth. In the case of refugee children, only the host State is in a position to register the child. It is particularly important for a refugee child, especially if unaccompanied, to be provided with clear documentation concerning the identity of parents and place of birth.

85. Families who reach a border are still very exposed and young girls and women who have been separated from their families are particularly vulnerable to exploitation and abuse from border guards and others. Even those who succeed in crossing a border have no guarantee of asylum. The 1951 Convention and the 1967 Protocol relating to the Status of Refugees may not fully cover those fleeing armed conflict. In cases of mass exodus from countries like Afghanistan and Viet Nam, many Governments were sufficiently flexible to grant temporary refuge. However, since the end of the cold war, many Governments have been more reluctant to grant asylum and have even sought to prevent asylum seekers from reaching their borders. As a minimum, Governments should grant temporary asylum pending the identification of a durable solution.

. . . .

7. Returning home and durable solutions

87. Long-term solutions for refugees involve voluntary repatriation, local integration or resettlement into new national communities. Whichever is chosen, procedures should be expeditious and carried out in the best interests of the child. The principles relating to voluntary repatriation and reintegration should also be applied to the return of internally displaced persons. These are to ensure that conditions of safety and dignity as well as national protection are available.

88. For refugee or internally displaced families and children returning to their home communities, reintegration may be very difficult. In countries disrupted by many years of conflict, there are often tensions between returnees and residents. For children in particular, one of the most important measures is to ensure education and the opportunity to re-establish family life and productive livelihoods.

....

C. Sexual exploitation and gender-based violence

1. Gender-based violence: a weapon of war

91. Rape poses a continual threat to women and girls during armed conflict, as do other forms of gender-based violence including prostitution, sexual humiliation and mutilation, trafficking and domestic violence. While abuses such as murder and torture have long been denounced as war crimes, rape has been downplayed as an unfortunate but inevitable side effect of war. Acts of gender-based violence, particularly rape, committed during armed conflicts constitute a violation of international humanitarian law. When it occurs on a massive scale or as a matter of orchestrated policy, this added dimension is recognized as it was at the most recent International Conference of the Red Cross and Red Crescent, as a crime against humanity.

....

94. Rape is not incidental to conflict. It can occur on a random and uncontrolled basis due to the general disruption of social boundaries and the license granted to soldiers and militias. Most often, however, it functions like other forms of torture and is used as a tactical weapon of war to humiliate and weaken the morale of the perceived enemy. During armed conflict, rape is used to terrorize populations or to force civilians to flee.

....

2. Child victims of prostitution and sexual exploitation

96. Poverty, hunger and desperation may force women and girls into prostitution, obliging them to offer sex for food or shelter, for safe conduct through the war zone or to obtain papers or other privileges for themselves and their families. Children have been trafficked from conflict situations to work in brothels in other countries, transported from Cambodia to Thailand, for example, and from Georgia to Turkey. In refugee camps in Zaire, the expert heard numerous reports of girls who had been pressured by their families to enter prostitution. Similarly, some parents among the internally displaced communities in Guatemala have been forced to prostitute their children. Other girls have done so in the hope of securing greater protection. In Colombia, for example, there have been reports of girls as young as twelve submitting themselves to paramilitary forces as a means of defending their families against other groups.

97. With time, different forms of gender-based violence experienced during armed conflicts become institutionalized, since many of the conditions that created the violence remain unchanged. Young girls who have become victims of prostitution for armies, for example, may have no other option but to continue after the conflict has ceased. In Phnom Penh, the number of child victims of prostitution continues to escalate with an estimated 100 children sold into prostitution each month for economic reasons.

98. Children may also become victims of prostitution following the arrival of peace-keeping forces. In Mozambique, after the signing of the peace treaty in 1992, soldiers of the United Nations Operation in Mozambique (ONUMOZ) recruited girls aged 12 to 18 years into prostitution. After a commission of inquiry confirmed the allegations, the sol-

diers implicated were sent home. In 6 out of 12 country studies on sexual exploitation of children in situations of armed conflict prepared for the present report, the arrival of peacekeeping troops has been associated with a rapid rise in child prostitution.

99. Sexual exploitation has a devastating impact on physical and emotional development. Unwanted and unsafe sex is likely to lead to sexually transmitted diseases and HIV/AIDS, which not only affect immediate health but also future sexual and reproductive health and mortality. In Cambodia, according to a study prepared for the present report, it is estimated that 60 to 70 per cent of the child victims of prostitution are HIV positive. Adolescent girls may nonetheless suffer in silence after the trauma of sexual exploitation; they often fear reprisals from those who attacked them or rejection by their families, not to mention the sheer personal humiliation and anguish which causes so many of them to withdraw into a shell of pain and denial. WHO has found that among rape victims the risk of suicide is high.

. . . .

3. Ending impunity

103. The failure to denounce and prosecute wartime rape is partly a result of its mischaracterization as an assault against honour or a personal attack rather than a crime against the physical integrity of the victim. The International Tribunal established to try war crimes committed in the former Yugoslavia has indicted eight people on specific charges of rape and sexual assault, despite estimates of up to 20,000 victims. This limited result underscores the difficulties in applying international human rights and humanitarian law to rape—difficulties which are reflected both in the codification and interpretation of national, and even international, law.

104. The widespread practice of rape as an instrument of armed conflict and ethnic cleansing must be ended and its perpetrators prosecuted. National and international law must codify rape as a crime against the physical integrity of the individual, national Governments must hold those who commit rape in internal conflicts accountable and must reform their national laws to address the substantive nature of the abuse. Unwanted pregnancy resulting from forced impregnation should be recognized as a distinct harm and appropriate remedies provided.

. . . .

4. Preventing gender-based violence

107. Prevention of gender-based violence should include a role for the military, and United Nations peacekeepers in particular. Senior officers often have turned a blind eye to the sexual crimes of those under their command, but they must be held accountable for both their own behaviour and that of the men they supervise. The 12 case studies on gender-based violence prepared for the present report found the main perpetrators of sexual abuse and exploitation to be the armed forces of parties to a conflict, whether governmental or other actors. Military training should emphasize gender sensitivity, child rights and responsible behaviour towards women and children. Offenders must be prosecuted and punished for acts against women and children.

108. Other preventive measures include the construction of shelter, water and sanitation facilities in camps which must be carefully designed to avoid creating opportunities for gender-based aggression against displaced women and children.

. . . .

109. Humanitarian responses have been largely inadequate. UNHCR, however, has published guidelines on prevention and response to sexual violence against refugees and

guidelines on evaluation and care of victims of trauma and violence. These are important efforts to ensure that relief workers are equipped to respond to the special needs of victims of sexual violence. Some effective programmes do exist, such as the "Women Victims of Violence" project in Kenya. This was initiated by UNHCR following the very large number of rapes committed by bandits and local security personnel in the Somali refugee camps of north-eastern Kenya.... Such programmes have been few and far between, however. To be effective, they should provide comprehensive services including economic assistance and psychosocial support, and they should not overtly identify the women as victims. If such initiatives are to succeed, the local community must be involved in their design and implementation.

....

F. Health and Nutrition

....

3. Disability

145. Millions of children are killed by armed conflict, but three times as many are seriously injured or permanently disabled by it. According to WHO, armed conflict and political violence are the leading causes of injury, impairment and physical disability and primarily responsible for the conditions of over 4 million children who currently live with disabilities. In Afghanistan alone, some 100,000 children have war-related disabilities, many of them caused by landmines. The lack of basic services and the destruction of health facilities during armed conflict mean that children living with disabilities get little support. Only 3 per cent in developing countries receive adequate rehabilitative care, and the provision of prosthetics to children is an area that requires increased attention and financial support. In Angola and Mozambique, less than 20 per cent of children needing them received low-cost prosthetic devices; in Nicaragua and El Salvador, services were also available for only 20 per cent of the children in need. This lack of rehabilitative care is contrary to article 23 of the Convention on the Rights of the Child, which lays out clearly the responsibilities of States Parties for ensuring effective access of disabled children to education, health and rehabilitation services.

4. Destruction of health facilities

146. In most wars, and particularly in internal conflicts, health facilities come under attack, in direct violation of the Geneva Conventions of 1949. During the armed conflict from 1982 to 1987 in Nicaragua, for example, 106 of the country's 450 health units were eventually put out of service as a result of complete or partial destruction, and a further 37 health posts were closed owing to frequent attacks. The intensity of the war also diverted much of the health service to the needs of immediate casualties.... Even health facilities that remain open during a conflict offer very restricted service. In Mozambique, between 1982 and 1990, about 70 per cent of health units were looted or forced to close down and the remainder were difficult to reach because of curfews.

....

5. Protecting health services and health workers

149. In actions at both global and national level, the health sector should continue to promote children's rights to survival and development while doing all it can to prevent and alleviate their suffering. In the midst of armed conflict, WHO urges that health facilities be respected as safe environments for the care of patients and as safe workplaces for health workers. The delivery of medical assistance should not be prevented or obstructed. Moreover, the health care system and the community should work together,

using health care wherever possible as an opportunity to gain access to children for other positive purposes.

....

151. Armed conflict is a major public health hazard that cannot be ignored. Any disease that had caused as much large-scale damage to children would long ago have attracted the urgent attention of public health specialists. When armed conflict kills and maims more children than soldiers, the health sector has a special obligation to speak out. Health professionals must be advocates of the rights of the child.

....

G. Promoting psychological recovery and social reintegration

....

    1. Psychosocial impact of violence on children

....

170. All cultures recognize adolescence as a highly significant period in which young people learn future roles and incorporate the values and norms of their societies. The extreme and often prolonged circumstances of armed conflict interfere with identity development. As a result, many adolescents—especially those who have had severely distressing experiences—cannot conceive of any future for themselves. They may view their lives very pessimistically, suffer from serious depression or, in the worst of circumstances, commit suicide. They may not wish to seek help or support from adults. Moreover, sudden changes in family circumstances, such as the death or disappearance of parents, can leave youth without guidance, role models and sustenance.... Despite all of this, adolescents, during or after wars, seldom receive any special attention or assistance. This is a matter of urgent concern.

....

VII. Conclusion

313. There is a clear and overwhelming moral case for protecting all children while seeking the peaceful resolution of wars and challenging the justification for any armed conflict. That children are still being so shamefully abused is a clear indication that we have barely begun to fulfil our obligations to protect them. The immediate wounds to children, the physical injury, the sexual violence, the psychosocial distress, are affronts to each and every humanitarian impulse that inspired the Convention on the Rights of the Child. The Convention commits States to meet a much broader range of children's rights, to fulfil the rights to health, to education and to growth and development within caring and supportive families and communities.

....

318. Let us claim children as "zones of peace". In this way, humankind will finally declare that childhood is inviolate and that all children must be spared the pernicious effects of armed conflict.

....

By focusing on children, politicians, Governments, the military and non-State entities will begin to recognize how much they destroy through armed conflict and, therefore, how little they gain. Let us take this opportunity to recapture our instinct to nourish and protect children. Let us transform our moral outrage into concrete action. Our children have a right to peace. Peace is every child's right.

Notes and Questions

1. The Machel report was a profoundly influential document. It achieved its purpose of providing a comprehensive analysis of children in armed conflicts, no doubt because it approached the problem in a multi-faceted way. It adopted a tone of moral outrage and urgency often lacking in the bureaucratic language of UN documents. Machel was able to present the problem of child soldiers as a global one, with common and tragic characteristics. What kinds of recommendations does Machel make? What does her primary objective seem to be? Does Machel appear to be assigning blame to any particular party or parties, or provide some other clear sense of causation? She describes the difficulties of reintegrating affected children into societies torn by these conflicts. Whose responsibility should it be to invest in the expertise required for this task?

2. The effect of warfare on children inevitably leads to a host of other violations of children's rights; sexual abuse, trafficking, and lack of access to education and health care, to name but a few. Machel was careful to take note of these related forms of abuse, in particular sex crimes against children, as an aspect of warfare. Did her report try to tackle too many problems at once?

B. Aftermath of the Machel Report

The Machel Report had the effect of making governments aware of the particular brutality of conflicts in which child soldiers were a significant factor. After the report was issued, virtually all writing on the subject began by reference to the galvanizing effect Machel had on international society. Several years after the report, an Optional Protocol to the UNCRC on children and armed conflict[1] was drafted and widely ratified, as will be discussed below. Networks of NGOs, notably the Coalition to End the Use of Child Soldiers, mobilized to bring attention to the plight of child soldiers, and have continued to document conditions in war zones where child soldiers play a prominent part.

The article that follows takes a somewhat different approach, and emphasizes the role of economic globalization in exacerbating the child soldier problem. Stephen Hick relies heavily on Machel's insights, but points to globalization as a major contributor to child-dependant conflicts. Is the author being true to the Machel Report, or using the occasion to make an entirely different set of arguments about the adverse effects of economic globalization?

Stephen Hick, *The Political Economy of War-Affected Children*
575 Annals of the American Academy of Political and
Social Science 106 (2001)

An international policy shift is required to meet the challenges of growing and protracted armed conflicts. This is occurring in the context of increasingly global economic structures, sometimes called globalization. Globalization as it is currently discussed is often perceived largely in economic and political terms. Here I examine globalization as the newest development in the expansion of global capitalism. It is a new manifestation of an old sys-

---

1. Optional Protocol to the Convention on the Rights of the Child on the Involvement of Children in Armed Conflict, G.A. Res. 54/263, Annex I, U.N. GOAR, 54th Sess., Supp. No. 49, U.N. Doc. A/54/49 (May 25, 2000), *available at* http://www2.ohchr.org/english/law/pdf/crc-conflict.pdf.

tem of market liberalism, only this time it is occurring on an international, rather than national, level. Globalization has had numerous negative impacts on people worldwide, one of which is a quantitative shift in the nature of warfare. Increased poverty, weapon sales, new economic relations, and corporate intrusion have contributed to changes in the nature of warfare. All the major armed conflicts in the world are now protracted civil wars in which the primary victims are women and children.

....

Globalization and War

At the 2000 International Conference on War-Affected Children in Winnipeg, Canada, Machel summed up the situation of the world's children caught up in wars:

> Wars have always victimized children and other non-combatants, but modern wars are exploiting, maiming and killing children more callously and more systematically than ever. Children today find themselves caught up in complex and confusing conflicts that have multiple causes and that lack clear prospects for resolution. Children are being sucked into seemingly endless endemic struggles for power and resources.

Machel identifies endemic struggles for power and resources as being at the core of modern wars. It was initially thought that the end of the Cold War would bring peace as the superpowers ceased to fight over control of different regions of the world. Instead, the number of wars has increased, and they have spread to all parts of the world. The wars, however, are different in nature. Instead of wars between nations, they are wars within nations. Mistakenly, these wars are often presented in the media as simply tribal conflicts or ethnic hostilities. But tribal and ethnic differences have always existed and cannot explain the rise of this new phenomenon. These new wars must be analyzed in the context of simultaneous changes that have occurred in the world's political and economic organization. The new wars should be examined within the changes taking place in the world economic organization.

These new wars—intranational wars—have recent and multiple roots, based primarily in the changing politics of economic globalization. Increased economic globalization has created important changes in the world that are resulting in new intranational wars. A review of the literature on recent trends in the global economy and analysis of the political and economic environment in new war-torn countries show three critical factors:

- free trade and direct foreign transnational corporation investment or incursion,

- forced structural adjustment, and

- diverging per capita incomes between countries.

Another factor, the end of the Cold War, has lent a hand in increasing international weapons sales as stockpiles of weapons are sold.

Part of the agenda of globalization is free trade. This aspect is embodied in the World Trade Organization's (WTO) 550-page document "Final Act of the 1986–1994 Uruguay Round." This element of globalization is opening countries to the entry of transnational corporations that are exploiting both people and resources and selling products such as luxury items and weapons. Securing access to resources and cheap labor within countries has involved the use of armies to protect resource-laden land areas and corporate interests. For example, in Angola, Congo, Sierra Leone, and Sudan, competing oil prospectors, gold and diamond miners, and private armies and security firms hired by prospectors are at the root of war. Global businesses not only have created the conditions necessary for many of the current wars but are also directly involved in those wars. In addition, the existence of markets for these products in richer countries has created complicity on the part of developed countries.

As part of free trade, global corporations are profiting from the new wars by selling the weapons that are used. The arms trade has flourished since the start of the 1990s, as corporations produce increased quantities of cheap assault rifles and small arms and as Cold War stockpiles of weapons are sold on the world market. Military spending globally in 1993 was estimated to be U.S.$790 billion, of which U.S.$121 billion was spent in developing countries.

The institutions of globalization, such as the International Monetary Fund, fuel the new wars by forcing countries into structural adjustment programs that weaken national economies and create the conditions for conflict. Rigorous programs of structural adjustment promise long-term market-based economic growth, but demands for immediate cuts in budget deficits and public expenditure only weaken already fragile states, leaving them dependent on forces and relations over which they have little control. It is clear that poverty and lack of development fuel and escalate wars and that decreases in world inequality would go far to help reduce conflicts.

Another aspect is the increased wealth gap created by globalization. The neoliberal economic theory that international trade will result in an equalization of incomes between countries is not being borne out. The adoption of trade liberalization policies and direct foreign investment, the two pillars of economic globalization, are having long-term social and economic impacts in the world. The number of children living in poverty continues to grow as globalization proceeds to expand markets across national boundaries and increase the incomes of a relative few.

The two-tiered world economy widens the gap between rich and poor countries and between rich and poor people within countries. Trends in income for the poorest 40 percent of countries have been "significantly downward since the mid-1960s." The increasing discrepancy between the rich and poor since the initiation of globalization illustrates this. In 1960, the richest 20 percent of the world's population had 70 percent of the world's wealth, and the poorest 2.3 percent. Today, the richest have 85 percent of the wealth, and the poorest have just 1.1 percent. Individual billionaires, numbering 358, have more wealth today than the combined yearly income of 45 percent of the world's people. Poverty is not only persisting in the age of globalization; it is becoming more entrenched. Woodward found that the per capita income of countries during the period of globalization has diverged. For example, between 1965 and 1995, the gross domestic product per capita of the sub-Saharan African countries was halved, and Latin America's fell by 30 percent. Even a recent WTO study confirmed this, finding that "richer countries have been growing faster on average than poorer countries, thereby increasing the global income disparity. These are the very countries that are increasingly finding themselves in civil war. These levels of poverty and misery represent a massive denial of human rights that can generate only more violence and conflict.

Machel has similarly identified several critical causes of the current wave of intranational wars:

1. The fight over natural resources is one cause. Diamonds have financed long-running wars in Sierra Leone and Angola. In Sudan, oil fuels the civil conflict. The profits from narcotics are at the heart of struggles in Afghanistan and Colombia.

2. None of these "economies of war" could flourish without markets in richer countries. Global businesses, some legal, some illegal, have spawned international complicity that makes war not just possible but highly profitable.

3. The wars themselves are perpetuated by international weapons sales, especially sales of small arms. Indeed, small arms are now so accessible that the poorest communities can gain access to deadly weapons capable of transforming any local conflict into a bloody slaughter.

4. Constrained by debt and structural adjustment programs, many developing countries have been forced to restructure their economies, cut basic services, and reduce the size of the public sector. In so doing, they have often weakened national economies and cleared the stage for other actors bent on power and profit.

. . . .

Prevention is the Best Medicine

The best way to protect children from wars is to stop wars from happening. Movement toward this goal could be attained by promoting equitable development, reducing the wealth gap between countries and within countries, stopping the proliferation of weapons sales from the developed to the developing countries, controlling the unchecked exploitation of resources of war-torn countries by transnational corporations, and finding peaceful ways to resolve conflict. While it is crucial to protect children from today's armed conflicts, it is just as important to prevent the outbreak of future wars. The only way of truly protecting children from the impact of armed conflict is to stop the conflicts from occurring. Once a war has started, children's suffering can only be mitigated.

The international community can lower the likelihood of transnational war by addressing these root causes. Corporations must be held accountable for their actions. Governments must lower the risk of armed conflict by demobilizing their societies and reducing the percentage of their gross domestic product spent on military expenditures. Tighter controls need to be placed on the international flow of weapons, and a halt must be put on the illicit trafficking in diamonds, narcotics, and other products that fuel so many conflicts. As a start, the International Labor Organization and other U.N. bodies need to strengthen enforcement of international labor rights as well as establish an enforceable corporate code of conduct. The operations of transnational corporations must be open to more effective citizen, governmental, and multilateral regulation.

Notes and Questions

1. Is there a real and genuine link between the Machel Report and Hick's analysis? Machel identifies a number of reasons why brutal conflicts have come to involve children to such a degree. Is Hick's view of the role of "globalization" in these conflicts convincing? Why or why not?

2. In her report, Machel writes: "The impact of armed conflict on children must be everyone's concern and is everyone's responsibility; governments, international organizations and every element of civil society." Machel Report, *supra*, at para. 317. Given what Hick argues, do you agree with this characterization? Does Hick's approach diminish our collective sense of social and political complicity in allowing the recruitment of child soldiers to continue? Is the search for a theoretical framework useful for solving the child soldier problem?

II. International Laws Relating to Children and Armed Conflict

The idea that children require special protection during times of armed conflict has a considerable history. A particular concern for child welfare during war was expressed in the humanitarian law—also called the "laws and customs of war"—of the early twentieth century. International humanitarian law has attempted to establish benchmarks for the humane conduct of war. As will be described in the readings below, the Geneva Conventions of 1949 elaborated on the obligations of national armies and armed groups, and sought to provide humane treatment to all non-combatants.[2] Children were singled out for special protection under the Fourth Geneva Convention, Articles 24 and 50, as described below.

The 1977 Protocols Additional to the Geneva Conventions referred more specifically to underage soldiers. Protocol I, Relating to the Protection of Victims of International Armed Conflicts, states in Article 77 that "Parties to the conflict shall take all feasible measures in order that children who have not attained the age of fifteen years do not take a direct part in hostilities and, in particular, they shall refrain from recruiting them into their armed forces. In recruiting among those persons who have attained the age of fifteen years but who have not attained the age of eighteen years, the Parties to the conflict shall endeavor to give priority to those who are oldest."[3] In Protocol II, Relating to the Protection of Victims of Non-International Armed Conflicts, Article 4 states that "children who have not attained the age of fifteen years shall neither be recruited in the armed forces or groups nor allowed to take part in hostilities."[4] While useful, these calls for special care and consideration for the needs of children were embedded within the complex objectives of international humanitarian law, and lacked specificity for application to modern child soldiers and their unique set of difficulties.

In recent years, a number of international instruments have developed and refined obligations towards vulnerable children during times of armed conflict. The UNCRC directly touches upon the problem of children and armed conflict in Article 38, which sets out a general rule that children under 15 should not be recruited to serve directly in armed conflicts. It also refers States Parties back to pre-existing humanitarian law obligations to protect children in armed conflicts. Clearly, many other rights articulated in the CRC (rights to be free of exploitation, rights to education and health care, to name but a few) are also of great relevance to the issue of children trapped within the dynamic of violent conflicts.

---

2. Geneva Convention for the Amelioration of the Conditions of Wounded and Sick in Armed Forces in the Field (First Geneva Convention), Aug. 12, 1949, 6 U.S.T. 3114, 75 U.N.T.S. 31; Geneva Convention for the Amelioration of the Conditions of Wounded, Sick and Shipwrecked Members of Armed Forces at Sea (Second Geneva Convention), Aug. 12, 1949, 6 U.S.T. 3217, 75 U.N.T.S. 86; Geneva Convention Relative to the Treatment of Prisoners of War (Third Geneva Convention), Aug. 12, 1949, 6 U.S.T. 3116, 75 U.N.T.S. 135; Geneva Convention Relative to the Protection of Civilian Persons in Time of War (Fourth Geneva Convention), Aug. 12, 1949, 6 U.S.T. 3516, 75 U.N.T.S. 287.

3. Protocol Additional to the Geneva Conventions of 12 August 1949, and Relating to the Protection of Victims of International Armed Conflicts (Protocol 1) art. 77, June 8, 1977, 1125 U.N.T.S. 3.

4. Protocol Additional to the Geneva Conventions of 12 August 1949, and Relating to the Protection of Victims of Non-International Armed Conflicts (Protocol II) art. 4, June 8, 1977, 1125 U.N.T.S. 609.

At least partially due to the impact of the Machel Report, there was a growing sense that the severe conditions faced by children caught up in warfare during the 1990s demanded a specialized international agreement. In 2000, an Optional Protocol to the UNCRC on the subject of child soldiers was finalized. (See the Optional Protocol on the Involvement of Children in Armed Conflict, reproduced in the Appendix.) It should also be recalled that recruitment of child soldiers found a place in the International Labor Organization's Worst Forms of Child Labor Convention,[5] the content of which was covered in the second chapter of this book. In addition, recruitment of child soldiers has come to be seen as a war crime, and has been included as such in international post-conflict criminal tribunals. This heightened awareness of child exploitation in armed conflicts, and legal recognition of the dire situation of child soldiers, has led to a number of prosecutions under international criminal laws. The problem of child soldiers in the context of regimes for post-conflict transitional justice has gained a great deal of attention, both from the point of view of criminal penalties for recruitment of child soldiers, and the contrasting problem of the culpability of juveniles for the commission of war crimes.

A. The Evolution of an International Law on Children and Armed Conflict

The following excerpt from an article by Nsongurua Udombana sets out the historical development of legal obligations to refrain from exploiting children in situations of armed conflict. It describes the development of a general principle of child protection during wartime, through the growing awareness in recent times of a severe global problem, and on to an—at least apparent—prioritizing of this problem within the United Nations.

Nsongurua J. Udombana, *War Is Not Child's Play! International Law and the Prohibition of Children's Involvement in Armed Conflicts*
20 Temple International & Comparative Law Journal 57 (2006)

....

III. International Law's Prohibition on the Involvement of Children in Armed Conflicts Pre-CRC Protocol

The sources of international law on the child are varied and include treaties, customs, and general principles. For ease of analysis, this section will discuss international law's prohibition of children's involvement in armed conflicts under four categories: IHL [international humanitarian law], human rights law, international criminal law, and international labor law. In practice, human rights law complements IHL, although the latter is more specialized and in many areas, more detailed than the former. Human rights norms usually become useful when a conflict does not meet the applicability requirements of the Geneva Conventions, in particular the Additional Protocols or Article 3 common to the four Geneva Conventions. The common foundation in both regimes is the respect that is owed to all human beings without any distinction. Both

---

5. Convention Concerning the Prohibition and Immediate Elimination of the Worst Forms of Child Labour (I.L.O. No. 182), June 17, 1999, 38 I.L.M. 1207.

seek to protect life, humanity, dignity, the rudiments of justice and freedom; one protects these values essentially during peace times, the other protects them essentially during war times.

A. Child Soldiers and IHL

Generally, the four Geneva Conventions and their two Additional Protocols form the core of modern IHL and provide standards for the treatment of persons not or no longer taking active part in hostilities during a state of armed conflict or occupation. Admittedly, most of today's conflicts are internal, whereas the Geneva Conventions regulate international conflicts. However, Article 3 common to the Geneva Conventions, which the ICJ regards as reflecting "elementary considerations of humanity," defines certain rules to be applied, "as a minimum," in armed conflicts of a non-international character. Article 3 also constitutes a minimum yardstick for international armed conflicts. The Additional Protocols, in turn, combine rules of war with rules protecting civilians, thereby filling in some of the shortcomings of the Geneva Conventions. The Second Protocol, which supplements and develops Article 3 common to the four Geneva Conventions, applies to all non-international armed conflicts taking place in a territory of a State party between its armed forces and dissident armed forces.

1. Defining a Child under IHL

.... In general, the Geneva laws establish the age of fifteen as the age below which a child must enjoy some special protection, although some laws set a higher threshold. The Fourth Convention's provision dealing with safety zones indicates, for example, that such zones may protect, in particular, children under fifteen years of age. Similarly, the provision of the Convention dealing with the free passage of relief consignments for the weakest categories of the population explicitly refers to children under the age of fifteen as being among its potential beneficiaries.

All of Article 24 of the Fourth Convention is devoted to children, particularly those under the age of fifteen who are orphaned or who are separated from their families as a result of war. It enjoins parties to "take necessary measures to ensure" that such children "are not left on their own resources, and that their maintenance, the exercise of their religion and their education are facilitated in all circumstances." It specifies that this task should be entrusted, as far as possible, to persons of the same cultural tradition, thus excluding any religious or political propaganda designed to wean children from their natural milieu. According to the Commentary of the International Committee of the Red Cross ("ICRC"), fifteen was chosen as an age limit for purposes of maintenance and education because, after that age, "a child's faculties have generally reached a stage of development at which there is no longer the same necessity for special measures."....

2. The Prohibition of Child Soldiers under IHL

One of the cardinal principles contained in the texts constituting the fabric of IHL is the protection of the civilian population and civilian objects and the distinction between combatants and non-combatants. The basic rule is stated in the First Protocol as: "In order to ensure respect for and protection of the civilian population and civilian objects, the Parties to the conflict shall at all times distinguish between the civilian population and combatants and between civilian objects and military objectives and accordingly shall direct their operations only against military objectives." A corollary of the principle of distinction is the prohibition on the deliberate attack on non-combatants. Although the performance of military actions might sometimes result in the death or injury of non-combatants—so-called "collateral damage"—it is never permissible for the object of military actions to be the harm of non-combatants.

. . . .

IHL affords children, as members of the civilian population, protection against inhumane treatment and directed attacks during armed conflicts, whether international or non-international. Article 3 of the Geneva Conventions lays down the following general principle:

> Persons taking no active part in hostilities, including members of armed forces who have laid down their arms and those placed hors de combat by sickness, wounds, detention, or any other cause, shall be treated humanely in all circumstances, without any adverse distinction founded on race, colour, religion or faith, sex, birth or wealth, or any other similar criteria.

Article 3 particularly prohibits "(a) violence to life and person, in particular murder, cruel treatment and torture; (b) hostage taking; (c) outrages upon dignity, in particular humiliating and degrading treatment; (d) the passing of sentences and the carrying out of executions in the absence of due process." The requirement of humane treatment is the fundamental principle underlying IHL, the one principle that led to the founding of the Red Cross movement and the conclusion of the Geneva Conventions. Regrettably, it is also the one principle that is more often breached than honored in the majority of intra-state armed conflicts.

IHL protects children in three specific aspects. First, they afford children special protection as a particularly vulnerable category of persons. Second, they question the use of children in military operations. Third, some provisions take into consideration children's immaturity if they commit offenses during armed conflicts. This principle—that children deserve special protection during armed conflict—can be said to be a norm of customary international law; *opinio juris* and state practice supports such a finding. With particular reference to their recruitment into armed conflicts, the First Protocol stipulates that children under the age of fifteen may not be enrolled in the armed forces or take part directly in hostilities. As for the older group of persons between fifteen and eighteen years of age, the First Protocol provides that recruitment priority should be given to those who are oldest. This formulation is less mandatory and was, according to the ICRC, "a compromise." The initial proposal on the limit on non-recruitment was eighteen years, but "the majority" rejected this proposal. The final formulation reflected governments' avoidance of entering into absolute obligations with regard to the voluntary participation of children in hostilities.

Although the obligation to refrain from recruiting children younger than fifteen years of age remains, voluntary enrollment is not explicitly mentioned in the First Protocol, an omission that probably was deliberate. According to the Rapporteur, the Working Group of Committee III noted that it would not be realistic to completely prohibit voluntary participation of children under fifteen, especially in occupied territories and in wars of national liberation....

. . . .

The First Protocol makes guidelines for "exceptional cases" where "under fifteens" are intent on participating in hostilities. In such situations, the authorities employing them should be conscious of the heavy responsibility they are assuming and should give such children "the appropriate instruction on handling weapons, the conduct of combatants and respect for the laws and customs of war." The First Protocol also commits parties to ensure that such children do not take "a direct part in hostilities," since this right is reserved only to members of the armed forces. There is, however, considerable lack of clarity in determining when civilians, including children, have participated in hostilities. The ICRC's commentaries state that "taking direct part in hostilities" means "acts of war which by their nature or purpose are likely to cause actual harm to the personnel and equipment of the enemy armed forces."....

The Second Protocol, which applies to non-international conflicts, provides that "children who have not attained the age of fifteen years shall neither be recruited in the armed forces or groups nor allowed to take part in hostilities." Unlike the First Protocol, the Second Protocol offers increased protection for children who fall within its scope, and it does not permit exceptions to the proscribed conduct, but extends the recruitment restrictions to groups other than the armed forces of the state. It could even be argued that knowingly recruiting, or allowing other states or armed opposition groups to recruit children into armed conflicts raises questions about the compliance of states with these obligations. The word "recruitment" covers any means, formal or *de facto*, by which a person becomes a member of the armed forces or of an armed group. It includes conscription, voluntary enlistment, and forced recruitment. This implies that parties must refrain from enrolling children under fifteen years of age even if they volunteer to join the armed forces.

Some commentators believe that the Additional Protocols have not yet acquired the status of customary law, as they do not enjoy the same universal ratification as the four Geneva Conventions; thus, their applicability depends upon whether one of the other protocols is applicable. In practice, this implies that the rules become applicable only if a state involved in the armed conflict, whether it be international or internal in scope, is a party to the protocols, and the conflict fulfills the conditions for its application. Customary international law may, however, still bind parties that have not ratified the relevant treaties, "once a pattern of practice or expectation is generally accepted or [becomes] extant." Indeed, the Appeals Chamber of the Special Court for Sierra Leone concluded that "many of the provisions of Additional Protocol II, including the fundamental guarantees, were widely accepted as customary international law by 1996." In any event, it is hopeful that state practice will continue to update the basis of IHL, given the shortcomings of the Geneva laws regarding the protection of children.

B. Child Soldiers and Human Rights Law

....

1. Defining a Child under Human Rights Law

.... The CRC defines a child as "every human being below the age of eighteen years unless, under the law applicable to the child, majority is attained earlier." Some commentators believe that the CRC's qualification of the upper limit of eighteen years by the attainment of majority under the law applicable to the child is to achieve flexibility, "considering that the age of eighteen years is not necessarily consonant with the age of majority in various countries, and that the application of the rights recognized in the CRC to a person who is no longer a minor could be incompatible with his or her legal status." In any event, the CRC's definition of a child pertains only to the child as a civilian, not as a combatant.

Unlike the CRC, the African Charter on the Rights and Welfare of the Child ("African Child Charter") does not set an upper age limit that states may manipulate, but defines a "child" uniformly as "every human being below the age of 18 years." The African Child Charter's provisions reflect Africa's peculiar context, circumstances and sensibilities; indeed, almost all African human rights instruments stress the virtues of Africa's cultural heritage, historical background, and civilization as factors that inspire and characterize Africa's conception of rights. The African Child Charter notes with concern, "that the situation of most African children remains critical due to the unique factors of their socio-economic, cultural, traditional and developmental circumstances, natural disasters, armed conflicts, exploitation and hunger, and on account of the child's physical and mental immaturity he/she needs special safeguards and care." Some of the peculiar problems confronting the African child include the potential to become handicapped or a refugee, or experience internal displacement; along with harmful social and cultural practices that affect the welfare, dignity, normal growth, and development of the child. The CRC does not address these sensitive areas, understandably, because most universal human rights treaties are products of compromises aimed at accommodating diverse cultures.

2. The Prohibition of Child Soldiers under Human Rights Law

. . . .

Article 38(1) of the CRC envisages two types of state obligations: "respect" and "ensure respect" for rules of IHL relevant to children in armed conflicts. This implies, in the words of Rachel Brett, "positive as well as negative duties both with regard to their own conduct in armed conflicts and also in relation to the conduct of others." The provision is also significant because it creates the possibility that the CRC Committee will examine states parties' compliance with their obligations under IHL relating to the rights of the child.

Article 38 of the CRC prohibits the use of children less than fifteen years of age in armed conflict, regardless of whether the child volunteered or was conscripted, whether the war is international or internal in scope, or whether the recruiting party is a government or opposition army. The relevant provision reads, "States Parties shall take all feasible measures to ensure that persons who have not attained the age of fifteen years do not take a direct part in hostilities." In recruiting among those persons between ages fifteen and eighteen, the CRC requires states parties to give priority to those who are oldest, thereby reiterating and reinforcing the First Protocol to the Geneva Conventions. It is worth noting that none of the ratifying states parties have made any reservation regarding Article 38, thus providing "compelling evidence that the conventional norm" is part of customary law.

By using the age of fifteen as the threshold for its prohibition of recruitment and precluding only direct participation in hostilities, the CRC contains an obvious anomaly....

Nonetheless, Article 38 is significant for bringing together IHL and human rights law, thereby "showing their complementarity." Article 38 is a mixture of the two Additional Protocols; and, since these protocols have not yet enjoyed universal ratification — due to their lack of uniformity, the CRC remains "the ideal context within which the states could declare their unqualified political will to raise those standards." The CRC is also significant in that it permits no derogation of its rights in times of state emergency, when rights are most vulnerable to being compromised. The CRC also contains an omnibus provision; to wit, nothing in its provision should be construed to override other provisions of international law that are more conducive to the protection of children's rights. This includes by implication IHL, in particular the First Protocol. However, the CRC does not contain enforcement mechanisms, making its enforceability dependent upon domestic laws of each State Party.

. . . .

C. Child Soldiers and International Criminal Law

Two recent developments stand out in considering international criminal law's prohibition of children's involvement in armed conflicts. The first is the Rome Statute of the ICC, which was adopted with 120 in favor, 7 against, and 21 abstentions. The second is the Statute of the Special Court for Sierra Leone's War Crimes, which is an integral part of the Agreement between the U.N. and the Government of Sierra Leone on the Establishment of a Special Court for Sierra Leone. The following sections examine each in turn.

1. The ICC Statute

The ICC, created under the Rome Statute of July 17, 1998 ("ICC Statute"), is arguably the most significant international organization to be created since the U.N. Its establishment is a landmark in international cooperation and possibly the greatest step towards multilateral justice since the Nuremberg and Tokyo tribunals. The direct descendant of these tribunals, as well as the more recent international criminal tribunals for the Former Yugoslavia and Rwanda, the ICC will prosecute genocide, crimes against humanity, and war crimes when national justice systems are either unwilling or unable to do so themselves....

The ICC Statute has paved the way for the prosecution of international and, to some extent, internal criminal atrocities. Article 8(1) of the Statute posits a jurisdictional threshold and provides: "The Court shall have jurisdiction in respect of war crimes in particular when committed as part of a plan or policy or as part of a large-scale commission of such crimes."....

The ICC Statute also includes, as war crimes, "violations of the laws and customs applicable in international armed conflict, within the established framework of international law," including "committing rape, sexual slavery, enforced prostitution, forced pregnancy, ... enforced sterilization, or any other form of sexual violence also constituting a grave breach of the Geneva Conventions." The inclusion of the phrase "or any other form of sexual violence" gives the provision an open-ended character, though this proviso is itself qualified by the fact that such violence must amount to a grace breach.

Most significant, the ICC Statute expressly states that "conscripting or enlisting children under the age of fifteen years into the national armed forces or using them to participate actively in hostilities" is a war crime in both inter-state and intra-state armed conflicts. The offense does not require any element of force and, as is generally the case with war crimes, the consent of the child is no defense to enlistment or conscription. Similarly, with respect to the level of knowledge that the accused must have regarding the age of the child, it has been argued that evidence of the accused's willful blindness of the child's age should be sufficient to establish liability under the ICC Statute. This means that "the *mens rea* requirement would for instance be met if the accused does not provide for safeguards and inquire the age of the child even though the child's age appears close to the protected minimum age."

The ICC Statute's criminalization of children's involvement in armed conflicts was "a balanced compromise after much intense negotiation" at the Rome Diplomatic Conference.

....

2. The Statute of Sierra Leone's Special Court

Another instrument of relevance to this discourse is the Statute of the Special Court for Sierra Leone's War Crimes ("Sierra Leone Statute"), which is unique in its attention to child soldiers, though it sets fifteen years of age as the threshold *vis-a-vis* the powers of the Special Court. The Sierra Leone Statute empowers the Special Court to prosecute persons who conscripted or enlisted children under the age of fifteen into armed forces or groups or used them to participate actively in hostilities. The original proposal referred to the crime of "abduction and forced recruitment of children under the age of 15 years into armed forces or groups for the purpose of using them to participate actively in hostilities." Recruitment of children age fifteen and older is not considered an offense under the Sierra Leone Statute. The Statute also gives the Special Court the power to prosecute persons who committed certain crimes under Sierra Leonean law, in particular, offenses relating to the abuse of girls under the Prevention of Cruelty to Children Act of 1926 ("1926 Act"). These provisions reflect the extensive recruitment of child soldiers and the conditions of their use and exploitation during the long-drawn civil war in Sierra Leone. The total number of children who have been officially disarmed in Sierra Leone is 6,904.

In *Prosecutor v. Norman*, the Special Court was confronted with the issue of its temporary jurisdiction in relation to the prohibition of bringing children under the age of fifteen "into armed forces or groups or using them to participate actively in hostilities." The Special Court upheld the legality and specificity of the Sierra Leone Statute's provisions relating to child enlistment. It held that all parties to the Sierra Leone conflict were bound by customary law's prohibition of child recruitment that existed before November 30, 1996, the date that determined the temporal jurisdiction of the Special Court. According to the Special Court:

> [O]ne can determine the period during which the majority of states criminalized the prohibited behaviour, which in this case, as demonstrated, was the period between 1994 and 1996. It took a further six years for the recruitment of children between the ages of 15 and 18 to be included in treaty law as individually punishable behaviour.

The Special Court does not, however, have jurisdiction over any perpetrator who was under the age of fifteen at the time of the alleged commission of the crime. The Sierra Leone Statute provides:

> Should any person who was at the time of the alleged commission of the crime between 15 and 18 years of age come before the Court, he or she shall be treated with dignity and a sense of worth, taking into account his or her young age and the desirability of promoting his or her rehabilitation, reintegration into and assumption of a constructive role in society, and in accordance with international human rights standards, in particular the rights of the child.

In the disposition of a case against a juvenile offender, the Special Court may order any of the following: 1) care, guidance, and supervision orders; 2) community service orders; 3) counseling; 4) foster care; and 5) correctional, educational and vocational training programs. It may also order entry into programs of disarmament, demobilization, and reintegration, or programs with child protection agencies, as appropriate.

D. Child Soldiers and International Labor Standards

The International Labor Organization ("ILO") establishes and supervises the application of international labor standards, including child labor standards. It first adopted the Minimum Age Convention in 1973 ("1973 Convention"), which laid the foundation for international action towards the eventual elimination of child labor. The 1973 Convention sets an age limit for entry into work, which is not less than the age of completion of compulsory schooling and, in any case, is not less than fifteen years of age. On June 17, 1999, the ILO took a further step towards the elimination of child labor by adopting the Convention Concerning the Prohibition and Immediate Action for the Elimination of the Worst Forms of Child Labour ("1999 Convention"). The 1999 Convention, which defines a child as a person under the age of eighteen, brings the problem of child labor to the front burner of international labor relations and policy.

....

The 1999 Convention is significant for being the first specific legal instrument to characterize child soldiering as a form of child labor and to set eighteen as the minimum age limit for the recruitment of children into armed conflicts....

IV. The CRC Protocol

The CRC Protocol is a significant milestone in the international community's attempt to elaborate norms to deal with the problem of children's recruitment into armed conflicts. In adopting this "groundbreaking piece of international legislation," as Nancy Morisseau has called it, the international community has acknowledged that the pre-existing fifteen-years-of-age standard for recruitment does not adequately protect children. The CRC's provision regarding child soldiers appears to have encouraged more daring recruitment, as evidenced by the increasing number of child soldiers. The proceeding sections examine the context and text of the CRC Protocol, including the obligations of states parties and the institutional mechanism for its implementation, the CRC Committee.

A. The Context

....

The CRC Committee also played a significant role in the processes leading to the drafting of the CRC Protocol. On October 9, 1992, the CRC Committee undertook "Children in Armed Conflicts" as the subject for its first general discussion and recommended the adoption of an optional protocol raising the minimum age for recruitment into the armed forces to eighteen years. The CRC Committee also proposed a study on children affected by armed conflicts. Pursuant to the recommendation of the CRC Committee, the U.N. General Assembly, in 1993, requested that the Secretary-General appoint an expert to study the impact of armed conflict on children. Graça Machel, widow of the late President Somora Machel of Mozambique and current wife of Nelson Mandela, was appointed for the exercise.

After two years of research, field visits, and consultations, Machel submitted her report, the most fundamental premise of which is that children simply should not have any part in warfare and that "war violates every right of a child." The Machel Report revealed the full extent of children's involvement in armed conflicts raging around the world and set out its findings and recommendations aimed at governments, U.N. entities, other inter-governmental bodies, civil society organizations, and individuals. It also recommended eighteen years as the minimum age for recruitment into armed forces or groups and for participation in hostilities.

A combination of unusual circumstances ultimately resulted in the establishment of the machinery for the drafting, completion, adoption and, subsequently, the entry into force of the CRC Protocol. Not surprisingly, the United States was the party most strongly opposed to raising the minimum age for child participation in armed conflict to eighteen years of age. The reason for U.S. opposition was arguably because of the U.S. practice of recruiting seventeen-year-olds and the sheer number of Junior Reserve Officers' Training Corps ("ROTC") programs operating in high schools throughout the country would directly violate such an age restriction. There were also concerns that such a treaty would impair the ability of the United States to deploy its seventeen-year-old recruits. International and domestic pressures, including pressure from the American Bar Association ("ABA"), forced the United States to recapitulate, and by March 2002, the Senate Foreign Relations Committee had held hearings on ratifying the CRC Protocol. On December 23, 2002, the United States joined the list of states that have ratified the Protocol, thereby agreeing to take "all feasible measures" to prevent the deployment of individuals under the age of eighteen in combat situations.

B. The Text

The adoption of the CRC Protocol was based on a conviction that raising "the age of possible recruitment of persons into armed forces and their participation in hostilities will contribute effectively to the implementation of the principle that the best interests of the child are to be a primary consideration in all actions concerning children." In other words, a coherent approach to the definition of a child had serious implications for children participating in armed conflict. It was necessary to amend the CRC, since it constituted a weakening of the IHL protection accorded to children in armed conflict. This segment examines the text of the CRC Protocol—in particular, its new standard—states' obligations under it, and its implementation by the CRC Committee.

1. Setting a New Standard

The CRC Protocol pays tribute to earlier international instruments touching upon the problem of child soldiers, such as the ICC Statute and the ILO Child Labor Convention, each of which have already been examined in this article. The CRC Protocol, more importantly, amends the CRC's minimum age for recruitment of persons into their armed forces from fifteen to eighteen years of age. It urges state parties to take "all feasible measures to ensure that members of their armed forces who have not attained the age of 18 years do not take a direct part in hostilities." The language of this Article falls short of the protection provided by Article 4(3)(c) of the Second Protocol, which prohibits any participation in hostilities. By limiting its prohibition to taking "a direct part in hostilities," the CRC Protocol appears to be a compromise. However, a broader prohibition, similar to that contained in the Second Protocol, should have been included to protect children not only from indirect participation in armed conflicts but also from pressures that, in practice, compel them to participate directly in armed conflicts. As this article has indicated, children often start out in support functions but become combatants over time or when the armed forces are under pressure. It seems that the Protocol, in mending one thing, has marred another: by removing old miseries it might have inadvertently produced new ones.

The CRC Protocol obligates states parties to "ensure that persons who have not attained the age of 18 years are not compulsorily recruited into their armed forces." Recognizing that children are the "easy prey" of non-governmental armed groups, the CRC Protocol extends the prohibition to "armed groups, distinct from the armed forces of a State," which "should not, under any circumstances, recruit or use in hostilities persons under the age of 18 years." States are obligated to criminalize such activities. The irony is that states have, by these provisions, bound potential opponents with stronger obligations than they are prepared to accept for themselves.

Nevertheless, the prohibition of recruitment of children into armed conflicts reflects an area where human rights law, as opposed to humanitarian law, has been extended to non-state entities, though such an extension is progressively being developed in other areas. Traditionally, human rights law is applied to states, while humanitarian law is applied to all parties in conflicts. This extension is a welcome development because the law should be dynamic, particularly in times of rapidly shifting values. Ideals are not immutable but must change with the accumulation of experiences and lessons derived from costly experiments tinkering with humanity. International law must constantly respond to change and must adapt itself to idiosyncrasies of contemporary armed conflicts.

There is no requirement that non-state groups be involved in armed conflicts before the CRC Protocol applies, meaning that questions of whether or not a situation amounts to an armed conflict are irrelevant. Recruitment prior to the start of a conflict is also covered and state parties must take all feasible measures to prevent such recruitment, "including the adoption of legal measures necessary to prohibit and criminalize such practices." This provision is rightly focused because military disciplinary procedures would normally apply only to government forces. Rachel Brett, however, has pointed out the practical problems with such a provision, specifically that "a government fighting a civil war is more likely to try for treason anyone it catches, rather than for under-aged recruitment."

As for voluntary recruitment of children, the CRC Protocol commits state parties to raise the minimum age of persons in their national armed forces to that set out in the CRC Protocol, taking account of principles contained in the CRC Protocol and recognizing that persons under eighteen are entitled to special protection under the CRC. On becoming a party to the Protocol, a state must set forth a binding declaration establishing its minimum voluntary recruitment age and safeguards adopted to comply with the Protocol....

State parties that permit voluntary recruitment of individuals under the age of eighteen into their national armed forces must maintain safeguards to ensure, as a minimum, that such recruitment is genuinely voluntary and is carried out with the informed consent of the person's parents or legal guardians. Such recruits must also be fully informed of the duties involved in military service and must provide reliable proof of age prior to acceptance into national military service. This provision on volunteers again appears to be a compromise, but it was unnecessary because the CRC Protocol is optional. States are not obliged to become parties if they do not want or if their existing laws or practices are not in conformity with it. The drafters appear to have been more cautious than courageous, shying from the opportunity to draft a protocol that significantly affects the existence of the problem that it was meant to address.

. . . .

V. Between Rhetoric and Reality

. . . .

B. Working to Ensure Scrupulous Compliance of IHL by States and Non-State Entities

The child soldier menace is largely the outcome of the international community's failure to ensure adequate compliance with its laws. A practical problem, of course, is how to enforce the provisions of the CRC Protocol relating to non-state entities, since, not being parties to it, they could argue that the CRC Protocol's provisions do not bind them. Such an argument misses the point that the rule *pacta tertiis nec nocent nec prosunt* has certain "apparent exceptions," one of which is that a treaty rule may bind non-parties if it becomes a part of international custom. This is not to say that the CRC Protocol has attained such a status. It is, at best, a progressive development of the law, but it has a propensity to become general international law in the future.

States must lead the way in implementing the CRC Protocol. When politicians and military leaders know that retribution is not only possible but also likely, then the inhuman and impersonal recruitment and slaughter of children carries a much more personal dimension. Those who violate children's rights or collude in such violations must be made to feel the repugnance of civilized people everywhere.

Emerging international case law already indicates that non-state entities, as parties to internal armed conflicts, are bound by certain humanitarian norms, including the special protection and non-recruitment of children. In 1995, the Appeals Chambers of the ICTY upheld the legality of prosecuting non-state entities for violations of the laws and customs of war, including violations of Common Article 3 and the Additional Protocols. Rebel leaders, in particular, are responsible for the conduct of their members and may be "held so responsible by opposing parties or by the outside world." In the realm of human rights, private actors are now being held liable for torturous human rights violations. As the U.S. Court of Appeals for the Second Circuit rightly held in *Kadic v. Karadzic*, "[a] private individual acts under color of law ... when he acts together with state officials or with significant state aid." International law must continue to adapt itself to the needs of the moment and must move from being a thermometer that records the ideas and principles of popular opinion to being a thermostat that transforms the mores of society.

....

Notes and Questions

1. Read through the sections of the Protocol Additional to the Geneva Conventions of 12 August 1949, Relating to the Protection of Victims of Non-International Armed Conflicts (Protocol II), reproduced in the Appendix. Protocol II deals specifically with non-international armed conflict. Also, review the Optional Protocol to the Convention on the Rights of the Child on the Involvement of Children in Armed Conflict. How do the emphases in these instruments differ? In what sense are they similar? According to Udombana, which aspects of Article 38 of the UNCRC led to the conclusion that a supplemental protocol was necessary?

2. To what extent does the Optional Protocol on children and armed conflict provide an international wake up call on the issue of child soldiers? What are ratifying states asked to do? Are the obligations clear enough? How does it purport to reach non-state actors, or does it? Could the Optional Protocol have offered more complete protection by covering more topics related to children and armed conflict?

3. How well does the existing international regime deal with the adolescent soldier who has been victimized, but who has also been the perpetrator of brutal attacks on civilians? Does the Optional Protocol offer any guidance on the vexed issue of juvenile culpability for atrocities committed in armed conflict?

B. Culpability of the Child Soldier: Should Juveniles Ever Be Treated as War Criminals?

While there are no hard and fast international law rules governing the age at which criminal responsibility should be set, it is clear that states are encouraged to recognize the fact that adolescents under the age of eighteen are not making decisions with a maturity comparable to an adult. The United Nations Standard Minimum Rules for the Administration of Juvenile Justice (Beijing Rules),[6] discussed at length in Chapter Five of this book, state that the age of criminal responsibility should not in any event be set too low, while allowing some flexibility for individual states to exercise discretion in this area.

The excerpt from the Nienke Grossman article that follows takes up the thorny question of post-conflict justice for child soldiers who have been involved in committing atrocities against civilians. To what extent should these juveniles be treated as culpable for their

---

6. United Nations Standard Minimum Rules for the Administration of Juvenile Justice (Beijing Rules), G.A. Res. 40/33, Annex, U.N. GOAR 40th Sess., Supp. No. 53, U.N. Doc. A/40/53 (Nov. 29, 1985).

criminal behavior? To what extent should we consider their age alone as indicative of diminished will and consent, not to mention the frightening circumstances under which they have acted? It stands to reason that conflicts that rely on large numbers of child soldiers are likely to be characterized by high levels of brutality, and thus war crimes. It is hardly surprising that armed groups that prey upon children are motivated by a desire to expand the reach of terror attacks against civilians.

Nienke Grossman, *Rehabilitation or Revenge: Prosecuting Child Soldiers for Human Rights Violations*
38 Georgetown Journal of International Law 323 (2007)

International law provides no explicit guidelines for whether or at what age child soldiers should be prosecuted for grave violations of international humanitarian and human rights law such as genocide, war crimes, and crimes against humanity. Due to increasing numbers of children participating in armed conflict and engaging in serious human rights breaches, a coherent policy response consistent with international legal standards, including states' duties to promote children's well-being and to prevent and prosecute human rights abuses, is necessary. This paper argues that the hundreds of thousands of children under age eighteen participating in armed conflicts around the globe should be treated primarily as victims, not perpetrators, of human rights violations and that international law may support this conclusion.

. . . .

I. The Basics on Child Soldiers

. . . .

Over 300,000 children under age eighteen actively participate in armed conflict in 41 countries across the globe, according to the Coalition to Stop the Use of Child Soldiers, a group of six nongovernmental organizations ("NGOs") including Amnesty International and Human Rights Watch. An additional 200,000 children are recruited into paramilitary and guerilla groups and civil militias in more than 87 countries. Paramilitary groups in Colombia have recruited children as young as eight years old; eleven-year olds have been drafted into the Northern Alliance in Afghanistan; and teenage boys are frequently forced from their villages into the national army in Myanmar. Despite demobilizations of child soldiers in Sierra Leone and Southern Sudan, the use of child soldiers is most prevalent in Africa, with more than 120,000 children engaged in active combat. Children are involved in soldiering in the developed world as well; about 7,000 children under the age of eighteen were in the British Armed Forces in June 2001. Children are increasingly participating in internal armed conflicts, and the more protracted the conflict, the higher the likelihood of child participation.

. . . .

The psychological trauma of soldiering is undoubtedly severe. Robbed of their childhood, these children witness the worst of humanity on a daily basis. One thirteen-year-old from Sierra Leone described his first day of combat with children eight and nine years old, dragging their AK-47's because they were too heavy to carry:

> I was in an ambush and bullets were flying back and forth, people were shooting. I didn't want to pull the trigger at all but when you watch kids ... being shot and killed and ... dying and crying and their blood was spilling all over your

face you just moved beyond, something just pushed you and you start pulling the trigger.

A Ugandan girl abducted by the Lord's Resistance Army in Uganda was forced to kill a boy who tried to escape, witnessed another boy hacked to death, and was beaten when she dropped a water container and ran for cover under gunfire. Brutal hazing practices include everything from torture and beatings inflicted upon the new recruit to forcing him or her to commit these atrocities on others. The Mozambican Resistance Organization's (RENAMO) training regimen included physical abuse, punishment for showing sympathy for victims of violence, and forced participation in killing. Children exposed to rampant violence and death through involvement in armed conflict may suffer flashbacks, nightmares, sleep disorders, and post-traumatic stress disorder, in addition to desiring revenge and fearing retribution from the communities they have hurt.

Although these children are themselves victims of violence, they are also perpetrators of atrocities. Once they become child soldiers, these children murder, maim, and plunder. Graça Machel, a former Expert of the Secretary General of the U.N. on the impact of armed conflict on children, wrote that children from countries including Afghanistan, Mozambique, Colombia, and Nicaragua, sometimes committed atrocities against their own families and communities. The children in Uganda's Lord's Resistance Army were both brutally abused and abusive, killing attempted escapees, captured government soldiers, and civilians, using everything from stones to axes. Children as young as five were accused of participating in the Rwandan genocide.

Deciding what to do with these children once the conflict ends is a daunting task; the government(s) involved must fulfill international humanitarian, human rights, and criminal law commitments to both the former child soldiers and their victims....

II. International Law on Prosecuting Child Soldiers
A. States' Obligations to Child Soldiers

International humanitarian law, or the "laws of war" that seek to regulate behavior during international and internal armed conflict, and the international law of the child explicitly prohibit the recruitment and use of children under age fifteen in armed conflict....

In recent years, various international treaties have sought to raise the age of permitted participation in armed conflict to eighteen years.

....

B. States' Duty to Prosecute Persons Who Commit Crimes
Under International Criminal Law

A state that fails to prosecute an individual—child or adult—who violates international criminal law may find itself in violation of international law. If a person commits certain international crimes, a state may be obligated to prosecute him or her under international treaty and customary law, even if these crimes are committed against the state's own nationals. For example, the Convention on the Prevention and Punishment of the Crime of Genocide explicitly binds states to "undertake to prevent and to punish" the crime of genocide. Similarly, the Convention Against Torture, and Other Cruel, Inhuman or Degrading Treatment or Punishment establishes that States Parties must criminalize torture under its domestic law and "shall make these offenses punishable by appropriate penalties which take into account their grave nature."

....

Nevertheless, some believe that during cases of internal strife, the decision to prosecute rests on domestic criminal law. Article 3 common to the four Geneva Conventions of 1949, although prohibiting parties to a conflict from harming unarmed civilians in an internal conflict, contains no "grave breaches" provision mandating criminal punishment, making the duty or decision to prosecute dependent on domestic law. Furthermore, Article 6(5) of the Protocol II to the Geneva Conventions, addressing the protection of victims during internal conflicts, seems to encourage amnesty over prosecution, implying a dissimilar duty to prosecute in internal rather than international conflicts: "At the end of hostilities, the authorities in power shall endeavour to grant the broadest possible amnesty to persons who have participated in the armed conflict, or those deprived of their liberty for reasons related to the armed conflict...."

Despite these interpretations of Article 6(5) of Protocol II and Common Article 3, the international community advocated for criminal tribunals in Rwanda and the former Yugoslavia, even though those conflicts were internal. This advocacy reflects a duty to prosecute serious violations of international humanitarian law. Furthermore, when the Special Representative of the U.N. Secretary General for Sierra Leone signed the Lome Peace Accord of 1999, he was instructed to add a disclaimer "to the effect that the amnesty provision contained in article IX of the Agreement ('absolute and free pardon') shall not apply to international crimes of genocide, crimes against humanity or other serious violations of international humanitarian law," explicitly rejecting the idea of a broad amnesty. Consequently, a state's failure to prosecute a child who commits a serious violation of international law may itself be in breach of international law.

C. The Minimum Age of Criminal Responsibility for Child Soldiers

At what age the duty to prosecute applies to international humanitarian crimes such as crimes against humanity and war crimes committed by children appears unresolved under the statutes of recent human rights tribunals and the Rome Statute. Although the International Criminal Tribunals for the Former Yugoslavia and for Rwanda do not address the minimum age of criminal responsibility, both stress the importance of prosecuting and punishing those responsible; their silence does not necessarily preclude prosecution of children under these mechanisms. The Report of the Secretary-General on the Establishment of a Special Court for Sierra Leone, however, explicitly allows for all persons aged fifteen and above to fall under the jurisdiction of the Court. The Rome Statute does not include persons under eighteen at the time of commission of a crime within its jurisdiction, although it is a war crime to conscript or enlist children under age fifteen into armed forces.

Treaty law on the treatment of juveniles undergoing ordinary domestic criminal prosecutions similarly acknowledges the lack of consensus on the minimum age of criminal responsibility, showing the absence of both treaty and customary norms. The CRC recognizes not only the differences of opinion regarding the definition of a "child," describing a child as "every human being below the age of eighteen years unless, under the law applicable to the child, majority is attained earlier," but also the broad scope of views regarding the age at which children may be prosecuted, and it calls on States Parties to set a minimum age. The U.N. Standard Minimum Rules for the Administration of Juvenile Justice ("Beijing Rules") echo the variety in the age of criminal responsibility among states:

> It should be noted that age limits will depend on, and are explicitly made dependent on, each respective legal system, thus fully respecting the economic, social, political, cultural and legal systems of Member States. This makes for a wide variety of ages coming under the definition of 'juvenile,' ranging from 7 years to

18 years or above. Such a variety seems inevitable in view of the different national legal systems and does not diminish the impact of these Standard Minimum Rules.

The Beijing Rules further add that the lower limit should not be set "at too low an age level, bearing in mind the facts of emotional, mental and intellectual maturity." In the same vein, although the most recent international treaty on juvenile delinquency defines a juvenile as any child under age eighteen, it requests that states determine "an age below which it should not be permitted to deprive a child of his or her liberty," while providing no direction for what that lower limit should be. A 1997 UNICEF report on the progress of the CRC illustrates the wide variety of the age of criminal liability: twenty in Japan, seven in India, South Africa, and Sudan, ten in England, thirteen in France, sixteen in Argentina, eighteen in Peru, and fourteen in China.

Despite the lack of an explicit consensus in the statutes of international criminal tribunals and the absence of a customary norm regarding the exact minimum age of criminal responsibility for international humanitarian crimes, interpretation of the CRC in light of the Vienna Convention on the Law of Treaties may point to a legal obligation to refrain from prosecuting at least children under fifteen for serious crimes arising from armed conflict. Article 31 of the Vienna Convention states as a "General Rule of Interpretation" that "[a] Treaty shall be interpreted in good faith in accordance with the ordinary meaning to be given to the terms of the treaty in their context and in the light of its object and purpose."

.... By setting the minimum age for recruitment and use at fifteen, the drafters of the CRC pointed to the need to protect children from the dangers of war, in accord with international humanitarian law. In addition to the psychological and physical dangers of war, the prohibition on both forced recruitment and use of children under age fifteen in direct hostilities suggests that the States Party to these treaties believed children under fifteen do not possess the mental maturity to express valid consent to join an armed group. If children under fifteen are not sufficiently mature to consent to engage directly in armed conflict and must be protected from the dangers of war under the CRC, they arguably are more like victims of armed conflict than its perpetrators. In agreement with this interpretation of the CRC, the Sierra Leone Report allows for the prosecution of only children aged fifteen and over while recognizing the victimhood of all child soldiers. Similarly, the Rome Statute makes it a war crime to conscript or enlist children under age fifteen in armed conflict.

The Rome Statute and the Optional Protocol to the CRC arguably demonstrate an emerging consensus that children aged fifteen to eighteen should also be shielded from criminal liability. Although it is a war crime to conscript or enlist children aged under fifteen according to the Rome Statute, the international community expressed a preference for not prosecuting persons aged fifteen through seventeen by limiting the ICC's jurisdiction to persons aged eighteen and over at the time of commission of a crime. Furthermore, since the Optional Protocol precludes States Parties from allowing children under eighteen to participate in direct hostilities, they should be protected from criminal liability if they are used in armed conflict. Finally, the CRC itself prefers the measures most "conducive to the realization of the rights of the child" when the CRC and domestic law or domestic treaty obligations differ, suggesting that the higher the age of allowable recruitment and criminal responsibility, the better.

D. Protective Guidelines for Children Undergoing Prosecution

In addition to the affirmative obligation to reintegrate former child soldiers into society as previously noted, if a state chooses to prosecute a former child soldier for violations of domestic or international criminal laws, he or she is entitled to special protections under international law. As delineated in Article 3 of the CRC, "in all actions concerning children, whether undertaken by public or private social welfare institutions, courts of law, administrative authorities or legislative bodies, the best interests of the child shall be a primary consideration." As well as providing a variety of procedural safeguards for children accused of criminal activity, such as presumption of innocence, knowledge of charges against him or her, and rights of privacy and appeal, Article 40 of the CRC articulates that such a child should be:

> treated in a manner consistent with the promotion of the child's sense of dignity and worth, which reinforces the child's respect for the human rights and fundamental freedoms of others and which takes into account the child's age and the desirability of promoting the child's re-integration and the child's assuming a constructive role in society.

Rule 5 of the Beijing Rules similarly establishes that the aims of juvenile justice should include an emphasis on the "well-being of the juvenile" and a consideration of the individual circumstances of the offense and the offender, including examination of individual social status, family situation, and gravity of the crime in fashioning an appropriate response. In the same vein, in describing the powers and duties of the Prosecutor of the International Criminal Court, Article 54 of the Rome Statute charges the Prosecutor with considering both incriminating and exonerating circumstances, which presumably might include the age of the alleged offender, in deciding whether to investigate and prosecute crimes. In deciding how a child offender should be punished, the CRC, the ICCPR, and the Beijing Rules specify that capital punishment shall not be imposed upon persons under age eighteen, and the CRC and Beijing rules state that deprivation of liberty of a child "shall be used only as a measure of last resort and for the shortest appropriate period of time."

If a state is obligated or chooses to prosecute a child who allegedly committed international crimes, the state must also ensure that the child meets the substantive intent requirements for commission of the crime. Since these often severely abused children frequently were forced to commit crimes under duress or to take desensitizing drugs, the requisite *mens rea* may not be present. Although in the commission of certain crimes the order of a supervisor ordinarily does not shield a suspect from liability, since children under fifteen presumably do not possess the mental maturity to volunteer to participate directly in armed conflict, they are probably insufficiently mentally developed to resist an order from a supervisor. If drugs were involved, the child likely did not possess the necessary will to perform the acts at all. Furthermore, in the case of genocide, the *mens rea* requirement is even more complex and difficult to fulfill; a child must possess the "intent to destroy, in whole or in part, a national, ethnic, racial or religious group." A child soldier under the age of fifteen or even eighteen may not satisfy this intent requirement because he or she may not understand the meaning of the crime itself.

. . . .

III. Policy Goals
A. Why Children Under Eighteen Should Not be Prosecuted

. . . .

Psychological studies show a child's understanding of the world is fundamentally altered during adolescence, suggesting he or she does not possess the same abilities to act independently or appreciate the rights of others as an adult and should be shielded from liability for crimes arising from war. A child's grasp of the political world changes dramatically between ages twelve or thirteen and fifteen or sixteen; a child's cognitive mode changes, his or her authoritarian views of the political system sharply decline, and he or she achieves a capacity for ideology. While older children are capable of shifting back and forth between concrete examples and abstract generalizations or principles, younger children are generally limited to concrete examples. Younger children are usually incapable of imagining social reality in the abstract; an early adolescent:

> enters adolescence with only the weakest sense of social institutions, or their structure and functions, or of that invisible network of norms and principles which link these institutions to each other. Furthermore, the failure to achieve abstractness does not permit him to understand, except in a most rough and ready way, those concepts essential to political thought—such ideas as authority, rights, liberty, equity, interests, representation, and so on.

. . . .

If a child does not understand that he or she may choose to disobey an order to protect community welfare or to avoid self-condemnation, it may be inappropriate to hold him or her accountable for crimes when ordered by a supervisor or in the context of collective armed action.

. . . .

Because of their youth and victimhood, post-conflict societies should focus on rehabilitation, rather than punishment of former child soldiers. These children have been more wounded by the world than vice versa. Even children who "volunteer" to join an armed group are driven to do so by hunger, poverty, political or cultural pressures, fear, and desire for protection. After being deliberately exposed to atrocious human rights violations like rape, murder, and maiming, or being forced to commit such violations themselves, many of them become completely desensitized to violence. Particularly in cases of abduction or forced recruitment, these children are ripped out of their community and familial networks; they live, suffer abuse or die at the whim of their superiors.

Instead of prosecuting children under age eighteen, post-conflict governments should seek alternative methods of addressing the needs of victims of child soldiers and their communities while rehabilitating the child soldiers themselves. Truth commissions may serve as a viable alternative to trials as long as procedures "(1) do not conflict with local healing methods, and (2) incorporate the supportive programs necessary to enhance the therapeutic value, and minimize any negative impact, that participating in a truth-seeking process might have on child victims, witnesses and perpetrators, and on their caregivers and communities."

In South Africa, the Truth and Reconciliation Committee chose not to elicit testimony from children for fear of inflicting more pain on them, although it did hear adults speak of their experiences as children. Neither truth commissions nor trials may ultimately be the answer to this quandary; the Machel Report highlights the importance of culturally appropriate, community-based methods for helping to heal child soldiers and encouraging communities to reintegrate them. Because some African cultures believe that accepting a person who has killed into the community will lead to evil spirits, any social reintegration and forgiveness process must include traditional healers and "cleansing" processes. In one village in Angola, after living with a former child soldier for one month, feeding him a special cleansing diet while advising the child on proper village behavior, a traditional healer convened the village for a ceremony where he buried a frequently used weapon such as a machete or an AK-47 and declared the boy's life as a soldier ended and life as a civilian begun. In Mozambique, a child taken by RENAMO at age eight participated in collective prayer and singing in a local church where he was welcomed back as a member of his community. No matter which specific methods are chosen for handling the reintegration of child soldiers into their communities in the wake of mass violence, the child's psychological and physical well-being and dignity must be taken into account. The focus should be on forgiveness when children are involved.

B. Applying International Relations Paradigms to the Child Soldier Quandary

....

... In Sierra Leone and Rwanda, domestic groups explicitly called for the prosecution of youth involved in mass violence; the Sierra Leone Report states,

> The Government of Sierra Leone and representatives of Sierra Leone civil society clearly wish to see a process of judicial accountability for child combatants presumed responsible for the crimes falling within the jurisdiction of the Court. It was said that the people of Sierra Leone would not look kindly upon a court which failed to bring to justice children who committed crimes of that nature and spared them the judicial process of accountability.[7]

The same report points out that child-focused NGOs were "unanimous in their objection" to judicial accountability for these children for fear it would endanger rehabilitation efforts. Liberals concerned with protecting former child soldiers must use the arguments at their disposal to convince the domestic population, find a way to have their views better represented in the governing elite, and encourage other states to pressure their elites.

....

When state interests converge around raising the age of criminal responsibility to eighteen and focusing efforts on the rehabilitation of former child soldiers, Institutionalism posits that states will seek to institutionalize their new understanding. States could make clear, either through the Optional Protocol to the CRC or otherwise, that children should be considered primarily victims of armed conflict and should not be prosecuted, or the Rome Statute could be changed to criminalize the use of child soldiers under the age of eighteen instead of fifteen, emphasizing child soldiers are victims until age eighteen. Once an expected behavior or rule is codified in a binding way, such as by modifying a treaty, the reputational costs of non-compliance are higher than prior to the existence of the codified change.

... [D]espite some signs of an emerging consensus around the age of eighteen as the minimum age of criminal responsibility for violations of international humanitarian law, the current focal point of fifteen may present a hurdle, or at least institutional drag. International humanitarian law's proscription of the use of children under age fifteen is a clear, recognized benchmark age around which states have expressed consensus in the past. Although the Rome Statute establishes the lower limit of criminal responsibility at age eighteen, the ICC's success is still in question, and the Rome Statute only criminalizes the use of child soldiers under the age of fifteen. Even though the Optional Protocol to the CRC prohibits any use of children under age eighteen in direct hostilities, it still allows children age fifteen and over to volunteer to join a Party's armed forces. Finally, in the Sierra Leone Report, the Secretary General used the age of fifteen as a minimum age

---

7. Report of the Secretary-General on the Establishment of a Special Court for Sierra Leone, UN Doc. S/2000/915 (4 October, 2000), ¶ 35, *available at* http://daccessdds.un.org/doc/UNDOC/GEN/N00/661/77/PDF/N0066177.pdf?OpenElement.

of criminal accountability, suggesting the current institutional framework, at least as embodied in the U.N. Secretary General's Report, considers prosecuting persons under age eighteen a legitimate, although unfortunate, measure.

....

Notes and Questions

1. For people living in a community that has endured civil war and the mass killing and maiming of civilians, how are arguments to the effect that juvenile offenders are more victims than criminals going to resonate? Whose perceptions are most important in such a scenario? What is to be gained, and what lost, by bringing former child soldiers to trial? Should the matter be decided via bright line tests as to age, or should there be a more flexible standard, based on the child's history and behavior?

2. What evidence does Grossman rely on to construct her argument in favor of protecting former child soldiers? Does she appear to have the weight of international opinion on her side?

The following statement by Amnesty International, which predates the Grossman article by several years, presents a somewhat different view of the matter. In this piece, Amnesty certainly does not accept underage status as a simple proxy for diminished responsibility. What accounts for the different approach taken by Amnesty?

Amnesty International, *Child Soldiers: Criminals or Victims?*

(2000), *available at* http://www.amnesty.org/en/library/asset/IOR50/002/2000/
en/f1883757-dc60-11dd-bce7-11be3666d687/ior500022000en.pdf

Amnesty International's position on the prosecutions of child soldiers.

Amnesty International supports the prosecution of any person who is responsible for serious crimes such as genocide, crimes against humanity and war crimes, as long as any trial takes place with all the appropriate fair trial standards in place, and without the possibility of the death penalty or other cruel, inhuman or degrading treatment or punishment being imposed.

Amnesty International considers that due to the nature of the conflicts in which child soldiers are most often used, it will be very clear in many cases that children were not acting voluntarily—in some cases, they were drugged against their will—and therefore may not be criminally responsible. In other cases they were threatened and might be able to assert a defense of duress or to have duress taken into account in mitigation of punishment. However, it is vitally important that in those cases where persons under 18 acted entirely voluntarily, and were in control of their actions, they should be held to account for their actions in an appropriate setting. Due weight should be given to their age and other mitigating factors, for example, if they were abducted and brutalized by their recruiters. The assessment of a child's awareness of the choices open to him or her, whether to join the armed groups or to commit atrocities, should be undertaken critically, with due consideration to a child's vulnerability and limited understanding. Such an assessment should contribute to mitigation of the child's responsibility.

Alongside the more complex cases, there may be examples of young commanders of units who committed mass atrocities, including murder and rapes, who were clearly willing and acted without coercion, and who may have forced other children to commit such acts. Where an individual can be held responsible for their actions, failure to bring them to justice will support impunity and lead to a denial of justice to their victims. It may even encourage the use of children to commit atrocities.

Does international law permit the prosecution of children?

International law has not addressed directly the issue of whether child soldiers should face prosecution for atrocities they committed during armed conflict. The recent Optional Protocol to the Convention on the Rights of the Child on the involvement of children in armed conflict does not contain any specific provisions on whether child soldiers should be prosecuted, or what would be an appropriate age of criminal responsibility (the age when a young person can be considered to appreciate right from wrong actions and to have some measure of responsibility for his or her acts; and when therefore it would be appropriate for a criminal investigation into such acts). Some child protection agencies working in Sierra Leone have opposed any prosecution of persons who were under 18 at the time the alleged crimes were committed on the grounds that they would be stigmatized and their rehabilitation into the community would be seriously compromised.

However, the Convention on the Rights of the Child does allow for young people to be prosecuted if the procedure can be fair and take into account the particular needs and vulnerabilities of young people. Article 3 of the Convention on the Rights of the Child requires that any legal action taken by the authorities must have the best interests of the child as a primary consideration. It is possible that in certain cases where a child soldier did act with full awareness of what he was doing and with full intent to commit atrocities, then it would be in his best interests to take responsibility for his acts, and the consequences of these acts, through a criminal process specially adapted for children. The principle of the best interests of the child requires that any criminal process involving children must have their needs at the heart. Other UN standards require that "The well-being of the juvenile shall be the guiding factor in the consideration of his or her case."

Prosecutions in an international criminal tribunal of those under 18 at the time of the offence.

Those who oppose the prosecution of child soldiers under any circumstances have argued that they should certainly not be prosecuted in international criminal courts, such as the proposed Special Court for Sierra Leone, because the International Criminal Court, when it has been set up, will not have jurisdiction over children. The Rome Statute states clearly that "the Court shall have no jurisdiction over any person who was under the age of 18 at the time of the alleged commission of a crime." However, this is a misunderstanding of the true position, because the Rome Statute provision was the result of a political compromise rather than a statement of principle.

The statutes of the *ad hoc* International Criminal Tribunals for the former Yugoslavia and Rwanda are silent on the subject of whether those under 18 can be tried, or whether a person under 18 could use his or her age as a defence to a criminal charge. Therefore, if allegations of sufficient seriousness were brought against an individual who committed crimes while under the age of 18, the Prosecutor could then use her or his discretion. Similarly, the Chambers of the International Military Tribunals for the Far East and at Nuremberg, Allied Control Council Law No.10 and the Draft Code of Crimes against the Peace and Security of Mankind of 1996 are silent on this issue. The Convention on the Rights of the Child does not define an appropriate age of criminal responsibility, but it does envisage trials of children under 18 in Article 40.

Most recently, the draft Statute for a Special Court in Sierra Leone has specified that accused persons who were between the ages of 15 and 18 at the time of the commission of the crimes may be prosecuted. However, it is unlikely that many children will be prosecuted in the Special Court, given that only the "most responsible"—particularly those who had a leadership role—will be prosecuted.

Amnesty International would not oppose such prosecutions of children between 15 and 18, as long as the court concerned implements fair trial guidelines for children in full, particularly, excluding the possibility of imposing the death penalty or life imprisonment without possibility of release. Any court in which children take part in proceedings must take into account the special needs of persons under 18 who may participate in the trial in any way, as defendants or as witnesses.

The UN Secretary-General has indicated that the prosecution of children might occur in exceptional circumstances, and has asked the Security Council to make the final decision on whether the Special Court for Sierra Leone should have jurisdiction over suspects aged between 15 and 18 years. If such cases arise in any court, the international community should respond by providing the necessary resources to ensure a fair trial for such children. It is particularly important that such children be dealt with in a fair international court with sufficient resources, as often domestic juvenile justice systems lack resources and often breach international standards for juvenile justice. For example, the juvenile justice system in Sierra Leone has been virtually destroyed by the civil war, and even when it was functioning, the juvenile justice system in Sierra Leone frequently sentenced boys to corporal punishments.

. . . .

Fair trial standards for children under 18: rehabilitation, not stigmatization

It has been argued that any prosecution of any child soldier will stigmatize all of them, and inhibit their reintegration into society. However, if persons under 18 are prosecuted, such trials will be extremely rare, as only the most serious cases will be prosecuted: therefore such prosecutions are unlikely to stigmatize all former child soldiers.

International standards relating to justice for children clearly state that the aim of prosecuting children under 18 must be to rehabilitate them, and their interests should be at the heart of the process. They also require that the child's privacy should be protected throughout the trial process, which means that if trials of children are undertaken fairly, then the child will not be publicly stigmatized. . . .

The age of criminal responsibility

. . . . Amnesty International considers that a minimum age limit for criminal responsibility should be set, and the fixing of any age should take into account the moral and psychological components of criminal responsibility—that is, whether a child has the discernment and understanding to choose certain acts and therefore be held legally responsible for those acts. A balance must be drawn between attributing responsibility appropriately and protecting children from a process they are too young to understand.

As well as setting a minimum age of criminal responsibility, the authorities dealing with criminal justice issues in the domestic and the international setting should also put in place guidelines and safeguards for protecting and rehabilitating children who have committed offences when they were below the age of criminal responsibility. Such children may often be dealt with by social care services or mental health service. Without appropriate safeguards, procedures to review progress and to appeal against decisions, there is a risk that children in the care of social services or the mental health care system may be detained for longer than is appropriate or not receive proper treatment.

...

Amnesty International's recommendations

Child soldiers should be seen primarily as victims of conflicts.

1. In the rare cases where it is in the interests of justice to prosecute child soldiers, the criminal process should be specially adapted, according to the provisions of the Convention on the Rights of the Child, and other international standards such as the Beijing Rules, to their needs and level of understanding. The best interests of the child should be the guiding principle in any criminal process. The international community should ensure that sufficient resources are made available to implement these standards.

2. Children should be held in detention as a last resort and for the shortest possible period of time. In such situations, a child should be held in appropriate conditions and kept separately from adult prisoners. No child should ever be sentenced to the death penalty, corporal punishment or other cruel, inhuman or degrading treatment under any circumstances.

Notes and Questions

1. Given the fact that children are now commonly used as soldiers, especially in the most brutal settings where aggressive military tactics are the norm, how well does international law deal with the problem posed by the older adolescent who commits atrocities? What is Grossman's position on this? What does Amnesty seem to be advocating? Is it possible to find a middle ground on this question? Is it possible to promulgate objective standards of juvenile culpability in the armed conflict context, given the fact that even the older children are terrorized and exploited by their very participation in warfare? On the question of the criminal culpability of the child soldier, which set of recommendations would be easier to implement, Grossman's or Amnesty International's?

III. Beyond the Legal Norms: Recent Global Reaction to Children and Armed Conflict

A. Have We Begun to Care?

In February 2008, a UNICEF press release indicated that, although certain conflicts characterized by the use of child soldiers had improved, the total number of armed groups and forces using children had risen.[8] In Sri Lanka, Chad, Sudan, Afghanistan and the Central African Republic, recruitment of children was on the upswing. It appears that, despite the enhanced monitoring of these situations and the new sense of international accountability, the moral vacuum described by Machel in 1996 is still evident.

Indeed, from around the time of the Machel report, there has been a flurry of UN initiatives around the problem of children in armed conflict. In December 1996, the Gen-

----

8. Press Release, UNICEF, Number of Armed Groups or Forces Using Child Soldiers Increases from 40 to 57 (Feb. 12, 2008), *available at* http://www.unicef.org/media/media_42833.html.

eral Assembly adopted resolution 51/77, which established the mandate of the Special Representative of the Secretary General for Children and Armed Conflict.[9] This mandate comes up for extension every three years. The principal tasks of the Special Representative are to advocate for vulnerable children, to raise awareness by visiting countries where children are being exploited in warfare, to gather data and present reports. As described above, the Optional Protocol to the UNCRC on Children and Armed Conflict was opened for ratification in 2000, and has to date been ratified by 127 countries. Further, a Security Council Working Group on Children and Armed Conflict was created in 2005 pursuant to Security Council resolution 1612 (2005).[10] The principal object of this Working Group is to monitor and review progress on the child soldier issue, and to make pertinent recommendations.

It is important to examine whether this high level of interest and activity on the part of the UN is being reflected in positive changes on the ground. Without question, states are more aware of the impermissibility of allowing the recruitment of child soldiers, and other forms of abuse and exploitation of children in the prosecution of war. In 2007, fifty-eight states formally adopted the so-called "Paris Commitments" and "Paris Principles"—agreements which aim to combat the recruitment and use of child soldiers— showing renewed determination to take firm action to eradicate reliance on children in armed conflict.[11] Despite all this international activity, it seems that just as one conflict is settled, others having the same characteristics of chaotic brutality appear.

This section will attempt to confront the question of how much the global public truly cares about this issue, and the degree to which the international community is investing in the relevant remedies and solutions. Various commentators assess the effectiveness of these international initiatives, and consider the number of children still adversely affected by their proximity to armed conflict. UN documents are included in the readings, to encourage comment and analysis as to their utility in drawing attention to continued exploitation of children in armed conflict situations.

It is of course highly difficult to measure "caring" in the child soldiers context. We have seen above how there has been a proliferation of legal norms dealing with children and armed conflict, including a specialized protocol to the UNCRC. Despite these legal norms, there are many barriers between the international community and those involved in situations of conflict and chaos that lead to large scale use of child soldiers. Should we measure "caring" by post-conflict prosecutions of those who recruit child soldiers? Or should it be measured by the level of international resources devoted to the rehabilitation of child soldiers? As is often the case, the UN is open to charges that it tends to measure progress by the number of declarations and resolutions passed on a particular subject. On the other hand, is it unfair to expect the UN to achieve rapid results in situations that result from complex historical realities?

In a 2005 news article, Jenny Kuper noted that "Throughout human history, children have been the unrecorded, and often unlamented, victims of warfare." It was her view that "now, finally, attention is being paid to their suffering. She wrote of a 2005 conference in the Hague, attended by the Chief Prosecutor for the International Criminal Court,

---

9. G.A. Res. 51/77, U.N. GOAR, 51st Sess., U.N. Doc. A/RES/51/77 (Feb. 20, 1997).
10. S.C. Res. 1612, U.N. Doc. S/RES/1612 (July 26, 2005).
11. Free Children from War Conference, Paris, Fr., Feb. 6, 2007, *The Paris Principles: The Principles and Guidelines on Children Associated with Armed Forces or Armed Groups*; Free Children from War Conference, Paris, Fr., Feb. 6, 2007, *The Paris Commitments to Protect Children from Unlawful Recruitment or Use by Armed Forces or Armed Groups*.

the deputy prosecutor for the International Criminal Tribunal for the former Yugoslavia, and the prosecutor for the Special Court for Sierra Leone, on a topic she found "astonishing"—namely, "International Criminal Accountability and the Rights of Children".

She stated that "Largely as a result of initiatives taken under the umbrella of the 1989 CRC, the UN has begun to take notice of children in armed conflict. The Security Council now has an annual day of discussion on this issue—and it has recently taken the hitherto unimaginable step of naming countries that use child soldiers and proposing measures both to sanction those countries and to put in place a monitoring system to track the situation of children involved in various armed conflicts, whether as civilians or combatants." She took stock of statements made by the various prosecutors at the conference, and wrote approvingly of David Crane, from the Special Court for Sierra Leone. Kuper wrote: "He asserted that one of the guiding principles of his work has been: 'If you go after women and children, you will pay the price.' And, indeed, he has put this principle into practice in Sierra Leone and been responsible for some ground-breaking cases against those who seemed, not very long ago, to be completely beyond the reach of international—or indeed national—law."

Interestingly, Kuper's view was that "It is encouraging to find that the endless meetings in international organisations such as the UN do sometimes bear fruit. And that their justified concerns are finding their way to some of the most remote regions of the world and to some of the most forgotten victims of violence." See Jenny Kuper, *We Have Finally Begun to Care about Child Soldiers,* Independent (U.K.), Mar. 29, 2005, available at http://www.essex.ac.uk/armedcon/story_id/000254.html.

Kuper stakes out a position that is cautiously optimistic. How can we know what sort of fruit is being borne, apart from yet more of what Kuper calls "endless meetings"? What is the best way to measure the success or failure of these initiatives?

———————

In the next article, how hopeful is P.W. Singer about the impact of ethical norm codification—that is, the production of more explicit norms prohibiting the use of child soldiers—on the actual phenomenon? Singer places emphasis on the purposefulness with which armed opposition groups employ child soldiers. He notes that these groups are perfectly aware that they are acting contrary to ethical principles, but do so for self-interested reasons. He seems far from certain that the proliferation of legal norms will coincide with behavioral changes. There are approaches he favors—criminalization of child soldier recruitment, and various forms of political and economic sanctions. How do Singer's suggested responses differ from those already taken by UN bodies? How effective do you think Singer's own proposed solutions would prove? Singer offers one further way of measuring the effectiveness of international action on the child soldier problem, including his version of a way forward, one that recognizes, but does not over-emphasize, international law rules. He suggests that effectiveness should not be measured by the implementation of moralistic norms, but on actual changes in the conditions that lead to conflict to begin with.

P.W. Singer, *Talk Is Cheap: Getting Serious about Preventing Child Soldiers*

37 Cornell International Law Journal 561 (2004)

. . . .

This Article looks at potential ways to prevent and deter the practice of child soldiers. To be effective, any effort against the use of child soldiers must seek to realistically understand the doctrine that drives it. Child soldiering stems from a set of deliberate choices and strategies designed to benefit from using children in war. By understanding the causes, as well as the resulting dynamics, one can develop more nuanced strategies that attack the very heart of the practice.

. . . .

II. Talk Is Cheap

Recently, in the academic literature that studies international relations, many experts have written about the importance of beliefs about right and wrong in shaping policy. They claim that beliefs shape actions, even when they conflict with one's interests. Such socially directed behavior is described as being guided by a "norm," or what anthropologist Paul Bohannan described as "a rule, more or less overt, which expresses 'ought' aspects of relationships between human beings."

This research about the power of beliefs extends into the military realm. Many have argued that "norms" about what is proper and improper behavior on the battlefield still matter today. They argue, for instance, that norms have limited the use of certain weapons that, while advantageous, are horrific. For example, chemical and biological attacks might have been quite useful in recent wars, but were considered so horrible in World War I that the vast majority of nations have since refrained. Most recently, activists have tried to harness this type of thinking by advocating the outlaw of weapons like the antipersonnel landmine.

However, the word "norm" can have two meanings. It can describe ethical beliefs about proper behavior, but it can also describe the most common practices of behavior, irrespective of ethics. Thus, while people writing about norms in international relations have focused on the positives of how ethics can lead to good behavior in warfare, they have ignored the second aspect. Experts have written little about the darker side of social behavior in warfare—the buildup of new, but malevolent, beliefs and common practices. These new standards prescribe malicious behavior.

Past decades of warfare have seen the breakdown of moral codes that guided behavior in war. This has increased the savagery toward innocent civilians, generally, and to children, specifically. Yet little of the new literature on norms confronts the issue of a proper response. Likewise, most analysts have incorrectly assumed that non-state actors play a purely positive role in developing the norms that direct common practice. Being separate from the state does not guarantee good behavior. It is true that some non-state actors positively affect policy, such as the actors behind the global campaign to eliminate landmines. However, immoral non-state actors also exist, such as the Lord's Resistance Army in Uganda, whose existence relies on the abduction and enslavement of children.

As the doctrine justifying the use of child soldiers has spread, the most basic ethical injunctions against using children in war have rapidly collapsed. Their failure was influenced primarily by technological and geopolitical changes, with the result that children are now regular actors on the battlefield. This indicates that the durability of ethical norms in the face of external forces is far less powerful than believed. If ethical norms are not sustainable, then their power is limited. Their failure also reinforces the argument that while common behavioral practices are often grounded in moral principles, their strength is influenced by very real contextual factors, such as the environment.

This weakening of constraints may be particularly strong for non-state armed groups, who are less influenced by moral norms. This conjecture is similar to the theory of "realist" international relations scholars, who feel that beliefs have no great role in politics. Instead, realists believe that power and interests can best explain actions.

However, there is one important caveat to the realist argument. While the rise of norms may be due to the power and interests of the strongest actors in the system (who receive most of the realists' focus), with the issue of child soldiers, the normative breakdown was caused by the innovations of some of the weakest actors in the international system. In fact, it was because of their weakness that such groups chose to violate the old norms against using children. Just as terrorist groups have revived fears of chemical and biological weapons use, the weaker parties have facilitated a new standard of behavior for using child soldiers in contemporary warfare.

III. Lost Norms and Child Soldiers

....

Despite international law's strong opposition to the practice, the child soldier doctrine spread widely in the 1990s. The international community's response, however, was to condemn the practice and codify the use of child soldiers as a specific violation of the law. The United Nations even created an office of the Special Representative of the UN Secretary-General for Children and Armed Conflict to investigate and lobby for children's rights in warfare. Former Ugandan diplomat Olara Otunnu currently holds this position.[12]

The major impetus behind these efforts was a group of geographically diverse NGOs, united under the umbrella of the *Coalition to Stop the Use of Child Soldiers*. The Coalition was formed in May 1998 by several leading nongovernmental organizations (NGOs): Amnesty International, Human Rights Watch, Defence for Children International, International Save the Children Alliance, Jesuit Refugee Service, the Quaker United Nations Office in Geneva, International Federation Terre des Hommes, and World Vision International. Over the next few years, it built up a global network of interested NGOs, aid agencies, research institutes, and other linked coalitions willing to stand against the use of child soldiers.

A major part of the Coalition's strategy was to generate consensus and enact treaties against the practice of child soldiering beginning at the state and regional levels. This endeavor was quite successful and eventually led to the mobilization of campaigns in over forty different countries. These efforts resulted in a series of regional agreements that currently encompass much of the globe, including:

- 1996 OAU Resolution on the Plight of African Children in Situation of Armed Conflicts,
- 1997 The Capetown Principles,
- 1998 European Parliament Resolution on Child Soldiers,
- 1999 Declaration by the Nordic Foreign Ministers Against the Use of Child Soldiers,
- 1999 Berlin Declaration on the Use of Children as Soldiers,
- 1999 Montevideo Declaration on the Use of Children as Soldiers,
- 1999 Maputo Declaration on the Use of Children as Soldiers,
- 2000 Organization of American States (OAS) Resolution on Children and Armed Conflict, and
- 2001 Amman Declaration on the Use of Children as Soldiers.

---

12. Radhika Coomaraswamy was appointed by UN Secretary-General Kofi Annan as Special Representative for Children and Armed Conflict in April 2006. She was reappointed by current UN Secretary-General Ban Ki-moon in February 2007.

The group successfully pushed for international condemnation of the practice. In 1999, the UN Security Council adopted Resolution 1261, which condemned the targeting of children in armed conflict, including their recruitment and use as soldiers. In 2000, the UN General Assembly adopted an "Optional Protocol to the Convention on the Rights of the Child." This protocol significantly amended the 1989 treaty in order to confront the issue of child soldiers. Principally, it raised the age at which direct participation in conflict is legally permitted from fifteen to eighteen years old. It also banned compulsory recruitment of any child younger than eighteen years old, and explicitly included non-state actors within its coverage. With intense lobbying, the treaty was quickly adopted and entered into force on February 12, 2002. As of February 2004, the treaty had been signed by 115 parties and ratified by 62.

Thus, as a result of the *Coalition to Stop the Use of Child Soldiers* and other international actors, a series of international regimes have buttressed the ethical norms against child soldiering. The UN Special Representative, Olara Ottunu, has also directly attempted to convince conflict groups to stop using children. He personally met with rebel group leaders in over twenty countries to negotiate the end of the practice. In January 2003, the treaty was followed up by UN Resolution 1460, which called on a list of specific child soldier groups in five countries (Afghanistan, D.R.C., Burundi, Liberia, and Somalia) to halt the practice and provide the Security Council with a report of the steps they have taken.

Ethical norms are clearly important in providing the standards that are intended to guide behavior. Proponents of the legal effort against child soldiering point to five key strengths of this activism: (1) it established an international standard on the employment of child soldiers; (2) codified legal norms; (3) set minimum age requirements that are more difficult to fabricate; (4) encouraged states to implement the laws; and (5) raised public awareness, both in the West and in areas where the child soldier groups were active—potentially empowering greater activism.

One should not, however, confound ethical norms with actual behavior or enforcement. Unfortunately, all of the international attention and condemnation of child soldiers has not translated into an end to the practice. Throughout the process, the use of child soldiers on an international scale did not diminish, but instead spread further still. Indeed, many of the same countries that signed the various treaties continue to flout their obligations. This is evidenced by the fact that while there are over 100 signatories, child soldiers still exist in roughly 85 countries. Indeed, some of the largest known users of child soldiers, such as the various child soldier groups fighting in Myanmar, Colombia, and Uganda, were not even on the specific Resolution 1460 list released by the UN in early 2003.

Moreover, the new protocol and the meetings with Mr. Ottunu have failed to sway the rebel groups from using child soldiers. Typically, after a period of public denial, these groups would pledge to stop using children as soldiers, in an effort to garner international goodwill and aid. However, they would not change their actual practices....

Indeed, the only change for some groups resulting from this lobbying effort against child soldiers was simply to try to better hide the practice. For example, when they first entered the Afghan civil war in 1994, the fundamentalist Taliban primarily recruited young Afghan refugees attending Pakistani madrassashs. Following international pressure, the leader of the Taliban, Mullah Omar, made a public decree in 1998 that any of his followers who had not yet grown a beard were too young and should leave the force. Omar declared that he would punish any commander who used child soldiers. Just one year later, the UN reported that Taliban offensives were using between 2,000 and 5,000 children bussed over from the religious schools, many preadolescent. Likewise, Renamo in

Mozambique steadfastly denied its use of children throughout its war with the government. At the war's end, though, many of its marchers in demobilization parades were children, including one sixteen-year-old who had been fighting since he was eight.

....

Consequently, while most groups no longer publicly extol their recruitment of children, the doctrine behind the use of child soldiers has continued to spread. Counterefforts have meant that the recruitment of children is no longer a source of pride (for example, the now defunct Farabundo Marti National Liberation (FMLN) in El Salvador once complained that it was excluded from an article in Time magazine about child soldier groups). All the same, however, groups continue to use children as soldiers.

IV. Turning Outrage into Action

....

The crux of the problem is that groups deciding to adopt the child soldier doctrine have never been ignorant about whether it was the ethical thing to do or confused as to what exactly was allowed under international law or norms of proper behavior. The codes against using children as soldiers have existed for thousands of years. Groups who have brought children into warfare know that they are violating a moral code. As just one illustration, the LTTE [Liberation Tigers of Tamil Eelam] has one of the most systemized approaches in its execution of the child soldier doctrine—ranging from sophisticated recruiting strategies using computer databases to a complicated structure of training camps and deployment strategies. However, even this group pointedly omits the dates of birth on the headstones of its child soldiers, knowing that history will harshly judge their exploitation of these children.

Those who use child soldiers are, by definition, willing to ignore and transgress longstanding ethical norms and will likely be unswayed by new ones. Those who abduct children, send them into battle, and force them to commit rape and murder are simply unlikely to be persuaded by moral appeals. One cannot shame the shameless.

Governments and groups interested in preventing the use of child soldiers must realize that the employment of children as soldiers reflects the use of a well-planned doctrine, resulting from conscious and deliberate decisions. Unless the international community can alter the real calculations and conditions that led to this choice, the prohibitions against child soldiering will be as empty and continually violated as the new, largely symbolic prohibitions against landmines. Groups will continue to use child soldiers. In short, making laws is not the same as finding ways to enforce them.

This realization may be sobering to the global activist movement, but all is not hopeless. Indeed, there are a number of feasible steps that could turn the ethical norms against child soldiers back into standard practice. Each represents a true possibility within the realm of policymaking; in general, they only lack the requisite level of attention and political will, which can be mobilized.

The first feature of a program to weaken the practice of child soldiers is that it must be smart and judicious. Any effort to stop a global practice inherently faces an uphill battle. Thus, if possible, a program must try to make the biggest difference in children's lives. One aspect of this is to focus on the worst abuses, as a shrewd use of the limited political capital and attention at hand. While all uses of children under the age of eighteen as soldiers are wrong, not all are equal.

The groups working to stop the use of child soldiers are motivated by noble ideals but too often have been distracted by other political agendas. Thus, they have often squandered their valuable energy and capital....

The focus of groups working to stop the use of child soldiers should turn from standard-setting and borderline issues to the heart of the matter. If the advocacy community hopes to ultimately make a difference, it must seek to change the present practices of the most offensive abusers. To accomplish this, it must move from moral excoriation to changing the political and economic calculations that actually lead to the exploitation of children. In military parlance, if it wants to defeat child soldier users, it must infiltrate their "decision cycle."

V. The Legal Angle

Groups do not accidentally choose to use child soldiers, nor are they motivated by pure malice. They have underlying interests and have deliberately set up special processes for the recruitment, indoctrination, and utilization of child soldiers because they believe they will draw certain advantages from the practice. These calculations must be altered in order to defeat the overall habit of using child soldiers.

One strategy is to criminalize the practice. The legal transgressions involved in child soldiering are almost too numerous to make an exhaustive list. The use of child soldiers has violated the laws of war for over four millennia. Indeed, as one expert notes of child soldier commanders in the D.R.C., "[t]hey know it's a war crime, but they seem to believe they'll never be brought to justice. There is a sense of rampant impunity." The problem is that, so far, these commanders have been correct.

Given the number of treaties and legal compacts that this practice violates, there is no need for additional international law in this arena. Rather, the full measure of international law needs to be applied to eliminate the sense of impunity enjoyed by those leaders who use child soldiers.

Two legal pathways offer hope in this area. Both entail treating the use of child soldiers as a war crime in and of itself and prosecuting the leaders responsible for the explicit recruitment and use of children. Both involve setting a legal precedent that punishes the practice.

Treating the practice itself as a war crime would also lower the bar for prosecution. That is, the widespread presence of child soldiers within an organization would be fairly easy to prove, as compared to the current high legal burden of proof that leaders must be aware of individual acts by their soldiers. For example, leaders of the Revolutionary United Front (RUF) or LRA may successfully distance themselves from certain massacres by saying they were elsewhere or didn't know of the actions committed by their subordinates. However, they could never claim ignorance of the fact that the majority of their soldiers were underage.

Moreover, the criminalization of the practice would make it binding on other states to turn over any leaders who have escaped across state boundaries. This would also apply to their assets, which might have been acquired through the use of child soldiers. Notably, non-state groups do not escape the jurisdiction of these laws. Like all governments, they are bound by the basic principles of international law and required to respect all four Geneva Conventions, even in internal conflicts.

. . . .

Thus far, the ad hoc tribunals have been geographically-centered, focusing on conflicts in Sierra Leone, Rwanda, and the former Yugoslavia. However, the reach of the tribunals transcends state borders. For example, the tribunals have indicted war criminals who took refuge outside the countries where their crimes originally took place. This provides the potential for a new mode in the use of ad hoc tribunals. One idea that merits exploration is the UN Security Council convening a new issue-centered tribunal that would tackle the international child soldier problem. The structure of such a tribunal would resemble previous tribunals, but the new version would seek out offenders regardless of where the crime was committed.

.... The purpose of this program of criminalization would be to affect the decisional calculus behind the use of child soldiers. The use of children as a weapon of war would become like the use of chemical or biological weapons—simply unacceptable to the entire world, under any circumstances. Those groups that consciously choose to transgress international law would then open themselves up to the risk of prosecutions, sanctions, and asset seizures. Such prosecution must be judicious enough to limit their focus to those who were in leadership positions, either politically or militarily, and not waste time and effort on followers. The idea behind criminalization and prosecution is not revenge, but deterrence.

....

VI. Taking Action, Indirectly but Effectively

....

Those armed groups that refuse to acknowledge and follow the prohibition of child soldiers violate one of the most basic tenets of international law, and accordingly, they should be denied recognition and legitimacy within the international community. This sense of legitimacy and respect is something that is surprisingly craved by many such warlords. International connections offer a boost to the leaders' egos and offer a means to distinguish themselves from their peers and deter subordinates and potential competitors.

... Finally, the rewards to child soldier groups that make only token demobilizations, such as the elevation of warlords in the Eastern Congo to statesmen, must end. Instead, the burden of proof must fall on these child soldier users and abettors to prove their compliance with international law, before they are accepted as legitimate players in the international arena.

NGOs and interested state governments should lobby and pressure the international community to withhold recognition and all the benefits that accrue (ranging from seats at the UN to international aid and trade) to any groups that seize power through the use of child soldiers or to those that aid them. This would send an effective message to other groups that they will not be able to achieve their aims if they continue to use child soldiers. Otherwise, humanitarian organizations should also hold them at a distance—as they would treat those who are actively engaged in ethnic cleansing or genocide. They should also pressure other groups and states to act similarly. NGOs and interested states might provide further incentives by connecting such efforts to proposals to broker agreements that connect the flow of aid to the ending of child recruitment.

These efforts may prove insufficient, because the decisional calculus of some child soldier groups, such as predatory groups and warlords, is driven by nonpolitical rationales. These groups will require other action to sway them. The payoffs of using children should be limited by proscribing trade with such groups, targeting corporate bodies and other trading links. Research has shown that the majority of "war economies" that reward local predators and warlords are linked to the global economy. The current international campaign against the market for "blood diamonds" from Sierra Leone and Angola provides a blueprint showing how to target these profits.

.... Finally, while they may be nonstate actors, many ultimately depend on the backing of certain states. An example was the LRA's use of Southern Sudan as a training refuge or the RUF's basing in Liberia, the equivalent of hiding a criminal in one's garage. The support or presence of such groups that use child soldiers should also render host states violators of the international law. This liability would open the host state up to outside pressure, including sanctions and asset seizures, which may indirectly hinder the practice of nonstate groups employing child soldiers.

Conclusions

While certainly well-intentioned, the present strategy of raising awareness and shaming child soldier users will only partially eliminate the exploitation and abuse of children as soldiers. For the practice to end, an additive of deterrence is required. Groups seeking to end the use of child soldiers need a new strategy. They no longer need to convince the international community that using child soldiers is ethically wrong. Instead, they must change another belief, the common thinking of many conflict group leaders that the benefits of using child soldiers outweigh the costs. By directly responding to the doctrine itself and its underlying political and economic rationales, groups seeking to end the use of child soldiers stand a far better chance of affecting the calculus of would-be child soldier users.

Notes and Questions

1. The Singer article takes up the old question of whether "ethical norm production", one of the main tasks of the United Nations, is likely to be translated into action. What is the basis for Singer's skepticism? In the case of child soldiers, how do ideal norms and human needs collide?

2. Singer provides a complex critique of the idea of "norms". Does international law reflect an awareness of the fact that there are behavioral, as opposed to legal, norms, according to which the expected behavior in combat is increasingly brutal? What does Singer mean by the need to "infiltrate the decision cycle" of armed groups that exploit children?

The fact that the Security Council, sitting as it does at the very center of the UN's power structure, has taken a major and very explicit interest in the child soldiers question is considered highly significant. Security Council Resolution 1612, reproduced below, demonstrates the Council's intention to involve itself in an ongoing monitoring of state behavior with respect to the use of child soldiers. What seems to be the Security Council's primary motivation for involvement in this issue? Does this Security Council initiative represent the major departure in action on child soldiers that it is often said to be?

Press Release, Security Council, *Security Council Establishes Monitoring, Reporting Mechanism on Use of Child Soldiers*

Unanimously Adopting Resolution 1612: Will Collect Timely, Reliable Information on Recruitment, Use; Calls on Offenders to Prepare Time-Bound Action Plans to Halt Practice, U.N. Doc. SC/8458 (July 26, 2005), *available at* http://www.un.org/News/Press/docs/2005/sc8458.doc.htm

. . . .

The ... text of resolution 1612 (2005) reads as follows:

"*The Security Council,*

"*Reaffirming* its resolutions 1261 (1999) of 25 August 1999, 1314 (2000) of 11 August 2000, 1379 (2001) of 20 November 2001, 1460 (2003) of 30 January 2003, and 1539

(2004) of 22 April 2004, which contribute to a comprehensive framework for addressing the protection of children affected by armed conflict,

"*While noting* the advances made for the protection of children affected by armed conflict, particularly in the areas of advocacy and the development of norms and standards, *remaining deeply concerned* over the lack of overall progress on the ground, where parties to conflict continue to violate with impunity the relevant provisions of applicable international law relating to the rights and protection of children in armed conflict,

"*Stressing* the primary role of national governments in providing effective protection and relief to all children affected by armed conflicts,

"*Recalling* the responsibilities of States to end impunity and to prosecute those responsible for genocide, crimes against humanity, war crimes and other egregious crimes perpetrated against children,

. . . .

"*Reiterating* its primary responsibility for the maintenance of international peace and security and, in this connection, its commitment to address the widespread impact of armed conflict on children,

"*Stressing* its determination to ensure respect for its resolutions and other international norms and standards for the protection of children affected by armed conflict,

"*Having considered* the report of the Secretary-General ...

"*Gravely concerned* by the documented links between the use of child soldiers in violation of applicable international law and the illicit trafficking of small arms and light weapons and stressing the need for all States to take measures to prevent and to put an end to such trafficking,

"1. *Strongly condemns* the recruitment and use of child soldiers by parties to armed conflict in violation of international obligations applicable to them and all other violations and abuses committed against children in situations of armed conflict;

"2. *Takes note* of the action plan presented by the Secretary-General relating to the establishment of a monitoring and reporting mechanism on children and armed conflict as called for in paragraph 2 of its resolution 1539 (2004) and, in this regard:

(a) underlines that the mechanism is to collect and provide timely, objective, accurate and reliable information on the recruitment and use of child soldiers in violation of applicable international law and on other violations and abuses committed against children affected by armed conflict, and the mechanism will report to the working group to be created in accordance with paragraph 8 of this resolution;

(b) underlines further that this mechanism must operate with the participation of and in cooperation with national government and relevant United Nations and civil society actors, including at the country-level;

. . . .

(d) also stresses that any dialogue established under the framework of the monitoring and reporting mechanism by United Nations entities with non-state armed groups in order to ensure protection for and access to children must be conducted in the context of peace processes where they exist and the cooperation framework between the United Nations and the concerned government;

"3. *Requests* the Secretary-General to implement without delay, the above-mentioned monitoring and reporting mechanism, beginning with its application, within existing resources, in close consultation with countries concerned, to parties in situations of armed conflict listed in the annexes to Secretary-General's report (S/2005/72) that are on the agenda of the Security Council, and then, in close consultation with countries concerned, to apply it to parties in other situations of armed conflict listed in the annexes to Secretary-General's report (S/2005/72), bearing in mind the discussion of the Security Council and the views expressed by Member States, in particular during the annual debate on Children and Armed Conflict ...

. . . .

"4. *Stresses* that the implementation of the monitoring and reporting mechanism by the Secretary-General will be undertaken only in the context of and for the specific purpose of ensuring the protection of children affected by armed conflict and shall not thereby prejudge or imply a decision by the Security Council as to whether or not to include a situation on its agenda;

. . . .

"7. *Expresses* serious concern regarding the lack of progress in development and implementation of the action plans called for in paragraph 5 (a) of its resolution 1539 (2004) and, pursuant to this, calls on the parties concerned to develop and implement action plans without further delay ...

"8. *Decides* to establish a working group of the Security Council consisting of all members of the Council to review the reports of the mechanism referred to in paragraph 3 of this resolution, to review progress in the development and implementation of the action plans mentioned in paragraph 7 of this resolution and to consider other relevant information presented to it; *decides further* that the working group shall:

(a) make recommendations to the Council on possible measures to promote the protection of children affected by armed conflict, including through recommendations on appropriate mandates for peacekeeping missions and recommendations with respect to the parties to the conflict;

(b) address requests, as appropriate, to other bodies within the United Nations system for action to support implementation of this resolution in accordance with their respective mandates;

"9. *Recalls* paragraph 5 (c) of its resolution 1539 (2004), and reaffirms its intention to consider imposing, through country-specific resolutions, targeted and graduated measures, such as, inter alia, a ban on the export and supply of small arms and light weapons and of other military equipment and on military assistance, against parties to situations of armed conflict which are on the Security Council's agenda and are in violation of applicable international law relating to the rights and protection of children in armed conflict;

. . . .

"11. *Welcomes* the efforts undertaken by United Nations peacekeeping operations to implement the Secretary-General's zero-tolerance policy on sexual exploitation and abuse and to ensure full compliance of their personnel with the United Nations code of conduct, requests the Secretary-General to continue to take all necessary action in this regard and to keep the Security Council informed, and urges troop-contributing countries to take appropriate preventive action including predeployment awareness training, and to take disciplinary action and other action to ensure full accountability in cases of misconduct involving their personnel;

"12. *Decides* to continue the inclusion of specific provisions for the protection of children in the mandates of United Nations peacekeeping operations, including the deployment, on a case-by-case basis, of child-protection advisers (CPAs) ...

"13. *Welcomes* recent initiatives by regional and subregional organizations and arrangements for the protection of children affected by armed conflict, and encourages continued mainstreaming of child protection into their advocacy, policies and programmes; development of peer review and monitoring and reporting mechanisms; establishment, within their secretariats, of child-protection mechanisms; inclusion of child-protection staff and training in their peace and field operations; sub- and interregional initiatives to end activities harmful to children in times of conflict, in particular cross-border recruitment and abduction of children, illicit movement of small arms, and illicit trade in natural resources through the development and implementation of guidelines on children and armed conflict;

"14. *Calls upon* all parties concerned to ensure that the protection, rights and well-being of children affected by armed conflict are specifically integrated into all peace processes, peace agreements and post-conflict recovery and reconstruction planning and programmes;

"15. *Calls upon* all parties concerned to abide by the international obligations applicable to them relating to the protection of children affected by armed conflict ...

"16. *Urges* Member States, United Nations entities, regional and subregional organizations and other parties concerned, to take appropriate measures to control illicit subregional and cross-border activities harmful to children, including illicit exploitation of natural resources, illicit trade in small arms, abduction of children and their use and recruitment as soldiers as well as other violations and abuses committed against children in situations of armed conflict in violation of international applicable law;

"17. *Urges* all parties concerned, including Member States, United Nations entities and financial institutions, to support the development and strengthening of the capacities of national institutions and local civil society networks for advocacy, protection and rehabilitation of children affected by armed conflict to ensure the sustainability of local child-protection initiatives;

....

"19. *Reiterates* its request to the Secretary-General to ensure that, in all his reports on country-specific situations, the protection of children is included as a specific aspect of the report, and expresses its intention to give its full attention to the information provided therein when dealing with those situations on its agenda;

"20. *Requests* the Secretary-General to submit a report by November 2006 on the implementation of this resolution;

....

———————

Note the language used by the UN in announcing the Security Council initiative to the world, in the press release below. The UN's Special Representative on the subject hails the move as the dawn of a new era in dealing with the problem of child soldiers.

Press Release, Office of the Special Representative for Children and Armed Conflict, *UN Security Council Establishes First Comprehensive Monitoring and Reporting System to Protect Children Affected by Armed Conflict*

(July 25, 2005), *available at* www.un.org/ children/conflict/pr/2005-07-25112.html.

In a major and ground-breaking development, the UN Security Council today voted unanimously for a series of measures, including the establishment of a comprehensive monitoring and reporting mechanism, to ensure the protection of children exposed to armed conflict.... The mechanism will monitor grave violations by all parties, both governments and insurgents, focusing particularly on:

- killing or maiming of children

- recruiting or using child soldiers

- attacks against schools or hospitals

- rape or other sexual violence against children

- abduction of children

- denial of humanitarian access for children

The Security Council has endorsed the continued naming and listing of all offending parties, both insurgents and governments, which are responsible for grave violations against children. In the same resolution, the Security Council ordered offending parties which have already been listed, to prepare and implement right away, concrete action plans and timelines for ending violations against children. The Security Council also decided to establish its own special Working Group to oversee implementation of these measures and to monitor progress in ending on-going violations against children. The adoption of this resolution by the Security Council followed several months of intensive negotiations on a package of measures and recommendations submitted to it by the Secretary General in his report (S-59/695) of February, 2005.

"We have now entered the 'era of application,'" commented UN Special Representative for Children and Armed Conflict, Olara A. Otunnu. "For the first time, the UN is establishing a formal, structured and detailed compliance regime of this kind. This brings together all the key elements we have been developing, in the last few years, to ensure accountability and compliance on the ground. This is a turning point of great consequence."

Under the new mechanism, UN-led task forces will be established in phases, ultimately covering all conflict situations of concern, to monitor the conduct of all parties, and to transmit regular reports to a central task force based at UN headquarters in New York. These reports will serve as triggers for action against the offending parties.

The Security Council has directed UN peacekeeping missions and UN country teams to enter into immediate dialogue with offending parties listed in the Secretary-General's latest report, in order to prepare and implement, concrete time-bound action plans for ending the violations for which they have been cited. The latest report lists 54 offending parties, governments as well as insurgents, drawn from 11 situations of conflict. These included: the Tamil Tigers (LTTE) from Sri Lanka; Fuerzas Armadas Revolucionarias de Colombia (FARC) from Colombia; Janjaweed from Sudan; the Communist Party of Nepal-Maoist (CPN-Maoist) from Nepal; Lord's Resistance Army (LRA) from Uganda; Karen National Liberation Army from Myanmar; and government forces from DRC, Myanmar and Uganda....

The Security Council's special Working Group, composed of all 15 members, will review reports and action plans, and consider targeted measures against offending parties, where insufficient or no progress has been made. Such measures might include travel restrictions on leaders, and their exclusion from any governance structures and amnesty provisions, the imposition of arms embargoes, a ban on military assistance, and restriction on the flow of financial resources to the parties concerned.

In his statement to the Security Council, Mr. Otunnu said, "The time has come for the international community to redirect its energies from the normative task of the elaboration of standards to the compliance mission of ensuring their application on the ground. Today, as never before, we have the necessary norms, institutions, and means to realize the 'era of application' for the protection of all children exposed to armed conflict."

In the last decade, 2 million children have been killed in situations of armed conflict, while 6 million children have been disabled or injured. Over a quarter of a million child soldiers are being abused and exploited today in situations of armed conflict around the globe. Since 2003, over 11 million children have been displaced within their own countries, and 2.4 million children were forced to flee conflict and take refuge outside their home countries. Abductions are becoming more widespread, as witnessed, for example, in Darfur, Northern Uganda, Nepal and Burundi. Thousands of children, particularly girls, are subjected to rape and other sexual abuses in situations of conflict. Landmines kill or maim 8, 000 to 10, 000 children every year.

Notes and Questions

1. Resolution 1612 set in motion a UN process that includes monitoring and reporting on conflicts involving the use of child soldiers. For those inclined to take the statements of the UN as fundamentally important, the Security Council's action was major step in the right direction. For critics of the UN, this sort of "document production" might be seen as a substitute for, rather than a spur towards, real action. How closely does the Security Council mandate reflect the suggestions contained in the Machel Report?

———————

As part of the monitoring mechanism described above, the Security Council receives reports from the Secretary-General on the global situation with regard to children and armed conflict. The excerpts below are taken from the 2007 report. Given all the international legal activity surrounding this issue, does the report reflect genuinely positive developments? Ten years having passed since the Machel Report, should we expect more in the way of concrete results, or is it unrealistic to look for major changes in the short term?

The Secretary-General, *Report of the Secretary-General on Children and Armed Conflict*

delivered to the Security Council and the General Assembly,
U.N. Doc. S/2007/757, A/62/609 (Dec. 21, 2007),
available at http://www.un.org/Docs/sc/sgrep07.htm

. . . .

II. Cross-cutting issues of concern

6. Recruitment of children and internal displacement are closely linked, such as in Colombia, as too often displacement becomes the only avenue left for families in certain areas to avoid their children's recruitment by armed groups. On the other hand, evidence suggests that refugee and internally displaced person camps are often prime recruiting grounds for child soldiers owing to the convenient concentration of vulnerable children. The lack of security around these camps is said to be an important factor that increases the likelihood of child recruitment. During the reporting period, there have been reports that the Karuna faction have abducted and recruited children from internally displaced person camps in Sri Lanka. In the Democratic Republic of the Congo, children have been recruited from internally displaced person camps in North Kivu Province by forces loyal to rebel leader Laurent Nkunda during the recent upsurge in violence.

7. The movement of armed groups across borders to recruit children from refugee camps continues to be alarming. Along the Sudan-Chad border, both Sudanese and Chadian armed groups are recruiting children from Sudanese refugee camps in eastern Chad, while Chadian refugee children are being recruited by Sudanese rebel groups in Darfur. Since January 2007, there has also been a surge in the recruitment and use of Congolese and Rwandan children in North Kivu from refugee camps and communities in Rwanda by forces loyal to Laurent Nkunda, as well as Ugandan children from the Democratic Republic of the Congo-Uganda border areas. The transportation of vulnerable children by both the Government and rebel groups across borders during armed conflict constitutes one of the worst forms of child trafficking.

8. Girls, and sometimes boys, are targeted with various forms of sexual and gender-based violence, including rape, during armed conflicts. The perpetration of sexual violence against children by State and non-State parties to conflict is prohibited by international humanitarian law and is a violation of human rights. In Darfur, rape is a method of warfare used by armed groups to deliberately humiliate and to force displacement of girls and their families. In the Great Lakes region, especially in the Democratic Republic of the Congo and Burundi, the United Nations High Commissioner for Human Rights indicated appalling levels of sexual and gender-based violence. For example, 60 per cent of the cases recorded in Kisangani, northern Democratic Republic of the Congo, involved victims between the ages of 11 and 17. It is imperative that perpetrators of acts of rape and other sexual violence which leave a long-term, devastating impact on the victims are prosecuted in accordance with the gravity of such crimes. The recent decision of the International Criminal Court to open an investigation in the Central African Republic on allegations of rape and other sexual crimes committed in the context of armed conflict between the Government and rebel forces is an important step towards that end.

9. Increasingly, we are also encountering cases of children being detained for alleged association with armed groups in violation of international standards, for example in Burundi, Colombia, the Democratic Republic of the Congo, Iraq, Israel and the Philippines. Many of the detained children are subjected to ill treatment, torture, forceful interrogation and deprivation of food and education. The children also lack recourse to prompt and appropriate legal assistance, and usually are not separated from adults. In certain situations, some of these children have been used as guides and informers for Government military operations, usually under coercion. During the reporting period, some children have been released owing to United Nations advocacy efforts, such as in Burundi and the Democratic Republic of the Congo; however, many children remain in detention centers, local prisons, interrogation centers and holding camps.

10. Systematic and deliberate attacks on schoolchildren, teachers and school buildings have, since the last reporting period, escalated in certain conflict situations, warranting the increased attention of, and action by, the international community. In Afghanistan, insurgents continue to burn down schools, especially girls' schools, in an effort to intimidate and prevent girls from accessing education. In Iraq, students are also targets of violent crimes and sectarian killings, especially in Baghdad and Mosul. Killings of teachers, closures of schools and children's fear of being abducted have contributed to a dramatic decrease in school attendance rates.

....

12. Since the last reporting period, important precedents have been set to end impunity for crimes against children, particularly the recruitment and use of children by Government forces or armed groups. These include the confirmation of charges by the

International Criminal Court against Thomas Lubanga Dyilo, founder and leader of the Union of Congolese Patriots in the Ituri region of the Democratic Republic of the Congo, for the conscription and enlistment of children under the age of 15 and the use of children for active participation in hostilities and the arrest warrants issued by the Court for five senior members of the Lord's Resistance Army (LRA), including its leader, Joseph Kony, who is charged with 33 counts of war crimes and crimes against humanity, including the forcible enlistment and use of children in hostilities. Furthermore, for the first time, a former head of State, Charles Taylor of Liberia, is undergoing trial in The Hague before the Special Court for Sierra Leone for 11 counts of war crimes and crimes against humanity, including conscripting or enlisting children into armed forces or groups and using them to participate actively in hostilities. Sentencing by the Special Court for Sierra Leone of Alex Tamba Brima, Brima Bazzy Kamara and Santigie Borbor Kanu of the Armed Force Revolutionary Council and the conviction of Allieu Kondewa of the Civil Defence Forces militia for the recruitment and use of child soldiers send an important message that such crimes against children will not be tolerated and that those who engage in the practice will be brought to justice. Notwithstanding international efforts, national authorities must also promptly commence appropriate national prosecutions for grave crimes against children.

. . . .

14. There has been less focus on the reintegration of children associated with armed groups than on disarmament and demobilization in post-conflict situations. As the prospects for recovery in most countries also depend on the successful reintegration of these children, peace building efforts should address children's protection and reintegration needs in the initial planning and implementation of peace building operations. Long-term recovery and development programmes, linked to disarmament, demobilization and reintegration, should be community based, in order to provide sustainable and successful reintegration for these children.

III. Information on compliance and progress in ending the recruitment and use of children and other violations against children

. . . .

17. Parties who fully comply with terms set forth in action plans and undertake verified measures to address all the other grave violations for which they have been cited, to the satisfaction of the country-level task forces on monitoring and reporting or United Nations country teams and the Task Force on Children and Armed Conflict, will be considered for de-listing from the annexes. De-listing does not in any way negate the requirement for continued monitoring of formerly listed parties by the country-level task force on monitoring and reporting or the United Nations country team. Should it be determined that de-listed parties recruit and use children at a later point in time or fail to allow continuous and unhindered access to the United Nations for verification, they will be re-listed onto the annexes and the Security Council alerted to non-compliance.

. . . .

A. Information on compliance and progress in situations on the agenda of the Security Council

Developments in Afghanistan

19. The security situation in Afghanistan has deteriorated during the reporting period, with children continuing to be the victims of the conflict between anti-Government elements, including the Taliban, and national and international security forces, namely,

the United States-led Coalition as well as the North Atlantic Treaty Organization-led International Security Assistance Forces (ISAF). Weak governance and judicial system, as well as the inadequate coverage by the Afghan security forces in insurgency-affected areas, have contributed to the lack of protection afforded to children affected by the conflict. Indiscriminate attacks and disproportionate use of force by the Taliban and other armed elements, including the use of car bombs, suicide attacks and improvised explosive devices, directed at national and international forces have caused a high number of child deaths and injuries. Many of these attacks have taken place in densely populated areas or in the vicinity of popular gatherings. From January to July 2007, there were at least 950 civilian deaths as a result of insurgency-related violence, out of which the United Nations Assistance Mission in Afghanistan has documented at least 49 deaths and 19 injuries to children. On 15 June 2007, a suicide attack against an ISAF convoy in Uruzgan Province that was distributing sweets and water to local children resulted in the deaths of four girls and seven boys, aged between 8 and 15 years.

. . . .

22. The United Nations remains disturbed by reports of children being used to perpetrate attacks and, in some cases, as human shields by the Taliban and other insurgents. There have been reports that the Taliban have recruited and used children in their activities, such as suicide attacks. This is a relatively new phenomenon, and the United Nations has documented several high-profile cases of children involved in attacks. In February 2007, a boy estimated to be between 12 and 15 years old killed himself and a guard and injured four civilians as he attempted to gain entry to a police station in Khost city, Khost Province. Additionally, a 14-year-old boy was caught wearing a suicide vest on his way to assassinate the Khost provincial governor. No commitments have yet been made by any of these groups to end this practice.

. . . .

Developments in Burundi

24. The reporting period was characterized by political instability and persistent tensions between the Government and political opposition parties following the President's unilateral Cabinet reshuffle on 13 July 2007. It was equally characterized by the impasse in the implementation of the Comprehensive Ceasefire Agreement signed by the Government and the armed rebel group Forces nationales de libération (FNL)-Agathon Rwasa on 7 September 2006. Children continue to be associated with FNL. The ongoing recruitment of children by the two factions of FNL-Agathon Rwasa and the smaller break away Jean Bosco (Gateyeri) was of serious concern. However, the FNL-Jean Bosco (Gateyeri) faction is now defunct. From October 2006 to July 2007, 85 cases of recruitment of children were reported throughout the country, with 60 cases occurring in the months following the signing of the Comprehensive Ceasefire Agreement.

. . . .

26. As a result of the ceasefire, the number of children killed and maimed in armed clashes between members of the armed forces (Forces de défense nationale (FDN)) and FNL from September 2006 to August 2007 decreased by 30 per cent in comparison with the last reporting period. A total of 40 cases of children killed and maimed by FDN and FNL was reported, with 80 per cent of the victims killed by grenade explosions during looting operations. On 11 December 2006, five children were killed in Taba, Gitega district, when three FDN soldiers threw a grenade into their residence.

. . . .

Developments in the Central African Republic

28. There have been numerous reported cases of recruitment of children by the Union des forces démocratiques pour le rassemblement (UFDR) rebel group, which controls parts of north-eastern Central African Republic. During UFDR attacks on the positions of the Government Forces armées centrafricaines (FACA) and French Army in Birao on 3 and 4 March, some of the rebels were identified as former students of the Birao governmental secondary school. Many of the children, between the ages of 12 and 17 years, who participated in these attacks, were killed. Further, two out of three schools were partially destroyed by FACA and UFDR following the attack.

29. On 16 June, a tripartite action plan between UFDR, the Government of the Central African Republic and the United Nations Children's Fund (UNICEF) for the reduction and elimination of the recruitment and utilization of child soldiers and their demobilization and reintegration was signed, following which the first group of approximately 200 children were symbolically released. Earlier, in April and May, over 450 children associated with UFDR, 75 per cent of whom were boys aged 13 to 17 years, were demobilized. All these children have since been reintegrated into their families and communities....

....

32. Owing to the heavy presence of rebel groups in the areas of the Batangafo-Kabo-Ouandago "triangle", there has been a 75 per cent increase in sexual and gender-based violence reported, compared with the number of cases reported in 2006. According to UNICEF, 15 per cent of women and girls in the northern region of the country have been raped. United Nations partners also report that between Batangafo and Bokamgaye, many young girls are forcibly taken as wives for rebels and forced to perform sexual favours in exchange for movement across the numerous checkpoints set up by these rebel groups.

....

Developments in the Democratic Republic of the Congo

38. There has been a decrease in the number of cases of recruitment of children in the reporting period, which can be attributed to several factors, including the progress made in the implementation of the disarmament, demobilization and reintegration programme for children, the army integration process, the decrease in the number of active fighting zones and persistent lobbying by child protection networks against the recruitment of children. Despite this overall trend, all the parties to conflict listed in my 2006 report (A/61/529-S/2006/826) continue to recruit, use and abduct children. The presence of children in the Forces armées de la République démocratique du Congo (FARDC) integrated and non-integrated brigades remains high, particularly in the Ituri district and the two Kivu Provinces.

....

44. Despite all the initiatives undertaken by the Government to counter sexual violence, including the adoption of two national laws on 20 July 2006, the number of incidents of rape and other sexual violence against children remains extremely high. From October 2006 to July 2007, 10,381 survivors of sexual violence, 37 per cent of whom are children, were identified by United Nations partners in the eastern region of the Democratic Republic of the Congo; a 4 per cent increase since the previous reporting period. In a one-year period until June 2007, at least 1,400 child victims of rape and other sexual violence were registered and received assistance from the United Nations and its partners in South Kivu alone, where the main perpetrators include elements of FARDC, the police and armed elements of FDLR.

....

Developments in Haiti

46. It should be noted that, pursuant to Security Council resolution 1780 (2007), the Council recognizes the grave violations committed against children affected by the armed violence in Haiti and requests their continued protection, as set out in resolution 1612 (2005). Following military operations by the Haitian National Police (HNP) and the United Nations Stabilization Mission in Haiti (MINUSTAH) since December 2006, as well as the arrest of several gang leaders and the dismantling of armed entities, security conditions have improved, especially in areas affected by armed violence, such as Cité Soleil and Martissant in Port-au-Prince. These armed entities vary in organizational structure, activities, motivation and degree of political affiliation. According to MINUSTAH, although these groups are currently essentially criminal in nature, their character and motivations may shift between criminal and political depending on the specific time and circumstances and may pose a threat to peace and security.

....

51. Gang rape and other sexual violence against girls and women are still extensively perpetrated by groups in Cité Soleil, Martissant and Carrefour Feuilles. Owing to the lack of official and aggregated data, the number of cases reported is indicative of a larger phenomenon of sexual violence against girls in Haiti. According to a United Nations partner, approximately 100 cases of child rape were registered from October 2006 to January 2007. Among these, a 3-year-old girl was raped by armed men from Cité Soleil on 9 November, and two cases of rape allegedly perpetrated by members of Evens's group were registered in January 2007. From January to June 2007, it was reported that 54 children, 10 of whom were victims of gang rapes, were raped by members of armed and criminal entities. On 7 May 2007, a 15-year-old girl was raped by six armed men of Bois Neuf, and on 10 May 2007, a 17-year-old girl was raped by six armed men in Grand Ravine, controlled by Base Galil.

....

Developments in Myanmar

62. The Government, through its Committee for the Prevention of Military Recruitment of Underage Children, has undertaken some efforts to address the issue of the recruitment and use of children, including the recent inclusion of preventing the recruitment of child soldiers in their national plan of action against trafficking. Furthermore, written law states that participation in the Government armed forces (Tatmadaw Kyi) is entirely voluntary and that the minimum age for recruitment is 18 years. However, reliable reports from United Nations partners indicate that forcible attempts to recruit children for Tatmadaw Kyi are still taking place. It is difficult to systematically verify the extent of recruitment or the number of children in military camps owing to access limitations. Lack of proper birth certification and local-level connivance in falsifying existing registration information also perpetuate the difficulty of verifying child recruitment.

....

Developments in Nepal

72. The Comprehensive Peace Agreement signed between the Seven Party Alliance (SPA) and the Communist Party of Nepal-Maoist (CPN-M) in November 2006, as well as the separate Agreement on Monitoring and Management of Arms and Armies signed in December 2006, prohibits both parties from recruiting or using persons under age 18....

73. With the end of active conflict, there has been a significant decrease in reports of grave violations of children's rights. Reports of violations by the Government's security forces have seen a particularly marked decrease, and large recruitment drives by CPN-M have come to an end. The Nepal country-level task force on monitoring and reporting documented over a thousand cases of children recruited by CPN-M and its affiliates between October and December 2006. Many of those children ended up in Maoist Army cantonments, and over 300 were released without follow-up or official documentation after spending a few days at these sites. Since January 2007, four cases of recruitment by the Maoist Army have been documented. Two of the children involved have since left the Maoist Army. There were also no new cases of arrest under the Terrorist and Disruptive Activities (Control and Punishment) Ordinance (TADO) reported. TADO expired at the end of September 2006 and was not renewed. Most children arrested under TADO during the conflict were released.

....

77. There are also serious concerns regarding the Government's commitment to ending impunity and ensuring accountability for serious human rights violations. An increasing number of reports indicate that the Nepal Police refuse to register or investigate serious crimes committed during and after the conflict. The Government believes that the Truth and Reconciliation Commission, as referred to in the Comprehensive Peace Agreement, will address the issues of ending impunity, if and when established.

Developments in the Occupied Palestinian Territory and Israel

78. The situation of Palestinian children in the Occupied Palestinian Territory, including East Jerusalem, remains grave, with continued Israeli military operations, incursions and raids throughout the territory, in addition to an escalation in internal hostilities resulting in intense fighting between rival Palestinian factions. During the reporting period, a total of 106 Palestinian children were killed in the Occupied Palestinian Territory; 58 per cent of whom were killed by the Israel Defense Forces (IDF). Seventy-four per cent of child deaths caused by IDF occurred in the Gaza Strip, mostly during military operations and artillery shelling. From 1 to 7 November 2006 alone, eight children were killed during the Israeli incursion, code-named "Operation autumn Clouds", into Beit Hanoun in the northern Gaza Strip.

....

82. Documenting the recruitment of children by Palestinian armed groups remains a challenge, and the extent of the phenomenon is not well known. Although there is no evidence of systematic attempts to recruit children for training or operations, militiamen from at least one Palestinian armed group have approached boys outside their school in Gaza requesting them to join paramilitary training. On 2 August 2007, the case of a 13-year-old boy recruited by Hamas militants in Gaza was reported. The boy had been asked by Hamas to monitor the streets and gather information on drug dealers and collaborators with Israel. On 30 August 2007, IDF soldiers on an anti-terror patrol in the northern Gaza Strip spotted a 16-year-old boy who was carrying two explosive devices intended to be detonated in a suicide bombing attack against them. In April 2007, during the mission of my Special Representative to the Middle East, Palestinian President Abbas and then Foreign Minister Abu Amr agreed to revive the code of conduct among Palestinian groups not to involve children in political violence, and to engage with UNICEF to devise a plan of action to prevent the use of children in such violence.

83. Reports also suggest that Shabak, Israel's security agency, continues to seek to recruit Palestinian children to be used as collaborators inside prisons or upon their release.

Data are extremely difficult to gather owing to the reluctance of child detainees to talk about these issues, especially while still in detention, and the lack of systematic monitoring. However, at least one case involving a 16-year-old boy was reported in 2007. Furthermore, IDF continues to force civilians, often minors, to enter potential zones of conflict before the soldiers in order to clear the area or limit casualties, although the Israeli Supreme Court has ruled that practice to be illegal.

....

86. At any given point during the reporting period, between 361 and 416 Palestinian children were being held in Israeli prisons and detention centers, including children as young as 12 years. Between 10 and 22 of those children were being held in administrative detention without charge or trial. The majority of prisoners were boys, while approximately 11 girls had been detained or were serving terms of imprisonment during this period. Over 90 per cent of children arrested, interrogated and charged before the military courts were convicted and sentenced to a term of imprisonment. There are reports that some children held in detention undergo physical beatings and psychological torture, including threats of sexual violence. The systematic transfer of Palestinian child prisoners outside the Occupied Palestinian Territory into Israel is in direct violation of the Fourth Geneva Convention.

....

Developments in Somalia

88. Reports indicate that both the Union of the Islamic Courts (UIC) and the Transitional Federal Government (TFG) recruited and used children during intense fighting for control of Mogadishu in November and December 2006. UIC publicly declared its intention to recruit from schools, and appointed Sheikh Fu'aad Mohamed Khalaf to be in charge of training the students. An intensive recruitment campaign of boys and girls under age 18 by UIC and its allied militias took place from schools in Mogadishu in that period. TFG militias as well as some clan militias have been widely reported to be using children to carry arms. In January 2007, a senior United Nations official visited Mogadishu and was an eyewitness to children training at Belidogle airport, where TFG has a military base. Since June 2007, however, the TFG administration in Jowhar has begun to release children from its ranks, and activities are being planned to reintegrate these children into their communities, with support from UNICEF. In August 2007, the Minister for Women's Development and Family Affairs agreed to play a role in an advocacy campaign to release children from TFG armed forces and prevent future child recruitment.

....

Developments in the Sudan

94. The overall situation in Southern Sudan has improved slightly since the last reporting period. The Government of National Unity and the Government of Southern Sudan made the following commitments during the visit of my Special Representative to the Sudan in January 2007: to allow UNICEF and the United Nations Mission in Sudan (UNMIS) access to the military barracks of the Sudan Armed Forces (SAF), Sudan People's Liberation Army (SPLA) and allied armed forces and groups to monitor and verify compliance; to adopt and implement national legislation to criminalize the recruitment of child soldiers in a timely manner; to allocate adequate resources for the reintegration of children associated with the armed forces; to establish jointly with the United Nations a task force on sexual violence and abuse against children; and to ensure the safety and protection of humanitarian personnel.

95. As a follow-up to those commitments, some important measures have been undertaken by the Government of Southern Sudan to address the situation of children, in-

cluding progressive legislative reform, structures to address sexual exploitation and abuse and other child protection concerns and a serious commitment to the disarmament, demobilization and reintegration of children.

. . . .

103. Rape continues to be widespread in Darfur, and is used as a method of warfare, with an increasing trend to specifically target younger girls. During the reporting period, there have been 23 confirmed reports of rape, with two of the victims being boys. The perpetrators include elements of SAF, CRP, Janjaweed and SLA/MM. Although the prosecution of perpetrators of rape is rare in Darfur, during the reporting period two CRP officers and one SAF soldier were prosecuted for the rape of children as young as 13 years old.

. . . .

B. Information on compliance and progress in situations not on the agenda of the Security Council or in other situations of concern

Developments in Chad

107. With the talks between the Government and the armed opposition in Tripoli, and the rainy season, fighting in eastern Chad has significantly decreased. The security situation, however, remains extremely volatile and tense owing to the unsuccessful integration of the United Front for Change (FUC) fighters in the national army following the peace agreement signed in December 2006 by the FUC leader, Mahamat Nour, and President Deby, and the build-up of Government forces. The prevailing insecurity in eastern Chad is also exacerbated by sporadic cross-border raids by Janjaweed militias from the Sudan and inter-communal violence. The decrease in clashes has not reduced the phenomenon of forced recruitment of children by both the State and non-State parties to the conflict. Reports indicate that children have been recruited into the Chadian National Army. Although the actual figures are unknown, approximately 400 child soldiers, 100 of whom are between the ages of 8 and 12, were found stationed at a Government training centre in central Mongo. On 9 May 2007, the Government of Chad and UNICEF signed an agreement for the demobilization of child soldiers throughout the country. As at 30 July, 425 children, all boys, had been released from Mongo and Moussoro military instruction centres and the N'Djamena main military camp, and transferred to five transit care centres in Abeche and N'Djamena. However, thousands of children in various locations in eastern Chad have yet to be released from armed forces and groups.

. . . .

Developments in Colombia

113. The Government of Colombia, through the Colombian Family Welfare Institute, has carried out programmatic efforts to prevent the recruitment of children and reintegrate children into their communities. To date, the Government's efforts have benefited 3,326 children previously associated with illegal armed groups.

114. The Fuerzas Armadas Revolucionarias de Colombia Ejército del Pueblo (FARC-EP) continues to recruit and use children. Cases have been reported in the Departments of Cauca, Antioquia, Sucre, Bolivar, Cundinamarca, Guaviare, Meta and Nariño. In Corinto, Cauca Department, members of FARC frequently visit schools to persuade children to join their ranks. Furthermore, despite current talks between the Government and the Ejército de Liberación Nacional (ELN) and demands by the National Council for Peace that ELN cease recruitment and release all children from its ranks immediately, this group also continues to recruit children. In December 2006, two girls aged 14 and 15 were forcibly recruited by ELN in Nariño, municipality of Guachavez-Santa Cruz.

115. Children have been used by Government armed forces for intelligence purposes despite official Government policy to the contrary. On 6 March 2007, the Colombian Ministry of Defence issued directive 30743, prohibiting all members of the armed forces from utilizing children for intelligence activities, especially children recovered from illegal armed groups. However, the Defensoría del Pueblo reported that in Cauca, a child demobilized from FARC was used by the XXIX Brigade as an informant for the armed forces in an operation and was later killed at the age of 19 years while in combat with FARC, in contravention of the Paris Principles and Guidelines on children associated with armed forces or armed groups.

. . . .

116. There are increasing concerns about reported violations and abuses committed against children by new organized illegal armed groups. These groups, such as the Aguilas Negras, Manos Negras, Organización Nueva Generación or the Rastrojos are largely involved in criminal activities related especially to drug trafficking. The Government considers these groups as criminal gangs. . . .

117. Positive efforts have been made by the Government in the demobilization of combatants from the Autodefensas Unidas de Colombia (AUC). According to official figures, 63 children were demobilized from AUC in 2006, compared with 17,581 adults. Those children, however, were not formally handed over as per the requirements of the collective demobilization process, and there are concerns that a number of children have been missed out in that process. The Colombian Family Welfare Institute reports that an additional 32 children were demobilized on an individual basis during the same period.

. . . .

Developments in Sri Lanka

126. From 1 October 2006 to 31 August 2007, UNICEF received confirmed reports of 339 children being recruited or re-recruited by the Liberation Tigers of Tamil Eelam (LTTE), of which 41 per cent were from Batticaloa, compared with 679 children recruited in the preceding 11 months. In the same period, LTTE released 226 children, compared with 171 children released in the preceding 11 months, predominantly from Kilinochchi. Of the children recruited, 78 per cent were boys and 22 per cent girls. The average age of the children recruited during the reporting period was 16 years. Among the 6,221 children registered on the UNICEF database as having been recruited since 2001, 1,469 cases remain outstanding, including 335 children currently under 18 years of age as at 31 August 2007. The reported cases may only be indicative of the actual number of children recruited given access limitations in LTTE-controlled areas. LTTE has designated its so-called Child Protection Authority as the interlocutor on child recruitment issues and Security Council resolution 1612 (2005), and weekly dialogue between UNICEF and the so-called Child Protection Authority continues. As at 22 August 2007, eight children continued to reside in the Educational Skills Development Centre, in violation of the recommendations of the Working Group of the Security Council. At the time of reporting, UNICEF was in the process of arranging the return of those eight children to their families.

. . . .

132. LTTE submitted a draft action plan on 28 March 2007 and a revised version on 19 July 2007, following dialogue with the country-level task force on monitoring and reporting. However, those drafts committed LTTE to a minimum age of recruitment of 17 years until 1 January 2008, at which point the minimum age of recruitment would be raised to 18 years. The delay in raising the minimum age of recruitment to 18 years is

contradictory to their previous commitments and international standards. At the time of reporting, LTTE had indicated that the minimum age of recruitment would be raised to 18 years. However, this has not translated into a commitment to release those between 17 and 18 years old at the present time.

....

Developments in Uganda

133. Although the Government of Uganda has no deliberate or systematic policy to recruit children, the lack of effective monitoring at the local level leads to children continuing to join some elements of the armed forces. During the reporting period there were 16 cases of recruitment and use of children aged 14 to 17 years by the Uganda People's Defence Forces (UPDF). Three cases were reported in Pader district in which children who had escaped from LRA were used for gathering intelligence before being released in February 2007. In that regard, UPDF did not make use of the agreed civilian reintegration structures in place.

....

136. Owing to the absence of LRA in Ugandan territory during the reporting period, no cases attributable to it have been recorded by the country-level task force on monitoring and reporting. LRA has not released any children from the Ri-Kwangba assembly point in Southern Sudan. However, since the signing of the Cessation of Hostilities Agreement in August 2006, approximately 70 children, 15 per cent of whom are girls, have returned from Southern Sudan to reception centres in Gulu, Kitgum, Pader and Lira. The majority of the children had either escaped or were captured by UPDF or SPLA forces, while six children were transferred from the Toto Chan reception centre in Juba, Southern Sudan. Those children have been successfully reintegrated into their communities through UNICEF-supported child protection programmes. A mechanism is currently in place to receive the remaining children still held by LRA. The country-level task force continues to advocate for the release of all children and women remaining in LRA captivity.

C. Sexual exploitation and abuse of children by United Nations peacekeeping and other United Nations personnel

137. During the reporting period, the United Nations continued to seek ways in which to strengthen the institutional framework to prevent and address sexual exploitation and abuse by peacekeepers and other United Nations personnel, with some initiatives directed specifically at preventing the abuse of children.

138. The ability of the United Nations to cover field locations grew considerably, and as at 31 July 2007, the Department of Field Support has established Conduct and Discipline Units to cover 18 peace operations. Those units are responsible for receiving, monitoring and tracking complaints of sexual exploitation and abuse against peacekeepers, developing and implementing prevention initiatives and enforcing standards of conduct.

....

140. In June 2007, allegations of sexual exploitation and abuse by a contingent of United Nations peacekeepers were reported in the United Nations peace operations in Côte d'Ivoire. Those allegations involved acts of abuse of young women and girls. OIOS was immediately informed and the investigation process was initiated. Owing to the seriousness of the allegations, the contingent concerned was cantoned. The Departments of Peacekeeping Operations and Field Support, together with the concerned Member State, remain actively seized of the matter.

141. Recognizing the importance of a strategy for victim assistance as a part of the comprehensive response to sexual exploitation and abuse, the General Assembly, in its resolution 61/291, established an ad hoc open-ended Working Group to consider a draft policy statement and comprehensive strategy on assistance and support to victims of sexual exploitation and abuse by United Nations staff and related personnel (see A/60/877, annex). That Working Group commenced its deliberations during the sixty-second session of the General Assembly. It is anticipated that, when endorsed by the Assembly, the strategy will provide an institutional framework that will give much-needed support to children who are victims of abuse or are born as a result of cases of abuse by United Nations staff and related personnel. In the interim, victims of abuse may receive emergency medical and psychosocial support facilitated by United Nations operations on the ground in conjunction with local service providers. In some peace operations, such as in Liberia, the United Nations peace operation has established a Rape and Sexual Assault Rapid Response Team to ensure that swift action is taken to aid women and children who are victims of abuse. That team, which embraces local partners, has helped some minors to receive safe housing and medical attention. This initiative was intended to minimize the risk of losing or damaging critical evidence and to reduce the exposure of survivors of abuse to further trauma. The challenge now is to create sustainable initiatives for victims' support. Implementing this strategy is of critical importance.

. . . .

143. Significant progress was made during the reporting period with the establishment of an effective legislative framework which members of national contingents are required to comply with. It is encouraging to note that in July 2007, the General Assembly unanimously endorsed recommendations to incorporate revisions on standards of conduct into the draft model memorandum of understanding between troop-contributing countries and the United Nations (see A/61/19 (Part III)). In addition to strengthening the accountability of uniformed contingent personnel, the revisions to the memorandum of understanding also emphasize the need to immediately collect forensic evidence in sexual exploitation and abuse cases in a manner which will be sufficient to prosecute perpetrators in their home country.

IV. Information on progress made in the implementation of the monitoring and reporting mechanism and mainstreaming of child protection in United Nations peacekeeping operations

144. As called for in paragraph 3 of Security Council resolution 1612 (2005), a monitoring and reporting mechanism on grave child rights violations has been established in situations of armed conflict, listed in annex I of the Secretary-General's 2006 report, that are on the agenda of the Security Council, namely Burundi, Côte d'Ivoire, the Democratic Republic of the Congo, Somalia and the Sudan; and in other situations of armed conflict, listed in annex II of the Secretary-General's 2006 report, that have voluntarily implemented the monitoring and reporting mechanism, namely, Chad, Nepal, Sri Lanka and Uganda. The Government of Myanmar has also agreed to cooperate in establishing a monitoring and reporting mechanism within the framework of resolution 1612 (2005).

145. Since its inception, monitoring and reporting has moved from a concept to a concrete United Nations system response. The establishment of the monitoring and reporting mechanism has allowed for systematic, reliable, timely and objective information to be gathered on the six grave violations against children in armed conflict, including the identification of offending parties, which feeds into my country-specific reports examined by the Working Group of the Security Council on Children and Armed Conflict.

The designation of these offending parties on the annexed lists of my annual reports has proven to have a deterrent effect and has allowed the relevant "destinations for action", such as the Working Group, to maintain political pressure and take action on parties to conflict who are found to be persistent violators of child rights. Reports generated through the monitoring and reporting mechanism process have also contributed significantly to increased international awareness on the issue of Children and Armed Conflict, particularly though their inclusion in Security Council resolutions and debates that have been generated in other United Nations forums.

146. There have been positive developments as a result of the recommendations and actions taken by the Working Group, including drawing the attention of the Security Council as well as its sanctions committees, where applicable, to the need to follow up on the recommendations addressed to them.

....

151. My Special Representative has undertaken several country missions to carry out high-level advocacy on issues of children and armed conflict and to assist the authorities, United Nations and civil society partners in improving the situation of children in armed conflict. Several of these country missions have been mandated by the Working Group. Cooperation from Governments in extending their invitation to my Special Representative has been instrumental in achieving those objectives. In the reporting period, missions to Sri Lanka (November 2006); the Sudan (January 2007); the Democratic Republic of the Congo (March 2007); Lebanon, Occupied Palestinian Territory and Israel (April 2007); and Myanmar (June 2007) were carried out by my Special Representative or, in the case of Sri Lanka, by the Special Adviser to the Special Representative....

....

V. Information on progress made in the development and implementation of action plans

156. Pursuant to Security Council resolutions 1539 (2004) and 1612 (2005), parties are called upon to develop and implement concrete time-bound action plans, in close collaboration with United Nations peacekeeping missions and/or United Nations country teams. During the reporting period, progress on action plans has been made with armed forces and groups in four country situations on the agenda of the Security Council, namely, the Central African Republic, Côte d'Ivoire, Myanmar and the Sudan; and two parties in country situations not on the Council's agenda, namely Sri Lanka and Uganda. In Chad, although an action plan has not been developed, the Government signed an agreement with UNICEF to demobilize child soldiers from the armed forces.

....

Notes and Questions

1. The report excerpted above, and its accompanying list of armed groups engaged in recruitment of child soldiers, indicates a daunting array of situations in which children continue to be used and abused as soldiers, and otherwise subjected to violence. Portions of the report were included to make clear how prevalent and persistent the child soldier problem—and related issues of child exploitation and abuse in armed conflict—really is. Of the various legal approaches discussed above, which if any seems most likely to induce adults to refrain from relying on children to achieve combat goals? Does the report presented to the Security Council tend to take for granted the effectiveness of the UN monitoring system?

2. In 2007, more than fifty nations united behind a set of principles designed to enhance the protection of children in armed conflicts. To this end, a major international conference entitled "Free Children from War" was held in Paris on 5 and 6 February 2007. The meeting, co-organized by the French Government and UNICEF, was attended by 58 countries, including dozens of government ministers, donors, the heads of UN agencies and many non-governmental organizations.

At the meeting, the 58 governments endorsed and pledged to respect the Paris Commitments and the Paris Principles.[13] The Commitments are a set of legal and operational objectives aimed at protecting children from recruitment or use in armed conflict. These complement legal and political mechanisms already in place. The "Paris Principles" are more detailed, and set forth a wide range of goals relating to the protection of children from recruitment or use in armed conflict, as well as their release and successful reintegration into civilian life. The principles also address the need for long term prevention strategies in order to definitively end children's involvement in armed conflict.

The meeting was the culmination of an 18-month process to review the "Cape Town Principles and Best Practice on the prevention of recruitment of children into the armed forces and on demobilization and social reintegration of child soldiers in Africa", adopted by non-governmental organizations at a conference in Cape Town in 1997. The review process was led by UNICEF and drew upon a wealth of experience gained by UN field staff, NGOs and other practitioners in this field. For a description of this recent initiative, see Jenny Barchfield, *Pledge Aims to Halt Child Soldiers*, St. Louis Post-Dispatch, Feb. 7, 2007, at A10. Barchfield writes that "Some nations hailed the text, which carries moral but no legal weight, as a breakthrough. But others said it may be no more than empty promises and that more than words are needed to rehabilitate children mentally and physically scarred by war." She quotes the Liberian deputy minister of education as saying that "We've lost a whole generation of children," a fact the minister termed "scary." The article states that at least 250,000 children are still fighting in various conflicts worldwide.

The eloquent young Sierra Leonean spokesman Ishamel Beah is quoted by Barchfield as expressing concern that the new documents would prove "just more empty promises," because they will not be "properly applied." African representatives discussed the difficulties of rehabilitation and the resentment of the local population when former child soldiers seem to be rewarded for their violent behavior during the conflicts.

3. The adoption of the Paris Principles and Paris Commitments may be taken as further evidence of the fact that there is a global effort underway to stop the recruitment of child soldiers. From the description provided, does it seem that these efforts have taken on a new emphasis, or is the international community engaged in more of the same "norm creation" seen as ineffective by Singer? How would Singer react to the recent indictment of warlord Thomas Lubanga by the ICC? See Former Congolese leader on trial at ICC, BBC news, http://news.bbc.co.uk/2/hi/programmes/newsnight/7853562.stm.

B. Machel at 10: Another Retrospective

The UN report immediately following was issued with the intention of reflecting on ten years of efforts by the international community to respond to the findings of the

---

13. *Paris Principles and Paris Commitments, supra* note 10.

Machel Report of 1997. Although it may be classified as yet one more attempt by the UN to summarize its efforts in this field, its specific focus is how the international community has internalized the Machel findings. Does the international community have anything to be pleased about as it provides this perspective on the adequacy of the international response? What are the international responses that the UN is most eager to feature?

Special Representative of the Secretary-General for Children and Armed Conflict, *Report of the Special Representative of the Secretary-General for Children and Armed Conflict ("Machel 10 Year Review")*
delivered to the General Assembly,
U.N. Doc. A/62/228 (Aug. 13, 2007), *available at*
http://www.un.org/children/conflict/english/reports.html

I. The Machel Study and the 10-year Strategic Review

"Children are both our reason to struggle to eliminate the worst aspects of warfare, and our best hope for succeeding at it." — Graça Machel

1. The landmark 1996 United Nations report "Impact of armed conflict on children" (A/51/306 and Add.1) proposed comprehensive actions to improve the protection and care of children affected by armed conflict. Known as the Machel study because of its author, the expert of the Secretary-General, Graça Machel, the report remains widely used as a foundation for programme and advocacy....

2. The present report results from a tenth-anniversary strategic review of the Machel study co-convened with UNICEF. This is the first review presented to the General Assembly since 1996 ...

3. ... A special consultation process reached more than 1,000 children and youths through focus groups in 18 war-affected countries, and an online survey reached more than 300 in another 91 countries.

4. As stated in the Machel study, "war violates every right of a child — the right to life, the right to be with family and community, the right to health, the right to the development of the personality and the right to be nurtured and protected". While the recruitment and use of children by armed forces and armed groups has dominated attention in the last decade, all impacts of armed conflict on children must be redressed.

5. Many conflicts last longer than the duration of childhood. The present report focuses on children, but at times analysis is extended to youth, defined by the General Assembly to be those aged 15 to 24. We should recognize the capacities and agency of children and youth, and avoid characterizing children and youth as vulnerable or as delinquents who pose a threat to security. Moreover, adults are responsible for environments of conflict and violence.

....

7. The Machel study galvanized significant action and progress for children in 10 years. Building on the foundation provided by the Convention on the Rights of the Child, which details comprehensive rights for children at all times, highlights of progress in the last decade include a strengthened international legal framework and the first prosecutions of perpetrators by international tribunals.

8. Much more remains to be done....

II. Changing Characteristics of Armed Conflict and Consequences for Children

9. The Machel study noted with concern how war tactics had changed, with civilians, including children, increasingly becoming targets of violence and atrocities. The last decade has featured growing recognition of the changes to the character of armed conflict. An emerging body of United Nations reports and research illustrates that changing characteristics of armed conflict have created new threats to children.

10. As stated by the Secretary-General "there is no universally applicable definition of 'armed conflict'". Analysis of reports monitoring battle deaths shows that the number of conflicts for 2005 ranged from 17 to 56 worldwide....

11. One-sided violence has become a feature of many of today's armed conflicts, with poorly resourced and lightly armed groups often preying on civilians. Yet as the Machel study reported, in addition to thousands of children being killed and wounded every year as a direct result of fighting, many more children in conflict contexts die from malnutrition and disease. The International Rescue Committee's mortality survey of conflict-affected provinces in the Democratic Republic of the Congo, covering a three-year period, reported that 86 per cent of deaths were caused by indirect consequences of war, with children disproportionately affected.

12. Another emerging understanding concerns "asset wars", where economic interests commercialize and prolong conflict. Misuse of natural resources, such as diamonds, or the scarcity of resources, such as water, can fuel conflict. Such conflicts often become self-perpetuating and protracted. The Secretary-General has noted, "the illicit exploitation of natural resources ... serve[s] to intensify the vulnerability of children in conflict situations, as well as in transitional and postconflict situations".

13. Many of today's conflicts involve non-State actors and shifting landscapes of transnational organized crime. Security vacuums feature an increase in paramilitary forces and the privatization of conflict. Situations of armed violence fall into grey areas as traditional definitions of armed conflict erode. Despite distinctions in legal frameworks, the experience for children is the same. The situation in Haiti clearly highlights how, in a conflict-affected State with extreme poverty and corruption, armed groups, many with links to political parties, can quickly move towards organized crime, including drug and arms trafficking. A child recruited by an armed group one day may be labelled a gang member the next as political realities evolve.

14. Over recent years, terrorism has come to define the security discourse. One of the most striking instances of terrorism aimed at children was the Beslan school hostage-taking in the northern Caucasus in 2004. Of great concern is the use of children in suicide attacks and the fact that such attacks are disproportionately against civilians, often perpetrated in places of worship, market squares and other public places....

15 ... the proliferation and accessibility of small arms and other improvised munitions continue to endanger children. The widespread availability and misuse of small arms and light weapons can contribute to a sustained culture of violence and the "rule of the gun". A variety of explosive devices continue to kill and maim children in about 85 conflict and post-conflict countries.

16. While new features of conflict may have emerged, the impact on children remains as brutal as ever....

17. The frame of grave violations in situations of armed conflict proposed by the Secretary-General for priority attention in global monitoring and reporting provides a starting point for examining the impacts of conflict on children.

18. The killing or maiming of children is defined as any action that results in death or permanent or disabling injury, scarring, disfigurement or mutilation. With increased blurring of the distinction between civilians and combatants, as described above, children bear a heavy toll of mortality. Often threats continue even after hostilities cease; hundreds of thousands of cluster bombs left in Lebanon in 2006 pose a particular risk to children, heavily contaminating school grounds and agricultural lands. Globally, more than a third of casualties from explosive remnants of war are children.

19. While at the normative level there has been significant progress in addressing the recruitment or use of child soldiers in the last decade, large numbers of boys and girls continue to serve as fighters, cooks, porters and messengers, and to be used for sexual purposes. Since 2002, the Secretary-General has listed parties that recruit or use children in situations of armed conflict in 18 countries. That estimate is at the lower end; in 2004 the Coalition to Stop the Use of Child Soldiers identified 43 countries where either illegal recruitment or use was "indicated".

20. Attacks against schools or hospitals, including the occupation, shelling or destruction of facilities, as well as harm to personnel, have risen dramatically in recent years. Such attacks not only directly harm the individuals involved but severely limit others' access to basic services. A recent study commissioned by the United Nations Educational, Scientific and Cultural Organization provides sobering statistics on attacks against schools, teachers and students. In Afghanistan, over 100 bombing, arson and missile attacks were made against educational facilities in the first half of 2006, and approximately 105,000 children were denied access to education because of insecurity.

21. Widespread rape or other grave sexual violence continues to be committed in virtually every conflict situation and can take the form of sexual slavery, forced prostitution, sexual mutilation or other forms of brutality. In the Democratic Republic of the Congo, a climate of impunity has resulted in rampant sexual violence, with children representing an alarming 33 per cent of victims. Gender based violence often leads to severe and long-lasting health problems, including early pregnancies, fistula, infections, HIV/AIDS and psychological trauma. Rape victims and children born as a result of rape are often marginalized. In Rwanda and the Democratic Republic of the Congo, for example, children born of rape are at times referred to as "children of hate" and at times even "the enemy's children".

22. Abduction of children can be politically motivated or for purposes of recruitment, sexual exploitation or forced labour. The number of abductions in northern Uganda since the onset of conflict is estimated at 25,000. Recent reports of the Secretary-General note abductions in Burundi, Chad, Côte d'Ivoire, the Democratic Republic of the Congo, Nepal, where some 22,000 students were abducted by Maoists between 2002 and 2006, Somalia, Sri Lanka and the Sudan.

23. The denial of humanitarian access for children, whether deliberate or the result of a deteriorating security situation, deprives children of assistance and violates their basic rights, including the right to life. In Chad, the Secretary-General reported that the theft of 118 humanitarian vehicles by armed persons in 2006 seriously deterred humanitarian efforts.

24. A number of other conflict-related issues not listed among the six grave violations have a significant impact on children's lives....

....

27. Children have increasingly been pulled into hazardous work, as parties to conflict seek new sources of revenue to sustain military campaigns. In the Democratic Re-

public of the Congo, where the United Nations Panel of Experts on the Illegal Exploitation of Natural Resources and Other Forms of Wealth of that country determined that the war was mainly about access to, control of and trade in key mineral resources, children are commonly found working in mines and used in trafficking or as security guards.

....

29. The disintegration of basic social services that accompanies conflict further weakens coping mechanisms. For instance, in Sierra Leone more than 60 per cent of rural health-care units were non-functional in the immediate aftermath of war. In Southern Sudan, inadequate attention to the nutrition status of adolescents at one point contributed to mortality rates above 20 per 10,000 people per day. For education in northern Uganda, classes of 200 or more are common; students sit in cramped conditions, with few books, listening to a teacher who has little professional training. In contexts such as Chad, Darfur and Iraq, reduced access to and availability of safe water and sanitation have increased endemic diarrhoea and affected school attendance, especially of girls.

30. Social protection systems are overstretched such that children who are orphaned, disabled or vulnerable in other ways may need special attention. Children and young people are not a homogeneous group. Young children are more vulnerable to visible health risks, adolescent girls may be targeted for sexual violence and boys may be singled out for recruitment. Conflicts and their aftermath can last the length of childhood and adolescence, compounding physical, social, emotional and cognitive risks.

....

III. Political Engagement and the Legal and Normative Framework

32. The Machel study launched global mobilization that yielded gains in the international political and legal spheres. However, widespread violations occur daily against children, demanding further concerted action and engagement. The General Assembly is uniquely placed to deepen its engagement by systematically addressing all violations against children and the full breadth of impacts faced by children in conflict situations.

....

34. Security Council resolution 1261 (1999) affirmed the protection of children as a peace and security concerned initiated the progressive consideration of children in armed conflict by the Council [sic]. Reports of the Secretary-General to the Council on children and armed conflict have since provided an essential base for situation specific actions required of Member States and other stakeholders.

35. An innovation in addressing the conduct of parties to conflict followed the adoption of resolution 1379 (2001), in which the Security Council recommended that the Secretary-General list parties recruiting and using children in armed conflict. In its resolution 1460 (2003) the Council called on parties to prepare and implement concrete, time-bound action plans for the cessation of all violations against children. Action plans provide a mechanism to engage parties in practical steps to fulfil their obligations in regard to children. Although the Council expressed its intention to take targeted measures against perpetrators on the lists, action in this regard remains a pressing challenge.

36. Another milestone was the adoption of resolution 1612 (2005), in which the Security Council established a monitoring and reporting mechanism and the Working Group on Children and Armed Conflict. By August 2007 that Working Group had considered 10 country reports, making specific recommendations for each context and taking such actions as public statements to parties by the Chairman. Resolution 1612 (2005) is result-

ing in progressive action by some countries, including Myanmar, Nepal, Sri Lanka and Uganda, to establish mechanisms, whether or not they are on the Council's agenda.

37. The continued success of the Working Group will depend on the potency of its recommendations. All States should ensure timely follow-up to the recommendations and conclusions of the Working Group. Further, whereas focus has been on the recruitment and use of child soldiers, all grave violations against children require comparable attention.

38. The Machel study urged regional and subregional bodies to formulate action plans to protect children. Though some progress has been achieved, the engagement of regional bodies remains inconsistent. The establishment of the child protection unit within the Economic Community of West African States in 2002 was a promising initiative, but the unit ceased to exist in November 2006....

39. The last 10 years have witnessed increased inclusion of children in a wide range of negotiations, agreements and peacekeeping and peacebuilding efforts. Children's concerns have also been more consistently included in peace agendas and treaties. Clauses on children in peace agreements should be specific and their goals achievable.

40. Challenges remain for enforcing compliance. For example, while in the Sudan the Comprehensive Peace Agreement included a specific benchmark to demobilize all child soldiers within six months of the signature of the Agreement, only an estimated 1,000 children had been released one year later, despite estimates of "the significant presence" of children within the armed forces and other armed groups. Robust monitoring mechanisms should be established and continuous dialogue maintained with all parties to ensure compliance with their commitments.

Legal and normative framework, instruments and standards

41. Significant advances have been made since the Machel study in both the development of the international legal and normative framework and the adoption of instruments at the national level.

42. Progress has been especially significant on the issue of the recruitment and use of children. While the recruitment of children under 15 and their direct participation in hostilities were prohibited by the Additional Protocols to the Geneva Conventions, the Optional Protocol to the Convention on the Rights of the Child on the Involvement of Children in Armed Conflict, adopted in 2000, detailed the standards against the use of children in armed conflict and raised the minimum age of participation to 18 years. International Labour Organization Convention No. 182, defining child soldiering as among the worst forms of child labour, and the African Charter on the Rights and Welfare of the African Child are other examples of progress.

....

44. The prosecution of crimes against children has advanced significantly. In 1998 the Rome Statute of the International Criminal Court established a vital tool to address impunity by codifying grave violations against children. The Court has charged Ugandan and Congolese commanders with recruiting and using children in hostilities.

45. Special tribunals have set important precedents in holding perpetrators accountable. The ruling by the Special Court for Sierra Leone that the recruitment or use of children under 15 in hostilities is a war crime under customary international law and its recent conviction of military commanders for recruiting children are notable achievements. The International Tribunal for the Former Yugoslavia and the International Criminal Tribunal for Rwanda set vital precedents by prosecuting sexual violence and rape as crimes against humanity and instruments of genocide.

46. Some national legal systems have also taken steps to hold perpetrators accountable. In March 2007, a local tribunal in the Democratic Republic of the Congo prosecuted and sentenced a military commander for the recruitment and use of children.

....

49. Despite the broad and rapid acceptance of international legal standards for the protection of children in armed conflict, a significant gap remains between the standards and their implementation. With specific regard to the Optional Protocol to the Convention on the Rights of the Child on the Involvement of Children in Armed Conflict, the enactment of national legislation is lagging. The work of the Committee on the Rights of the Child in reviewing country reports and delineating implementation actions at the national level is important in bridging this gap. Though States are obliged to report on implementation, many country reports are overdue. States should meet reporting obligations to the Committee and ensure timely and sustained follow-up at the national level of the Committee's recommendations.

....

52. Related to the need for specific actions to control the illicit trade in small arms and light weapons, as called for in Security Council resolutions 1460 (2003), 1539 (2004) and 1612 (2005), an international arms trade treaty establishing common international standards for the import, export and transfer of conventional arms could help reduce the illicit trade in small arms and light weapons and its adverse impact on children.

53. The troubling dichotomy between the advances in norms at the international level and the prevalence of serious violations of children's rights on the ground points to the continuing need to translate political engagement and legal norms into tangible gains for children.

IV. System-level Developments

54. The past decade has featured significant system-wide developments related to children affected by armed conflict.

....

56. Where the Machel study found troubling denial regarding sexual exploitation and abuse, the Secretary-General's bulletin "Special measures for protection from sexual exploitation and sexual abuse" has institutionalized consistent disciplinary measures for United Nations peacekeepers and staff members, and influenced a number of other actors to create their own codes of conduct.

57. The Integrated Disarmament, Demobilization and Reintegration Standards (2006) and Paris Principles and Guidelines on Children Associated with Armed Forces or Armed Groups (2007) represent major progress and now require effective implementation. As part of this, child disarmament, demobilization and reintegration, rights training and justice concerns need to be systematically incorporated into emerging work on security system reform.

....

Monitoring, reporting and analysis

73. As noted, the monitoring and reporting mechanism set up pursuant to Security Council resolution 1612 (2005) is a milestone in terms of meeting the information needs for Security Council action....

....

V. Towards a Comprehensive Response

....

Strengthening protection systems and support

....

89. A major issue addressed in the Machel study was the tracing and reunification of unaccompanied minors and separated children. Significant progress has been made in this area, including strong coordination among actors, culminating in the Inter-Agency Guiding Principles. Prevention of and response to the separation of children remain priority activities in all stages of a crisis.

90. Consensus on good practice for children's mental health and psychosocial well-being has been a point of progress since the Machel study. The Inter-Agency Standing Committee guidelines in this area indicate an age-appropriate, multisectoral approach. Strengthening of social support systems, provision of opportunities for play and development and clinical services for specific problems all constitute aspects of programming in this area. Sport, music and drama activities have been shown to play an important role in providing children with a sense of normalcy and routine.

....

Addressing special concerns

....

94. Reintegration is commonly thought of as the final component of disarmament, demobilization and reintegration, but in reality encompasses much more, and for children, it requires programming outside of formal disarmament, demobilization and reintegration processes....

95. Too often, reintegration efforts inappropriately single out children who in the past were recruited, thereby perpetuating stigma. Likewise, cash benefits for returning children can be seen as rewarding their involvement in violence. To the extent possible, reintegration efforts should benefit all affected children, rather than select groups. A useful approach in the Democratic Republic of the Congo and Sierra Leone has involved the provision of materials to schools accepting demobilized children, thus benefiting all students.

96. Girls often suffer stigmatization whether formerly associated with armed forces or armed groups, or as victims of sexual violence. Response should prevent further harm and provide confidential access to reintegration supports. Addressing a range of long-term needs entails health care, including reproductive health, fistula treatment and provision of post-exposure prophylaxis; legal support; and psychosocial care. Centers that provide comprehensive health, legal and psychosocial support and care to victims and their families in safety and confidentiality have been shown to be effective. Sustainable livelihood opportunities for young girls are a priority, to limit the risk of sexual exploitation and violence.

97. Local approaches to justice and reconciliation are increasingly playing a role in transitional justice strategies, building upon traditional norms to strengthen the protection of children in communities. In research conducted in Sierra Leone for this review, local actors cited the most positive reconciliation experiences as those that included traditional approaches. Children compelled to commit atrocities during the conflict reported that they had gained acceptance in their communities through dialogue based on traditional healing mechanisms. The feasibility of involving children in traditional approaches to justice and enhancing their role in community reconciliation requires further attention.

....

99. The subject of reintegration brings with it the question of what young people are returning to, which is usually an impoverished, subsistence-based environment. Most vocational training programmes result in more young hairdressers, tailors or carpenters than the market can absorb, yet research has found significant positive outcomes in terms of new identities and self-esteem. Increased support for child and youth livelihoods is essential; however, broader economic recovery and investment allowing small businesses to survive is equally vital. The education and livelihood aspects of reintegration programming require greater investment and identification of effective models.

....

VI. Looking Ahead: A Platform of Recommendations

102. The most effective way of protecting children's rights is to prevent conflict and promote peace.

....

Notes and Questions

1. How does the Machel 10 Year Review report divide up and categorize the international community's "achievements" in the effort to eliminate the child soldier phenomenon? Which accomplishments seem to you the most important? In what way does the UN reveal its tendency to over-emphasize placing items on the "agenda," or passing resolutions? Like the original Machel Report, the ten-year retrospective aims to set out broad themes. How urgent is the tone in the Machel 10 Year Review?

2. Machel originally pointed to such factors as social and economic collapse when analyzing the brutality of conflicts that rely on child soldiers. In the Machel 10 Year Review, these factors seem to be as omnipresent as ever, and the conflicts as chaotically violent as before. If this is the case, how can ICC prosecutions, for instance, have any effect on the actual precipitating factors?

IV. Child Soldiers in Particular Conflicts

Consider how the following reports and case studies reflect the themes set out in the original Machel report; that is, political conflict, social collapse, civil war characterized by massive brutality against civilians, and unbridled exploitation of children, including their use as combatants and sex slaves. What "causes" of the armed conflict and the recruitment of children in particular do the following reports present? Are there common elements in the methods of recruitment of child soldiers? Are there clear motivations expressed by any children for joining an armed group, assuming that not every child soldier is forcibly abducted? What methods for the re-establishment of peace and order have been tried in each conflict? How successful are efforts at post-conflict rehabilitation of children? In light of the Singer article's emphasis (see section III above) on self-interested motivation on the part of those who recruit child soldiers, which such factors are at work in the conflicts described in the following readings?

A. The Case of Uganda

1. Background to the Tragedy

Although the long running conflict in Uganda seems to be finally winding down, it has been the scene of some of the worst abuses of children for use in combat. With its potent mix of ethnicity, political power struggles and religion, the conflict at its height saw traumatized and terrorized children unable even to sleep in their own homes, but instead marching at dusk to sleep in crowded public places for their own safety. At the time of this writing, although the Ugandan government and the rebel forces of the "Lord's Resistance Army" have taken steps in the direction of a permanent ceasefire agreement, it appears that any such "peace" established will be precarious at best.

Interestingly, in a conflict characterized by egregious levels of brutality and cruelty, and the constant terrorizing of children, one of the outstanding issues across Ugandan society is what should happen to those leaders of the rebellion who have been accused of war crimes. As will be discussed below, the International Criminal Court (ICC) has issued arrest warrants for several of these leaders. At the same time, it is likely that the rebel forces are hoping that a peace agreement will obviate the need for such prosecutions to go forward. A tragic aspect of this twenty-year conflict is that, despite the intense level of concern shown by the international community, the children of northern Uganda were essentially left to fend for themselves for years on end. Their own communities were powerless to help them, as night time raids saw the abduction of children from their own homes. In desperation, rural communities began sending their children on marches into the towns to sleep together in relative safety each night, to return with the morning light to their own villages. Although the threat of international prosecutions seems to have encouraged moves towards the signing of a peace deal, some have questioned the practical utility of prosecuting key figures long after the fact, apart from the abstract goal of establishing principles and legal norms. Seen separately from the atrocities committed by the rebel fighters, it should be borne in mind that the international community failed to protect thousands of children who were forced to live in great fear for many years. In essence, the worst crimes against them were allowed to go unchecked for what must have seemed an eternity to the children.

Excerpts from an article by Hema Chatlani, below, describes the historical background to the Ugandan civil war; colonization by the British, followed by a violent struggle for power by representatives of Uganda's different geographical regions and ethnic groups. The British colonial tradition of "divide and rule" is at least in part responsible for the severity of modern day ethnic conflict in Uganda. The Human Rights Watch report that follows the Chatlani article outlines the nature of the civil war and the techniques of child exploitation relied on by the Lord's Resistance Army. A later report by Human Rights Watch shows that the brutal abuses continued for many years after HRW's initial assessment.

Hema Chatlani, *Uganda: A Nation in Crisis*

37 California Western International Law Journal 277 (2007)

I. History

Uganda's current civil war began in 1986, but the controversy has its roots in conflicts arising after the country seceded from decades of British colonization in 1962. The British had divided the nation into a northern and southern region, and attempted to maintain order by pitting the two areas against each other. They recruited northerners into the armed forces, and employed southerners in civil service. As a result, the South prospered and contained the majority of Uganda's educated citizens, while the North, where the Acholis reside, became poor and undeveloped.

This "divide and rule" policy stirred resentment and animosity between the two regions, resulting in a polarized nation ripe for conflict. Ethnic groups within the North and South vied for political and economic power, and feared political domination by a singular regional group.

Succeeding presidents utilized this division to their benefit, causing the polarization to linger long after Uganda gained its independence. Milton Obote, Uganda's first post-colonial president, continued to pit the regions against each other, and exploited the Ugandan Army to create a reign of corruption and suspended rights. Obote's use of the military backfired, as his reign ended in 1971 by a military coup led by Colonel Idi Amin.

Amin embarked on a regime notorious for its political violence, beginning with an order demanding the murder of Obote supporters. Amin eventually targeted his brutality on the northern Acholi and Lango tribes, whose members comprised a majority of the Ugandan Army during Obote's reign. Dissatisfaction and frustration under Amin's reign resulted in the creation of several rebel and anti-government groups, which were successful in overthrowing Amin in 1978. For the next few years, Uganda suffered through several governments, with each collapse adding to the fragility of the nation. The indifference and failure of successive governments to create a unified nation contributed to northern Uganda's instability, setting the stage for further rebellions and insurgencies.

By 1986, the National Resistance Army (NRA), an organization created in 1981 by President Yoweri Museveni, had gained control of Uganda. Members of previous governments fled to northern Uganda and neighboring Sudan and formed the Uganda People's Democratic Army (UPDA), a military group that waged a war against the NRA in northern Uganda for two years.

During this time, several splinter groups formed, consisting mostly of members of the Acholi tribe, who were growing resentful and frustrated by the constant chaos and lack of security in the North. The Holy Spirit Mobile Forces was the most powerful and successful new organization. Alice Auma Lakwena, a spiritual medium, led the rebellion, proclaiming that a holy spirit told her to fight against the government and protect the Acholi people from the atrocities suffered for the past few years. Her army was successful for a short period, but met its defeat at the hands of the NRA in 1987.

The Holy Spirit Mobile Forces was highly influential on the Lord's Resistance Army (LRA), which grew in strength shortly after Lakwena's defeat. Joseph Kony, the LRA's leader, claimed to have inherited the spirit of Lakwena, and marketed himself as a "messenger of God and a liberator of the Acholi people."

The LRA fused politics and religion, and drew on a mixture of Christian, Islamic, and animist beliefs to validate its actions. Despite its spiritual similarity to Lakwena's group, the LRA did not gain popular support at the outset, and initially faced rejection by Acholi leaders. Because of his early rejection, Kony grew hostile towards the civilian population, and organized attacks on villages he feared were conspiring against him.

Although the LRA has professed a desire to overthrow the Ugandan government, its motivation, ideology, and exact political agenda are unclear. Kony's extreme brutality against the Acholi people contradicts his occasional promises of Acholi liberation and emancipation. His rebels have killed, kidnapped, raped, and maimed thousands of northern Ugandan civilians, including many belonging to the Acholi tribe. "The LRA routinely cuts off lips, ears, and breasts; gouges eyes; and amputates limbs" under the pretense of avoiding a betrayal. Perhaps the most astonishing atrocity is the LRA's frequent kidnapping of Ugandan children to serve as child soldiers and sex slaves. Reports estimate that the LRA currently consists of approximately two hundred armed commanders and three thousand child soldiers.

Child abductees are immediately taught to fight, kill, and steal for the LRA, and are forced to participate in the abduction of other children. The LRA initiates the children by beating them with sticks and machetes, and smearing their bodies with shea-nut oil in the sign of a cross under the pretense of hardening them for life as soldiers. To instill fear and crush their spirits, the LRA then forces the new recruits to commit atrocious acts, such as killing children who attempted to escape, disobeyed orders, or were too weak to fight. A nine-year-old ex-abductee gave the following gruesome account of his life with the LRA:

> There is nothing that I liked there. They collect all the children together and make you beat someone to death. Once there were about seven who tried to escape, including two girls. The commander decided not to kill the girls. He picked one boy to be killed.... [and] placed his head on a piece of wood. He told one of the girls to.... chop this boy into small pieces. She started.... to cut his head off, but was not doing a good job. The other boys were told to help. When they had almost taken the head off, they had to chop the body into small pieces. Then they were told to play with the dead person's head. The boys had to throw it in the air four times and the girls three times. The girls were bare-chested. After that, they commanded the girls to smear blood of the dead boy on their chest. [Then the LRA] put the head.... in a central place, put clubs all over it covering the head, and informed us that anyone who tries to escape will have the same thing. These child soldiers are both perpetrators and victims, ironically forced to commit violent acts against Acholi villages in the name of Acholi nationalism. Escape does not bring peace to former abductees, as they continue to suffer from ongoing physical and psychological injuries. The trauma arising from their own injuries and memories of having to kill and torture civilians makes it difficult for the children to reintegrate into society. Girls often return with sexually transmitted diseases and young children fathered by LRA commanders.

To avoid capture, thousands of children have become "night dwellers." Every night, up to 25,000 Ugandans, mostly children, walk miles into town to sleep in verandas or shelters to escape LRA attacks. At dawn, they make the trek back home on empty stomachs and return to their villages in time for school or the start of the workday.

. . . .

II. The Government's Response

A. Military Efforts

The Ugandan government has made several attempts to disband the LRA and halt the violence in northern Uganda. In 1991, it launched Operation North, a military offensive that succeeded in greatly weakening the LRA. To follow up on its military action, the government initiated formal peace talks with the remaining rebel leaders in 1994. Although the initial peace process was promising, it did not succeed because both sides grew distrustful of each other. After this first failed attempt at peace, the LRA grew in strength, renewed by support from neighboring Sudan. For the next several years, violence in northern Uganda intensified, intimidating any large-scale efforts at disbanding the LRA.

By 2001, relations between Uganda and Sudan improved, allowing the Ugandan government to launch Operation Iron Fist in 2002 with the support of the Sudanese government. Under this new initiative, Sudan permitted Ugandan troops to cross the border and attack LRA campsites located in southern Sudan. The troops successfully destroyed numerous camps but did not eradicate the LRA, as several rebels fled further into Sudan or returned to northern Uganda. In response to Operation Iron Fist, the LRA increased the severity and frequency of its attacks on civilians, spreading the violence into the non-Acholi districts of Lira and Soroti.

In 2004, Uganda launched Operation Iron Fist II, again with the support of the Sudanese government. Similar to the first military operation, the LRA met Iron Fist II with increased violence, and this time concentrated its attacks on displaced persons' camps.

B. Protected Camps

In an effort to shield villagers from LRA pillaging, the government of Uganda created a number of protected camps. LRA raids have forced approximately three-quarters of the Acholi population into these protected camps. Despite the violence faced at home, several Ugandans protested leaving their villages, and have complained that the government ignored their objections, and mandated that they move into the camps.

Living conditions in the protected camps are squalid. Displaced persons residing in camps grapple with a loss of community and livelihood, and must rely on humanitarian aid for provisions. The government has not provided enough food for the thousands of displaced persons, causing the residents to resort to looting and prostitution for sustenance. Many have died from hunger, disease, and malnutrition.

Although designed to provide refuge from the LRA, the camps have failed to protect civilians from violence. Between June and September of 2003, the LRA attacked sixteen protected camps in the Gulu, Kitgum, and Pader districts. Several residents claim Ugandan soldiers fled and told the civilians to protect themselves when the rebels attacked. The military provides little security, and, in fact, has been responsible for additional acts of violence. Acholi religious leaders report that soldiers raped over twenty-seven women and girls between June and December 2002. The actual number is probably greater, as women are reluctant to report these crimes because of the social stigma attached to being a rape victim, and from fear of angering the soldiers.

. . . .

Note that the selections from the Human Rights Watch report that follow are relevant to the sections of the Machel Report dealing with refugees and internally displaced children, children in camps, health and nutrition, especially with regard to communicable diseases, and the destruction of health facilities. While the situation has improved in recent years, it is important to consider the years of fear and insecurity endured by the people of northern Uganda, particularly children. Why were there few, if any, calls for effective humanitarian intervention in the Ugandan crisis?

Human Rights Watch, *The Scars of Death: Children Abducted by the Lord's Resistance Army in Uganda*

(1997), *available at* http://www.hrw.org/sites/default/
files/reports/ uganda979.pdf

....

Other Effects Of The Conflict In The North

....

Northern Uganda today faces an acute humanitarian crisis. The two northern districts of Gulu and Kitgum, the homeland of the Acholi people, have been hardest hit: relief agencies estimate that over 240,000 people are currently displaced from their homes and villages, while some local officials estimate that the figure is as high as two million displaced people. In Kitgum, nearly half of the displaced people are children, and more than a third of those children have been orphaned by the war.

The infrastructure in Gulu and Kitgum is in a state of collapse. The constant danger of land mines and rebel ambushes has made many of the region's few roads unsafe for travel. Rebel attacks destroyed thousands of homes. Agriculture has come to a standstill in parts of the region, since the insecurity has forced people to flee their homes and abandon their fields.

Education, too, has stopped in many places. The rebels target schools and teachers, and in the last year, in Gulu alone, more than seventy-five schools have been burnt down by the rebels, and 215 teachers have been killed. Many more teachers have been abducted or have fled the region. An estimated 60,000 school-aged children have been displaced, and during 1996, the number of functioning schools in Gulu fell from 199 to sixty-four.

Attacks on schools are an efficient way for the rebels to abduct many children at once. In October 1996, for instance, the rebels raided St. Mary's, a Catholic girls' boarding school in the town of Aboke, in Apac district. The rebels arrived in the middle of the night, and entered the school through a window. They destroyed a school vehicle, ransacked the school clinic, attempted to burn down a number of school buildings, and abducted 139 girls, aged mostly fifteen to seventeen. The scale of the Aboke abductions was unusual, as was the rebel incursion into Apac, but the rebel tactic of raiding schools is typical, and has gravely disrupted the north's educational system.

The health care system in the north, always rudimentary, has almost collapsed. Many of those who are wounded in the fighting receive little or no medical attention; as a result, figures giving the number of dead and wounded are almost certainly too low, since many deaths and injuries never come to the attention of the authorities. Rebel raids on clinics and dispensaries have diminished the store of medicines available, and the instability has caused many health workers to flee. This has disrupted most basic non-emergency services, including immunization campaigns. Officially, there are thirty rural health units in Gulu, but as of May 1997, only fourteen remained in operation.

.... The health crisis has been greatly exacerbated by the government policy of encouraging civilians to leave rural areas and move to "protected camps" near Uganda People's Defense Force military installations. The rationale behind the protected camps is straightforward: by concentrating the civilian population in a few well-defined areas, the army hopes both to simplify the task of protecting people from rebel attacks and make it harder for the rebels to find food by raiding villages. But in practice, the protected camps have been, at best, a mixed blessing for the internally displaced people of Gulu and Kitgum: tens of thousands of them thronged to the camps, only to find that virtually no provision had been made for sanitation or sustenance.

In the protected camp at Pabbo, in Gulu district, for instance, a displaced population of over 30,000 relies for water on only two boreholes ... Along with the paltry water supply in Pabbo, no latrines had been created for the camp. And Pabbo is not unusual; according to the Gulu Disaster Management Committee, "[T]he whole situation is pathetic.... Suffering in long queues, and swamps of flies over the stinking garbage and human excreta is the order of the day in most camps."

Unsurprisingly, limited water, poor sanitary facilities and minimal provision of medical care in the protected camps has led to thousands of deaths each month. Ten of the twenty-four camps in Gulu district are situated in areas with no health care facilities at all, and a recent survey in three of the camps found that 41.9 percent of the children were malnourished. Epidemics of measles, malaria and dysentery kill off many of the weakest in the camps. In Pabbo alone, there were more than four thousand deaths during the month of February 1997 ...

A local doctor's words give some sense of the scope of the humanitarian crisis in the north:

> ....

> The majority of children come to us because of the indirect effects of the war. When there is inadequate food, children are usually the first to become ill. We see epidemics, malnutrition, malaria, and most of the outbreaks start in the protected camps. More children are sick, and those who are sick are sicker than usual. Now the malnutrition wards are full of children from the camps. In the camps, children are very sick; many of them are dying. Most of them never get to the hospital.

> The government thought that protected camps would deny the rebels access to support and information, but it was done in such a hurry, and without planning, that really it was a source of great suffering to the people. Last year, when people began surging to the towns, the population in Gulu town swelled by 70,000 people, and a measles epidemic struck. About 20 percent of the children brought into the hospital died. In the villages, maybe half of the children who got sick died, because they got no medical care.

> If there had been prior planning, if there had been planning for sanitation, food, water, and medicines.... but by herding people into the camps, just like that, this cost a lot of lives. Some of the camps have only a few soldiers nearby, and people say, "They are using us as human shields." So if the rebels try to attack the soldiers, it is civilians who are killed. And if the people leave the camp, if they even just go home for a day to try to find food, then they are targeted by the rebels for having gone to the camps. Many people lose their lives that way.

> The problem is that we don't see an end to the problem. When you have a problem and you think it's coming to an end, then you say, let's persevere. But I really don't see how this is going to end. I foresee unlimited suffering.... the last two years have been the worst in ten years. We cannot do anything, we cannot go outside in the community, we cannot do our work. We are trapped, we can't move on the roads. So now the sense of hopelessness is the biggest problem with the people. And this is the easiest situation for the rebels to operate in. The people have no will except to surrender.

> It has to stop, it must stop. It is painful to live in a place where the rebels are around, and you have to hide your own children in the bush and bring food to

them, to try to keep them safe. The rebels' main interest is in the children, it's how they recruit. Children are malleable, they can be easily managed. The rebels don't care if some die: they just abduct more. And there is really no protection for these children. If they were taking adults, I would not care as much, I would perhaps say that this kind of thing is just part of the problem with us here in Uganda—but these children are just used. They are not the ones who voted for Museveni. If our country is troubled the fault is not theirs.

When you are in the medical field, you are trained always to look for solutions. But I cannot see one here.

. . . .

Notes and Questions

1. A 2003 follow up report by Human Rights Watch, entitled *Stolen Children: Abduction and Recruitment in Northern Uganda*, available at http://www.hrw.org/sites/default/files/reports/uganda0403.pdf, made clear that the Lord's Resistance Army continued to abduct and recruit children and to rely on them to assist in assaults on the Ugandan people for years after the earlier report. Uganda, manipulated both during the colonial and Cold War periods, rife with residual ethnic tension and resentment, became a "perfect storm" for abuse of children in the ensuing armed conflict. The intensity of their suffering makes this one of the most severe examples of the exploitation of children to attain adult aims in an armed conflict context.

2. The conflict between the Ugandan government and the LRA cost tens of thousands of lives and uprooted more than a million people from their homes. Starting in 2005, it became more difficult for the LRA to find refuge in southern Sudan, and all parties began to engage in peace overtures. Joseph Kony, the LRA leader famous for his brutality, went into hiding in a remote area of Congo. He is currently under criminal indictment by the International Criminal Court, but LRA leaders have made withdrawal of the charges a condition for signing peace agreements with the Ugandan government. The ICC has continuously refused to withdraw the warrants for arrest. For a discussion of these events, see Felix Osike, *Kony Must Face Trial*, Global Policy Forum, July 17, 2007, http://www.globalpolicy.org/intljustice/icc/investigations/ uganda/2007/0712facetrial.htm.

3. The Ugandan conflict, which has run for more than twenty years, seems a textbook example of what Graça Machel was describing in her 1996 report. What aspects of these conflicts make them so difficult to solve, despite ten years of attention and discussion by the international community?

---

2. Legal Response to the Ugandan Conflict

Nations faced with trying to restore order and public trust in the wake of violent civil conflict have two essential choices: prosecution of those identified as having carried out illicit forms of violence, or adoption of a process of reconciliation, through the establishment of a truth and reconciliation commission, for example. It is also possible to adopt a hybrid approach, though the goals of retributive justice and reconciliation often seem to be opposed to one another.

The creation of the permanent and independent International Criminal Court, established under a treaty accepted by over one hundred countries, was hailed by those who hoped to see enhanced enforcement mechanisms for international criminal law.[14] The ICC is charged with prosecuting war crimes and crimes against humanity in the event that the country in which such criminals are located proves unable or unwilling to do so. In a world reluctant to step in and prevent or stop violence against civilians, the emphasis on post-conflict tribunals has been striking. To date, the United States has resisted ratification of the treaty establishing the ICC on grounds that politically motivated prosecutions could be brought against U.S. officials or military personnel.

Press Release, International Criminal Court,
Warrant of Arrest Unsealed against Five LRA Commanders
(Oct. 14, 2005), *available at* http://www2.icc-cpi.int/NR/exeres/ 4BCE015E-9F70-4CD1-8AC2-4CACDB6070B6.htm

On 13 October 2005, Pre-Trial Chamber II unsealed the warrants of arrest for five senior leaders of the Lord's Resistance Army (LRA) for Crimes against Humanity and War Crimes committed in Uganda since July 2002. The Chamber concluded that "there are reasonable grounds to believe" that Joseph KONY, Vincent OTTI, Okot ODHIAMBO, Dominic ONGWEN and Raska LUKWIYA, "ordered the commission of crimes within the jurisdiction of the Court".

The warrants of arrest were issued under seal by Pre-Trial Chamber II on 8 July 2005 to "ensure the safety or physical or psychological well-being of" and to "prevent the disclosure of the identity or whereabouts of any victims, potential witnesses and their families". The Chamber also issued requests for arrest and surrender of the five LRA commanders named in the warrants and decided that they would be transmitted by the Registrar of the International Criminal Court to the Government of Uganda.

Pre-Trial Chamber II decided on 13 October to unseal the arrest warrants, noting that "the overall plan in respect of the situation in Uganda for the security of witnesses and victims in the field has been completed and implemented; and that by the assessment and advice of the Prosecutor and the Victims and Witness Unit the overall plans provide the necessary and adequate protective measures for all concerned at this stage".

The warrants of arrest are the first to be issued by the International Criminal Court since its creation by an international treaty, the Rome Statute adopted on 17 July 1998. The aim of the Court is to help end impunity for the most serious crimes of concern to the international community.

Background

According to the allegations set out in the warrants of arrest, the LRA is an armed group which "has established a pattern of brutalization of civilians by acts including murder, abduction, sexual enslavement, mutilation, as well as mass burnings of houses and looting of camp settlements; that abducted civilians, including children, are said to have been forcibly recruited as fighters, porters and sex slaves and to take part in attacks against the Ugandan army (UPDF) and civilian communities".

The specific allegations are that in mid-2002 Joseph Kony ordered LRA forces to begin a campaign of attacks against civilians in Uganda.

---

14. *See* Rome Statute of the International Criminal Court, July 17, 1998, 2187 U.N.T.S. 90, *available at* http://www.icc-cpi.int/NR/rdonlyres/EA9AEFF7-5752-4F84-BE94-0A655EB30E16/0/Rome_Statute_English.pdf.

It is alleged that during the last quarter of 2003 Kony issued orders to kill, loot and abduct civilian populations, including those living in camps for internally displaced persons ("IDP"). In response, senior LRA commanders and all of the brigade commanders, including the persons named in the warrants of arrest, began attacking several regions in Uganda. The direct involvement of the persons whose arrest and surrender are sought in the objectives and strategies of the campaign is supported by evidence submitted by the Prosecutor.

The Counts

The warrant of arrest for Joseph Kony lists thirty-three counts on the basis of his individual criminal responsibility (Articles 25(3)(a) and 25(3)(b) of the Statute) including:

- Twelve counts of crimes against humanity (murder—Article 7(1)(a); enslavement—Article 7(1)(c); sexual enslavement—Article 7(1)(g); rape—Article 7(1)(g); inhumane acts of inflicting serious bodily injury and suffering—Article 7(1)(k)), and;

- one counts of war crimes (murder—Article 8(2)(c)(i); cruel treatment of civilians—Article 8(2)(c)(i); intentionally directing an attack against a civilian population—Article 8(2)(e)(i); pillaging—Article 8(2)(e)(v); inducing rape—Article 8(2)(e)(vi); forced enlisting of children—8(2)(e)(vii)).

The warrant of arrest for Vincent Otti lists thirty-two counts on the basis of his individual criminal responsibility (Article 25(3)(b) of the Statute) including:

- Eleven counts of crimes against humanity (murder—Article 7(1)(a); sexual enslavement—Article 7(1)(g); inhumane acts of inflicting serious bodily injury and suffering—Article 7(1)(k)), and;

- Twenty-one counts of war crimes (inducing rape—Article 8(2)(e)(vi); intentionally directing an attack against a civilian population—Article 8(2)(e)(i); forced enlisting of children—8(2)(e)(vii); cruel treatment of civilians—Article 8(2)(c)(i); pillaging—Article 8(2)(e)(v); murder—Article 8(2)(c)(i)).

The warrant of arrest for Okot Odhiambo lists ten counts on the basis of his individual criminal responsibility (Article 25(3)(b) of the Statute) including:

- Two counts of crimes against humanity (murder—Article 7(1)(a); enslavement—Article 7(1)(c)), and;

- Eight counts of war crimes (murder—Article 8(2)(c)(i); intentionally directing an attack against a civilian population—Article 8(2)(e)(i); pillaging—Article 8(2)(e)(v); forced enlisting of children—8(2)(e)(vii)).

The warrant of arrest for Dominic Ongwen lists seven counts on the basis of his individual criminal responsibility (Article 25(3)(b) of the Statute) including:

- Three counts of crimes against humanity (murder—Article 7(1)(a); enslavement—Article 7(1)(c); inhumane acts of inflicting serious bodily injury and suffering—Article 7(1)(k)), and;

- Four counts of war crimes (murder—Article 8(2)(c)(i)); cruel treatment of civilians—Article 8(2)(c)(i); intentionally directing an attack against a civilian population—Article 8(2)(e)(i); pillaging—Article 8(2)(e)(v)).

The warrant of arrest for Raska Lukwiya lists four counts on the basis of his individual criminal responsibility (Article 25(3)(b) of the Statute) including:

- One count of crimes against humanity (enslavement—Article 7(1)(c)), and;

- Three counts of war crimes (cruel treatment of civilians—Article 8(2)(c)(i); intentionally directing an attack against a civilian population—Article 8(2)(e)(i); pillaging—Article 8(2)(e)(v)).

The readings that follow explore the inherent limitations on the actions of the International Criminal Court. A major issue in this context is how the "justice seeking" actions of the Court can and should interact with national efforts at conflict resolution. How can amnesties offered to former combatants, for instance, be reconciled with the drive towards high profile international criminal prosecutions?

Noah Benjamin Novogrodsky, *Challenging Impunity*
New Internationalist, Dec. 2005, at 20

In mid-October this year the International Criminal Court (ICC) issued indictments for the arrest of Joseph Kony and four other leaders of Uganda's Lord's Resistance Army (LRA). The LRA is notorious for a 21-year campaign of terror in Northern Uganda—including the abduction of thousands of children and the widespread use of child soldiers. Kony and the other LRA leaders are charged with 'crimes against humanity' and 'war crimes'.

The case against the LRA is a test of the power and limits of the ICC just three years after its birth. The new legal body taking shape at The Hague is a direct legacy of the Nuremberg tribunals which tried Nazi war criminals after World War Two. But unlike Nuremberg the ICC contains the promise of a universal court for universal crimes.

It is this elusive goal that sustains the victims of human rights abuses hungry for individual accountability, the diplomats who negotiated the Court's creation in Rome during the summer of 1998, and the international lawyers and activists who desperately want such an institution.

Supporters of the Court believe it is the most significant advance in international human rights law in the last half-century. In addition to Northern Uganda, the ICC has begun investigations into atrocities in the Congo and, most recently, in Darfur, Sudan. The Chief Prosecutor, Luis Moreno-Ocampo, is an Argentinean with a domestic record of successful prosecutions of corrupt politicians, organized criminals and the generals responsible for mass 'disappearances' during Argentina's 'dirty war' of the 1970s and early 1980s.

Naming war criminals

But what can the Court really do? The ICC has no police force connected to its operations, so it can't directly arrest indicted suspects. If the prosecutor can persuade UN peacekeepers or sympathetic states to arrest suspects, the Court will provide criminal justice for a select number of the world's worst killers. In the process the ICC hopes to destigmatize warring communities and rid them of collective guilt by assigning blame to individuals. For victims and their families the Court offers the possibility of retribution through law—a forum where they can bear witness to the atrocities they've experienced—and a compensation fund. Equally important, the ICC aims to influence international politics by naming and isolating war criminals....

Even without its enforcement problems, the Court will have to overcome external enemies and internal deficiencies. The fact that the ICC's first cases are all in Africa has led to the predictable charge that the Court represents the selective imposition of Western values on poor states.

The Court is an international anomaly — an institution created by treaty among 99 states that functions without the co-operation of a few key actors, many of whom are openly hostile to it. That treaty — the 1998 Rome Statute — is the product of compromise. In the end, the Treaty created a court capable of prosecuting only three universal offences: war crimes, genocide and crimes against humanity.

The result is a codification of international criminal norms which will stop the creation of ad hoc UN criminal tribunals — like the ones for the former Yugoslavia and Rwanda. The Court's statute identifies rape and torture as crimes against humanity and provides clear definitions of liability for officers in command positions who are barred from arguing that they were simply 'following orders'. The statute also guarantees defendants substantial 'due process' protections (for the accused) and preserves a right of appeal. Despotic heads of state from signatory states are stripped of the immunity that allowed Idi Amin, Uganda's one-time dictator, to retire in luxury. The Court also entrenches the principle of 'complementarity' — which means the ICC will step aside if legitimate national courts decide to try war criminals.

The ICC has the power to investigate human rights abuses on the territory of states that have signed and ratified the treaty or when the suspect hails from a signatory state. If the Security Council refers a matter to the Court, as it did belatedly in response to the slaughter in Darfur, the ICC may take jurisdiction even where the affected state objects to the presence of outside investigators. But more often cases will come from a state that is unable or unwilling to prosecute serious crimes committed on its own soil. In Uganda, for example, the Government is all too willing to let the ICC prosecute the LRA. (If the Court were to indict Government soldiers for their abuses, the picture might look very different). Any mass crime, committed in a signatory state unable to mount a genuine prosecution, can come before the ICC.

Of course, the Court only binds those states (and, by extension, individuals from those states) that sign and ratify the treaty. In theory, however, the Court could exercise jurisdiction over an individual from a non-state party who commits grave violations on the territory of a signatory state. Peacekeepers or foreign forces from non-state parties are potentially bound to the Court if they are arrested for crimes committed on the soil of a signatory state.

Bilateral Deals

. . . .

The Court's focus on consensus definitions of war crimes and genocide limits its range of potential cases and leaves it, quite literally, fighting the last war. The ICC thus reflects the tragedy of Bosnia in 1993, not Afghanistan in 2005. Post 9/11, suspected non-state terrorists are detained by U.S. forces in legal limbo at Guantanamo Bay. And human smugglers operate unchecked in states with underdeveloped legal systems, instead of being sent to the ICC.

Finally, the ICC faces the very real problem that it is powerless to address abuses arising from many of the world's great powers. Russia, China, Iraq, India, Pakistan, Iraq, Saudi Arabia and Indonesia have joined the U.S. in refusing to sign the Rome Treaty. Much of this is due to domestic concerns — Iran has no interest in allowing an international body to examine the horrors of Iranian prisons. But the cost to the international community is significant. China and India are burgeoning economic and geopolitical powers; their absence from a court capable of trying individuals according to common standards erodes the notion of universal justice. At present, sex traffickers, arms dealers, even international terrorists, from countries that have not signed the Rome Statute, are beyond the Court's reach.

The ICC is left to prosecute 'crimes against humanity', 'genocide' and 'war crimes' in states that have joined the Court. In addition to Uganda, the list of signatories where such crimes may have been committed since 1 July 2002 includes the Democratic Republic of Congo, Liberia, Colombia and Sierra Leone. Civil wars may explain why each of those states has joined—they are undoubtedly hoping the Court will prosecute rebel forces—but the legal hook remains. Sadly, there is little current evidence that the spectre of ICC prosecutions has changed the behaviour of human rights abusers on the ground. In Northern Uganda many human rights advocates fear that the ICC will complicate efforts to achieve a negotiated settlement after decades of fighting.

The challenge will be to conduct fair and transparent trials in the face of criticism that the Court is merely a vehicle for Northern states to condemn select crimes in the South—not an instrument of universal justice. Over time the states that have joined the ICC hope to persuade the others. The goal is to lead by example, prosecuting humanity's worst crimes effectively and reversing the past century's culture of impunity.

Continued U.S. opposition hurts but, as the Uganda indictments demonstrate, the Bush Administration has been unable to derail the ICC. Likewise, a change in the U.S. position will not guarantee the Court's future success. For that, its fortunes may well turn on an expansion in the list of crimes within its authority and the involvement of emerging powers as members.

. . . .

Notes and Questions

1. Is the prosecution of war criminals involved in the Ugandan civil war meant to address, at least in part, the horrific suffering of children? If so, do such prosecutions fulfill their purpose? Is there a difference between post-conflict tribunals in the aftermath of a war in which the international community intervened to stop the suffering, versus in a conflict where the prosecutions only take place after the conflict has run its course?

———————

Manisuli Ssenyonjo, *Accountability of Non-State Actors in Uganda for War Crimes and Human Rights Violations: Between Amnesty and the International Criminal Court*
10 Journal of Conflict & Security Law 405 (2005)

. . . .

3. The LRA: War Crimes and Human Rights Violations

3.1 General Overview

. . . .

As shown below, the conduct of the LRA rebels is in violation of international law applicable to non-international armed conflicts. The alleged crimes being committed in the region (e.g. conscription or enlisting of children under fifteen years into the army, willful killing, rape, sexual slavery, forced pregnancy and forced displacement of civilians) may constitute crimes against humanity (under article 7 of the Rome Statute) and/or war crimes (under article 8 of the Rome Statute).

3.2 Geneva Conventions and the LRA

Although the four Geneva Conventions of 12 August 1949 were concerned with (grave breaches in) international armed conflict, common article 3, which applies to any case of 'armed conflict not of an international character' requires 'as a minimum' that persons taking no active part in hostilities be 'treated humanely' and prohibits:

> (a) [V]iolence to life and person, in particular murder, cruel treatment and torture; (b) hostage taking; (c) outrages upon dignity, in particular humiliating and degrading treatment; (d) the passing of sentences and the carrying out of executions in the absence of due process.

These minimum safeguards are meant to protect human life and dignity and bind both the government and rebel forces. By article 8(1) of the Rome Statute of the ICC:

> The Court shall have jurisdiction in respect of war crimes in particular when committed as part of a plan or policy or as part of a large-scale commission of such crimes.

'War crimes' for purposes of the above article include in the case of an armed conflict not of an international character, such as the conflict between the LRA and the Ugandan government:

> [S]erious violations of article 3 common to the four Geneva Conventions of 12 August 1949, namely, any of the following acts committed against persons taking no active part in the hostilities, including members of armed forces who have laid down their arms and those placed hors de combat by sickness, wounds, detention or any other cause:
>
> (i) Violence to life and person, in particular murder of all kinds, mutilation, cruel treatment and torture;
>
> (ii) Committing outrages upon personal dignity, in particular humiliating and degrading treatment;
>
> (iii) Taking of hostages;
>
> (iv) The passing of sentences and the carrying out of executions without previous judgement pronounced by a regularly constituted court, affording all judicial guarantees which are generally recognized as indispensable.

In addition, 'war crimes' include other serious violations of the laws and customs applicable in armed conflicts not of an international character, within the established framework of international law. These include 'intentionally directing attacks against the civilian population as such or against individual civilians not taking direct part in hostilities'; 'intentionally directing attacks against buildings, material, medical units and transport, and personnel using the distinctive emblems of the Geneva Conventions in conformity with international law'; 'committing rape, sexual slavery, enforced prostitution, forced pregnancy, ... enforced sterilization, and any other form of sexual violence also constituting a serious violation of article 3 common to the four Geneva Conventions' and 'conscripting or enlisting children under the age of fifteen years into armed forces or groups or using them to participate actively in hostilities'. As shown...., the LRA rebels have often committed several war crimes. In particular they have directed intentional attacks against civilians not taking direct part in hostilities; attacked civilian objects; committed sexual violence and conscripted children under the age of fifteen into rebel armed forces. These are some of the most serious crimes of concern to the international community as a whole, over which the ICC has jurisdiction.

The safeguards listed in common article 3 for the four Geneva Conventions of 12 August 1949 were developed by Protocol II, 1977, (the Protocol) which by virtue of article 1 applies to all non-international armed conflicts which take place in a territory of a State party between its armed forces and dissident armed forces. The Protocol developed the common article 3 safeguards by prohibiting violence to life, health and physical and mental well-being of persons, including torture; collective punishment; hostage-taking; acts of terrorism; outrages upon personal dignity, including rape and enforced prostitution and pillage. It also protects children, civilians, treatment of prisoners and detainees and the wounded and sick. However, Protocol II is confined to civil wars in which both sides control tracts of territory. Since the LRA does not exercise control over a part of Uganda's territory, it would appear that it is not bound by Protocol II, but bound by common article 3....

....

3.3.3 Legislative Measures: Amnesty Act, 2000

....

... [T]he government has used legislative measures in an attempt to end the armed conflict. This has been manifested partly in the form of granting amnesty to the LRA rebels who renounce rebellion in accordance with the Uganda's Amnesty Act, 2000.

The Amnesty Act, 2000, was enacted 'to provide for an Amnesty for Ugandans involved in acts of a war-like nature in various parts of the country and for other connected purposes'. The Amnesty Act, 2000, was based on what its preamble termed 'the expressed desire of the people of Uganda to end armed hostilities, reconcile with those who have caused suffering and rebuild their communities' and 'the desire and determination of the Government to genuinely implement its policy of reconciliation ...'. Under Uganda's Amnesty Act, 2000, 'Amnesty' means 'pardon, forgiveness, exemption or discharge from criminal prosecution or any other form of punishment by the state'. Accordingly, the Act provided:

> An Amnesty is declared in respect of any Ugandan who has at any time since the 26th day of January, 1986 engaged in or is engaging in war or armed rebellion against the government of the Republic of Uganda by
>
> (a) actual participation in combat;
>
> (b) collaborating with the perpetrators of the war or armed rebellion;
>
> (c) committing any other crime in the furtherance of the war or armed rebellion; or
>
> (d) assisting or aiding the conduct or prosecution of the war or armed rebellion.

The aim of the Amnesty Act was to forgive and reconcile with those involved in armed rebellion and thus end the conflict and eliminate 'unnecessary suffering'. It was provided that a person in the above category:

> [S]hall not be prosecuted or subjected to any form of punishment for the participation in the war or rebellion for any crime committed in the cause of the war or armed rebellion.

The above provision makes it clear that once a person has been granted amnesty, such a person 'shall not be prosecuted' for war crimes unless a new crime is committed. To qualify for amnesty, the Act requires that a person:

> (1) reports to the nearest Army or Police Unit, a Chief, a member of the Executive Committee of a local government unit, a magistrate or a religious leader within the locality;

(2) renounces and abandons involvement in the war or armed rebellion;

(3) surrenders at any such place or to any such authority or person any weapons in his or her possession and

(4) is issued with a Certificate of Amnesty ...

It was believed that immunity from prosecution would enable 'the Government to genuinely implement its policy of reconciliation in order to establish peace, security and tranquillity throughout the whole country'. The Act then provided (sections 3–16) for an Amnesty Commission to promote the granting of amnesty under the legislation and a Demobilisation and Resettlement Team (DRT) to carry out disarmament and encourage reintegration into the community of those who sought amnesty under the legislation.

In the context of the LRA, amnesty may be considered necessary because many LRA combatants were children abducted and forced to fight and might not have had chances to either escape or surrender. Such children were abducted because of the government's failure to provide security against rebel abductions. In this respect, amnesty offers an opportunity at reconciliation and a greater respect for future human rights of formerly abducted children. In such a context, Additional Protocol II to the Geneva Conventions encourages States to grant the 'broadest possible amnesty' at the end of hostilities in non-international armed conflicts. The Amnesty Act commenced on the 21 January 2000, was initially to remain in force for a period not exceeding six months subject to ministerial extension. The Act has since been extended several times to enable rebels to surrender and continues to be in force. According to the chairman of the Amnesty Commission, Peter Onega, since the Commission was set up in 2000, up to 9717 rebels had surrendered by September 2003. They included 3824 former LRA combatants. By June 2005, more than 15,000 former combatants and abductees of the LRA had taken advantage of the Amnesty Act. As a result of this apparent success of the amnesty legislation, some Ugandan political opposition groups (such as the Forum for Democratic Change) and religious/conflict resolution groups (e.g. the Acholi Religious Leaders' Peace Initiative) remain supportive of amnesty as a plausible route to peace. Even the government's Amnesty Commission is of the view that the amnesty process will be badly damaged if the ICC prosecutes leaders of the LRA since such an action could even lead to another rebellion.

While the effect of the Amnesty Act should be applauded since amnesty has the potential of providing a strong framework for peace and reconciliation, the key question that arises from Uganda's Amnesty Act is whether the immunity from prosecution granted to any rebel who renounces and abandons involvement in the armed rebellion is a bar to prosecution by the ICC. For example, if the LRA top commanders—Joseph Kony, Vincent Otti—are granted amnesty by the Ugandan government, would this operate as a bar to prosecution by the ICC? If Uganda's domestic amnesty law is not a bar to prosecution by the ICC, does this mean that the ICC statute is counterproductive to domestic amnesty and the peace building process? Can the ICC, for example, prosecute any of the several leaders of the LRA rebels—including Brigadier Sam Kolo (former chief spokesman for the LRA)—who have taken advantage of, and have surrendered under, the amnesty law?

4. The ICC and the LRA

4.1 General Overview

By article 1 of the Rome Statute of the ICC, the ICC is established as a permanent institution with 'the power to exercise its jurisdiction over persons for the most serious crimes of international concern, ... and shall be complementary to national criminal jurisdictions'. Article 5(1) limits the jurisdiction of the ICC to the following crimes: '(a) The crime of genocide; (b) Crimes against humanity; (c) War crimes; (d) The crime of aggression'. Under article 7(1) 'crime against humanity' means any of the following acts when committed as part of a widespread or systematic attack directed against any civilian population, with knowledge of the attack:

(a) Murder; (b) Extermination; (c) Enslavement; (d) Deportation or forcible transfer of population; (e) Imprisonment or other severe deprivation of physical liberty in violation of fundamental rules of international law; (f) Torture; (g) Rape, sexual slavery, enforced prostitution, forced pregnancy, enforced sterilization, or any other form of sexual violence of comparable gravity; (h) Persecution against any identifiable group or collectivity ... ; (i) Enforced disappearance of persons; (j) The crime of apartheid; (k) Other inhumane acts of a similar character intentionally causing great suffering, or serious injury to body or to mental or physical health.

.... [T]he LRA rebels under Joseph Kony have systematically attacked civilians and committed several crimes in northern Uganda, which may constitute crimes against humanity under the Rome Statute. In particular, 'many women and girls in the conflict areas have been victims of violence, including abduction and sexual slavery'. This may constitute crimes against humanity in terms of article 7(1)(g) under the Rome Statute for which those responsible—LRA top commanders—must be investigated with a view to being prosecuted.

Similarly, under article 8(1), the Court has jurisdiction in respect of 'war crimes' in particular when committed as part of a plan or policy or as part of a large-scale commission of such crimes. As noted..., the LRA rebels have often committed several war crimes falling within the jurisdiction of the ICC. The Court's jurisdiction only arises with respect to crimes committed after the entry into force of this Statute. Uganda signed the ICC Statute on 17 March 1999 and ratified it on 14 June 2002 without any interpretative declaration or reservation. The Ugandan government published the ICC Bill to implement the ICC Statute in domestic law but the Bill had not been enacted by the end of 2004. The ICC's investigation into the armed conflict pertains to crimes committed in the conflict since 1 July 2002, when the court came into force. As noted..., the government of Uganda referred the situation concerning the LRA in northern Uganda to the ICC in December 2003. The decision to open a formal investigation was taken in July 2004. In August 2004, a team of ICC investigators arrived in Uganda to begin their probe, shortly after the LRA had burned, shot or bludgeoned to death an estimated 337 people in Barlonyo IDP camp in Lira district, 180 km north of Uganda's capital, Kampala. According to the ICC Prosecutor, Louis Moreno-Ocampo, investigation 'will include the analysis of all alleged crimes within the jurisdiction of the court committed in northern Uganda'. The prosecutor stressed that:

In accordance with the policy and strategy of the office of the prosecutor, the investigation and prosecutions will focus on those limited number of individuals who bear greatest responsibility for committing the most serious crimes within the jurisdiction of the court.

As noted above, in 2000, the Ugandan government instituted an Amnesty Act, effectively pardoning any rebel who denounced the insurgency and voluntarily surrendered to the Ugandan government authorities. The key question, however, is how to reconcile amnesty with the pending investigation of the rebels and threats of prosecution by the ICC. According to the Acholi leaders the prosecutor has to ensure that 'whoever has already benefited from amnesty will not be investigated or prosecuted by the ICC'. As noted by the chairman of the Acholi Religious Leaders Peace Initiative (ARLPI), Archbishop John Baptist Odama, 'How can we tell the LRA soldiers to come out of the bush and receive amnesty when at the same time the threat of arrest by the ICC hangs over their heads?'. Seen from this perspective, investigation of the LRA leadership by the ICC or excluding them from possible amnesty may jeopardise the possible peaceful resolution of the northern Uganda armed conflict. Given the approach of the LRA to the conflict, it is likely that this may lead the LRA to intensify its atrocities. It is, therefore, suggested that the government, at the very least, will need to make effective military plans to forestall as much of the violence and protect as many civilians in the north as possible.

4.2 Reinforcing Accountability of the LRA: Legal Obligations to Prosecute

The key question here is can rebel movements ignore human rights as long as governments don't hold them accountable? To put the question in context, if the Ugandan government granted amnesty to the top leaders of the LRA and decided that it no longer required the assistance of the ICC in the conflict and asked the ICC to withdraw, would the ICC stop its work regarding the LRA? At the outset it must be pointed out that this is a complex question that is open to different views. This is mainly because the relationship between prosecution, on the one hand, and amnesties, on the other, is not addressed directly in the ICC Statute.

Regarding the relationship between Uganda's Amnesty Act and the ICC, President Museveni stated in June 2005 that 'If we told the ICC that we had found an internal solution, they would be happy' and that if Joseph Kony (LRA commander most responsible for crimes against humanity and war crimes) surrendered, he would benefit from the amnesty. President Museveni is further reported to have stated that leaders of the LRA could cease fighting and 'engage in internal reconciliation mechanisms put in place by the Acholi community such as *mataput* or blood settlement'. He added that if this were to occur, '[t]he State could withdraw its case [in the ICC]'. Two questions arise here. First, would such grant of amnesty (as an 'internal solution') be inconsistent with the ICC Statute? If so, can the government withdraw its referral from the ICC under the ICC Statute?

It should be noted that the reported statement by President Museveni that he intended that members of the LRA, which include some of those most responsible for crimes against humanity and war crimes, participate in traditional reconciliation procedures instead of facing investigation and possible prosecution in Ugandan independent and impartial courts confirms that Uganda is neither able nor willing genuinely to investigate and prosecute such crimes, whether committed by the LRA members or by the members of government forces. It indicates clearly the State's inability to detain the LRA commanders and demonstrates its willingness to shield the persons concerned from criminal responsibility for crimes within the jurisdiction of the ICC. In the face of the continuing failure of Uganda to investigate and prosecute these crimes, the ICC may exercise its jurisdiction under article 17 of the Rome Statute over all crimes against humanity and war crimes committed in the northern part of the country, regardless whether they were committed by members of the LRA or of government forces.

From an international law perspective, domestic amnesties are strictly a matter for national authorities and do not act as a bar to an investigation by the ICC. Generally, for international treaties to be effective, State obligations must be 'reflected in the content of the domestic law'. It is generally agreed that irrespective of the system through which international law is incorporated in the domestic (or national or municipal) legal order…, following ratification of an international instrument, it is 'binding' upon the parties and must be performed in 'good faith' and given full effect in the domestic legal order. It follows that States are under a general obligation to act in conformity with the rules of international law and will bear responsibility for breaches of it, whether committed by the legislative, executive or judicial organs. This follows from a well-established principle of international law that States cannot invoke their domestic legal systems—internal laws and procedures—(such as Uganda's Amnesty Act) as justification for not complying with international treaty obligations (such as the obligation to prosecute arising under the ICC statute). Generally States are obliged not to condone or encourage human rights violations. The ICC Statute affirmed that 'it is the duty of every State to exercise its criminal jurisdiction over those responsible for international crimes'. This is necessary 'to put an end to impunity for the perpetrators of these crimes and thus to contribute to the prevention of such crimes'. Gerhard Werle observes that 'the duty to prosecute follows from the duty of states to guarantee human rights and ensure effective legal protection'. Therefore to the extent that international law creates a duty to prosecute and punish the most serious crimes, general amnesties that offer exemption from criminal responsibility are impermissible. Indeed 'as international crimes constitute attacks on universal values, no single State should arrogate to itself the right to decide to cancel such crimes, or to set aside their legal consequences … the requirement to dispense justice should trump the need to respect State sovereignty'. As noted rightly by the chairman of the Uganda's Amnesty Commission:

> Since the ICC takes precedence over our national laws, even people already granted amnesty could be taken for trial before the ICC—if this happens, the amnesty process and the law will be rendered useless.

As noted above, Uganda referred the LRA rebel activities to the ICC in accordance with the ICC Statute. The ICC Statute does not provide for withdrawal of referrals as such. Therefore, the ICC, given its mandate, must generally insist on the prosecution of the LRA top commanders who bear the greatest responsibility for committing the most serious crimes within the jurisdiction of the court. It is essential (for the Ugandan government) to recognise that the ICC has responsibilities to carry out its independent mandate and that the prosecutor answers to the Court and its judges, not to the authorities of the State that has ceded a specific area of sovereignty. The crimes committed by the LRA rebels under international law deeply shock the conscience of humanity and are thus not limited to the domestic realm of Uganda. Instead the effects of the acts of the LRA are directed against the interests of the international community as a whole. It follows from this universal nature of crimes that the international community (through the ICC) is empowered to prosecute and punish these crimes, regardless of the domestic amnesty. As pointed out in the Preamble to the ICC Statute 'the most serious crimes of concern to the international community as a whole must not go unpunished and … their effective prosecution must be ensured by taking measures at the national level and by enhancing international cooperation'.

However, in accordance with the ICC Statute, the prosecutor has the power to reconsider a decision to investigate and prosecute in the light of 'new facts or information'. If there is willingness for the leadership of the LRA rebels to conclude a peace agreement with the Ugandan government, then the prosecutor has discretion under article 53(4) of the Court's statute to reconsider his decision to prosecute. If that point is reached, it will be in the interest of justice and much more feasible for the prosecutor to suspend prosecution if 'a genuine, robust and credible reconciliation and accountability process is in prospect as part of a negotiated settlement'. In this context, it would not be in the interests of justice to interfere with a reconciliation mechanism to bring an end to the nearly two decades of the conflict. Nevertheless, this should only be seen as a question of timing and not a bar to future prosecution since 'a blanket amnesty for international crimes would be the antithesis of the purpose of the ICC and should never enjoy deference from the Court'.

A blanket amnesty is also difficult to reconcile with the fundamental principles underpinning the protection, promotion and enforcement of human rights. Accountability is an essential element in the observance of human rights. It demands that those who violate human rights must not do so with impunity whether that impunity is conferred by law or otherwise. Such individuals must be prosecuted and punished, whether under national or international law....

By contrast, ... The view that non-State actors (NSAs) are beyond the direct reach of international human rights law threatens to make a mockery of much of the international system of accountability for human rights violations. Today, NSAs—including armed opposition groups such as the LRA—have committed, and continue to commit, massive human rights violations. As shown..., the rights of women and children have suffered serious violations within the context of armed conflicts involving NSAs. Such developments, among others, provide a basis for the horizontal extension of the application of human rights to NSAs. As the UN General Assembly recognised in 1970, human rights 'continue to apply fully in situations of armed conflict'. It is in this context that there is increasing recognition that 'it is essential to ensure human rights obligations fall where power is exercised', whether it is in the rebel movement or elsewhere.... It follows, therefore, that those who violate human rights (whether States or NSAs) must not do so with impunity whether that impunity is conferred by law or otherwise. In this respect, the LRA leaders should be pursued locally and internationally and brought to justice.

....

Secondly, NSAs—such as the LRA—should take into account the human rights dimension of their policies and activities. In the context of rebel movements, they are obliged not to commit the most serious crimes of concern to the international community as a whole. They must refrain from the following crimes: the crime of genocide; crimes against humanity; war crimes and the crime of aggression. Otherwise, individuals responsible must be investigated for the purpose of determining whether one or more specific persons should be charged with the commission of such crimes.

5. Conclusion

....

... [I]n the light of the war crimes committed in the conflict, it is also necessary to find a justice and accountability strategy that involves better understanding by the government of the ICC's independent responsibilities and objectives while striving to take into account the related objectives of peace, reintegration and reconciliation. It must be noted that domestic amnesties are strictly a matter for national authorities and do not act as a bar to an investigation by the ICC. In accordance with article 5 of the 1998 Rome Statute for the ICC, the ICC jurisdiction extends to the 'most serious crimes of concern to the international community as a whole' being genocide, crimes against humanity, war crimes and aggression. Such direct criminalisation of acts (of NSAs) which violate human rights represent a higher level of human rights protection. It makes space in the legal regime to take account of the role of NSAs for human rights violations, one of the biggest and most critical challenges facing international law today. All States parties to the ICC Statute should, therefore, support the prosecution of those who bear the greatest responsibility for crimes committed in the course of the conflict, which have caused gross human rights violations. This follows from the fact that the 'rules concerning the basic rights of the human person' are *erga omnes* obligations and that there is a United Nations Charter obligation to promote universal respect for, and observance of, human rights and freedoms. Any investigation of the war crimes and crimes against humanity in northern Uganda must be part of a holistic and comprehensive plan to end impunity for all such crimes, regardless of whether the crimes were committed by the LRA rebels or the Ugandan government's soldiers and of the level of the perpetrator.

Under article 25(2) of the ICC Statute, a person who commits a crime within the jurisdiction of the Court 'shall be individually responsible and liable for punishment' in accordance with the Statute. It is in this respect that the ICC should focus its investigation and prosecutions on those limited number of individuals in the LRA/M command who bear the greatest responsibility for committing the most serious crimes within the jurisdiction of the court. Such commanders may be prosecuted for ordering the commission of war crimes/crimes against humanity, or at least for being negligent to take necessary and reasonable measures to prevent crimes committed by their subordinates (abducted children) or to punish the perpetrators thereof. Since the majority of the LRA rebels were children abducted and forced to fight and commit war crimes, the ICC should categorise them as victims who should benefit from amnesty.

Notes and Questions

1. This article highlights a potentially deadly combination—a national desire for peace and reconciliation in the aftermath of horrific violence, and the stated commitment of an international court to proceed with prosecution of war criminals. Who should have the final say in this matter? What are the implications of allowing one or the other to make the final determination on the prosecution issue? Does the fact that so many of Kony's victims were children tilt the scales in any particular direction, or should the situation be analyzed in the same way as any other post-conflict scenario?

There is often profound disagreement about the desirability of the international community moving in on a conflict to "seek justice" by prosecuting war criminals. Often the people who have suffered the most are wary of reigniting violence, and understandably fearful of jeopardizing fragile peace agreements. The following editorial from a Ugandan newspaper expresses such a view.

Maggie Alerotek, *Bad Timing: ICC Justice Should Wait*
Monitor (Uganda), Nov. 23, 2005

The recently issued warrant of arrest for LRA leaders Joseph Kony, Vincent Otti, Raska Lukwiya, Odhiambo Okot and Dominic Ogwen by International Criminal Court (ICC) … is doing nothing other than scaring the rebels and jeopardising [Betty] Bigombe's initiative to a peaceful resolution of the 19 year old conflict that has raged on and continued to terrorize many lives and inflict pain on the people of Acholi.[15]

---

15. Betty Bigombe is a former Minister in the Ugandan Parliament. She is an ethnic Acholi and has been involved in peace negotiations to end the LRA insurgency since 1993. In 2004, she acted as

The questions we should ask ourselves are: What is the priority of a 20 year old born amidst a bloody war characterised by massive abductions, devastating IDP camp life?

Does such a person want to see peace first or justice? Believe me, though he/she maybe interested in seeing that justice takes its course and the perpetrators "pay" for the so much sufferings they caused, the poor boy or girl who lives in constant fear and with no peace of mind, craves for peace and wonders every hour if it is achievable.

The war that has lasted two decades, poses a big challenge to many who desire to see an end to it. Over the years, the government of Uganda that continues to pursue the rebels militarily, launched two offensives (Iron Fist I &II) against the rebellion, and even put money on Kony's head, but all failed and the cult movement masterminded by Joseph Kony goes on with its evil mission. (Of course I am not overlooking some of the military successes registered).

Then the ICC, though it has issued the arrest warrant, must be at a dilemma of how the perpetrators will be caught. So what is the next option of resolving the war? Against such a background, shouldn't one think that peaceful resolution deserves a chance?

It cannot be refuted that in every society where crimes are committed against the innocents, justice must rule and perpetrators stand up to their actions. However, for tangible justice to be executed, certain considerations must be looked into especially if the political situation in the particular society like is the case of northern Uganda, is still volatile and the people in whose names justice is being pursued continue to suffer.

World sustenance

Rabban Shimon ben Gamliel, author of Mishnah, and father of Judah HaNasi argues that the world is sustained by three things: By justice, truth and by peace. Shimon advances his arguments that justice speaks of the purposes for which God created the world, whereas truth speaks of principles which sustain it, and prevents it from collapsing.

Critically looking at this argument, it is obvious that strife and war are destructive of society and according to his philosophy, justice and truth are important values in sustaining peace in any peace-loving society. However, one thing we should put at the back of our minds is that these two values normally work against the realisation of peace in a war-stricken society like northern Uganda.

When parties are in dispute, peace between them maybe best settled by both sides agreeing on certain things with help of a mediator, rather than advocating for strict justice, which even if is the correct thing to do, usually leaves one party (the perpetrators) feeling injured and angry, which in most cases provoke them to committing more atrocities.

When people normally turn to law courts, there is no peace as defaulters, well aware of what their fate is, will cause worse harm than before. The decision of offering mediation as an alternative to court is always meritorious. Therefore for the sake of real peace, justice can for now be left out until the wounds have completely healed and the sufferers begin to live as human beings once again!

I clearly remember when the ICC team just began their preliminary investigation into the crimes against humanity committed in the region. Bannie Afako, a brilliant lawyer, was contracted by Save the Children in Uganda to explain to the Acholi community what

---

chief mediator between the LRA and the government of Uganda, until those peace talks fell through in 2005. Her meetings with Kony and other LRA leaders became known as the "Bigombe talks." Her negotiations laid the ground work for the current round of talks.

ICC is all about, and implications of its operation in as far as the peace processes are concerned but also its goodness.

Already many had expressed their fears about the ICC's interference with the different peace initiatives including the Acholi traditional system of settling disputes which is believed to be very effective. I still vividly remember an elderly man and the remarks he made on learning about ICC and what its intentions in the conflict are.

The old man said, "It is good that they want the criminals to pay, but how will it be done when the war is still going on? We cannot afford to continue suffering because of the existence of a law. Besides, this ICC knows nothing about the dynamism of this war."

Prosecutor wrong

He said that the prosecutor went against their advice during the pre-investigation stage that if ICC went ahead to issue arrest warrants, it would be a challenge arresting the perpetrators considering that ICC has no army of its own, and besides, may lead to an escalation of the situation. The unanswered question is, do the government of Uganda, ICC and any other established legal system want to see tangible justice, or a just hazy one?

My take is, it would be better for ICC to consider the role that the Acholi traditional way of executing justice, which they prefer to call reconciliation and forgiveness. Culturally, the Acholi look at their traditional means as the best mechanisms for managing conflict and most appropriate and accepted non violent way of resolving conflict.

Cultural forgiveness

According to the Acholi culture, when one commits crimes against another, there is an established institution called Reconciliation Council which brings together perpetrators and victims to reconcile done through painful experiences called "makoput". This is the drinking of bitter herbs as a demonstration of true forgiveness, and bending of spears to show that there will be no fighting between the two parties.

However, if the perpetrators continue with the crimes, there is what is called Elders' Institution which is highly respected. The elders will curse the person and when that happens, it is believed the person's punishment is death which comes mysteriously. Isn't this a better way of healing wounds other than leaving one party so bitter?

Much as every person wants to see that justice is done for the sake of those who have undeservedly suffered, one thing we must remember is that the perpetrators will not feel the pain of their actions on the victims since it may be just a question of serving the specified sentence and who knows, eventually walk away free.

Violence breeds more violence. So let's work towards a peaceful resolution of any conflict.

Notes and Questions

1. The newspaper article excerpted above leads us to ask the question: What role should public opinion have in determining the relative merits of prosecution versus reconciliation? In violent civil wars, it will always be the case that even the worst perpetrators belong to one ethnic or cultural group or the other. How can prosecution, even if satisfying to writers on international law, successfully deal with the wounds left at the end of such conflicts? If one could determine that international prosecutions had essentially no deterrent effect on the behavior of combatants in civil wars, would there remain any compelling arguments in their favor?

2. For a detailed discussion of the ICC and the role of reparations in "doing justice," see Adrian Di Giovanni, *The Prospect of ICC Reparations in the Case Concerning Northern Uganda: On a Collision Course with Incoherence?* 2 Journal of International Law & International Relations 25 (2006). The author makes a number of important points with regard to the limited potential of reparations, especially with respect to long running civil wars. The article makes clear that in a war "by children against children," the goal of reparations is highly problematic.

Luis Moroeno-Ocampo is the Chief Prosecutor of the International Criminal Court. The following remarks were presented at a conference on "International Criminal Tribunals in the 21st Century" hosted by the War Crimes Research Office of the Washington College of Law, American University, on September 30, 2005.

Luis Moreno-Ocampo, Keynote Address, *Integrating the Work of the ICC Into Local Justice Initiatives*
21 American University International Law Review 497 (2006)

Let me start by explaining to you why I believe the topic of this event—International Criminal Tribunals in the 21st Century—is so important. The Rome Statute creates a system that is not only about the ICC—it is about national systems. It is important that we have almost one hundred states committed to preventing and punishing crimes against humanity, genocide, and war crimes. I believe that the most important work is not what has happened in The Hague; the most important work is what has happened in these one hundred states. This is a way in which we can really succeed and use the Court to help change the world. We have to investigate and to prosecute, but the issue is how we can have an impact on national systems.

. . . .

The final challenge that I would like to present to you is a classic one—the interaction between peace and justice. Normally, peace and justice are integrated; but they do not necessarily follow a linear peace-then-justice trajectory. However, let me present to you one example of how people have a different view on the issue.

When I started the Uganda case, I received a visit from an ambassador. He tried to explain to me that investigation was wrong; that I was destroying the chances of making peace in Uganda. I listened to him carefully, and I said to him that the Statute says that I have to respect the interests of victims. This may mean that I can delay an investigation, if it is in the interests of victims. We start here to integrate the concepts of peace and justice. It is the judges who may then review my decision.

I told the ambassador that he would have to give me evidence that the peace effort will stop the violence and would thus be in the interests of victims. The ambassador explained to me, however, that it was not something where one could provide evidence. A peace process is like a little light at the end of the tunnel.

What we did was the following. My duty is to investigate and to prosecute. We decided to investigate and to prosecute, but to conduct the investigation in a very low-key way, and try not to interfere with the peace efforts. At the end, the peace efforts collapsed, but not because of our investigation. It collapsed because the rebels were not really ready to make peace. So in this way, we allowed them to negotiate peace efforts. I then discussed the role of the prosecutor with the local leaders. I explained to them that we have to respect the victims and that if they can do this, then they could proceed with their negotiations. I had to keep my investigation going, but I would not interfere with the peace process. The solution that we found was to combine peace and justice.

However, what happens if they one day reach an agreement? What happens when the leaders of a rebel group are ready to stop the massacres, return the weapons and dismantle the groups, but call for an end to the investigation? What, then, do I have to do?

Can we do an informal survey here now? Please raise your hand if you believe that I should stop my investigation on the condition that the rebel leaders are ready to stop the massacres, return the weapons, and dismantle the groups? Please raise your hand if you believe that I cannot do that?

I see that there are many neutral people here. There is a slight "no" majority, but it varies. Even this informal survey illustrates that people are uncertain about what to do. One of the challenges that we face in relation to peace and justice is that we have to develop criteria.

We must first understand the meaning of the interests of victims. There is an article in the Rome Statute, Article 53(2), that refers to "the interests of victims." The interests of victims are not just about peace. They can also include security, for instance. Take the following situation. If I decide that the only way to proceed with a case is if I am sure that no one will be killed, this means that any rebel or any State could kill twenty people to stop me from proceeding with the case. If, on the contrary, I ignore the killings, then I do not respect the interests of victims. How can I manage this? What is the meaning of "the interests of victims" ? People say that because we proceed with the case, we serve the interests of victims in the long run. They say that in any event, the guerrillas will kill people and not to worry about this. But I have to worry, because people could be killed because of my decision. So again, what is the standard? What are the criteria?

I would now like to address the issue of local justice initiatives. Our investigation and prosecution is just one piece of the justice activities. For instance, in northern Uganda, the crimes were committed there for the last nineteen years, but we can investigate only those committed after July 1, 2002. We decided to investigate only those who bear the greatest responsibility. What about the other perpetrators? What do we do with the other crimes? What is the role of local justice initiatives?

Amnesties are an example of local justice. Allow me to illustrate to you a challenge that we face with regards to amnesties. A couple of months ago, I attended the meeting on Guidelines for United Nations Representatives in Certain Aspects of Negotiations for Conflict Resolution. The Guidelines prohibit amnesties for war crimes, crimes against humanity, and genocide. The U.N. has since reiterated this key principle in other public reports and documents. However, there is a real disconnect between legal scholars and the practitioners making peace.

For instance, I received in the same week two letters that illustrate these two very different perspectives on the issue of amnesties. One letter came from Amnesty International, telling me to ignore the amnesty law in Uganda because international law, which does not recognize amnesties for serious violations, must prevail. In the same week, I received a letter from a paramount chief. He said that the amnesty law is a decision of the local people to reintegrate the children that were abducted and forced to become child soldiers. I must respect the amnesty law, he continued, because the amnesty law is not impunity. He said that they will apply traditional African mechanisms based on truth, reconciliation, and compensation.

The issue for me is how to integrate these different elements. In other words, how do we integrate the activity of the Court to prosecute the leaders with other initiatives, such as local mechanisms, because we cannot prosecute every single perpetrator. What is the right standard? We must understand this dynamic between legal scholars and practitioners and develop standards for those implementing peace and those pursuing prosecutions.

Another area in which discussions are needed is in relation to a decision not to prosecute, pursuant to Article 53 of the Rome Statute. What, then, is the role of local justice initiatives?

Let me now turn to the issue of impartiality. What is the meaning of impartiality to an international prosecutor? There are allegations of crimes committed by the UPDF, the Ugandan army. Some people say that the only way to retain our impartiality is to prosecute both the LRA and the UPDF. However, I think that impartiality means that we apply the same criteria equally to all sides. A major criterion is gravity. There is no comparison of gravity between the crimes committed by the Ugandan army and by the LRA—the crimes committed by the LRA are much more grave than those committed by the Ugandan army. I continue to collect information on allegations against the UDPF. Then I will determine whether the gravity and complementarity requirements of the Statute are met for an investigation.

What I present to you today are some of the issues that I have to define or decide each and every day. Legal scholars must understand and discuss these examples, and develop standards with regards to selection, peace and justice, and local justice initiatives.

Academic debate is needed, because the Court is a new system. The Court is based on different assumptions than a normal court. We have a treaty, we have committed States, and we are independent. The issues that I face as an international prosecutor are different than those of a national prosecutor. A prosecutor in the United States does not have to convince the Senate to support his activities, nor convince the chief of police to follow his instructions. He has a police force at his disposal. I have none of this. In effect, I am a stateless prosecutor.

This difference is also illustrated by the fact that any criminal court is based on the idea that there is State control over the territory and over its forces. We have a case only when the State has no control over the forces and when groups are killing people. This is the best scenario: when no one controls the forces. The worst scenario is when the State has a monopoly of forces, but the State is killing people. In both cases, we need other actors to cooperate with us. Of course, States Parties have treaty obligations of cooperation, but we need support going beyond that.

My activities must be based on understanding the situation and on convincing other actors to work closely with us. I have to explain to them that I only prosecute the leaders; they can deal with the other perpetrators. I have to keep in my role of prosecutor, but I have to interact with other actors so that we can combine our efforts. We intend to be clear about this and about how we go about doing this.

And of course, each time that I do this, I talk openly, but I do not look like a prosecutor. People ask, "Why is the prosecutor talking about peace? Why is the prosecutor talking with the president of the country? Why is the prosecutor meeting with traditional leaders? It is not his role." But it is necessary to carry out my mandate. This is part of the challenge that I face.

Outreach then becomes a very important issue. It is not about putting something in the media; it is about understanding different actors from local to international areas and to have them support the investigation. This is an important part of my role.

I would like to finish by reiterating that I have six years and eight months remaining of my work as chief prosecutor of the Court. In the next six years, we will probably do six to eight cases, which will demonstrate how the Court works. The Court will evolve.

I also hope that we can dramatically reduce the occurrence of massive crimes, in which millions of people are displaced and millions of people die. I think that in seven or ten years the Court will have an impact. We can stop genocide, prevent crimes against humanity, and prevent massive crimes. This is an incredibly difficult goal.

We need your support to achieve this: scholars and others must help to develop standards, and engage other actors to think not just about the elements of crimes or cross-examination, but also about an integrated approach. We have to think more about what the political scientists are saying and about what the economists are saying. In order to integrate different initiatives, we must think about how to integrate our views with the views of other actors.

I will conclude by stressing once again the need for an integrated approach. Ninety percent of the members of the LRA are children who have been abducted. They are forced to kill people in their own village and to destroy their relations with their local community. Girls are forced to become sex slaves. It is an awful situation. There are stories about a few children that have escaped from the LRA and who returned to their village, but were not welcomed. They have nothing. They cannot find a place to stay. They have no choice but to return to the LRA. We cannot offer these children anything better than the LRA.

Even if we succeed using different initiatives to stop the crimes and to prosecute those responsible, someone else has to train these children, to offer them job opportunities, a family, and a community. National issues are not just about prosecution, nor are they just a job for lawyers. National issues are the job of an entire community. This is why we must think about an integrated approach and how to combine justice with other areas, such as rehabilitation and development, in order to produce better communities.

Notes and Questions

1. Luis Moreno-Ocampo is clearly more aware than most of the serious implications of choosing a "peace" or a "justice" model. How does he present the concept of "interests of the victims"? Is Moreno-Ocampo successful in his attempt to synthesize international law and local justice initiatives?

2. Even in the relatively chaotic and fast-changing Ugandan situation, we can see the emergence of a stark question: Is it helpful, and does it truly deliver justice, when an international court attempts to impose criminal penalties on the perpetrators of terrible violence in a conflict like that which has raged in Uganda? For international lawyers, there is a great temptation to say yes, that the criminal law should identify the guilty at all costs. On the other hand, to the extent that arrest warrants and threats of imprisonment can serve to make rebel leaders wary of revealing their whereabouts, and thus resistant to dealing with the national government to establish a peace agreement, many people on the ground feel aggrieved by this externally derived "justice." Who pays the price if the ICC and its supporters are wrong, and criminal prosecution of war criminals like Joseph Kony prove ineffectual in the longer term? Is the international community too eager to impose a Nuremberg type solution on every conflict? Do such prosecutions make sense when the conflict is still ongoing, or could be easily revived? Do the alternative peace and justice models leave out the best solution of all—serious prevention and/or intervention by the international community to ensure that this kind of exploitation does not occur?

Is the current debate something of a distraction for the real question: Why are these abuses allowed to continue for so long?

3. For a description of how a peace deal between the LRA and the Ugandan government broke down in 2008, see *Peace Deal in Central Africa Fails*, International Herald Tribune, Apr. 12, 2008, at 4, explaining that Kony refused to sign the deal in the face of pressure over his indictment by the ICC.

Interestingly, attempts to capture Joseph Kony after the breakdown of the peace deal have led to further, and extremely brutal, violence against civilians in Congo where Kony is believed to be in hiding. Human Rights Watch has had to issue warnings against the perpetration of human rights abuses in the name of locating Kony. See *HRW Warns against Violence on Civilians as Great Lakes Hunts Kony*, Afrol News, Dec. 16, 2008, http://www.afrol.com/articles/32019. Uganda's government has insisted that a peace deal, understandably much desired by the general public, can coexist with the ICC prosecution. See Katy Glassborow, *Uganda Insists Peace Not at Odds with ICC*, Institute for War and Peace Reporting, Apr. 14, 2008, *available at* http://iwpr.net/?p=acr&s=f&o=344125& apc_state=henh.

B. The Case of Sierra Leone

1. Background to the Conflict

The civil war in Sierra Leone, raging over much of the 1990s, was one of the very worst conflicts from the point of view of child exploitation. Child soldiers recruited by the warring factions took a prominent part in the severe atrocities committed during that war. The conflict became notorious for the manner in which rebel groups arbitrarily hacked off the limbs of even the youngest non-combatants as a means of keeping civilian populations cowed and compliant.

In the aftermath of this almost unspeakable violence, the Sierra Leonean Government established a Truth and Reconciliation Commission (TRC) in 2000. A primary objective of the Commission was to create an impartial historical record of violations and abuses of human rights and humanitarian law during the armed conflict, from its beginning in 1991 to the signing of the Lomé Peace Agreement in July 1999. Public hearings, which began in April 2003, were aimed at addressing impunity, breaking the cycle of violence, providing a forum for both victims and perpetrators of human rights violations to tell their stories, and gaining a clear picture of the recent past. The Commission's purpose was to lay foundation for reconciliation and healing after eleven years of horrific internal conflict. Thus, identification of victim and victimizer was only part of the process. The section excerpted below from the very lengthy Truth and Reconciliation Commission Report addresses the historical causes of the civil conflict in Sierra Leone. As a model of the type of conflict that tends to create many child soldiers, note its characteristics, and ask yourself how Sierra Leone fits into the "Machel paradigm."

Excerpts from the Truth and Reconciliation Report provide one explanation as to why the behavior of the combatants became so brutal and merciless during the civil war in Sierra Leone—namely, the failed politics of the post-colonial era. Recall that Stephen Hick, in an article earlier in this chapter, pointed to economic globalization as a root cause of these child-dependent conflicts. How might the Commission respond to Hick's assessment of the causes of recent civil wars? Are the two views of the cause of conflict mutually exclusive?

The final TRC report consisted of 1,500 pages in addition to 3,500 pages of transcripts of testimonies. It contained an executive summary and several sections: the historical antecedents of the war; the causes of the war; its nature, with a focus on such atrocities as amputations and sexual slavery; the role of external actors, and circumstances that fuelled the war, such as mineral resources; the impact of warfare on women and children; the relationship between the Commission and the Special Court for Sierra Leone (a tribunal to be discussed in detail below); and the efforts made to help the country reconcile with its past. It also offers a detailed set of recommendations, including a call to abolish the death penalty. Statements were taken from more than seven thousand people from across the country, with special efforts made to specifically include children.

Interestingly, in light of the many children directly involved in the conflict, there is a child-friendly version of the same report. It is the first time a truth and reconciliation committee has written an entirely separate report aimed at children, using less complicated jargon and easy-to-understand concepts. The children's version of the report can be viewed at http://www.trcsierraleone.org/pdf/kids.pdf. Indeed, there is an entire website on the conflict designed especially for Sierra Leonean children: http://www.trcsierraleone.org/children/index.html.

Truth and Reconciliation Commission of Sierra Leone, *Witness to Truth: Report of the Sierra Leone Truth and Reconciliation Commission*

(2004), *available at* http://www.trcsierraleone.org/pdf/FINAL %20VOLUME%20TWO/VOLUME%202.pdf

Volume 2: Chapter 1: Executive Summary

....

Historical Antecedents to the Conflict

7. How did a peace-loving nation become engulfed, seemingly overnight, in horror? What events occurred in the history of the country to make this conflict possible? Explanations put forward have varied from 'bad governance' and 'the history of the post-colonial period in Sierra Leone' to 'the urge to acquire the country's diamond wealth' and the roles of Libya or the Liberian faction leader Charles Taylor. The international community initially dismissed the war as just another example of tribal conflict in Africa; another failed state imploding in the context of environmental degradation and acute economic crisis.

8. In order to "compile a clear picture of the past" the Commission devoted considerable resources towards examining the pre-conflict history of the country. These efforts were intended to locate causes of conflict in Sierra Leone's past, place the conflict within its proper historical context and offer explanations for what went wrong.

9. The Commission identified social trends that spawned division and confrontation between the various groups that make up Sierra Leone. It picked out fault lines and key events that created the structural conditions for conflict. It highlighted decisions on the part of the political elite that were designed to strengthen their grip on power at the expense of common benefit, progress and ultimately peace.

10. Central to the Commission's study of history was the social and political interaction among Sierra Leone's constituent groups. The nature and extent of such interaction—often negative and limited—influenced people's perceptions of the state in which they lived and their own places within it. These perceptions in turn presented the great-

est challenge to the concepts of nationhood and citizenship. They undermined the positive sense of national identity needed to build a strong and unified independent nation.

11. The Commission examined the colonial period and the first few years of independence together under the section entitled 'The Historical Evolution of the Sierra Leonean State'. In this section, four distinct phases proved crucial to understanding the roots of the conflict and some of the challenges that the country still faces today:

- *The Colony and the Protectorate.* Rather than constructing a unified Sierra Leonean state, the colonial government effectively created two nations in the same land. The colonial capital Freetown, known as the Colony, and the much larger area of provincial territory, known as the Protectorate, were developed separately and unequally. The colonial government formalised the common law practised in the Colony yet neglected the development of customary law in the Protectorate, thus producing two separate legal systems that persist to the present day. The impact of colonial policies and practices, including those relating to citizenship, ownership of land, land tenure rights and conflict of laws, was far-reaching. People in the Colony enjoyed vastly superior social, political and economic development and access to vital resources such as education. The divide between the two entities bred deep ethnic and regional resentment and destabilised the traditional system of Chieftaincy.

- *The Era of Party Politics.* In 1947, a new Constitution was proposed in order to prepare Sierra Leone for independence. This Constitution amalgamated the Colony and the Protectorate into a single political entity, but divided their elite representatives into opposing factions, each dedicated to protecting the interests of its own people. In due course these factions formed themselves into narrow, regionally based political parties with little or no national agenda. Party politics became the greatest obstacle to national cohesion and identity. Party allegiance was just as divisive as ethnicity, class or regional prejudice in the battle over who should succeed the British. On the cusp of independence in 1961, the ten-year-old Sierra Leone People's Party (SLPP) was joined in the political arena by the All People's Congress (APC), which would become its main rival in contesting elections.

- *The Sierra Leone People's Party (SLPP) in Power.* The SLPP majority party formed the first post-colonial government in 1961. The 1962 elections then revealed the depths of ethnic and regional polarisation in Sierra Leone and the superficiality of the ideological differences between the opposing parties. The SLPP retained power by winning most of its seats in the South and East of the country, which were predominantly populated by Mende people. The SLPP government was therefore labelled as a Mende government. This image polarised public opinion in the country, introduced notions of cronyism in many state institutions and laid the foundations for military involvement in politics. The period had terrible, albeit foreseeable consequences on the unity of the young state and served to deepen existing cleavages.

- *The 1967 Elections and their Aftermath.* The elections of 1967 were scarred by bitter power struggles based on ethnicity, personality and party affiliation. Although the APC won the most seats, the leadership of the SLPP stoutly refused to concede defeat. The resultant standoff signalled a watershed in the political fortunes of the country and ultimately led to the destruction of the multi-party system. The head of the Army sabotaged the swearing-in of the APC Prime Minister and declared martial law. When it became apparent that this move was engineered to favour the SLPP leadership, junior-ranking soldiers staged a coup. The consequent period of military rule served to narrow the political space in Sierra Leone and compelled others to seek alternative routes to power that did not depend on free and fair elections. It set the scene for multiple further coup attempts in the following decades.

12. In the second section of the chapter, the Commission focused on the prolonged period in power of the All People's Congress (APC). The APC government used concerns about internal security as a pretext to stifle the nascent democratic culture. All the institutions of the state were subjected to strict party control and Siaka Stevens, the new President of the Republic of Sierra Leone, adopted an increasingly authoritarian approach.

13. Under the APC, central government sustained itself through corruption, nepotism and the plundering of state assets. These practices were replicated at regional and local levels, where Chieftaincy became synonymous with power, patronage and control of resources. When Sierra Leone adopted a one-party constitution in 1978, any semblance of accountability or effective opposition had already been eliminated. Historical trends like economic decay and fragmentation of the national spirit were exacerbated under the one-party system and became key causes of the conflict.

14. Neither the SLPP nor the APC made any genuine effort to attend to the debasement of the post-independence politics and economy of the country. On the contrary, history speaks of a systemic failure, whereby all the members of the political elite belonged to the same failing system. While they claimed to be ideologically different, in reality the two parties shared a brand of politics that was all about power and the benefits it conferred. Tragically these characteristics persist today in Sierra Leone.

15. The final section of this chapter traces past dynamics at District level in order to help explain the manner in which the war unfolded across the nation. There were undercurrents of conflict in many areas, from the border Districts that served as 'gateways' for the fighting forces, to the strategically located 'heartland' Districts that initially supported the insurgency to overthrow the APC. At local level as at national level, many of the answers as to why and how this conflict happened are to be found in its historical antecedents.

. . . .

Notes and Questions

1. Like Uganda, the colonial past and sharply divided ethnic identifications of the populace were factors that contributed to Sierra Leone's civil war. It is plain from the brief discussion provided by the Commission that successive governments of Sierra Leone made no attempt to live up to the needs and expectations of the population generally, and that political power became a sphere to be fought over, like any other resource or advantage. What does the Sierra Leonean situation tell us about the role of the state in fostering a climate of fear and competition that can lead to extreme brutality in civil wars?

It is important to note that Sierra Leone is an important source of the world's diamonds. The wealth represented by the diamond mines goes a long way towards explaining the ferocity of the civil war. Having gained independence from Britain in 1961, it was entirely predictable that a diamond industry that had been controlled by European interests would be a magnet for internal conflict among Sierra Leoneans. A succession of coups and notorious corruption in the 1970s and 1980s predisposed Sierra Leone to the kind of brutal, all-out civil war that followed from the early 1990s onward.

Sierra Leone's colonial past gave rise to a complex host of relentless characters. In 1991, a rebel group calling itself the Revolutionary United Front (RUF) launched an insurgency from neighboring Liberia. Two of the leaders of this extremely violent group were to become especially notorious for the death and destruction they wrought within Sierra Leone: Foday Sankoh and Charles Taylor. While Sankoh was Sierra Leonean, Taylor had been a rebel leader and later head of state in his native Liberia. Taylor served as president of Liberia between 1997 and 2003.

In 1992, yet another Sierra Leonean coup, led by Captain Valentine Strasser, installed a junta calling itself the National Provisional Ruling Council (NPRC). The NPRC attempted, to no avail, to deal with the RUF, both politically and militarily. In 1996, it seemed there would be a peace agreement between the warring factions, though this also failed to come to fruition. International peace keepers were dispatched to Sierra Leone, but were unable to contain the violence. Strasser was himself ousted in a coup in 1996, with elections held soon after. Ahmad Kabbah was elected president and moved to sign a peace deal with the rebel RUF. This deal quickly fell apart and Kabbah was deposed in 1997 by the Armed Forces Revolutionary Council (AFRC), only to return to power with the assistance of Nigeria the next year. The AFRC, joining forces with the RUF, pursued their cause during a period characterized by senseless and frenzied violence against the civilian population.

In 1999, UN peace keeping troops arrived to enforce a cease fire agreement. Timely intervention by the British also helped contain the worst of the violence. The process of bringing the war to a definitive end, however, took until early 2002. Elections took place, and Kabbah's Sierra Leone People's Party emerged the winner. The year 2002 also saw the establishment of the joint UN and Sierra Leonean government Special Court for Sierra Leone (SCSL). While awaiting trial for war crimes at the SCSL, rebel leader Foday Sankoh died in prison in 2003. Charles Taylor was arrested in Nigeria in 2006 and turned over to the SCSL to face prosecution. His trial, which is wrapping up at the time of this writing, was moved to the Hague to allow prosecutors to avail of the facilities of the ICC.

The Human Rights Watch reports excerpted below were written at the height of the fighting in the Sierra Leonean civil war. They are included to give a sense of the multifaceted nature of the violence, the type of atrocities endured by the civilian population, and the role of random brutalization in attempts by the various factions, especially the RUF, to gain power. As with the Uganda reports, consider the effects on young children of the type of terror unleashed by rebel groups against the civilian population. Could the same humanitarian principles that have led to post-conflict prosecutions have prompted the international community to act in a preventative manner before or during the hostilities?

Human Rights Watch, *Sowing Terror: Atrocities Against Civilians in Sierra Leone*

(1998), *available at* http://www.hrw.org/en/reports/
1998/07/29/sowing-terror

Summary

Since losing political power in February 1998, members of the Armed Forces Revolutionary Council (AFRC) and the Revolutionary United Front (RUF) have been engaging in a war of terror against civilians in Sierra Leone. With no recognizable political platform, the AFRC/RUF rebel alliance is committing widespread and egregious atrocities against unarmed civilians in an attempt to regain power. As the violence in Sierra Leone continues, grave abuses continue to take place.

....

Many thousands of Sierra Leonean civilians have been raped; deliberately mutilated, often by amputation; or killed outright in a campaign by the AFRC/RUF between February and June 1998 alone. Men, women and children, probably numbering in the thousands, have been abducted by the AFRC/RUF for use as combatants, forced laborers, or sexual slaves. Women have been actively targeted through sexual violence, including rape and sexual slavery. Children have been targets of killings and violence and are forcibly recruited as soldiers. In addition to various forms of physical abuse, innumerable Sierra Leoneans suffer from psychological trauma due to intentionally cruel methods of inflicting harm against these individuals and their communities.

These atrocities committed against civilians are the latest cycle of violence in the armed conflict that has devastated Sierra Leone for seven years. The fighting has caused the displacement of more than a million Sierra Leoneans. Most have become internally displaced, while hundreds of thousands have fled the country as refugees, predominantly to neighboring Guinea and Liberia.

The AFRC—led by a group of military officers—took power forcibly on May 25, 1997. During the nine months it was in power, the AFRC joined forces with the armed rebel group, the RUF, to form a regime characterized by serious human rights violations and a complete breakdown of the rule of law. In February 1998, a Nigerian-led peacekeeping force, the Economic Community of West African States Monitoring Group (ECOMOG), forced the AFRC/RUF out of power and reinstated former President Ahmad Tejan Kabbah, who had been elected president in March 1996 in the first multi-party elections for almost three decades in Sierra Leone. Since the reinstatement of Kabbah, the AFRC has joined forces with the RUF to wage a war against ECOMOG and the Kabbah government.

Since independence in 1961, Sierra Leone has endured a series of military regimes and rebellions in struggles over economic and political power. However, the latest round of violence is unique in the scale and grotesque nature of the attacks on civilians. Much of rural Sierra Leone is inaccessible due to the ongoing war, and information is available for the most part only through health facilities where victims seek care in Sierra Leone and through the testimonies of witnesses and survivors in neighboring Guinea and Liberia. Of the hundreds of testimonies collected by Human Rights Watch, many described situations in which the interviewee was the sole survivor among many victims. The cases reported in this document represent only a small fraction of the actual number of victims. The true number may never be known.

Human Rights Watch compiled information regarding the experiences of more than 500 survivors of atrocities committed in Sierra Leone between February and June of 1998. The vast majority of these abuses were perpetrated by members of the AFRC/RUF. Of this number, over 425 survivors of gunshot wounds, amputations and other mutilations, or rape were registered in Connaught, Magburaka, and Makeni hospitals in Sierra Leone. Approximately eighty-two survivors of the same types of abuse were identified in Guinea at Conakry, Faranah, Kissidougou, and Guéckedou hospitals during roughly the same period. In the Liberian refugee camps, Human Rights Watch interviewed victims of the conflict and former AFRC/RUF combatants living alongside one another.

Forces fighting on behalf of President Kabbah have also committed human rights abuses and violations of international humanitarian law. Civilian Defense Forces (CDFs), civilian militias who support the Kabbah government, have committed numerous abuses including indiscriminate killings and torture. These killings are on a smaller scale than those carried out by the AFRC/RUF and are of a different nature: the CDFs were created in order to assure local security, and they generally limit their abuses to those they claim are AFRC/RUF combatants and to a lesser extent, those perceived as their supporters. The largest and most powerful of the CDFs, the Kamajors,[16] have been responsible for the majority of abuses committed by those fighting on behalf of the Kabbah government since February 1998. In addition to killings and torture, Kamajors have also been responsible for obstructing humanitarian assistance and demanding money or other payment at roadblocks. There are many child soldiers among the Kamajors, and despite promises by the government to demobilize all combatants under the age of eighteen, recent reports indicate that the CDFs continue to recruit children.

. . . .

The atrocities that drive civilians into flight are only the first chapter of hardship for many Sierra Leoneans affected by the crisis. Approximately one-quarter million Sierra Leoneans have fled to refugee camps in neighboring Guinea and Liberia to escape the abuses and fighting. The location of the camps in border areas presents problems of security for and access to the camps, which in turn have impaired assistance and protection for refugees. Security conditions in many of the camps are precarious, and humanitarian assistance has been hampered by difficult access to the camps, a lack of resources at the disposition of the United Nations High Commissioner for Refugees (UNHCR) and aid agencies, and in some instances, poor coordination of relief efforts.

Protecting refugees in this context remains a challenge for UNHCR and other humanitarian agencies. In the Guinean camps, many unaccompanied women, children, and other war victims suffer from inadequate protection. Delays in the distribution of identity cards for refugees have led to restricted movement for refugees, as well as extortion and arbitrary arrest by Guinean authorities. Despite repeated requests from UNHCR and the International Committee of the Red Cross (ICRC), the Guinean authorities have denied access to detained asylum seekers they are holding as suspected combatants.

. . . .

Sierra Leone has been largely ignored by much of the international community, with the exception of those attempting to exploit its rich diamond and mineral deposits. This mix of exploitation and indifference, combined with a history of weak respect for the rule of law and democratic institutions, has repeatedly permitted military leaders to hold power and divert revenue from the mines for their own benefit. In attempts during recent years to gain political and economic control, both government and rebel groups have sought to tip the balance of power by employing private security firms or mercenaries, often in exchange for lucrative contracts and mining concessions.

. . . .

Human Rights Abuses Committed By Members of the AFRC/RUF

A War of Terror against Civilians

Human Rights Watch took testimony from dozens of survivors and witnesses of gross violations of human rights committed by the AFRC/RUF, involving the physical mutilation,

---

16. The Kamajors were the so-called "traditional hunters," a civilian defense group created to respond to the attacks of the RUF against the civilian population.

torture and murder of Sierra Leonean civilians. They included: amputations by machete of one or both hands, arms, feet, legs, ears and buttocks and one or more fingers; lacerations to the head, neck, arms, legs, feet and torso; the gouging out of one or both eyes; rape; gunshot wounds to the head, torso and limbs; burns from explosives and other devices; injections with acid; and beatings. Human Rights Watch also received unconfirmed reports of sexual mutilation such as the cutting off of breasts and genitalia, among other atrocities.

This is a war being waged through attacks on the civilian population. AFRC/RUF soldiers typically capture civilians, round them up from their hiding places in the forest or in villages and commit atrocities against them in an effort to instill terror. The AFRC/RUF appears to use this campaign of fear as a means of exerting political and military control. They often summarily execute civilians, accusing them of being Kabbah or Kamajor supporters, or Kamajor relatives. The soldiers further terrorize their victims by forcing them to participate in their own mutilation, asking them to make choices about which finger, hand or arm, for example, to have amputated. They also use mutilation and other forms of physical abuse as punishment for refusing to follow their instructions.

The AFRC/RUF uses the civilians it abuses to "send messages" to its opponents. Victims of amputations or other mutilations are frequently told that they should take their amputated limb and a verbal or written message to ECOMOG or the Kabbah government. The messages are typically demands that ECOMOG should "leave the country to Sierra Leoneans" or that Kabbah should replace the limbs of amputees. The AFRC/RUF also state that they will keep fighting until Kabbah is gone and their leaders are restored to power. They call for the release of RUF leader Fodey Sankoh, imprisoned in Nigeria. According to testimony from other victims and witnesses, many victims die from complications related to their wounds before their messages of horror can be heard.

Since February 1998, attacks on civilians have occurred in almost all regions of the country but with a particularly high concentration in the Koidu diamond-mining area in the east, where the AFRC/RUF maintain a strong presence. The vast majority of victims are males between the ages of sixteen and forty-five, but women, children, and the elderly are not spared. For example, testimonies collected by Human Rights Watch included male and female amputees over the age of sixty, as well as from a three-year-old boy with a gunshot wound. Attacks on villages or civilians hiding in the forest are seemingly carried out without regard for ethnic or religious affiliation. Perpetrators and victims come from diverse ethnic and religious groups, and ethnicity is seldom invoked as a motivating factor in killings or abuse.

Men of voting and fighting age are particularly targeted in order to discourage them from giving political or military support to President Kabbah or the Kamajors. When the RUF committed atrocities prior to elections in 1996, they told victims that their hands were being amputated so that they could not vote. Women and girls are also frequently subject to rape and other forms of gender-based violence, including sexual slavery. Pregnant women and nursing mothers are also targets of the AFRC/RUF.

The AFRC/RUF led at least two loosely organized campaigns of terror, "Operation No Living Thing" and "Operation Pay Yourself." These campaigns, both of which originated in the Koidu area in February 1998 and then spread throughout the country, were designed to loot, destroy, or kill anything in the path of the combatants. Operation Pay Yourself included AFRC/RUF roadblocks where civilians were forced to place their belongings into two piles, one for civilians to keep, to "pay themselves," and one to be handed over to the soldiers. One witness who fled Koidu described what happens at the road blocks:

> Ten of them [AFRC/RUF soldiers] in a van with weapons—RPGs, AK47s—stopped us and told us to put down our bags. They searched us from shirt to pants. They told us to make two piles and put all the best of what we had—money, rice—into one pile, and the rest in another. They took all the best and gave us the one that wasn't good. That's "Operation Pay Yourself!"

These operations were apparently designed to force the local populations to provide them with economic support and to assert their position as political and military players in Sierra Leone.

Although the attackers claim to be seeking out supporters of President Kabbah or the Kamajors, which have fought on behalf of Kabbah, there is often no distinction being made by AFRC/RUF forces. A small minority of victims are, in fact, Kabbah supporters or Kamajors; most are subsistence farmers, miners or small merchants with no history of political activity. One witness to atrocities near Koidu said, "They don't ask you if you're a Kabbah supporter; they just kill randomly ... they just kill anyone. But if they know you are a Kabbah supporter, they will kill you faster."

....

Atrocities Against Children

Children are the frequent targets of brutal, indiscriminate acts of violence by the AFRC/RUF. Children are murdered, mutilated, tortured, beaten, raped, enslaved for sexual purposes, forced to work, and forced to become soldiers by the AFRC/RUF.

In addition to violating the instruments of international humanitarian law cited above, these crimes violate the Convention on the Rights of the Child, which makes explicit children's right to life and freedom from sexual abuse, abduction and forced recruitment, among other rights.

Examples of these types of violations were frequent. Sam R., a farmer in the Koidu area, saw six of his children and his wife attacked in front of his house ... He recalled:

> They accused me of being a Kamajor. When they want to kill you, they accuse you of anything. There is no reason. I am a farmer. I don't vote. I have no money. They burnt my house.
>
> At about 4:00 a.m., I heard bombs and gunshots outside my house. The rebels came and banged on the door. They said they would kill us all outside. My wife took five of the children outside. I stayed inside with one. My wife threw herself on top of two of the children to protect them. They shot my wife, killed two of the children, shot my seven-year-old through the stomach, and cut another one on the buttocks. Two got away.

Human Rights Watch received documentation on dozens of similar cases. According to medical records, out of 265 war wounded patients admitted to Connaught hospital from April 1 though June 20, approximately one-quarter were children. According to reports from humanitarian agencies, 111 children died between February 15 and 24, 1998 during AFRC/RUF attacks in the Bo area.

Gender-based Violence

Women and girls are the primary targets of widespread rape, sexual slavery, and other forms of sexual violence. Although the exact number of those raped will never be known, testimonies from survivors confirm that sexual violence has been widespread, against thousands of women and girls. Furthermore, no comprehensive medical statistics have been compiled on rape-related injuries or on pregnancies as a result of rape. Those who have witnessed, or endured and survived these and other atrocities are suffering enormous psychological trauma.

Women and girls are brutally raped and gang-raped at gunpoint and knife point by AFRC/RUF soldiers or raped with objects, such as sticks. Often, the rapes occur in front of family members and others, and in some cases relatives are forced to rape their sisters, mothers or daughters. Women and girls are frequently abducted individually or collectively and kept as so-called "wives" for members of the AFRC/RUF. Some suffer rape or gang rape multiple times as they escape one AFRC/RUF group, only to be caught by another. Rape is also used as an immediate punishment for refusing to follow instructions or in retaliation for the acts of others held in captivity.

. . . .

The crimes of sexual violence committed by the AFRC/RUF against women and girls are often accompanied by other forms of violence. Murder or mutilation frequently follows these rapes. Many are forced to work as porters for the AFRC/RUF and witness their children being abducted, abused, or killed. Some women and young girls are abducted to care for the many young children captured by the AFRC/RUF.

Pregnant women are not spared from attacks by the AFRC/RUF. In light of the gruesome nature of the atrocities committed against them, these women seem to be targeted because of their status as pregnant women. Witnesses report having seen the mutilated bodies of pregnant women whose fetuses had been cut out of their wombs or who died of gunshot wounds to the abdomen. Some pregnant women are also forced into labor due to the extreme physical hardship of having to flee their homes, and at times die in flight due to complications in childbirth.

The AFRC/RUF's rape and enslavement of women and girls for sex is not only a vicious expression of power over the individual, but also a means of expressing dominance over the community. Throughout the world, sexual violence is routinely directed against women and girls during situations of armed conflict as a weapon to terrorize a community and to achieve a political end. The humiliation, terror and pain inflicted by the rapist is meant to harm not only the individual victim but also to strip the humanity from the larger group of which she is a part. The rape of one person can be translated into an assault upon the community through the emphasis placed in every culture on women's sexual virtue; the shame of the rape humiliates the family and all those associated with the survivor.

. . . .

Forced Recruitment

The AFRC/RUF is using and forcibly recruiting children and young men to engage in armed attacks against Sierra Leone civilians, Civilian Defense Forces, and ECOMOG soldiers. Many witnesses told Human Rights Watch that they had seen AFRC/RUF soldiers abducting and holding young men and boys to use as child soldiers and that child soldiers had been among their AFRC/RUF attackers.

The forced recruitment of boys as child soldiers by the AFRC/RUF in Sierra Leone is not new. As armed conflict in Sierra Leone has intensified in recent years, the social fabric of the country has unraveled, and children have increasingly seen their rights erode. Many children have lost or been separated from their parents in the fighting, do not have enough to eat and do not have schools and other basic structures in place to meet their needs. They are particularly vulnerable to forced recruitment and have clearly been targeted by the AFRC/RUF as it seeks to reinforce its ranks.

Young boys are targeted in part because their captors consider them to be less afraid to fight; they likely do not have children or wives to consider in risking their lives. They are readily manipulated because they are vulnerable and without protection. Child soldiers are often placed at the front line and forced to commit atrocities against their own communities. This establishes a sense of culpability in them, as well as traumatization, and makes it less possible for them to be accepted back into society or to be psychologically prepared to return.

Little is known about the condition of the young men and children abducted since February by the AFRC/RUF for use as soldiers; few have escaped to tell the story. Over the past few years, however, child recruits were typically provided with food, mind-altering drugs and firearms and were forced to fight and commit atrocities alongside the AFRC/RUF soldiers. The demobilization, rehabilitation and reintegration of these children will ultimately present an enormous challenge to all those involved in healing the wounds of war and building a future for Sierra Leone.

. . . .

Abuses Committed By Members of Civilian Defense Forces (CDFs)

. . . .

The largest and most powerful of these groups, the Kamajors, were responsible for the majority of the most serious abuses committed by those fighting on behalf of the Kabbah government since February 1998. In recent months, Kamajors have also been responsible for obstructing humanitarian assistance and demanding money or compensation at roadblocks.

Humanitarian and United Nations organizations complain that Kamajors frequently obstruct the delivery of aid to IDPs and civilian groups in need. Humanitarian agency vehicles were frequently commandeered by Kamajors, and aid workers were occasionally detained by Kamajors, two as recently as June 1998. Groups providing assistance to the interior of Sierra Leone reported in June that the Kamajors had become increasingly demanding at checkpoints, often insisting that they be compensated for having "liberated" the country from the AFRC/RUF.

Killings and Mutilation

The scale and nature of abuses committed by Kamajors and other members of CDFs differ significantly from atrocities carried out by the AFRC/RUF, but the abuses are often no less horrific. Many witnesses of abuses committed by Kamajors spoke of the grotesque nature of killings, at times including disembowelment followed by consumption of vital organs, such as the heart. Acts such as these were intended to transfer the strength of the enemy to those involved in the consumption. Killings by Kamajors usually targeted people they believed to be members of the AFRC/RUF and their civilian supporters.

. . . .

Recruitment of Child Soldiers

CDFs, especially the Kamajors, have contributed to one of the most urgent human rights problems involving children in Sierra Leone: the recruitment of child soldiers. Children have been recruited by the CDFs for many of the same reasons that the AFRC/RUF abduct them into their ranks: children are often easily indoctrinated, fearless, have little sense of what is morally right or wrong, and, according to Kamajor leaders, are more likely to be "unadulterated." While no one knows the number of children fighting among the CDF forces, one field commander estimated that their forces in the eastern Kailahun district alone numbered 3,000.

The situation for child combatants provoked a mission to Sierra Leone from Special Representative of the Secretary-General for Children in Armed Conflict Olara Otunnu. Otunnu urged that "the international community make Sierra Leone a pilot project for a more concerted and effective response to the needs of children affected by war." During his visit, Otunnu obtained commitments from the government to assure that the CDFs would cease recruitment of children under the age of eighteen, begin demobilization of child soldiers, provide special protection to child combatants, and create a Joint Task Force comprising representatives from the government, ECOMOG, U.N. agencies, and relevant NGOs. On June 25, in an interview with Human Rights Watch, the Deputy Minister of Defense, Hinga Norman, also declared that the government was committed to demobilizing CDF child combatants. In mid-July, however, aid agencies and press reports concurred that the CDFs were still recruiting children in northern Sierra Leone.

National and international human rights and humanitarian workers in Sierra Leone expressed their concern to Human Rights Watch that Civilian Defense Forces, such as the Kamajors and loosely organized bands of youths, represent a serious and growing human rights issue in Sierra Leone today. Like the AFRC/RUF, these groups are able to act largely with impunity. This trend, when considered in the context of past practices of armed groups in Sierra Leone, underscores the need to develop a comprehensive program to disarm, demobilize and reintegrate all combatants into the new national army or Sierra Leonean society.

. . . .

————————

Children are affected by armed conflict in many ways that go beyond recruitment into armed forces. Recall that the original Machel Report also addressed the issue of armed conflict and child refugees. These displaced children are especially vulnerable to violence and sexual exploitation; the Human Rights Watch report below describes the living conditions of Sierra Leonean children who lived in refugee camps in Guinea.

Human Rights Watch, *Forgotten Children of War: Sierra Leonean Refugee Children in Guinea*

(1999), *available at* http://www.hrw.org/reports/1999/guinea/

I. Summary

Sierra Leonean refugee children in Guinea are among the most vulnerable children in the world. They have lived through an extremely brutal war—most have witnessed or suffered unspeakable atrocities including widespread killing, mutilation, and sexual abuse. The human rights abuses that drove these children into flight are only the first chapter of hardship for many Sierra Leoneans affected by the crisis. Even after traveling across an international border to seek refuge in Guinea, they remain vulnerable to hazardous labor exploitation, physical abuse, denial of education, sexual violence and exploitation, cross-border attacks, militarization of refugee camps, and recruitment as child soldiers.

Guinea is host to one of the largest refugee populations in the world, including more than 300,000 Sierra Leoneans, up to 65 percent of whom are estimated to be under age eighteen. Most of these children have been in Guinea since early 1998, when Revolutionary United Front (RUF) rebels embarked upon a massive reign of terror after being ousted from power in Sierra Leone. Those who arrived in 1998 have largely settled in the more than sixty camps in the Gueckedou area of southeastern Guinea, which forms a peninsula-like territory stretching into eastern Sierra Leone. Their situation is characterized by the United Nations High Commissioner for Refugees (UNHCR) as one of "care and maintenance" (i.e. normal operations), following the initial "emergency" phase from February to December 1998 when refugees poured into Guinea, sometimes at a rate of thousands per day.... Until true peace, security, and respect for human rights can be guaranteed in Sierra Leone, the refugee children are likely to remain at great risk in the refugee camps.

Children in all the refugee camps may face serious protection concerns at the hands of their caregivers including physical abuse, sexual abuse and exploitation, denial of food, hazardous labor exploitation, and denial of education. These concerns are particularly acute for children who have become separated from their parents during the war, commonly referred to as "separated children" and "unaccompanied minors," most of whom have been taken in by families whom one child described as "forced caretakers." ... Some of these caregivers say that it is common practice for families to accept children in need into their homes. However, many cautioned that they should not be expected to treat these children as well as they treat their own.

While it is a positive development that these children are being cared for by families rather than in institutions, it is essential that their treatment be monitored. Through implementing partners, UNHCR has established a network of refugee social workers, which is supplemented by UNHCR protection and community services officers, for this purpose. However, social workers interviewed by Human Rights Watch were frequently shocked to learn that the separated children they were responsible for had suffered abuse. In fact, social workers have not even identified or registered the majority of separated children in the camps and, consequently, cannot be expected to monitor their care or intervene on the children's behalf. While these social workers are well-meaning, they lack training in international standards and UNHCR guidelines on refugee children, and how to identify and address child abuse and exploitation....

In addition, Human Rights Watch documented sexual violence against girls in the camps, a problem that remains largely unaddressed. Neither UNHCR nor the Guinean government had made sufficient efforts to determine the scale of, prevent, or respond to incidents of sexual violence in the camps. Guinean authorities are not known to have brought any prosecutions for crimes of sexual violence against refugees before the Guinean courts....

Human Rights Watch also identified a serious problem of child prostitution in the camps, where girls as young as twelve said that they feel compelled to "play sex for money" in order to support themselves and, in some cases, their families. As with the problem of sexual violence, very little has been done by UNHCR to understand the problem of child prostitution in the camps in Guinea or to prevent it. In addition, little has been done to protect the human rights of girls forced into the practice, including their rights to education and reproductive health care.

. . . .

Human Rights Watch also documented the presence of combatants in refugee camps, with large numbers of child soldiers in their ranks. The Kamajors, a Sierra Leonean government civil defense force, maintain a presence in at least two refugee camps, which they have used as a base for military activities. The presence of combatants with children in their ranks in the camps violates international standards mandating the civilian character of refugee camps and prohibiting the use of child soldiers. It is not clear whether armed groups have actively recruited children from the refugee camps. However, the potential for large-scale recruitment of child soldiers, depending on the turn of events in the

Sierra Leonean civil war, has been real and was acknowledged to Human Rights Watch by a Kamajor commander.

Many of these protection concerns, particularly the various forms of hazardous labor exploitation, are directly linked to a lack of food security. Refugees and assistance workers in several camps told Human Rights Watch that they had not received food distributions for up to three months; that the distributions they received were inadequate; that some refugees were not able to register and, consequently, to receive any distributions; and that assistance did not always reach separated children and other vulnerable refugees....

One alarming result of this is that many refugees, primarily those in camps close to the border, feel compelled to cross into nearby Sierra Leone in search of food to feed themselves and their families. Despite the obvious safety risks involved, caregivers frequently have frequently sent adolescents across the border to forage for food. Human Rights Watch interviewed one seventeen-year-old boy who was abducted by RUF rebels while searching for food in Sierra Leone. Several other children told Human Rights Watch that they encountered rebel soldiers, but managed to escape back to Guinea.

Despite the facts that these children have suffered enormously and that they remain extremely vulnerable, their plight has largely been ignored by the international community. UNHCR, the primary actor responsible for the assistance and protection of refugee children, has developed extensive policies and guidelines over the past several years aimed at ensuring respect for the rights of refugee children facing these difficulties. Nevertheless, there remain significant shortcomings in the implementation of these policies in refugee camps in Guinea.

....

[T]he failure to adequately protect the rights of refugee children can only partially be attributed to a lack of resources. The international community has failed to identify vulnerable children; to monitor children for abuse and exploitation; to protect girls from sexual abuse and exploitation; to move the refugees to safe locations away from the border; to preserve the humanitarian character of the refugee camps; and to prevent refugee children from serving as child soldiers.

....

Notes and Questions

1. The fighting in Sierra Leone was officially declared over in 2002, leaving behind a civilian population marked by the civil war's trademark amputations. Direct attacks against children appear to have played a significant role in terrorizing the civilian population, in order to facilitate the insurgency's plans. As in other conflicts of this kind, many of the atrocities were carried out by children against children. In terms of its main characteristics, how does the Sierra Leonean civil war compare with the Ugandan conflict? From a child protection point of view, what lessons ought the international community learn from these conflicts? As you read the material below on the legal response to the Sierra Leonean conflict, consider why the international community places so much emphasis on war crimes prosecutions of particular individuals in the wake of such devastating events. Is this attention appropriate, or inordinately weighted in favor of legal process removed from the roots of the conflict itself?

2. *Legal Response to the Conflict in Sierra Leone*

As in Uganda, the people of Sierra Leone have pursued the dual, and often conflicting, objectives of national reconciliation and post conflict justice in the form of war crimes prosecutions. The main players in the Sierra Leonean conflict have been put on trial through the establishment of a unique hybrid court, created through an agreement between the United Nations and the government of Sierra Leone. It is seated in Freetown, Sierra Leone. (The high profile Charles Taylor trial, however, has been moved to The Hague, to allow the Court to avail of the facilities of the International Criminal Court.) In 2000, the UN Security Council called on the General Assembly to move forward with the creation of the Special Court for Sierra Leone, in order that there could be a "credible system of justice and accountability" that would strike a balance between the truly international court concept and the often inadequate national courts.

As the readings below will demonstrate, the relationship between the Sierra Leonean Truth and Reconciliation Commission and the Special Court has been a difficult one. As in Uganda, the general population tends to be understandably more interested in the reestablishment of peace than with the naming of war criminals.

S.C. Res. 1315, U.N. Doc. S/RES/1315

(Aug. 14, 2000), *available at* http://daccessdds.un.org/doc/
UNDOC/GEN/N00/605/32/PDF/N0060532.pdf?OpenElement

The Security Council:

Deeply concerned at the very serious crimes committed within the territory of Sierra Leone against the people of Sierra Leone ... and at the prevailing situation of impunity,

. . . .

Noting also the steps taken by the Government of Sierra Leone in creating a national truth and reconciliation process, as required by Article XXVI of the Lomé Peace Agreement (S/ 1999/ 777) to contribute to the promotion of the rule of law,

Recalling that the Special Representative of the Secretary-General appended to his signature of the Lomé Agreement a statement that the United Nations holds the understanding that the amnesty provisions of the Agreement shall not apply to international crimes of genocide, crimes against humanity, war crimes and other serious violations of international humanitarian law,

Reaffirming the importance of compliance with international humanitarian law, and *reaffirming further* that persons who commit or authorize serious violations of international humanitarian law are individually responsible and accountable for those violations and that the international community will exert every effort to bring those responsible to justice in accordance with international standards of justice, fairness and due process of law,

Recognizing that, in the particular circumstances of Sierra Leone, a credible system of justice and accountability for the very serious crimes committed there would end impunity and would contribute to the process of national reconciliation and to the restoration and maintenance of peace,

Taking note in this regard of the letter dated 12 June 2000 from the President of Sierra Leone to the Secretary-General ...

Recognizing further the desire of the Government of Sierra Leone for assistance from the United Nations in establishing a strong and credible court.

. . . .

1. *Requests* the Secretary-General to negotiate an agreement with the Government of Sierra Leone to create an independent special court consistent with this resolution, and expresses its readiness to take further steps expeditiously upon receiving and reviewing the report of the Secretary-General referred to in paragraph 6 below;

2. *Recommends* that the subject matter jurisdiction of the special court should include notably crimes against humanity, war crimes and other serious violations of international humanitarian law, as well as crimes under relevant Sierra Leonean law committed within the territory of Sierra Leone;

3. *Recommends further* that the special court should have personal jurisdiction over persons who bear the greatest responsibility for the commission of the crimes referred to in paragraph 2, including those leaders who, in committing such crimes, have threatened the establishment of and implementation of the peace process in Sierra Leone;

. . . .

6. *Requests* the Secretary-General to submit a report to the Security Council on the implementation of this resolution, in particular on his consultations and negotiations with the Government of Sierra Leone concerning the establishment of the special court, including recommendations, no later than 30 days from the date of this resolution;

7. *Requests* the Secretary-General to address in his report the questions of the temporal jurisdiction of the special court, an appeals process including the advisability, feasibility, and appropriateness of an appeals chamber in the special court or of sharing the Appeals Chamber of the International Criminal Tribunals for the Former Yugoslavia and Rwanda or other effective options, and a possible alternative host State, should it be necessary to convene the special court outside the seat of the court in Sierra Leone, if circumstances so require;

8. *Requests* the Secretary-General to include recommendations on the following:

(a) any additional agreements that may be required for the provision of the international assistance which will be necessary for the establishment and

functioning of the special court;

(b) the level of participation, support and technical assistance of qualified persons from Member States of the United Nations, including in particular, member States of ECOWAS and the Commonwealth, and from the United Nations Mission in Sierra Leone that will be necessary for the efficient, independent and impartial functioning of the special court;

(c) the amount of voluntary contributions, as appropriate, of funds, equipment and services to the special court, including through the offer of expert personnel that may be needed from States, intergovernmental organizations and non-governmental organizations;

(d) whether the special court could receive, as necessary and feasible, expertise and advice from the International Criminal Tribunals for the Former Yugoslavia and Rwanda;

. . . .

The following articles are taken from the Statute of the Special Court for Sierra Leone. The stated objective of the Court was to try the major players in the conflict, those with the greatest responsibility for committing the outrages listed in the statute.

Statute of the Special Court for Sierra Leone

Jan. 16, 2002, 2178 U.N.T.S. 145, *available at*
http://www.sc-sl.org/LinkClick.aspx?fileticket=uClnd1MJeEw%3d&tabid=176

Article 2: Crimes against humanity

The Special Court shall have the power to prosecute persons who committed the following crimes as part of a widespread or systematic attack against any civilian population:

a. Murder;

b. Extermination;

c. Enslavement;

d. Deportation;

e. Imprisonment;

f. Torture;

g. Rape, sexual slavery, enforced prostitution, forced pregnancy and any other form of sexual violence;

h. Persecution on political, racial, ethnic or religious grounds;

i. Other inhumane acts.

Article 3: Violations of Article 3 common to the Geneva Conventions and of Additional Protocol II

The Special Court shall have the power to prosecute persons who committed or ordered the commission of serious violations of article 3 common to the Geneva Conventions of 12 August 1949 for the Protection of War Victims, and of Additional Protocol II thereto of 8 June 1977. These violations shall include:

a. Violence to life, health and physical or mental well-being of persons, in particular murder as well as cruel treatment such as torture, mutilation or any form of corporal punishment;

b. Collective punishments;

c. Taking of hostages;

d. Acts of terrorism;

e. Outrages upon personal dignity, in particular humiliating and degrading treatment, rape, enforced prostitution and any form of indecent assault;

f. Pillage;

g. The passing of sentences and the carrying out of executions without previous judgement pronounced by a regularly constituted court, affording all the judicial guarantees which are recognized as indispensable by civilized peoples;

h. Threats to commit any of the foregoing acts.

Article 4: Other serious violations of international humanitarian law

The Special Court shall have the power to prosecute persons who committed the following serious violations of international humanitarian law:

a. Intentionally directing attacks against the civilian population as such or against individual civilians not taking direct part in hostilities;

b. Intentionally directing attacks against personnel, installations, material, units or vehicles involved in a humanitarian assistance or peacekeeping mission in accordance with the Charter of the United Nations, as long as they are entitled to the protection given to civilians or civilian objects under the international law of armed conflict;

c. Conscripting or enlisting children under the age of 15 years into armed forces or groups or using them to participate actively in hostilities.

Selections from an article by Stephanie Bald highlight some of the potential weaknesses of the "hybrid" court form chosen by the government of Sierra Leone for prosecution of civil war criminals. On balance, do the strengths of the Special Court—its proximity to the people of Sierra Leone and its stated role in helping to develop a strong national system of justice, outweigh its defects?

Stephanie Bald, *Searching for a Lost Childhood: Will the Special Court of Sierra Leone Find Justice for Its Children?*
18 American University International Law Review 537 (2002)

....

II. Analysis

The novel structure of the Special Court of Sierra Leone is a direct response to the successes and failures of previous tribunals such as the International Criminal Tribunal of Yugoslavia ("I.C.T.Y.") and the International Criminal Tribunal of Rwanda ("I.C.T.R."). As a result, the creation of the Special Court represents an innovative attempt by the United Nations to establish a more efficient and effective international criminal tribunal.

While the United Nations was criticized for situating the I.C.T.R. and I.C.T.Y. outside of Rwanda and Yugoslavia, the Special Court will sit in Freetown, the capital of Sierra Leone.

Because one objective of the Special Court is to help Sierra Leone rebuild a strong national judicial system, the Court's establishment in Sierra Leone is critical to its success. Since the judicial process will be both visible and accessible to the people of Sierra Leone, the Special Court will have the potential to send the important message that "international and domestic trials are complementary parts of an integrated, holistic, and multifaceted approach to justice."

Notwithstanding the benefits of the Special Court's location, many structural and procedural inadequacies of the Special Court are likely to hinder the Court's efforts to bring those responsible for the recruitment of child soldiers to justice. Limitations on the Special Court's jurisdiction, the United Nations' decision not to grant the Special Court Chapter VII powers, the amnesty provision of the Lomé Peace Agreement, and substantial funding restraints will most likely present significant obstacles to holding accountable all persons responsible for the recruitment of children into armed conflict in Sierra Leone.

A. Temporal and Personal Jurisdiction

Limitations placed on the Special Court's jurisdiction are likely to prove prohibitive in prosecuting persons responsible for the recruitment of child soldiers....

The Court's personal jurisdiction, which extends only to those individuals who bear the greatest responsibility for serious violations of international humanitarian law and Sierra Leonean law committed in the territory of Sierra Leone since November 30, 1996, will further limit the Court's prosecutorial potential. By restricting personal jurisdiction to those who bear the greatest responsibility, the Special Court will not bring to justice all persons responsible for the recruitment of child soldiers. While the United Nations recommended that jurisdiction be extended to "persons most responsible" so that the Special Court would have more prosecutorial power, the original phrasing has not been changed. As a result, the personal jurisdiction of the Special Court will only reach a very small number of the many persons responsible for the atrocities committed in Sierra Leone.

The Statute for the Special Court provides that persons who bear the greatest responsibility include "those leaders who, in committing such crimes, threatened the establishment of and implementation of the peace process in Sierra Leone." In Sierra Leone, not only the highest-ranking leaders were responsible for serious human rights abuses against children. In fact, persons of all ranks in armed groups and militias contributed to the atrocities. Thus, by limiting personal jurisdiction to the most notorious perpetrators, the Special Court for Sierra Leone will never try many of the individuals guilty of violations of international and domestic law. Because the people of Sierra Leone believe that all individuals guilty of crimes during the war should be held accountable, this jurisdictional limitation is likely to undermine the legitimacy and effectiveness of the Special Court.

B. Chapter VII Powers

The United Nations' decision not to grant Chapter VII Security Council powers to the Special Court of Sierra Leone presents another challenge to holding individuals accountable for the recruitment of child soldiers. Chapter VII, Article 48 of the U.N. Charter obligates all member state national courts to comply with Security Council decisions, rather than just the national court of the state in which the international tribunal is operating. Therefore, by establishing the ad-hoc I.C.T.Y. and I.C.T.R. tribunals under Chapter VII, these tribunals enjoyed primacy and concurrent jurisdiction with respect to all national member courts.

In contrast, Sierra Leone Special Court's primacy is limited to the national courts of Sierra Leone because the United Nations did not grant the Special Court of Sierra Leone Chapter VII powers. As a result, other countries are not required to comply with the Special Court's requests for evidence. Crucially, the lack of Chapter VII powers means that other states have no obligation to arrest an accused individual who has fled Sierra Leone seeking safe harbor in another state.

The failure of the United Nations to grant the Special Court Chapter VII powers is likely to substantially inhibit the prosecution of those responsible for the recruitment of child soldiers. Many R.U.F. commanding officers fled Sierra Leone to fight in Liberia, and many more openly express their intention to leave Sierra Leone before the Special Court becomes operational. As a result, without Chapter VII powers, it is likely that many of the leaders most culpable for the systematic recruitment of child soldiers will escape unscathed by Sierra Leone's Special Court.

. . . .

Notes and Questions

1. The Special Court was created with a number of inherent limitations on its freedom to act. On the other hand, was there some benefit to the Court's special "hybrid" structure—neither totally national nor fully international? Does the nature of a tribunal hearing war crimes prosecutions matter when it comes to ultimate acceptance of the criminal approach in post-conflict situations? Is it more likely that a nationally-based court

will find greater favor with a population weary of conflict than a more distant international court?

2. Note that, despite arguments raised to the effect that the recruitment of child soldiers was not an internationally recognized crime in 1996, the Special Court's Appeals Chamber ruled that, in fact, a prohibition against such practices had crystallized into a principle of customary international law by that time. See the news item explaining this below. Also see Elizabeth Blunt, *Child Recruitment 'Was War Crime'*, BBC News, June 1, 2004, *available at* http://news.bbc.co.uk/2/hi/africa/3767041.stm, explaining that the Court's finding paved the way for the "first ever prosecution for child recruitment at an international war crimes tribunal."

Press Release, Special Court for Sierra Leone, Appeals Chamber Rules Recruitment of Child Combatants a Crime under International Law

June 1, 2004, *available at* http://www.sc-sl.org/LinkClick.aspx?
fileticket=9gSfvaPyPUY%3D&tabid=113

The Appeals Chamber of the Special Court for Sierra Leone, in a majority decision, held Monday that the recruitment of child soldiers was a crime throughout the period of the Court's temporal jurisdiction.

The Special Court is mandated to try those deemed to bear the greatest responsibility for atrocities committed in Sierra Leone after 30th November 1996.

Defence Counsel argued on behalf of Sam Hinga Norman, who is currently in the Court's custody in Freetown, that it was not a crime under international law to recruit child soldiers at the time of the acts alleged in the indictment.

The Justices looked at both customary law and international conventions in reaching their conclusion.

In a summary of the decision, the Appeals Chamber stated:

> "Prior to November 1996, the prohibition on child recruitment had crystallized as customary international law, as demonstrated by the widespread recognition and acceptance of the norm prohibiting child recruitment in these international instruments, reiterated in the 1990 African Charter on the Rights and Welfare of the Child."

The Appeals Chamber found that child recruitment was criminalized before it was explicitly set out as an international crime in treaty law and certainly by the time frame relevant to the indictments. "The principle of legality and the principle of specificity are both upheld."

Justice George Gelaga King, in a separate opinion, found that the Defence had failed in its duty to explain what it meant by "at the times relevant to the indictment". For this reason, Justice King felt unable to grant the declaration requested.

In a dissenting opinion, Justice Geoffrey Robertson found that the recruitment of child soldiers was not a crime under international criminal law until July 1998 with the adoption of the Rome Statute that established the International Criminal Court.

The Preliminary Motion was dismissed in accordance with the decision of the majority which means that alleged members of the Civil Defence Forces, whose trial begins in

Freetown on Thursday, will face charges of child recruitment under Article 4(c) of the Court's Statute as set out in the indictments against them.

3. The war crimes trials in the Special Court began in March 2005. Members of the military government were charged with murder, rape, sexual slavery and recruiting child soldiers. *See S. Leone War Crimes Trial Starts*, BBC News, Mar. 7, 2005, *available at* http://news.bbc.co.uk/2/hi/africa/4325763.stm. Special Court judges announced the first verdicts in June 2007. Human Rights Watch hailed them as "the first time that an international court has issued a verdict on child recruitment." *See First S. Leone War Crimes Verdicts*, BBC News, June 20, 2007, available at http://news.bbc.co.uk/2/hi/africa/6221112.stm.

4. Sam Hinga Norman, a member of the Civilian Defense Forces (CDF) fighting on the side of the Sierra Leonean government, was considered by many to be a hero. Though not comparable in brutality, the abuses by the CDF were also considerable. Norman's trial brought the vexed question of the relationship between the Special Court and the national Truth and Reconciliation Commission into sharp focus. There was a tragic failure to coordinate the work of the two bodies, such that valuable testimony that could have aided the TRC was never obtained. For a detailed discussion of this problem, see Michael Nesbitt, *Lessons From the Sam Hinga Norma Decision of the Special Court for Sierra Leone: How Trials and Truth Commissions Can Co-Exist*, 8 German Law Journal 977 (2007). What rules should obtain when criminal defendants could add a great deal to the record being established by a truth and reconciliation process?

————————

At the very least, it would seem that the convictions at the Special Court for recruitment of child soldiers will set an invaluable international precedent. In the brief news item that follows, note the fact that international tribunals look to one another for guidance as the international law relating to children in armed conflict evolves.

Lisa Clifford & Katy Glassborow,
ICC Examines Child Solider Convictions
Institute for War and Peace Reporting, June 22, 2007, *available at* http://iwpr.net/?p=acr&s=f&o=336525&apc_state=henh

The conviction of three Sierra Leonean military leaders this week for conscripting child soldiers will have a major impact on upcoming prosecutions at the International Criminal Court, ICC, say observers interviewed by IWPR.

The guilty verdicts on 11 counts of war crimes and crimes against humanity were the first from the Special Court for Sierra Leone and the first by an international court for the recruitment of children to fight in an armed conflict.

The Special Court's first-ever prosecutor told IWPR that the verdict will be closely examined by the ICC as child soldier recruitment also features heavily in its cases in Uganda and the Democratic Republic of Congo.

"Our colleagues in the ICC have been following our work in West Africa with great interest and have been emboldened by the fact that we've moved forward on child soldiers," said David Crane, who signed the original Special Court indictments and is now a law professor at Syracuse University in New York state.

"It's all part of the jurisprudence that's building up. Each of the tribunals follows the other's precedents, so clearly this [verdict] will have a huge impact.

"This sends an incredible notice to cynical warlords round the world who are using children and abusing children in their armed forces that they can now be prosecuted and convicted for this."

Human rights campaigners agreed that the June 20 verdicts delivered in a Special Court courtroom in Freetown were significant for ICC prosecutors.

"This verdict is a very concrete demonstration of criminal prohibition of the conscription of child soldiers," said Jo Becker, children's rights advocacy director at Human Rights Watch. "These prosecutions are a major step towards bringing justice to hundreds of thousands of children worldwide. And hopefully this will be the first of many."

In Uganda, the ICC has charged four LRA leaders with numerous war crimes, including some relating to child soldier recruitment. In DRC — where more indictments are expected within the next few weeks — militia leader Thomas Lubanga Dyilo faces similar child soldier allegations.

Beck Bukeni Waruzi, director of Ajedi-Ka /Child Soldiers Project, an NGO in eastern DRC, sees the convictions as a victory for African children.

"It is very positive that a court in Africa, for the first time, has touched on the important issue of youth in Africa. In every conflict on the continent, children are involved as both victims and perpetrators," he said.

Alex Tamba Brima, Brima Bazzy Kamara and Santigie Borbor Kanu were also found guilty of crimes including rape, murder, enslavement, pillage and extermination. All three were members of the Armed Forces Revolutionary Council, AFRC, made up primarily of soldiers from the Sierra Leone army.

Prosecutors alleged the AFRC joined with the rebel Revolutionary United Front, RUF, which fought against the government-backed Civil Defence Forces, CDF, wreaking havoc on Sierra Leone during an 11-year civil war that claimed tens of thousands of lives and displaced millions.

Prosecutors told the trial that attacks were carried out against civilians to terrorise and punish those who didn't support the rebel militias. Physical mutilations, including the amputation of hands and feet, were common.

Civilians were routinely abducted while captured women were raped and used as sex slaves or forced labour. Abducted boys and girls were given combat training and used in battle.

....

The Special Court in Freetown is slowly winding down with all trials and appeals due to be completed by the end of 2008.

Its final — and arguably most high profile — case against Liberia's former president Charles Taylor began earlier this month in an ICC courtroom in The Hague.

The ICC is hosting the trial because of fears of unrest if the case is heard in Sierra Leone. Taylor — who prosecutors say supported the RUF rebels — faces 11 counts of war crimes and crimes against humanity including murder, rape and conscripting child soldiers.

....

For Sierra Leone, the impending closure of the Special Court will likely mark the end of prosecutions for crimes committed during the civil war.

The peace deal that ended the war granted amnesty for war crimes and crimes against humanity. A South Africa-style Truth and Reconciliation Commission was held, but

Christopher Hall, senior legal advisor in Amnesty's international justice project, said many of its recommendations have yet to be implemented.

. . . .

Notes and Questions

1. The conflicts in Uganda and Sierra Leone, though hardly identical, have common roots in colonial domination and ethnic rivalry. In both cases, children became central targets, finding themselves brutalized and forced to brutalize others. In the aftermath of these conflicts, characterized by competition for national power and natural resources, both states have struggled with the question of whether to invest more heavily in structures of reconciliation or legal accountability. What is the role of the international community in the post-conflict reality of these states? Does international law have a meaningful role to play?

C. The Case of Colombia

1. Background and Description of the Conflict

Children have been exploited in conflicts all around the world. In Latin America, children have been recruited in large numbers to serve the needs of parties to civil wars arising out of classic left-right ideological conflicts. In states with massive economic disparities and histories of oppression of indigenous communities, rebel movements have found rich soil for the recruitment of juveniles into service. Likewise, right wing paramilitary groups have forced children to engage in violent activities.

As in all conflicts that exploit children as soldiers, the techniques of recruitment in Latin America are based on fear and manipulation. Leftist rebel groups, however, have been able to present participation in their cause as politically attractive, noble, and principled. That being said, once in, these children find it as impossible to escape as was the case in the other conflicts that have been examined in this chapter. The brutal methods of initiation and forced loyalty are very similar to what occurred in the African conflicts, already described. Sexual exploitation and desensitization are inevitably core characteristics of armed conflicts that use large numbers of very young people. In the Human Rights Report on civil war in Colombia, note the nature of the armed group's organization, the ideological gloss put on its activities, and the particular treatment of girls. See Human Rights Watch, *"You'll Learn Not to Cry": Child Combatants in Colombia* (2003), http://www.hrw.org/en/reports/2003/09/18/you-ll-learn-not-cry.

The Colombian civil war drags on, albeit with less ferocity in recent times. Against the backdrop of U.S. involvement in the Colombian 'war on drugs', and indeed the infiltration by drug cartels into Colombian social and political life, the decades-long ideological battle described by Human Rights Watch continues to claim victims. In recent months, the Colombian government has successfully lured leftist rebels away from their insurgent groups by offering economic and educational assistance. This represents a new departure for the Colombian government, after an endless series of punitive responses that have failed to wipe out the leftist rebel movement.

As in the African conflicts already considered, factions struggling for power in Colombia have relied on child soldiers for their compliance with orders and willingness to take risks. In all these conflicts, the exploitation of children seems to be the end product after years of social breakdown and political frustration. All conflicts that rely heavily on child soldiers also have a component of callous targeting of civilians. The Human Rights Watch report notes that "[c]hildren are an especially vulnerable group in Colombia's triangular war between guerrillas, paramilitaries, and government security forces. Their lives and welfare are at risk even if they do not join an armed group. Children and their mothers make up the majority of the Colombian families forcibly displaced by war, and number in the hundreds of thousands. Children face reprisals, the destruction of their homes, and kidnapping. In Colombia's cities, stray bullets from guerrilla-paramilitary street wars and military clean-up operations claim the lives of dozens of children, even as they sit in their homes."

Commentators on Colombia describe a political situation in which the national government has learned the language of international law (norm internalization), while maintaining all the elements that lead, almost inevitably, to conflicts likely to exploit young children. See, for example, Veronica Escobar, *Reclaiming the "Little Bees" and the "Little Bells": Colombia's Failure to Adhere to and Enforce International and Domestic Laws in Preventing Recruitment of Child Soldiers*, 26 Fordham International Law Journal 785 (2003). Escobar writes that

> It is recognized that internal armed conflicts take an enormous toll on a country's ability to protect its citizens and enforce its laws. This has certainly been the case with Colombia. Yet, it must be recognized that a long-standing weak and corrupt government is to blame for Colombian citizens' current predicament — they are prisoners and victims in a conflict they did not create, but where they have suffered the most harm. Colombians face a beleaguered and overwhelmed government who is seemingly unable to assist them. The Colombian government may truly be incapable of controlling the movements and actions of the armed insurgents because of the groups' admitted military and financial strength, but the government does have control when it comes to what is first on its national agendas. Alongside the much publicized peace process and multi-billion U.S. dollar war against narcotics trafficking, the Colombian government should be concerning itself with the welfare and peace of its children.

> In a country where fifty percent of the population lives below the poverty line and lack of access to basic education is common, many Colombian children, especially those in rural areas, struggle to make it through childhood. The armed internal conflict and the resulting forced displacements of people, have only aggravated the already precarious situation by preventing Colombian children from living in stable environments, where education and basic amenities are readily available. While it is noteworthy that the Colombian government has taken steps to protect the rights of its children in national legislation, it must be acknowledged that these are merely first steps.

> Colombia's most significant legal instrument, its Constitution, emphasizes, promotes, and guarantees Colombian children's basic and inalienable rights. In addition, it proclaims that Colombian children will enjoy the rights contained within international treaties ratified by the country. It declares that Colombian children's rights are above those of all other Colombian citizens. Unfortunately, the rights of the "others," Colombian civilians, have been repeatedly violated during the past fifty years of internal armed conflict. The rights of Colombian children have not fared any better, for they have been repeatedly trampled on

and ignored. Colombian children have yet to enjoy the rights set forth in their own Constitution, much less those in international treaties.

Yet, the Colombian government should be credited for signing and ratifying some of the most important international humanitarian law treaties. By ratifying these treaties, Colombia has held itself up to the world as a Nation that will protect the rights of its citizens during armed conflict. Unfortunately, proclaiming to do something and actually following through are two different things—and Colombia is failing in the latter respect.

It has also been pointed out that, as a party to the UNCRC and the Optional Protocol on the involvement of children in armed conflicts, Colombia should provide a far more systemic and generous system for the demobilization of child soldiers. On this point, see the submission of the NGO Vides International to the United Nations Human Rights Council, entitled *Colombia Child Soldiers: Victims not Criminals* (2008), *available at* http://lib.ohchr.org/HRBodies/UPR/Documents/Session3/CO/VI_COL_UPR_S3_2008_Vides International_uprsubmission.pdf.

Notes and Questions

1. The leftist militias in Colombia are especially reliant on strict codes of conduct and rigid decision-making structures. Despite their emphasis on political and military "discipline," how do these groups attempt to justify their use of children and combatants? What role does extreme poverty play in predisposing children in Colombia to recruitment by rebel groups? Is it plausible that parents would consider life in such a group to be "safer" than life in a village for their children, as the Human Rights Watch report suggests? It is of interest that Manuel Marulanda, leader of the FARC, a faction notorious for its reliance on child soldiers, died of a heart attack in 2008, having evaded capture by the Colombian government for many years.[17] For purposes of comparison, also read the Human Rights Watch report on the situation of child soldiers in Burma, now known as Myanmar, *My Gun Was as Tall as Me: Child Soldiers in Burma* (2002), *available at* http://www.hrw.org/reports/2002/burma/ Burma0902.pdf.

In Burma, unlike in other conflicts described above, most of the thousands of child soldiers are forcibly recruited by the official army, though some children are also exploited by the insurgent armies of various ethnic groups. In Burma, because the national army requires large numbers of compliant children to help maintain the power of an extremely repressive government, techniques of recruitment are also different from those used in other conflicts.

The dominant techniques used in Burma are fear, coercion and violence; few of the recruits seem to wish to join the army, most are kept in the army through threats and punishments. Young soldiers assist the Burmese army in its campaign of intimidation against villagers, forcing people around the country to provide free labor to the state. Children separated from their families for any reason are especially vulnerable to sudden "recruitment", a fate no child in Burma seems to wish for, but one few are strong enough to resist.

2. What social legacy is left behind by the wide scale reliance on child soldiers, whether by insurgencies in civil wars, or by the national army? In which situations does it seem

---

17. Simon Romero, *Manuel Marulanda, Top Commander of Colombia's Largest Guerrilla Group, is Dead*, N.Y. TIMES, May 26, 2008, *available at* http://www.nytimes.com/2008/05/26/world/americas/26marulanda.html.

that it would be hardest to eradicate this phenomenon? In which of the armed conflicts described in the readings above would it be easiest to eliminate reliance on children? Why?

3. It is clear from the reports on Uganda, Sierra Leone and Colombia that adults caught up in civil wars invest a great deal of energy in breaking down the will of children, brutalizing them, and forcing them to act according to the needs of the commanders. Apart from the fact that children are said to be more compliant than adults in combat situations, what other motivations might the leaders of rebel groups have in thus exerting ultimate control over children? How could it be that all ideas of nurture and protection can disappear so completely as to lead to prolonged and widespread exploitation of children? How does analysis of the Colombian situation further our understanding of motivations and root causes?

D. Effect of Economic Sanctions on Children

While children who are directly involved in armed conflict as combatants or refugees tend to receive most of the attention, children are also severely impacted by international economic sanctions. Ironically, such sanctions are often seen as a more humane alternative to armed attack, yet over time, sanctions take a huge toll in terms of child nutrition and health care. Graça Machel, in her ground breaking report on children and armed conflict devoted a section of her report to this problem, and urged the international community to consider the needs of child victims of sanctions. Machel's recommendations, if followed, would make it far more difficult for states to impose sanctions against any particular state without first determining what the effects on children would be. She called for "child impact assessments" to be a regular part of the UN sanctions process. This portion of her report is excerpted immediately below.

Graça Machel, *Impact of Armed Conflict on Children*
U.N. Doc. A/51/306 (Aug. 26, 1996), *available at*
http://www.unicef.org/graca/a51-306_en.pdf

E. Sanctions

127. The present report focuses on armed conflict, but a closely-related issue that also has a serious impact on children is the imposition of economic sanctions. In recent years, economic sanctions have been seen as a cheaper, non-violent alternative to warfare. In his follow-up report to "An Agenda for Peace" (A/50/60), the Secretary-General of the United Nations recognized that sanctions raise the ethical question of whether suffering inflicted on vulnerable groups in the target country is a legitimate means of exerting pressure on political leaders. Since 1991, under Article 41, Chapter VII of the Charter of the United Nations, the international community has collectively imposed sanctions on Iraq, the Federal Republic of Yugoslavia (Serbia and Montenegro), the Libyan Arab Jamahiriya and Haiti. In addition, countries can and have employed bilateral sanctions. In the post-cold war era, it seems likely that sanctions will play an increasingly important part in international policy. Governments are reluctant to commit troops and funds to international military intervention and see sanctions as a safer recourse that can be applied at lower cost to the embargoing power. While not necessarily the case, sanctions also appear less deadly than military action for the population of the target country.

1. Humanitarian exemptions

128. In theory, most sanctions regimes exempt critical humanitarian supplies from general embargoes. In practice, sanctions have so far proved blunt instruments. Humanitarian exemptions tend to be ambiguous and are interpreted arbitrarily and inconsistently. They often cause resource shortages; disrupt the distribution of food, pharmaceuticals and sanitation supplies; and reduce the capacity of the public health system to maintain the quality of food, water, air, and medicine. Delays, confusion and the denial of requests to import essential humanitarian goods cause resource shortages. While these effects might seem to be spread evenly across the target populations, they inevitably fall most heavily on the poor. Those with power and influence will usually have ways of acquiring what they need, while the general population struggles to survive with what remains. While adults can endure long periods of hardship and privation, children have much less resistance, and they are less likely to survive persistent shortages. Studies from Cuba, Haiti and Iraq following the imposition of sanctions each showed a rapid rise in the proportion of children who were malnourished. In Haiti after 1991, for example, one study indicated that the price of staple foods increased fivefold and the proportion of malnourished children increased from 5 to 23 per cent.

129. Even when exemptions are permitted, the conditions applied may be unacceptable to the Government in power. Indeed, those Governments and authorities against which sanctions are imposed are rarely personally affected and may be precisely those less responsive to the plight of their people. Iraq since 1990 has experienced the most comprehensive regime ever imposed. In order to mitigate some of the effects on health and nutrition, the Security Council adopted resolution 706 (1991) to permit the use of frozen Iraqi funds to purchase food and medicine, stipulating that these supplies had to be purchased and distributed under the supervision of the United Nations. The Iraqi Government considered these conditions unacceptable and only started to discuss them in 1995. Meanwhile, the situation for children has deteriorated.

Over the past five years, infant mortality is thought to have tripled....

130. In the interests of children, the international community should cease to impose comprehensive economic sanctions without obligatory and enforceable humanitarian exemptions and agreed mechanisms for monitoring the impact of sanctions on children and other vulnerable groups. Any measures taken should be precisely targeted at the vulnerabilities of the political or military leaders whose behaviour the international community wishes to change. These actions could include an arms embargo, the freezing of all corporate and individual overseas assets, the stopping of certain kinds of economic transactions, the suspension of air links and other forms of communication and the isolation of countries from the rest of the world through cultural, academic and economic boycotts.

2. The need for child impact assessments and monitoring

131. Sanctions should be judged against the standards of universal human rights, particularly the Convention on the Rights of the Child. The primary consideration must always be the potential human impact, which should influence the imposition and choice of sanctions, the duration, the legal provisions and the operation of the sanctions regime. Sanctions should not be imposed without advance assessment of the economic and social structure of the target country and the ability of the international community to sustain continuous monitoring.

132. Monitoring systems make it possible to assess the impact of the embargo on health and well-being. At minimum, such assessments should measure changes in access to es-

sential medicines and medical supplies (especially items that may serve both civilian and military purposes such as chlorine for water purification or lab reagents for health screening and testing), water quality and quantity, the nutritional state of children and the infant mortality rate.

133. When targeted sanctions are imposed, humanitarian exemptions should be formulated with clear guidelines. At the same time, in order to help vulnerable groups, the established agencies should formulate appropriate humanitarian assistance programmes. If essential humanitarian goods are denied to the population, the sanctioning powers have a responsibility to assure new sources of supply. When the Security Council imposes sanctions, it should also simultaneously provide resources to neutral, independent bodies to monitor the situation of vulnerable groups. In the event that the position of children deteriorates, the United Nations should assume responsibility for redressing the situation.

134. Since many of the effects of sanctions, particularly the health impact, may only become evident over a period of years, no sanctions regime should be allowed to continue indefinitely. When the Security Council imposes sanctions, it should also clearly define the circumstances under which they should be lifted. If the sanctions fail to produce the desired result within a predetermined period, they should be replaced by other measures.

3. Specific recommendations on sanctions

135. The expert submits the following recommendations on sanctions:

(a) The international community should ensure that whenever sanctions are imposed they provide for humanitarian, child-focused exemptions. The international community should establish effective monitoring mechanisms and child impact assessments. These must be developed with clear application guidelines;

(b) Humanitarian assistance programmes of the United Nations specialized agencies and of NGOs should be exempt from approval by the Security Council Sanctions Committee;

(c) A primary concern when planning a targeted sanctions regime should be to minimize its impact on vulnerable groups, and particularly children. Sanctions or other measures taken by the Security Council should be precisely targeted at the vulnerabilities of those whose behaviour the international community wishes to change;

(d) The Security Council Sanctions Committee should closely monitor the humanitarian impact of sanctions and amend sanctions immediately if they are shown to cause undue suffering to children.

Amy Howlett, in the article excerpted below, describes recent instances of U.S.-imposed economic sanctions, and the way in which these sanctions harmed the well-being of civilians, including children. To what extent would her theory limit freedom of action in the imposition of these sanctions? Is it likely that U.S. policy makers would ever agree to such sweeping humanitarian limitations?

Amy Howlett, *Getting "Smart": Crafting Economic Sanctions That Respect All Human Rights*

Note, 73 Fordham Law Review 1199 (2004)

Introduction

.... The United States has imposed economic sanctions to punish violations of civil and political human rights abroad with increasing frequency in recent years. This increased use has contributed to establishing international human rights norms indicating that the behavior of the sanctioned country—usually violations of civil and political rights—is unacceptable under international law. But where economic sanctions cause severe human suffering, they jeopardize the economic, social, and cultural rights ("ESC rights") of civilians living inside the sanctioned country by, for example, destroying jobs, contributing to poor health conditions, and increasing hunger and poverty. Thus, the same sanctions that are imposed to end human rights violations of a civil and political nature are causing human rights violations of an economic, social, and cultural nature, in the same country.

. . . .

As a solution, the United States should only impose economic sanctions when it can be sure sanctions will not jeopardize ESC rights, through the use of narrowly tailored "smart" sanctions. Sanctions legislation should also be drafted with a nod toward ESC rights by phrasing violations in rights-based language that clearly implicates ESC rights rather than merely citing civil and political violations as impetus for sanctions.

. . . .

I. The Human Rights Idea and International Human Rights Law

. . . .

E. Enforcement of Human Rights Violations Through Economic Sanctions

When an international human right is violated, states and, in some circumstances, individuals have recourse to various domestic, regional, and international forums for enforcement, such as the International Criminal Court and the International Court of Justice. Unfortunately, there are significant barriers to international human rights law enforcement, and overall, the enforcement arm of international human rights law remains underdeveloped and often impotent. In light of these barriers, countries and international bodies have turned to economic sanctions to economically coerce governments to comply with international human rights standards.

Gary Clyde Hufbauer, Jeffrey J. Schott, and Kimberly Ann Elliot, in their comprehensive study of 116 sanctions regimes, define economic sanctions as "the deliberate, government-inspired withdrawal, or threat of withdrawal, of customary trade or financial relations." Withdrawals of trade relations, known as "trade sanctions," encompass embargoes (bans on exports to a target state) and boycotts (bans on imports from a target state). Withdrawals of foreign assistance are accordingly referred to as "financial sanctions," which include measures such as the freezing of government assets, bans on loans from banks and international lending institutions, and visa denials. Economic sanctions also can include bans on foreign investment and denials of foreign aid.

Sanctions literature refers to the primary country or organization imposing sanctions as the "sender," and the country on which sanctions are imposed as the "target." The sender can be one country acting alone (unilateral sanctions), a country acting in concert with several other states (collective sanctions), or an international organization such as the United Nations (multilateral sanctions).

Senders employ sanctions with the assumption that the sanctions will cause severe hardship within the target. Traditionally, sanctions have targeted countries, and thus the expected scenario is that the population-at-large, experiencing severe hardship caused by sanctions, will rise up against its leaders to demand change. In another scenario, the leaders acquiesce to the demands of sanctions out of guilt.

More recently, "smart" sanctions have targeted only the individuals responsible for the reprehensible behavior a sender wishes to punish, such as terrorist groups or specific leaders, instead of entire countries. The assumption here is that the leaders or elite members of society affected by sanctions will demand or make changes to end their own suffering. To achieve these results, "smart" sanctions could involve some form of limited financial sanctions such as visa denials or freezing assets of targeted individuals....

3. Iraq

On August 2, 1990, the United States imposed economic sanctions on Iraq, which included a comprehensive trade ban and a ban on financial relationships with Iraq. The United Nations also imposed economic sanctions on Iraq later that year with U.N. Security Council Resolution 661, calling upon member states to impose trade and financial sanctions against Iraq. The goal of the U.N. sanctions against Iraq was to get Saddam Hussein to withdraw from Kuwait, which Iraq had recently invaded. The U.S. sanctions shared this goal, and in addition, were imposed to "condemn [ ].... gross violations of internationally recognized human rights in Kuwait, including widespread arrests, torture, summary executions, and mass extrajudicial killings." And though not mentioned in either sanctions policy, human rights organizations were concerned at the time with Saddam Hussein's gassing of Kurdish civilians at Halabja where, according to Human Rights Watch, "most likely tens of thousands—of civilians were killed during chemical and conventional bombardments stretching from the spring of 1987 through the fall of 1988."

Despite these brutal acts against the Kurds, Iraq, prior to sanctions, "was a relatively prosperous nation with a sophisticated health and welfare system.... and ample food and water." Eric Hoskins has assessed pre-sanctions Iraq as follows:

> Iraq's investment in its own economic and social development had a visible effect on the living conditions and health status of the civilian population. Iraq's medical facilities and public health system were well developed.... By 1990, nearly all urban dwellers and 72 percent of rural residents had access to clean water, while 93 percent of Iraqis had access to health services.

4. Haiti

In 1991, President George H.W. Bush imposed economic sanctions against Haiti, one of the most impoverished countries in the western hemisphere. The sanctions were aimed at forcing a military coup to step aside and restoring the democratically elected leader, Jean-Bertrand Aristide, to power. In the words of Sarah Zaidi in her assessment of the Haiti sanctions, "[t]he coup unleashed a campaign of terror and repression.... including extrajudicial executions, disappearances, torture, rape, limitations on freedom of association and assembly, and disruption in personal and professional activities."

5. Burma

More recently, in 2003, the United States imposed sanctions on Burma. A host of other countries and organizations have joined the United States by imposing sanctions on Burma in response to Burma's human rights violations:

> Condemnation by U.N. bodies, monitoring, reporting, and widely-publicized awards by international organizations and NGOs, withholding of diplomatic relations, denials of loans and foreign assistance, visa blacklists, domestic litigation, corporate withdrawals and consumer boycotts [have all been imposed on Burma] ...

U.S. legislation authorizing sanctions describes the specific behavior the United States condemns via sanctions. The ruling military regime, the State Peace and Development Council ("SPDC"), failed to honor the results of a free election held in 1990. Then, in 2003, the SPDC "brutally attacked [democracy] supporters.... and arrested democracy.... activists." Further, the SPDC "continues egregious human rights violations" such as torture, conscription of child soldiers, ethnic cleansing against minorities in Burma, and the government-sponsored use of forced and slave labor. The sanctions will not be lifted until, inter alia, "[t]he SPDC has made measurable.... progress toward implementing a democratic Government including.... releasing all political prisoners;.... allowing freedom of speech and the press;.... allowing freedom of association;.... [and] permitting the peaceful exercise of religion."

Like Haiti, but unlike Iraq and South Africa, Burma's economy and public infrastructure on the eve of sanctions were already in ruins. In Burma, wealth was concentrated tightly in the hands of the ruling military regime. The ruling military junta monopolized benefits from foreign trade and investment and spent an inordinate amount of money on its military infrastructure rather than on public programs.

....

II. The Tense Relationship Between International Human Rights Law and Economic Sanctions

....

A. The Effects of Economic Sanctions on Civilians

Scholars have condemned economic sanctions for being inhumane and destructive diplomatic measures that jeopardize human rights in target countries. Daoudi and Dajani, in their book about economic sanctions, provide a harsh critique: "Like cancer, international economic sanctions kill minute cells within the economic structure of the target nation." Geoff Simons has summarized some of the negative effects of economic sanctions on the population-at-large in countries targeted by sanctions:

> [T]o deny a nation the means to purify water or to treat sewage.... encourage[s] the spread of disease.... To deny a nation access to antiseptics, antibiotics and other essential medical supplies.... render[s] disease untreatable.... To deny people adequate electricity for hospitals and factories, to deny people—including pregnant women, babies, infants, the sick, the old—sufficient food and clean water is.... undeniably a gross violation of humanity.

Others have criticized the very rationale behind sanctions as inhumane and contrary to international human rights law. Where the expected scenario is that sanctions will cause severe civilian suffering inspiring either guilt-driven reforms by the target's leaders or the population-at-large to revolt in response, such sanctions are, by definition, inhumane.

General economic sanctions have been criticized as blunt mechanisms, analogous to blowing up an entire airplane with innocent passengers on board to kill just one terrorist. Richard Haass, in his comprehensive book on U.S. economic sanctions notes: "Political leaders and other elites often are able to shield themselves from the worst effects of broad sanctions, something most of the population is unable to do."

Such criticism has led to the development of "smart" sanctions, which focus on the specific individuals the United States wishes to punish by narrowly tailoring sanctions to affect just these guilty few. However, general economic sanctions are still commonly used by the United States and others....

3. Iraq

Less than a year after initial imposition of sanctions, Iraq had no substantial food stockpiles—meat stockpiles were negligible, feed for chickens was almost exhausted, and cooking oils and vegetables were in short supply. In the years following the Persian Gulf War, the situation deteriorated further. The war completely devastated the country, leaving the people in abject poverty with minimal infrastructure. Then, according to Simons, the sanctions exacerbated the problem. They blocked Iraq from importing much-needed food, a serious impediment as prior to sanctions food imports had accounted for seventy percent of national requirements.

After the Gulf War, international organizations warned of grave humanitarian disasters in Iraq if then-present conditions were left unassuaged. For the duration of the sanctions policy, there were reports of: "malnutrition, diarrhoea [sic] and dehydration among children, [and] sick people being given contaminated drinking water...." Simons reports children drinking contaminated water, making them susceptible to "severe malnutrition, marasmus, gastrointestinal illnesses and other diseases." Despite such warnings and reports, economic sanctions remained firmly in place, which, according to critics, further contributed to the health crisis. The ban on food imports was contributing to malnutrition by blocking the flow of food into the starving country, and the health situation for children was particularly severe. The infant mortality rate tripled in 1991, the mortality rate for children under five nearly quadrupled, and items such as baby food, incubators, and catheters for babies were not allowed into the country.

4. Haiti

The Haiti sanctions have been similarly criticized for "wreaking severe damage" on the country's civilian population. Among other provisions, the sanctions suspended thirty million dollars in U.S. aid to Haiti—money earmarked for public works projects "to build roads, help farmers and improve medical care." The United States did take steps to assuage the situation by maintaining a humanitarian stream of money to nongovernmental organizations in Haiti. Nonetheless, "[t]he U.S. cutoff of direct aid.... coupled with the cancelled loans by multilateral organizations, cost Haiti $150 million, economists say—the equivalent of the annual budget." As a result, prices nearly doubled, unemployment skyrocketed, and the minimum wage fell to three dollars a day in towns and less in rural areas.

Reductions in spending also made food very expensive, reduced the availability of medicine and medical supplies, stopped garbage collection and the maintenance of sewage treatment plants, and decreased the supply of drinking water.

5. Burma

Preliminary reports have indicated negative effects on the civilian population of Burma as a result of the sanctions. The sanctions have already reportedly caused 400,000 layoffs in the textile industry, and reports predict that 100,000 Burmese—mainly women working in the textile industry—stand to lose their jobs as a result of sanctions. Many women who have already lost their jobs in the textile industry have been forced into prostitution. As Nicholas Kristof has pointed out, this will cause many of these women to die from AIDS.

. . . .

III. Economic Sanctions Strengthen Civil and Political Rights but Weaken ESC Rights

. . . .

B. Putting Economic, Social, and Cultural Rights in U.S. Sanctions Policy

It is time for the United States to send a message to the world that civilized nations should not contribute to poverty, hunger, and poor health conditions through economic sanctions. To do so, the United States must take the following course of action: (1) It must only employ narrowly targeted smart sanctions, thus affirming the idea that ESC rights cannot be subjugated to civil and political goals; and (2) The United States must articulate its sanctions policies using ESC-rights language in order to give credence to ESC rights. Such measures will nurture the development of ESC rights into CIL and help garner respect for the notion that countries are obligated to respect these rights both domestically and extraterritorially.

1. Only Impose Smart Sanctions

First, the United States should only impose smart sanctions. Smart sanctions are narrowly tailored to minimize civilian suffering through measures such as visa denials and the freezing of assets. This will prevent or at least minimize violations of ESC rights in target countries. The United States should formalize this foreign policy decision by articulating it clearly in legislation authorizing sanctions. In this way, the United States will contribute to state practice that pays homage to, and consequently strengthens, ESC rights.

. . . .

Notes and Questions

1. Howlett identifies the ironic fact that economic sanctions are generally imposed as a response to human rights violations by the "target" country, but that they tend to result in violations of economic, social and cultural (ESC) rights within the target country. If in fact sanctions are always imposed in order to get a result through the imposition of hardship, should anyone be surprised if sanctions cause suffering among the civilian population? Does Howlett make a compelling case that most economic sanction regimes are in fact violations of important human rights? What if the objective of the sanctions is to prevent greater harm being carried out by the target country? Is it acceptable to take the "long view" and assume that the sanctions will eventually fulfil a good purpose? Or is it impermissible under international law to make civilians pay the price for such a long term goal?

2. Who is to blame for the fact that under the sanctions regime against Iraq, the child mortality rate in that country quadrupled? Is there any mechanism in place to ensure that someone takes responsibility for these outcomes?

───────────

Robin Geiss, *Humanitarian Safeguards in Economic Sanctions Regimes: A Call for Automatic Suspension Clauses, Periodic Monitoring, and Follow-Up Assessment of Long-Term Effects*
18 Harvard Human Rights Journal 167 (2005)

I. Introduction

. . . .

Initially praised as the new method to guarantee effective Security Council action while avoiding the costs and risks of military engagement, it soon became evident that sanctions had a number of unintended side effects, predominantly a devastating impact on the civilian population. Most strikingly, albeit by no means exclusively, these consequences became conspicuously evident in Iraq, after the most severe economic sanctions employed in Security Council history were implemented in response to Iraq's occupation of Kuwait.

Today there is widespread consensus that the comprehensive sanctions regimes of the past amounted to a rather blunt instrument and that future sanctions must be designed more humanely. Building on these experiences, Security Council measures of the type adopted against Afghanistan in 1999 and in response to the diamond trade in Liberia in 2001 have arguably managed to strike a more tolerable balance between the necessary degree of effectiveness and the injuries imposed. Similarly, arms embargoes, albeit often flawed and ineffective, have generally proved selective enough to spare the population grave injury and have not featured an overall impact on the socioeconomic structure of a state similar to that attributed to economic sanctions.

Nevertheless, even with the development of these more recent measures—so-called "smart sanctions".... the humanitarian impact of sanctions regimes demands further consideration given the extent of the current use of sanctions and the potential length of each regime....

. . . .

III. Recent Improvements, Remaining Shortcomings, and Prospective Solutions

. . . .

A. Smart Sanctions: Recent Improvements and Remaining Shortcomings

Since the adoption of Security Council Resolutions 661 and 687, a number of improvements in the design of sanctions, commonly known as "smart sanctions," have been adopted. By contrast to the comprehensive sanctions regime imposed against Iraq in the early 1990s, these smart sanctions regimes take into account humanitarian factors and unintended side effects. They do so either by (1) targeting specific actors and sectors of the economy ab initio, or (2) including humanitarian exemption clauses that make provision for products essential to meeting humanitarian needs. Neither approach has significantly limited the effectiveness of a sanctions regime. To the contrary, practitioners and analysts agree that focused targeting and humanitarian exemption clauses have actually increased the effectiveness of various sanctions regimes. It is thus a misconception that comprehensive sanctions are necessarily the most effective ones.

1. Targeted Sanctions

. . . .

First, directing measures against governments or particular actors will not necessarily protect the population from devastating side effects. Even selective sanctions such as travel bans and financial measures will inevitably have far-ranging effects if imposed over a significant period of time. While targeting sanctions helps to limit their adverse effects from the outset, given the complexity of state economies and welfare systems, even a focused ban on air flights or the supply of petroleum could adversely affect a state's population in troubling ways. This effect is amplified if sanctions are imposed during a time of crisis, caused for example by famine or war. The case of Haiti vividly exemplifies the complex and often unintended effects economic sanctions may have. Despite humanitarian relief clauses contained in the sanctions regime imposed against Haiti, the fuel embargo— in and of itself raising no specific humanitarian concerns—nevertheless led to an increase in transportation costs that in turn caused a dramatic increase in food prices.

Second, while individual or sector-specific sanctions may be effective and humane in some instances, they do not cover the entire spectrum of instances in which sanctions may have to be imposed. Sanctions must be tailored to the particular circumstances and idiosyncrasies of each situation, and some situations still call for more comprehensive sanctions. A targeted sanction, such as an arms embargo, would arguably be adequate if the primary objective of the international community was to decrease the level of violence in an armed conflict. But when sanctions are employed to coerce a change in state behavior, they may have to be more comprehensive. For example, if sanctions become necessary against Iran, it may be that a regime of a more comprehensive kind will be needed. Iran has not responded so far to threats of economic enforcement measures and seems prepared to endure the consequences of a sanctions regime rather than end its nuclear program. In such instances, the Security Council may be left with few alternatives other than to implement a relatively comprehensive, coercive sanctions regime....

2. Humanitarian Exemption Clauses

If more comprehensive sanctions cannot be ruled out, the inclusion of effective humanitarian exemption clauses only increases in importance. Generally speaking, humanitarian exemption clauses exclude certain categories of goods—typically, food and medical supplies—from the sanctions regime....

....

... [H]umanitarian exemption clauses manifest ... general deficiencies. They have been criticized as too marginal and too narrowly focused—i.e., they merely take into account the transactional aspect of welfare delivery, leaving aside other aspects relevant to the limitation of adverse humanitarian consequences. These other relevant considerations include whether there is an adequate infrastructure in place for the distribution of humanitarian supplies. Even if certain goods are provided, lack of transportation or exorbitant prices may render them inaccessible or unaffordable. These deficiencies in humanitarian exemptions are a continuing source of concern and figure prominently in current debates about how to make smart sanctions smarter.

Additional humanitarian concerns in the use of sanctions remain unaddressed. One problem concerns the fact that sanctions are not usually short-term measures. Initially, a target state either changes its behavior in view of a credible threat of sanctions, or, for whatever reason, it prepares to endure the regime rather than alter its policies. Thus, when sanctions are finally implemented, it is likely—as recent sanctions regimes have confirmed—that they will remain in place for a significant period of time, ranging from a few years to more than a decade. Two important implications flow from this.

First, if sanctions regimes are imposed over a significant period of time, they will most likely have a prolonged negative impact on the socioeconomic structure of the target states, arguably severely impeding future attempts at economic development and democratic transition. Nonetheless, not a single Security Council resolution, including Resolution 1483 ending the sanctions regime in Iraq, has provided for follow-up assessment of the aftereffects of sanctions. At present, there is no monitoring nor are there any proposals for monitoring. Perhaps most problematically, there is not even a significant debate over the adverse long-term implications of economic enforcement measures.

Second, it is true that humanitarian exemption clauses can help fine-tune sanctions regimes over time, by permitting the import of medical or food supplies. However, given the deficiencies laid out above, it is unlikely that humanitarian exemption clauses as currently structured will be able to address the more extensive humanitarian needs that arise in times of severe crisis. A natural catastrophe or the commencement of military operations, for example, would likely severely distort the initial proportionality assessment and demand a more profound adjustment of the sanctions regime than the humanitarian exemption clauses could provide. In short, multiple factors unanticipated at the time of implementation can significantly enhance the negative impact of sanctions. Hyperinflation, the cumulative effects of military operations, the collapse of government institutions, a natural disaster, or the targeted state's own behavior can all transform a sanctions regime intended to be moderate into a devastating means of coercion by drastically augmenting its adverse impact. The humanitarian exemption clauses currently employed are simply not up to the task of preventing a dramatic, adverse impact on the population of the target state with any degree of certainty. As such, the consequences of war or a similarly severe crisis (events which, like a natural disaster, can be described as "a public emergency threatening the life of the nation") may render the continued imposition of sanctions disproportionate.

B. Proposals for Structural Improvements in the Design of Sanctions

In light of the remaining shortcomings discussed above, I propose the following improvements to sanctions regimes: (a) include automatic suspension clauses triggered by a humanitarian emergency, (b) implement monitoring mechanisms that will periodically assess the humanitarian situation in the target state, and (c) assess the significant aftereffects of sanctions, which have thus far been overlooked in evaluating the proportionality of sanctions regimes.

1. Automatic Suspension Clauses

....

... [I]n the event of war, famine, natural catastrophe, or state collapse, the Security Council should suspend economic sanctions until it can assess the humanitarian situation on the ground and make adequate provisions to protect the right to life. The most significant problem in designing suspension clauses is how to minimize the procedural obstacles to a decision to suspend in the face of severe and disproportionate infringements of the right to life—without enabling states to suspend for improper reasons. A suspension of sanctions by individual states independent of any U.N. decision could in many cases seriously undermine the effectiveness of a sanctions regime. Individual states might try to legitimate violations of a sanctions regime by claiming, for example, that famine had broken out. Given the idiosyncrasies of decision-making by the Security Council and its subsidiary organs, no solution will be perfect. However, one possible response might be to define the circumstances that trigger suspension in the initial Security Council resolution authorizing the sanctions regime. Then, under article 27(2) of the Charter, the Security Council could characterize the actual decision as to whether the triggering circumstances exist as a procedural one, which only requires majority support in the Security Council or the sanctions committee.

....

2. Periodic Monitoring of the Humanitarian Impact of Sanctions

....

The obligation not to deprive anyone arbitrarily of his or her life.... implicates an obligation to institute mechanisms to monitor the humanitarian impact of sanctions. Without any form of monitoring, the adverse consequences of a sanctions regime will either not come to the attention of the Security Council, or will do so only belatedly. An automatic suspension clause, the triggering of which depends on certain circumstances on the ground, is rendered meaningless if the conditions on the ground are not monitored.

Similarly, sanctions committees need accurate data about the humanitarian situation in a target state in order to make informed decisions regarding whether to grant a humanitarian exemption, or whether to pursue a stricter or more lenient policy with the target state. The meaningful functioning of these humanitarian safeguards depends on a regular assessment of the circumstances on the ground.

. . . .

Notes and Questions

1. Robin Geiss seems skeptical as to whether sanctions regimes can be tweaked in such a way as to ensure consistency with humanitarian objectives. Geiss presents us with a conundrum: namely, whether it is ever permissible to weaken the economic foundations of a state in order to secure some long term political objective, *i.e.*, changing the behavior of the target state. While the lives of all persons living within the target state should be considered, it is particularly disturbing when economic sanctions, normally entered into with great moralistic fanfare, leads to the untimely deaths of young children. Should the norms of international children's rights have something more explicit to say about this problem?

Chapter Seven

Enforcement of Children's Rights through Regional Human Rights Systems

Given the sheer scale and complex nature of the violations of children's rights, it is difficult to be optimistic that effective remedies can be found to parallel the development of international children's rights norms. Embedded as the UNCRC is in historical, economic and cultural realities that pose intractable difficulties, it is understandable that some have seen the Convention as a mythic or symbolic document, one whose terms are, at best, merely aspirational. As a general matter, the human rights system of the United Nations often seems remote from national realities. It would be difficult to prove that the UNCRC's "reporting system" has done a great deal to improve the situation of vulnerable children, despite its intended role in promoting better child welfare policies at the national level. At the margins, such improvements are occasionally discernible, but viewed globally, the overwhelming impression is of continued impunity as children's rights are violated at many levels.

By contrast with the international norms and procedures, regional human rights systems may offer important models for the enforcement of human rights principles against nation states. Neither as remote or mistrusted as the "international human rights system," nor as subject to political pressure as domestic constitutional systems, regional mechanisms have the advantage of being close to home in the cultural sense, but also to a large extent independent of national governments and institutions. Of the world's existing regional systems, the Council of Europe's human rights mechanism, based on the European Convention on Human Rights,[1] and the European Court of Human Rights (ECHR)[2] that enforces it, is by far the best developed. One might not always agree with the conclusions of the ECHR, but as an experiment in meaningful enforcement of regional human rights norms against state governments, the European human rights system is clearly an impressive model. Indeed, there is no comparable example of nation states recognizing, and agreeing to act upon, the human rights-related decisions of an external judicial body.

The Council of Europe, on which the European human rights system is based, is an intergovernmental system dating back to the late 1940s. It has produced Europe-wide agreements on a variety of subjects, but it is in the human rights sphere that it has commanded extraordinary respect and compliance. Each member state of the Council of Eu-

---

1. Convention for the Protection of Human Rights and Fundamental Freedoms, Nov. 4, 1950, E.T.S. No. 5, 213 U.N.T.S. 222, *as amended* by Protocol No. 11, *available at* http://www.echr.coe.int/nr/rdonlyres/d5cc24a7-dc13-4318-b457-5c9014916d7a/0/englishanglais.pdf.
2. Article 19 of the Convention mandated the establishment of the ECHR. *Id.* art. 19.

rope, a more diverse group than that of the European Union,[3] has accepted the need for compliance with the decisions of the European Court of Human Rights (ECHR)—no small achievement in light of the fact that actions brought by citizens in this high profile forum can and do prove embarrassing to national governments. It is a measure of the power of the post-World War II vision of a Europe based on the rule of law that acceptance and compliance are as high as they are. To a lesser extent, as will be explored later in this chapter, the Inter-American human rights system is proving important to the development of a human rights culture in Latin America. Again, this system has the distinct advantage of appearing to be "home grown," yet free of the partisan political divisions that too often beset the interpretation of national constitutions. In addition, Africa is in the process of creating a regional human rights system of its own, with a separate set of human rights norms, as well as its own enforcement mechanism. Finally, the Association of South East Asian Nations (ASEAN) has been engaged in discussions concerning the possible future formation of a regional human rights body as well.[4]

Each of these systems will be explored in turn in the readings that follow, with the greatest attention paid to the European model—not because it is more important than the others, but simply because it is far better developed, and has a sophisticated case law firmly in place. Ironically, given the state of European economic development, the violations of children's rights in the European states may be said to be comparatively less egregious than in other parts of the world. In this sense, when it comes to children's issues, the ECHR at times gives the appearance of dealing not so much with human rights violations as with questions of family law. Nevertheless, the fact that so many European states take the Court's judgments seriously and accept the idea of a regional set of human rights norms is noteworthy. It may be that regional human rights tribunals are the best positioned to apply concepts that derive from international human rights instruments when the international instruments lack a direct link to national political and social realities.

I. The Emerging Role of Regional Human Rights Systems in the Enforcement of Children's Rights

The article excerpted below describes the regional enforcement of international principles as a contemporary "trend" in the enforcement of children's rights. The author,

---

3. The Council of Europe comprises 47 member states. Council of Europe, The Council of Europe's Member States, http://www.coe.int/T/e/com/about_coe/member_states/default.asp. They are: Albania, Andorra, Armenia, Austria, Azerbaijan, Belgium, Bosnia and Herzegovina, Bulgaria, Croatia, Cyprus, Czech Republic, Denmark, Estonia, Finland, France, Georgia, Germany, Greece, Hungary, Iceland, Ireland, Italy, Latvia, Liechtenstein, Lithuania, Luxembourg, Malta, Moldova, Monaco, Montenegro, The Netherlands, Norway, Poland, Portugal, Romania, Russia, San Marino, Serbia, Slovakia, Slovenia, Spain, Sweden, Switzerland, Macedonia, Turkey, Ukraine, and the UK. *Id.* By contrast, the European Union is comprised of 27 member states. The EU at a Glance, European Countries, http://europa.eu/abc/european_countries/index_en.htm. Current EU members include Austria, Belgium, Bulgaria, Cyprus, Czech Republic, Denmark, Estonia, Finland, France, Germany, Greece, Hungary, Ireland, Italy, Latvia, Lithuania, Luxembourg, Malta, The Netherlands, Poland, Portugal, Romania, Slovakia, Slovenia, Spain, Sweden, and the UK. *Id.*

4. *See, e.g.,* Working Group for an ASEAN Human Rights Mechanism, http://www.aseanhrmech.org/.

Berdardine Dohrn, finds common elements in regional human rights tribunals and in those national courts that have been willing to recognize and apply international children's rights norms.

She is particularly enthusiastic about the approach of the ECHR, since it both applies the European Convention on Human Rights and invokes the principles of the UNCRC. Dohrn also notes the "internationalizing" jurisprudence of the Inter-American Court of Human Rights and national courts in South Africa and Canada. While acknowledging the role played by international principles in the *Roper* death penalty case, discussed in Chapter Five, Dohrn suggests that the United States has not demonstrated a comparable willingness to embrace children's rights.

Bernardine Dohrn, *Something's Happening Here: Children and Human Rights Jurisprudence in Two International Courts*
6 Nevada Law Journal 749 (2006)

I. Introduction

Children's rights are undergoing an unprecedented expansion in multiple domains as varied as corporal punishment, deprivation of liberty, rape, participation, juvenile justice, adoption, abduction, street children, child protection, and custody—a case law jurisprudence of human rights barely known within the United States. In particular, two regional human rights courts are cautiously but substantively creating a body of case law developed from the right of individual petition under human rights treaties that is becoming a new "children's common law": the European Court of Human Rights ("ECHR") and the Inter-American Court of Human Rights ("IACHR"). Both enabling treaties are "adult treaties"; they mention children explicitly numerous times, but are focused on the human rights of all persons. Yet a growing cohort of children's rights attorneys, NGOs, and ordinary lawyers are bringing a rainbow of cases involving the children's rights to these two courts.

. . . .

II. The International Human Rights of the Child: Cases from the European Court of Human Rights

Because the ECHR has been functioning for more than five decades, the cases analyzed below do not represent the full range of decisions involving children's rights, particularly in the area of domestic relations, custody, and family law. Here, the discussion will focus on targeted areas of children's rights, noting particularly the ECHR's recent discussions of children's rights in relationship to their role in families. Specific areas include juveniles deprived of their liberty, violence against children (including torture, corporal punishment, and abuse/neglect), and family law as it relates to adoption, abduction, and visiting or contact with parents. Of particular note are the ECHR's growing references to the Convention on the Rights of the Child as interpretive of the European Convention on the Protection of Human Rights and Fundamental Freedoms.

The ECHR may order damages and costs, and enforceability of the court's judgments includes both the obligation to put an end to the violation and to redress its effects, subject to supervision by the European Committee of Ministers.

A. Rights of Children Tried as Adults/Effective Participation and Sentencing

The sensational British child murder case ("the Bulger case") involved the abduction of a two-year-old child from a shopping mall by two children aged ten. The baby, James

Bulger, was bludgeoned to death and left on a railroad track. Appealed to the ECHR, the twin judgments of 1999 are known as *T. v. United Kingdom and V. v. United Kingdom.* The two children were tried as adults in Old Bailey where they were placed in a specially raised dock for their three-week trial. The media covered the trial extensively, and hostile crowds gathered during the transport of the child defendants to and from court, at one time surrounding and rocking the van in which they were placed. In violation of British law, the tabloids published the children's names and photos.

The minimum criminal age of responsibility in England and Wales is ten years, below which no one can be found guilty of a criminal offense. Generally, children under eighteen are tried in the specialist Youth Court, with informal procedures and the exclusion of the general public. The exceptions are those children charged with murder, manslaughter, or an offense punishable by a sentence of fourteen years or more if committed by an adult; those are tried in the (adult criminal) Crown Court before a judge and jury.

The ECHR held that neither the attribution of criminal responsibility nor the (adult) criminal trial of young children, in and of itself, gave rise to a violation of the Convention, under Article 3. However, the ECHR did conclude the requirement of effective participation in the trial mandated that the trial court take full account of the defendants' ages, levels of maturity, and intellectual and emotional capacities, and that steps be taken to promote their ability to understand and participate in the proceedings. In the instant cases, the young defendants suffered traumatic effects during and after the trial; there was no serious argument that the boys were able to follow or participate in the proceedings. The ECHR suggested that appropriate procedures for very young defendants might include informal procedures such as the judges and barristers not wearing wigs or gowns, taking frequent breaks, having a social worker sit with the children to explain the proceedings, and conducting "the hearing in such as way as to reduce as far as possible their feelings of intimidation and inhibition."

. . . .

Subsequent to the *T.* and *V.* judgments, the ECHR again addressed the right of a child to participate effectively in his trial, pursuant to Article 6(1) of the Convention for the Protection of Human Rights and Fundamental Freedoms in the *Case of S.C. v. United Kingdom.* S.C. at the age of eleven was charged with attempted robbery of an eighty-seven-year-old woman who was knocked to the ground in an attempt to take her handbag. His fourteen-year-old co-defendant stayed with the victim. S.C.'s defense was that he acted under duress, being threatened by the fourteen-year-old. He was sentenced to a two-year supervision order and placed with foster parents. One month later, the Youth Court reviewed the defendant's history of delinquency, which included robbery, burglary, theft, and arson, and concluded that he should be tried in the (adult) Crown Court.

S.C.'s defense counsel obtained two expert reports: the first, from an adolescent forensic psychiatrist who spoke to him for twenty minutes before S.C. terminated the interview; and a second by a consultant clinical psychologist. The reports included a full scale IQ of fifty-six, learning delays, impaired reasoning skills, conduct disorder of the unsocialized type, disrupted educational career, cognitive abilities in the range of six years and two months to eight years and two months, rather than his eleven years.

The Crown Court adjusted the hearing based on the child's age. The child was accompanied by a social worker, was not required to sit in the dock, and the court dispensed with wigs and gowns and took frequent breaks. The Crown Court sentenced S.C. to two-and-a-half years' detention. He appealed on the grounds that he had been deprived of a fair trial due to his age and impaired intellectual ability, and gave new testimonial evidence by the social worker who had been with him in Crown Court. The British court dismissed the appeal, noting S.C. had made improvements in behavior and work while incarcerated, which therefore must be in his best interests.

Despite the special protections put in place by the trial judge, the European Court concluded that S.C. was unable to fully comprehend or participate in the trial process and could not adequately give instructions. Although Article 6(3)(c) does not require that a child understand every point of law or evidence, effective participation "presupposes that the accused has a broad understanding of the nature of the trial process and what is at stake for him or her, including the significance of any penalty that may be imposed." Participation must include understanding the general thrust of what is said in court. The defendant should be able to follow what is said by the prosecution witnesses and, if represented, to explain to his own lawyers his version of events, point out any statements with which he disagrees and make them aware of any facts which should be put forward in his defense.

In effect, the court in the *S.C.* judgment retrieves and breathes new life into the decisions in *T.* and *V.* by giving substance to the requirement that children tried in adult proceedings must be able to effectively participate in their trial....

Clearly, this 5–2 decision narrows the ability to try extremely young, incapacitated, or emotionally—or intellectually—challenged children in adult criminal court because such defendants must be able to effectively participate in their trials.

....

B. Violence Against Children

The ECHR addresses a range of cases involving violence against children by state authorities, schools, private parties, and families. A growing jurisprudence articulates the special obligation of the state to protect the young and to take age into account in determining the impact and consequences of violence. Issues of gender and rape are being clarified, and traditional biases degrading girls and women are rejected. The Convention on the Rights of the Child is cited as a basis for interpreting relevant Articles in the European Convention for the Protection of Human Rights and Fundamental Freedoms. Cases range from the torture, disappearance, and police rape of children to corporal punishment in British boarding schools and parental neglect, and articulate the state's clear obligation to provide due process to the parents of children alleged to be in need of removal of parental authority and/or denial of access (visiting).

1. Torture/Rape

In the case of *Aydin v. Turkey*, the ECHR held for the first time that rape by a public official of a person in custody amounts to torture. Aydin, a seventeen-year-old girl, was seized at her home by four security officials, along with her father and sister-in-law, taken to the town square, blindfolded, and transported to the district gendarmerie headquarters. Aydin, who had never traveled outside her village, was separated from her family, taken upstairs to a "torture room", stripped, and put into a car tire and spun. Later, she was again stripped and this time raped in a locked room and beaten for an hour. The gendarmerie released her into the mountains four days later, and she made her way back to her village, where she complained to the public prosecutor of the rape and beatings.

Within a week, authorities sent Aydin to two doctors to establish whether she was a virgin and if there were marks of physical violence or injury; the results were inconclusive. The gendarmerie headquarters denied that she—or anyone—had been in custody but declared that the "investigation" was ongoing. The applicant married and left the jurisdiction, looking for work.

The ECHR concluded that to be raped by an official of the state is an especially grave and abhorrent form of ill-treatment that amounted to torture because it was deliberate inhuman treatment causing very serious and cruel suffering. Based on the hearings and investigations conducted by the Commission, the court concluded that Aydin was held for three days; blindfolded; in a constant state of physical pain, mental anguish, and apprehension; beaten; paraded naked; and pummeled with high-pressure water.

Rape, the court noted, exploits the vulnerability and weakened resistance of the victim, involves the acute pain of forced penetration, and leaves one feeling debased, with deep psychological scars. The judgment, which never refers to Aydin as a child, a girl, or even a female person, concludes for the first time that "having regard to her sex and youth and the circumstances under which she was held," the accumulation of acts of physical and mental violence, and the especially cruel act of rape amounted to torture in breach of Article 3.

Torture recognizes no exception, no derogation, even in the case of a public emergency threatening the life of a nation or any suspicion, however well-founded, that a person may be involved in terrorist or other criminal activities.

. . . .

3. Corporal Punishment

One of the most dynamic areas extending children's human rights is the evolving protection of children from corporal punishment in three domains: criminal corporal punishment by the state, corporal punishment in schools (both public and private), and parental corporal punishment as reasonable chastisement or punishment.

In *Tyrer v. United Kingdom*, the ECHR concluded that judicial corporal punishment for delinquent crimes by an adolescent on the Isle of Man violated Article 3's prohibition of degrading punishment—even though the "strokes" had been reaffirmed in a democratic referendum by the population of the Isle of Man. Tyrer was a fifteen-year-old arrested and convicted after a school fight. The punishment of "birching," which raised welts on his skin, was administered by authorities on his bare buttocks the same day the punishment was announced. The ECHR held that while the punishment did not meet the level of severity that amounted to torture or inhuman punishment, it did violate Article 3's prohibition of degrading punishment. The judgment noted that all of England, Wales, the rest of the U.K., and Europe had abolished corporal punishment of children as a judicial sentence for delinquency.

Thirteen years later, a closely divided ECHR (5–4) upheld the private school "slippering" of a seven-year-old boy for talking in the corridor in *Costello-Roberts v. United Kingdom*. Five years before this case, England had abolished corporal punishment in public (independent) schools by removing the defense of reasonable chastisement for teachers (1987); the brochure of this private school gave parents notice only that the school believed in strict punishment. Although the seven-year-old new student received three "whacks" on his bottom through his shorts with a slipper, it was in the privacy of the headmaster's office and with no evidence of severe or long-lasting effects. *Costello-Roberts* concludes that ill-treatment must attain a minimum level of severity to fall within Article 3 (citing *Tyrer*) and that the determination of a violation is relative, depending upon all the circumstances of case.

Thus, the majority of the ECHR held that this school corporal punishment did not reach the minimum level of severity to violate Article 3, although the ECHR expressed "certain misgivings" about the automatic nature of the punishment for three demerits and the three-day wait before the "whack" was administered.

The dissent pointed out that Europe and U.K. independent schools have progressively outlawed corporal punishment, that the school gave no notice to the mother and sought no consent from parents, and that the three-day delay and the ritualized nature of the corporal punishment were of concern. *Costello-Roberts*, the dissent concluded, was a borderline decision and not to be taken as approval in any way of the retention of corporal punishment as part of the disciplinary regime of a school.

In the case of *A. v. United Kingdom*, just seven years later, the ECHR unanimously held that harsh parental corporal punishment of a nine-year-old boy violated Article 3. Furthermore, by that time the U.K. had abolished corporal punishment in all schools (1998). In this case, A.'s stepfather had previously been reported to the child protection registry (when still a boyfriend of the mother). He was charged with assault for beating A. with a garden cane with considerable force on more than one occasion, but the court acquitted the father based on the parental defense of reasonable chastisement or correction.

The government of the U.K. asked the ECHR not to make a general statement about corporal punishment of children but to limit the judgment to the facts of the *A.* case. The U.K. accepted that the case of *A.* violated Article 3 and stated that its law providing for the parental defense of reasonable chastisement must be amended. Yet the ECHR concluded that the U.K. failed to meet its affirmative obligations under Article 3 by protecting A. and not holding accountable the perpetrator of the assaults.

. . . .

C. Family Law and Children's rights

1. Adoption/Parental Rights

In *Pini v. Romania*, involving the Hague Convention on Protection of Children and Cooperation in Respect of Intercountry Adoption, as well as the European Convention and Romanian law, two Italian families each adopted a girl from Romania. Both children had been abandoned at a young age and were being cared for by a private institution for orphans, the Poiana Soarelui Educational Centre in Brasov ("CEPSB"). The adoptive couples met the girls at the institution when the children were approximately nine years old. The adoption was ordered, appealed by the Romanian Committee for Adoption, but the court rejected the appeal and entered final orders. There followed two years of efforts by the adoptive parents to have the orders enforced, including sending a bailiff to the orphanage door, and filing a criminal complaint against CEPSB, which was not prosecuted.

The children, now aged eleven, filed to have their adoptions revoked, with the Director of the CEPSB as their guardian, arguing that they expressly wished to remain in the family-like environment in which they were growing up and being educated, and that they never met their adoptive parents nor do they speak Italian. Intervenors, including the Baroness Nicholson of Winterbourne, a British national and rapporteur for the European Parliament, provided evidence that the CEPSB was an excellent and family-like institution and that the girls were well and personally cared for. At the same time, the Baroness's report to the European Parliament on Romania's application for membership of the European Union noted that the fate of Romanian children in institutions remained a "major cause for concern and a problem in terms of fundamental rights, with an impact on the accession procedure." The Director of the CEPSB was quoted in the media as saying that it was time "to stop exporting Romanian children."

The ECHR found a violation of Article 8, noting that the Article must be interpreted in light of the Convention on the Rights of the Child and the Hague Convention on Protection of Children and Cooperation in Respect of Intercountry Adoption, as well the European Convention on the Adoption of Children. The ECHR concluded that the final order of adoption and the adoptive parents' reliance established a relationship of family life and that that relationship was violated by the failure of the national authorities to take the necessary steps to implement that right. At the same time, the ECHR recognized the competing interests of the adoptive parents and the adopted children and firmly put the expressed wishes of the children and the children's best interests ahead of formal law. "There are unquestionably no grounds, from the children's perspective, for creating emotional ties against their will between them and people to whom they are not biologically related and whom they view as strangers."

The best interests of the child will override the interests of the parents, and "adoption is a means of providing a child with a family, not a family with a child." Once the children turned ten, their consent was required under Romanian law, and the ECHR held that they are also entitled to have their adoption order revoked once they reach that age. The court deplored the adoption process, the lack of effective contact between the children and adoptive parents before the adoption, and the absence of psychological support to prepare the children for departure. It was remarkably forgiving, however, of the lengthy proceedings and resistance to enforcing the adoption order, and in fact explicitly noted the possibility of a fresh examination of the evidence at a later stage when required. The children's consistent refusal to be adopted after reaching the age of ten carried weight and led to the ECHR's conclusion that there was no violation of Article 8.

Instead, the ECHR concluded that Romania violated Article 6(1) by failing to take effective measures to comply with final, enforceable judicial decisions for more than three years. Noting with regret the "probably irreversible consequences of the passage of time for the potential relationship between the applicants and their adopted daughters," the ECHR concluded that the now thirteen-year-old girls remained strongly opposed to being adopted and moving to Italy.

. . . .

III. The International Human Rights of the Child: Cases from the Inter-American Court of Human Rights

Unsurprisingly, the cases from the IACHR involving children focus more on state violence against children and the failure of the state to protect children than on private party disputes as to custody and access. The IACHR has been hearing cases since 1978, twenty years less than the ECHR. Nonetheless, the IACHR has produced an emerging line of children's rights cases that balance complex interests with a powerful delineation of children's interests and needs.

A. Violence Against Children: Police

The first landmark children's rights case decided by the IACHR is known as the "Bosques case," or the case of *Villangrán Morales v. Guatemala*. The abduction, torture, and murder of five young men (including seventeen-year-old Anstraum Villagrán and two other children ages fifteen and seventeen) who were street children in Las Casetas, a high crime area of Guatemala City, by members of the Fifth National Police Corps in 1990 resulted in total impunity. The accused were acquitted on all charges, and appeals were upheld. The IACHR found that in the years following their deaths, the Guatemalan government never undertook proper investigations or prosecutions. The court unanimously held that Guatemala violated the Rights of the Child (Article 19) as well as Articles 4 (Right to Life), Article 5 (Right to Humane Treatment), Article 7 (Right to Personal Liberty), Article 8 (Right to a Fair Trial), and Article 25 (Right to Judicial Protection). The IACHR ordered reparations to be paid to the families of the murdered children and youth, based on the individual situations of each family.

Three elements stand out in this case about the murder of street children by state agents and the subsequent impunity for the crimes. First, the IACHR engaged in an explicit discussion of the Convention on the Rights of the Child, signed by Guatemala at the time of the Bosques murders but not then ratified. The IACHR used the state obligations specified in the CRC to interpret Article 19 of the ACHR [American Convention on Human Rights] Rights of the Child provision. The Court concluded that the state did not take adequate measures to protect street children, but rather made them outcasts.

This incorporation of the subsequently-ratified CRC into the ACHR provision on the Rights of the Child illustrates the indivisibility of human rights standards in the sense that it begins a process of integrating the provisions of one international human rights treaty with another, in this case using the greater depth of the CRC on matters involving children to interpret and give substance to an article about children in an adult treaty, the ACHR. Perhaps more significantly, *Villangrán Morales* expands enforceable substantive and procedural rights for children, by incorporating the substance of the CRC into the individual right of petition in the ACHR.

Second, the petition was submitted by the parents of the murdered children. The IACHR discussed the suffering and agony of the parents at several points of the ruling and noted the torture of the street children (e.g., burns, eyes gouged out, tongue cut out), the length of time between the abduction and their deaths, and the humiliation and dismissal of the parents and families of the deceased in the investigation, trials, and appeals within the Guatemalan legal system. The principal remedy in *Villagrán Morales* was reparations to the family. At no point did the IACHR consider the limitations of the families or their inability to protect their children during their lifetime.

Third, a noted Central American NGO, Casa Alianza, brought the case and provided the team of attorneys. It took nine years to obtain a measure of justice. Casa Alianza worked to have the members of the police indicted and tried, appealed the cases, brought in expert witnesses, challenged the evidence, and ultimately brought the case to the international human rights system for a ruling at the IACHR. This model of sustained NGO advocacy was required to obtain the (delayed) justice of *Villagrán Morales*.

Similar children's rights cases of abductions, beatings, torture, and murder by police with subsequent impunity at the IACHR have continued and expanded this line of findings of children's human rights abuses.

. . . .

Bulacio v. Argentina involved a youth detained and beaten by police, who then failed to notify the child's parents. Walter David Bulacio was repeatedly hospitalized due to his injuries and eventually died. After ten years of criminal charges against the police captain, the Argentinian courts never reached a decision. A human rights case was filed with the IACHR, and the parties reached a friendly settlement in 2003, limiting the case at the IACHR to the question of reparations to the next of kin. The IACHR held that Argentina violated Articles 4, 5, 7 and 19 (Rights of the Child), as well as Articles 8 and 25, and concluded that Argentina must continue its investigation of the case, enact preventive legislation, and pay reparations and legal fees to the victim and next of kin.

In a subsequent case of "forced disappearance" of a fourteen-year-old boy, kidnapped from his parents' home by members of the Guatemalan Army in 1981, the IACHR declared that Guatemala violated Articles 4, 5, 7, 8, 17 (Rights of the Family), 19 (Rights of the Child) and 25 in the death of Marco Antonio Molina Theissen. The IACHR ordered the state to pay reparations to each family member (mother, deceased father, and three sisters) according to their relationship, and ordered other actions as remedies for past violations.

This line of cases involving state violence against children continued in the case of *Serrano Cruz Sisters v. El Salvador* (2005), where two young girls were forcibly disappeared by soldiers, and their whereabouts remain unknown. The IACHR concluded they could not hear the initial violation by state actors because El Salvador had not yet availed itself of the IACHR's jurisdiction, but it would hear the case on procedural and investigative defects that occurred after the incident when El Salvador had accepted the Court's jurisdiction. The state violated Articles 5, 8 and 25, due to the harm inflicted on the Serrano Cruz sisters and their family by the defective investigation.

B. Violations of the Rights of Children in Detention; Incarceration with Adults and Trial as Adults

In *Minors in Detention v. Honduras*, the Inter-American Commission on Human Rights ("the Commission") took up the unlawful detention of juveniles in adult prison facilities. This case involved the unlawful arrest of street children, orphans, and vagrants who were incarcerated in Tegucigalpa's central prison and held in an adult facility, sometimes with approximately eighty adult prisoners in each cell. The Commission found first, that taken together, the provisions of the American Convention, Article 19 (Rights of the Child), international treaties and rules, and the Honduran Constitution, Article 122(2) require the state to keep juveniles separate from adult inmates. Article 37 of the CRC provides that "... every child deprived of liberty shall be separated from adults unless it is considered in the child's best interest not to do so...." The Honduran Constitution provides that "[n]o juvenile under the age of 18 shall be confined in a jail or a prison."

Further, the Commission concluded that "Honduras has an administrative practice of allowing children of both sexes under the age of eighteen to be deprived of their freedom and confined to penal institutions for adults." A Honduran Supreme Court ruling *en banc* initiated the practice when it adopted the practice as a temporary measure to cope with rising juvenile delinquency and lack of security at juvenile facilities. The Honduran Supreme Court revoked their ruling on November 29, 1995, but the Commission concluded that the general practice of detaining children together with adults had continued after the revocation. Rape, physical assault, and abuse of the detained children had been well documented. Despite Honduras' assertion that the children in adult prisons were being held separately from adults in those prisons, the Commission concluded that

> the practice of incarcerating minors under the age of 18 in adult penal institutions, thus placing their physical, mental and moral health in serious peril, is a violation of Article 19 of the Convention, which stipulates the obligation to provide special protection for children, a non-derogable obligation echoed in the Constitution and laws of Honduras.

The Commission concluded that Article 5(5) taken together with Article 19 prohibits the state from housing detained minors in the same facility as those housing adults. "[M]inors shall be housed separately from adults, in other words, in special juvenile facilities." Citing abuse, beatings, sexual violations, and subhuman conditions, "[t]he Commission considers that the cohabitation of juvenile and adult inmates is a violation of the human dignity of these minors and has led to abuses of the juveniles' personal integrity."

Again, the Commission took note of Article 37 of the CRC, concluding that the Honduran practice of incarcerating children in adult prison facilities violated the duty to provide special protection to children.

In addition, the state of Honduras violated Article 7 of the American Convention by failing to guarantee the non-criminalized children's right to personal liberty and right to be free from arbitrary arrest and imprisonment. In a strongly-worded opinion, the IACHR stated that children who are abandoned, orphaned, or vagrant cannot be incarcerated simply because they are at risk and that incarcerating them constituted a serious violation of human rights. Children may not be "protected" by the state by being deprived of their liberty.

Minors in Detention cites Article 39 of the CRC, the Beijing Rules, the Riyadh Guidelines, and the Havana Rules, as well as Article 37 of the Convention on the Rights of the Child ("[t]he arrest, detention or imprisonment of a child shall ... be used only as a measure of last resort"). In summary, the IACHR identifies a clear tendency in international human rights law to provide greater protection to minors than to adults and to limit the role of punishment. "This is why States are required to afford them greater guarantees in the event of their detention, which should only be an exceptional measure."

Here, as well as in *Villangrán Morales*, decided by the IACHR the same year, the IACHR affirmatively asserted its duty to refer to "other international instruments that contain even more specific rules regarding the protection of children." Citing Article 29 of the American Convention, the IACHR affirmed the use of a "combination of the regional and universal human rights systems for purposes of interpreting the Convention."

Importantly, the Commission held that Honduras violated Article 8(e) of the American Convention by failing to provide the right to a public defender to the incarcerated juveniles if they had not engaged private representation. Again, the Commission read the American Convention in conjunction with Article 37(d) and Article 40 of the CRC.

Finally, the Commission held that one of the principal rules of international law in the matter of children's rights is the prohibition against prosecuting children as adults. Citing Article 5(5) of the American Convention, requiring the state to bring minors "before special tribunals, as speedily as possible, for trial," the Commission held that there is an obligation to create a special jurisdiction "which shall be the only court competent to prosecute minors." The Commission concluded that the Honduran Constitution, Article 122, taken together with Article 19 of the American Convention's obligation to provide special protection for children results in distinct and specialized jurisdiction for juvenile justice.

Five years later, the Inter-American Court of Human Rights found similar human rights violations against Paraguay, where conditions at juvenile detention facilities subjected the children to inadequate conditions. The children's detention system of Paraguay was overpopulated, had poor health care, lacked infrastructure, and had insufficient competent staff. Following fires in the facility that killed twelve students, the state dispersed the remaining children throughout the adult penitentiaries, even those not yet sentenced, and separated them from their families. The IACHR held that the state of Paraguay violated international law and standards, including Articles 2, 4, 5, 8 and 25 of the American Convention, and violated the children's personal integrity and judicial rights, and the Court ordered reparations to the families.

IV. Integration of International Human Rights by National Courts

Harold Koh, now Dean of Yale Law School, has written that the enforceability of international human rights law depends on the establishment of a set of norms, the formalization of those norms into a structure, the legal ratification and acknowledgement of international standards, and most effectively, the integration or absorption of international standards into domestic law.

In that regard, it is worth noting that nations as distinct as South Africa, Canada, and the United States have decided children's rights cases with reference to international human rights law and the cases discussed above. These three examples are a modest selection of such integration or domestication of children's human rights into national law.

Perhaps most remarkably, the new Constitutional Court of South Africa ("Constitutional Court") has issued judgments in a series of children's rights cases involving the right to housing, the right to health care treatment, and the right to be free from judicial corporal punishment. In *State v. Williams*, the Constitutional Court reviewed the long history of the abolition of judicial whipping and beatings throughout the world, reviewed international law and treaties, and then analyzed the new South African Constitution, drawing in large part on human rights standards. The Constitutional Court concluded that children have the right to be free from cruel, inhuman, and degrading punishment and that corporal punishment as a sentence for criminal activities by minors will no longer be constitutional.

In *Canadian Foundation for Children, Youth and the Law v. Canada*, the Canadian Supreme Court took up the issues of both school and parental corporal punishment of children. Under scrutiny was Article 43 of the Criminal Code which provided a defense of reasonable chastisement to assault charges where the parent or person in the position of parental authority used reasonable force as an instructional measure.

The Supreme Court concluded, almost without discussion, that corporal punishment by teachers was not constitutional but created a patchwork of criteria for reasonable chastisement by parents. For example, the Canadian Supreme Court prohibited the hitting of a child under the age of two, disabled children, and children over the age of twelve (since adolescents respond to physical force with anger and violence). The Court similarly forbade hitting a child with an implement or about the head or face. In the course of its analysis, the Canadian Supreme Court noted the trend toward abolishing corporal punishment of children altogether, citing ECHR cases and commentary by the Committee on the Child.

The U.S. Supreme Court in *Roper v. Simmons* engaged in a surprising four-page discussion of international law and human rights standards, the law of other nations, and the law of England and Wales in regard to the execution of juvenile offenders. While not determinative, the U.S. Supreme Court noted international treaties, law, and practice is "instructive" of our own laws and traditions, particularly regarding an interpretation of the Eighth Amendment's prohibition against "cruel and unusual" punishment as indicated by "evolving standards of decency."

V. Conclusions of Common Law Analysis Jurisprudence by Regional Human Rights Courts

The cases discussed in this article are a mere sample of the rich array of case law being developed by international human rights courts in the arena of children's rights. Several remarkable steps have been taken, almost without commentary. First, cases involving children as petitioners, victims and subjects are being brought to the European Court of Human Rights and the Inter-American Court of Human Rights in increasing numbers. Second, the regional treaties that provide the basis for jurisdiction are being interpreted and expanded through the analytical use of other international human rights treaties and laws involving children — treaties for which there is no individual right of petition. Thus courts draw upon the Convention on the Rights of the Child, the Hague Convention on the Protection of Children and Co-operation in Respect of Intercountry Adoption, and the Hague Convention on Child Abduction to give substance and content to the rights of the child to protection, safety, survival, family life, and regard for the dignity of the person embodied in the general language of the regional treaties. Third, age, gender, and developmental competence are being deemed relevant factors in deciding violations of human rights. Fourth, children's right to participation, their right to be heard, and their right to express their opinions are being acknowledged, recognized, and elevated in the courts' analyses. Fifth, the body of jurisprudence is becoming a form of common law, distinguishable on the facts but relied upon both for principles of law and for methodological analysis.

Finally, in the contested zone of parental rights and children's rights, the careful balancing of competing interests is undergoing interesting developments. Both the ECHR and the IACHR recognize the margin of appreciation due to the nation state and its legal traditions and procedures. Both give great weight to the particular rights of family life and parental ties to and interest in their children. It is increasingly noted that states have the obligation to assure that parents must be given a full right to participate in and have access to relevant information and have timely decision-making when their parental interests in recognition, custody, access, enforcement, and decision-making are involved. Parents' interests prevail over state convenience, cost, or frustration.

At the same time, giving meaning to "best interests of the child" is being steadily, if cautiously, approached. Children's best interests trump parents' interests in the balance. Children's ability to participate must be negotiated. Children's wishes must be heard and taken into account, with due regard to their age and development. Children have a right to know and have access to their parents. They have a right to protection against the harshness of adult law, incarceration, institutions, and a right to special protection against violence.

....

Perhaps this somewhat capricious array of human rights decisions by regional human rights courts will provide a spark to encourage children's lawyers in the U.S. to look to developments at the ECHR and the IACHR for standards, concepts, and trajectories that will strengthen the rights of children in families.

Notes and Questions

1. Dohrn, a former student radical and now director of the Children and Family Justice Center at Northwestern University Law School, has become a major voice in the debate over children's rights in the United States. In the article excerpted above, she argues that the regional human rights model has the capacity to guide the development of U.S. law in the area of child rights, while acknowledging that U.S. legal institutions are largely ignoring this model. While full of enthusiasm for what she sees as this evolving phenomenon, does she address any problems or limitations that the regional approach might present? What might those problems be?

II. The Enforcement of Human Rights in Europe

We have already seen that the European Court of Human Rights plays a major part in determining the scope of children and family rights in the Council of Europe states. The readings that follow place the ECHR and the European Convention on Human Rights in a larger "rule of law" context in Europe. The European Union, comprised of a smaller number of states than the Council of Europe, and supranational as opposed to intergovernmental, nevertheless has had a major role in creating an atmosphere of orderly adherence to transcendent principles of law and a common European legal tradition. The Dinah Shelton article, excerpted below, explains the larger structures by which human rights law is applied and enforced in Europe as a whole.

A. Overview of the European Human Rights System

Dinah Shelton, *The Boundaries of Human Rights Jurisdiction in Europe*

13 Duke Journal of Comparative and International Law 95 (Winter 2003)

Over the past half-century, complex systems of norms, institutions and procedures have regionalized many aspects of human rights law in Europe. The Contracting Parties to the European Convention on Human Rights, for example, have repeatedly lengthened the list of guaranteed rights and expanded individual access to the European Court of Human Rights. The result ... is that "there is no aspect of national affairs which can be said to be without implications for one or other of the rights protected by the Convention, [and consequently] there is no matter of domestic law and policy which may not eventually reach the European Court." Those issues that might escape jurisdiction of the ECHR may still be scrutinized if they fall within the jurisdiction of the European Union's Court of Justice (ECJ) or the mandate of the bodies and procedures established in the framework of the Organization for Security and Cooperation in Europe (OSCE).

The strengthening and proliferation of European regional bodies monitoring the human rights performance of their Member States raise fundamental issues of governance. While the need for regional human rights protection is unquestioned in Europe, views diverge about the appropriate division of jurisdiction and authority between the Member States and regional bodies and among the different regional institutions....

I. EUROPEAN REGIONAL INSTITUTIONS

Jurisdiction over human rights matters within Europe is conferred on three entities of partially overlapping membership: the Council of Europe, the European Union (EU) and the OSCE. None of them is concerned exclusively with human rights, but each one considers the topic essential to achieving its objectives.

A. The Council of Europe

A little over 50 years ago, 10 northern and western European countries created the Council of Europe, the first post-war European regional organization. Europe had been the theater of the greatest atrocities of the Second World War and felt compelled to press for international human rights guarantees as part of its reconstruction. Faith in western European traditions of democracy, the rule of law and individual rights inspired belief that a regional system could be successful in avoiding future conflict and in stemming post-war revolutionary impulses backed by the Soviet Union. The Statute of the Council provides that each Member State must "[a]ccept the principles of the rule of law and of the enjoyment by all persons within its jurisdiction of human rights and fundamental freedoms."

A year later, these same states, self-described as "like-minded and hav[ing] a common heritage of political traditions, ideals, freedom and the rule of law," agreed to take the "first steps for the collective enforcement of certain of the rights stated in the Universal Declaration (of Human Rights)" and adopted the Convention for the Protection of Human Rights and Fundamental Freedoms (hereinafter European Convention). Today, membership in the Council is *de facto* conditioned upon adherence to the European Convention and cooperation with its supervisory machinery, a condition met by all of the 44 Member States. In addition, accession requires free and fair elections based upon national suffrage, freedom of expression, protection of national minorities and observance of the principles of international law. Several new Member States also have entered into additional and specific commitments during the examination of their request for membership.

... The original Convention set forth a short list of civil and political rights and a single and opening statement of the obligation of Contracting Parties: "The High Contracting Parties shall secure to everyone within their jurisdiction the rights and freedoms defined in Section I of this Convention." ...

The Court today is composed "of a number of members equal to that of the High Contracting Parties" to the European Convention. The judges are elected for a six-year renewable period by the Parliamentary Assembly of the Council of Europe from a list of three nominees submitted by each Member State. The judges serve in their individual capacities and must be persons of "high moral character" who "possess the qualifications required for appointment to high judicial office or be persons of recognized competence." The judges do not have to be nationals of the Member States of the Council of Europe. They serve full-time during their term and may not undertake any activity incompatible with their judicial functions. They must retire at age 70. The permanent Court has its seat in Strasbourg, also the seat of the Council of Europe, and judges are expected to live in the area. The Court has a Registry and legal secretaries to assist it. The Registrar is the chief clerk of the Court.

Although the European Convention initially created an independent Commission and Court, the drafters made the Court's jurisdiction optional. They also established, but again made optional, the world's first individual petition procedure for human rights violations. The "normal" procedure thus envisaged was one of inter-state complaints brought through the Commission to the Committee of Ministers. The Commission would meet in closed sessions, undertake fact-finding, attempt a friendly settlement of the matter, and report its findings to the Committee of Ministers for decision. Only the Commission or the state could refer a matter to the Court, if the state in question had accepted the Court's jurisdiction. Enforcement of judgments of the Court and decisions of the Committee of Ministers lay with the Committee itself, which could suspend a state from its rights of representation or ask it to withdraw from the Council for serious violations of its obligations.

During the intervening half century, this rather modest system has undergone evolutionary, sometimes revolutionary, changes. The Council of Europe has adopted 13 protocols to the European Convention, and in the process expanded the list of guaranteed civil and political rights. The first Protocol added a right to property, a right to education and the undertaking by the Contracting Parties to hold free and secret elections at reasonable intervals. Protocol No. 4 enlarged the list further by prohibiting deprivation of liberty for failure to comply with contractual obligations, by guaranteeing the right to liberty of movement, and by barring forced exile of nationals and the collective expulsion of aliens. Protocol No. 6 abolished the death penalty except during wartime and Protocol No. 7 requires states to accord aliens various due process safeguards before they may be expelled from a country where they reside. The instrument also provides for rights of appeal in criminal proceedings, compensation in cases of miscarriage of justice, protection against double jeopardy, and equality of rights and responsibilities between spouses. Protocol No. 12 augments the non-discrimination guarantee in Convention Art. 14 by providing that "the enjoyment of any right set forth by law shall be secured without discrimination on any ground," adding that "no one shall be discriminated against by any public authority." Protocol No. 13, adopted by the Committee of Ministers on February 21, 2002, abolishes the death penalty under all circumstances.

Other protocols gradually enhanced the role and status of the individual before the Court and eliminated the discretion of Member States to accept the jurisdiction of the Court and the right of individual petition. In 1990, Protocol No. 9 enabled individuals to take cases to the Court in certain circumstances. Protocol No. 11 fundamentally restructured the system, eliminating the Commission and providing the new full-time Court with compulsory jurisdiction over interstate and individual cases brought against Contracting Parties to the Convention. Today the states are locked into a system of collective responsibility for the protection of human rights, a system in which the jurisdiction of the Court provides the centerpiece. Pursuant to Article 34 of the Convention, the Court now may receive applications from "any person, non-governmental organization or group of individuals claiming to be the victim of a violation … of the rights set forth in the Convention or the protocols thereto."

. . . .

B. The European Union

[The author describes the development of a commitment to fundamental rights within the European Union, including in the jurisprudence of the European Court of Justice. The Council of Europe, of course, is intergovernmental, and is institutionally distinct from the European Union.]

. . . .

II. JURISDICTION AND ROLE OF THE EUROPEAN COURTS

The litigation-based human rights system of the Council of Europe is undoubtedly the best known aspect of its monitoring of the human rights performance of Member States. Similarly, the EU developed its human rights doctrine through the jurisprudence of the ECJ. In recent years, however, other procedures have emerged and become important, including the inspection process of the European Torture Convention, the conciliation work of ECRI [European Commission Against Racism and Intolerance], and the country reports of the European Parliament. To some extent, these new procedures reflect the borrowing of successes from other national and international institutions. They also reflect a shift of power as the Parliamentary Assembly and European Parliament increasingly demand and play a role. To some extent their expanding functions may also respond to concerns about transparency and democratic participation in regional organizations.

For the European Court of Human Rights, Protocol No. 11 fundamentally changed the system, abolishing the Commission and giving individuals direct access to the Court to bring actions against any State Party to the Convention. Protocol 11 also introduced a limited "appellate" procedure. A Grand Chamber of 17 judges now has jurisdiction to review decisions of any seven member Chamber if the case raises a "serious question affecting the interpretation or application of the Convention or protocols thereto, or a serious issue of general importance" and a panel of five judges of the Grand Chamber decides that it is appropriate to do so after a request from one of the parties. Although there is no explicit reference to intra-Chamber conflicts in interpreting and applying the Convention, the Grand Chamber could serve to ensure consistency of jurisprudence by resolving any such conflicts. The Grand Chamber conducts *de novo* review of cases referred to it, including admissibility of the complaint if the issue is raised.

....

A. General Rules of Interpretation and the Specificity of Human Rights Treaties

....

The European Court of Human Rights describes the ECHR as a "living instrument which must be interpreted in the light of present day conditions" rather than remain static. It also holds that the object and purpose of the ECHR, which is to emphasize the protection of human rights, requires that limitations or qualifications of the rights granted be narrowly construed.

The Court clearly struggles with questions of uniformity and diversity in judging whether a given state practice falls below ECHR standards. The Court has stated that it will search for "common European standards" based upon domestic law and practice, other international or European instruments and the Court's own case law. The Court has engaged in such searches to determine the legality of corporal punishment of juveniles, the distinctions between legitimate and illegitimate children, criminalization of homosexual conduct, and the regulation of blasphemy. The Court will often defer to the state when it finds no general consensus on an issue, but it has also served notice that state law and practice cannot remain static while European standards evolve towards greater human rights protection. Thus, in the *Selmouni* case the Court announced that

> certain acts which were classified in the past as "inhuman and degrading treatment" as opposed to "torture" could be classified differently in future. [The Court] takes the view that the increasingly high standard being required in the area of the protection of human rights and fundamental liberties correspondingly and inevitably requires greater firmness in assessing breaches of the fundamental values of democratic societies.

While it may appear from *Selmouni* that states are judged by ever-changing standards, the Court in fact gives great weight to its precedents. Although neither the Convention nor the Rules of Court expresses the principle of *stare decisis*, the Rules make abandonment of precedent one of the grounds for a Chamber to relinquish jurisdiction in favor of a Grand Chamber. The Court's stated approach is to follow its precedents "in the interests of legal certainty and the orderly development of the Convention case law." It will depart from an earlier decision if it finds the earlier interpretation erroneous or for another "cogent reason" including the need to "ensure that the interpretation of the Convention reflects societal change and remains in line with present day conditions."

The European Court of Human Rights has made clear that the principle of effectiveness is a fundamental principle of interpretation. It requires that the provisions of the Convention be interpreted "so as to make its safeguards practical and effective," protecting the individual in a real and practical way as regards those areas with which it deals. The principle of effectiveness has led the Court to expand protections in a number of areas. For example, in *Soering v. United Kingdom* and other cases concerning extradition or deportation, the Court has admitted petitions when violations were imminently threatened, but had not yet occurred.

....

B. Margin of Appreciation

The concept of a margin of appreciation is extremely important to the work of the European Court of Human Rights. It determines the scope of judicial review of state action and the degree of deference afforded to states in deciding on the implementation and application of rights guaranteed in the European Convention. To a large extent, it reflects and encapsulates the principle of subsidiarity that is much more prevalent in and associated with the EU and ECJ. The margin of appreciation acts both as a standard of review and as a substantive norm for interpreting the Convention....

The doctrine of margin of appreciation was articulated in the first case to come before the Court, *Lawless v. Ireland*, in connection with the scope of judicial review of a declared state of emergency in Ireland. It was discussed in more detail in the *Handyside* case, in reviewing a ban on publication in order to protect the morals of minors. In the latter judgment, the Court refers to its role as subsidiary to the national system safeguarding human rights because the Convention leaves to each contracting state, in the first place, the task of securing the rights and liberties it enshrines. In particular, in assessing restrictions and limitations on rights, the Court gives deference to the state, because according to the Court, "by reason of their direct and continuous contact with the vital forces of their countries, state authorities are in principle in a better position than the international judge to give an opinion on the ...'necessity' of a 'restriction' or 'penalty'... [I]t is for the national authorities to make the initial assessment of the reality of the pressing social need implied by the notion of 'necessity' in this context." Consequently, a margin of appreciation is given to the domestic legislator and to the local courts or other bodies called upon to interpret and apply the law adopted.

The margin of appreciation is not unlimited, however. The Court, being responsible for ensuring the observance of state obligations, is empowered to give the final ruling on whether a restriction is compatible with rights guaranteed by the Convention. "The domestic margin of appreciation thus goes hand in hand with European supervision. Such supervision concerns both the aim of the measure challenged and its 'necessity;' it covers not only the basic legislation but also the decision applying it, even one given by an independent court."

. . . .

The Court's use of inter-state comparisons to give content and scope to Convention norms is sometimes in tension with the margin of appreciation. The Court often finds an emerging or established consensus on evolved standards that it may apply to all states, not just those that have moved in that direction. In other cases, where the Court finds wide divergence in practice, it is likely to rely upon the margin of appreciation to permit divergent political determinations, while calling on states to interpret and apply the Convention "in the light of current circumstances," having regard particularly to scientific and societal developments.

. . . .

C. Implied Rights

. . . .

The ECHR has implied rights as part of its "doctrine of effectiveness." In the *Golder* case, the applicant was denied permission to see a lawyer in order to bring an action against a prison warden. The European Court of Human Rights found that the government violated Article 6, the right to a fair trial, because that right must be held to imply a right of access to a court where a fair trial could be obtained. The ECHR found this interpretation based on "the very terms of the first sentence of Article 6(1), read in its context and having regard to the object and purpose of the convention, a lawmaking treaty ... and to general principles of law." Similarly, the ECHR held in *Airey v. Ireland*, that where no legal aid was available and the costs of litigation were prohibitive, the government violated the right of access to a court as part of the right of a fair trial. In *Luedicke, Belkacem and Koç* the ECHR found an obligation to provide free interpretation for foreign-language defendants in criminal cases implied in the right to a fair trial.

The European Court of Human Rights also implied positive obligations with respect to certain rights, including the right to life and the right to family life. The right to freedom of assembly may also require positive measures to ensure that others do not interfere with the exercise of the right to freedom of assembly. The European Court of Human Rights has accepted that pollution and other environmental harm can lead to violations of rights guaranteed by the Convention, particularly Article 8 which provides for respect for home and private life.

. . . .

E. Remedial Powers and Enforcement

Article 41 of the European Convention is cryptic and does not make clear whether the Court may order remedial measures when a violation is found. Throughout most of its history, the ECHR has interpreted its powers narrowly and declared that it is for the respondent state to decide upon the measures needed to fulfill the state's obligations and comply with the judgment declaring the state's law or action incompatible with the Convention. Judgments always involve a declaration judging whether or not a violation has been proven. Where a violation is found, Article 41 allows the ECHR to give "just satisfaction" to the injured party, including pecuniary and moral damages, as well as reimbursement of costs, expenses, and attorneys' fees. The ECHR's judgments on remedies have been inconsistent and are rarely accompanied by reasoned opinions.

The judgments of the ECHR are legally binding on the respondent state. The Committee of Ministers, a political body, has the responsibility to ensure compliance with the ECHR's decisions. Article 8 of the Statute of the Council of Europe empowers the Committee of Ministers to suspend or expel from membership any State that has seriously violated Article 3 of the Statute. Systematic human rights violations or non-compliance with judgments of the Court would likely be seen as such a breach.

The ECJ indicated its approach to remedies for breach of Community law in *Brasserie du Pecheur v. Germany*. The ECJ applied the principle that the state is liable for damage caused in accordance with its national law, stating that:

> Reparation for loss or damage caused to individuals as a result of breaches of Community law must be commensurate with the loss or damage sustained so as to ensure the effective protection for their rights. In the absence of relevant Community provisions, it is for the domestic legal system of each Member State to set the criteria for determining the extent of reparation. However, those criteria must not be less favorable than those applying to similar claims based on domestic law and must not be such as in practice to make it impossible or excessively difficult to obtain reparation.

Applying this test, the ECJ found that the limitations of German national law were incompatible with Community law. In other cases, the ECJ also has exercised supervisory power over the remedies provided by Member States, using the principle of subsidiarity in favor of its jurisdiction. In several cases, for example, the Court has held that the prohibition of discrimination must be enforced by sanctions that have a real deterring effect.

F. Gross and Systematic Violations

The ECHR has been fortunate in having few cases of gross and systematic violations. Those cases that have been brought indicate the limitations of the judicial process in resolving systemic failure of the rule of law. In this respect, the ECHR faces the same problem the United States Supreme Court did when it decided *Brown v. Board of Education* in the face of long-standing and widespread *de jure* discrimination, legally founded and often supported by the majority of citizens. Without the full support of the executive, which required calling out the military to enforce the decision at one point, the United States Supreme Court's judgment would have been toothless.

. . . .

In recent years, when there have been serious or widespread violations, some states have challenged the authority of the European Court of Human Rights' judgments with regard to either the just satisfaction awarded or specific measures required of them by the judgments. The Committee of Ministers' position remains firm that states have an unconditional obligation to comply with judgments of the Court. Confidential scrutiny of a state during the Committee of Ministers' meetings can lead to direct contacts by the Chairman, public resolutions may be adopted to convey the Committee of Ministers' concerns, and other states, organizations, and parties can pressure the recalcitrant government. If there are serious obstacles to execution, the Committee of Ministers may adopt a more strongly worded interim resolution urging the authorities to take the necessary steps to comply. The Committee of Ministers has been urged by the Rome Ministerial Conference and by the Parliamentary Assembly to study what else may be done. The problem is extremely serious because non-compliance is a threat to the entire system. As time passes and compliance is not forthcoming, the credibility of the system is put in question.

Notes and Questions

1. It is clear from the article above that the European Court of Human Rights enjoys broad powers to enforce its vision of human rights within the member states of the Council of Europe. This is a major legal accomplishment, and is virtually without parallel anywhere else in the world. Is there any down side to a regional court taking on such a role? Might such a strong emphasis on a regional system impede the development of national constitutional innovations?

2. What is the "margin of appreciation" recognized by the ECHR? What are the positive aspects of this idea? What obstacles might it create to the uniform enforcement of human rights in Europe? Why is it an especially important concept in the children's rights realm?

———

The following summary is from the European Court of Human Rights website. It provides a concise and convenient timeline for the development of European human rights law and practice.

Council of Europe, European Court of Human Rights

Information Document on the Court (2006), http://www.echr.coe.int/NR/
rdonlyres/981B9082-45A4-44C6-829A-202A51B94A85/0/ENG_Infodoc.pdf

I. History and development of the Convention system

A. A system in continuous evolution

1. The Convention for the Protection of Human Rights and Fundamental Freedoms was drawn up within the Council of Europe. It was opened for signature in Rome on 4 November 1950

and entered into force in September 1953. Taking as their starting point the 1948 Universal Declaration of Human Rights, the framers of the Convention sought to pursue the aims of the Council of Europe through the maintenance and further realisation of human rights and fundamental freedoms. The Convention represented the first steps for the collective enforcement of certain of the rights set out in the Universal Declaration.

2. In addition to laying down a catalogue of civil and political rights and freedoms, the Convention set up a mechanism for the enforcement of the obligations entered into by Contracting States. Three institutions were entrusted with this responsibility: the European Commission of Human Rights (set up in 1954), the European Court of Human Rights (set up in 1959) and the Committee of Ministers of the Council of Europe, the last of these being composed of the Ministers of Foreign Affairs of the member States or their representatives.

....

The Protocols to the Convention

7. Since the Convention's entry into force fourteen Protocols have been adopted. Protocols Nos. 1, 4, 6, 7, 12 and 13 added further rights and liberties to those guaranteed by the Convention. Protocol No. 2 conferred on the Court the power to give advisory opinions, a little used function that is now governed by Articles 47–49 of the Convention.... Protocol No. 9 allowed individuals to seek referral of their case to the Court. Protocol No. 11 radically transformed the supervisory system, creating a single, full-time Court to which individuals can have direct recourse. Protocol No. 14, which was adopted in 2004 and is currently in the process of ratification, will introduce a number of institutional and procedural reforms, with the main objective being to expand the Court's capacity to deal with clearly inadmissible complaints as well as admissible cases that can be resolved on the basis of well established case law ... The other Protocols, which concerned the organization of and procedure before the Convention institutions, are of no practical importance today.

B. Mounting pressure on the Convention system

8. In the early years of the Convention, the number of applications lodged with the Commission was comparatively small, and the number of cases decided by the Court was much lower again. This changed in the 1980s, by which time the steady growth in the number of cases brought before the Convention institutions made it increasingly difficult to keep the length of proceedings within acceptable limits. Adding to the problem was the rapid increase in the number of Contracting States from 1990 onwards, rising from twenty-two to the current total of forty-six. The number of applications registered annually with the Commission increased from 404 in 1981 to 4,750 in 1997, the last full year of operation of the original supervisory mechanism. By that same date, the number of unregistered or provisional files opened each year in the Commission had risen to over 12,000. Although on a much lower scale, the Court's statistics reflected a similar story, with the number of cases referred annually rising from 7 in 1981 to 119 in 1997.

....

10. This enormous case load has raised concerns over the continuing effectiveness of the Convention system. Further changes to the system were agreed in 2004, when Protocol No. 14 [improving the efficiency of the Court] was adopted and opened for signature.... By mid-2006, all but a handful of States had ratified it. Although Protocol No. 14 will allow the Court to deal more rapidly with certain types of case, it cannot lessen the flow of new applications. It is widely agreed that further adaptation of the system is necessary.

At the Third Summit of the Council of Europe in Warsaw in May 2005, the Heads of State and Government present decided to convene the Group of Wise Persons, composed of eminent legal personalities, to consider the steps that might be taken to ensure the system's continuing viability and make proposals ...

II. The European Court of Human Rights

A. Organisation of the Court

11. The Court, as presently constituted, was brought into being by Protocol No. 11 on 1 November 1998. This amendment made the Convention process wholly judicial, as the Commission's function of screening applications was entrusted to the Court itself, whose jurisdiction became mandatory. The Committee of Ministers' adjudicative function was formally abolished.

12. The provisions governing the structure and procedure of the Court are to be found in Section II of the Convention (Articles 19–51). The Court is composed of a number of judges equal to that of the Contracting States.... Judges are elected by the Parliamentary Assembly of the Council of Europe, which votes on a shortlist of three candidates put forward by Governments. The term of office is six years, and judges may be re-elected. Their terms of office expire when they reach the age of seventy, although they continue to deal with cases already under their consideration.

Judges sit on the Court in their individual capacity and do not represent any State. They cannot engage in any activity which is incompatible with their independence or impartiality or with the demands of full-time office.

....

B. Procedure before the Court

1. General

19. Any Contracting State (State application) or individual claiming to be a victim of a violation of the Convention (individual application) may lodge directly with the Court in Strasbourg an application alleging a breach by a Contracting State of one of the Convention rights. A notice for the guidance of applicants and the official application form are available on the Court's internet site. They may also be obtained directly from the Registry.

20. The procedure before the European Court of Human Rights is adversarial and public. It is largely a written procedure. Hearings, which are held only in a very small minority of cases, are public, unless the Chamber/Grand Chamber decides otherwise on account of exceptional circumstances. Memorials and other documents filed with the Court's Registry by the parties are, in principle, accessible to the public.

21. Individual applicants may present their own cases, but they should be legally represented once the application has been communicated to the respondent Government ... The Council of Europe has set up a legal aid scheme for applicants who do not have sufficient means.

....

2. The handling of applications

....

28. All final judgments of the Court are binding on the respondent States concerned.

29. Responsibility for supervising the execution of judgments lies with the Committee of Ministers of the Council of Europe. The Committee of Ministers verifies whether the State

in respect of which a violation of the Convention is found has taken adequate remedial measures, which may be specific and/or general, to comply with the Court's judgment.

. . . .

Notes and Questions

1. How important do you imagine the individual petition to be in the overall functioning of the European human rights system? While individual states may tend to feel threatened and criticized by the international human rights bodies, why is it that the states of the Council of Europe have consented to such a binding, high profile system of enforcement? Does this system provide a genuine model for other regions of the world, or is Europe unique in its ability to embrace these transcendent regional structures?

———————

B. The European System as a Model for American Advocates for Children's Rights

The following article compares the approach taken by the U.S. Supreme Court in cases touching on children's rights with that taken by the ECHR. It points out conceptual limitations in U.S. Supreme Court jurisprudence, and indicates how the ECHR's method could benefit American children. Tania Schriwer is particularly critical of the fact that U.S. constitutional concepts often leave children unprotected, especially in the areas of child abuse and neglect.

Tania Schriwer, *Establishing an Affirmative Governmental Duty to Protect Children's Rights: The European Court of Human Rights as a Model for the United States Supreme Court*
34 University of San Francisco Law Review 379 (2000)

... The United States Supreme Court has consistently refused to recognize an affirmative governmental duty to protect the rights of its most vulnerable citizens: children.

. . . .

The European Court shows a greater willingness than the United States Supreme Court to establish affirmative governmental duties for its Member States. The European Court is the highest tribunal enforcing the European Convention on Human Rights ("Convention").... One important feature of the European Human Rights System is "its creation of an individual's right to bring petitions seeking relief from a state's human rights violations." The European Commission on Human Rights is the first body to rule on a claim brought by a plaintiff once he or she has exhausted all avenues of relief provided by the Member State. It may then be reviewed by the European Court, which acts as the ultimate arbiter of the Convention, the same way the United States Supreme Court reviews constitutional claims. In this role, unlike the United States Supreme Court in its interpretation of the Constitution, the European Court has declared that the Convention imposes an affirmative duty on the Member States to protect its children from abuse.

Proponents have stated that "[t]he European Human Rights System is the most highly developed regional system for the protection of human rights." This System, which has established the most developed body of international human rights law, may serve as an example for the creation of affirmative governmental duties for the protection of children in the United States.

This comment suggests that the United States Supreme Court should follow the lead of the European Court and impose an affirmative duty on the states to protect children.

. . . .

I. Background

The United States Supreme Court has taken a "narrow view of judicial power to protect individual rights." According to the Supreme Court, the state merely has a duty to refrain from interfering with the rights of the individual. In stark contrast to the Supreme Court, the European Court has consistently recognized a government's affirmative obligation to protect its citizens' rights, even from invasion by private actors. The European Member State has the obligation to take positive steps to alter its laws when they are found to interfere with Convention rights.

Juxtaposing the European Court's decision in *A. v. United Kingdom* against the United States Supreme Court's decision in *DeShaney v. Winnebago County Department of Social Services*, the courts' opposing views are clear. The European Court held the United Kingdom government responsible for its failure to take affirmative steps to protect a fourteen-year-old boy from caning by his stepfather, which caused severe marks and bruises. The Supreme Court, in contrast, held the State of Wisconsin was not responsible for its failure to protect a four-year-old boy from beatings by his father, which caused severe mental retardation.

A. The Laws of the United Kingdom and the European Court of Human Rights

1. Imposing Affirmative Duties on Member States

The European Court has imposed affirmative governmental duties on its Member States. The European Court has imposed not only the negative obligation of refraining from the interference with private citizens' rights, but has also established an affirmative governmental duty to protect private citizens' rights. In Article 1 of the Convention, the contracting parties agree not only to refrain from conduct interfering with citizens' rights, but also agree to "secure to everyone within their jurisdiction the rights and freedoms defined in Section I of this Convention." This protection, espoused by the Convention, extends not only to state action, but also to private acts.

The European Court's case law shows a willingness to impose affirmative obligations upon Member States to alter their laws when they violate citizens' rights. In *Johnston v. Ireland*, the European Court stated "there may ... be positive obligations inherent in an effective 'respect' for family life" mandated by Article 8 of the Convention. In other cases, the European Court has also found the United Kingdom has a duty to make available the supervision records of a child committed to public care and that the applicant has a vital interest in receiving such information. Ireland was told it should provide legal aid for individuals seeking judicially recognized marriage separations. The European Court ordered the Belgian government to take the affirmative acts necessary to end the discriminatory treatment the domestic law was imposing upon illegitimate children with respect to their legal relationship with their parents and their inheritance rights.

The European Court has also imposed affirmative obligations on Member States to prevent violations of Convention rights by private parties. The European Court has stated that a state's positive obligations under Article 8 "may involve the adoption of measures designed to secure respect for private life even in the sphere of the relations of individuals between themselves." The European Court has similarly stated that Article 11, which guarantees freedom of assembly and association, "sometimes requires positive measures to be taken, even in the sphere of relations between individuals." In this vein, the European Court held that the Dutch Government had a duty to adopt criminal law provisions where fundamental values and essential aspects of private life are at stake, such as in a case of the rape of a mentally retarded girl. The European Court articulated a state's responsibility to protect children from private actors in a case involving the corporal punishment of a seven-year-old boy by the headmaster of a private boarding school, which received no financial support from the state. This expansive human rights view of the Convention ultimately enabled the European Court to find that the United Kingdom violated Article 3 of the Convention when it failed to protect a young boy from beatings at the hands of his father.

2. A Judgment by the European Court of Human Rights: *A. v. United Kingdom*

In May 1990, A., a year-old British citizen, was placed in his local Child Protection Register because of "known physical abuse." He was removed from the Register approximately one and a half years later. In February 1993, the head teacher at A.'s school reported to the local Social Service Department that A.'s stepfather was beating him with a stick. That same month a pediatrician found marks and bruises on the boy's body "consistent with the use of a garden cane, applied with considerable force, on more than one occasion." A. complained to the European Court of Human Rights that the state had failed to protect him from abuse by his stepfather in violation of Article 3 of the Convention.

In September 1998, the European Court of Human Rights declared that

> the obligation on the High Contracting Parties under Article 1 of the Convention to secure to everyone within their jurisdiction the rights and freedoms defined in the Convention, taken together with Article 3, requires States to take measures designed to ensure that individuals within their jurisdiction are not subjected to torture or inhuman or degrading treatment or punishment, including such ill-treatment administered by private individuals.

The European Court noted that "[c]hildren and other vulnerable individuals, in particular, are entitled to State protection, in the form of effective deterrence, against such serious breaches of personal integrity." The European Court found the laws of the United Kingdom failed to protect the boy, and thus the State was responsible for the stepfather's beating of A.

B. The Laws of the United States

1. No Affirmative Duties on States

Judge Richard Posner's declaration that the "Constitution is a charter of negative rather than positive liberties" encapsulates the Supreme Court's refusal to require the state or federal governments to protect citizens' fundamental rights against infringement by private actors. This view of the Constitution in general, and the Due Process Clause of the Fourteenth Amendment in particular, has led the Supreme Court to recognize only "negative rights, which require the government to refrain from certain conduct, as opposed to positive rights, which impose affirmative duties on the government to take actions or expend resources to meet the needs of certain citizens."

. . . .

2. *DeShaney v. Winnebago County Department of Social Services*

In January 1982, the Winnebago County Department of Social Services ("DSS") received notice that Joshua DeShaney's father, Randy DeShaney, "had previously 'hit the boy causing marks and [was] a prime case for child abuse.'" In January 1983, when Joshua was treated in the hospital for multiple bruises and abrasions, the physician suspected child abuse and notified the DSS. Joshua was taken into protective custody for three days. The DDS found "that there was insufficient evidence of child abuse."

Despite the lack of evidence, Joshua's return to his father's custody was subject to a voluntary agreement to comply with measures to protect Joshua. The protective measures included enrolling Joshua "in a preschool program, providing his father with certain counselling services, and encouraging his father's girlfriend to move out of the home."

. . . .

In March 1984, Randy DeShaney beat four-year-old Joshua so badly that "he suffered brain damage so severe that he is expected to spend the rest of his life confined to an institution for the profoundly retarded." When the DSS caseworker was told about the beating, she said, "'I just knew the phone would ring some day and Joshua would be dead.'"

Joshua and his mother brought an action under 42 U.S.C. § 1983 against Winnebago County, DSS, and various DSS employees. They claimed the state and its agency were liable for their failure to intervene and protect Joshua against the risk of violence by his father—the state knew, or should have known, of the risk of severe injury. Joshua and his mother argued that in failing to intervene, the state deprived Joshua of his liberty without due process of the law, in violation of his Fourteenth Amendment rights.

On February 22, 1989, the United States Supreme Court held there is no deprivation of the constitutional right to liberty when the state fails to protect a child from harm inflicted by a private citizen. The Court declared the Fourteenth Amendment "confer[s] no affirmative right to governmental aid, even where such aid may be necessary to secure life." The Court stated that although the text of the Due Process Clause "forbids the State itself to deprive individuals of life, liberty, or property without 'due process of law,'... its language cannot fairly be extended to impose an affirmative obligation on the State to ensure that those interests do not come to harm through other means." The Court reasoned that, since the Due Process Clause does not impose a duty upon the state to provide citizens with protective services, the state cannot be held accountable for injuries that could have been avoided had it provided them. Only in limited circumstances, where the state has created or assumed a "special relationship" with respect to a certain individual or where the harm an individual suffers occurs while in state custody, does the state have an affirmative duty to protect that person.

. . . .

II. The Problem

Many arguments have been proffered to support the troubling holding in *DeShaney*. Those who agree with the decision argue that it is supported by the text of the Constitution, its history, the Framers' intent, the concept of federalism, American philosophical heritage, and the common law. In addition, proponents of *DeShaney* argue that the fear of opening the floodgates of litigation, as well as the fear of sliding down the proverbial slippery slope, support the decision. There are, however, equally persuasive arguments for overturning *DeShaney* and finding an affirmative governmental duty to protect individual rights.

The debate becomes an academic exercise in a particularly even-handed game of ping-pong. For every argument against finding affirmative governmental duties, there is a matching and equally compelling reason to do so. Thus, as Justice Blackmun noted, the question really is an open one. The Court, however, shows a strong preference in favor of those parties who oppose finding affirmative duties. Instead of openly declaring a tie, the Court hides its tendency towards favoring no governmental duty behind conclusory labels such as "positive rights, or government action."

. . . .

III. The Solution

Neither the Constitution nor policy reasons compelled the Court's decision in *De-Shaney*. The Court simply made a value judgment that favored a negative rights view of the Constitution. If the Supreme Court allows itself to be guided by the European Court's standards of interpretation and its substantive law on human rights, it may move closer to accepting some affirmative governmental duties.

The Supreme Court "take[s] a narrow view of judicial power to protect individuals' rights," while the European Court broadly interprets the provisions of the Convention and the rights protected by it. The Supreme Court should adopt the European Court's policy, which looks beyond the text of the written instrument and considers contemporary moral values in determining what human rights are protected and who should protect them.

The European Court in particular, and international human rights law in general, have consistently recognized an affirmative governmental obligation to protect individual rights. The Supreme Court should use the international human rights law as a guide in evaluating the extent to which United States jurisprudence requires human rights reform.

A. The Supreme Court Should Adopt the Broad Standard of Interpretation of the European Court

1. The European Court Adopts a Broad Standard of Interpretation

Although the European Court often relies on the ordinary meaning of the words of the Convention as its guide in interpreting its provisions, it has consistently adopted a broad standard of interpretation of Convention rights. The European Court interprets the Convention by considering the context of the Convention's entire text, as well as its object and purpose. By adopting this dynamic system of interpretation, the European Court has expanded on the broad language of Convention rights and ensured full protection to the individual in the face of changes in European political and social attitudes. Article 3, in particular, is deemed to require a contextual interpretation. This fundamental right must be considered in light of the context of the conduct involved and present-day circumstances. It is this kind of vigorous interpretation of Article 3 which served as the impetus for finding a positive duty on behalf of the United Kingdom to protect a young boy from severe beatings at the hands of his father.

. . . .

b. The European Court Considers Contemporary Standards of Morality

The European Court refuses to be bound by the Convention Framers' original intentions and instead looks at contemporary attitudes. This energetic approach to interpretation takes into account evolving political, social, and economic circumstances. The European Court interprets particular Member States' concerns in the "broader context of evolving, European-wide standards and practices," and is less willing to defer to the concerns of a particular country. Thus, the European Court noted in *Tyrer v. United Kingdom* that there "had developed a European standard excluding corporal punishment ... from which only the [United Kingdom] and the Republic of Ireland continued to deviate." Despite the strong sentiment by the inhabitants of the Isle of Man in favor of corporal punishment, the European Court declared that "Article 3 established absolute obligations from which there could be no retreat even to take ... account [of] local circumstances."

The European Court's broad interpretation of the Convention—in terms of looking beyond the text toward evolving trends across Europe—effectively moves all the Member States toward human rights reforms. The contracting states did not intend to solely protect those human rights threats that were prevalent at the time of drafting the Convention. Rather, "[t]heir intention was to protect the individual against the threats of the future, as well as the threats of the past." A dynamic interpretation of the European Convention is consistent with the Convention's general "purpose of promoting human rights, rather than merely maintaining them." In employing the principles of Articles 1 and 3 of the Convention, the European Court was able to find an affirmative duty to protect the children of the Member States from violence in the non-public realm.

. . . .

Notes and Questions

1. This article makes clear that there is a divide between the U.S. Supreme Court and the ECHR when it comes to the notion of the affirmative duty of officials to prevent private violence. Why is this issue so important in the realm of children's rights? Can a high level of child rights protections be achieved in the absence of such a jurisprudential idea? To what does the author attribute the Supreme Court's unwillingness to apply such an approach to official obligations? Is U.S. culture a factor? Could U.S. judicial reluctance in this regard be overcome?

2. As described above, in the late 1990s, an English boy known as "A" made an application under the European human rights procedures in place at the time. His complaint was that he had not been protected from repeated brutal beatings by his stepfather, who had used a garden cane on him. When the case went to the English court, the stepfather was found not guilty by virtue of the defense of "reasonable chastisement." As we know, the case went against the UK at the European level, where the Commission and Court held that the boys' right not to experience torture or degrading treatment or punishment under Article 3 of the European Convention had been violated. These institutions faulted UK law for not providing an adequate level of protection for children experiencing such treatment. In particular, the European bodies emphasized the fact that the member states of the Council must take adequate measures to ensure that everyone within their jurisdictions can exercise their rights under the Convention. What is the significance of this case? Realistically, how would a State Party go about complying with such a ruling? Is the Court saying that the UK must criminalize corporal punishment of children in the home, or something milder than that? How far has the Court gone in ensuring that a protective human rights standard governs state behavior, even as regards treatment of children within their own homes? What is it that the UK authorities were required to do?

C. The European Human Rights System and the UNCRC

In the article that follows, Ursula Kilkelly reflects the theory put forward by Bernardine Dohrn, to the effect that regional human rights bodies may apply both regional and international child rights principles, making international law norms far more effective. Kilkelly describes the ECHR as a court that actually interprets and applies the UNCRC as a complement to the European Convention on Human Rights, and in a manner befitting European needs and concerns. Is she overly optimistic about this process of synthesis, or perhaps overly eager to see the UNCRC "saved" by the ECHR?

Ursula Kilkelly, *The Best of Both Worlds for Children's Rights? Interpreting the European Convention on Human Rights in the Light of the UN Convention on the Rights of the Child*
23 Human Rights Quarterly 308 (2001)

I. Introduction

The European Convention on Human Rights (ECHR) has always operated successfully as a regional mechanism of human rights protection. Now, following the ECHR's incorporation into the legal systems of the vast majority of Council of Europe States, including, most recently, the United Kingdom, its potential to influence law and policy can be realized at the domestic as well as the regional level. The Convention's scope for enforcing and protecting the rights of children is not immediately evident given that it contains few specific references to the rights of the child. However, the European Commission of Human Rights and the European Court of Human Rights have made a considerable contribution to European law and practice in the areas of private and public family law, the protection of children from abuse and neglect and, most recently, juvenile justice and detention. They have done this, it is submitted, through a variety of inventive methods of interpretation, including the practice of drawing on the provisions of the UN Convention on the Rights of the Child (CRC). While it is not apparent that the Court (or the Commission, up to its abolition in 1998) has followed a consistent strategy to refer to the Convention on the Rights of the Child in all children's cases, it has been making such references with increasing frequency and with significant effect. This article analyzes the Court's approach to interpreting the ECHR in the light of the CRC and identifies the features of each treaty, which encourage this approach. It examines two specific areas of the Court's practice in this regard—physical punishment and juvenile justice—and concludes with some suggestions as to how this approach might be developed further in a way that offers greater scope for the protection and promotion of children's rights in Europe.

II. The UN Convention on the Rights of the Child

... Any assessment is made more difficult by the fact that the Convention lacks a powerful system of enforcement to allow for the adjudication of complaints of individual children, resulting in a lack of case law applying Convention standards to individual cases. Instead, implementation of the Convention's principles and provisions is monitored by a panel of international experts whose success depends largely on the willingness of national governments to take its criticisms and recommendations seriously. The approach of the UN Committee on the Rights of the Child to the promotion and protection of children's rights is thus advisory and non-adversarial in nature and its success relies on diplomacy rather than legal sanction. Despite its potential to advance protection of children's rights, this is a mechanism which clearly has long-term, rather than short-term, goals. However, in addition to its legally binding nature, the CRC also enjoys a certain moral force derived from its unanimous approval by the General Assembly in 1990, as well as the status it has since acquired as the most highly ratified instrument in international law.

....

One of the CRC's outstanding features is the comprehensive nature of its provisions. It is arguably by putting these to effective and imaginative use that the Convention can play an influential and dynamic role in the protection of the rights of children and young people. For example, the CRC sets out the rights to be secured to children and young people in many aspects of their lives and in a variety of circumstances. Its provisions are both numerous and detailed and combine civil and political rights, such as the right to liberty and the right to a fair trial; and social, economic, and cultural rights, including the right to education, the right to an adequate standard of living and health care, and the right to play. Many Convention provisions reflect those of other, more general human rights instruments, but there are also new provisions which recognize, *inter alia*, the right to identity and the rights of vulnerable children to special protection. The Convention breaks fresh ground by providing for child-specific versions of existing rights, like the freedom of expression and the right to a fair trial. It also establishes new standards by codifying for the first time the right of the child to be heard, both in general and, more specifically, in all proceedings that affect the child. This right to participate, together with the principles of non-discrimination in Article 2 and provision for the child's best interests in Article 3, form the guiding principles of the Convention, which reflect the vision of respect and autonomy which the drafters wished to create for all children.

In light of these two opposing factors—the CRC's weak enforcement mechanism and its impressive substantive content—it is important to look for alternative methods to maximize its potential for vindicating the rights of children. One such approach is to combine it with the successful system of individual petition which operates under the ECHR. This approach, whereby the principles and provisions of the Children's Convention are invoked, where relevant, to offer guidance on the interpretation and application of the ECHR, would help to fulfill the potential of both treaties to protect and promote children's rights at the international level and at the domestic level where the ECHR is part of domestic law.

III. Children and the European Convention on Human Rights

Although children's rights are essentially absent from the ECHR, this does not necessarily lessen its relevance to children and its potential use for protecting their rights. Nevertheless, it is an obvious observation that the text of the ECHR contains few express references to either children or their rights. Minors or juveniles (the text is inconsistent in its use of relevant terminology) appear only twice in the main body of the Convention, first in Article 5 concerning the right to liberty, and finally in Article 6 in relation to the right to a fair trial....

Although the ECHR is short on substantive rights for children, a number of its features make the use of the CRC as an interpretive guide both possible and valuable. First, many of the ECHR's provisions are phrased in broad terms, allowing them to be interpreted in an expansive and imaginative way. ECHR Article 8, for example, which guarantees the right to respect for private and family life, has been and continues to be very dynamically interpreted. For instance, among the rights found to fall within the scope of Article 8 are the right to physical integrity, the right to a healthy environment, and the right to parental leave allowance. Thus, the broad nature of Convention provisions facilitates their adaptation in a way which takes account of the particular needs and rights of the child.

Secondly, one of the significant features of the ECHR is its existence as a living instrument that must evolve so as to maintain relevance to current legal and social conditions. This approach recognizes that the Convention cannot operate in isolation from surrounding legal and social influences. Indeed, the Court has always drawn on factors outside of the ECHR in applying the Convention's standards. This is evident from the Court's application of the margin of appreciation according to which contracting states are allowed a certain degree of discretion when they take legislative, administrative, or judicial action in the area of a Convention right. The exercise of this discretion is subject to European supervision and the European Court of Human Rights has applied it to mean that where issues in a particular case touch on areas where there is little common ground among member states, the respondent state must be afforded a wide margin of appreciation within which to guarantee Convention rights. Consequently, then, states will enjoy less discretion where their approach is out of line with commonly accepted standards and norms both within the Council of Europe and beyond....

Article 1 of the ECHR guarantees Convention rights and freedoms to "everyone," and this provision has a central role in the way in which the Convention is interpreted and applied. The child's equal entitlement under the Convention is enforced further by Article 14, which prohibits discrimination in the enjoyment of Convention rights on numerous grounds, including the unenumerated ground of age. In theory, then, Convention rights are guaranteed to all, and there is little, other than the obvious practical difficulties, to prevent their application to children. Moreover, in practice, the Commission and Court of Human Rights have refrained from placing express or general limits on the application of the Convention in children's cases. Frequent reference to the standards of the CRC have encouraged this approach and generally raised the profile of children's rights in ECHR proceedings, as well as at the domestic level where such cases necessarily originate.

. . . .

IV. Reliance on The Convention on the Rights of the Child by the European Court of Human Rights

While the reference by the Strasbourg institutions to other regional and international treaties is important, the use of the CRC is a particularly significant development, given the detailed and specific nature of its provisions and the fact that they are widely accepted and legally binding internationally. Both the Commission and the Court have referred to provisions of the CRC in children's cases since it came into force in 1990....

A. Protection of the Child from Physical Punishment and Abuse

One of the areas of Strasbourg case law in which the influence of the CRC is clearly evident is in relation to cases of physical punishment and abuse. In fact, one of the first references to the CRC was made by the Court in the *Costello-Roberts* case, which concerned the physical punishment meted out to a seven-year-old boy in a private school in the United Kingdom. The boy complained that his treatment violated both Article 3 of the ECHR, which prohibits inhuman or degrading treatment, as well as Article 8, which requires respect for private life, of which the right to physical integrity is an important part. Although both of the boy's substantive complaints failed before the Court, the case established for the first time that the state could be held responsible for breaches of the ECHR which occur in the private sphere. In reaching this conclusion, the Court gave particular regard to the educational context of the dispute and recalled the state's obligation to secure to children their right to education under Article 2 of the First Protocol. In this regard, it was noted that the provisions of the ECHR must be read as a whole. The Court held that functions relating to the internal administration of school, like discipline, cannot be said to be ancillary to the education process. Importantly, support for the Court's proposition that the disciplinary system of a school falls within the ambit of the right to education was found in Article 28 of the CRC. Thus, the Court went on to cite paragraph 2 of that provision, which places an obligation on states to take all measures to ensure that school discipline is administered in a manner consistent with the child's human dignity and in conformity with the CRC. The Court relied on this provision to conclude that the state cannot absolve itself from responsibility by delegating its obligations to private individuals or bodies.

. . . .

Even though the Court agreed with the Commission's conclusion in the *A* case, its judgment is phrased in more general terms, not least because the Government did not contest proceedings before the Court. The Court confined its references to the CRC to the question of state responsibility where it recalled that children are entitled to state protection against serious breaches of personal integrity *a propos* Articles 19 and 37 of the CRC.

. . . .

B. Juvenile Justice

Article 6 of the ECHR guarantees the right to a fair trial in criminal and civil matters before an independent and impartial tribunal within a reasonable time. The second and third paragraphs set out the additional safeguards which are to apply to criminal trials, such as the right to be considered innocent until proven guilty, the right to a lawyer, and the right to have witnesses cross-examined. With the exception of the reference in Article 6 paragraph 1 to the need to protect juveniles from adverse publicity, the provision offers no special protection for the rights of young people involved in criminal proceedings. However, Article 6 has been found to include other rights which are an inherent part of the fair trial process, such as the right to access and participate effectively in such proceedings. These have obvious significance for minors. Although the main content of Article 40 — the equivalent fair trial provision in the CRC — is little different from ECHR Article 6, fundamentally, Article 40 provides that children in conflict with the law must be treated in a way that promotes the child's sense of dignity and worth and takes the child's age into account. Neither the Commission nor the Court of Human Rights has ever attempted to limit the application of Article 6 in children's cases. However, it is only recently that the institutions have expressly recognized the importance of treating children in the juvenile justice system in an appropriate manner. The confirmation of this approach as a firm ECHR principle would, it is submitted, have been unlikely without the guidance offered, directly or indirectly, by the CRC.

. . . .

The European Convention organs have rarely been faced with issues regarding the application of Article 6 to juveniles and the search for balance between applying special considerations to young persons in conflict with the law and refraining from any dilution of the fundamental guarantees of Article 6 if their criminal trial continues. The Commission was the first institution to deal with this issue head on in the cases of *T & V v. UK*, which involved the trial for murder of two eleven-year-old boys in an adult court. According to the facts, the accused were provided with defense counsel and the assistance of a social worker and the court sittings were shortened to take their limited concentration span into account. Despite these "not inconsiderable safeguards," the boys were subjected to the full rigors of the adult, public court in their trial for murder. The Commission regarded the trial process in an adult court with attendant publicity as a severely intimidating procedure for a child and it went on to conclude that these conditions must have seriously impinged on the boys' ability to participate in the proceedings in any meaningful way. The end result was a violation of their right to a fair trial under Article 6. While the Commission did not refer expressly to the CRC in its application of ECHR Article 6 (nor, incidentally, did it refer to the special provision in Article 6 itself which allows for excluding the press or public from a trial in the interests of juveniles) its opinion clearly reflects both the CRC's principles—the best interests principle under Article 3 as well as the child's right to participate in proceedings concerning him under Article 12—and its provisions on juvenile justice, particularly Article 40. Indeed, Mr. Bratza, in his concurring opinion, made express reference not only to the importance of the best interests principle in Article 40 of the CRC, but also to Article 14 § 4 of the International Covenant on Civil and Political Rights as well as the Beijing Rules (UN Standard Minimum Rules for the Administration of Juvenile Justice) to drive the point home.

The Court, in its December 1999 judgment, agreed with the Commission's conclusion that the accused were unable to participate effectively in their criminal trial and that this gave rise to a violation of Article 6. In particular, it reiterated the Commission's view that "it is essential that a child charged with an offence is dealt with in a manner which takes full account of his age, level of maturity and intellectual and emotional capacities, and that steps are taken to promote his ability to understand and participate in the proceedings."

Importantly, this involved two factors: the fundamental question of the children's ability to participate in the proceedings and the related factor of publicity. In relation to the latter, the Court found that in respect of a young child charged with a grave offence attracting high levels of media and public interest, it is necessary to conduct the hearing in such a way as to reduce as far as possible the child's feelings of intimidation and inhibition. In this regard, the Court referred to a number of international instruments advocating the protection of the privacy of child defendants, including the Beijing Rules, the CRC and a recommendation adopted by the Committee of Ministers of the Council of Europe in 1987. The Court observed that where it is considered appropriate in view of the age of the child and the surrounding circumstances, this need to protect the defendants' privacy could be balanced with the general interest in the open administration of justice by using a modified reporting procedure, including selected attendance rights and judicious reporting. As the trial in this case was conducted in a blaze of publicity, which led to the release of the defendants' names following the trial's conclusion, the case raised a clear issue of compatibility with Article 6. In relation to the more fundamental issue of the boys' participation in the trial, the Court noted that it was highly unlikely in the charged atmosphere of the courtroom that they could have consulted with their lawyers. It also held that the boys' immaturity and disturbed psychological state made it unlikely that they would have been capable of cooperating with their lawyers outside the courtroom in the preparation of their defense. The combination of these factors meant that the accused were unable to participate effectively in the criminal proceedings against them, giving rise to a breach of their right to a fair trial under Article 6 § 1.

While the Court did not rely directly on the CRC in formulating the right of the child to participate effectively in his own criminal trial, the judgment's wording and context indicate that the Court was informed by the Convention's juvenile justice provisions and other, more general standards, including the best interests principle in Article 3. This is highly significant given that it is the first time the Court has dealt squarely with the issue of what constitutes a fair trial for juveniles. It is clear from the judgment that certain modifications to the adult trial court and procedures are necessary to take into account the age and understanding of the accused and his ability to participate in his own trial to ensure compatibility with the CRC. In particular, this suggests the Court's firm support for Article 40 § 3 of the CRC, which requires states to seek the promotion of legal procedures and authorities specifically designed for dealing with children in conflict with the law. However, the Court did not find that the attribution of criminal responsibility to the eleven-year-old defendants breached the Convention and was unconvinced that the Beijing Rules and Article 40 § 3 of the CRC required more than the establishment of a minimum age of criminal responsibility, without specifying the relevant age in this respect....

The *T and V* judgments are clearly landmark in nature and provide valuable and necessary guidance as to the compatibility of juvenile criminal proceedings and the sentencing of juveniles with Article 6 and other ECHR provisions. Direct references to the standards of the CRC are frequent and meaningful throughout the judgments. What is more significant, however, is that the judgments as a whole are informed by and consistent with the provisions and principles of the CRC. There is thus firm evidence that the CRC's standards in the area of juvenile justice have been accepted by the Court, which, as an international tribunal, is in a position to enforce them.

V. The Future of this Approach

....

Another area in which reference to the provisions of the CRC may be influential is in relation to the child's right to identity, contained in Articles 7 and 8 of the Convention on the Rights of the Child. The Court's consideration of this issue thus far has been hesitant. In *X, Y and Z*, for example, the Court appeared to postpone consideration of whether it is in the child's interests to have the name of a person who is not the biological father on his birth certificate, arguably due, *inter alia*, to concerns for the child's right to identity. Were the Court to revisit this issue, reference to the CRC might play a positive role in the context of formulating the entitlement to birth information. Useful guidance could be sought from its provisions, as well as the UN Committee's positive interpretation of them, in the event of future challenges to such identity issues, including the policies of anonymity which operate as part of the adoption and artificial reproduction systems, in the light of their compatibility with respect for private and family life.

Notes and Questions

1. The Kilkelly article, above, makes it clear that the Council of Europe's human rights system embraces the UNCRC unequivocally. This is indicative of the fact that European states and institutions have shown much less resistance to the imposition of international legal norms than has the United States. Kilkelly argues that the UNCRC, being weak on enforcement, has been augmented by the reliance of the ECHR on its substantive content. Does her theory require that we see a direct link between the content of the UNCRC and the European Convention and corresponding jurisprudence, or is it enough to accept her vision of a less than fully demonstrable, yet important, link between the two systems?

2. Is the ECHR doing what it should do, as a regional human rights court, when it reaches beyond its own mandate to apply what it sees in the UNCRC? Is the Court reading children's rights issues into the European Convention on Human Rights that in fact are just not there, or is this process of cross-fertilization judicially permissible — perhaps even necessary? In order to further enhance the implementation of children's rights in Europe, in 1996 the Council of Europe created a separate convention, the European Convention on the Exercise of Children's Rights, available at http://conventions.coe.int/Treaty/en/Treaties/Html/160.htm.

3. Particular ECHR cases may appear to be about family law matters, only revealing their children's rights dimension on further examination. For a case that is superficially about administrative rules and access to documents, there is in fact a significant link with the child's right to an identity. See *Gaskin v. United Kingdom*, 160 Eur. Ct. H.R. (ser. A) (1989).

D. The European System in Focus

Most of the ECHR cases that center on the interests of children involve Article 3, Article 8 or Article 14 of the Convention, as reproduced below. At least in part because European society is economically advanced, most of the child rights cases that come before the Court actually involve family relationships, as opposed to egregious child rights violations. To that extent, these cases on children's rights might be seen by some as family law cases, although analyzed through the prism of fundamental rights. As you read on, consider the manner in which the ECHR has taken broad and general human rights prescriptions and applied these to often fairly specific questions of access, authority and inheritance.

Convention for the Protection of Human Rights and Fundamental Freedoms

Nov. 4, 1950, 213 U.N.T.S. 222, *available at* http://www.echr.coe.int/nr/ rdonlyres/d5cc24a7-dc13-4318-b457-5c9014916d7a/0/englishanglais.pdf

Article 3 — Prohibition of torture

No one shall be subjected to torture or to inhuman or degrading treatment or punishment.

Article 8 — Right to respect for private and family life

1. Everyone has the right to respect for his private and family life, his home and his correspondence.

2. There shall be no interference by a public authority with the exercise of this right except such as is in accordance with the law and is necessary in a democratic society in the interests of national security, public safety or the economic well-being of the country, for the prevention of disorder or crime, for the protection of health or morals, or for the protection of the rights and freedoms of others.

Article 14 — Prohibition of discrimination

The enjoyment of the rights and freedoms set forth in this Convention shall be secured without discrimination on any ground such as sex, race, colour, language, religion, political or other opinion, national or social origin, association with a national minority, property, birth or other status.

Article 41 — Just Satisfaction[5]

If the Court finds that there has been a violation of the Convention or the protocols thereto, and if the internal law of the High Contracting Party concerned allows only par-

---

5. Prior to the amendments contained in Protocol 11 to the Convention, which entered into force on Nov. 1, 1998, the "just satisfaction" provision appeared at Article 50. *See* Protocol No. 11 to the Convention for the Protection of Human Rights and Fundamental Freedoms, May 11, 1994, E.T.S. 155, 33 I.L.M. 943. Article 50 formerly provided:

> If the Court finds that a decision or a measure taken by a legal authority or any other authority of a High Contracting Party, is completely or partially in conflict with the obligations arising from the present convention, and if the internal law of the said Party allows only partial reparation to be made for the consequences of this decision or measure, the decision of the Court shall, if necessary, afford just satisfaction to the injured party.

Convention for the Protection of Human Rights and Fundamental Freedoms art. 50, Nov. 4, 1959, 213 U.N.T.S. 222, *as amended by* Protocols Nos. 1–10.

tial reparation to be made, the Court shall, if necessary, afford just satisfaction to the injured party.

──────────

What follows is a representative sample of cases from the ECHR, across a range of child-related subjects. The first of these is the seminal *Marckx v. Belgium*, which dealt with the problem of legal discrimination against non-marital children. In this case and those that follow, the Court applies European Convention principles, such as the right to a family life, that, while not necessarily drafted with children's rights in mind, prove useful in bringing about a pan-European vision of fairness in such relationships. As you read each of the following cases, consider how the ECHR is promoting the interests of children, often in opposition to traditional concepts deriving from national legal systems.

Marckx v. Belgium
31 Eur. Ct. H.R. (ser. A) (1979)

[The applicants, Paula Marckx and her infant daughter Alexandra, complained that certain aspects of the illegitimacy laws in Belgium—including the requirement that maternal affiliation could be established only by a formal act of recognition, and the existence of limitations on the mother's capacity to give or bequeath, and the child's capacity to take or inherit, property—contravened Article 8 of the European Convention on Human Rights (right to respect for family life) taken alone and in conjunction with Article 14 (right to be secured without discrimination) and Article 1 of the First Protocol (right to peaceful enjoyment of possessions) alone and together with Article 14. It was also claimed that Articles 3 (prohibition of degrading treatment) and 12 (right to marry and found a family) had been infringed. By a majority, the Commission formed the view that there had been violations of all the articles relied upon, except for Articles 3 and 12, and referred the case to the Court.

Specifically, the court held that the legislation failed to respect the applicants' family life, as protected by Article 8, and constituted discrimination in violation of Article 14 by virtue of the lack of any objective and reasonable justification for the differences of treatment between the legitimate and illegitimate family. The limitations on the mother's right to dispose of her property amounted to a violation of Article 1 of the First Protocol taken in conjunction with Article 14.]

. . . .

AS TO THE FACTS

A. Particular circumstances of the case

8. Alexandra Marckx was born on 16 October 1973 at Wilrijk, near Antwerp; she is the daughter of Paula Marckx, a Belgian national, who is unmarried and a journalist by profession. Paula Marckx duly reported Alexandra's birth to the Wilrijk registration officer who informed the District Judge as is required by ... the Belgian Civil Code in the case of 'illegitimate' children.

. . . .

10. On 29 October 1973, Paula Marckx recognised her child in accordance with Article 334 of the Code. She thereby automatically became Alexandra's guardian; the family council, on which the sister and certain other relatives of Paula Marckx sat under the chairmanship of the District Judge, was empowered to take in Alexandra's interests various measures provided for by law.

11. On 30 October 1974, Paula Marckx adopted her daughter pursuant to Article 349 of the Civil Code. The procedure, which was that laid down by Articles 350 to 356, entailed certain enquiries and involved some expenses. It concluded on 18 April 1975 with a judgment confirming the adoption, the effect whereof was retroactive to the date of the instrument of adoption, namely, 30 October 1974.

. . . .

13. The applicants complain of the Civil Code provisions on the manner of establishing the maternal affiliation of an 'illegitimate' child and on the effects of establishing such affiliation as regards both the extent of the child's family relationships and the patrimonial rights of the child and of its mother. The applicants also put in issue the necessity for the mother to adopt the child if she wishes to increase its rights.

B. Current law

(1) Establishment of the maternal affiliation of an 'illegitimate' child

14. Under Belgian law, no legal bond between an unmarried mother and her child results from the mere fact of birth: whilst the birth certificate recorded at the register office suffices to prove the maternal affiliation of the married woman's children..., the maternal affiliation of an 'illegitimate' child is established by means either of a voluntary recognition by the mother or of legal proceedings taken for the purpose (action en recherche de maternité).

Nevertheless, an unrecognised 'illegitimate' child bears its mother's name which must appear on the birth certificate ... The appointment of its guardian is a matter for the family council which is presided over by the District Judge.... Many unmarried mothers—about 25% according to the Government, although the applicants consider this an exaggerated figure—do not recognise their child.

Proceedings to establish maternal affiliation may be instituted by the child within five years from its attainment of majority or, whilst it is still a minor, by its legal representative with the consent of the family council ...

(2) Effects of the establishment of maternal affiliation

. . . .

(b) Rights of a child born out of wedlock and of his mother in the matter of inheritance on intestacy and voluntary dispositions

17. A recognised 'illegitimate' child's rights of inheritance on intestacy are less than those of a 'legitimate' child.... [A] recognised 'illegitimate' child does not have, in the estate of its parent who dies intestate, the status of heir, but solely that of 'exceptional heir' (successeur irrégulier): it has to seek a court order putting it in possession of the estate (envoi en possession). [It] is the sole beneficiary of its deceased mother's estate only if she leaves no relatives entitled to inherit ... ; otherwise, its maximum entitlement—which arises when its mother leaves no descendants, ascendants, brothers or sisters—is three-quarters of the share which it would have taken if 'legitimate'... Furthermore, its mother may, during her life-time, reduce that entitlement by one-half. Finally, [the Belgian Civil Code] denies to the 'illegitimate' child any rights on intestacy in the estates of its mother's relatives.

18. Recognised 'illegitimate' children are also at a disadvantage as regards voluntary dispositions, since [the Belgian Civil Code] provides that they 'may receive by disposition inter vivos or by will no more than their entitlement under the title "Inheritance on Intestacy".

Conversely, the mother of such a child, unless she has no relatives entitled to inherit, may give in her lifetime or bequeath to it only part of her property. On the other hand, if the child's affiliation has not been established, the mother may so give or bequeath to it the whole of her property, provided that there are no heirs entitled to a reserved portion of her estate (héritiers réservataires). The mother is thus faced with the following alternative: either she recognises the child and loses the possibility of leaving all her estate to it; or she renounces establishing with it a family relationship in the eyes of the law, in order to retain the possibility of leaving all her estate to it just as she might to a stranger.

(3) Adoption of 'illegitimate' children by their mother

19. If the mother of a recognised 'illegitimate' child remains unmarried, she has but one means of improving its status, namely, 'simple' adoption. In such cases, the age requirements for this form of adoption are eased.... The adopted child acquires over the adopter's estate the rights of a 'legitimate' child but, unlike the latter, has no rights on intestacy in the estates of its mother's relatives ...

Only legitimation ... and legitimation by adoption ... place an 'illegitimate' child on exactly the same footing as a 'legitimate' child; both of these measures presuppose the mother's marriage.

C. The Bill submitted to the Senate on 15 February 1978

[The Court notes that a bill had been submitted to the Belgian legislature that would establish equality in law between all children, regardless of the marital status of their mother.]

....

AS TO THE LAW

....

II. On the merits

28. The applicants rely basically on Articles 8 and 14 of the Convention. Without overlooking the other provisions which they invoke, the Court has accordingly turned primarily to these two articles in its consideration of the three aspects of the problem referred to it by the Commission: the manner of establishing affiliation, the extent of the child's family relationships, the patrimonial rights of the child and of her mother.

29. [The Court here notes the language of Article 8 of the Convention.]

30. The Court is led in the present case to clarify the meaning and purport of the words "respect for ... private and family life", which it has scarcely had the occasion to do until now ...

31. The first question for decision is whether the natural tie between Paula and Alexandra Marckx gave rise to a family life protected by Article 8.

By guaranteeing the right to respect for family life, Article 8 presupposes the existence of a family. The Court concurs entirely with the Commission's established case law on a crucial point, namely, that Article 8 makes no distinction between the 'legitimate' and the 'illegitimate' family. Such a distinction would not be consonant with the word "everyone", and this is confirmed by Article 14 with its prohibition, in the enjoyment of the rights and freedoms enshrined in the Convention, of discrimination grounded on "birth". In addition, the Court notes that the Committee of Ministers of the Council of Europe regards the single woman and her child as one form of family no less than others....

Article 8 thus applies to the "family life" of the 'illegitimate' family as it does to that of the 'legitimate' family. Besides, it is not disputed that Paula Marckx assumed responsibility for her daughter Alexandra from the moment of her birth and has continuously cared for her, with the result that a real family life existed and still exists between them.

It remains to be ascertained what the "respect" for this family life required of the Belgian legislature in each of the areas covered by the application.

By proclaiming in paragraph 1 the right to respect for family life, Article 8 signifies first that the State cannot interfere with the exercise of that right otherwise than in accordance with the strict conditions set out in paragraph 2. As the Court stated in the "Belgian Linguistic" case, the object of the Article is 'essentially' that of protecting the individual against arbitrary interference by the public authorities … Nevertheless, it does not merely compel the State to abstain from such interference: in addition to this primarily negative undertaking, there may be positive obligations inherent in an effective "respect" for family life.

This means, amongst other things, that when the State determines in its domestic legal system the régime applicable to certain family ties such as those between an unmarried mother and her child, it must act in a manner calculated to allow those concerned to lead a normal family life. As envisaged by Article 8, respect for family life implies in particular, in the Court's view, the existence in domestic law of legal safeguards that render possible, as from the moment of birth, the child's integration in its family. In this connection, the State has a choice of various means, but a law that fails to satisfy this requirement violates paragraph 1 of Article 8 without there being any call to examine it under paragraph 2.

Article 8 being therefore relevant to the present case, the Court has to review in detail each of the applicants' complaints in the light of this provision.

32. [The language of Article 14 is cited.]

The Court's case-law shows that, although Article 14 has no independent existence, it may play an important autonomous role by complementing the other normative provisions of the Convention and the Protocols: Article 14 safeguards individuals, placed in similar situations, from any discrimination in the enjoyment of the rights and freedoms set forth in those other provisions. A measure which, although in itself in conformity with the requirements of the Article of the Convention or the Protocols enshrining a given right or freedom, is of a discriminatory nature incompatible with Article 14, therefore violates those two articles taken in conjunction. It is as though Article 14 formed an integral part of each of the provisions laying down rights and freedoms …

Accordingly, and since Article 8 is relevant to the present case (see para. 31 above), it is necessary also to take into account Article 14 in conjunction with Article 8.

33. According to the Court's established case-law, a distinction is discriminatory if it "has no objective and reasonable justification", that is, if it does not pursue a "legitimate aim" or if there is not a "reasonable relationship of proportionality between the means employed and the aim sought to be realised" …

. . . .

A. On the manner of establishing Alexandra Marckx's maternal affiliation

. . . .

1. The alleged violation of Article 8 of the Convention, taken alone

36. [The Court describes the complex process of "affiliation" by which illegitimate children are brought into a legal relationship with their mothers.]

....

[T]he necessity to have recourse to such an expedient derived from a refusal to acknowledge fully Paula Marckx's maternity from the moment of the birth. Moreover, in Belgium an unmarried mother is faced with an alternative: if she recognises her child (assuming she wishes to do so), she will at the same time prejudice it since her capacity to give or bequeath her property to it will be restricted; if she desires to retain the possibility of making such dispositions as she chooses in her child's favour, she will be obliged to renounce establishing a family tie with it in law ... Admittedly, that possibility, which is now open to her in the absence of recognition, would disappear entirely under the current Civil Code ... if, as is the applicants' wish, the mere mention of the mother's name on the birth certificate were to constitute proof of any 'illegitimate' child's maternal affiliation. However, the dilemma which exists at present is not consonant with "respect" for family life; it thwarts and impedes the normal development of such life ... Furthermore, it appears ... that the unfavourable consequences of recognition in the area of patrimonial rights are of themselves contrary to Article 14 of the Convention, taken in conjunction with Article 8 and with Article 1 of Protocol No. 1.

The Court thus concludes that there has been a violation of Article 8, taken alone, with respect to the first applicant.

37. [The Court states that the time consuming legal procedure necessary for affiliation could mean along period during which mother and child would remain legally separated.].... This system resulted in a lack of respect for the family life of Alexandra Marckx who, in the eyes of the law, was motherless from 16 to 29 October 1973. Despite the brevity of this period, there was thus also a violation of Article 8 with respect to the second applicant.

2. On the alleged violation of Article 14 of the Convention, taken in conjunction with Article 8

38. The Court also has to determine whether, as regards the manner of establishing Alexandra's maternal affiliation, one or both of the applicants have been victims of discrimination contrary to Article 14 taken in conjunction with Article 8.

39. The Government, relying on the difference between the situations of the unmarried and the married mother, advance the following arguments: whilst the married mother and her husband "mutually undertake ... the obligation to feed, keep and educate their children"..., there is no certainty that the unmarried mother will be willing to bear on her own the responsibilities of motherhood; by leaving the unmarried mother the choice between recognising her child or dissociating herself from him, the law is prompted by a concern for protection of the child, for it would be dangerous to entrust it to the custody and authority of someone who has shown no inclination to care for him; many unmarried mothers do not recognise their child ...

In the Court's judgment, the fact that some unmarried mothers, unlike Paula Marckx, do not wish to take care of their child cannot justify the rule of Belgian law whereby the establishment of their maternity is conditional on voluntary recognition or a court declaration. In fact, such an attitude is not a general feature of the relationship between unmarried mothers and their children; besides, this is neither claimed by the Government nor proved by the figures which they advance. As the Commission points out, it may happen that also a married mother might not wish to bring up her child, and yet, as far as she is concerned, the birth alone will have created the legal bond of affiliation.

Again, the interest of an 'illegitimate' child in having such a bond established is no less than that of a 'legitimate' child. However, the 'illegitimate' child is likely to remain motherless in the eyes of Belgian law. If an 'illegitimate' child is not recognised voluntarily, it has only one expedient, namely, an action to establish maternal affiliation … A married woman's child also is entitled to institute such an action…, but in the vast majority of cases the entries on the birth certificate … or, failing that, the constant and factual enjoyment of the status of a legitimate child (une possession d'état constante) render this unnecessary.

40. The Government do not deny that the present law favours the traditional family, but they maintain that the law aims at ensuring that family's full development and is thereby founded on objective and reasonable grounds relating to morals and public order (ordre public).

The Court recognises that support and encouragement of the traditional family is in itself legitimate or even praiseworthy. However, in the achievement of this end recourse must not be had to measures whose object or result is, as in the present case, to prejudice the 'illegitimate' family; the members of the 'illegitimate' family enjoy the guarantees of Article 8 on an equal footing with the members of the traditional family.

. . . .

43. The distinction complained of therefore lacks objective and reasonable justification. Accordingly, the manner of establishing Alexandra Marckx's maternal affiliation violated, with respect to both applicants, Article 14 taken in conjunction with Article 8.

B. On the extent in law of Alexandra Marckx's family relationships

[The Court find a further violation of Articles 8 and 14 with respect to the fact that illegitimate children, including adopted illegitimate children, are essentially "strangers to their parents' families." The Court also finds a violation in the distinction drawn between legitimate and illegitimate children in the matter of "patrimonial rights" to inherit property under rules of intestate succession.]

. . . .

56. Unlike a 'legitimate' child, Alexandra has at no time before or after 30 October 1974 had any entitlement on intestacy in the estates of members of Paula Marckx's family … Here again, the Court fails to find any objective and reasonable justification.

. . . .

59. To sum up, Alexandra Marckx was the victim of a breach of Article 14, taken in conjunction with Article 8, by reason both of the restrictions on her capacity to receive property from her mother and of her total lack of inheritance rights on intestacy over the estates of her near relatives on her mother's side.

. . . .

Notes and Questions

1. What do you perceive to have been the rationale behind the Belgian laws of parental and family affiliation? Was the Court justified in sweeping the effect of the national laws away? Was its reasoning persuasive? What European values are served by this judgment?

2. What exactly was the disadvantage to non-marital children that the Court focused on? Under the legal regime Marckx complained of, what was she required to do before her relationship with her child would be treated on the same footing as that between mar-

ital children and their parents? To what degree did the decision of the Court ensure that equality of status? Does the Court give any indication that it had a wider agenda than just laws of maternal affiliation? Did the Court go far enough?

—————

The following case had the effect of spotlighting divergences in Irish law from the European mainstream with respect to divorce and remarriage. It should be noted that, as was perhaps inevitable, the Irish Constitution was amended following a popular referendum in 1995 to allow for the freedom to divorce. The referendum was hotly contested, but unlike an earlier vote on the same question, and despite some collective misgivings, its passage reflected significant social change. Divorce in Ireland is now neither uncommon nor socially controversial.

It is interesting to note that in *Johnston*, while the subtextual question is certainly the right to marry, the legal problem is not framed by the applicants in that way. As you read this famous case, consider where the Court stands on Irish social issues, family life and, for our purposes, the rights of children.

Johnston v. Ireland
112 Eur. Ct. H.R. (ser. A) (1986)

. . . .

AS TO THE FACTS

I. THE PARTICULAR CIRCUMSTANCES OF THE CASE

10. The first applicant is Roy H. W. Johnston, who was born in 1930 and is a scientific research and development manager. He resides at Rathmines, Dublin, with the second applicant, Janice Williams-Johnston, who was born in 1938; she is a school-teacher by profession and used to work as director of a play-group in Dublin, but has been unemployed since 1985. The third applicant is their daughter, Nessa Doreen Williams-Johnston, who was born in 1978.

11. The first applicant married a Miss M. in 1952 in a Church of Ireland ceremony. Three children were born of this marriage, in 1956, 1959 and 1965.

In 1965, it became clear to both parties that the marriage had irretrievably broken down and they decided to live separately at different levels in the family house. Several years later both of them, with the other's knowledge and consent, formed relationships and began to live with third parties. By mutual agreement, the two couples resided in self-contained flats in the house until 1976, when Roy Johnston's wife moved elsewhere.

In 1978, the second applicant, with whom Roy Johnston had been living since 1971, gave birth to Nessa. He consented to his name being included in the Register of Births as the father.

12. Under the Constitution of Ireland, the first applicant is unable to obtain, in Ireland, a dissolution of his marriage to enable him to marry the second applicant. He has taken the following steps to regularise his relationship with her and with his wife and to make proper provision for his dependents.

(a) With his wife's consent, he has consulted solicitors in Dublin and in London as to the possibility of obtaining a dissolution of the marriage outside Ireland. His London solicitors advised that, in the absence of residence within the jurisdiction of the English courts, he would not be able to do so in England, and the matter has therefore not been pursued.

(b) On 19 September 1982, he concluded a formal separation agreement with his wife, recording an agreement implemented some years earlier. She received a lump-sum of IR£8,800 and provision was made for maintenance of the remaining dependent child of the marriage. The parties also mutually renounced their succession rights over each other's estates.

(c) He has made a will leaving his house to the second applicant for life with remainder over to his four children as tenants in common, one half of the residue of his estate to the second applicant, and the other half to his four children in equal shares.

(d) He has supported the third applicant throughout her life and has acted in all respects as a caring father.

(e) He contributed towards the maintenance of his wife until the conclusion of the aforementioned separation agreement and has supported the three children of his marriage during their dependency.

(f) The second applicant has been nominated as beneficiary under the pension scheme attached to his employment.

(g) He has taken out health insurance in the names of the second and third applicants, as members of his family.

13. The second applicant, who is largely dependent on the first applicant for her support and maintenance, is concerned at the lack of security provided by her present legal status, in particular the absence of any legal right to be maintained by him and of any potential rights of succession in the event of intestacy. As is permitted by law, she has adopted the first applicant's surname, which she uses amongst friends and neighbours, but for business purposes continues to use the name Williams. According to her, she has felt inhibited about telling employers of her domestic circumstances and although she would like to become an Irish citizen by naturalisation, she has been reluctant to make an application, not wishing to put those circumstances in issue.

14. The third applicant has, under Irish law, the legal situation of an illegitimate child and her parents are concerned at the lack of any means by which she can, even with their consent, be recognised as their child with full rights of support and succession in relation to them. They are also concerned about the possibility of a stigma attaching to her by virtue of her legal situation, especially when she is attending school.

15. The first and second applicants state that although they have not practised any formal religion for some time, they have recently joined the Religious Society of Friends (the Quakers) in Dublin. This decision was influenced in part by their concern that the third applicant receives a Christian upbringing.

II. RELEVANT DOMESTIC LAW

A. Constitutional provisions relating to the family

16. The Constitution of Ireland, which came into force in 1937, includes the following provisions:

. . . .

> 41.1.1° The State recognises the Family as the natural primary and fundamental unit group of Society, and as a moral institution possessing inalienable and imprescriptible rights, antecedent and superior to all positive law.

> 41.1.2° The State, therefore, guarantees to protect the Family in its constitution and authority, as the necessary basis of social order and as indispensable to the welfare of the Nation and the State.

(…)

41.3.1° The State pledges itself to guard with special care the institution of Marriage, on which the family is founded, and to protect it against attack.

41.3.2° No law shall be enacted providing for the grant of a dissolution of marriage.

. . . .

17. As a result of Article 41.3.2° of the Constitution, divorce in the sense of dissolution of a marriage (divorce a vinculo matrimonii) is not available in Ireland. However, spouses may be relieved of the duty of cohabiting either by a legally binding deed of separation concluded between them or by a court decree of judicial separation (also known as a divorce a mensa et thoro); such a decree, which is obtainable only on proof of commission of adultery, cruelty or unnatural offences, does not dissolve the marriage. In the remainder of the present judgment, the word "divorce" denotes a divorce a vinculo matrimonii.

It is also possible to obtain on various grounds a degree of nullity, that is a declaration by the High Court that a marriage was invalid and therefore null and void ab initio. A marriage may also be annulled by an ecclesiastical tribunal, but this does not affect the civil status of the parties.

. . . .

B. Recognition of foreign divorces

19. Article 41.3.3° of the Constitution provides:

"No person whose marriage has been dissolved under the civil law of any other State but is a subsisting valid marriage under the law for the time being in force within the jurisdiction of the Government and Parliament established by this Constitution shall be capable of contracting a valid marriage within that jurisdiction during the lifetime of the other party to the marriage dissolved."

20. A series of judicial decisions has established that the foregoing provision does not prevent the recognition by Irish courts, under the general Irish rules of private international law, of certain decrees of divorce obtained, even by Irish nationals, in another State. Such recognition used to be granted only if the parties to the marriage were domiciled within the jurisdiction of the foreign court at the time of the relevant proceedings … ; however, since 2 October 1986 a divorce will be recognised if granted in the country where either spouse is domiciled …

. . . .

C. Legal status of persons in the situation of the first and second applicants

1. Marriage

22. Persons who, like the first and second applicants, are living together in a stable relationship after the breakdown of the marriage of one of them are unable, during the lifetime of the other party to that marriage, to marry each other in Ireland and are not recognised there as a family for the purposes of Article 41 of the Constitution.

2. Maintenance and succession

23. Such persons, unlike a married couple, have no legal duty to support or maintain one another and no mutual statutory rights of succession. However, there is no impediment under Irish law preventing them from living together and supporting each other and, in particular, from making wills or dispositions inter vivos in each other's favour. They can also enter into mutual maintenance agreements, although the Government and the

applicants expressed different views as to whether these might be unenforceable as contrary to public policy.

In general, the married member of the couple remains, at least in theory, under a continuing legal obligation to maintain his or her spouse. In addition, testamentary dispositions by that member may be subject to the rights of his or her spouse or legitimate children under the Succession Act 1965.

....

D. Legal situation of illegitimate children

1. Affiliation

25. In Irish law, the principle mater semper certa est applies: the maternal affiliation of an illegitimate child, such as the third applicant, is established by the fact of birth, without any requirement of voluntary or judicial recognition.

The Illegitimate Children (Affiliation Orders) Act 1930, as amended by the Family Law (Maintenance of Spouses and Children) Act 1976 and the Courts Act 1983, provides procedures whereby the District Court or the Circuit Court may make an 'affiliation order' against the putative father of a child directing him to make periodic payments in respect of the latter's maintenance and also whereby the court may approve a lump-sum maintenance agreement between a person who admits he is the father of an illegitimate child and the latter's mother. Neither of these procedures establishes the child's paternal affiliation for all purposes, any finding of parentage being effective solely for the purposes of the proceedings in question and binding only on the parties.

26. Under the Registration of Births and Deaths (Ireland) Act 1863, as amended by the Births and Deaths Registration (Ireland) Act 1880, the Registrar may enter in the register the name of a person as the father of an illegitimate child if he is so requested jointly by that person and the mother. The act of registration does not, however, establish paternal affiliation.

2. Guardianship

27. The mother of an illegitimate child is his sole guardian as from the moment of his birth (section 6(4) of the Guardianship of Infants Act 1964) and has the same rights of guardianship as are jointly enjoyed by the parents of a legitimate child. The natural father can apply to the court under section 11(4) of the same Act regarding the child's custody and the right of access thereto by either parent; however, he cannot seek the court's directions on other matters affecting the child's welfare nor is there any means whereby he can be established as guardian of the child jointly with the mother, even if she consents.

3. Legitimation

28. An illegitimate child may be legitimated by the subsequent marriage of his parents, provided that, unlike the first and second applicants, they could have been lawfully married to one another at the time of the child's birth or at some time during the preceding 10 months (section 1(1) and (2) of the Legitimacy Act 1931).

....

6. Succession

31. [In this section, it is noted that under Irish law illegitimate children do not inherit from the father where the father dies intestate. They may inherit from their mother in the same situation, but only where the mother has no legitimate children as heirs.]

....

PROCEEDINGS BEFORE THE COMMISSION

38. The application of Roy Johnston, Janice Williams-Johnston and Nessa Williams-Johnston (no. 9697/82) was lodged with the Commission on 16 February 1982. The applicants complained of the absence of provision in Ireland for divorce and for recognition of the family life of persons who, after the breakdown of the marriage of one of them, are living in a family relationship outside marriage. They alleged that on this account they had been victims of violations of Articles 8, 9, 12 and 13 of the Convention and also of Article 14 (taken in conjunction with Articles 8 and 12).

39. The Commission declared the application admissible on 7 October 1983.

In its report adopted on 5 March 1985..., the Commission expressed the opinion that:

—there was no breach of Articles 8 and 12 in that the right to divorce and subsequently to re-marry was not guaranteed by the Convention (unanimously);

—there was no breach of Article 8 in that Irish law did not confer a recognised family status on the first and second applicants (twelve votes to one);

—there was a breach of Article 8 in that the legal regime concerning the status of the third applicant under Irish law failed to respect the family life of all three applicants (unanimously);

—there was no breach of the first applicant's rights under Article 9 (unanimously);

—there was no breach of Article 14 in conjunction with Articles 8 and 12 in that the first and second applicants had not been discriminated against by Irish law (twelve votes to one);

—it was not necessary to examine the third applicant's separate complaint of discrimination;

—there was no breach of Article 13 (unanimously).

....

FINAL SUBMISSIONS MADE TO THE COURT

40. The applicants invoked before the Court the same Articles as they did before the Commission, other than Article 13.

....

AS TO THE LAW

....

II. SITUATION OF THE FIRST AND SECOND APPLICANTS

A. Inability to divorce and re-marry

1. Articles 12 and 8

49. The first and second applicants alleged that because of the impossibility under Irish law of obtaining a dissolution of Roy Johnston's marriage and of his resultant inability to marry Janice Williams-Johnston, they were victims of breaches of Articles 12 and 8 of the Convention. These provisions read as follows:

Article 12

"Men and women of marriageable age have the right to marry and to found a family, according to the national laws governing the exercise of this right."

[The Court goes on to cite the provisions 8, which is reprinted above.]

This allegation was contested by the Government and rejected by the Commission.

50. The applicants stated that, as regards this part of the case, the central issue was not whether the Convention guaranteed the right to divorce but rather whether the fact that they were unable to marry each other was compatible with the right to marry or remarry and with the right to respect for family life, enshrined in Articles 12 and 8.

The Court does not consider that the issues arising can be separated into watertight compartments in this way. In any society espousing the principle of monogamy, it is inconceivable that Roy Johnston should be able to marry as long as his marriage to Mrs. Johnston has not been dissolved. The second applicant, for her part, is not complaining of a general inability to marry but rather of her inability to marry the first applicant, a situation that stems precisely from the fact that he cannot obtain a divorce. Consequently, their case cannot be examined in isolation from the problem of the non-availability of divorce.

(a) Article 12

[The Court here agrees with the Commission that there is no right under Article 12 to obtain a divorce, and that the "right to marry" refers only to the "formation of marital relations," not to their dissolution.]

....

(b) Article 8

55. The principles which emerge from the Court's case-law on Article 8 include the following.

(a) By guaranteeing the right to respect for family life, Article 8 presupposes the existence of a family ...

(b) Article 8 applies to the "family life" of the "illegitimate" family as well as to that of the "legitimate" family.

(c) Although the essential object of Article 8 is to protect the individual against arbitrary interference by the public authorities, there may in addition be positive obligations inherent in an effective "respect" for family life. However, especially as far as those positive obligations are concerned, the notion of "respect" is not clear-cut: having regard to the diversity of the practices followed and the situations obtaining in the Contracting States, the notion's requirements will vary considerably from case to case. Accordingly, this is an area in which the Contracting Parties enjoy a wide margin of appreciation in determining the steps to be taken to ensure compliance with the Convention with due regard to the needs and resources of the community and of individuals ...

56. In the present case, it is clear that the applicants, the first and second of whom have lived together for some fifteen years, constitute a "family" for the purposes of Article 8. They are thus entitled to its protection, notwithstanding the fact that their relationship exists outside marriage ...

The question that arises, as regards this part of the case, is whether an effective "respect" for the applicants' family life imposes on Ireland a positive obligation to introduce measures that would permit divorce.

57. It is true that, on this question, Article 8, with its reference to the somewhat vague notion of "respect" for family life, might appear to lend itself more readily to an evolutive interpretation than does Article 12. Nevertheless, the Convention must be read as a whole and the Court does not consider that a right to divorce, which it has found to be excluded from Article 12 ..., can, with consistency, be derived from Article 8, a provision of more general purpose and scope. The Court is not oblivious to the plight of the first and second applicants. However, it is of the opinion that, although the protection of private or family life may sometimes necessitate means whereby spouses can be relieved

from the duty to live together…, the engagements undertaken by Ireland under Article 8 cannot be regarded as extending to an obligation on its part to introduce measures permitting the divorce and the re-marriage which the applicants seek.

58. On the point, there is therefore no failure to respect the family life of the first and second applicants.

2. Article 14, taken in conjunction with Article 8

59. The first and second applicants complained of the fact that whereas Roy Johnston was unable to obtain a divorce in order subsequently to marry Janice Williams-Johnston, other persons resident in Ireland and having the necessary means could obtain abroad a divorce which would be recognised de jure or de facto in Ireland … They alleged that on this account they had been victims of discrimination, on the ground of financial means, in the enjoyment of the rights set forth in Article 8, contrary to Article 14 …

[The court here notes the text of Article 14.]

This allegation, contested by the Government, was rejected by the Commission.

60. Article 14 safeguards persons who are "placed in analogous situations" against discriminatory differences of treatment in the exercise of the rights and freedoms recognised by the Convention …

The Court notes that under the general Irish rules of private international law foreign divorces will be recognised in Ireland only if they have been obtained by persons domiciled abroad … It does not find it to have been established that these rules are departed from in practice. In its view, the situations of such persons and of the first and second applicants cannot be regarded as analogous.

61. There is, accordingly, no discrimination, within the meaning of Article 14.

3. Article 9

62. The first applicant also alleged that his inability to live with the second applicant other than in an extra-marital relationship was contrary to his conscience and that on that account he was the victim of a violation of Article 9 of the Convention, which guarantees to everyone the "right to freedom of thought, conscience and religion".

The applicant supplemented this allegation, which was contested by the Government and rejected by the Commission, by a claim of discrimination in relation to conscience and religion, contrary to Article 14 taken in conjunction with Article 9.

63. It is clear that Roy Johnston's freedom to have and manifest his convictions is not in issue. His complaint derives, in essence, from the non-availability of divorce under Irish law, a matter to which, in the Court's view, Article 9 cannot, in its ordinary meaning, be taken to extend.

Accordingly, that provision, and hence Article 14 also, are not applicable.

4. Conclusion

64. The Court thus concludes that the complaints related to the inability to divorce and re-marry are not well-founded.

B. Matters other than the inability to divorce and re-marry

65. The first and second applicants further alleged that, in violation of Article 8, there had been an interference with, or lack of respect for, their family life on account of their status under Irish law …

….

68. It is true that certain legislative provisions designed to support family life are not available to the first and second applicants. However, like the Commission, the Court does not consider that it is possible to derive from Article 8 an obligation on the part of Ireland to establish for unmarried couples a status analogous to that of married couples.

The applicants did, in fact, make it clear that their complaints concerned only couples who, like themselves, wished to marry but were legally incapable of marrying and not those who had chosen of their own volition to live together outside marriage. Nevertheless, even if it is circumscribed in this way, the applicants' claim cannot, in the Court's opinion, be accepted. A number of the matters complained of are but consequences of the inability to obtain a dissolution of Roy Johnston's marriage enabling him to marry Janice Williams-Johnston, a situation which the Court has found not to be incompatible with the Convention. As for the other matters, Article 8 cannot be interpreted as imposing an obligation to establish a special regime for a particular category of unmarried couples.

69. There is accordingly no violation of Article 8 under this head.

III. SITUATION OF THE THIRD APPLICANT

A. Article 8

70. The applicants alleged that, in violation of Article 8, there had been an interference with, or lack of respect for, their family life on account of the third applicant's situation under Irish law. In addition to the points mentioned ... above, they cited, by way of illustration, the following matters:

(a) the position regarding the third applicant's paternal affiliation ... ;

(b) the impossibility for the first applicant to be appointed joint guardian of the third applicant and his lack of parental rights in relation to her ... ;

(c) the impossibility for the third applicant to be legitimated even by her parents' subsequent marriage ... ;

(d) the impossibility for the third applicant to be jointly adopted by her parents ... ;

(e) the third applicant's succession rights vis-à-vis her parents ... ;

(f) the third applicant's treatment for the purposes of capital acquisition tax and the repercussions on her of her parents' own treatment for fiscal purposes.

The Government contested this allegation. The Commission, on the other hand, expressed the opinion that there had been a breach of Article 8, in that the legal regime concerning the status of the third applicant under Irish law failed to respect the family life of all three applicants.

71. Roy Johnston and Janice Williams-Johnston have been able to take a number of steps to integrate their daughter in the family. However, the question arises whether an effective "respect" for family life imposes on Ireland a positive obligation to improve her legal situation ...

72. Of particular relevance to this part of the case, in addition to the principles recalled in paragraph 55 above, are the following passages from the Court's case-law:

> "... when the State determines in its domestic legal system the regime applicable to certain family ties such as those between an unmarried mother and her child, it must act in a manner calculated to allow those concerned to lead a normal family life. As envisaged by Article 8, respect for family life implies in particu-

lar, in the Court's view, the existence in domestic law of legal safeguards that render possible as from the moment of birth the child's integration in his family. In this connection, the State has a choice of various means, but a law that fails to satisfy this requirement violates paragraph 1 of Article 8 without there being any call to examine it under paragraph 2." ...

"In determining whether or not a positive obligation exists, regard must be had to the fair balance that has to be struck between the general interest of the community and the interests of the individual, the search for which balance is inherent in the whole of the Convention ... In striking this balance the aims mentioned in the second paragraph of Article 8 may be of a certain relevance, although this provision refers in terms only to 'interferences' with the right protected by the first paragraph — in other words is concerned with the negative obligations flowing therefrom" ...

As the Government emphasised, the *Marckx* case related solely to the relations between mother and child. However, the Court considers that its observations on the integration of a child within his family are equally applicable to a case such as the present, concerning as it does parents who have lived, with their daughter, in a family relationship over many years but are unable to marry on account of the indissolubility of the existing marriage of one of them.

. . . .

74. ... As it observed in its above-mentioned *Marckx* judgment, "respect" for family life, understood as including the ties between near relatives, implies an obligation for the State to act in a manner calculated to allow these ties to develop normally ... And in the present case the normal development of the natural family ties between the first and second applicants and their daughter requires, in the Court's opinion, that she should be placed, legally and socially, in a position akin to that of a legitimate child.

75. Examination of the third applicant's present legal situation, seen as a whole, reveals, however, that it differs considerably from that of a legitimate child; in addition, it has not been shown that there are any means available to her or her parents to eliminate or reduce the differences. Having regard to the particular circumstances of this case and notwithstanding the wide margin of appreciation enjoyed by Ireland in this area ..., the absence of an appropriate legal regime reflecting the third applicant's natural family ties amounts to a failure to respect her family life.

Moreover, the close and intimate relationship between the third applicant and her parents is such that there is of necessity also a resultant failure to respect the family life of each of the latter. Contrary to the Government's suggestion, this finding does not amount, in an indirect way, to a conclusion that the first applicant should be entitled to divorce and re-marry; this is demonstrated by the fact that in Ireland itself it is proposed to improve the legal situation of illegitimate children, whilst maintaining the constitutional prohibition on divorce.

76. There is accordingly, as regards all three applicants, a breach of Article 8 under this head.

77. It is not the Court's function to indicate which measures Ireland should take in this connection; it is for the State concerned to choose the means to be utilised in its domestic law for performance of its obligation under Article 53 ... In making its choice, Ireland must ensure that the requisite fair balance is struck between the demands of the general interest of the community and the interests of the individual.

. . . .

IV. THE APPLICATION OF ARTICLE 50[6]

80. Under Article 50 of the Convention,

> "If the Court finds that a decision or a measure taken by a legal authority or any other authority of a High Contracting Party is completely or partially in conflict with the obligations arising from the ... Convention, and if the internal law of the said Party allows only partial reparation to be made for the consequences of this decision or measure, the decision of the Court shall, if necessary, afford just satisfaction to the injured party."

The applicants sought under this provision just satisfaction in respect of material loss, non-pecuniary loss and legal costs and expenses.

A. Material loss

[Because the Court found that the applicants' arguments with respect to both material and non-pecuniary loss derived from the inability of the man and woman to marry under Irish law, these claims were rejected. Applicants were awarded legal costs and expenses of 12,000 Irish pounds.]

FOR THESE REASONS, THE COURT

. . . .

2. Holds by sixteen votes to one that the absence of provision for divorce under Irish law and the resultant inability of the first and second applicants to marry each other does not give rise to a violation of Article 8 or Article 12 of the Convention;

3. Holds by sixteen votes to one that the first and second applicants are not victims of discrimination, contrary to Article 14 taken in conjunction with Article 8, by reason of the fact that certain foreign divorces may be recognised by the law of Ireland;

. . . .

6. Holds unanimously that the legal situation of the third applicant under Irish law gives rise to a violation of Article 8 as regards all three applicants;

. . . .

8. Holds unanimously that Ireland is to pay to the three applicants together, in respect of legal costs and expenses referable to the proceedings before the Commission and the Court, the sum of twelve thousand Irish pounds (IR£12,000), together with any value added tax that may be chargeable;

. . . .

Separate Opinion, Partly Dissenting and Partly Concurring, of Judge de Meyer (Translation)

I. The impossibility for the first applicant to seek the dissolution of his 1952 marriage and the resultant inability of the first and second applicants to marry each other

1. As the Court observes, in paragraph 50 of the judgment, these two questions cannot be separated: in fact, they come down to a single question, namely the first.

The fact that the first and second applicants are unable to marry each other so long as the first applicant's 1952 marriage is not dissolved cannot, of itself, constitute a violation of their fundamental rights.

---

6. The court decided this case prior to the adoption of Protocol 11, which replaced and amended Article 50 with Article 41. *See supra* note 5 and accompanying text. Although the language of Article 50 was altered, the concept of "just satisfaction" remains the same.

It is only the fact that the first applicant cannot seek the dissolution of his 1952 marriage that may constitute such a violation. It may, of itself, do so, as regards the first applicant, because he is a party to that marriage. It may also do so, as regards the second as well as the first applicant, because it necessarily means that neither of them can marry the other during the lifetime of the first applicant's wife.

....

5. We are thus faced with a situation in which, by mutual consent and a considerable time ago, two spouses separated, regulated their own and their children's rights in an apparently satisfactory fashion and embarked on a new life, each with a new partner.

In my view, the absence of any possibility of seeking, in such circumstances, the civil dissolution of the marriage constitutes, first and of itself, a violation, as regards each of the spouses, of the rights guaranteed in Articles 8, 9 and 12 of the Convention. Secondly, in that it perforce means that neither spouse can remarry in a civil ceremony so long as his wife or husband is alive, it constitutes a violation of the same rights as regards each of the spouses and each of the new partners.

The absence of the aforesaid possibility is consonant neither with the right of those concerned to respect for their private and family life, nor with their right to freedom of conscience and religion, nor with their right to marry and to found a family.

In fact, it seems to me that in cases like the present the effective exercise of these rights may require that the spouses be allowed to apply not only to be relieved of their duty to live together but also to be completely released in civil law from their marital ties, by means of legal recognition of their definitive separation.

The prohibition, under the Constitution of the respondent State, of any legislation permitting the dissolution of marriage is, as seems already to have been recognised in 1967 by a Committee of that State's Parliament, "coercive in relation to all persons, Catholics and non-Catholics, whose religious rules do not absolutely prohibit divorce in all circumstances" and "at variance with the accepted principles of religious liberty as declared at the Vatican Council and elsewhere". Above all, it is, as that Committee stated, "unnecessarily harsh and rigid".

In what the Convention, in several provisions and notably those concerning respect for private and family life and freedom of conscience and religion, calls "a democratic society", the prohibition cannot be justified.

On more than one occasion, the Court has pointed out that there can be no such society without pluralism, tolerance and broadmindedness: these are hallmarks of a democratic society.

In a society grounded on principles of this kind, it seems to me excessive to impose, in an inflexible and absolute manner, a rule that marriage is indissoluble, without even allowing consideration to be given to the possibility of exceptions in cases of the present kind.

For so draconian a system to be legitimate, it does not suffice that it corresponds to the desire or will of a substantial majority of the population: the Court has also stated that "although individual interests must on occasion be subordinated to those of a group, democracy does not simply mean that the views of a majority must always prevail: a balance must be achieved which ensures the fair and proper treatment of minorities and avoids any abuse of a dominant position".

In my opinion, this statement must also be applicable in the area of marriage and divorce.

6. The foregoing considerations do not imply recognition of a right to divorce or that such a right, to the extent that it exists, can be classified as a fundamental right.

They simply mean that the complete exclusion of any possibility of seeking the civil dissolution of a marriage is not compatible with the right to respect for private and family life, with the right to freedom of conscience and religion and with the right to marry and to found a family.

7. I also believe that there is discrimination as regards the exercise of the rights involved.

Although it totally prohibits divorce within Ireland itself, the respondent State recognises divorces obtained in other countries by persons domiciled there at the time of the divorce proceedings.

Thus, Irish citizens who move abroad and stay there long enough for it to be accepted that they intend to remain there permanently escape their inability to obtain a divorce in Ireland.

This state of affairs is in unfortunate contradiction with the absolute character of the principle of indissolubility of marriage, in that the principle thus appears to warrant observance only in Ireland itself and not elsewhere.

The distinction so made between Irish citizens according to whether they are domiciled in Ireland itself or elsewhere appears to me to lack an objective and reasonable justification.

8. Unlike the majority of the Court, I am therefore of the opinion that in the present case the first and second applicants rightly complain of a violation of their right to respect for their private and family life, of their right to freedom of conscience and religion and of their right to marry and to found a family, as well as of discrimination in the exercise of these rights.

....

Notes and Questions

1. Does it seem that the real question in this case was the one the Court showed the least interest in dealing with: the lack of divorce in Ireland? As mentioned, Irish voters did in fact approve of removing the Constitutional prohibition against divorce in a 1995 referendum. How could the child's family status be seen in human rights terms, while her parents remained legally unable to marry?

2. In both the *Marckx* case and the *Johnston* case, the ECHR tells European countries to eliminate at least some of their rules on family formation. On what basis does the Court exercise such powers, especially given the fact that the Convention is so broad and general in its approach? Can you identify common themes or myths relied on by the Court as it reasons its way through these problems?

The ECHR has never ruled directly on the contentious question of human rights and international adoption. In the following case, however, the Court looked at the rights of older Romanian children who were opposed to being adopted abroad. As you read the case, try to determine if there are indications of the Court's position on intercountry adoption generally. On its facts, does the case seem broadly representative of the core issues in intercountry adoption or not?

Pini and Bertani and Manera and Atripaldi v. Romania
2004 Eur. Ct. H.R.

[The applicants were two Italian couples who had obtained orders for the adoption of two Romanian children, Florentina and Mariana, who were judicially declared to have been abandoned. The children were nine years old when the adoption orders were made and in the care of the CEPSB [Poiana Soarelui Educational Centre in Brasov], a private institution approved by the Brasov Child Protection Department. CEPSB's function was to provide a home for orphaned and abandoned children, to take care of them and provide them with an education. The District Court granted the adoption orders in September 2000 and ordered the children's birth certificates to be amended. An appeal by the Romanian Adoptions Board was dismissed and the orders became final. The applicants sought to enforce the orders but the CEPSB refused to hand over the children's birth certificates or transfer custody. Court bailiffs tried in vain to enforce the orders, while the CEPSB lodged various objections to enforcement and unsuccessfully applied to annul the adoptions.

In September and November 2002 the children brought proceedings to revoke their adoptions on the ground that they did not know their adoptive parents and did not wish to leave the CEPSB. Florentina's application was dismissed on the ground that it was not in her interests for the adoption order to be revoked but the court granted Mariana's application after noting that she was receiving a sound education and living in good conditions at the CEPSB and had not formed any emotional ties with her adoptive parents.

Relying on Article 8 of the Convention, the applicants complained that the Romanian authorities' failure to enforce the adoption orders had deprived them of all contact with their adopted children. They also argued that the authorities' refusal to permit their daughters to leave the country breached Article 2(2) of Protocol No.4. They claimed just satisfaction under Article 41.]

. . . .

THE LAW

I. ALLEGED VIOLATION OF ARTICLE 8 OF THE CONVENTION

1. The applicants complained of the failure to execute the domestic courts' final decisions concerning the adoption of Florentina and Mariana, and submitted that this amounted to an infringement of their right to respect for their family life as guaranteed by Article 8 of the Convention . . .

[Here the court recounts the text of Article 8, which is reprinted above.]

A. The parties' submissions

1. *The applicants*

(a) Whether there was a bond amounting to "family life" within the meaning of Article 8 § 1 of the Convention

2. The applicants submitted that the relationship established between them and their respective adopted daughters constituted a family tie, protected by Article 8 of the Convention, which was therefore applicable in the present case. They referred to *Abdulaziz, Cabales and Balkandali v. the United Kingdom* . . . , *Eriksson v. Sweden* . . . , *Marckx v. Belgium* . . . and *Ignaccolo-Zenide v. Romania*. . . .

3. They submitted that the Court had already held that the word "family" applied to the relationship between two people who believed themselves to be married and genuinely wished to cohabit and lead a normal family life, on the ground that the committed relationship

thus established was sufficient to attract the application of Article 8 ... On the basis of the final adoption orders, they argued that the relationship between them and their respective adopted children *a fortiori* amounted to a family tie.

4. Furthermore, they pointed out that they had met Florentina and Mariana and that, although the CEPSB had denied them the right to pay them further visits, they had constantly thought of them, showing them affection and frequently sending them letters and presents.

5. Referring in particular to their visit on 3 August 2000, they disputed Florentina's and Mariana's allegations and doubted that they had actually been made by the children, bearing in mind the atmosphere of hostility and resistance fostered by the CEPSB. They pointed out that a video recording proved that the girls had been pleased with their visit and had expressed the desire to join them as they had appreciated spending time with them.

6. While accepting that the girls had been able to develop emotional ties with the other children in the CEPSB or with the "substitute mothers", they argued that children needed support when they had to leave surroundings which they had regarded for years as their real life in order to join their new family; however, no such support had been provided in the present case. In the applicants' submission, the very foundations of the institution of adoption suggested that children should be assisted in this delicate stage of their lives.

(b) Whether their "family life" was respected

7. The applicants pointed out that all the international treaties on children's rights stated unequivocally that the family provided the best environment for the development of the child's personality. Referring in addition to a European Parliament report..., they noted that one of the areas given priority by the Romanian government with a view to European Union accession was the question of children in institutions. Notwithstanding the CEPSB's qualities, they considered that the centre could not under any circumstances replace a family in so far as it merely provided the children in its care with "contract substitute mothers", who were nothing but ordinary employees and could be dismissed or resign at any moment.

8. In any event, the applicants contended that the role of such an institution was not to hinder the adoption process; nor should it engage in a smear campaign by making unsubstantiated allegations against adoptive parents, which the newspapers had taken up using the epithet "child traffickers".

9. The centre's intention to discredit at all costs those foreigners who wished to adopt Romanian children raised doubts, in the applicants' submission, as to its qualities, particularly as it would have sufficient opportunity to find other children to replace those who left as a result of adoption orders made by the competent authorities. They submitted that such doubts were further reinforced by the recent conviction of one of the centre's employees for sexually abusing three of the children in its care ...

10. Lastly, they noted that if the girls had not become aware of the adoption orders until 3 September 2002 and only "by chance", as they had alleged, that proved that the centre had never told them about the orders.

11. With regard to the CEPSB's alleged lack of consent to the adoptions, they emphasised that the procedures for adopting Florentina and Mariana had complied with Romanian legislation and with the relevant international treaties, seeing that pursuant to section 8 of Government Emergency Ordinance no. 26/1997, parental rights over children who had been judicially declared to have been abandoned had been exercised by the Brasov Child Welfare Board and that the Board had given its approval to the children's adoption and

had reiterated that position before the court that had ruled on the applicants' applications for adoption orders.

2. The Government

(a) Whether there was a bond amounting to "family life" within the meaning of Article 8 § 1 of the Convention

12. The Government argued, as their main submission, that Article 8 of the Convention did not apply to the circumstances of the applicants, who could not claim that there was "family life" meriting protection under that provision. They submitted that, although the applicants had been acknowledged as the adoptive parents of Florentina and Mariana in final judicial decisions, that fact alone should not be regarded as bringing their cases within the scope of Article 8, seeing that no family life had ever existed in practice. They observed in that connection that the applicants had never met their adopted daughters in their capacity as parents and had never enjoyed genuine family relations with them.

13. Although they had visited the CEPSB on 3 August 2000, the visit could not in the Government's opinion be taken to have created any bond that was sufficiently deep to amount to family life. They submitted that the adoptions had been arranged through the C. association and that the children had never lived with the applicants and had never regarded them as their parents.

14. The Government contended that the applicants had not in fact shown any real interest in getting to know the girls or in ensuring that their well-being came first. They observed in that connection that, during the adoption process, the first applicant couple had travelled to Romania on only five occasions, and the second applicant couple on only three; just one of those visits had taken place before the adoption order had been made on 28 September 2000.

15. They argued that the applicants were still in the position of "prospective" parents, as there were no blood ties and no *de facto* family life binding them to their children. That being so, the existence of a formal family tie established by a court decision should not, they maintained, enjoy the protection of Article 8, the Convention institutions having always favoured an approach based on substantive aspects rather than a formal approach based on the definition of the concept of family in domestic law.

. . . .

16. The Government submitted in conclusion that the concept of family life within the meaning of Article 8 could not apply to a relationship based on adoption, which only the adoptive parents viewed as a family tie while the child refused to live with them.

(b) Whether the applicants' "family life" was respected

17. In the alternative, the Government maintained that the particular circumstances of the present cases effectively altered the scope of the positive obligations arising for the State from the concept of "respect for family life". They pointed out in the first place that the family ties established between Florentina and Mariana and the CEPSB staff did not equate merely to the relationship between a social worker and her clients but had attained the same depth as the bonds developed in a traditional parent/child relationship. The girls' respective "mothers" and "aunts" at the centre had "witnessed" their growing up, having shared in the most significant moments of their childhood; this, in the Government's submission, was of great significance for their personal development.

18. The Government submitted that the girls' feelings towards these people and the other children in the centre were extremely warm, sincere and strong. The sudden and delib-

erate severing of such ties, which had built up over time, could have devastating consequences for the children's psyche.

19. Pointing out that the centre's management made efforts to trace the biological parents of the children in its care, the Government considered that there were major issues at stake in the present case, as it concerned intercountry adoption. They noted in that connection that the possibility for the children to see their biological parents or their close friends from the CEPSB would be greatly reduced if they were adopted and taken to Italy, and that the suffering resulting from their separation from those people would be heightened in a foreign environment, in view of the cultural and religious differences and the lack of familiar reference points.

20. The Government further observed that the girls were not treated in an "institutionalised" or "arithmetical" manner at the centre but that, on the contrary, they lived there as in a family, without fearing that they might be thrown out when they reached adulthood, since they knew that they would receive support from the centre until the point where they took control of their own lives. They also pointed out that the centre provided the girls with all the necessary conditions for pursuing their own vocations. In particular, the Government noted that Florentina was attending the College of the Arts, where she was taking violin and piano lessons, while Mariana was being encouraged to develop her skills in dance and sport.

21. All those aspects, together with the girls' consistent attitude towards their adoption, had a strong bearing, in the Government's submission, on the steps that should be taken by the authorities to ensure respect for the applicants' family life. They argued in that connection that the two children had always been opposed to moving to Italy, as was clear, for example, from their applications to have the adoption orders revoked and from the statement made by Florentina in the course of criminal proceedings instituted by the applicants against the centre's director for false imprisonment of the girls ...

22. The Government submitted, lastly, that no breach of Article 8 could be made out in the instant case, since that provision could not be construed as requiring the State to take radical steps to enforce an adoption order with police assistance or to use other means of psychological preparation to develop a family relationship while court proceedings to determine the children's interests were still pending.

B. Submissions of the third parties

1. Whether there was a bond between the applicants and the children amounting to "family life" within the meaning of Article 8 § 1 of the Convention

. . . .

23. Florentina and Mariana submitted, in particular, that it had not been until 3 September 2002 that they had learned, quite by chance, of the existence of a final and binding decision on the basis of which their respective adoptive parents were seeking to force them to leave their country and the family within which they had been living at the CEPSB for eight and four years respectively. They pointed out that they were not related to the applicants by blood or by *de facto* family ties and argued that the applicants' alleged visit to the centre on 3 August 2000, of which they had no recollection, could not be regarded as a sufficiently close bond to commit them to a new family life.

. . . .

C. The Court's assessment

1. Applicability of Article 8 of the Convention

. . . .

24. With regard in particular to the obligations imposed by Article 8 of the Convention on the Contracting States in the field of adoption, and to the effects of adoption on the relationship between adopters and those being adopted, they must be interpreted in the light of the Hague Convention of 29 May 1993 on Protection of Children and Cooperation in respect of Intercountry Adoption, the United Nations Convention of 20 November 1989 on the Rights of the Child and the European Convention on the Adoption of Children, opened for signature in Strasbourg on 24 April 1967.

25. In this connection, the Court would refer to an older line of case-law to the effect that, although the right to adopt is not, as such, included among the rights guaranteed by the Convention, the relations between an adoptive parent and an adopted child are as a rule of the same nature as the family relations protected by Article 8 of the Convention ...

26. In the instant case the Court notes that the applicants are able to rely on final and irrevocable decisions by the domestic courts, which allowed their applications for adoption and acknowledged them as the parents of Florentina and Mariana.

27. It must be pointed out that the adoption orders conferred on the applicants the same rights and obligations in respect of their adopted children as those of a father or mother in respect of a child born in lawful wedlock, while at the same time ending any rights and obligations existing between the adopted children and their biological father or mother or any other person or body, as is clear from Article 10 of the European Convention on the Adoption of Children, which Romania ratified on 18 May 1993. The Court further notes that the relevant domestic legislation, in particular section 1 of Government Emergency Ordinance no. 25/1997, approved by Law no. 87 of 25 April 1998, which replaced the former Article 75 of the Family Code, likewise makes no distinction between the parents of children born in lawful wedlock and adoptive parents ...

28. Admittedly, by guaranteeing the right to respect for family life, Article 8 presupposes the existence of a family..., a requirement which does not seem to have been met in the instant case as the applicants did not live with their respective adopted daughters or have sufficiently close *de facto* ties with them, either before or after the adoption orders were made. However, this does not mean, in the Court's opinion, that all intended family life falls entirely outside the ambit of Article 8. In this connection, the Court has previously held that Article 8 may also extend to the potential relationship between a child born out of wedlock and his or her natural father..., or apply to the relationship that arises from a lawful and genuine marriage, even if family life has not yet been fully established ...

29. There is no reason in the instant case to cast doubt on the compliance of the adoption orders with domestic legislation or with the relevant international treaties. The national authorities established that the children, who had been judicially declared to have been abandoned, were eligible for adoption, and considered that intercountry adoption would be in their best interests, having obtained the consent of the prospective adopters and of the Brasov Child Welfare Board, which exercised parental rights over the children, in accordance with section 8 of Government Emergency Ordinance no. 26/1997 ...

30. It is true that the children's consent was not obtained by the courts that allowed the applicants' applications for adoption. The Court observes, however, that that was not an omission. As the children were nine and a half years old on the date on which the national courts ruled on the applications for adoption, they had not yet reached the age at which their consent should have been obtained for the adoption order to be valid, set at ten years under the domestic legislation. Such a threshold does not appear unreasonable, since the relevant international treaties leave the national authorities some discretion as

to the age from which children are to be regarded as sufficiently mature for their wishes to be taken into account ...

31. Lastly, the Court notes that, although family life has not yet been fully established in the instant case, seeing that the applicants have not lived with their respective adopted daughters or had sufficiently close *de facto* ties with them either before or after the adoption orders were made, that fact is not attributable to the applicants. In selecting the children solely on the basis of a photograph without having had any real contact with them that would have served as preparation for the adoption, the applicants were simply following the procedure put in place by the respondent State in such matters.

32. It further appears from the evidence before the Court that the applicants always viewed themselves as the girls' parents and behaved as such towards them through the only means open to them, namely by sending them letters written in Romanian ...

33. In the light of the foregoing, the Court considers that such a relationship, arising from a lawful and genuine adoption, may be deemed sufficient to attract such respect as may be due for family life under Article 8 of the Convention, which accordingly is applicable.

2. Compliance with Article 8 of the Convention

34. The Court reiterates that the essential object of Article 8 is to protect the individual against arbitrary action by the public authorities. There are, in addition, positive obligations inherent in effective "respect" for family life. In both contexts regard must be had to the fair balance that has to be struck between the competing interests of the individual and of the community as a whole; and in both contexts the State enjoys a certain margin of appreciation ...

35. As regards the State's obligation to take positive measures, the Court has repeatedly held—where it has established the existence of family relations based on descent or on existing emotional ties—that Article 8 includes a parent's right to the taking of measures with a view to his or her being reunited with the child and an obligation on the national authorities to take such action ...

36. However, the obligation on the national authorities to take measures to that end is not absolute—even in the case of family relations based on descent—especially where the parent and child are still strangers to one another ... The nature and extent of such measures will depend on the circumstances of each case, but the understanding and cooperation of all concerned will always be an important ingredient. While the national authorities must do their utmost to facilitate such cooperation, any obligation to apply coercion in this area must be limited since the interests and the rights and freedoms of all concerned must be taken into account, and more particularly the best interests of the child and his or her rights under Article 8 of the Convention. Where contact with the parent might appear to threaten those interests or interfere with those rights, it is for the national authorities to strike a fair balance between them ...

37. What is decisive in this case is therefore whether the national authorities took the necessary steps to enable the applicants—who had been acknowledged as the adoptive parents of Florentina and Mariana and had in both cases obtained a court order, on an urgent application, requiring the CEPSB, a private institution, to hand over the child to them—to establish family relations with each of the children they had adopted.

38. As the Government stated, at issue here are the competing interests of the applicants and of the adopted children. There are unquestionably no grounds, from the children's perspective, for creating emotional ties against their will between them and people to whom they are not biologically related and whom they view as strangers. It is clear from

the facts of the case that at present Florentina and Mariana would rather remain in the social and family environment in which they have grown up at the CEPSB, into which they consider themselves to be fully integrated and which is conducive to their physical, emotional, educational and social development, than be transferred to different surroundings abroad.

39. The adoptive parents' interest derived from their desire to create a new family relationship by forging ties with Florentina and Mariana, their adopted children.

40. Although such a desire on the part of the applicants is legitimate, the Court considers that it cannot enjoy absolute protection under Article 8 in so far as it conflicts with the children's refusal to be adopted by a foreign family. The Court has consistently held that particular importance must be attached to the best interests of the child in ascertaining whether the national authorities have taken all the necessary steps that can reasonably be demanded to facilitate the reunion of the child and his or her parents. In particular, it has held in such matters that the child's interests may, depending on their nature and seriousness, override those of the parent ...

41. The Court considers that it is even more important that the child's interests should prevail over those of the parents in the case of a relationship based on adoption, since, as it has previously held, adoption means "providing a child with a family, not a family with a child ..."

42. It must be pointed out that in the instant case the children rejected the idea of joining their adoptive parents in Italy once they had reached an age at which it could reasonably be considered that their personality was sufficiently formed and they had attained the necessary maturity to express their opinion as to the surroundings in which they wished to be brought up ... The Court further notes that Romanian law expressly affords them the opportunity to express their opinion on the matter since, firstly, children who are the subject of adoption proceedings are required to give their consent from the age of 10 onwards and, secondly, children who have already been adopted are entitled to apply to have the adoption order revoked once they have reached that age.

43. Admittedly, it is not in doubt that the children's interests were assessed by the relevant authorities in the course of the adoption proceedings. In the Court's opinion, however, that does not rule out the possibility of a fresh examination of all the relevant evidence at a later stage where this is required by specific circumstances and where the child's best interests are at stake ...

44. In this connection, the Court notes, as the Government did, that after 28 September 2000 the applicants' relationship with the girls was recognised on a purely formal basis and was not accompanied by any real ties. They have never truly known the children, since the adoption was carried out through the C. association and the children had not lived with them beforehand and did not regard them as their parents. The girls, who at the time of their adoption were nine and a half years old and were thus close to the age from which their consent to the adoption would have been compulsory, did not accept this relationship and were opposed to it.

45. They also lodged applications in their own name to revoke the adoption orders on the ground that they did not wish to leave the country and the surroundings in which they had been raised and into which they felt fully integrated. It is of some significance here that Mariana's application was successful and the order for her adoption has now been revoked in a final decision [that had immediate effect].

46. The Court also notes that for a number of years after the decisions of 28 September 2000 in the applicants' favour, various other sets of proceedings were pending in the na-

tional courts to have the adoption orders declared void on the ground that, among other things, provisions of the international treaties on the subject had been infringed. The Court does not find it unreasonable that the authorities awaited the conclusion of those proceedings, whose outcome could not have been foreseen, before taking measures of a permanent nature that were likely to create a new family life for the applicants.

47. Indeed, in so far as allegations of irregularities in adoption procedures were the subject of proceedings before the competent courts, the authorities had a duty to ensure that any uncertainty as to the lawfulness of the adoption was dispelled. That conclusion is particularly valid in the present case as the enforcement of the decisions in the applicants' favour, with the children moving to Italy, would have made it difficult for the children and harmful to their interests to return to Romania in the event of a subsequent court decision setting aside or revoking the adoption orders.

48. The Court deplores the manner in which the adoption proceedings were conducted, in particular the lack of real, effective contact between the interested parties before the adoption, a state of affairs made possible by shortcomings in the relevant domestic legislation at the material time. It finds it particularly regrettable that the children clearly did not receive any psychological support capable of preparing them for their imminent departure from the centre which had been their home for several years and in which they had established social and emotional ties. Such measures would probably have made it possible for the applicants' interests to converge with those of their adopted children, instead of competing with them as occurred in the present case.

49. Nevertheless, in the circumstances of the case, given that the applicants' interests were weaker as they had been acknowledged as the adoptive parents of children aged almost 10 without having any genuine pre-existing ties with them, there could be no justification for imposing on the Romanian authorities an absolute obligation to ensure that the children went to Italy against their will and irrespective of the pending judicial proceedings instituted with a view to challenging the lawfulness and well-foundedness of the initial adoption orders. The children's interests dictated that their opinions on the subject should have been taken into account once they had attained the necessary maturity to express them.

The children's consistent refusal, after they had reached the age of 10, to travel to Italy and join their adoptive parents carries a certain weight in this regard. Their conscious opposition to adoption would make their harmonious integration into their new adoptive family unlikely.

50. In the light of the foregoing, the Court concludes that the national authorities were legitimately and reasonably entitled to consider that the applicants' right to develop ties with their adopted children was circumscribed by the children's interests, notwithstanding the applicants' legitimate aspirations to found a family.

51. There has therefore been no violation of Article 8 of the Convention.

II. ALLEGED VIOLATION OF ARTICLE 6 § 1 OF THE CONVENTION

52. The Court considers it necessary in the circumstances of the case to examine the applicants' complaint about the failure to execute final decisions relating to the adoption of Florentina and Mariana under Article 6 § 1 of the Convention, the relevant parts of which provide:

> "In the determination of his civil rights and obligations . . . , everyone is entitled to a fair and public hearing within a reasonable time by an independent and impartial tribunal . . ."

A. The parties' submissions

53. The applicants submitted that the Romanian State had for several years failed in its duty to execute final and irrevocable judgments. They referred in particular to the bailiff's report of 3 September 2002, which stated that the attempt to enforce the final judgments had resulted, through the intervention of the centre's doormen, in their being unlawfully detained, together with the bailiff and their lawyer ...

. . . .

B. The Court's assessment

54. The Court notes that the judgments delivered on 28 September 2000 by the Brasov County Court — involving the determination of the applicants' civil rights, namely their recognition as the adoptive parents of Florentina and Mariana — and the subsequent orders by the same court requiring the CEPSB to hand the children over have yet to be enforced, despite being final and irrevocable.

55. It reiterates that the enforcement of decisions of this kind requires urgent handling as the passage of time can have irremediable consequences for relations between children and parents who do not live with them ...

56. The Court would further reiterate its settled case-law to the effect that Article 6 also protects the implementation of final, binding judicial decisions, which, in States that accept the rule of law, cannot remain inoperative to the detriment of one party. Accordingly, the execution of a judicial decision cannot be prevented, invalidated or unduly delayed ...

57. In the instant case the Court notes that the proceedings to enforce the decisions in the applicants' favour have been pending since September 2000. It observes at the outset that this situation is not in any way attributable to the applicants, who have made approaches to the national authorities to put an end to it and have regularly taken steps to have the children and their birth certificates handed over to them.

58. The Court also notes, as the Government did, that the bailiffs have not remained inactive either. Outside the periods during which execution of the decisions in issue has been stayed by the national courts, they have put the CEPSB on notice to comply with the final and binding judicial decisions in the applicants' favour ...

59. It must be recognised, however, that all the attempts by the bailiffs to enforce the adoption orders have met with manifest opposition on the part of the private institution where the children live, and have remained unsuccessful.

60. It would therefore appear that, in the circumstances of the case, the failure to execute the decisions granting the applicants' applications for adoption was due solely to the actions of the CEPSB staff and its founder members, who consistently opposed the children's departure to Italy by lodging various objections to enforcement or by thwarting the steps taken by the bailiffs.

61. While the Government argued that they could not be blamed for the actions of a private institution, the Court should look behind appearances to assess whether the State may be held responsible for the situation complained of. A number of facts are particularly striking in this regard.

62. The Court notes, firstly, that in spite of the efforts by the bailiffs to ensure the execution of the decisions in question, their actions were wholly ineffective in the instant case. The events recorded by the bailiff in his report of 3 September 2002 are a significant example, since the attempt at enforcement on that date appears to have resulted in the bailiff himself, the applicants and their lawyer actually being detained within the CEPSB building ...

63. The Court considers that such conduct towards bailiffs, who work to ensure the proper administration of justice and thus represent a vital component of the rule of law, is incompatible with their position as law-enforcement officers and that action should be taken against those responsible. In this connection, it is for the State to take all the necessary steps to enable bailiffs to carry out the task they have been assigned, particularly by ensuring the effective participation of other authorities that may assist enforcement where the circumstances so require, failing which the guarantees enjoyed by a litigant during the judicial phase of the proceedings will be rendered devoid of purpose ...

64. In the instant case the Court observes that the uncomfortable situation in which the bailiff responsible for enforcing the decisions in the applicants' favour found himself on 3 September 2002, when he was detained inside the CEPSB building, resulted directly from the police authorities' failure to assist the enforcement, and that no subsequent action has been taken.

65. In that connection, the Court notes that a wide range of legislative measures have been implemented by the Romanian government in order to comply with European and international treaties on adoption. Its attention has been drawn in particular to Decisions nos. 502 and 770, governing the organisation and functioning of the Romanian Committee for Adoption and the National Authority for Child Protection, which are, among other things, empowered to suspend or terminate activities that endanger children's health or physical or psychological development, for example by withdrawing the operating licences of the bodies responsible.

66. However, in spite of those domestic legal provisions, the Court observes that no sanctions have been taken in respect of the lack of cooperation of the private institution in question with the authorities empowered to enforce the adoption orders made in the instant case. It further notes that the CEPSB director's refusal to cooperate with the bailiffs has had no repercussions for him in almost three years.

67. The Court agrees with the Government that the use of force to execute the final decisions in question would have been a very delicate matter in the present case. Nevertheless, as the orders for the adoption of the two children have become final but have not been executed, they have been deprived of their binding force and have remained mere recommendations. Such a situation contravenes the principles of the rule of law and of legal certainty, notwithstanding the existence of special reasons potentially justifying it, the Government having cited the obligations on the respondent State with a view to its future accession to the European Union legal order.

68. By refraining for more than three years from taking the effective measures required to comply with final, enforceable judicial decisions, the national authorities deprived the provisions of Article 6 § 1 of the Convention of all useful effect.

That conclusion is made all the more necessary in the present case by the probably irreversible consequences of the passage of time for the potential relationship between the applicants and their adopted daughters. Here, the Court notes with regret that the prospects of that relationship flourishing now appear if not seriously jeopardised, then at least highly unlikely, particularly as the children, now aged 13, recently indicated that they were strongly opposed to being adopted and moving to Italy.

69. There has consequently been a violation of Article 6 § 1 of the Convention.

. . . .

IV. APPLICATION OF ARTICLE 41 OF THE CONVENTION

[The court here notes the text of Article 41 of the Convention.]

A. Damage

[Pecuniary and non-pecuniary damages were sought by the applicants, in light of expenses incurred in travelling to Romania and frustration caused by the failure of the authorities to execute a decision in their favor over several years.]

. . . .

70. As regards non-pecuniary damage, [the Court] does not find it unreasonable to conclude that the applicants undoubtedly sustained some damage—particularly on account of the frustration caused by the failure to execute final and binding decisions in their favour for several years, and of the probably irreversible consequences of that situation—for which the mere finding of a violation cannot constitute sufficient redress. However, the amounts claimed under this head are excessive.

71. In these circumstances, having regard to all the evidence before it and making its assessment on an equitable basis as required by Article 41 of the Convention, the Court awards the first applicant couple EUR 12,000 and the second applicant couple EUR 10,000, in respect of all heads of damage taken together.

B. Costs and expenses

72. The applicants sought reimbursement of all the costs which they had incurred in the proceedings before the Romanian authorities and before the Court, which they broke down as follows, submitting vouchers in support of their claim:

(a) EUR 868 (the first applicant couple) and EUR 868.36 (the second applicant couple) for translation costs;

(b) EUR 8,754 (the first applicant couple) and EUR 7,133.28 (the second applicant couple) for their lawyer's fees in the proceedings before the Court; and

(c) EUR 5,002 (the first applicant couple) and EUR 652.18 (the second applicant couple) for their lawyers' fees in the proceedings before the national authorities.

They further sought reimbursement of EUR 35,107 (the first applicant couple) and EUR 36,824.63 (the second applicant couple) in respect of "provisional costs linked to the outcome of the proceedings", without giving further details.

73. The Government objected to the award of the sums claimed by the applicants in respect of "provisional costs", submitting that such a description was unclear. They disputed that those amounts had actually been incurred and pointed out that they had not been substantiated as required by the Court's case-law in relation to Article 41 of the Convention.

74. The Court has assessed the claims in the light of the principles set forth in its case-law ...

75. Applying these criteria to the present case, and making its assessment on an equitable basis as required by Article 41 of the Convention, the Court considers it reasonable to award EUR 7,000 to the first applicant couple and EUR 6,000 to the second applicant couple in respect of all their costs and expenses.

FOR THESE REASONS, THE COURT

1. *Holds* by five votes to two that there was a bond between the applicants and the adopted children amounting to "family life" within the meaning of Article 8 § 1 of the Convention, which is applicable in the present case;

2. *Holds* by six votes to one that there has been no violation of Article 8 of the Convention;

3. *Holds* by four votes to three that there has been a violation of Article 6 § 1 of the Convention;

...

5. *Holds* by five votes to two

(a) that the respondent State is to pay the applicants, within three months from the date on which the judgment becomes final according to Article 44 § 2 of the Convention, the following amounts:

(i) EUR 12,000 (twelve thousand euros) to the first applicant couple and EUR 10,000 (ten thousand euros) to the second applicant couple in respect of pecuniary and non-pecuniary damage;

(ii) EUR 7,000 (seven thousand euros) to the first applicant couple and EUR 6,000 (six thousand euros) to the second applicant couple in respect of costs and expenses;

(iii) any tax that may be chargeable on the above amounts;

(b) that from the expiry of the above-mentioned three months until settlement simple interest shall be payable on the above amounts at a rate equal to the marginal lending rate of the European Central Bank during the default period plus three percentage points;

6. *Dismisses* unanimously the remainder of the applicants' claims for just satisfaction.

Notes and Questions

1. Both opponents and proponents of international adoption hailed this decision when it was handed down. In fact, what is the position taken by the Court here on the validity of international adoption? Why would parties on both sides have been pleased with the judgment?

2. Had the family been a biological, rather than an adoptive one, would the result have been the same? Could it have been? Does this suggest that the reasons given by the Court for its decision may not be the real ones, or at least may not provide the complete picture?

3. Also see the case *Ignaccolo-Zenide v. Romania*, 2000 Eur. Ct. H.R. Though framed in terms of a parent's right to be reunited with children, it is also implicitly concerned with the parallel right of children to their parents, and to receiving the truth about their parents. In that case, a non-Romanian mother had been shut out of the lives of her children by their Romanian father, with the apparent cooperation of the Romanian authorities. The ultimate question considered had to do with the state's obligation to provide access to children by their parents. It is doubtful whether the tone taken by the ECHR in *Ignaccolo-Zenide* captures the tragedy of the tale, and whether the judgment deals successfully with the discriminatory policy being pursued by the Romanian authorities.

With regard to that case, what seemed to be going on in Romania that allowed the children's father to shun contact with their mother for so long? What motivations can you detect in the behavior of the Romanian authorities?

The case, perhaps more than others, seems to represent an exact fit between the human rights as set out in the Convention and the specific violation being described. For the mother in *Ignaccolo-Zenide*, though, was any remedy actually possible? Could any pronouncement of the Court assist her in improving the situation? Was the Court hard enough on Romania and its state apparatus in its conclusions?

———————

The following case presents the vexing question of whether European states should allow legalized, confidential child abandonment. Whereas the French position is that this saves lives and offers biological parents the right to sever all ties with their children, such a system will eventually, and inevitably, be confronted by the children who, when adults themselves, seek information about their biological parents. It should be stated that the idea of child "safe havens", or anonymous abandonment, is not unique to France. A number of American states have experimented with this idea, as has Japan. As a point of interest, one of the unintended consequences of this type of mechanism is that parents tend to use it to relinquish older children, rather than the infants for which it was intended. Critics of adoption also tend to take a negative view of these anonymous "drop off" systems, insofar as the convenience of adults at a particular point in time is given priority, as opposed to the need of children to maintain critical links with their origins.

Odièvre v. France
2003-III Eur. Ct. H.R. 1

. . . .

THE FACTS

I. THE CIRCUMSTANCES OF THE CASE

9. The applicant is a French national who lives in Paris.

10. She was born in the fourteenth administrative district of Paris on 23 March 1965. Her mother requested that the birth be kept secret and completed a form at the Health and Social Security Department abandoning her after signing the following letter:

> "I abandon my child Berthe Pascale. I certify that I have been informed that after one month the abandonment of my child will become irreversible and that the authorities reserve the right to have her adopted.
>
> I decline the assistance that has been offered to me.
>
> I request that this birth be kept secret.
>
> I certify that I have received the form setting out information on abandonment.
>
> Paris, 24.5.[deleted] Berthe"

11. The applicant was placed with the Child Welfare Service at the Health and Social Services Department (*Direction de l'action sanitaire et sociale*—"the DASS") and registered on 1 July 1965 under no. 280326 as being in the care of the *département* of Seine. Subsequently, a full adoption order was made on 10 January 1969 in favour of Mr and Mrs Odièvre, under whose name she is now known ...

12. In December 1990 the applicant consulted her file as a person formerly in the care of the Children's Welfare Service of the *département* of Seine and managed to obtain non-identifying information about her natural family:

> "Record of information on a child admitted to the Saint-Vincent-de-Paul Hospital and Nursing Home provided by: CONFIDENTIAL
>
> *Date of admission* [date deleted]
>
> *Detailed explanation of the reasons for the child's admission (if the child has been or may be abandoned, provide full information on such matters as the mother's, and if possible the father's, physical appearance, mental outlook, health, social background and occupation in order to enable the authorities to find the best possible placement)*

Abandonment: The parents have been cohabiting for seven years. Two children have been born of their relationship: an elder child, who is 21 months old, and Pascale, whom the mother has today abandoned and placed in our care. The couple have been put up by a woman for two years, but she now faces eviction. The father is a Spanish national and works as a painter and decorator. His monthly wage is approximately 1,200 [French] francs. He is married and has a legitimate daughter, who is being brought up by her mother. According to Pascale's mother, her partner refuses to have anything to do with Pascale and says that he cannot take on this new burden. She (Ms Berthe) appears to have no will of her own and is content to go along with her partner's wishes. She has not visited her daughter at the clinic, saying that she does not wish to become attached. She did not see her daughter until today and greeted their separation with total indifference. Ms Berthe does not work and looks after her son and her landlady's child.

A request has been made for the birth to remain secret.

Description of the mother: 1.63 m tall, slim, regular features, clear-skinned, heavily made-up brown eyes, long, thick brown hair, in good health, ambivalent attitude, very limited intellect.

Description of the father: average height, blond hair, brown eyes, in good health, sober.

Pascale was born 1 3/4 months premature and weighed 1,770 grams. She now weighs 3,100 grams. Her stay in the incubator room at ... was trouble-free. She has now reached term and presents no neurological or organic anomalies. Information noted on the medical certificate supplied to the nursery department ..."

13. On 27 January 1998 the applicant applied to the Paris *tribunal de grande instance* for an order for the "release of information about her birth and permission to obtain copies of any documents, birth, death and marriage certificates, civil-status documents and full copies of long-form birth certificates". She explained to the court that she had learned that her natural parents had had a son in 1963 and two other sons after 1965, that the DASS had refused to give her information concerning the civil status of her siblings on the ground that disclosure would be a breach of confidence, and that, now that she knew of her siblings' existence, she was entitled to seek an order for the release of information about her own birth.

14. On 2 February 1998 the court registrar returned the case file to the applicant's lawyer with the following letter of explanation:

"Following examination of your file by Mrs B., Vice-President of the First Division, it appears that the applicant should consider applying to the administrative court to obtain, if possible, an order requiring the authorities to disclose the information, although such an order would in any event contravene the law of 8 January 1993."

II. RELEVANT DOMESTIC LAW AND PRACTICE

A. A brief historical background to the system of anonymous births in France and its evolution

15. The *mater semper certa est* rule has not found acceptance in French law. There is an ancient tradition in France that enables newborn babies to be abandoned in accordance with a set procedure. The practice can be traced back to the time of Saint Vincent de Paul, who introduced the use of the *tour*, a sort of revolving crib housed in the wall of a charitable institution. The mother would place the child in the crib and ring a bell. On that

signal someone on the other side of the wall would cause the *tour* to pivot and collect the infant. The aim of Saint Vincent de Paul in setting up the Foundlings Home (*Œuvre des Enfants trouvés*) in 1638 was to prevent infanticide, abortion and babies being exposed.

....

... [A 1941] legislative decree allowed the mother to give birth anonymously and to receive free medical care during the month preceding and the month following the birth in any public hospital able to provide her with the care her condition required. [Later decrees were ultimately reflected in] the current Article L. 222-6 of the Social Action and Families Code:

> "The costs of accommodation and confinement of women who, on being admitted to a public institution or approved private institution, request that their identity remain secret shall be borne by the Child Welfare Service in the *département* in which the institution's head office is located.
>
> At their request or with their agreement the women referred to in the first sub-paragraph shall receive psychological support and practical advice from the Child Welfare Service.
>
> The first sub-paragraph shall apply without any means of identification being required or inquiry conducted.
>
> ..."

The system of anonymous births was embodied in Law no. 93-22 of 8 January 1993 "amending the Civil Code as regards civil status, the family and the rights of the child and instituting the office of family judge", which introduced new provisions concerning the secret abandonment of children. For the first time, choosing to give birth in secret had an effect on the determination of filiation, as Articles 341 and 341-1 of the Civil Code created an estoppel defence to proceedings to establish maternity: there was no mother in the legal sense of the word:

> "An action to establish maternity may be brought subject to the application of Article 341-1. The child bringing the action shall be required to prove that he or she is the child to whom the alleged mother gave birth. The case may be proved only by strong presumptions or circumstantial evidence.
>
> On giving birth, the mother may request that her admission to hospital and identity shall remain secret."

In addition ... information about a child's origins may also be confidential under another provision. Provided the child is less than a year old, its parents may entrust it to the Child Welfare Service and request that their identity be kept secret ... The filiation stated in the civil-status documents is annulled and a fictitious birth certificate, known as a provisional civil-status certificate, issued in lieu.

16. Since the adoption of the law of 1993, several official reports have suggested that a reform of the system of anonymous births would be desirable.

....

B. Law no. 2002-93 of 22 January 2002 on "access by adopted persons and people in State care to information about their origins"

17. This statute is the final stage in the process of reform described above. It does not call into question the right to give birth anonymously but allows arrangements to be made for disclosure of identity subject to the mother's and the child's express consent being

obtained. It does, however, abolish the parents' right to request confidentiality under Article L. 224-5 of the Social Action and Families Code ...

....

D. Comparative law

19. It is relatively rare for mothers to be entitled to give birth anonymously under European domestic legislation, as Italy and Luxembourg stand alone in not imposing a statutory obligation on the natural parents to register a newborn child or to state their identity when registering it. Conversely, many countries make it obligatory to provide the names, not only of the mother, to whom the child is automatically linked, but also of the father....

The current trend in certain countries is towards the acceptance, if not of a right to give birth anonymously, then at least of a right to give birth "discreetly". An example of this is provided by Belgium, where a debate has begun, largely as a result of the large number of women crossing the border to give birth anonymously in France. In an opinion delivered on 12 January 1998 the Consultative Committee on Bioethics set out the two lines of argument that were defensible from an ethical standpoint: the first considered it unacceptable for children to be brought into the world without parents; for that reason its proponents proposed that facilities for "giving birth discreetly" should be provided, without completely closing the door on all attempts to trace the parents. Proponents of the second line of argument considered that the ethical dilemma posed by the right to give birth anonymously did not result from the need to resolve the conflict arising out of the clash between the respective rights of "the child to filiation" and "the mother in distress", but from the more fundamental confrontation of two values: the life of the child on the one hand and the right of everyone to know his or her natural mother on the other. They contended that in the face of that dilemma, the primary concern had to be the protection of the life and of the development of the child. For that reason, they considered that giving birth anonymously was perfectly legitimate and acceptable from an ethical standpoint. Likewise, in Germany, in view of the rising number of abandoned newborn infants, the first "baby box" (*Babyklappe*)—a system that allows the mother to leave her child, ring a bell and leave without giving her identity—was installed in Hamburg approximately two years ago. Since then, other "baby boxes" have been installed in other towns ... Yet another example is provided by Hungary, where mothers may decide to remain anonymous by abandoning their newborn child in a special, unsupervised room in the hospital.

THE LAW

....

II. ALLEGED VIOLATION OF ARTICLE 8 OF THE CONVENTION

24. The applicant complained that she was unable to obtain identifying information about her natural family and had thereby been prevented from finding out her personal history. She alleged a violation of Article 8 of the Convention ...

[The court provides the text of Article 8 here.]

A. Applicability of Article 8

1. *The parties' submissions*

25. The applicant maintained that her request for information about strictly personal aspects of her history and childhood came within the scope of Article 8 of the Convention. Establishing her basic identity was an integral part not only of her "private life", but also of her "family life" with her natural family, with whom she hoped to establish emotional ties were she not prevented from doing so by French law.

26. The Government excluded the latter possibility, contending that the guarantee of the right to respect for family life under Article 8 presupposed the existence of a family ... Although the case-law did not require cohabitation between the various members of the "family", there had to be at the very least close personal ties. The existence of ties demonstrating an emotional relationship between two beings and a desire to pursue that relationship was essential so far as the Convention institutions were concerned. The Convention institutions had even held that in the absence of close personal ties between those concerned a mere biological link was insufficient to constitute family life within the meaning of Article 8. Thus, the Commission had expressed the opinion that the situation in which a person donated sperm only to enable a woman to become pregnant through artificial insemination did not of itself give the donor a right to respect for family life with the child ... In the instant case, the Government maintained that no family life within the meaning of Article 8 of the Convention existed between the applicant and her natural mother, as the applicant had never met her mother, while the latter had at no point expressed any interest in the applicant or regarded her as her child. The applicant's natural mother had expressly manifested an intention to abandon the applicant and had agreed to her adoption by others. Only the applicant's family life with her adoptive parents could come within the scope of Article 8.

. . . .

2. The Court's assessment

28. In the instant case, the Court notes that the applicant's purpose is not to call into question her relationship with her adoptive parents but to discover the circumstances in which she was born and abandoned, including the identity of her natural parents and brothers. For that reason, it considers it necessary to examine the case from the perspective of private life, not family life, since the applicant's claim to be entitled, in the name of biological truth, to know her personal history is based on her inability to gain access to information about her origins and related identifying data.

29. The Court reiterates in that connection that "Article 8 protects a right to identity and personal development, and the right to establish and develop relationships with other human beings and the outside world.... The preservation of mental stability is in that context an indispensable precondition to effective enjoyment of the right to respect for private life" ... Matters of relevance to personal development include details of a person's identity as a human being and the vital interest protected by the Convention in obtaining information necessary to discover the truth concerning important aspects of one's personal identity, such as the identity of one's parents ... Birth, and in particular the circumstances in which a child is born, forms part of a child's, and subsequently the adult's, private life guaranteed by Article 8 of the Convention. That provision is therefore applicable in the instant case.

B. Compliance with Article 8

1. The parties' submissions

(a) The applicant

30. The applicant said that she defended the rights of the child. In France it was possible to act as if the mother did not exist, whereas in most countries in the world birth automatically created parental ties between the mother and the child she had brought into the world. By a legal fiction and because she had expressly sought confidentiality, the applicant's mother was deemed never to have given birth. The applicant described how difficult it was for her to live without knowing her original identity and complained not

only of the arbitrary interference in her life as an ordinary citizen caused by the system used to preserve confidentiality, but also of culpable failure on the part of the domestic authorities through their refusal to disclose the requested information even though it was available in the file.

31. The applicant maintained that giving birth anonymously was not a woman's right, but an admission of failure. She said that women who asked for the birth and their identity to be kept secret found themselves in that position mainly through a lack of autonomy, problems related to youth, difficulties in gaining access to the job market, the isolation and financial predicament of single-parent families and domestic violence. In her submission, an anonymous birth therefore constituted an act of violence that was easily avoidable: concerns for the health of mother and child could be addressed without any need to rely on a right to confidentiality that would prevent the child from finding out its origins. In most cases the distress of a mother who was unable to care for her child could be alleviated by providing her with the necessary help or enabling her to make her child available for adoption, not by promising her anonymity. The days when women did not express their feelings after abandoning a child were over. Many women had now formed associations. Society had been given an insight into the trauma that followed from their accounts of their experiences. Despite appearances to the contrary, the child often represented an "emotional investment", the page was rarely turned and life did not simply go on as if nothing had happened. The argument that it was necessary to reassure the mother in order to prevent infanticide was a thing of the past and unconvincing when the situation in countries which did not allow mothers to give birth anonymously was examined. The health of mother and child was protected in many countries without resorting to a right to confidentiality which prevented the child from ever being able to find out its origins.

32. In the applicant's submission, the fact that the child was taken into care and could be adopted speedily had absolutely no bearing on the issue of confidentiality, since those consequences followed directly from the child's abandonment, whether or not the mother requested anonymity. It was the irrational fear of certain adoptive parents and adoption agencies that had encouraged the belief that children without a past were easier to adopt. However, adoptive parents could easily be reassured if they were reminded that legal filiation by a full adoption order was irrevocable. As to the emotional tie, an understanding by the adoptive parents of their child's desire to know his or her natural parents and support for him or her in that quest could only serve to strengthen it.

....

35. Lastly, the applicant criticised France for its isolated stance on the subject. Admittedly, in *X, Y and Z v. the United Kingdom* ..., which concerned a conflict between the right of a child born through medically assisted procreation and the anonymity promised to the sperm donor, the Court had ruled that the respondent State had a wide margin of appreciation, as the law on that subject was in a transitional phase. However, the problem posed by secret births was very different: a State could not be afforded a margin of appreciation if, despite the fact that the child's best interest was at stake, it chose to differ from the shared views of the member States of the Council of Europe on the subject. Such was the position with France's legislation on the right to give birth anonymously, even after the enactment of the law of 22 January 2002.

(b) The Government

36. The Government maintained that a woman's right to request that the birth and her identity be kept secret was laid down by Article 341-1 of the Civil Code and amounted to an interference prescribed by law. The interference pursued a legitimate aim, namely

alleviating the distress of mothers who did not have the means of bringing up their children. By affording them the option of confidentiality, the French State sought to encourage women in that position to give birth in favourable conditions, rather than alone with the attendant risk that they may not tend to the child's needs. Such situations of distress were by no means rare in France (the number of births to mothers of unknown identity was approximately 600 a year). The Government observed that until the 1960s, when the applicant's natural mother had taken the decision to request that her identity remain secret, neither contraception nor abortion were legal in France. Nowadays, there were three main categories of women who chose to give birth anonymously: young women who were not yet independent, young women still living with their parents in Muslim families originating from North African or sub-Saharan African societies in which pregnancy outside marriage was a great dishonour, and isolated women with financial difficulties (the youngest, many of whom were under 25, were single mothers; many of the older women were over 35 and for the most part separated or divorced or had been abandoned, some being victims of domestic violence, with several children to look after). As to what drove women to seek confidentiality, the Government said that the stated reasons sometimes concealed more serious problems, such as rape or incest, which were not always revealed by those concerned.

. . . .

38. The Government observed that, even before the adoption of the law of 2002, the French legislation had sought to reconcile the competing interests in three respects.

(i) By trying to encourage mothers to assume responsibility for the birth of their children

Alternative systems offering psychological and social support had long been established by law to encourage mothers to keep their children despite the difficult position in which they found themselves. Former Article 62 of the Family Code had imposed a duty on social services to inform mothers of the various measures available to assist them in bringing up their children themselves. Social services were also under a duty to inform mothers of the time-limits and conditions that had to be complied with if they wished to take their children back.

(ii) By affording such children access to certain information

The right to obtain non-identifying information about their mother, father and even other members of their natural family had been made generally available to abandoned or adopted children by the law of 17 July 1978, thus enabling them to reconstruct their personal histories.

(iii) By providing that the mother could waive confidentiality

Since the enactment of a law of 5 July 1996 it had become easier for mothers to waive a decision to request confidentiality, as provision had been made for a mother who had requested confidentiality under Article 62 of the Family Code to be informed that in addition to supplying non-identifying information she could reveal her identity by contacting the president of the council of the *département*, who would keep her identity secret until such time as it was expressly requested by the child or her descendants.

Through all those provisions domestic law had struck a careful balance between the woman's interest in not disclosing the birth and the child's interest in gaining access to information about its origins.

39. The Government submitted, lastly, that the law of 2002 had considerably reinforced the prospects of securing a waiver of confidentiality. The applicant was free to make use of the provisions of the new legislation and to apply to the National Council for Access

to Information about Personal Origins. The machinery established under the legislation satisfied the proportionality requirements contained in the Court's case-law, as the French State took into account the child's interest by regulating access to information about the child's origins while making it easier for the mother to waive confidentiality. Firstly, the mother was invited, as soon as she had given birth, to leave particulars of her identity in a sealed envelope together with non-identifying information, to which the child would have access if it wished. Secondly, considerable efforts were made to trace the mother and to seek her consent to disclosure of her identity to the child. Professional help was also available, both to persons trying to discover their origins and to the natural parents. The Government submitted that a fair balance had therefore been struck between the competing interests.

2. The Court's assessment

. . . .

44. The expression "everyone" in Article 8 of the Convention applies to both the child and the mother. On the one hand, people have a right to know their origins, that right being derived from a wide interpretation of the scope of the notion of private life. The child's vital interest in its personal development is also widely recognised in the general scheme of the Convention ... On the other hand, a woman's interest in remaining anonymous in order to protect her health by giving birth in appropriate medical conditions cannot be denied. In the present case, the applicant's mother never went to see the baby at the clinic and appears to have greeted their separation with total indifference ... Nor is it alleged that she subsequently expressed the least desire to meet her daughter. The Court's task is not to judge that conduct, but merely to take note of it. The two private interests with which the Court is confronted in the present case are not easily reconciled; moreover, they do not concern an adult and a child, but two adults, each endowed with her own free will.

In addition to that conflict of interest, the problem of anonymous births cannot be dealt with in isolation from the issue of the protection of third parties, essentially the adoptive parents, the father and the other members of the natural family. The Court notes in that connection that the applicant is now 38 years old, having been adopted at the age of four, and that non-consensual disclosure could entail substantial risks, not only for the mother herself, but also for the adoptive family which brought up the applicant, and her natural father and siblings, each of whom also has a right to respect for his or her private and family life.

. . . .

48. The Court observes that in the present case the applicant was given access to non-identifying information about her mother and natural family that enabled her to trace some of her roots, while ensuring the protection of third-party interests.

49. In addition, while preserving the principle that mothers may give birth anonymously, the system recently set up in France improves the prospect of their agreeing to waive confidentiality, something which, it will be noted in passing, they have always been able to do even before the enactment of the law of 22 January 2002. The new legislation will facilitate searches for information about a person's biological origins, as a National Council for Access to Information about Personal Origins has been set up. That council is an independent body composed of members of the national legal service, representatives of associations having an interest in the subject matter of the law and professional people with good practical knowledge of the issues. The legislation is already in force and the applicant may use it to request disclosure of her mother's identity, subject to the latter's con-

sent being obtained to ensure that her need for protection and the applicant's legitimate request are fairly reconciled. Indeed, though unlikely, the possibility that the applicant will be able to obtain the information she is seeking through the new Council that has been set up by the legislature cannot be excluded.

The French legislation thus seeks to strike a balance and to ensure sufficient proportion between the competing interests. The Court observes in that connection that the States must be allowed to determine the means which they consider to be best suited to achieve the aim of reconciling those interests. Overall, the Court considers that France has not overstepped the margin of appreciation which it must be afforded in view of the complex and sensitive nature of the issue of access to information about one's origins, an issue that concerns the right to know one's personal history, the choices of the natural parents, the existing family ties and the adoptive parents.

Consequently, there has been no violation of Article 8 of the Convention.

. . . .

CONCURRING OPINION OF JUDGE RESS, JOINED BY JUDGE KŪRIS *(Translation)*

I entirely agree with the majority's reasoning, but there are one or two points I should like to underline.

. . . .

4. There is not merely a conflict between the child's right to know its origins and the mother's interest in keeping her identity secret. A further factor to be taken into account is the State's interest in offering a solution to mothers in distress while at the same time protecting the life of the unborn child. The State has to take into account those three aspects. It would be too simple to reduce the conflict solely to the relationship between the mother and child after the latter's birth. In my opinion, in cases of multiple relationships such as the present one, the State enjoys a margin of appreciation. The concern to avoid or reduce the number of abortions is an aspect of the protection of life, and is closely connected to the situation of the mother and her unborn child. The State is entitled in such situations of distress for the mother to give precedence to her interest over the child's right to know its origins. The introduction of the system in which anonymity, that is to say confidentiality, shall cease on a decision by a commission may have disastrous consequences for the entire system and the protection of life. Persons who seek disclosure at any price, even against the express will of their natural mother, must ask themselves whether they would have been born had it not been for the right to give birth anonymously. That concern serves and may legitimately serve as the basis for the State's decision to introduce and uphold such a system.

. . . .

JOINT DISSENTING OPINION OF JUDGES WILDHABER, Sir Nicolas BRATZA, BONELLO, LOUCAIDES, CABRAL BARRETO, TULKENS AND PELLONPÄÄ *(Translation)*

We disagree with the majority's opinion that there has been no violation of Article 8 of the Convention and wish to explain our reasons for so doing.

. . . .

7. As a result of the domestic law and practice, no balancing of interests was possible in the instant case, either in practice or in law. In practice, French law accepted that the mother's decision constituted an absolute defence to any requests for information by the applicant, irrespective of the reasons for or legitimacy of that decision. In all circumstances, the mother's refusal is definitively binding on the child, who has no legal means

at its disposal to challenge the mother's unilateral decision. The mother thus has a discretionary right to bring a suffering child into the world and to condemn it to lifelong ignorance. This, therefore, is not a multilateral system that ensures any balance between the competing rights. The effect of the mother's absolute "right of veto" is that the rights of the child, which are recognised in the general scheme of the Convention..., are entirely neglected and forgotten. In addition, the mother may also by the same means paralyse the rights of third parties, in particular those of the natural father or the brothers and sisters, who may also find themselves deprived of the rights guaranteed by Article 8 of the Convention. In view of these considerations, we cannot be satisfied by the majority's concession that "the applicant was given access to non-identifying information about her mother and natural family that enabled her to trace some of her roots while ensuring the protection of third-party interests" ...

8. At various points, the Court seems to regard the fact that the applicant is an adopted child as decisive..., thereby implying that in the circumstances her search for her natural mother—who had abandoned her at birth—was superfluous and even unhelpful. We do not share that view. It has been shown that adopted children often consider it their duty to trace their original parents. Even if it has been adopted, a child who is unable to gain access to any type of information about its family origins is made to endure a form of suffering, and that suffering may leave scars. As to the need to protect the adoptive parents, a factor also relied on by the majority, there is nothing in the case file to suggest that they were opposed to the applicant's actions.

9. As regards the general interest, the Court relied, *inter alia*, on the need to avoid illegal abortions ... However, it should be noted that at present there is no reliable data to support the notion that there would be a risk of an increase in abortions, or even of cases of infanticide, if the system of anonymous births was abolished. In addition, that risk has to be assessed in the light of the situation obtaining in countries which do not operate a system of anonymous births. It has not been established, in particular by statistical data, that there has been a rise in the number of abortions or cases of infanticide in the majority of the countries in the Council of Europe that do not have legislation similar to that existing in France. In many countries, and indeed in France, the development of contraception and family planning has played a significant role in raising awareness among prospective parents. As to the "right to respect for life, a higher-ranking value guaranteed by the Convention" relied on by the majority, which they say is "thus one of the aims pursued by the French system"..., we cannot accept the proposition implicit therein, namely that within all the countries in the Council of Europe the French system is the only one that ensures respect for the right to life as guaranteed by Article 2 of the Convention.

....

Notes and Questions

1. In the above case, the Court speaks of striking the proper balance between the rights of the applicant to information about her background and the objectives of the French law in preserving confidentiality. Do you think the Court got this balance right? Is there a subtext to this case, in terms of the real nature of the applicant's dissatisfaction with the French law being challenged?

2. What are the strongest arguments against allowing "anonymous births?" How are arguments concerning the relative importance of biological links presented in this case?

3. Japan recently enacted a law similar to the French one, making it legal to leave children in "baby hutches". The first child left there, however, was not a newborn infant, but rather a toddler.[7] How should such a situation be resolved? For further information on the Japanese law, see *Don't Want Your Baby, Drop It Off*, Japan Times, Nov. 10, 2006, http://search.japantimes.co.jp/cgi-bin/nn20061110a3.html.

4. Also consider the case of *Evans v. the United Kingdom*, 2007 Eur. Ct. H.R. 264, in which a woman turned to the ECHR in a last ditch effort to save her frozen embryos. The woman and her partner had broken up, and her partner refused to give consent for them to be implanted, exercising an option he clearly had under their original agreement. While not about children's rights *per se*, the case did confront issues of reproductive freedom and the right to life. Mothers' versus fathers' rights were also a theme in the case. There are many painful ironies in the case; for one thing, the woman had had her ovaries removed after the extraction that led to the creation of the embryos, making it certain that she would not conceive in the future. Also, the ECHR looked for, and failed to find, a "European consensus" on this issue. Of what interest could that be to a person in her position? Is it sensible to think of the man's interest as equal to that of the woman's in such a situation?

III. The Inter-American Human Rights Systems

A. Overview of Regional Human Rights in Latin America

By comparison with the European Court of Human Rights, which has reviewed a range of national laws on the family, corporal punishment and juvenile justice as part of its human rights remit, the Inter-American Court of Human Rights has issued a small number of high profile decisions involving extreme and egregious violations of children's rights. While these rulings have brought attention to the plight of marginalized children in Latin America, the role of the Inter-American Court has been confined to condemning only the very worst forms of abuse by the state. This distinction is in line with the greater degree of political and legal integration in Europe generally. The idea of "American" integration is more problematic. It is the case, though, that the Inter-American Court has reflected trends within the Latin American states towards accountability on the part of officials for human rights abuses.

The Organization of American States (OAS), another creation of the immediate post-World War II era, consists of all countries of the Americans[8] — north, central and south — and is based on the OAS Charter,[9] its foundational document. The OAS, with headquarters in Washington, DC, is largely focused on issues of democracy, human rights and the rule of law in the Americas. The main human rights instruments of the organization are

---

7. *Japanese "Baby Drop Box" Service Abused*, ASSOC. PRESS, May 17, 2007, http://www.msnbc.msn.com/id/18709944/.

8. *See* OAS Member States, http://www.oas.org/documents/eng/memberstates.asp. All 35 "independent" countries of the Americas belong to the Organization and all have ratified the OAS Charter. *Id.* Interestingly, Cuba remains a member, but its government has been excluded from participation in the OAS since 1962. *Id.*

9. Charter of the Organization of American States, Apr. 30, 1948, 2 U.S.T. 2394, 119 U.N.T.S. 3.

the 1948 American Declaration of the Rights and Duties of Man[10] and the American Convention on Human Rights,[11] which came into force in 1969. The Convention, of course, covers a much broader range of rights, including civil, political, economic, social and cultural rights. While there is extensive ratification of the Convention across Latin America, it has not been ratified by Canada or the United States.

The bodies established to enforce "Inter-American" human rights standards include the Inter-American Commission on Human Rights, and the Inter-American Court of Human Rights, created in 1979. In contrast to the European Court of Human Rights, the Inter-American Court can only hear cases referred to it by the "gate-keeping" Inter-American Commission or by one of the States Parties to the American Convention on Human Rights. It is the Inter-American Commission that accepts petitions from individuals or NGOs, and attempts to reach a settlement between the parties, before, in some instances, it decides to turn the matter over to the Inter-American Court. Note that the Inter-American Court may only exercise jurisdiction where the defending state has ratified the Inter-American Convention, and accepted the contentious jurisdiction of the Court. The United States, of course, has not done either.

The readings below introduce the workings of the Inter-American human rights system, explaining its role in the evolving democratization of Latin America.

Víctor Rodríguez Rescia & Marc David Seitles, *The Development of the Inter-American Human Rights System: A Historical Perspective and a Modern-Day Critique*
16 New York Law School Journal of Human Rights 593 (2000)

INTRODUCTION

The Inter-American human rights system is composed of a series of international documents. The principal human rights tools include: the American Convention on Human Rights, and its accompanying protocols; the Additional Protocol to the American Convention on Human Rights in the Area of Economic, Social and Cultural Rights; and the Protocol to the American Convention on Human Rights to Abolish the Death Penalty. In addition, three regional inter-American conventions seek to broaden the scope of protected human rights: the Inter-American Convention to Prevent and Punish Torture; the Inter-American Convention on Forced Disappearance of Persons; and the Inter-American Convention for the Prevention, Punishment, and Eradication of Violence Against Women.

The American Declaration of the Rights and Duties of Man also plays a significant role in the protection of human rights in the Americas. In fact, the impact of the American Declaration should not be understated as it binds countries that have ratified the American Convention and those who have not. The American Declaration operates as a source for common rights, and replaces serious juridical lacunae that exist in the case of economic, social and cultural rights.

....

---

10. Organization of American States, American Declaration of the Rights and Duties of Man, O.A.S. Res. XXX, 9th Int'l Conf. of Am. Sts., OEA/Ser.L/V/II.23, doc. 21 rev. 6 (May 2, 1948).

11. Organization of American States, American Convention on Human Rights, Nov. 22, 1969, O.A.S.T.S. No. 36, 1144 U.N.T.S. 123, *available at* http://www.oas.org/juridico/English/treaties/b-32.html.

The goal of this Article is to review the development of human rights in the Americas so that it may be possible to analyze specific aspects of this protective system that need serious repair....

....

II. THE INTER-AMERICAN COMMISSION ON HUMAN RIGHTS

A. The Commission Before the American Convention

1. A Brief History

The Inter-American Commission on Human Rights was created in 1959 during the Fifth Meeting of the Consultation of Secretaries of Foreign Affairs in Santiago, Chile. On May 25, 1960, the Council of the OAS approved the Commission's Statute. A month later, the Commission was fully operative. Pursuant to Article 18 of the Statute, the Inter-American Commission included the following tasks: stimulating an awareness of human rights among Pan-American cities; formulating recommendations to governments so that they may adopt progressive measures; preparing studies or reports that they consider useful; requesting reports from governments on human rights measures that they adopt; serving as an advisory body for the OAS on human rights.

Other functions of the Commission include preparing individualized country reports documenting the general state of human rights. All OAS member countries are required to participate. At present, more than forty country reports have been completed. Although no single procedural norm exists to investigate a State Parties conduct, the practice has been consistent since its origin....

The structure of the Commission goes hand in hand with that of the OAS, in that each body was concerned with not intruding on the domestic affairs of member countries. It was initially designed to operate as a promotional and educational body for human rights through the enactment of studies, symposiums, and general meetings, but without interfering in a particular country's policies toward human rights.

Nevertheless, the Commission interpreted that it had been granted the authority to overlook, protect, defend, and promote the observance of human rights throughout the Americas. It was obvious to the Commission that the inadequate faculties conferred upon it made it difficult to fulfill its mission. Therefore, the Commission began to carry out activities not explicitly provided for in its Statute, but which it considered necessary for the best execution of its tasks. In fact, it was the submission of numerous petitions against various governments that stimulated the Commission to carry out an extensive revision of its Statute. The OAS did not question these undertakings, which implied a tacit acceptance of their validity.

Through this plan, the main function of the Commission was to deal with the problem of the massive and systematic violations of human rights, rather than to investigate isolated violations. This structure paralleled the European human rights system. The purpose was to document the existence of human rights violations in a country and to place pressure on that government to improve its general human rights record. The procedure was characterized by its flexibility to be able to become cognizant of human rights abuses in the Americas, to request information from governments, and to formulate final recommendations. More specifically, and in descending order of importance, the characteristics of that process were as follows: to put forth a procedural decree that did not examine the requirements of the admissibility of the accusation; to exercise a very active role in the request of information and to investigate by using all its available resources (witnesses, newspapers, non-governmental organizations, on-site visits, etc.); to publicize the facts to pressure governments; to send the results of investigations to the political bodies within the OAS for their review and approval; and to prevent from draining the domestic resources of the jurisdiction.

In 1965, Resolution XXII of the Second Special Inter-American Conference authorized the Commission to examine and investigate *individual* communications and to formulate recommendations to individual countries. Contrary to previous practice, in this new phase the Commission was required to verify the exhaustion of internal remedies.

. . . .

2. Rights to Protect

Article 1(2) of the Commission's Statute established that "human rights are understood to be the rights set forth in the American Declaration on the Rights and Duties of the Man." Some have attempted to undermine the irrefutable character of the rights contemplated in the American Declaration through contrasts with the American Convention, the latter being an international treaty, the former only an international declaration of human rights principles. However, the fact that the Declaration has been adopted unanimously by the participating members of the OAS contributes to its character as customary law, at least within the context of the inter-American system. Further, aside from being a source of international rights, regularly invoked by the participating OAS countries, it is also often used by State Parties to create national legislation.

In addition, the Inter-American Commission (similar to that of the Inter-American Court) has a great ability to interpret "other treaties concerning the protection of the human rights in the countries in the Americas." In their advisory opinion OC-1/82, the Inter-American Court interpreted the phrase "other treaties" mentioned, in the following way:

> "the advisory jurisdiction of the Court can be exercised, in general, with regard to any provision dealing with the protection of human rights set forth in *any international treaty in the American States, regardless of whether it be bilateral or multilateral, whatever be the principal purpose of such a treaty, and whether or not non-Member States of the inter-American system are or have the right to become parties thereto."*

3. Procedures for Country Reports

Country reports serve as an important function of the Commission in analyzing human rights situations of particular countries. The procedures utilized in conducting such an investigative report include the following: to seek reports from the State or other governmental institutions; to conduct hearings of witnesses and experts; to carry on individual communications; to undertake in loco observations, where the Commission requests permission from the State or suggests to the State to invite the Commission; to conduct public or private interviews of people, groups or institutions; to make visits to jails and interview persons privately detained; to mediate for the resolution of specific cases.

. . . .

III. THE INTER-AMERICAN COURT OF HUMAN RIGHTS

. . . .

In 1959, at the Fifth Meeting of Consultation, the Inter-American Council of Jurists was instructed to prepare two conventions: one on "human rights" and the other on the creation of an "Inter-American Court of Human Rights," and other organs appropriate for the protection and observance of those rights.

The Council of Jurists completed its project during the Fourth Meeting in Santiago, Chile, in 1959. The Council prepared a draft convention, which included substantive provisions on human rights. Moreover, they developed institutional and procedural regulations with regard to those rights, which entailed the creation and operation of the Inter-American Court and the Inter-American Commission on Human Rights.

. . . .

In 1979, in La Paz, Bolivia, the OAS General Assembly approved the Statute of the Court through Resolution 448. Article 1 of the Statute defines the Court as "an autonomous judicial institution whose purpose is the application and interpretation of the American Convention on Human Rights."

In May 1979, during the seventh special session period of the OAS General Assembly, the participating State Parties of the Convention elected the first seven judges of the Court. On September 3, 1979, the inaugural judges were officially elevated to their positions at the Court's seat in San Jose, Costa Rica.

. . . .

A. Procedural Role of the Court

In conformity with the American Convention, the Court exercises contentious and advisory jurisdiction. These functions are highlighted in the rules that govern these respective processes. When exercising their contentious role, the Court analyzes a specific demand, establishes the truthfulness of the asserted facts, and decides if they constitute a violation of the American Convention. The advisory role, when enacted, is different in its content and aptitude. When analyzing a petition of an advisory nature, the Court interprets the international right, not the specific facts. Consequently, there are no facts to prove.

Also, while the contentious function materializes into a judicial process of contradicting positions, the essential elements of the advisory function are less adversarial. Further, the contentious jurisdiction of the Court is dependent on its previous acceptance by State Parties, which then must respect the Court's judgment. In contrast, the advisory function of the Court does not depend on the consent of the interested States. Lastly, a difference exists in the Court's juridical role. In contentious cases, the Court issues judgments and orders concluding whether or not there was a violation of an international right, and whether the Court is capable of judicially resolving the conflict that has emerged between the petitioner and the State Party. On the other hand, in the case of the advisory role, the Court submits an opinion, which does not have the characteristics of an executable sentence.

Hence, it can be said that the Court's contentious jurisdiction represents a medium to resolve conflicts. The Court's advisory jurisdiction, in contrast, serves to prevent disputes between the members and organs of the inter-American system and is a means to perfect existing human rights instruments in a manner in which the agreements are respected and followed.

B. Phases of a Contentious Case

. . . .

2. Merits Phase

The Merits Phase begins with the presentation of the case before the Court by the Commission or through a participating country. If the suit fulfills all the elements contained within Article 34 of the Court's Rules of Procedure, the President authorizes a formal notification to the responding State. The State, in turn, is granted four months to answer. This period often increases up to three or four months as countries usually request extensions of time to gather evidence, hire an agent, etc.

Once the responding country replies to the petition or if the term lapses without an answer, the parties could request the Court's President to require further written presentations. If necessary, the President could request the parties to present other pertinent writings. During the public hearing, the Court listens to witnesses and experts regarding the matter at issue. In the final oral argument phase, known as the "final conclusions," the parties in the case can propose what they want the court to consider. Also, in several cases, the Court has conducted public hearings with the sole purpose of listening to allegations regarding specific claims, such as objections to witnesses.

After the conclusion of the oral process, the Court deliberates in private on the underlying issue and presents a definitive opinion that cannot be appealed. The Court may only proceed to reevaluate its judgments by a request from the parties involved. For legal purposes, the Court has left open the possibility of case revisions, but only in very rare circumstances, such as the findings of new evidence that could modify the final result of the sentence.

3. Reparations Phase

The Court has the ability to dictate reparations that it considers necessary if they have found a violation of the American Convention. These reparations can be ordered at the time of the verdict, but this matter is generally reserved for a later stage. The existence of this separate stage provides for the ordering of compensatory damages and/or other reparations.

4. Supervision and Execution of Judgments

. . . .

If the State party does not comply with the Court's judgment, the victims or their relatives could execute the judgment in the country concerned in accordance with domestic procedure governing the execution of judgments against the State. Further, victims or their relatives may inform the Court, who in turn, will inform the General Assembly. The General Assembly shall specify the cases in which a State has not complied with its judgments, making any pertinent recommendations. It is important to indicate that the mechanism to execute judgments by the Court via Article 68 is unparalleled, as the European system contains no such provisions. Therefore, at least in theory, the Court's judgments are effective juridical instruments. However, a problem could arise regarding non-monetary damages such as the restoration of a victim's rights, the further investigation of a particular matter, and the sanction of those responsible.

. . . .

C. The Victim Before the Inter-American Court

A topic that deserves a more in-depth review, particularly in the inter-American system, is the role of the victim. Unlike the human rights system in the Americas, the European Court of Human Rights provides the victim with direct access. Article 61 of the American Convention limits the jurisdiction of the Court to "[o]nly the State Parties and the Commission." Hence, until recently, neither the victim nor its representatives were part of the process before the Inter-American Court.

A fundamental change was introduced in the new Rules of Procedure of the Court, which became effective on January 1, 1997. The change refers to the participation of victims or their representatives in the process before the Court. The Court now recognizes the importance of the victim's role in the reparations phase. During this phase, representatives of the victims or its relatives are able to present their own arguments in developing a theory for appropriate damages.

D. Advisory Opinions

According to Article 64 of the American Convention, the Inter-American Court is qualified to be consulted with in regards to the interpretation of the Convention or of other related treaties concerning the protection of human rights in the Americas. Hence, this Article has been interpreted to guide the Court's advisory opinions. According to these pronouncements, the advisory function of the Court extends to the interpretation of a treaty whenever it is directly implicated in the protection of human rights in a participating country of the inter-American system. This wide interpretation covers treaties and other human rights instruments that have been subscribed outside the regional inter-American system, including the Universal Declaration of Human Rights. It also authorizes the Court to interpret the American Declaration on the Rights and Duties of Man, as several references are made to it in the American Convention and in the Charter of the Organization of American States.

Similarly, the Court, by request of a participating State in the OAS, will be able to provide opinions based on the compatibility between a State Parties' internal law and the aforementioned international documents.

. . . .

V. EVALUATION OF THE INTER-AMERICAN SYSTEM FOR HUMAN RIGHTS

As discussed throughout this Article, the operation of the inter-American system for the protection of human rights functions through two protective bodies; the Inter-American Court of Human Rights and the Inter-American Commission for Human Rights. The role of these bodies has greatly enhanced the development of international human rights law. Nevertheless, these bodies have been presented with structural, normative, and procedural challenges that have affected their operation.

A. Structural Problems

1. Number of Ratified Countries

One of the most pressing issues facing the inter-American human rights system is the number of member countries of the OAS that have neither ratified the American Convention nor accepted the contentious jurisdiction of the Inter-American Court. In reality, the Americas have a Latin American system of human rights not an inter-American system. The United States and Canada have not yet ratified the American Convention,[12]

---

12. The United States signed the Convention in 1977, but has not ratified it. See the Inter-American Commission on Human Rights, Basic Documents—Ratifications of the Convention, http://www.cidh.org/Basicos/English/Basic4.Amer.Conv.Ratif.htm for a list of those countries that have ratified the American Convention on Human Rights and have recognized the jurisdiction of the Inter-American Court. Canada considered ratification, but presumably decided not to because the Convention's right to life provisions conflict with Canada's domestic laws allowing abortion. *See* Enhancing Canada's Role in the OAS: Canadian Adherence to the American Convention on Human Rights, http://www.parl.gc.ca/37/2/parlbus/commbus/senate/com-e/huma-e/rep-e/rep04may03-e.htm.

and other countries, especially in the Caribbean, have not accepted the Court's contentious jurisdiction. It is critical that State Parties that have ratified the American Convention also accept the contentious jurisdiction of the Inter-American Court. Thus, the recent commitment of Brazil and Mexico to accept the Court's contentious jurisdiction is encouraging.[13]

The inter-American system requires great persistence and a continual effort on behalf of the political bodies of the OAS to get member countries to ratify the American Convention and accept the contentious jurisdiction of the Inter-American Court. The resolution of the General Assembly that approves the Annual Report of the Court found that the system needs greater participation from member countries to become truly an inter-American system.

. . . .

3. Headquarters of the Protective Bodies

The different locations of the headquarters of each representative body deepens the problems of miscommunication and lack of coordination. Further, the long geographical distance between the two bodies increases the costs related to all the resulting activity between them. The only valid reason for the Commission to remain in Washington D.C. lies in its historical roots.

The Commission and the Inter-American Court concur that ideally both headquarters should be in the same place. The most appropriate headquarters for both the Commission and the Court would be San José, Costa Rica, since it is halfway between the continents of the Americas. However, until the implementation of such a geographical change for one of these human rights bodies, it is essential that the Commission establish an office or branch in San José. This step would immediately improve communication and coordination efforts, a necessary requisite to satisfy the protective purpose of the inter-American human rights system.

4. Time Delay for Cases to Proceed Through the Inter-American System

Only upon the exhaustion of domestic remedies may a case be presented before the Inter-American Court. In fact, prior to the commencement of this process, a case must proceed before the Inter-American Commission, which takes an average of three to four years. If the Commission decides to present the case before the Inter-American Court, the process often takes another four years to be completely resolved. Hence, in real terms, the victim of a violation of human rights becomes a victim of the inter-American system. The delay to resolve the demands of human rights abuses, the duplicity of processes, the loss of evidence, and the anguish of having to relive often horrific events after eight or ten years contradicts the purpose of a system which seeks to emotionally and economically compensate victims.

. . . .

5. The Inter-American Court and Commission Must Function Permanently

Considering the extraordinary length of time for a case to proceed through the inter-American system it is difficult to hold a state responsible for unjustified delay in its own

---

The U.S. is not a party to the Convention, and likely on account of the same right to life provisions; however, it seems U.S. resistance stems from its use of capital punishment.

13. These countries recognized and accepted the jurisdiction of the Court in 1998. Inter-American Commission on Human Rights, Basic Documents—Ratifications of the Convention, http://www.cidh.org/Basicos/English/Basic4.Amer.Conv.Ratif.htm .

domestic processes. In order to truly reform the inter-American system, the Court and the Commission must be provided with the necessary resources to function as permanent bodies.

Given the increased caseload before the Court and the Commission, the fact that these bodies continue to meet only three or four times a year, each time for a period of two or three weeks, adversely hinders the quality of reports and judgments. A firmer commitment is also needed from the judges and the commissioners toward their international tasks....

While the Court remains a temporary institution, an intermediate solution would be to require the President to reside at the Court's headquarters, essentially allowing him/her, with the aid of the Secretariat, to resolve the most pressing matters, particularly, all urgent provisional measures in cases of extreme graveness. The Commission has already put in place a similar system, as the President resides permanently in the country of the headquarters.

. . . .

7. The Role of the Commission in the Process of Individual Petitions

As stated earlier, when a case is presented before the Commission, certain procedural requirements must be exhausted. Since the Commission is not an international tribunal, the process, the review of evidence and its final reports, do not have judicial characteristics. Thus, when a matter is brought before the Court, it results in procedural duplicity, as the Court, a judicial body, must reach a legal judgment without considering the decision of the Commission.

One solution is for the Court to accept some of the Commission's proven facts as undisputed. A more radical approach is for the Commission to be the sole finder of fact. These may be viable alternatives in terms of procedural economy, but it would be inadequate because the function of a human rights tribunal requires extensive knowledge of a case to make factual determinations that are intimately connected to an individual's rights.

Further, suggesting that the facts determined by the Commission remain undisputed would likely reduce the credibility of the inter-American human rights system. Since the Commission is not a tribunal, it would be difficult for the parties to understand why a judicial body would be bound by the Commission, a non-legal entity. In fact, it is not necessary for the Commission to have any judicial characteristics. Moreover, the Commission, which would have previously functioned as the sole fact-finding body, would then serve as the accuser in the same matter before the Court, a clear conflict of interest to one or more of the parties.

However, if the Commission, upon reaching a decision, respects due process, the right to a defense, and all the rights of the parties, and the State Party does not object to its decision, the Commission's decision would achieve a presumption of validity.

Although presently the system continues to function in a relatively fluid manner, it is still advisable to "rethink" the role of the Commission in regard to the individual petitions process and to eliminate many of the dual functions of the system. Quite simply, there is no reason why a human rights victim has to be subjected to two different international processes, as the system was designed to protect the victim, not to serve as a tool for further victimization.

Therefore, the process of presenting individual petitions before the Commission should be eliminated where State Parties have ratified and accepted the American Convention and the contentious jurisdiction of the Court. In a sense, it is a basic step toward granting the victim direct access to the Court. The Commission would continue its role in the process as a third party agent and would maintain the important responsibilities that the OAS Charter and its Statute assign to it. This would allow the Commission to strengthen its ability to develop an awareness of human rights among the peoples of America, a delicate and critical task. The Commission would also retain its primary functions carried out through on-site visits, country reports and the protection of citizens from State Parties within the OAS, including from those States who have not accepted the Court's contentious jurisdiction.

. . . .

C. Procedural Problems

. . . .

2. Admissibility of a Case Before the Court

State Parties often use preliminary exceptions to review the admissibility of a case brought against them. To eliminate this practice, the norm should require all State Parties to argue issues of admissibility only before the Commission, with the exception of cases involving a statute of limitations issue. The Inter-American Court has repeatedly found that if a State Party does not present a preliminary exception before the Commission for failure to exhaust domestic remedies, then it cannot later be presented as an objection before the Court.

. . . .

4. Criteria for Submitting Cases Before the Court

There is no definitive guideline of how the Commission submits cases to the Court nor how it decides to publish a particular report pursuant to Article 51 of the American Convention. What is clear is that the approaches should not be political. During the external session of the Hague Convention that took place in San José, Costa Rica, Judge A. Cançado-Trindade proposed the following guidelines in regards to the submission of cases before the Court: cases that entail serious human rights violations; cases that review matters which are susceptible to prompt judicial solution; cases which involve State Parties from throughout the Americas; cases whose resolution allows the judicial interpretation of the Convention and of other treaties.

. . . .

5. Locus Standi

The Court modified its Rules of Procedure so that the victims or their relatives could present independent requests for reparations before the Commission. The doctrine and practice mandate the recognition of locus standi for an individual throughout the process before the Court. Without having to reform the American Convention, the Court could further reform its Rules of Procedure to allow a victim or its relatives to argue their cases independent of the Commission. The formula is not unique and it has proven to be a success in the European system, which allows direct access to the European Court without proceeding before the European Commission.

. . . .

CONCLUSION

The improvement and reformation of the inter-American human rights system should not be solely viewed with respect to the reformation of the inter-American instruments. On the contrary, there are many ways for the human rights bodies to apply the American Convention and interpret it in a more effective manner. Progressive reformation of the Rules of the Commission and of the Court, more coordinated efforts, the use of advisory opinions to clarify points that necessitate interpretation, and the increased political will of the OAS member countries are a few tools at the disposition of those interested in reforming the effectiveness of the Inter-American human rights system. In addition, the political bodies of the OAS and its member countries must stop continuing the "double talk" that has characterized yearly budgetary discussions. The member countries must manifest a commitment to human rights in the Americas by approving these bodies' annual budgets. This would allow the Court and the Commission to sustain the adequate levels of work and activities necessary to function properly. The implementation of such measures would avoid having to appeal for more complex reformations of the system, which would likely be counterproductive.

. . . .

Notes and Questions

1. What do you see as the strengths and weaknesses of the Inter-American system? Europe no longer has a human rights "gatekeeper" in the form of a human rights commission, but allows applications directly to the ECHR, assuming the prior exhaustion of national remedies. Is this merely a question of procedural emphasis, or does it represent a further step in Europe towards full enforceability for human rights norms? How do the respective roles of the Inter-American Commission and Court differ? What is the likelihood that the Inter-American system will ever evolve into as influential a mechanism as that created by the Council of Europe?

———————

The brief excerpt that follows presents an "insider's" analysis of the functioning of the Inter-American human rights system. Christina Cerna's focus is on the relationship between political democracy and the human rights system that should serve to support it. Note her understanding of how the Inter-American system has evolved along with the trends of history. On balance, she seems optimistic that, over time, the Inter-American system might come to resemble the European human rights system.

Christina M. Cerna, *The Inter-American System for the Protection of Human Rights*
16 Florida Journal of International Law 195 (2004).

. . . .

II. What Is the Inter-American System for the Protection of Human Rights?

. . . .

Currently, the Inter-American Commission on Human Rights has a professional staff of seventeen lawyers, of which I am one, and carries out basically two functions. The first is the examination and preparation of draft decisions of individual petitions, and the second is the performance of on-site visits and the preparation of draft country reports on the situation of human rights in the member states of the hemisphere. During approximately the first thirty years of the Inter-American Commission's history, from 1959 to 1989, that second function was really its primary function. The Inter-American Commission's reputation was built on the importance of its on-site visits and the seriousness of the approximately two or three hundred page country studies that analyzed the human rights situations in these member states.

Since the entry into force of the American Convention and the creation of the Inter-American Court of Human Rights, the Inter-American Commission's functions regarding individual petitions have increased in importance as its on-site visits and country reports have faded. Since 1965, the Inter-American Commission has opened approximately 12,500 cases, whereas the Inter-American Court has taken decisions in approximately 45 cases since its first judgments were issued in 1987....

The Inter-American Commission on Human Rights was not given explicit authority to carry out on-site visits; it created that competence by dint of its own initiative. The Inter-American Commission's Statute, which is prepared by the member states of the OAS, authorized it to hold meetings in any state in the hemisphere, and the Commission converted that authorization into a mandate to conduct monitoring and the preparation of a report on the human rights situation in the country visited. These reports dominated the agenda of the OAS General Assemblies for many years, especially during the long period of military dictatorships in the region, when the Inter-American Commission critically reviewed the behavior of these states as regards their failure to respect human rights norms.

After the initial period of on-site visits and country reports (1959–1989), the period from 1989 to the present, which can be called the second period, has been characterized by the creation of the Inter-American Court of Human Rights. The Inter-American Court was created in 1979, but did not issue its first decisions on the merits in contentious cases until 1988–1989. This second period has been dominated by the processing of individual petitions. As a result of the re-democratization of the Americas, the barrier to the presentation of petitions, which is the exhaustion of domestic remedies, has been easier to overcome since there are now domestic remedies to exhaust. States tend to answer complaints that the Inter-American Commission sends them, which for years they did not do, or did so erratically. The Inter-American Court took approximately ten years to begin to function properly. From 1979–1986, it received no contentious cases. But since 1986, the Inter-American Commission has been presenting cases regularly to the Inter-American Court.

Any individual may present a petition to the Inter-American Commission on Human Rights, alleging the violation of a right set forth either in the American Convention, for state parties thereto, or in the American Declaration, for those OAS member states that are not parties to the Convention. The violation must be attributable to agents of the state, or the failure of the state to act, for example, as in the investigation of a crime, or in the execution of a judicial sentence. Before the Inter-American Commission will consider a petition, the alleged victims must have exhausted domestic remedies at the national level. This requirement is crucial and underlines the general principle of international law that the international system plays a subsidiary role and is triggered by the failure of national law to function properly. If every member state had a functioning and effective Bill of Rights as part of its Constitution that included all the rights adopted at the international level, then the inter-American machinery would be redundant. It is the failure to observe human rights at the national level that has created the necessity for the adoption of international standards and mechanisms. If there has been a manifest denial of justice, then the exhaustion requirement is waived. A manifest denial of justice occurs: 1) if the state fails to act or provide a remedy for the alleged violations; 2) if the judicial system does not function, and there has been an unwarranted delay in reaching a decision in the national courts; or 3) if the alleged victims have been denied access to the remedy.

. . . .

On balance, today there are twenty-four state parties to the American Convention on Human Rights, which includes all of Spanish-speaking Latin America and Brazil. Of those twenty-four state parties, twenty-one have accepted the contentious jurisdiction of the Inter-American Court of Human Rights, including all the Spanish-speaking countries, as well as Brazil, Suriname, and Haiti. Grenada and Jamaica have ratified the American Convention but have not accepted the Inter-American Court's jurisdiction. Barbados and Trinidad and Tobago have ratified the Convention and accepted the Inter-American Court's contentious jurisdiction, but Trinidad and Tobago denounced the Convention on May 26, 1998, over the issue of the death penalty—the first country to do so. That denunciation went into effect one year later, and, consequently, there are now twenty-four (rather than twenty-five) state parties to the American Convention and twenty-one (rather than twenty-two) states that currently accept the Inter-American Court's contentious jurisdiction. As mentioned earlier, neither the United States nor Canada has ratified the American Convention.

III. What Have We Learned from Looking at the History of the System?

The Inter-American Commission's greatest contribution to the inter-American system has been in de-legitimizing nondemocratic governments by means of the monitoring conducted during its on-site visits, and as a result of the presentation of its country reports to the OAS political organs and to hemispheric public opinion in general. These country reports are presented to the political organs and have dominated the agendas of the OAS General Assemblies for many years. The documentation presented by an intergovernmental organization of human rights violations committed by states against their own populations has a credibility not achieved by reports issued by nongovernmental organizations, and every state will fight not to be censured by its peers. In 1980, Argentina, for example, threatened to pull out of the OAS fearing censure because of the Inter-American Commission's report on human rights violations in that country, which focused, *inter alia*, on the military regime's policy of "forced disappearances."

Also, it has been one of the first acts of governments that have made the transition from dictatorship to democracy to ratify the American Convention on Human Rights, as was the case with Nicaragua, Argentina, and Chile. In the past two decades, we have also seen a dramatic increase in the number of states accepting the contentious jurisdiction of the Inter-American Court of Human Rights, with ten states accepting its jurisdiction in the 1980s, and another eleven in the 1990s. Barbados is the first to accept the Inter-American Court's jurisdiction in this decade (June 4, 2000) which we hope is an auspicious sign suggesting increased participation by the English-speaking states in the system.

The democratization of the hemisphere is the central political advance in the region during the twentieth century, and the Inter-American Commission's role in this political development has been crucial. In 1991, the OAS General Assembly adopted Resolution 1080, which has now evolved into a treaty, the Inter-American Democratic Charter, which attempts to guarantee democracy in the Americas. The obligations incumbent upon member states under this Charter require the convocation of a meeting to discuss collective action in the case of any interruption of the democratic process in any member state in the region.

The fact that the region now attempts to guarantee democracy has also brought about a change in the nature of the violations presented to the Inter-American Commission on Human Rights. Whereas the earlier period (1959–1989) of the Inter-American Commission's history was replete with petitions concerning forced disappearances, extrajudicial executions and torture, petitions presented in recent years concern problems common to most democratic states, such as violations of due process, delays in judicial proceedings, disputes over property rights, and status questions (e.g. loss of employment, decrease in pension, and the like). One might even characterize this change as the Europeanization of the inter-American system. At the same time, the European system, (which, since Protocol 11 now comprises only a single organ, the European Court of Human Rights, with the European Commission having been fused into the new European Court), also is dealing with different violations due to the composition of the newly democratic governments of the new member states of the Council of Europe. The membership of the Council of Europe now, in July 2003, comprises forty-five member states, and the conflicts occurring in these states, such as the conflict in Russia with Chechen rebels, and the incidents of torture in Turkey, might justify characterizing this development as the Latin-Americanization of the European system.

But there are many things that the inter-American system can still learn from the European model. The inter-American system is on the road set by the Europeans and if it continues to function as it is at present, it can be assumed that there will also be an eventual fusion of the Inter-American Commission on Human Rights and the Inter-American Court of Human Rights. The President of the Inter-American Court, the distinguished Brazilian jurist, Antonio Cancado Trindade, in his public appearances during the past few years, has called for a Protocol 11 for the inter-American system and direct access for alleged victims to the Inter-American Court. I do not see this happening tomorrow, but I see it clearly on the horizon.

What have we learned? We have learned that, in general, the member states of the Organization, the state parties to the American Convention, have accepted this system of monitoring and supervision. They have accepted the judgments of the Inter-American Court of Human Rights and, this is surprising, because the decisions of the Commission still generally remain unobserved in comparison.

. . . .

The most remarkable development in the evolution of the inter-American human rights system, and I cannot emphasize this enough, is that it has become accepted. All of the Latin countries in the hemisphere have ratified the American Convention. I can recall approximately twenty-two years ago, Cesar Sepulveda, a distinguished Mexican jurist and member of the Commission, telling me, "Christina, this system was not made for supervising the human rights performance of our countries," meaning Mexico and the United States. In his view, the inter-American system was designed to monitor small countries that are considered insignificant on the world stage, but not big countries such as Mexico, Brazil, and the United States; that view has now been totally superseded. Brazil and Mexico are state parties to the American Convention and have accepted the contentious jurisdiction of the Inter-American Court, whereas the United States, although it signed the Convention during the Carter Administration, still has not ratified it. The struggle for legitimacy of the inter-American human rights system has been largely won in Latin America but has yet to be won in the English-speaking states in the region.

IV. What Can We Say About State Compliance and State Noncompliance with the Recommendations of the Inter-American Commission on Human Rights and the Judgments of the Inter-American Court of Human Rights?

The American Convention provides that the judgments of the Inter-American Court of Human Rights are legally binding. A court judgment generally consists of two parts: 1) the reparations, which includes both material and moral damages, and costs and expenses, and 2) the obligation to investigate, try, and punish those responsible for the violation. Given that Latin America has now demonstrated ownership of the system, and approximately forty-five cases have been decided by the Inter-American Court, some preliminary critical observations are in order. In most cases, the state is prepared to pay the pecuniary reparations ordered by the Inter-American Court, but only in the rarest case is it willing to investigate, try and punish the perpetrators, and in those rare cases where it does punish them, they tend to be released from prison after short periods, or never serve prison terms at all.

This climate of impunity characterizes the Americas, and amnesty laws have proliferated throughout the region. The Inter-American Commission on Human Rights, in 1992, was the first international human rights body to declare in two cases, dealing with victims in Argentina and in Uruguay, that amnesty laws were incompatible with the obligations of a state in the inter-American system. These were, perhaps, the Inter-American Commission's most important decisions, and their effects are still being felt. The Inter-American Commission also took the issue to the Inter-American Court of Human Rights in the context of the Peruvian amnesty laws in *Barrios Altos*, and in a judgment issued on March 14, 2001, accepted the Commission's arguments that the amnesty laws were incompatible with the state's obligations under the American Convention.

The Commission amended its Rules of Procedure in 2001 in order to give greater normative value to their decisions which, according to the American Convention, are not explicitly defined as legally binding. The most important amendment has been in Rule 44, which provides that if the state has not complied with the Inter-American Commission's recommendations as set forth in the merits report on the case, the case shall be sent to the Inter-American Court of Human Rights, unless four members of the Commission take a reasoned decision that it should not be sent. This change in the Rules will undoubtedly lead to a greater number of cases being sent to the Inter-American Court. In this year alone, ten cases had already been sent as of July, whereas in all of last year only seven cases were sent to the Inter-American Court.

The Inter-American Court of Human Rights also amended its Rules of Procedure, and the most significant amendment was to Rule 23, which grants autonomy to the representatives of the victims. Whereas previously the alleged victims could only speak before the Inter-American Court through the Inter-American Commission on Human Rights, except for the reparations stage of the proceedings, now they are autonomous throughout the entire proceedings. Unlinking the alleged victims from the Inter-American Commission will doubtless also result in a change in the role of the Commission before the Inter-American Court. Until now, the Inter-American Commission's role was that of a quasi-judicial organ when the case was pending before it; when it decided the case, it was transformed into the advocate of alleged victims before the Inter-American Court. The representatives of alleged victims, in many ways the true party to the case, were euphemistically known as the assistants of the Inter-American Commission's delegates. Now, the courtroom will be reconfigured and alleged victims and the state will have their respective seats before the Inter-American Court as the parties to an individual case, whereas the Inter-American Commission is a party only in the procedural sense, and will modify its role, foreseeably, to that of defender of the best interests of the system.

....

Notes and Questions

1. The Inter-American human rights system, whatever its procedural and budgetary limitations, has had a major impact on the development of a human rights consciousness in Latin America. The Rescia & Seitles and Cerna articles above note that in reality there is no "Inter-American" system, but rather a "Latin American" human rights system, to the extent that the United States and Canada have not ratified the Convention on Human Rights and have not accepted the contentious jurisdiction of the Inter-American Court. Does this mean that the system can only be partially successful? Or is it perfectly fine, and perhaps preferable, that the system is only fully effective with regard to the Latin American countries?

2. What can the Inter-American system offer victims of human rights violations in Latin America that the domestic constitutional order cannot? Is it your impression from the readings that the Inter-American human rights system is capable of bringing about extensive change in the legal and political culture of Latin America?

———————

B. The Inter-American System in Focus

Only Article 19 of the American Convention, reproduced below, directly addresses the rights of the child. In this sense, it resembles the European Convention on Human Rights, which says little specific about child rights *per se*. In the remainder of this section, which presents readings on the Inter-American Court and children's rights, note the way in which the Inter-American Court interprets the general articles of the Convention in relation to children.

Organization of American States, American Convention on Human Rights

Nov. 22, 1969, O.A.S.T.S. No. 36, 1144 U.N.T.S. 123, *available at* http://www.oas.org/juridico/English/treaties/b-32.html

Article 19. Rights of the Child

Every minor child has the right to the measures of protection required by his condition as a minor on the part of his family, society, and the state.

Ann Birch, *State of Guatemala Condemned in Historic Court Case*

NACLA Report on the Americas, Jan.–Feb. 2000, at 46

SAN JOSE—The Inter-American Court on Human Rights, based in San Jose, Costa Rica, has condemned the State of Guatemala for the brutal murder and torture of five

Guatemalan street youth by at least two National Police officers in 1990. In a unanimous decision, the Court found that Guatemala had violated seven articles of the American Convention on Human Rights, the international legal instrument for the protection of human rights in the Americas, including the right to life and the rights of the child. Guatemala was also found guilty of violating several articles of the Inter-American Convention for the Prevention and Punishment of Torture.

The case of the five youths has gone into the legal history books as being the first ever before the Court involving children. "All too often we forget about the children who are victims of wars and violence created by adults," said Bruce Harris, the Regional Director of Casa Alianza/Covenant House Latin America. The childcare agency, which is dedicated to the care and rehabilitation of street children, helped bring the landmark case before the Court. The Court, which is the highest court of appeals in the Americas, is expected to recommend that compensation be paid to the families of the victims. Casa Alianza says it will call for an investigation into the judges involved in the original legal case in Guatemala who acquitted the police officers.

Note that in the following landmark case, the Inter-American Court relied heavily on the main international human rights instruments, including the UNCRC. As you read the case, consider how the Court uses these other agreements to bolster its analysis. This case was hailed for its value as a "message" sent to countries where the national police had brutalized marginalized youth with impunity for many years. The unanimous decision was the first before the Inter-American Court to deal with this widespread problem. See Serge F. Kovaleski, *Guatemala Held Liable in Case of Slain Youths*, Washington Post, Dec. 5, 1999, at A42.

How is the general issue of street children framed and presented by the Court in the case? How are the victims described?

Case of the "Street Children" (Villagrán-Morales et al.) v. Guatemala

1999 Inter-Am. Ct. H.R. (ser. C) No. 63, Judgment, (Nov. 19, 1999), *available at* http://www.corteidh.or.cr/docs/casos/articulos/ seriec_63_ing.pdf

I
Introduction of the Case

1. On January 30, 1997, the Inter-American Commission on Human Rights (hereinafter "the Commission" or "the Inter-American Commission") submitted to the Court an application against the Republic of Guatemala (hereinafter "the State" or "Guatemala") deriving from a petition (No. 11, 383) received by the Secretariat of the Commission on September 15, 1994.

2. When presenting the case to the Court, the Commission invoked Articles 50 and 51 of the American Convention on Human Rights (hereinafter "the Convention" or "the American Convention") and Articles 32 *et seq.* of the Rules of Procedure. The Commission referred this case for the Court to determine whether Guatemala had violated the following Articles of the Convention: 1 (Obligation to Respect Rights), 4 (Right to Life), 5 (Right to Humane Treatment), 7 (Right to Personal Liberty), 8 (Right to a Fair Trial) and 25 (Right to Judicial Protection). According to the application, these violations were the result of

the abduction, torture and murder of Henry Giovanni Contreras, Federico Clemente Figueroa Túnchez, Julio Roberto Caal Sandoval and Jovito Josué Juárez Cifuentes; the murder of Anstraum [Aman] Villagrán Morales; and the failure of State mechanisms to deal appropriately with the said violations and provide the victims' families with access to justice.

3. As two of the victims, Julio Roberto Caal Sandoval and Jovito Josué Juárez Cifuentes, were minors when they were abducted, tortured and murdered, and Anstraum Aman Villagrán Morales was a minor when he was killed, the Commission alleged that Guatemala had violated Article 19 (Rights of the Child) of the American Convention. The Commission requested the Court to order the State to take the necessary steps to conduct a prompt, impartial and effective investigation into the facts "so that [the individual responsibilities for the alleged violations may be] recorded in an officially authorized report" and "those responsible may be punished appropriately". It also requested the Court to order the State "to vindicate the names of the victims and make fair payment to the persons affected by the violations of the aforementioned rights" and to pay costs to the victims and their representatives. In its application, the Commission also cited the violation of Articles 1, 6 and 8 of the Inter-American Convention to Prevent and Punish Torture (hereinafter "Convention against Torture").

II
Competence of the Court

4. The Court is competent to hear this case. Guatemala has been a State Party to the American Convention since May 25, 1978, accepted the contentious jurisdiction of the Court on March 9, 1987, and ratified the Convention against Torture on January 29, 1987.

III
Proceedings before the Commission

5. On September 15, 1994, the Center for Justice and International Law (CEJIL) and Casa Alianza presented the formal petition corresponding to this case to the Inter-American Commission. The petition was based on "the death of five youths and the alleged denial of domestic justice in the case". On September 20, 1994, the Commission opened case No. 11,383, transmitted the pertinent parts of the petition to the State and requested it to provide information on the facts contained in this communication within a period of 90 days.

. . . .

[The Commission made several recommendations to the State requesting their immediate implementation. Guatemala did not comply with Commission's requests. After a series of hearings, the Commission referred the case to the Inter-American Court in January 1997.]

. . . .

IV
Proceedings before the Court

. . . .

[The Commission submitted a formal application to the Court. Guatemala responded to the application by objecting to the jurisdiction of the Court, but this objection was dismissed by the Court.]

. . . .

56. On January 28 and 29, 1999, the Court received the statements of the witnesses and the reports of the expert witnesses proposed by the Commission and heard the final oral arguments of the parties in a public hearing on the merits of the case.

....

V
The Evidence

A) DOCUMENTARY EVIDENCE

59. The Commission presented a copy of documents related to the following, as annexes to the application and as evidence:

a. Domestic judicial proceedings relating to the homicide of Henry Giovanni Contreras, Federico Clemente Figueroa Túnchez, Julio Roberto Caal Sandoval and Jovito Josué Juárez Cifuentes and to the homicide of Anstraum Aman Villagrán Morales.

....

b. The processing of the case before the Inter-American Commission on Human Rights.

c. The issue of "street children" in Guatemala at the time the facts that originated this case occurred.

60. The State did not contest or object to the documents presented by the Commission nor did it question their authenticity, so the Court considers them to be valid.

61. The State did not present any evidence in its reply to the application or at any time during the preliminary objections and merits phases.

....

B) TESTIMONIAL EVIDENCE

65. During the public hearing, the Court received the following testimonies:

a. Testimony of Ana María Contreras, mother of Henry Giovanni Contreras

She declared that, during 1989 and 1990, her son sometimes lived on the streets of Guatemala City, specifically on 18th, 9th and 17th streets. In June 1990, when he was abducted, he was spending some periods of time with her in her house and others in Casa Alianza. Moreover, during this time her son worked in a printing workshop.

On June 15, 1990, between nine and ten in the morning, Henry Giovanni Contreras left his home to obtain an identity card as he had recently had his 18th birthday. When about 15 days had elapsed and he had not returned, the witness went to look for him "on the streets". She asked in a café located in front of a place called "the Zocalo", on 18th Street, showing a photograph of her son. The woman who worked in the café told her that "he had been taken away in a pickup truck with some other boys".

The following day, she went to the Guatemalan National Police Force (hereinafter "National Police Force") where the death of Henry Giovanni Contreras was confirmed and she was shown a half-length photograph of "the body [of her son] with a bullet wound". Furthermore, she was told that she should go to Mixco, where she could find out more details of what had happened. In Mixco, they explained to her that Henry Giovanni Contreras had been found dead in the San Nicolás Woods and she was questioned about this. She declared that she was also summoned by a court or tribunal, which she only referred to as a "court", where "they questioned" her about her son, although she does not remember the exact nature of the questions.

....

She added that, following her statements to the courts, she received an anonymous threatening letter. This frightened her and she said that she was also afraid to be making a statement on the events to the Inter-American Court.

....

b. Testimony of Matilde Reyna Morales García, mother of Anstraum Aman Villagrán Morales

She declared that Anstraum Aman Villagrán Morales attended school up to sixth year and, when he was 15 years of age, he abandoned his studies and began to work in the "La Parroquia" market. From then on, he helped his family financially and was like the man of the house. In 1990, Villagrán Morales "lived" with her and his siblings. However, she indicated that he ceased to live with them "on a permanent basis" when he began to work....

In the early morning of June 26, 1990, her daughter told her that she had been advised by the morgue employees that Anstraum Aman Villagrán Morales was dead. She went to the morgue with her daughter and identified his body. They were given no information about the circumstances of death. When she left the morgue, a youth of about 17 years of age approached her and told her that he had been a friend of her son. He added that, when he was having a cup of coffee in a sector of 18th Street, he saw three men go past shooting at Anstraum Aman Villagrán Morales and that one of the bullets killed him.

[Here similar testimony is given as the previous mother indicating that she did not take steps before the authorities on account of her fear.]

c. Testimony of Bruce Harris, Regional Director for Latin America of Casa Alianza

He declared that Casa Alianza is an organization that executes educational and support programs for "street children" in Mexico, Guatemala, Honduras and Nicaragua. He heard about the case of the four bodies found in the San Nicolás Woods through Aída Cámbara Cruz, a "street child" who took part in the organization's program. He knew the victims because they also participated in Casa Alianza programs. He stated that Anstraum Aman Villagrán Morales and the four youths who were murdered in the San Nicolás Woods were a group of friends who could often be seen on 18th Street.

Regarding the events relating to the abduction and homicide of the four youths, he declared that, from what he saw in photographs that he was shown when he identified the victims before the National Police Force, "they had suffered tremendously [...], they had been tortured, abused [...] and [...] had [received several shots] in the head." Byron Gutiérrez, an investigator from the Ombudsman's Office (*Procuraduría de Derechos Humanos*), told him that the boys showed signs of "torture, typical of the State security forces". He also stated that the area called "Las Casetas" in 18th Street, is known to be a very dangerous area and that he had heard from the Casa Alianza street educators that Anstraum Aman

Villagrán Morales "was apparently drinking beer with two men who were identified or recognized as police agents from the Fifth Corps, apparently [there was] some kind of discussion, shots were heard and the two men ran off and Anstraum [...] died there from the shots."

....

He stated that the file at the Mixco Magistrate's Court was composed of "a few pages" and made no reference to the torture that he had seen in the National Police Force's identification photographs....

While he was the private prosecutor in the case ... the judge never summoned him. Moreover, not all the witnesses that he proposed were summoned, and the information that he contributed to the proceeding was not used in the investigation....

He stated that both the Judiciary and the National Police Force took an excessive time to investigate the events.

He stated that he was frightened as a result of the denunciations made in the case.... In July 1991, three men came to look for him in an armored vehicle without license plates and, as he was not at Casa Alianza, "they covered the façade of our building with bullet holes"....

He added that Casa Alianza is handling 392 cases of alleged crimes against "street children", of which approximately 50 are for murder. Of the 392 cases, less than five per cent have been finalized by the courts, and almost half of them have been closed. Most of the perpetrators of these crimes were members of the National Police Force or other State security forces, or private police agents who were also under the aegis of the Ministry of the Interior. He knew of no training programs for police agents in Guatemala on how to treat children.

d. Testimony of Rosa Angélica Vega, "street child" at the time the events occurred

She declared that she was a friend of the five youths in this case. In 1990, she worked at night in the kiosk of Julia Griselda Ramírez López on 18th Street. On the day of the events she saw how three police agents abducted the four youths later found dead in the San Nicolás Woods. She stated that they were held up at gunpoint and taken away in a black "pick-up". The police agents were dressed in civilian clothes, but she knew they were policemen because of the heavy-caliber arms that they carried. Following the event, she went to the Identification Section of the National Police Force to see the photographs of the bodies.

She stated that on the night of the murder of Anstraum Aman Villagrán Morales, she saw him drinking beer with a young man with curly-hair wearing "tight denim trousers and boots", who she did not know. The young man urged Villagrán Morales to leave; then the two of them walked to the corner and she heard a shot. When she left the kiosk to see what was happening, she saw Villagrán Morales running and then "he bumped into some boards and fell there, face up". Because she was afraid, she waited for people to approach Villagrán Morales' body before she herself went to look at it....

....

The witness was afraid of the threats of the National Police Force when she was a "street child" and, even today, she is afraid to make statements on the case, such as before this Court. Consequently, when on April 12, 1991, she make [sic]

a statement before the Judge of the Guatemalan Second Criminal Trial Court, she said nothing about what she had seen because she feared for her life ... She stated that she identified the man who accompanied Anstraum Aman Villagrán Morales in the kiosk in photographs before the Guatemalan court....

....

In general, regarding her experience as a "street child", she declared that she was afraid of the police because they told her companions and herself that "if they did not [...] disappear from there, [they would take them] prisoner", they would beat them and, "as [they] were good for nothing", they would be better dead....

e. Testimony of Julia Griselda Ramírez López, who worked in a kiosk on 18th Street in Guatemala City

f.

[The witness gives testimony about the shooting of one of the victims.]

....

f. Testimony of Osbelí Arcadio Joaquín Tema, former Guatemalan National Police Force investigator

He declared that, in 1990, he worked as an investigator in the Homicide Unit of the National Police Force ... It was his responsibility to "collect the physical evidence and interview the persons who were present". He was in charge of the preliminary investigation in the case of Anstraum Aman Villagrán Morales....

He stated that he was able to observe when a person ... found a bullet head "of unknown caliber" about a meter from the body.... [H]e calculated that it could have been a .30 or .38 caliber. At that time, the National Police Force used .38 special revolvers. The shot had been fired from a distance of five to six meters from the victim....

He stated that he interviewed three children who were at the scene of the crime and also a woman who attended a food kiosk. However, no one could identify the dead youth and no one said that they had directly seen the perpetrator of the act. At that time, he concluded that some event might have occurred among the children themselves that led to the crime.

....

[Here similar testimony of another National Police Force expert is recounted.]

....

h. Testimony of Roberto Marroquín Urbina, former chief of the Minors' Section of the National Police Force

He declared that his function, when he was Chief of the Minors' Section of the National Police Force, was to investigate both abuses against children and offenses committed by children. He initiated the investigation of the San Nicolás Woods case. In the context of those proceedings, he interviewed [a young girl], who was a "street child" and who told how she had been abducted together with other "street children" a few days before the abduction of the four youths whose bodies were found in the San Nicolás Woods....

He was also in charge of the investigations in the case of Anstraum Aman Villagrán Morales and he declared that two witnesses ... had identified the police

agents from the Fifth National Police Unit, Néstor Fonseca López and Samuel Rocael Valdez Zúñiga, as those responsible for the murder....

... He added that police agents had been responsible for other cases of the abuse
and murder of "street children".

i. Testimony of Ayende Anselmo Ardiano Paz, National Police Force investigator

... He indicated that, according to the ballistic test, the bullet head found near
the body of Anstraum Aman Villagrán Morales coincided with fragments in
Samuel Rocael Valdez Zúñiga's revolver. In his report, he concluded that Néstor
Fonseca López and Samuel Rocael Valdez Zúñiga were responsible for the murder of Anstraum Aman Villagrán Morales "because of the interviews and the certainty of the persons that [he] interviewed and also because of the ballistic test
on the arm that [Samuel Rocael Valdez Zúñiga] carried, since there were sufficient elements to be sure that he was responsible" ...

C) EXPERT WITNESS EVIDENCE

66. The Court heard the reports of the expert witnesses that are summarized below in a
public hearing:

a. Report of Roberto Carlos Bux, Deputy Director of the Bay County Forensic
Center, San Antonio, Texas

....

Regarding the youths found dead in the San Nicolás Woods, he declared that the
forensic analysis report in the case contained important information, such as
the fact that the youths had not been killed in the place where the bodies were
found. He stated that two of the victims, those who were found on June 16,
1990, had died that day before 3.30 a.m. or at 5.30 a.m. at the latest; the other
two, whose bodies were found the following day, were also killed on June 16,
1990, but after 3.30 a.m., approximately 12 hours later. He stated that the two
groups of youths that were found died at different times.

[He gave further evidence concerning the nature of the gunshot wounds, as well
as the premeditated characteristics of the killing.]

....

b. Report of Alberto Bovino, Expert in criminal law, criminal procedural law
and human rights

....

He stated that the police investigation conducted into the case was in no way exhaustive and did not comply with the obligations established in the Guatemalan
Criminal Procedural Code in force, because all the witnesses who could have
identified the suspects were not summoned to make a personal identification
(only four of them were summoned); neither were all the facts that had been
denounced investigated (for example, the threats that several witnesses had received and the torture). As an example of the flaws, he indicated that there was
no attempt to establish the identity of "Pele", a child who, according to the statements of various witnesses, saw Villagrán Morales murdered.

He mentioned other elements that show negligence in the investigation such as
the fact that the judge issued the order for the investigation into the Anstraum
Aman Villagrán Morales case six months after the murder had occurred; no

order was issued to search the homes of the defendants, although this might have allowed the arm of Néstor Fonseca López to be found ...

He added that there was no investigation of the contradictions between the ledger in the National Police Force armory, in which is was recorded that, on the night of the homicide, the arm that was allegedly used was there, and the ballistic test, that showed that the said arm was the one used to kill the victim. He also stated that there was a contradiction as regards the time at which Samuel Rocael Valdez Zúñiga left the National Police Force barracks, and the judge did not take steps to clarify this. Furthermore, the judge did not take into consideration the contents of two official communications that indicated that on June 15, 1990, the day the four youths were abducted, Mr. Fonseca López absconded from the National Police Force school with another person at 5.00 p.m., and they returned together at 6.00 a.m. the following morning.

....

He affirmed that the judge had disqualified a great many testimonies because of his partiality ... As examples of this, he mentioned that the judge rejected witnesses for the sole reason that they were the victims' mothers and this procedure did not correspond to Guatemalan law.... He mentioned that the court also rejected the testimony of Bruce Harris, because he was the Director of Casa Alianza ... Finally, with regard to the ballistic report, he established that the homicide bullet was fired by the revolver belonging to Samuel Rocael Valdez Zúñiga; despite this the judge disqualified the report because this man went off duty at 8.00 p.m. that day.

....

He indicated that, from the evidence produced, the responsibility of Samuel Rocael Valdez Zúñiga and Néstor Fonseca López could have been established for the death of Anstraum Aman Villagrán Morales....

VI
Evaluation of the Evidence

....

72. Regarding testimonial evidence, this Court has said

the criteria for evaluating evidence in an international human rights tribunal are endowed with special characteristics, so that the investigation into a State's international responsibility for human rights violations bestows on the Court a greater latitude to use logic and experience in evaluating the oral testimony that it hears on the pertinent facts.

....

74. With specific regard to the evidence of torture, the Court deems it pertinent to state that, in order to establish if torture has been inflicted and its scope, all the circumstances of the case should be taken into consideration, such as the nature and context of the respective aggressions, how they were inflicted, during what period of time, the physical and mental effects and, in some case, the sex, age and state of health of the victims.

75. Lastly, the Court has maintained that

[u]nlike domestic criminal law, it is not necessary to determine the perpetrators' culpability or intentionality in order to establish that the rights enshrined in the

Convention have been violated, nor is it essential to identify individually the agents to whom the acts of violation are attributed. The sole requirement is to demonstrate that the State authorities supported or tolerated infringement of the rights recognized in the Convention. Moreover, the State's international responsibility is also at issue when it does not take the necessary steps under its domestic law to identify and, where appropriate, punish the author of such violations.

VII

Proven facts

76. After examining the documents, the statements of the witnesses and the reports of the expert witnesses, together with the arguments of the State and the Commission during this proceeding, the Court considers that the facts referred to in this section have been proved.

77. The alleged victims, Henry Giovanni Contreras, 18 years of age; Federico Clemente Figueroa Túnchez, 20 years of age; Julio Roberto Caal Sandoval, 15 years of age, Jovito Josué Juárez Cifuentes, 17 years of age, and Anstraum Aman Villagrán Morales, also 17 years of age, were "street children", friends, and lived on 18th Street, between 4th and 5th Avenues in Zone 1 of Guatemala City; in this general area they particularly frequented the sector known as "Las Casetas", where there were kiosks selling food and drinks, and where the facts of this case took place.

78. When the facts occurred, the area of "Las Casetas" was notorious owing to the high rate of crime and delinquency; it also sheltered a large number of "street children".

79. In Guatemala, at the time the events occurred, there was a common pattern of illegal acts perpetrated by State security agents against "street children"; this practice included threats, arrests, cruel, inhuman and degrading treatment and homicides as a measure to counter juvenile delinquency and vagrancy ...

> a. Abduction and murder of Henry Giovanni Contreras, Federico Clemente Figueroa Túnchez, Julio Roberto Caal Sandoval and Jovito Josué Juárez Cifuentes

80. During daylight hours of June 15, 1990, in the area of "Las Casetas", a pick-up truck approached the youths, Contreras, Figueroa Túnchez, Caal Sandoval and Juárez Cifuentes; armed men descended from the vehicle, obliged the youths to enter the vehicle and took them away.

81. The bodies of the youths Juárez Cifuentes and Figueroa Túnchez were found in the San Nicolás Woods on June 16, 1990, and the bodies of the youths Contreras and Caal Sandoval were discovered in the same place, the following day. In all cases, the official cause of death was attributed to injuries produced by gunshots in the head.

> b. Torture of Henry Giovanni Contreras, Federico Clemente Figueroa Túnchez, Jovito Josué Juárez Cifuentes and Julio Roberto Caal Sandoval

82. The youths Juárez Cifuentes and Figueroa Túnchez were in the power of their abductors for at least 10 hours while the other two, Contreras and Caal Sandoval, were kept by the abductors for at least 21 hours.

> c. Murder of Anstraum Aman Villagrán Morales

83. At approximately midnight on June 25, 1990, Anstraum Aman Villagrán Morales was killed by a gunshot in the "Las Casetas" sector.

....

[Here the Court reviews the procedural history of the case as it made it way through Guatemala's national court system: from the Magistrate's Court, to the Criminal Trial

Courts and the Court of Appeal, and then finally to the Supreme Court of Justice of Guatemala where the defendants were ultimately acquitted. The Court then outlines the evidence admitted at trial and the rulings of the various judges, highlighting all the while the procedural and substantive inadequacies.]

....

VIII
Violation of Article 7
(Right to Personal Liberty)

122. In the application, the Commission alleges that Article 7 of the Convention has been violated since Henry Giovanni Contreras, Federico Clemente Figueroa Túnchez, Julio Roberto Caal Sandoval and Jovito Josué Juárez Cifuentes were illegally and arbitrarily deprived of their liberty by National Police Force agents.

123. When it answered the application, the State did not offer any defense with regard to the violation of Article 7 of the Convention....

....

125. In particular, the Commission stated that the former officers Néstor Fonseca López and Samuel Rocael Valdez Zúñiga, who they allege are the perpetrators of the abduction and retention, did not make a report on the detentions, did not present the youths before the competent judicial authority and, therefore, did not allow them to file a petition for habeas corpus. It also stressed that the right to personal liberty is an essential condition for the exercise of the other fundamental rights and that, as the alleged victims were retained clandestinely, they had no defense against the violation of the rights to receive humane treatment and to life that they also suffered.

....

127. Article 7 of the Convention provides that

1. Every person has the right to personal liberty and security.

2. No one shall be deprived of his physical liberty except for the reasons and under the conditions established beforehand by the constitution of the State Party concerned or by a law established pursuant thereto.

3. No one shall be subject to arbitrary arrest or imprisonment.

[...]

5. Any person detained shall be brought promptly before a judge or other officer authorized by law to exercise judicial power and shall be entitled to trial within a reasonable time or to be released without prejudice to the continuation of the proceedings. His release may be subject to guarantees to assure his appearance for trial.

6. Anyone who is deprived of his liberty shall be entitled to recourse to a competent court, in order that the court may decide without delay on the lawfulness of his arrest or detention and order his release if the arrest or detention is unlawful. In States Parties whose laws provide that anyone who believes himself to be threatened with deprivation of his liberty is entitled to recourse to a competent court in order that it may decide on the lawfulness of such threat, this remedy may not be restricted or abolished. The interested party or another person in his behalf is entitled to seek these remedies.

[...]

128. In the instant case, there is abundant concurring evidence that the abduction of the four youths was perpetrated by State agents and, more specifically, by members of the National Police Force. Indeed:

- according to witnesses, those who deprived them of their liberty did so in daylight, in the street, without hiding their faces and they moved about freely within sight of numerous persons;

- the abductors had efficient means of mobilization and aggression: they arrived at the site in a pick-up truck, armed with firearms that they used to threaten the youths, and they left the site in the same vehicle, taking those abducted;

- several witnesses, who made statements during the domestic judicial proceedings, provided the investigators with detailed physical descriptions of the abductors and identified them in personal and photographic identification procedures. The persons identified by the witnesses were members of the National Police Force. Several of those who made statements mentioned that those agents frequented the area of "Las Casetas".... and

- one witness declared that the National Police Force agents who were identified as the perpetrators of the detention of the youths had taken part in a similar abduction of "street children" from the "Las Casetas" area a few days earlier, and that she was one of the victims ...

129. The investigations of the National Police Force itself ... arrived at the conclusion that the four youths had been apprehended by the two agents identified by the witnesses....

130. The said conclusion is confirmed by abundant information on the ... unlawful and violent actions against the "street children" by various types of State security agents. These actions include several that are very similar to those that constitute the facts of the instant case.

. . . .

132. It is clear that, contravening the provisions of Article 7.2 of the Convention, the four youths were arrested although the causes or conditions established by the Guatemalan Constitution, in force since January 14, 1986, were not present. Article 6 of the Constitution establishes that a person may only be deprived of his liberty "under an order issued according to the law by a competent judicial authority" or because he is caught *in fraganti* while committing a crime or offence. Neither of these two grounds was present in this case.

133. Moreover, they were not "brought before the competent judicial authority within six hours", as the said Article 6 of the Guatemalan Constitution orders. What is more, this article expressly establishes that those arrested "may not be subject to any other authority". If we compare the facts of this case with this basic procedural regulation, it is clear that it was not complied with.

134. Consequently, we can conclude that neither the material nor the formal aspect of the legal rules for detention were observed in the detention of the four youths.

135. The European Court of Human Rights (hereinafter "European Court") has remarked that the emphasis on the promptness of judicial control of arrests is of special importance for the prevention of arbitrary arrests. Prompt judicial intervention allows the detection and prevention of threats against life or serious ill-treatment that violate fundamental guarantees contained in the European Convention for the Protection of Human Rights and Fundamental Liberties (hereinafter "European Convention") and the American Con-

vention. The protection of both the physical liberty of the individual and his personal safety are in play, in a context where the absence of guarantees may result in the subversion of the rule of law and deprive those arrested of the minimum legal protection. In this respect, the European Court particularly stressed that the failure to acknowledge the arrest of an individual is a complete negation of these guarantees and a very serious violation of the article in question.

136. Consequently, this Court concludes that the State violated Article 7 of the American Convention on Human Rights, in relation to Article 1.1 of the Convention, to the detriment of Henry Giovanni Contreras, Federico Clemente Figueroa Túnchez, Julio Roberto Caal Sandoval and Jovito Josué Juárez Cifuentes.

IX
Violation of Article 4
(Right to Life)

137. In the application, the Commission maintained that Guatemala had violated Article 4 of the Convention because two National Police Force agents murdered Henry Giovanni Contreras, Federico Clemente Figueroa Túnchez, Julio Roberto Caal Sandoval, Jovito Josué Juárez Cifuentes and Anstraum Aman Villagrán Morales. The Commission emphasized that "[t]he right to life cannot be annulled" and that "[t]he violation of that norm […] has not been the object of any corrective".

138. The State did not offer any defense on this point in its answer to the application …

139. In its final arguments, the Commission underscored the *ius cogens* nature of the right to life and the fact that it is the essential basis for the exercise of the other rights. The Commission stated that compliance with Article 4 in relation to Article 1.1 of the Convention, not only presumes that no person shall be deprived of his life arbitrarily (negative obligation), but also requires the States to take all necessary measures to protect and preserve the right to life (positive obligation). It concluded, therefore, that the State had violated two aspects of the said right because, when the events took place, the "street children" were the object of different types of persecution, including threats, harassment, torture and murder. In consequence, there were a great many complaints to which the State should have responded with effective investigations, prosecutions and punishment; however, the State agents who were responsible were rarely investigated or convicted, and this gave rise to the *de facto* impunity that allowed, and even encouraged, the continuation of these violations against the "street children", increasing their vulnerability.

. . . .

141. Article 4.1 of the Convention stipulates:

> Every person has the right to have his life respected. This right shall be protected by law and, in general, from the moment of conception. No one shall be arbitrarily deprived of his life.

142. In the instant case there is extensive concurring evidence that it was State agents and, more specifically, members of the National Police Force, who murdered Henry Giovanni Contreras, Federico Clemente Figueroa Túnchez, Julio Roberto Caal Sandoval, Jovito Josué Juárez Cifuentes and Anstraum Aman Villagrán Morales. [Here the Court reviews the salient facts indicating the involvement of State agents.]

. . . .

143. As State agents perpetrated the five homicides, the Court must necessarily conclude that they may be attributed to the State.

144. The right to life is a fundamental human right, and the exercise of this right is essential for the exercise of all other human rights. If it is not respected, all rights lack meaning. Owing to the fundamental nature of the right to life, restrictive approaches to it are inadmissible. In essence, the fundamental right to life includes, not only the right of every human being not to be deprived of his life arbitrarily, but also the right that he will not be prevented from having access to the conditions that guarantee a dignified existence. States have the obligation to guarantee the creation of the conditions required in order that violations of this basic right do not occur and, in particular, the duty to prevent its agents from violating it.

. . . .

146. The Court wishes to indicate the particular gravity of the instant case since the victims were youths, three of them children, and because the conduct of the State not only violated the express provision of Article 4 of the American Convention, but also numerous international instruments, that devolve to the State the obligation to adopt special measures of protection and assistance for the children within its jurisdiction ...

147. Based on the foregoing, the Court concludes that the State violated Article 4 of the American Convention on Human Rights, in relation to Article 1.1 of the Convention, to the detriment of Henry Giovanni Contreras, Federico Clemente Figueroa Túnchez, Julio Roberto Caal Sandoval, Jovito Josué Juárez Cifuentes and Anstraum Aman Villagrán Morales.

X
Violation of Article 5
(Right to Humane Treatment)

. . . .

155. Article 5 of the American Convention stipulates that

1. Every person has the right to have his physical, mental, and moral integrity respected.

2. No one shall be subjected to torture or to cruel, inhuman, or degrading punishment or treatment. All persons deprived of their liberty shall be treated with respect for the inherent dignity of the human person.

[...]

. . . .

157. In the instant case, there is considerable, concurring evidence that the physical integrity of these four youths was violated and that, before they died, they were victims of serious ill-treatment and physical and psychological torture by the State agents and, more specifically, members of the National Police Force.

158. The bodies of the youths were found dead with signs of serious physical violence that the State has been unable to explain. The file contains photographs of the faces and necks of the bodies of the youths. Different injuries are very visible in these photographs, including those made by the bullets that were the cause of death and other signs of physical violence. The four autopsies mention the approximate location of the shot wounds and, in two case[s], refer to other injuries that can be clearly seen in the photographs, or are located in other parts of the bodies, attributing them generically to "animal bites". The size of the wounds is not specified or their depth, the type of animal that could have produced them, or whether they occurred before or after death. The autopsies of the other two youths provide no explanation of the injuries to their bodies.

159. An Amnesty International report, included with the file…, which was not contested by the State, mentions that

> the bodies presented signs of torture: the ears and tongues had been cut off, and the eyes had been burned or extracted. Furthermore, it appears that some kind of burning liquid had been thrown on the chest and chin of [Caal Sandoval]. According to the Prosecutor-General's office, the mutilations to which the four had been subjected correspond to the treatment that the police usually use on those who inform against this security force. The mutilation of the ears, eyes and tongue signifies that the person had heard or seen or spoken of something inadvisable.

. . . .

162. It should be remembered that the youths were retained clandestinely by their captors for between 10 and 21 hours. This lapse of time occurred between two extremely violent circumstances: forced seizure and death due to the impacts of a firearm while defenseless, which the Court has already declared proved … It is reasonable to conclude that the treatment they received during those hours was extremely aggressive, even if there was no other evidence in this regard.

163. While they were retained, the four youths were isolated from the external world and certainly aware that their lives were in danger. It is reasonable to infer that, merely owing to this circumstance, they experienced extreme psychological and moral suffering during those hours.

. . . .

166. Furthermore, it is worth recalling, as this Court has already stated, that a persons who is unlawfully detained is in an exacerbated situation of vulnerability creating a real risk that his other rights, such as the right to humane treatment and to be treated with dignity, will be violated.

167. Lastly, from the documents and testimonies that are included in the probative material, it is clear, as we have already stated, that the facts in this case occurred in a context of great violence against children and youths who lived on the streets…, violence that very often included different types of torture and ill-treatment.

. . . .

169. The Court believes that the ill treatment and torture was practiced by the same persons that abducted and killed the youths. Since the Court has established that those responsible for these acts were member of the National Police Force, it is pertinent to conclude that the perpetrators of the ill-treatment and torture carried out in the time between the seizure and the murders, were State agents, whether they were those investigated and charged in the domestic proceedings or others.

. . . .

177. Owing to the foregoing, the Court concludes that the State violated Article 5.1 and 5.2 of the American Convention on Human Rights, in relation to Article 1.1 of the Convention, to the detriment of Henry Giovanni Contreras, Federico Clemente Figueroa Túnchez, Jovito Josué Juárez Cifuentes and Julio Roberto Caal Sandoval, …

XI
Violation of Article 19
(Rights of the Child)

178. In the application, the Commission alleged that Guatemala had violated Article 19 of the American Convention by omitting to take adequate prevention and protection

measures in favor of Julio Roberto Caal Sandoval, 15 years of age, Jovito Josué Juárez Cifuentes, 17 years of age and Anstraum Aman Villagrán Morales, also 17 years of age.

179. The Commission stated that the crimes committed against these minors "are an example of the serious human rights violations that Guatemalan street children suffered at the time the complaint in the case was made".

180. To this should be added, according to the Commission, the "serious risk for their development and even for their life […] itself" to which "street children" were exposed, in view of their abandonment and social exclusion, a situation that "was exacerbated in some cases by the extermination and torture to which they were subjected by death squadrons or by the Police Force itself".

181. In particular, the Commission believes that the State omitted to take measures destined to "safeguard the development and the life of the victims", to investigate and end the abuse, to punish those responsible, and "to train and impose adequate disciplinary measures and penalties on its agents". All this, despite being aware that "street children" were the object of acts of violence, particularly by members of the police force, based on reports presented to the State by several international organizations and complaints submitted by non-governmental organizations.

182. In its answer to the application, the State remained silent on this point …

183. In its final arguments, the Commission indicated that Guatemala signed the United Nations Convention on the Rights of the Child (hereinafter "Convention on the Rights of the Child") on January 26, 1990, and deposited the respective instrument of ratification on June 9, 1990 — this Convention entered into force on September 2, 1990. In 1995, during the hearings before the Committee on the Rights of the Child, a supervisory body created by this Convention, Guatemala presented a report in which it stated that "it could only provide information on the situation [of "street children"] as of 1994" and added that "although the number of complaints about police brutality suffered by street children had declined, the problem had not been resolved and the police force had not been completely restructured". Moreover, it stated that, in Guatemala, there was "a violent culture and that the police force did not receive training on how to deal with these children'". Lastly, the State "acknowledged that 84 children had been murdered in the first three months of 1996 and that, according to available information, there had only been seven [convictions]". The Commission asserted that this declaration was a unilateral acknowledgement of facts generating international responsibility.

184. The Commission described the three child victims of the facts of this case as persons who lived in extremely precarious socio-economic conditions and who fought to survive alone and fearful of a society that did not include them, but rather excluded them. Furthermore, it stated that, as the State abstained from taking effective measures to investigate and prosecute the perpetrators, it exacerbated the risk of violations of the rights of "street children" in general, and the victims of this case, in particular.

185. The Commission stated that the reason for Article 19 of the Convention arose from the vulnerability of children and their incapacity to personally ensure the respect of their rights. It also declared that while the consequent protection responsibilities correspond to the family in principle, State measures are necessary in the case of at risk children. According to the Commission, this special State obligation encompasses the protection of a wide range of social, economic, civil and political interests of the child.

. . . .

187. Article 19 of the Convention stipulates that "[e]very minor child has the right to the measures of protection required by his condition as a minor on the part of his family, society, and the State".

188. Article 19 of the American Convention does not define what is meant by "child". However, the Convention on the Rights of the Child (Article 1) considers every human being who has not attained 18 years of age to be a child, "unless, by virtue of an applicable law, he shall have attained his majority previously". According to the Guatemalan legislation in force at the time of the facts of this case, those who had not attained 18 years of age were also minors. Using this criteria, only three of the victims, Julio Roberto Caal Sandoval, Jovito Josué Juárez Cifuentes and Anstraum Villagrán Morales, were children. However, in this judgment, the Court is using the colloquial expression "street children" to refer to the five victims in this case, who lived on the streets, in a risk situation.

189. In this judgment, the Court has also recognized as a notorious and public fact that, at the time the facts of this case occurred, there was a systematic practice of aggression against 'street children' in Guatemala carried out by members of State security forces; this included threats, persecution, torture, forced disappearance and homicide.

190. Based on the different reports on the issue of "street children" in Guatemala, and the characteristics and circumstances of this case, the Court believes that the events that culminated in the death of the minors, Caal Sandoval, Juárez Cifuentes and Villagrán Morales, are linked to the prevailing pattern of violence against "street children" in Guatemala at the time the facts occurred.

191. In the light of Article 19 of the American Convention, the Court wishes to record the particular gravity of the fact that a State Party to this Convention can be charged with having applied or tolerated a systematic practice of violence against at-risk children in its territory. When States violate the rights of at-risk children, such as "street children", in this way, it makes them victims of a double aggression. First, such States do not prevent them from living in misery, thus depriving them of the minimum conditions for a dignified life and preventing them from the "full and harmonious development of their personality", even though every child has the right to harbor a project of life that should be tended and encouraged by the public authorities so that it may develop this project for its personal benefit and that of the society to which it belongs. Second, they violate their physical, mental and moral integrity and even their lives.

. . . .

194. Both the American Convention and the Convention on the Rights of the Child form part of a very comprehensive international *corpus juris* for the protection of the child that should help this Court establish the content and scope of the general provision established in Article 19 of the American Convention.

195. The Convention on the Rights of the Child contains various provisions that relate to the situation of the "street children" examined in this case and, in relation with Article 19 of the American Convention, it throws light on the behavior that the State should have observed towards them....

[The Court outlines relevant provisions of the CRC including Articles 2(1), 2(2), 3(2), 6(2), 20(1), 20(2), 27(1), 27(3) and Article 37.]

196. These provisions allow us to define the scope of the "measures of protection" referred to in Article 19 of the American Convention, from different angles. Among them, we should emphasize those that refer to non-discrimination, special assistance for children deprived of their family environment, the guarantee of survival and development

of the child, the right to an adequate standard of living, and the social rehabilitation of all children who are abandoned or exploited. It is clear to the Court that the acts perpetrated against the victims in this case, in which State agents were involved, violate these provisions.

197. The file contains documentary references to the fact that one of the three children in this case, Jovito Josué Juárez Cifuentes, was registered in the "criminal archives" of the Identification Office of the National Police Force. In this respect, the Court considers that it is relevant to stress that, if the State had elements to believe that "street children" are affected by factors that may induce them to commit unlawful acts, or has elements to conclude that they have committed such acts, in specific cases, it should increase measures to prevent crimes and recurrence. When the State apparatus has to intervene in offenses committed by minors, it should make substantial efforts to guarantee their rehabilitation in order to "allow them to play a constructive and productive role in society". In this case, it is clear that the State seriously infringed these directives.

198. In view of the foregoing, the Court concludes that the State violated Article 19 of the American Convention on Human Rights, in relation to its Article 1.1, to the detriment of the minors, Julio Roberto Caal Sandoval, Jovito Josué Juárez Cifuentes and Anstraum Aman Villagrán Morales.

XII
Violation of Articles 25, 8 and 1(1)
(Rights to Judicial Protection and a Fair Trial)

[Based on the detention, torture and ultimate murder of the youths, the Court finds violations of these rights as well.]

. . . .

XIII
Violation of Articles 1, 6 and 8 of the Inter-American
Convention to Prevent and Punish Torture

239. In its application, the Commission alleged that the State had also violated Articles 1, 6 and 8 of the Convention against Torture, which "define more precisely and extensively the mechanisms of protection established in Article 5 of the American Convention", to the detriment of Henry Giovanni Contreras, Federico Clemente Figueroa Túnchez, Julio Roberto Caal Sandoval and Jovito Josué Juárez Cifuentes. Furthermore, it added that, in violation of the provisions of the Convention against Torture, "an investigation was never initiated, nor were the perpetrators [of this crime] prosecuted or punished" although the State was fully and opportunely aware of the events through "[c]ompetent [national] authorities" who "examined and recovered the bodies from the site in the San Nicolás Woods"....

240. Just as the State did not make any reference to the violation of Article 5 of the American Convention in its answer to the application, neither did it allude to the violation of Articles 1, 6 and 8 of the Convention against Torture....

. . . .

244. Article 1 of the Convention against Torture stipulates:

The State Parties undertake to prevent and punish torture in accordance with the terms of this Convention.

245. Article 6 of the Convention against Torture establishes

In accordance with the terms of Article 1, the States Parties shall take effective measures to prevent and punish torture within their jurisdiction.

The States Parties shall ensure that all acts of torture and attempts to commit torture are offenses under their criminal law and shall make such acts punishable by severe penalties that take into account their serious nature.

The States Parties likewise shall take effective measures to prevent and punish other cruel, inhuman, or degrading treatment or punishment within their jurisdiction.

246. Lastly, Article 8 of the Convention against Torture adds:

The States Parties shall guarantee that any person making an accusation of having been subjected to torture within their jurisdiction shall have the right to an impartial examination of his case.

Likewise, if there is an accusation or well-grounded reason to believe that an act of torture has been committed within their jurisdiction, the States Parties shall guarantee that their respective authorities will proceed properly and immediately to conduct an investigation into the case and to initiate, whenever appropriate, the corresponding criminal process.

After all the domestic legal procedures of the respective State and the corresponding appeals have been exhausted, the case may be submitted to the international fora whose competence has been recognized by that State.

....

250. It is clear from the documents, testimonies and expert witness reports in the file, that the Guatemalan administrative and judicial authorities did not adopt any formal decision to initiate a criminal investigation into the alleged perpetration of the crime of torture, neither did they investigate it in practice, although a great deal of concurring evidence was collected on the cruel treatment and torture of the victims when the homicides were investigated.

251. Article 8 of the Convention against Torture expressly embodies the State's obligation to proceed *de oficio* and immediately in cases such as this one, and the Court has declared that "in proceedings on human rights violations, the State's defense cannot rest on the impossibility of the plaintiff to obtain evidence that, in many cases, cannot be obtained without the State's cooperation". However, the State did not act in accordance with these provisions.

252. Therefore, the Court concludes that the State violated Articles 1, 6 and 8 of the Inter-American Convention to Prevent and Punish Torture to the detriment of Henry Giovanni Contreras, Federico Clemente Figueroa Túnchez, Julio Roberto Caal Sandoval and Jovito Josué Juárez Cifuentes.

XIV
Operative Paragraphs

253. Therefore,

THE COURT

DECIDES

unanimously,

1. to declare that the State violated Article 7 of the American Convention on Human Rights, in relation to its Article 1.1, to the detriment of Henry Giovanni Contreras, Fed-

erico Clemente Figueroa Túnchez, Julio Roberto Caal Sandoval and Jovito Josué Juárez Cifuentes;

2. to declare that the State violated Article 4 of the American Convention on Human Rights, in relation to its Article 1.1, to the detriment of Henry Giovanni Clemente Figueroa Túnchez, Julio Roberto Caal Sandoval, Jovito Josué Juárez Cifuentes and Anstraum Aman Villagrán Morales;

3. to declare that the State violated Article 5.1 and 5.2 of the American Convention on Human Rights, in relation to its Article 1.1, to the detriment of Henry Giovanni Contreras, Federico Clemente Figueroa Túnchez, Jovito Josué Juárez Cifuentes and Julio Roberto Caal Sandoval;

. . . .

5. to declare that the State violated Article 19 of the American Convention on Human Rights, in relation to its Article 1.1, to the detriment of Julio Roberto Caal Sandoval, Jovito Josué Juárez Cifuentes and Anstraum Aman Villagrán Morales;

6. to declare that the State violated Articles 8.1 and 25 of the American Convention on Human Rights, in relation to its Article 1.1, to the detriment of Henry Giovanni Contreras, Julio Roberto Caal Sandoval, Jovito Josué Juárez Cifuentes, Federico Clemente Figueroa Túnchez and Anstraum Aman Villagrán Morales and their immediate next of kin;

7. to declare that the State violated Articles 1, 6 and 8 of the Inter-American Convention to Prevent and Punish Torture to the detriment of Henry Giovanni Contreras, Federico Clemente Figueroa Túnchez, Julio Roberto Caal Sandoval and Jovito Josué Juárez Cifuentes;

8. to declare that the State violated Article 1.1 of the American Convention on Human Rights regarding the obligation to investigate, that the State should conduct a real and effective investigation to determine the persons responsible for the human rights violations referred to in this judgment and eventually punish them; and

9. to open the phase of reparations and costs and authorize the President to adopt the corresponding procedural measures.

. . . .

So ordered.

Notes and Questions

1. On 26 May 2001, the Court ordered the State of Guatemala to build a school with a plaque in memory of the victims, pay compensation to the victims' families, investigate the facts of the case and identify and sanction those responsible, and change its domestic legislation in accordance with Article 19 of the American Convention. Guatemala adopted these measures in the months following. On 19 December 2001 it paid compensation to the victims' families. It also established an educational centre with a plaque dedicated to the memory of the five boys. The Minors Code which had been in force since 1979 was abolished, and the national Congress passed a new Code for Children and Young People which would enter into force one year later. However, as a result of various delays, the law did not enter into force as planned. Finally, and thanks to pressure from civil society, on 4 June 2003, the Law of Integral Protection of Children and Young People (Ley de Protección Integral de la Niñez y Adolescencia) was passed.[14]

---

14. Child Rights Information Network, Street Children: Villagrán Morales and Others v. Guatemala, http://www.crin.org/Law/ instrument.asp?InstID=1072.

2. What is the principal value of a decision like that in the "Street Children" case? How can it influence state behavior? Is its main effect as a warning to other states? A vindication of the interests of a long disadvantaged population? Political catharsis? What does litigation of this type add to the other forms of "blame and shame" characteristic of the international human rights system?

———————

In the case above the Inter-American Court addressed the issue of street children and their brutal treatment at the hands of the state. The following article explains how the Commission and the Court might also be relied on in similar fashion to address the issue of child labor. Bearing in mind our discussion of child labor in Chapter Two of this book, why are abuses relating to economic exploitation more difficult to improve via existing human rights mechanisms? What difficulties are cited by Jennifer Bol in her article?

Jennifer Bol, *Using International Law to Fight Child Labor: A Case Study of Guatemala and the Inter-American System*
13 American University International Law Review 1135 (1998)

....

V. THE INTER-AMERICAN SYSTEM FOR THE PROTECTION AND PROMOTION OF HUMAN RIGHTS

....

C. Taking Child Labor to the Inter-American System

Taking the issue of child labor in Guatemala through the Inter-American system would first require a petition to the Inter-American Commission alleging a violation of a right or rights enunciated in the American Convention or the American Declaration, the key human rights instruments in the Inter-American arsenal.

By creating binding treaty obligations, the American Convention is the most important of these instruments. Unfortunately, it is primarily a document on civil and political rights. Article 26, the obligation of progressive development, is the only right under the rubric of economic and social rights. Under this Article, states pledge only to "adopt measures ... with a view to achieving progressively, by legislation or other appropriate means, the full realization of the rights implicit in the economic, social, educational, scientific, and cultural standards set forth in the Charter of the Organization of American States...." While this may appear to limit the usefulness of the American Convention in the realm of child labor, many of the provisions under the heading of civil and political rights can be interpreted to apply to the child labor problem in Guatemala.

Most importantly, Article 19 of the American Convention imposes a positive obligation on the state to provide a minor with "the measures of protection required by his condition as a minor on the part of his family, society, and the state." Although this is obviously a vague obligation, the measures of protection that a state must take under Article 19 can be interpreted using the rights enumerated elsewhere in the American Convention, as well as Guatemala's other international obligations....

Thus, in a child labor case, the prohibition against forced and compulsory labor in Article 6(2) and the right to physical integrity in Article 5 may be relevant. The Commission has recognized these rights as applying to incidences of forced overtime in the maquilas. Likewise, the right to life in Article 4 and the right to physical, mental, and moral integrity in Article 5 applies where children are working in inherently dangerous occupations, particularly where children are more likely to suffer injury or death due to their physical or mental immaturity. Freedom of association in Article 16 may also be relevant. Anyone old enough to work legally in Guatemala has the right to join a trade union. In reality, the exercise of this right is severely restricted. The rule also disenfranchises thousands of underage workers who cannot join unions. Finally, Article 25 of the American Convention guarantees judicial protection of an individual's rights. The court system in Guatemala, as noted above, is unable or unwilling to enforce the rights of individuals, including child laborers.

The scope of Guatemala's obligation to protect children in Article 19 can be further clarified by examining its commitments to children under other international instruments. Guatemala is a party to the Economic Covenant that provides the right to just and favorable conditions of work including fair wages and the right to education. Article 10(3) provides that:

> Children and young persons should be protected from economic and social exploitation. Their employment in work harmful to their morals or health or dangerous to life or likely to hamper their normal development should be punishable by law. States should also set age limits below which the paid employment of child labour should be prohibited and punishable by law.

Guatemala has also ratified ILO Convention No. 138 on a minimum age for employment. This Convention prohibits countries from allowing children under the age of completion of primary schooling to work and, in developing countries, children younger than fourteen years of age cannot work. Finally, Guatemala ratified the UNCRC, which provides for the right of children to be protected from economic exploitation and from performing any work that is likely to be hazardous, interfere with the child's education, or be harmful to the child's health or physical, mental, spiritual, moral, or social development. This provision goes further than the Economic Covenant since it requires states' parties to ensure the implementation of this right, including, providing a minimum age of admission to employment, providing appropriate regulation of hours and conditions of work, and providing appropriate penalties or other sanctions.

Article 19 of the American Convention should also be interpreted bearing in mind the provisions of the American Declaration. Article XI of the American Declaration provides every person with the right to the preservation of health through sanitary and social measures. Article XII states that every person has the right to an education that will prepare him to attain a decent life, to raise his standard of living, and to be a useful member of society. Finally, Article XIV provides that every person has the right to work, under proper conditions, and that every working person has the right to receive remuneration in proportion to his capacity and skill in order to assure a standard of living suitable for himself and for his family.

Relevant economic and social rights are laid out in detail in the Additional Protocol to the American Convention on Human Rights in the Area of Economic, Social, and Cultural Rights ("Protocol of San Salvador").[1] This instrument, however, has not yet come into force.[2] Nonetheless, Guatemala is a signatory, thereby indicating its willingness to abide by its objects and purposes. The Additional Protocol contains detailed provisions on the right to work, the right to just, equitable, and satisfactory conditions of work, and trade union rights. In particular, Article 7(f) of the Protocol provides that states parties must guarantee in their legislation:

---

1. *Available at* http://www.oas.org/juridico/English/sigsla-52.html.
2. [It came into force in November, 1999.]

The prohibition of night work or unhealthy or dangerous working conditions and, in general, of all work which jeopardizes health, safety, or morals, for persons under 18 years of age. As regards minors under the age of 16, the work day shall be subordinated to the provisions regarding compulsory education and in no case shall work constitute an impediment to school attendance or a limitation on benefiting from education received.

The obligation to protect children under the American Convention and the American Declaration "have not been subject to particularly close scrutiny or analysis by the Commission or Court." In fact, like most other rights, neither the Inter-American Commission nor the Inter-American Court has ever addressed the issues of children's rights and labor rights outside the context of individual cases of violence. Any petition on child labor, therefore, must present a strong case to compensate for the novelty of the claim.

The best route is likely in the form of a small class action, whereby an NGO brings forward several egregious examples of child labor engaging several of the specific articles of the American Convention mentioned above, as well as Article 19. For example, the class might include a child worker injured in an agricultural accident, an underage maquila worker who was locked in the factory overnight on several occasions, and children working in inherently dangerous occupations such as mining and prostitution. The petition should present cases of the youngest children working full-time in each sector since child labor at a very young age is in itself considered to be a particularly egregious form of child labor.

The procedure for such a petition is straightforward. The petition must first meet certain technical requirements, including the identity of the petitioner(s), the facts of the complaint, evidence of exhaustion of domestic remedies, and an assurance that the incident is not before any other international body.

In order to satisfy the exhaustion of domestic remedies prerequisite, these cases must first be taken before a Guatemalan tribunal. The exhaustion threshold, however, has not been held to be an onerous burden. In the *Velasquez Rodriguez* case, the Court held that only those domestic remedies that are "adequate" and capable of producing the desired result need be exhausted. In an advisory opinion, the Inter-American Court also held that the exhaustion threshold may be met where the victim is too poor to obtain a lawyer and the state does not provide legal aid, or where the victim cannot obtain legal representation because of a general fear of violent reprisals for taking the case. The failure of the Guatemalan courts to effectively deal with the complaints would also raise concerns under Article 25 of the American Convention as a ground for the complaint.

When a petition is deemed admissible, the Commission sends the relevant information to the government involved. Under Article 48(1)(a), the government must provide information on the allegations within a reasonable period. In the Regulations of the Commission, the government must supply the requested information within ninety days, but a state may request an extension of thirty days for justifiable cause as long as the time does not extend beyond one hundred eighty days in total. If there is no response, or the response is inadequate, the Commission may deem the allegations in the petition to be true.

If the Commission decides to proceed, it may hold a full hearing or request the parties to provide additional written information. The Commission may also carry out an on-site visit to investigate the case. Under the American Convention, the Commission must also "place itself at the disposal of the parties concerned with a view to reaching a friendly settlement." If a friendly settlement is not reached, the Commission draws up a report that is sent to the state party in confidentiality.

Within three months of submitting this report, the affair may be settled or the Commission may decide to send the case to the Court for a binding judgment. If neither of these occur, the Commission writes a second report containing the facts, its conclusions and recommendations, and a time limit for implementation. If the government involved does not implement the recommendations within the time frame determined by the Commission, the report may be published in the Commission's Annual Report.

The recommendations of the Commission do not have the force of binding judgments. Their biggest impact lies in the threat of publicity. Additionally, the Annual Report of the Commission is addressed by the OAS General Assembly, raising the theoretical possibility of political pressure on non-complying states. It is the discretion of the Commission, however, to refer cases to the Court for a binding judgment that offers the real incentive for states to comply with the Commission's recommendations.

The Commission is supposed to send controversial cases or cases on matters of importance to the hemisphere to the Court. It is questionable whether a child labor petition would meet these criteria. The Court examines the case *de novo* and makes a judgment that is final and binding. Under Article 63 of the American Convention, the Court is authorized to award remedies. The scope of the right to a remedy is of considerable importance in the case of child labor and will be discussed further in Part VI.

VI. LIMITATIONS OF INTERNATIONAL LITIGATION

A. Limitations of the Inter-American System

. . . .

Commentators have criticized the legal reasoning and the irregularity of the procedural rules applied by the Commission. They have also reproached the lack of publicity surrounding activities of the Commission and the Court. Publicity is, of course, one of the major reasons for taking a child labor petition forward in the first place. Other criticism has focused on political problems, which always arise in a system designed as part of a political organization. One observer commented that political considerations may be more difficult to escape in the Inter-American Court with its seven judges than in the European Court, which has thirty-two judges. Financial difficulties also limit the effectiveness of both the Commission and the Court. The Commission sits for only two sessions a year and receives only 2% of the budget of the OAS.

Having a two-tiered system also creates lengthy delays. In the *Velasquez Rodriguez* case, it took four and a half years from the petition until the case was referred to the court and another four years until the judgment was rendered. Cases cannot be taken to the court without first going through the Commission. Judge Rodolfo Piza Escalante commented in his concurrence in the case *In re Viviana Gallardo*: "they hobbled [the court] by interposing the impediment of the Commission, by establishing a veritable obstacle course that is almost insurmountable, on the long and arduous road that the basic rights of the individual are forced to travel."

A central problem is that, unlike the Commission, individuals and NGOs do not have standing to bring contentious cases before the Court. Cases must arise between states, or the Commission must send cases to the Court. Although some have advocated for a change in this regard, resource restrictions, as well as the lesser degree of acceptance of the Court's jurisdiction compared to the European Court, make this change unlikely in the near future. This means that the Commission has unlimited discretion to decide what cases to refer to the Court. Due to the progressive nature of obligations to ensure economic rights and the arguably less serious nature of child labor compared to political killings, the Commission may not see the referral of a child labor petition as appropriate or necessary.

B. Hurdles to Using International Litigation

While choosing to litigate child labor in an international forum may be more effective than leaving the issue to diplomatic questioning under a United Nations treaty body, international litigation presents more general difficulties. These difficulties include the need to prove state responsibility; the reticence of international law to hold states accountable for economic, social, and cultural rights, and the question of flexibility of remedies.

1. State Responsibility

International law governs the behavior of states, not private individuals. The responsibility of the state must be addressed before Guatemala can be held accountable for violations of the American Convention or other international obligations relating to child labor. In most cases, however, children who are exploited work for private employers or even their own families.

The *Velasquez Rodriguez* case, decided by the Inter-American Court in 1988, held that states can be held responsible for the actions of private individuals in some cases. The *Velasquez* case involved the responsibility of the state for the disappearance of Rodriguez at the hands of one of the notorious Latin American death squads. The Court found that, even if the state was not directly involved in the rights violation, responsibility could still arise from the state's response or lack of response to a consistent pattern of gross human rights violations. The Court, in that case, was interpreting Article 1(1) of the American Convention, a key provision which puts a positive obligation on the state to respect and ensure the rights contained in the Convention. The Court held that Article 1(1) encompassed three distinct obligations for the state: the obligation to refrain from violating rights, the obligation to prevent the violation of rights, and the obligation to investigate and punish violations which have occurred. Although the *Velasquez* case arose in the context of a disappearance at the hands of a Latin American death squad—a terrible and frequent occurrence in Latin American countries during the 1970s—there is no principled reason why this interpretation of Article 1(1) should not apply to all cases where human rights violations occur consistently.

Thus, even if a state has not been guilty of directly using child labor, it can still be held responsible for failing to prevent it and for failing to investigate and punish those who are responsible.

....

2. Litigating Economic and Social Rights

Until now, the Inter-American system has focused almost exclusively on the egregious violations of civil and political rights committed under authoritarian regimes in Latin America. The Commission and the Court have examined the right to life and the right to physical integrity. The European Court of Human Rights and the Human Rights Committee similarly have rarely delved into economic rights. The exclusion of economic rights is partly a reflection of the fact that civil and political rights have been separated from economic and social rights under international law. This division is evident in the existence of two International Covenants, one for civil and political rights and another for economic, social, and cultural rights. It is also noticeable in the lack of explicit attention directed to economic and social rights in the American Convention. According to Chinkin and Wright, "One unfortunate consequence of the perceived division of human rights law into these two areas has been a priority accorded to civil and political rights to the detriment of economic and social rights."

. . . .

3. Remedies

"It is a principle of international law, which jurisprudence has considered 'even a general concept of law,' that every violation of an international obligation that results in harm creates a duty to make adequate reparation." In the American Convention, this principle is codified in Article 63 (1), which states:

> If the Court finds that there has been a violation of a right or freedom protected by this Convention, the Court shall rule that the injured party be ensured the enjoyment of his right or freedom that was violated. It shall also rule, if appropriate, that the consequences of the measure or situation that constituted the breach of such right or freedom be remedied and that fair compensation be paid to the injured party.

Broadening the scope of the Inter-American system to deal with economic, social, and cultural rights such as child labor will require an expanded view on how this right to a remedy should be interpreted.

All of the cases before the court thus far have involved actual or presumed loss of life for which reparation must be in the form of monetary compensation. In the *Velasquez Rodriguez* case, the wife sought, in addition to pecuniary compensation, several other remedies. These additional measures included: an end to the forced disappearances, an investigation into other similar cases, a complete and truthful public report on what happened, a public act to honour the disappeared, and guarantees to respect the work of humanitarian and family organizations.

. . . .

Merely requiring the government to enforce legislation on child labor cannot solve the problem ... In fact, it may make a bad situation worse since children would be forced to find work in the informal economy to survive.... [B]y making their economic role illegal, children become even more difficult to protect from exploitation. Moreover, addressing child labor concerns on an individual basis would reach only the few complainants whose stories are brought forward. Even if the victims could be adequately compensated, the restitution would do nothing to change the underlying problems that contribute to child labor for thousands of others. Such a conclusion would be contrary to the point of bringing such a petition forward in the first place.

Even if broad remedies were available, it would be difficult to determine an appropriate remedy in a child labor petition because it goes to the heart of the disagreement over what causes child labor and how it can be best eliminated. An appropriate remedy, however, would necessarily require a whole range of approaches. For example, the Court should order the government to improve its enforcement of domestic labor laws and its health and safety regulations. It should also order the government to allow underage workers to join unions if they desire. More importantly, the government should be required to increase the proportion of its budget spent on education and other social programs to at least the median of other countries in the region. A reasonable timetable for the increase of the adult minimum wage to a level consistent with the amount required to meet basic needs, as well as other plans for addressing the inequitable distribution of wealth and the extreme poverty faced by the country, should be required. A flexible remedy certainly would need to combine both orders and prescriptions for progressive change to reflect the nature of the rights at issue. Thus, freedom from violence and the right to organize should be recognized as core rights that cannot be derogated from, while other remedies, such as poverty alleviation, must leave the state with some margin to implement remedies as it chooses.

Despite the decision in *Velasquez* to limit reparations to monetary compensation, the right to such a broad remedy is not inconsistent with the American Convention. Note that Article 63 provides that the Court, on finding a violation "shall rule that the injured party be ensured the enjoyment of his right or freedom that was violated [and shall rule] if appropriate, that the consequences of the measure or situation that constituted the breach of such right or freedom be remedied...." Thus, the Court could use such broad remedies if it determined that they were necessary to ensure the enjoyment of the right by the injured party or as a way of remedying the consequences of the situation that caused the breach.

. . . .

––––––––––

The following article by Israel de Jesús Butler describes two other cases involving children that came before the Inter-American Court. The author praises the Court for its ultimate decisions, but criticizes it for its lack of analysis. As we have seen, child rights-related cases at the Inter-American Court have tended to involve extreme violations of children's rights, at least by comparison with the European Court of Human Rights.

Israel de Jesús Butler, *The Rights of the Child in the Case Law of the Inter-American Court of Human Rights: Recent Cases*
5 Human Rights Law Review 151 (2005)

1. Introduction

The present commentary considers two cases decided in 2004 by the Inter-American Court of Human Rights (the Court) concerning the rights of the child as protected by Article 19 of the American Convention on Human Rights (the Convention). In the first of these cases the Court takes a nuanced approach to Article 19, incorporating its requirements into the other substantive rights of the Convention rather than examining it in isolation. In the second case the Court considers the torture and extrajudicial execution of two minors during an anti-terrorism campaign in Peru in 1991. This judgment reinforces the State's obligation to respect human rights even when combating terrorism, which is pertinent given the current global 'war' on terror.

2. Case Concerning the Children's Rehabilitation Institute

The 'Panchito Lopez' Institute near Asuncion, Paraguay was a severely overpopulated and under-resourced government detention centre for minors. Considering the general conditions of detention, particular incidents involving injury to, and loss of life by, inmates (resulting from fires and acts of violence) and the inadequacy of local remedies, the Court determined that Paraguay had violated Articles 2 (duty to implement the Convention guarantees), 4(1) (right to life), 5(1), 5(2), 5(6) (right to humane treatment), 8(1) (right to a fair trial), in conjunction with Article 1(1) (duty to respect the Convention rights) and in light of Article 19 (rights of the child); and Article 25(1) (right to judicial protection) in conjunction with Article 1(1) in relation to various inmates of the Institute, as well as Article 5(1) with Article 1(1) in relation to their families.

The Court accorded Article 19 a parasitic character, considering it in terms of what it added to other Convention rights, rather than as an isolated provision. Although this is consistent with its previous approach to Article 19, the Court has, in the past, been less express in adopting this method. The Court indicated in the present decision that the parasitic approach taken in this instance might not be applied in future cases.

At the outset the Court underlined the importance of the economic and social dimensions of the rights of the child, particularly in relation to the rights to life (Article 4) and physical integrity (Article 5(1)). The Court's incorporation of these considerations meant a wide reading of and holistic approach to these rights, making a separate examination of the issues under Article 26 (the obligation to progressively implement economic, social and cultural rights) unnecessary. The Court had express recourse to the United Nations Convention on the Rights of the Child 1989 (CRC), and the Additional Protocol to the American Convention on Human Rights in the area of Economic, Social and Cultural Rights 1988 (the 'San Salvador Protocol') in interpreting the Convention.

The Court made a general note that as detainees are completely subject to State control and unable to realise their basic needs of their own accord, there exists a special relationship between them and the State. As guarantor of their rights, the State must ensure the necessary conditions for a dignified life. The Court acknowledged that although the restriction of certain rights (such as the right to privacy and family life) was inherent in the deprivation of liberty, any such restriction should be kept strictly to the minimum necessary in a democratic society. Furthermore, the restriction of rights which are unconnected to a situation of detention (such as the right to life, personal integrity, religious freedom and due process) is completely unjustifiable.

A. The Rights to Life and Physical Integrity of Minors

The Court held that in fulfilling its obligations with respect to the rights to life and physical integrity of detainee minors, the State should assume its position of guarantor with even greater care and responsibility than it must generally. Firstly, the State must conform to the principle of the 'best interests of the child'. Secondly, the State must pay particular attention to the quality of life enjoyed by minors while in detention. Referring to Articles 6 and 27 of the CRC, the Committee on the Rights of the Child General Comment 5 on General Measures of Implementation of the Convention on the Rights of the Child of the UN Committee on the Rights of the Child; and the UN Rules for the Protection of Juveniles Deprived of their Liberty, the Court found that the State, as part of its obligations to secure the rights to life and physical integrity, is obliged to provide for the health and education of minors so as to secure their physical, mental, spiritual, moral, psychological and social development.

The Court entered into a preliminary consideration of whether the defendant State had successfully guaranteed a dignified life to both adult and minor detainees at the Institute, examining the general conditions of detention. The Institute was seriously overpopulated and under-resourced. Inmates were without adequate sanitation, medical, psychological or dental care, and were malnourished. Specialised medical treatment was unavailable for those with physical disabilities, mental illnesses and drug addiction problems. Inmates had insufficient opportunity to take exercise or engage in recreational activities. Due to an inadequate supply, many of them were obliged to share beds, blankets or mattresses, which facilitated incidences of sexual abuse among them. Furthermore, the administration made frequent use of cruel and violent forms of punishment prohibited by Article 5(2), such as isolation, beatings and torture.

. . . . The Court then moved on to consider whether the general conditions of detention disclosed violations of Articles 4 and 5, specifically in relation to the minors detained in the Institute. The Court held that special measures of protection were necessary to provide for their health and education. This was of particular importance given that minors are at a crucial stage of physical, mental, spiritual, moral, psychological and social development, which can have consequences for their 'project of life'. Minors were not assured the regular medical supervision required to ensure the detainees' normal development. While there existed a formal programme of education at the Institute, there were insufficient teachers and resources for its implementation, drastically limiting the opportunities for acquiring a basic education or learning a trade. This deficiency was all the more serious since the children in question came from marginalised sections of society, limiting the prospect of their successful re-entry into society or fulfilment of their 'project of life'. In light of the general conditions of detention, as well as the particular lack of special measures to ensure adequate healthcare and education, the Court found violations of Articles 4(1) (protection of the right to life), 5(1) (the right to physical, mental and moral integrity), 5(2) (freedom from torture or to cruel, inhuman, or degrading punishment or treatment), and 5(6) (obligation to rehabilitate detainees) in conjunction with Article 1(1), read in the light of Article 19. The State had also patently failed in its duties under Article 5(5) (the separation of child and adult detainees) by transferring inmates to adult prisons as a form of punishment. Within these adult prisons the children were not separated from adult detainees, which was damaging to their development and made them vulnerable to abuse. The Court's decision could have benefited from an exposition of what measures the State would need in place to satisfy the requirements of Articles 4 and 5, especially with regard to the provision of healthcare and education, since these are relatively undeveloped dimensions of the rights to life and physical integrity.

The Court next considered particular instances of death and injury at the Institute over the period in question. During 2000 and 2001 there were three fires resulting in several deaths and injuries among the inmates, the last of which provoked the permanent closure of the Institute. It had been well known that the Institute was inadequately equipped (without even fire alarms or extinguishers) and the guards untrained to respond to a fire, despite the fact that inmates routinely lit fires for cooking and tattooing. As guarantor of the rights of the detainees, the State was responsible for introducing measures to prevent critical situations which could endanger the lives of inmates. Accordingly, the Court found that the State's failure to prevent the deaths of inmates in these fires amounted to extreme negligence, which violated Article 4(1) in conjunction with Article 1(1), read in the light of Article 19. The survivors who were injured in the fires experienced, and continued to experience, intense physical and mental suffering. The burns, injuries and smoke poisoning to which they were subject, whilst in the care of the State, constituted a violation of Articles 5(1) (the right to physical, mental and moral integrity), and 5(2) (freedom from torture or cruel, inhuman, or degrading punishment or treatment) in conjunction with Article 1(1), in the light of Article 19.

The deaths of three inmates formed the basis for further examination by the Court. Two of these died as a result of wounds inflicted during separate incidents of violence between inmates in the young offenders' block of an adult prison, to which they had been transferred from the Institute. The third minor died as a result of a gunshot wound inflicted by a State agent at the Institute. In relation to the first two inmates, despite the fact that State agents were not implicated in the deaths and that prompt medical assistance was given, the Court found that the State had violated Article 4(1) in conjunction with Article 1(1), read in the light of Article 19, because it had failed to create conditions of detention which limited, as far as possible, the risk of fights between inmates. The Court also found a violation of Article 4(1) in respect of the third minor.

The Court's judgment leading to these findings under Article 4 are open to criticism. The Court should have offered a more concrete analysis of the first two deaths by considering conditions in the adult prison where the incidents took place. It does not seem appropriate for the Court to rely on its account of conditions in the Institute as the basis for a decision regarding events in another prison. In relation to the third death it made no analysis of the incident beyond the fact that the victim died. There was no enquiry into whether the use of force by the State had been necessary or proportionate. It may be that the Court simply inferred that the use of lethal force was not justified in the circumstances given the propensity of the prison guards to use excessive force. It might be implied that the use of lethal force against detainee minors can never be justified and will always violate Article 4. However, the Court did not make such an indication.

. . . .

B. The Obligation of the State to Adopt Domestic Measures of Implementation and the Right to a Fair Hearing in Relation to Minors

Formerly, Paraguayan law subjected all persons from 14 years of age to the criminal jurisdiction of the ordinary courts. It was not until 1998 that a separate criminal procedure was introduced in favour of minors and not until 2001 that a specialised juvenile jurisdiction was developed. Drawing on its Advisory Opinion 17 and Article 40(3) of the CRC, the Court found that Article 8 of the Convention, read in light of Article 19, requires the establishment of a specialised court system and procedure for the implementation of juvenile criminal justice. In light of Article 40(3)(b) of the CRC and the UN Standard Minimum Rules for the Administration of Juvenile Justice (Beijing Rules), the Court found that a specialised juvenile jurisdiction should have some flexibility in its powers in relation to minors. Firstly, it should have the ability to adopt non-judicial measures. Secondly, where a judicial process was necessary, the national court should be able to provide psychological support for the minor during the trial; monitor the manner in which evidence was obtained from the minor; and regulate publicity surrounding the trial. Thirdly, it should have wide powers of discretion over the conduct of all stages of the trial and the administration of the sentence, enabling it to tailor them to the facts of the particular case. Fourthly, the decision-makers in a system of juvenile justice should be specially prepared and trained in the human rights of the child and infant psychology in order to avoid any abuse of discretion and ensure that any measures ordered are suitable and proportionate. Such measures were lacking in Paraguayan law until at least 2001, and, therefore, there had been a violation of Articles 2 and 8(1), in conjunction with Articles 19 and 1(1), in relation to all those detained in the Institute over the period in question.

The Court's explanation of the necessary elements of a juvenile justice system is welcome. However, the Court did not engage in any analysis, or examine in any detail, the adequacy of the changes introduced into Paraguayan law after 2001. While the question of Paraguay's reforms may have post-dated the dispute under examination—as the dispute related to a period regulated largely by the old law—the Court could have examined Paraguay's reforms ex officio. This might avoid a future dispute arising out of the same reforms. Although the Court acknowledged the efforts of Paraguay in reforming its law, it also impliedly acknowledged (in the section of the judgment relating to reparations) that the present law was still defective in respect of the State's failure to separate child and adult detainees and sentenced and non-sentenced detainees, and the absence of adequate education, medical and psychological services.

C. The Right to Personal Liberty

The Court did not expressly refer to Article 19 in its analysis of Article 7 (right to personal liberty), but it did consider the special measures of protection required by virtue of the vulnerability of minors. The Court stated that pre-trial detention, as it was the most severe measure applicable to an accused, should be used as a matter of exception, limited by the presumptions of innocence, necessity and proportionality in a democratic society. It must be limited in time to a period which is reasonable and does not go beyond the continued existence of the circumstances which made it necessary. Rather than rely on such circular reasoning, the Court could have explained which factors are relevant to determining whether pre-trial detention is reasonable and whether Article 7 imposes an upper limit on the length of detention. Where minors are concerned, pre-trial detention should be even more rigorously regulated. The Court continued that measures other than pre-trial detention should be considered, including close supervision, permanent escort, foster care, transfer to an educational institute, as well as care, guidance and supervision orders, counselling, probation, education and vocational training programmes and other alternatives to internment. The Court seems to establish its own set of alternatives to detention and then lists those contained in Article 40(4) of the CRC (to which it refers) wholesale without regard for the obvious overlap between them. It might have been more helpful for the Court to go into detail and explain the alternatives and their distinguishing features. The Court went on to state that pre-trial detention for minors should conform to Article 37(b) of the CRC, which reads:

> No child shall be deprived of his or her liberty unlawfully or arbitrarily. The arrest detention or imprisonment of a child shall be in conformity with the law and shall be used only as a measure of last resort and for the shortest appropriate period of time.

D. The Right to Judicial Protection

In 1993 a non-governmental organisation (the Tekojojá Foundation) sought to complain about the conditions of detention in the Institute (rather than to request the release of any detainees) by way of a generic writ of habeas corpus. In 1998, the writ was granted in favour of the detainees named therein (all those who had been present in the Institute in 1993 when the writ was sought), and the State was ordered to transfer them to a place of detention which accorded with standards required by human dignity. However, no action was taken by the State.

The Court recalled that for a remedy to be effective it must be capable of establishing if a violation has occurred and then provide the necessary remedy. This will not be the case if, as on the facts, the remedy cannot be delivered in time to relieve the violation. The delay of five years in the present case patently exceeded this limit. Furthermore, the late arrival of the remedy made it ineffective for many of those named in the writ who had, in all probability, left the Institute by 1998. There had, therefore, been a violation of Article 25(1), which provides for the right to 'simple and prompt recourse'. Additionally, the fact that the order of the Paraguayan Court was not then carried out violated Article 25(2)(c).

E. Further Comments

....

By way of general comment on the Court's judgment in this case, the Court's holistic approach to Articles 4 and 5, through the incorporation of economic and social considerations derived from Article 13 of the San Salvador Protocol, is to be welcomed. However, it might have been helpful if the Court had made some comments on Article 26 of the Convention (on economic and social rights) to give some substance to this vague provision. The fact that the Court believed Article 26 raised no separate issues from those considered under Articles 4 and 5 at least implies that the requirements of adequate education and healthcare also form part of Article 26 of the Convention and will therefore bind States Parties who are not also party to the San Salvador Protocol.

Following past practice, the Court made extensive use of the provisions of the CRC and other non-binding UN instruments to continue to flesh out the meaning of Article 19 of the Convention. From the point of view of human rights protection the Court is performing an admirable role in the protection of the rights of the child, promoting an expansive understanding of Article 19 and complementing the role of the UN Committee on the Rights of the Child. However, States Parties to the Convention might object that the Court is effectively supervising the provisions of the CRC under the guise of Article 19 of the Convention. While all Parties to the Convention are also Parties to the CRC, they have only consented to supervision of their obligations by the UN Committee on the Rights of the Child, not the Court.

3. The 'Gómez-Paquiyauri Brothers' v. Peru

Between 1984 and 1993 Peru underwent a period of internal conflict, during which the State systematically carried out extrajudicial executions of suspected 'subversives'. In 1991 the Gómez-Paquiyauri brothers (14 and 17 years of age) were seized, tortured and summarily executed by State agents searching for suspected terrorists. Their relatives were subsequently harassed by the State. Only some of the State agents responsible were criminally prosecuted and even then they were not properly punished. The Court found that Peru had violated Article 4(1) (right to life), Article 7 (right to personal liberty), Article 5 (right to humane treatment), Articles 8 and 25 (right to a fair trial and judicial protection), and Article 19 (rights of the child), all in conjunction with Article 1(1) (duty to implement Convention obligations) of the Convention, as well as Articles 1 (duty to punish torture), 6 (duty to prevent and punish torture), 9 (duty to compensate victims) and 8 (duty to investigate allegations of torture) of the Inter-American Convention to Prevent and Punish Torture ('Torture Convention'), in relation to the brothers. Furthermore, the State had violated Article 5, Articles 8 and 25, and Article 11 (the right to family life), all in conjunction with Article 1(1) in relation to their relatives.

A. The Right to Personal Liberty in States of Emergency

The brothers were arrested, tortured and found dead approximately one hour after their arrest. The flagrant nature of the acts in question meant that the Court had little to add to its existing case-law on Article 7, though it did have occasion to reaffirm the *Bulacio* judgment where it found that in the case of minors the right of a detainee to make contact with a relative on being taken into custody was all the more important and included contact immediately upon arrest in order to be effective.

Of greater significance is that the Court stated in its consideration of Article 7 that the existence of a state of emergency could not be invoked in the present case. The Court stated simply that any suspension of Convention guarantees must conform to the strict necessities of the circumstances and not go beyond the limits of the Convention. It should be noted that Article 27 of the Convention which governs the suspension of Convention guarantees in situations of emergency does not allow for any derogation from Articles 4 or 5 which protect the right to life and humane treatment and which were obviously violated in the present case. However, it does permit States to derogate from Article 7 on personal liberty. The Court did not consider whether the detention and absence of judicial supervision which resulted from the suspension of Article 7 guarantees were necessary or proportionate in the circumstances existing in Peru at the time. Rather, it seemed to consider that because the torture and execution resulted from the detention and absence of judicial control, the measure of detention without charge or judicial supervision must, in themselves, have been unjustifiable. This would imply that where conduct in a case affects rights which may not be suspended under Article 27, the Court can ignore the existence of a state of emergency as a legally relevant fact altogether. It would have been helpful if the Court could have addressed this question with greater clarity.

B. Freedom from Torture

Reaffirming past case-law, the Court stated that the fact that detention is arbitrary, even if it is brief, is enough to imply without any other evidence that the victim has suffered inhuman and degrading treatment. It also reaffirmed the subjective and relative nature of treatment constituting torture, the non-derogable nature of the prohibition of torture—which extends to the so-called 'fight against terrorism'—and its status as a rule of *jus cogens*. The mere act of being placed in the boot (trunk) of a police car was enough to violate Article 5. In the present case the brothers received physical and mental mistreatment, being hurled to the ground, kicked, stood on, hooded, beaten with rifle butts and shot repeatedly. The Court interpreted the definition of torture contained in Article 2 of the Torture Convention widely as the infliction of suffering for whatever ends, which extended in the present case to the systematic use of torture with the objective of intimidating the general population. Consequently, the State had violated Article 5 in conjunction with Article 1(1) of the Convention as well as Articles 1, 6 and 9 of the Torture Convention (the duties to prevent and punish torture and compensate victims). The Court did not discuss which particular facts of the case violated Articles 1, 6, and 9 of the Torture Convention. It is submitted that such a discussion is all the more necessary in the case of these Articles, because of the questionable nature of the Court's jurisdiction over violations of the Torture Convention.

....

C. The Right to Life

The Court stated that the obligation to protect the right to life disclosed special obligations in the case of minors, although it did not elaborate on this. The failure of the State to punish the police officers responsible for the killings, in particular the agent who ordered the acts, created a situation of impunity. The State is under a duty not only to take measures to prevent, try and punish deprivations of life, but also to prevent extrajudicial executions committed by its agents. Drawing on the jurisprudence of the European Court of Human Rights, the Court stated that the right to life, coupled with the State's obligation to implement the Convention, implies a duty to establish domestic procedures to monitor the use of lethal force by State agents as a matter of routine, by way of an effective official investigation.

The Court asserted that State-sponsored or -tolerated extrajudicial killings violated a rule of *jus cogens*. However, it did not provide any examination of relevant authorities for this. While it is a welcome finding, the absence of any legal reasoning or examination of the sources of international law to substantiate this pronouncement undermines the prestige of the Court as an international judicial institution.

D. The Right to a Fair Trial and Judicial Protection

In 1993 the national courts sentenced two of the perpetrators to terms of imprisonment and ordered them to pay compensation to the brothers' family. However, the compensation was not paid and by 1994 and 1995, respectively, the two perpetrators had been granted partial liberty and conditional liberty. Although the Court would not examine the domestic legislation regarding the granting of such forms of release of prisoners, it did say that the State must ensure that they should be regulated in such a way as to prevent impunity. A third State agent, responsible for ordering the killings, had been found guilty but had hitherto evaded custody, despite the fact that he continued to present communications to the domestic courts through his attorney in an attempt to take advantage of amnesty laws and statutes of limitation. Furthermore, the State had not investigated the possible existence of other culprits.

The aforementioned circumstances had created a situation of impunity. The State was under a duty to conduct ex officio a serious, impartial and effective investigation to clarify the facts surrounding the detention, torture and execution of the brothers, and to identify those responsible. The failure of the State to conduct such an investigation and punish all those responsible violated Articles 8 and 25 of the Convention in conjunction with Article 1(1) with respect to the brothers and their relatives, and Article 8 of the Torture Convention with respect to the brothers.

Most of the issues which the Court examined in relation to Articles 8 and 25 centre around the lack of an investigation by the State and the consequent problem of repetition of the offence and impunity, rather than the inadequacy of the trials which were conducted. Judge Medina Quiroga in her partially dissenting opinion noted that the Court was in the habit of blurring Articles 8 and 25. Article 8 sets out the requirements of a fair hearing for an aggrieved person, while Article 25 establishes the right to an effective remedy before national authorities for violations of Convention rights. If the failure to conduct an effective investigation falls under any of these Articles, it surely falls under Article 25 rather than Article 8. However, since the duty to prevent, investigate and punish torture had already been discussed under the Court's consideration of Articles 4 and 5 of the Convention, it would seem more sensible for it not to have repeated its analysis by examining the same failures under Articles 8 and 25 as well.

E. The Rights of the Child

The Court reaffirmed that the measures of protection required by Article 19 of the Convention in favour of minors must be based on the principle of the best interests of the child. Noting the widespread ratification of the CRC, the Court concluded that the guarantees embodied therein formed part of the body of international law which it should use to give meaning to Article 19 of the Convention. Minors should be treated in accordance with the rules of non-discrimination (Article 2, CRC), as well as respect for the right to life (Article 6, CRC) and the right to humane treatment (Article 37, CRC). Consequently, the detention of minors should be an exceptional measure and be as brief as possible; where the alleged victim is a minor a stricter standard will be applied in determining the qualification of mistreatment as torture; and the State must take special measures to ensure that the right to life of minors is secured (though the Court does not elaborate on these). The State's flagrant failure to respect these requirements meant that it had violated Article 19 in relation to the two brothers.

. . . .

G. Further Comments

The Court noted that the State's international responsibility for violating the Convention was aggravated on two counts. Firstly, because there existed systematic human rights violations, including extrajudicial executions carried out by State agents, which infringed a rule of jus cogens. Secondly, because the alleged victims were minors. As to the first of these counts, it does not seem to follow that the State's international responsibility for violations towards the victims should be aggravated by virtue of the fact that they took place in the context of a systematic practice of extrajudicial executions committed in respect of other people. A determination of State responsibility based on the existence of widespread or systematic violations where specific victims are not parties to a legal dispute is surely more appropriately dealt with under the function of State reporting or country visits, carried out by the Inter-American Commission on Human Rights.

4. Conclusion

In both the cases reviewed, the Court effectively imported provisions of the CRC into the Convention through the back door. It is, of course, desirable for the purposes of harmony and universality in international human rights law for the Court to ensure that its rulings are in keeping with prevailing international standards. Furthermore, the CRC offers any tribunal a rich source of material to draw from when interpreting the rights of the child. Therefore, in the long run, one would expect that the case law of the Court should be consistent with, and build upon, the standards elaborated in the CRC. However, rather than drawing incrementally upon the CRC or offering its own independent interpretation of Article 19 of the Convention, which it can then support by reference to the CRC, the Court has adopted the custom of simply quoting relevant tracts of the CRC as the starting point for its analysis. It is submitted that there is an important, even if subtle, distinction between employing the CRC to interpret Article 19 and simply asserting that the standards elaborated in the CRC can be implied wholesale into Article 19. The importance of not overtly and directly introducing other international standards through the Convention is this: in a human rights protection system without a specialised enforcement body to supervise the implementation of its judgments, the Court should be wary of handing States reasons to question the legal integrity of its decisions.

Notes and Questions

1. The decisions of the Inter-American Court support the view that regional human rights systems can act as conduits for the importation of international human rights principles; in this instance, those of the UNCRC. Do the children's rights cases taken up by the Inter-American Court to date set out an "inter-American" vision of the child, or are the facts of the relevant cases simply part and parcel of larger problems of democracy and due process in Latin America?

IV. The African Human Rights System

A. Overview of the African Human Rights System

In a region beset by severe human rights abuses, the African human rights system has enormous potential to raise awareness and promote good governance. The system is based on the 1986 African Charter on Human and Peoples' Rights,[15] an innovative instrument

---

15. Organization of African Unity, African Charter on Human and Peoples' Rights, June 27, 1981, 21 I.L.M. 58, *available at* http://www.africa-union.org/root/au/Documents/Treaties/Text/Banjul%20Charter.pdf.

that sets out both individual and collective rights. To date, the system remains largely symbolic, with little power as yet to influence events within Africa.

The following article describes the development of the African human rights system, and indicates what its future role might be in curbing abuses of rights on that continent.

Christof Heyns, *The African Regional Human Rights System: The African Charter*
108 Penn State Law Review 679 (2004)

I. Introduction

While the term "human rights" is of relatively recent currency on the continent, people have been struggling for freedom, dignity, equality, and social justice for centuries in Africa. In Africa, as is the case elsewhere, that which is now called human rights finds its foundations in the struggle to assert these core values of human existence.

Today, the term human rights is used widely in the African context. The written constitutions of every country in Africa recognise the concept; the inter-governmental organisation of African states, the African Union, regards the realisation of human rights as one of its objectives and principles; and the record of ratification of the human rights treaties of the United Nations by African countries is on a par with practices around the world. There is wide acceptance that the future of Africa will have to be based on that which is internationally known as human rights.

.... A significant number of African constitutions explicitly recognise a direct right, located in the people, to protect constitutional and human rights norms, if need be, through political struggle. The foundational document of the African Union uniquely provides for a right of humanitarian intervention in member states by the Union, in cases of grave human rights violations. The African Charter on Human and Peoples' Rights also reflects in many ways a reaction to the continental experience of slavery and colonialism, for example by recognising a "peoples'" right to self-determination. Human Rights in this context, it could be said, is seen as "a demand by citizens backed by a threat"—the threat of struggle.

However, the struggle for human rights on the African continent is far from over or complete. The continent is plagued by widespread violations of human rights, often on a massive scale. The process to establish effective institutional structures that will help to consolidate and to protect the hard earned gains of the freedom struggles of the past has become a struggle in its own right. No doubt, the most important task in this regard is to establish legal and political systems on the national level that protect human rights. But regional attempts to change the human rights practices of the continent, and to create safety nets for those cases not effectively dealt with on the national level, are assuming increased importance.

This Article describes the institutional human rights structures created on a continental level in Africa. The specific focus is on the general human rights treaty of Africa, the African Charter on Human and Peoples' Rights, as the legal foundation of a system that could potentially play the same role as is the case with the regional human rights systems in Europe and the Americas. The underlying question is how this could be achieved in the most effective way.

II. Sources

The African regional system has been developed under the auspices of the Organization of African Unity ("OAU"), which was transformed in 2002 into the African Union

("AU"). While the Charter of the OAU of 1963 made only passing reference to the concept of human rights, the Constitutive Act of the AU of 2001 has now placed human rights squarely on the agenda of the new regional body.

The central document of the African regional system, the African Charter on Human and Peoples' Rights ("African Charter"), was opened for signature in 1981 and entered into force in 1986. It has been ratified by all fifty-three member states of the OAU/AU. The sole supervisory body of the African Charter currently in existence is the African Commission on Human and Peoples' Rights ("African Commission"). The African Commission was constituted and met for the first time in 1987. The Commission has adopted its own Rules of Procedure (amended in 1995) and Guidelines for State Reporting (amended in 1998).

The Protocol to the African Charter on Human and Peoples' Rights on the Establishment of the African Court on Human and Peoples' Rights ("African Human Rights Court Protocol") was adopted in 1998. The Protocol entered into force January 25, 2004 after receiving the necessary fifteen ratifications.

The Annual Activity Reports of the Commission, which reflect the decisions, resolutions, and other acts of the Commission, are submitted each year for permission to publish to the meeting of the Assembly of Heads of State and Government ("Assembly") of the OAU/AU, which takes place in June or July of the following year ... A Protocol to the African Charter on Human and Peoples' Rights on the Rights of Women in Africa was adopted at the African Union Summit in Maputo in July 2003.

In addition to the African Charter, the African regional human rights system is comprised of the OAU Convention Governing the Specific Aspects of Refugee Problems in Africa ("African Refugee Convention") of 1969, which entered into force in 1974 (44 ratifications); and the African Charter on the Rights and Welfare of the Child ("African Children's Charter") of 1990, which came into force in 1999 (32 ratifications). A special monitoring body for the African Children's Charter has been created. The African Committee on the Rights and Welfare of the Child had its first meeting in 2002 in Addis Ababa, Ethiopia.

The relatively unknown Cultural Charter for Africa of 1976 came into force in 1990 (33 state parties). There are also two African treaties dealing with the environment, although not from a human rights perspective.

....

The African Human Rights Court ... is clearly intended to be an independent judicial body, but as a result the political impact of its decisions is uncertain. The NEPAD African Peer Review Mechanism, on the other hand, is largely political and as such could potentially, in the short term, have a stronger impact, but it remains an open question to what extent such a political body could be expected to protect the human rights of the weak in an independent fashion. The African Commission, as a quasi-judicial body, occupies a position somewhere in between, and could potentially share either the positive or the negative aspects of the other two bodies depending on how it is managed.

III. The African Charter

A. Background

.... The African Charter recognises a wide range of internationally accepted human rights norms, but also has some unique features, elaborated upon below. Several reasons have been advanced for why only a Commission, and not a Court, was provided for in the African Charter in 1981 as the body responsible for monitoring compliance of state parties with the Charter. On the one hand there is the more idealistic explanation that the traditional way of solving disputes in Africa is through mediation and conciliation, not through the adversarial, "win or lose" mechanism of a court. On the other hand there is the view that the member states of the OAU were protective of their newly found sovereignty, and did not wish to limit it by means of a supra-national court.

The notion of a human rights court for Africa would be taken up by the OAU thirteen years after the adoption of the African Charter when, in 1994, the Assembly adopted a resolution requesting the Secretary-General of the OAU to convene a Meeting of Experts to consider the establishment of an African Court on Human and Peoples' Rights. This eventually led to the adoption of the African Human Rights Court Protocol in Addis Ababa, Ethiopia in 1998.

Ostensibly, the concept of human rights was accepted widely enough in Africa in the early 1990s for the decision to be made to give more "teeth" to the African human rights system in the form of a Court. This came in the wake of the different waves of democratisation on the national level, epitomised by the watershed elections in Benin in 1991 and the advent of democracy in South Africa in 1994. Worldwide, of course, the idea of human rights also gained prominence after the end of the Cold War.

B. Norms Recognised

We now turn to a consideration of the norms recognised in the African Charter and the nature of its enforcement mechanisms.

The civil and political rights recognised in the African Charter are in many ways similar to those recognised in other international instruments, and these rights have in practical terms received most of the attention of the African Commission.

The Charter recognises the following rights as individual rights: freedom from discrimination; equality; bodily integrity and the right to life; dignity and prohibition of torture and inhuman treatment; liberty and security; fair trial; freedom of conscience; information and freedom of expression; freedom of association; assembly; freedom of movement; political participation; and property.

A number of possible shortcomings in respect to civil and political rights in the African Charter could be noted. There is, for example, no explicit reference in the Charter to a right to privacy; the right against forced labour is not mentioned by name; and the right to a fair trial and the right of political participation are given scant protection in comparison with international standards.

In addition, the way in which the Charter deals with gender issues has been a bone of contention. Article 18(3) provides as follows: "The state shall ensure the elimination of every discrimination against women and also ensure the protection of the rights of the woman and the child as stipulated in international declarations and conventions."

This lumping together of women and children in an article that deals primarily with the family, re-enforces outdated stereotypes about the proper place and role of women in society and has been partially responsible for the drive to adopt the Protocol to the African Charter on the Rights of Women in Africa.

The way in which the African Charter deals with restrictions on all rights, including civil and political rights, presents a significant obstacle. The African Charter does not contain a general limitation clause (although, as is noted below, article 27(2) is starting to play this role). This means that there are no general guidelines on how Charter rights should be limited—no clear "limits on the limitations," so to speak. A well-defined system of limitations is important. A society in which rights cannot be limited will be ungovernable, but it is essential that appropriate human rights norms be set for the limitations.

A number of the articles of the Charter setting out specific civil and political rights do contain limiting provisions applicable to those particular rights. Some of these internal limitations clearly spell out the procedural and substantive norms with which limitations should comply, while others only describe the substantive requirements that limitations must meet.

....

A unique feature of the Charter is the inclusion of socio-economic rights in a regional human rights treaty, alongside the civil and political rights mentioned above.

The inclusion of socio-economic rights in the Charter is significant, in that it emphasises the indivisibility of human rights and the importance of developmental issues, which are obviously important matters in the African context. At the same time, the fact that only a modest number of socio-economic rights are explicitly included in the Charter should be noted. The Charter only recognises "a right to work under equitable and satisfactory conditions," a right to health, and a right to education. Some prominent socio-economic rights are not mentioned by name, such as the right to food and water (or nutrition), social security, and housing.

It is also somewhat surprising that the socio-economic rights that are recognised are not explicitly made subject to the usual internal qualifiers that apply to such rights in most international instruments—such as the provision that the state is only required to ensure progressive realisation, subject to available resources, etc. This is made more problematic by the absence of a general limitation clause in the Charter, as discussed above. A selected few socio-economic rights, stated in near absolute terms, are recognised, while other obvious candidates for inclusion are not present.

The socio-economic rights in the Charter have received scant attention from the Commission, but in a prominent case the Commission dealt with the issue and in effect held that the internationally recognised socio-economic rights that are not explicitly recognised in the Charter should be regarded as implicitly included.

The so-called *SERAC v. Nigeria* decision dealt with the destruction of part of Ogoniland by a petroleum company acting in co-operation with the government of Nigeria. In an extraordinary decision, the Commission held that the presence of an implicit right to "housing or shelter" in the Charter has to be deduced from the explicit provisions on health, property and family life in the Charter. Similarly, a right to food has to be read into the right to dignity and other rights. It was accepted, without argument, that the Ogonis constituted a "people."

As with the claw-back clauses, the approach of the Commission in filling in the gaps in the Charter in the *SERAC* case could be seen as a creative and bold move on the part of the Commission, but it leaves the Charter exposed as an outdated document in need of revision to ensure that it actually says, loud and clear, what it has been interpreted by the Commission to say. The current discrepancy between the wording of the Charter and the interpretation of the Commission undermines the principle of the rule of law above the rule by people.

There are other, more exotic features of the Charter that have attracted their fair share of academic and political commentary but have figured less in the pronouncements of the Commission.

The Charter, for example, recognises "peoples' rights." All "peoples," according to the Charter, have a right to be equal; to existence and self-determination; and to freely dispose of their wealth and natural resources. Clearly a major part of the motivation for the recognition of "peoples' rights" lies in the fact that entire "peoples" have been colonised and otherwise exploited in the history of Africa and have had to engage in protracted struggles to realise their human rights.

This concept has been referred to in some of the cases before the Commission, including the following two cases.

In a case concerning Katangese secessionists in the former Zaire, a complaint was brought on the basis that the Katangese people had a right, as a people, to self-determination in the form of independence. The Commission ruled against them on the basis that there was no evidence that a Charter provision had been violated because widespread human rights violations or a lack of political participation by the Katangese people had not been proven. This seems to suggest that if these conditions were met, secession by such a "people" could be a permissible option.

In a case concerning the 1994 *coup d'etat* against the democratically elected government of The Gambia, the Commission held that this violated the right to self-determination of the people of The Gambia as a whole.

The Charter recognises duties in addition to rights. For example, individuals have duties towards their families and society, and state parties have the duty to promote the Charter.

Perhaps the most significant provision under the heading "Duties" is article 27(2), which reads as follows: "The rights and freedoms of each individual shall be exercised with due regard to the rights of others, collective security, morality and common interest." This provision has now in effect been given the status of a general limitation clause by the African Commission. According to the Commission: "The only legitimate reasons for limitations to the rights and freedoms of the African Charter are found in article 27(2)...."

The Commission's use of article 27(2) as a general limitation clause seems to confirm the view that the concept of "duties" should not be understood as a sinister way of saying rights should first be earned, or that meeting certain duties is a precondition for enjoying human rights. Rather, it implies that the exercise of human rights, which are "natural" or valid in themselves, may be limited by the duties of individuals. Rights precede duties, and the recognition of duties is merely another way of signifying the kind of limitations that may be placed on rights.

The African Charter does not contain a provision either allowing or disallowing derogation from its provisions during a state of emergency. This has led the Commission to the conclusion that derogation is not possible. This conclusion is unfortunate because it means that in real emergencies the Charter will be ignored and will not exercise a restraining influence.

C. Enforcement Mechanism: The African Commission

....

1. The Complaints Procedure

Both states and individuals may bring complaints to the African Commission alleging violations of the African Charter by state parties.

The procedure by which one state brings a complaint about an alleged human rights violation by another state has only been used once in a case. Currently that case is pending before the Commission.

The so-called individual communication or complaints procedure is not clearly provided for in the African Charter. One reading of the Charter is that communications could be considered only where "serious or massive violations" are at stake, which then triggers the rather futile article 58 procedure described below. However, the African Commission has accepted from the start that it has the power to deal with complaints about any human rights violations under the Charter, provided the admissibility criteria are met.

The Charter is silent on the question of who can bring such complaints, but the Commission's practice is that complaints from individuals as well as non-governmental organizations are accepted. The individual complaints procedure is used much more frequently than the inter-state mechanism, although not as frequently as one might have expected on a continent with the kind of human rights problems like Africa's. The potential of this mechanism has not nearly been exhausted.

As with other complaints systems, the African Charter imposes certain admissibility criteria before the Commission may entertain complaints. These criteria include the important requirement of exhausting local remedies. The Commission may be approached only once the matter has been pursued in the highest court in the country in question without success or the prospect of success. Uniquely, there is also a requirement that the communications are "not written in disparaging or insulting language directed against the state concerned and its institutions or to the Organization of African Unity."

When a complaint is lodged, the state in question is asked to respond to the allegations against it. If the state does not respond, the Commission proceeds on the basis of the facts as provided by the complainant. If the decision of the Commission is that there has indeed been a violation or violations of the Charter, the Commission sometimes also makes recommendations that continuing violations should stop (e.g., prisoners be released) or specific laws be changed; but mostly the recommendations are rather vague, and the state party is merely urged to "adopt measures in conformity with the decision."

....

2. Consideration of State Reports

Each state party is required to submit a report every two years on its efforts to comply with the African Charter. Although it is not provided for in the African Charter that the reports should be submitted specifically to the African Commission, the Commission recommended to the Assembly that the Commission be given the mandate to consider the reports. The Assembly has endorsed this recommendation. Non-governmental organizations ("NGOs") are allowed to submit shadow or alternative reports, but the impact of this avenue is diminished by the NGOs' lack of timely access to the state reports to which they are supposed to respond. The reports are considered by the Commission in public sessions. Reporting by state parties under the African Charter has to be done in accordance with the guidelines mentioned above.

Reporting under the Charter, as in other systems, is aimed at facilitating both introspection and inspection. "Introspection" refers to the process when the state, in writing its report, measures itself against the norms of the Charter. "Inspection" refers to the process when the Commission measures the performance of the state in question against the Charter. The objective is to facilitate a "constructive dialogue" between the Commission and the states.

Reporting has been very tardy, with approximately half of the state parties not submitting any reports. In 2001, the Commission started to issue concluding observations in respect to reports considered.

....

4. Site Visits

Since 1995, the Commission has conducted a number of on-site visits. These involve a range of activities, from fact-finding to general promotional visits.

5. Resolutions

The Commission has adopted resolutions on a number of human rights issues in Africa. In addition to country-specific and other more ad hoc resolutions, they have adopted resolutions on topics such as the following: fair trial; freedom of association; human and peoples' rights; education; humanitarian law; contemporary forms of slavery; anti-personnel mines; prisons in Africa; the independence of the judiciary; the electoral process and participatory governance; the International Criminal Court; the death penalty; torture; HIV/AIDS; and freedom of expression.

NGOs have a special relationship with the Commission. Large numbers have registered for affiliate status. NGOs are often instrumental in bringing cases to the Commission; they sometimes submit shadow reports, propose agenda items at the outset of Commission sessions, and provide logistical and other support to the Commission, for example by placing interns at the Commission and providing support to the special rapporteurs and missions of the Commission. NGOs often organise special NGO workshops just prior to Commission sessions and participate actively in the public sessions of the Commission. NGOs also collaborate with the Commission in developing normative resolutions and new protocols to the African Charter.

....

IV. The African Human Rights Court

Once the African Human Rights Court is in place, it will "complement" the protective mandate of the Commission under the Charter. The Court will consist of eleven judges, serving in their individual capacities, nominated by state parties to the Protocol, and elected by the Assembly. Only the president will be full-time.

The Protocol provides that the judges will be appointed in their individual capacities, and their independence is guaranteed. Special provision is made that "[t]he position of judge of the Court is incompatible with any activity that might interfere with the independence or impartiality of such a judge...." A judge will not be allowed to sit in a case if that judge is a national of a state that is a party to the case. The seat of the Court is still to be determined by the Assembly.

In respect to the Court's findings, the Protocol determines that "[i]f the Court finds that there has been a violation of a human or peoples' right, it shall make appropriate orders to remedy the violation, including the payment of fair compensation or reparation." The Court is explicitly granted the powers to adopt provisional measures.

By ratifying the Protocol, states accept that the Commission and the states involved will be in a position to take a case that has appeared before them to the African Human Rights Court to obtain a legally binding decision. Individuals and those who act on their behalf will be able to take cases to the Court only in respect to those states that have made an additional declaration specifically authorising them to do so. In such instances, the case will have to be taken "directly" to the Court, presumably bypassing the Commission.

Article 3(1) reads as follows:

> The jurisdiction of the Court shall extend to all cases and disputes submitted to it concerning the interpretation and application of the Charter, this Protocol and any other relevant human rights instrument ratified by the states concerned.

The phrase "any other relevant human rights instrument ratified by the states concerned," according to most commentators, means that adjudication in respect to even United Nations and sub-regional human rights instruments will fall within the jurisdiction of the African Human Rights Court, provided that such treaties have been ratified by the states concerned.

It is submitted that nothing is wrong with the African Human Rights Court interpreting the Charter in view of international standards. However, if cases could be brought to the African Human Rights Court on the ground that, for example, United Nations treaties have been violated, with no reference to the African Charter, this will lead to jurisprudential chaos, and it will undermine the unique nature of the African Charter. Instead, the word "relevant" human rights instrument should be understood to restrict the jurisdiction of the Court beyond the Charter and the Protocol only to those instances where the instrument in question has explicitly provided for the jurisdiction of the Court—for example as is the case in the Draft Protocol on the Rights of Women.

V. Conclusion

Much remains to be done to make the African human rights system effective. I would venture to say there are a number of determinants for the effectiveness of any regional human rights systems, which include the following.

An adequate level of compliance with human rights norms on the domestic level must occur in a significant number of the state parties. Working national human rights systems are the building blocks of an effective regional system. If the level of respect for human rights norms on the domestic level is low, and domestic courts are not effective in implementing these norms, there can be little hope for supra-national enforcement.

The necessary political will must be present in the regional organisation of which the system forms part, to ensure that the system really works and is not an empty façade. The regional organisation is the primary body through which peer pressure must be channelled. The all-important selection process of Commissioners and Judges must be taken seriously by the regional body. The budgets allocated to human rights organisations also often have an important influence on how effective they are. The system must be properly serviced and able administrators appointed.

Publicity for the work of the monitoring body or bodies of the system is essential. The decisions and resolutions of these bodies must be available, and disseminated on the national and regional level, to have an impact. Publicity is needed so that those who want to comply voluntarily know what is expected of them, but it is also necessary to ensure that shame or peer pressure can be mobilised against recalcitrant states. Peer pressure can change behaviour by inducing shame, or if that does not work, by mobilising stronger forms of sanctions against states. All of this is possible only when there is sufficient publicity. The responsibility to see to it that there is publicity lies on the regional system, the states, and civil society alike.

. . . .

The African regional human rights system is faced with almost insurmountable challenges: massive violations on a continent of immense diversity, where a tradition of domestic compliance with human rights norms is still to be established. The trade and communication links that are necessary to exercise influence over member states in many cases do not exist.

Moreover, the system itself is also not currently well equipped to face these challenges. The African Charter has severe shortcomings and is in need of reform. The shortcomings in the African Charter relate to the norms recognised (the omission of important civil and political as well as socio-economic rights, the inclusion of concepts that are not easy to translate into legal terms, and the absence of adequate rules in respect to restrictions on rights) as well as the monitoring mechanism itself (none of the main monitoring procedures allowed by the Commission—individual communications, state reports, and special rapporteurs—are provided for explicitly in the Charter, and the provisions concerning secrecy and massive violations should be scrapped). The African Charter should be reformed to keep abreast of the times.

. . . .

Notes and Questions

1. A seat for the African Court, in Arusha, Tanzania, has now been chosen. The first eleven judges were elected by the African Union in 2006, and the Court held its first meeting in 2006 as well. However, the Court is still not fully operational and no cases have been brought before it. *See* African International Courts and Tribunals, http://www.aict-stia.org/court_conti/achpr/achpr_home.html.

2. For further reading on restrictions and problems in bringing the Court's mission to reality, see Rebecca Wright, *Finding An Impetus for Institutional Change at the African Court on Human and Peoples' Rights*, 24 Berkeley J. Int'l L. 463 (2006).

Vincent O. Nmehielle, *Development of the African Human Rights System in the Last Decade*
11:3 Human Rights Brief 6 (Spring 2004)

. . . .

THE CHILD RIGHTS CHARTER[16]

An early evidence of the inadequacy of the normative content of the African Human Rights Charter was the adoption of the Child Rights Charter CITE thirteen years ago to specifically provide for the protection of children as a particular class of persons that was not adequately protected under the Human Rights Charter. The Child Rights Charter was Africa's enlistment to the ideals of the UN Convention on the Rights of the Child (UN Child Rights Convention) but with an African emphasis because of the perceived exposure of the African child "to a particular set of dangerous circumstances" as stated by Gino Naldi ... The charter deals with all aspects of children's rights, ranging from civil, political, social, and economic rights to the prohibition of child soldiers, the prohibition of harmful social and cultural practices, the recognition of the best interest of the child principle, protection from child labor, protection from sexual exploitation, etc.

The Child Rights Charter entered into force in 1999 and has a supervisory mechanism; an eleven-member African Committee of Experts on the Rights and Welfare of the Child (African Child Rights Committee), whose functions are akin to that of the African Commission. The first members of the committee were elected on July 10, 2001, and had their first meeting from April 29 to May 3, 2002. Among other functions, the committee

---

16. Organization of African Unity, African Charter on the Rights and Welfare of the Child, July 11, 1990, OAU Doc. CAB/LEG/24.9/49, *available at* http://www.africa-union.org/root/au/Documents/Treaties/treaties.htm.

receives periodic reports from states parties on implementing measures they have taken within two years of becoming a party and every three years thereafter. Under Article 44 of the Child Rights Charter, the committee is also mandated to receive communications "from any person, group or non-governmental organization recognized by the Organization of African Unity, by a Member State, or the United Nations relating to any matter covered by this Charter."

The recognition of the rights of the child as a component norm of the African System was an idea that was welcomed. However, the monitoring mechanism continues to be criticized as needless duplication that should have been adequately covered under the mandate of the African Commission, particularly because of the lack of adequate resources, which has been a handicap of the African System. This situation has been described as an instance of lack of harmonization among human rights instruments and institutions. It does not appear that there [has been] any change of mind in this regard. The African Child Rights Committee, it appears, is here to stay and has taken steps to entrench itself as part of the African Human Rights System....

....

Notes and Questions

1. As of June 2007, 41 nations had ratified the African Charter on the Rights and Welfare of the Child. The Committee completed its tenth meeting in the fall of 2007. Moreover, States are due to submit their country reports two years after ratification and every three years thereafter. However, since the Committee began its work in 2001, and as of December 2006, only Egypt, Mauritius, Rwanda and Nigeria have submitted reports. Some on-site visits have been conducted. *See generally* African Committee of Experts on the Rights of the Child, http://www.africa-union.org/child/home.htm.

———————

B. The African System in Focus

The full text of the African Children's Charter can be found in the appendix. The Thoko Kaime article below demonstrates the benefit of having the Children's Charter in addition to the African Charter on Human and Peoples' Rights. Chapter Four of this book discussed refugee children and unaccompanied minors, and Chapter Six addressed the problem of refugee and internally displaced children in the context of children and armed conflict. Kaime's article shows the relevance of the Children's Charter to children living in those difficult circumstances in Africa.

African Charter on the Rights and Welfare of the Child
OAU Doc. CAB/LEG/24.9/49 (1990), *available at*
http://www.africa-union.org/official_documents/Treaties_%20
Conventions_%20Protocols/A.%20C.%20ON%20THE%20
RIGHT%20AND%20WELF%20OF%20CHILD.pdf

Article 23: Refugee Children

1. States Parties to the present Charter shall take all appropriate measures to ensure that a child who is seeking refugee status or who is considered a refugee in accordance with

applicable international or domestic law shall, whether unaccompanied or accompanied by parents, legal guardians or close relatives, receive appropriate protection and humanitarian assistance in the enjoyment of the rights set out in this Charter and other international human rights and humanitarian instruments to which the States are Parties.

2. States Parties shall undertake to cooperate with existing international organizations which protect and assist refugees in their efforts to protect and assist such a child and to trace the parents or other close relatives or an unaccompanied refugee child in order to obtain information necessary for reunification with the family.

3. Where no parents, legal guardians or close relatives can be found, the child shall be accorded the same protection as any other child permanently or temporarily deprived of his family environment for any reason.

4. The provisions of this Article apply mutatis mutandis to internally displaced children whether through natural disaster, internal armed conflicts, civil strife, breakdown of economic and social order or howsoever caused.

Thoko Kaime, *From Lofty Jargon to Durable Solutions: Unaccompanied Refugee Children and the African Charter on the Rights and Welfare of the Child*
16 International Journal Of Refugee Law 336 (2004)

1. Introduction

At the end of 2001, the total refugee population in Africa was estimated at approximately 3.6 million refugees. Fifty-six percent of these refugees are children under the age of eighteen. Nearly five percent (or two hundred thousand) of the refugee children are unaccompanied refugee children. Due to the factors such as the absence of an older guardian or their young age, unaccompanied refugee children face a myriad of risks over and above those faced by other refugee children. These risks include unlawful military recruitment, sexual exploitation and abuse, child labour, denial of access to education and basic assistance and even death. Due to their heightened vulnerability, it has always been accepted that unaccompanied refugee minors require a raised level of protection and assistance in order to find durable solutions for their particularly tragic situation.

However, despite the existence of multitudes of unaccompanied refugee minors on the continent and the recognition of their vulnerable status, the African human rights system did not provide for a special protection regime for addressing their particular plight. The entry into force of the African Charter on the Rights and Welfare of the Child ('the African Children's Charter' or 'the Charter') brought fundamental and profound changes in the protection of children generally and unaccompanied refugee minors especially. Although the African Children's Charter's provisions relating to protection of unaccompanied refugee children is substantially similar to that of the Convention on the Rights of the Child (CRC), its strength lies in the extension of protection to internally displaced children, 'something which the CRC does not do' and in the formal synergies that it creates between itself and other authoritative international instruments.

....

2. General Principles of Protection

Although the rights and duties in the African Children's Charter cover almost every aspect of a child's life, there are three principles that are so fundamental that they may be thought of as underpinning the entire Charter. These include the rule against non-discrimination, the 'best interests' rule, and the rule requiring the child's participation. Since these are crosscutting principles, they apply to all considerations relating to the protection of unaccompanied refugee minors.

2.1 Non-discrimination

Article 3 of the Charter guarantees every child the enjoyment of the rights set forth in it without discrimination. This provision obligates state parties to ensure to all children within their jurisdiction the rights guaranteed in the Charter. This not only implies that states must prevent discrimination, but that they must also ensure the positive enjoyment of the rights which enable children to be recognised as equally valuable members of the society. In other words, every child within a state's jurisdiction holds all the rights guaranteed under the Charter without regard to political opinion, citizenship, immigration status or any other status.

In relation to unaccompanied refugee children, the Charter's position is even more unequivocal and obligates states to ensure that necessary measures are taken to enable refugee children to enjoy the rights set forth in the Charter as well as other international human rights instruments to which the states are parties. Thus, unaccompanied refugee children are entitled to the enjoyment of the full range of the rights contained in the Charter.

By ensuring the non-discrimination of refugee children, the African Charter has moved the level of protection to a higher plane. It is submitted that this approach takes into cognisance the vulnerability and special needs of the unaccompanied refugee child. Such an approach also augurs well with the 'best interests' approach.

2.2 Best Interests of the Child

Article 4 of the Charter provides that in all actions affecting the child, the primary consideration shall be the best interests of the child. This provision obligates states to accord the primary consideration to the best interests of the child. This obligation, however, does not entail the adoption of a paternalistic or know-all attitude on the part of authorities, parents or guardians. Since the list of factors competing 'for the core of the child's best interests is almost endless and will vary depending on each particular factual situation', the provision requires and indeed demands that careful and objective assessment of the child's competing needs are made.

In relation to unaccompanied refugee children, the best interests of the child require that durable solutions be found as quickly as possible. Durable solutions are those which positively contribute to the refugee child's survival, protection and development and encompass considerations such as the child's need for 'bodily and mental health, normal intellectual development, adequate material security, stable and non-superficial interpersonal relationships and a fair degree of liberty'. In short, the state is bound to facilitate the quickest possible normalisation of the child's situation.

By championing the best interests approach, the Children's Charter has prescribed a uniform standard relating to the treatment of unaccompanied refugee children and African states that are parties to the Charter must ensure that they comply with this standard.

2.3 Participation

Implicit within the best interests approach is the requirement for individual determination of each particular child's situation and needs. The African Children's Charter concretises this approach by making provision for the child's participation rights, namely the right of the child to be heard in all proceedings affecting that child and the right of the child to freely express his or her opinions. The obligation of states under these provisions is to ensure that appropriate mechanisms for the channelling of the child's views are put in place. Such mechanisms must be child-centred and non-threatening.

In relation to child refugees, children's participation rights require that in the determination of their status and in any aspect of providing durable solutions, the child's views should feature prominently. The body entrusted with the task of finding the durable solutions must solicit the views of the refugee child in determining the child's status and such views must be taken into account in any subsequent decisions relating to the child. The obligation also requires the state to provide the unaccompanied child with a guardian or adviser who is well trained in child welfare matters and who will promote decisions in the best interests of the child and positively contribute to the quest for durable solutions.

Thus, the right of participation is critical in determining the best interests of the child and ensuring mechanisms that enable unaccompanied children to exercise this right is the positive step towards affording them effective protection and assistance.

3. Primary Considerations for Unaccompanied Refugee Children

The African Children's Charter identifies two key responses with respect to unaccompanied refugee children, namely the 'trac[ing] of the parents or other close relatives ... in order to obtain information necessary for reunification with the family' and, where such parents or relatives cannot be found, the placement of such child in alternative care. Decisions regarding whether to reunite the child with its family or to place him or her in alternative care must be non-discriminatory, must take into account the child's views and, above all, must be predicated on the child's best interests.

3.1 Family Reunification

Although the African Children's Charter gives individual rights to children, it also emphasises relationships. In this regard, the African Children's Charter proclaims the family as 'the natural unit and basis of society' and entitles every child 'to the enjoyment of parental care and protection'. These affirmations are strengthened by the placement of children's rights within the context of parental rights and duties and community responsibilities. The recognition of the centrality of the family in the upbringing of a child forms the basis of the prioritisation of family reunification as a primary response in situations of separation.

International law and refugee policy also emphasise that the first priority in caring for unaccompanied children is family reunification. This is because children are generally better protected from risks such as sexual exploitation and abuse, military recruitment, child labour, denial of access to education and basic assistance and detention within the context of family protection. Thus, it is not surprising that the Charter advocates family reunion as the first option. However, the most important addition to the protection framework is the incorporation of the best interests standard in the resolution of the matter. Reunification is thus not an automatic response that should be dogmatically pursued. It is a factor which is subsumed under the inquiry to determine the best interests of the particular child. This is because there will be situations where reunification may not be in the best interests of the child. In this regard, the durability of the relationship between the minor and the family must be carefully assessed to determine whether they should remain together. For example, reunification would not be advisable where the remaining parent or relatives were responsible, partly or otherwise, for the minor's flight. Similarly, where a child flees from a social practice such as forced or early marriage, and which implicates family members, reunification must be considered with very great circumspection. Further, where a minor has developed a great degree of attachment to a foster family, the disruptive effect of ultimate family reunification must be weighed against the need for continuity and stability.

It is also important to note that reunification does not only entail sending the unaccompanied minor to his or her country of origin but may also involve organising the reunification around the child if this is in his or her best interests. For example, it would not be in the best interests of the child to send her back where hostilities were still going on. Similarly, if minors are targeted for military recruitment by authorities or other parties in the country of origin, reunification should be organised within the host country or another third party state.

3.2 Alternative Care

Article 23(3) provides that where parents or legal guardians or close relatives cannot be found, the unaccompanied refugee minor must be accorded the same protection as any other child who has been permanently or temporarily deprived of his or her family environment for any reason. The extent of the state's obligations must, therefore, be sourced from article 25 of the Charter which obligates states to accord special protection and assistance to any child who is permanently or temporarily deprived of his or her family environment. Since the Charter already accords special protection and assistance to all children, the implication from this provision is that children without families are entitled to an additional level of protection and assistance above that of other children.

The obligation of states under these provisions is to ensure that children who are parentless or permanently deprived of their family environment must 'be provided with alternative family care' which may take the form of adoption, foster placement or placement in suitable institutions for the protection and care of children. Further, when considering such alternative family care for the child, states are required to have the best interests of the child as the primary consideration and to pay due regard to the desirability of continuity in the child's upbringing and to the child's ethnic, religious or linguistic background.

In relation to the provision of alternative care for unaccompanied refugee children, it is noteworthy that the Charter demonstrates an unspecified preference for placements which maintain the child's previous, ethnic, religious, cultural and linguistic background. Furthermore, the Charter also prescribes an analogous preference to continuity in the child's upbringing. However, the most notable aspect of article 25 is that it does not prescribe an overall standard for choice of placement, leaving the ultimate choice to be predicated on the best interests of the child. Thus, the unaccompanied refugee child's ethnic, religious, cultural and linguistic background are not the primary consideration, but rather are 'subsumed under the larger issue whether the particular placement meets his or her best interests'.

Under this obligation, states must put in place effective adoption and foster care arrangements as well as monitoring mechanisms for such arrangements and must in all circumstances ensure that the process is directed at ensuring the best interests of the child and not the disposal of the affected children to their country of origin. These considerations apply whether the refugee population is in camps or otherwise, and the search for durable solutions may involve the arrangement of foster placement within the host country or in third countries.

4. Complementary Rights

The process of establishing durable solutions for the unaccompanied child within the parameters of family reunion and alternative family care must be informed by guarantees of the rights of identity, rights of protection, and rights of support. The guarantee of these complementary rights not only takes cognisance of the vulnerability of unaccompanied refugee minors, but also ensures the achievement of solutions which are in their best interests. Thus, in designing response systems to deal with unaccompanied refugee children, states must ensure that these complementary rights are observed.

4.1 Rights of Identity

Article 6 of the Children's Charter guarantees every child the right to a name, the right to be registered immediately after birth, and the right to acquire a nationality. The obligation of states under this article is to put in place appropriate mechanisms to ensure the registration of children immediately after birth and to ensure that children are not unlawfully deprived of their names or family background. It goes without saying that these rights are crucial to a child's identity because 'only by registration is it guaranteed that the existence of a [child] is legally recognised'.

The preservation of a child's identity also includes within its purview the protection of the child's cultural, racial, linguistic and religious identity and, in this regard, the African Children's Charter guarantees every child the right to participate freely in cultural life and the right to freedom of religion.

In relation to unaccompanied refugee minors, rights of identity are of fundamental importance. Registration of children will assist in the tracing of family members for the purpose of reunification and the protection of the child's cultural, racial, linguistic and religious identity, which in turn will inform the process of determining the child's best interests. These provisions obligate states to identify, register and document unaccompanied minors as soon as possible. To this end, an active search must be undertaken to find unaccompanied children, including those living with unrelated adults. The best interests of the child and the preservation of the child's identity require that unaccompanied children be registered and their personal history properly documented. Further, if the minor's parents or relatives cannot be traced, proper mechanisms must be built into the alternative care mechanisms to ensure that children are not unlawfully deprived of their identity.

4.2 Rights of Protection

Due to their age or the absence of an older guardian, unaccompanied children face a great number of risks which include sexual exploitation and abuse, forced military recruitment, child labour, and denial of access to education and health services.

To ensure the child's well-being and development by preventing the above harm, the African Children's Charter protects all children from all forms of torture, physical or mental injury and abuse, neglect or maltreatment. The child also has the right to be protected from sexual exploitation as well as economic exploitation and from performing any work that is likely to be harmful to the child's health or physical, mental, spiritual, moral or social development. Further, children under the age of eighteen have protection against military recruitment and direct involvement in military hostilities.

Thus, in ensuring the best interests of the child and securing for them durable solutions, states must ensure that the protection accorded by the above provisions is extended to unaccompanied children. Failure to ensure this entails failure to provide special protection and assistance to unaccompanied refugee children as required by the Charter.

4.3 Rights of Support

The quest for durable solutions may be described as an endeavour towards normalcy. In this respect, the guarantee of rights of support is crucial as it ensures not only the child's best interests, but also his or her rights to normal growth and development.

These rights of support include the child's right to education, rest, leisure and play and to the highest attainable state of health. State parties are thus obliged to accord unaccompanied refugee children access to education and adequate healthcare services. Further, states must desist from measures which impact adversely on the child's right to play such as the detention of unaccompanied children.

5. Conclusion

An analysis of the extent of state obligations emanating from the duty to provide protection and assistance to unaccompanied refugee children demonstrates just how onerous the duties assumed under these provisions of the Charter are. The economic implications of guaranteeing these rights to refugee children by states may lead to their totally shirking from the duty to protect and provide assistance to unaccompanied child refugees. However, the plight of these vulnerable children demands no less. Further, the immediacy of the various responses required of states demonstrates the necessity of states guaranteeing these rights for their own children. Thus, the duty to protect and provide assistance to unaccompanied children will be discharged more easily if the state already ensures the rights and the protections provided by the Charter for its own children.

Where there are economic, institutional or administrative hurdles in affording protection and assistance to unaccompanied refugee children, it is imperative that states cooperate with other governments and international organisations as envisaged by the Charter instead of ignoring their duties under the Charter. Unless that is done, the lofty jargon of the Charter shall remain that: jargon; and will not result in durable solutions for this vulnerable section of our society.

Notes and Questions

1. Given what the readings in this book have shown about the problems of child soldiers, child refugees and street children in Africa, will the African Children's Charter prove to be just more words on a page? How does the African regional system try to address problems of domestic capacity-building, if at all? What would a regional human rights system in South Asia look like? What about North America? As regional systems fall between domestic constitutional systems and distant international principles, what opportunities do you see for bringing children's rights "close to home" culturally, without compromising on high standards and rigorous application?

Index